Dictionary of Literary Biography

1 *The American Renaissance in New England*, edited by Joel Myerson (1978)

2 *American Novelists Since World War II*, edited by Jeffrey Helterman and Richard Layman (1978)

3 *Antebellum Writers in New York and the South*, edited by Joel Myerson (1979)

4 *American Writers in Paris, 1920–1939*, edited by Karen Lane Rood (1980)

5 *American Poets Since World War II*, 2 parts, edited by Donald J. Greiner (1980)

6 *American Novelists Since World War II, Second Series*, edited by James E. Kibler Jr. (1980)

7 *Twentieth-Century American Dramatists*, 2 parts, edited by John MacNicholas (1981)

8 *Twentieth-Century American Science-Fiction Writers*, 2 parts, edited by David Cowart and Thomas L. Wymer (1981)

9 *American Novelists, 1910–1945*, 3 parts, edited by James J. Martine (1981)

10 *Modern British Dramatists, 1900–1945*, 2 parts, edited by Stanley Weintraub (1982)

11 *American Humorists, 1800–1950*, 2 parts, edited by Stanley Trachtenberg (1982)

12 *American Realists and Naturalists*, edited by Donald Pizer and Earl N. Harbert (1982)

13 *British Dramatists Since World War II*, 2 parts, edited by Stanley Weintraub (1982)

14 *British Novelists Since 1960*, 2 parts, edited by Jay L. Halio (1983)

15 *British Novelists, 1930–1959*, 2 parts, edited by Bernard Oldsey (1983)

16 *The Beats: Literary Bohemians in Postwar America*, 2 parts, edited by Ann Charters (1983)

17 *Twentieth-Century American Historians*, edited by Clyde N. Wilson (1983)

18 *Victorian Novelists After 1885*, edited by Ira B. Nadel and William E. Fredeman (1983)

19 *British Poets, 1880–1914*, edited by Donald E. Stanford (1983)

20 *British Poets, 1914–1945*, edited by Donald E. Stanford (1983)

21 *Victorian Novelists Before 1885*, edited by Ira B. Nadel and William E. Fredeman (1983)

22 *American Writers for Children, 1900–1960*, edited by John Cech (1983)

23 *American Newspaper Journalists, 1873–1900*, edited by Perry J. Ashley (1983)

24 *American Colonial Writers, 1606–1734*, edited by Emory Elliott (1984)

25 *American Newspaper Journalists, 1901–1925*, edited by Perry J. Ashley (1984)

26 *American Screenwriters*, edited by Robert E. Morsberger, Stephen O. Lesser, and Randall Clark (1984)

27 *Poets of Great Britain and Ireland, 1945–1960*, edited by Vincent B. Sherry Jr. (1984)

28 *Twentieth-Century American-Jewish Fiction Writers*, edited by Daniel Walden (1984)

29 *American Newspaper Journalists, 1926–1950*, edited by Perry J. Ashley (1984)

30 *American Historians, 1607–1865*, edited by Clyde N. Wilson (1984)

31 *American Colonial Writers, 1735–1781*, edited by Emory Elliott (1984)

32 *Victorian Poets Before 1850*, edited by William E. Fredeman and Ira B. Nadel (1984)

33 *Afro-American Fiction Writers After 1955*, edited by Thadious M. Davis and Trudier Harris (1984)

34 *British Novelists, 1890–1929: Traditionalists*, edited by Thomas F. Staley (1985)

35 *Victorian Poets After 1850*, edited by William E. Fredeman and Ira B. Nadel (1985)

36 *British Novelists, 1890–1929: Modernists*, edited by Thomas F. Staley (1985)

37 *American Writers of the Early Republic*, edited by Emory Elliott (1985)

38 *Afro-American Writers After 1955: Dramatists and Prose Writers*, edited by Thadious M. Davis and Trudier Harris (1985)

39 *British Novelists, 1660–1800*, 2 parts, edited by Martin C. Battestin (1985)

40 *Poets of Great Britain and Ireland Since 1960*, 2 parts, edited by Vincent B. Sherry Jr. (1985)

41 *Afro-American Poets Since 1955*, edited by Trudier Harris and Thadious M. Davis (1985)

42 *American Writers for Children Before 1900*, edited by Glenn E. Estes (1985)

43 *American Newspaper Journalists, 1690–1872*, edited by Perry J. Ashley (1986)

44 *American Screenwriters, Second Series*, edited by Randall Clark, Robert E. Morsberger, and Stephen O. Lesser (1986)

45 *American Poets, 1880–1945, First Series*, edited by Peter Quartermain (1986)

46 *American Literary Publishing Houses, 1900–1980: Trade and Paperback*, edited by Peter Dzwonkoski (1986)

47 *American Historians, 1866–1912*, edited by Clyde N. Wilson (1986)

48 *American Poets, 1880–1945, Second Series*, edited by Peter Quartermain (1986)

49 *American Literary Publishing Houses, 1638–1899*, 2 parts, edited by Peter Dzwonkoski (1986)

50 *Afro-American Writers Before the Harlem Renaissance*, edited by Trudier Harris (1986)

51 *Afro-American Writers from the Harlem Renaissance to 1940*, edited by Trudier Harris (1987)

52 *American Writers for Children Since 1960: Fiction*, edited by Glenn E. Estes (1986)

53 *Canadian Writers Since 1960, First Series*, edited by W. H. New (1986)

54 *American Poets, 1880–1945, Third Series*, 2 parts, edited by Peter Quartermain (1987)

55 *Victorian Prose Writers Before 1867*, edited by William B. Thesing (1987)

56 *German Fiction Writers, 1914–1945*, edited by James Hardin (1987)

57 *Victorian Prose Writers After 1867*, edited by William B. Thesing (1987)

58 *Jacobean and Caroline Dramatists*, edited by Fredson Bowers (1987)

59 *American Literary Critics and Scholars, 1800–1850*, edited by John W. Rathbun and Monica M. Grecu (1987)

60 *Canadian Writers Since 1960, Second Series*, edited by W. H. New (1987)

61 *American Writers for Children Since 1960: Poets, Illustrators, and Nonfiction Authors*, edited by Glenn E. Estes (1987)

62 *Elizabethan Dramatists*, edited by Fredson Bowers (1987)

63 *Modern American Critics, 1920–1955*, edited by Gregory S. Jay (1988)

64 *American Literary Critics and Scholars, 1850–1880*, edited by John W. Rathbun and Monica M. Grecu (1988)

65 *French Novelists, 1900–1930*, edited by Catharine Savage Brosman (1988)

66 *German Fiction Writers, 1885–1913*, 2 parts, edited by James Hardin (1988)

67 *Modern American Critics Since 1955*, edited by Gregory S. Jay (1988)

68 *Canadian Writers, 1920–1959, First Series*, edited by W. H. New (1988)

69 *Contemporary German Fiction Writers, First Series*, edited by Wolfgang D. Elfe and James Hardin (1988)

70 *British Mystery Writers, 1860–1919*, edited by Bernard Benstock and Thomas F. Staley (1988)

71 *American Literary Critics and Scholars, 1880–1900,* edited by John W. Rathbun and Monica M. Grecu (1988)

72 *French Novelists, 1930–1960,* edited by Catharine Savage Brosman (1988)

73 *American Magazine Journalists, 1741–1850,* edited by Sam G. Riley (1988)

74 *American Short-Story Writers Before 1880,* edited by Bobby Ellen Kimbel, with the assistance of William E. Grant (1988)

75 *Contemporary German Fiction Writers, Second Series,* edited by Wolfgang D. Elfe and James Hardin (1988)

76 *Afro-American Writers, 1940–1955,* edited by Trudier Harris (1988)

77 *British Mystery Writers, 1920–1939,* edited by Bernard Benstock and Thomas F. Staley (1988)

78 *American Short-Story Writers, 1880–1910,* edited by Bobby Ellen Kimbel, with the assistance of William E. Grant (1988)

79 *American Magazine Journalists, 1850–1900,* edited by Sam G. Riley (1988)

80 *Restoration and Eighteenth-Century Dramatists, First Series,* edited by Paula R. Backscheider (1989)

81 *Austrian Fiction Writers, 1875–1913,* edited by James Hardin and Donald G. Daviau (1989)

82 *Chicano Writers, First Series,* edited by Francisco A. Lomelí and Carl R. Shirley (1989)

83 *French Novelists Since 1960,* edited by Catharine Savage Brosman (1989)

84 *Restoration and Eighteenth-Century Dramatists, Second Series,* edited by Paula R. Backscheider (1989)

85 *Austrian Fiction Writers After 1914,* edited by James Hardin and Donald G. Daviau (1989)

86 *American Short-Story Writers, 1910–1945, First Series,* edited by Bobby Ellen Kimbel (1989)

87 *British Mystery and Thriller Writers Since 1940, First Series,* edited by Bernard Benstock and Thomas F. Staley (1989)

88 *Canadian Writers, 1920–1959, Second Series,* edited by W. H. New (1989)

89 *Restoration and Eighteenth-Century Dramatists, Third Series,* edited by Paula R. Backscheider (1989)

90 *German Writers in the Age of Goethe, 1789–1832,* edited by James Hardin and Christoph E. Schweitzer (1989)

91 *American Magazine Journalists, 1900–1960, First Series,* edited by Sam G. Riley (1990)

92 *Canadian Writers, 1890–1920,* edited by W. H. New (1990)

93 *British Romantic Poets, 1789–1832, First Series,* edited by John R. Greenfield (1990)

94 *German Writers in the Age of Goethe: Sturm und Drang to Classicism,* edited by James Hardin and Christoph E. Schweitzer (1990)

95 *Eighteenth-Century British Poets, First Series,* edited by John Sitter (1990)

96 *British Romantic Poets, 1789–1832, Second Series,* edited by John R. Greenfield (1990)

97 *German Writers from the Enlightenment to Sturm und Drang, 1720–1764,* edited by James Hardin and Christoph E. Schweitzer (1990)

98 *Modern British Essayists, First Series,* edited by Robert Beum (1990)

99 *Canadian Writers Before 1890,* edited by W. H. New (1990)

100 *Modern British Essayists, Second Series,* edited by Robert Beum (1990)

101 *British Prose Writers, 1660–1800, First Series,* edited by Donald T. Siebert (1991)

102 *American Short-Story Writers, 1910–1945, Second Series,* edited by Bobby Ellen Kimbel (1991)

103 *American Literary Biographers, First Series,* edited by Steven Serafin (1991)

104 *British Prose Writers, 1660–1800, Second Series,* edited by Donald T. Siebert (1991)

105 *American Poets Since World War II, Second Series,* edited by R. S. Gwynn (1991)

106 *British Literary Publishing Houses, 1820–1880,* edited by Patricia J. Anderson and Jonathan Rose (1991)

107 *British Romantic Prose Writers, 1789–1832, First Series,* edited by John R. Greenfield (1991)

108 *Twentieth-Century Spanish Poets, First Series,* edited by Michael L. Perna (1991)

109 *Eighteenth-Century British Poets, Second Series,* edited by John Sitter (1991)

110 *British Romantic Prose Writers, 1789–1832, Second Series,* edited by John R. Greenfield (1991)

111 *American Literary Biographers, Second Series,* edited by Steven Serafin (1991)

112 *British Literary Publishing Houses, 1881–1965,* edited by Jonathan Rose and Patricia J. Anderson (1991)

113 *Modern Latin-American Fiction Writers, First Series,* edited by William Luis (1992)

114 *Twentieth-Century Italian Poets, First Series,* edited by Giovanna Wedel De Stasio, Glauco Cambon, and Antonio Illiano (1992)

115 *Medieval Philosophers,* edited by Jeremiah Hackett (1992)

116 *British Romantic Novelists, 1789–1832,* edited by Bradford K. Mudge (1992)

117 *Twentieth-Century Caribbean and Black African Writers, First Series,* edited by Bernth Lindfors and Reinhard Sander (1992)

118 *Twentieth-Century German Dramatists, 1889–1918,* edited by Wolfgang D. Elfe and James Hardin (1992)

119 *Nineteenth-Century French Fiction Writers: Romanticism and Realism, 1800–1860,* edited by Catharine Savage Brosman (1992)

120 *American Poets Since World War II, Third Series,* edited by R. S. Gwynn (1992)

121 *Seventeenth-Century British Nondramatic Poets, First Series,* edited by M. Thomas Hester (1992)

122 *Chicano Writers, Second Series,* edited by Francisco A. Lomelí and Carl R. Shirley (1992)

123 *Nineteenth-Century French Fiction Writers: Naturalism and Beyond, 1860–1900,* edited by Catharine Savage Brosman (1992)

124 *Twentieth-Century German Dramatists, 1919–1992,* edited by Wolfgang D. Elfe and James Hardin (1992)

125 *Twentieth-Century Caribbean and Black African Writers, Second Series,* edited by Bernth Lindfors and Reinhard Sander (1993)

126 *Seventeenth-Century British Nondramatic Poets, Second Series,* edited by M. Thomas Hester (1993)

127 *American Newspaper Publishers, 1950–1990,* edited by Perry J. Ashley (1993)

128 *Twentieth-Century Italian Poets, Second Series,* edited by Giovanna Wedel De Stasio, Glauco Cambon, and Antonio Illiano (1993)

129 *Nineteenth-Century German Writers, 1841–1900,* edited by James Hardin and Siegfried Mews (1993)

130 *American Short-Story Writers Since World War II,* edited by Patrick Meanor (1993)

131 *Seventeenth-Century British Nondramatic Poets, Third Series,* edited by M. Thomas Hester (1993)

132 *Sixteenth-Century British Nondramatic Writers, First Series,* edited by David A. Richardson (1993)

133 *Nineteenth-Century German Writers to 1840,* edited by James Hardin and Siegfried Mews (1993)

134 *Twentieth-Century Spanish Poets, Second Series,* edited by Jerry Phillips Winfield (1994)

135 *British Short-Fiction Writers, 1880–1914: The Realist Tradition,* edited by William B. Thesing (1994)

136 *Sixteenth-Century British Nondramatic Writers, Second Series,* edited by David A. Richardson (1994)

137 *American Magazine Journalists, 1900–1960, Second Series,* edited by Sam G. Riley (1994)

138 *German Writers and Works of the High Middle Ages: 1170–1280,* edited by James Hardin and Will Hasty (1994)

139 *British Short-Fiction Writers, 1945–1980,* edited by Dean Baldwin (1994)

140 *American Book-Collectors and Bibliographers, First Series*, edited by Joseph Rosenblum (1994)

141 *British Children's Writers, 1880–1914*, edited by Laura M. Zaidman (1994)

142 *Eighteenth-Century British Literary Biographers*, edited by Steven Serafin (1994)

143 *American Novelists Since World War II, Third Series*, edited by James R. Giles and Wanda H. Giles (1994)

144 *Nineteenth-Century British Literary Biographers*, edited by Steven Serafin (1994)

145 *Modern Latin-American Fiction Writers, Second Series*, edited by William Luis and Ann González (1994)

146 *Old and Middle English Literature*, edited by Jeffrey Helterman and Jerome Mitchell (1994)

147 *South Slavic Writers Before World War II*, edited by Vasa D. Mihailovich (1994)

148 *German Writers and Works of the Early Middle Ages: 800–1170*, edited by Will Hasty and James Hardin (1994)

149 *Late Nineteenth- and Early Twentieth-Century British Literary Biographers*, edited by Steven Serafin (1995)

150 *Early Modern Russian Writers, Late Seventeenth and Eighteenth Centuries*, edited by Marcus C. Levitt (1995)

151 *British Prose Writers of the Early Seventeenth Century*, edited by Clayton D. Lein (1995)

152 *American Novelists Since World War II, Fourth Series*, edited by James R. Giles and Wanda H. Giles (1995)

153 *Late-Victorian and Edwardian British Novelists, First Series*, edited by George M. Johnson (1995)

154 *The British Literary Book Trade, 1700–1820*, edited by James K. Bracken and Joel Silver (1995)

155 *Twentieth-Century British Literary Biographers*, edited by Steven Serafin (1995)

156 *British Short-Fiction Writers, 1880–1914: The Romantic Tradition*, edited by William F. Naufftus (1995)

157 *Twentieth-Century Caribbean and Black African Writers, Third Series*, edited by Bernth Lindfors and Reinhard Sander (1995)

158 *British Reform Writers, 1789–1832*, edited by Gary Kelly and Edd Applegate (1995)

159 *British Short-Fiction Writers, 1800–1880*, edited by John R. Greenfield (1996)

160 *British Children's Writers, 1914–1960*, edited by Donald R. Hettinga and Gary D. Schmidt (1996)

161 *British Children's Writers Since 1960, First Series*, edited by Caroline Hunt (1996)

162 *British Short-Fiction Writers, 1915–1945*, edited by John H. Rogers (1996)

163 *British Children's Writers, 1800–1880*, edited by Meena Khorana (1996)

164 *German Baroque Writers, 1580–1660*, edited by James Hardin (1996)

165 *American Poets Since World War II, Fourth Series*, edited by Joseph Conte (1996)

166 *British Travel Writers, 1837–1875*, edited by Barbara Brothers and Julia Gergits (1996)

167 *Sixteenth-Century British Nondramatic Writers, Third Series*, edited by David A. Richardson (1996)

168 *German Baroque Writers, 1661–1730*, edited by James Hardin (1996)

169 *American Poets Since World War II, Fifth Series*, edited by Joseph Conte (1996)

170 *The British Literary Book Trade, 1475–1700*, edited by James K. Bracken and Joel Silver (1996)

171 *Twentieth-Century American Sportswriters*, edited by Richard Orodenker (1996)

172 *Sixteenth-Century British Nondramatic Writers, Fourth Series*, edited by David A. Richardson (1996)

173 *American Novelists Since World War II, Fifth Series*, edited by James R. Giles and Wanda H. Giles (1996)

174 *British Travel Writers, 1876–1909*, edited by Barbara Brothers and Julia Gergits (1997)

175 *Native American Writers of the United States*, edited by Kenneth M. Roemer (1997)

176 *Ancient Greek Authors*, edited by Ward W. Briggs (1997)

177 *Italian Novelists Since World War II, 1945–1965*, edited by Augustus Pallotta (1997)

178 *British Fantasy and Science-Fiction Writers Before World War I*, edited by Darren Harris-Fain (1997)

179 *German Writers of the Renaissance and Reformation, 1280–1580*, edited by James Hardin and Max Reinhart (1997)

180 *Japanese Fiction Writers, 1868–1945*, edited by Van C. Gessel (1997)

181 *South Slavic Writers Since World War II*, edited by Vasa D. Mihailovich (1997)

182 *Japanese Fiction Writers Since World War II*, edited by Van C. Gessel (1997)

183 *American Travel Writers, 1776–1864*, edited by James J. Schramer and Donald Ross (1997)

184 *Nineteenth-Century British Book-Collectors and Bibliographers*, edited by William Baker and Kenneth Womack (1997)

185 *American Literary Journalists, 1945–1995, First Series*, edited by Arthur J. Kaul (1998)

186 *Nineteenth-Century American Western Writers*, edited by Robert L. Gale (1998)

187 *American Book Collectors and Bibliographers, Second Series*, edited by Joseph Rosenblum (1998)

188 *American Book and Magazine Illustrators to 1920*, edited by Steven E. Smith, Catherine A. Hastedt, and Donald H. Dyal (1998)

189 *American Travel Writers, 1850–1915*, edited by Donald Ross and James J. Schramer (1998)

190 *British Reform Writers, 1832–1914*, edited by Gary Kelly and Edd Applegate (1998)

191 *British Novelists Between the Wars*, edited by George M. Johnson (1998)

192 *French Dramatists, 1789–1914*, edited by Barbara T. Cooper (1998)

193 *American Poets Since World War II, Sixth Series*, edited by Joseph Conte (1998)

194 *British Novelists Since 1960, Second Series*, edited by Merritt Moseley (1998)

195 *British Travel Writers, 1910–1939*, edited by Barbara Brothers and Julia Gergits (1998)

196 *Italian Novelists Since World War II, 1965–1995*, edited by Augustus Pallotta (1999)

197 *Late-Victorian and Edwardian British Novelists, Second Series*, edited by George M. Johnson (1999)

198 *Russian Literature in the Age of Pushkin and Gogol: Prose*, edited by Christine A. Rydel (1999)

199 *Victorian Women Poets*, edited by William B. Thesing (1999)

200 *American Women Prose Writers to 1820*, edited by Carla J. Mulford, with Angela Vietto and Amy E. Winans (1999)

201 *Twentieth-Century British Book Collectors and Bibliographers*, edited by William Baker and Kenneth Womack (1999)

202 *Nineteenth-Century American Fiction Writers*, edited by Kent P. Ljungquist (1999)

203 *Medieval Japanese Writers*, edited by Steven D. Carter (1999)

204 *British Travel Writers, 1940–1997*, edited by Barbara Brothers and Julia M. Gergits (1999)

205 *Russian Literature in the Age of Pushkin and Gogol: Poetry and Drama*, edited by Christine A. Rydel (1999)

206 *Twentieth-Century American Western Writers, First Series*, edited by Richard H. Cracroft (1999)

207 *British Novelists Since 1960, Third Series*, edited by Merritt Moseley (1999)

208 *Literature of the French and Occitan Middle Ages: Eleventh to Fifteenth Centuries*, edited by Deborah Sinnreich-Levi and Ian S. Laurie (1999)

209 *Chicano Writers, Third Series*, edited by Francisco A. Lomelí and Carl R. Shirley (1999)

210 *Ernest Hemingway: A Documentary Volume*, edited by Robert W. Trogdon (1999)

211 *Ancient Roman Writers*, edited by Ward W. Briggs (1999)

212 *Twentieth-Century American Western Writers, Second Series*, edited by Richard H. Cracroft (1999)

213 *Pre-Nineteenth-Century British Book Collectors and Bibliographers*, edited by William Baker and Kenneth Womack (1999)

214 *Twentieth-Century Danish Writers*, edited by Marianne Stecher-Hansen (1999)

215 *Twentieth-Century Eastern European Writers, First Series*, edited by Steven Serafin (1999)

216 *British Poets of the Great War: Brooke, Rosenberg, Thomas. A Documentary Volume*, edited by Patrick Quinn (2000)

217 *Nineteenth-Century French Poets*, edited by Robert Beum (2000)

218 *American Short-Story Writers Since World War II, Second Series*, edited by Patrick Meanor and Gwen Crane (2000)

219 *F. Scott Fitzgerald's* The Great Gatsby: *A Documentary Volume*, edited by Matthew J. Bruccoli (2000)

220 *Twentieth-Century Eastern European Writers, Second Series*, edited by Steven Serafin (2000)

221 *American Women Prose Writers, 1870–1920*, edited by Sharon M. Harris, with the assistance of Heidi L. M. Jacobs and Jennifer Putzi (2000)

222 *H. L. Mencken: A Documentary Volume*, edited by Richard J. Schrader (2000)

223 *The American Renaissance in New England, Second Series*, edited by Wesley T. Mott (2000)

224 *Walt Whitman: A Documentary Volume*, edited by Joel Myerson (2000)

225 *South African Writers*, edited by Paul A. Scanlon (2000)

226 *American Hard-Boiled Crime Writers*, edited by George Parker Anderson and Julie B. Anderson (2000)

227 *American Novelists Since World War II, Sixth Series*, edited by James R. Giles and Wanda H. Giles (2000)

228 *Twentieth-Century American Dramatists, Second Series*, edited by Christopher J. Wheatley (2000)

229 *Thomas Wolfe: A Documentary Volume*, edited by Ted Mitchell (2001)

230 *Australian Literature, 1788–1914*, edited by Selina Samuels (2001)

231 *British Novelists Since 1960, Fourth Series*, edited by Merritt Moseley (2001)

232 *Twentieth-Century Eastern European Writers, Third Series*, edited by Steven Serafin (2001)

233 *British and Irish Dramatists Since World War II, Second Series*, edited by John Bull (2001)

234 *American Short-Story Writers Since World War II, Third Series*, edited by Patrick Meanor and Richard E. Lee (2001)

235 *The American Renaissance in New England, Third Series*, edited by Wesley T. Mott (2001)

236 *British Rhetoricians and Logicians, 1500–1660*, edited by Edward A. Malone (2001)

237 *The Beats: A Documentary Volume*, edited by Matt Theado (2001)

238 *Russian Novelists in the Age of Tolstoy and Dostoevsky*, edited by J. Alexander Ogden and Judith E. Kalb (2001)

239 *American Women Prose Writers: 1820–1870*, edited by Amy E. Hudock and Katharine Rodier (2001)

240 *Late Nineteenth- and Early Twentieth-Century British Women Poets*, edited by William B. Thesing (2001)

241 *American Sportswriters and Writers on Sport*, edited by Richard Orodenker (2001)

242 *Twentieth-Century European Cultural Theorists, First Series*, edited by Paul Hansom (2001)

243 *The American Renaissance in New England, Fourth Series*, edited by Wesley T. Mott (2001)

244 *American Short-Story Writers Since World War II, Fourth Series*, edited by Patrick Meanor and Joseph McNicholas (2001)

245 *British and Irish Dramatists Since World War II, Third Series*, edited by John Bull (2001)

246 *Twentieth-Century American Cultural Theorists*, edited by Paul Hansom (2001)

247 *James Joyce: A Documentary Volume*, edited by A. Nicholas Fargnoli (2001)

248 *Antebellum Writers in the South, Second Series*, edited by Kent Ljungquist (2001)

249 *Twentieth-Century American Dramatists, Third Series*, edited by Christopher Wheatley (2002)

250 *Antebellum Writers in New York, Second Series*, edited by Kent Ljungquist (2002)

251 *Canadian Fantasy and Science-Fiction Writers*, edited by Douglas Ivison (2002)

252 *British Philosophers, 1500–1799*, edited by Philip B. Dematteis and Peter S. Fosl (2002)

253 *Raymond Chandler: A Documentary Volume*, edited by Robert Moss (2002)

254 *The House of Putnam, 1837–1872: A Documentary Volume*, edited by Ezra Greenspan (2002)

255 *British Fantasy and Science-Fiction Writers, 1918–1960*, edited by Darren Harris-Fain (2002)

256 *Twentieth-Century American Western Writers, Third Series*, edited by Richard H. Cracroft (2002)

257 *Twentieth-Century Swedish Writers After World War II*, edited by Ann-Charlotte Gavel Adams (2002)

258 *Modern French Poets*, edited by Jean-François Leroux (2002)

259 *Twentieth-Century Swedish Writers Before World War II*, edited by Ann-Charlotte Gavel Adams (2002)

260 *Australian Writers, 1915–1950*, edited by Selina Samuels (2002)

261 *British Fantasy and Science-Fiction Writers Since 1960*, edited by Darren Harris-Fain (2002)

262 *British Philosophers, 1800–2000*, edited by Peter S. Fosl and Leemon B. McHenry (2002)

263 *William Shakespeare: A Documentary Volume*, edited by Catherine Loomis (2002)

264 *Italian Prose Writers, 1900–1945*, edited by Luca Somigli and Rocco Capozzi (2002)

265 *American Song Lyricists, 1920–1960*, edited by Philip Furia (2002)

266 *Twentieth-Century American Dramatists, Fourth Series*, edited by Christopher J. Wheatley (2002)

267 *Twenty-First-Century British and Irish Novelists*, edited by Michael R. Molino (2002)

268 *Seventeenth-Century French Writers*, edited by Françoise Jaouën (2002)

269 *Nathaniel Hawthorne: A Documentary Volume*, edited by Benjamin Franklin V (2002)

270 *American Philosophers Before 1950*, edited by Philip B. Dematteis and Leemon B. McHenry (2002)

271 *British and Irish Novelists Since 1960*, edited by Merritt Moseley (2002)

272 *Russian Prose Writers Between the World Wars*, edited by Christine Rydel (2003)

273 *F. Scott Fitzgerald's* Tender Is the Night: *A Documentary Volume*, edited by Matthew J. Bruccoli and George Parker Anderson (2003)

274 *John Dos Passos's* U.S.A.: *A Documentary Volume*, edited by Donald Pizer (2003)

275 *Twentieth-Century American Nature Writers: Prose*, edited by Roger Thompson and J. Scott Bryson (2003)

276 *British Mystery and Thriller Writers Since 1960*, edited by Gina Macdonald (2003)

277 *Russian Literature in the Age of Realism*, edited by Alyssa Dinega Gillespie (2003)

278 *American Novelists Since World War II, Seventh Series*, edited by James R. Giles and Wanda H. Giles (2003)

279 *American Philosophers, 1950–2000*, edited by Philip B. Dematteis and Leemon B. McHenry (2003)

280 *Dashiell Hammett's* The Maltese Falcon: *A Documentary Volume*, edited by Richard Layman (2003)

281 *British Rhetoricians and Logicians, 1500–1660, Second Series*, edited by Edward A. Malone (2003)

282 *New Formalist Poets*, edited by Jonathan N. Barron and Bruce Meyer (2003)

283 *Modern Spanish American Poets, First Series*, edited by María A. Salgado (2003)

284 *The House of Holt, 1866–1946: A Documentary Volume*, edited by Ellen D. Gilbert (2003)

285 *Russian Writers Since 1980,* edited by Marina Balina and Mark Lipoyvetsky (2004)

286 *Castilian Writers, 1400–1500,* edited by Frank A. Domínguez and George D. Greenia (2004)

287 *Portuguese Writers,* edited by Monica Rector and Fred M. Clark (2004)

288 *The House of Boni & Liveright, 1917–1933: A Documentary Volume,* edited by Charles Egleston (2004)

289 *Australian Writers, 1950–1975,* edited by Selina Samuels (2004)

290 *Modern Spanish American Poets, Second Series,* edited by María A. Salgado (2004)

291 *The Hoosier House: Bobbs-Merrill and Its Predecessors, 1850–1985: A Documentary Volume,* edited by Richard J. Schrader (2004)

292 *Twenty-First-Century American Novelists,* edited by Lisa Abney and Suzanne Disheroon-Green (2004)

293 *Icelandic Writers,* edited by Patrick J. Stevens (2004)

294 *James Gould Cozzens: A Documentary Volume,* edited by Matthew J. Bruccoli (2004)

295 *Russian Writers of the Silver Age, 1890–1925,* edited by Judith E. Kalb and J. Alexander Ogden with the collaboration of I. G. Vishnevetsky (2004)

296 *Twentieth-Century European Cultural Theorists, Second Series,* edited by Paul Hansom (2004)

297 *Twentieth-Century Norwegian Writers,* edited by Tanya Thresher (2004)

298 *Henry David Thoreau: A Documentary Volume,* edited by Richard J. Schneider (2004)

299 *Holocaust Novelists,* edited by Efraim Sicher (2004)

300 *Danish Writers from the Reformation to Decadence, 1550–1900,* edited by Marianne Stecher-Hansen (2004)

301 *Gustave Flaubert: A Documentary Volume,* edited by Éric Le Calvez (2004)

302 *Russian Prose Writers After World War II,* edited by Christine Rydel (2004)

303 *American Radical and Reform Writers, First Series,* edited by Steven Rosendale (2005)

304 *Bram Stoker's* Dracula: *A Documentary Volume,* edited by Elizabeth Miller (2005)

305 *Latin American Dramatists, First Series,* edited by Adam Versényi (2005)

306 *American Mystery and Detective Writers,* edited by George Parker Anderson (2005)

307 *Brazilian Writers,* edited by Monica Rector and Fred M. Clark (2005)

308 *Ernest Hemingway's* A Farewell to Arms: *A Documentary Volume,* edited by Charles Oliver (2005)

309 *John Steinbeck: A Documentary Volume,* edited by Luchen Li (2005)

310 *British and Irish Dramatists Since World War II, Fourth Series,* edited by John Bull (2005)

311 *Arabic Literary Culture, 500–925,* edited by Michael Cooperson and Shawkat M. Toorawa (2005)

312 *Asian American Writers,* edited by Deborah L. Madsen (2005)

313 *Writers of the French Enlightenment, I,* edited by Samia I. Spencer (2005)

314 *Writers of the French Enlightenment, II,* edited by Samia I. Spencer (2005)

315 *Langston Hughes: A Documentary Volume,* edited by Christopher C. De Santis (2005)

316 *American Prose Writers of World War I: A Documentary Volume,* edited by Steven Trout (2005)

317 *Twentieth-Century Russian Émigré Writers,* edited by María Rubins (2005)

318 *Sixteenth-Century Spanish Writers,* edited by Gregory B. Kaplan (2006)

319 *British and Irish Short-Fiction Writers 1945–2000,* edited by Cheryl Alexander Malcolm and David Malcolm (2006)

320 *Robert Penn Warren: A Documentary Volume,* edited by James A. Grimshaw Jr. (2006)

321 *Twentieth-Century French Dramatists,* edited by Mary Anne O'Neil (2006)

322 *Twentieth-Century Spanish Fiction Writers,* edited by Marta E. Altisent and Cristina Martínez-Carazo (2006)

323 *South Asian Writers in English,* edited by Fakrul Alam (2006)

324 *John O'Hara: A Documentary Volume,* edited by Matthew J. Bruccoli (2006)

325 *Australian Writers, 1975–2000,* edited by Selina Samuels (2006)

326 *Booker Prize Novels, 1969–2005,* edited by Merritt Moseley (2006)

327 *Sixteenth-Century French Writers,* edited by Megan Conway (2006)

328 *Chinese Fiction Writers, 1900–1949,* edited by Thomas Moran (2007)

329 *Nobel Prize Laureates in Literature, Part 1: Agnon–Eucken* (2007)

330 *Nobel Prize Laureates in Literature, Part 2: Faulkner–Kipling* (2007)

331 *Nobel Prize Laureates in Literature, Part 3: Lagerkvist–Pontoppidan* (2007)

332 *Nobel Prize Laureates in Literature, Part 4: Quasimodo–Yeats* (2007)

333 *Writers in Yiddish,* edited by Joseph Sherman (2007)

334 *Twenty-First-Century Canadian Writers,* edited by Christian Riegel (2007)

335 *American Short-Story Writers Since World War II, Fifth Series,* edited by Richard E. Lee and Patrick Meanor (2007)

336 *Eighteenth-Century British Historians,* edited by Ellen J. Jenkins (2007)

337 *Castilian Writers, 1200–1400,* edited by George D. Greenia and Frank A. Domínguez (2008)

338 *Thomas Carlyle: A Documentary Volume,* edited by Frances Frame (2008)

339 *Seventeenth-Century Italian Poets and Dramatists,* edited by Albert N. Mancini and Glenn Palen Pierce (2008)

340 *The Brontës: A Documentary Volume,* edited by Susan B. Taylor (2008)

341 *Twentieth-Century American Dramatists, Fifth Series,* edited by Garrett Eisler (2008)

342 *Twentieth-Century American Nature Poets,* edited by J. Scott Bryson and Roger Thompson (2008)

343 *Mark Twain's* Adventures of Huckleberry Finn: *A Documentary Volume,* edited by Tom Quirk (2009)

344 *Nineteenth-Century British Dramatists,* edited by Angela Courtney (2009)

345 *American Radical and Reform Writers, Second Series,* edited by Hester Lee Furey (2009)

346 *Twentieth-Century Arab Writers,* edited by Majd Yaser Al-Mallah and Coeli Fitzpatrick (2009)

347 *Twenty-First-Century "Black" British Writers,* edited by R. Victoria Arana (2009)

348 *Southeast Asian Writers,* edited by David Smyth (2009)

349 *Herman Melville's* Moby-Dick: *A Documentary Volume,* edited by Jean-François Leroux (2009)

350 *Twenty-First-Century American Novelists, Second Series,* edited by Wanda H. Giles and James R. Giles (2009)

351 *Ralph Waldo Emerson: A Documentary Volume,* edited by Ronald A. Bosco and Joel Myerson (2010)

352 *Twentieth-Century British Humorists,* edited by Paul Matthew St. Pierre (2010)

353 *Twenty-First-Century Central and Eastern European Writers,* edited by Steven Serafin and Vasa D. Mihailovich (2010)

354 *Norwegian Writers, 1500 to 1900,* edited by Lanae H. Isaacson (2010)

Dictionary of Literary Biography Documentary Series

1 *Sherwood Anderson, Willa Cather, John Dos Passos, Theodore Dreiser, F. Scott Fitzgerald, Ernest Hemingway, Sinclair Lewis,* edited by Margaret A. Van Antwerp (1982)

2 *James Gould Cozzens, James T. Farrell, William Faulkner, John O'Hara, John Steinbeck, Thomas Wolfe, Richard Wright,* edited by Margaret A. Van Antwerp (1982)

3 *Saul Bellow, Jack Kerouac, Norman Mailer, Vladimir Nabokov, John Updike, Kurt Vonnegut,* edited by Mary Bruccoli (1983)

4 *Tennessee Williams,* edited by Margaret A. Van Antwerp and Sally Johns (1984)

5 *American Transcendentalists,* edited by Joel Myerson (1988)

6 *Hardboiled Mystery Writers: Raymond Chandler, Dashiell Hammett, Ross Macdonald,* edited by Matthew J. Bruccoli and Richard Layman (1989)

7 *Modern American Poets: James Dickey, Robert Frost, Marianne Moore,* edited by Karen L. Rood (1989)

8 *The Black Aesthetic Movement,* edited by Jeffrey Louis Decker (1991)

9 *American Writers of the Vietnam War: W. D. Ehrhart, Larry Heinemann, Tim O'Brien, Walter McDonald, John M. Del Vecchio,* edited by Ronald Baughman (1991)

10 *The Bloomsbury Group,* edited by Edward L. Bishop (1992)

11 *American Proletarian Culture: The Twenties and The Thirties,* edited by Jon Christian Suggs (1993)

12 *Southern Women Writers: Flannery O'Connor, Katherine Anne Porter, Eudora Welty,* edited by Mary Ann Wimsatt and Karen L. Rood (1994)

13 *The House of Scribner, 1846–1904,* edited by John Delaney (1996)

14 *Four Women Writers for Children, 1868–1918,* edited by Caroline C. Hunt (1996)

15 *American Expatriate Writers: Paris in the Twenties,* edited by Matthew J. Bruccoli and Robert W. Trogdon (1997)

16 *The House of Scribner, 1905–1930,* edited by John Delaney (1997)

17 *The House of Scribner, 1931–1984,* edited by John Delaney (1998)

18 *British Poets of The Great War: Sassoon, Graves, Owen,* edited by Patrick Quinn (1999)

19 *James Dickey,* edited by Judith S. Baughman (1999)

See also DLB 210, 216, 219, 222, 224, 229, 237, 247, 253, 254, 263, 269, 273, 274, 280, 284, 288, 291, 294, 298, 301, 304, 308, 309, 315, 316, 320, 324, 338, 340, 343, 349, 351

Dictionary of Literary Biography Yearbooks

1980 edited by Karen L. Rood, Jean W. Ross, and Richard Ziegfeld (1981)

1981 edited by Karen L. Rood, Jean W. Ross, and Richard Ziegfeld (1982)

1982 edited by Richard Ziegfeld; associate editors: Jean W. Ross and Lynne C. Zeigler (1983)

1983 edited by Mary Bruccoli and Jean W. Ross; associate editor Richard Ziegfeld (1984)

1984 edited by Jean W. Ross (1985)

1985 edited by Jean W. Ross (1986)

1986 edited by J. M. Brook (1987)

1987 edited by J. M. Brook (1988)

1988 edited by J. M. Brook (1989)

1989 edited by J. M. Brook (1990)

1990 edited by James W. Hipp (1991)

1991 edited by James W. Hipp (1992)

1992 edited by James W. Hipp (1993)

1993 edited by James W. Hipp, contributing editor George Garrett (1994)

1994 edited by James W. Hipp, contributing editor George Garrett (1995)

1995 edited by James W. Hipp, contributing editor George Garrett (1996)

1996 edited by Samuel W. Bruce and L. Kay Webster, contributing editor George Garrett (1997)

1997 edited by Matthew J. Bruccoli and George Garrett, with the assistance of L. Kay Webster (1998)

1998 edited by Matthew J. Bruccoli, contributing editor George Garrett, with the assistance of D. W. Thomas (1999)

1999 edited by Matthew J. Bruccoli, contributing editor George Garrett, with the assistance of D. W. Thomas (2000)

2000 edited by Matthew J. Bruccoli, contributing editor George Garrett, with the assistance of George Parker Anderson (2001)

2001 edited by Matthew J. Bruccoli, contributing editor George Garrett, with the assistance of George Parker Anderson (2002)

2002 edited by Matthew J. Bruccoli and George Garrett; George Parker Anderson, Assistant Editor (2003)

Concise Series

Concise Dictionary of American Literary Biography, 7 volumes (1988–1999): *The New Consciousness, 1941–1968; Colonization to the American Renaissance, 1640–1865; Realism, Naturalism, and Local Color, 1865–1917; The Twenties, 1917–1929; The Age of Maturity, 1929–1941; Broadening Views, 1968–1988; Supplement: Modern Writers, 1900–1998.*

Concise Dictionary of British Literary Biography, 8 volumes (1991–1992): *Writers of the Middle Ages and Renaissance Before 1660; Writers of the Restoration and Eighteenth Century, 1660–1789; Writers of the Romantic Period, 1789–1832; Victorian Writers, 1832–1890; Late-Victorian and Edwardian Writers, 1890–1914; Modern Writers, 1914–1945; Writers After World War II, 1945–1960; Contemporary Writers, 1960 to Present.*

Concise Dictionary of World Literary Biography, 4 volumes (1999–2000): *Ancient Greek and Roman Writers; German Writers; African, Caribbean, and Latin American Writers; South Slavic and Eastern European Writers.*

Dictionary of Literary Biography® • Volume Three Hundred Fifty-Four

Norwegian Writers, 1500 to 1900

ISSN 1096-8547

Dictionary of Literary Biography® • Volume Three Hundred Fifty-Four

Norwegian Writers, 1500 to 1900

Edited by
Lanae H. Isaacson

A Bruccoli Clark Layman Book

GALE
CENGAGE Learning

**Dictionary of Literary Biography,
Volume 354: Norwegian Writers,
1500 to 1900**
Lanae H. Isaacson

Founding Editors:
  Matthew J. Bruccoli, Editorial Director
    (1931–2008)
  C. E. Frazer Clark Jr., Managing Editor
    (1925–2001)

Advisory Board: John Baker,
  William Cagle, Patrick O'Connor,
  Trudier Harris, Alvin Kernan

Editorial Director: Richard Layman

@ 2010 Gale, Cengage Learning

ALL RIGHTS RESERVED. No part of this work covered by the copyright herein may be reproduced, transmitted, stored, or used in any form or by any means graphic, electronic, or mechanical, including but not limited to photocopying, recording, scanning, digitizing, taping, Web distribution, information networks, or information storage and retrieval systems, except as permitted under Section 107 or 108 of the 1976 United States Copyright Act, without the prior written permission of the publisher.

This publication is a creative work fully protected by all applicable copyright laws, as well as by misappropriation, trade secret, unfair competition, and other applicable laws. The authors and editors of this work have added value to the underlying factual material herein through one or more of the following: unique and original selection, coordination, expression, arrangement, and classification of the information.

For product information and technology assistance, contact us at
Gale Customer Support, 1-800-877-4253.
For permission to use material from this text or product, submit all requests online at **www.cengage.com/permissions**
Further permissions questions can be e-mailed to
permissionrequest@cengage.com

While every effort has been made to ensure the reliability of the information presented in this publication, Gale, a part of Cengage Learning, does not guarantee the accuracy of the data contained herein. Gale accepts no payment for listing; and inclusion in the publication of any organization, agency, institution, publication, service, or individual does not imply endorsement of the editors or publisher. Errors brought to the attention of the publisher and verified to the satisfaction of the publisher will be corrected in future editions.

EDITORIAL DATA PRIVACY POLICY. Does this publication contain information about you as an individual? If so, for more information about our editorial data privacy policies, please see our Privacy Statement at www.gale.cengage.com

LIBRARY OF CONGRESS CATALOGING-IN-PUBLICATION DATA

Norwegian writers, 1500 to 1900 / edited by Lanae H. Isaacson.
  p. cm. — (Dictionary of literary biography ; v. 354)
"A Bruccoli Clark Layman book."
Includes bibliographical references and index.
ISBN-13: 978-0-7876-8172-2
ISBN-10: 0-7876-8172-5
1. Authors, Norwegian—16th century—Biography. 2. Authors, Norwegian—17th century—Biography. 3. Authors, Norwegian—18th century—Biography. 4. Authors, Norwegian—19th century—Biography. 5. Authors, Norwegian—16th century—Bio-bibliography. 6. Authors, Norwegian—17th century—Bio-bibliography. 7. Authors, Norwegian—18th century—Bio-bibliography. 8. Authors, Norwegian—19th century—Bio-bibliography. 9. Norwegian literature—16th century—Bio-bibliography. 10. Norwegian literature—17th century—Bio-bibliography. 11. Norwegian literature—18th century—Bio-bibliography. 12. Norwegian literature—19th century—Bio-bibliography.
I. Isaacson, Lanae H.
  PT8405.N67 2009
  839.82—dc22
  [B]
                                          2009039164

ISBN-13: 978-0-7876-8172-2   ISBN-10: 0-7876-8172-5
ISSN 1096-8547

Gale
27500 Drake Rd.
Farmington Hills, MI 48331-3535

Printed in the United States of America
1 2 3 4 5 6 7 13 12 11 10 09

*In Loving Memory of Those Who Have
Gone Before . . .
Kareen Isaacson
James LeConte Isaacson
Ruby Runnels Isaacson*

Contents

Plan of the Series xv

Introduction xvii

Ivar Aasen (1813–1896) 3
   Eirik Helleve

Peter Christen Asbjørnsen (1812–1885) 13
   Donna H. Stockton

Absalon Pederssøn Beyer (1528?–1575) 20
   Lanae H. Isaacson

Bjørnstjerne Bjørnson (1832–1910) 25
   Ann Schmiesing

Niels Krog Bredal (1732–1778) 39
   Lanae H. Isaacson

Johan Nordahl Brun (1745–1816) 44
   Lanae H. Isaacson

Sophus Bugge (1833–1907) 49
   Lanae H. Isaacson

Camilla Collett (1813–1895) 56
   Donna H. Stockton

Petter Dass (1647–1707) 70
   Lanae H. Isaacson

Hans Egede (1686–1758) .82
   Lanae H. Isaacson

Kristian Elster (1841–1881) 87
   Lanae H. Isaacson

Dorothe Engelbretsdatter (1634–1716) 93
   Laila Akslen

Claus Fasting (1746–1791) 100
   Lanae H. Isaacson

Arne Garborg (1851–1924) 104
   Jan Sjåvik

Hulda Garborg (1862–1934) 118
   Torild Homstad

Maurits Hansen (1794–1842) 123
   Bjørn Tysdahl

Gunnar Heiberg (1857–1929) 130
   Tanya Thresher

Henrik Ibsen (1828–1906) 136
   Astrid Sæther

Hans Jæger (1854–1910) 151
   Dean Krouk

Drude Krog Janson (Judith Keller) (1846–1934) . . 158
   Ingrid K. Urberg

Alexander L. Kielland (1849–1906) 163
   Hans H. Skei

Jens Kraft (1720–1765) 171
   Carl Henrik Koch

Vilhelm Krag (1871–1933) 175
   Henning Howlid Wærp

Magnus Brostrup Landstad (1802–1880) 188
   Lanae H. Isaacson

Jonas Lie (1833–1908) 195
   Milda Ostrauskaite

Jørgen Moe (1813–1882) 210
   Aaron Schmitt

Andreas Munch (1811–1884) 216
   Henning Howlid Wærp

Johan Storm Munch (1778–1832) 224
   Lanae H. Isaacson

Sigbjørn Obstfelder (1866–1900) 228
   Jan Sjåvik

Alvilde Prydz (1846–1922) 234
   John Eason

Dagny Juel Pryzbyszewska (1867–1901) 239
   Lanae H. Isaacson

Per Sivle (1857–1904) 246
   Eirik Helleve

Amalie Skram (1846–1905) 252
   Katherine Hanson and Judith Messick

Contents

Mattis Størssøn (ca. 1500–1569)............... 267
Lanae H. Isaacson

Magdalene Thoresen (1819–1903)............. 270
Lorna Selley

Christian Braunmann Tullin (1728–1765) 275
Lanae H. Isaacson

Johan Vibe (1748–1782) 280
Lanae H. Isaacson

A. O. Vinje (1818–1870) 283
Jan Sjåvik

Nils Collett Vogt (1864–1937) 288
Hans H. Skei

Johan Sebastian Welhaven (1807–1873) 292
Jan Sjåvik

Henrik Wergeland (1808–1845) 301
Ann Schmiesing

Books for Further Reading 315
Contributors 317
Index 321

Plan of the Series

... Almost the most prodigious asset of a country, and perhaps its most precious possession, is its native literary product—when that product is fine and noble and enduring.

Mark Twain*

The advisory board, the editors, and the publisher of the *Dictionary of Literary Biography* are joined in endorsing Mark Twain's declaration. The literature of a nation provides an inexhaustible resource of permanent worth. Our purpose is to make literature and its creators better understood and more accessible to students and the reading public, while satisfying the needs of teachers and researchers.

To meet these requirements, *literary biography* has been construed in terms of the author's achievement. The most important thing about a writer is his writing. Accordingly, the entries in *DLB* are career biographies, tracing the development of the author's canon and the evolution of his reputation.

The purpose of *DLB* is not only to provide reliable information in a usable format but also to place the figures in the larger perspective of literary history and to offer appraisals of their accomplishments by qualified scholars.

The publication plan for *DLB* resulted from two years of preparation. The project was proposed to Bruccoli Clark by Frederick G. Ruffner, president of the Gale Research Company, in November 1975. After specimen entries were prepared and typeset, an advisory board was formed to refine the entry format and develop the series rationale. In meetings held during 1976, the publisher, series editors, and advisory board approved the scheme for a comprehensive biographical dictionary of persons who contributed to literature. Editorial work on the first volume began in January 1977, and it was published in 1978. In order to make *DLB* more than a dictionary and to compile volumes that individually have claim to status as literary history, it was decided to organize volumes by topic, period, or genre. Each of these freestanding volumes provides a

*From an unpublished section of Mark Twain's autobiography, copyright by the Mark Twain Company

biographical-bibliographical guide and overview for a particular area of literature. We are convinced that this organization—as opposed to a single alphabet method—constitutes a valuable innovation in the presentation of reference material. The volume plan necessarily requires many decisions for the placement and treatment of authors. Certain figures will be included in separate volumes, but with different entries emphasizing the aspect of his career appropriate to each volume. Ernest Hemingway, for example, is represented in *American Writers in Paris, 1920–1939* by an entry focusing on his expatriate apprenticeship; he is also in *American Novelists, 1910–1945* with an entry surveying his entire career, as well as in *American Short-Story Writers, 1910–1945, Second Series* with an entry concentrating on his short fiction. Each volume includes a cumulative index of the subject authors and articles.

Between 1981 and 2002 the series was augmented and updated by the *DLB Yearbooks*. There have also been nineteen *DLB Documentary Series* volumes, which provide illustrations, facsimiles, and biographical and critical source materials for figures, works, or groups judged to have particular interest for students. In 1999 the *Documentary Series* was incorporated into the *DLB* volume numbering system beginning with *DLB 210: Ernest Hemingway*.

We define literature as the *intellectual commerce of a nation:* not merely as belles lettres but as that ample and complex process by which ideas are generated, shaped, and transmitted. *DLB* entries are not limited to "creative writers" but extend to other figures who in their time and in their way influenced the mind of a people. Thus the series encompasses historians, journalists, publishers, book collectors, and screenwriters. By this means readers of *DLB* may be aided to perceive literature not as cult scripture in the keeping of intellectual high priests but firmly positioned at the center of a nation's life.

DLB includes the major writers appropriate to each volume and those standing in the ranks behind them. Scholarly and critical counsel has been sought in deciding which minor figures to include and how full their entries should be. Wherever possible, useful references are made to figures who do not warrant separate entries.

Each *DLB* volume has an expert volume editor responsible for planning the volume, selecting the figures for inclusion, and assigning the entries. Volume editors are also responsible for preparing, where appropriate, appendices surveying the major periodicals and literary and intellectual movements for their volumes, as well as lists of further readings. Work on the series as a whole is coordinated at the Bruccoli Clark Layman editorial center in Columbia, South Carolina, where the editorial staff is responsible for accuracy and utility of the published volumes.

One feature that distinguishes *DLB* is the illustration policy—its concern with the iconography of literature. Just as an author is influenced by his surroundings, so is the reader's understanding of the author enhanced by a knowledge of his environment. Therefore *DLB* volumes include not only drawings, paintings, and photographs of authors, often depicting them at various stages in their careers, but also illustrations of their families and places where they lived. Title pages are regularly reproduced in facsimile along with dust jackets for modern authors. The dust jackets are a special feature of *DLB* because they often document better than anything else the way in which an author's work was perceived in its own time. Specimens of the writers' manuscripts and letters are included when feasible.

Samuel Johnson rightly decreed that "The chief glory of every people arises from its authors." The purpose of the *Dictionary of Literary Biography* is to compile literary history in the surest way available to us—by accurate and comprehensive treatment of the lives and work of those who contributed to it.

The *DLB* Advisory Board

Introduction

Nordic literary historians often refer to the literature written during the four-hundred-year union between Denmark and Norway as *fælleslitteratur* (shared literature), as though the two countries were literary twins and had a single culture, history, and heritage under the hegemony of the Danish monarchy. While it is true Denmark and Norway shared cultural, educational, and religious values, the two cultures were distinct; they may have been twins in some ways but they were hardly identical. Norway had an independent literary voice before, throughout, and after the union; it could lay claim to its own identity, its own place in a larger world, and its own connections to a distant Europe. Norwegians also helped shape the literature of Denmark. Ludvig Holberg, born in Bergen, is regarded by many as the father of Danish theater, and the poets Christian Braunmann Tullin (1728–1765) and Johan Herman Wessel and the folklorists Magnus Brostrup Landstad (1802–1880), Peter Christen Asbjørnsen (1812–1885), and Jørgen Moe (1813–1882) made contributions to Danish literature, folklore, and literary history. (Both Danes and Norwegians lay claim to Holberg and Wessel as literary sons; see *DLB 300: Danish Writers from the Reformation to Decadence, 1550–1900* for essays on these authors.)

The term *fælleslitteratur* fits in part–and only in part–if the *fælles* half of the term is restricted to the language used in writing. If, on the other hand, one considers the content of the literature, its subjects, themes, descriptions, and goals, then the idea of a single literature for both countries breaks down–and a disservice is done to each. Much of the literature written in Norway between 1500 and 1900 expressed and developed themes, subjects, and settings that could only be Norwegian. To gain a deeper and a broader understanding of the literature of the region, one must go beyond the simplifying designation of *fælleslitteratur*.

Through the biographies of forty-one authors, *DLB 354: Norwegian Writers, 1500–1900* surveys Norwegian literature from the humanism of the vibrant, worldly Hanseatic city of Bergen in the sixteenth century to the symbolism, expressionism, and fin-de-siècle poetry and prose associated with Europe and with Christiania, a capital city at the end of the nineteenth century on the verge of taking its place among major modern European cities. (Christiania is now known as Oslo, the name originally given to the town founded circa 1000 on the Bjørvika inlet. After a devastating fire in 1624, Oslo was rebuilt, slightly relocated, and renamed Christiania by King Christian IV. The name was spelled *Kristiania* from 1874 to 1925, when it was changed back to Oslo. To avoid confusion, Christiania is used throughout this volume.) Norway came into its own as a literary powerhouse in the nineteenth century, a period of literary ferment when most of the authors covered in this volume lived. This introduction places the authors covered in this volume in a chronological framework, except that Henrik Ibsen (1828–1906), whose status as one of the great authors of the world requires special treatment, is discussed last.

The story told by *DLB 354* begins with a man who left nothing in the way of manuscripts or personal papers or books and is not a subject for an entry: Geble Pederssøn (1490–1557). The last Catholic bishop and first Lutheran superintendent in Bergen, Pederssøn played the role of literary father to the Bergen humanists Mattis Størssøn (circa 1500–1569) and Absalon Pederssøn Beyer (1528?–1575). He founded the Bergen Cathedral Latin School, an institution central to the education of Beyer and other civic and religious leaders. Under Pederssøn's influence, Bergen achieved primacy as the center for humanism in Norway, the place where the lamp of learning flamed most brightly. The steps Pederssøn took to promote learning and the study of Norwegian history led in large part to Størssøn's *Norske Kongers Krønicke* (1594, The Norwegian Royal Chronicle) and Beyer's *Oration om Mester Geble, 1571* (1963, Oration on Master Geble, 1571), a biography of the superintendent, and *Om Norgis Rige* (1780, On the Kingdom of Norway). All three of these works–written in the Danish of the day by well-educated pillars of the community–deal with the Norway of the past and of their day.

The seventeenth century in Norway is represented by two colleagues and friends, poets who carried on an extensive correspondence across considerable geographical distance: Dorothe Engelbretsdatter (1634–1716) in Bergen and Petter Dass (1647–1707), far to the north in Alstahaug, Helgeland. Engelbretsdatter, the first woman writer of note in Norway, gave the Norwegian religious community hymns that are still included in *Norsk Salmebok* (1985, Norwegian Hymns), the current hymnal. Engelbretsdatter also wrote elegies and eulogies for important members of her community as well as poems on current events in Bergen. Dass, the bishop of Alstahaug, was known for his contributions to religious, ceremonial, and celebratory poetry of the day. His most important literary legacy by far is *Nordlandstrompet* (1739, The Trumpet of the North), a record of an excursion through the far north of Norway that provides a valuable examination of the region. At once poetry and an effort to portray people, *Nordlandstrompet* is a work that resonates with modern readers as well as literary historians.

The eighteenth century brought an age of inquiry and enlightenment to Norway and the rest of Europe. Scientific and philosophical societies flourished, and universities began to develop new approaches to teaching and learning; scholars exchanged ideas and posited new theories about culture and how human beings operated and behaved in societies. Jens Kraft (1720–1765), a professor of mathematics and philosophy at the Sorøe Ridder-Akademie in Denmark, became a founder of scientific anthropology. Hans Egede (1686–1758) earned a niche in Danish and Norwegian history as the Apostle of Greenland and as the leader of an important trade mission that secured Danish/Norwegian commerce in the face of fierce competition from the Dutch. Egede's claim to literary fame rests with his studies and accounts of life and work among the Inuit on Greenland. Going beyond the scientific and philosophical approach, eighteenth-century authors also viewed nature in emotional and personal terms. The poets Tullin and Johan Nordahl Brun (1745–1816) depict the experience of communing with nature as a glorious idyll. Tullin's poetry served the needs of a Christiania aristocracy for elegant, refined *leilighetsdiktning* (occasional poetry), while Brun created songs that revealed a pride in Norway that all felt. Literary historians have sometimes seen the stirrings of Norwegian nationalism in Brun's songs, and his work was such that more revolutionary minds may well have used Brun's words as rallying cries in the cause. But though Brun was first and foremost a Norwegian patriot, a man with a deep love for his homeland, he was also fiercely loyal to the Danish monarch in Copenhagen.

Working with the Italian composer Guiseppe Sarti, Niels Krog Bredal (1732–1778) is credited with creating the first Danish national heroic play, the *syngespil* (musical drama) *Gram og Signe* (1756, Gram and Signe), as well as the first Danish *pastoreller* (pastoral), *Eremiten* (1758, The Hermit). Wildly popular with the royal court and courtly audiences, the *syngespil* and *pastoreller* of the Bredal-Sarti team combined the alexandrines of French poetry with popular Italian opera. Such plays either served as the main fare for an evening at the theater or were intermezzi between longer plays and operas. From 1761 to 1770 Bredal served as mayor of Trondheim, a progressive, lively city. He returned to Copenhagen in 1770 and, after the success of his new *syngespil* collaboration with Sarti, *Tronfölgen i Sidon* (1771, The Royal Succession in Sidon), he was appointed director of Det Kongelige Teater (The Royal Theater).

Despite its popularity with the upper echelon of Copenhagen society, *Tronfölgen i Sidon* failed to win critical acclaim. Peder Rosenstand-Goiske, a nineteen-year-old law student, thoroughly panned the piece in the first issue of his periodical *Den Dramatiske Journal,* finding fault with virtually every aspect of the play. For the performance of *Tronfölgen i Sidon* on 25 November 1771 Bredal wrote a one-act retort to Rosenstand-Goiske's criticism, a biting satire titled *Den Dramatiske Journal, eller Critik over* Tronfölgen i Sidon (The Dramatic Journal; or Criticism over *The Royal Succession in Sidon*) and arranged for a military guard to be present. A conflict broke out between members of the militia and rioting students who championed their peer, Rosenstand-Goiske, and his critical approach to dramatic performances. The protests over Bredal's *Tronfölgen i Sidon* signaled the end of the line for the *syngespil* as well as the emergence of critical audiences and a new organ for reviewing and critiquing dramatic performances.

The eighteenth century marked the onset of modern literary criticism and a new style of writing Norwegian prose. Claus Fasting (1746–1791), the mayor of Bergen, tried his hand at both poetry and drama, but he found his niche as a literary critic and historian with impeccable taste and as an essayist and editor with considerable savoir faire. Fasting's collections of essays and reviews, *Provinzialblade* (1778–1781, Provincial Leaves) and *Provinzialsamlinger* (1791, Provincial Collections), served scholars, students, and other readers in Bergen. A gifted pianist and a talented composer, Fasting also contributed to the musical and cultural life of his community. His awareness of European literary and cultural trends enabled him to broaden the interests and insights of his community.

The Age of Enlightenment led to the founding of literary societies in many towns and cities in Denmark and Norway. In Copenhagen, Norwegian scholars, students, and poets began to meet informally at Madame Juel's Café on Læderstræde; one of them, Owe Gierløv Meyer, began a literary society that adopted rules and bylaws and took the name Det Norske Selskab (The Norwegian Society) on 30 April 1774. The society moved with Madame Juel to Sværtegade 7, to Wessels Kro, the *stamcafé* (home café) of one of its most illustrious members, Wessel. During the period of ascendancy and its *Gullalder* (Golden Age) Det Norske Selskab was led by Wessel and Johan Vibe (1748–1782), a true *bon esprit* whose short life, lived under the cloud of death, was devoted to wine, women, and song. Vibe's legacy lies in his drinking and celebratory songs and in his remarkable leadership of Det Norske Selskab, a group that included Brun and Fasting, as well as Wessel, among its members.

An undeveloped, even unexplored country of a less than a million souls on the fringe of Europe, Norway in the year 1800 hardly seemed like a country poised for a literary century. During the nineteenth century the country was under the political thumbs first of Denmark and then of Sweden. Nevertheless, in this seemingly unpromising milieu Norwegian literature emerged and attained a reputation far beyond its own borders. In the course of the century Norway became a European country, sharing its culture and perspective with other European countries. It became fully its own country at the beginning of the twentieth century.

The son of two of Norway's most illustrious families, the Munchs and the Storms, Johan Storm Munch (1778–1832) followed a ministerial calling and rose to the position of bishop of Kristiansand Diocese. Pursuing his studies of Old Norse sagas and Norwegian rural dialects, Munch founded and edited the journal *Saga* and wrote poetry showing his love for the natural surroundings of his homeland as well as its culture and history. Munch's poetry is at its lyrical best in his sole collection, *Fjeldblomster* (1813, Mountain Flowers), and in some monologues from *Præsten i Hallingdal* (1825, The Parson of Hallingdal), a play that never made it to the stage. Munch stood at the crossroads between the shared Danish/Norwegian literary past and the emergence of a Norwegian national literature. He was an inspired student of the new Romantic poetry of German and Danish poets, especially Friedrich Schiller and Adam Oehlenschläger, whom he met during his theological studies in Copenhagen.

With the home rule provided by the Treaty of Kiel in 1814, Norway came into its own–to a degree. The country was under the Swedish monarch in Stockholm instead of the Danish monarch in Copenhagen, but in the transition it had gained a measure of independence: a *Storting* (Parliament) in Christiania. Students at the new University of Christiania aimed to create a Norwegian national literature. One of their number was the gifted storyteller Maurits Hansen (1794–1842), whose tales of Norwegian country people inspired later writers, among them Bjørnstjerne Bjørnson (1832–1910). As a teacher, Hansen pioneered the idea of a Norwegian language distinct from Danish in vocabulary and grammar; he contributed several textbooks used in the schools along with stories that dealt with Norwegians in Norway in innovative ways and a detective story that has a legitimate claim to being the first of a kind.

Hansen's work suggested directions that Norway might take in developing and refining its own written language. In the early decades of the nineteenth century, the issue of language became paramount among Norwegian scholars, literary historians, and authors. Two gifted poets, Johan Sebastian Welhaven (1807–1873) and Henrik Wergeland (1808–1845), engaged in a sometimes acrimonious debate over language and aesthetics, especially on the role of Denmark and Danish cultural hegemony in the new Norway. Both were ardent patriots, but their patriotism and their poetry took vastly different paths. Welhaven believed in maintaining the cultural ties and traditions shared with Denmark; he was related to the preeminent Danish literary critic and dramatist Johan Ludvig Heiberg, and he proposed retaining the literary values that the Hegelian Heiberg espoused. Wergeland was a socially engaged activist whose views were evident in his poetry. Wergeland opposed Danish cultural hegemony and a provision in the Norwegian Constitution that barred Jews from entering Norway; he also fought for the common people and felt their traditions and culture should form the basis for the new nation. The literary and aesthetic polemic between Wergeland and Welhaven was complicated by the romantic interest that Wergeland's younger sister Camilla felt for Welhaven, who was ambivalent about pursuing a relationship with the sister of his literary and cultural rival.

When her relationship with Welhaven came to an end, Camilla married the politician and literary critic Peter Jonas Collett. As Camilla Collett (1813–1895) she proved to be a fine novelist. Her novels and short stories, especially her chef d'oeuvre, *Amtmandens Døttre* (1854, 1855, The District Governor's Daughters), explored the condition of women in Norway, their subjugation to men, and the inequities they had to endure. She has been called Norway's first feminist writer.

The popular German folktales published as *Kinder- und Hausmärchen* (1812, 1815, Children's and Household Tales; translated as *German Popular Stories*, 1823, 1826), by Wilhelm and Jacob Grimm, profoundly influenced the Norwegian poets Landstad, Asbjørnsen, and Moe. Asbjørnsen and Moe collected folktales and legends from rural people, drawing on an oral literature and history removed from the world of books and formal education. The men dedicated themselves to preserving folk literature and history faithfully, publishing *Norske Folkeeventyr* (1841–1844, Norwegian Folktales) at the crest of the National Romanticism movement in Europe. Landstad, a pastor as well as a poet, collected ballads and folk songs in the Telemark region of Norway from informants such as Maren Ramskeid whose variants of *Draumkvædet* (The Dream Ballad) and other medieval ballads connected the people to their cultural history. With the aid of a local voice teacher in Telemark, Olea Crøger, Landstad recorded both the music and the lyrics of the living ballad tradition. Landstad also collected folk narrative of all sorts, particularly *sagn* (legends) and produced a hymnal that served the Norwegian Church for more than a hundred years. Asbjørnsen, Moe, and Landstad worked to preserve folk culture as a way of affirming Norway's links to a history that predated its union with Denmark, to a time when the country sang its own tune. Such efforts were closely connected to the growing interest in and support for the idea of an independent Norway.

Norwegian folk traditions, the ballads and legends of rural Norway–specifically of the Telemark region–also caught the attention of the academic community and the leading literary scholar and historian of his generation, the venerable professor Sophus Bugge (1833–1907). Bugge's first book, *Gamle norske Folkeviser* (1858, Old Norwegian Ballads) appeared as a scholarly–and personal–response to Landstad's work and to the first volume of his friend and colleague Svend Grundtvig's *Danmarks gamle Folkeviser* (1853, Denmark's Old Folk Ballads). Bugge went on to publish many works, exploring a wide range of interests, including folk narrative, legends, and riddles; *Guldhornene* (runic inscriptions); Nordic and Germanic philology and etymology; and the *Eddas* and Old Norse sagas. Bugge opened new vistas on Old Norse literature and was admired for his serious approach to literary study, his fine writing, and the excellence of his teaching.

Ivar Aasen (1813–1896), a fine composer of songs, as he called his poems, was a founding father of Landsmål, or Nynorsk, which became one of Norway's two official languages. His poems appeared in a single collection, *Symra* (1863, The Anemone), the first book to use Landsmål exclusively. Most of Aasen's works were nonfiction and concerned the grammar and vocabulary of the language he built from dialects, especially from the dialects in Telemark. Another Landsmål poet, Aasmund Olafsson Vinje (1818–1870), came from the rural population in Telemark. The son of a tenant farmer, Vinje was known as a journalist, satirist, conversationalist, inveterate traveler, and essayist, as well as a poet. He bridged the gap between rural and urban–between the socially forgotten and the social elite–in mid-nineteenth-century Norway.

At midcentury, halfway between Welhaven and Wergeland, on the one hand, and Bjørnson and Ibsen, on the other, stood the dramatist and poet, the preeminent writer of his day, Andreas Munch (1811–1884), the son of Johan Storm Munch. Munch's historical plays were performed to critical acclaim in theaters in Denmark, Norway, Germany, and England. His poetry was popular with readers, and he was respected as an insightful art and literary critic and editor. His home was the focal point for writers, musicians, poets, critics, and artists; when he moved to Copenhagen, he served as host for a crowd of artists and writers, just as he had done in Christiania. A young Knut Hamsun revered Munch and acknowledged the older writer's literary acumen and expertise.

Born in Fredericia, Denmark, Magdalene Thoresen (1819–1903)–a Norwegian by choice if not by birth–was acclaimed in her day as a poet, dramatist, and writer of stories. Thoresen also enjoyed close familial ties to Ibsen as the stepmother of his wife, Suzannah, and a "spiritual marriage" to Bjørnson. Thoresen came to Norway as Magdalene Kragh, a governess for the children of the widowed parson of Herøy, Hans Conrad Thoresen; she went on to marry Thoresen, who supported and encouraged her in a writing career, even moving to Bergen so she could have a fair chance. The Thoresen home in Bergen was an enlightened one, and Thoresen blossomed in such surroundings. Her fame did not endure far into the twentieth century, however.

One of the literary lions of the second half of the nineteenth century, Bjørnson combined an interest in social, cultural, and political issues with literary and critical talents that enabled him to write plays, poetry, essays, articles, commentaries, and literary criticism. Bjørnson was a Norwegian first and foremost, but he was also well known–and well regarded–abroad for his social engagement and for his plays and poems. Bjørnson was one of what the Copenhagen publisher Gyldendal termed "de fire store" (the four great ones), the other three being Ibsen, Alexander L. Kielland (1849–1906), and Jonas Lie (1833–1908). Kielland was second only to Ibsen as a representative of the Modern Breakthrough, a literary movement championed by the Danish literary critic Georg Brandes. The Modern Breakthrough promoted realism and naturalism as means of addressing social problems. Kielland's novels dealt with contemporary conflicts and controversies, treating human flaws and failings, including unethical business practices, in urban settings. The novelist Lie stood a little to the side of the Modern Breakthrough as his stories incorporated elements of mysticism and folklore, legends from northern Norway, and fantasy. Lie also concentrated on depicting families and bourgeois homes, but his focus on magic and mystery, on the blend of fantasy and reality, put his work at odds with the thrust of the Modern Breakthrough.

With his insightful analysis of the psyche and the heart, his insistence on letting his characters tell their own stories, and his poetic descriptions of the natural surroundings and climate of Vestlandet, the western coast of Norway, Kristian Elster (1841–1881) contributed to the development of the novel and novella in Norway. Elster was also an intensely practical man who served as a forest manager in the Trondheim district, all the while keeping abreast of the cultural and literary scene in Europe and writing perceptive, astute literary criticism for those keen on following literary trends. Elster did not live long enough to write many works, but he made his mark with such stories and novels as "Solskyer" (1877, Sun Clouds), *Tora Trondal* (1879), and *Farlige Folk* (1881, Dangerous People).

Three women writers born the same year expanded the themes and motifs of nineteenth-century Norwegian literature. Alvilde Prydz (1846–1922) combined elements of realism with romanticism and a penchant for symbols in her many novels. She focused on the entrapment of women in a male-dominated society that denied their potential and independence. Drude Krog Jansson (1846–1934) expanded the scope of Norwegian literature by writing of the Norwegian community in the American Midwest. Her novels are based on her experiences in the United States, on the struggles involved in making new lives in a new land. Amalie Skram (1846–1905) took the idea of writing realistically, of presenting social and personal problems boldly and baldly, to heart; her novels were shocking to her contemporaries as she refused to shy away from attacking the hypocrisies of the church, social and sexual inequities, and the evils of the class system. Skram is known for her graphic treatment of marriage in "marriage novels," for her descriptions of mental hospitals based on her own experience with such institutions, and for her four-volume series of novels, *Hellemyrsfolket* (1887–1898, The People of Hellemyr).

A contemporary of "de fire store," Arne Garborg (1851–1924) was well known and considered "den femte store" (the fifth great one) during his lifetime. Garborg made his reputation with Realistic/Naturalistic novels in Nynorsk, most notably *Bondestudentar* (1883, Peasant Students), *Hjaa ho Mor* (1890, Living with Mama); *Trætte Mænd* (1891; translated as *Weary Men*, 1999), and *Fred* (1892; translated as *Peace*, 1929). His novels were well known in Europe, and his work was considered of uniformly high caliber. Garborg also wrote an extraordinary, truly Norwegian poem, *Haugtussa* (1895, The Hill Maiden) that blends legends, folk beliefs and fantasy, with glorious nature poetry, capturing the essence of Norway in a song cycle that the composer Edvard Grieg set to music. Garborg's wife, Hulda Bergersen Garborg (1862–1934) pursued a literary career in her own right, writing nonfiction works on Norwegian folk ballads, folk dancing, customs, *bunad* (regional dress), and novels, short stories, and plays that were staged successfully at the Christiania Theater.

An anarchist, extremist, and bohemian, Hans Jæger (1854–1910) managed to outrage and alienate the solid bedrock of Christian bourgeoisie in Norway. Jæger entered the *sedelighetsdebatt* (debate about morality) on the side of sexual freedom and social revolution. As a result of his efforts to expose hypocrisy and the failings of Christian morality, Jæger served time in prison for blasphemy and obscenity. His writings were vehicles for the expression of his radical, anarchist views. Much of his work was censored or confiscated outright, but his influence extended to a younger generation in Scandinavia. His novel *Fra Kristiania-Bohêmen* (From the Christiania Bohemia) was confiscated by the Norwegian government on publication in 1885.

The poems of Per Sivle (1857–1904), once critically acclaimed and appreciated, no longer attract the interest of Norwegian readers. Sivle's tragic life was punctuated by an irregular family life, poor health, dependency on others, and poverty. As he sought stability and tranquility, he dreamed of independence for Norway. He committed suicide shortly before Norway achieved its independence.

Following in the footsteps of two of "de fire store," Ibsen and Bjørnson, Gunnar Heiberg (1857–1929) became the most successful Norwegian playwright after Ibsen. His plays have not stood the test of time despite the fact that they were insightful, well crafted, and thoughtful. Heiberg was also a gifted stage director and reviewer for theater. His writings on drama provide remarkable insights into late-nineteenth-century literature.

Nils Collett Vogt (1864–1937) lived "Et liv i dikt" (A Life in Poetry), a phrase used as the title of his collected poems published in 1930. He began his career in the late 1880s, a time when most writers were addressing social problems and conflicts in prose. With his emphasis on the inner world of his own thoughts and feelings, Vogt led the way into a new decade and helped usher in a New Romanticism in Norway. A sharp contrast to Vogt is provided by the career of Sigbjørn Obstfelder (1866–1900), whose symbolist poetry was confined to the single decade of the 1890s. Obstfelder delved into the themes of isolation and alienation, insanity, and frenetic mania over female sexuality. Obstfelder's poems "Jeg ser" (I Look) and "Roser" (Roses) took the Norwegian and Scandinavian literary world by storm, and the poet is still held in high esteem in Norway, in large part because of his influence on later modernist poets. He has not won the attention of the English-speaking world.

Dagny Juel Przybyszewska (1867–1901) was one of a group of bohemian authors and artists who in the 1890s gathered at Zum schwarzen Ferkel (At the Black Piglet), a pub in Berlin, including Obstfelder, as well as Edvard Munch, Gunnar Heiberg, Gustav Vigeland, Holger Drachmann, Stanisław Przybyszewski, and August Strindberg. A gifted pianist from Kongsvinger, Dagny Juel went to study music in Berlin, where she married Przybyszewski. Her work contributed to a renewal of poetry and drama, as it paved the way for literary expressionism in the late plays of Ibsen and Strindberg. A dynamic, sexually assertive, modern woman, Przybyszewska was nevertheless unable wholly to leave behind the traditions of family and home to pursue the modern order she envisioned in her plays and poems. A true fin-de-siècle artist, Przybyszewska pointed to the future while remaining enveloped in the past.

One writer in *DLB 354* bridges the late nineteenth and early twentieth centuries. Vilhelm Krag (1871–1933) was a modernist poet, a dramatist and storyteller, an advocate for Sørlandet (the southern coastal region of Norway), and a memoirist of his youth.

Ibsen is undoubtedly the central figure of nineteenth-century Norwegian literature. Norway, the source of his inspiration, played a significant role as the setting and background for nearly all of his plays and poetry. But Ibsen, much more than the most important writer in his own country during his lifetime, became a writer of international importance, and his significance has only increased in the century since his death. Like William Shakespeare, Ibsen has transcended time and place as his plays still stimulate the modern imagination. What is there about *Brand* (1866; translated, 1891), *Peer Gynt* (1867; translated, 1892), *Et Dukkehjem* (1879, A Doll's House; translated as *Nora*, 1882), *Gengangere* (1881; translated as *Ghosts*, 1888), *Vildanden* (1884; translated as *The Wild Duck*, 1890), *Hedda Gabler* (1890; translated as *Hedda Gabler*, 1890) or any of Ibsen's other masterpieces that causes modern audiences to watch and listen so intently, to debate and discuss long after the applause has ended? The answer, perhaps, is that Ibsen, more than just treating the bourgeoisie in Norway, focused on what it means to be a human being and what it means to be part of a society. As he put it himself in discussing *Et Dukkehjem*, Ibsen focused on the problems of humanity. Like Shakespeare, Ibsen asked the hard questions, the essential questions with which everyone must come to grips: What is my purpose in life? How should I treat others in my world? How do I respond to the way they treat me? What is my value to myself and others? With Ibsen, Norwegian literature moved beyond the boundaries of time, place, and language to become world literature.

–Lanae H. Isaacson

Acknowledgments

This book was produced by Bruccoli Clark Layman, Inc. George Parker Anderson, Philip B. Dematteis, and Penelope M. Hope were the in-house editors.

Senior editor is Philip B. Dematteis.

Production manager is Janet E. Hill.

Administrative support was provided by Carol A. Cheschi.

Accountant is Ann-Marie Holland.

Copyediting supervisor is Phyllis A. Avant. The copyediting staff includes Candice Gullett and Rebecca Mayo. Freelance copyeditors are Brenda L. Cabra, Jennifer Cooper, David C. King, and Katherine E. Macedon.

Pipeline manager is James F. Tidd Jr.

Permissions editor is Dickson Monk.

Office manager is Kathy Lawler Merlette.

Digital photographic copy work and photo editing was performed by Dickson Monk.

Systems manager is James Sellers.

Typesetting supervisor is Kathleen M. Flanagan. The typesetting staff includes Patricia M. Flanagan.

Graphics compositor is Patricia M. Flanagan. She was assisted by Kathleen M. Flanagan.

Library research was facilitated by the following librarians at the Thomas Cooper Library of the University of South Carolina: Elizabeth Sudduth and the rare-book department; circulation department head Tucker Taylor; reference department head Virginia W. Weathers; reference department staff Marilee Birchfield, Karen Brown, Mary Bull, Gerri Corson, Joshua Garris, Beki Gettys, Laura Ladwig, Tom Marcil, Bob Skinder, and Sharon Verba; interlibrary loan department head Marna Hostetler; and interlibrary loan staff Robert Amerson and Timothy Simmons.

The editor would like to express her gratitude to contributors who shared their talents and wisdom with each other; participants in the 1987 NEH Summer Seminar at Harvard and her Harvard colleagues Joseph Harris, Thomas Hill, and Stephen Mitchell; former colleagues and students at the department of Scandinavian Studies, University of Wisconsin–Madison, most especially professors Niels and Faith Ingwersen and Harald S. Næss; and to kindhearted, selfless librarians at Det Kongelige Bibliotek in Copenhagen and Nasjonalbiblioteket in Oslo, as well as at Stanford University and the University of California, Berkeley.

The editor also wants to thank her enablers, who smoothed her way and helped her to see: Nejleh T. Abed, Boyd W. Seaman, and John H. Sullivan. And friends who followed the path and pointed the way: Kirsten M. Bentzen and Jens Bo Jørgensen (in memory of her Danish family), James Cathey, and Charlotte and Ken Gray. Finally, a special note of appreciation to Jan Sjåvik for going above and beyond and saving the day.

Dictionary of Literary Biography® • Volume Three Hundred Fifty-Four

Norwegian Writers, 1500 to 1900

Dictionary of Literary Biography

Ivar Aasen
(5 August 1813 – 23 September 1896)

Eirik Helleve
Nynorsk kultursentrum

BOOKS: *Fem Viser i søndre Søndmørs Almuesprog* (Eegsæt, 1842);

Det norske Folkesprogs Grammatik (Christiania: Det kongelige norske Videnskabs-Selskab, 1848);

Ordbog over det norske Folkesprog (Christiania: Det kongelige norske Videnskabs-Selskabs Foranstaltning, 1850);

Søndmørsk Grammatik eller kortfattet Underretning om Bygdemaalet paa Søndmør (Eegsæt: Aarflot, 1851);

Prøver af Landsmaalet i Norge (Christiania: Printed by C. C. Werner, 1853);

Ervingen: Sangspil i een Akt (Christiania: Det norske Theaters Forlag, 1855);

Norske Ordsprog: Samlede og oordnede af Ivar Aasen (Christiania, 1856; revised edition, Christiania: Malling, 1881);

Fridtjofs Saga: I Omskrift i det nyere Landsmaal ved Ivar Aasen (Christiania: Selskabet for Folkeoplysningens Fremme, 1858);

Symra: Tvo Tylvter med nya Visor, anonymous (Christiania: Malling, 1863); translated by Kjetil Myskja as *Symra* (Fjærland: Norske Bokbyen, 2002);

Norsk Grammatik (Christiania: Malling, 1864);

Norsk Ordbog med Dansk Forklaring (Christiania: Malling, 1873);

Heimsyn: Ei snøgg Umsjaaing yver Skapningen og Menneskja, tilmaatad fyre Ungdomen, anonymous (Christiania: Det Norske Samlaget, 1875);

Norsk Navnebog eller Samling af Mandsnavne og Kvindenavne (Christiania: Malling, 1878);

Om grunnlaget for norsk målreising: Seks Artiklar av Ivar Aasen (Voss: Vestanbok Forlag, 1984);

Sunnmørsgrammatikkane av Ivar Aasen, edited by Jarle Bondevik, Oddvar Nes, and Terje Aarset (Bergen: Norsk Bokreidingslag, 1992);

Ivar Aasen (Den Store Danske <http://www.denstoredanske.dk/ Samfund,_jura_og_politik/Sprog/Nordiske_filologer/ Ivar_Aasen?highlight=Aasen,%20Ivar>)

Målsamlingar frå Sunnmøre av Ivar Aasen, edited by Bondevik, Nes, and Aarset (Bergen: Norsk Bokreidingslag, 1994);

Målsamlingar frå Bergens Stift av Ivar Aasen, edited by Bondevik, Nes, and Aarset (Bergen: Norsk Bokreidingslag, 1995);

Målsamlingar frå Christiansands og Agershuus Stifter av Ivar Aasen, edited by Bondevik, Nes, and Aarset (Bergen: Norsk Bokreidingslag, 1997);

Målsamlingar frå Trondhjems og Tromsø Stifter av Ivar Aasen, edited by Bondevik, Nes, and Aarset (Bergen: Norsk Bokreidingslag, 1998);

Målsamlingar 1851–1854 av Ivar Aasen, edited by Bondevik, Nes, and Aarset (Bergen: Norsk Bokreidingslag, 1999);

Dansk-norsk Ordbog, edited by Bondevik, Nes, and Aarset (Bergen: Norsk Bokreidingslag, 2000);

Målsamlingar 1855–1861 av Ivar Aasen, edited by Bondevik, Nes, and Aarset (Bergen: Norsk Bokreidingslag, 2001);

Målsamlingar 1862–1883 av Ivar Aasen, edited by Bondevik, Nes, and Aarset (Bergen: Norsk Bokreidingslag, 2001);

Mellom Bakkar og Berg, music by Ludvig M. Lindeman (Oslo: Musikk-forlaget, 2005);

Namnesamlingar av Ivar Aasen, edited by Bondevik, Nes, and Aarset (Bergen: Norsk Bokreidingslag, 2006);

Symrasongar, music by Lorents Aage Nagelhus (Oslo: Musikk-forlaget, 2006).

Collections: *Udvalgte Skrifter,* edited by Vetle Vislie (Christiania: Malling, 1896);

Folke-Udgave av Ivar Aasens Skrifter i Udvalg (Christiania: Malling, 1899);

Skrifter i Samling, 3 volumes, edited by Knut Liestøl (Christiania & Copenhagen: Gyldendalske Boghandel / Nordisk Forlag, 1911–1912);

Norske Minnestykke, edited by Jens Lindberg (Christiania: Norsk Folkeminnesamlag, 1923);

Skrifter: Eit utval, edited by Olav Hr. Rue (Oslo: Det Norske Samlaget, 1976);

Mellom bakkar og berg, edited by Magne Myhren (Stabekk: Norske Bokklubben, 1980);

Ivar Aasens beste, edited by Rue (Oslo: Det Norske Samlaget, 1991);

Det er vondt å tru alle; det er verre å tru ingen (Oslo: Det Norske Samlaget, 2002).

Edition in English: "On Our Written Language, on Culture and Norwegianness: Recollections from the Language Debate of Autumn 1858," translated by J. Peter Burgess, in his *Ivar Aasen's Logic of Nation: Toward a Philosophy of Culture* (Volda: Høgskolen i Volda, 1999).

PLAY PRODUCTIONS: *I Marknaden,* Christiania, Christiania Norske Theater, February 1854;

Ervingen, Christiania, Christiania Norske Theater, April 1855.

Well over a century after his death, Ivar Aasen remains a household name in Norway. He is recognized as the father of Landsmål (today's Nynorsk), one of Norway's two official languages, and as a linguist he is held in very high esteem. But he also had a talent for writing poetry and has the rare distinction of being admired both for his scholarly works and for his poems. A deep respect for the common people is the foundation for all his work, both the linguistic and the poetic.

Aasen grew up in Hovdebygda in Sunnmøre, where he was born on 5 August 1813, the ninth and final child in the family. Even though the family farm, Åsen, was located in the valley between two villages, Ørsta and Volda, there were no immediate neighbors. Aasen lost his parents at an early age: his mother died in 1816, and his father a decade later. As is common in Norway, the oldest son inherited the farm. In later years, Aasen referred to the years he lived and worked for Jon, his oldest brother, as five hard years. He took part in the daily routines, but he was not made for heavy physical work.

Aasen's formal education was brief. Like the other children in the area, he went to school ten days each year for six years. Reading and writing came easy to him, and he enjoyed reading the religious books found in the family home. On his confirmation day, at the age of fifteen, he was top of the class. When compiling the list of that year's confirmants in the church records, the vicar drew the figure of a head close to Aasen's name. In later years, that drawing was commonly taken as a proof that the vicar was impressed by Aasen's mind.

Already in his youth Aasen showed a talent for systematizing and cataloging. Like many young boys, Aasen tried to catch thrushes, which could be sold as a delicacy; he made a list of all the thrushes he caught, sorted by date and color. He kept such a list from 1826 until 1840. For other gifted youths in rural Norway at that time, it was difficult to find intellectual stimuli. Aasen was luckier than most, as he grew up only a half hour's walk from the Eikset farm, which the owner, Sivert Aarflot, had turned into an oasis of learning. As early as 1797, Aarflot had donated 104 of his own books for a public library located on his own farm–probably the first public library in rural Norway. Aarflot received permission to start his own printing company in 1809; the next year he started *Norsk Landboeblad,* only the seventh newspaper in Norway and the first outside the big cities. By the time of Aarflot's death the library owned 550 books. Aasen was a frequent guest at Eikset, spending a great deal of time with the books, and he also got a chance to read newspapers from Christiania, thereby gaining knowledge about the world outside his home area. The Aarflot family remained important to Aasen; Sivert Aarflot's grandson, also called Sivert Aarflot, was probably the closest friend and ally Aasen had in his youth. The distance between their homes was not far, but even so they communicated through letters, possibly as a way of practicing writing. When the younger Sivert died in 1836, Aasen wrote a memorial poem,

"Ved Efterretningen om den unge Sivert R Aarflots død" (At the news of young Sivert R Aarflot's death), printed in *Norsk Landboeblad* on 26 March 1836. Throughout his life, Aasen remained close to the younger Sivert's brother, Maurits Aarflot, who spent the years from 1854 to 1888 in Christiania as a representative in Stortinget, the Norwegian parliament.

Prior to the construction of permanent school buildings, education in rural Norway took place in an ambulatory school, where the teacher traveled through the area, staying at farms for a week or two. At the age of eighteen, Aasen got a job as a teacher at such an ambulatory school in Ørsta, a position he held for two years. He felt the need for more education, so he contacted H. C. Thoresen, who was the dean in the parish at Herøy, a community closer to the coast. Thoresen was known for letting young teachers stay at his house for further teacher training, and in 1831 Aasen moved in with the Thoresen family. Thoresen quickly realized that Aasen was a willing student and allowed him to stay for two years, teaching him Latin, geography, history, rhetoric, and even poetry. Thoresen offered to help Aasen financially, to give him the chance of studying at the University of Christiania, but Aasen declined, believing that a university degree would create a barrier between himself and the farmers of Norway. (Thoresen's daughter Suzannah later married Henrik Ibsen.)

In 1835 Aasen moved to the farm Solnør in Skodje, still in the Sunnmøre region. Solnør was owned by Ludvig Daae, the brother of Thoresen's wife. There were six children in the family, and Aasen was to become their teacher. His stay at Solnør was a pleasant one. He got on well with the family, and in his spare time he made good use of the book collection in the house and also found time to pursue his interest in botany. Many a day was spent hiking in the local outdoors, all the time collecting plants for his own herbarium. Eventually, Aasen's herbarium included well over five hundred plants. His other passion was language, for which he had exceptional talent. Daae subscribed to newspapers and magazines from Christiania, and Aasen took special interest in discussions of the language situation in Norway. It had been two decades since Norway had won independence from Denmark, but there was still no sign of a written Norwegian language, Danish being the only written language used in Norway. The historian Peter Andreas Munch and the poet Henrik Wergeland were among those who sought ways to design a Norwegian language, but Aasen was not happy with their suggestions. In his article "Norsk Sprogreformation" (Norwegian Language Reform) Munch proposed using one of the Norwegian dialects as the foundation for written Norwegian, while Wergeland, in his article "Om norsk Sprogreformation" (On

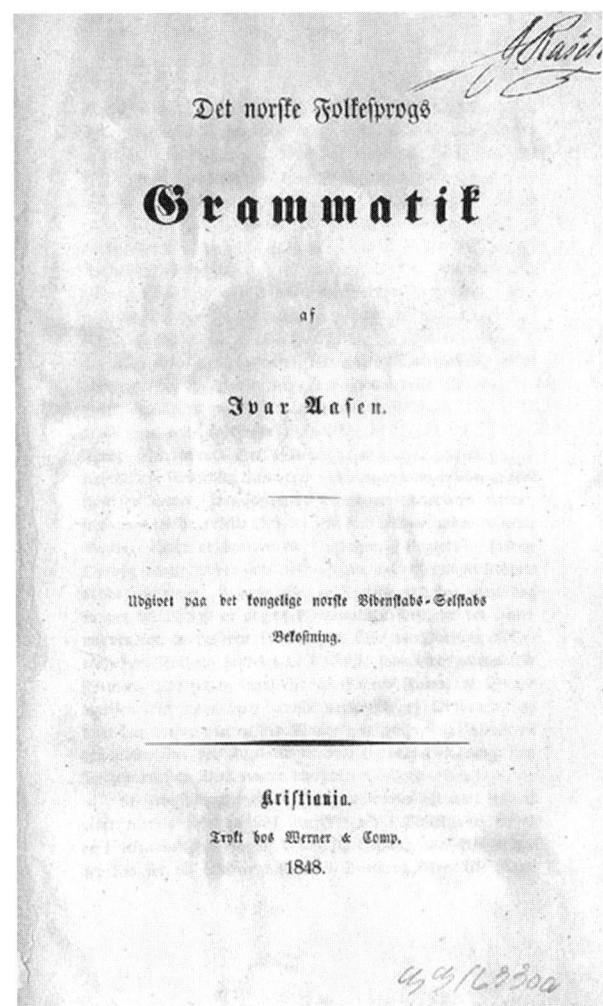

Title page for Aasen's grammar of Norwegian folk language (Sprakradet [the Norwegian Language Council] <http://www.sprakrad.no/upload/9284/gr1b.jpg>)

Norwegian Language Reform), argued for the inclusion of words from Norwegian dialects in Danish.

Aasen's solution to the language debate was a far more democratic one. In his essay "Om vort Skriftsprog" (1909, On Our Written Language), written in January 1836 (possibly as a paper to H. C. Thoresen), he argued that it was impossible to use Danish as a starting point for a Norwegian language as Wergeland suggested. Using just one dialect would also be unfair to those using the many other dialects in Norway. Aasen suggested that the new Norwegian language should be based on a comparison of all Norwegian dialects. Remarkably, Aasen was only twenty-two when he wrote "Om vort Skriftsprog," and even more remarkably, he devoted his life to implementing the solutions suggested in this essay. The work remained unpublished until after his death, when it was discovered

Manuscript for Aasen's poem "Dei gamle fjelli" (translated as "The Old Mountains"), published in his collection Symra (The Anemone; translated as Symra, 2002) in 1863 (Ivar Aasen Center) among his manuscripts and notes; it is now considered one of the key documents in the history of Nynorsk.

Aasen was an ambitious young man. Even though he enjoyed his stay at Solnør, he felt that he did not face enough intellectual challenges there. On two occasions Aasen made short visits to bigger cities, hoping to meet somebody who could help him obtain more important positions. In 1840 he visited the dean in Molde in order to show him the herbarium he had collected. Nothing came of this trip, as the dean was too busy to meet extensively with Aasen. The following year Aasen traveled to Bergen, and this trip proved far more fruitful. With help from an acquaintance, Aasen got an appointment with Bishop Neumann. In addition to his herbarium, Aasen also brought along the manuscript for a grammar for his own dialect, a work he had completed in 1839 but that was not published until 1851. Neumann did not show much interest in the plants but was much impressed with the grammar and told Aasen that he would do what he could to help him. Neumann asked Aasen to write a short autobiography for publication in a local paper. In this article Aasen devoted much space to his thoughts about language and included the query: "Hvorfor, tænkte jeg, blive ikke de norske dialekter behandlede ligesom andre Sprog? Ere ikke vore dialekter, de gamle og ægte norske sprog, en grundigere behandling værdig? Et saadant arbeide, tænkte jeg, kan kun udføres af en som er født og opvokst i en bondes hytte" (Why should not the Norwegian dialects be treated as other languages? Are not our dialects, the old and pure Norwegian language, worthy of a more thorough study? Such a work can be done only by somebody born and bred in a farmer's cabin). The passage can easily be read as an application for a vacant position, and Aasen got the job: he returned to Solnør after two weeks in Bergen, and in July 1842 the Royal Norwegian Science Society in Trondheim informed Aasen that he would receive a grant to study the rural dialects of Norway. He received the first installment of the grant on 12 September. Within a week he resigned as teacher at Solnør and traveled to his brother's farm in Ørsta, where he spent a week preparing for his travels. He headed south on 29 September, embarking on a trip that lasted four years.

Aasen was not on the move constantly. He sought out smaller towns, where he would stay for some weeks, in some cases longer, and he made detours into the surrounding areas. His normal practice was to encourage the people to talk freely, while he took notes on how words were pronounced and inflected. Whenever he did not acquire adequate information from listening to people talk, he would ask direct questions concerning the dialect in question. Aasen was required to hand in reports to the Science Society twice each

The 1871 photograph that led Aasen to write in his diary, "Hos Fotografen. Slet Humør" (At the Photographers'. In a sad mood). He did not have his picture taken again for years (Ivar Aasen Center).

year. In return, he would receive money for the next six months. In June 1843 he reached Litlebergen in Meland, a little north of Bergen. His stay there lasted longer than intended, as he did not hear from the Science Society and thus ran out of money. He traveled to Bergen for the expected letter from Trondheim no fewer than nine times before finally receiving the money for further travels in March 1844.

The important issue for Aasen was listening to ordinary people. His intention was to create a language for everyone in Norway, something with which all Norwegians could feel at home, as it would include words from all the dialects. Aasen's project was extremely democratic, and his efforts to raise the self-esteem of ordinary people cannot be underestimated. He traveled all over southern Norway, going by boat, by horse and buggy, or simply walking. He made notes of how people dressed, noticed differences in architecture, wrote down folk melodies and folktales, collected local proverbs, drew simple maps of some of the areas, and certainly gathered information on more than just the dialects. In November 1845 he made a stop in Trondheim, getting to know his sponsors, and he also made plans for what he would do with the materials he had collected. The Science Society suggested that he also travel through the area north of Trondheim, and in spring 1846 he hit the road again, eventually going as far north as Helgeland. Aasen returned to Trondheim in December 1846. He immediately started work on a grammar and, when the grammar was finished, a dictionary.

In September 1847 Aasen moved to Christiania. His grammar, *Det norske Folkesprogs Grammatik* (Grammar of the Norwegian Folk Langauge) was published in 1848, and the dictionary, *Ordbog over det norske Folkesprog* (Dictionary for the Norwegian Folk Language), followed two years later. Aasen's research and completion of two major books in such a short time prove that he was an energetic and dedicated worker. Both books received much praise. The historian Munch, who was one of the leading Norwegian intellectuals of the time, wrote that the grammar was a work in which the entire nation could take pride and that the dictionary was filled with clear and precise definitions. In August 1850, two months after the publication of the dictionary, Aasen moved back to the family farm in Ørsta. The following year the government gave him a lifelong grant to enable him to continue his studies of the Norwegian dialects. In summer 1851 Aasen traveled north, all the way to Tromsø, before he turned south again to Ørsta. In October he again moved to Christiania, and the capital remained his home for the rest of his life.

Aasen's grants from the Science Society were intended to fund his documentation of the various Norwegian dialects. For Aasen, however, another issue was just as important. In "Om vort Skriftsprog," the unpublished essay from 1836, Aasen argued for a written Norwegian language based on a comparison of all dialects. He intended to use the material collected on his travels in designing the new written langauge. As early as 1849 Aasen had used the term *landsmål* (the language of the country) for this new language, and in 1853 the first book in Landsmål was published, *Prøver af Landsmaalet i Norge* (Examples of the Norwegian Landsmål), a collection of texts written in various dialects. In this book, Aasen suggested a norm that he was hardly to alter. The term *Landsmål* remained in use until 1929, when the Norwegian parliament opted for the term *nynorsk* (New Norwegian).

Aasen realized that his new language, like all languages, needed three foundations to survive. His published dictionary and grammar were the first two, but he still needed the third foundation, the users. The praise he had received for his scholarly works was welcome, of course, but those books would be read mainly by scholars. If his language was to reach a bigger audience, it needed texts intended for all. Aasen reached a wider range of readers with the publication of *Prøver af Landsmaalet i Norge,* but he still needed to show that Landsmål could be used in all fields of literature. In early 1854 Aasen wrote *I Marknaden* (On the Market), a five-page play that consisted of a conversation between persons from three different areas in Norway and ended with praise for the politicians of Stortinget. *I Marknaden* was performed in early February 1854 at Christiania Norske Theater. But his real entry to the world of drama came in April 1855, when his play *Ervingen* (The Heir) premiered. *Ervingen* lauds rural life and farming as a vocation as well as old habits and traditions. Aasen's play was successful and was performed several times in his lifetime, including in Paris in 1879, and often after his death.

The 1850s, the first decade after Aasen finished his dictionary, did not produce many new writers of Landsmål. Apart from Aasen, the first prominent writer of Landsmål was Aasmund Olavsson Vinje (1818–1870), a very colorful character and journalist originally from the Telemark region. In 1858 Vinje started *Dølen,* the first newspaper in Landsmål, which he published until his death in 1870. Vinje became one of Aasen's closest friends, and at times Aasen gave Vinje a helping hand with his newspaper, both in discussions of language and by writing articles and poems for the paper.

Aasen came to realize that his grammar needed a complete revision. He regretted that he had not provided a final norm for Landsmål. In some cases, he had left the future writers of Landsmål with too many options, and he realized that the language needed to have stricter rules. After settling in Christiania in 1851, Aasen spent most summers until 1868 on shorter or longer journeys, collecting more material, and becoming better acquainted with the various dialects. He visited some parts of the country many times; with the possible exception of Eilert Sundt, a sociologist, Aasen probably knew more about daily life in rural Norway in the nineteenth century than anyone else.

In 1859 Aasen began revising his grammar, with the intention of finishing in one year. The work was a lot harder than he anticipated; it actually took him an entire year to write the chapter on inflectional termination. He was not ready to publish the new grammar until 1864. The title of the book no longer mentioned a Norwegian folk language; instead, the title was simply *Norsk Grammatik* (Norwegian Grammar). With its well-written introductory chapter, this work is still important for all those interested in Norwegian language.

Having finished the new edition of his grammar, Aasen started preparing for a new and extended version of his dictionary, another project that lasted much longer than intended. His first dictionary was published in 1850, and his many travels in the following years had given him a larger supply of words. His 1850 dictionary included twenty-five thousand words; when published in 1873, the new dictionary included forty-five thousand words. As was the case with the grammar, the new dictionary had a new title, *Norsk Ordbog med Dansk Forklaring* (Norwegian Dictionary). In his diary Aasen often complained about how long it took him to finish his dictionary. He noted every time he finished one of the notebooks in which he wrote his manuscript, allowing scholars to follow his progress.

Aasen's diary entry for 4 December 1869 reads "Færdig med Ø (Side 3453). Dermed Slut" (Done with Ø [page 3453]. Consequently it's over). Aasen underlined the words, and just to mark the big event, the next day he added: "Forrige dag sluttet Ordbogen" (Yesterday the dictionary ended). However, he still had a lot of work to do, as the 3,453-page manuscript needed proofreading. He started proofreading in September 1870, and, with some breaks, kept at it until June 1873, the same month the entire dictionary was finally printed. In a letter to his brother Jon Aasen, dated 15 June 1872, Aasen calls the dictionary "det største og fornemste af mine Arbeider" (the greatest and most distinguished of my works). It certainly was a huge achievement, and his final big undertaking.

In 1875 Aasen published *Heimsyn* (A Look at the World), a short encyclopedia for which he wrote articles about the universe, the earth, and various forms of life on earth. The book was intended to provide information on various subjects for young people. Three years later, Aasen finished another book, *Norsk Navnebog* (Book of Norwegian Names). This book also had a clear purpose, as Aasen felt that too many Norwegians gave their children Danish names, and that this could spell the end for many Norwegian names. Munch had worked on a similar project, and their efforts were not in vain, as it became more common to use Norwegian names.

Aasen's final book was a revised edition of *Norske Ordsprog* (Norwegian Proverbs) published in 1881, twenty-five years after the first edition. The new edition contained approximately the same number of proverbs; the biggest difference was in the way the proverbs are grouped together.

Several writers of Landsmål saw the need to use the language in religious texts. In 1854 Aasen emphasized the need for caution in introducing Landsmål to the field of religion. He experimented with brief translations of religious texts in 1855, and he discussed various translations of catechisms. Det Norske Samlaget, a publishing house established in 1868 to publish books in Landsmål, proposed publishing the New Testament in Landsmål. From the early 1880s Aasen was involved in this project, together with Elias Blix, Matias Skard, and Johs. Belsheim. In December 1890 the New Testament was published. The entire Bible was first published in Landsmål in 1921.

Drawing by Johan Nordhagen of Aasen in 1896, the year of his death (Store Norske Leksikon <http://snl.no/.bilde/ Aasen%2C_Ivar_(portrett)>)

Aasen's body of work is dominated by nonfiction, but he also wrote fiction and poetry. He wrote his first poems at an early age but soon realized that most of these were of poor quality. In 1845, in a letter to Maurits Aarflot, who was in charge of the printing press at Eikset, Aasen stipulated that none of the poems written before 1840, all of which were in Danish, should be printed again. Aasen intended Landsmål to be used in all fields of literature. When he made a list of future projects in 1852, he mentioned "Symra. Samling af nye Sange" (The Anemone. A Collection of New Songs). In a similar list written two years later, he even listed the titles of twelve poems to be included in *Symra*. When *Symra* was eventually published in 1863 (translated as *Symra*, 2002), some of these twelve poems were included. The anemone is one of the first flowers to appear in spring, and this was, of course, Aasen's reason for choosing such a title. *Symra* was the first book of poetry in Landsmål, and included twenty-four poems. It was published anonymously; but the author was soon well known, as few people wrote in Landsmål as early as 1863.

Aasen considered his poems to be songs. They were all written to various melodies, and he included these melodies at the back of his volume. Several of Aasen's poems are still well-known songs; the most popular, "Nordmannen" (The Norwegian), still ranks as one of the most popular Norwegian songs and is regarded as an alternative national anthem for the Nynorsk movement.

The first eight poems in *Symra* deal with the country ("Gamle Noreg" [Old Norway], "Nordmannen"), nature ("Dei gamle fjelli" [The Old Mountains]), and with three of the four seasons ("Vårdagen" [Spring Day], "Sumarkvelden" [Summer Evening], "Haustvisa" [Autumn Song]). From the ninth poem ("Hugen" [The Mind]), the poems deal more and more with people's inner feelings, gradually becoming more serious and even slightly sad. Throughout the book, Aasen's respect for the common man is obvious. *Symra* sold well, and was republished in slightly altered versions in 1867 and in 1873. Few people were used to reading Landsmål in the 1860s, and according to an account in *Dagbladet* published six days after his death in 1896, Aasen was once asked if he would be willing to translate the poems for a Danish edition. He lay motionless on his couch for twenty minutes before his guest repeated his question. After another ten silent minutes, Aasen replied "Jeg tenker ikke, det er værdt" (I don't think it is worth it).

Symra was Aasen's only collection of poems in Landsmål, but he wrote several other individual poems. Some were included in his plays; some were published in magazines or newspapers; and others remained unpublished until his death. In "Lovtale yver Culturen" (A Eulogy for Culture), Aasen revealed his talent for comedy. In this long poem published in *Dølen* Aasen pokes fun at all the foreign words in Dano-Norwegian. Just to make sure that he drove his humor home, he used the pen name Ohle Ohlzén.

Aasen was a hard worker, but he also knew how to take his mind off work. Every day, as a break from writing, and a way of getting exercise, Aasen would venture from his home to a small café, where he enjoyed a cup of coffee or a glass of beer, read the papers, and met people. Aasen enjoyed the theater, and in his diaries he mentions the more than six hundred plays he had seen. Aasen enjoyed lighter farces the most; he only saw two plays by Ibsen. He had a wide range of friends and saw them frequently. When in the right mood, Aasen could be the focus of gatherings, constantly entertaining the others with stories of all kinds. His diaries mention those he met; a great number of other writers of Landsmål were regular guests. Aasen became quite wealthy, and he happily shared what he had with others, even with beggars, who were not always welcome, as they distracted him from his work.

Aasen never married. His only known serious affair was in the 1830s, with the servant Berte Paulsdotter Vike at Herøy. According to the local tradition, they became engaged, but that seems unlikely, though apparently the two were still a couple when Aasen left Herøy. Some time after Aasen moved to Solnør, Vike went to see him. By then he had lost interest in her and avoided her by staying in the woods and looking for plants for his herbarium. The humiliated Vike became the laughingstock of the Daae family, and returned to Herøy without even talking to Aasen. The two never met again.

Later in life, Aasen proposed to three women. All three proposals were written, as was customary in those days, and the letters are all included in the collection of Aasen's letters published in the 1950s. They make for sad reading, especially the final one, written in 1861, where he, after having introduced the matter at hand, lists reasons why the recipient should decline his offer. One of these reasons, that he felt that he looked "gammel og styg" (old and ugly), may explain why he kept postponing his first visit to a photographer. He finally had his picture taken in 1871, and when he picked up the picture a couple of days later, he was not thrilled with the results. In his diary entry that day he wrote, "Hos Fotografen. Slet Humør" (At the Photographers'. In a sad mood). In later years he twice had his photograph taken again. Three photographs taken on the street without his knowledge also exist. In his final years he posed for two artists, the painter Lars Osa and the sculptor Augusta Finne.

In May 1885 Aasen tasted one of his sweetest victories. Stortinget, the Norwegian parliament, passed a bill stating that "det norske Folkesprog sidestilles med vort almindelige Skrift- og Bogsprog" (the Norwegian folk language should be equal with our ordinary book language). This must have been a glorious day for Aasen after his hard work; amazingly, he did not mention the passage of the bill in his diaries. He frequently wrote of his ill health; he must have been relatively healthy, however, even given his constant smoking habit. In the 1890s his health gradually declined, and he arranged for a younger relative, Jon Fagerhol, to rent a room in his building. Fagerhol assisted him in his daily life, took notes, read the papers, went on errands, and supported or even carried him on the few occasions that Aasen left his home in his final years. Aasen died on 23 September 1896 and is buried in Vår Frelsers Gravlund in Oslo.

At his death Aasen was a wealthy man. He had received a government grant from 1851 on, and he never incurred large expenses. He never bought his own house but lived in modest quarters; never had a family; and, through the years, he managed to save quite a bit of money. When he passed away, he had more than 31,000 NKR, roughly the equivalent of 1.8 million NKR today. As he had no descendants and as he survived all his sib-

Front-page report of Aasen's death, published on the day he died (Ivar Aasen Center)

lings, his belongings were split between more-distant relatives, most of whom were still living in the Sunnmøre region. Jon Aasen, the oldest son of the family at Aasen's childhood farm, wrote a letter to the administrator of Aasen's estate, requesting that all of Aasen's belongings be brought to the Åsen farm, where they would remain as a monument to him. This letter, written sixteen days after Aasen's death, was the foundation for the first Norwegian museum devoted to the life and work of only one person. Everything Aasen owned was shipped to Ørsta, where a small wooden building was erected in 1898. The only exceptions were Aasen's manuscripts, which were given to the University Library in Christiania.

The collection of effects sent to Åsen is still preserved and provides a fascinating insight into the life of the writer, who owned approximately 2,500 books, in at least fifteen languages, covering a broad range of subjects, but surprisingly few items apart from his books. The small wooden building, which was not even big enough to house Aasen's book collection, remained the Ivar Aasen Museum until 1946, when a stone building was erected next to it. This new building was bigger and also had electricity, meaning that the condition for storing the books was much improved. The late 1900s brought an increasing interest in Aasen's life and work, and in 1996, the one hundredth anniversary of his death, more than a thousand large and small events took place all over Norway to honor his work.

In 2000 a third museum building named after Aasen was erected. This new building, also located on the Åsen farm, was designed by the renowned architect Sverre Fehn and is much more than a museum. The building, which contains a library, exhibits, archives, and an amphitheatre, is run by Nynorsk kultursentrum, an organization dedicated to the importance of Nynorsk.

Ivar Aasen's importance in the history of Norway cannot be underestimated. The language he created is still one of Norway's two official languages. Though the work of most other Norwegian scientists from the 1800s has now been forgotten, Aasen's work is still referred to and discussed today. Aasen is regarded as the finest linguist Norway has ever produced, and as a poet he is also held in high esteem, even if the number of poems he wrote is somewhat limited.

Letters:

Brev til vener i heimbygda, edited by M. A. E. Aarflot (Volda: Aarflots Prenteverks Forlag, 1950);

Brev og dagbøker, 3 volumes, edited by Reidar Djupedal (Oslo: Det Norske Samlaget, 1957–1960).

Bibliographies:

Jostein Fet, *New Norse Literature in English Translation 1880–1982: A Bibliography* (Volda: Møreforsking, 1985);

Ivar Aasen-Tunet <www.aasentunet.no> [accessed 13 August 2009].

Biographies:

Johs. Belsheim, *Ivar Aasen: En Levnetsskildring* (Christiania: Dybwad, 1901);

Arne Garborg, *Ivar Aasen* (Oslo: Norigs ungdomslag og Student-maallaget, 1902);

Ivar Mortensson-Egnund, *Ivar Aasen–Ein norsk kulturmann* (Christiania: Jensen, 1903);

Anders Hovden, *Ivar Aasen i kvardagslaget* (Trondheim, 1913);

Garborg, Anders Hovden, and Halvdan Koht Hovden, *Ivar Aasen: Granskaren, maalreisaren, diktaren. Eit minneskrift um livsverket hans* (Christiania, 1913);

Lars Eskeland, *Ivar Aasen: Ei folkeskrift* (Bjørgvin [Bergen]: Lunde, 1923);

Knut Liestøl, *Ivar Aasen* (Oslo: Noregs Boklag, 1963);

Stephen J. Walton, *Ivar Aasens Nedre halvdel* (Oslo: Det Norske Samlaget, 1991);

Jostein Krokvik, *Ivar Aasen: Diktar og granskar, sosial frigjerar og nasjonal målreisar* (Bergen: Norsk Bokreidingslag, 1996);

Kjell Venås, *Då tida var fullkomen: Ivar Aasen* (Oslo: Novus Forlag, 1996);

Venås, *Livssoga åt Ivar Aasen* (Oslo: Ivar Aasen-året 1996);

Walton, *Ivar Aasens kropp* (Oslo: Det Norske Samlaget, 1996).

References:

J. Peter Burgess, *Ivar Aasen's Logic of Nation: Toward a Philosophy of Culture* (Volda: Høgskolen i Volda, 1999);

Ivar Eskeland, *Halvtanna hundreår med Ivar Aasen* (Oslo: Noregs Mållag, 1964);

Ottar Grepstad, *Viljen til Språk* (Oslo: Det Norske Samlaget, 2006);

Kaare Haukaas, *Lista yver Ivar Aasen-boksamlingi* (Volda: Aarflots, 1946);

Geir Hjorthol, ed., *Forteljingar om Ivar Aasen: Aasenresepsjonen i fortid og notid* (Volda: Høgskolen i Volda, 1997);

Oddmund Løkensgaard Hoel, "Ordbøkene til Ivar Aasen. Prinsipp og metodar for innsamling og utval av ord," *Maal og Minne,* 1, nos. 3–4 (1994): 147–166;

Magne Myhren, ed., *Ei bok om Ivar Aasen: Språkgranskaren og målreisaren* (Oslo: Det Norske Samlaget, 1975);

Jostein Nerbøvik, ed., *Ivar Aasen-senteret: Eit nasjonalt Senter for nynorsk skriftkultur* (Volda: Senteret, 1992).

Peter Christen Asbjørnsen
(15 January 1812 – 6 January 1885)

Donna H. Stockton
University of Colorado at Boulder

BOOKS: *Nor: en Billedbog for den norske Ungdom,* by Asbjørnsen and Bernt Moe (Christiania: Guldberg & Dzwonkowski, 1837);

Billedmagazin for Børn (Christiania: Guldberg & Dzwonkowski, 1838);

Naturhistorie for ungdommen, 6 volumes (Christiania: Guldberg & Dzwonkowski, 1838–1849);

Norske Folkeeventyr, 4 parts, by Asbjørnsen and Jørgen Moe (Christiania: Johan Dahl, 1841–1844; revised and enlarged, 1 volume, 1852); translated by George Webbe Dasent as *Popular Tales from the Norse* (Edinburgh: Edmonston & Douglas, 1859); Norwegian version revised (Christiania: Dybwad, 1866; revised again, 1868; revised again, 1874);

Norske Huldreeventyr og Folkesagn: 1 Samling (Christiania: Fabritius, 1845; revised and enlarged, 1859);

Norske Huldreeventyr og Folkesagn: 2 Samling (Christiania: Fabritius, 1848; revised and enlarged, 1866);

Juletræet for 1850: en Samling af Norske Folke-og Børne Eventyr (Christiania: Dzwonkowski, 1850);

Juletræet 1866: Norske Folke- og Børne Eventyr (Christiania: Dybwad, 1866);

Norske Folkeeventyr: Ny Samling, by Asbjørnsen and Moe (Christiania: Dybwad, 1871; revised and enlarged edition, Christiania: Gyldendal, 1876); translated by Dasent as *Tales from the Field: A Series of Popular Tales from the Norse* (London: Gibbings, 1896);

Norske Folke- og Huldre-eventyr i Udvalg (Copenhagen: Gyldendal, 1879);

Eventyrbog for Børn: norske Folkeeventyr, 2 volumes (Copenhagen: Gyldendal, 1883);

Erotiske Folkeeventyr, by Asbjørnsen, Moe, and Knut Nauthella, edited by Oddbjørg Høgset (Oslo: Universitetsforlaget, 1977).

Editions and Collections: *Norske Folkeeventyr: Fællessamlingen,* 2 volumes, edited by Moltke Moe (Christiania: Aschehoug, 1896, 1899);

Udvalgte Folkeeventyr: Ny Samling, edited by Moe (Christiania: Gyldendal, 1907);

Norske Huldreeventyr og Folkesagn, revised by Moe and Anders Krogvig (Christiania: Aschehoug, 1914);

Peter Christen Asbjørnsen (Store Norske Leksikon <http://snl.no/ .bilde/Asbj%C3%B8rnsen%2C_Peter_Christen_(foto)>)

Barne-eventyr, edited by Moe (Christiania: Aschehoug, 1920);

Norske Huldreeventyr og Folkesagn, 2 volumes, edited by Knut Liestøl (Oslo: Tanum, 1949).

Editions in English: *A Selection from the Norse Tales for the Use of Children,* translated by George Webbe Dasent (Edinburgh: Edmonston & Douglas, 1862);

Round the Yule Log: Norwegian Folk and Fairy Tales, translated by H. L. Brækstad (London: Sampson, Lowe, Marston, Searle & Rivington, 1881);

Norwegian Fairy Tales, translated by Abel Heywood (London & New York: Routledge, 1895);

Norwegian Fairy Tales, translated by Helen Grade and John Grade (London: Milford, 1924; New York: American-Scandinavian Foundation, 1924);

Norwegian Folk Tales, translated by Pat Shaw Iversen and Carl Norman (New York: Viking, 1960; London: Allen & Unwin, 1963);

Norwegian Fairy Tales, translated by Brenda Romskaug and Reidar Romskaug (London: University of London, 1961; Chester Springs, Pa.: Dufour, 1961;

Folktales of Norway, translated by Iversen (London & Chicago: Chicago University Press, 1964);

A Time for Trolls: Fairy Tales from Norway Told by Asbjørnsen and Moe, translated by Joan Roll-Hansen (Oslo: Tanum-Norli, 1964).

OTHER: *Hjemmet og vandring: En Asbjørnsen bog for 1848,* edited by Asbjørnsen (Christiania: Asbjørnsen, 1848);

Ydale: et vinterskrift, edited by Asbjørnsen (Christiana: Feilberg & Landmark, 1851);

Nyttårsbog, edited by Asbjørnsen (Christiania: Werner, 1854).

TRANSLATIONS: *Juletrold: Udvalgte Folke- og Børne-Eventyr* (Christiania: Brøgger, 1851);

Eventyr fra fremmede Lande (Christiania: Steensballes, 1860).

Peter Christen Asbjørnsen is remembered today for his contributions to Norwegian folk literature. The folktales and legends collected by Asbjørnsen and Jørgen Moe in the rural districts of mid-nineteenth-century Norway are the most widely read literature ever produced in that country. The tales, told by people living in a landscape of deep waters, thick forests, and rugged mountains where mythological beings were believed to dwell, form the literary foundation of Norwegian cultural identity. They have been in print since the first collection was published in 1841.

Asbjørnsen was born on 15 January 1812 in Christiania (later Oslo), the capital of Norway, to Andreas Asbjørnsen, a glazier, and Thurine Elisabeth Bruen. He was sent to the Cathedral School in Christiania to prepare for a classical university education, but he preferred reading fairy tales and adventure stories by authors such as Sir Walter Scott to studying Latin grammar. When he was fourteen, his father enrolled him in a school in Ringerike, the district northwest of Christiania, for a course of intensive preparation for his *examen artium* (university entrance examination), but Asbjørnsen chose to wander the countryside rather than study. He also became close friends with a fellow student, Moe, the son of a prosperous farmer. The two became blood brothers, mixing their blood as they imagined was done in the days of the Vikings. They shared a love of writing, finding inspiration in the Gothic tales and stories from the Norwegian countryside by the Romantic writer Mauritz Hansen. After a year, Asbjørnsen's father brought him home. He resumed his studies at the Cathedral School and helped his father build metrological instruments. He and Moe corresponded after Asbjørnsen returned to Christiania.

Asbjørnsen spent much time fishing and hunting in Nordmarken, the woods above Christiania, becoming a self-trained naturalist and expert on the flora and fauna of the region. He enjoyed chatting and exchanging stories with strangers he met in his father's shop or in the forest. He also wrote, honing skills for what became a lifelong career as a freelance author. But he again neglected his formal academic studies and failed his first attempt to pass his university entrance examination in 1833. He then took a position as a resident tutor for a family in Romerike, a region of forests and farms northeast of Christiania. During the three years he spent there he recorded stories and legends he heard from the country people, and he wrote detailed descriptions of the natural surroundings. He became engaged to a woman named Caroline Marianne Gründer, but her parents did not consider him a good match for her. He returned to Christiania in 1835, passed his examination, and enrolled at the Royal Frederik University in Christiania. Moe was already a student there.

The year Asbjørnsen entered the university a revised second edition of *Norske Sagn* (Norwegian Legends), by the minister Andreas Faye, was published under the title *Norske Folke-sagn* (Norwegian Folk Legends). In the first edition, published two years earlier, Faye had deplored the superstitions of the peasants, such as their belief in supernatural beings such as *jutuler* (giants) and *nøkker* (water spirits). Like other clergymen and scholars of the Enlightenment, he believed that exposing the falsehood of these notions would lead to their eradication. In the second edition Faye's viewpoint changed. Influenced by the ideas of Romanticism and the folktale work of the brothers Jacob and Wilhelm Grimm in Germany, Faye introduced the word *folke* to describe those he now saw as nature's noblemen rather than as ignorant peasants. Although Faye wrote in Danish rather than the vernacular of his informants, he attempted to record their accounts accurately, and his collection included legends not found elsewhere. Although Faye showed a kinder attitude toward his sources in his second edition, he conveyed their legends in a dry and lackluster manner.

Asbjørnsen had contributed legends to Faye's second edition; but when it was published, he publicly criticized Faye's presentation as unnecessarily moralizing. Inspired by a growing interest among the educated elite of Norway in the national heritage represented by rural cultural traditions, Asbjørnsen and Moe began work on their own collection of Norwegian folktales. Their initial goal was to reproduce the oral tales of Norway faithfully, just as the Brothers Grimm claimed to have done with the German tales in their *Kinder und Hausmärchen* (1812, 1815, Children's and Household Tales; translated as *German Popular Stories*, 1823, 1826). They already had material that Asbjørnsen had collected in Romerike and Moe had collected in Ringerike, but they needed more. In the summer of 1837 they went on field trips to Ådalen and Valdres, the first of several journeys to various districts to find tales for their planned collection.

Meanwhile, Asbjørnsen and Bernt Moe, a cousin of Jørgen Moe, published an illustrated children's book, *Nor: en Billedbog for den norske Ungdom* (Mite: A Picture-Book for Norwegian Children), at Christmas 1837. The first part of the book, by Moe, consisted of stories about heroes of Norwegian history and sagas; in the second part Asbjørnsen presented folktales. In "Egebergkongen" (The King of Egeberg) he recalls his childhood memories of legends children living near Ekeberg Mountain on the southeast outskirts of Christiania had told. "Egebergkongen" opens with a man hiking down the mountain. His walk brings to mind the legends of the *underjordiske* (subterranean beings) who, the children believe, live inside the mountain. The king of the *underjordiske* asks a human midwife to assist his queen in giving birth. The children born to the queen are always ugly, with red faces and oversized heads, so some of the *underjordiske* sneak above the ground and go down into the city to kidnap a human infant. In its place they leave the queen's ugly infant as a *bytting* (changeling). "Egebergkongen" concludes by suggesting methods a mother can employ to force the kidnappers to return her baby. Similar stories appear in many Norwegian legends.

"Mathias Skytters Historier" (Mathias the Hunter's Stories) combines legends from Romerike about *underjordiske*, *huldre-folk* (beings who live near humans and sometimes appear in human form), *puslinger* (small, weak creatures), and *nisser* (small-statured house guardians). To frame the legends Asbjørnsen creates a local storyteller, the hunter Mathias, who relates them to a visitor from the city on a nighttime ramble through a moonlit forest where such beings are supposed to live. Asbjørnsen adopted this technique of framing legends from a German translation of Crofton Croker's *Fairy Legends and Traditions of the South of Ireland* (1825) that he frequently checked out of the university library. Mathias explains the origins of the *underjordiske*: when God cast the evil angels out of heaven, some fell down to hell; those who had not sinned so greatly dwelt in the air, under the earth, and in the sea. He tells

Decorative binding for the second edition (1896) of Asbjørnsen and Jørgen Moe's 1879 collection of folktales (Library of Congress)

the city dweller of several occasions when he encountered one *hulder*, a beautiful wood nymph who looked human except for her tail. Once he met an old man with three legs who disappeared down a hole in the ground. Occasionally, the educated visitor interjects a doubtful comment about the existence of *underjordiske*; Mathias ignores him and continues with yet another legend. One Christmas Eve he and his little brother were playing on a rock outcrop. When it got dark, the rock started shouting at them to go home. He also tells of meeting a *nisse* one evening when he went to the stable to feed the family horse. He climbed up to the hayloft and grabbed a bunch of hay. In it he saw two eyes so red that they glowed like hot coals. He threw the hay to the stable floor below. He looked for what he had seen hidden in the hay but could not find it. As he was leaving the stable something tripped him, and he fell flat on his face. He looked back over his shoulder to see a *nisse* standing at the stable door, laughing so hard that its pointed red hat shook. In all of the stories Mathias tells of meeting *huldre*, *puslinger*, and *nisser* no permanent harm results, although his brother went insane for a time after an encounter with a group of *huldre-folk*. According to the legends, these beings live more or less peacefully on the fringes of human habitation in the forests and agricultural regions of eastern Norway.

Asbjørnsen's tales in *Nor* attracted favorable comment. While no copies of the book are known to have survived, the legends related in it are known from their inclusion in his *Norske Huldreeventyr og Folkesagn: 1 Samling* (1845, Norwegian Hulder Tales and Folk Legends: First Collection). The positive response encouraged Asbjørnsen and Moe to continue their research and writing, but they had important decisions to make about content, form, and language before they could start organizing their material for publication. Folk narratives were differentiated into two categories, although the terms often overlap. *Folkeeventyr* (folktales) do not purport to be true. They are international, told in variants from one country to another; in Norway they begin with the phrase "Det var en gang . . ." (Once upon a time . . .). They are often about peasants and their encounters with evil trolls or beautiful princesses. The lazy farm boy Askelad, who would prefer to spend his days sitting by the fire rather than working, is an unlikely hero in many Norwegian folktales. *Sagn* (legends), on the other hand, are narratives that are claimed to be true by the people who tell them. They are often quite brief. The subjects of legends may be beings such as the *huldre-folk* of "Mathias Skytters Historier," trolls, or *jutuler*. Historical tales also fall into the category of *sagn*.

Asbjørnsen and Moe's initial goal was to provide accurate records of folk literature, but they found that while they could faithfully record the words of the storytellers, they could not replicate the gestures, expressions, and cadences that made the telling of a tale a performance; also, sometimes an unskilled storyteller would tell an incomplete or garbled version of a story. In such cases Asbjørnsen and Moe edited the texts to convey the mannerisms of the speaker or to improve the story. But although they rewrote or combined the folktales and legends they collected, they never invented narratives out of whole cloth. All of their published folktales and legends are based on material they collected in the field.

The status of language in Norway presented another challenge to Asbjørnsen and Moe's goal of accuracy. The written language of Norway was Danish, which had been the language of administration and literature during the centuries when the country was under the Danish crown. Most educated people considered their spoken Dano-Norwegian superior to the provincial dialects of Asbjørnsen and Moe's informants. Those dialects were based on Old Norse, which had been spoken long before Norway fell under foreign rule. In addition, there were many unique local expressions that would not be easily understood by outsiders. Asbjørnsen and Moe attempted to maintain the vocabulary and local turns of phrase of the spoken versions of the tales, while still making them understandable. They preserved more of the original language in the legends than in the folktales, since they considered the legends to have stronger ties to the places where they were told. The two men thus abandoned their original goal of scientifically recording and presenting Norway's oral-cultural heritage.

In writing up the *sagn* Asbjørnsen refined the technique he had used in "Mathias Skytters Historier." A narrator sets the scene for the legends, which are told by a local person who has either experienced the events or has heard of them from someone else. The narrator, who is typically an educated city dweller, occasionally interjects comments, and he brings the story to a close. Specific place-names and detailed descriptions of the natural setting draw the reader into the story.

Asbjørnsen and Moe tried to finance publication of their first collection by soliciting subscriptions—an uncommon practice in Norway at the time. Moe's prospectus referred to the scientific and national importance of the folktales, the richness of the poetry of the people, and the urgent need to record this literature before it disappeared. There was little response. Finally, the publisher Johan Dahl agreed to fund the publication of *Norske Folkeeventyr* (Norwegian Folktales) in 1841 as a ninety-eight-page pamphlet with a plain blue-gray cover that lacked the title or the names of the authors and the publisher. The simple volume received surprisingly good reviews. Encouraged by the reception, Asbjørnsen and Moe went on to collect material from the more distant districts of Røyken and Telemark to the west of Oslo and Gudbrandsdalen to the north.

Asbjørnsen was on such an expedition when he met Camilla Collett on a boat on Lake Mjøsa in 1842. They talked for hours, and she later sent him a folktale she had heard from her nanny, Lisbeth-Marie, during her childhood. Still later, she introduced Asbjørnsen to Lisbeth-Marie, who told him many tales and legends. Asbjørnsen used much of her material in his collections and incorporated her into his work as the storyteller Anne-Marie.

The year after meeting Collett, Asbjørnsen anonymously published the tale "Fuglesang og Huldreæt" (Bird Songs and Huldre Families) in the newspaper *Den Constitutionelle* (The Constitutional). A man and woman are walking in the hills of Romerike when it suddenly begins to rain, and they take shelter in a rundown hut. To pass the time, the woman tells a legend. Then the weather clears, and the tour continues with a breathtaking description of the woods after the rain and the view across hills and valleys. Collett had contributed short stories, some situated in Romerike, to the paper, and many attributed "Fuglesang og Huldreæt" to her. As a joke, Collett wrote a tale titled "Badeliv og Fjelliv" (1843, Life at the Spa and Life in the Mountains) in Asbjørnsen's style for the paper.

Three more *Norske Folkeeventyr* pamphlets were published in 1844. Collett and her husband, Jonas, had helped Asbjørnsen prepare the legends for publication, and several of the frame narratives in the pamphlets are the anonymous work of Camilla Collett. The collections were highly praised by the majority of Norwegian reviewers, although some wondered how tales that they had heard in the nursery or on the farm could be considered literature. The works quickly gained the attention of folklorists in other countries; German critics declared that the Norwegian folktale collections were the best ever produced. Historians claim that they marked the beginning of Norway's National Romantic or National Breakthrough period, which led to Norwegian independence in 1905.

Asbjørnsen and Moe continued to work on their project throughout the 1840s but also pursued individual interests. Asbjørnsen wrote a six-volume textbook series, *Naturhistorie for ungdommen* (1838–1849, Natural History for the Young). He frequently combined his interests in folklore, science, hunting, and fishing by teasing a local legend out of a fellow hunter or making notes on flora and fauna while recording a folktale.

Asbjørnsen published several other stories based on legends in *Den Constitutionelle*, acquainting readers in Christiania's intellectual circles with his new method of presenting the material. These pieces were included in *Norske Huldreeventyr og Folkesagn,* published in 1845. Reviewers praised Asbjørnsen's fresh and entertaining portrayal of rural life and nature, as well as his technique for telling the legends. A second collection of *Norske Huldreeventyr og Folkesagn* was published in 1848. Henrik Ibsen borrowed legends from the two collections for his *Peer Gynt* (1867; translated, 1892): the first two first acts of Ibsen's play are from the stories "En søndagskveld til seters" (Sunday Evening at the Mountain Dairy) and "Rensdyrjakt i Rondane" (Reindeer Hunt in the Rondane Mountains). Reidar Thoralf Christiansen's *Folktales of Norway* (1964) is the most accurate English translation of material from the 1845 and 1848 editions of *Norske Huldreeventyr og Folkesagn*. Written for adult readers, it includes a representative selection of folktales and legends about spirits of the air, water, farms, forests, and mountains; ghosts; shape-shifters; witches; the devil; and historical persons and events.

Asbjørnsen and Moe returned to *Norske Folkeeventyr* in 1852, adding more material and editing their pre-

Dust jacket for the 1960 English translation of a selection of Asbjørnsen and Moe's folktales (Richland County Public Library)

vious work. The 1852 edition is better written and reproduces spoken dialects more accurately than the 1841 and 1844 pamphlets. It was translated into English by George Webbe Dasent in 1859 as *Popular Tales from the Norse*. Dasent was the first of many English translators who used material from the 1852 edition.

After the 1852 edition was completed, Asbjørnsen and Moe went their separate ways and did not work together again. Moe entered the ministry, and Asbjørnsen focused his interest on natural science. He wrote and translated articles and textbooks, and in 1856 he enrolled in a two-year forestry course in Germany. Afterward, he held government positions managing forests and peat bogs that provided him with a regular income, so that he was no longer dependent on the marginal revenues from his publications. He took an early interest in Charles Darwin's theory of evolution by natural selection and published an article about it in the journal *Budstikken* in 1861, two years after *On the Origin of Species* appeared.

Asbjørnsen did not abandon his work with folklore, however. He translated folktales from other languages into Norwegian and collected new tales and legends when he was on scientific field trips. He published revised and enlarged editions of *Norske Huldreeventyr og Folkesagn* in 1859 and 1866. While not participating directly, Moe sent Asbjørnsen all of his remaining material in 1865. Asbjørnsen used this material in *Norske Folkeeventyr: Ny Samling* (1871, Norwegian Folktales: New Collection). In 1876 Moe's son, Moltke, a folklore scholar in his own right, joined Asbjørnsen in publishing an enlarged edition of the 1871 collection; it was translated by Dasent in 1896 as *Tales from the Field: A Series of Popular Tales from the Norse*. In 1879 Asbjørnsen and Moltke Moe published *Norske Folke- og Huldre-eventyr i Udvalg* (Norwegian Folk- and *Huldre*-Tales: A Selection), with illustrations by eight of Norway's most prominent artists: Peter Arboe, Hans Gude, V. St. Lerche, Eilif Peterssen, A. Schneider, Otto Sinding, August Tidemann, and Erik Werenskiold. The illustrations, along with drawings by Theodore Kittelsen, were republished in later collections of folktales and have created an image of how *troll, nisser, huldre,* and other *underjordiske* beings should look. The drawings also help to preserve the nineteenth-century landscape of Norway in the memories of Norwegians, as well as to create an image of Norway for people all over the world.

International interest in Norwegian folktales steadily increased, and two collections for children were translated into English during Asbjørnsen's lifetime: Dasent's *A Selection from the Norse Tales for the Use of Children* in 1862 and H. L. Brækstad's *Round the Yule Log: Norwegian Folk and Fairy Tales* in 1881. Among the many popular children's tales in the two volumes are "East of the Sun and West of the Moon," The Man Who Kept House," "The Three Billy Goats Gruff," and "Why the Bear is Stumpy-Tailed."

Although Norse folktales for children were published in English in 1862, twenty-one years passed before a children's collection appeared in Norway. Asbjørnsen had contributed tales for children to magazines and annuals, but no book-length work had been published since his and Bernt Moe's *Nor* in 1838. In 1883, however, he brought out the first two volumes of *Eventyrbog for Børn: Norske Folkeeventyr* (Tales for Children: Norwegian Folktales) with illustrations by Werenskiold and Kittelsen. They were Asbjørnsen's last works; he died on 6 January 1885. A third volume was completed two years later by Moltke Moe.

Asbjørnsen left all of his notes and manuscripts to Moltke Moe, as did Jørgen Moe when he died in 1882. They also granted him the right to carry on their work. The younger Moe continued to refine the forms of the folktales and legends. He also added more of the flavor of the various dialects, in accordance with Asbjørnsen's instructions to change the language of the stories along with the vernacular of the people so that the folktales and legends would remain fresh for new readers. When one reads "Mathias Skytters Historier" in an updated version today, the visitor from the city speaks in modern literary Bokmål while Mathias tells the local legends in *kav romeriksdialekt* (thick Romerike's dialect).

When Moltke Moe died in 1912, he bequeathed the handwritten and printed folklore material in his possession to the government. It formed the basis for the Norsk Folkeminnesamling (Norwegian Folklore Archives) at the University in Oslo. Material collected by other folklorists has since been added, and these archives are the primary source for Norwegian folklore studies today.

There had long been rumors that erotic tales were to be found in these archives. Asbjørnsen had been known to enjoy telling a spicy story on occasion, and his tales of this nature occasionally showed up in print outside of Norway. In 1943 Christiansen, who had access to the archives, privately printed thirteen copies of three of Asbjørnsen's tales with illustrations by Thorbjørn Egner. In the early 1970s Oddbjørg Høgset began searching the folklore archives for erotic tales collected by Asbjørnsen, Jørgen Moe, and other folklorists. She found virtually untouched material in the form of field notes by Asbjørnsen and Moe and in 1977 published the first erotic folklore collection freely available to Norwegians: *Erotiske folkeeventyr* (Erotic Folktales). She points out that much of the material was subjected to censorship from the time it was collected: Asbjørnsen frequently wrote "svinsk–ubrukelig–obscønt" (filthy–unusable–obscene) in the margins of his notes. Today the tales seem more comical than shocking.

Peter Christen Asbjørnsen's folktale work has had a profound influence on the history of Norway and the language and self-image of the Norwegian people. His and Moe's folktale and legend collections were the most widely read literature in nineteenth-century Norway. Asbjørnsen's frame narratives, with their detailed, painterly descriptions of the natural surroundings, contributed to the development of Norwegians' deep affinity for the rural landscapes of their homeland. The language used by the two writers in their early editions, in which they strove to find a middle ground between written Danish and the spoken dialects of Norway, established a form from which Bokmål, the most widely used written Norwegian, evolved. Asbjørnsen's stipulation in his bequest to Moltke Moe that future editions be rewritten in the language of their time assured that the collections have continued to be accessible to new generations, and their language has become, as Asbjørnsen and Moe originally wished, a realistic rendition of the dialects of the regions where the tales were collected. Finally, Asbjørnsen and Moe presented the folktales from the countryside in a form that made them appealing to educated readers; as a result, folk literature became an integral element in the building of a Norwegian national identity, which led to Norway's becoming an independent nation in 1905. Asbjørnsen and Moe's folktales and legends, illustrated by well-known artists, have a central place in Norway's cultural heritage.

Biographies:

Hans Hansen, *Peter Christen Asbjørnsen* (Oslo: Aschehoug, 1932);

Knut Liestøl, *P. Chr. Asbjørnsen: Mannen og livsverket* (Oslo: Tanum, 1947);

Truls Gjefsen, *Peter Christen Asbjørnsen: Diger og folkesæl* (Oslo: Andresen & Butenschøn, 2001).

References:

Marte Hvam Hult, *Framing a National Narrative: The Legend Collections of Peter Christen Asbjørnsen* (Detroit: Wayne State University Press, 2003);

Reimund Kvideland and Henning K. Sehmsdorf, *Scandinavian Folk Belief and Legend* (Minneapolis: University of Minnesota Press, 1988);

Daniel Popp, *Asbjørnsens Linguistic Reform* (Oslo: Universitetsforlaget, 1977);

Ellisiv Steen, *Diktning og Virkelighet: en studie i Camilla Colletts forfatterskap* (Oslo: Gyldendal, 1947);

Egil Sundland, *"Det var en Gang–et Menneske": Tolkninger av Asbjørnsen og Moes Undereventyr som Allegorier på Menneskelig Innsikt og Erkjennelse* (Oslo: Cappelen akademisk forlag, 1995).

Papers:

Peter Christen Asbjørnsen's letters, papers, field notes, and manuscripts are archived in the Norsk Folkeminnesamling in the Institutt for Kulturstudier og Orientalske Språk at the University of Oslo.

Absalon Pedersson Beyer
(1528? – 1575)

Lanae H. Isaacson

BOOKS: *Om Norgis Rige* (Bergen, 1780);

Liber Capituli Bergensis: Absalon Pedersson Beyers Dagbog over Begivenheder, især i Bergen 1552–1572, edited by Nicolay Nicolaysen (Christiania: Johan Dahl, 1860);

Oration om Mester Geble 1571 (Oslo: Det Norske Sprog og Litteraturselskap/Universitetsforlaget, 1963).

Absalon Pedersson Beyer was at the forefront of the small group of humanists who set the literary, cultural, and religious tone in Bergen during the sixteenth century. Following in the footsteps of his patron and mentor, Geble Pedersson, Beyer served as a *lektor i teologi* (teacher) at Bergen Latin (Cathedral) School. He was an active member of the Bergen Cathedral Chapter, and he arranged and directed the didactic *skoledramaer* (religious dramas) performed by the students of the school. Beyer assumed Geble Pedersson's position of castle chaplain and bishop for Bergenhus (Bergen Castle) under the Danish royal regent and governor, Erik Rosenkrantz. Beyer secured a place in literary history as a reporter of events great and small in Bergen; as the writer of *Om Norgis Rige* (1780, On the Kingdom of Norway), a work combining history, commentaries on current events, and political statement; and as a biographer of the first Lutheran bishop in Bergen, *Oration om Mester Geble 1571* (1963, Oration on Master Geble, 1571). *Norges Litteraturhistorie* (1982, History of Norwegian Literature) calls Beyer's works "spirene til en moderne norsk nasjonalfølelse" (the roots for a modern feeling of Norwegian nationalism). It is perhaps more accurate to consider Beyer's writings as evidence of a feeling of *hjemstavnskærlighed* (regional connection) and of an abiding love for the local intellectual and religious community, Beyer's humanist colleagues, and the culture in Bergen that Beyer helped build.

Not much is known about Beyer's early years, and not much more can be learned by going to the logical source for such information, *Liber Capituli Bergensis: Absalon Pederson Beyers Dagbog over Begivenheder, især i Bergen 1552–1572* (1860, Book of the Bergen Chapter: Absalon Pedersson Beyer's Diary of Events, Particularly in Bergen, 1552–1572). Beyer's work offers surprisingly little autobiographical information about the leader of the Bergen religious and intellectual community, the man who inherited Geble Pedersson's position in the Lutheran Church and Latin School. Beyer was born in Aurlandsfjorden, Sogn, in 1528. At an early age Beyer lost both parents and was sent by his uncle to study in Bergen. There he entered Bergen Latin School and became the foster son of the Lutheran Superintendent, Mester Geble Pedersson, Bergen's religious constant during the transition from Catholicism to Lutheran Evangelicalism. (Geble Pedersson was Bergen's last Catholic priest, as well as the town's first Protestant bishop.) Without a doubt, the young orphan received the finest education available at the time: Beyer finished his studies at Bergen Latin, and, under the sponsorship and watchful guidance of Mester Geble, he studied for five years in Copenhagen, earning the degree of *magister* (master) while staying in the home of Peder Palladius, the bishop of Sjælland and Denmark's foremost humanist. Beyer continued his studies in Wittenberg, where he attended lectures by eminent church leader Philip Melanchton. In 1552 Beyer returned home to Bergen, where he assumed the post of teacher of theology and rector for Bergen Latin School. His lectures on the sermons of Danish theologian Niels Hemmingsen at Bergen Latin School suggest an additional influence beyond that of Palladius and Melanchton. Beyer died in 1575 and was survived by his widow, Anne Pedersdotter, who was burned as a witch in 1590; as Peter Kirkegaard noted, her fate was not uncommon in a time of superstition, violence, and general mayhem.

The Bergen of Beyer's diary bears little resemblance to the life and the progressive city of the late twentieth and early twenty-first centuries. The Bergen that Beyer knew and wrote about was evidently a wild place, a community where violence, petty theft, civil unrest, assault, and conflict were the order of the day. Beyer may have presided over a group of humanist intellectuals, valued and beloved (or feared) community leaders, the finest minds of the day, and the pillars of society. His diary suggests that Beyer also played a role in maintaining civility, law, and order in a community where, Kirkegaard notes, "humaniteten... kunne være nok så skrøbelig" (humanity... could definitely be very miserable). The entries in the diary amply suggest a dark undercurrent of conflict and dissension running alongside the brighter stream of Geble Pederssøn's and Beyer's enlightened Humanism.

The diary is divided chronologically and lingually: the entries from 1552 to 1561 are exclusively in Latin. From 1561 until concluding the work in 1572, Beyer wrote in Danish and Latin or exclusively in Danish. The diary is replete with everyday events, the births, baptisms, marriage, deaths, and burials of the townspeople. (Virtually the only family to escape–or nearly escape–mentioned in the work was Beyer's own. Beyer did mention his wife and sons in passing, but he was remarkably silent about himself.) Generally, the entries in the diary fall into four categories: single-sentence notices on the passage of lives and the religious observances attending such rites de passage; remarks on Beyer's duties for the Church, the Bergen Latin School, the government in Copenhagen, and its Royal Regent, Erik Rosenkrantz; reports on everyday events, unacceptable or antisocial behavior, inexplicable tragedies, *pestis* or *pestelentze* (illnesses), accidents, and natural phenomena that strike Bergen as evidence of the town's wickedness and as a warning–for example, "Væ dig Bergen du fule Sodoma oc Gomorrhæ søster" (Woe onto you Bergen, you sister of Sodom and Gomorrah); and cryptic reports, almost asides, on the continual violence and civil unrest that Beyer and his colleagues tried to hold in check.

Most of the entries in the diary are brief, a line or two in length, and matter-of-fact, shockingly so when the crimes–and the punishments–are so drastic and horrific. Occasionally, however, the entries in Beyer's diary develop into dramatic episodes, complete with background narrative or explication, dialogue attributed to various individuals, complications, and resolutions. Such dramatic episodes offer a much more involved picture of the community and its members. The entries for 1 to 17 April 1562 concern one Jacob Olufson (later named Jacob Christiernson), who announces his decision to resign his post as schoolmaster of Sancte Michels Skole:

> 1562. April: 1. . . . Oc sagde der hoes J sistis ieg var paa Capitelit gaff ieg oc tilkenne, at ieg vilde icke haue den Skole lenger end til paaske. Dette suar gaue vi byspen tilkende. Liden stund (same dag) der effter, gick for Jacob atter sielff igen op til doctor oc gaff hannom dette tilkende och sagde sig aff med Scholen.

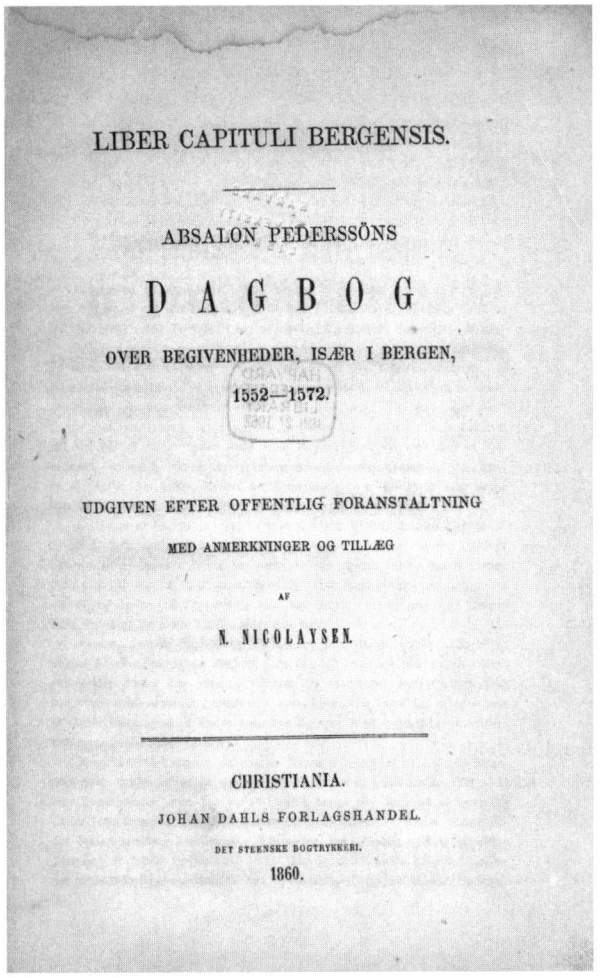

Title page for Absalon Pederssøn Beyer's Bergen diary
(Widener Library, Harvard University)

(. . . And then Jacob said "I went to the Chapel and gave notice that I did not want to run that school any longer after Easter." We let the Bishop know this answer. A little while later [the same day] Jacob came up to the Doctor again and informed him of this and said he was finished with the school.)

Christiernson's abrupt decision leads on into an extended discussion and systematic review of the employment, compensation, duties, taxes, and working conditions of schoolmasters and educators. After Jacob's resignation is announced, the committee of the whole, led by Beyer, turns the tables on the schoolmaster, declaring him unfit for the job and–what is worse–derelict in his religious duties:

> hand er icke saa fulkommen i den lerdom som en Scholemester bør at vere fulkommen vdi som skal oplere vngdomen, huilked ieg kand beuise, med hans egen schrifft, om behoff gøris. . . . Ieg kand icke forfare

at hand haffuer giort stoer frucht siden hand tog den Schole.... Haffuer hand skicket sig saa i sine ord oc gerning att hand haffuer wheld aff huer Mand Oc alle dømer hannom at vere wduelig oc wskickelig thil een Scholemester... Haffuer hand forsømmit Musicam figuratiuam i denne Neruerendes paaske høgtid oc sielden søgt kircken.

(he is not as versed in the knowledge a schoolmaster should possess if he is going to teach the youth; I can demonstrate this with his own writing, if need be.... I can not affirm that he has accomplished very much since he took over the school.... He has demonstrated in word and deed that he deals poorly with everyone and that all deem him to be incompetent and unsuitable as a schoolmaster ... He has neglected his duties as Musicam figuratiuam in the Easter High Holy Days and he has not attended church since.)

In many respects, the diary is a record of crime in the community, a sixteenth-century police blotter that underscores Beyer's role as a judge and magistrate in civil as well as church cases. (The separation of church and state was far into the future; in the Lutheran theocracy of sixteenth-century Bergen, Beyer and his colleagues dealt routinely with crime and sin, and they did not differentiate clearly between the two. Both brought on the wrath of the civil society and that of God.) The entry in the diary for 12 October 1562 may seem amusing; there is nothing amusing, however, about the chaos that results from a minor affront:

October. 1562. Dies 12 Wart en tyske skreddere ille martlerit aff en bysseskyttere som tiente paa slottet, huilken som først hug honnom vdi houedit med en rapir, och gick saa heden, och der hand fornam at der var liff vdi honnom, gick hand op vdi gen i lofftid och stack honnom vdi tarmerne och hug honnom vdi henderne och I kroppen alleuegne, och vndkom saa, at mand ved ei huort. Det kom der aff at skredderen hafde købt sig j kanne øl, och begynte at quede, huilked den anden ei vilde fordrage, di stod hand fraa bordet, ligeruis som han vilde gonged heden, drog saa veried och hug honnom offuer hoffuedet.

(A German tailor was savagely attacked by a rifleman who served at the castle, [he] first struck him in the head with a rapier, and went away at it, and when he discovered that there was still life in him [the tailor], he carried on and struck him in the intestines and the hands and all over his body, one does not know where else. It all started when the tailor bought himself a beer and began to sing, the other could not stand that [singing], so he got up from the table as though he was going to leave, pulled his weapon and struck him on the head.)

One thing is clear from a glance at the entries in Beyer's diary: violence rapidly escalates over the most trivial of causes. A minor infraction—or perceived infraction—quickly turns into major assaults and violence. Beyer sometimes plays a role in arbitration, but, in most instances, he is a reporter of faits accomplis, deeds that have already occurred. Individuals handle and resolve disputes without much ado, with the maximum force at their disposal.

One aspect of life in sixteenth-century Bergen connects the town to the modern Norwegian city: even during the 1500s, Bergen looked south and west to the Atlantic for commerce and intellectual and cultural enrichment. Bergen was a cosmopolitan city bustling with foreigners and immigrant communities, with entrepreneurs and wheeler-dealers, with charlatans and victims, with scholars from every academic corner of Europe. As a member of the Hanseatic League (a trading monopoly) of Northern German and Frisian towns and cities, Bergen's economic and cultural life was enriched beyond measure by the Hanseatic community. The Hanseatic League had a vested interest in maintaining a strong presence in "Bryggen," the harbor area controlled by the German Hansa. At the same time, the Bergen community had developed *en høj kultur* (a high culture) distinct from that of the Hansa economic powerhouse.

As the lecturer in theology and rector of Bergen Latin School, Beyer played a major role in arranging *skoledramaer* and in directing student performances of the verse dramas. Some of the dramas illustrated precepts from the Bible; they were known as *Adamsspillene* (the Adam plays) and attracted audiences in many European cities and towns. The dramas may have curbed the crime and violence endemic at that time. Beyer probably wrote such dramas as well as arranging and directing their performance; the diary refers to four such dramas: "et spel som jeg Mester Absalon lot agere her på kirkegården med stor umak og bekostning om Adams fall" (a play on the Fall of Adam that I, Master Absalon, took great care and expense to arrange for performance here in the churchyard); two Norwegian comedies, "en som kalles 'Studentum'" (one called "Student"); and a tragedy dealing with "billedstrid" (the conflict over the pictures), a piece concerned with the remnants of Catholicism, the elaborate decorations, paintings, and religious icons adorning the walls of Bergen's churches.

Beyer's principal work, *Om Norgis Rige,* combines an historical account of Norway's past, a description of the land and its people, and a political statement concerning Norway's current and future state. Beyer was clearly influenced by the works of Saxo Grammaticus and Olaus Magnus, as well as by the chroniclers of French, Italian, German, and Scottish history. *Om Norgis Rige* is also a political gesture in writing, a way for Beyer to assert Norwegian cultural and social autonomy and—for the Danish regent governor, Erik Rosenkrantz—a means to hold the Hanseatic League in check, to tip the balance of political power away from the economic concentration at "Bryggen" and toward the Royal (Danish) authority at Bergenhus.

Ironically, Beyer took his historical account, *Om Norgis Rige,* in a slightly different direction than Rosenkrantz may have intended. Beyer moved in step with contemporary ideas about history and the art of writing history, with the humanists who linked Norway's history with the history of the individual human being; Beyer viewed Norway in entirely human terms: "Norgis rigis stat kand mand skiffte vdi hendes alder, huilken ligeruis som it menniske haffuer haft sin wdspring fremgang oc end" (The state of Norway changed with her age, like a person, she had a period of formation, of progress and of culmination).

Beyer went on to describe the golden age of Norway, the time when Norway formed alliances, conducted wars, acquired territories abroad, held sway throughout Europe, and Norway extended its own political power far beyond its boundaries—to Britain, the Atlantic, Paris, and even the Mediterranean. Beyer interwove evidence of Norway's former glories, elaborate descriptions of cathedrals such as that at Trondheim, a beacon for the Christian faith, into his account of Norway at its prime; the prime was symbolized by the Monarch, the Royal Realm:

Memorial stone to Beyer in the Vangen churchyard in Aurland (from <http://members.virtualtourist.com/m/p/m/2459c4/>)

> Aff diße historier, bygning, krig, loug *etc.* kand mand vel forfare at Norgis rige haffuer standit vdi sin blomster oc verit eit sterckt oc mandeligt kongerige, oc bevist sin mandoms störcke ifra kong Harald haarfagre hin store oc indtil den sidste konge som gifftedis med drotning Margrete vdi fem hundret aars tid, huilcken som er viß oc seduanlig termin. . . . Ifra den dag, Norge kom vnder Danmarck oc miste sine egne herrer oc konger, saa haffuer det oc mist sin mandoms styrcke oc mact, oc begynner nu at bliffue gammel oc graaherit oc saa tung, at det ey kan bere sin egen vld.
>
> (From these stories, buildings, wars, laws *etc.* we can see that Norway once flowered and was a strong, manly realm and gave proof of the strength of its manly power from the time of King Harald Fair-Haired the Great until the last King, who married Queen Margrete [of Denmark], for five hundred years, which is surely the usual time frame for kingdoms. . . . From the day that Norway came under Denmark and lost its own lords and kings, it also lost its manly strength and power, and it began to be old and gray-haired and so heavy that its own mantle weighed upon it.)

To Beyer, Norway's decline as a nation was linked to the loss of the independent monarch. (While Erik Rosenkrantz looked to Beyer to assert the power of the Danish monarch against the Hansa, Beyer saw the Danish monarch as the endgame, the turning point for Norway's life as a nation. From the loss of a national monarch, it was all downhill for Norway, as far as Beyer could see.) Beyer noted how important it was for the citizens of the country to see their king. The monarch's regular progress through Norway was another example of gesture politics, a powerful sign that all was well and a way for king and country to connect, an affirmation of the vitality of all Norway.

Despite Beyer's assertion that the loss of an independent Norwegian monarch marked decline and tottering old age for Norway, *Om Norgis Rige* includes a virtual song of praise of the representative of the Danish monarch, Erik Rosenkrantz. Beyer seems to have viewed Rosenkrantz as both ordained and rewarded by God and as the representative of Norwegian nobility, since he lived in Bergenhus and was surrounded by the trappings and material symbols of royalty:

> [g]ud vnde hannom [Erich Rosenkrantz] oc hans börn det [godz] til lycke oc salighed, oc dette rige til ornament oc verdighed, effterdi at hand er nu med sine

elskelige börn oc brödre det ypperste blomster aff Norgis rigis adel. Amen

(God grant him [Erich Rosenkrantz] and his children that [property] in joy and blessing, in praise and glory for this realm, since he is now with his beloved children and brothers the finest flower of Norway's nobility. Amen)

Nonetheless, *Om Norgis Rige* amply suggests that the union of Norway and Denmark under a single monarch spelled an end to the life of the country. Despite such a gloomy assessment of Norway's current status, Beyer never gave up hope for Norway's future, for the day when Norway reclaimed its own king: "Dog kunde vel Norge vogne op aff söffue en gang, der som hun finge en regenter offuer sig, thi hun er icke aldeles saa forfalden oc foremectit at hun io kunde komme til sin mact oc herlighed igien" (And yet Norway could awaken from her sleep, if she could find a regent over her, as she is not so completely fallen and conquered that she could not come to her power and glory again).

Beyer also functioned as a cultural historian, describing the traditions, legends, beliefs and superstitions of the people, and he added the role of topographer to his work on Norway. Beyer devoted much attention to the natural environment and to the products—and produce—that Norway furnished in abundance. The physical features—the trees, lakes, mountains, and farming valleys of Norway—receive their due in Beyer's multifaceted work. *Om Norgis Rige* also functioned as the newspaper, the reporter, of the day. The work ebbs into a catalogue of leaders, kings, and administrators. Beyer carefully described the cathedrals and churches that dotted the Norwegian landscape and provided the cultural and community life of the country. For a cleric like Beyer, the cathedrals were more than buildings; they were also visual links to Christianity and Christians throughout Europe.

Beyer's final work, *Oration om Mester Geble,* sings the praises of the first—and greatest, according to the author—Lutheran superintendent in Bergen, Geble Pederssøn, a man who was astute enough to spot Beyer's intellectual talents and steer him into positions of authority within the Church and the Bergen Latin School. Beyer's biography dwells extensively on the Catholic bishops who preceded Master Geble before turning to a fairly complete account of Master Geble's life in school and church. As is typical of much of Beyer's work, *Oration om Mester Geble* punctuates a rather dry chronological presentation with incidents and events that quickly reveal the character and personality of the man who steered Bergen through the Reformation and Beyer to his place in the next generation of scholars and churchmen. Beyer personalized his story, carefully linking his subject (Master Geble) to his own life and the events of the time and praising the munificence of his esteemed mentor: "hand med sit Gods oc Pændinge kunde forfremme Guds Ære oc Menniskens Salighed, oc være sit Fæderneland til Ære oc Prydelse, oc andre til et got Exempel" (with his property and money he could enhance the honor of God and the blessedness of men and live for the honor and glory of his fatherland and in order to be an example for others).

Absalon Pedersson Beyer made his literary mark as an astute, perceptive witness to events and incidents within his community, as an engaged historian and social/political commentator and as a biographer of the humanist and Reformation leader in Bergen, Mester Geble Pederssøn. While Beyer apparently did not leave much of a paper trail of his own life, he succeeded in leaving an account of what life—both the prosaic aspects and the more prominent—was like for many of his contemporaries in sixteenth-century Bergen.

Biographies:

H. F. J. Estrup, *Absalon som helt, statsmand og biskop: et biographisk forsøg* (Sorøe: Holm, 1826);

Axel Larsen, *Absalon: Historisk Skildring* (Copenhagen: Hagerup, 1899);

Vilhelm Madsen, *Biskop Absalon: fædrelandets fader* (Copenhagen: Nyt Nordisk Forlag/Arnold Busck, 1928).

References:

Edvard Beyer, *Utsyn over Norsk Litteratur* (Oslo: Cappelen, 1983), pp. 34–35;

Nils Gilje, *Heksen og humanisten: Anne Pedersdatter og Absalon Pederssøn Beyer. En historie om magt og trolldom i Bergen på 1500-tallet* (Bergen: Fagbokforlaget, 2003);

Ludvig Holm-Olsen and Kjell Heggelund, *Norges Litteraturhistorie,* volume 1, third edition (Oslo: Bokklubben Nye Bøker, 1982), pp. 357–364;

Peter Kirkegaard, "Dansk-Norsk Fælleslitteratur 1536–1807," in his *Norsk Litteratur i Tusen År. Teksthistoriske Linjer* (Oslo: Landslaget for Norskundervisning / Cappelen, 1994), pp. 139–141;

Kathleen Stokker, "Oral Tradition, Humanism, and the Baroque," in *A History of Norwegian Literature,* edited by Harald S. Næss (Lincoln & London: University of Nebraska Press, 1993), pp. 44–45.

Bjørnstjerne Bjørnson
(8 December 1832 – 26 April 1910)

Ann Schmiesing
University of Colorado at Boulder

See also the Bjørnson entry in *DLB 329: Nobel Laureates in Literature, Part 1: Agnon–Eucken.*

BOOKS: *Synnøve Solbakken* (Christiania: Johan Dahl, 1857); translated by Mary Howitt as *Trust and Trial* (London: Hurst & Blackett, 1858);

Mellem Slagene: Drama i 1 Akt (Christiania: Dybwad, 1858);

Halte-Hulda: Drama i tre Akter (Bergen: H. J. Geelmuydens, 1858);

Arne (Bergen: H. J. Geelmuydens, 1859); translated anonymously as *Arne; or, Peasant Life in Norway: A Norwegian Tale* (Bergen, 1860);

Småstykker (Bergen: Giertsen, 1860)–includes "Min første Fortælling," *Mellem Slagene, Ei faarleg Friiing,* "Faderen," *Ørneredet,* and "En glad Gut";

Kong Sverre (Copenhagen: Gyldendal, 1861);

Sigurd Slembe (Copenhagen: Gyldendal, 1862); translated by William Morton Payne as *Sigurd Slembe: A Dramatic Trilogy* (Boston: Houghton, Mifflin, 1888);

Maria Stuart i Skotland (Copenhagen: Gyldendal, 1864);

De Nygifte (Copenhagen: Gyldendal, 1865); translated by Theodore Soelfeldt as *The Newly-Married Couple* (London: T. H. Lacy, 1868);

Fiskerjenten (Copenhagen: Gyldendal, 1868); translated by M. E. Niles from the author's German version as *The Fisher-Maiden: A Norwegian Tale* (New York: Leypoldt & Holt, 1869);

En glad Gut (Copenhagen: I Commission hos Gad, 1868); translated by Sivert Hjerleid and Elizabeth Hjerleid as *Ovind: A Story of Country Life in Norway* (London: Simpkin, 1869);

Digte og Sange (Copenhagen: Gyldendal, 1870); translated by Arthur Hubbell Palmer as *Poems and Songs* (New York: American-Scandinavian Foundation, 1915);

Arnljot Gelline (Copenhagen: Gyldendal, 1870);

Sigurd Jorsalfar (Copenhagen: Gyldendal, 1872);

Brude-Slaatten (Copenhagen: Gyldendal, 1873);

Bjørnstjerne Bjørnson (photograph by Karl Anderson; Herman H. J. Lynge & Søn, Denmark)

Redaktøren: Skuespil i fire Handlinger (Copenhagen: Gyldendal, 1874);

En Fallit: Skuespil i fire Handlinger (Copenhagen: Gyldendal, 1874);

Kongen (Copenhagen: Gyldendal, 1877);

Magnhild: En Fortælling (Copenhagen: Gyldendal, 1877);

Det ny system: Skuespil i fem handlinger (Copenhagen: Gyldendal, 1879);

Leonarda: Skuespil i fire handlinger (Copenhagen: Gyldendal, 1879);

Kaptejn Mansana: En Fortælling fra Italien (Copenhagen: Gyldendal, 1879);

Af mine Foredrag om Republiken (Kristiania: I Kommisjon for Norge / Selskabet for Folkeskrifters Udbredelse, 1880);

Over ævne: Første stykke (Copenhagen: Gyldendal, 1883); translated by W. Wilson as *Pastor Sang* (London: Longmans, Green, 1893);

En hanske: Skuespil (Copenhagen: Gyldendal, 1883); translated by H. L. Brækstad as *A Gauntlet* (London & New York: Harper, 1890);

Det flager i byen og på havnen (Copenhagen: Gyldendal, 1884); translated by Cecil Fairfax as *The Heritage of the Kurts* (London: Heinemann, 1892);

Geografi og kærlighed (Copenhagen: Gyldendal, 1885);

På Guds veje (Copenhagen: Gyldendal, 1889); translated by Elizabeth Carmichael as *In God's Way* (London: Heinemann, 1890);

Over ævne: Andet Stykke (Copenhagen: Gyldendal, 1895);

Paul Lange og Tora Parsberg (Copenhagen: Gyldendal, 1898); translated by Brækstad as *Paul Lange and Tora Parsberg* (London & New York: Harper, 1899);

Laboremus (Copenhagen: Gyldendal, 1901); translated anonymously as *Laboremus* (London: Chapman & Hall, 1901);

På Storhove (Copenhagen: Gyldendal, 1902);

Daglannet (Copenhagen: Gyldendal, 1904);

Mary (Copenhagen: Gyldendal, 1906);

Når den ny vin blomstrer (Christiania: Gyldendal, 1909); translated by Lee M. Hollander as *When the New Wine Blooms* (Boston: R. G. Badger, 1911);

Kongebrødrene (Oslo: Gyldendal, 1932)—comprises *Kong Eystein* and *Sigurd Jorsalfar*.

Editions and Collections: *Samlede værker: Folkeudgave*, 11 volumes, edited by Carl Nærup (Copenhagen: Gyldendal, 1900-1902);

Bjørnstjerne Bjørnsons fortællinger: Jubileumsudgave, 2 volumes (Christiania: Gyldendal, 1907);

Samlede værker: Mindeutgave, 5 volumes (Christiania: Gyldendal, 1910-1911);

Artikler og taler, 2 volumes, edited by Christen Collin and H. Eitrem (Christiania: Gyldendal, 1912, 1913);

Bjørnson's Synnøve Solbakken, edited by George T. Flom (Minneapolis: Free Church Book Concern, 1918);

Samlede Digter-Verker: Standardutgave, 9 volumes, edited by Francis Bull (Christiania: Gyldendal, 1919-1920);

Samlede Digte, edited by Bull (Oslo: Gyldendal, 1926);

Digte og sange, edited by Bull (Oslo: Gyldendal, 1957);

Selvstændighetens Æresfølelse: Artikler og taler i utvalg 1879-1905, edited by Knut Johansen (Bergen: Eide, 1974);

De gode gjerninger redder verden: Tanker og idéer, råd og dåd (Oslo: Gyldendal, 1982);

Jeg velger meg April! 95 dikt, edited by Rolf Jacobsen (Oslo: Gyldendal, 1982);

Bondefortellinger; Dikt i utvalg; Skuespill (Oslo: Gyldendal, 1989);

Verker i samling, 3 volumes, edited by Edvard Beyer (Stabbekk: Den Norske Bokklubben, 1993);

Fortellinger i utvalg (Oslo: Aschehoug, 1996).

Editions in English: *Arne: A Sketch of Norwegian Country Life*, translated by Augusta Plesner and Susan Rugeley-Powers (London & New York: Strahan, 1866);

Love in Wedlock, translated by W. and C. Wilkinson (Lowestoft, U.K., 1869);

Love and Life in Norway, translated by Plesner and Augusta Bethell (London: Cassell, Petter & Galpin, 1870);

The Happy Boy, translated by Helen R. Gade (Boston: Sever, Francis, 1870);

Bjørnstjerne Bjørnson's Works, 7 volumes, translated by Rasmus B. Anderson (New York: Doubleday, Page, 1882)—comprises volume 1, *Synnove Solbakken;* volume 2, *The Bridal March; Captain Mansana;* volume 3, *Arms; Early Tales; Sketches;* volume 4, *A Happy Boy; Later Sketches;* volume 5, *The Fisher Maiden;* and volume 6, *Magnhild; Dunt;*

The Novels of Bjørnstjerne Bjørnson, 13 volumes, edited by Edmund Gosse (New York: Macmillan, 1895-1909)—comprises volume 1, *Synnövé Solbakken*, translated by Julie Sutter (1895); volume 2, *Arne*, translated by William Low (1895); volume 3, *A Happy Boy*, translated by Mrs. W. Archer (1896); volume 4, *The Fisher Lass* (1896); volume 5, *The Bridal March & One Day* (1896); volume 6, *Magnhild & Dust* (1897); volume 7, *Captain Mansana & Mother's Hands* (1897); volume 8, *Absalom's Hair & A Painful Memory* (1898); volumes 9 and 10, *In God's Way*, translated by Elizabeth Carmichael (1908); volumes 11 and 12, *The Heritage of the Kurts*, translated by Cecil Fairfax (1908); and volume 13, *Mary*, translated by Mary Morison (1909);

Three Comedies, translated by R. Farquharson Sharp (London: Dent / New York: Dutton, 1912)—comprises *The Newly-Married Couple, Leonarda,* and *A Gauntlet;*

Plays, translated by Edwin Björkman (New York: Scribners, 1913)—comprises *The Gauntlet, Beyond Our Power,* and *The New System;*

Plays: Second Series, translated by Björkman (New York: Scribners, 1914; London: Duckworth, 1914)—comprises *Love and Geography, Beyond Human Might,* and *Laboremus;*

Three Dramas, translated by Sharp (London: Dent / New York: Dutton, 1914)–comprises *The Editor, The Bankrupt,* and *The King.*

PLAY PRODUCTIONS: *Mellem Slagene,* Christiania, Christiania Theater, 27 October 1857;

Kong Sverre, Christiania, Christiania Norwegian Theater, 9 October 1861;

Sigurd Slembe, Trondheim, Trondheim Theater, 30 September 1863;

Sigurds første Flugt, Christiania, Christiania Theater, 27 August 1865;

Halte-Hulda, Christiania, Christiania Theater, 4 November 1865;

De Nygifte, Copenhagen, Det Kongelige Theater, 23 November 1865;

Maria Stuart i Skotland, Christiania, Christiania Theater, 29 March 1867;

Sigurd Jorsalfar, Christiania, Christiania Theater, 10 April 1872;

En Fallit, Stockholm, Nya Teater, 19 January 1875; Christiania, Christiania Theater, 29 January 1875;

Redaktøren, Stockholm, Nya Teater, 17 February 1875;

Det ny system, Berlin, Residenztheater, 19 December 1878;

Leonarda, Christiania, Christiania Theater, 22 April 1879;

En hanske, Hamburg, Stadttheater, 11 October 1883;

Geografi og kærlighed, Christiania, Christiania Theater, 21 October 1885;

Over ævne: Første stykke, Stockholm, Nya Teater, 3 January 1886;

Over ævne: Andet Stykke, Christiania, Christiania Theater, 23 December 1895;

Paul Lange og Tora Parsberg, Copenhagen, Dagmar Theater, 28 April 1901;

Laboremus, Christiania, National Theater, 29 April 1901;

Kongen, Christiania, National Theater, 11 September 1902;

På Storhove, Christiania, National Theater, 4 November 1902;

Daglannet, Christiania, National Theater, 31 August 1905;

Når den ny vin blomstrer, Christiania, National Theater, 29 September 1909.

TRANSLATION: Victor Hugo, *Århundredenes legende* (Oslo, 1911).

A man of inestimable influence on Norwegian culture in the second half of the nineteenth century, Bjørnstjerne Bjørnson was a poet, dramatist, essayist, literary critic, journalist, editor, theater director, orator,

Bjørnson as a young man (Store Norske Leksikon <http://www.snl.no/.bilde/Bj%C3%B8rnson,_ Bj%C3%B8rnstjerne_(ungdomsbilde)>)

and activist. In these and other roles he concerned himself with social and cultural issues involving politics, literature, language, religion, pedagogy, and national identity. He was both a Norwegian patriot and a cosmopolite, and for his literary works and his social engagement he was celebrated both within Norway and beyond its borders. Both his contemporaries and subsequent commentators have observed that few writers in any time or any country can match Bjørnson's many and wide-ranging contributions to the intellectual and social fabric of his nation. The Danish critic Georg Brandes said that to utter Bjørnson's name was tantamount to hoisting the Norwegian flag.

Bjørnstjerne Martinius Bjørnson was born on 8 December 1832 at Bjørgan vicarage in Kvikne, a small mountain district in eastern Norway. He was the first child of Peder Bjørnson, a pastor, and Inger Elise Bjørnson, née Nordraak, the daughter of a merchant from Kragerø. His parents named him Bjørnstjern (Bear Star), but in early adulthood he began adding an *e* to the end of the name.

Bjørnson's principal friends during his childhood were the animals on his father's farm–particularly the colt Blakken (a name commonly given to a dun-colored horse), whom Bjørnson memorializes in his autobiographical story "Blakken" (1868; translated, 1882). As Bjørnson notes in the story, Kvikne had a rough reputation. The previous pastor had fled, and another predecessor had found it necessary to have his pistols with him at all times. Winters were harsh, and Bjørnson recalled hesitating to open the front door for fear his fingers might freeze to the iron latch.

When Bjørnson was six, the family moved to Romsdal in western Norway, where his father became the pastor of Nesset parish. As an adult, Bjørnson described his upbringing in Romsdal in idyllic terms. Nature lay at his doorstep, and the climate was milder than in Kvikne. In "Blakken" he portays the Nesset parsonage as "en av de skjønneste gårder i landet, som den ligger der bredbarmet mellom to møtende fjorder, med grønt fjell over seg, fossefall og gårder på den motsatte strand, bølgende marker og liv inne i dalbunnen, og utover langs fjorden fjell med nes i nes skytende ut i sjøen og en stor gård ute på hvert" (one of the finest gards in the country, lying broadbreasted between two arms of the fjord, with green mountains above and cataracts and gards on the opposite shore, with undulating fields and eager life in the heart of the valley, and out along the fjord mountains, from which naze after naze, with a large gard on each, project out into the water). Bjørnson grew into a strong boy with an outgoing, though at times stormy, temperament, which bore features of both of his parents' personalities. His father was strict, once taking the nine-year-old Bjørnson to see an execution as a warning not to stray from the path of virtue. Though not nearly as stern as his father, Bjørnson shared with him a lifelong obsession with justice, while his perennial optimism was likely influenced by his loving and congenial mother. Bjørnson found many metaphors for his own personality in the natural surroundings of Romsdal, describing himself later in life as a boat on a fjord during a storm, or as a fjord itself.

From 1843 to 1849 Bjørnson attended school in the little fishing town of Molde. There he became acquainted with the writings of the Norwegian patriot Henrik Wergeland, on whom he later modeled his own social activism and nationalist sentiments. In Molde he also first proclaimed his intention to become a writer. In early 1850 he moved to Christiania (now Oslo) to prepare for admission to the university there. He lived with his uncle, Georg Nordraak, a gilder and decorative painter, who introduced him to the theater in addition to nurturing his budding republican sentiments. Bjørnson entered the university in 1852 but was far more interested in writing than in his studies, and he never received a degree. In 1854 he began to write for the paper *Krydseren*. His other journalistic work at this time included working as a correspondent for *Christiania-Posten*, for which he reported on the Lagting (upper house) of the Norwegian parliament, and, beginning in 1856, as an anonymous drama critic for *Morgenbladet*.

Bjørnson's criticism was influenced by the writings of the Danish Hegelian philosopher Johan Ludvig Heiberg, the French critic Jules Janin, the German journalist and literary historian Heinrich Julian Schmidt, and the eighteenth-century German dramatist Gotthold Ephraim Lessing. The Christiania Theater was at that time dominated by Danish actors and the Danish director Carl Peter Borgaard. Although French and Danish pieces made up most of the repertoire, even the few Norwegian plays produced at the theater were performed almost exclusively by Danish actors and in Danish pronunciation. As a critic Bjørnson turned his attention to promoting young Norwegian acting talent. The most promising Norwegians at the Christiania Theater were the young actresses Laura Svendsen (who later became Laura Gundersen) and Lucie Johannesen (later Wolf), both of whom were natives of Bergen. But, as Bjørnson complained in *Krydseren* (1 March 1854), Borgaard repeatedly cast Svendsen and Johannesen in insignificant parts while giving even youthful female roles to the theater's main tragedienne, the aging Danish actress Augusta Schrumpf. Not wishing to be accused of hotheaded nationalism, however, Bjørnson claimed that it was a mere coincidence that Schrumpf was Danish and Svendsen and Johannesen were Norwegian; he insisted that his foremost goal was the integrity of the acting at the theater. Nevertheless, although he claimed that he would have supported the young actresses even if they had been Danish, clearly he regarded the middle-aged Dane, Schrumpf, as a symbol of the past and the young Norwegian actresses as symbols of Norway's bright future.

While Bjørnson wanted to promote Norwegian acting and Norwegian drama, he was not a hotheaded nationalist. He frequently disparaged the stereotypical portrayals of Norwegian peasants and historical figures in Norwegian drama. A historical play titled *Valborg* that he himself had written in this style had been accepted for production by the Christiania Theater, but Bjørnson had withdrawn it before it was performed. In a review of the anonymously written *Fiskerhjemmet* (The Fisherman's Home) he complained that Norwegian dramatists had sought to imbue their peasant characters with the ruggedness and steely wills allegedly possessed by the Vikings, with the result that their characters appeared as stereotypical braggarts or scoundrels. Bjørnson's skepticism with regard to the nationalists' agenda is also evident in his comments in *Krydseren* (16 September 1854) regarding the Christiania Norske Dramatiske Skole (Christiania Norwegian Dramatic

School), which was founded in 1852 as a theater in which Norwegian acting and the Norwegian language would be promoted: "Heller ikke er det Lokkemad nok, at det *norske* Theater aabnes; thi Folk har ikke og *bør* ikke have Interesse for Andet end hvad der er godt, selv om det er 10 Gange nationalt; ja det bør allermindst vænnes til at taale det Slette der, hvor det Nationale bydes, fordi dette er et Begreb, som skal staa rent og tillokkende i Folkets Bevidsthed, slet ikke være behæftet med nogen Biforestilling om Kjede eller Skamfuldhed" (Nor is it sufficient bait that the *Norwegian* Theater has been opened, for the people do not have and *should not* have an interest for anything other than that which is good, even if it is ten times national; yes, they should accustom themselves least of all to tolerating inferiority where the national is offered, because the national should be pure and attractive in the people's consciousness, instead of burdened with any accompanying feeling of boredom or shamefulness).

Some intellectuals in Christiania, most notably the Hegelian philosopher Marcus Jacob Monrad, believed that only the Christiania Norwegian Dramatic School, which was renamed the Christiania Norske Theater (Christiania Norwegian Theater) in 1854, could eventually throw off the yoke of Danish cultural tutelage and become Norway's national theater. Bjørnson, however, continued to work to transform the Christiania Theater from a Danish show house into a Norwegian cultural institution. His disgust at Borgaard's treatment of the Norwegian actors surged again when, in May 1856, Borgaard hired the Dane Ferdinand Schmidt. Formerly a brush maker, Schmidt had little acting experience. Though he and his wife had been promised acting positions at the Christiania Theater, according to the official account they were only visiting. Bjørnson was outraged both at the subterfuge and at Borgaard's practice of hiring even the most untalented Danes rather than cultivating Norwegian talent. In protest, he and his followers attempted to disrupt Schmidt's debut at the theater on 6 May by whistling in the audience. Although this protest was not particularly successful, a second demonstration on 8 May was significantly larger and more effective.

Defending the protests in his essay "Pibernes Program" (The Whistlers' Program) in *Morgenbladet* (8 May 1856), Bjørnson portrayed himself as a successor to the Norwegian poet and patriot Wergeland. He described a national theater as "Nationalitetens Forpostvagt mod Utlandet" (nationality's outpost guard against foreign countries) and the capital city as the place where the break between the native and the foreign occurs. He explained that this break was not meant as a rejection of the growing calls in the 1850s for closer political ties among the Scandinavian countries, but rather was a

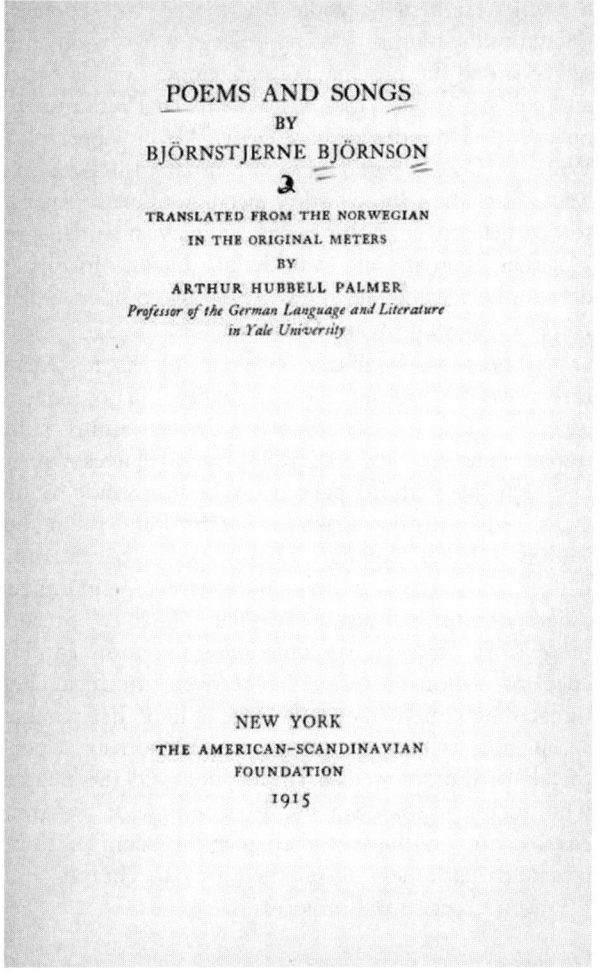

Title page for the English translation of Bjørnson's 1870 collection, Digte og Sange *(University of California Libraries)*

necessary precondition to Pan-Scandinavian union: "I en Tid, hvori man prædiker Sammensmeltning, maa man vel mindes, at først naar hvert enkelt Land er blevet et udviklet Statsindivid, kan en sund, til Fællesarbeide skikket, Formæling tænkes paa. Ikke saameget i vort mindre Folkeantal, ikke saameget i alt dette udvortes, som man stadig ser fremholdt, men netop i, at vi endnu ikke fuldstændig er bleven Nation, ligger den rette Grund til, at den skandinaviske Tanke møder mindre Velvilje hos os" (In a time when one preaches union, one must be reminded that only when each individual nation has become a developed national entity can a healthy wedding take place which is suited for collaboration. The actual reason for why the Scandinavian idea is greeted with less acceptance among Norwegians lies not so much in our smaller population, not so much in all such superficial matters [although one constantly sees this maintained], but precisely in the fact that we still have not fully become a nation). Reflecting on the protests, the author Jonas Lie observed to Reidar

Marum, "Hermed begyndte den Bjørnsonske épopée" (With this the Bjørnsonian epopee began). Bjørnson himself regarded the protests as the beginning of his social and political activism as a writer, as he later indicated in his essay "Hvorledes jeg blev Dikter" (How I Became a Writer) in *Ny Illustreret Tidende* (2 February 1882). A few weeks after the 1856 whistle concerts took place, Bjørnson participated in meetings of Scandinavian students in Uppsala, Kalmar, and Stockholm. In the following decades he became one of the best-known proponents of Pan-Scandinavianism and Pan-Germanism.

The most significant event in Bjørnson's early career was the publication on 10 August 1857 of his *bondefortelling* (peasant tale) *Synnøve Solbakken* (Sunny Hill; translated as *Trust and Trial,* 1858). Synnøve lives a quiet and pious life with her parents on the sunny side of the valley, while Torbjørn, whose family home is on the sunless side, is stubborn, easily provoked, attends dances, and engages in frequent fistfights. Despite their different temperaments, the two fall in love. By the end of the story Torbjørn has come under the positive influence of Synnøve; when he recovers from a life-threatening knife wound suffered in a fight, her parents accept him as their daughter's fiancé. Bjørnson's portrayals of the Norwegian countryside and the people who inhabit it possess a simple, if somewhat romanticized, beauty. In the second chapter, for example, Torbjørn and his father are on their way to church, and Bjørnson observes of Torbjørn:

> Litt eldre må han gjete til fjells; men når han den vakre, duggfulle søndagsmorgen sitter på stenen med kreaturerne nedenfor seg og hører kirkeklokkene over deres bjeller, da blir han tungsindig. Ti der klinger i dem noe lyst, lett, lokkende dernedefra, tanke om kjenninger ved kirken, glede, når man er der, enda større når man har vært der, god mat hjemme, far, mor, søskende, lek på volden den glade søndagskveld, og det lille hjerte gjør opstand i brystet. Men det ender dog alltid med at det var kirkeklokkene som lød; han husker seg om og finner til sist en halv salmestubb han kan; den synger han med foldede hænder og et langt øye ned i dalen, sier så en liten bønn ovenpå, springer opp, er glad og støter i luren, så det skraller i fjellene.

(When he is older he will have to herd the goats in the mountains. But when he then on a beautiful, dew-filled Sunday morning sits on a rock with the animals below him and hears the church bells ringing above the tinkling of their bells, he will grow melancholy. For in the church bells ringing down below there is something bright, cheerful, and coaxing, the thought of acquaintances at church, the joy one feels when one is there, which is greater still after one has been there, good food at home, father, mother, siblings, games in the meadow on happy Sunday afternoons, and his little heart thumps in his chest. But in the end it is always the church bells that he heard. He thinks a bit and at last remembers just a snatch of a psalm. He sings it with folded hands and a longing look down into the valley, and then says a little prayer, jumps up happily, and blows his alpine horn so it peals in the mountains.)

In the preface to his 1918 edition of *Synnøve Solbakken* for American college students George T. Flom observes that modern Dano-Norwegian—known in the nineteenth century as *riksmål* (official language) and today as *bokmål* (book language)—virtually began with *Synnøve Solbakken,* while Clemens Petersen, a prominent Danish critic and close friend of Bjørnson's, declared that Norwegian literature itself began with the story. The Swedish poet Verner von Heidenstam's memorial ode to Bjørnson begins with the words, "Gråt, Synnøve, gråt!" (Weep, Synnøve, weep!). Bjørnson's famous portrayal of Synnøve as a beautiful girl with a red ribbon in her blond hair has been interpreted by several artists. The story remains the best-known of Bjørnson's works and has long been a staple of the Norwegian literature school curriculum.

Bjørnson's career as a dramatist began when Borgaard produced his *Mellem Slagene* (Between the Battles) at the Christiania Theater in October 1857. The one-act play portrays Sverre Sigurdsson before his ascent to the throne in 1184. Sverre, who disguises himself in the play as Øystein, wishes to be king not for the power it brings but out of an unselfish desire to shape Norway. Recalling the achievements of past Norwegian kings in uniting Norway and bringing law and Christianity to it, Sverre observes that the present king, Magnus, has done neither good nor ill for the country. He prays that he, as king, will be able to influence Norway more positively: "Den være konge som har noe han vil være konge for" (May he be king who has something he wants to be king for). As Harald Noreng observes in his seminal 1954 study of Bjørnson's dramatic works, in this piece Bjørnson introduces the themes of self-assertion and service to society that run through his plays and yield insights into his view of himself as a leader in Norwegian society.

Bjørnson completed his play *Halte-Hulda* (published 1858, produced 1865, Lame Hulda) in 1857 while visiting his parents in Søgne, where his father had been pastor since June 1853. The work is set in the thirteenth century. Hulda, whose father was killed by the Aslak clan and whose mother died of grief soon afterward, has been raised by the Aslak clan to atone for their deed. Although lame, she has grown into a beautiful woman and has been married against her will to Gudleik Hustadvik. The chieftain, Eyolf Finsson, murders Gudleik, and he and Hulda become lovers. Eyolf then murders Hulda's former father-in-law, Aslak.

Aulestad, the farm in Østre Gausda that Bjørnson bought in 1875 (photograph by Axel Lindahl; Norwegian Folk Museum)

When Hulda learns that Eyolf intends to leave her to marry Svanhilde, an attendant to the queen, she tells Gudleik's brothers, who wish to avenge Gudleik's and Aslak's deaths, where to find him that evening. They surround and set fire to the chamber where Eyolf and Hulda are conversing. They call to Hulda to come out, but she decides to stay and burn to death with Eyolf.

In November 1857 Bjørnson accepted the position of director of the Norwegian Theater in Bergen, which had been founded in 1850 by the violinist Ole Bull. Bjørnson's predecessor, Henrik Ibsen, had been at the Bergen theater since 1851 and was leaving to become artistic director at the Christiania Norwegian Theater. In Bergen, Bjørnson became known for his attempts to improve the repertoire. He produced works by William Shakespeare, Ludvig Holberg, Adam Oehlenschläger, Andreas Munch, and Johan Herman Wessel. In addition, he presented Ibsen's *Hærmændene paa Helgeland* (1858; translated as *The Vikings at Helgeland*, 1890) and his own *Mellem Slagene*. Nevertheless, Bjørnson found it difficult to make the theater artistically and commercially successful. Bergen had a population of just twenty-five thousand, and the resources Bjørnson had at his command were meager. His insights into character and plot motivation were praised, though some theatergoers and critics alleged that the actors did not play their characters but played Bjørnson playing the characters. Some even insisted that the actors had begun to pronounce their lines in Bjørnson's Romsdal accent.

In Bergen, Bjørnson became acquainted with Karoline Reimers, also known by her stepfather's surname as Karoline Jahn. Reimers had some acting experience and had signed on as back-up help at the theater in Bergen, though she met Bjørnson not at the theater but at a social gathering. On 16 May 1858 he proposed to her in Trondheim, where the Bergen troupe was on tour. One day later, he delivered his first Constitution Day speech.

That summer Reimers and a friend accompanied Bjørnson to Eikesdal in Romsdal, where the women spent their days reading, picking berries, and fishing, while Bjørnson worked on his novel *Arne* (1859; translated as *Arne; or, Peasant Life in Norway: A Norwegian Tale*, 1860). The title character is born out of wedlock, though his mother, Margit, later marries his father, Nils, a tailor, after Nils suffers severe injuries in a fight with Baard Bøen. Nils is often drunk, and he abuses Margit physically and verbally. When he threatens during one such episode to choke her, Arne grabs an axe and rushes toward him. Before Arne can reach him, Nils falls on top of Margit, dead from a heart attack. Arne wishes to leave the countryside, but Margit implores him to stay, lest she be completely alone. She hides letters to him from his friend Christian, who left to become a sailor. Arne grows to view himself as a coward who long ago should have intervened to stop his father from abusing his mother and should now have the courage to leave home as Christian had. He worries about what others think of him and shuns social interactions. His fondness for Eli Bøen, the daughter of the man who crippled his father, grows when Baard Bøen hires him as a carpenter. Despite its many dark passages, the story ends happily with the marriage of Arne and Eli.

Bjørnson and Reimers were married on 11 September 1858 in Søgne. The following year Bjørnson accepted an offer to become coeditor of *Aftenbladet,* the successor to *Krydseren,* in Christiania. In October 1859 he published his poem "Ja, vi elsker dette Landet" (Yes, We Love This Land) in *Aftenbladet;* five years later, it was named Norway's national song. Though "Ja, vi elsker dette Landet" is by far Bjørnson's best-known poem, many of the verses that appear in his peasant tales also proved popular and were set to music by prominent composers. On 15 November 1859 Karoline gave birth to a son, Bjørn, after which she lay ill for several months with puerperal fever. The Bjørnsons went on to have five more children, one of whom died shortly after birth.

In 1859 Bjørnson and Ibsen cofounded Det Norske Selskabt (The Norwegian Society). Bull played Norwegian folk music at the first meeting of the society on 22 November. Among the stories Bjørnson wrote during this time is "En glad Gut" (1860; translated as *A Happy Boy,* 1882), a cheerful account of a boy who grows up to attend an agricultural school and marry his beloved, Marit.

Amid debates over whether the office of viceroy of Norway should be abolished, Bjørnson resigned as coeditor of *Aftenbladet.* The viceroy was appointed by the Swedish king, and Bjørnson was among those who believed that the position should be eliminated. He spent three years in Europe after receiving a travel stipend from the Storting (Parliament). His principal literary works during his travels were dramas. Both *Kong Sverre* (1861, King Sverre) and *Sigurd Slembe* (1862, Sigurd the Bad; translated as *Sigurd Slembe: A Dramatic Trilogy,* 1888) take place in the twelfth century. The former play depicts Sverre, the hero of *Mellem Slagene,* after his ascent to the throne; the latter, one of Bjørnson's best dramatic works, portrays the pretender Sigurd as a complex man—noble yet despotic, self-assured yet self-doubting, unsatisfied and always longing for achievement: "Jeg trer aldri inn i en liten kirke uten å tenke meg en stor, aldri i en av tre uten å lenges til hine av marmor.... Således står jeg heller aldri i en liten handling uten å tenke meg en stor, i mange tusens overvær, i lysning av et kveld" (I never enter a small church without picturing a large one, never a wooden one without longing for those of marble.... So I never do a small deed, without thinking of great ones, done in the sight of thousands, in the glow of song). The trilogy follows Sigurd from the time he learns that he is the son of Magnus Barefoot and leaves to become a crusader, through his adventures in Scotland, to his return to Norway, where he murders his half brother, Harald Gille, for the crown. His attempt to secure the throne ends in failure, and at the end he awaits capture and certain death.

In addition to emphasizing his support of the Danes in their emerging struggle against Germany over Schleswig-Holstein, the letters Bjørnson wrote while touring Europe frequently refer to theaters and performances. Observations in his correspondence concerning the state of the Christiania Theater indicate that he still fervently hoped for the establishment of a Norwegian national theater. After his return to Norway, he continued to be engaged in the future of the Christiania Theater, which was amalgamated with its erstwhile rival, the Christiania Norwegian Theater, in 1863. Also in 1863 Bjørnson became the first person to receive an author's salary from the Norwegian government.

On 1 January 1865, after lengthy negotiations, Bjørnson became artistic director of the Christiania Theater. During his tenure he experienced considerable discord with the theater management, and he also encountered a public that was often at odds with his vision for the theater. Although the troupe was, at last, composed overwhelmingly of Norwegian actors, their lines still tended to be spoken with Danish pronunciation and in what was regarded as a Danish acting style. Instead of producing only musical plays and nationalistic pieces, Bjørnson wanted to show that Norwegian actors were capable of performing dramatic masterpieces.

In addition to producing many of his own and Ibsen's works, Bjørnson staged plays by Shakespeare, Lessing, and Holberg. One of his first productions was Shakespeare's *A Midsummer Night's Dream* (circa 1595), translated by Oehlenschläger and with the music of Felix Mendelssohn. Although critics were displeased with the acting and the sets, it was perhaps the most significant production of his tenure. He produced his own *De Nygifte* (1865; translated as as *The Newly-Married Couple,* 1868) and *Maria Stuart i Skotland* (published 1864, produced 1867, Mary, Queen of Scots). *De Nygifte* had the distinction of being the first Norwegian play to be produced simultaneously in Christiania, Copenhagen, and Stockholm. Laura, who is newly married to Axel, finds it difficult to see herself as a wife first and a daughter second. Against her and her parents' wishes, Axel moves away with her. Over the following year Laura grows ever colder toward Axel for separating her from her parents, even though he does everything he can to make her feel comfortable—including decorating their home with furnishings identical to those in her parents' home. Laura's friend Mathilde secretly writes a book in which Laura and Axel's unhappy relationship is mirrored. Laura and Axel do not realize until the end of the play who wrote the book, but it leads them to reflect on their marriage. Meanwhile, Mathilde persuades Laura's parents to visit, and they are reconciled with Axel on seeing how hard he has worked to make Laura feel at home even while away from them. Seeing how fond they now are of Axel, Laura realizes that she has been unfair and proclaims her love for him.

Maria Stuart i Skotland depicts Mary as she struggles in her roles as woman and queen in her interactions with her husband, Henry Stewart, Lord Darnley, whose love she does not return; with her secretary, David Rizzio; and with James Hepburn, fourth Earl of Bothwell. She exclaims in a soliloquy, "Å, hvorfor kom jeg til dette land! Ingen venn, ikke en beskytter, alle forrædere mot meg, og jeg er blott en kvinne!" (Oh, why did I come to this country! No friend, not one protecter, every traitor against me, and I am just a woman!).

In 1866 Bjørnson became editor of *Norsk Folkeblad*. He resigned from the Christiania Theater at the end of the 1866–1867 season. Despite the strife he had experienced as director, he is generally credited with transforming the Christiania Theater into an acclaimed Norwegian cultural institution whose repertoire included the classics of both the Norwegian and the European dramatic canons.

In the autumn of 1867 Bjørnson and his family visited Copenhagen. Shortly before he departed, a Danish publisher asked him to contribute a poem about April to a calendar in which each month of the year would be accompanied by poetry about that month. As Bjørnson scholars have often pointed out, the poem Bjørnson wrote for the calendar aptly describes his own temperament (many have noted the coincidence that Bjørnson died in April). The poem begins emphatically with the line "Jeg velger meg April!" (I choose April!) and proceeds to portray the month as one of dynamic change in which the old falls and the new sprouts; a month of storms and showers, of melting snow and the promise of the summer yet to come. It is a tumultuous month; but peace is not the best thing, the speaker says. It is better that people have desires and goals that force them to act.

The main character in Bjørnson's novel *Fiskerjenten* (1868; translated as *The Fisher-Maiden: A Norwegian Tale*, 1869), on which he worked in Copenhagen, also bears features of his personality–first and foremost, his passion and drive. Indeed, in response to questions as to the identity of the actress on whom he modeled the fisher-maiden, Bjørnson insisted that she was based on no one but himself. The title character is a poor girl who disgraces herself and her mother by deceiving three suitors, each of whom believes she has promised him her hand. Aided by a man who, unbeknownst to

Bjørnson and his wife, the former Karoline Reimers, at Aulestad in 1897 (Store Norske Leksikon <http://www.snl.no/.bilde/ Bj%C3%B8rnson%2C_Bj%C3%B8rnstjerne_(med_Karoline)>)

her, is her father, she flees from her small town to Bergen. There she grows enamored of the theater, and at the end of the novel she realizes her dream of becoming an actress. Bjørnson devotes several passages in the second half of *Fiskerjenten* to overturning church associations of the theater with immorality. In many of his subsequent literary works and speeches he expressed exasperation with the failures of organized religion and–influenced in the 1870s by the theology of N. F. S. Grundtvig–advocated an open and affirming Christianity that would be true to Christ's teachings of brotherly love.

In the summer of 1869 Bjørnson traveled to northern Norway, where he gave many lectures. His growing engagement in the controversial political issues of the day earned him both acclaim and derision.

Though Ibsen denied that he had modeled the character of Stensgaard in *De unges Forbund* (1869; translated as *The League of Youth,* 1919) on Bjørnson, Bjørnson was deeply insulted by the portrayal. But despite being frequently branded a demagogue and a populist, Bjørnson continued to devote himself to social activism. In this respect he differed greatly from Ibsen, who, reflecting on his miserable experiences at the theaters in Bergen and Christiania, had written in a letter to Bjørnson in 1867 that theater directing is like an abortion that takes the life of the writer's unborn literary works. Bjørnson, by contrast, viewed being a writer as a public role that should go hand in hand with other public roles such as directing and engaging in politics.

In 1870 Bjørnson was elected chairman of the Studentersamfundet (Students' Association) and became the director of a small group of actors who had broken from the Christiania Theater and were performing at the Møllergaten Theater in the same city. The latter venture lasted about a year and a half. Perhaps his most enduring public achievement of 1870 was his organization of a children's parade for the Constitution Day celebration on 17 May. Processions of flag-waving Norwegian children are still a feature of Constitution Day celebrations; Bjørnson came to be known as "barnetogets far" (the father of the children's parade). Also in 1870 his *Digte og Sange* (translated as *Poems and Songs,* 1915) and his saga-inspired epic poem, *Arnljot Gelline,* were published.

In 1871 Bjørnson went on a lecture tour of Sweden. In many of his speeches and writings of 1871 and 1872 he advocated closer ties between the Scandinavian countries and Germany, though his Pan-Germanic viewpoint was at odds with the sentiments of many Scandinavians—particularly since Germany's defeat of Denmark in the 1864 war over Schleswig-Holstein. While vacationing with his family in Florence in the summer of 1873 he wrote a drama, *Kong Eystein* (King Eystein), that he intended as the first installment of a two-part drama of which *Sigurd Jorsalfar* (1872, Sigurd the Crusader) would form the second part. But he never made *Kong Eystein* public, and it did not appear in print until 1932. *Kong Eystein* is nevertheless significant in that it represents the last of Bjørnson's literary works dealing with historical themes. *Sigurd Jorsalfar* became a popular piece on the stage, where it was accompanied by music composed by Edvard Grieg.

In *Redaktøren* (1874; translated as *The Editor,* 1914), also written in Florence, Bjørnson turned to contemporary social drama. The title character is an unscrupulous journalist whose scathing columns contribute to the ill health of a politician, Halvdan Rejn, and tarnish the reputation of his brother, Harald, who aspires to carry on Halvdan's work. Harald's engagement is threatened when his fiancée's parents, who are friends of the editor, seek to distance themselves from Harald; in the end, however, they see that the editor has acted with evil intentions. Halvdan dies toward the end of the play of a massive hemorrhage while reading one of the editor's columns. In condemning the editor's actions Bjørnson condemns a culture in which only hard-hearted men who have purged themselves of all feeling can survive the media's attacks. He also criticizes individuals such as the fiancée's parents, who are more concerned with what people think of Harald than with his actual character.

Although *Redaktøren* deals with contemporary issues, it is not commonly regarded as the breakthrough to the drama of social realism in the Nordic countries; that distinction is held by Bjørnson's *En Fallit* (published 1874, produced 1875; translated as *The Bankrupt,* 1914). The businessman Henning Tjælde finds himself bankrupt but ultimately manages to repay his creditors, in large part because of the hard work of his family members and his loyal clerk, whose betrothal to Tjælde's daughter Valborg ends the play on a happy note.

In 1875 Bjørnson bought the farm Aulestad in Østre Gausdal, where he wrote *Kongen* (published 1877, produced 1902; translated as *The King,* 1914). Many of the characters in the play voice republican sentiments; one of them, Flink, says that monarchy is "en assuransekasse, rett og slett! En del prester, embetsmenn, adel, godseiere, grosserere, militære har aksjer i den" (nothing more or less than an insurance business in which a whole crew of priests, officials, noblemen, landed proprietors, merchants and military men hold shares). Even the king expresses support for democratic government, describing monarchy as having become "så stor en løgn at det tvinger selv de rettskafneste til å nærme seg det i løgn" (so all-pervading a lie that it infects even the most upright of men). Among these upright men the king includes Christians, who, he suggests, should take far more interest in attempting to prevent the abuse of power that is inherent to monarchical systems of government. When his desire for change is thwarted, the king commits suicide.

The novel *Magnhild: En Fortælling* (Magnhild: A Tale; translated as *Magnhild,* 1882), written during Bjørnson's stay in Italy but not published until 1877, was as controversial as *Kongen,* though for different reasons. The sole survivor of a landslide that killed the rest of her family, Magnhild is raised by the local pastor as a ward of the parish. She is coerced into marrying Skarlie, a saddler who is much older than she, and soon comes to despise him. Her talent for music, first displayed when she lived with the pastor's family, is reawakened when she rents a room in her and Skarlie's home to a composer, Tande. Tande is having an affair with a married lodger across the road, but he breaks it off when he falls in love with Magnhild. Magnhild realizes that she loves Tande, too; but instead of pursuing the illicit relationship she temporarily leaves home, and Tande departs for Germany. Several years pass; Magnhild grows ever more dejected and neglectful of her appearance. Finally, at the end of the novel she gains the courage to leave Skarlie and travel with a friend to America. Bjørnson's view that marriage must be based on love, not duty, was considered radical.

Bjørnson's condemnation of social hypocrisy appears in a different context in *Det ny system* (1879; translated as *The New System*, 1913). The director-general of railroads institutes a "new system" that is challenged by a young engineer, who claims that it is costing the country millions of kroner. In the ensuing debate, others begin to doubt the efficacy of the system, and the director-general himself privately expresses reservations. He holds onto his belief in the system because of his chief clerk's faith in it—but then finds out that the clerk is also dubious but has clung to his faith in the system because of the director-general's apparent confidence. Bjørnson thus criticizes the keeping up of appearances and praises those who, like the young engineer, have the courage to live a life guided by truth.

In the play *Leonarda* (1879; translated, 1912) Bjørnson attacks social mores regarding women's conduct and reputations. Leonarda has a bad reputation because of her friendship with General Rosen, who is viewed by the community as morally dissolute. Leonarda's neice, Aagot, whom she has raised, falls in love with Hagbart, who shares the common view of Leonarda. In a conversation with the bishop, Leonarda argues that she is merely exercising Christian compassion toward Rosen; the assertion is not enough to sway the bishop to accept her conduct. Hagbart eventually decides that Leonarda does not deserve her ill repute and finds that he is more in love with her than with her niece. Leonarda is drawn to Hagbart, too, but to avoid hurting Aagot she leaves on a journey with Rosen—who, it is revealed, is her former husband. The bishop and other characters come to the realization that they have done Leonarda a grave injustice.

Kaptejn Mansana: En Fortælling fra Italien (Captain Mansana: A Tale from Italy; translated as *Captain Mansana*, 1882), was also published in 1879. Early in the novel the title character attends a memorial service for his father. Reflecting on his father's life, he realizes that the pursuit of honor and glory—or, as he puts it, conspiracy and revenge—condemns the pursuer to a life of emptiness and restlessness and forces his women and children to make do on their own. But he is incapable of applying this lesson to his own life. His ego leads him to want to possess the princess Theresa Leaney, and he

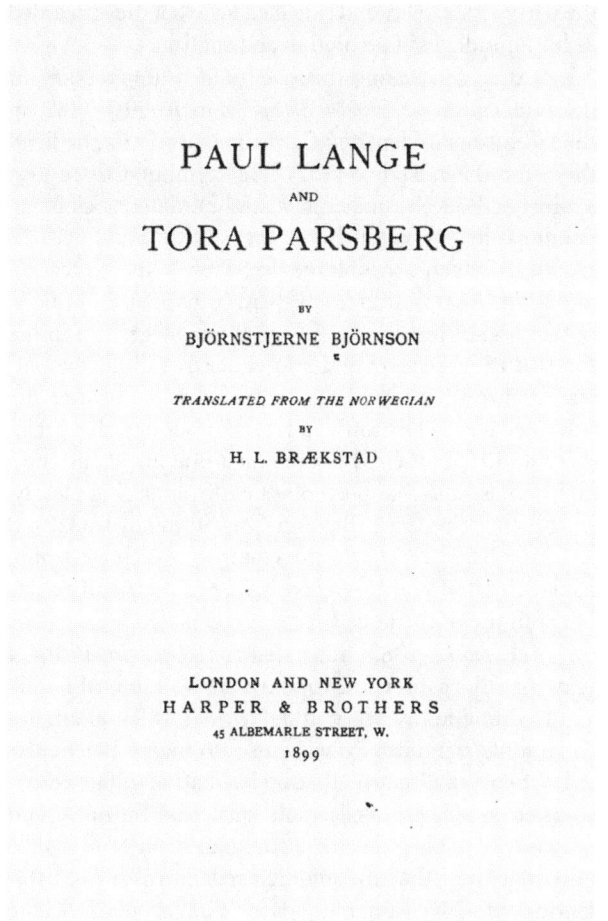

Title page for the English translation of Bjørnson's play Paul Lange og Tora Parsberg. *The original was published in 1898 and produced in 1901 (University of Michigan Libraries).*

becomes engaged to her. But he fears that marrying someone of her high station will transform him into little more than a manager of her property and a servant of her whims, and he breaks off the engagement to pursue Amanda Brindini, a young woman who is far beneath his class. The pursuit fails, and he returns to Theresa. She recognizes that he has suffered from a mental illness and marries him. Like Mansana, the male characters in Bjørnson's works often live in a world of dreams and ideals and come perilously close to losing their foothold in reality. They must either learn to recognize these fantasies and prevent themselves from acting on them or be led back to the path of virtue and restraint by a strong female such as Theresa Leaney.

In 1880 Bjørnson traveled to America, where he gave lectures in New England and the Midwest. He returned to Norway in 1881. His campaigning for the Venstre (Left) Party proved indispensable to its success in the election of 1882. Nevertheless, he was viewed by many in the party as a liability and ridiculed for what they regarded as his unbridled self-promotion and egotism.

After celebrating the twenty-fifth anniversary of the publication of *Synnøve Solbakken* in August 1882, in the fall Bjørnson departed Christiania for Paris; he lived there for the next five years. He continued to protest against orthodoxy, intolerance, and outdated social conventions in works such as the story "Støv" (1882, Dust), in which a couple neglect their sons' education and allow a servant to teach them romanticized notions of death and the afterlife. When the boys get lost in the forest during a storm and subsequently fall ill, the parents realize their error; the mother dies soon after the boys recover. Bjørnson's narrator describes the prejudices and romanticized notions that one instills in one's children as dust that prevents them from seeing clearly. In the play *Over ævne* (Beyond Our Strength; translated as *Pastor Sang*, 1893), the first part of which was published in 1883 and produced in 1886, Bjørnson rejects belief in the miraculous.

En hanske (1883; translated as *A Gauntlet*, 1890), a play that Bjørnson wrote to mark the occasion of his silver wedding anniversary in September 1883, examines the double standard. Svava refuses to marry her fiancé, Alf, when she discovers that he has had an affair with a married woman. Intellectuals such as Brandes and August Strindberg sneered at the moralism of *En hanske* and suggested that the middle-aged Bjørnson was forgetting his own amorous past. The ensuing debate between the so-called moralists and immoralists over sexual mores came to be known as the *Hanskestriden* (*Gauntlet* Feud). Not everyone counted Bjørnson among the moralists: to many social conservatives the questions explored in *En hanske* and in Ibsen's *Et Dukkehjem* (1879; translated as *A Doll's House*, 1889) and *Gengangere* (1881; translated as *Ghosts*, 1888) constituted an attack on the institution of marriage.

Bjørnson continued to protest against social conventions regarding gender roles and marriage in the novel *Det flagger i byen og på havnen* (1884, Flags are Flying in Town and by the Harbor; translated as *The Heritage of the Kurts*, 1892). Tomasine Rendalen struggles to raise her son, Tomas, to avoid the dissolute ways of his father and the father's family. Tomas becomes an upstanding man and joins his mother in founding a school for girls. Bjørnson inserts many references to pedagogical theory into the work. At the end of the novel a young woman who has been seduced and jilted by a man confronts him with their child on the day he is to wed another woman. Far more lighthearted is the play *Geografi og kærlighed* (1885, Geography and Love; translated as *Love and Geography*, 1914), which, though not one of Bjørnson's stronger works, was for a long time one of his most popular plays on the stage.

While vacationing in Norway in the summer of 1886, Bjørnson proclaimed himself a socialist. Bjørnson's socialism was not revolutionary in nature but emphasized tolerance and love of one's fellow human beings. This emphasis comes to the fore in his novel *På Guds veje* (1889; translated as *In God's Way*, 1890), which depicts the rivalry between a freethinking doctor, Edvard Kallem, and his childhood friend, pastor Ole Tuft, who marries Edvard's sister, Josephine. While Josephine, unlike her brother, views herself as a Christian, she takes issue with what she views as her husband's too literal presentation of Scripture in his sermons and to their son. When Ole and Josephine wrongly suspect Kallem's wife, Ragni, of having an affair with her friend Karl Meek, they cut off contact with the Kallems and even decline to visit Ragni when she is dying of tuberculosis. Only when Ole and Josephine's son grows gravely ill and is successfully operated on by Kallem is contact reestablished. After his son's recovery, Tuft gives a sermon in which he states:

aldri mer skal ordene bli det øverste for meg, ikke heller tegnene; det skal livets evige åpenbaring være. Aldri mer skal jeg fryse fast i en lære, men la livsvarmen løse min vilje. Aldri skal jeg dømme mennesker efter dogmer ut av forrige tiders rettferd, når den ikke holder kjærlighetens mål i vår tid. Aldri for Gud! Og det, fordi jeg tror på ham, livets gud, hans uavlatelige åpenbarelse i livet.

(never again shall either words or signs be for me the most important; but, contrariwise, the everlasting revelation of life. Never again will I let myself be immured in any doctrine; but will let my will be set free by the warmth of life. Never again will I judge mankind by the codes of an old-world justice, if the justice of our day cannot use the language of love. Before God never! And this because I believe in Him, the God of life, and His incessant revelation in life.)

On learning that Ragni was not guilty of an affair and had not, until shortly before her death, even known that she was suspected of having had one, Josephine is plagued with guilt for having misjudged her. She views herself as Ragni's murderess, but she is forgiven by Edvard. In the final lines of the novel Bjørnson issues a plea for tolerance and understanding. Ole is pondering God's ways as he, Josephine, and Edvard walk slowly homeward together. Edvard says that he still does not share Ole's faith, to which Ole replies, in typical Bjørnsonian fashion: "Nei, nei, nei, nei . . . der bra folk går, der er Guds veie!" (No, no, no, no . . . there where good people walk, those are God's ways!).

Bjørnson's socialist ideals manifest themselves strongly in the second part of *Over ævne* (1895; translated as *Beyond Our Power*, 1913), in which he contrasts "true" or "pure" Christianity with the institutionalized religion that the leaders of industry manipulate in their exploitation of their workers. Opposing the practices of his fellow capitalists, the character Anker says: "Den ansvarsløshet, den ryggesløshet hvormed rikfolk ødsler vekk millioner, som var den ingen annen til i landet enn de selv og de som hjelper dem med å more seg–den er likså anarkisme, et opprør mot Guds og menneskets lov" (This irresponsibility, this dissoluteness with which the wealthy squander millions as if there were no one else in the country except for themselves and those who enable them to amuse themselves–this, too, is anarchy, a revolt against the law of God and the human being).

The tragedy *Paul Lange og Tora Parsberg* (published 1898, produced 1901; translated as *Paul Lange and Tora Parsberg*, 1899) was written in reaction to the suicide of the politician Ole Richter in Stockholm on 15 June 1888, for which many blamed Bjørnson. Bjørnson had withdrawn his support of Prime Minister Johan Sverdrup, with whom he differed on church matters, and he believed that his longtime friend Richter would collaborate with him in defeating Sverdrup. For Richter the stress grew too great to bear, especially after Sverdrup accused him of misusing his authority and Bjørnson betrayed Richter's confidence by publishing a private letter from him. In Bjørnson's play minister of state Paul Lange is planning on resigning his post when he is called on by the king's chamberlain to give a speech in opposition to a proposed vote of no confidence in the government. The chamberlain notes that Lange has maintained that the current head of government, while not perfect, is still the best man available to bring the country forward. As an added incentive, the chamberlain offers Lange the post of ambassador to Britain. Lange accepts, and he and Tora Parsberg decide that they will marry and travel to London together. But Lange's support of the government results in a political maelstrom, and he is denounced as dishonest and unethical. Unable to bear the opprobrium, he commits suicide. Tora laments in the final lines of the play: "Å, hvorfor skal det være så at de gode så ofte blir martyrer? Kommer vi aldri så langt at de blir førere?" (Oh, why must it be that good men are so often martyrs? Shall we never see the day when they become our leaders?).

Laboremus (1901; translated, 1901), its sister play *På Storhove* (1902, At Storhove), and *Daglannet* (published 1904, performed 1905) address family conflict and rivalry rather than politics. The best of the three is *Daglannet,* in which a father opposes his engineer son's plan to build a factory near a waterfall on the family farm. The father tells the son that he will never inherit the farm or be allowed to buy it. The son's plans to develop the land are blocked by political developments, and father and son are reconciled at the end of the play.

Bjørnson won the Nobel Prize in literature in 1903. In the speech he gave on his receipt of the prize on 10 December he stressed his belief that the mission of the writer must be rooted in moral values.

Bjørnson's last play, *Når den ny vin blomstrer* (1909; translated as *When the New Wine Blooms,* 1911), explores modern marriage. In a conversation with their uncle, Pastor Hall, Helene and Marna reject biblical teachings on marriage–particularly the notion that a wife must be subservient to her husband. Hall is in love with Helene and proposes to her; she accepts, leading to discussions by various characters about the advanges and disadvantages of a younger woman marrying an older man. Marna returns to the family home when her marriage breaks down after only five months, and Helene and Marna's parents also experience a breakdown of their marriage when the father, Arvik, leaves for Australia. His wife feels remorse for doting on their children and neglecting his needs. Even before reaching the harbor, Arvik realizes that he cannot turn his back on his wife and family. The play ends with the parents' reconciliation.

To the end, Bjørnson's life and writings demonstrated his belief that the mission of the writer in society must be rooted in moral values. In a conversation with the Swedish writer Ellen Key, Bjørnson emphasized that although his political activism resulted in fewer completed literary works and less income, "Jeg vil dikte et nytt og bedre Norge" (I want to write a new and better Norway)–an utterance that supplies the title of one of Per Amdam's biographies of Bjørnson. In the last decade of his life, Bjørnson's endeavors to write not only a better Norway but also a better world were particularly palpable in his commitment to pacifism, self-government, and human rights. He spoke out in support of Alfred Dreyfus in the Dreyfus Affair in France in 1898, criticized the German discrimination of Danes in Schleswig, denounced the Hungarians' oppression of the Slovaks in 1904, and, as earlier in his life, supported Norway's steps toward independence from Sweden. The union was dissolved in 1905. Bjørnson died in Paris of complications from a stroke on 26 April 1910. On his deathbed he wrote, "De gode gjerninger redder verden" (Good deeds save the world).

In a tribute written in 1882 for the twenty-fifth anniversary of *Synnøve Solbakken* Ibsen had proclaimed of Bjørnstjerne Bjørnson that "Hans liv var hans beste diktning" (His life was his finest work). It is true that the ideas and passions that Bjørnson embodied in his life, more than his writings, have been of lasting influence on Norwegian society. Whereas Ibsen's dramas have endured, Bjørnson's plays and other writings, apart from the national song and school readings of works such as *Synnøve Solbakken,* largely have not. While many of his works are overly sermonizing, to Bjørnson speaking out—whether in a literary work, as a theater director, at a political rally, or in the pages of a newspaper—constituted the sole manner in which one could effect change in a world rife with injustice and narrow-mindedness.

Letters:

Aulestad breve til Bergliot Ibsen, second edition (Christiania & Copenhagen: Gyldendal, 1911);

Gro-tid: Brev fra årene 1857–1870, 2 volumes, edited by Halvdan Koht (Christiania: Gyldendal, Nordisk, 1912);

Brytningsår: Brev fra årene 1871–1878, 2 volumes, edited by Koht (Christiania: Gyldendal, Nordisk, 1921);

Bjørnstjerne Bjørnsons breve til Alexander L. Kielland, edited by Francis Bull (Oslo: Gyldendal, 1930);

Kamp-liv: Brev fra årene 1879–1884, 2 volumes, edited by Koht (Oslo: Gyldendal, 1932);

Bjørnstjerne Bjørnsons brevveksling med danske, 1875–1910, 3 volumes, edited by Bull, Øyvind Anker, and Torben Nielsen (Copenhagen: Gyldendal Boghandel / Oslo: Gyldendal, 1953);

Din venn far, edited by Dagny Bjørnson Sautreau, foreword by Bull (Oslo: Gyldendal, 1956);

Breve til Karoline 1858–1907, edited by Sautreau, introduction by Bull (Oslo: Gyldendal, 1957);

Bjørnstjerne Bjørnsons brevveksling med svenske 1858–1909, 3 volumes, edited by Anker, Bull, and Örjan Lindberger (Oslo: Gyldendal, 1960–1961);

Land of the Free: Bjørnstjerne Bjørnson's America Letters, 1880–1881, edited and translated by Eva Lund Haugen and Einar Haugen (Northfield, Minn.: Norwegian-American Historical Association, 1978);

"Og nu vil jeg tale ut," "Men nu vil jeg også tale ud": Brevvekslingen mellom Bjørnstjerne Bjørnson og Amalie Skram 1878–1904, edited by Anker and Edvard Beyer (Oslo: Gyldendal, 1982);

Bjørnstjerne Bjørnson und Maximilian Harden: Briefwechsel, edited by Aldo Keel (Frankfurt am Main: Peter Lang, 1984);

Bjørnstjerne Bjørnsons Briefwechsel mit Deutschen, 2 volumes, edited by Keel (Basel: Helbing & Lichtenhahn, 1986, 1987);

God morgen, Rosalinde! Brev til Rosalinde Thomsen (Oslo: Cappelen, 1990).

Bibliography:

Arthur Thuesen, *Bjørnson-bibliografi,* Småskrifter for bokvenner 76, 78, 79, 82, 85 (Oslo: Damm, 1948–1957).

Biographies:

Christen Collin, *Bjørnstjerne Bjørnson: Hans barndom og ungdom,* 2 volumes (Christiania: Aschehoug, 1907);

Gerhard Gran, *Bjørnstjerne Bjørnson* (Copenhagen: Schønbergske, 1916);

Francis Bull, *Bjørnstjerne Bjørnson* (Christiania: Aschehoug, 1923);

Christian Gierløff, *Bjørnstjerne Bjørnson* (Oslo: Gyldendal, 1932);

Per Amdam, *Den unge Bjørnson: Diktningen og barndomslandet* (Oslo: Gyldendal, 1960);

Amdam, *Bjørnson og kristendommen 1832–1875: Selverkjennelse, selvhedelse* (Oslo: Universitetsforlaget, 1969);

Amdam, *Bjørnson og kristenarven, 1875–1910: Selvhedelse, selverkjennelse* (Oslo: Universitetsforlaget, 1977);

Amdam and Aldo Keel, *Bjørnstjerne Bjørnson,* 2 volumes (Oslo: Gyldendal, 1993, 1999).

References:

Per Amdam, *Bjørnstjerne Bjørnson—han som ville dikte et nytt og bedre Norge* (Oslo: Cappelen, 1979);

Øyvind Anker, *Boken om Karoline: Karolines Bjørnson og Bjørnsons Karoline* (Oslo: Aschehoug, 1982);

Fredrik Engelstad, *Kjærlighetens irrganger: Sinn og samfunn i Bjørnsons og Ibsens diktning* (Oslo: Gyldendal, 1992);

Astrid Finsland, *Bjørnstjerne Bjørnson og fredssaken inntil 1900* (Oslo: Gyldendal, 1948);

Einar Haugen, *The Vocabulary of Bjørnson's Literary Works: A Word Index and Word Count of a Norwegian Author* (Oslo: Universitetsforlaget, 1978);

Bjørn Hemmer, *Ibsen og Bjørnson: Essays og analyser* (Oslo: Aschehoug, 1978);

Aldo Keel, *Bjørnson in Deutschland: Ein Materialienband* (Frankfurt am Main: Peter Lang, 1985);

Harold Larson, *Bjørnstjerne Bjørnson: A Study in Norwegian Nationalism* (New York: King's Crown Press, 1944);

Helge Lervik, *Bjørnstjerne Bjørnsons politiske agitasjon 1880–1884* (Oslo: Universitetsforlaget, 1969);

Herluf Møller, *Fem år: Studier i Bjørnsons ungdomsdiktning* (Oslo: Gyldendal, 1968);

Harald Noreng, *Bjørnstjerne Bjørnsons dramatiske diktning* (Oslo: Gyldendal, 1954);

Øystein Sørensen, *Bjørnstjerne Bjørnson og nationalismen* (Oslo: Cappelen, 1997);

Olaf Øyslebø, *Bjørnsons "bondefortellinger": Kulturhistorie eller allmennmenneskelig diktning?* (Oslo: Gyldendal, 1982).

Papers:

Most of Bjørnstjerne Bjørnson's manuscripts and other papers are in the Bjørnsonsamling (Bjørnson Archives) at the Nasjonalbiblioteket (National Library) in Oslo.

Niels Krog Bredal

(6 September 1732 – 26 January 1778)

Lanae H. Isaacson

BOOKS: *Gram og Signe; eller Kierligheds og Tapperheds Mesterstykker* (Copenhagen, 1756);

Eremiten: Et nyt musicalsk Hyrde-Spil. Indrettet som en Pastorelle, udi tvende Afhandlinger. I Anledning af Vores allernaadigste Arve-Herre og Konge, Kong Friderich den Femtes høistvelsignede Fødsels-Fest som til alle troe Undersaatters Glæde indfaldt den 31 Martii 1757, til den kongelige danske Skuepladses Brug (Copenhagen: Nicolaus Møller, 1758);

Det kræsne Val: En original dansk Pastorelle udi tvende Afhandlinger indrettet som en Intermezzo, til den kongelige danske Skuepladses Brug (Copenhagen: Nicolaus Møller, 1758);

Den tvivlraadige Hyrde eller Den vovelige Prøve: Et originalt Synge-Spil i tvende Afhandlinger, indrettet som en Intermezzo til den Kongelige Danske Skue-Pladses Brug (Copenhagen: Nicolaus Møller, 1758);

Den lykkelige Hververe, et originalt dansk Synge-Spil udi tvende Afhandlinger indrettet som et Intermezzo, til den kongelige danske Skuepladses Brug (Copenhagen: Nicolaus Møller, 1758);

Beileren efter Moden, eller Den romanske Jomfrue: Et original Synge-Spil udi tvende Afhandlinger indrettet som et Intermezzo til den Kongelige Danske Skuepladses Brug (Copenhagen: Nicolaus Møller, 1758);

En musicalsk Prologus i Anledning af H.K.H. Kron-printz Christians Fødsels-fest den 29 Januar 1759 (Copenhagen, 1759);

Breve efter Rabernes Maade (Copenhagen: Møllmann, 1759);

Ode til den fuldkomne Ina (Copenhagen, 1760);

Allerunderdanigst Taksigelse til Deres Kongelige Majestæt Kong Friderich den Femte . . . da Deres Majestæt den 27 August 1760 benaadede det Asiatiske Compagnie med sin allerhøjeste Nærværelse . . . udført i en Samtale imellem Irene, Gudinde for Freed, og Mercurius, Gud for Handelen (Copenhagen, 1760);

Hr Joh. Andr Cramer, Kongelig tydsk Hof-Prædikant i Kiøbenhavn, hans Afhandling om Smaae-koppernes Indpodning eller Inoculation, nu paa Dansk oversat, samt forøget med adskillige Anmærkninger uddragne af de beste Skribentere om Indpodningens Historie ved Niels Krog Bredal (Copenhagen & Trondheim, 1762);

Ufuldkomne Tanker ved Hiertets følelser ved den sande og indbildte Lyksalighed i Anledning af Ægte Foreening mellem Chr Fr Hagerup, Pastor til Skiærstad og Anna Margrethe Catherine Vestermann 20 September 1764 paa Torget i Norlandene (Trondheim, 1764);

Lykønsknings-Ode til Georg Friderich von Krogh, Chef for første Tronhiemske Inf. Regimente da han med Marg Lerche fortsatte sin Hiem-reyse (Trondheim, 1765);

Korte Sørge-Tanker ved en høyagtet Vens uformodentlige Dødsfald, da den veledle og velvüse Hr Christian Brauman Thullin, fordum Kongel. Majestæts velbestaltede Raadmand udi Christiania, midt paa Ærens Bane, midt i Udødeligheds Haab ved en salig Død ble henkaldet fra det Jordiske (Trondheim: Jens Christensen Winding, 1765);

Tanker efter Niels Klims Maade, eller en opmærksom reysende Amerikaners Efterretning, til en Borger i Maanen, om et vist Land og Folk paa vores Jordkugle (Copenhagen: Hans Mikkelsens Halvbroder, 1767);

Tale over Aage Schavland, forhen Sognepræst til vor Frue Kirkes Menighed i Trondhjem holden den 16de Maii 1768 (Trondheim, 1768);

Tronfölgen i Sidon: En original lyrisk tragi-comedie udi to handlinger, til den kongelige Danske Skuespladses Brug (Copenhagen: Bibliotheca Danica, 1771);

Den dramatiske Journal, eller Critik over Tronfölgen i Sidon: *Et efterstykke i een Handling* (Copenhagen: Møller, 1771);

Passions Oratorium, som i Fasten opføres af det musikalske Sælskab, poesien af Bredal, Musiken af Scheibe (Copenhagen, 1771);

Ephemeron, eller det gamle døende Insect (Copenhagen: Svare, 1771).

PLAY PRODUCTIONS: *Gram og Signe; eller Kierligheds og Tapperheds Mesterstykker,* Copenhagen, Bryggergaarden, 21 February 1757;

Eremiten: Et nyt Musikalsk Hyrde-Spil. Indrettet som en Pastorelle, Copenhagen, Bryggergaarden, 31 March 1757;

Den tvivlraadige Hyrde eller Den vovelige Prøve, Copenhagen, Det Kongelige Teater, 13 February 1758;

Den lykkelige Hververe, et originalt dansk Synge-Spil udi tvende Afhandlinger, indrettet som en Intermezzo, Copenhagen, Det Kongelige Teater, 2 May 1758;

Beileren efter Moden eller Den romanske Jomfrue: Et original Synge-Spil, Copenhagen, Det Kongelige Teater, 4 October 1758;

Det kræsne Val: En original dansk Pastorelle udi tvende Afhandlinger indrettet som en Intermezzo, Copenhagen, Det Kongelige Teater, 8 November 1758;

Tronfölgen i Sidon: En original lyrisk tragi-comedie, Copenhagen, Det Kongelige Teater, 4 April 1771;

Den dramatiske Journal, eller Critik over Tronfölgen i Sidon: *Et efterstykke i een Handling,* Copenhagen, Det Kongelige Teater, 25 November 1771.

TRANSLATIONS: Albrecht von Haller, *Doc. Albrecht von Hallers Poetiske Tanker om det Ondes Oprindelse: Oversat til Danske Vers* (Copenhagen, 1751);

Publii Ovidii Nasonis Metamophoses, oversatte i Danske Vers (Copenhagen, 1758);

G. F. Poullain de St. Foix, *Deucalion og Pyrrha: Comedie med Arier* (Copenhagen, 1771?);

Charles Georges Fenouillot De Falbaire, *De tvende Giærrige: Comedie i 2 Handlinger* (Copenhagen: Bibliotheca Danica, 1774);

Jean François Marmontel, *Skov-Byggeren: En lyrisk Comodie i een Handling* (Copenhagen, 1775);

Michel-Jean Sedaine, *Deserteuren, eller Den rømmende Soldat: En lyrisk Tragi- Comoedie i tre Handlinger* (Copenhagen, 1775);

Sedaine, *Venskab paa Prøve: En lyrisk Comedie i 2 Handlinger, tagen af Marmontels Fortællinger* (Copenhagen: Bibliotheca Danica, 1775);

Charles-Simon Favart, *Bondepigen ved Hoffet: En lyrisk Comedie i to Handlinger* (Copenhagen, 1776);

Nicolas Etienne Framery, *Colonien eller den nye-bebyggede Øe: En lyrisk Comedie i to Handlinger* (Copenhagen, 1778);

Sedaine, *Den forstilte Tvistighed, eller den Franske: Rose og Collas, et comisk Synge-Spil i een Handling* (Copenhagen: Gyldendal, 1778).

OTHER: *Tale over Sti Tønsberg de Schøller af Niels Krog Bredal 20 Junii 1769 Trondheim,* in *Samling af Minde-Taler, holdne i det Kongelige Norske Videnskabers Selskab over adskillige af dets afdøde Medlemmer, 1805,* edited by Hans Jacob Wille (Copenhagen: Norske Videnskabers Selskab / J. H. Schubothe, 1805), pp. 21–40.

Active in creating and promoting Danish musical drama and poetry, Niels Krog Bredal served as the director of Det Kongelige Teater (The Royal Theater) in Copenhagen from 1771 until his death in 1778. In collaboration with the Italian impresario, court composer, and musical director Guiseppe Sarti, Bredal composed *syngespil* (operettas) and *pastoreller* (pastorals) that combined Nordic themes and settings, French structure and alexandrine verse, and Italian melodies. A language purist, Bredal also sought to provide Danish theater audiences with plays in Danish based on Danish history. Bredal is credited with composing the first national heroic drama in Danish: *Gram og Signe; eller Kierligheds og Tapperheds Mesterstykker* (1756, Gram and Signe; or, Masterpieces of Love and Bravery)—although, in fact, the play represents a synthesis of domestic and European elements. Bredal enlivened the dramatic scene with his intermezzi and *syngespil*. He also wrote occasional poetry and verses, celebratory addresses to the monarch and other members of Danish high society, eulogies of writers, and essays on noteworthy events and discoveries of the day. His works, however, have not generally stood the test of time or secured a permanent niche in the Danish repertoire. Bredal is remembered today mainly for a riot that broke out at Det Kongelige Teater at a performance of his wildly popular but critically panned *Tronfölgen i Sidon* (1771, The Royal Succession in Sidon).

Bredal was born on 6 September 1732 in Trondheim, a thriving mercantile center and a focal point of the Enlightenment, to Thomas Bredal, an attorney, judge, and poet, and Anna Dorothea Krog; his father died when Bredal was six. In 1747 he completed his studies at Trondheim Latin Cathedral School and entered the University of Copenhagen, where he studied theology and law and translated German, French, and Latin works into Danish. During his student years he met the historian and judge Caspar Peter Rothe, whose interest in *sprogrensning* (language purification) touched a responsive chord in him.

Bredal completed his law degree in 1755. That year his association with the newly appointed court kapellmeister Sarti led to the composition of *Gram og Signe,* which was first performed in an apartment in Bryggergaarden for students of the University of Copenhagen on 21 February 1757 with music by Sarti and decorations by the theater artist Peter Cramer, who also sang one of the parts.

Despite Bredal's boast of having written "det allerførste Danske Synge-Spil" (the very first Danish operetta), *Gram og Signe* is an elaborate pastiche or meld of French and Italian opera. The play's claim to national dimensions and foundations rested on its links to the medieval historian Saxo Grammaticus's *Gesta Danorum* (circa 1204, The History of the Danes) and its use of Nordic names and references. A play about disguise and deception and obstacles to true love, it resembled the Italian opera that the court and high society favored. The Danish king, Gram, is involved in a war with Sumble, the king of Finland, when he falls in love at first sight with Sumble's daughter, Signe. Gram promises an end to the hostilities if he is allowed to replace his consort, Gro, with Signe. Sumble agrees to the match but subsequently promises Signe to King Henrich of Saxony. Gram disguises himself as a physician, travles to the Finnish court, and issues a dire prediction concerning Henrich's fate. During the wedding supper Gram reveals his true identity, kills Henrich, and claims Signe as his bride.

Gram og Signe moved on to formal presentation at Det Kongelige Teater, and Bredal and Sarti quickly became the darlings of the stage. Bredal touted his play as an example of "Saxos gamle 'ukunstlede skaldekunst,' som han gleder seg over å gi danskene del i" (Saxo's old "unaffected skaldic art" that he was pleased to share with the Danes). The style that Bredal considered unaffected, simple, and skaldic later became the target of parody by the Dano-Norwegian playwright Johan Herman Wessel, who wrote the biting satire *Kierlighed uden Strømper* (1772, Love without Stockings) in response to the facetious, pretentious language Bredal used in *Gram og Signe* and, later, in *Tronfölgen i Sidon*.

Gram og Signe was such a success that Bredal quickly completed what he called "den første danske pastorelle" (the first Danish pastoral), *Eremiten: Et nyt musicalsk Hyrde-Spil. Indrettet som en Pastorelle* (The Hermit: A New Musical Shepherd-Play. Organized as a Pastorale). It premiered on King Frederik's birthday, 31 March 1757, and attracted the crème de la crème of Danish society. Also in 1757 Bredal was given the title of vice mayor of Trondheim but remained in Copenhagen.

A call went out for more *syngespil;* the first to answer was the playwright C. A. Thielo, who offered *Det Ubekiendte Land: En Heroisk Musikalsk Comoedie* (1758, The Unknown Land: A Heroic Musical Comedy). Bredal responded with a series of intermezzi, slight pastorals about love between shepherds and country girls: *Den tvivlraadige Hyrde eller Den vovelige Prøve* (1758, The Irresolute Shepherd or The Daring Test), *Den lykkelige Hververe* (1758, The Happy Recruiter), *Beileren efter Moden, eller Den romanske Jomfrue* (1758, The Proper Suitor; or, The Romantic Maiden), and *Det kræsne Val* (1758, The Discerning Choice). But the homegrown product could not compete with popular Italian operas sung by visiting troupes of Italian singers–troops solicited by Sarti

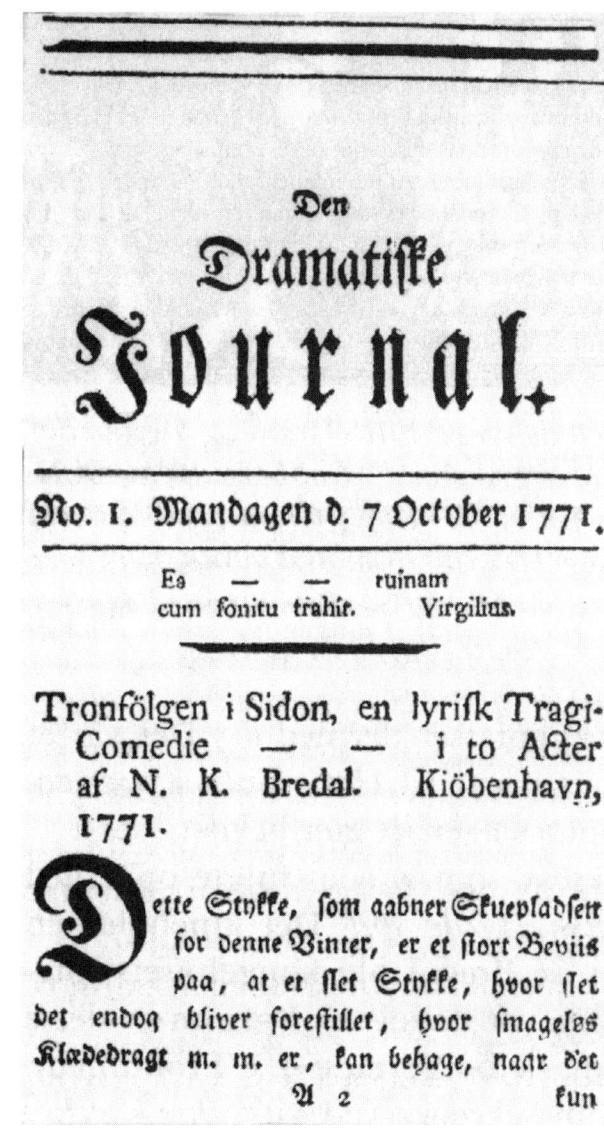

Front page of the first issue of Niels Krog Bredal's periodical (The Dramatic Journal) that established the field of drama criticism in Denmark (from Edvard Beyer, ed., Norges Litteratur Historie, volume 1 [Oslo: Cappelen, 1974]; University of Kansas Libraries)

himself. In 1761 Bredal returned to Trondheim, of which he had been appointed mayor. There he became a founding member and first secretary of Det Kongelige Norske Videnskabers Selskab (The Royal Norwegian Academy of Sciences) and took part in various literary and musical events. But he missed the theater in Copenhagen, and he returned to the city in 1770. He remained titular mayor of Trondheim until he formally surrendered the appointment in 1774.

On 4 April 1771 *Tronfölgen i Sidon* premiered at Det Kongelige Teater. Bredal drew on an Italian opera, Pietro

Metastasio's *Il Re Pastore* (1751, The Shepherd King), while Sarti composed entirely new arias for the play. Abdolonimus is offered the crown of Sidon and peace for his people if his daughter, Euphemia, marries Cleobulus. He accepts, thereby breaking his promise to Euphemia that she will marry Agathocles. At the moment that the marriage is to take place, Agathocles staggers into the scene, declares his love for Euphemia, and stabs himself. Cleobulus sings that he regrets forcing Euphemia to marry him. After half an hour of songs of regret and accusation, Agathocles springs to his feet: he did not stab himself after all. The drama ends happily with Cleobulus's retreat and the marriage of Agathocles and Euphemia.

Tronfölgen i Sidon was a huge success; according to Rolf Gaasland, Bredal and Sarti had created precisely the kind of melodramatic musical play that appealed to "den fornemme hoffsmaken representert ved losjenes publikum" (the refined courtly taste represented by the public in the loges). The two men also found Danish performers who were adept at handling the singing parts—in particular, the young actress Caroline Halle, who played Euphemia. Audiences returned to the Danish *syngespil,* and Bredal and Sarti pleased such courtly audiences with their 1771 collaboration.

Because of the success of the play, Bredal was named director of Det Kongelige Teater. He mounted a new production of *Tronfölgen i Sidon* on Monday, 7 October. That day Peder Rosenstand-Goiske, a nineteen-year-old law student at the University of Copenhagen, published the first issue of his *Den Dramatiske Journal* (The Dramatic Journal) and established the field of drama criticism in Denmark. Rosenstand-Goiske wrote a scathing review of *Tronfölgen i Sidon,* calling it "et elendigt misfoster, en parodi, der viser, at Hr. Bredal ikke er skabt til en dramaforfatter" (a miserable deformed fetus, a parody that proves that Mr. Bredal is not designed to be a playwright). He attacked the improbable plot, the music, the lyrics, the costumes, and the acting—even Halle did not escape his criticism. Rosenstand-Goiske decried the unheroic nature of the young lovers; attacked the play for not following the unities of French classic drama—when, in fact, *Tronfölgen i Sidon* was never intended to be a classic drama but a tragicomedy; and ignored the fact that Bredal had followed pastoral tradition in writing his *syngespil*.

Bredal immediately appended to *Tronfölgen i Sidon* a one-act *efterstykke* (afterpiece), *Den Dramatiske Journal, eller Critik over* Tronfölgen i Sidon (The Dramatic Journal; or, Criticism over *The Royal Succession in Sidon*), a dialogue between the actors and the critics in which the latter are ridiculed. Bredal scheduled the *efterstykke* to conclude the evening performance of *Tronfölgen i Sidon* on 25 November 1771, and he arranged for military officers to be present. The result was a violent confrontation between the students who supported Rosenstand-Goiske and his new journal and the armed guards; the students were forcibly evicted. In the aftermath of the riot a debate over Bredal's play and afterpiece was carried on for some time in the pages of *Adresse-Avisen* and *Den Dramatiske Journal*. In fact, the *syngespil* was running out of time as an entertainment form of the courtly, aristocratic classes. Bredal and Sarti had pleased the courtly class with plays such as *Gram og Signe, Eremiten,* and *Tronfölgen i Sidon,* but a new, more critical, and more discerning public was starting to attend plays. According to Gaasland, "*Tronfölgen i Sidon* blir dermed ikke bare offer for estetiske dommer, men også for sosio-økonomiske konjunkturer. Idet den kritiske offentlighet gradvis erstatter den representative, og kritikeren eller 'kunstdommeren' dermed gradvis erstatter 'den besyngende undersått,' faller også eneveldets foretrukne genre– nemlig syngespillet" (*Tronfölgen i Sidon* becomes not only a victim of negative aesthetic judgment thereby but also of socioeconomic conjunctures. As the critical public gradually replaces the representative, and the critic or "judge of art" gradually replaces "the artistic subject," the preferred genre of the aristocracy—namely, the song-drama—falls).

As the acrimony over *Tronfölgen i Sidon* continued, Bredal moved on to organize a competition for the best original Danish tragedy; Johan Nordahl Brun received the award for his play *Zarine* in 1772 (produced 1792). He also tried to ensure that fledgling dramatists received all the receipts for premieres of their plays at Det Kongelige Teater. And he translated plays by French playwrights such as Michel-Jean Sedaine, Charles-Simon Favart, Nicolas Etienne Framery, and Charles Georges Fenouillot De Falbaire into Danish for performance at Det Kongelige Teater. Bredal died in Copenhagen on 26 January 1778.

Niels Krog Bredal's *syngespil* and *pastoreller* have vanished from the Danish repertoire. He came from a vibrant, energetic, fairly egalitarian community, Trondheim, which was advancing the arts and sciences, and as mayor he encouraged those advances. He then moved on to a Copenhagen that was on the cusp of the Enlightenment. Yet, he made little use of his background and his milieu in his art. Instead, as volume 4 of *Dansk Litteratur Historie* (1983) summarizes, he chose to create for a social and cultural elite whose own day was drawing to a close:

> Bredal fungerede som skribent helt på den bestående ordens betingelser. Disse betingelser var af en sådan art, at de fuldstændig afskar ham fra hans egne erfaringer. Født i et fremdriftigt borgermiljø, hensat i København i et begyndende oplysningsmiljø, fanget ind af den patriotiske sprogbestræbelse og siden forfremmet til borgmester for byen med de driftige

borgere: hvad kunne det ikke være blevet til? Men alt dette blev udgrænset, fordi de former, der bød sig til for Bredals musik-dramatiske lidenskab, var af en sådan karakter, at de afskar ham fra enhver mulighed for at komme til bevidsthed om sig selv som borger.

(Bredal functioned as a writer in accordance with the established order. The preconditions were such that they completely cut him off from his own experiences. Born into a milieu with a progressive citizenry, sent to Copenhagen at the start of an Enlightenment, ensnared by patriotic efforts on behalf of language and then promoted to mayor for the very town with the daring citizens: what could that not have led to? But everything was ruled out because the forms that were available for Bredal's passion for music and drama were such that they cut him off from every possibility of becoming aware of himself as a citizen.)

References:

Johan Fjord Jensen and others, *Dansk Litteratur Historie*, volume 4: *Patriotismens Tid, 1746–1807* (Copenhagen: Gyldendal, 1983), pp. 124–128;

Rolf Gaasland, "Verdien af Niels Krog Bredals *Tronfölgen i Sidon*," in *Mellom europeisk tradisjon og national bevissthet: Det norsk-klassiske drama 1750–1814*, by Gaasland and Erik Aarseth (Oslo: Spartacus, 1999), pp. 79–91;

Søren Kjær-Jensen, *Den feudale Klappen og den borgerlige Piben. Tronfølgefejden i 1771 set som et sammenstød imellem den Repræsentative offentlighed og den borgerlige offentlighed* (Copenhagen: Copenhagens Universitet, 1980).

Johan Nordahl Brun

(21 March 1745 – 26 July 1816)

Lanae H. Isaacson

BOOKS: *Jomfru Pecunia,* anonymous (Trondheim, 1768);

Naturens Navnedag, i Anledning af Skabelsens 2 Cap. 19 Vers, for at lykønske Hans Høiærværdigheds Hr. Biskop Gunneri Hjemkomst fra sin Nordlandske Reise (Trondheim: Jens Christensen Winding, 1769);

En øm Faders Betragtninger ved sin dødfødde Søns Lüg-Stene (Trondheim: Jens Christensen Winding, 1770);

Zarine, et sørgespil i fem optog: opført paa den kongelige danske Skueplads første gang den 17 Februarii 1772 af de kongelige danske Skuespillere (Copenhagen: Godiche, 1772);

Einer Tambeskielver: et Sørgespil i fem Optog til Brug for den kongelige danske Skueplads (Copenhagen: Godiches Efterleverske, 1772);

Til Nordmænd om Troeskab mod Kongen og Kierlighed til Fædrenelandet: i Anledning Af Einer Tambeskielver (Trondheim: Jens Christensen Winding, 1773);

Det Kongelige Norske Videnskabers Selskabs Tab ved Hans Høyærværdigheds Hr Biskobs John Ernst Gunneri Død (Trondheim: Jens Christensen Winding, 1773);

Tvende hellig Taler: holdne i Korskirken første Søndag i Advendt (Bergen: H. Dedechens Efterleverske, 1779);

Hellige taler i Anledning af Ungdommens Confirmation (Copenhagen: Gyldendal, 1782);

Toldbetienten: et Syngestykke i tre Handlinger (Copenhagen: Gyldendal, 1783);

Væveriet: et Skuespil i fem Handlinger (Copenhagen: Gyldendal, 1783);

Lovens eller De Ti Buds Kraft, i Christi Kirke: forestillet i en Prædiken 6te Søndag efter Trinitas i Korskirken (Bergen: Rasmus Dahl, 1785);

Vore gamle Kirke-Skikke, forsvarede mod Hr Confessionarius og Doktor Bastholm (Bergen: Rasmus Dahl, 1785);

Evangeliske Sange (Bergen: Hans Kongl. Majests. Priviligerede Bogtrykkerie, Rasmus Dahl, 1786);

Endres og Sigrids Brøllup: et Syngestykke i tre Handlinger (Copenhagen, 1791);

Samling af Johan Nordahl Bruns mindre digte (Copenhagen: Møller, 1791);

Johan Nordahl Brun (portrait by Paul Ipsen, 1791; Store Norske Leksikon <http://snl.no/.bilde/Brun%2C_Johan_Nordahl_(portrett-tegning%2C_profil)>)

Republikken på Øen: et skuespil i fem handlinger bestemt til den 28 januari 1793 (Bergen: Rasmus Dahl, 1793);

Hellige taler, 2 volumes (Bergen: R. Dahls Efterleverske, 1796);

Jonathan: et Digt i ti Sange (Bergen: R. Dahls Efterleverske, 1796);

Officieren: et Skuespil i fem Handlinger (Bergen: R. Dahls Efterleverske, 1802);

Samling af minde-taler holdne i det Kongelige Norske Videnskabers-selskab over Adskillige af dets afdøde medlemmer (Copenhagen: J. H. Schubothe, 1805);

Tolv hellige Taler (Bergen: R. Dahls Efterleverske, 1806);

Tanker til nærmere Eftertanke om vort synkende Pengevæsen m.m. (Bergen, 1815).

Editions and Collections: *Mindre digte,* edited by Christen Brun (Christiania: Jacob Lehmann, 1818);

Johan Nordahl Bruns Evangeliske Sange (Bergen: Chr. Dahl, 1834);

Johan Nordahl Bruns Hellige Taler (Christiania, 1836);

Selskaps- og leilighetssanger, edited by G. Stoltz (Bergen: Privately printed, 1944).

PLAY PRODUCTIONS: *Zarine, et sørgespil i fem optog,* Copenhagen, Den kongelige Danske Skueplads, 17 February 1772;

Endres og Sigrids Brøllup: en Syngestykke i tre Handlinger, Trondhiem, Rotvold, 14 September 1790;

Republikken på Øen: et skuespil i fem handlinger, Bergen, 28 January 1793.

SELECTED PERIODICAL PUBLICATION–UNCOLLECTED: "Hr Lieutenant Ferrys og Jomfrue Nordahls Brudevielses Tale holden af J. N. Brun udi Bergen d. 27 December 1774," *Personalhistorisk tidsskrift,* 3 (1774): 161.

Johan Nordhal Brun wrote plays, religious poems, *lejlighedsdigte* (occasional songs), *selskabssange* (society songs), tracts, articles, addresses, and sermons that were collected in his *Evangeliske Sange* (1786, Evangelical Songs), *Samling af Johan Nordahl Bruns mindre digte* (1791, Collection of Johan Nordahl Brun's Smaller Poems), and *Hellige taler* (1796, Holy Talks). Much of this work, especially his religious writing, has fallen by the wayside; today he is remembered mainly for composing Norway's first–unofficial–national anthem, "Norges Skaal: For Norge, Kjæmpers Fødeland" (1772, For Norway, Birthplace of Warriors); for his Easter hymn "Jesus lever, Graven brast" (1786, Jesus Lives, the Grave has Burst); for his tribute to Bergen, "Udsigter fra Ulrikken" (1791, Views from Ulrikken), popularly known as "Jeg tog min nystemte Cithar i Hænde" (I Took my Newly Tuned Zither in Hand); and for his play about a Norwegian national hero, *Einer Tambeskielver: et Sørgespil i fem Optog* (1772, Einer Tambeskielver: A Tragedy in Five Scenes).

Brun was born in Byneset (which was incorporated into the municipality of Trondheim in 1964) on 21 March 1745 to Svend Busch Brun, a merchant, and Mette Catharina Nordhal. When he was four, the family moved to a farm in Klæbu. Brun became a junior officer in the Nordenfjeldske Skiløperkorps (Nordenfjeld Ski Guard) at twelve and entered Trondheim Cathedral Latin School in 1760. There he studied history with the rector, Gerhard Schøning, and graduated in 1763 with an *examen artium* (examination qualifying students for university study). He worked as a house tutor, studying theology on his own, before entering the University of Copenhagen. He completed his second-level student examination in 1764 and obtained his degree in theology in 1767. He returned to Trondheim, resumed teaching, and began writing. His first publication, the comedy *Jomfru Pecunia* (Miss Pecunia), appeared anonymously in 1768.

Brun made his debut as a poet in 1769 with *Naturens Navnedag, i Anledning af Skabelsens 2 Cap. 19 Vers, for at lykønske Hans Høiærværdigheds Hr. Biskop Gunneri Hjemkomst fra sin Nordlandske Reise* (The Name-Day of Nature, with Reference to Genesis Chapter 2, Verse 19, Written to Welcome Home His Highly Esteemed Lord Bishop Gunnerus, from his Journey to Nordland). The poem begins with a depiction of the beginning of time, which seems a bit grandiose for a poem commemorating the return of the Johan Ernst Gunnerus, the bishop of Bergen, from a trip to the extreme northern part of Norway. The poem suggests the Enlightenment view of creation as the work of a divine but distant clock maker who set the marvelous timepiece running in one momentous instant. Brun declares that neither the wonders of spring in the far north nor the poetic rendering of spring by Christian Braunmann Tullin in *En Maij-Dag* (1758, A May Day) can compare with the first day of the world. Adam, the recipient of God's creation, was endowed with a wise soul that enabled him to see God in nature. But the human "Opfindingskraft" (power of invention) can lead one astray: the individual can use divine reason for evil purposes. In such cases one must turn away from impetuosity to caution and reason, using the gifts of nature as wisdom and virtue dictate:

> Men, himmelsk Viisdom! Du, som bedst veilede kan,
> Som har saa tit oplyst en taagemørk Forstand;
> En Straale af dit Lys kan endnu Veien lære,
> Ved Dig man Gud endnu kan i Naturen ære,
> Du splitter Taagen hist, som Synet dunkelt gjør;
> For nyttig Indsigt Dig man ene takke bør.

> (But, heavenly Wisdom! You, who can best guide,
> Who has so often enlightened a fog-darkened Understanding;
> A beam of your Light can still teach the Way,
> By You man can still honor God in Nature,
> You divide the Fog there, where the Sight darkens;
> For useful Insight, man ought to thank you alone.)

At the end of his tribute to nature and to God's gift of divine reason to humanity Brun launches into a wide-ranging tour of the glories and wonders of flora and fauna and the deeds of great heroes. Finally, he focuses on his subject, the safe return of Bishop Gunnerus from Nordland. The conclusion of *Naturens Navnedag* dwells

Brun in 1774, the year he became parish provost of Korskirken in Bergen (painting by Andreas Bergius; from Edvard Beyer, ed., Norges litteratur historie, volume 1 [Oslo: Bokklubben Nye Bøker, 1982]; Library of the University of California, Berkeley)

on Brun's deep and abiding love for his homeland and its beauty:

> Naar fra Forglemmelse man redder Mark og Eng
> Og døber Skjønheder, som voxte op i Flæng,
> Mit kjære Fødeland! Saa seer Du nu den Dag,
> Som med sit blanke Smiil forklare skal din Sag,
> Og sige Verden, at blandt Norske Fjelde findes
> De Blomster, som ei kan i Skjønhed overvindes,
> Der fødes ogsaa den, som kjender deres Værd,
> Og ei forgjæves bær det store Navn af lærd.

> (When from Oversight one saves Fields and Meadows
> And baptizes Beauties that grow up helter-skelter,
> My dear Birthplace! Then You will see the Day,
> Which with its bright Smile will enlighten your Cause,
> And say to the World that among Norwegian Mountains are found
> Those Flowers that cannot be bested in Beauty,
> One is also born who knows their Worth,
> And does not bear the great Name of learned in vain.)

This theme is also found in his later national songs such as "Den gamle Nordmand eller Gjenlyd fra Norge" (1776, The Old Norwegian; or, Echo from Norway) and "Norges Herlighed" (1791, Norway's Glory). Given these sentiments, it might seem logical to view Brun as an early nationalist and proponent of independence for Norway. But Brun was as loyal to the monarch in Copenhagen as he was proud of his Norwegian homeland.

In 1771 Brun was named Bishop Gunnerus's secretary. He accompanied the bishop's delegation to Copenhagen on a mission to reform Danish universities and—Gunnerus secretly hoped—to lay the groundwork for a Norwegian university. During his stay in Denmark, Brun completed a patriotic song, "Norges Skaal . . . For Norge, Kjæmpers Fødeland" (Toasts to Norway . . . For Norway, the Birthplace of Warriors), that became a rallying cry for Norwegian students at the University of Copenhagen. In contrast to the loving, euphoric descriptions of the natural beauty of Norway in *Naturens Navnedag*, the stanzas of "Norges Skaal . . . For Norge, Kjæmpers Fødeland" are aggressive and strident and border on advocating national independence—and so it was considered by the Norwegian students and the Danish authorities:

> For Norge, Kjæmpers Fødeland,
> Vi denne Skaal vil tømme,
> Og naar vi først faae Blod paa Tand,
> Vi sødt om Frihed drømme;
> Dog vaagne vi vel op engang
> Og bryde Lænker, Baand og Tvang;
> For Norge, Kjæmpers Fødeland,
> Vi denne Skaal udtømme!

> (For Norway, Birthplace of Warriors,
> We'll drink this Toast,
> And when we first have Blood on our Teeth,
> We'll sweetly dream of Freedom;
> Yet we'll awaken one time for certain
> And break our Fetters, Bonds and Coercion;
> For Norway, the Birthplace of Warriors,
> We'll drink this Toast!)

It soon became apparent to Gunnerus that Brun would be unable to function as a secretary to the mission—not because of his patriotic songs and sentiments but because of his feeble command of German, the diplomatic language of the time. Brun resigned his position and turned to playwriting. He won a competition for the first Danish original tragedy with *Zarine, et sørgespil i fem optog* (1772, Zarine, a Tragedy in Five Scenes). Based on the French dramatist Voltaire's *Zaïre* (1733) and written in strict alexandrine verse, *Zarine* is the story of the love of the Meder army commander Stryange and the captured Sacer queen, Zarine. To hide from Zarine the fact that he is married to Rhetea, the Meder king's daughter, Stryange has Rhetea abducted. Zarine, however, meets Rhetea and rejects Stryange. A short time later, Stryange receives a message falsely claiming that his wife has died. In shame and despair, he kills himself. The play ends with the two mourning women standing over his corpse.

In the preface to *Zarine* Brun expressed his hope that Norway would "besynge Nordens egne Helte" (sing the North's own heroes). Four months after the first performance of *Zarine* on 17 February 1772, Brun completed the tragedy *Einer Tambeskielver* for performance. Based on the work of the medieval Icelandic historian Snorri Sturluson and written in alexandrines, Brun's second play depicts the loss of Norwegian independence through union with Denmark. It was rejected for performance; Ivar Havnevik explains that

> litteraturhistorien har gjerne lagt stor vekt på at stykket er gjennomført "norsk," med mange verdiutsagn som lovpriser norske fenomener: frihet, fjell, tapperhet og liknende. Disse ingrediensene gjorde at stykket ikke kunne oppføres, med tanke på at det kunne oppfordre til utbredelsen av norske selvstendighetsideer.
>
> (literary history has emphasized that the piece is solidly "Norwegian" with many important addresses that praise Norwegian phenomena: freedom, mountains, bravery, and so forth. These ingredients led to the piece not being performed, as the idea was that the piece could lead to the dissemination of ideas of Norwegian independence.)

In 1772 Brun was called to the position of resident chaplain of Byneset. After 1772 he turned to writing hymns characterized by clear, concrete images and scenes, such as "Jesus lever, Graven brast." He defended *Einer Tambeskielver* in a pamphlet, *Til Nordmænd om Troeskab mod Kongen og Kierlighed til Fædrenelandet: i Anledning Af Einer Tambeskielver* (1773, To Norwegians on Loyalty to the King and Love of the Fatherland: With Reference to *Einer Tambeskielver*), in which he argues that love of Norway was inextricably linked to loyalty to the Danish king. On 2 September 1773 he married Ingeborg Lind. In 1774 he became parish provost of Korskirken in Bergen. In his poem "Under Tullins Portrait" (1782, Under Tullin's Portrait) Brun acknowledges his debt to the Christiania nature poet and laments a young star that faded much too soon:

> For tidlig døde Du, for tidlig Danmark haver
> Forbrudt sig mod dit Støv, og sat en *Evalds* Gaver
> Fremfor det Liv og Lys, som hædrede din Sang.

Title page for a collection of Brun's minor poems (Bøger & Kuriosa, Denmark)

> *Tullin!* Fornuft tiltrods Du fik dog *anden* Rang;
> Men naar man vaagner op af disse søde Drømme,
> Naar Mørkhed, Qvalm og Damp for sund Forstand maae rømme,
> Naar Folk igjen faae Lyst at læse og forstaae,
> Da skal Du *første* Sted blandt Sjaldre hidtil faae.
>
> (Too soon You died, too soon has Denmark
> done harm to your Dust, and placed the Gifts of an *Evald*
> Ahead of the Life and Light that glorified your Song.
> *Tullin!* Contrary to Reason You received but *second* Place;
> But when one wakes from these sweet Dreams,
> When Darkness, Unease and Excess must flee in the face of sound Understanding,
> When People again have the Desire to read and understand,
> Then You shall have *first* Place among Skalds.)

Brun's play *Endres og Sigrids Brøllup* (Endres and Sigrid's Wedding) was produced in 1790 and published the following year. His 1791 poem "Paa Kongens Fødselsdag" (On the King's Birthday) links Norway's welfare, peace, and bounty to the benevolent Danish monarch:

Saa var blandt Dagene Landsfaders Fødselsdag:
Vær glad ved Kongens Held, det er din egen Sag;
Thi vor Lyksalighed er hans Regjerings Maal,
Og derfor *leve Christian,* vor bedste Skaal!

(So was the Birthday of the Father of the Country among Days
Be glad for the King's Good Fortune, that is your own Affair,
Because our Happiness is the Goal of his Reign,
And therefore, *long live Christian,* our best Toast.)!

Also in 1791 Brun published "Udsigter fra Ulrikken," in which he describes Bergen as seen from the highest of the seven mountains that surround the city:

Herfra fortryllende Syner jeg skuer,
Lungegaards Vandet, den Slette saa blaa,
Nyegaards Alleens løvkronede Buer,
Derunder prydede Skjønne at gaae,
Deromkring Markens den festlige Dragt,
Det Guld i det Grønne den blomstrende Pragt.
. . . .
Bedre frem Bergen, det Handelens Sæde,
Strækkende Arme om seilbare Vaag.
Derhen høifarmede Jægter med Glæde
Rustes hver Sommer til dobbelte Tog;
Derfra gaae Skibe saa vide om Land;
Der kjøber, der sælger, der handler hver Mand.

(From here I spy enchanting Sights,
Nyegaard's Alléé's leaf-crowned Arches,
Under them decorated Beauties walk,
There around the Fields the festive Apparel,
The Gold in Green, the blossoming Glory.
. . . .
On and forward Bergen, the Seat of Commerce,
Stretching its Arms on sea-worthy Bays.
There high-mast Ketches with Joy
Are outfitted every Summer with double Loads;
From there Ships go far about the Land;
Buying, selling, every Man is trading.)

Brun closes his song with the lines: "Held for vort Bergen, vort Fødeland Held! / Gid alting maa blomstre, fra Fjere til Fjeld!" (Good Luck for our Bergen, our Birthplace Good Luck! / If only everything may bloom, from Seas to Mountains!).

Brun's play *Republikken på Øen* (Republic on the Island) was published and produced in 1793. That same year he was appointed provost of the Lutheran congregation in Bergen; the following year he was named a member of the Bishop's Council. His last poetic work, *Jonathan* (1796), deals with a biblical subject in alexandrine verse; he considered it the chief poem of his oeuvre.

In 1804 Brun became bishop of Bergen. Conservative, paternalistic, and unyielding, he was a stern opponent both of the Deism of the Enlightenment and of the Pietist movement; he tended to view Christ as a divine warrior and Christians as soldiers of God. A lifelong supporter of the Danish monarchy, Brun opposed Norway's union with Sweden but acquiesced when the union was a fait accompli in 1814. He died 26 July 1816.

Johan Nordahl Brun was not a nationalist and certainly not a revolutionary, but some of his works were used as rallying cries by Norwegian nationalists and revolutionaries in Copenhagen and in Norway. He was a true lover of his homeland who followed in the footsteps of Christian Braunmann Tullin and wrote poetry that captures the beauty—and the divinity—of Norway's natural surroundings.

Biography:

A. H. Winsnes, *Johan Nordahl Brun* (Bergen: Universitetet i Bergen, 1919).

References:

Edvard Beyer, *Utsyn over Norsk Litteratur* (Oslo: Cappelen, 1983), pp. 47–48;

Bjarne Fidjestøl, *Norsk Litteratur i Tusen År. Teksthistoriske Linjer* (Bergen: Landslaget for Norskundervisning / Cappelen akademisk forlag, 1994), pp. 180–181;

Ivar Havnevik, *Dikt i Norge: Lyrikkhistorie 200–2000* (Oslo: Pax, 2002), pp. 154–156.

Sophus Bugge
(5 January 1833 – 8 July 1907)

Lanae H. Isaacson

BOOKS: *Gamle norske Folkeviser* (Christiania: Feiberg & Landmark, 1858);

Folkeviser fra øvre Telemarken (Copenhagen: Folkes, 1859);

Forbindelse mellem Grógaldr og Fjölsvinnsmál: oplyst ved Sammenligning med den dansk-svenske Folkevise om Sveidal (Christiania, 1861);

Norrøne Skrifter af Sagnhistorisk Indhold, 3 volumes (Christiania: Norske Oldskriftselskabs Samlinger/Brøgger & Christie, 1864–1873)—comprises volume 1, *Hálfs saga, Norna-Gests þáttr* (1864); volume 2, *Volsunga saga* (1865); volume 3, *Hervarar saga og Heidreks Konungs* (1873);

Norrœn fornkvædi: Islandsk Samling af Folkelige Oldtidsdigte om Nordens Guder og Heroer. Almindelig Kaldet Sæmundar Edda hins Fróda (Christiania: Malling, 1867);

To nyfundne norske Rune-indskrifter fra den ældre Jærnalder (Christiania: Videnskapsselskabets Forhandlinger, 1872);

T. Macci Plavti Mostellaria: Plautus's Spøgelse-Komedie (Christiania, 1873);

Om Runeskriftens Oprindelse (Christiania: Forhandlinger i Videnskabs-Selskabet i Christiania, 1873);

Hamdismál: aus dem Vorarbeiten zu einer neuen Ausgabe der sogenannten Sæmundar Edda (Christiania, 1876);

Rune-indskriften paa ringen i Forsa Kirke i Nordre Helsingland (Christiania: H. J. Jensen, 1877);

Sproglige Oplysninger om Ord i Gamle Nordiske Love (Copenhagen, 1878);

Altitalische Studien (Christiania: Gesellschaft der Wissenschaften zu Christiania / A. W. Brøgger, 1878);

Bidrag til den Nordiske Balladedigtnings Historie (Christiania & Copenhagen, 1879);

Die Flexion des Pali in ihren Verhältniss zum Sanskrit (Christiania: Universitäts Programm für das erste Halbjahr, 1881);

Studier over de nordiske Gude- og Heltesagns Oprindelse, 3 volumes (Christiania: Cammermeyer, 1881–1889; republished, 1 volume, 1889);

Sophus Bugge (Den Store Danske <http://www.denstoredanske.dk/Samfund,_jura_og_politik/Sprog/Nordiske_filologer/Sophus_Bugge?highlight=BUGGE>)

Der Ursprung der Etrusker durch zwei lemnische Inschriften erläutert (Christiania: Forhandlinger i Videnskabs-Selskabet, 1886);

Studien über das Beowulfsepos (Halle, 1887);

Om Runeindskrifterne paa Røk-Stenen i Østergøtland og paa Fonnaas-Spænden fra Rendalen i Norge: Kungliga Vitterhets Historie och Antiqvitets Akademiens Handlingar, Ny Följd 11, 3 (Stockholm: Norstedt, 1888);

Beiträge zur Etymologische Erläuterung der armenische Sprache (Christiania: Dybwad, 1889);

Etruskisch und Armenisch: Sprachvergleichende Forschungen, Erste Reihe (Christiania: Aschehoug, 1890);

Runverser: undersökning af Sveriges metriska runinskrifter (Stockholm: Antiqvarisk Tidskrift för Sverige, 1891);

Nyere forskninger om Irlands gamle aandskultur og digtning i dens forhold til Norden (Christiania: Videnskabs-Selskabet, 1892);

Bidrag til den ældste Skaldedigtnings Historie (Christiania: Aschehoug, 1894);

To runestene fra Sønderjylland og deres historiske betydning (Christiania, 1894);

Kungssonen av Norigsland: en folkevise fra Telemarken (Christiania: Norge, 1895);

Helge-digtene i den Ældre Edda, deres hjem og forbindelser: Studier over de nordiske gude- og heltesagns oprindelse, 2. Række (Copenhagen: Gad, 1896); revised by Bugge with a new introduction, translated by William Henry Schofield as *The Home of the Eddic Poems, with Especial Reference to the Helgi-Lays* (London: Nutt, 1899; New York: AMS Press, 1972);

Torsvisen i sin norske Form: Udgivet med en Afhandling om dens Oprindelse og Forhold Til de andre Nordiske Former (Christiania: Aschehoug, 1897);

Erpr og Eitill: et lidet Bidrag til den nordiske Heltedigtnings Historie (Christiania: Dybwad, 1898);

Tale ved Rigsmaalsmødet 28 November 1899 (Christiania, 1900);

Sagaen om Ravnkel Frøisgode (Christiania: Aschehoug, 1901);

Norsk sagafortælling og sagaskrivning i Irland (Christiania: Grøndahl, 1901);

Et Benstykke med Runeskrift fundet i Trondhjem (Trondheim: Aktietrykkeriet, 1902);

Hønen-runerne fra Ringerike (Christiania: A. W. Brøgger, 1902);

Samhold i Norden: Tale i det Norske Studentersamfund den 7de februar 1903 (Christiania: Schibsted, 1903);

Fricco, Frigg und Priapos: Forhandlinger I Videnskabsselskabet i Christiania (Christiania: Dybwad, 1904);

Historiske Skrifter tilegnede og overleverede professor dr. Ludvig Daae paa hans Syttiende fødselsdag den syvende december 1904 af venner og disciple (Christiania: Aschehoug, 1904);

Landsmaal eller Rigsmaal? Tale ved Rigsmaalsmødet 28 November 1899 (Christiania, 1904);

Bidrag til Tolkning af danske og tildels svenske Indskrifter med den længere Rækkes Runer, navnlig paa Guldbrakteater (Copenhagen: H. H. Thieles, 1906);

Runerne paa en sølvring fra Senjen (Christiania: Dybwad / A. W. Brøgger, 1906);

Om nordiske folkenavn hos Jordanes (Stockholm: Fornvännen, 1907);

Norske eventyr og segnir, edited by Rikard Berge and Johanna Bugge Berge (Copenhagen & Christiania: Gyldendal/Nordisk, 1909);

Das Verhältnis der Etrusker zu den indogermanen und der vorgriechischen Bevölkerung Kleinasiens und Griechenlands: Sprachliche Untersuchungen (Strasbourg: K. J. Trübner, 1909);

Der Runenstein von Rök in Östergötland, Schweden, edited by Magnus Olsen, Axel Olrik, and Erik Brate (Stockholm: Hæggström, 1910);

Norske folkevisur: av samlingane etter Sophus Bugge, edited by Rikard Berge and Johanna Bugge Berge (Christiania: Dybwad, 1911);

Norske eventyr og segnir: 2. Samling, edited by Rikard Berge and Johanna Bugge Berge (Christiania: Dybwad, 1913; Copenhagen: Gyldendal, 1913);

Norges Indskrifter med de ældre Runer (Christiania: Det Norske Historiske Kildeskriftfond, 1917);

Gaader samlede i Telemarken af Sophus Bugge, edited by Rikard Berge (Risør: Norsk folkekultur, 1925).

Collections and Editions: *Norges Indskrifter med de ældre Runer. Norske Indskrifter indtil Reformationen: 1ste afdeling*, 4 volumes (Christiania: Brøggers, 1891–1924);

Lykische Studien, 2 volumes (Christiania: Dybwad, 1897, 1901);

Norges Indskrifter med de yngre Runer, 2 volumes (Christiania: Det norske Kildeskriftfond, 1902, 1906)—comprises volume 1, *Hønen: Runer fra Ringerike*; volume 2, *Runerne paa En Sølvring fra Senjen*;

Populær Videnskabelige Foredrag: Efterladte Arbejder (Christiania: Alexander Bugge, 1907);

Norske eventyr og sagn, 2 volumes, edited by Rikard Berge and Johanna Bugge Berge (Christiania: Gyldendal, 1909, 1913);

Norsk folkedigtning, med opskrifter fra Sophus Bugges utrykte samlinger, illustreret med Norsk folkekunst, 2 volumes (Christiania & Copenhagen: Nordisk, 1909, 1913).

SELECTED PERIODICAL PUBLICATIONS—UNCOLLECTED: "Om Consonant-Overgange i det norske Folkesprog," *Norsk Tidsskrift for Videnskab og Litteratur*, 5 (1852): 201–216;

"Zur Erklärung der oskischen Sprachdenkmäler," *Zeitschrift für vergleichende Sprachforschung*, 2 (1853): 382–385;

"Mythologiske Oplysninger til Draumkvædi," *Norsk Tidsskrift for Videnskab og Litteratur*, 7 (1854): 102–121, 192;

"Zur bantinischen Tafel," *Zeitschrift für verleichende Sprachforschung*, 3 (1854): 419–426;

"Altnordische Namen," *Zeitschrift für vergleichende Sprachforschung*, 3 (1854): 26–34;

"Guldhorn-Indskriften," *Tidsskrift for Philologi og Pædagogik*, 6 (1865): 317–318;

"Sjældne ord i norrön skaldskap," *Tidsskrift for Philologi og Pædagogik*, 6 (1865): 87–103;

"Bidrag til Tydning af de ældste Runeindskrifter," *Tidsskrift for Philologi og Pædagogik*, 7 (1867): 211–252, 312–363; 8 (1869): 163–204;

"Efterslæt til min Udgave af Sæmundar Edda," *Aarbøger for nordisk Oldkyndighed og Historie* (1869): 244–276;

"Lidt om de ældste nordiske Runeindskrifters sproglige Stilling," *Aarbøger for nordisk Oldkyndighed og Historie* (1870): 187–216;

"Bemærkninger om runeindskrifter på guldbrakteater," *Aarbøger for nordisk Oldkyndighed og Historie* (1871): 172–226;

"Remarques sur les inscriptions runiques des bracteates enor," translated by L. Morillot, *Société des Antiquités du Nord* (1871): 362–384;

"Altlateinische Wörter und Wortformen bey Festus und Paulus," *Neue Jahrbuch für Philologi und Pädagogik* (1872): 106;

"Altitalische Studien I, Primare und secundare Personalendungen des oscischen und umbrischen Verbs," *Zeitschrift für vergleichende Sprachforschung*, 22 (1875): 385–466;

"Biskop Bjarne Kolbeinsson og Snorres Edda," *Aarbøger for nordisk Oldkyndighed og Historie* (1875): 210–246;

"Run-inskrifter på marmorlejonet från Piræeus," *Kungl. Vitterhets Historie og Antiquvitets Akademiens Månadsblad* (1875): 43, 98–102;

"Reseberättelse," *Kungl. Vitterhets Historie og Antiquvitets Akademiens Månadsblad* (1878): 69–70;

"Tolkning af Runeindskriften på Rökstenen i Östergötland. Et Bidrag til Kundskab om svensk Sprog, Skrift og Skaldekunst i Oldtiden," *Antiqvarisk tidskrift för Sverige*, 5 (1878): 1–148, 211–215;

"Beiträge zur Erforschung der etruskischen Sprache," *Beiträge zur Kunde der indo-germanischen Sprachen*, 10 (1885); 11 (1886);

"Etymologische Studien über germanische Lautverschiebung," *Beiträge zur Geschichte der deutschen Sprache und Literatur* (1887): 400–430; (1888): 168–201, 312–339;

"Om versene i Kormaks saga," *Aarbøger for nordisk Oldkyndighed og Historie* (1889);

"Bidrag til nordiske navnes historie," *Arkiv for nordisk filologi*, 1 (1889);

"Etymologische Studien über germanische Lautverschiebung," *Beiträge zur Geschichte der deutschen Sprache und Literatur*, 13 (1891): 312–339;

"Fyrunga-indskriften," *Arkiv för nordisk filologi*, 9 (1895): 318–359;

"Bronsspänne med runinskrift funnet vid Skabersjö i Skåne," *Svenska fornminnesföreningens tidskrift*, 10 (1897);

"Runeindskrift på en stol fra Lillhärdal," *Svenska fornminnesföreningens tidskrift*, 10 (1898): 30–37;

"Beiträge zur vorgermanischen Lautgeschichte," *Beiträge zur Geschichte der deutschen Sprache und Literatur*, 24 (1899): 425–463;

"En olddansk Runeoptegnelse i England," *Aarbøger for nordisk Oldkyndighed og Historie* (1899): 264–272;

"En nyfunden götlandsk Runesten," *Svenska fornminnesföreningens tidskrift*, 11 (1900): 115–124;

"Flistad-indskriften," *Arkiv för nordisk filologi*, 14 (1900): 1–16;

"Runeindskriften paa en Guldmedaljon funden i Svarteborgs Sogn," *Svenska fornminnes-föreningens tidskrift*, 11 (1900): 110–113;

"Bidrag til Forklaring af norske Stedsnavne," *Arkiv for nordisk filologi*, 16 (1904): 334–357;

"Bidrag til Tolkning af danske og tildels svenske indskrifter med den længere Rækkes Runer, navnlig paa Guldbrakteater," *Aarbøger for nordisk Oldkyndighed og Historie* (1905): 142–328.

During his academic career at the University of Christiania (today the University of Oslo) Sophus Bugge gave the fields of comparative Indo-European languages, runic studies, Old Norse literature, and folklore their scholarly underpinnings. He stimulated the enthusiasm of students and colleagues for Old Norse studies, expanded the teaching of comparative philology, and established contact with Nordic scholars of philology and folklore. Bugge was a pioneer in research into the Indo-European Languages, the *Eddas* (Old Norse Poetry and Literature), runic inscriptions, and the folk narratives and poems that are still current in rural districts such as Telemark. Like other folklorists of his generation, such as Olea Crøger, Magnus Brostrup Landstad, Peter Christen Asbjørnsen, and Jørgen Moe, Bugge also responded to the national Romantic impulse to collect medieval ballads; the result was his first book, the masterful *Gamle norske Folkeviser* (1858, Old Norwegian Ballads).

Elseus Sophus Bugge was born on 5 January 1833 in Larvik, Vestfold, to Alexander Bugge, a timber dealer, and Maren Kirstine Sartz. He finished his admission examination for the University of Christiania in 1848. His teachers at the university included the Latin professor L. C. M. Aubert, who taught comparative languages and textual criticism, and the historians P. A. Munch and Rudolf Keyser, who lectured on Old Norse and historical source analysis.

In his early twenties Bugge formed a close friendship and collaboration with Svend Grundtvig, the edi-

Title page for Bugge's first book (Old Norwegian Ballads), a collection of folk songs collected in Telemark in 1856–1857 (University of Michigan Libraries)

tor of the first edition of *Danmarks gamle Folkeviser* (1853, Denmark's Old Folk Ballads); Bugge contributed reliable Norwegian variants of the Danish ballads for Grundtvig's seminal work, which later influenced and guided the Harvard scholar Francis James Child in preparing *The English and Scottish Popular Ballads* (1882–1898). (*Danmarks gamle Folkeviser* was brought to a conclusion in 1976 in twelve volumes with a total of 539 ballads compiled and edited by the scholars, field researchers, and archivists at the Dansk Folkemindesamling [Danish Folklore Archives].) In addition to his contributions to *Danmarks gamle Folkeviser,* Bugge began his career with a series of short pieces on Germanic, Italian, and Norse philology for scholarly journals in Germany and two articles for *Norsk Tidsskrift for Videnskab og Litteratur* (Journal of Science and Literature): "Om Consonant-Overgange i det norske Folkesprog" (1852, On Consonant Changes in Norwegian Rural Language), which drew on studies by the poet and proponent of Norwegian language reform Ivar Aasen, and "Mythologiske Oplysninger til Draumkvædi" (1854, Mythological Information on The Dream Ballad), which was influenced by Landstad's *Norske Folkeviser* (1853, Norwegian Folk Ballads).

Spurred by the work of Crøger, Landstad, and Grundtvig, Bugge applied for and received several grants to collect ballads and folklore in Telemark in 1856–1857. He completed his *cand. mag.* degree in 1857. His work in Telemark resulted in 1858 in *Gamle norske Folkeviser.*

One of the tenets of fieldwork, collection, and editing that guided Landstad, Grundtvig, and Bugge was absolute accuracy in recording and publishing what storytellers and singers of ballads actually performed. Bugge was particularly strict with respect to the oral nature of folk tradition, excluding from his collection ballads in folk language that originally appeared in written form.

The works Bugge collected for *Gamle norske Folkeviser* range from single strophes to complete, highly involved narrative songs. In many cases the ballads were Norwegian variants of what Grundtvig had published in *Danmarks gamle Folkeviser,* and they fell into the same categories of magical, courtly, and historical ballads that Grundtvig had used. One ballad that Crøger, Landstad, and Bugge encountered was unique not only to Norway but to the Telemark district: *Draumkvædet* (The Dream Ballad) recounts the visions of Olav Åkneson, who fell asleep on Christmas Eve and wandered through heaven and hell before awakening to share his experiences and send a warning to worshipers at church. Bugge and his contemporaries sought to trace the origins of the ballad, beginning a research path that continues to unwind to the present day. *Draumkvædet* became a powerful symbol for the emerging Norwegian nation, and scholars have focused on it again and again. The variant of *Draumkvædet* that Bugge collected from Anne Skålen of Mo, Telemark, in 1857 was one of the most complex versions, turning from visions of hell to commentaries on the rewards and glories awaiting the pious and righteous. Scenes of horror and dread alternate with glimpses of the lives and fates of the virtuous and the damned. The lengthy ballad alternates between third-person narration and Olav's own account of his visions. A constant refrain that combines eerie moonshine and the long, lonely, winding roads Olav travels in his trance accompanies the song.

Other ballads in *Gamle norske Folkeviser* include *Bendik og Årolilja* (Bendik and Årolilja) and *Agnete og bergemannen* (The Ordinary Mortal and the King of the Mountains). In the former Bendik falls in love with

Årolilja, the princess of Denmark. Her father, the king, takes Bendik prisoner and places him in sturdy bands that Bendik breaks as though they were thread. But a band made of "eitt hår av Årolilja" (a hair from Årolilja) holds Bendik fast. He is killed, and Årolilja joins him in death. The formulaic final scene describes the union of Bendik and Årolilja for eternity. *Agnete og bergemannen* is a *trylleviser* (magical ballad) dealing with an encounter between a human being and a supernatural creature. The *bergemannen* spirits Antonetta away, marries her, and fathers seven children with her. Antonetta begs to leave the mountain and return home for a visit; she receives permission but immediately breaks the rules that prohibit her undoing her red hair, telling her mother about her life in the mountain, or kneeling before the altar in church. The *bergemann* enters the church, seizes Antonetta, carries her back to the mountain, and uses a spellbinding wine from a magic chalice to erase her memory of her former life with her mortal family.

Gamle norske Folkeviser led to Bugge's election as the youngest member of the newly established Videnskabs-Selskabet i Christiania (Scientific Society of Christiania). It also opened the door to study abroad: he received a fellowship in Indo-European languages and Old Norse for advanced study in Berlin and Copenhagen, where he attended lectures by the German professor of Indo-European languages Franz Bopp and the Danish classical philologist J. N. Madvig. In Denmark, Bugge began planning his next project, a critical edition of Eddic poetry and sagas associated with the *Eddas*. He returned to Telemark for more fieldwork in the summer of 1859. In 1860 he received his first academic appointment at the University of Christiania, a fellowship in comparative languages and Sanskrit. He became a lecturer in comparative Indo-European languages and Old Norse in 1864. In a short article, "Guldorn-Indskriften" (1865, The Gold Horn Inscription), Bugge suggested that the language of runic inscriptions was not Gothic, as his teacher Munch (and others) had assumed, but "den germanske dialekt som språkene i de nordiske land hadde utviklet seg fra, ur-nordisk" (the Germanic dialect from which the languages in the Nordic countries derived, Ur-Nordic). He was appointed extraordinary professor of comparative Indo-European languages and Old Norse in 1866.

In 1867 Bugge edited and published *Norrœn fornkvædi* (Old Norse Songs), the first truly critical edition of the *Eddas;* it still serves as an invaluable aid to scholars. The work includes an introduction in which Bugge ties the *Eddas* to Norway and to an oral poetry that predates their collection into written texts:

> Den Samling af Oldtidskvæder, som her gives i ny Udgave, er i sit fulde, her foreliggende Omfang ikke

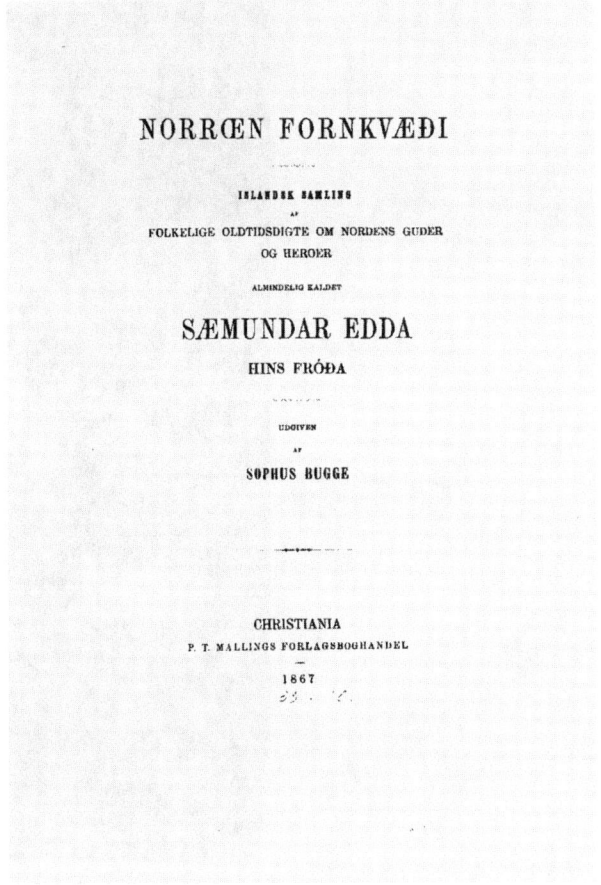

Title page for Bugge's collection of the Eddas *(Oxford University Libraries)*

gammel. De fleste af disse Digte vare dog allerede i den tidlige Middelalder paa Island forenede til én Samling, som vi nu især kjende fra to Haandskrifter. Denne Samling indeholder Kvæder i det gamle norske Sprog, som behandle Æmner af Nordens mythiske og heroiske Digtning; de ere digtede i det simpleste og oprindeligste nordiske Versemaal; ved intet af dem er Forfatter nævnt. Alle disse Kvæder have lydt fra Folkets Mund, før de bleve optegnede.

(This collection of Old Songs, now given in a new edition, is not old in its present complete form. The majority of these poems were already compiled into a collection in the early Middle Ages, and we are familiar with them in two manuscripts. The present collection contains songs in the old Norwegian language and deals with subjects from Nordic myth and heroic poetry; they are composed in the simplest and most original Nordic verse; in none of them is an author mentioned. All these songs have been sung by the people before they were written down.)

By connecting the poetry to Norway, Bugge sought to enhance the country's role as the home of Norse culture and literature and its uniqueness as a nation.

Oil painting of Bugge in 1889 by Wilhelm Holter (Store Norske Leksikon <http://snl.no/.bilde/Bugge%2C_Sophus_ (portrett%2C_malt_av_Holter%2C_utsnitt)>)

On 6 July 1869 Bugge married Karen Sophie Schreiner. Their son, Alexander, followed in his father's footsteps to become a professor at the University of Christiania; their daughter, Johanna, and her husband, Rikard Berge, edited Bugge's unpublished works after his death, and Johanna illustrated them and also painted his portrait.

Bugge published several works concerned with runic inscriptions found in various locales in Scandinavia. They include "Lidt om de ældste nordiske Runeindskrifters sproglige Stilling" (1870, A Little on the Language Situation in the Oldest Nordic Runic Inscriptions), *To nyfundne norske Rune-indskrifter fra den ældre Jærnalder* (1872, Two Newly Found Norwegian Runic Inscriptions from the Older Iron Age), *Om Runeskriftens Oprindelse* (1873, On the Origin of Runic Inscriptions), *Norges Indskrifter med de yngre Runer* (1902, 1906, Norwegian Inscriptions with Younger Runes), and the posthumously published *Norges Indskrifter med de ældre Runer* (1917, Norwegian Inscriptions with Older Runes).

Bugge's *Studier over de nordiske Gude- og Heltesagns Oprindelse* (Studies of the Origins of the Legends of the Nordic Gods and Heroes) appeared in three parts from 1881 to 1899; a second series was published in one volume in 1896. It caused considerable controversy. Bugge proffered the theory that the heroic legends and sagas derived from Greek, Roman, and biblical legends and stories that heathen or half-heathen Norse living in the British Isles during the Viking era had learned from monks and men educated in monasteries. He won support among a few stalwart scholar friends in Uppsala, Adolf Noreen among them. He went on to assert in *Bidrag til den ældste Skaldedigtnings Historie* (1894, Contributions to the History of the Oldest Skaldic Poetry) that *skaldedigtning* (skaldic poetry) was not nearly as ancient as his colleagues believed but that its roots were to be found in the Viking era, as well.

In addition to his works on Old Norse poetry and literature, Nordic gods and heroes, connections between various ancient and modern Indo-European languages, and Nordic runic inscriptions, Bugge wrote treatises on place and personal names in Scandinavia and lectured frequently at universities, archives, institutes, and scholarly societies in all of the Nordic countries. He was a member of many international scholarly societies, received an honorary doctorate from Uppsala University on the occasion of its four hundredth anniversary in 1877, and was honored with two festchrifts. He became a knight of the Order of St. Olav in 1877, a commander of the order in 1890, and a holder of the order's Most Distinguished Cross in 1896. He died on 8 July 1907 in Tynset, Hedmark.

The foremost philologist and comparative linguist of his generation, Sophus Bugge expanded the intellectual horizons of his country and the Nordic region. His interests in literature were closely tied to the emergence of Norway as a modern nation with an honored heritage; he represented the scholarly side of the national Romantic movement, the trend that echoed through Norwegian belles lettres. Bugge probed the heritage of Norway and made it accessible and relevant to his students and colleagues throughout Scandinavia. A man of many talents, eager to learn from others and willing to share what he had discovered, he was equally at home in the archives and libraries of Christiania and Copenhagen and in the rural homes of singers and storytellers in the Telemark region of Norway.

Letters:

K. Aubert, "Breve fra Sophus Bugge til Svend Grundtvig," *Maal og minne* (1909): 52–64;

A. Jakobsen, "Sophus Bugge i brevveksling med Adolf Noreen," *Maal og minne* (1957): 1–24;

Brev, 1855–1907, 2 volumes, edited by Alfred Jakobsen (Øvre Ervik: Alvheim & Eide Akademisk Forlag, 1990, 1992);

Sophus Bugges brev, 3 volumes, edited by Kristoffer Kruken (Øvre Ervik: Alvheim & Eide Akademisk Forlag, 2004).

References:

Ludwig Holm-Olsen, *Lys over norrøn kultur: Norrøne studier i Norge* (Oslo: Cappelen [Reistad & Sønn], 1981);

Lanae H. Isaacson, "'Draumkvædet': The Structural Study of an Oral Variant," *Jahrbuch für Volksliedforschung,* 25 (1980): 51–66;

Sproglige og Historiske Afhandlinger viede Sophus Bugges minde. Med tillæg: To Undomsbreve fra Sophus Bugge; Fortegnelse over Sophus Bugges trykte arbeider (Christiania: Aschehoug, 1908), pp. 285–294.

Camilla Collett
(23 January 1813 - 6 March 1895)

Donna H. Stockton
University of Colorado at Boulder

BOOKS: *Amtmandens Døttre: en Fortælling,* 2 volumes, anonymous (Christiania: Dahl, 1854, 1855); translated by Kirsten Seaver as *The District Governor's Daughters* (Norwich, U.K.: Norvik, 1991);

Fortællinger, anonymous (Christiania: Steensballe, 1861)–includes "Eventyr Sara og Hendes Datter," translated by Katherine Hanson as "Storyteller Sara," in *An Everyday Story: Norwegian Women's Fiction,* edited by Hanson (Seattle: Seal, 1984);

I de lange Nætter, anonymous (Christiania: Cappelen, 1863; revised edition, Copenhagen: Cammermeyer, 1892);

En undersøisk Parlament, anonymous (Christiania: Privately printed, 1863);

Under ljusa dagar, anonymous, translated by Anne Marie Lidfors (Stockholm: Hiertas, 1866);

Sidste Blade: Erindringer og Bekjendelser af Forfatterinden til "Amtmandens Døttre," anonymous (Copenhagen: Gyldendal, 1868);

Sidste Blade: Erindringer og Bekjendelser. Anden og tredje Række, anonymous (Christiania: Privately printed, 1872);

Sidste Blade: Erindringer og Bekjendelser. Fjerde og femte Række (Christiania: Malling, 1873);

Fra de Stummes Ljer (Christiania: Malling, 1877);

Et Lyst Billede i en mørk Ramme (Copenhagen, 1878);

Mod Strømmen (Copenhagen: Schous, 1879);

Ekko i Ørkenen: En Hilsen fra Norden til Mrs. Josephine Butler (Copenhagen: Prior, 1880);

Mod Strømmen: Ny Række (Copenhagen: Schous, 1885).

Editions and Collections: *Samlede Skrifter,* 8 volumes (Christiania: Cammermeyer, 1892–1893);

Samlede verker: Mindeutgave, 3 volumes (Christiania: Gyldendal, 1913);

Dokumentasjonsprosjektet, Tekstsamling, Camilla Collett <http://www.dokpro.uio.no/litteratur/collett> [accessed 31 August 2009]–comprises *I de Lange Nætter; Fortællinger; Amtmandens Døttre; Paa et gammelt Herresæde; En undersøisk Debat; Sidste Blade, 1ste Række; Sidste Blade, 2den og 3dje Række; Sidste Blade, 4de og 5te Række, Fra de Stummes Ljer; Mod Strømmen, Første Række; Mod Strømmen; Anden Række; Efterslæt, Camilla Wergelands Optegnelser 1831–1837; Senere Optegnelser og Breve vedrørende Camilla Wergelands Ungdomshistorie; Camilla Wergelands Brev.*

Camilla Collett (1839 oil painting by Johan Gørbitz; Oslo City Museum)

OTHER: "Kongsgaard," in *Hjemmet og Vandring–en Aarbog for 1847,* edited by Peter Christian Asbjørnsen (Christiania, 1846);

"Et Gjensyn," in *Ydale: Et vinterskrift,* edited by Asbjørnsen (Christiania: Feilberg & Landmark, 1851); translated by Leslie Grove and Diane Oatley as "Meeting Again," in *Female Voices of the North:*

An Anthology, volume 2, edited by Inger M. Olsen and Sven Hakon Rossel (Vienna: Praesens, 2006).

Camilla Collett is remembered by her countrymen as the most prominent female personality in nineteenth-century Norway. She was the author of the first realistic family novel in Norway and was Norway's first feminist. Her experiences during her formative years shaped the themes she wrote about in her adult years. She was the daughter of Nicolai Wergeland and the younger sister of Henrik Wergeland. As these male members of her family struggled for the independence of Norway, she later struggled for the independence of Norwegian women. Her major work of fiction, the novel *Amtmandens Døttre* (1854, 1855; translated as *The District Governor's Daughters,* 1991), is a critical portrayal of how upper-class families in the Norway of her era raised their daughters. Her other published works range from fiction and autobiography to collections of essays on a variety of topics. In each genre the major theme of her work is the condition of women. Collett was a prolific writer whose cause gave her life significance and purpose. At Collett's request, her personal letters and diaries were published only after her death. These documents serve to give deeper insight into how she matured as a writer by means of sorrow and self-doubt. Her writings, no matter in what genre, frequently express a sense of indignation, which she balances by an ironic sense of humor.

Jacobine Camilla Wergeland was born on 23 January 1813 in Christiansand, one of the five children of Nicolai and Alette Thaulow Wergeland. At the time of her birth, Norway was on the verge of an historic turning point, the beginning of its emergence as a modern independent nation, after centuries of control by Denmark. In May 1814 a Constitutional Assembly with representatives from all parts of Norway met at the village of Eidsvoll to draw up a constitution. On 17 May 1814 the Assembly declared Norway a free and autonomous nation, although the country did not gain complete independence until 1905. Wergeland's father was a representative at the Eidsvoll Constitutional Assembly. Later, her older brother Henrik played an active role in the debates about the future political and cultural identity of the Norwegian people. Camilla Wergeland called for improved legal and social rights for women.

Nicolai Wergeland was a proponent of Enlightenment ideals and a student of French language, thought, and literature. He was a serious, reflective man, with a tendency to brood. He took an active interest in the upbringing and education of his children, whom he raised according to the theories of philosopher Jean-Jacques Rousseau. Rousseau's argument was that nature tells human beings what is best, and that the education of a young person should draw on the individual's natural goodness rather than on corrupting civilization. Wergeland's mother was from a prominent family that valued knowledge, art, and artistic creativity. She was outgoing and fun loving, and enjoyed performing in amateur theatrical productions. In contrast to her husband, Alette was impulsive and straightforward in her dealings with others.

The Wergeland children grew up in an ideal setting to develop according to Rousseau's ideas. In 1816 Nicolai Wergeland became the priest of a large and wealthy parish seated in Eidsvoll, where the Constitutional Assembly had taken place. After the historic events of 1814, Eidsvoll reverted to a quiet, country backwater. The combination of an educated father and an artistic mother, a secure standard of living, and life in the country furnished an environment for the growth of children according to their own natures. Therefore, all five children were characterized by their tutors as bright but stubborn. Wergeland confirmed this viewpoint in her memoirs, recalling that their dispositions and aptitudes, flaws and passions flourished like the trees they planted in their gardens.

Growing up in the country, the Wergeland children were exposed to the folktales and legends of the rural population. The children's nanny, Lisbeth-Marie, was the daughter of a storyteller called Sara Trænese (Sara Wooden-Nose). Sara entertained her own children with her wide store of tales, and Lisbeth-Marie in turn told them to the Wergeland children. These stories contributed to the children's poetic education and developed their appreciation for the wealth of oral stories originating in rural districts. Camilla Wergeland later wrote several folktales based upon the stories she had heard as a child.

Wergeland was an imaginative child who enjoyed making up and staging her own plays. She had problems persuading her playmates to participate, however, so she often had to perform all the parts herself. Wilhemine Knudsen, in her memoir titled *Minner fra Eidsvoll* (1945, Memories from Eidsvoll), remembered her childhood friend as a happy, towheaded little girl. Always the leader in the childish pleasures they thought up, she improvised, declaimed, sang, and was a happy child. Wergeland's childhood was a time of undisciplined play that fostered her creative abilities.

Although known as a proponent of equality, Rousseau posited a difference between the formal education afforded boys and that given to girls. Rousseau felt that young men should be educated to become free, independent thinkers according to their nature, while young women should prepare for subordination to men. Separate schools and different modes of education were customary at that time. In her letters and diaries, Wergeland described how the beginning of her formal education at the age of twelve marked the end of her carefree childhood. Her father first enrolled her at Jomfru Pharos Pigeskole (Miss Pharo's School for Young Ladies) in Christiania (Oslo). She felt out of place and was homesick, and she left the school before completing her studies.

Searching for a more suitable school, her father enrolled her in the Moravian Congregation School in Christiansfeld, Denmark. Christiansfeld was a highly organized religious community. There were boarding schools for both boys and girls that attracted students from all of the Lutheran countries of Scandinavia. The students' days were devoted to education and religious activities, which gave little free time for private pursuits. Compared to Lutheranism, the Moravian philosophy was a milder form of Christianity with a focus on the joyful experience of a good and merciful God who was present in all forms and aspects of life. Important for Wergeland and other young Scandinavian women who were exposed to the Moravian teachings was the belief that men and women were equal under God. Each adult individual had an obligation to develop his or her spiritual potential to the fullest.

In a letter to the school, Wergeland's father stated that he desired a moral and intellectual education for his daughter. He first described her character. She was a sensible young woman, with a kind heart. He discussed her good educational background, her abilities and talents, emphasizing that she had the potential to excel. He then listed what he wanted her to learn: in addition to the school's standard curriculum, she was to have classes in German and French, as well as music and drawing; her drawing lessons were to focus on landscapes and portraiture; she was to be trained to play the piano tastefully and sing in a pleasant manner while accompanying herself. He concluded his instructions with his views on her character development. He hoped that his daughter would develop into a virtuous, well-mannered, and accomplished young woman. He was preparing her for a future as a member of Norway's finest social circle.

During this era, now termed the Romantic Age, the education of young women from the upper middle class in Europe emphasized the acquisition of social accomplishments that would make them pliable wives and pleasant drawing-room ornaments. Modest behavior and gracious manners were highly valued, and knowledge of French, music, and drawing were essential accomplishments.

Writing later about her two years at Christiansfeld in her memoirs, *I de lange Nætter* (1863, In the Long Nights), Collett concluded that the school did not suit a child of her temperament and reinforced her tendency to feel shy. She was a lonely young woman, far away from home in a foreign country where the teaching language was German. She initially withdrew into herself, but during her second year she formed a close and emotionally intense friendship with a fellow student, Christiane v. Schoulz. At the end of the term, Schoulz suddenly died after entering a state of religious exaltation. Wergeland completed her education shortly thereafter and left Christiansfeld, grieving her friend's death. After her return to Norway, she felt that the school's cloister-like setting had not given her the social skills and ease of manner she would need to negotiate the world of drawing rooms, balls, and courtship as a marriageable young woman of her class. Later in life, however, she realized that the Moravians' belief in women's spiritual potential as equal to that of men and their teachings that women also had rights and responsibilities in secular life had inspired the feminist movement in late-nineteenth-century Scandinavia. As she grew older, her personal faith became stronger, and in her final years she came to value the religious education she had received in Christiansfeld.

Wergeland returned to her family home in Eidsvoll at age sixteen. Aside from confirmation studies with her father, her formal education ended. She had been prepared for a life in the domestic sphere. She spent her time on domestic duties or took long, solitary walks in the countryside. She led an isolated existence, which she relieved by writing letters and keeping a diary. Important for her continued intellectual development, she had access to her father's library with his collection of French literature.

The Wergelands believed that the best way to secure both their daughters' futures was to develop their charm, character, and accomplishments so that they would be able to find the best possible husbands. Nicolai painted a series of miniatures of Wergeland in 1830–1831. One of these portrays a dreamy, delicate young woman with charming curls framing her face, sitting in an idyllic flower garden. Another shows her, again beautifully dressed, with a bonnet and curls framing her glaring eyes and tight-lipped mouth. The first miniature portrays the idealized young woman of the time; the second reveals the woman that Wergeland was to become, one who was ready to fight for her causes.

Shortly after Wergeland's return to Eidsvoll, her older sister, Augusta, was married. Under pressure from her parents, she married a much older suitor who was a clergyman. They considered him a suitable husband for their daughter. Augusta, however, loved a local farm boy, and she was never happy in her marriage.

Her fate mirrored the lives of many other women of her era who were forced into arranged marriages. Wergeland herself personally knew of, or heard gossip about, many unhappy wives in loveless unions with brutal or unfaithful husbands. She resolved to marry for love.

The three Wergeland brothers were sent to the capital city, Christiania, to complete classical academic studies. In the capital they were also exposed to the political and cultural pulse of the new nation. When their educations were complete, they would be prepared for lives as independent adults. Nicolai Wergeland gave his wholehearted support to his sons' education, work, and careers, especially Henrik's. Nicolai could see the dimensions of Henrik's gifts and abilities and encouraged their development. He was, however, blind to the fact that he had a daughter with far above average potential who wanted more than a life devoted solely to home and family.

In a letter to her brother Oscar while he was a cadet at a military academy, Wergeland first noted that she envied his future freedom. She then wrote of her own hopeless future, one without the faintest possibility of accomplishing anything of significance in life. As a young woman of marriageable age, Wergeland clearly saw the limitations imposed on women. In a letter to a friend, she wrote of her hopes of having an independent life, but she had only a vague notion of finding some kind of position. All women of her class were financially dependent on men, either on a husband they did or did not love or on other male family members if they were single or widowed.

At age sixteen Wergeland made her social debut in Christiania, where she attended parties and balls with others of an upper social class composed of senior civil servants and their families. The sheltered young woman felt awkward and shy in this new social situation. Many others, however, remembered her in their memoirs as a legendary beauty, with a shy grace and good nature that won the affection of all who met her. She has been described as a stylish and charming young woman, well trained in drawing-room accomplishments. Her lively wit, intelligence, and wealth of knowledge quickly attracted many suitors. She became infatuated with poet and intellectual Welhaven. They met in 1830, when Wergeland was seventeen years old, and their relationship lasted for seven years, during which time neither of them publicly acknowledged it. They frequently saw each other at balls or as guests in the homes of mutual friends. They were attracted to each other, enough that rumors about them began to flourish. Wergeland's infatuation grew into a lifelong obsession. Welhaven wrote poems about her and initiated a correspondence with her, but he was unsure of his feelings for her. At the same time, Welhaven was embroiled in a public, ideological conflict with her older brother, Henrik, about the nature of Norway's cultural identity. The men were the two most prominent participants in this debate, which engaged the intellectual elite of the new nation. Their exchanges were passionate, personal, and contentious. They became archenemies.

Wergeland kept silent about her romantic feelings for Welhaven, as well as her ideological support for his views. As a woman, her words had no place in a public debate, and, as a Wergeland, her family ties demanded her tacit loyalty. After attending a ball in 1833 at which Welhaven was present, she felt such a need to express her feelings that she made Emilie Diriks her confidante. At this point, Wergeland had given up hope of ever marrying Welhaven. The two young women became close friends and correspondents. Wergeland often visited Diriks in Christiania, and when Wergeland was at home in Eidsvoll, they wrote each other letters. Wergeland and Diriks's correspondence is preserved in *Breve fra Ungdomsaarene* (1930, Letters from Youthful Years, volume 2 of a four-volume collection of Wergeland's correspondence from this phase of her life, edited by Leiv Amundsen and published approximately one hundred years after the letters were written). Many of the letters between Wergeland and Diriks were about Welhaven, while others described the daily lives of two young women of Norway's upper social class. They frequently discussed books they were reading. Wergeland's commentaries often had a humorous and witty tone that she carried into her future authorship. As the two women corresponded with each other, Wergeland's writing technique improved; she added artistry to the documentary style of her letters. Her attraction for Welhaven dominated her thoughts, but her writings revealed that she was always unsure of his feelings for her.

Five years after they met, Welhaven initiated a secret correspondence with Wergeland using a mutual friend, Bernhard Herre, as an intermediary. Herre, speaking for Welhaven, wrote that Welhaven had previously been in love with her but had forced himself to give up pursuing a romantic relationship since an engagement between them was impossible. Instead, Welhaven wished to establish a relationship as friends. Any exchange of letters between them, he insisted, must be confidential. Thus, their secret correspondence began. Welhaven was careful to speak of friendship. He considered his cause to be more important than any personal relationship, although he referred to a profound unity in their natures.

Wergeland believed that they were meant for each other, that their union was ordained by God and higher than any ideological cause. Welhaven rejected this idea. He alluded to romantic feelings for her, but

Paperback cover for the English translation (1991) of Collett's first book, the novel Amtmandens Døttre, *published in two volumes in 1854 and 1855 (Amazon.com)*

then retracted what he had written. Beneath his vacillation was an undertone of suppressed passion. He wrote poems about her, and in one, "Den sidste september-dag" (The Last September Day), he recalled her tears falling in the whirlwind of the dance and her hopes withering, rekindling his own sorrow and the longings of his own heart. Here he acknowledged her pain and his own wavering desire. After they had corresponded for two years, Wergeland realized that their relationship was going nowhere and broke off all contact. Welhaven had never clearly declared his intentions. Later, he fell deeply in love with another woman. Welhaven had been attracted to Wergeland; whether he had loved her or not is unclear.

Wergeland's experience led her to reflect on how differently men and women experience love, as well as on women's lot in life: women's feelings were neither valued nor respected—not by their own families, not by the men they loved, and not by a society that censured young women who expressed their own desires. In a letter to Welhaven in April 1835 she had written that the distance between the ideal of womanly love that she anticipated and what the world arranged for her was as great as the space between heaven and earth. Both her own belief in all-encompassing love and his irresolution influenced her future ideas and her writings.

Searching for an explanation for why her romance with Welhaven had failed, Wergeland later wrote that reason had triumphed over emotion. Higher value was placed on reason, equated with the masculine, in the public sphere. Indeed, it appears from Welhaven's letters that his public debate against her brother Henrik was more important to him than his feelings for Camilla, while Wergeland's focus was on love and personal relationships. Emotion was associated with the feminine. Thus, women and feminine qualities were silenced and relegated to the domestic sphere. She later used this insight to define her own feminist cause.

Wergeland invested profound emotions into her relationship with Welhaven. Over time the uncertainty of the relationship affected her physical and mental health, leaving her in a state of depression. In retrospect, she remembered their relationship with a sense of betrayal and humiliation. To help her recover and to expose her to Europe's cosmopolitan centers, her father arranged for her to take two trips abroad, first to Paris and later to Hamburg, where she met members of German literary circles. The latter trip stimulated her admiration of the works of young German writers and encouraged her own ambition to become a writer.

After Wergeland's return to Norway in 1837, she and her friend Diriks decided to publish a magazine titled *Forloren Skildpadde* (Mock Turtle). The title referred to the finest dish created in Norwegian kitchens. Their goal was to produce the equivalent in literature, since they would never master the art of cooking. At least six issues of this handwritten magazine are known to have been produced. Wergeland's budding talent as a writer was visible in one of the articles, "Otte Dage i Hamburg" (Eight Days in Hamburg). Her prose displayed attention to form and style. Her language was conversational and simplified. Her keen observations and characterizations of the people she met combined with warm, sensitive feelings and ironic reflections in this piece point to narrative qualities later found in her published writings.

Wergeland also met her future husband, Peter Jonas Collett, at this time. He gave new optimism and vitality to the disillusioned young woman. They were engaged in 1839 and married two years later. During their engagement, Wergeland arranged all the letters, diaries, and notes from her relationship with Welhaven in chronological order. She then gave them to her future husband to read so that nothing about the cause of the emotional pain she still carried with her would be hidden from him. She asked him to burn them after he had read them, but he saved them. Twenty years later, she let Welhaven read the material. Although she originally had intended this collection to remain private, she later asked her son, Alf Collett, to arrange for its publication after her death. He never acted upon her request. The material was published more than thirty years after her death under the title *Opptegnelser fra Ungdomsaarene* (1926, Writings from Younger Years). It is volume 1 of the four volumes of her personal writings edited by Amundsen. The central theme of her diary was the expression of her feelings of love for Welhaven as well as her subjective experience of their relationship. In addition, she kept a journal in which she revisited and interpreted events that had occurred months or even years before. She inserted the letters she received from both Herre and Wergeland in chronological order. The collection is reminiscent of a documentary novel. Wergeland's prose was nuanced, powerful, and deft. She mitigated her emotional expressions of pain and her self-searching with an ability to view her situation with irony and wit.

The third and fourth volumes of the series edited by Amundsen are titled *Frigjørelsens aar* (1932, The Liberating Years) and *Før bryllupet* (1933, Before the Wedding). These volumes include the correspondence between Wergeland and Collett. Their early correspondence suggests that she loved Collett, and as they got to know each other better through their exchange of letters her affection for him grew. He had a stable personality and was a thoughtful and dependable man. She developed a wiser and deeper love for him than she had felt for Welhaven. Nevertheless, she continued to suffer from bouts of depression, especially if she was separated from Collett for any length of time. Collett encouraged her to share her sorrows with him. He believed that she needed to write about her dark memories in order to put them behind her and achieve mental stability. On the contrary, reliving her affair with Welhaven only renewed the intensity of her suffering. Wergeland's letters indicate that she felt most alive when suffering, and suffering was the means by which she accessed her creative ability. No matter how much she wanted to forget the pain of her unrequited love, a cure by means of writing it out of her mind was doomed to fail. Collett was, however, a positive and stabilizing influence, and Wergeland looked forward to a happy future as his wife. Their love was a meeting of souls that formed a solid foundation for their marriage. She evoked caring and protective qualities in her husband, and she became dependent on him to ease her ongoing struggle to maintain her emotional equanimity.

At the time of her engagement to Collett, Wergeland was painted by Johan Gørbitz. It is her most famous portrait. She radiated beauty and repose. Youth and passion were behind her, but her face was not etched by the sorrows and battles life would bring later.

Wergeland and Collett were married on 14 July 1841. The couple was able to marry when Jonas Collett became a *lektor* (lecturer) in law at Norway's one university, located in the capital city. Following in his father's footsteps, he had studied law, despite his greater interest in literature and the humanities. He was a member of both academic and literary circles in Christiania, and, through him, Camilla Collett became acquainted with influential writers and intellectuals of the time. Her husband recognized her talent for composition in her letters, and he encouraged her to try her hand at writing fiction for publication. He possessed a discerning literary taste and was a literary critic for the daily newspaper *Den Constitutionelle*.

The Colletts' marriage can be seen in part as a period of literary collaboration. Camilla Collett's husband valued her intellectual needs as being as important as his own. They enjoyed discussing literature and ethics, and his education and knowledge helped her clarify her own ideas. Through him she gained access to the *Læsselskabet Athenaeum* (Athenaeum Subscription Library) with its collection of newly published works. She was especially interested in works by Karl Ferdinand Gutzkow and other writers of the Young Germany movement, as well as Scandinavian authors, among them Maurits Hansen, Thomasine Gyllembourg, and Søren Kierkegaard.

Jonas encouraged Camilla to write, and he read and commented on her drafts, helping her to refine her prose. She had great respect for his literary and artistic talent. He was a frequent contributor to *Den Constitutionelle*. The couple also collaborated on articles for *Den Constitutionelle* that were published under his name. This collaboration gave Camilla the opportunity to express her views in a public forum. Careful readers can detect which pieces were written jointly because of differences in their writing styles. The first article believed to be written by the two of them was a travel depiction, published in the journal two weeks after they were married. It is titled "En Dag ved Eidsvoldsbrønden" (1841, A Day at the Eidsvoll Well). The couple had spent a day at this spa while on their honeymoon. Their piece was a witty portrayal of the rundown spa and its self-absorbed visitors, which they contrast with the beautiful natural landscape surrounding it.

Neither of the Colletts would admit to writing "Et Stykke av en norsk Dames Brev til en Dansk" (An Excerpt of a Norwegian Lady's Letter to a Dane), which was printed anonymously in *Den Constitutionelle* in 1842. It was a critical review of a novella titled *Nær og Fjern* (1841, Near and Far), published anonymously. This review was not included in any of Camilla Collett's later collections of her works. She had, however, a good reason for denying authorship. Danish writer Thomasine Gyllembourg was later identified as the author of the novella. Not only did Collett have a high regard for Gyllembourg, but she had also become a close friend of the author's son, J. L. Heiberg. Heiberg was also a writer, and Collett later turned to him for advice when she wrote her first novel. Although no supporting evidence existed, several scholars maintained–and still maintain–that this uncomplimentary article was written by the Colletts.

Gradually, Camilla Collett developed her own style, and her talent came to surpass that of her husband and mentor. Several pieces that she wrote independently–and included in later collections–appeared anonymously in *Den Constitutionelle*. The essay "Nogle strikketøybetraktninger" (1842, A Few Reflections While Knitting) was an early example of both her writing technique and the opinions expressed in her later works. She considered this article to be the beginning of her career as a writer. Both the title and the author's point of view clearly indicate that this anonymous essay was written by a woman. The article begins as a humorous chat, but the humor soon turns to satire. Collett writes from the position of a mere woman thinking about her superiors as she knits, referring to them as "our lords." Examples follow of how men fail to live up to these superlatives, concluding with a young woman's complaint that the men at a ball were so dreadfully dull. Collett argues that men are boring in their exchanges with women because they expect little from the weaker sex. Women respond with passivity and silent resignation. Basing her discussion on the popular view that men have the ability to reflect and women to feel, and that each sex should teach the other, Collett criticizes men for not keeping their part of the bargain. She attacks the privileged minority of men who have access to higher education. She accuses them of intellectual elitism, of unwillingness to share their knowledge with others. Men maintain their air of self-satisfaction, while women remain stunted, tragic figures. Collett's initially humorous, and then satirical, article ends on a melancholy note.

"Nogle strikketøybetraktninger" was an attack on the same intellectuals who had founded *Den Constitutionelle,* the journal in which her article was published. The article was printed because of her husband's association with the periodical, but its publication marked the beginning of a social change in ideas about the roles of men and women. Three readers wrote letters in response to the article. The first, by a man, stated that "Madam" was too harsh in judging all men alike. The second, by a woman, praised and complimented the author of the article but also asserted that to use the boring behavior of some gentlemen at balls as a norm for men's attitude toward women was unfair. The third article was signed by a well-known man of letters, Rolf Olsen. He satirized the article, cleverly comparing it to knitted fabric: the article was long, open at both ends, and full of holes. He accused the writer of anticipating emancipation, then concluded with a chauvinistic joke. Collett's article struck a chord because, despite her generalizations, she accurately portrayed the unbalanced relationship between men and women.

Collett turned from essays to short portrayals of nature and people in "Badeliv og Fjeldliv" (1843, Life at the Spa and Life in the Mountains) and "En Vandring og et Eventyr" (1844, A Ramble and an Adventure). Both of these were published anonymously in *Den Constitutionelle,* and Collett later included them in her anthologies. Readers of articles and stories that were published anonymously enjoyed guessing the names of the authors. In "Badeliv og Fjeldliv," a young man returns to Eidsvoll, where he spent his childhood. As he wanders in the region, he recalls the accident that robbed the storyteller Sara of her nose. This story of an individual's tragic fate touched many who read it, and it received high praise in a review by folklorist Jørgen Moe. Moe believed, however, that the short story had been written by his fellow folklorist Peter Christen Asbjørnsen, and that belief may have influenced his opinion.

Asbjørnsen and Moe had traveled together in the Norwegian countryside where they collected folktales and legends. They published their collection under the title *Norske Folkeeventyr* (1843–1844, Norwegian Folktales). Their work recognized Norway's oral narrative tradition, which had been preserved and passed down through generations of storytellers. When converting the oral material to written form, they attempted to replicate as accurately as possible the spoken words in rural dialects, languages quite different from the standard Danish-influenced Norwegian spoken by the educated classes in the capital.

Jonas Collett reacted against the language choice in *Norske Folkeeventyr,* and, with his wife's help, he tried his hand at writing and refining one of Lisbeth-Marie's tales. His goal was to bring an elegance of form and a finer style to the rural dialects used in stories and thereby to develop a national literature of high poetic quality. When "En Vandring og et Eventyr" was published, Moe reacted with a combination of rage and humor. By refining Lisbeth-Marie's language, the Colletts sacrificed the qualities that made the tale uniquely Norwegian; it became a tale with an international flavor. Later, a friendship grew between the Colletts and the folklorists, in part because of this incident.

With her own store of tales that she had heard as a child, Camilla Collett became a source and a collaborator for Asbjørnsen, whom she had met earlier while traveling in the Eidsvoll district. She introduced him to Lisbeth-Marie, as well as Peter, the sexton of Eidsvoll Church. Both furnished Asbjørnsen with folktales and legends. Collett also wrote introductions to folktales Asbjørnsen published under the title *Norske Huldreeventyr og Andre Folkesagn* (Norwegian Huldre Tales and Other Folk Legends, 1845). Here, Asbjørnsen and Collett used their nearly identical writing styles–a coincidence that had fooled Moe–to their own advantage. Camilla Collett's first two published novellas were included in Asbjørnsen's collections. Both "Kongsgaard" (1846, The King's Estate) and "Et Gjensyn" (1851, Meeting Again) dealt with young love betrayed. The quality of these two pieces showed Collett's potential as an author. The novellas demonstrated her ability to write longer pieces and were important steps on the way to her first novel.

Collett's main focus during this decade was on her role as wife and mother. She had heavy responsibilities. She gave birth to four sons–Robert, Alf, Oscar, and Emil–within seven years. Her husband worked long hours as a lecturer and later as a professor. He had always suffered from poor health, and his professional obligations exhausted him. Camilla herself was still prone to bouts of depression. During this period, her mother died, then her brother Henrik, followed by her father. Looking for enjoyable and productive activities to keep his wife from brooding, Jonas encouraged her interest in reading and helped her develop her writing skills. He no longer had time to read anything other than material related to his work. So, in the evenings, Camilla would describe and interpret the literature she read for both of them. This sharpened her ability to express ideas clearly. The Colletts' home in Christiania was open to Jonas's colleagues from the university as well as friends from the literary circle of which they both were members. Jonas encouraged his wife to participate in the intellectual life he himself enjoyed. Many of those who knew the Colletts believed they were unhappily married. Camilla was characterized as demanding and pretentious. She was also criticized for being a poor homemaker. She took part in men's literary discussions; she read serious works of literature; and she wrote articles that appeared in print, apparently neglecting her domestic duties. In reality, Camilla had been well-trained in household management by her mother. She enjoyed having a well-furnished home and frequently purchased items from country auctions.

Camilla Collett was especially criticized by members of the Collett family. When Jonas died of brain fever ten years after their marriage in 1851, one of his cousins claimed that he had died from her lack of care. Several literary historians have written that he was under a constant strain to make her happy, and his efforts drove him to an early death. Her biographer, Ellisiv Steen, concedes that the couple's correspondence can lead to this conclusion, since their letters discuss their struggles during their married years with the pressures of raising four young children, physical illness, and her depressions. Steen points out that their shared intellectual interests, their collaboration on articles, as well as their mutual devotion indicate otherwise. Collett herself later spoke of their marriage as a conversation, saying they never tired of sharing their ideas and opinions.

Jonas Collett's own ideas about the role of women in society supported his wife's statement that they were friends and equals in their marriage. He was an early believer in improved rights for women. Privately, he encouraged his wife to live up to her artistic and intellectual potential. During his career, he coauthored a legal draft that proposed changes in Norway's laws governing inheritance. The draft corrected an inequity in the law that allowed a sister to inherit only one-half of what her brother received. Legalized financial inequity between the sexes portended the situation his widow later faced.

Jonas Collett's death marked the end of ten rich years for his wife and children. She lost her soul mate, and the family's economic situation was dire. Her widow's pension did not give her enough money to maintain a household with four children. Her brothers-in-law, Johan and Carl Collett, offered their support. In their letters to her, they made clear to her that they expected her to lead a reclusive life and devote herself to her children. They were kind but conservative men who had never understood her temperament or need to write. Fearing she would lose her freedom if she became financially dependent on them, she refused their help. Johan then offered to adopt Robert, who had great potential, so that he could give the boy the education he deserved.

During this time when she was facing poverty and had to make difficult decisions, Collett was in a state of deep grief and suffered from a growing anxiety. She accepted Johan's offer. She then sold her home and moved to Copenhagen, taking Alf and Oscar with her. She temporarily left the youngest, Emil, with one of her own relatives. Carl Collett later took on the responsibility of raising Oscar. Only Alf and Emil lived with their mother until they were adults. She never realized her dream of creating a new home and reuniting her family. She became distant from her children, not only because she did not keep them together but also because of her discontented nature. Alf remained loyal to her, and she depended on him for practical help. Nothing indicates, however, that they were close to each other. After she lost Jonas, she was never truly close to another person again. She was lonely the rest of her life.

Collett was driven by her anxiety and her search for inner peace from rooming house to rooming house in Copenhagen and Christiania. She always carried all of her letters, diaries, journals, essays, and other writings in a black case when she traveled. In Copenhagen, away from the traumatic memories and cruel gossip of Christiania, she took her first step toward recovery. In this isolated and restless phase of her life, she revisited her past in her writing. Drawing on the material from her youth, she began to work on her novel, *Amtmandens Døttre,* which was published in 1854–1855.

Amtmandens Døttre focuses on a taboo subject: the reasons why young, upper-middle-class women end up in loveless marriages. Collett portrays the personal tragedy that results when a young woman of the era, one filled with romantic longings and expectations, begins the search for a suitable husband; either she pursues the search alone, or her parents take charge of the search, thereby exerting their influence over the rest of her life. Collett also criticizes the inadequate education that women receive; their program of studies leads women to guide their own daughters into making poor choices. Collett's *Amtmandens Døttre* was the first Norwegian novel to address a contemporary social problem. The novel employs a woman's voice and places women's issues on the literary agenda. In this novel, women become the subject, not the object. Collett's arguments concerning emotions and the selection of a marriage partner are expressed by a fictional woman in a letter to a male friend:

> Når det er mulig, burde mennene aldeles ikke velge. De velger mest efter sanselige innskytelser; de setter besidelse over alt.
>
> . . . Kvinnene burde heller ikke velge. De er så lite utviklet at de ikke engang kan velge fornuftig av fornuft. Man ville forferdes ved å se de motiver der ofte beveger dem til å ta imot et tilbud.
>
> Det er blott ett, der i sannhet bør velge, og det er den kvinnelige kjærlighet.
>
> (Whenever possible, men clearly should not choose. They generally follow their sensual desires; they value possession above all else.
>
> . . . Women should not choose, either. They are so immature that they can't even make a rational choice based on common sense. One would be shocked if one knew the motives that often inspire them to accept a proposal.
>
> There is only one, which truthfully should choose, and that is woman's love.)

Collett argues that neither men nor women are capable of choosing a mate. Men are attracted by women's physical attributes and the desire to possess them; women become sexual objects. A young woman who has not been adequately educated to make a mature decision is in danger of choosing a husband based on motives Collett refers to as "shocking." The novel later shows that women's motives are often related to social position and financial security; however, young women want to follow their hearts in choosing a husband. The paradox is that, according to the social norms of the time, a young woman was expected to hide her romantic feelings and silently wait for the man of her choice to express his feelings for her. In the final sentence in the above quote, Collett states that women's love is the only true authority. Collett argues that feminine emotion must be allowed expression and that it must be valued.

Collett's authorial strategy was a direct attack on social norms, written from a woman's point of view. Her novel portrayed several tragic fates in which young women's romantic dreams were never realized. Rather, harsh reality brought loveless marriages. None of the four daughters of the district governor finds lasting happiness. Sophie, the central character in the novel, is based on the young Camilla Wergeland. She falls in love with Georg Cold. He loves her, too, but an accident of fate destroys their relationship. Two of Sophie's sisters are forced by their mother into unhappy marriages. The fourth sister marries the man she loves, but their happiness does not survive the pressures of everyday life. Typical of the outcome of these marriages is this self-commentary by one of the governor's married daughters: "The woman who can neither love nor respect the man she is tied to, little by little loses her self-respect." Unhappily married women in this novel have brutal, drunken, unfaithful husbands. The women age quickly, or they die young. Worse, they live to inflict their miserable fates upon their own daughters, whom they force into unsuitable unions for the wrong reasons.

When the first volume of the novel was published, word had already spread in Christiania that the anonymous author was a woman, most likely Camilla Collett. Half of the six hundred copies sold immediately. Members of the small upper class in Christiania, where everyone knew everyone, were curious about whom they would recognize among Collett's characters. The book attracted great interest and was reviewed in many newspapers. The author was praised for the most part for the quality of her prose. The book was also recognized for its significance as Norway's first novel. The subject, however, was difficult for reviewers to accept. The contents were considered too radical, possibly inciting women to demand emancipation. After the initial sensation, sales dropped. The first edition of *Amtmandens Døttre* was not a financial success, but many editions have since been published. There has been a continuous interest in the novel.

In the author's preface to the third edition, published in 1879, Collett spoke of the "uproar" caused by her novel when it was first published. It had been criticized for its pessimistic view of life. In her rebuttal, Collett stated that she used care in telling her *kvinnehjertets historie* (story of the female heart), since she suspected that it would be risky to tear away too suddenly the veil hiding conditions that people deliberately chose to ignore. Comparing novels to reality, she stated that the romantic novel had become the repository for beautiful, romantic feelings that are denied young women in their own lives. These novels were often written abroad, which she felt gave Norwegian readers the impression that such feelings were distant and removed from reality. Collett's purpose was to write a realistic novel about the beauty of feminine emotion situated in the reality of Norwegian life.

Collett's next piece of fiction, with the simple title *Fortællinger* (Stories) was published in 1861. It is a collection of short stories, including "Kongsgaarden" and "Et Gjensyn," which date back to the 1840s. All were edited for this collection, resulting in texts with tighter composition and a more polished style. Collett was a perfectionist who made a practice of revising her previous work. Collett drew upon her own memories of folktales to compose these stories. They were influenced by national romanticism and designed to continue the oral storyteller tradition in written form. "Eventyr Sara og Hendes Datter" (Storyteller Sara and Her Daughter; translated as "Storyteller Sara," 1984) tells how Sara lost her nose and acquired the name Sara Trænese. A high-kicking dancer broke off her nose, and her fiancé no longer wanted her. A widower with many children married her, and he carved her two wooden noses. The family was poor, and there were many nights when the children did not have enough to eat. Sara told them wonderful stories to take their minds off their hunger. Sara was a poor woman with a wooden nose, but she personified the will to prevail despite a cruel turn of fate.

In the tale "Langs Andelven" (Along Duck River) Lisbeth-Marie tells the story of a prince who has been changed to a bear. Only the princess whom he visits in the night can rescue him from his fate. This story develops in the classic fairy-tale form. The princess disobeys a command, and the prince is then revealed to her in

Statue of Collett by Gustav Vigeland in the Royal Park, Oslo (University of Oslo)

his animal form and runs away. She follows him and passes three tests, freeing the prince from the spell he is under. In this tale, the woman challenges fate and takes on the role of hero.

Collett's descriptions of nature and the milieu in which her female protagonists live create a romantic, but melancholy, frame for the tales. In the final piece from *Fortællinger,* one titled "Octoberphantasier" (October Fantasies), four women sit together at dusk, silently watching the comet Donati cross the skies. They begin to talk about folk beliefs tied to comets; then, strangely inspired, each reveals her disapproval of a variety of social values in Norway. The comet falls below the horizon, and the women fall silent again. "Octoberphantasier" builds from an idle discussion to a polemic. Collett wrote and organized this collection of tales of women's lives to point out that women must be given the freedom to participate in public life and take responsibility for their own lives.

Fortællinger was reviewed by literary critic J. R. Monrad in *Morgenblad,* an Christiania newspaper. Comparing the collection to *Amtmandens Døttre,* he found these tales to be less tendentious. He praised Collett's beautiful descriptions of settings and the powerful moods she evoked. He found the collection well written and able to capture the reader's interest. He criticized, however, an air of discontent in the tales, which he felt was unjustified.

Around the time Collett was working on *Fortællinger,* she was living in Christiania. She had a small circle of women friends, among them Josephine Welhaven, the wife of Johan Welhaven. Josephine knew of the earlier relationship between her husband and Collett. Since that time, they had avoided meeting each other. Josephine encouraged the two to attempt reconciliation. They were both members of a small social and intellectual circle in Christiania, and more than twenty years had passed since they had broken off their correspondence. After much persuasion, Collett sent Johan Welhaven the diaries, letters, and journals that she had arranged for her husband, Jonas. When Welhaven read the collection, he wrote Collett that he had been unable either to let her go or to hold her tight. Only through reading the material she sent him did he come to understand how much she had loved him. Welhaven admitted guilt and asked for her forgiveness.

Their reconciliation was short-lived. Collett and Welhaven met each other in the homes of mutual friends, but the meetings created an uncomfortable situation for Collett and her friend Josephine. The man that Welhaven had become was also not the man Collett remembered. Time had created a distance between them. She decided again to refuse to meet him socially. Despite this resolve, their attempt to settle the past was partially successful for Collett. She was released from much of her bitterness toward Welhaven. Afterward, she wrote that she had found the thread of her life again. By letting go of old memories she was able to reconnect to her past and her old feeling of purpose.

Collett picked up the threads of her life in her 1863 memoir, *I de lange Nætter.* She framed her autobiography in the storyteller tradition: during sleepless nights, Collett tells sixteen stories to others who cannot sleep in order to shorten the long, dark hours. Much of what is known about Collett's early years is taken from this book. She first writes about her lively, happy childhood at Eidsvold and the members of her family. She intertwines her portraits of her family with episodes from their lives. Several folktales are also included, because listening to them was part of her happy memories. These tales also serve to point out parallels in her own life. A tale in which the heroine looks into a shattered mirror reflects the imagery of her own life. As she loses those people she loved when young, either to separation or death, her life becomes fragmented. Left alone, she becomes one of the sleepless.

This collection of memoirs not only gives a vivid description of Collett's early life among the historical personalities of her time; it is also an inspired piece of literature that plays on moods ranging from humor to despair. Monrad, the literary critic, again reviewed Collett's work in *Morgenblad.* Praising *I de lange Nætter,* Monrad stated that her memoirs were the most satisfying he had read in a long time. He also commented that the writer now seemed more reconciled to her life, a fact that made her work more appealing. *I de lange Nætter* has withstood the test of time. It is the second most sold work in Collett's oeuvre and is still read in Norway today.

Later that year, Collett wrote a short polemic that was published as a pamphlet with the title *En undersøisk Parlament* (1863, An Underwater Parliament). The work is written in the same style as "Strikketøysbetraktninger" and "Octoberfantasier." *En undersøisk Parlament* begins as a fable, with a cook's helper finding objects in the gut of a fish. Among the objects are the minutes of the Fish Parliament. The tale builds in fantasy and irony as a lobster, an eel, an oyster, and other sea creatures debate how large a pension a widow deserves. This story is a satire on the debate in the Norwegian *Storting* (Parliament) on the same topic. The underwater debate is interrupted when the flying fish, who has flown around the world observing the condition of human widows, returns. He reports that the widows of Norway, burdened with the task of raising their children alone with little money, cry endless tears. He concludes that the widows of India are more fortunate, since they die on their husbands' funeral pyres.

After writing this piece, Collett, like the flying fish of her polemic, left Norway to find inspiration abroad. She found the intellectual circles in Christiania too conservative. She first visited Copenhagen and then traveled to Berlin and Paris. The intellectual circles she hoped to join in these cities were not always open to her. Their rejection was partly the result of the insularity of their members, but it also was the result of her reputation for being overbearing. She spent much time exploring and writing about Berlin and Paris, and then she sent her travel descriptions back to Christiania for publication in *Illustreret Nyhedsblad* (Illustrated New Magazine). The publication gave her some income to finance her journey. Collett continually lacked funds. While she was traveling, the Norwegian *Storting* awarded her a small pension. It was not given in recognition of her own achievements, however, but rather her father's and brother's.

In 1866 Collett's collected travel letters were published in Stockholm under the title *Under ljusa dagar* (Under the Light of Days). These were later published in Christiania in the first of a series of five essay collections titled *Sidste Blade 1–5: Erindringer og Bekjendelser af Forfatterinden til "Amtmandens Døttre"* (1868, Last Leaves 1–5: Memoirs and Confessions by the Author of *The District Governor's Daughters*). These five volumes, published from 1868 to 1873, are a collection of travel descriptions, essays, articles and open letters. The 1873 volumes were the first of her writings to be published under her own name, rather than as anonymous. By now, Collett had for the most part abandoned writing fiction. She felt that she could better express herself in essay form. The primary theme of her writings continued to be the situation of women in Norwegian society. No matter what readers felt about the content of her writings, Collett was consistently praised for the high quality of her prose.

The publication in 1869 of *Kvindernes Underkuelse*, the literary critic Georg Brandes's translation into Danish of *The Subjection of Women* (1869) by John Stuart Mill, was a turning point for Collett. She had long felt isolated in her fight for women's personal freedom, but now others were taking up their pens to critique women's social and political status. The women's rights movement in Norway had begun. Collett was an active participant through her writing in the press as well as through her essay collections.

The title of Collett's next work, *Fra de Stummes Ljer* (1877, From the Encampment of the Mutes), was a salvo in the fight for equality. Collett first challenges women to act, employing inflammatory phrases, referring to human rights that lay trampled in the dust. She then employs her wit and humor to discuss how male European novelists compare women to food, sometimes to a ripe piece of fruit, sometimes to another delicacy to tempt the palate. She cites a reference to appetizing, white, female flesh in a German novel. By reading novels, women can find out what men desire of them. Female readers can then decide if being a tasty dish will bring them self-respect. Collett had become bolder; she was a powerful polemicist.

Fra de Stummes Ljer created an instantaneous and powerful controversy. Collett received high praise from both old and new admirers of her work, while she was attacked by male reviewers in the daily press and other publications. The debate raged for months in Copenhagen, where Collett's work became the catalyst for a debate about women's rights. To clarify her own standpoint, Collett published a pamphlet titled *Et Lyst Billede i en mørk Ramme* (1878, A Light Picture in a Dark Frame) and distributed it in Copenhagen. In Christiania, Collett's polemic received little attention aside from the initial reactions when it was published. Rather, the debate about women's emancipation centered on Henrik Ibsen's *Samfunnets Støtter* (1877; translated as *Pillars of Society*, 1880) and Bjørnson's *Magnhild* (1877, translated,

1897). Although Collett was exhausted from the controversy her work had generated in Copenhagen, she realized that her name was now known to many new readers. She decided to publish again quickly.

Collett contacted Schous forlag (Schou's Publishing House) in Copenhagen, where she signed the contract for the revised 1879 edition of *Amtmandens Døttre*. She also arranged for publication of a new book, *Mod Strømmen* (1879, Against the Current). This collection of articles was tied together by a theme from a folktale titled "Kjerringa mod Strømmen," collected by Asbjørnsen, her folklorist friend. The tale is about a farmer's wife who always contradicts him. One day, he becomes so angry that he throws her into the river. She then floats upstream, against the current. Collett is encouraging the women of Norway to live up to their heritage and do what the farmer's wife has done. Each article in the collection is based on an actual incident or social convention that demeans women. In one article, Collett challenges the idea that "housewives should economize," connecting it to a debate over pensions in the *Storting*, where it was repeatedly asserted that women did not need as large a pension as men since they ate less and did not need as many of life's luxuries. Collett also points out that the few women who work hold menial positions and earn less. In the most controversial article, "Privligerte Rovmord" (Robbery and Murder by the Privileged), Collett attacks the sale of pornographic pictures and books. These deprive all women of their modesty. While Collett encouraged women's personal development and equal status in her earlier works, she exposes social conditions affecting their lives in "Privligerte Rovmord." She challenges women to speak out against institutionalized male privilege.

Like most of Collett's previous works, *Mod Strømmen* received negative critiques in the daily press. One reviewer, however, highly praised the work and its author and correctly predicted that in one hundred years Collett's name would still be honored and live on in the memories of the Norwegian people. This review was printed in *Smaalenenes Amtstidende*, a local newspaper in Halden, a town far to the south of Christiania. It was signed by a woman who a few years later became one of Norway's most controversial authors, Amalie Skram.

In 1880 Collett published a pamphlet, *Ekko i Ørkenen: En Hilsen fra Norden til Mrs. Josephine Butler* (Echo in the Desert: A Greeting from the North to Mrs. Josephine Butler), in support of the priests of Christiania and others who were fighting against officially-sanctioned prostitution. Collett had previously read the Danish translation of Josephine Butler's *Une voix dans le désert* (1875, A Voice in the Desert) and had been inspired by the Englishwoman's fight against prostitution in Europe and England. Collett's pamphlet condemning the sexual double standard was an important contribution that encouraged those who were combating a human tragedy that continually played out in the streets of major Norwegian cities. Five years later, official prostitution ceased in Christiania.

Collett's final work, *Mod Strømmen: Ny Række* (Against the Current: New Series), was published in 1885. During the period between the publication of the two essay collections with the same title, Collett spent time in Germany, Italy, and France. She especially enjoyed a long visit with her close friends, Henrik and Suzannah Ibsen, in Sorrento. In Italy, she met other Scandinavian artists and writers who lived abroad. She returned to Norway in 1883 to celebrate her seventieth birthday but left soon after for Copenhagen. She finally settled into lodgings in Christiania the next year, where she lived the rest of her life.

In the forward to *Mod Strømmen. Ny Række,* Collett writes that Henrik Ibsen had encouraged her to rescue all her writings that lay hidden and forgotten in magazines and newspapers from *"ørkendøden"* ("death in the desert"). The result is a loose collection of articles she wrote after 1879 mixed with some earlier attempts at poetry and a few previously unpublished essays and critiques of literature. The collection is a display of the many nuances and moods in her authorship. It also shows her still-powerful engagement in the fight for women's rights. Literary critics took advantage of the occasion of the publication of *Mod Strømmen: Ny Række* to praise Collett for her contributions to Norwegian literature, culture, and women's rights. Several critics pointed out that women had won their emancipation, that their fight belonged in the past. Brandes used the opportunity, however, to hold Collett responsible for the war between the sexes, and, at the same time, he defended August Strindberg's attacks on women. Steen states, "Av all den kritikk Camilla Collett i sitt lange liv hadde måtte fordøye, var dette den mest ondskapsfulle og forståelsesløs, og den vittigste" (Of all the criticism Camilla Collett had to swallow during her long life, this was the most evil and incomprehensible, and the wittiest). Collett replied in an open letter to Brandes, which was printed in Copenhagen and Christiania. She employed sharp sarcasm to refute his assertions, pointing out that a man, John Stuart Mill, had initiated the struggle for women's rights. She did not need to remind Brandes that he had translated Mill's *The Subjection of Women* (1869) into Danish in 1869 and thereby brought the cause into Scandinavia. Collett then reiterated that her fight was never against men; instead, it was against the social system that encouraged women's servility.

Before a second edition of *I de lange Nætter* was published in 1892, Collett, as was her custom, took the opportunity to edit and revise her earlier work. She put more emphasis on her marriage and widowhood in her revisions. She added to the story of "Eventyr Sara og Hendes Datter," including the tale from *Fortællinger* of the fiancé who failed Sara and the husband who gave her life purpose. She replaced "Paa et gammelt Herresæde" with the story "Ved Badet og i Dalen" (At the Spa and in the Valley). "Ved Badet" was written by her husband, Jonas. In this tale, the sick visitors to the spa in Eidsvoll dress up for the nightly ball. They hide their illness behind their jewels and gowns. Suddenly, intruders come and threaten to spoil the evening. A description of nature is also added to the second edition: nymphs are driven away by a dark cloud of smoke rising from the earth: a train line has come to the valley. The intruders at the ball and the train intruding on the peaceful valley are metaphors for death, whose appearance ruins everything. By 1892 Collett had been a widow for forty years, or half of her life. In her new edition of *I de lange Nætter,* she placed greater emphasis on the difficult lives women lead after their roles of wives, the only acceptable one in the social order, ends. Collett focused on her own experiences as a lonely widow on the fringes of society.

The next year, however, an official celebration of her eightieth birthday was arranged. When she was told of the event, the sharp-tongued old woman recalled all the years when she had been shut out in the cold before her fame had finally opened hearts to her late in life. Her birthday brought her the recognition and honor she had long deserved. After this event, she found a measure of inner peace. Two years later, on 6 March 1895, she passed away with the knowledge that the fight for women's rights would be carried forward by younger women.

In 1911 a statue of Collett was erected on the grounds of the royal palace in Oslo (formerly Christiania). The sculptor Gustav Vigeland had long debated how he would portray her: as a charming young debutante; as a woman in the prime of life; or as an aged woman formed by her own life's struggle. The statue shows an aged woman holding a shawl tightly around her, her back turned toward the wind. Her head is bowed. The pose has been interpreted in several ways: as an expression of resignation, of indignation, or of determination. When most Norwegians recall Collett, the image captured in this statue comes to mind.

During the twentieth century the reputation of Camilla Collett as a bitter and difficult woman faded. The publication of her diaries and correspondence in the late 1920s and early 1930s gave new insight into what formed her character and motivated her life's work. The depth of expression in these personal papers served to enhance her reputation as a writer. In the

1970s, a decade marked by a new wave of women demanding rights, Collett became a symbol of their struggle and their determination to succeed against all odds. Today, Collett is still remembered for her life story, her literary production, and her struggle on behalf of the women of Norway. Had she written in one of Europe's major languages, the quality of her life's work might have brought her international recognition.

Letters:

Opptegnelser fra Ungdomsaarene, edited by Leiv Amundsen (Oslo: Gyldendal, 1926);

Breve fra Ungdomsaarene, edited by Amundsen (Oslo: Gyldendal, 1930);

Frigjørelsens aar, edited by Amundsen (Oslo: Gyldendal, 1932); republished as *Camilla Collett og Peter Jonas Collett: Dagbøker og Breve* (Oslo: Gyldendal, 1932);

Før bryllupet, edited by Amundsen (Oslo: Gyldendal, 1933).

Biographies:

Lilly Heber, *Camilla Collett* (Christiania, 1879);

Clara Bergsøe, *Camilla Collett: et livsbilde* (Christiania: Gyldendal, 1902);

Alf Collett, *Camilla Collett Livs Historie: belyst ved hendes Breve og Dagbøker* (Christiania: Gyldendal, 1911);

Aagot Benterud, *En skjebne og et livsverk* (Christiania: Dreyer, 1947);

Ellisiv Steen, *Diktning og virkelighet: En Studie i Camilla Collett's forfatterskap* (Oslo: Gyldendal, 1947);

Steen, *Den lange strid: Camilla Collett og hennes senere Forfatterskap* (Oslo: Gyldendal, 1954);

Torill Steinfeld, *Den unge Camilla Collett: Et kvinnehjertets historie* (Oslo: Gyldendal, 1996);

Kristin Ørjasæter, *Camilla: Norges første feminist* (Oslo: Cappelen, 2003).

References:

Sigurd Aage Aarnes, *Søkelys på Amtmandens Døttre* (Oslo: Universitetsforlag, 1977);

Janet Garton, *Norwegian Women's Writing: 1850-1990* (London: Athlone, 1993);

Steinar Gimnes, *Sjølbiografiar: skrift, fiksjon og liv* (Oslo: Det Norske Samlaget, 1998);

Jorunn Hareide, *Skrift, kropp og selv: nytt lys på Camilla Collett* (Oslo: Emilia, 1998);

Joan Templeton, *Ibsen's Women* (Cambridge: Cambridge University Press, 1997);

Agnes Mathilde Wergeland, *Leaders in Norway and Other Essays* (Freeport, N.Y.: Books for Libraries Press, 1966).

Papers:

Camilla Collett's papers are held by the Nasjonalbibliotek (National Library) in Oslo.

Petter Dass
(1647 – September 1707)

Lanae H. Isaacson

BOOKS: *Den nordske Dale-Viise: siungis med den Thone: Bonden Hand acter paa Tiden etc.* (Copenhagen: Utgitt anonymt, 1683);

D. Mart Luthers lille Catechismus Forfattet I beqvemme Sange under føyelige Melodier (Christiania, 1715);

I Jesu Navn. Episteler og Evangelier/Sangviis Forfattet udi beqvemme Melodier Componeret, Epistlerne af Hr. Steen Wirtmand, Medtiener til Alstahoug, Evangelierne af Hr. Peder Dass, Sogne-Præst der (Christiania, 1722);

Trende Bibelske Bøger, nemlig: Ruth, Esther, og Judiths Udi Danske Riim forfattet af Peder Dass (Copenhagen: Bockenhoffer, 1723);

Nordlandstrompet (Copenhagen, 1739); also published as *Nordlands Beskrivelse: som er Helgelands, Saltens, Lofodens, Westeraalens, Senniens og Tromsens Fogderier, med dets Beliggende oc hvorudi enhvers Næring og Brug bestaar, saa og Hvad slags Fugle i Luften og svemmende Dyr i Havet sig der opholder, samt om dets Horizont, Elementer og Veyrlig, item om Finderne og Lapperne/forfattet af Peder Dass, 1678–1692* (Bergen: Kong. Majests. Privil. Bogtryckerie, 1739);

Aandelig Tids-Fordriv, eller Bibelske Viise-Bog (Christiania: Jens Berg, circa 1750).

Editions and Collections: *Samlede skrifter*, 3 volumes, edited by A. E. Eriksen (volume 1, Christiania: Den norske historiske forenings forlag, 1874; volumes 2 and 3, Christiania: Cappelen, 1875, 1877);

Viser og rim, 2 volumes, edited by Didrik Aarup Seip (Oslo: Aschehoug, 1934, 1950);

Samlede verker (Oslo: Gyldendal, 1997);

Nordlandstrompet, foreword by Nils Magne Knutsen (Oslo: Gyldendal, 2007);

Petter Dass. Tekstsamling. Dokumentasjonsprosjektet. <http://www.dokpro.uio.no/litteratur/dass> [accessed 1 September 2009].

Petter Dass (identification uncertain; detail of a 1684 painting in Melhus Church; Store Norske Leksikon *<http://snl.no/.bilde/Dass%2C_Petter_(portrettmaleri%2C_1684)>)*

The first literary voice of northern Norway was that of Petter Dass, the priest of the most important parish in the region, Alstahaug. Dass was one of the major writers of the Norwegian baroque and a colleague and correspondent of the remarkable hymn writer Dorothe Engelbretsdatter. Not only was Dass the primary church leader of northern Norway, he was also an important businessman and trader, a successful farmer and owner of fishing fleets, and a notable public administrator and official—in a word, "en herre" (a gentleman). Dass also became the stuff of local and national legend, story, and history.

Dass wrote didactic religious poetry with a special sensitivity to the rural people and the region that was part of his own history; he provided all sorts of *leilighetsdiktning* (occasional poetry) for the formal rites de passage and the more informal celebrations and gatherings of both king and country folk; and he offered poetry and songs that made the teachings of Martin Luther understandable, immediate, memorable, and meaningful for ordinary, often illiterate, people far from the centers of seventeenth-century learning, Bergen and Copenhagen. Dass's major work, *Nordlandstrompet* (1739, The Trumpet of the North), was—and still is—one of the most remarkable achievements in Norwegian literature, a work that gracefully combines topography, zoology, cultural history, ethnology, folklore, autobiography, and travel account in rhyme. It reveals Dass to be the first master at describing both the natural and the human settings in northern Norway. Dass has remained at the center of much literary and scholarly discussion; he has also lived on in the hearts and minds of many ordinary Norwegians, attaining heroic stature as the first—and some might say, the best—poet of the far north.

Dass was born in the year 1647 at Farstuen, Nord-Herøy, Alstahaug Parish, Helgeland. His father, Peiter Don Dass, was the son of a Scottish entrepreneur, who received *utliggerborgerskap* (foreigner's citizenship) and permission to trade goods in Nord-Herøy in 1635; his mother, Maren Falch, was the daughter of a local magistrate and sheriff. Dass was barely seven when his father died in 1654, and he and his four younger siblings were farmed out to relatives in the area. Dass landed at the home of his maternal aunt, Anna Falch, who was married to the parish priest of Nærø in Namdalen, Nils Mikkelssøn Arctander. Dass shared his home tutor with his first cousin, Peter Jesperssøn, who quickly became and remained his closest friend. At the age of thirteen, Dass was sent to Bergen to live with a paternal aunt and study at Bergen Latin Cathedral School, one of the finest schools in western Norway, while Peter Jesperssøn went on to study in Trondheim. (The paths of the two cousins crossed again in Copenhagen.) Dass spent five years at Bergen Latin Cathedral School, principally under the direction of Edvard Edvardssøn. He then moved on to theological studies at the University of Copenhagen where he studied an additional three years, until he earned the title of priest.

In 1669 Dass returned to Helgeland and took the position of home teacher for Sthen Wirtmand, son of the priest in Vefsn, Jacob Wirtmand. (Sthen Wirtmand later was Dass's chaplain and colleague.) Dass became engaged to Wirtmand's stepdaughter, Margreta Andersdatter; in the year they married, 1673, his wife gave birth to the first of their two sons, and he received the appointment of personal chaplain for the priest in Nesna, Henrik Dinclow. Dass's years in Nesna were difficult. Dass was routinely passed over for Wirtmand's post in Vefsne when the older priest died in 1678, and he suspected that money had changed hands and played a role in securing the appointment for someone else. The ambitious Dass lingered on as a servant to the servants of others, living in dire financial straits and frustrated by the lack of opportunity. In 1681 Dass assumed the post of chaplain in Nesna after the death of Henrik Dinclow. And on 18 May 1689, after twenty years of striving to make ends meet, personal struggles, and frequent sea voyages to make pastoral visits throughout Nordland, Dass returned to Helgeland and the influential post of parish priest of Alstahaug. He remained in the position until his son took over in 1704.

Dass's fortunes improved dramatically with his new, more important church position. He became the chief administrator of the largest parish in the north, which later was divided into several smaller units. As was true for many church and civic leaders of the time, Dass acquired more property in addition to the church farm that he ran and owned. He supervised the work of all the farmworkers on his estates. He also owned at least two ships and soon acquired more vessels so that he could supply church needs for fish and also conduct fishing trade with merchants in Bergen. He was actively engaged in the education—generally religious education—of the local people in the region. Because of his own history of struggles, he lent a sympathetic ear to the farmers and fishermen who took on the often violent forces of Nature to earn their daily bread. He also wrote poetry and sought to keep in touch with the newest books and literary trends, in an area where the postman rang twice a year:

> Han var jo alt i den tid opptatt av sin diktning, når han iblant fant stunder til det, og det er forståelig at han kan ha savnet den adgang til biblioteker han hadde hatt i studieårene. Men for øvrig var det vel så, at det i hans slekt og vennekrets ble brukt noenlunde like meget av skrift og bøker som ellers i landet, selv om det var langt mellom hver gang landsdelen hadde sine postforbindelser. Som sogneprest til Alstahaug fikk han rikelig anledning til å skaffet seg mest mulig av den litteratur han i de fattige ungdomsårene hadde ønsket å eie. Han hadde de kirkelige plikter å vareta i sitt store sokekall med de mange båtreiser, han syslet med sin diktning, var fullt fortrolig med sitt folk, og uløselig knyttet til sitt kjære Helgeland, hvor han i ett og alt følte seg hjemme.

> (He was in all that time occupied with his poetry, when he found time for it, and it is understandable that he might have missed the accessibility of libraries that he had had during his student years. But, on the other hand, it was the practice in his family and circle of friends to use as much writing and as many books as

anywhere in the country, even though a long time passed between each connection to the post. As the parish priest at Alstahaug, he had a rich opportunity to acquire most of the works that he had wished for in his poverty-stricken student years. He had church duties and many boat trips to attend to in his large parish, busied himself with his poetry, was very well acquainted with his people, and was inextricably connected to his dear Helgeland, where he felt at home in all respects.)

By the late 1670s or early 1680s Dass had written his first major work, the only one published in his lifetime: *Den nordske Dale-Viise* (1683, The Norwegian Dale-Song); first published in 1683; and, he was also hard at work on *Nordlandstrompet,* which began circulating in handwritten and privately published copies even before it was finished. While the remoteness of the region made the formal publication of Dass's works difficult and accounts for the many years that passed between their composition and publication, Dass was not unknown and uncelebrated during his lifetime, though he framed it that way in a rhymed letter to Engelbretsdatter, quoted in *Norsk Litteratur i Tusen År* (Norwegian Literature for a Thousand Years):

> En ydmyg Salutats
> Forresten vil jeg sende
> Mitt Navn er Peter Dass
> Som bor mot Verdens Ende.

> (A humble salutation
> I will send by the way
> My name is Petter Dass
> the one who lives at the end of the world.)

Dass's poems received considerable local attention; they were memorized and recited by local people who were often illiterate or too poor to afford the luxury of books. His work was passed hand to hand and mouth to ear for years, even decades, before finally being published.

A depiction of folklife that anticipates *Nordlandstrompet, Den nordske Dale-Viise* initially offers a series of scenes or episodes, all leading to small minidramas on daily life in a rural community. The reader catches glimpses of the hardscrabble lives of those who build boats for fishermen and plant and harvest crops. Dass's depiction of rural life is neither especially heroic or monumental nor romanticized. Hard work inevitably leads to even harder work, as the struggle to survive in a harsh climate and hostile land never lets up. The initial scene of industrious boatbuilding, of hard work in the forest for slim rewards, leads to a contrasting scene, a short glimpse of another forest worker who "holder sig kun slet" (who keeps himself shabbily). Dass then focuses on the beauty and fertility of the valley in the fjord:

> Bønder som boer ind i Fiorde,
> Part haffver hærlige Jorde,
>   Eng oc grønne Volde,
>   Blant Knolde,
> Fructbar Korne-Land,
> Som vel nære kand
> Rundelig sin Mand,
> Ligger for et Spand,
> Er dog god for Tvende,
>   Ja Trende,
> Føder Qveg oc Faar uden Ende.

> (Farmers who live within the Fjord,
> Some have glorious lands,
>   Meadows and green banks,
>   Among knolls,
> Fertile fields of grain,
> That can sustain life well,
> Amply supply their man,
> Lie ready for the plow,
> Are good for Two,
>   Yes, Three,
> Feed Cattle and Sheep without End.)

This rather placid, pastoral scene, a relief from the description of forest workers, quickly leads to the first drama of *Den nordske Dale-Viise,* the conflict between two farmers who live too close for comfort:

> Aamund og Gudmund hans Grande,
> Boer paa en Gaard, heder Sande,
>   Disse Toe paa Leye,
>   Mon eye,
> Hver af dem et Pund,
> Trætter dog hver Stund
> Om sin Gaard og Grund,
> Ret som Kat og Hund,
> Skiendis, handis, kivis,
>   Og rivis.
> Hvoraf stor Forargelse givis.

> (Aamund and Gudmund his Neighbor,
> Live on a Farm named Sande,
>   These two on Rent,
>   May own,
> Each of them a Pound,
> Fighting Each and Every Hour
> Over their Farm and Lands,
> Just like Cats and Dogs,
> Fighting, swearing, arguing,
>   And striking blows,
> That lead to much Offense.)

Dass constructs this first dramatic episode in *Den nordske Dale-Viise* as a series of escalating conflicts and ever more drastic resolutions. Aamund and Gudmund start as enemies, quibbling and quarreling over everything. (There is a lesson here for Dass's parishioners; undoubtedly a didactic purpose underscores *Den nordske Dale-Viise,* as Dass offers examples of sin, waywardness, and wrongdoing as well as suggestions on how to live and secure the necessary blessings of God.) The initial situation leads to a resolution in which the two neighbors swear to be "Evig gode Venner og hulde" (eternally good friends and true). But this truce does not last long, for the conflict escalates to blows. Aamund and Gudmund proceed on course to the next level of justice, a magistrate who decides that Gudmund will pay fines in three days' time or else surrender his livestock. Gudmund tarries—and suffers the consequences:

> Saa maat' Gudmund see
> Hvor de tog hans Fæ.
> Det var den betalning,
>   Den Galning
> Fick for sin motvillig Forhalning.

> (Then Gudmund had to see
> Them take away his Livestock.
> That was the fine,
>   That Idiot
> Got for his contrary Delay.)

Den nordske Dale-Viise then proceeds to the lives of Halvar and Malfri. Their pedestrian activities—slaughtering cattle for food and hides, churning butter and cream, and cooking up a storm—become the focus of another series of scenes of farm life and farmers in the far north. The rich details of the stanzas may not strike much of a responsive chord with city dwellers, but they do reveal that it's another world out there in the countryside. In the middle of the series on Halvar and Malfri, Malfri's sausage-making moves center stage, as the narrator shares what seems to be a visit in Malfri's kitchen with the reader, his friend and companion on the journey. The tone is a humorous one, for the narrator—or traveler—adds a bit of timely, earthy advice on the fare in Malfri's home:

> Men end om Pølsen er blandet
> Med noget udaf det andet,
>   At forstaa: de Krommer,
>   Som kommer
> Udaf Vommen trind
> Stengt for med en Pind,
> Æd du dem kun blind.
> Tag dem frilig ind,
> Hvad som ey dit Øye
>   Ser nøye,
> Kandst du uden Harme fordøye.

> (But even though the Sausage is mixed
> With something from somewhere else,
>   Know this: the Parts,
> That come
> Dripping from the Gut
> Stuffed in with a Skewer,
> Eat them only blind.
> Take them in without a Worry,
> What your Eye doesn't
>   See so clearly,
> You can digest with no harm.)

At this point in *Den nordske Dale-Viise,* the connection between Dass's poem and his later, longer work, *Nordlandstrompet,* is clear. The poem is changing from a somewhat detached, bookish description of rural life and rural people to an actual journey related by a narrator. The narrator starts *Den nordske Dale-Viise* as an outside observer, making general observations on rural activities and the surroundings. With Aamund and Gudmund, he moves to the position of eyewitness and court reporter. By the time he reaches Malfri's kitchen, he is a traveler and guest, giving practical travel tips to the reader and enduring the honors—such as they are—and the hazards of rural life in the far north. The immediacy Dass creates by involving his narrator in the action greatly enlivens *Nordlandstrompet.*

The narrator of *Den nordske Dale-Viise* continues on with Halvar and Malfri a bit longer, describing more farm work and drudgery as well as Malfri's corporal punishment of a servant girl for stealing some cream and then blaming the theft on the farm boy. No longer is the narrator the detached commentator who started *Den nordske Dale-Viise;* he has changed into a participant, eating food spiced or laced with flies and insects, sleeping under lice-infested blankets, enjoying—or rather suffering—the hospitality of the earthy peasants and of one formidable Fru Gurru:

> Som jeg saae Dagen fremliuse,
> Bød jeg Farvel udi Huuset;
>   Gurru bad mig tøve,
>   Mad prøve:
> Faa den Skam det giør!
> Icke jeg det tør.
> Jeg har været der før,
> Kiender vel jers Skiør;
> Gid det i jers Tarme
>   Med Harme
> Stod indtryckt med Ild og med Varme!

> (As I saw the light of Day,
> I bid the House Goodbye;
>   Gurru bade me stay,
>   And try the Food;
> You take What it does!
> I don't dare.
> I've been there before,
> I know your Devices;
> If only it were in your Belly
>   And doing Harm
> Stuffed in with Fire and with Heat!)

The last family described in *Den nordske Dale-Viise* is Harald and his twelve lusty young sons, who cause their father no end of worry, emptying his wallet to pay fines and for girls who have been "besoffven" (bedded) and have grown a little wider about the waist. The narrator describes the situation with amusing understatement: "Haralds Penger sprunge, Hans Punge Bleffve siden icke saa tunge" (Harald's Money vanished, His Money Purse was then not so heavy). There is considerable humor in *Den nordske Dale-Viise,* another quality that carries over into *Nordlandstrompet.* The traveling narrator captures the spirit of the places he visits, the way events just seem to happen and people interact with each other willy-nilly. The sense of spontaneity, the thought that anything can happen around the next bend in the road or past the next sea cliff or island, is also a feature of *Nordlandstrompet,* enlivening an already lively account and contrasting markedly with the dour admonitions and fervent prayers of Pastor Dass. The final strophe of *Den nordske Dale-Viise* is a heartfelt prayer for God's blessing on the humblest of Christian souls, the farmer in the far north. With his prayer—so common in Dass's poetry—the priest reveals his keen insight into the lives of ordinary folk, his empathy for their lot, and the strong roots connecting him to his native Helgeland:

> Slutningen denne skal bliffve:
> Herre GUD Kornet os giffve,
>   Snuus og Tobackstuden
>   Foruden
> Vi nock være kan.
> GUD signe Haff oc Land,
> GUD signe Strand oc Vand,
> Oc oplad din Hand,
> At den stackels Bunde
>   Hand kunde
> Nyde din Velsignelser runde.
>
> (This shall be the End:
> Lord GOD give us wheat
>   Snuff and Tobacco butts
>   Without which
> We can surely be.
> GOD bless the Sea and Land
> GOD bless the Strand and Water,
> And raise your Hand
> So the poor Farmer
>   Can
> Enjoy your Blessings so bounteous.)

Den nordske Dale-Viise is included in Dass's *Samlede skrifter* (1874–1877, Collected Writings), with the occasional poems that Dass often wrote in service to his parishioners, to the community at large, and to the country beyond the borders of Helgeland. Not only a kind of literary prototype for *Nordlandstrompet, Den nordske Dale-Viise* was also an independent depiction of Dass's pastoral calling and the Norway he and his contemporaries recognized.

Dass's salutations to his fellow countrymen opens his most exceptional, multifaceted contribution to Norwegian literature, *Nordlands Beskrivelse* (Description of Nordland), or, as it was entitled in the Danish edition, *Nordlandstrompet.*

> Vær hilset, I, Nordlands bebyggende Mænd
> Fra Verten i Huset til trælende Svend,
>   Vær hilset, I, Kofte-klæd Bønder!
> Ja samtlig saa vel ud til Fiære som Field
> Saa vel den der bruger med Fisken paa Gield
>   Som salter Graae-Torsken i Tønder.
> Vær hilset, I Geistligheds hederlig Lius
> Prælater, og Orden i Helligdoms Huus,
>   Hver I sin Bestilling hin gieve!
>
> (Greetings, You Men who dwell in Nordland
> From the Host in the House to the toiling Lad,
>   Greetings, you Cloak-clad Farmers!
> Yes, the same to Sea as Mountain
> To the One who trades in Fish for Geld
>   Who salts down Gray-Cod in Barrels.
> Greetings, You Venerable Lights of the Church,
> Prelates, and Orders in the Holiest House,
>   Each to his Position most worthy!)

This beginning clearly shows that the pastor wrote with engagement, energy, and intense enthusiasm; he included all his fellow countrymen in his address, and he intended his work for those who worked the lands—and plied the seas—in the far north. Dass began his major work while still struggling to find his own place in the sun; he knew all too well the hardships involved in earning a living in a place of great natural beauty amid the fierce forces of nature. Pastoral visits on land and sea had taught Dass a great deal about his own region, Helgeland, and the north. When Dass finished *Nordlandstrompet* in the early 1690s, his own finances had improved and his stature had soared dramatically, but he had not forgotten the essential truth of life in the north. And he shared that knowledge with an eagerness and exuberance—and a respect—that still resonate today.

Nordlandstrompet is organized as a poetic journey of discovery, a voyage through mysterious and otherworldly lands and waters that Dass knew firsthand. Dass's opening includes an address to the book itself, a good wish for the work as it begins its own voyage to readers in Norway: "Hermed jeg dig befaler Gud, / Og dine Reyser ind og ud, / Og alle dem, dig ynder, / Men allermeest vor Adels-Mand, / Som udi din fornedret Stand, / Vil være din Formynder" (Herewith I commend you to God, / And to your travels to and fro, / And to all those who sustain you, / But most of all to our Nobleman, / Who in your diminished State, / Will be your Protector). An address to the reader follows hard by, a promise to tell the unvarnished truth, as "een Nordlands Mand" (a Man of the North Country), or rather as a son of Helgeland. Veracity is a key quality in the work, and Dass admits to not having seen it all; what lies beyond his dear Helgeland is a mystery for him too. In its early stages—or pages—*Nordlandstrompet* establishes his voice, offering a vibrant, lively account by an observant traveler, a well-read and experienced clergyman who has retained respect and empathy for those who till the soil and ply the seas. Having learned from writing *Den nordske Dale-Viise,* Dass is more engaged than ever in telling his adventures. He creates a dynamic and dramatic narrative as he moves from scene to scene, episode to episode, coming full circle in the end. Dass masterfully uses the crowing of a cock, "Saa galer dog min Hane" (Thus crows my Cock) to open and close his work.

Nordlandstrompet is organized into logical sections that parallel a sea voyage to the far north. From the onset it is clear that Nature plays a double role in *Nordlandstrompet*: it is the source of whatever wealth the people of the region possess; it is also a constant threat to that very wealth and to the lives of the people. The harsh, unforgiving climate, the rocky soil, the seasonal flooding, the failing of light, the sheerness of the inland fjords, the tempestuous seas, even the wildlife—all both define and threaten the people of the region, blessing and bruising them by turns. The narrator of *Nordlandstrompet* makes it clear that he plans a full description of the north for the enjoyment or pleasure of his reader:

> I Pennen at føre jeg haver i agt,
> Om Nordland, hvorledes det findes udstragt
> Med liggende Lotter og Lunder;
> Om Klipper at skrive, baad' gammel og graae,
> Om Snee, som evindelig ligger derpaa,
> Om Bakker, om Elver og fleere;
> Hvad Landmanden haver for Næring og Brug,
> Hvad Spiise de pleyer at sette paa Dug,
> Med anden Omstændighed meere.
> Slig Skrifter, om Bugen ey mættes derved,
> De Sindet dog nogen Fornøyelighed
> Den elskelig Læser kand bringe.
>
> (I intend to take Pen in Hand,
> Over Nordland, how it stretches so far
> With Vales and Groves;
> To write of Cliffs, both old and gray,
> Of Snows, that lie on them forever,
> Of Hills, of Rivers and more;
> On what the Countryman has for Food and his Use,
> What they usually set on the Table,
> And on other Circumstance as well.
> Such Writings, if they do not fill the Stomach,
> Can bring Some Enjoyment to the Mind
> Of the Beloved Reader.)

Title page for Dass's major work (The Trumpet of the North), which combines topography, zoology, cultural history, ethnology, folklore, autobiography, and travel writing, all in rhyme
(Petter Dass Museum, Alstahaug)

Dass proceeds to a general discussion of the Nordland region that covers its topography and geography; its people, their manners and customs; and the abundant flora and fauna. A myriad of details, incidents, and events fill sections titled "Nordlands Beliggende" (Nordland's Location), "Nordlands Horizont, Elementer og Veyrligt" (Nordland's Horizon, Elements and Climate), "Allehaande Fugler og flyvende Dyr I Nordlandene" (All Sorts of Birds and Flying Creatures in the North Countries), "Svemmende Dyr i det Nordlandske Hav" (Swimming Creatures in the Nordland Sea), and "Om Land og Lands Brug" (On the Land and Agriculture). Dass proceeds to an elaborate description of each and every region, adding more records and recollections, tales, stories, and observations from his journey. *Nordlandstrompet* offers a dizzying array of background information in a linear narrative that encompasses Dass's own story as well as the stories of many others. Dass relates all these stories from a position of pastoral authority: he is the Copenhagen-educated cleric who "knows what is best" for his religious charges. However, Dass is also keenly aware of the ominous plight, the fleeting pleasures, and the sure pride of his parishioners who somehow eke out a life under the harshest of circumstances–or die trying.

In the section "Nordlands Horizont, Elementer og Veyrligt" Dass refers to one of the many losses that the sea inflicts on those who venture out for their livelihood. The sense of futility, of risking all for naught, is palpable in Dass's account:

> Mig mindes og vel den ulykkelig Stund,
> Da henved fem Hundrede Kropper til Grund
>   Omkomme for Uveyr paa Folden
> Hvor ey kunde føres en Traad eller Klud;
> Af tusinde Siæle, som seylede ud,
>   Kom neppe tre hundred beholden.
> Jeg tiend' vil gange den Fare forbi,
> Indbyggerne var geraaden udi
>   Der Vester ved Loefodens Side
> Hvor mange en Broder for anden kom bort,
> Og etlige Qvinder til Enker blev giort,
>   Sligt giør elementer ublide.
> Saa kand hver fornuftig vel dømme ved sig,
> Naar Mennisker friske saa legges I Liig,
>   Hvad Ynk da maa være paa færde!

> (I remember well that unhappy Hour,
> When nearly Five Hundred Bodies to the Depths
>   Died in the Storm at Folden
> How neither Thread nor Cloth could be traced;
> Of the thousand Souls, who sailed out,
>   Scarcely three hundred returned safe and sound.
> I will pass silently by the Danger,
> The Inhabitants know full well
>   There West of Loefoden's Coast
> How many a Brother was lost to the other,
> And Women made Widows,
>   Such do the elements unkind inflict.
> Every sensible man can judge for himself,
> When young Men are turned to dead Bodies,
>   What Misery must be on the way!)

Dass makes it abundantly clear that the sea is both an extreme danger to the people of Nordland and a bounteous, nearly never-ending source of sustenance. Danger and prosperity–or at least survival–go hand and hand in the north. And the fate of all rest in the hands of God: God determines the happy outcome or the disastrous misfortune of those who combine farming–an occupation with its own set of risks and dangers–with the even chancier test on the seas.

Indications are, according to Dass, that the old days brought more reward than danger; sadly, the times have changed. Dass repeatedly returns to a lament for the past, a desire to recapture distant better times.

> O! ville vor Herre velsigne det Hav,
> Og unde den Lykke, han fordum os gav
>   Langt hen i Forfædrenes Minde;
> Hvor glædeligt var det i Landet at boe,
> Hvor lystigt var det paa Vandet at roe,
>   Naar Folk kunde Næringen finde!

> (Oh! If Our Lord wanted to bless the Sea,
> And grant us the Luck, he used to give us
>   Far back in the Memory of Our Ancestors;
> How wonderful it would be to dwell on the Land,
> How merry it was to row on the Water,
>   When Folks could find Sustenance!)

Along with the often made contrast between the bounty and the brutality that Nature affords, the remembrance of better things past is a major theme in Dass's work.

The narrator of *Nordlandstrompet* reveals an infectious sense of humor and an enthusiasm for each of the teeming topics he addresses. His work covers everything from whale stranding to quarrels between unhappy neighbors; from the Black Death to Trondheim Cathedral; from fisticuffs to death-dealing storms; from physical features of the landscape–Torghatten, for example–to strange phenomena or sights; from the Sámis (Lapplanders) to the newest of newlyweds and the oldest of lovers. One of the most amusing sections of *Nordlandstrompet* is devoted to fish–the flounder, cod, salmon, and trout–that feed the local populace and give them something to trade in Bergen. Dass creates mini-odes to two specific species unique to Norway, the "Qyæite" and the "Sey," managing to find beauty, poetry, and grace in their lives. His words of praise may strike the modern reader as amusing, perhaps a bit pompous, but there is no denying the importance of such fish for the fishermen of the far north, which Dass fully understood and honored:

> Du smukeste Qyæite, du Dronning i Vand,
> Hvor flad er din Boelig paa dybeste Sand,
>   Hvorpaa du fremskrider saa sagte!
> Du farer spagfærdig paa Grunden omkring,
> Og hviler, naar andre de kiøre i Ring,
>   Det kan vore Fisker' vel agte . . .

> Du spralende Sey! See jeg nær hadde glemt
> Din hoppende Springen og lystige Skiemt
>   Udi mine Skrifter at teigne:
> Hvor smuk er din Dands alt om Mid-Sommers Tiid,
> Naar Soelen er skinnend' og Væjret er bliid
>   Et Menniskes Hierte maa qveigne!

> (You most beautiful "Qyæite," you Queen of the Water,
> How flat is your Palace on the deepest Sand,
>   Where you float by so silently!
> You swim so quietly around on the Bottom,
> And rest, when others speed by in circles,
>   Our Fisherman surely prize that! . . .

You jumping "Sey"! See I nearly forgot
Your hopping Springs and merry Cavorts
   To note in my Writings:
How lovely your Dance at Midsummer's Time,
When the Sun is shining, and the Weather so mild
   A Human Heart must tremble!)

One of the most interesting sections of *Nordlandstrompet*, "Om Lapperne og Findene" (On Lapps and Finns), deals with the mysterious minorities of the north, who live "blant Klipper og Knold, / Og haver i høyeste Tinder Tilhold / Blant u-kiendte Stier og Trapper" (among Cliffs and Knolls, / And have Dwellings in the Highest Peaks / on unknown Paths and Trails). Dass devotes considerable attention to the activities of the Lapps, their trade in reindeer at midsummer, their clothing and shoes of reindeer hide, their feasts of bear meat, their wanderings and occasional meetings, and their sharp-eyed, "dwarf-like" appearance. Once again a note of pessimism creeps in to Dass's description, as he laments the old days when everyone—even the eerie Lapps and Finns—enjoyed plenty and the forests were full of game and timber:

Thi Skovene giøres nu tomme.
Hos dem, som hos andre er Handelen alt
Fordervet, forkarvet og lider Gevalt,
   Udarmet er vorden de fleeste;
Jo ældre Verden hun bliver af Aar,
Jo verre, jo slemmer' er Menniskens Kaar,
   Vi have alt levet det beste.

(Now the Forest is emptied,
With them, as with others, Commerce is
Ruined, finished, and suffers Reverses,
   Most of us have grown poor,
The older the World gets
The worse, the more pathetic are the Conditions for People,
   We have all lived the best.)

Dass is a rather cautious, even suspicious commentator on the Lapps. Their strange ways, their unusual appearance, their unintelligible language, and their position outside his religious and social community raise the cleric's fears that the Lapps engage in heathen practices, even that they go so far as to consort with the devil. Dass offers a fairly complete view of the Lapps, adding details and episodes that only partly obscure the fact that he is a fearful reporter peering in on a culture he fervently hopes to change or to see change:

Det er at beklage; den Lappiske Slægt
Er meget med Hedenske Taage bedægt,
   Hvor vel deres Præster formane
Med Trusler og Ord som retsindige Tolk'.

Maae man dog ugierne fornemme det Folk
   Vil elske Forfædrenes Vane,
Og give! Vi vare bemægtige saa,
Det Lappiske Tungemaal til at forstaae,
   Som Norsk eller Dansk til at tale!
Da kunde der blive Forhaabninger om,
At faa dem omvendt, men o! HERRE saa from,
   Vi ville dig Dommen befale!

(It is lamentable; the Lapp Family
Is well cloaked in a Heathenish Fog,
   Whereby their Priests force them on
With Threats and Words like righteous Leaders;
One does not want to believe that such Folk
   Will always love the Ways of their Forefathers.
O if only! We were so empowered,
To understand the Lapp Language,
   Those of us who speak Norwegian or Danish
Then there could be hope
Of converting them, but o! LORD so righteous,
We leave you to Judge!)

Dass is certainly no modern-day ethnologist, careful to tread lightly on the beliefs and practices of others. The Lapps come across in Dass's record as in need of immediate conversion, of someone to show them the way out of darkness and into the light. Of course, that someone will not be Dass as the task is one for God.

As the narrator of *Nordlandstrompet*, Dass is a man for all seasons: teacher, clergyman, astute businessman; tourist and tourist guide; ethnologist and zoologist; topographer and geographer. At times he addresses the reader as a comrade on the journey, as someone who plies the coast in a small ketch with Dass and discovers wonders along the way. At other times Dass plays the role of patriarch for the church, recalling the countless pastoral visits he made over the years throughout the north. Dass dons many hats and plays many roles, several simultaneously, in describing the north for his own family and community and for those beyond the boundaries of the region. At times his tone is rollicking, fun, and imaginative as he brings the mysteries and magic of the place to life for one and all.

Throughout *Nordlandstrompet* Dass incorporates the dialogue of other characters to move the dramas of the moment along. Generally, however, Dass's characters—the people who cross his path or guide his ketch to safe harbor and respite—turn out to sound too much like Dass himself. Quarrels between two farmer neighbors, for example, are framed in Dass's poetry, and no attempt is made to realize the distinctive voices of the rural characters:

Vor Asmund fremkalded' sin Grande saa brat
   At svare sin Sag udi Rette;
Han sagde: du haver u-førmed min Grund,
Da svared, den anden: du løgst i din Mund,

Frontispiece for Dass's Aandelig Tids-Fordriv, eller Bibelske Viise-Bog (circa 1750, Spiritual Hourly Pursuits; or, The Bible Songbook), a collection of pieces based on the teachings of Martin Luther (Petter Dass Museum, Alstahaug)

Saa toeg de Kompaner at trætte.

(Our Asmund summoned his Neighbor so quick
    To answer his Cause in Law;
He said: you have ruined my Land,
Then the other answered: You're lying,
    So then those Neighbors began to fight.)

A bit further on in the same section, "Om Land og Lands Brug," however, Dass creates a passage that could conceivably have been spoken by a farmer and not by the well-educated cleric:

Blant andet kom en med et Spørsmaal for Dag,
Han sagde: Goe Skrivar Æg hæve ey Sag
    Angaaende meg og min Granne.
I giær nu vel at j græi os den ut:
Æg kiøbte ei Møll-Qvæin og Grannen eit Skiut
    I fælleslag skulle di stande;
Æg sa: min goe Grande brug Qvæinna me meg,
Saa gaaer eg halvparten i Skiute med deg,
    Og bytte saa, qva vi forqværva;
Saa kom eg for skaen, eg seia de maae.
Gu naae den, som Kors og Modgangen fæll paa!

(Among other things someone came forward with a Question that Day,
He said: Good Master I have a Cause
    Concerning me and my Neighbor.
You'll do well now if you sort it out:
I bought a Milk-Cow and my Neighbor a Skiff
    They would be shared between us:
I said: My good Neighbor use the Cow with me,
And I'll go half-part in the Skiff with you,
    And we'll share what we acquire;
But I came to harm, I must saw.
God's mercy to him that the Cross and Adversity fall on!)

Dass is at his most vivid when he describes his own home region in "Helgelands Beskrivelse" (Description of Helgeland). While he makes it clear that Helgeland has its own share of trials and tribulations, Dass's deep affection for the place shines through. *Nordlandstrompet* may be said to build to a tribute, a song of praise for Helgeland that is the emotional highpoint of the poem:

Blant Nordlandske Provstier regnes du først,
I Skatte-Mandtallene vises du størst,
    Du giver saa mangen en Sæde!
I dig er jeg baaren og svøbet i Klud,
I dig har jeg holdt mange Tørninger ud,
    Ja haft baade Velstand og Møye,
Men hvad det har vært, enten Fryd, eller Ach!
Saa skee for altsammen min Skabermand Tak!

(Among Nordland Provinces you are considered the first,
In Numbers of Taxable Men you are shown to be the greatest,
    You yield so many a Pace!
In you I was born and swaddled in Garb,
In you I have withstood many a Trial,
    Yes, I've had both Wealth and Hard Care,
But whatever has come, whether Joy or Woe!
For all of it, Thanks to my Maker!)

In Dass's description of Helgeland, each and every church and chapel—and all the churchmen attending the region—receive their due, with his own parish of Alstahaug first on the agenda. The physical features of the region—extraordinary cliffs and rocks such as Torghatten "som seer med usovendes Øye" (that sees with a nonsleeping Eye) and the remarkable mountain peaks, "Syv Søstre, som fletter sin' Lokker I Snee . . . Og ses i Havet saa vide"(Seven Sisters, who braid their locks in snow . . . And are seen out so far to Sea)—catch the wonder and stir the imagination of the natives as well as the narrator and his reader. Dass describes the area as one of bounty but also one of tragedies such as the Black Death, failing crops, and financial reversals as the result of natural forces. Invoking one of his main themes, Dass suggests that the good times have passed and that now everyone has clearly fallen on hard times:

> Mens Bønderne seyled' og Jægterne foer,
> Da stode Nordlandene deilig I floer,
> Men anderleds lyder nu Piben;
> Thi Verden sin Pelts har no snoet omkring,
> De strippende jager saa kunstrig i Ring,
> At Bonden er kommen i Kniben.

> (When the Farmers sailed and the Ketches rushed about
> Then the North Lands were all in flower,
> But now the Pipe plays another Tune:
> For the Old World has turned its Pelt inside out,
> The Culprits so deftly turn all about,
> And so the Farmer is caught in the Pinch.)

Before moving on to other regions even further north (Salten, Loefoden, Vesteraalen, Senjen, Tromsø), Dass directs his attention to the curious behavior of the puffins of Helgeland, their penchant for linking together to face danger and thereby falling victim to hunters. Dass describes the puffins in quite human terms, much as he did the fish in his earlier account, presenting a "march of the Puffins" to the mind's eye:

> At hvert Creatur det vil holde til Ven
> Sin' egne og dennem forsvare,
> Thi kniber en Lunde ved anden sig fast,
> I Tanker at hindre den myrdende Gast,
> Men kommer derover i Fare.

> (Every Creature will hold to its Friend
> His own and them defend,
> Therefore a Puffin with latch fast to another,
> With the Idea of hindering a murdering Attacker,
> But therefore he comes to Danger.)

Dass closes his varied portrait of his home in Helgeland, its past and present, with a heartfelt prayer for God's blessings and mercy. Such prayers are rather like formulas and occur at the close of every section, along with a recognition that God determines who will win and lose in the battle for survival. A bit of the fatalist, Dass knows that the ways and will of God are sometimes an even greater mystery than those he has encountered on his journey and described for his reader. The predetermined life of man seems to be one of strife, struggle, and suffering: "Thi maae vi for Synden det lide!" (For we must suffer for the Sin!).

Dass's journey through the far north ends as it began, with thanks to God, with prayers for God's mercy—Dass being the proper patriarch and pastor at Alstahaug—and with thanks for those who share his home and their own lives with him. In a graceful allusion to the beginning of *Nordlandstrompet* so many accounts, stories, and descriptions ago, Dass closes with his Nordland cock ending its own song:

> Men alle, saa mange, som under mig vel,
> Forynskes Guds Naade til Liv og til Siel,
> Far vel! Med et broderlig Vale!
> Far tusindfold vel, og hav tusindfold Tak!
> Og her med jeg ender min Nordlandske Snak
> Min Hane hold op til at gale!

> (But to all, so many, who wish me well,
> Are wished God's Mercy on your Life and Soul,
> Farewell! With a Brotherly Laud!
> A Thousand Farewells, and a Thousand Thanks!
> And herewith I end my Talk of the North
> My Cock cease to crow!)

For Dass, more was definitely better. *Nordlandstrompet* is a true treasure trove of stories as well as the memoir of a man who achieved prominence, glory, and eventual prosperity. The work introduces so many sides to the story of Nordland that it may overwhelm the reader. Dass was, when all is said and done, a man in love with the world he knew and, in spite of his rather formidable Lutheran foundation, in love with poetry. As is observed in *Norsk Litteratur i Tusen År*, "For Dass er intet fænomen upoetisk i sig selv" (For Dass no phenomenon was unpoetic in and of itself). His history in rhyme—expansive, florid, robust—inspired a willing audience in his own time and, remarkably, still inspires readers in Norway today.

In addition to his great work *Nordlandstrompet*, Dass was active in spreading the gospel and making it come alive for people with no access to books and learning. As the patriarch for Alstahaug and the surrounding parishes in Helgeland, Dass wrote religious poems, stories, and songs based on Martin Luther's teachings that were eventually published in four separate volumes: *D. Mart Luthers lille Catechismus* (D. Mart Luther's Little Catechism, 1715), *Aandelig Tids-Fordriv, eller Bibelske Viise-Bog* (circa 1750, Spiritual Hourly Pursuits; or, The Bible Songbook), *I Jesu Navn* (1722, The Name of Jesus), and *Trende Bibelske Bøger, nemlig: Ruth, Esther, og Judiths Udi Danske Riim* (1723, Three Bible Books, Namely: Ruth's, Esther's, and Judith's, in Danish Rhymes). The final category of Dass's oeuvre is that of *leilighetsdiktning*, a sort of catchall category that included celebratory songs, eulogies, rhymed correspondence, even rhymed addresses from the pastor to his flock, as well as songs of praise, mourning, marriage, baptisms, inaugurations, and crownings. Dass wrote such poetry with the intention of teaching his

Dass's wife, Margreta Andersdatter, whom he married in 1673 (Petter Dass Museum, Alstahaug)

parishioners in a simple, direct manner. Composers have long been and continue to be inspired by Dass's verses, in Norden and beyond, including the national composers Edvard Grieg, David Monrad Johansen, Ole Olsen, and Rolf Karlsen.

Dass's didactic religious poetry includes works such as "Første jule-dag Evangelium LUC. 2.C.V.1. Christi naaderige fødsell" (First Christmas-Day Evangelical LUC. 2.C.V.1. The Merciful Birth of Christ) and "De Ti Buds Bud-Ord. Det Første Bud" (The Ten Commandments. The First Commandment). Using his knowledge of the fishers and farmers of Alstahaug–their concerns, life-and-death struggles, the poverty and misfortune they endured as well as their great love of songs and stories–Dass played on their cultural background to get his rather stern Lutheran message across.

"Aften-Suk," one of the poems in the category of *leilighetsdiktning*, suggests a spiritual shepherd's simple, heartfelt prayer for his flock. After his rambles, discoveries, adventures, and recollections in *Nordlandstrompet*, Dass's celebration of poetry-for-poetry's sake, the call to God in humility and fear, offers an intertextual contrast between two genres of his oeuvre:

O store Gud, som hjælpe kan,
Hvis Sti er i den store Vand,
    Kast ud dit Guddoms Åie
Til alle dem, paa Havet er,
Bevare dem fra Grund og Skjær,
    Lad Veir og Vind dem føie!

Lad dine Engle følge dem
Beholden vel til Hus og Hjem!
    Velsigne Landsens Næring,
Giv Fisk og Sild af Havsens Grund,
Giv daglig Brød for hver mands Mund,
    Giv fattig' Folk sin Tæring!
Forlad vor Synd, o Fader god,
For hans Skyld, som paa Korset stod,
    Tænk paa dit gamle Rygte!
Lad os i Landet bo med Fred
Og med en god Samvittighed
    Dig, Herre Gud, at frygte!

(Oh, Great God, who can help,
Whose Path lies in the great Waters,
    Cast out your Divine Eye
To all who are on the Sea.
Preserve them from Ground and Skerries,
    Let the Wind and Weather carry them on!

Let your Angels follow them
Preserve them well to House and Home!
    Bless the Foods of the Land,
Give Fish and Herring from the Sea Bottom,
Give daily Bread for each Man's Mouth,
    Give poor Folks their Sustenance!
Forgive our Sin, oh Father good,
For his Sake who hung on the Cross,
    Think of your ancient Glory!
Let us live in the Land in Peace
And with a good Conscience
    You, Lord God to fear.)

Dass continued writing poetry to the end of his life, even after he turned over his position at Alstahaug to his son and went into semiretirement. He had suffered a crushed leg in a fall, and he was plagued with severe kidney stones for seven years before his death. (He even wrote a poem about kidney stones!) He died in September 1707 and was buried at Alstahaug on 18 September 1707. Dass had made such an imprint on the land and on the people of all Norway that he rose to legendary status, and tales were told of the pastor who held special magic powers. The legends focus either on Dass as a poor orphan who managed to bootstrap his way to the highest pastoral calling in the north or on Dass as the man of God who outwitted the very devil and forced Satan to carry him all the way to Copenhagen on his back so that Dass could deliver a Christmas sermon in 1695. It was believed–or told–that Dass knew the contents of the Black Book of Wittenberg and that he was able to bind evil, using the Black Book for good purposes.

With *Nordlandstrompet* Petter Dass gave the far north a poetic voice for the first time. Dass knew his home, and he knew the people who lived, loved, and died surrounded by the wonder, beauty, and terrible power of Nature in the far north. And he could write what he knew. Dass's use of contrasts, of telling details, of poetry to describe and portray almost everything, connect him to the Norwegian baroque, to his notable colleague and friend, Dorothe Engelbretsdatter. His remarkable chef d'oeuvre, *Nordlandstrompet*, occupies a secure place in the Norwegian literary canon.

Biographies:

Harald Beyer, ed., *Petter Dass 1647–1947* (Bergen: Eide, 1947);

Sverre Inge Apenes, *Rapport om Petter Dass–presten som diktet makt til folket* (Oslo: Gyldendal, 1978);

Sigmund Nesset, ed., *Herr Petter 350 År: Et festskrift fra Universitetet i Tromsø,* Skriftserie Ravnetrykk, No. 13 (Tromsø: Universitetet i Tromsø, 1997);

Karl Erik Harr, *Mit Navn er Petter Dass som Boer mot Verdens Ende* (Stamsund: Orkana, 2007).

References:

Laila Akslen, *Norsk barokk: Dorothe Engelbretsdatter og Petter Dass i retorisk Tradisjon,* Landslaget for Norskundervisning Skriftserie, no. 109 (Oslo: Landslaget for norskundervisning/Cappelens Akademisk Forlag, 1997);

Edvard Beyer and others, *Norges Litteraturhistorie,* volume 1 (Oslo: Cappelen, 1995), pp. 427–441;

Asle K. Brovoll, *Dynastiet: "een ydmyg Salutatz"* (Sandnessjøn: Asle K. Brovoll, 2007);

Karl Erik Harr, *Mit Navn er Petter Dass som Boer mot Verdens Ende* (Stamsund: Orkana, 2007);

Lanae H. Isaacson, "Petter Dass: Story-Teller, Moralist, and Student: The Changing Narrator of 'Nordlandstrompet,'" *Edda: Nordisk Tidsskrift for Litteraturforskning,* 5 (1980): 297–306;

Peter Kirkegaard, "Dansk-Norsk Fælleslitteratur 1536–1807," in *Norsk Litteratur i Tusen År. Teksthistoriske Linjer* (Oslo: Landslaget for Norskundervisning/Cappelen, 1994), pp. 155–157;

Hanne Lauvstad, *Helicons Bierge og Helgelands Schiar: Nordlands Trompets Tekst, Repertoar og Retorikk* (Oslo: Universitetet i Oslo, 2007);

Knut Mykland, "Skriver, fut og prest," in *Norges Kulturhistorie,* volume 3, edited by Ingrid Semmingsen and others (Oslo: Aschehoug, 1984), pp. 173–196;

Kathleen Stokker, "Oral Tradition, Humanism, and the Baroque," in *A History of Norwegian Literature,* edited by Harald S. Næss (Lincoln & London: University of Nebraska Press, 1993), pp. 51–52;

Johan Sebastian Welhaven, "Digteren fra Alstadhoug, Peder Dass," *Nordisk Universitets-Tidsskrift,* 2–3 (1856): 365–392.

Hans Egede
(21 January 1686 – 5 November 1758)

Lanae H. Isaacson

BOOKS: *En skrift- og fornuftgrundet Resolution og Erklaring om de Objectioner og Forhindringer angaaende det Forsæt til de hedenske Grønlænderes Omvendelse* (Vågan: Hans Egede, 1715);

Det gamle Grønlands nye Perlustration, eller en kort Beskrivelse om de nordske Coloniers Begyndelse og Undergang i Grønland (Copenhagen: J. C. Groth, 1729); revised as *Det gamle Grønlands nye Perlustration eller Naturel-Historie og Beskrivelse over det gamle Grønlands Situation, Luft, Temperament og Beskaffenhed* (Copenhagen: J. C. Groth, 1741);

Kort Beretning om den Grønlandske Missions Beskaffenhed (Copenhagen, 1737);

Omstændelig og udførlig Relation, Angaaende Den Grønlandske Missions Begyndelse og Fortsættelse (Copenhagen: J. C. Groth, 1738);

Grønlands ABC og Læsebog (Copenhagen: Seminarium Groenlandicum, 1739);

Erindring til Missionairerne (Copenhagen: Seminarium Groenlandicum, 1739);

Elementa fidei Christianæ Grønlandice (Copenhagen: Seminarium Groenlandicum, 1742);

Grönlændernes förste præsts Hans Egedes aftensamtaler med sine diciple, forfattet af Johan Christian Mørch: Kaladlit Pelleserkãngoæta Hans Egedib Okallõutèi Unnukorsiutit, edited by Peter Kragh (Copenhagen: Fabritius de Tengnagels Bogtrykkeri, 1837);

Egedes dagbog i udtog: Tillægshefte til Folkevennen, 9, edited by Eilert Sundt (Christiania: Malling, 1860);

Apostelens dagbok: fra Hans Egedes dagboksnotater, edited by Karl Erik Harr (Harstad: Aas & Søn, 1998).

Hans Egede (painting by Johan Hörner, 1740; Store Norske Leksikon <http://snl.no/.bilde/ Egede%2C_Hans_(Portrettmaleri_fra_V%C3%A5gan_kirke)>)

Hans Egede made his mark in Danish and Norwegian history as "Grønlands apostel" (Greenland's Apostle), the missionary who sought to convert the Inuit to Christianity and secure Danish economic and political power against growing Dutch trade with the island. Egede kept a remarkably detailed diary of his experiences and efforts in Greenland: *Omstændelig og udførlig Relation, Angaaende Den Grønlandske Missions Begyndelse og Fortsættelse* (1738, Detailed and Complete Account Concerning the Beginning and Continuation of the Greenland Mission). He also provided a similarly detailed description of Greenland's history, geography, and people for the benefit of later missionaries and researchers on the Inuit in *Det gamle Grønlands nye Perlustration, eller en kort Beskrivelse om de nordske Coloniers Begyndelse og Undergang i Grønland* (1729, Old Greenland's New Presentation; or, A Short Description of the Beginning and Demise of the Norwegian Colonies in Greenland).

Hans Poulsen Egede was born at Harstad Gård, Trondenes, in Troms on 21 January 1686. His parents were the parson Poul Hansen Egede, whose family included civil servants from Vester Egede on Sjælland (Denmark), and Kirsten Jensdatter Hind, the daughter of the former minister at Trondenes. Egede received his early education from his maternal uncle, Peter Hind, the chaplain in Sand, and from Niels Schielderup in Hamarøy. Egede entered the University of Copenhagen in 1704 and received a degree in theology with the notation "mediocrem" (mediocre) in August 1705. He returned to Norway after completing his education in Copenhagen and served as a tutor for his younger brothers until he was appointed chaplain of Vågan by Peter Krog, the bishop of Trondheim, in 1707.

Egede encountered both personal and professional difficulties in Vågan. The young chaplain was expected to marry Dorothea de Fine, the widow of his predecessor; instead, he chose a somewhat older girl he knew from his childhood, Gertrud Nielsdatter Rasch. De Fine did not accept the rejection graciously; instead, she caused trouble for the couple, who were her immediate neighbors. Egede managed to win the support of the congregation at Vågan, but this accomplishment proved a mixed blessing: the parish priest, Jacob Svensson Parelius, who was Egede's superior, was denied admission to Vågan Church by the congregation. The congregation's clear preference for Egede led to fines against him and a reprimand from church officials. Egede remained minister to the Vågan congregation until 1718.

Early on in his call to Vågan, Egede showed an interest in Greenland and the Christian mission established by Norwegian and Icelandic missionaries during the Middle Ages. Egede's interest was deepened by his reading of Paster Peder Claussøn Friis's *Om Grønland: En kort Extract af Norges Krønike* (1632, On Greenland: A Short Extract of the Chronicle of Norway), as well as by the reports of his brother-in-law Niels Rasch, who had sailed with whalers to Greenland and worked as a merchant on the island. Egede wrote several proposals to bishops in Bergen and Trondheim, soliciting their support for a new mission to Greenland. His appeals were motivated by a personal calling and by the belief of the time that it was the duty of Christian monarchs to evangelize their subjects in territories and colonies.

In *Omstændelig og udførlig Relation, Angaaende Den Grønlandske Missions Begyndelse og Fortsættelse* Egede describes his concern for the spiritual state of affairs on Greenland, suggesting his motivation for seeking a post among the Inuit:

Denne Relation virkede udi mig en hiertelig Commiseration over disse arme Menneskers elendige Tilstand, at de tilforne havde været Christne og udi den Christelige Troe oplyste, men af Mangel paa Lærere og Undervisning vare da igien forfaldne udi hedensk Blindhed og Vildhed.

(This account caused within me a heartfelt commiseration over the miserable state of these poor people, that they had previously been Christian and informed in the Christian faith but, because of a lack of teachers and education, had again fallen into heathen blindness and savagery.)

In 1715 Egede presented yet another tract in support of the mission to Greenland, *En skrift- og fornuftgrundet Resolution og Erklaring om de Objectioner og Forhindringer angaaende det Forsæt til de hedenske Grønlænderes Omvendelse* (A Written and Wisely Formulated Resolution and Explanation Concerning the Objections and Obstacles to the Proposal for the Heathen Greenlanders' Conversion), the only such proposal that was published. Despite repeated rejections of his proposals, Egede went to Bergen in 1717 in order to find financial and clerical support for his mission and to propose the establishment of a Bergen Merchant Trading Company with Greenland as its focus. Egede proposed to serve as an officer of the company on Greenland as well as leader of the Christian mission. In 1719 Egede traveled to Copenhagen to present his plan to King Fredrik IV. As is clear from *Omstændelig og udførlig Relation, Angaaende Den Grønlandske Missions Begyndelse og Fortsættelse*, Egede's appeal to the king for establishment of a mission to Greenland wove arguments for increased trade with Greenland around expressions of serious concern for the souls of the Greenlanders:

Grønlænderne har været oplyste udi den Christelige Tro . . . Efter Margrethes død kom de i forglemmelse . . . Landet [var] i forglemmelse . . . [saa] havde andre fremmede Nationer søgt at betiene sig af Farten til Grønland . . . den hollandske Nation i faa Aar har draget all Handelen til sig . . . Grønland er ikke saa armt og fattigt, at der jo var en utroelig Fordeel at hente for vores Nation . . . maatte det ikkun Allernaadigst behage Deres Kongelige Majestæt at forunde Compagnier som sig her til ville resolvere visse Privilegier . . . [at] de hedenske Grønlandernes Omvendelse skulle lettere og lyckeligere udfalde end den udi Ost-Indien, er det icke uden Grund, thi mand skulde haabe at det endnu skulde findes nogen Levninger af den forfaldne Christendom.

(The Greenlanders have been taught in the Christian faith . . . After the death of Margrethe they were forgotten . . . The land [was] forgotten . . . [so] other foreign nations have tried to make use of the journey to Greenland . . . the Dutch nation has in just a few years drawn all the commerce to it . . . Greenland is not so poor and

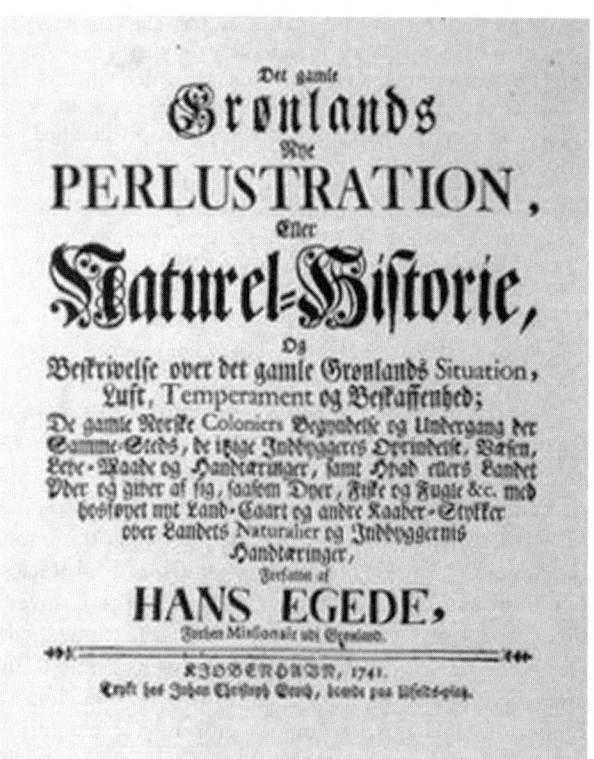

Title page for the revised edition of Egede's description of the natural history of Greenland, originally published in 1729 (Mandøes Antikvariat, Denmark)

miserable that there [is not] an unbelievable advantage to secure for our nation . . . may it most respectfully please Your Most Benevolent Royal Majesty to grant companies that will resolve this certain privileges . . . [that] the heathen Greenlander's conversion should be easier and more successful than that in East-India is not without foundation because we should hope that there might be found some remnants of now-defunct Christianity.)

Egede's two-pronged approach, his deliberate linkage of pecuniary interests, national prestige and standing, and Christian missions to the Inuit won the day and full support from the king, whom Egede quotes: "Da er vores allernaadigste Villie og Befaling, at indfalde for Eder de Negotierende der sammensteds, og fornemme deres Meening, om Handelen derfra paa Grønland med nogen Fordeel kand drives . . . den 17. November 1719" (Therefore It is Our Most Munificent Will and Order to designate you to attend to the negotiations in the same place, and discern the Opinion concerning whether commerce from Greenland can be conducted with Any Advantages . . . the 17th of November 1719). Less than a year and a half later, Egede and his family left Bergen for Greenland:

Saa blev da Reisen i den Herres Jesu navn foretaget den 3 May 1721, da vi med Skibet Haabet og indeværende Mandskab, i alt 46 Mennisker, min Familie inclusive (foruden den med os følgende Galliot) gik fra Bergen, i det faste Haab, lykkeligen til Grønland at ankomme.

(So the Journey was undertaken in the Lord Jesus' Name on 3 May 1721, when we with the ship The Hope and the company, in all 46 people, my family included [in addition to our companion Galliot], left Bergen, in the firm hope of arriving happily in Greenland.)

It was the start of a fifteen-year mission fraught with difficulties and challenges.

In discussing the medieval Christian colonies in Greenland, Egede claimed rather vaguely that the former Norse settlements, the Greenlandic Inuit converts, and the land itself "kom i forglemmelse" (came into forgetfulness). As he writes in *Det gamle Grønlands nye Perlustration*, Egede saw part of his mission to be the rescue and restoration of "de gamle øde Pladser med nye Bebyggere, til Kongens og Landes store nytte" (the old abandoned places with new residents, to the greater usefulness of the King and lands). Research on the earlier Greenland colonies now suggests that their decline and disappearance resulted from several factors: a mini–Ice Age on Greenland; general ill health and malnutrition; the strict, unbending social dictates of the Church fathers, and the unwillingness and inability of the colonists to abandon their European lifestyle and agricultural practices. By contrast, the Inuit lived a life in harmony with the natural environment, based on hunting and fishing, and so were able to survive changes in the climate.

Egede initially encountered great difficulty communicating with the Inuit. But his two sons, Poul Hansen Egede and Niels Rasch Egede, quickly mastered the language and helped their father on his difficult, often trying excursions among the Greenlanders. (Egede never mastered spoken Inuit as his sons did.) *Omstændelig og udførlig Relation, Angaaende Den Grønlandske Missions Begyndelse og Fortsættelse* is a record of constant energetic activity, with Egede assuming the role of church and civic leader in the community. Egede's writings make clear the price paid by his family, particularly his wife, Gertrud, who feared that the mission might lead to ruination for everyone in the family. In the end, Gertrud Egede died from overwork after a devastating smallpox epidemic.

Egede devoted considerable time and effort to his extensive study of Greenland, which is most fully presented in the 1741 second edition of *Det gamle Grønlands nye Perlustration*. In this work Egede expressed particular concern for the lost Christian colonies, the earlier Norse sites that had fallen on hard times after the reign of Margrethe I. He included detailed information on history, geography, flora and fauna, climate, and topography as well as the Inuit. Despite his concern for the people, Egede as an educated European of his time viewed the Inuit as inferior, hapless heathens:

> . . . her er intet at melde, hverken om faste eller velbebygde stæder og Byer, ej heller om en vel indrettet Politie, herlige Konster og Viidenskaber og saadant mere, men allene om nogle eenfoldige, fattige og vanvittige hedninger, som lever som de kand og giør sig Landet saa nyttig, som de allerbest veed og forstaar.
>
> (. . . here there is nothing to mention, nothing on the order of solid or well-built cities and towns, nor anything like a well-designed system of civil control, glorious arts or sciences or the like, but there are only some simple, poor and ignorant heathens, who live as they can, and make the best use of the land that they know and understand.)

Egede, however, did not ignore the Inuit beliefs. He wove Greenlandic oral history and legends, what he called "Fabler" (fables), into his record of the past, making the work—at least in part—a key to the Inuits' own view of their past and, on occasion, using their oral history to strengthen contemporary conjectures and claims:

> Man haver for denne Tid være i Tanke, at Grønland paa den Nord-Ost Siide ogsaa grenzer lige hen til Asien og Tartariet, ja lige til Rysland, i hvilken Meening man uden Tvivl er bleven bestyrket af en Grønlands Fabel, om en ved navn Harald Geed, som til Lands og over Bierge og Klipper, skal have reyst fra Grønland til Norge, førende med sig en Geed, af hvis Melk hand levede og opholdte sig paa Reysen, hvorfore hand og siden blev kaldet Harald Geed.
>
> (For this time we have come to think that Greenland borders right up to Asia and Tartaria, indeed to Russia, on the northeast, in which opinion we are no doubt supported by a Greenlandic fable about a man by the name of Harald Goat who shall have crossed lands and mountains and cliffs and traveled from Greenland to Norway leading a goat whose milk sustained and nourished him on the journey, whereupon he was ever after called Harald Goat.)

In his observations of the natural world, the merchant-missionary sometimes relied on the stories and descriptions the Inuit provided, but he also revealed a degree of skepticism and a tendency to discount some of their stories as unbelievable:

> Grønlænderne har ellers fortalt os om et andet slags skadelige Diur, som de kalde Anarok, og skal tragte baade efter Mennesker og Diur, men som ingen hav selv kunde sige mig at have seet det Diur, man har ikkun haft det efter andres Beretning, disligeste, at fordi vore egne Folk, som vel har gaaet vitt nok omkring i Marken ikke heller, har seet sligt et Diur, holder jeg det ikkun for en Fabel.
>
> (The Greenlanders have also told us about another sort of harmful creature that they call Anarok, one that forages for both people and other animals, but one that none of them could tell me he had seen, they only had it from the accounts of others, therefore, because our own people, who have gone far afield, have not seen such a creature either, I hold it to be just a fable.)

Det gamle Grønlands nye Perlustration describes the Inuits' way of life, their social customs and family traditions, their physical attributes, their environment and the wildlife on which they depended. It features drawings, maps, and sketches of remarkable detail, prepared by Egede's son, Poul, who proved to be a talented artist and illustrator of his father's works. While Egede's descriptions of the physical appearance of the Inuits reflect his cultural bias, Egede also provides insights into a way of life notable for its music, dance, levity, and strong sense of community:

> De have en liden Tromme, som er en Ring af Træ eller et stokke af et Hvalfiske Ribbeen, med Skafft paa, overtrækket med tynd skind, paa den slaaer en af dem med en stok og siunger derhos nogle Viiser, angaaende enten deris Haandteringer i Almindelighed, eller hans egen i Særdelished, Med ham istemer det hele Chor, Mand Og Qvinder.
>
> (They have a little drum that is a ring of wood or a stalk from the rib of a whale, with a shaft on it, covered with thin skin, one of them strikes it with a stalk and sings some songs, either dealing with their deeds in general or his in particular. The whole choir, men and women, join in.)

Egede evidently described his encounter with another culture, another way of living and thinking, as accurately as his experience, expertise, and personal resources allowed.

In 1727 the Bergen Trading Company supporting the mission to Greenland failed in the face of fierce competition from the Dutch and their vast fleet of merchant vessels. Frederik IV stepped in to support Egede's work, but the king's death soon left the trade mission up in the air. Egede managed to persuade the new king, Christian VI, to renew support for the mission, but the management of the venture was transferred from Egede to Jacob Severin, a powerful merchant entrepreneur in Copenhagen. Egede also faced competition on the missionary front, as two Hernnhut missionaries, members of an even stricter sect than Egede's own, were given permission to proselytize in Greenland. In 1734 the Inuit congregation that Egede had worked so hard to build was nearly wiped out by smallpox brought from Denmark;

their numbers decreased from seven thousand to around four thousand. Egede's wife was weakened by her nursing efforts and died in December 1735. Egede viewed all these reversals as evidence of God's displeasure at his efforts, and in 1736 he left Greenland for good.

Egede's work on behalf of the mission to Greenland did not cease, however. In 1737 he established a seminary to train missionaries for Greenland, Seminarium Groenlandicum, which he directed until 1747. He published not only *Omstændelig og udførlig Relation, Angaaende Den Grønlandske Missions Begyndelse og Fortsættelse* and the second edition of *Det gamle Grønlands nye Perlustration* but also explanations of Inuit grammar and vocabulary and instruction books for the missionaries: *Grønlands ABC og Læsebog* (1739, Greenland's ABC and Reader), *Erindring til Missionairerne* (1739, Memoir for the Missionaries), and *Elementa fidei Christianæ Grønlandice* (1742, Elements of the Christian Faith). In 1739 Egede married the widow Mattea Trane, and the following year he was named titulary bishop for Greenland. He was offered several important clerical offices, but he declined, as he wrote in *Det gamle Grønlands nye Perlustration,* in favor of "de arme vanvittige Menniskers Opliusning og saliggiørelse. Som ønskes allertroehiertigst af" (the poor ignorant people's education and salvation, which is most heartily desired).

For some years Egede and his second wife lived with her son-in-law in Vardal, Norway. In 1751 the couple moved to Stubbekøbing on Falster, Denmark, where Egede died on 5 November 1758 during an epidemic. He was buried alongside his first wife in Nikolaj Kirkegård in Copenhagen.

Hans Egede provided the first solid studies of the Inuit and their land, with *Det gamle Grønlands nye Perlustration* being his most important work. While his own European cultural heritage and values are apparent in his accounts, he was a dedicated scholar who wrote honestly of his encounter with a new and largely unknown world. Egede was instrumental in converting many Inuit to a new faith and expanding their cultural horizons beyond their isolated island home. His studies of the Inuit language and oral literature prepared the way for those who would follow in his footsteps. While serving the commercial interest of his king and country, Egede performed the more valuable service of opening the minds of his countrymen to a remarkable land and its people.

Bibliography:

Holger Ehrencron-Müller, "Hans Egede," in his *Forfatterlexicon omfattende Danmark Norge og Island indtil 1814,* volume 2 (Copenhagen: Aschehoug, 1925), pp. 405–406.

Biography:

Liv Randi Bjørlykke, *Hans Egede* (Oslo: Lunde, 1976).

References:

Torstein Aarthun, *Hans Poulsen Egede: en studie av hans motivasjon og dens praktiske utslag i misjonsvirksomheten på Grønland 1721–1736* (Stavanger: Misjonshøgskolen, 2002);

Knut Bergeland and Jørgen Rischel, eds., *Pioneers of Eskimo Grammar: Hans Egede's and Albert Top's Early Manuscripts on Greenlandic* (Copenhagen: Linguistic Circle of Copenhagen, 1986);

Niels Fenger, *Palasé: Hans Egede i Grønland* (Copenhagen: Wöldike, 1971);

Karl Erik Harr, *Hans Egedes opptegnelser og begynnelsen på hans Grønlandsferd* (Oslo: Kolofonen, 1992);

Mogens Hindsberger, *Den grønlandske kristendomsopfattelse fra Hans Egede til vore dage* (Copenhagen: Museum Tusculanum, 1997);

Katherine Kjærgaard, *Hans Egede: et studie i kirkehistorisk ikonografi, 1728–2005* (Copenhagen: Reitzel, 2006);

Lone Klem, *Grønland civiliseres: Kulturmodsætninger under Hans Egedes Grønlands-mission 1721–1736* (Kronborg-Hensingør: Maritime studier tilegnet Knud Klem, 1966);

O. Kolsrud, "Hans Egede og Grønland," *Norvegia Sacra: aarbok til kunnshap am den Norske kirke i fortid og samtid* (1921): 76–86;

Olav Guttorm Myklebust, *Hans Egede. Studier til 200-årsdagen for hans død* (Oslo: Egede Instituttet, 1958);

Kristian Nissen, *Hans Egede som Grønlandsk geograf og kartograf* (Oslo: Egede Instituttet, 1959);

Thomas Strack, *Exotische Erfahrung und Intersubjektivität: Reiseberichte im 17. und 18. Jahrhundert. Genregeschichtliche Untersuchung zu Adam Olearius, Hans Egede, Georg Forster* (Paderborn: Igel, 1993);

Hans-Jørgen Wallin, *"Social Work" and Missionary Work as Part of the Power Game: A Discussion through Two Examples. Hans Egede Missionary in Greenland 1721–1736 and the Norwegian Saami Mission in Finnmark: The Period of Establishment of Missions and Social Services 1888–1900* (Lund: Lunds Universitet, 1999);

Margarethe Ølberg, *Missionspionér fra Nord: Hans Egedes Misjonssyn og Praksis* (Stavanger: M. Ølberg, 2006).

Kristian Elster
(4 March 1841 – 11 April 1881)

Lanae H. Isaacson

BOOKS: *Tora Trondal: Fortælling* (Copenhagen: Gyldendal, 1879);
Farlige Folk: fortælling (Copenhagen: Gyldendal, 1881);
Solskyer: udvalgte Fortællinger, edited by Alexander L. Kielland (Copenhagen: Gyldendal, 1881);
En fremmed Fugl (Copenhagen: Gyldendal, 1884);
Kjeld Horge (Copenhagen: Gyldendal, 1884);
Samlede skrifter, 2 volumes (Copenhagen: Gyldendal, 1903);
Fra det moderne gjennombrudds tid: litteraturkritikk og artikler 1868–1880, edited by Willy Dahl (Bergen: Eide, 1981).
Edition: *Farlige folk: en korsgang,* introduction by Ivar Holm (Oslo: Gyldendal, 1968).

PLAY PRODUCTION: *Eystein Meyla,* Christiania, Christiania Norske Teater, 13 August 1863.

SELECTED PERIODICAL PUBLICATION–UNCOLLECTED: "Om Modsætningen mellem det vestlige og østlige Norge: ved Tusindaarsfesten til Minde om Norges Samling som Rige," *For Idé og Virkelighed,* 2 (1872): 97–152.

Kristian Elster (from Edvard Beyer, ed., Norges Litteratur Historie, *volume 3 [Oslo: Cappelen, 1975]; University of Kansas Libraries)*

Despite his early death at forty, Kristian Elster made an indelible mark on the Norwegian literary scene. He was a gifted novelist and storyteller with special insights into the psyches of his characters; an observer of the turbulent social fabric of his time; and a lyric poet capable of invoking the extraordinary beauty of natural surroundings, especially of Vestlandet, the western coast and skerries of Norway, and of capturing the loveliness and symbolic and real power of weather and water, flora and fauna, and signs and seasons in beautiful, memorable words. He was a keen critic, essayist, and commentator on contemporary literary trends and writers and their works. He was also a moderator and mediator who introduced Norwegian literati to Scandinavian and European writers, social thinkers, philosophers, and cultural leaders–Søren Kierkegaard, Georg Brandes, Ivan Turgenev, and Charles Darwin among them. Elster insisted on literary realism, on letting his characters tell the tale, and on fidelity to life as lived in a Norway divided by class and cultural differences.

Kristian Mandrup Elster was born on 4 March 1841 in Namdalen, Overhalla, Nord-Trøndelag, to Christen Christensen Elster, a sheriff, and Elen Sophie Alstrup. In 1853 his father received an appointment as civil magistrate in Sunnfjord, and the family moved to Førde. At fifteen Elster was sent to Christiania (today Oslo) to study at Nissen's School to become a military officer, but myopia prevented him from finishing his training.

In 1860 Elster submitted a play, *Fra Fjorden* (From the Fjord), to Henrik Ibsen, director of the Christiania Norske Teater, but withdrew it almost immediately and also ended a stint as an apprentice actor. He prepared to take the *examen artium* (examination qualifying a student to study at a university), but a severe case of nerves and a poor foundation in Latin forced him to withdraw twice; he eventually abandoned a third attempt. Elster submitted and withdrew a play about the Norwegian Middle Ages, *Audun Hugleikson,* in 1863. His *Eystein Meyla* premiered and closed on 13 August 1863 after a cool reception from the critics; Ibsen was especially hostile. Elster submitted two short stories to popular journals: "En Lægpredikant" (1865, A Lay Preacher) to *Illustreret Nyhedsblad* and "Trodals-Rakel" (1869, Rachel of Trodal) to *Norsk Folkeblad*. In the middle of seeing these stories through to publication, Elster left Christiania to study forestry in Giessen, Germany, where he received a diploma as a forest superintendent in 1868. In 1869 he returned to Christiania, where he worked as a literary critic and and translator of novels by such writers as Turgenev, Berthold Auerbach, and Friedrich von Spielhagen for *Aftenbladet* and *Norsk Folkeblad*. Elster followed Jonas Lie as the Norwegian correspondent for the Copenhagen journal *For Idé og Virkelighed,* to which he contributed the short story "En Korsgang" (1871, A Cross to Bear). Based on an actual event in Elster's home district, "En Korsgang" is the story of Salbjørg, who on discovering that her son, Jon, is a thief and murderer, faces the painful choice of living with her knowledge of the crime or turning him over to the authorities. It is set in the natural surroundings that figure so prominently in Elster's works:

Men her, i det indre Liv, som ligger truet med Døden oppe paa Vidderne, begynder man dog at finde Menneskespor og at føle, at den samme Sag føres for Gud heroppe i Fokket som der, hvor Naturen ødsler med Gaver. Forunderligt arter vel ofte Sjælelivet sig under saadanne Kaar; man finder baade Dværgbirkens forvoxne Former og dens haarde Ved; men Ingen tvivler længer paa, at det er den samme Nød, som herjer Livet her som overalt, den samme Grundsorg, som breder Tungsind over det, og det samme Solhaab, som faar det til at grønnes og spire. . . . Og naar det strømmer over En af Fortællinger om Vildskab og Blodtørst fra de store Kamppladse, da finder man ogsaa de samme vilde Drifter her; og raabes en Heltegjerning ud med tusinde Tunger fra de store Verdenslejre, da finder man ogsaa her det samme Heltemod, om ogsaa dets eneste Daad var en stille Korsgang, som Ingen taler om.

(But out here in the vast wide expanses, one begins finding human tracks within an inner life that is threatened with death, and one feels that the same divine cause is involved up here in the wilderness as in places where Nature abounds in gifts. It is strange how the life of the soul develops in such a place; one finds both the spent forms of the dwarf birch and its hard wood; but no one doubts any longer that the same need puts life to the test here as everywhere else, the same fundamental sorrow leads to a heavy heart, and the same sunny hope causes verdant new growth and fresh branches. . . . And when stories of violence and blood thirst stream in over you from the great battlefields, you also find the same violent acts here; and if heroic deeds are declaimed in a thousand foreign tongues from the battlefields of the great, wide world, you will also find the same heroic courage here, even though the act of courage may mean silently bearing a cross that no one speaks about.)

Salbjørg's husband, Gjest, is a dishonest horse trader. Jon follows in his father's footsteps, quickly learning that money is what matters most. Jon murders a wandering merchant and steals his money; Salbjørg discovers him in the act of covering his tracks and counting his ill-gotten gains. Salbjørg begins a series of appeals: to her husband, who has served as Jon's accomplice in spirit if not in deed; to Jon himself; and finally to the pastor. Her efforts are met with Gjest's rebuff and Jon's decision to leave home. The pastor feebly advises Salbjørg to do what she believes the Lord would command. And so she brings the law down on Jon and testifies against him. In the end she witnesses the return of the snows and the loss of any possibility of happiness in her life:

Hun gik forbi sit gamle Hjem, hvor hendes første Vaardrøm var kommen under de lysløvede Birke, uden et Suk for den tunge Løvfaldstid, som havde fulgt; men da hun var kommen op paa Hejerne og saa sit Hjem og tænkte paa, at nu var ikke bare Sneen føgen høj om hendes Hus, men ogsaa om hendes Liv, da sank hun dødstræt ned på Vejkanten; hu, da saa hun i et eneste Syn det hele Øde, som laa foran hende, og da kjendte hun lige i sit Inderste Iskulden af det Liv, som stod igjen. Hun havde fulgt sit eget Livshaab til Graven, og nu havde hun Tid til at græde over sit Tab.

(She went by her old home, where her first spring-dream had come with the fresh young birches, without a sigh for the heavy fall of autumn leaves that followed; but when she came up on the heights and saw her home and thought that the snow had not only settled high up around her house but also around her life, then she sank down dead-tired by the edge of the road; oh, then she saw at once the entire desolation that lay before her, and she sensed to the depths of her being the ice-cold life that remained. She had followed her own hope for life to the grave, and now she had the time to cry for her loss.)

In 1872 Elster contributed to *For Idé og Virkelighed* the essay "Om Modsætningen mellem det vestlige og østlige Norge: ved Tusindaarsfesten til Minde om Norges Samling som Rige" (On the Differences between Western and Eastern Norway: On the Occasion of the Millennium of Norway's Royal Unification). The piece demonstrates his mastery in depicting nature with words. He draws clear distinctions between the characters, cultures, standards of living, and topographies of the regions and expresses hope for stronger agreement between the regions for their mutual strength.

In early spring of 1873 Elster paid a visit to Copenhagen, where he had the opportunity to hear a lecture by the leading European literary historian, Brandes. That year Elster was appointed to the forestry service in Valdres; while working as a forester, he contributed articles on forestry and essays and literary reviews to *Throndhjems Stiftsavis* and the liberal/radical paper *Dagsposten*.

On 17 August 1874 Elster married Sanna Fasting. The couple had three sons; born a few weeks before his father's death in 1881, the youngest, Kristian, became an author and literary critic and is generally referred to as Kristian Elster d.y. (*den yngre* [the younger]). His father, in turn, is frequently designated Elster d.e. (*den eldre* [the older]).

Elster's "Solskyer: fra en Bygdelæge til en Ven" (Sun Clouds: From a Village Doctor to a Friend) first appeared in *Nordisk Tidsskrift for almendannende og underholdende Læsning* in 1877; it was republished in subsequent editions of Elster's works, including an 1881 collection of novellas and short stories for which it formed the title piece. It masterfully interweaves lyrical descriptions of the west country with an effort to delve into the psyche and emotions of the characters; it has a fascinating protagonist, Elina, with whom two men fall in love. Elster's frequent use of a love triangle linking an independent, strong woman with two weaker men of varying temperaments, intellects, and backgrounds reflects the influence of Turgenev. Returning home from medical studies abroad, Henrik falls in love with Elina, and his love is returned. The sun seems to smile through and illuminate the clouds; images of clouds underscore the ebb and flow of the love of Henrik and Elina. Elina realizes that Holt, her guardian and uncle, has fallen in love with her and that she loves him. But she is torn because of her love for Henrik and her anticipation of the world he has opened to her. Henrik leaves to start a medical practice beyond the reaches of the valley. On his return, Elina breaks with him in an encounter filled with longing, regret, and sorrow for what they once had together, the most beautiful time in her life. Many years later, Henrik learns that Holt and Elina were returning from a business meeting when their boat capsized and both drowned. The bearer of the sad tidings relates that Elina accepted her death calmly:

Elster's tombstone in Førde (County Archives of Sogn og Fjordane)

> "Da Holt mærkede, at han ikke sad sikker med hende, sagde han: 'Elina, tag dig sammen–det gjælder Livet.'–'Lad mig fare,' sagde hun; 'det er det samme, nu er det ikke tungt at dø.' Hun talte maaske i Vildelse; men jeg har dog ogsaa tænkt, at hun forraadte et lønligt Ønske–Og hun, som engang sagde: 'Det er dejligt at leve!'"

> ("When Holt noticed that he no longer had a firm hold on her, he said: 'Elina, get yourself together–it's a question of life.'–'Let me go,' she said, 'it's just as well, now, it's not hard to die.' Perhaps she was speaking incoherently, but I also believe that she hid a secret wish.–And she was the one who once said: 'It's lovely to live!'")

Henrik's last reflections and recollections concern the sun clouds on the western horizon.

Elster's novel *Tora Trondal* (1879) depicts another love triangle. The title character is courted by Hans

Ejd–a genuine man of the west, a fearless man who stands on the foundation of truth and love for the fatherland–and District Attorney Erik Gran, a hero in conversation but lacking inner substance. The two suitors represent the conflict between the civil elite and the traditional rural culture based on personal and social responsibility and respect for the land. In the end, Ejd wins Tora. With its open discussion and presentation of the two cultures, *Tora Trondal* provided the impetus for contemporary debate on the direction Norwegian society might take; the novel also served as a precedent for literary works dealing with the rifts within Norwegian society, among them Arne Garborg's *Bondestudentar* (1883, Peasant Students).

Elster's next work, the short story "En fremmed Fugl" (1881, A Foreign Bird), most clearly reflects Kierkegaard's views concerning aesthetic versus ethical "stages on life's way." Paul Horst, an aesthete, is an editor and writer who settles on an outlying western island with the idea of writing about the local people from the viewpoint of an outsider. He falls in love with another of Elster's unusual female protagonists, the lively, fiery redheaded Julie, who is the exact opposite of the wealthy merchant's daughter to whom he is engaged. Julie is already being courted by the pastor Holk and a surveyor, Einar Borg; she chooses the latter. The aesthete returns to his intended, but he has learned something about life and love in a community far from the urban scene; he has, moreover, become aware of values, choices, and responsibilities that are remote from his world of privilege and power, a world where everything is taken for granted. For lack of courage, Horst retreats from the happiness he knew on the island. His retreat means that he is doomed to a life of longing. Horst is the bird of the title, *en fremmed fugl* condemned to seek "nye Omgivelser, altid nye" (new surroundings, always new). "En fremmed Fugl" is replete with masterful poetic descriptions of the natural world Horst discovers:

> Himlen ligger stille i dets Dybder, og Mennesket gribes af Længsel efter at føle det lunt og ømt om sig. Men det frister ogsaa til at drømme,–at drømme om en dulgt herlig Verden, som ikke er til. Hvor det taber sig i det Fjerne i let henaandede, fine rosenfarvede Florskyer, munder det ud i det altid eftertragtede, aldrig opdagede Lykkens Eventyrland.

> (The sky lay still in its depths, and one was gripped by a longing to feel soft and warm. But there was also a temptation to dream,–to dream of a hidden, glorious world, that did not exist. Where everything lost in the distance in lightly wispy, fine, rose-colored floral clouds opened out onto the eternally sought and never discovered Adventure Land of Joy.)

Elster's principal novel, *Farlige Folk* (Dangerous People), did not appear until a few weeks after his death from pneumonia or lung disease on 11 April 1881. The novel combines a love story that almost ends on an upbeat with a rather detailed account of social turmoils and class struggles in a smaller coastal town. *Farlige Folk* opens:

> Et stort Dampskib styrer ind mod en norsk Kystby. Længe har man ombord blot seet Vand og Berg, afblæst, vejrbleget Berg. Endelig er der en Forandring. Klipperne er tildels bedækkede med kaffebrun Lyng, og man ser hist og her en ensom Furru med alle Grene vredne fortvilet mod Land. Efter at Damperen har strøget forbi et Utal af ubeboede Udøer, opdager man nogle hvide Pletter paa en graa Strand. Det er Byen. . . . Dampbaaden nærmer sig Indløbet til Havnen . . . Man ser Byen gjennem et Net af Skibsrigge. Nederst ved Søen, Væg i Væg, en Rad brede Søboder. Ovenfor dem ligger de øvrige Huse terrassevis opover det skraanende Fjeld, længst nede samlede i Rækker, men øverst oppe spredt uregelmæssigt om. . . . Op over alle andre Huse rager Kirken og Latinskolen.

> (A large steamship steers in toward a Norwegian coastal town. For a long time on board one sees only water and mountains, windblown, weather-worn mountains. Finally, there's a change. The peaks are partially covered with coffee-brown heather, and here and there one sees a lonely fir with all its branches turned uncertainly toward the land. After the ship has passed countless uninhabited islands, one discovers some white flecks on a gray coast. That's the town. . . . The ship nears the entrance to the Harbor. . . . One sees the town through a net of ship riggings. Closest to the sea, wall to wall, a row of broad shops. Above these lie the remaining houses in terraces up over the steep peaks, the lowest grouped in rows, the rest spread about irregularly. . . . Above all the other houses stand the church and the Latin School.)

On board the steamship is the young physician Knut Holt, who is returning home after years of study and travel in Europe and North and South America. Once an avid democrat, he has given up his idealism after witnessing the harsh reality of the struggle for life in distant climes. The world to which Knut returns is controlled by the banker and financier Klaus Hamre and the editor of the newspaper and director of the Latin School, Kristoffer Bjørnholt, at the expense of the workers, fishermen, and shipbuilders.

Arne Holt, Knut's father, identifies with those who work in his shipyard and tries to treat them fairly. Starting with nothing but his ingenuity, the older Holt has thrived in adversity but has forgotten his roots and fearlessly attacks his "betters" on behalf of the workers.

Knut's idealism is reawakened by the love and courage of a strong woman, Kornelia Vik, the daughter of Arne Holt's old enemy and rival, Jacob Vik. Kornelia's idealism is reawakened by Knut:

> "Men det ved jeg, at jeg i Deres Sted ikke vilde bukke og smile, ikke sidde ledig et eneste Minut. Hvordan kan De udholde det med Deres Tro? Om jeg vidste, at mit Ord, min Daad idag skulde være glemt imorgen, jeg maatte dog raabe af alle Kræfter, arbejde saalænge jeg kunde røre en Haand. Om jeg fortvilede over, at ikke hele Verden kan reformeres og Millionerne hjælpes, jeg maatte dog kjæmpe til Døden for ialfald at faa en eneste Fordom dræbt, et eneste uretfærdigt Forhold forandret, en eneste nødlidende reddet. Jeg vilde forgaa af Skam, af Sorg og Smerte, ifald jeg ikke gjorde det. Den, der spørger: 'hvad kan det hjælpe,' vil ikke hjælpe."

> (But I know this, that I would not bow and smile if I were in your place, not sit still a single minute. How can you stand that with your belief? If I knew that my words, my deeds would be forgotten tomorrow, I would still have to cry out with all my strength, work as long as I could move my hand. If I doubted whether the entire world could be reformed and millions helped, I would still fight to the death to put one prejudice to death, to change a single unfair condition, to save a single desperate soul. I would die of shame, of sorrow and pain, if I didn't do that. He who asks: 'What can that help,' does not want to help.")

Full of life, passion, and compassion for the suffering of others, Kornelia is the strongest character in *Farlige Folk*. It appears that the love story will end on a happy note. But in a moment of indiscretion in Argentina years before, Knut promised marriage to a half-Norwegian girl. He thought her long dead, but she has wandered through Europe searching for him; she now turns up and demands her due. Knut acquiesces and gives up the love of his life for a girl he hardly knows or remembers. He retreats from his hometown with his new wife to embark a medical career in another town. Arne's workers turn against him in the mistaken belief that he has betrayed them; they attack his home and try to destroy the shipyard. Kornelia Vik and Arne Holt die. At the end of the novel Bjørnholt declares that Arne and Knut Holt "var farlige folk" (were dangerous people). But the supposedly "dangerous people" in the community have been neutralized–they are dead or departed–and the real "farlige folk" still hold sway over the hearts and minds of the people.

Elster's final work was the novella *Kjeld Horge* (1884). The last member of the Horge family, Kjeld turns away from the pastoral calling of his father and forefathers. Kjeld's mother aids and abets his dreams; she believes that something grand is in the offing for her son. Kjeld purchases a farm in the neighboring village and marries a local girl, Aase. His neighbors see him putting on airs, living a lifestyle that they consider

Cover for Elster's collected writings, published in 1903 (County Archives of Sogn og Fjordane)

too grandiose for his station in life. The political leader Hall Huk proposes that Kjeld run for a seat in Parliament and become a spokesman for his party. The plan suits Kjeld's ambition, and he runs and wins. Since Huk's talents for public speaking are modest, he suggests that Kjeld prepare an opening address and proposal for consideration, and Kjeld agrees. Tension mounts as Kjeld rehearses his remarks; the reader senses that he is heading for disaster and humiliation, but he seems unaware of his impending doom until the evening before his speech:

> Han prøvte at tænke igjen; men den Rædsel, som meldte sig i samme Stund, drev Tankerne fra hverandre. Han læste igjennem den lune Begyndelse og den lynende Slutning, som før altid havde trøstet ham; men nu syntes han, Begyndelsen var søvnig og Slutten stakaandet. Han forstod ikke længer, at han nogentid kunde have haft Længsel efter Udfærd. Nu gav han gjerne en Konge-Krone for et Fristed under det lave, kjemlige Tag.

> (He tried to think again; but the fear that announced itself in the same moment drove his thoughts apart from each other. He read through the warm beginning

and the lightning ending which had always comforted him before; but now he thought that the beginning was sleepy and the end breathless. He no longer understood that he could have longed for travel. Now he would have given a royal crown for a free place under his low, home roof.)

Things go as Kjeld fears: his memory fails completely when he tries to deliver the speech. He returns home in disgrace and realizes that Aase has borne the brunt of his dreams and schemes.

The early death of Kristian Elster was a huge loss for Norwegian literature and literary criticism. Elster charted the course for the modern Norwegian novel and novella, wrote discerning criticism and essays, and was keenly aware of literary and cultural trends in Norway, Scandinavia, and Europe. Few could match the beauty of Elster's descriptions of his home district, Sunnfjord in western Norway; few could create such lovely poetry to describe natural surroundings, wind and weather, and the flora and fauna he knew so well. He also offered keen insights into the psyche of the individual and sought to free his characters to speak from the depths of their souls.

Biography:

Josef Nilsson, *Kristian Elster, 1841–1881* (Lund: Gleerups, 1942).

References:

Edvard Beyer, *Utsyn over Norsk Litteratur* (Oslo: Cappelen, 1983), pp. 94–95;

Willy Dahl, *Kristian Elster: veien fra Grundtvig til Marx* (Oslo: Gyldendal, 1977);

Kjell Heggelund, Simon Skjønsberg, and Helge Vold, "Kristian Elster," in *Forfatternes Litteraturhistorie*, volume 1: *Fra Maurits C. Hansen til Arne Garborg* (Oslo: Gyldendal, 1980), pp. 153–161;

Ivar Holm, "Om natur og menneskesinn: refleksjoner over et essay til tusenårsfesten i 1872," *Samtiden*, 68, no. 8 (1959): 476–484;

Tor Otterholt, *Kristian Elster d.e's ungdomsdiktning: historiske skuespill* (Oslo: University of Oslo, 1975);

Ellinor Reichelt, *Natur og menneske: en sammenlikning av: Jonas Lie: Den Fremsynte; Kristian Elster d.e: Solskyer; Knut Hamsun: Pan; Martin A. Hansen: Løgneren* (Oslo: Reichelt, 1992).

Dorothe Engelbretsdatter
(16 January 1634 – 19 February 1716)

Laila Akslen

BOOKS: *Siælens Sang-Offer: Indeholdende Gudelige Sange paa de Fornemste Fester, tillige med andre sær Himmelske Sange, saa og om Syndernis Forladelse og Fortrøstning paa Guds Naade mod Fortuilelse og Utaalmodighed* (Copenhagen, 1678);

Taare-Offer Gudelige Siæle til Underviißning/der vil vide hvad Pœnitentzis Fagter formaar (Copenhagen: Aar, 1685);

Tvende ny aandelige Psalmer: den første: en Morgen-Sang/Nu er det Tid at vaage . . . ; Dend anden: En Aften-Sang/ Dagen viger og gaar bort (Copenhagen, 1708);

Tvende skiønne aandelige Sange: den første: Sorrig og Glæde de vandrer tilhaabe . . . : Den anden: Naar du O Herre tugter mig . . . , by Engelbretsdatter and Thomas Kingo (Copenhagen, 1708).

Editions and Collections: *Samlede skrifter,* 2 volumes, edited by Kristen Valkner (Oslo: Aschehoug, 1955, 1956);

Tekster i utvalg: salmer, rimbrev og leilighetsdikt, edited by Egil Pettersen and Elisabeth Aasen (Bergen: Eide, 1996).

Dorothe Engelbretsdatter (from a 1681 edition of Siælens Sang-Offer; *Norway National Archives)*

Dorothe Engelbretsdatter was considered a great poet by her contemporaries. The many editions, excerpts, and reprints of her texts and the inclusion of her hymns in religious books all attest to her work's being constantly read and used. In literary circles, Engelbretsdatter was praised and admired, as honorary poems by colleagues and well-known individuals also suggest. Engelbretsdatter's verse technique was elegant and intelligent; she used simple meters in her strophes, according to the contemporary rules for poetry in the vernacular, and her rhythms and rhymes show complete mastery of the newly discovered accent principles for Germanic languages.

Engelbretsdatter's themes were popular in the inspirational literature of the day. She did not exaggerate when she called herself "The first Female Poet in the Hereditary Monarchy's Lands." The high regard that Engelbretsdatter enjoyed in her own time was also underscored by her holding royal copyrights on her principal work and by her eventually paying no taxes.

Her success as a female writer led to admiration and criticism, both during her lifetime and afterward. Some of the criticism and her responses to it are reflected in her occasional secular poetry. Her hymns have remained popular with ordinary Norwegians into the twenty-first century. No fewer than forty-five different folk melodies have been linked to twenty-two of her texts, and Magnus Brostrup Landstad's hymnal, *Kirke-salmebog efter offentlig Foranstaltning samlet og udarbeidet ved M. B. Landstad* (1869, Common Hymns of the Church, Collected and Edited by M. B. Landstad) included four

Frontispiece and title page for an edition of Engelbretsdatter's principal work (The Song-Offer of the Soul), originally published in 1678 (J. W. Cappelen Auction Catalogue 45, 14 December 2006)

of her hymns, while *Norsk Salmebok* (1985, Norwegian Hymns) includes two of them.

Engelbretsdatter was born 16 January 1634 in Bergen. She was the daughter of the rector, later parish priest of Bergen Cathedral, Engelbret Jørgenssønn, and Anna Wrangel, daughter of the civil legal magistrate, Hans Wrangel. Engelbretsdatter grew up in what was then the largest and most international city in Norway, within an upper-class milieu well versed in theoretical knowledge; one can assume that the setting for her early years provided opportunities in many areas, even though she received no formal education. As a child Engelbretsdatter spent nearly three years in Copenhagen, the scene of an even richer literary life. She enjoyed her associations with the Norwegian poet Petter Dass and the Danish writer Thomas Kingo.

In 1652 Engelbretsdatter married co-rector and chaplain, later parish priest, Ambrosius Hardenbeck. Hardenbeck was the son of a German organist in Bergen, and through him Engelbretsdatter came into contact with the German theological and musical tradition in Bergen. She had nine children, seven of whom preceded her in death, even before she had completed her first work. Of her two surviving sons, one fell in war against the Turks and the other vanished. Engelbretsdatter's first work, *Siælens Sang-Offer* (The Song-Offer of the Soul), appeared in 1678. Her husband died in 1683. Her life as a widow was difficult. She wrote her second work, *Taare-Offer* (1685, Offering of Tears), after becoming a widow. After her year in mourning, she went to Copenhagen to find a publisher for her second work and to receive recognition as a great poet. At the end of this journey she returned to Bergen, where she lived the rest of her life, at times under difficult and trying circumstances. She lost her house in a fire in 1702; after many appeals to the king, she managed to secure a new house only four years before her death. Engelbretsdatter died in Bergen on 19 February 1716.

Engelbretsdatter's poetry was securely traditional, written according to a Christian rhetorical tradition with roots in antiquity and the first centuries of the Christian era. The purpose of her poetry was to teach, challenge, comfort, and to offer thanks and praises to God. Originality was not a goal of her writing. However, while she used traditional literary ideals and subjects, she also reformulated them in her own manner, creating her own poetry built on a foundation of tradition for inspirational purposes. The unusual quality of Engelbretsdatter's work resided in her manner of using and restyling traditional materials. She also pioneered writing in the vernacular, which, for her, was Danish with occasional Norwegian words and expressions. She helped develop and refine written Dano-Norwegian until it became a living literary language for a broad spectrum of the public.

Engelbretsdatter's poetry belongs to the category of inspirational literature–works used in religious services, worship in the home and private settings, burials, and instruction in Christianity. Her hymns were seldom read or sung in isolation; they were part of Bible reading, liturgies, sermons, religious texts, and other songs. The details known of her life, the books she left, and her poems indicate that she belonged to Reform Orthodoxy. She was clearly influenced by German and English religious writings, particularly religious sermons by writers such as Lewis Bayly, Heinrich Müller, Valentin Wudrian, and Johan Arndt. Some of the texts in *Siælens Sang-Offer* can be characterized as verse translations of excerpts of Bayly's *Praxis pietatis* (1611, The Practice of Piety). Traces of medieval mysticism are also found in her poetry, with special emphasis on the mystique concerned with the Passion and the Bride; however, Engelbretsdatter followed acceptable Lutheran practice in using this mysticism.

Siælens Sang-Offer includes several genres of hymns. *Perikopesalmene* (pericopes) are songs written to Bible texts and used for Christian holy days: Christmas, New Year's, Easter, Ascension, and Whitsuntide. Typical for Engelbretsdatter's treatment of the Bible texts was to use them for sources of meditation and reflection rather than for paraphrase. She entered the world she found in the texts, or she formed her song as a response to a biblical text and the pictures she created from the text. Engelbretsdatter let the religious congregation meet the biblical Christ, and she designed the message and teaching on Christ from that basis. To the congregation she left the task of responding with praise and thanks, prayer, queries, and confessions. She expressed a personal dedication to the work of salvation, and her own feelings and experiences played an important role in such work, as did the feelings and experiences of others. The images of meditation that she created provided opportunities for highly personal, emotional prayers, addresses, praise, and thanksgiving.

Engelbretsdatter's interest in meditation, salvation, and personal connection to God was reflected in her style. Her language, rhetoric, character portrayals, and images built bridges over time and space and between individuals; readers and singers became participants in what was happening in the Biblical texts. At the same time, she found inspiration in texts on faith and learning, and she argued for central Lutheran doctrine in a clear, lively style:

> Een Krybbe var hans Vugge,
> Hand lader sig ey rugge,
>   Endog hand var Guds Søn,
> Saa Verdens stolte facter,
> Aldelis hand foracter,
>   Om de end siunis skiøn.
> . . . .
> Du Jesu vilde stige,
> Her ned til Jorderige,
>   I saadan ussel Stand,
> At hielpe os aff vaade,
> Ved din bondløse Naade,
>   Som voris Frelser Mand.
>
> (A Manger was his Cradle,
> He was not rocked into sweet slumber,
>   Although he was the Son of God,
> All the proud Glories of the World,
> He scorned in full measure,
>   Although they were thought beautiful.
> . . . .
> You, Jesus, wanted to come,
> Down here to Earth,
>   In such a humble Condition,
> To help us when we're in harm's way,
> By your boundless Mercy,
>   As our Savior.)

Engelbretsdatter used images with strong inner warmth and rich nuances that lent a calm but deep intensity to feelings and expressions of faith. She looked inward, to the faith of believers and their emotional space, but her *Perikopesalmene* also belonged within the context of religious worship.

Engelbretsdatter's Good Friday hymn, "Jesu Christ hellige Pinis og Døds Salige Brug og Tilegnelse" (Jesus Christ's Holy Suffering and Death's Glorious Purpose and Dedication) is a typical hymn for the Passion and follows the pattern for such hymns and for the Passion celebration of the time. The title of the hymn already provides a clue to its purpose: Christ's suffering and its purpose are passion laden and internalized for the individual believer. With its meditative style and thirty-four stanzas, the hymn is intended for personal worship. The first two strophes are an introduction presenting the theme and providing for a first-person response from a believer as to why Jesus had to suffer. The answer is an expression in allegory borrowed from bridal mysticism that records the experience of Jesus Christ's suffering within the context of the individual soul, and it offers an ultimate guarantee of union between Jesus and the soul in eternal life:

> Jesus som af Kierlighed,
>   Fra sit høje Himmel-sæde,
>   I Fornedring vilde træde,
>   Og kom her saa usel ned,
>   Hand for vore Synder lider,
> Fattigdom og Verdens skam,
>   Mod alt saadant hand ey strider,
> Men er taalig som it Lam.
>
> Din forsmædelse, min Gud,
>   Og din ringe verslig ære
>   Til it Klenod vil jeg bære,
> Paa mit Hierte, som een Brud,
>   Om end Stolthed sig indsniger,
> Da har jeg dit Smycke paa,
>   Saa det Lyde skamfuld viger,
> Og sin fremgang ey kand faa.
>
> (Jesus who out of Love,
>   From his High Seat in Heaven
>   In Disgrace wanted to descend,
> And came down here in misery,
>   He suffered for our Sins,
> Poverty and the shame of the World,
>   Against all that he did not fight,
> But was meek as a Lamb.
>
> Your disgrace, my God,
>   And your poor worldly esteem
>   I will bear as a Treasure,
> On my Heart, as a Bride,
>   Even though Pride should creep in,
> I will still have your Jewel on,
>   So the Flaw will give way in shame,
> And will not go forth.)

The subsequent strophes of "Jesu Christ hellige Pinis og Døds Salige Bruge og Tilegnelse" are built in pairs: one strophe depicts a stage or event on Jesus' path of suffering, and the next strophe offers a first-person answer to that depiction. The answers all interpret the suffering of Jesus as a gift for the believer and as an example for followers; Jesus' suffering and death are atonement for sins and a sign of his grace and presence to believers as well as an indication of comfort and hope for eternal glory. The suffering and death of Christ are a mirror for believers to learn and experience what it will mean to follow Jesus after this life. The last two strophes of the hymn serve as a summary: the first is a triumphant summary of all Jesus had to experience, which is now past. Now is the poet's own time, when Jesus' glory impresses all in the congregation and demands thanks and praise from all Christians. The song of praise and promise to follow Jesus in passive suffering fills the entire final strophe:

> Jesu nu er Striden dempt,
>   Nu er Angsten offvervuden,
>   Nu er spaat og hug forsvunden,
> Nu er Torne Kronen glemt,
>   Nu er borte blodig Smerte,
> Nu er lægte dine Saar,
>   Nu er ledsked vel dit Hierte,
> Nu er Kaarsit dig ey svaar.
> . . . .
> Loffved være dig Guds Søn,
>   Som saa mandelig har kiemped,
>   Alle Fiender du ned demped,
> Og gick self for os i Bøn,
>   Verdens Jammer bør vi lide,
> Som er Timelig og læt,
>   Og for Paradisit stride,
> Til det sidste Aandedræt.
>
> (Jesus, now the Battle is won,
>   Now Fear is overcome,
>   Now scorn and blows have vanished,
> Now the Crown of Thorns is forgotten,
>   Now the bloody Pain is far away,
> Now your Wounds are healed,
>   Now your Heart is comforted,
> Now the Cross no longer burdens you.
>
> Praise to you, Son of God,
>   Who have fought so bravely,
>   All Enemies you have vanquished
> And have gone in Prayer on our behalf,
>   The Woes of the World we must suffer,
> Which are Timely and hard,
>   And for Paradise we must strive,
> To our last Breath.)

Many of Engelbretsdatter's hymns can be characterized as hymns of repentance. Repentance consists of recognition of sin, open acknowledgment of sin, penitence and prayers for forgiveness, belief in the grace and love of Jesus, and the absolute certainty of life everlasting and glorious for those who repent. These texts provide many powerful depictions of sin and the wages of God's wrath, of the penitent's experience of misdeeds and powerlessness before the forces of evil, and of the prayers necessary for forgiveness. Just as powerful and abundant are the expressions of joy, comfort, and love that Christ bestows on the penitent, and heavenly ecstasy is described with brilliant, ecstatic pictures and often with the allegories of bridal mysticism. Engelbretsdatter's sacramental hymns, among them "Gudelig beredelse til Herrens hellige Nadere" (Divine Prepara-

 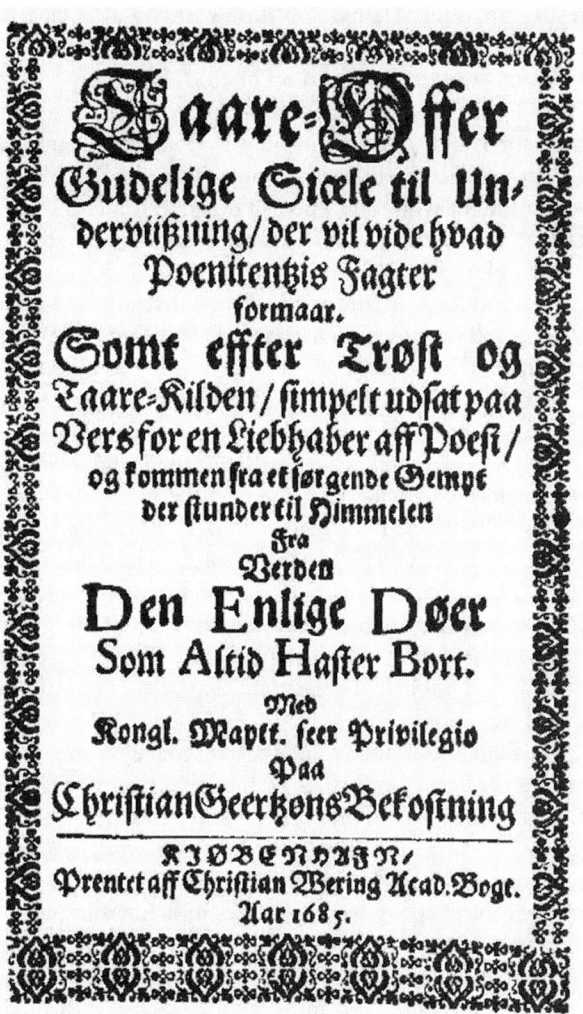

Frontispiece and title page for Engelbretsdatter's second book (Offering of Tears), a free rendering of a Danish translation of a German work (National Archives of Norway)

tion for the Communicants of the Lord) and "Tacksigelse effter Christi hellige Legoms og Blods Annammelse" (Thanksgiving after the Partaking of the Holy Body and Blood of Christ), can also be considered hymns of repentance, with a definite nod to the elements of mysticism connected to the Passion.

Much of Engelbretsdatter's verse is a form of *ars moriendi* (art of dying) poetry, concerned with living and dying in a way that can be termed beatified. A keynote for many of Engelbretsdatter's texts is that life always has death within it, that everything is transient. But she also expresses a belief in the good, simple life in eternity. The duty of everyone was to live in such a way as to earn participation in life everlasting. This kind of poetry connects Engelbretsdatter to a broad tradition with roots in the literature of solace in Antiquity and with medieval art and literature. Engelbretsdatter shared certain themes with this earlier literature: vanity of human life and the renunciation of the world, the inconstancy of *Fortuna* (fortune) and the world, memento mori, and Death and the Dance of Death. But just as important as these themes were the victory of Jesus over the world, sin, the devil, and death, and the prospect of eternal bliss awaiting those who die in Christ. The hymn "Om Verdens Vstadighet" (On the Inconstancy of the World) presents many of these themes and examples of them. The world is depicted as a woman (Lady World) with two faces and two sides: a smiling face and a face covered with tears; a good side and an evil one. No one can ever know which side Lady World will turn toward him or her, as she is hypocritical, deceitful, and unreliable. In the same hymn, there are other symbols of inconstancy and vanity: water drops, swallows, shadows, and weather. People have to know to turn away from this world of fleeting pleasure and pain and seek the eternal bliss that only

Jesus can offer. Hatred for this world is also clearly apparent in the hymn, "De som er til Guds Rige fød" (Those Born for the Kingdom of God).

Death is depicted in "En Sang om Døden" (A Song of Death), and many motifs from the Dance of Death are included. Death is personified as a skeleton and a knight who mows people down and seizes them, taking well-born and lowly, rich and poor, all being equal before Death. The power of Death or Vanity furnishes motifs in many texts. In the hymn "Tenck at Døden Liffvet ender" (Think that Death Ends Life), for example, Engelbretsdatter included many motifs connected to vanity and *memento mori*. She also used many biblical themes and exempla.

One of Engelbretsdatter's morning and evening hymns has won a special place with the passage of time and is still included in revised editions of *Norsk Salmebok*: namely, "Dagen viger og gaar bort" (The Day Ebbs and Fades Away). This hymn and all her other morning and evening hymns reflect the patterns of the genre at that time, but they also suggest the poet's private life and have a more personal tone than was common at that time.

Engelbretsdatter's poetic language and style reflect the ideals and rules of her time. Knowledge of the Bible and insight into biblical allegories are essential to interpreting and understanding her works. Many allusions to the Bible and its complex of involved allegories can cause the modern reader difficulties in understanding the texts. On the other hand, insight into the complex of allegories can open a wealth of images that are lovely, intense, and meaningful, especially through the allegorical images in religious hymns and similar texts inspired by the Bible.

Taare-Offer is a poetically free rendering of selections from *Taare- og Trøste-Kilde* (1677, Sources of Tears and Solace), a Danish translation by Norwegian priest Peder Møller of a German work. The German edition, *Thränen- und Trostquelle* (1675), was written by well-known German theologian Heinrich Müller. The work was built on the Bible text Luke 7:36–50, and Engelbretsdatter followed church tradition in calling the nameless woman at Jesus' feet Mary Magdalene and making her the example of a penitent Christian. As the title suggests, the work concerns tears of penitence. But tears come in many kinds: tears of regret for a sinful life, tears of prayer for forgiveness, and tears of love. Tears can express the loss of joy, or sorrow and the pain caused by a vile and hard life; they can also constitute an appeal to God to spare someone deserving punishment. Tears can stay the fires of God's wrath and persuade God to give comfort and blessing, and they can also signify love. Jesus' love for humans' souls can cause them to weep, and such "Tears of Love" can calm, bless, and drive all fear away. Tears will end, if not here, then in Heaven.

An expression used about Mary Magdalene in *Taare-Offer* is "sinful Bride." Engelbretsdatter depicts not only "The Sinner" but also "the Bride" in her work. The woman at Jesus' feet renounces herself as an offering to the Bridegroom of the Soul, Jesus, and the flame of his love releases her own passion. Engelbretsdatter depicted the life in Christ as a union in love, in this world and in the world everlasting. Belief and love are indivisible, and love is a sure sign of penitence. But those who love only with limits will be forgiven only in part.

The texts titled "Siste Sanger" (Final Songs) in Kristen Valkner's edition of Engelbretsdatter's poems (1955, 1956), repeat many of her earlier themes, but these texts also provide glimpses into her life as an aging widow. In "Efterfølgende Liig-Sang" (Eulogy), a song to be sung over her grave, she calls herself "Bergen's Deborah" and identifies with the singing women in the Bible whom she hoped to meet in Heaven. She also provided for an "Efftterfølgende Grafskrift" (Final Tribute) to be engraved on her casket and to record her work as a poet and express her longing for Heaven, "where my husband and children will embrace me."

Many of Engelbretsdatter's occasional poems have disappeared, and the texts remaining span forty years. Some of these poems are associated with Engelbretsdatter's stay in Copenhagen from 1684 to 1685. The occasional poems often have a different tone and style from her religious poems; they express worldly, often aggressive, thoughts and blunt assessments of her male detractors. Two illegal printings of her work and malevolent, unwarranted accusations of plagiarism incited her anger and efforts to defend herself.

Engelbretsdatter's tone is entirely different in the texts she wrote for her friends, poems such as "Tack til Madame Bladt for Bindebrevet" (Thanks to Madame Bladt for the Letter-Leaflet") and "Til Christian Geersøn" (To Christian Geersøn): these poems are personal, warm, and enhanced by wordplay and cheerful asides. By contrast, Engelbretsdatter's poems for the Royal Family, "Amindelse Over Den Stormægtigste og Højbaarne Monach Christian den Femte" (Eulogy for the Most Mighty and High-Born Monarch Christian the Fifth) and "Stormægtigste og Højbaarne Himmelgiven Monach, Friederich den Fierde" (Most Mighty and High-Born Heaven-Sent Monarch Friederich the Fourth), are markedly pompous, in accordance with the style of the time, while her written requests and acknowledgments to the king and queen, "Dend Stormægtigste, Høybaarne MONACH CHRISTIAN den Femte" (The Most Mighty, High-Born MONARCH CHRISTIAN the Fifth) and "Dend

Stormægtigste og Højbaarne DRONNING CHARLOTTA AMALIA" (The Most Mighty and High-Born QUEEN CHARLOTTA AMALIA), provide touching and interesting glimpses of her everyday life. Engelbretsdatter left few eulogies and memorial poems; however, her poem in memory of her husband, "Sidste Ære-Mindis smertelig Dict Over min allerkiæriste salig Hosbond Den Guds Mand Ambrosius Hardenbeck, Skreved med angst-bevrende Haand af Dorothe Engelbretz-Datter" (A Last Remembrance's Painful Poem for [my] most beloved and blessed Husband the Man of God Ambrosius Hardenbeck, Written with a Hand shaking with Fear by Dorothe Engelbretz-Datter), and the charming memorial for Kingo, with whom she would sing "triumph and a song of jubilee before the throne," "Simpell Quindelig Erindring over Den Vitt berømte Poet DOCTOR THOMAS KINGO" (Simple Womanly Memorial for the Widely Known Poet DOCTOR THOMAS KINGO), are notable. The poem Engelbretsdatter wrote for her neighbors in Bergen after the fire in 1686, "Dikt over brannen i Bergen: Medlidig Trøst til Jndvaanerne i Bergen over den Jammerlige Jldebrand som Aar 1686, d. 27 Sept. lagde en stor deel af Byen i Aske" (Poem on the Fire in Bergen: Heartfelt Solace for the Inhabitants of Bergen after the Horrific Fire which on the 27 September Left a Great Deal of Bergen in Ashes), follows the pattern for this genre, but at the same time it is marked by theological reflection, personal empathy, and feelings of solidarity.

Measured against criteria for good poetry that date from the Romantic era, Dorothe Engelbretsdatter's poetry has been disparaged by literary critics from the Romantic breakthrough until our own time; works on literary history from both Denmark and Norway suggest as much. Literary critics have especially found fault with her "overworked" and unappealing style, her melodramatic floods of tears and her sorrow-laden laments. Research based on criteria for good literature that predate the Romantic era and on interdisciplinary studies of all the texts that remain and all aspects of such texts will surely give a more complicated and positive picture of the first well-known woman writer of Norway.

Biography:

Laila Akslen, *Feminin barokk: Dorothe Engelbretsdatters liv og diktning* (Oslo: Universitetsforlaget, 1970).

References:

Laila Akslen, *Femfaldig festbarokk: norske perikopedikt til kyrkjelege høgtider* (Sofiemyr: L. Akslen, 2002);

Akslen, *Norsk barokk: Dorothe Engelbretsdatter og Petter Dass i retorisk tradisjon* (Oslo: Landslaget for norskundervisning / Cappelen akademisk Forlag, 1997);

Akslen, "Norwegische Kirchenlieder im 17. Jahrhundert im Kontext der deutsch-nordischen Erbauungsliteratur," in *Skandinavische Literaturen der frühen Neuzeit*, volume 3, edited by Jürg Glauser and Barbara Sabel (Tübingen: Francke, 2002), pp. 75–96;

Hubert Seelow, "'Ellers er ieg bar af Bøger,' Zur Editionsgeschichte von Dorothe Engelbretsdatters Siælens Sang-Offer," *Beiträge zur nordischen Philologie*, 2 (2002): 335–350;

Thomas Seiler, "'. . . med en Pen i Graad Poleret,' Weinen, Weiblichkeit, Schrift in der Dichtung Dorothe Engelbretsdatters," in *Skandinavische Literaturen der frühen Neuzeit*, volume 3, pp. 319–334;

Inger Vederhus, "'Saa foor han Melancholisk frem,' Sentrale biletkrinsar i salmar av Dorothe Engelbretsdatter," *Kirke og Kultur*, 1 (1995): 45–56.

Claus Fasting
(29 October 1746 – 25 December 1791)

Lanae H. Isaacson

BOOKS: *Harmonisang: verdners Liv og Aanders Glæde* (Bergen: Det musicalske Selskab, 1769);

Et musicalsk Hyrde-Stykke opført i anledning af Hans Kongelige Majestæt Kong Christian den Syvendes Fødsels Fest av Det musicalske Selskab i Bergen (Bergen: Det musicalske Selskab / H. Dedechen, 1771);

Hermione: et Sørgespil i fem Optog (Copenhagen: August Friedrich Stein, 1772);

Forsøg til originale Danske Fortællinger efter Hr. Fontaines Maade (Copenhagen: Nicolaus Møller, 1772);

Provinzialblade, 4 volumes (Bergen: Claus Fasting / H. Dedechen, 1778–1781);

Sørgekantate, til Erindring av Salig Hr. Justizraad og Rektor Boallh, opført af det Kongelige Harmoniske Akademie (Bergen: Det Kongelige Harmoniske Akademie, 1780);

Til Erindring af Høyædle Velbyrdige Frue Justitzraadinde Boallh, begravet i Bergen den 10de Junii 1785 (Bergen: Claus Fasting, 1785);

Provinzialsamlinger (Bergen: Claus Fasting, 1791);

Actierne, eller De Rige: et Lystspil (Bergen: Johan Dahl, 1797);

Udvalg af Claus Fastings forhen trykte og ytrykke Skrifter, med Bidrag til hans Biographie af L. Sagen (Bergen: Johan Dahl, 1837);

Samlede Skrifter, 3 volumes, edited by Sverre Flugsrud (Oslo: Gyldendal, 1963–1979);

"*Samdhed og retskaffenhed*": *Claus Fastings politie-actorat 1784–1791,* edited by Bjørn Kvalsvik Nicolaysen (Bergen: Senter for Europeisk Kulturstudier, 1996);

Claus Fastings fablar og aforismar, edited by Nicolaysen (Bergen: Nordisk Institutt/Universitetet i Bergen, 1998).

PLAY PRODUCTION: *Actierne, eller De Rige: et Lystspil,* Copenhagen, Det Kongelige Teater, 9 October 1788.

TRANSLATIONS: Salomon Gessner, *Evander og Alcimna: Hyrdestykke i tre Optog* (Copenhagen: August Friedrich Stein, 1767);

Claus Fasting (University of Bergen Library)

Christoph Martin, *Musarion, eller Gratiernes Philosophie: et Poem i tre Bøger* (Copenhagen: Gyldendal, 1776).

Claus Fasting of Bergen made his mark as the preeminent literary critic, essayist, historian, reviewer, and editor of the last decades of the eighteenth century. Fasting tried his hand at verse-drama but found his niche as an essayist and prose writer, adept at following and illuminating the literary and cultural trends of Bergen and beyond. Fasting was strongly influenced by the Dano-Norwegian dramatist Ludvig Holberg and the

French writer and philosopher Voltaire. As editor and principal writer of the collected essays, stories, poems, and reviews published annually as *Provinzialblade* (1778–1781, Provincial Leaves), Fasting entertained, educated, and offered a wider European world to the citizens, scholars, and schoolchildren of Bergen. Few writers and readers of his day knew European literary and cultural trends as well as Fasting.

The son of Bergen parish pastor Frederik Fasting and Gerhardine von Güllich, Fasting was born 29 October 1746. He received his earliest education from Ole Camstrup, a colleague of Holberg, and from the scholar J. S. Cammermeyer. Fasting's father was determined that his son follow in his footsteps and enter the ministry; with that goal in mind, Fasting studied from 1759 to 1761 with Jens Boalth and Fredrik C. H. Arentz at the Bergen Latin School. He finished a degree in philosophy in 1762, after only one year at the University of Copenhagen. His father continued to pressure him into studying for the ministry, and Fasting dutifully returned to Copenhagen and completed the required entrance examination in 1766. During his student years he wrote poems such as "Sørgetanker over Livet" (1766, Mournful Thoughts about Life), published in *Adresseavisen* in Copenhagen; "Pans Fest" (1768, Pan's Celebration); and *Harmonisang: verdners Liv og Aanders Glæde* (1769, Harmony Song: The Life of Worlds and the Joys of Souls). Fasting also served as editor for several student literary journals, among them *Kritisk Journal* (Critical Journal) in 1773 and *Kritisk Tilskuer* (Critical Observer), in 1775–1776.

In 1768 Fasting returned to Bergen to comply with his father's demand that he enter the ministry, but he abandoned theology permanently on the death of his father in 1769. In 1770 he returned to Copenhagen, where he joined and became a leader of Det Norske Selskab (The Norwegian Society). His quick wit, gift for writing epigrams, solid knowledge of contemporary and older European literature, and fine talent for criticism secured him a leading role in the Copenhagen intellectual community.

Fasting's short poems or epigrams focus on the failures and foibles as well as the gifts and glories of ordinary people. Fasting could write poetic lines and thoughts with the best. He does not stint in praising an entirely unknown Elise, a paragon of beauty and grace immortalized in one of his poems: "Dyd, Skjønhed og Forstand, Alt med Elise dør; / Og Gratierne strax blev tre igjen, som før" (Honor, Beauty and Wisdom, All dies with Elise; / And the Graces become three once again, just as before).

Fasting could also use irony and biting wit to expose those who claimed talents and gifts they did not possess. He also displayed a fierce anticlericalism akin to that of his hero Voltaire; this bias may have been a reaction to the pressure he had felt to enter the ministry and please his father. In the epigram "Over et Syngespil, hvortil Poesien var en Fruetimmer" (On a Song-Play, with Poetry being a Woman), Fasting shows his talent for cutting to the core:

> *Hun* skrev et Syngespil;
> *Han* satte Musikken til;
> Nu trættes begge om, at det ei lykkes vil.
> Hun dømmer hans Musik, han dømmer Texten slet;
> Jeg dømmer: De har begge Ret.
>
> (*She* wrote a Song-Play;
> *He* set it to Music;
> Now they're both arguing because it won't work.
> She blames his Music, he calls the Text poor;
> I'll be the Judge: They're both right.)

Fasting's epigrams also touch on writers who were making their mark in Copenhagen such as the Dano-Norwegian dramatist J. H. Wessel, author of *Kierkighed uden Strømper* (1772, Love without Stockings), for whom he wrote a short, poignant eulogy: "Sku Wessels Grav og Glædens Tempel øde! / Sku Latter selv i Graad, fordi dens Fader døde!" (Behold Wessel's Grave and the Ruins of the Temple of Mirth! / Behold Laughter itself in Tears, because its Father is Dead!).

In addition to epigrams, Fasting wrote drinking and toasting songs that express the joie de vivre that Fasting and his comrades enjoyed in Copenhagen and Bergen. In "Kom Brødre! Kom! Nu vil vi til at drikke! (Come Brothers! Come! Now We're ready to Drink!), one of his best-known poems, he touches on a certain carefree nonchalance and devil-may-care spirit in the face of the brevity of life:

> Kom Brødre! Kom! Nu vil vi til at drikke!
> Lad ingen Sorg forstyrre denne Fest!
> I Bacchi Navn vi Fanerne udstikke;
> den største Helt er den, der tørster meest.
>
> (Come Brothers! Come! Now We're ready to Drink!
> Let no Sorrow disturb this Celebration!
> In the Name of Bacchus, We'll unfurl the Banners,
> The Greatest Hero is He who is most Thirsty.)

In 1772, in an effort to increase the repertoire of Danish plays, Det Kongelige Teater (The Royal Theatre) Copenhagen proposed a competition for the best original tragedy. Fasting entered *Hermione,* based on Jean Racine's tragedy *Andromaque* (1667). While Fasting's play matched Johan Nordahl Brun's winning entry, *Zarine* (1772), it fell far short in terms of composition and narrative.

Disappointed by the failure of *Hermione,* Fasting did not give up but wrote a second play, *Actierne, eller De Rige* (performed 1788, published 1797, Financiers; or, The Wealthy). Highly critical of "profitørene under den nordamerikanske frihetskrig" (profiteers during the North American War of Independence), *Actierne* made it as far as performance at Det Kongelige Teater in 1788, but had little long-term success.

In 1777 Fasting returned to Bergen, where he remained for the rest of his life. He applied for the position of overseer of fisheries but was rejected. He took on a private student, Alette Sophie Rohde, who was thirteen. Teacher and student fell in love, but Henrica Rohde, who competed with her daughter for Fasting's affections, took Alette away from Bergen and painted Fasting as a dangerous seducer. Fasting never recovered from the affair; he remained unmarried, and the tragedy may have led to his early death.

In 1781 Fasting secured the position of commissioner of police; in that capacity he proved himself to be rather strict and severe with the more affluent members of Bergen high society but tolerant and understanding of those who struggled to make ends meet, as he often did himself. In 1778 he began publishing *Provinzialblade,* a far-ranging collection of essays, reviews, cultural and literary studies, reports on current events, and social commentary; he wrote most of the contributions to the collection, which grew to four annual volumes.

The essays, reviews, and commentaries in *Provinzialblade* were read widely. They delved into the mysteries of science and discussed the arts and belles lettres in Europe. They reveal competence and dedication to scholarly research and enthusiasm for teaching and learning and demonstrate Fasting's intellectual links to the wider European world of Holberg, Nicolas Boileau-Despreaux, Alexander Pope, and–first and foremost–Voltaire. *Provinzialblade* served as a model for lucid, refined prose, addressing the same sort of educated readers as Fasting's models, *The Spectator* in England and *Sneedorffs Patriotiske Tilskuer* (Sneedorff's Patriotic Observer) in Denmark. *Provinzialblade* included commentaries on noteworthy and newsworthy events, from the American War of Independence to scientific discoveries concerning electricity and natural occurrences such as volcanic eruptions and earthquakes; tributes and elegies to poets and philosophers; reviews of new works of poetry and drama; poems and one-act plays by the editor; travelogues; tales of mystery, miracles, and suspense; and proposals for civic improvements and the founding of such institutions as a conservatory for the arts and a college of commerce in Bergen. Fasting attacks public officials whose ethical and moral standards fall short of the mark. *Provinzialblade* also published letters to the editor and responses. The essay "Om Adskillige Nationers Musik" (On the Music of Diverse Nations) surveys the invention and use of musical instruments, the songs and dances, and the performance norms in the "exotic locales" of Egypt, India, Mongolia, the Philippines, and Turkey. Fasting concludes that music is in a primitive stage of development in lands beyond Europe in which clerics play a large role in the daily lives of the citizenry:

> Tyrkernes Musik er endnu i sin Barndom, ligesom alle deres Videnskaber. Man kan endog tvivle om den nogen Tid kommer at opnaae nogen Grad av Fuldkommenhed. Deres Præster giøre sig al Flid for at giøre den forhadt for den almindelige Mand, og de klogere blant Nationen, som ikke troe paa Præster, ere saa faae, at deres Antal er ikke tilstrækkeligt at opveye Mængden. I Konstantinopel har man vel en Art av Luth med 3 Strenge, som man spiller med Færdighed, endskiønt uden Smag og Takt, men Fløyter synes for Resten at være det eneste Instrument, som Trykernes Øren endnu, med Præsternes Tilladelse, tør lade sig fornøye ved.
>
> (The music of the Turks is still in its infancy, just like all their sciences. We may doubt whether it will ever reach any degree of perfection. The priests do everything in their power to make music detestable to the average man, and the wiser people of the nation, those who don't believe the priests, are so few that their numbers are insufficient to raise the majority. In Constantinople they have a kind of lute with three strings that some play with dexterity but without taste or tact, but other than that flutes seem to be the only instrument that the ears of the Turks dare allow themselves to appreciate, with the permission of the priests, of course.)

There is no particular organization in *Provinzialblade*: "Om Adskillige Nationers Musik" is sandwiched between an account of an individual whose life includes one horrific, harrowing calamity after another, "Et Eksempel paa et besynderligt Forsyn" (An Example of a Curious Turn of Fate), and a lengthy discourse on commerce, trade, and industry in Holland. "Et Eksempel paa et besynderligt Forsyn" ends with Fasting's assurance that the story is "en uforfalsket Beretning" (an unfalsified account)–an attempt to counter the tale's obvious improbability.

In 1783 Fasting became vice mayor of Bergen; he later secured the position of mayor and, with the post, freedom from financial worries. In 1791 he began a new annual, *Provinzialsamlinger* (Provincial Collections), which followed the form and format of the highly acclaimed and popular *Provinzialblade*. He published only one volume before his death on 25 December 1791. Fasting left his small but select library to the

Nykirkens Fattigskole (New Church School for the Poor) in Bergen for the use of the public.

Despite his own slight poetic and dramatic gifts, Claus Fasting secured a firm niche in Norwegian literary history as an essayist and editor with extraordinary expertise, insight, acumen, and impeccable taste. Fasting contributed much to the cultural and musical life of Bergen as an active member of Det musicalske Selskab/Det Kongelige Harmoniske Akademie, as a pianist and music teacher and as a composer. He supported many educational endeavors including a conservatory of the arts, a college of commerce and trade, and an institute for drawing and painting connected to Det Kongelige Harmoniske Akademie. Fasting's *Provinzialblade* and *Provinzialsamlinger* signaled refinements of Norwegian prose and provided new standards for literary criticism and cultural commentary in eighteenth-century Norway.

Bibliographies:

Fortegnelse over afgl. Raadmand Claus F. Fastings efterladte og af ham til offentlig Brug testamenterede Bogsamling (Bergen: Johan Dahl, 1792);

Index Librorum Bibliothecae Fastingianæ (Bergen: Johan Dahl, 1847).

Biographies:

Johan Nordahl Brun, *Fastings Æreminde: i en Tale holden den 5te Januarii 1792 paa De Frievillige Hamonisters Academie af J.N. Brun og besvaret paa Stedet af S. T. Hr. Stiftbefalingsmand og Kammerherre von Hauch* (Bergen: Johan Dahl, 1792);

L. Sagen, *Udvalg af Claus Fastings forhen trykte og utrykte Skrifter, med Bidrag til Hans Biographie af L. Sagen* (Bergen: Johan Dahl, 1837);

R. Schreiner, ed., *Syv norske digtere fra forrige aarhundrede: Christian Braunman Tullin; Claus Fasting* (Christiania: Haffner & Hille, 1897).

References:

Leiv Amundsen, *Norskhet i sproget hos Claus Fasting* (Christiania, 1921);

Aage Skavlan, *Claus Fasting: til Bergens historie* (Bergen: Grieg / Bergensposten, 1877).

Arne Garborg
(25 January 1851 – 14 January 1924)

Jan Sjåvik
University of Washington

BOOKS: *Smaa-Stubber,* as Alf Buestreng (Tvedestrand, Norway: Lærer-standens avis, 1873);

Den ny-norske Sprog- og Nationalitetsbevægelse (Christiania: Cammermeyer, 1877);

Ein Fritenkjar (Christiania: Cammermeyer, 1881);

Bondestudentar (Bergen: Nygaard, 1883);

Forteljingar og Sogur (Christiania: O. Huseby & O. Olsen, 1884)–includes "Døy," translated by James McFarlane as "Dying," in *Slaves of Love and Other Norwegian Short Stories,* edited by McFarlane and Janet Garton (New York: Oxford University Press, 1982), pp. 22–29; and "Ungdom," translated by Leslie Ann Grove as "Youth," in *Short Stories from Norway 1850–1900,* edited by Henning K. Sehmsdorf, WITS: Wisconsin Introductions to Scandinavia II, no. 3 (Madison: Department of Scandinavian Studies, University of Wisconsin-Madison, 1986), pp. 27–41;

Mannfolk (Bergen: Nygaard, 1886);

Uforsonlige: Skuespil I Fire Akter (Copenhagen: Philipsen, 1888);

Hjaa ho Mor (Bergen: Mons Litleré, 1890);

Kolbotnbrev og andre Skildringar (Bergen: Mons Litleré, 1890);

Trætte Mænd (Christiania: Aschehoug, 1891); translated by Sverre Lyngstad as *Weary Men* (Evanston, Ill.: Northwestern University Press, 1999);

Fred (Bergen: Mons Litleré, 1892); translated by Philips Dean Carleton as *Peace* (New York: Norton, 1929);

Fra det mørke Fastland (Christiania: Olaf Norli, 1893);

Jonas Lie (Christiania: Aschehoug, 1893);

Haugtussa (Christiania: Aschehoug, 1895);

Læraren (Christiania: Aschehoug, 1896);

Den burtkomne Faderen (Christiania: Aschehoug, 1899); translated by Mabel Johnson Leland as *The Lost Father* (Boston: Stratford, 1920);

I Helheim (Christiania: Aschehoug, 1901);

Fjell-luft og andre smaastykke (Christiania: Aschehoug, 1903);

Knudahei-brev (Christiania: Aschehoug, 1904);

From the frontispiece for Erik Lie, Arne Garborg: en livsskildring, *1914; Robarts Library, University of Toronto*

Jesus Messias (Christiania: Aschehoug, 1906);

Den burtkomne Messias (Christiania: Aschehoug, 1907);

Heimkomin Son (Christiania: Aschehoug, 1908);

Politik (Christiania: Aschehoug, 1919);

Straumdrag (Christiania: Aschehoug, 1920);

Dagbok 1905–1923, 6 volumes, edited by Hulda Garborg (Christiania: Aschehoug, 1924–1927);

Tankar og utsyn: Artiklar, 2 volumes, edited by Johannes A. Dale and Rolv Thesen (Oslo: Aschehoug, 1950).

Editions and Collections: *Skriftir i Samling,* 7 volumes (Christiania: Aschehoug, 1908–1909);

Skriftir i Samling: Jubilæumsutgave, 7 volumes (Christiania: Aschehoug, 1921–1922);

Skriftir i Samling, 8 volumes (Oslo: Aschehoug, 1944);

Skriftir i Samling, 8 volumes (Oslo: Aschehoug, 1951);

Verk, 12 volumes (Oslo: Aschehoug, 1980);

Skrifter i Samling, 12 volumes (Oslo: Aschehoug, 2001);

Bondestudentar (Bryne: Time Kommune, 2007);

Fred (Oslo: Aschehoug, 2007);

Haugtussa (Bergen: Vigmostad & Bjerke, 2008).

TRANSLATIONS: Homer, *Odyssevskvædet* (Christiania: Aschehoug, 1918);

Ludvig Holberg, *Jeppe paa Berget* (Christiania: Aschehoug, 1920);

Valmiki, *Rama-kvædet* (Christiania: Aschehoug, 1922).

A novelist, poet, essayist, journalist, and dramatist, Arne Garborg is one of Norway's best-known writers. Active mostly in the 1880s and 1890s, he was the contemporary of the so-called four great writers in Norwegian literature—Bjørnstjerne Bjørnson, Henrik Ibsen, Alexander Kielland, and Jonas Lie—and is sometimes referred to as "den femte store," or Norway's fifth great author. While his reputation falls far short of that of the dramatist Ibsen, his significance is now considered equal to or greater than that of the other three. During his lifetime he was very well known both in the other Scandinavian countries and Germany, but he did not make much of an impact in the English-speaking world even though two of his novels were translated in the 1920s. His most significant novel, *Trætte Mænd* (1891), was published in translation as *Weary Men* in 1999, and American scholars have made important contributions to Garborg criticism since the 1970s.

Some readers think of Garborg primarily as the author of the beautiful nature poetry of *Haugtussa* (1895, The Hill Maiden) and its continuation, *I Helheim* (1901, In the Realm of Hell). Others associate him with a series of four realistic/naturalistic novels centered on life in Norway's capital city of Christiania in the 1870s and 1880s, *Bondestudentar* (1883, Peasant Students), *Mannfolk* (1886, Menfolk), *Hjaa ho Mor* (1890, Living With Mama), and *Trætte Mænd*. Others remember the penetrating analysis of religion found in the novel *Fred* (1892; translated as *Peace*, 1929), and the play *Læraren* (1896, The Teacher), as well as the novels *Den burtkomne Faderen* (1899; translated as *The Lost Father*, 1920) and *Heimkomin Son* (1908, The Returned Son). Many people know Garborg primarily as a political radical and crusader for Nynorsk (New Norwegian)—a form of Norwegian, established in the second half of the nineteenth century, that emphasized the rural dialects in opposition to the Danish-inspired speech of the major cities—and recall the masterful intellect displayed by his essays and his incisive political commentary. Garborg is thus notable for both the breadth and the depth of his contribution to Norwegian letters.

Born on 25 January 1851 into a rural family on the farm Garborg in Time Parish, at Jæren, a district to the south of the city of Stavanger, Garborg was the oldest son of Eivind Aadneson and Ane Oline, née Jonsdatter, Garborg. His earliest childhood years were happy ones, but when he was eight, his father turned toward a pietistic and very strict form of Christianity that emphasized man's sinful nature and the need to keep the devil at bay through hard work and sacrifice. The family also spent much time in family devotionals that focused on the reading of both Scripture and orthodox religious books, but Arne was able to read secular literature only on the sly. Both intellectually gifted and drawn toward religion, young Garborg wrote hymns and dreamed of becoming a writer. He also struggled with his own conversion to Christianity but was unable to share his father's beliefs and considered himself guilty of hypocrisy when submitting to confirmation in Norway's Evangelical Lutheran State Church at the age of fifteen.

Confirmation was a necessary rite of passage, however, and especially so because Garborg sought admission to a brief training program for teachers conducted by the sexton of Time Parish, after which—and still only fifteen years old—he got a job as a schoolmaster. In 1868 he was admitted to the Normal School at Holt near the town of Tvedestrand; he graduated in 1870. That same year his father committed suicide. The result of severe depression, of which his religious obsessions were but one of several symptoms, the father's suicide was perhaps also motivated by his son's rejection of his allodial rights to the family farm. Garborg believed that it was, at any rate, and carried lifelong feelings of guilt concerning the matter. Some of that guilt may have stemmed from emotional problems similar to those of his father.

After a year of teaching in the area of Søndeled, near the town of Kragerø, Garborg quit his career as a teacher and focused his attention on a paper called *Lærerstandens Avis* (News of the Teaching Profession) that he published between 1871 and 1873. In 1872 he also assumed the editorship of the paper *Tvedestrandsposten* (The Tvedestrand Post). He gave up his work on both newspapers to move to Christiania (now

Oslo), where he attended a school run by the scholar Henrik Anton Sehjø Heltberg to prepare himself for admission to the university. In 1875 he received superb marks both on his matriculation certificate and on the so-called second examination, a battery of general education tests required before admission to study in the major field. Rather than continuing his studies, however, Garborg accepted employment with the newspaper *Aftenbladet* (The Evening Post) in January 1876.

Garborg had reviewed Ibsen's play *Kejser og Galilæer* (1873; translated as *The Emperor and the Galilean,* 1876) soon after it was published. Influenced by the writings of the Danish philosopher Søren Kierkegaard, he also published a series of articles about Ibsen's play *Peer Gynt* (1867; translated 1892), which was being performed at the Christiania Theater in 1876. Much in the spirit of Kierkegaard, he regarded it as an anti-Romantic work. The following year he published *Den ny-norske Sprog- og Nationalitetsbevægelse* (1877, The New Norwegian Movement for Language and Nation), in which he argued that Norwegian cultural development would be well served if both writers and other citizens were to adopt the use of Nynorsk, a written form of Norwegian constructed by Ivar Aasen on the basis of Norwegian dialects, that differed considerably from the Danish-influenced written Norwegian of most educated Norwegians. Also in 1877 Garborg started the paper *Fedraheimen* (Home of the Fathers), which was published in Nynorsk and had as its purpose the promotion of national sovereignty. Most of Garborg's journalism and essays were first published in this newspaper.

During the 1870s Garborg also managed to shed what still remained of the religious orthodoxy and general conservatism with which he had been raised. An important statement of his recently broadened outlook was found in his article "Um Taalsemd i Tru og Meiningar" (About Tolerance in Faith and Opinion), which was serialized in *Fedraheimen* in July 1878. Garborg later attacked such advocates of orthodoxy as pastor Johan Christian Heuch, the author of *Vantroens Væsen* (1883, The Essence of Infidelity). His radicalism became increasingly evident in the short novel *Ein Fritenkjar* (A Freethinker), which was serialized in *Fedraheimen* in 1878 and published in book form three years later.

Ein Fritenkjar is the story of Eystein Hauk, a theologian who has come to doubt some of the tenets of State Church Lutheranism. When sharing his qualms about religion with other theologians, however, he does not receive the pastoral care that he had hoped for but is instead vilified and treated with dishonesty and malice. Rather than helping Hauk work through his concerns so as to aid him in arriving at a religious position characterized by honesty and integrity, his "brethren" label him a freethinker and assassinate his character in order to render him harmless in the struggle between traditionalism and modernity. His former friends and fellow believers avoid responsibility for their actions by claiming that his life has been ruined in consequence of God's chastening hand rather than because of their own evil acts. The story ends as Hauk's son, who has become an orthodox minister, condemns his father in a sermon at Hauk's funeral. Garborg wanted to show that the enmity of the church reaches beyond death and the grave.

Ein Fritenkjar is clearly an apprentice piece. The characters are portrayed with little nuance, and the author's didacticism mars the story line. Garborg's ethical seriousness was admirable, however, and his crusade against hypocrisy, guile, and dissimulation is reminiscent of Kierkegaard. There can be little doubt that Garborg was still largely a pamphleteer rather than a fully fledged literary artist, though, and this impression is confirmed by such short stories from the late 1870s as "Av Laak Ætt" (1878, From a Bad Family), "Hemn" (1878, Vengeance), and "Seld til den Vonde" (1879, Sold to the Evil One), all of which were first published in *Fedraheimen.*

Garborg's finest early literary effort is the short story "Stordaad" (1878, A Great Deed), which is set in Christiania and tells about two young children who try to earn a little money singing and playing a hand organ in the streets. Garborg's sympathy with the poor is conveyed through the response of a student who feels so sorry for the two children that he gives them his last coin. The great deed of the story's title, however, is not the student's gesture but an act of self-denial on the part of the two children. Rather than getting hot meals for themselves, they bring the coin home to their mother, who is sick in bed.

The depiction of urban poverty in "Stordaad" points toward a significant theme in Garborg's breakthrough as a writer, the novel *Bondestudentar*. Its protagonist, Daniel Braut, is the young son of a farmer from Garborg's home district of Jæren, who, motivated by his dislike for the hard physical labor of the farm, regards a university education as his ticket to a life of honor and ease. A quick study, Daniel cobbles together a college-prep education by attending a local course for teachers, the Latin School in neighboring Stavanger, and finally Heltberg's school in Christiania, the same crammer that Garborg had attended. Throughout this process Daniel is exposed to many of the educational and political ideologies present in contemporary Norwegian life, ranging from the enthusiastic worship of ancient Scandinavia advocated by

Nikolaj Frederik Severin Gruntvig to the pragmatic approach to exam preparation adhered to by Heltberg, who is portrayed as a gifted teacher. Garborg offers a cross section of Norwegian society at the time, providing a realistic portrait of social and economic conditions in Norway.

As was pointed out by the Danish critic Georg Brandes, *Bondestudentar* can be read largely as a story about the societal consequences of Norway's poverty. Set in the 1860s, it shows how Norwegian farmers were struggling to free themselves from both economic and social domination by the middle class, which consisted primarily of government officials, merchants, and large landowners. An intellectually gifted young man, Daniel Braut is seen by others as someone who may develop into a leader in this struggle, but instead he ends up joining the middle class through marriage to one of its daughters, a woman he does not love.

Before getting to this point, however, Daniel's high expectations have been significantly deflated. He had been attracted to the idea of intellectual labor—his ambition is to become a minister in the Norwegian State Church—by his basic indolence, and he approaches his university education with a distinct lack of enthusiasm. Encouraged or even required to think for himself in philosophical and political matters, he finds welcome relief in the study of theology, the dogmatism of which frees him from the obligation to reason independently. His attachment to religious authoritarianism is confirmed through a conversion experience during a brief period of illness.

One of Daniel's most serious problems is that his financial situation is utterly precarious. His father has borrowed money to help him get an education, thus bringing honor to the family, but he soon dies. Some reasonably well-to-do individuals lend him money directly, but it is not enough for him to live on. After his conversion he goes to the well-known pietistic head of a home for students, a man nicknamed Pater Omnipotens, who helps him financially. His finances are not secure, however, until he becomes a tutor in the home of a large landowner with a daughter named Hanna, who is well past her prime and in need of a husband.

By agreeing to marry Hanna, Daniel finally secures the funds that allow him to live in a manner that he considers suitable for a person in his position. Daniel's engagement marks his successful incorporation into the middle class, but it also entails a betrayal of both his own rural origins and the trust of many of those who have helped him financially and educationally. Instead of being in the process of becoming a liberal friend to Norway's rural population, Daniel is well

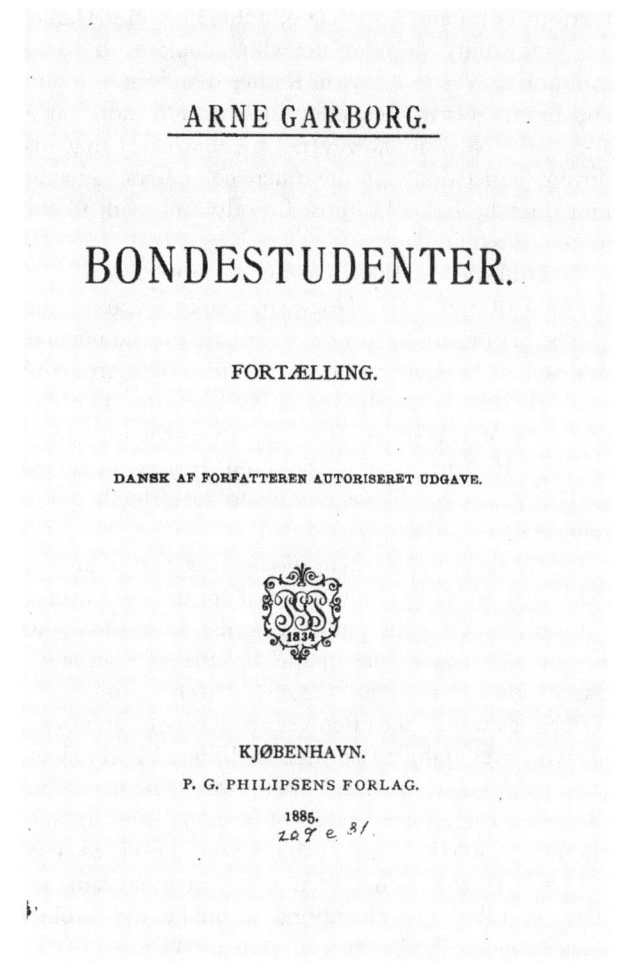

Title page for an edition of Garborg's novel (Peasant Students), originally published in 1883, about a farm boy who rises to the middle class (Oxford University Libraries)

on his way to turning into one of its conservatively minded exploiters.

In addition to its depiction of Daniel Braut's personal tragedy as a parable of the broken hopes held by Norway's progressives at the time, *Bondestudentar* also offers vivid portraits of some of the leading figures in Norwegian cultural life in the 1860s. One of these is the character Dølen, modeled on the Norwegian poet and journalist Aasmund Olafsson Vinje, whose use of irony parallels Garborg's own ironic portrayal of Daniel. Another is Professor Darre, who in real life was the Hegelian professor of philosophy Marcus Jacob Monrad; in *Bondestudentar* he is the proponent of an extreme form of idealism that Daniel wishes to emulate but that Garborg shows to be untenable because Darre is fundamentally out of touch with the realities of his students' lives. A third such character is Fram, modeled on the radical and anticlerical Olaus

Fjørtoft. Fram and his circle of adherents offer Daniel an opportunity to associate with people with backgrounds similar to his own. Rather than joining Fram and his friends in their efforts to create a more open society in Norway, however, Daniel worries that his flirting association with them may come back to haunt him once he has sold himself, body and soul, to the middle class.

Published in 1883, *Bondestudentar* depicts part of the background for the Norwegian culture wars of the 1880s. Set mostly in Norway's capital city, the novel is referred to by some critics as the first of a group of four Christiania novels written by Garborg. The second novel in this series, *Mannfolk,* covers the time from autumn 1879 to autumn 1880 and depicts the social and economic conditions that led to the struggle of the mid 1880s.

As first presented in *Bondestudentar* but further discussed in *Mannfolk,* the cultural conflict was primarily one between the public officials, merchants, and landowners, who later made up the Conservative Party (Høire), and the somewhat more progressive farmers as well as the often very progressive intellectuals who eventually constituted the Liberal Party (Venstre). The main political issue was whether King Oscar II, the joint monarch of Sweden and Norway, should be able to form a cabinet whose policies were contrary to the wishes of the Storting (Parliament). The liberals were attempting to make the cabinet responsible to the Parliament, thus establishing parliamentarism as a fundamental aspect of the Norwegian system of government. Although the Liberal Party had the votes to pass the reform measure, King Oscar II repeatedly vetoed their bill. A key vote in 1880 was also vetoed, and the 1882 election became a referendum on whether this veto was legal. The Liberal Party impeached the conservative cabinet in 1884, an event that is generally acknowledged as the beginning of parliamentarism in the Norwegian political system.

Against this background of political conflict, Norwegian society was also struggling with how to redefine the relationship between men and women—a conflict that pitted the radical intelligentsia against just about everyone else. As one of the leaders of the radicals, Garborg held that the marriage practices of the middle class had perverted the natural relations between the sexes. For economic reasons, young men postponed marriage until they finished their educations and became established in their careers while in the meantime relying on the companionship of prostitutes. Young women were raised to regard sex as something dirty, a belief that was used by their parents to dissuade them from entering into sexual relationships prior to marriage. Such an attitude, in turn, caused many women to become the type of wives that provided their husbands with justification for seeking continued solace outside the home. The radicals blamed conservatives for their mixed messages about sex as well as for other aspects of the deplorable conditions that they saw in the relations between men and women. They hoped that destroying the power of the conservatives would lead not only to greater political freedom but also to greater personal liberty for all people but were disappointed when the new liberal government turned out to be less progressive than they had expected.

Mannfolk is an attempt by Garborg both to depict sexual relations as they existed in Christiania at the beginning of the 1880s and to offer a naturalistic explanation of why there are inherent—and intractable—problems in the relationships between men and women. *Mannfolk* can be regarded as an early example of the collective novel in that it contains a large number of characters who are of approximately equal significance to the story. It differs from the collective novel proper, however, in that these characters are not regarded as a united group but as individuals whose specific histories can be used to illuminate the common theme of how the relationship between the sexes should be changed in order to promote human happiness.

As the title indicates, Garborg's focus in *Mannfolk* is on the male characters, all of whom, with the exception of Georg Jonathan, are in principle in favor of the institution of marriage. Most of them are not particularly happy in their marriages, though. The only happily married character, Markus Olivarius Markussen, is reputed to have entered into the state of matrimony largely because he was proposed to by his wife, Helga, née Thorsen. (Garborg's use of the motif of the woman who proposes to a man is most likely a way for him to pay his respects to the Norwegian early feminist writer Camilla Collett, who in her novel *Amtmandens Døttre* [1854, 1855; translated as *The District Governor's Daughters,* 1991] insisted that the woman's attraction to the man should form the basis for marriage, rather than the other way around.) The proponents of marriage are divided pretty much equally between married and unmarried men. Such married champions of marriage as the characters Bøckmann, Hummelvik, and Daniel Braut—the protagonist in *Bondestudentar* who recurs in a more limited role in *Mannfolk*—are all dissatisfied with their wives for various reasons. The unmarried men are single because of lack of money—for example, the painter Bjølsvik and the students Laurits Kruse and Nils Bugge—or for other reasons, such as the syphilis that affects medical student Kvaale or the seemingly pathological indecisiveness that plagues junior government official Gabriel Gram.

Garborg apparently created his cast of female characters to exemplify the sexual options available to women at the time. The woman characters are equally divided between those committed to and not committed to the idea of marriage, although their sense of commitment is not as much the result of a free choice as it is a consequence of their limited options. With the exception of Nina Bøckmann, who has taken Georg Jonathan as her lover, the women who see marriage as a realistic possibility are all committed to fidelity to a single partner. Most of the women for whom marriage is not an option have several partners, and eventually all of these women end up as full- or part-time prostitutes, usually after they experience one or more sexual relationships without monetary compensation. The exception is a young girl named Julie Lindner, who first becomes Georg Jonathan's lover and then his wife, but who loses his affection as soon as she has talked him into marriage.

The core of the narrative in *Mannfolk* consists of several case studies of the love lives of both men and women. In addition, there are several minor characters whose histories are touched on only briefly. The novel opens by describing the fate of the holdover from *Bondestudentar,* Daniel Braut. Through retrospective narration it becomes clear that Daniel had used the financial resources provided by his engagement to Hanna to live a life of unbridled sexual promiscuity while completing his degree in theology. After marrying Hanna and taking a job as a teacher at a girls' school, he fathers two daughters, becomes bored with both his marriage and his job, and begins to fantasize about his wife's servant girl. Rationalizing his lack of responsiveness to Hanna's desire for him by trying to convince her that sexual passion is incompatible with the idea of Christian marriage, Daniel reveals himself as an adulterer in spirit as well as a hypocrite.

Georg Jonathan is Garborg's foremost exponent of the idea of free love, an article of faith among the radical intelligentsia in Norway at the time. Georg first falls in love with Nina Grundt (who later marries the merchant Bøckmann), but she has been raised to regard sex as filthy and is frightened by his passion for her. The apparently less passionate Bøckmann seems a much safer choice. After a long relationship with Julie Lindner–a relationship that both of them claim has the spiritual force of a marriage–Georg becomes the now disillusioned Nina's lover. Although later married to Georg, Julie lacks the support of a loving husband and seems an easy prey for an unscrupulous man.

The ugliest–but in some respects not atypical–example of dysfunction in the relationship between men and women is the story of the young student Laurits Kruse. Laurits's studies are financed by a relative who exercises almost complete control over him, and the young man responds by becoming devious and sneaky. A boarder in the home of Daniel and Hanna Braut, Laurits becomes sexually involved with Helene, the object of Daniel's illicit fantasies. After getting her pregnant, he is sent away to a mountain community in order to serve as a tutor in the home of a friend of his benefactor. As he learns about the pregnancy and the baby's subsequent birth, he fervently hopes that the little girl–named Gunda–will die and thus absolve him of his financial and social responsibility. When he gets his wish and returns to town, he renews his relationship with Helene, whose interest in him now has a distinctly mercenary component. While sexually involved with Helene, Laurits also cultivates a close friendship with the young and chaste Dagmar Dyring, who is in love with the painter Bjølsvik without having the experience to decipher the true nature of her feelings. Dagmar and some of her girlfriends have entered into a pact not to marry men who have taken sexual advantage of powerless and unfortunate women. When, at the end of *Mannfolk,* Laurits proposes to Dagmar, she upholds her part of the bargain and asks him if he has ever been sexually involved with anyone. True to the nature of the middle-class marriage he seeks to establish, Laurits responds with a bald-faced lie.

Two of the saddest cases in *Mannfolk* are those of the low-level bureaucrat Gabriel Gram and the medical student Kvaale. Gram, who returns as a character in *Hjaa ho Mor* and as the narrator-protagonist in *Trætte Mænd,* is an example of a university-educated man who has not managed to break with the habit of visiting prostitutes. When first presented in *Mannfolk,* he is frantically washing because he fears that he has picked up a sexually transmitted disease, having been on a drinking binge and visited a house of prostitution. Almost destroyed by his alcoholism, Gram tries to lessen the chance of infection by arranging for a kept woman, whom he shares with a couple of other men, while constantly talking about solving his sexual problems through marriage. He cannot decide to commit to marriage, however, because he fears that he would end up with a boring wife.

When he is first encountered, Gram's friend Kvaale has been engaged to a proper bourgeois woman for several years. She apparently loves him deeply, but middle-class morality makes any sexual contact between them unacceptable prior to marriage. Kvaale has gone to prostitutes and has been infected with syphilis. Incurable at the time, it is a disease that Kvaale knows he will pass on to his fiancée if he marries her. If he does not marry her, he will have caused her to waste the best years of her life and perhaps be unable to find a husband because she has spent so much time waiting for him. He will have ruined her life in either case. Garborg's portrait of the relationship between men and women is unremittingly bleak.

Garborg's focus on the problems of love and marriage was continued in his next novel, *Hjaa ho Mor.* This book is thematically similar to *Mannfolk,* but its form is quite different. While the action in *Mannfolk* covers approximately one year, the beginning of the story in *Hjaa ho Mor* can be dated to April 1865 and its end to shortly before 5 June 1885. This twenty-year span of time is necessary for the depiction of the development of the protagonist in *Hjaa ho Mor,* Fanny Holmsen. Considerable attention in the novel is also devoted to the life story of Fanny's mother.

The story begins when Fanny is a little girl, living with her mother at the fictitious small town Kristiansborg, which is modeled on Hamar, a town in south-central Norway. Mrs. Holmsen is the divorced mother of three children, but only her youngest child, Fanny, lives with her. Fanny's father, a lawyer by training, is quite well off but is extremely irresponsible. Mrs. Holmsen had sought her divorce because she feared for her safety while living with her husband, and his desire for revenge keeps him from providing appropriate financial support for his children, the oldest two of whom live with his girlfriend.

Fanny grows up in abject poverty. Only the charity of Mrs. Holmsen's friends makes it possible for her to keep Fanny, and there are intimations that the mother is literally or figuratively prostituting herself. There is even a hint that she bears a child who is given up to be raised by acquaintances—a scandal that, together with the rest of Mrs. Holmsen's questionable sexual behavior, almost causes Fanny to despair at the thought of being able to live a morally responsible life.

Fanny's story is modeled on the early life of Garborg's wife, Hulda Bergersen, a novelist and dramatist in her own right who after her husband's death claimed to have actually written the first third of *Hjaa ho Mor.* Although this claim is neither generally known nor accepted by a majority of Garborg critics, the story of Fanny's childhood is told with great sensitivity and insight appropriate to a woman novelist writing about a young girl. Fanny's psychosexual development is depicted according to the ideas of naturalism, her social interactions with both peers and adults is described with great verisimilitude, and the force and hypocrisy involved in her religious training reveal the corrosive influence of the church in the lives of ordinary people. One of the bright spots in Fanny's life is her association with Mrs. Kahrs, the proprietor of a girls' school that Fanny gets to attend free of charge. Mrs. Kahrs is too broad-minded to suit the tastes of the local clergy, who, in effect, destroy her social position and her school. While Mrs. Holmsen's treatment of her daughter is narrated in a highly critical manner, the narrator also excuses the mother with reference to her own social background and life experiences.

As a teenager Fanny moves to Christiania with her mother, and there she becomes acquainted with a local theater and wants to become an actress. As her horizons broaden, she is torn between the promise of a life of freedom and responsibility and the demands of the religion in which she has, at least nominally, been raised. Garborg shows that the power of the church depends on the clergy's ability to scare young people into an obsession with the ideas of spiritual pollution and eternal punishment. In particular, Fanny is indoctrinated with the idea that her budding sexual feelings are identical with the Bible's concept of the evil spirit. She accepts the teachings of the church and becomes particularly zealous in her religious devotion at precisely those moments in her life when she feels great personal insecurity.

Garborg–whose correspondence shows that he had come to believe there was a strong connection between religious and erotic impulses–depicts religion as a crutch for the believer, the result of the clergy's pious deceptions and crass lies. Some of his presentation of religion as a phenomenon is quite funny, however, particularly the portrait of a small congregation called the Ansgar Mission, a group led by a Swedish lay preacher named Andersson. This circumstance leads the congregation's Norwegian members to witness to each other in Swedish, which because of Andersson they consider is more sacred than their own language. Fanny withdraws from fellowship with this group when she begins to suspect that Andersson's interest in her is not limited to the state of her soul. Her repulsion at Andersson's interest–expressed solely in writing, however–presages the tragic turn in her life at the end of *Hjaa ho Mor.*

As Fanny approaches physical maturity, her mother begins to look for opportunities to marry her off in a socially and economically advantageous manner. Fanny experiences several infatuations with boys near her own age, but her mother wants her to marry a man old enough to be her father–in fact, of Mrs. Holmsen's own vintage–a customs official named Ryen. One of the funniest scenes in the book occurs when Fanny confronts her mother with the idea that Ryen, a frequent guest in their home, is actually hoping to marry Fanny's mother. Mrs. Holmsen's consternation is such that the reader wonders which option seems the worse to her, gaining Ryen as a husband or losing him as a son-in-law. One suspects the latter, as having him as a son-in-law would give Mrs. Holmsen almost the same financial advantages as having him as a husband without any of the obligations of marital life.

In spite of the example of her older sister Lea, who marries according to Mrs. Holmsen's wishes, Fanny manages to resist her mother's pressure and remains single. The consequence is that as soon as she has gone through the rite of confirmation in the State Church, she has to work hard in order to support herself and help support her mother, which takes a severe toll on her health. At first, she helps her married sister to take care of her child, but later, and well into her twenties, she waits on customers in a store. Her social life is quite limited, but she becomes acquainted with several reasonably well-educated young men, with whom she carries on conversations about social issues, politics, and art. However, she soon discovers that, because of her sex, her opinions are not taken seriously. A couple of unwanted marriage proposals—her body seems to be in greater demand than her mind—leave her dismayed. Fearful of her own sexuality and interested in obtaining some kind of education, she does not feel ready for marriage. She becomes infatuated with a young medical student named Aas, but he gets engaged to one of her girlfriends, much to Mrs. Holmsen's dismay.

Since standing all the time at work undermines her health, Fanny manages to borrow money to become trained as an elementary-school teacher. The pay is low, however, and she has to be careful not to offend the priests who make up the school board. This circumstance is particularly grievous to her because she has become politically radicalized and has adopted the stance of the Liberal Party, a set of ideas considered anathema by the clergy. She feels robbed of her integrity by the religious doctrines that she is compelled to transmit to her students.

At the time Fanny becomes politically liberal she also meets the man who seems destined to become the love of her life, Gabriel Gram, who was introduced in *Mannfolk* and there served as one of Garborg's prime examples of the demoralizing influence of the conservative approach to life. The Gram the reader knows in *Mannfolk* is a promiscuous drinker who neglects his work as a junior government official. In *Hjaa ho Mor* Gram both fascinates and frightens Fanny during their first brief encounter because he is a freethinker. A few years later—shortly after 27 February 1884, according to what is said about the impeachment of the government—she gets to know him quite well and falls in love

Title page for Garborg's novel (translated as The Lost Father, *1920) about a banker who returns to Norway from America and adopts the simple Christian life of his brother (University of Wisconsin–Madison Libraries)*

with him. According to information about Gram's age given in *Mannfolk*, Gram would be about thirty-eight.

Despite his mature years and relatively secure finances, Gram has changed little from *Mannfolk*; he remains in the grip of alcohol, and his indecisiveness has not allowed him to marry. Fanny's love for him is beautiful and unselfish, but Gram is unable to reciprocate fully because he worries that she is not good enough for him. Since *Hjaa ho Mor* is narrated largely from Fanny's perspective, Gram's thoughts are not presented in detail, but the first part of Garborg's next novel, *Trætte Mænd,* makes it clear that he is concerned about her reputation and her possible earlier sexual involvement with other men.

Hjaa ho Mor ends when Gram suggests to Fanny that they should become lovers without the benefit of marriage—an idea in line with the views of the Christiania bohemians, a group of mostly young men who wanted to radically change society and with which

Garborg was briefly associated. Fanny, however, finds such a proposition extremely offensive, regarding it as an expression of contempt. Deeply wounded, she flees to her mother. After receiving a letter in which Gram indicates that he will attempt a marriage of convenience to a woman who is his equal socially, Fanny despairs and agrees to marry Ryen.

Garborg's purpose in *Hjaa ho Mor* was to show that marital happiness was nearly impossible to achieve in Norway in the 1870s and early 1880s. The teachings of the church, the patriarchal attitudes of parents toward their daughters, and the social expectations placed on young men combined to create unhappiness for both women and men. While *Mannfolk* had offered a series of brief accounts of the problem, *Hjaa ho Mor* constituted an extended narrative analysis of the fate of a young woman who is, in every material respect, normal and healthy in both body and mind. Garborg's chief villains are priests and parents, against whose power the individual child is helpless. *Hjaa ho Mor,* along with his earlier novels *Bondestudentar* and *Mannfolk,* showed Garborg to be committed to the literary doctrine of naturalism. The unhappy fate of the various characters is plainly the result of biological and environmental factors, and the individual is shown to have little or no freedom to affect his or her own fate.

While Garborg continued to ply naturalism as a literary approach, he was aware of a significant change in literary fashion occurring in Scandinavia. More and more in the fin de siècle, writers were turning away from naturalism, which many believed exhausted of its artistic possibilities. Naturalism, with its emphasis on determinism, natural science, and objective truth, was gradually being replaced by an idealist and individualist outlook on life.

Garborg, who did not share in the new admiration for idealism, took an ironic and satirical view of it. While his intellectual curiosity was excited by the new decadent literature emerging, particularly in France, his political beliefs—he was a progressive who regarded socialism as the best hope for the future—were fundamentally incompatible with what he referred to as neo-idealism. At the same time that he wanted to express his reservations about the new literary trend, he also wanted to treat the subject seriously. His next novel, *Trætte Mænd,* allowed him to have it both ways by providing an ironic portrait of a decadent neo-idealist.

By choosing Gabriel Gram as the narrator-protagonist of *Trætte Mænd* and also using other characters from his previous works, Garborg was able to write *Trætte Mænd* quickly and to anchor it firmly—in its setting and theme—in his previous naturalist novels.

In terms of form, however, *Trætte Mænd* was different from anything Garborg had previously written, as it had the look and feel of a diary novel. The first-person form allowed him to test out the subjectivism of the new literary fashion and to create a character who reveals himself as being in the grip of the decadent forces of the age.

In a personal narrative that begins at midnight on 5 June 1885, in a section titled "Introduction," Gram shows himself to be a man who is fundamentally weary with life. Suffering from dipsomania, bad nerves, and suicidal thoughts, he is identical to the way he is presented by the omniscient narrators of *Mannfolk* and *Hjaa ho Mor*. The thoughts and feelings recorded in his diary document his inner turmoil–Garborg's nod to the new literary fashions–as well as his social environment, as is characteristic of naturalistic literature. The diary form is used with a twist, however, as Gram soon turns to a project that is primarily subjective but that also has a significant objective component. During the previous year and a half he had drafted a large body of notes and other jottings, most of which had Fanny as their chief stimulus. To cope with the break from Fanny and to keep from destroying himself with alcohol, he begins to rearrange and edit the previously recorded notes. He puts them in their objective chronological order and occasionally adds brief bracketed comments. Indicating that this labor may well result in a novel, Gram describes adding chapter numbers and labeling the entire corpus of notes "Part One." The result of Gram's labor is thus "Part One" of *Trætte Mænd,* which corresponds to the portion of Fanny's story that is told in the last two chapters of *Hjaa ho Mor.*

Gram's editorial work comes to an end on 26 July 1885, when in the first entry in "Part Two" of *Trætte Mænd* he offers a retrospective view of how his relationship with Fanny came to its unhappy end, including how it caused her to sell herself into marriage to a rich old man. He continues to record his thoughts and impressions in the form of diary entries, however, and these entries continue his story until April 1889, almost four years after the date of the "Introduction." Gram's life during these years is described as fundamentally unhappy as he struggles to deal with his attraction to Fanny.

Part Two of *Trætte Mænd* tells about few external events. In typical decadent fashion, the city of Christiania is portrayed as a destructive environment that claims people as victims. A vacation trip to Hitterdal is described with the nostalgia of those exhausted by modern city life. It is noteworthy, however, that these manifestations of decadence are found in a text for which Gram—rather than Garborg—is formally responsible, and it should not be taken to indicate that Garborg had bought into Gram's fundamentally anti-naturalist view. The characters are relatively few, and most of them are borrowed from Garborg's previous novels. Georg Jonathan represents the kind of scientific empiricism that informed naturalism; Dr. Kvaale–the syphilitic medical student first encountered in *Mannfolk*–commits suicide and thus represents one possible response to modern exhaustion; while Dr. Thisted and Pastor Løchen favor an anthropology that offers hope through a belief in, respectively, free will and Christianity.

Jonathan and Kvaale represent the old-fashioned scientific and objective worldview, while Thisted and Løchen embody its opposite subjective and spiritual pole. Although torn and indecisive, Gram gradually moves away from objectivity to the subjective standpoint. Kvaale's suicide is a powerfully motivating factor, but Garborg–who had first discovered the relationship between the erotic and the religious in *Hjaa ho Mor*–shows that Gram's attraction to Fanny provides the pull that finally causes him to break with Jonathan and completely side with Thisted and Løchen.

Garborg thus manages to tell a story that is largely in conformity with the ideas of impressionist and decadent writing as practiced in the late 1880s and 1890s while simultaneously anchored in the aesthetics and worldview of the naturalists. The ironic distance between Garborg and Gram is achieved both thematically and formally. The erotic motivation for Gram's attraction to the church is the most important ironic thematic element, while striking discrepancies in the form of Gram's diary chronology in Part Two reveal that he is not as transparent as he at first seems to be.

When the chronology of the supposed diary in Part Two of *Trætte Mænd* is analyzed carefully, it becomes clear that the events that are narrated do not fit the dates that are given in the entries. While the story is continuous, the year 1886 has been used twice. This kind of mistake is literally impossible in an actual diary, and it is a mistake that should be regarded as having been made by Gram, not Garborg. When, through the reader's suspension of disbelief, the matter is viewed from a perspective located within the fictional world, the most likely explanation for the lapse is that *Trætte Mænd* is not a story that is naively told by Gram in his diary but rather a conscious and sophisticated reworking of actual experience produced by Gram in the form of a novel. As observed by the Norwegian critic Geir Mork, it is a testament to the sophistication of Garborg's narrative skill that the chronological irregularities in *Trætte Mænd* were not noticed until almost a hundred years after the book's appearance. It is now possible to realize that there is a great deal of narrative distance in *Trætte Mænd* between Garborg, whose commitments are largely those of naturalism, and Gram, a literary character created by Garborg in order to illuminate the decadent tendencies in contemporary European literary culture.

Garborg's commitment to naturalist aesthetics is also evident in *Fred*, in which the author is clearly attempting to come to terms with his father's suicide many years earlier. Set in Garborg's home district of Jæren, *Fred* focuses on Enok Hòve, whose ultimate tragedy is the inevitable result of having inherited his tendencies toward depression from his mother and living under social and economic conditions that further the progression of his illness. At the beginning of the novel, Enok is shown as a hardworking and prosperous farmer with a wife and several young children. He is a troubled man, however, as he is worried both about the status of his soul before God and financial risks he has taken. His metaphysical commitments lead him to see the hand of God in all things, from the death of a neighbor to aspects of the weather. His spiritual uncertainty is heightened by his experience of economic life, which is rapidly changing from old-fashioned self-sufficiency among the farmers to participation in a monetary economy founded on credit and banking. Enok feels socially and economically powerless when faced with these structural changes over which he has no control, and he interprets every economic reversal as evidence of God's displeasure with him.

Enok's fundamental problem, however, is that he shuts himself off from other human beings while brooding on the state of his soul. During periods of relative health he is a trusted member of the local community and participates actively in its political life. While in the grip of his depression, on the other hand, he tries to cope by controlling everything and everybody around him. He withdraws from the fellowship of his parish and insists on serving as a priest in his own family, conducting devotionals and keeping his children away from activities that he regards as vain and sinful. Such innocent pleasures as play and reading of nonreligious books is forbidden. The devil is to be conquered through prayer and hard work, and Enok's demands almost break the health of his wife, Anna. The work is particularly harsh because Enok wants to adhere to the old ways rather than use modern labor-saving farming methods and tools. His oldest son and allodial heir to the farm, Gunnar, becomes sneaky in order to endure his father's tyranny.

When Enok faces his final emotional crisis, he has cut himself off from every source of social, emotional, and spiritual support. Gunnar announces that he plans to emigrate to America, and Enok's deep depression turns to psychosis—he sees little grey men who are trying to get him—leading to his suicide by drowning. The most extreme form of Enok's illness is, however, logically connected with the rest of it, as it is his tendency to interpret the world and his experiences in it privately that lies at the root of his condition. There is not that much difference between seeing little grey men and discerning the hand of God in a lightning strike. Garborg seems to say that Enok's tendency to perceive the divine in his life idiosyncratically is unhealthy because there is no social dimension to his experience.

Garborg avoids making *Fred* into an utterly depressing story by adding a subplot involving a family of Roma (Gypsies). Fante-Tomas, the head of this family, is a stereotypically dishonest and deceptive person. He is also somewhat of an untutored thinker who likes to share his highly personal understanding of the world with anyone who will listen to him. His son, Carolus Magnus, becomes a close friend, playmate, and corrupter of Enok's son Gunnar. Garborg's naturalistic portrait of this family is extreme—even to the point of including a fair amount of text in Romani in the book—but their story is also told with warmth and humor. Fante-Tomas is a counterpart to Enok in that his understanding of the world is shared by hardly anyone else, but his emphasis on communicating his ideas to others opens him up to their criticism and correction. Only when Fante-Tomas plans a crime spree, in which secrecy is of the essence, do he and his family get into serious trouble, including incarceration. Keeping matters private thus constitutes the undoing of both Enok Hòve and Fante-Tomas.

Writing *Fred* seems to have been an act of personal liberation for Garborg, as painful memories from his childhood and youth became transmuted into an artistically satisfying literary work. His youthful desire to get away from home was now replaced by a wish to memorialize Jæren as he knew it from his earliest childhood, before its people became subject to pietistic religiosity and its farmland was capitalized. Garborg's means to this end was the poetic cycle *Haugtussa*.

The central character in *Haugtussa* is the young woman Veslemøy, who is gifted with an unusually clear perception of reality and truth, bordering on clairvoyance. By drawing heavily on both published and unpublished folklore, Garborg used traditional concepts and motifs as symbols of the workings of the human mind. Veslemøy suffers greatly when dealing with the evils of existence, but she has the strength to overcome her challenges without giving up on her primary values, genuine love and true knowledge. She is perhaps the greatest example of a truly human being in Garborg's oeuvre.

While Garborg had been known primarily as a novelist, he achieved a reputation as one of Norway's great poets with the publication of *Haugtussa*. His command of metrics, rhythm, rhyme, and alliteration were regarded as superb. He was also admired for his considerable stanzaic variation, ranging from approximations of Old Norse forms to those verse forms favored by his contemporaries. While Garborg had previously written brilliant descriptions of nature in prose—the introductory chapter in *Fred* being the outstanding example—*Haugtussa* showed that he was able to bring the same sensibility to his nature lyrics. The Norwegian composer Edvard Grieg used texts from *Haugtussa* for some of his best-known *Lieder,* or art songs.

Ever since the publication of *Ein Fritenkjar,* Garborg had been a sworn enemy of the Norwegian State Church, and he had also rejected the more popular pietistic movement, which he had excoriated in *Fred*. He did not reject such Christian ideals as genuine community and brotherly love, but he accused the men of the Church of having glossed over Jesus' true message in their lust for power. In his play *Læraren* he decided to depict what might happen in contemporary society to a person who tried to follow the ethical example set by Jesus and described in the New Testament.

The protagonist in *Læraren* is Paulus Hòve, a younger son of Enok Hòve of *Fred*. By teaching his followers that people should live according to a kind of Christian socialism that would be the end of the old farm society and its reliance on allodial rights, he offends both the farmers in his Jæren community and such local representatives of the government as the State Church minister and the sheriff. While the idealistic Paulus is generally sensitive to the needs of those around him, he is unable to see how difficult his teachings are for his wife, Helga, who, as the daughter of a rich farmer, is strongly attached to the old ways and who is carrying the child that might well become the allodial heir to their own farm. Also troubled by her husband's relationship with a young woman named Evelinde—with whom Paulus is in love without understanding it himself—Helga commits suicide.

Helga's suicide provides the civil and ecclesiastical authorities with enough leverage to get rid of Paulus by having him arrested and tried for his part in the tragedy. Daniel Braut, the dispicable protagonist of Garborg's novel *Bondestudentar,* has managed to become a parish priest in his home district and is one of the leaders in condemning the religious movement that Paulus has started. He is assisted by the district physician, Doctor Aas, who in *Hjaa ho Mor* appears as one of Fanny's admirers and Gabriel Gram's friend, as well as other representatives of the status quo. At the conclusion of *Læraren,* Paulus becomes a martyr to the cause of the powerless and the poor.

Paulus is considered dangerous by the authorities not only because he represents an alternative to their conservative politics but also because he renounces power altogether. He seeks to serve other people rather than rule over them, and this idea, which Garborg considered the vital point of Christianity, is utterly subversive to the efforts of those who will pay any price to obtain power and dominion. Garborg also shows, however, that Paulus has weaknesses of his own, and this is what makes *Læraren* a true tragedy in the Aristotelian sense. Paulus is just as human as Braut, Aas, and the rest of those who oppose him, and they, conversely, are just as human as Paulus. Human weakness, including that particular subcategory of human weakness that leads to a lust for power, is everywhere in evidence in Garborg's world.

In a retrospective entry in his diary, Garborg refers to several literary works starting with *Fred* as "*Fred*-Rekkja" (the *Fred* series), a structural counterpart to his Christiania novels. Like the books centered on life in Christiania, the works in the *Fred* series are connected to each other by several recurring literary characters, many of them members of the Hòve family. *Læraren* was the second work in this group, and it was followed by two short novels, *Den burtkomne Faderen* and *Heimkomin Son,* both of which have the form of selections from a diary.

Den burtkomne Faderen was the first book Garborg wrote at his summer cottage, Knudaheio (now a museum), which was located close to his father's farm at Jæren. Garborg had wanted to return to Jæren, but his wife, Hulda, who had her roots in the farming district north of Christiania, was reluctant to settle down permanently so far from her friends and professional associates. They reached a compromise when they purchased a permanent home at Labraaten in Asker, close to Christiania, at the same time that Garborg got his Jæren cottage. *Den burtkomne Faderen* marks a homecoming of sorts for its author.

Den burtkomne Faderen is narrated by Gunnar Hòve, Enok's oldest son, who has spent most of his adult life in America, where he worked in the banking industry. As a servant of Mammon he is the antithesis of his brother Paulus. Gunnar's health has suffered because of his unnatural and stressful life, and he returns to Norway and Jæren in order to reconnect with his emotional and spiritual roots. With the biblical story of the prodigal son as an important parallel,

Cover for Garborg's novel (Jesus Messiah), published in 1906 (New York Public Library)

Den burtkomne Faderen depicts Gunnar's efforts to find his way back to his childhood religion. He gradually becomes taken with the simple Christian life of his brother, who rejects all concern with doctrine in favor of the ethical dictum that people should help each other. The book ends with a postscript in which Gunnar's death and funeral are described.

Heimkomin Son, also centered on the teachings of Paulus Hòve, is largely made up of selections from notes made by Haavard Haatun, a farmer at Jæren who in his youth had been a schoolmaster. A footnote refers to "Bokmeistaren" (the Book Master), who made the selections from Haatun's notes that have been included in *Heimkomin Son*. Although the narrative situation is fairly complex, the emphasis is on what the text reveals about Paulus Hòve's religious ideas, which seem to be completely in line with Garborg's own thinking. *Heimkomin Son* might best be read as a fictionalized exposition of Garborg's ideas about Christianity. Part of the text consists of brief discourses based on specific scriptural passages, while the rest is more traditional narrative in which Paulus's views are presented.

Heimkomin Son amplifies and further explains the core ideas presented in *Den burtkomne Faderen*. While it can be read as a significant cultural and theological essay, its literary quality is greatly inferior to such earlier Garborg novels as *Bondestudentar, Trætte Mænd,* or *Fred*. There is a noticeable change in Garborg's oeuvre around the year 1900; as the author turns away from imaginative literature in favor of the essay and the treatise. Garborg evidently came to prefer the direct communication of the essay to the indirect and often ironic way he expressed himself through his novels.

Garborg's poetic powers also seemed to be on the wane. *I Helheim,* a continuation of the *Haugtussa* cycle, is generally considered an inferior poetic work. His essayistic *Knudahei-brev* (1904, Letters from Knudahei), a counterpart to his earlier *Kolbotnbrev og andre Skildringar* (1890, Letters from Kolbotn and other Portraits), includes musings on both his personal life and more general topics. While these works can read with interest, they lack the poetic power of the novels. *Jesus Messias* (1906, Jesus Messiah) and *Den burtkomne Messias* (1907, The Lost Messiah) are theological works that amplify some of the ideas in his *Fred* series, but are otherwise of limited interest. Strongly influenced by the American economist Henry George, Garborg viewed the biblical battle between good and evil in economic terms. The powers of darkness were allied with high capitalism and the Kingdom of God was to be seen as a metaphor for social justice.

During his many years in artistic decline, Garborg kept busy with tasks such as writing articles on historical and political topics, translating works of world literature into Nynorsk, and preparing a collected edition of his works. Ever the perfectionist, he made many changes, both great and small, in his texts. He also kept up a diary, *Dagbok, 1905–1923* (1924–1927), that was clearly intended for publication as a continuation of *Knudahei-brev,* and that was published with a lengthy introduction by his wife after his death. The diary mentions several writing projects that never came to fruition. He likewise published collections of earlier essays about politics and literature, *Politik* (1919, Politics) and *Straumdrag* (1920, Currents). Garborg experienced a great deal of loneliness during his later years and fought hard to maintain his emotional equilibrium.

At his death on 25 January 1924, Garborg was worn out by personal and cultural struggles. He had long been regarded as a leader by Norway's radical youth, and by the end of his life he had been embraced by even conservative forces as a major—and now unthreatening—writer. His family was pressured into allowing him to receive a state funeral, arranged by a church to which Garborg did not belong and on which he had heaped scorn through most of his life.

Arne Garborg's critical reputation rests primarily on his novels and some of the poetry in *Haugtussa*. He is also highly regarded as an essayist, and selections of his essays have been included in the collected editions of his works since 1980. There is wide critical agreement that he is one of Norway's most intellectually sophisticated writers, and *Trætte Mænd* is viewed as an interesting contribution to European decadent literature. Norway's reading public knows him first and foremost as the author of *Bondestudentar,* long a staple in the secondary-school reading curriculum, and as one of the early leaders in the Nynorsk movement.

Letters:
Mogning og manndom: Brev, 2 volumes, edited by Johannes A. Dale and Rolv Thesen (Oslo: Aschehoug, 1954).

Bibliography:
Thor M. Andersen, *Garborg litteratur 1866–1942: Ein bibliografi* (Oslo: Fabritius & Sønner, 1945).

Biographies:
Erik Lie, *Arne Garborg: en livsskildring* (Christiania: Aschehoug, 1914);

Ivar Mortensson Egnund, *Arne Garborg: Ein fyretalsmann* (Christiania: Norli, 1924);

Rolv Thesen, *Arne Garborg: Frå jærbu til europear* (Oslo: Aschehoug, 1933);

Thesen, *Arne Garborg: Europearen* (Oslo: Aschehoug, 1936);

Thesen, *Arne Garborg: Europear og jærbu* (Oslo: Aschehoug, 1939);

Thesen, *Ein diktar og hans strid: Arne Garborgs liv og skrifter* (Oslo: Aschehoug, 1945);

Finn Thorn, *Arne Garborg og kristendommen* (Oslo: Aschehoug, 1972);

Tor Obrestad, *Arne Garborg* (Oslo: Gyldendal, 1991).

References:
Agnete Jørstad Andersen, *Et essay fra en brytningstid: en analyse av Arne Garborgs Kolbotnbrev* (Oslo: Universitetet i Oslo, 2007);

Per Thomas Andersen, *Dekadanse i nordisk litteratur 1880–1900* (Oslo: Aschehoug, 1992);

Gudleiv Bø, ed., *Søkelys på Arne Garborgs bøker om Hoveætta* (Oslo: Universitetsforlaget, 1978);

Johannes A. Dale, *Garborg-studiar* (Oslo: Det Norske Samlaget, 1969);

Dale, *Studiar i Arne Garborgs språk og stil* (Oslo: Aschehoug, 1950);

Ine Westlye Fintland, "Å setja ord på vennskap: brevvekslinga mellom Kitty Kielland og Arne Garborg 1885-1891," in *18.06.46: Festskrift til Sveinung Time på 61-årsdagen*, edited by Leif Johan Larsen, Per Arne Michelsen, and Dag Orseth (Bergen: Høgskolen i Bergen Bodoni forlag, 2007), pp. 24-35;

Martin Humpál, "Irony Revisited: Arne Garborg's *Trætte Mænd*," *Brünner Beiträge zur Germanistik und Nordistik*, 15 (2001): 165-170;

Lanae H. Isaacson, "*Haugtussa:* Interweaving Traditional Theme, Character, and Motif," *Edda: Nordisk Tidsskrift for Litteraturforskning*, 82 (1982): 325-339;

Isaacson, "*Kolbotnbrev:* Poetic Prelude to *Haugtussa*," *Edda: Nordisk Tidsskrift for Litteraturforskning*, 84 (1984): 145-156;

Isaacson, "The Poetry of the Past: Reminiscence and Recollection in Arne Garborg's Lyric Prose," *Edda: Nordisk Tidsskrift for Litteraturforskning*, 85 (1985): 49-61;

Isaacson, "'Son et lumière' in Arne Garborg's Poetry and Prose," *Scandinavica: An International Journal of Scandinavian Studies*, 23 (May 1984): 39-50;

James Massengale, "*Haugtussa:* From Garborg to Grieg," *Scandinavian Studies*, 53 (1981): 131-153;

Geir Mork, *Den reflekterte latteren: På spor etter Arne Garborgs ironi* (Oslo: Aschehoug, 2002);

Gunhild Haugstad Obrestad, *"Es gibt ein Ziel aber keinen Weg," zum Topos und Problem der Heimkehr in Texten von Franz Kafka und Arne Garborg* (Bergen: Universitetet i Bergen, 2007);

Jan Sjåvik, "Arne Garborg: *Trætte Mænd*. En retorisk og genetisk analyse," *Edda: Nordisk Tidsskrift for Litteraturforskning*, 82 (1982): 1-22;

Sjåvik, *Arne Garborgs Kristiania-romaner: En berettertenisk studie* (Oslo: Aschehoug, 1985);

Sjåvik, "Form and Theme in Garborg's *Mannfolk* and *Hjaa ho Mor*," *Selecta: Journal of the Pacific Northwest Council on Foreign Languages*, 1 (1980): 87-90;

Sjåvik, "Hulda Bergersen, Arne Garborg, and the Rhetoric of *Hjaa Ho Mor*," *Scandinavian Studies*, 55 (1983): 134-148;

Sjåvik, "Intensjon og genre i Arne Garborgs *Bondestudentar*," *Edda: Nordisk Tidsskrift for Litteraturforskning*, 78 (1978): 333-339;

Sjåvik, "Intersubjektiv interpretasjon: Donald Davidson, triangulering og forfatterens rolle," *Nordlit: Arbeidstidsskrift i litteratur*, 16 (Fall 2004): 71-93;

Sjåvik, "Reading Arne Garborg's Irony: *Bondestudentar, Trætte mænd, Fred*," *Scandinavian Studies*, 72 (2000): 63-88;

Idar Stegane, "Angsten i Arne Garborgs *Fred*, I Høve til Søren Kierkegaards Begrebet Angest," in *18.06.46: Festskrift til Sveinung Time på 61-årsdagen*, pp. 36-53;

Siri Garborg Talle, *Kjære Bror! Arne Garborg og slekten* (Oslo: Aschehoug, 2000).

Papers:

Most of Arne Garborg's papers, including the manuscripts of *Trætte Mænd* and *Fred*, are in the Nasjonalbiblioteket (National Library) in Oslo.

Hulda Garborg
(22 February 1862 – 5 November 1934)

Torild Homstad
St. Olaf College

BOOKS: *Et frit Forhold* (Bergen: Litlere, 1892);
Mødre (Christiania: Feilberg & Landmark, 1895);
Rationelt Fjøsstell (Christiania: Feilberg & Landmark, 1896);
Hos Lindelands (Christiania: John Fredriksen, 1899);
Noahs Ark (Christiania: John Fredriksen, 1899);
Heimstell (Christiania: "Den 17de Mai," 1899);
Sovande Sorg (Christiania: Aschehoug, 1900);
Fra Kolbotnen og andetsteds (Christiania: Aschehoug, 1903);
Liti Kersti: Eventyrspel med song og Dans i tvo Vendingar (Christiania: Aschehoug, 1903);
Norske folkevisor: med utgreiding um vise-dansen av Hulda Garborg, I (Christiania: Norigs ungdomslag og Studentmaallaget, 1903);
Norsk klædebunad: (fraa ymse bygdir) (Christiania: Norigs ungdomslag og Student-maallaget, 1903);
Song-Dansen i Nord-Landi (Christiania: Aschehoug, 1903);
Kvinden Skabt av Manden: Studie af en Kvinde, i anledning av Dr. Otto Weiningers' bog "Geschlecht und Charakter," anonymous (Christiania: Aschehoug, 1904);
Edderkoppen (Christiania: Aschehoug, 1904);
April (Christiania: Aschehoug, 1905);
Fru Evas Dagbog (Christiania: Aschehoug, 1905);
Kongens Kone (Christiania: Aschehoug, 1906);
Matstell paa Landsbygdi (Christiania: Norigs ungdomslag og Student-maallaget, 1907);
Sigmund Bresteson (Christiania: Det norske samlaget, 1908);
Mann av Guds Naade (Christiania: Aschehoug, 1908);
Rousseau og hans Tanker i Nutiden (Christiania & Copenhagen: Gyldendal, 1909);
Rousseau (Christiania: Norigs ungdomslag og Student-maallaget, 1910);
Under Bôdhitræet: En Drom i fire billeder, anonymous (Christiania: Aschehoug, 1911);
Eli (Christiania: Aschehoug, 1912);
Barn i By (Christiania: Aschehoug, 1913);
Norske dansevisur (Christiania: Aschehoug, 1913);
Mot Solen (Christiania: Aschehoug, 1915);

Hulda Garborg (<http://www.heimen.net/aboutus.cfm>)

Tyrihans (Christiania: Aschehoug, 1915);
Gaaden (Christiania: Aschehoug, 1916);
Den store Freden (Christiania: Aschehoug, 1919); translated by Samual Garborg as *Hiawatha's Vision* (Minneapolis: Augsburg, 1927);
Mens dansen gaar (Christiania: Aschehoug, 1920);
I huldreskog (Christiania: Aschehoug, 1922);
Naar heggen blomstrer (Christiania: Aschehoug, 1923);
Grågubben (Christiania: Aschehoug, 1925);
National kost (Oslo: Fabritius, 1925);

Trollheimen (Oslo: Aschehoug, 1927);

Helenes historie (Oslo: Aschehoug, 1929);

Kornmoe (Oslo: Aschehoug, 1930);

Hildring (Oslo: Aschehoug, 1931);

Symra (Oslo: Aschehoug, 1934);

Barndomsminne (Oslo: Aschehoug, 1935);

Dagbok 1903–1914, edited by Karen Grude Koht and Rolv Thesen (Oslo: Aschehoug, 1962).

PLAY PRODUCTIONS: *Mødre,* Christiania, Christiania Theater, 23 October 1895;

Rationelt Fjøsstell, Christiania, Christiania Theater, 7 April 1897;

Noahs Ark, Christiania, Centralteatret, 16 September 1897;

Vaar, Christiania, Centralteatret, 17 March 1899;

Hos Lindelands, Bergen, Den Nationale Scene, 1 September 1899;

Edderkoppen, Christiania, Nationaltheatret, 19 October 1904;

Sovande Sorg, Christiania, Fahlstrøms Theater, 7 June 1910;

Tyrihans, Christiania, Det Norske Teatret, 26 December 1914;

Liti Kersti, Christiania; Det Norske Teatret, 10 July 1919;

Sigmund Bresteson, Oslo: Det Norske Teatret, 15 March 1932.

Photographs of Hulda Garborg often show her wearing a *bunad,* the Norwegian national costume. Known for her marriage to one of Norway's greatest national poets, Arne Garborg, Hulda Garborg is also strongly identified with the movement to revive Norwegian folk culture in the early part of the twentieth century. She was the first to write a book about the Norwegian national costume, *Norsk klædebunad* (1903, The Norwegian National Costume). She traveled to the Faroe Islands to search for the roots of Norwegian folk dance and published several books on the subject. She promoted the use of Nynorsk, especially in the theater, not only writing plays herself but also acting, directing, and organizing theater groups. At the same time, she provided the necessary peace and support that enabled Arne Garborg to work, in spite of his ill health, and also wrote novels, plays, and books on homemaking.

Karen Hulda Bergersen was born on 22 February 1862 in Stange, Hedmark. Shortly thereafter, her father, Christian Fredrik Bergersen, went bankrupt, and her parents divorced. Hulda and her two older sisters moved to Hamar with their mother. From living on a large farm in wealthy circumstances they were reduced to sharing one rented room, with Hulda's mother barely eking out a living for them by taking in sewing. Christian Bergersen provided support for Hulda's older sisters, who later lived with him in Christiania (renamed Oslo in 1925), but he showed little interest in or concern for Hulda's welfare.

Her childhood experiences in Hamar, especially as a scholarship student at Kristian Gløersen's girls' school, greatly influenced Hulda Bergersen's intellectual and personal development. Gløersen's pedagogy was inspired by the ideals of Nikolai Grundtvig and Jean-Jacques Rousseau and by all accounts might be considered progressive even in the twenty-first century. It was through Gløersen that Hulda Garborg's ideas about the importance of the national culture and about the complexity of the role of women in society were encouraged. Garborg chronicles her early life in Hamar in her memoirs and diaries. Arne Garborg also used material from Hulda's childhood memories in *Hjaa ho mor* (1890, At Mother's House).

When she was thirteen, Bergersen and her mother moved to Christiania. After one more year of school, she was confirmed. Then she went to work as a clerk for Dobloug & Co., a dry goods firm, where she remained for seven and a half years. Mikkel Dobloug introduced the young Hulda Bergersen to the Christiania Arbeidersamfunn (Christiania Workers' Society), which provided a stimulating intellectual environment in the spirit of Norwegian patriots such as Henrik Wergeland and Bjørnstjerne Bjørnson and also discussions of radical European politics, especially ideas from France and Russia. She began seriously to read literature written in New Norwegian and to learn to write it herself. In the fall of 1885 she began to study New Norwegian formally in Ivar Mortensson's language school. Many of her works for the theater are written in New Norwegian, especially those with rural settings and themes, while most of her major novels are written in Dano-Norwegian.

The Christiania Arbeidersamfunn also provided a lively social environment and contact with other young people. She first met Arne Garborg at a meeting as they both were part of a circle of young radical intellectuals engaged in the political and cultural debates of the day—debates concerning sexual morality, the nature and role of women in society, and the New Norwegian language movement. She and Arne Garborg were married in 1887, and in the spring of 1888 their only son was born. She describes amusingly the early years of their marriage when they lived in an isolated summer cabin and she was just beginning to learn the arts of cooking and homemaking in *Fra Kolbotnen og andetsteds* (1903, From Kolbotnen and Other Places).

In 1889 the Garborgs left Kolbotnen and traveled to Germany, settling temporarily in Diessen, near Munich. The next several years they spent much time

Title page for Garborg's novel (The Puzzle) about the conflict between love and work (Thorsens Antikvariat)

abroad, not only in Germany but also in France and Italy before settling down at Labråten, outside of Christiania, in fall 1898. During their years abroad Hulda Garborg learned both German and French; her later promotion of a national Norwegian culture rested solidly on a foundation of internationalism.

Arne Garborg was already an established author when Hulda Garborg made her literary debut in 1892 with the novel *Et frit Forhold* (An Open Relationship). A naturalistic novel, it tells the story of a naive young country girl, Dina Halvorsen, who had come to Christiania to work in a shop. She is seduced by the shop owner, becomes pregnant, and bears a child who is sent to live with foster parents and eventually dies of neglect and malnutrition. Characteristic of naturalism, the fate of each of the characters is determined by their economic and social condition. The title of the novel is ironic, as none of the characters is truly free to break out of his or her circumstances. Dina Halvorsen may be a victim, but she is not a passive victim: she continues trying to manipulate her circumstances to the bitter end. *Et frit Forhold* is amazingly frank in its depiction of female sexuality.

As a child Hulda Garborg dreamed of becoming an actress, and she was involved with the theater throughout her life, primarily as a playwright and as a promoter of New Norwegian in the theater. After the publication of her first novel Garborg turned to writing for the theater; and in 1895 her first play, *Mødre* (1895, Mothers), was produced at Christiania Theater. Her next play, *Rationelt Fjøsstell* (1896, Rational Farming), is a farce about a young woman, Inger Bøan, who comes home from school, bringing with her modern ideas about diet, health, and housekeeping, which she tries to impose on everyone else with disastrous results. A true bluestocking, she has even cut her hair short. In this conflict between modern ideas and old rural customs, it is the traditional values that win out in the end. *Rationelt Fjøsstell* was Hulda Garborg's most successful play. It was produced more than eighty times at the Christiania Theater between 1897 and 1899, more than any other play by a woman in the nineteenth century.

Rationelt Fjøsstell was followed by two other comedies: *Noahs Ark,* produced at Centralteatret in 1897 and published in 1899, and *Hos Lindelands* (At the Lindelands), published and produced in 1899. With *Vaar* (Spring), produced in 1899 and published in 1905 as *April,* Hulda Garborg turned her attention to treating the theme of eros and love as serious drama. Another play written in this vein was *Sovande Sorg* (1900, Sleeping Sorrow), which was not produced until 1910.

As she continued to write for the theater, Garborg in the next few years also published a collection of recipes and homemaking advice, *Heimstell* (1899, Homemaking); two books on folk song and dance, *Norske folkevisor: med utgreiding um vise-dansen av Hulda Garborg, I* (1903, Norwegian Folk Songs: With an Explanation of the Song-Dance by Hulda Garborg, I) and *Song-Dansen i Nord-Landi* (1903, The Song Dance in Northern Lands); and her book on the Norwegian national costume, *Norsk Klædebunad.* Concerned that the song-dance tradition had essentially died out in Norway, Garborg traveled to the Faroe Islands to study this tradition, where it had been unbroken since the Middle Ages. She founded and encouraged folk dance groups in Norway and the preservation of Norwegian folk culture.

Kvinden Skabt av Manden: Studie af en Kvinde, i anledning av Dr. Otto Weiningers' bog: "Geschlecht und Charakter" (Woman Made by Man: Study by a Woman, in Reference to Dr. Otto Weininger's Book: "Sex and Character"), published anonymously in 1904, went through ten printings and sold ten thousand copies in the first year. It soon became known that Garborg was the author of this scandalous novel. Leading advocates for women's rights found the book reactionary, while other critics, including Knut Hamsun, praised it highly. The novel was written in response to Weininger's claim that woman's nature is primarily sexual, and that women lack intellectual, spiritual, or moral qualities. The first-person narrator, relating the story of her relationship with her husband and with another man with whom she falls in love, reflects on a woman's needs for both sexual fulfillment and love. The protagonist's story is framed by an introductory essay on Weininger and a concluding chapter on the essential nature of woman.

In the sequel, *Fru Evas Dagbog* (1905, Eva's Diary), the unhappy Eva retreats to a small island in the Faroe Islands in order to find her identity as an individual and as a woman, wife, and mother. Because the island's inhabitants live in accord with nature, the relationships between men and women are harmonious and uncomplicated, and there is no need for emancipation. Also on the island are an elderly scientist who resembles Eva's husband and a younger misogynist poet who represents the ideas of Weininger. In her discussions and interactions with the other characters Eva attempts to understand how the healthy and natural relationship between the sexes she finds in this isolated location can be transmitted to modern society.

In 1908 Garborg completed *Mann av Guds Naade* (Man by the Grace of God). In many ways this novel, written in New Norwegian, is a tribute to the neighbors who provided so much practical help and support to the Garborgs in the early years of their marriage. It includes descriptions of rural culture and customs.

Garborg's interests, however, were not confined to Norwegian folk culture. She was also well traveled in Europe and international in her outlook. She had been given a copy of Rousseau's *Emile* (1762) when her son was born and was interested in his ideas on pedagogy. In 1909 she published *Rousseau og hans Tanker i Nutiden* (Rousseau and His Ideas Today), a work that combined a short biography with a presentation of some of Rousseau's ideas and Garborg's own philosophy of life. The following year she published *Rousseau*, a collection of articles written in New Norwegian that had appeared in *Syn og Segn*.

Garborg wrote thirteen plays in all, seven of them in New Norwegian. She wrote classical drama, tragedies, comedies, and plays based on folk motifs that incorporated music and dance. Although plays written in New Norwegian were not well received by bourgeois theater audiences at the time, Garborg worked tirelessly to bring serious New Norwegian theater before the public. She founded Det Norske Spellaget, a theater troupe that toured the country performing plays in New Norwegian between 1910 and 1913. Garborg arranged performances and raised funds for the company while

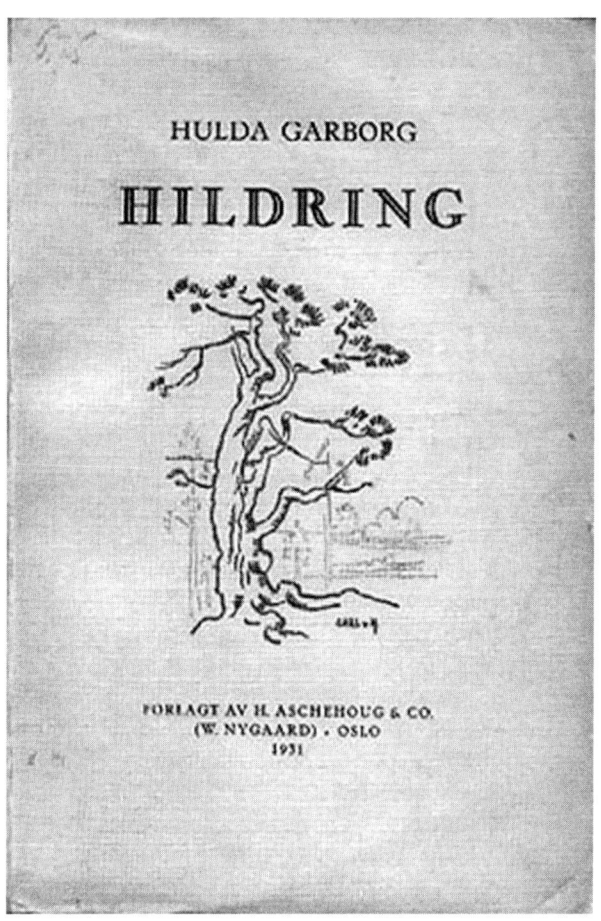

Title page for Garborg's last novel (Illusion), set in the Norwegian countryside (Wangsmo Antikvaria)

also acting in and directing some of its productions. The class schism between rural and urban interests was exemplified by the conflict between the use of Dano-Norwegian and New Norwegian. This conflict was so intense that many of their performances caused riots. In 1913 Garborg was also the driving force behind the founding of Det Norske Teatret (The Norwegian Theater), the only professional, permanent theater to use New Norwegian as its official language.

Two plays Garborg wrote arose out of her fascination for other cultures. *Under Bôdhitræet: En Drøm i fire billeder* (1911, Under the Buddha Tree: A Dream in Four Pictures), published anonymously and never produced, shows her interest in Eastern philosophy, which she read and studied for many years. In 1913, on a visit to the United States, where she had been invited to be a guest at the unveiling of a monument to Ivar Aasen in Fargo, North Dakota, Garborg saw a dramatization of Henry Wadsworth Longfellow's *The Song of Hiawatha* (1855). Already fascinated by Native American life and culture, she wrote a series of articles based on her encounters with Indians in the United States. In Hiawatha's vision of an organization of United Indian Nations that would maintain peace among the tribes she recognized an idea applicable to her own time. *Den store Freden* (1919, The Great Peace), written during World War I, presents Hiawatha's ideals in the form of a dramatic poem. The play was translated into English by her brother-in-law, Samuel Garborg, and published in the United States under the title *Hiawatha's Vision* (1927).

Garborg was one of the intellectual women of the time who believed that women are essentially different from men. For her, woman's capacity for love—both as woman and as mother—was the deepest and most essential part of the female nature. She believed that it was by fulfilling her role both as lover and as mother that a woman reached self-fulfillment. To deny woman's essential biological and spiritual attributes was to deny the true nature and role of woman. *Kvinden Skabt av Manden* was a response not only to Weininger but also to those women who believed that all gender differences were only a product of social conditioning and that women and men should be treated equally. In her own life and in many of her novels, however, Garborg indicates also that women need to develop their creativity and be able to engage in meaningful work. Novels such as *Eli* (1912), *Mot Solen* (1915, Toward the Sun), and *Gaaden* (1916, The Puzzle) demonstrate the conflict she sees between love and work. In her series of Hedmark novels, *Mens dansen gaar* (1920, While the Dance Goes On), *I huldreskog* (1922, In the Huldre Forest), *Naar heggen blomstrer* (1923, When the Chokecherry Blossoms) and *Grågubben* (1925, Graybeard), Garborg writes about a single woman who runs her own family farm and takes responsibility for others in the community as well. She is a strong woman and appears to live a fulfilling life; yet, she remains essentially lonely.

In the novel *Helenes historie* (1929, Helene's Story) Garborg returns to her youthful experiences, and especially her difficult relationship with her mother. The story of Helene Ravn provides a glimpse of what Hulda's life might have been like during her first years in Christiania, a constant struggle with economic hardship and loneliness but also filled with many suitors, young love, and intellectual and spiritual awakening. Her last novel, *Hildring* (1931, Illusion), set in the rural milieu, is one of only two of her novels written in New Norwegian. All of her other novels were written in Dano-Norwegian, though some had strong elements of dialect, especially the Hedmark novels. *Barndomsminne* (Childhood Memories) was published posthumously in 1935.

Hulda Garborg is remembered primarily today for her idealization of rural life and values and for promoting a form of national identity based upon traditional rural culture. Her efforts to revive and preserve traditional Norwegian folk music and the use of the national costume have overshadowed her important literary accomplishments. With *Kvinden Skabt av Manden* and many other of her literary works, however, she made a significant contribution to debates on the central issues of her time.

Biographies:

Johs. A. Dale, *Hulda Garborg* (Oslo: Noregs, 1961);

Tor Obrestad, *Hulda* (Oslo: Gyldendal, 1992);

Sønnøv Sem Borse, *Den myke Hulda: slik Garborg elsket henne* (Posgrunn: Forskningsstiffelsen Bics, 2006).

References:

Kari Fjørtoft, "Bohem i Bunad: Hulda Garborg (1862–1934)," in *Norsk kvinnelitteraturhistorie*, volume 2: *1900–1945*, edited by Irene Engelstad and others (Oslo: Pax, 1989), pp. 61–66;

Fjørtoft, "Den fiktive sjølvbiografien og den sjølvbiografiske fiksjonen: Om Hulda Garborgs *Barndomsminne* (1935) og Kvinnen skapt av mannen (1904)," *Edda: Nordisk Tidsskrift for Litteraturforskning*, 2 (1991);

Fjørtoft, "Sprogkamp og fredssag på scenen: Om Hulda Garborg," in *Nordisk kvinnelitteraturhistorie*, volume 3: *Vide verden 1900–1960*, edited by Elisabeth Møller Jensen and others (Copenhagen: Munksgaard-Rosinante, 1998), pp. 161–166;

Ivar Havnevik, "1904 og 1905–Hulda Garborg: Kvinnen skapt av mannen, Fru Evas dagbok," in *Norske Forfattere på Norsk Forlag: Aschehoug-bøker i tiden rundt 1905* (Oslo: Aschehoug, 1905), pp. 142–158;

Idar Stegane, "Kvinner i den nynorske litterære institusjonen," in *Norsk kvinnelitteraturhistorie*, volume 2: *1900–1945*, pp. 50–61.

Maurits Hansen
(5 July 1794 - 16 March 1842)

Bjørn Tysdahl
University of Oslo

BOOKS: *Digtninger* (Christiania: Privately published, 1816)–includes "Emil, en Roman i Breve" and "Fødselsdagsgaven";

Othar af Bretagne, et Riddereventyr (Christiania: Hartmanns, 1819);

Theodors Dagbog: en Fortælling (Christiania, 1820);

Forsøg til en Grammatik i Modersmaalet (Christiania: Hviid, 1822);

Digtninger: Samlede 1825, 2 volumes (Trondheim: T. A. Høeg, 1825)–includes "Skizzerede Nationale Fortællinger," "Nor og Gor," and "Keadan eller Klosterruinen";

Practisk Veiledning i Modersmaalet (Christiania: Hviid, 1825);

Materialier til en epideiktisk Undervisnings-Methode (Christiania: Hviid, 1828);

Eventyret ved Rigsgrændsen (Christiania: Hviid, 1828);

Første Omrids af Grammatiken (Christiania, 1830);

Norsk Idyllekrands (Christiania: Lehmann, 1831);

Omrids af Geografien til Brug for Begyndere (Christiania: Winther, 1831);

Kortfattet latinsk Lexicon (Christiania, 1831);

Det latinske Sprogs Syntaxis (Christiania: Roshauw, 1832);

Skolegrammatik i det franske Sprog (Christiania: Hviid, 1834);

Practisk Veiledning i Modersmaalet (Christiania: Hviid, 1836);

Samlede Noveller (Copenhagen: Den norske Boghandels Forlag, 1836);

Almindelig Verdenshistorie fra de ældste indtil vore Tider (Christiania: Winther, 1838);

Mordet paa Maskinbygger Roolfsen (Christiania: Winther, 1840);

Den Forskudte: en Novelle (Christiania: Wulfsburg, 1841);

Udvalg af M. C. Hansens Romaner og Noveller, 3 volumes (Bergen: Prahl, 1841–1843)–includes "Polykarps supplerede Manuskripter";

Forsøg til en hensigtmæssig Barnets første Bog (Christiania: Hviid, 1842);

Fremmed-Ordbog (Christiania, 1842);

Maurits Hansen (Dag Og Tid <http://www.dagogtid.no/ nyhet.cfm?nyhetid=941>)

Tone: Maurits C. Hansens sidste Novelle (Christiania: Malling, 1843).

Editions and Collections: *Noveller og Fortællinger: Efter Forfatterens Død samlede og ordnede,* 8 volumes, edited by C. N. Schwach (Christiania: Chr. Tønsberg, 1855–1858);

Noveller i Udvalg, edited by Henrik Jæger (Christiania: Aschehoug, 1882).

Maurits Hansen is a founding father of Norwegian fiction. After the great period of saga writing in the late Middle Ages, Norwegian cultural life suffered a sharp decline. The country was particularly hard hit by the Black Death, and the subsequent union with Denmark meant that the economic and cultural center for both countries was Copenhagen. The Norwegian economy only recovered in the eighteenth century: towns grew rapidly, and the number of people who could read soared. When Norway became a separate country once again in 1814, the ground was laid for a renaissance of literature. Hansen was one of a group of bright students in Christiania (today Oslo) whose aim was to create a literature that was Norwegian, not Danish.

Hansen grew up with Danish literature at a time when the two languages were virtually identical on the printed page. He also read German, French, and English, in addition to the Greek and Latin he had studied at school. When he turned to fiction writing, he wanted to use techniques and themes from European literature in stories set in Norway and focused on central aspects of local life. Between 1816 and 1842 he wrote short stories and a few novellas and novels that were all widely read and that made his name central and highly respected in literary circles in Christiania. Hansen was also active as a literary editor, giving other young writers an outlet for their work. As a teacher he was keenly interested in how pupils could learn other languages and produced several grammars for use in schools. His more theoretical works introduced Norwegians to current thinking in European linguistics.

Maurits Christopher Hansen was born on 5 July 1794 in the township of Modum in eastern Norway. The family soon moved to Porsgrunn, where his father had been made vicar, and in 1806 to Skedsmo, a rural district close to Christiania. On his father's side Hansen came from a line of Lutheran clergymen. His mother was the daughter of a Norwegian merchant. The home in which he grew up as one of the two children who survived early childhood was marked by a loving atmosphere, as well as by a lively interest in literature. As was often the case in Norway in the early nineteenth century, Hansen was taught central school subjects at home by his father until he was fifteen. His mother and an aunt who lived with the family encouraged his interest in fairy tales and other kinds of popular literature. Hansen even tried his hand at various kinds of poetry before he left home. In later years he came to believe that he would have been more diligent at school and the university if his early education had been more demanding.

In 1809 Hansen was sent to the Cathedral School in Christiania. Until the University of Christiania was established in 1811, the Cathedral School was the intellectual center of eastern Norway. Hansen thus found himself in a stimulating academic climate. The school library was good, and he read widely in Danish and German literature. His teachers soon realized that he was an exceptionally bright pupil. He passed his matriculation examinations ("examen artium") in 1814 with top marks; his papers on Norwegian literature were singled out for particular praise. A professor at the recently established university told him that he was an obvious candidate for a lectureship in aesthetics.

As it happened, this moment was the apex of Hansen's academic reputation. Enjoying the freedom he had as a student, he took an active part in the social and cultural life of the new capital of Norway. He acted in comedies, contributed poems to small collections edited by a friend, wrote occasional poetry for parties given by town dignitaries and for other local events, and helped to start a student society at the university. He also spent half a year in Copenhagen, the home of his father's family. In a far richer cultural climate than Christiania could offer, he met Danish authors such as the theologian and historian N. F. S. Grundtvig and the short-story writer B. S. Ingemann, both of whom impressed him deeply. In Copenhagen, Hansen also further developed his taste for the theater which, however, he never turned into serious attempts to write his own plays.

Hansen's studies suffered. Following the encouragement he had been given earlier, he started on courses in philology and philosophy, but he never sat for the final examinations. He had fallen in love with Helvig Leschly, the daughter of a customs officer, and they were married in 1816. The home they set up together remained a closely knit and happy one, but neither husband nor wife had private means, and from then on Hansen's life was marked by a tiresome struggle to make enough money to support the family. Even before he got married, he had taken a position as teacher and librarian at a military college, and in 1817 he and his wife started a school for girls in Oslo. He wanted to continue his studies, but he found virtually no time for them. In 1820 he realized that he needed a more settled income and sought and obtained a position as a teacher at a public boys' school in Trondheim. Taking stock of his career, he sadly found that his early ambitions had come to nothing: he had not taken the examinations normally required for a university career, nor was he qualified for most other government positions, whether in the best schools, in public administration, or in the church. The life he could envisage was one of hard teaching in schools that did not pay him well, combined with literary work in the small hours.

All his life Hansen had the desire to be a writer, and, even in the busy first years of his marriage, he

Kongsberg in eastern Norway, where Hansen lived from the mid 1820s until his death in 1842 (from Edvard Beyer, ed.,
Norges Litteratur Historie, *volume 2 [Oslo: Cappelen, 1974]; University of Kansas Libraries)*

found time for writing. Apart from occasional poetry, he wrote short stories and his first novel, *Othar af Bretagne, et Riddereventyr* (1819, Othar of Bretagne: A Fairy Tale about Knights). The narrative technique of *Othar af Bretagne, et Riddereventyr,* with its play on the fantastic, owes much to German writer Friedrich de la Motte Fouqué. The novel is, as the title says, a "fairy tale," set on the Continent. But, like fairy tales generally, *Othar af Bretagne* explores moral and existential questions: themes from the New Testament inform the narrative to the effect that *Othar af Bretagne* becomes a Christian allegory. As such, it is marked by considerable vigor and coherence. Parts of the story can also be read as an exploration of ambivalent feelings about sexuality. Hansen's frank depiction of lust may well have contributed to the popularity of the novel. It was translated into several other languages. Translations in the book markets of northern Europe were difficult to track, and the German version was on one occasion translated back into Norwegian.

Hansen wrote a few other stories in the manner of Fouqué, but around 1820 he realized that he was more at home as a writer in another narrative style: his *Digtninger: Samlede 1825* (1825, Poetic Works: Collected 1825) does not evince a full-fledged realism, but its central cycle of stories, "Skizzerede Nationale Fortællinger" (Sketches of National Stories), places the newly independent Norway on the literary map without any elements of the fantastic or the supernatural. In the first story, "Luren" (The Lur), a young couple communicate over long distances by the means of the old Norse instrument, a type of horn, that has given the story its title; and the girl's father, a wealthy old farmer, has Snorri Sturluson's *Sagas* on his bookshelf. The poor young man and the farmer's daughter are involved in a common situation in the period: they have a child without being married. The happy ending serves as a tribute both to the faithfulness and the perseverance of the young and to the humanity of the proud descendant of the Vikings who finally does allow his daughter to marry her lover. In intricate patterns of similarities and differences, these seven stories, set in different parts of the country, explore what Hansen considered basic themes in the lives of people in the countryside as well as in towns. What initiates the action of *Digtninger* is most often the problems young people have in finding their place in society. Ensuing events illustrate the relationships between the classes (there is a fair amount of social mobility even in the countryside); the moral dilemmas of the main characters (virtue is most often rewarded); and the cultural richness of the new country (seen both in the respect paid to its medieval literature and in the various artistic achievements of the present). Hansen has been criticized for lack of depth in his characterizations, but there are, in fact, portraits in *Digtninger* of the way human beings behave under pressure. These "sketches" inspired later writers; the most famous was Bjørnstjerne Bjørnson, whose *Bondefortellinger* (1857–1863, Stories about Farmers) owe much to Hansen.

After six years in Trondheim, Hansen was appointed headmaster of the "middle school" in the little town of Kongsberg in eastern Norway. "Middle schools" taught a wide variety of subjects at a relatively high level, but they did not take their pupils as far as the university matriculation examinations; for this education young people had to go to a cathedral school or a so-called Latin school. Hansen spent the rest of his life in Kongsberg. He never got the more-advanced and better-paid jobs that he hoped for. But life as a headmaster gave him interesting opportunities. He was an energetic and highly respected pedagogue and developed his interests, awakened in Trondheim, in the study of both the structure and the teaching methods of the languages on the school syllabus.

Hansen's *Forsøg til en Grammatik i Modersmaalet* (1822, Attempt at a Grammar of the Mother Tongue) appeared in five later editions, with emendations and additions, and it remained a popular textbook in schools for nearly forty years. Hansen pioneered the idea that Norwegian would develop both a vocabulary and a structure that would gradually remove it from Danish. In later editions his grammar included a vigorous attempt to establish Norwegian as a separate language. He also encouraged spelling reforms to reduce the distance between the written and the spoken forms of Norwegian. Hansen's writings on linguistic issues show how wide his interests were. In addition to his Norwegian grammar, he wrote textbooks for the teaching of French and Latin. His Latin grammar fully explicated his own theoretical model for linguistics: Hansen inherited the belief that a "universal grammar" could be established from the Port Royal philosophers in France. Once mastered, this grammar would be a key to the learning of all languages. His own version of the universal grammar relied on ideograms and geometrical figures to indicate connections between lexical elements. The result would, he believed, be a written language that could be used internationally. In reports from his school he insisted, probably correctly, that his students found the system helpful—they had an enthusiastic teacher. But Hansen's work was not well received at the university, and a lectureship in philosophy established in 1839 to which he aspired was given to a poet with no background in philosophy. Still, Hansen continued refining his system for the rest of his life. He also had the energy needed to produce textbooks in other subjects while in Kongsberg; one in geography appeared in 1831, and a world history, in 1838. He adapted a German Latin dictionary for use in Norway (1831), and a Norwegian *Fremmed-Ordbog* (Dictionary of Foreign Words) was first published in 1842. It remained a standard reference work for more than a generation.

Hansen's family life was a pleasant enclave in an exhausting career. Two girls and a boy grew up in their home, and their father liked to teach them. He even prepared one of his daughters for the matriculation examinations, something virtually unheard of at that time. In later years, Hansen's children remembered evenings at home with great pleasure. It was, said one of them after Hansen's death, impossible "to appreciate something beautiful if Father did not read it aloud."

In addition to being a devoted father, a keen pedagogue, a school administrator, and a professional linguist, Hansen found time and had the energy to continue his literary career in these years. He wrote a steady flow of stories of varying lengths. He also continued for a long time as editor of literary magazines, something that both helped and hindered him. It took time away from actual writing, but it also gave him opportunities to publish his shorter tales. In letters to friends, Hansen expressed his anxieties: he wrote everything in haste and could not see when he would be able to hone his texts with the care they deserved.

One of the central themes in Hansen's work is the complex relationship between appearance and reality. This theme provides a starting point for many of the "Skizzerede nationale Fortællinger," and several other early short stories hinge on misunderstandings that often create comic confrontations. The first more extended treatment of this theme is found in "Moderen" (1832, The Mother), a truncated novel published in *Bien,* a literary magazine that Hansen did not edit. This work about recent Norwegian history is ambitious, with portraits of well-known politicians and academics. His depiction of a fictitious party where many such leaders meet has been rightly praised; other chapters of "Moderen" give sharp glimpses of the lower levels of Norwegian society. Characterization, too, is a model of efficiency: characters that are psychologically unimportant are flat, whereas detailed studies of more important characters are subtle and convincing. The opening of "Moderen" is dramatic: "Paa en mørk, stormende Sommerdag i Aaret 1790 krydsede temmelig nær Højden af Færder et vel bemandet, sterkt ladet Skib" (On a dark, stormy summer's day in the year 1790 a well manned, heavily laden ship tacked [northwards] quite near Færder [the lighthouse at the opening of the Oslo Fjord]). What follows is a spirited account of a dangerous confrontation between the captain and the mate on board the ship, on the one hand, and customs officers on the other. Not only is the immediate danger of the expedition stressed in the first sentence, but a "trust-not-appearances" theme is also indicated: the Oslo Fjord was, and is, widely known for its pleasant summers, but its reputation is also deceptive. Storms can come quickly, and with its reefs the Færder archipelago is always a danger to shipping.

Subsequent chapters of "Moderen" concentrate on meetings between the main characters, placed as they are in widely different social circumstances. In one such case, the host of a grand dinner party, someone who is both a scientist and a financial magnate, invites his most famous guests to tell those present about memorable incidents in their lives. When the turn comes back to him, the host relates how moved he was when he signed the membership protocol of the Royal Society in London and found Isaac Newton's name on the same page. He continues to give the party brief accounts of his visits to Vesuvius and Pompeii. They sound like conventional tourist reports until the reader realizes their half-hidden symbolism: the host's own youth has been as eruptive as the volcano, and this period is now a buried part of his life. Will it, like Pompeii, be revealed? The rest of the story becomes an exploration of this mysterious past. After the opening chapters set in 1790, the reader is taken twenty years back, to events in Denmark that begin to explain the present. But there are still loose ends; the most conspicuous is the limited role of the mother, who has given the novel its title. The main reason for such lacunae illustrates Hansen's precarious position in a little town at some distance from the capital: the editor of *Bien* suddenly told him that the novel could not be published in the format Hansen intended, and a third of the projected story had to be reduced to a few pages. Though incomplete, "Moderen" is still a poignant and deeply moving story.

The appearance-and-reality theme becomes more and more firmly associated with a retrospective narrative technique in the course of Hansen's career. Stories tend to be set in a present in which life is so intriguing that questions about the past come naturally; and what is gradually revealed is a skeleton in the cupboard. "Schachten" (1833, The Shaft) is an interesting example. It has sometimes been sharply criticized as depending too heavily on an open air versus hidden shaft dichotomy. Predictably, the shaft turns out to hide the key to the secrets of the past, and some of the revelations are somewhat melodramatic. Still, "Schachten" illustrates how subtle Hansen's symbolic use of paraphernalia can be: dangers above ground are surprisingly balanced, not against cave horrors but against a life in the shaft marked by common sense and responsibility for others. The story becomes a fascinating study of men and women under pressure (male sexual roles are given special attention).

Often, as in the early novella "Keadan eller Klosterruinen" (1825, Keadan or the Ruined Monastery), what is revealed is a murder. Replete with its outlaws and hideouts, "Keadan eller Klosterruinen" reflects Hansen's enthusiasm for the novels of Sir Walter Scott. In "Jutulskoppen. En norsk Kriminal-Fortælling" (1836, Jutulskoppen. A Norwegian Crime Story) an intelligent woman solves the crime and thereby proves the innocence of a man suspected of murder. In 1840 Hansen published "Mordet paa Maskinbygger Roolfsen" (The Murder of Engineer Roolfsen), a narrative that combines all the hallmarks of the classic detective story. First, the tale concerns an unsolved mystery, the inexplicable disappearance and possible murder of a well-known man in town. Second, an honest, intelligent detective (traditionally male), inside or outside the public administration of justice, investigates the case. In Hansen's story the Kongsberg police chief, Barth, is the protagonist. Barth is aided by a scientist—in this case the town pharmacist—who also plays a part common to the genre. The powerful director of the famous silver mining company in town interferes with the investigation, but Barth guards his independence and trusts his own judgment. Third, suspicion centers on more than one possible culprit; the three prime suspects in "Mordet paa Maskinbygger Roolfsen" are a small grocer and his son and, as Barth gradually realizes, the director of the mine, who cunningly tries to turn suspicion away from himself. The fact that the story came out in 1840 has historical significance. Edgar Allan Poe's "The Murders in the Rue Morgue," which appeared in *Graham's Magazine* in 1841, is generally considered the first example of detective fiction. Hansen might have been recognized as a forerunner had he written in a larger language community.

The denouement of "Mordet paa Maskinbygger Roolfsen" comes as something of an anticlimax: Roolfsen is not dead; he had left Kongsberg suddenly because his fiancée began an affair with somebody else. Still, the story does not suffer unduly as a result, and for two reasons. One is that Barth's investigation does reveal crimes, though nothing as serious as murder. More important is the overall effect of the muted last pages. They suggest that the process of detection reveals something more important than a spectacular climax would. In the course of his work, Barth realizes that an investigation not only involves sharp observations and intelligent deductions; it may also lead to public riots based on vague but violent feelings as well as confrontations with authorities using their power to protect their own positions. Barth's pharmacist friend sums up this aspect of the events: "The higher ranks were supposed to be spared." But he exaggerates. What Hansen suggests in "Mordet paa Maskinbygger Roolfsen" is that local financial muscle is something to be reckoned with, but it is not an obvious winner in a confrontation with an honest administration of the law.

Avoidance of simplified attitudes is something that characterizes Hansen's fictional reports from his own country. As in the "Skizzerede nationale Fortællinger," Hansen throughout his career shows a deep respect for a newly liberated country that struggles to achieve an independence based on sound, incorruptible government and necessary thrift. But this respect does not make him blind to shortcomings of various kinds. The narrative perspective he adopts reflects this awareness. Stories told in the first person and stories with a named, fictitious narrator nearly always have in common a voice that represents common sense, sound critical judgments, and sometimes a schoolmasterly tendency to point out what is wrong. Hansen has been criticized for the upper-class allegiance that this perspective seems to involve: the narrator belongs to the cultural and economic establishment, and he looks down, directly or indirectly, on the natives of Norwegian valleys and small towns. But such critics forget that Hansen's own social position was insecure, placed as he was in a middle layer of society above the working classes but definitely below the cultural and economic elite. This insecurity is often reflected in his style and motifs. Novelist Camilla Collett, whose respect for Hansen was considerable, noticed what she thought was a lack of taste as well as a ludicrous clumsiness in his descriptions of the highest classes, but, significantly, "at the same time you hear painful sobs between the lines, you are taken aback and listen—you do not laugh."

Hansen's longest narrative, "Polycarps supplerede Manuskripter" (1841–1842, Polycarp's Manuscripts, with Supplements), describes the narrator's struggle to put together a family history partly from various written sources. The story that is unraveled stretches from the 1770s to 1814, the years in which the ground was laid for Norwegian independence. The novel sums up many of Hansen's main concerns. Moral weaknesses are exposed, not least, lack of responsibility in close family relations. The poverty and vulnerability of the country is stressed: with fluctuating trade in a Europe ravaged by war, businesses easily go bankrupt, and starvation threatens, but life is also marked by thrift and inventiveness. The main character, Gandel, has great buoyancy and energy. Toward the end he is eighty-four years old and is in charge both of the local sawmill and the local school. Other parts of the novel are set abroad in events that are starkly melodramatic (Hansen tends to describe other countries in black and white), but the rich gallery of characters from all levels of society and the ways their life stories interweave create a many-sided and intriguing narrative.

In exploring the past, Hansen reveals an increasingly keen interest in cultural history. This interest is reflected in Polycarp, the combined narrator and assembler of manuscripts in "Polycarps supplerede Manuskripter." Polycarp is a superficial young man who wants to become a poet, a career choice that seems unrealistic to the reader; but the family story that he writes and edits gives him credit. In its main themes and motifs the story is a wide-ranging and balanced cultural and economic history of forty formative years in the history of a new nation. One of the salient themes in the novel, the many possibilities of social mobility, reflects the author's view of Norway as a liberal country in a period of rapid development.

Some of Hansen's most intimate studies of local culture are found in stories set in Kongsberg and its surroundings. In "Fru Birthe" (1834, Mrs. Birthe), the narrator is fascinated by a nearby country estate with a strange painting on one of the walls and by an old, overgrown garden not far away. Both the painting and the garden represent first impressions of the past, enigmatic as in the painting and difficult to reconstruct as in the garden. The mystery that is unraveled hinges on a sexual escapade, but here as in other stories, sex is a trigger mechanism setting in motion events that reveal other aspects of life. "Fru Birthe" is a study of social ambition; of the way warfare disrupts ordinary life; of faithfulness versus fickle selfishness; and of the different ways in which creativity, artistic and otherwise, makes life richer.

Hansen died on 16 March 1842, after months of suffering from a terminal disease. His admirers soon circulated the idea that he had been killed by the exhausting struggle for money that had marked his life. Many felt that the novelist had been given short shrift by Norwegian officialdom. Some of his colleagues in the literary trade wrote moving tributes to his courageous life and to his importance in literary history. Later in the nineteenth century, Hansen tended to be overshadowed by authors such as Bjørnson and Henrik Ibsen. Hardline realists in the next generation criticized Hansen for lack of psychological depth, a judgment that is definitely unhistorical in its blindness to other ways in which human life can be depicted, and in particular to Hansen's unobtrusive symbolism and his shrewd use of analogies between characters. In the second half of the twentieth century, Hansen's place in literary history has been more fully acknowledged.

Maurits Hansen is important not only for his pioneering work but also for what he meant to the next generation of Norwegian writers. Ibsen read Hansen, and there can be no doubt that the dramatist known for his retrospective technique owes something to the stories of his forerunner who often lets the secret in the past have an explosive effect in the present. As a writer of stories about ordinary people in the Norwegian countryside, Hansen pioneered a tradition that later generations of novelists continued and developed; and his descriptions of Norwegian landscape, in narrative techniques learned from Scott, set the trend for many later writers.

Letters:

"Af Maurits Hansens Breve til C. N. Schwach," in *Historiske Samlinger*, volume 2, published by Den norske historiske Kildeskriftcommission (Christiania: Broggers, 1907), pp. 355–449.

References:

Ludvig Daae, "M. C. Hansens Ungdomsaar indtil hans Ansættelse i Throndhjem: Et Udkast," in *Historiske Samlinger*, volume 2, published by Den norske Kilderskriftkommission (Christiania: Broggers, 1907), pp. 470–484;

Arne Fretheim, *Livets kolde prosa: Maurits Hansen og hans samtid* (Oslo: Aschehoug, 2006);

P. L. Stavnen, "Maurits Hansens ungdomsår," *Edda: Nordisk Tidsskrift for Litteraturforskning*, 2 (1914): 250–280;

Paulus Svendsen, "Maurits Christopher Hansen," *Det Kongelige Norske Videnskabers Selskaps Forhandlinger*, 15 (1942): 37–79;

Bjørn Tysdahl, *Maurits Hansens fortellerkunst* (Oslo: Aschehoug, 1988);

Olaf Øyslebø, *Maurits Hansen som forteller: en studie av fortellemåter, språk og stil i de første romaner fra norsk miljø etter 1814* (Oslo: Solum, 2001).

Gunnar Heiberg
(18 November 1857 – 22 February 1929)

Tanya Thresher
University of Wisconsin–Madison

BOOKS: *Kants fornuftkritik og En soirée dansante,* by Heiberg and Hans Jæger (Christiania, 1878);

Tante Ulrikke (Copenhagen: Philipsen, 1884);

Kong Midas (Copenhagen: Schubothes Boghandel, 1890);

Kunstnere (Copenhagen: Schubothes Boghandel, 1893);

Balkonen (Copenhagen: Gyldendal, 1894); translated by Edwin Johan Vickner and Glenn Hughes as "The Balcony," *Poet Lore,* 33 (Winter 1922): 475–496;

Gerts have (Christiania & Copenhagen: Cammermeyer, 1894);

Det store Lod (Copenhagen: Philipsen, 1895);

Folkeraadet (Copenhagen: Gyldendal, 1897);

Harald Svans mor (Copenhagen: Gyldendal, 1899);

Pariserbreve (Christiania: Aschehoug, 1900);

Kjærlighed til næsten (Copenhagen: Gyldendal, 1902);

Kjærlighedens tragedie (Copenhagen: Gyldendal, 1904); translated by Edwin Björkman as "The Tragedy of Love," in *Chief Contemporary Dramatists,* edited by Thomas H. Dickinson (Boston: Houghton Mifflin, 1921), pp. 687–716;

Jeg vil værge mit land (Christiania: Aschehoug, 1912);

Paradesengen (Christiania: Aschehoug, 1913);

Set og hørt (Christiania: Aschehoug, 1917);

Ibsen og Bjørnson paa scenen (Christiania: Aschehoug, 1918);

Franske visitter (Christiania: Aschehoug, 1919);

Norsk teater (Christiania: Aschehoug, 1920);

1905 (Christiania: Aschehoug, 1923);

Salt og sukker (Christiania: Aschehoug, 1924);

I frihetens bur (Oslo: Aschehoug, 1929);

Hugg og stikk, introduction by Einar Skavlan (Oslo: Aschehoug, 1951);

Artikler om mange ting, edited by Hans Heiberg (Oslo: Aschehoug, 1972);

Artikler om teater og dramatikk, edited by Hans Heiberg (Oslo: Aschehoug, 1972).

Collection: *Samlede dramatiske verker,* 4 volumes (Christiania: Aschehoug, 1917–1918).

PLAY PRODUCTIONS: *Kong Midas,* Copenhagen, Det Kongelige Teater, 17 January 1890;

Gunnar Heiberg (Gyldendal Norsk Forlag)

Kunstnere, Copenhagen, Det Kongelige Teater, 1 November 1893;

Balkonen, Copenhagen, Fri Theater, January 1894;

Det store Lod, Christiania, Carl Johanteatret, 4 October 1895;

Folkeraadet, Christiania, Christiania Theater, 18 October 1897;

Harald Svans mor, Christiania, Nationaltheatret, 26 September 1899;

Tante Ulrikke, Christiania, Nationaltheatret, 8 January 1901;

Kjærlighed til næsten, Christiania, Nationaltheatret, 18 February 1903;

Kjærlighedens tragedie, Christiania, Nationaltheatret, 16 January 1905;

Jeg vil værge mit land, Christiania, Nationaltheatret, 8 February 1912;

Gerts have, Christiania, Nationaltheatret, 31 January 1917;

Paradesengen, Stockholm, Dramatiska teatern, 3 May 1920.

An enduring representative of the intellectual radicalism prevalent in Norway in the 1870s and 1880s, Gunnar Heiberg is best known for continuing the dramatic tradition of Henrik Ibsen, the father of modern drama. He was the most noteworthy playwright of the generation succeeding that of Ibsen and Bjørnstjerne Bjørnson; yet, while his plays were always highly provocative, they are seldom produced in Norwegian theaters today. Heiberg's acquaintance with many of the prominent Nordic authors and artists of his time, his stage directing, and his many theater reviews and essays on the arts and politics have given scholars valuable insights into the cultural climate of late-nineteenth-century Norway and Europe.

Gunnar Edvard Rode Heiberg was born in Gamlebyen, Christiania, 18 November 1857 to appellate court judge Edvard Omsen Heiberg and Vilhelmine (Minna) Augusta Rode, who had married in 1856. He was the eldest of eleven children. Heiberg's maternal family was highly artistic and included the well-known poet Helge Rode. The Heiberg family spent summers with relatives in Denmark and were exposed to the culturally more refined city of Copenhagen. Edvard Heiberg was a lawyer, like his own father, Edvard Christie Heiberg; but he was interested in literature and history at an early age, and throughout his life he was actively involved in cultural issues. As a member of the board of Christiania Theater, Edvard Heiberg often took his family to dramatic performances. This practice affected his eldest son in particular; the boy visited the theater whenever he could, often with a friend, and spent time behind the scenes. He even kept a diary, which has since been lost, in which he wrote about his theater visits and his appreciation of the art of acting. In fact, Heiberg's first drama review can be dated to a diary entry on 10 April 1872 and dealt with Bjørnson's *Sigurd Jorsalfar* (1872, Sigurd the Crusader).

At the age of five Heiberg enrolled at Nissen's School in the center of the city, where he was unremarkable as a pupil. He was interested in sports instead and was successful in athletic competitions. Nevertheless, even as a young boy he belonged to a literary club and was active in discussions of cultural events. After graduating from Nissen's in 1874, Heiberg studied at King Fredrick's University in Christiania. He earned the *Cand. Philos* in 1875 and then began studying law. He was employed in the law office of Vilhelm Heiberg, one of his uncles, but law never truly engaged the young Heiberg, who dreamed of becoming an actor. Heiberg sought the company of actors such as Bjarne Lund, who was employed at the Christiania Theater, and Arnoldus Reimers, whom he greatly admired. Heiberg, however, was not considered a handsome man and believed his own opportunities for a career on the stage were limited.

As a student Heiberg was inspired by Johan Sverdrup, a politician who later became the prime minister of Norway, and Georg Brandes, a Danish writer and critic who originated a movement he called the "Modern Breakthrough," which sought to address social problems through literary naturalism. The former inspired in Heiberg a strong feeling of nationalism and awakened his social conscience, and the latter encouraged his development of a European awareness and his willingness to question authority, particularly the authority of the state church. After hearing Brandes lecture, Heiberg wrote a letter to the great orator, dated 6 August 1875, in which he included a poem, "En Søndags-Formiddag" (A Sunday-Morning), asking that it be published in Brandes's journal *Det nittende aarhundrede* (The Nineteenth Century). Brandes's rejection of the poem did not weaken Heiberg's regard for the critic. Regarding Brandes's movement as part of his own journey to personal emancipation, Heiberg was engaged in the evolving debate about love, relations between the sexes, and marriage and was caught up in the radical and anti-Christian spirit of the 1870s and 1880s.

Heiberg began working on the characters of his first play, *Tante Ulrikke* (1884, Aunt Ulrikke), as early as 1877, but his first publications were two poems. In 1878 he published "Menneskets Genesis" (The Genesis of Mankind) in the radical *Nye norske tidsskrift* (New Norwegian Magazine). "Menneskets Genesis" is a long philosophical poem in the spirit of the Romantic poets Henrik Wergeland and George Gordon, Lord Byron. The poem discusses the fall from grace of Adam and Eve in the Garden of Eden and hails Cain and his descendents as the personification of a free human spirit. While the form of the poem is traditional, the ideas expressed were considered so revolutionary in conservative circles that his law professor requested that he be expelled from the university. Heiberg avoided expulsion by withdrawing from his law studies and traveling to Italy.

Before he left Norway, Heiberg published another poem anonymously in *Kants fornuftkritik og En soirée dan-*

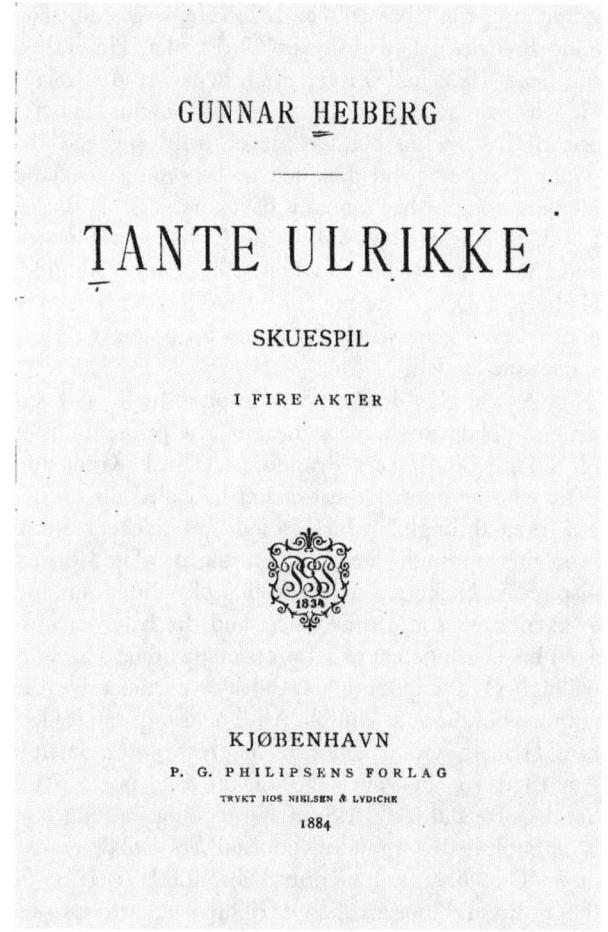

Title page for Heiberg's first play (Aunt Ulrikke), about a family divided by politics (Widener Library, Harvard University)

sante (1878, Kant's Critique of Reason and An Evening Party with Dance). Heiberg wrote the thirty-page poem "En soirée dansante," and Hans Jæger, the most prominent representative of the Christiania Bohême, was responsible for the philosophical essay on Immanuel Kant. The framework for the poem is a party during which two men and two women discuss the meaning of life and praise liberty and reason above all else. The style is free and reminiscent of a young Wergeland.

In fall 1878 Heiberg set out on his first trip abroad, having been given some money by his Danish aunt, Margrethe Vullum, who was a strong supporter of the arts. While he was disappointed in Rome, his stay there provided him the opportunity to become well acquainted with Ibsen and the Danish writer J. P. Jacobsen. Heiberg venerated Ibsen throughout his life. While in Rome, he staunchly supported Ibsen's advocacy of giving female members of the Scandinavian Club the right to vote. Jacobsen, who shared his interest in the works of Charles Darwin, was slowly working on his novel *Niels Lyhne* (1880), which he recited to Heiberg.

Heiberg returned to Christiania in fall 1879, traveling via Munich, where he came in contact with several Norwegian artists in the city and became friends with Erik Werenskiold. While the trip did not result in any notable literary output, it provided Heiberg with inspiration and admittance into the most influential and provocative cultural circles of the time.

Back in Christiania, Heiberg worked as a journalist, writing theater reviews for the *Christiania Intelligenssedler* (Christianian Intelligencer), a periodical edited by a good family friend, Hartvig Lassen. He also worked for *Ny Illustreret Tidene* (New Illustrated Ages), a weekly paper known for its high quality, and later for *Dagbladet* (The Daily Newspaper), the national paper of the left wing. Heiberg worked for *Dagbladet* for almost two years, during which time the newspaper faced severe financial difficulties. Heiberg was most interested in writing about theater, and unlike his more conservative colleagues, he enthusiastically reviewed Ibsen's *Gengangere* (translated as *Ghosts*, 1888) when it was published in 1881. He also took part in the emerging prostitution debate that was instigated by his old friend Jæger. After writing a eulogy for the actress Johanne Juell Reimers, Heiberg left *Dagbladet* and went to Copenhagen, where he lived with his maternal aunt, Othilie Hansen, for more than a year. In Copenhagen he met many writers, including Brandes and Erik Skram, and saw new art exhibitions, notably the great Nordic Exhibition of 1883. Heiberg also frequented the Royal Dramatic Theater, which was of superior quality to the emerging theaters in his home country. Heiberg completed work on his play *Tante Ulrikke* before returning to Norway at the end of July 1883.

Tante Ulrikke was published in 1884 and quickly established Heiberg's reputation as a dramatist of stature. This realistic problem drama was in the style of Ibsen, and the central character is, like Ibsen's Lorna Hessel in *Samfundets Støtter* (1877; translated as *The Pillars of Society*, 1888), modeled on the pioneering women's rights campaigner, Aasta Hansteen, the sister of Heiberg's uncle by marriage. Much of the action was based on the first socialist meetings that were taking place at Tyveholmen; the student agitator Fredriksen is loosely based on the socialist Olaus Fjørtorft. The setting is the home of Professor Blom, who is encouraged by friends to become involved in parliament. When his middle-aged sister-in-law, Ulrikke, arrives with the intention of taking part in an upcoming socialist rally, he attempts to dissuade her because her association with radicals may undermine his advancement. Blom's daughter, Helene, is unable to refrain from defending her beloved aunt, and she subsequently defies her father and also participates in the rally. This conflict leads to her breaking with her father, who in the final act decides to run for election. The balance between pathos and satire in the play and the intimate understanding of the nascent Workers' Movement portrayed were something quite new to Norwegian theater. Nevertheless, the Christiania Theater rejected the play on the grounds that it was too controversial. It was later accepted by Den Nationale Scene (The National Scene), or DNS, in Bergen in 1884, although Heiberg himself withdrew it after he accepted the position of artistic director at the theater on 8 March the same year. It was not performed until seventeen years later at the Nationaltheatret (National Theater).

Heiberg held the position of artistic director at DNS for four years and, like his predecessors Ibsen and Bjørnson, who had also worked at the theater, he gained valuable practical experience, although the demands of the job precluded any dramatic composition. After the death of his father in November 1884, Heiberg married the principal actress of the theater, Didrikke (Didi) Tollefesen from Bergen, on 1 April 1885. While at the theater Heiberg directed the premieres of several prominent plays, most notably Ibsen's *Vildanden* (1884; translated as *The Wild Duck,* 1890) on 9 February 1885, with Didi as Hedvig and Lars Michelsen as Hjalmar Ekdal, and *Rosmersholm* (1886; translated, 1889) on 17 January 1887, with Didi as Rebekka West and Nicolai Halvorsen as Rosmer. Economic hardship for the theater, along with disagreements as to the repertoire often led to difficulties for Heiberg, who went so far as to threaten to resign at the board's refusal to allow the performance of Bjørnson's *Kongen* (1877; translated as *The King,* 1914). Heiberg left his post in 1888 and never again held a full-time position at a theater, although he occasionally worked as a guest director.

Kong Midas (1890, King Midas) was Heiberg's first play to be performed, initially at Det Kongelige Theater (The Royal Theater) in Copenhagen on 17 January 1890 and later, in April, at Tivoli Teater (Tivoli Theater) in Christiania with Didi in the starring role of Anna Hielm. Unlike *Tante Ulrikke,* the play was completed quickly–in twenty-eight days. This comedy depicts the descent into seeming madness of Anna Hielm, a widow whose courage in starting a new relationship with the fifty-year-old editor and politician Ramseth is crushed when, in the spirit of truthfulness, he reveals he was unfaithful to her. The public saw Ramseth as a caricature of Bjørnson with his outspoken views on moral and political truth. Because of their respect for Bjørnson, the leaders of the Christiania Theater rejected the play, leading to protests. The writer Knut Hamsun announced to the nation that he was returning his complimentary tickets to the theater.

The relationship between Heiberg and his wife worsened because of her increasing drinking problem; they separated in February 1892, when he left unannounced for Copenhagen. In the same year he was granted an author's scholarship and completed *Kunstnere* (1893, The Artists), a five-act play about what it means to be an artist. The failure of the play, which premiered at Det Kongelige Teater in Copenhagen on 1 November 1893, was a disappointment for Heiberg, who had by then moved to Berlin. Many prominent Nordic artists lived in Berlin at the time, among them August Strindberg, Edvard Munch, and Christian Krohg. Heiberg became good friends with Krohg's wife, Oda, and she is said to have given him the inspiration for the play *Balkonen* (1894; translated as "The Balcony," 1922).

Balkonen is a stylized play characteristic of the neo-Romantic period in Norwegian literature. It opens with the lovers Julie and Abel declaring their passion and Julie introducing her lover to her old, sickly husband, Ressman, who is subsequently killed when he falls from a balcony. Social activism takes over Abel's time, and Julie, who fails to renounce her ideal of an all-consuming love, finally submits to the advances of a younger, more impulsive man, Antonio. Abel eventually leaves, and Julie asks whether Antonio will also civilize the love out of his body. The play was first performed at the Fri Theater in Copenhagen at the end of January 1894. Similar to *Balkonen* is *Gerts have* (Gert's Garden), a light comedy that also takes as its subject matter eroticism and all-consuming love. While it was published in the autumn of 1894, it was not performed until 1917 at the Nationaltheatret.

Det store Lod (1895, The Great Lottery Prize) examines the fate of an impoverished young student, Haller, who is the leader of a group of urban workers. Haller's father is killed in self-defense by the prime minister, whom the father had discovered with his wife. On the verge of exposing the prime minister, Haller wins the Spanish lottery and decides to remain silent. Having failed to win the love of the prime minister's niece, Ilka, Haller gives away all of his lottery money. When he tries to speak out at a revolutionary meeting, Haller is shot, having been identified as a traitor to the workers. The play premiered in October 1895 at Carl Johanteatret in Christiania under the direction of Heiberg himself.

In 1896 Heiberg's divorce was finalized, and the following year he became the Paris correspondent for the newspaper *Verdens Gang* (World Time), a position he held for five years. Generally he submitted about three articles each month to the paper, mostly concerning theater but also on politics. Oda Krohg left her husband and joined Heiberg in Paris. Heiberg was also busy completing the play *Folkeraadet* (The People's Council), and he returned to Norway with a finished manuscript in 1897. A political comedy in the style of Aristophanes, in which parliament is the main character, the satirical *Folkeraadet* succeeds in criticizing all political standpoints, from conservative to liberal. Clearly inspired by actual historical events, the play depicts parliament as the would-be defender of the country when it is threatened by a neighboring army. Rather than fight the incoming soldiers, however, the politicians argue among themselves and end up killing each other. The hotel boy, Rype, saves the day by destroying the threat and is consequently elected the new leader of the people. *Folkeraadet,* which was dedicated to Oda Krohg, was the first Heiberg play the Christiania Theater accepted, and it was performed there in October 1897 with music by the English composer Fritz Delius.

When Ibsen turned seventy in March 1898, there were great celebrations. As an indication of how highly Heiberg was regarded by his fellow artists, his was the only speech on the program for a party for the great playwright on 23 March. In the speech Heiberg expressed his great admiration and gratitude to Ibsen for having taught the Norwegian people both to respect and disrespect. While Heiberg was disappointed at Ibsen's failure to acknowledge his speech, he continued to support the dramatist and remained his friend until Ibsen's death in 1906.

Heiberg returned to Paris in May 1898 and remained there for the next year working both as a journalist and on his next play, *Harald Svans mor* (1899, Harald Svan's Mother), a comedy that highlights the problems of the press and the threats facing the integrity of journalists. The central character is a young journalist, Josef Ildberg, who slowly sinks deeper and deeper into corruption. This play was the first new Norwegian play to be preformed at the Nationaltheatret after it opened in the autumn of 1899, with the famous actress Johanne Dybwad in the lead female role.

In 1900 a collection of Heiberg's most successful articles on Paris life, art, theater, and politics—in particular the Dreyfus espionage affair—was published as *Pariserbreve* (Letters from Paris). His essays were clear and concise and frequently employed humor, even when he delved carefully and deeply into serious issues. In spite of his love of Paris and the bohemian lifestyle the city offered, Hieberg missed his home country. In 1901 he returned to Christiania where he started work on his next play, *Kjærlighedens tragedie* (1904; translated as "The Tragedy of Love," 1921). Before completing that play, though, he published *Kjærlighed til næsten* (1902, Love of One's Neighbor), a comedy about inauthentic altruism and the ways in which seemingly selfless dedication to the truth and well-being of another may serve as a disguise for self-love. It was first performed at the Nationaltheatret in February 1903. Heiberg returned to the French capital in 1902 and experienced the deterioration of his seven-year relationship with Oda Krohg, who eventually left him that year. Heiberg was devastated and returned home in 1904 with the finished manuscript of *Kjærlighedens tragedie*.

The sister play to *Balkonen, Kjærlighedens tragedie* concerns the relationship between Karen and Erling Kruse and examines the differences in how each character experiences love. For Karen, love is all-consuming and outranks even death in importance, while Erling is happy to settle into a mundane married existence with her. The politically active Erling does not recognize Karen's unhappiness and considers her eroticism madness. Karen eventually sacrifices her life for love. The poet of the play, Hatrvig Hadeln, asks whether it is not more beautiful for love to kill than to die itself. Inspired by Ibsen's *Når vi døde vågner* (1899; translated as *When We Dead Awaken,* 1900), the play is considered Heiberg's most personal and his most rich. It premiered at the Nationaltheatret on 16 January 1905, with Dybwad as Karen, Egil Eide as Hadeln, and Halvdan Christensen as Erling. While the play was praised by liberals, conservatives found the depiction of erotic love all too revolutionary, and yet again a Heiberg play aroused much public debate.

In the early years of the new century Heiberg became personally involved in the major political question of his day: the possible dissolution of Norway's union with Sweden. Heiberg spoke at rallies and was at the forefront of the Christiania agitators for a Norwegian Republic. He did not support the referendum that Sweden had called for concerning the dissolution and was also against the proposed disarmament of border fortresses. While ultimately disappointed in Norway's failure to secure a republic such as the one Heiberg so admired in France, the author was happy to celebrate the independence of his home country on 7 June 1905 when he was in Paris. His many essays about this political situation were collected and published in *1905* (1923).

In 1908 Heiberg made the acquaintance of Birgit Blehr, thirteen years his junior, the sister of his friend Hans Blehr. They married in 1911 in Christiania. The marriage was happy and allowed Heiberg both some economic security and entrance into younger artistic circles where he met such authors as Nini Roll Anker, Olaf Bull, and Helge Krog. It also gave Heiberg a renewed sense of confidence in his talents. The play *I frihetens bur* (In the Cage of Freedom) was completed in 1910 and submitted to the Nationaltheatret for performance, but on the recommendation of friends Heiberg withdrew it. It was never produced but was published after his death in 1929. Heiberg's next play to be published, *Jeg vil værge mit land* (1912, I Will Defend My Country), was dedicated to Georg Stang and revealed Heiberg's disappointment in how the Norwegian people had dealt with the events of 1905. This play was followed by the comedy *Paradesengen* (1913, Bed of State), a play that examines how the children of a famous artist, Jørgen Alfsøns, deal with his death and sell the film rights to his final moments. It was inspired by events following the death of Bjørnson in 1910.

The final years of Gunnar Heiberg's life were spent quietly with his family in Oslo, where he enjoyed financial security for the first time in his career and was finally recognized for his great artistic contribution. Collections of his many journalistic endeavors were published: *Set og hørt* (1917, Seen and Heard), *Ibsen og Bjørnson paa scenen* (1918, Ibsen and Bjørnson on the Stage), *Franske visitter* (1919, French Visits), *Norsk teater* (1920, Norwegian Theater), and *Salt og sukker* (1924, Salt and Sugar). There were great celebrations on his sixtieth and seventieth birthdays, the latter of which occasioned the publication of his collected works. In 1923 Heiberg was awarded a writer's scholarship from the Norwegian government. He died 22 February 1929 and is buried at the Vestre Gravlund cemetery in Oslo.

Biography:
Einar Skavlan, *Gunnar Heiberg* (Oslo: Aschehoug, 1950).

References:
Carl Fredrik Engelstad, "Gunnar Heiberg," in his *Fire norske diktere* (Oslo: Aas & Wahl, 1972);

Lars B. Haaland, "Gunnar Heibergs etterliv som dramatiker," *Norsk litterær årbok* (1999): 68–78;

Leif Longum, *To kjærlighetsromantikere* (Oslo: Universitetsforlaget, 1960);

Ragnvald Moe, "Gunnar Heiberg," *Samtiden* (1957): 599–606;

Knut Nygaard, *Gunnar Heiberg Teatermannen* (Bergen: Universitetsforlaget, 1975).

Papers:
Gunnar Heiberg's correspondence is held by Det Kongelige Bibliotek (The Royal Library), Copenhagen; Universitetsbibliotek (The University Library), Oslo; and Teaterarkivet ved Nordisk Instituttet (The Theater Archive at the Nordic Institute), University of Bergen.

Henrik Ibsen

(20 March 1828 – 23 May 1906)

Astrid Sæther
University of Oslo

BOOKS: *Catilina,* as Brynjolf Bjarme (Christiania: Steensballe, 1850); translated by Anders Orbeck as *Catiline* (New York: American-Scandinavian Foundation, 1921);

Gildet paa Solhoug (Christiania: Tønsberg, 1856); translated by William Archer and Mary Morison as *The Feast at Solhoug* (London: Heinemann, 1908);

Fru Inger til Østerraad (Christiania: H. J. Jensen, 1857); translated by Archer as *Lady Inger of Östrat* (London: Walter Scott, 1890);

Hærmændene paa Helgeland (Christiania: H. J. Jensen, 1858); translated by Archer as *The Vikings at Helgeland* (London: Walter Scott, 1890);

Kjærlighedens Komedie (Christiania: Illustreret Nyhedsblad, 1862); translated by C. H. Herford as *Love's Comedy* (London: Duckworth, 1900; Chicago: Charles H. Sergel, 1900);

Kongs-Emnerne (Christiania: Johan Dahl, 1864); translated by Archer as *The Pretenders* (London: Walter Scott, 1890);

Brand (Copenhagen: Gyldendal, 1866); translated by William Wilson as *Brand* (London: Methuen, 1891); translated by Herford as *Brand: A Dramatic Poem* (New York: Scribners, 1894);

Peer Gynt (Copenhagen: Gyldendal, 1867); translated by William Archer and Charles Archer as *Peer Gynt: A Dramatic Poem* (London: Walter Scott / New York: Scribners, 1892);

De unges Forbund (Copenhagen: Gyldendal, 1869); translated by R. Farquarson Sharp as *The League of Youth* (London: Dent, 1919);

Digte (Copenhagen: Gyldendal, 1871); translated by Brian Sourbut as *Poems* (York, U.K.: York Settlement Trust, 1993);

Kejser og Galilæer (Copenhagen: Gyldendal, 1873); translated by Catherine Ray as The *Emperor and The Galilean: A Drama in Two Parts* (London: Tinsley, 1876);

Samfundets Støtter (Copenhagen: Gyldendal, 1877); translated by William Archer, edited by Havelock Ellis as *The Pillars of Society: A Play in Four Acts* (London: Walter Scott / New York: Thomas Whittaker, 1888);

Henrik Ibsen (Det Kongelige Bibliotek)

Et Dukkehjem (Copenhagen: Gyldendal, 1879); translated by Henrietta Frances Lord as *Nora: A Play* (London: Griffith & Farran / New York: Dutton, 1882);

Gengangere (Copenhagen: Gyldendal, 1881); translated by William Archer as *Ghosts* (London: Walter Scott, 1888);

En Folkefiende (Copenhagen: Gyldendal, 1882); translated by William Archer as *An Enemy of the People* (London: Walter Scott, 1890);

Vildanden (Copenhagen: Gyldendal, 1884); translated by William Archer as *The Wild Duck* (London: Walter Scott, 1890);

Rosmersholm (Copenhagen: Gyldendal, 1886); translated by Louis Napoleon Parker as *Rosmersholm: A Play in Four Acts* (London: Griffith Farran Okenden & Welsh, 1889);

Fruen fra Havet (Copenhagen: Gyldendal, 1888); translated by Eleanor Marx Aveling as *The Lady from the Sea* (London: Unwin, 1890);

Hedda Gabler (Copenhagen: Gyldendal, 1890); translated by Edmund Gosse as *Hedda Gabler* (London: Heinemann, 1890; Boston: Walter H. Baker, 1890);

Bygmester Solness (Copenhagen: Gyldendal, 1892); translated by Gosse and William Archer as *The Master Builder* (Boston: Walter H. Baker, 1893);

Lille Eyolf (Copenhagen: Gyldendal, 1894); translated by William Archer as *Little Eyolf* (Chicago: Stone & Kimball, 1895; London: Heinemann, 1895);

John Gabriel Borkman (Copenhagen: Gyldendal, 1896); translated by William Archer as *John Gabriel Borkman* (New York: Stone & Kimball, 1897);

Når vi døde vågner (Copenhagen: Gyldendal, 1899); translated by William Archer as *When We Dead Awaken* (Chicago: Herbert S. Stone, 1900; London: Heinemann, 1900);

Kjæmpehøien (Bergen: Bergenske Blade, 1902); translated by Orbeck as *The Warrior's Barrow* (New York: American-Scandinavian Foundation, 1921);

Olaf Liljekrans (Copenhagen: Gyldendal, 1902); translated by Orbeck as *Olaf Liljekrans* (New York: American-Scandinavian Foundation, 1921);

Efterladte Skrifter, 3 volumes, edited by Halvdan Koht and Julius Elias (Christiania: Gyldendal, 1909);

Sancthansnatten (Christiania: Gyldendal, 1909).

Collections: *Samlede Værker*, 10 volumes, edited by J. B. Halversen (Copenhagen: Gyldendal, 1898–1902);

Samlede digterverker, 6 volumes, edited by Didrik Arup Seip (Christiania: Gyldendal, 1922);

Samlede verker: Hundreårsutgave, 21 volumes, edited by Seip, Francis Bull, and Halvdan Koht (Oslo: Gyldendal, 1928–1957);

Samlede verker, 7 volumes, edited by Bjørn Hemmer, Paulus Svendsen, and others (Oslo: Gyldendal, 1978);

Henrik Ibsens skrifter, 31 volumes published, edited by Vigdis Ystad and Narve Fulsås (Oslo: University of Oslo/Aschehoug, 2005–).

Editions in English: *The Collected Works of Henrik Ibsen*, 13 volumes, edited by William Archer (New York: Scribners, 1906–1912);

The Collected Works of Henrik Ibsen, 12 volumes, edited by Archer and C. H. Herford (London: Heinemann, 1911–1920);

The Oxford Ibsen, 8 volumes, translated and edited by James W. McFarlane (London: Oxford, 1960–1977);

The Complete Major Prose Plays, translated by Rolf Fjelde (New York: Farrar, Straus & Giroux, 1978).

PLAY PRODUCTIONS: *Kjæmpehøien*, Christiania, Christiania Theater, 26 September 1850;

Sancthansnatten, Bergen, Det Norske Teatret, 2 January 1853;

Fru Inger til Østerraad, Bergen, Det Norske Teatret, 2 January 1855;

Gildet paa Solhoug, Bergen, Det Norske Teatret, 2 January 1856;

Olaf Liljekrans, Bergen, Det Norske Teatret, 2 January 1857;

Hærmændene paa Helgeland, Christiania, Christiania Norske Teater, 24 November 1858;

Kongs-Emnerne, Christiania, Christiania Theater, 17 January 1864;

De unges Forbund, Christiania, Christiania Theater, 18 October 1869;

Kjærlighedens Komedie, Christiania, Christiania Theater, 24 November 1873;

Peer Gynt, Christiania, Christiania Theater, 24 February 1876;

Samfundets Støtter, Odense, Odense Theater, 14 November 1877;

Et Dukkehjem, Copenhagen, Det Kongelige Teater, 21 December 1879;

Catilina, Stockholm, Nya Teatern, 3 December 1881;

Gengangere, Chicago, Aurora Turner Hall, 20 May 1882;

En Folkefiende, Christiania, Christiania Theater, 13 January 1883;

Vildanden, Bergen, Den nationale Scene, 9 January 1885;

Brand, Stockholm, Nya Teatern, 24 March 1885;

Rosmersholm, Bergen, Den nationale Scene, 17 January 1887;

Fruen fra Havet, Christiania, Christiania Theater, 12 February 1889;

Hedda Gabler, Munich, Residentztheater, 31 January 1891;

Bygmester Solness, London, Theatre Royal, 7 December 1892;

Lille Eyolf, Berlin, Deutsches Theater, 12 January 1895;

Kejser og Galilæer, Leipzig, Leipzig Stadttheater, 5 December 1896;

John Gabriel Borkman, London, Avenue Theatre, 14 December 1896;

Når vi døde vågner, London, Theatre Royal, 16 December 1899.

Henrik Ibsen is the world's most frequently performed dramatist after William Shakespeare, and the founder of modern theater. Every year there are hundreds of Ibsen productions throughout the world, many of them adapted to meet the needs of local cultures. Ibsen is performed on every continent and in many different languages, and his ideas have energized social movements in countries as diverse as Bangladesh, China, and Nigeria. His dramas are studied in classrooms all over the world and discussed at international conferences in Europe, North America, and Asia. Each year brings an outpouring of scholarly work devoted to his life, times, and plays.

While the cultural property of humanity as a whole, Ibsen's oeuvre has its roots in Norway, a small northern European nation that during Ibsen's lifetime was barely coming into its own economically, socially, and politically. All but two of Ibsen's dramas have their setting in Norway, but the provincial nature of Norwegian life in the nineteenth century compelled Ibsen to take up residence abroad for most of his career. Living in Italy and Germany for a total of twenty-seven years, Ibsen drew heavily on continental European cultural resources in his work. That a writer from a small, peripheral, and poverty-stricken country should become an epoch-making dramatist is one of the happy accidents of literary history.

Henrik Johan Ibsen was born in Skien on 20 March 1828. His father, Knud, was a wealthy merchant and importer, and his mother, Marichen Altenburg, came from an affluent family. Skien is a coastal town in the province of Telemark; at the time of Ibsen's birth it was prospering from a boom in the shipping trade. Henrik was the oldest surviving child; his elder brother, Johan Altenburg Ibsen, died at the age of only one and a half years, three weeks before Henrik's birth. Knud and Marichen Ibsen had four more children in the next seven years: Johan Andreas in 1830, Hedvig Cathrine in 1831, Nicolai Alexander in 1834, and Ole Paus in 1835.

The Ibsen family lived in a spacious villa, well suited for a grand life and entertaining. Portraits of Marichen Ibsen preserved in newspaper clippings suggest that she was a beautiful woman. This opulent life ceased when Knud Ibsen's failures in financial speculations led to bankruptcy. Henrik was seven when the villa was sold and the family was forced to move to the large farm they owned, Venstøp, several miles out of town. Henrik's mother turned to religious musings and pursuits; his father started to drink excessively; and the Ibsen children were isolated from their former milieu. Henrik, the sensitive, vulnerable oldest son, became increasingly introverted. Encouraged by his mother, he started to stage puppet theater. He also read widely, drew, and painted. He felt himself an outsider, and suffered from his family's reduction in wealth, lack of unity, loss of happiness, and pervading sense of sorrow. Ibsen later described his childhood and boyhood in a short biographical fragment, "Fra Skien til Rom" (From Skien to Rome) written in 1881, the only one existing from his own hand. He was advised not to complete it by his Copenhagen publisher, Frederik Hegel. Despite its brevity, the fragment throws interesting light on the dramatist's upbringing, showing the fear and sorrow he felt when his happy childhood collapsed. Recent research on Ibsen's life is also casting new light on his childhood and youth, suggesting that they may not have been as bleak, desolate, lonely, and unhappy as previously posited.

Shortly after Christmas 1844—the year he was confirmed—the fifteen-year-old Ibsen left Skien aboard the coastal ferry *Lykkens Prøve* (The Lucky Chance) for Grimstad, another small town, further down the southern coast, where his father had arranged for him to become an apothecary's apprentice. The plan was for him to study medicine later. Although overburdened with work and having almost no money, he made some great friends and was able to read extensively, including classics by Shakespeare and Ludvig Holberg, by borrowing books from both private and public collections. In Skien the young Ibsen had been thought overly proud and arrogant, but he was accepted in Grimstad and became well acquainted with its eight hundred residents. His comrades invited him into their homes and provided him with contacts that later proved invaluable. While he was more interested in literature than in pharmacy, Ibsen studied and worked hard. His was a curious, inquiring nature, and he spent time gathering plants and herbs and studying their effects on the body.

In Grimstad and its beautiful surroundings, Ibsen began to write. He met a girl, Clara Ebbel, to whom he wrote his first love poems; some of them have survived. (Altogether, thirty poems have been preserved from the Grimstad period.) Ibsen's platonic relationship with Ebbel was of short duration and was followed by a more prosaic and physical relationship with the apothecary's servant woman, Else Sophie Jensdatter. Ten years older than Ibsen, Jensdatter was from a good family that, like Ibsen's, had suffered financial reverses and adversity. In 1846 Ibsen became the father of Jendatter's child, a boy she named Hans Jacob Henriksen. Ibsen's illegitimate son, who never had a relationship with his father, became a skilled blacksmith. Henriksen married three times; he died destitute, as did his mother.

The year 1848 brought revolution to France and Europe, a subject of deep interest to Ibsen and his intellectual friends. Inspired by the intrigue of contemporary events, Ibsen wrote his first play, which was about the Roman rebel and conspirator Catiline. Through the efforts of his friends in Grimstad, *Catilina* (1850; translated as *Catiline*, 1921), a blank-verse tragedy, was published just as Ibsen was getting ready to leave Grimstad and settle in the capital city, Christiania (now Oslo). Before he made this move, Ibsen visited his family in Skien, probably for the last time. Ibsen broke with his entire family, keeping in contact only with his sister, Hedvig. In Christiania, Ibsen decided to take the entrance examinations to study at the university. His failures in Greek and mathematics may have deprived the world of a doctor but decided the future path of the young playwright.

Ibsen thereafter devoted himself exclusively to his writing. In Christiania he continued to receive support from his friends from the Grimstad period, and he met new friends, such as Bjørnstjerne Bjørnson and the young philologist Paul Botten-Hansen, a country lad who became his greatest friend. Together with another country genius, Aasmund Olavson Vinje, Botten-Hansen and Ibsen started a periodical, *Andhrimner*, named after the cook for the gods in Nordic mythology. The three young writers made a productive trio, reporting on everything from debates in parliament and theater performances to skiing competitions. Work as a journalist gave Ibsen valuable insights into contemporary society as well as experiences he drew on in his later writings.

Ibsen wrote several new poems in the 1850s. In one of these, "Bjergmanden" (The Miner), originally published in the 1 June 1851 issue of *Andhrimner,* the hero of the poem hammers his way through the rock of the earth to reach the heart of Nature—clearly a metaphor for Ibsen's vision of the work of the literary artist. Critics have linked this early poem, which Ibsen twice revised, to his 1896 play about a miner's son, *John Gabriel Borkman* (translated, 1897).

Ibsen wrote about the Christianization of Norway in his play *Kjæmpehøien* (translated as *The Warrior's Barrow*, 1921), which was staged at Christiania Theater in September 1850 but not published until 1902. He submitted it under the same pseudonym as he had used for *Catilina*, Brynjolf Bjarne. Encouraged by the successful staging of *Kjæmpehøien,* Ibsen started to work on a third play, "Rypen I Justedal" (The Ptarmigan of Justedal),

Ibsen's wife, Suzannah, née Thoresen, whom he married in 1858 (from Halvdan Koht, The Life of Ibsen, *1931; Thomas Cooper Library, University of South Carolina)*

about a small girl in Jostedal who is the only person to survive the Black Death, but did not complete it.

In 1851 Ole Bull, a violinist and composer Ibsen had met in Christiania, appointed Ibsen to the position of "theater poet," or playwright-in-residence, at the newly established Det Norske Teatret (The Norwegian Theater) in Bergen, Norway's second largest city. The theater was an important element in the effort to create a new awareness of Norway's own cultural heritage and language. Ibsen held the post of dramatist while also serving as stage manager for the next six years. During these apprentice years Ibsen traveled to Copenhagen and Dresden on a scholarship to study stage direction, learned about dramaturgy, staged his own productions and those of others, and drew designs for costumes and the stage. By contract, he was also required to produce a new drama for performance each New Year. Because of the theater's radical repertoire and its lack of an artistic ensemble, Ibsen faced hardships and failures also during this period.

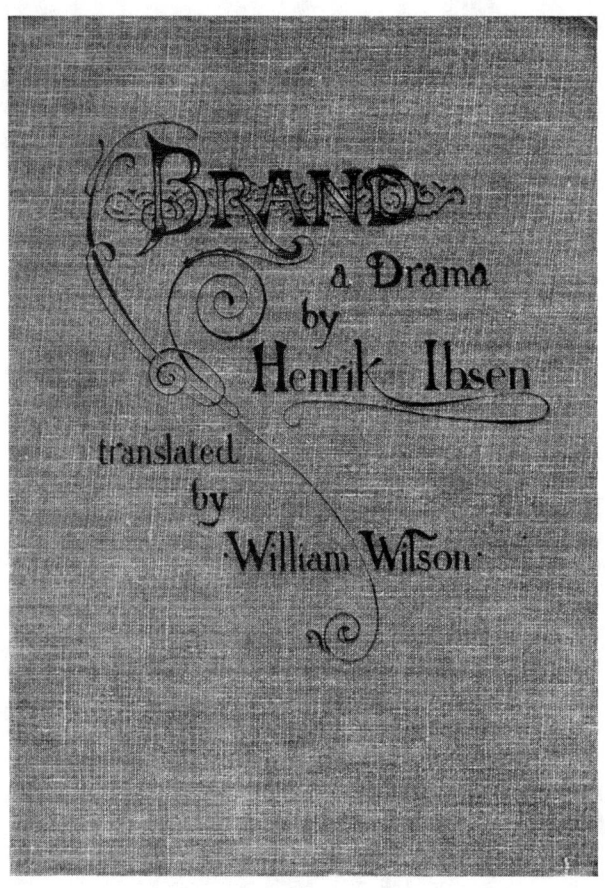

Cover for the 1891 English translation of Ibsen's 1866 dramatic poem about a country pastor who sacrifices his humanity in his uncompromising service to God (Thomas Cooper Library, University of South Carolina)

To escape from the pressures of running, directing, and writing for the theater, Ibsen in the spring of 1853 began an affair with fifteen-year-old Henrikke Holst. Some of Ibsen's most beautiful love poems stem from his infatuation with Holst. The affair ended abruptly when Holst's father discovered their secret meetings. Recognized as an outsider and rebel in town, Ibsen was nevertheless invited to the literary salon of Magdalene Thoresen; she was the second wife of the dean of Korskirken (Cross Church) in Bergen, Hans Conrad Thoresen, and the mother of nine children, five of whom were the offspring of Pastor Thoresen's first wife. One of her stepdaughters was Suzannah Daae Thoresen, born in 1836.

Ibsen first met Suzannah Thoresen in her family home in January 1855. They were married in June 1858, one week after her father's death. Ibsen's twenty-two-year-old bride came from an extraordinary family. Her father was a kind-hearted intellectual, and her stepmother was untraditional, provocative, and passionately interested in theater, literature, and art while also being a loving mother to her large family of children and stepchildren. The Thoresens' library and the small theater they built in their backyard provided the children with possibilities and cultural privileges. The intellectual and artistic atmosphere the Thoresens cultivated appealed to Ibsen. This family of strong-willed individuals openly discussed a wide range of topics, from art and science to the question of equality for women to the development of democracy. Ibsen's beautiful proposal poem for Suzannah–with the final line "til mine tankers brud" (to the bride of my thoughts)–seems an indication of the quality of their relationship. The night of their marriage they left Bergen for Christiania by a steamship that brought them around the coast past the towns of Grimstad and Skien. Ibsen had been offered the position of theater manager for the Christiania Norske Teater (Christiania Norwegian Theater), which he held for two years.

During his Bergen period, Ibsen had completed five plays, four of which were produced at Det Norske Teatret: *Sancthansnatten* (1909, St. John's Night), a comedy inspired by Norwegian folklore, first performed on 2 January 1853; *Fru Inger til Østerraad* (1857; translated as *Lady Inger of Östrat*, 1890), a historical drama set in Trondheim in 1528, performed on 2 January 1855; *Gildet paa Solhoug* (1856; translated as *The Feast at Solhoug*, 1908), a ballad drama about a woman who married for money, performed on 2 January 1856; and *Olaf Liljekrans* (1902; translated, 1921), based on a medieval folksong, performed on 2 January 1857. The fifth play, *Hærmændene paa Helgeland* (1858; translated as *The Vikings at Helgeland*, 1890), based on an old saga, was Ibsen's first work performed at the Christiania Norske Teater, on 24 November 1858. Although they develop conflicts that anticipate Ibsen's later work, these apprentice works, which may be generally characterized as historical dramas, are seldom revived. The one exception is the oft-produced *Fru Inger til Østerraad*, which deals with Norway's last chance to gain independence from the union with Sweden and Denmark. In this well-structured play of political intrigue with excellent dialogue, Lady Inger fails to carry through her plan to liberate her country.

Ibsen's six difficult years in Bergen were followed by another six years of even greater obstacles and challenges. The Christiania Norske Teater was supposed to present new, Norwegian dramas and, at the same time, earn enough money to pay off the debts arising from an expansive and expensive building program. The theater gradually went under financially and finally closed in 1862; as a result, Ibsen's own situation became desperate. As a family man with a wife and a son–Sigurd, who had been born on 23 December 1859–to take care of,

Ibsen did not meet either artistic or familial expectations. He took to drinking and was on the verge of giving up several times. He later admitted that his sheer survival at that time was a wonder.

Despite the desperate situation he was in during his association with the Christiania Norske Teater, Ibsen managed to compose two highly esteemed epic poems during these years: "Paa Vidderne" (On the Heights), which appeared in print in 1860, and "Terje Vigen," published in 1862. The first-person narrator in "Paa Vidderne" is an artist, struggling to become independent and pursue his vocation. "Terje Vigen" tells the story of an old sailor, full of bitterness and thoughts of revenge. Terje is haunted and deeply marked by his past, but he chooses to forgive those who have trespassed against him. In his next drama, *Kjærlighedens Komedie* (1862; translated as *Love's Comedy,* 1900), which was not produced until 1873, Ibsen for the first time questioned the rationale for marriage, as his protagonist chooses to remain free and not marry. Critics noted that his play suggested a strange attitude for a newly married man. Suzannah, however, remained his ardent supporter, "the only one who understood me," as Ibsen said later on. The last play Ibsen wrote before leaving Norway was *Kongs-Emnerne* (1864; translated as *The Pretenders,* 1890), a historical drama that was staged successfully in 1864, a short time before Ibsen moved to Rome, where he was joined by his wife and son, who had been staying in Copenhagen. Most of the family's personal belongings were left behind and sold at auction. Ibsen's voluntary exile from the Norwegian theatrical scene lasted for twenty-seven years.

In Rome, Ibsen was able to escape circumstances that had almost destroyed him and start anew. With a contract from the Danish publishing house Gyldendal and support from fellow writers, Ibsen set his family up in a small apartment in the foreign quarter in Rome, close to the *Circolo Scandinavo* (Scandinavian Circle), a group of fellow Scandinavian authors and artists. Suzannah took great interest in her husband's work. She learned Italian and borrowed works of modern literature from various libraries, keeping notes on what she read. In the four years he spent in the Italian city (1864 to 1868) Ibsen developed the genius that transformed him from an obscure Scandinavian author to the master builder of European drama, from being a poor and rejected writer to being the creator and diagnostician of the modern Western sensibility.

The first work Ibsen completed in Rome was *Brand* (1866; translated, 1891), a dramatic poem in rhyming verse that was not intended for the stage. This story about a dynamic, idealistic country pastor who forsakes his humanity in his uncompromising service to God went through many reprintings and won Ibsen fame far beyond Norway and Scandinavia. The poem ends with Brand being crushed in an avalanche, while a voice calls through the thundering roar: "He is the God of Love." After *Brand,* Ibsen received many assurances from friends and critics that Norwegians took pride in his achievements. He also received a substantial grant from the Norwegian government that enabled him to continue his work in Italy. Ibsen in part used his character Pastor Brand as a means of expressing his anger about the failure of the theater in Christiania; a lonely, passionate tower of a man, Brand, despite being misguided, in some ways was a model for the hero Ibsen wanted to be.

In the fantasy *Peer Gynt* (1867; translated, 1892)—like *Brand* a dramatic poem that was not intended for the stage—Ibsen tells the story of Brand's opposite, a charming country lad whose adventures and escapades are recorded in verse and prose. In a letter to his publisher in Copenhagen, Ibsen wrote that his protagonist in *Peer Gynt* was a figure from the recent past of the Norwegian peasantry, a half-mythical adventurer. Irresponsible, poetic, wild, and reckless, Peer as a young man is just the opposite of stern, unbending, uncompromising Brand. Through the love of Solveig, a much older Peer is saved from the consequences of his selfishness. Although Ibsen shows great empathy in depicting Peer's search for his "real" self, he was thoroughly criticized for his unconventional style and for shifting between reality and fantasy. The criticism stung Ibsen, and he wrote to his colleague Bjørnson: "Min Bog *er* Poesi" (My book *is* poetry).

The success of *Brand* and *Peer Gynt* changed Ibsen's life, attitudes, and manners. Having earned enough money to pay off his debts, he threw away his well-worn clothes and began to dress like a gentleman. He gained courage, and even his handwriting became more regular. Although his time in Rome had been happy, Ibsen decided in 1867 that the time was right to leave Italy. The family was cramped in their flat of one and a half rooms, and the Ibsens wanted their only son to receive a proper education in better surroundings. A sensitive, handsome, precocious boy, Sigurd had been allowed to roam all over Rome, visiting ruins, museums, and galleries.

The Ibsens left Rome in June 1868 for Dresden, Germany, a city with a relatively low cost of living in a country in which the theaters were beginning to show interest in Ibsen's work. Ibsen had started work on a new play, intended for the stage, *De unges Forbund* (1869; translated as *The League of Youth,* 1919), a realistic sociopolitical satire with a contemporary setting. The Ibsens settled in a nice area and lived comfortably and pleas-

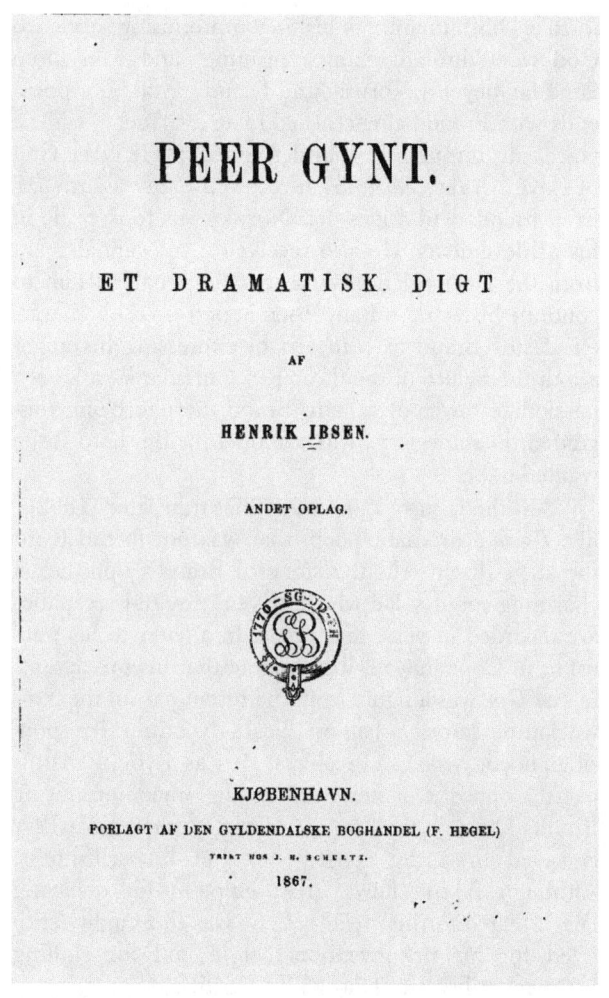

Title page for Ibsen's dramatic poem (translated, 1892) about a wild and reckless country lad who, as an adult, is saved from the consequences of his selfishness by a woman's love (Widener Library, Harvard University)

antly, as he wrote to one of his old friends. A new grant from the government enabled Ibsen to travel to Sweden in 1869, leaving his wife and son behind in Dresden. Later that year, Ibsen was invited to visit Egypt as the guest of the khedive. While he was traveling and enjoying his growing fame, Ibsen received word that *De unges forbund,* which had opened at the Christiania Theater on 18 October, had met with organized whistling and boos. Ibsen's provocative portraits of contemporary Norwegian political life—interpreted as attacks on liberal politicians—resulted in broken friendships and hatred. His relationship with Bjørnson was problematic for the rest of their lives. Nevertheless, Ibsen also made new friends, among them the Danish critic Georg Brandes, who had discovered the Norwegian dramatist in 1868 and had written a long essay about his early works. When the two men met for the first time in Dresden in 1870, their discussions of books and politics ended with their shaking hands and promising each other friendship and a common fight for everything new and radical.

In 1871 Ibsen's revisions of his early poems along with new verse were published as *Digte* (translated as *Poems,* 1993). One of his new poems—a long, technically intricate rhymed letter of admiration to the Danish actress Johanne Luise Heiberg—was highly praised by Brandes. The reviews of Ibsen's poems were generally positive, though some critics compared Ibsen's work to Bjørnson's and maintained that the latter was the more gifted poet. Ibsen, who believed that poems were meant for visions and prose for ideas, was henceforward to concentrate on ideas.

Ibsen, who enjoyed arguments, discussions, and the expression of varying viewpoints, frequently became involved in controversies. The 1860s and 1870s were a period of great intellectual ferment. The ideas of philosophers such as Georg Wilhelm Friedrich Hegel and Arthur Schopenhauer were much discussed. Karl Marx's study of materialism laid the foundation for the Workers' Movement, which was gaining strength in the late 1860s. Works such as Charles Darwin's *On the Origin of Species by Means of Natural Selection* (1859) and John Stuart Mill's *The Subjection of Women* (1869) sparked intense debate. Although Ibsen was certainly aware of the intellectual crosscurrents of his times, literary historians cannot say with certainty how deeply he studied such issues or where he stood on many controversies. When Brandes remonstrated with him for not having adequate knowledge of new achievements in science, Ibsen replied that he had the power derived from his senses and instincts—these were his "tools" as he participated in the struggle around him. One should not, however, take such a sentiment to imply that Ibsen was anti-intellectual.

In Rome, Ibsen had extensively studied art and art history, literature, and architecture. One of the historical figures who attracted his intense interest was the Roman Emperor Julian, who had turned against Christianity. Ibsen had abandoned the project of writing about Julian when he was in Rome, but in Dresden he resumed his work on the historical period in which Julian lived. He felt deep kinship with rebels, especially those who suffered defeat. Inspired by the thought of Schopenhauer and Hegel, Ibsen was interested in the possibilities of presenting a new kind of human being, who embodied both pagan and Christian ideals. Ibsen's play in ten acts, *Kejser og Galilæer* (1873; translated as *The Emperor and Galilean,* 1876), was built on the idea that a New World, the "third kingdom," was arising. Although Julian tries to bring this kingdom into being, his tyrannical rule and conflict with Christianity leads to the entrenchment of the religion on which he had turned his back.

The publication of *Kejser og Galilæer*, which was not produced until 1896, did not create the same level of controversy as did *De unges Forbund*. At the time—contrary to Ibsen's intent—people were inclined to interpret the play from a Christian perspective. Some critics, perhaps dismayed by how Ibsen's radical thinking had stirred the Norwegian public, stated that he was unloved and unpopular; critics suggested Ibsen was a doubter and a seeker, but his works lacked inner balance. Ibsen did not respond to this criticism. He spent summer 1873 in Vienna as a judge representing Norway in the art division of the World Exposition. Ibsen was quite famous by then. His books were being translated into German, and theaters outside Scandinavia were producing his plays.

In 1874 Ibsen and his family visited Norway for the first time since 1864. The visit was peaceful, and the Ibsens may have considered returning to the country permanently. Ibsen was affronted when he learned that old friends were critical of his political view of Norway. Ibsen decided to leave Norway again and, choosing not to return to Dresden, took his family to Munich, a city in which there were many Norwegian painters and authors. Ibsen's association with Brandes and the Norwegian writer Camilla Collett, regarded as the country's first feminist, gave new impetus to his progressive ideas. In the next few years Ibsen was troubled by the discrepancy between advancement in public life and the lack of a free inner life for the individual—a primary concern in the poem "Langt Borte" (Far Away). In the poem, Ibsen describes sailing with a corpse in the cargo. The visions of corpses and ghosts represent obstacles to freethinking and action.

Ibsen's next play, *Samfundets Støtter* (1877; translated as *The Pillars of Society*, 1888), took up the topic of the "corpse in the cargo," the old, rotten ethics of society being the main theme of this play set in a small Norwegian port town. The first in a series of twelve works that came to be known as Ibsen's "prose plays," *Samfundets Støtter* is focused on a wealthy local businessman, Consul Karsten Bernick, believed to be a man of high moral character. In the climactic scene Bernick, who nearly destroyed everything he loves, reveals his own hypocrisy and corruption in a public confession that renews his sense of self. After he has cleansed his soul with his honest declaration, Bernick turns to the "true and faithful women" who have continued to support him—his wife, his sister-in-law, his sister—calling them the "pillars of society." His sister-in-law, Lorna Hessel, corrects his "poor wisdom" with the final words of the play: "The spirits of Truth and Freedom—they are the Pillars of Society."

After the truth has made Consul Bernick a new man, he calls his sister, Martha, to him, telling her, "it

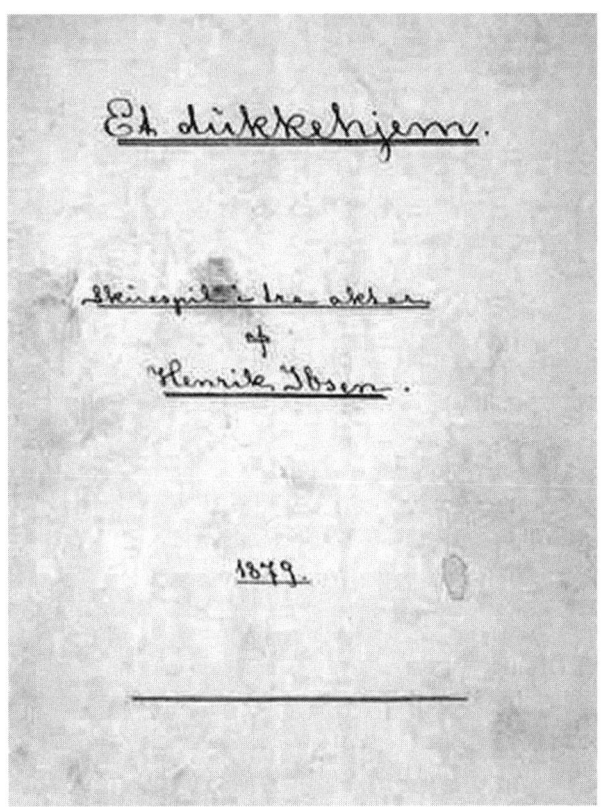

Title page of the manuscript for Ibsen's controversial play (A Doll's House; translated as Nora, *1882) about a woman who defies and, finally, walks out on her husband, slamming the door behind her (from <http://www.ibsen.net/index.gan?id=94&subid=0>)*

seems as though I had never seen you in all these years." Lorna Hessel responds that his society has been one of "bachelor-souls" and that he had "no eyes for Woman." Her words might very well have been spoken by Collett, who had reproached Ibsen for neglecting women's issues. Collett found a kindred spirit and voice of great authority in Suzannah Ibsen. The question of women's emancipation became Ibsen's subject in one of his most important dramas.

In March 1878 the Ibsens returned to Rome. While his son began studying law at the university, Ibsen was working on a new play. A first draft of the play was finished in October of the same year. Ibsen at the time commented on the theme of his work: "There are two kinds of spiritual law, one for men and quite a different one for women. [Men and women] do not understand each another; but women are always judged in practical matters by men's law, as though they were not women but men." A woman could not be herself in contemporary society, Ibsen stated, because society was exclusively male. In his personal life Ibsen behaved paternalistically. His wife

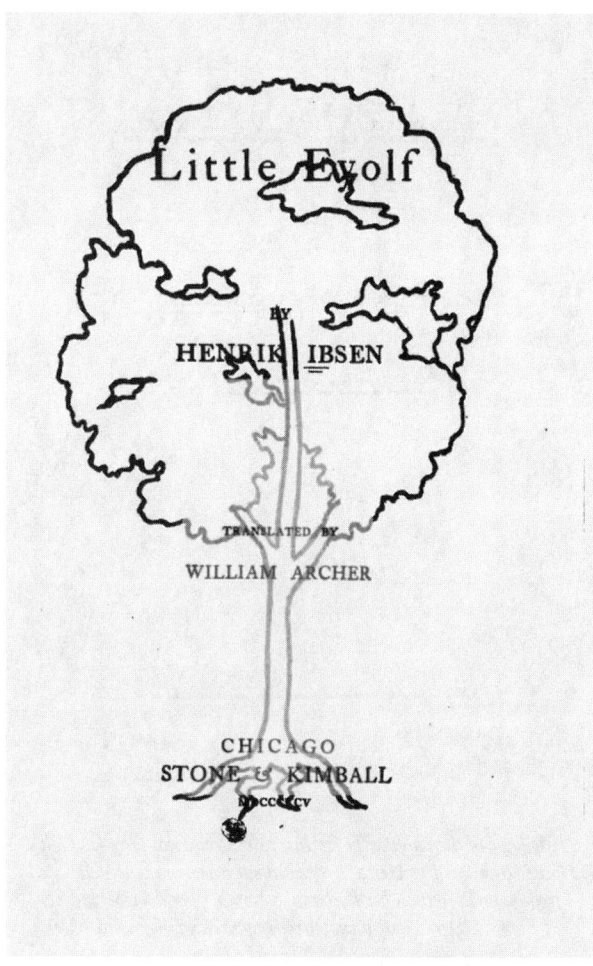

Title page for the U.S. edition of the English translation (1895) of Ibsen's 1894 play about the differing reactions of a mother and father to the crippling of their son (Widener Library, Harvard University)

was not at all self-effacing, but she did devote herself to his talents.

Ibsen's *Et Dukkehjem* (1879, A Doll's House; translated as *Nora*, 1882), first performed in Copenhagen on 21 December 1879, was his most controversial play and with time has been recognized as both his most beloved and his most "dangerous" work. The story treats the relationship of a seemingly loving married couple, Nora and Thorvald Helmer, who have three children. In the course of a few days at Christmas, the family experiences events that lead to the breakup of the Helmer marriage and the departure of Nora, who famously slams the door as she leaves the home. Nora's action caused shock waves throughout the world, for it challenged firmly held ideas, such as the sanctity of marriage and the absolute authority of the man in the home. Suzannah Ibsen was adamant about the ending of *Et Dukkehjem:* "If you don't let Nora go, then I'll have to leave." Dramatically speaking, Nora's slamming the door was necessary; psychologically, it was not. Nora in the course of the play had already proved herself to be the stronger person in the marriage.

The reaction of the press to *Et Dukkehjem* was hostile; some critics even wrote that the works of the Norwegian dramatist were not suitable for performance. German theaters did not want to stage the play, and Ibsen went so far as to write an alternative ending in which Nora returns home. (This ending was not used again.) The role of Nora Helmer is one of the most famous female roles in world theater. Nora's complex charm and attractive human foibles resemble those of Peer Gynt. Ibsen's opening the curtains on a family living room for scrutiny by strangers was so shocking that even Nora's struggle to become a grown-up and a human being were of secondary importance to theater audiences of the time.

Ibsen's next play, *Gengangere* (1881; translated as *Ghosts*, 1888), which dealt openly with syphilis (though not mentioned by name), defended free love, and even implied that an incestuous marriage might not have been a bad thing, shocked contemporary audiences so much that bookshops and theaters rejected it. The play, though, was popular among young people, who arranged readings in secret, out-of-the-way places. The first performance of *Gengangere*, in Norwegian for an audience of Scandinavian immigrants, took place in Chicago on 20 May 1882. Ibsen lost money on the play as it simply did not sell. Nevertheless, Ibsen continued his fight against hollowness and provincialism: he waged war against the negative impact of the past on people's minds, and he stressed the need for each individual to find his or her own freedom. Ibsen warned against the danger of renouncing love in the name of duty, as Helena Alving did in *Gengangere*. In self-defense and in defense of his play, Ibsen wrote in January 1882 to his publisher in Copenhagen, predicting that all the fading and decrepit individuals who spat on his work would one day reap the crushing judgment of future historians: "My book contains the future," Ibsen said in ending his letter.

Only one year passed between the publication of *Gengangere* and *En Folkefiende* (1882; translated as *An Enemy of the People*, 1890). The story in *En Folkefiende* is timeless and relevant to any society, for it concerns a person of principle standing against the perceived self-interest of the group. Dr. Stockman, a physician at a small spa in Norway, discovers that the baths on which the town's prosperity depend are contaminated. Consequently, the spa closes for several years, and Stockman is declared an enemy of the people. He is abandoned by his patients; his daughter is fired from her teaching position; and a mob breaks his windows.

Ibsen agreed with Mill's definition of the public and their opinions as "the mass," or the collective mediocrity. All wise and noble things must come from individuals, Ibsen maintained, first and foremost from one individual. Ibsen's belief was in accord with Dr. Stockman's message, and he realized it was an unpopular viewpoint. In a 3 January 1883 letter to Brandes, Ibsen concluded: "I firmly believe that an intellectual pioneer can never gather a majority behind him." In *Brand* Ibsen had his main character cry out: "It is horrible to stand alone." In *En Folkefiende* Stockman states: "the strongest man in the world is he who stands most alone."

En Folkefiende and its message received mixed reviews; in the twenty-first century the play continues to be criticized, though the grounds for the objections have shifted. In recent years the play has been frequently performed in countries where pollution and economic degradation are major issues. In such situations, Stockman is portrayed unequivocally as a hero. Some of the opinions that Stockman expresses, however, his contempt for the opinions of the masses, and his assertion that the "minority is always right"—come across as authoritarian and antiliberal.

Ibsen felt himself to be far ahead of "the masses," and he was right: a crowd was standing where he had stood when he had begun his career as a writer, but he was no longer with them. Ibsen had become an avant-garde artist. To Ibsen, "truths" had only limited duration; they were not everlasting. There is a bitter undertone in *En Folkefiende*. In Stockman's words, critics have recognized Ibsen's contempt for the ordinary man. But even more, Ibsen had uttered his contempt for petty politicians and town councils and pillars of society. After the outcry against him, Ibsen began to reconsider his own attitudes and his view of humanity and human life. Referring to this stage in Ibsen's dramatic production, the literary critic and historian Halvdan Koht in his introduction to *Samfundets Støtter* wrote that Ibsen "could not find firm ground under his feet, he became uncertain of his opinions and perplexed about all human existence." Ibsen continued to defend himself against accusations, telling Brandes in a 12 June 1883 letter that he felt an unrelenting compulsion to press forward.

In *Vildanden* (1884; translated as *The Wild Duck*, 1890), written in Rome and Gossensass, Gregers Werle, in the interest of "Truth," interferes in the marriage of his friend, Hjalmar Ekdahl, by informing him that Gina, Hjalmar's wife, has given birth to a child who is not his. When Hjalmar confronts Gina—the former mistress of Werle's father—she confesses that she does not know who is the father of their daughter, Hedvig. The festering family tension leads to a tragic ending, as Hedvig, encouraged by Werle to shoot the wild duck she loves to prove her love for her father, kills herself instead. The fanatic Gregers Werle shares some qualities with the uncompromising Pastor Brand, especially his search for the ideal. But the focus in *Vildanden* is as much on the family in distress and desperation. With a marriage breaking apart, the child is shown to be a vulnerable victim. The catastrophic conclusion of *Vildanden* linked the play to classical Greek drama, but at the same time the play contained some of the most humorous and charming scenes in all of Ibsen's plays. Ibsen's juxtaposition of comedy and tragedy functioned as one of the hallmarks of the drama.

Contemporary critics, readers, and audiences were often bewildered by *Vildanden,* which in its use of symbolism—especially that of the wild duck of the title—marked a definite change in Ibsen's writing. In his subsequent works, darker in mood and even more difficult for audiences, Ibsen seemed to be asking how far one can go in searching for the truth, how much one needs illusions, or "life lies." Ibsen increasingly pondered and posed such questions in the plays that were to follow.

Encouraged by Suzannah, who with Sigurd had made the long trip to Norway in 1884, Ibsen started planning his own journey to Norway in April 1885. On this first trip "home" in more than ten years, Ibsen and Suzannah traveled about the country for more than four months, visiting Trondheim, Molde, Ålesund, Bergen, and Christiania. The tour greatly affected Ibsen's life and work. He wrote to his editor Frederik Hegel at Gyldendal in Copenhagen that he had once toyed with the idea of buying a small villa in the vicinity of Christiania, someplace overlooking the fjord, but that this visit had caused him to change his mind. He returned to Germany introverted and distressed; he had left behind broken friendships and unpleasant confrontations with Norwegian officials. He was disappointed in the new liberal government. In short, Ibsen definitely did not want to move back to Norway.

With Sigurd serving in the foreign ministry of Sweden-Norway as an attaché in Washington, D.C., Ibsen rented a spacious and elegant flat in Munich, with plenty of room for his newly acquired paintings, bought in Italy. While he and Suzannah were well situated, the Ibsens' marriage was at a critical juncture. Suzannah suffered from bouts of rheumatism, and Ibsen, fifty-seven years old, had an eye for younger, more-attractive women, though his interest in women is believed to have been more of an artistic than a sexual nature. He was starting work on a new drama based on impressions he had received during the summer months in Norway and followed what had become his writing regimen. He wrote from nine o'clock in the morning until

Cover for the British edition of the English translation (1900) of Ibsen's last play, Når vi døde vågner (1899), about the unhappy marriage of an aging sculptor and his beautiful young wife (Thomas Cooper Library, University of South Carolina)

the lunch hour; then he read, had his dinner, and went for walks. Normally, Ibsen wrote in the summer, gathering his material and drafting his plots in the winter. In winter 1886 he started gathering material and plotting his drama; he wrote during the spring and summer in Munich, finishing his new play, *Rosmersholm* (1886; translated as *Rosmersholm*, 1889), in September 1886.

The action in *Rosmersholm* takes place in contemporary Norway at the remote Rosmer estate, Rosmersholm, on the western coast in a remote area. The main characters are the widowed former clergyman Johannes Rosmer and Rebekka West, a young woman who resides at the estate. Having turned his back on the church, Rosmer is devoted to his new, radical ideas of "enoblement." He believes the people in his former parish need to become free spirits, unbound by society's norms and regulations.

Robert Ferguson describes *Rosmersholm* as a play that connects two worlds previously kept apart in Ibsen's production: the public, quasi-political world of *De unges Forbund, Samfundets Støtter,* and *En Folkefiende* and the private, family world of *Et Dukkehjem, Gengangere,* and *Vildanden*. Ibsen's fascination with Rebekka—a complex character who is both manipulative and noble—adds her to the list of his best female characters, joining Helena Alving and Nora Helmer. Although Rosmer learns that Rebekka played a role in precipitating the suicide of his former wife, Beate, he still wants to marry her. When the couple end their lives by throwing themselves into the millrace at the same spot where Beate killed herself, the reader is left with a great puzzle. Readers and theatergoers were even more confused by *Rosmersholm* than they had been by *Vildanden*, but the characterization was undeniably powerful. Years later, Sigmund Freud was drawn to the psychological complexity of the drama and commented at length on Rebekka.

In the summer of 1887 the Ibsens went to Denmark and settled for some weeks at a seaside village, where Ibsen started working on *Fruen fra Havet* (1888; translated as *The Lady from the Sea,* 1890). He finished it in Munich in 1888. The main character is Ellida Wangel, the wife of an elderly doctor, who suffers from neuroses and lack of sleep. She cannot free herself from the memories of her former lover, a sailor who disappeared long ago. When he suddenly returns, Ellida faces a crisis and struggles to decide what to choose: her present, safe life with the reliable doctor and her stepdaughters or a new life with the attractive intruder, a lover who can promise nothing but excitement.

Like *Rosmersholm*, *Fruen fra Havet* failed on the stages of Europe. One reason for both failures was that the plays delve into complicated psychological problems that audiences found difficult to come to grips with. A second, more particular reason was that the parts and roles of Rebekka and Ellida Wangel made great demands on the actresses. When the roles were performed by the great Italian actress Eleonora Duse, the plays won great acclaim. The same situation pertained to Ibsen's next famous female character, Hedda Gabler.

Hedda Gabler (1890; translated, 1890), written in Munich, was set in contemporary bourgeois Christiania. Many critics have suggested that the character Hedda Gabler, the daughter of a general, was inspired by Emilie Bardach, a young woman Ibsen met during his summer stay in Gossensass. Ibsen's drafts of the play are interesting for their general comments on the psychology of women. In a 4 December 1890 letter to the French translator of the play, Ibsen explained why he chose not to use "Tesman," Hedda's married name to title the play: ". . . I wanted to indicate that as a personality she is to be regarded more as her father's daughter than her husband's wife." Later in the same letter, Ibsen explained his intention in the play: "I have not really tried to deal with so-called problems. My main purpose has been to describe human beings, human moods and human fates on the basis of certain conditions and views prevalent in society."

Bored in her life as the wife of the young, dull academic Jörgen Tesman, Hedda at the beginning of the play is pregnant but does not want to be so. When her former admirer, Eilert Løvborg, reappears, she feels all the more desperate in her inactivity and lack of meaning. Caught up in her own machinations, Hedda becomes the target of Judge Brack, who is blackmailing her to become his mistress. Feeling she has nothing to live for, Hedda at the end of the drama takes her own life with one of her father's pistols. First performed in Munich on 31 January 1891, *Hedda Gabler* created a great stir. Audiences could not understand Ibsen's interest in what they regarded as abnormal psychology. Hedda was a darker figure than any of Ibsen's previous women, and the critics all around in Europe were shocked.

Hedda Gabler was Ibsen's last play written abroad. In 1891 he moved into Viktoria Terrasse, a fashionable new apartment building in Christiania. While Suzannah was in Italy, traveling with Sigurd and searching for relief from rheumatism, Ibsen sought the companionship of the Sontums, a family he knew from Bergen, and especially the company of the young daughter of the house, Hildur Andersen. Often seen as his companion in Christiania, she became "his little princess." There were rumors about a romance between the two, but Andersen left Christiania to continue her musical studies in Vienna. When Suzannah returned, Ibsen was in the midst of composing a new drama, *Bygmester Solness* (1892; translated as *The Master Builder*, 1893). A poem Ibsen wrote in March 1892, collected in *Samlede Værker* (1899, Collected Works), speaks to one of the motifs in the play:

> They sat there, those two, in so snug a house
> through autumns and chill Decembers.
> Then fire destroyed it. Mere rubble to douse.
> The pair have to rake the embers.
>
> For under it all lies a hidden gem,
> a gem that's impervious to burning.
> And if they keep looking, either of them
> might find it by raking and turning.
>
> But even if the blaze-ravaged pair should find
> that priceless, fire-proof jewel,
> *she'll* not recover her peace of mind,
> nor *he* find bright joy's renewal [translated by John Northam].

The poem, which describes the situation between Halvald and Aline Solness in the play, probably had relevance for the Ibsen marriage. (The Ibsens, however, did have reason for celebration that year, as Sigurd married Bjørnson's daughter, Bergljot. In July 1893 she gave birth to the Ibsens' grandson, Tancred. The young family was happy, and their parents were—at least on the surface—reconciled.)

In *Bygmester Solness* Halvald Solness, a self-made man and respected architect in contemporary Christiania, is locked in a damaged marriage and mired in business concerns when he is unexpectedly visited by Hilde Wangel, an attractive young woman who is the catalyst in the play. Ibsen told a friend that he based the character on Emilie Bardach, describing her as a "little bird of prey" who delighted in stealing away the husbands of other women. In the play Wangel reminds Solness that ten years before, when she was a girl attending a ceremony celebrating the completion of a church tower in her town, he had kissed her and promised to return to offer her a "kingdom." Laying claim to her kingdom, Wangel is able to work her will upon her "Master Builder." In the climax she encourages Solness, who fears heights, to climb to the top of a high tower he has designed. The memory of Solness atop the tower—even though the triumph is momentary and he then falls to his death—gives her a sense of ecstasy. No less than in *Hedda Gabler*, *Bygmester Solness* deals with the nature of power, particularly the power to influence and impose oneself on other people; but while *Hedda Gabler* is a study in the demonic, *Bygmester Solness* is a study in the erotic. The mysterious capacity to exert power is the theme connecting these two plays.

Bygmester Solness puzzled many critics, though its reception was far more positive than that for *Hedda Gabler*. In a statement he made at the time, Ibsen insisted that he drew real, living people and did not write symbolically. Such a patently false repudiation of any suggestion of symbolism may have been owing to his desire to court the Norwegian playgoing public, even as he was still economically dependent on German audiences.

Ibsen's next play, *Lille Eyolf* (1894; translated as *Little Eyolf*, 1895), was first performed in Berlin on 12 January 1895. Set in contemporary Norway, the play describes the marriage of Rita and Alfred Allmers, a wealthy couple whose nine-year-old son is crippled, the result of an accidental fall when he was a baby. The estranged mother and father react in different ways to their guilt over the boy's condition, as Alfred loses himself in work and Rita gives in to bouts of jealousy. When their son drowns in a fjord, however, the couple is able to achieve a kind of reconciliation, as they then decide to devote themselves to the needy children in their village. This "happy ending" has been discussed and argued over since the play was first performed.

While many critics cite *Lille Eyolf* as one of Ibsen's greatest plays, it is rarely staged successfully.

In 1895 the Ibsens moved to Arbinsgate, a few blocks away from Viktoria Terrasse, where he wrote *John Gabriel Borkman*. The title character–an industrious, creative son of a miner–betrays the love of his life, Ella Rentheim, by forsaking her to marry her twin sister, Gunhild, and attain a position as a bank manager. Borkman loses his banking position when he is convicted of fraud and is imprisoned for several years. Borkman is a lover of poetry and music, but his heart has hardened and his spirit is drying out. Borkman helplessly witnesses his own gradual change into a "living corpse." He dies of a stroke, and the estranged twins, whom he betrayed in different ways, reunite over his corpse. The play was Ibsen's most popular since *Et Dukkehjem*.

Ibsen's seventieth birthday in March 1898 was celebrated in Norway and around the world. He received gifts and flowers from all over and personal greetings from the king, and theaters in Norway and many other countries staged his plays. At the official banquet on 23 March 1898, Ibsen spoke of his plans to write a prose work, a book that would bring his life and his writing together in an explanatory whole. He added that such a task would seem almost like a holiday–and that he had hardly had a holiday since he left Norway in 1864. This year of celebrations did not allow Ibsen time for writing a new play. He started collecting notes, however, and in spring 1899 began writing the play he called an "Epilogue." Ibsen explained what he meant by this term in the 12 December 1899 issue of the newspaper *Verdens Gang*, the month his new play was published, after it had mistakenly been reported that he thought of the play as his last:

> No, that is an over-hasty conclusion. The term "epilogue" does not refer to any such thought on my part. Whether I come to write something more is another matter. What I meant by the term epilogue in this connection is simply that the play forms an epilogue to a number of my dramas, beginning with "A Doll's House," and ending now with "When We Dead Awaken." The latter work comes under the experiences I have wanted to describe in these plays. They form a unity, a whole, and thus I have finished. If I come to write something more hereafter, it will all be in quite a different connection, and perhaps in a different form as well.

In *Når vi døde vågner* (1899; translated as *When We Dead Awaken*, 1900)–which did turn out to be Ibsen's last play–an aging sculptor, Professor Arnold Rubek, returns to his home country after a lifetime spent abroad. Rich and famous, he is married to a young, beautiful woman, Maja, who has become bored by her life of wealth and dependence on her husband. The Rubek marriage is unhappy, as marriages usually are in Ibsen's writings.

During the Rubeks' stay at a sanatorium, Rubek meets his former model, Irene, who has become mentally unbalanced. He had once used Irene as the model for a masterpiece sculpture and then had summarily discarded her. The artist's separation from his former model, once the object of his sexual desire, proved traumatic for Irene. Overwhelmed by their encounter and also by Irene's accusations that he betrayed artistic ideals he cherished as a young man, Rubek starts on a symbolic ascent of the nearby mountain with Irene. The play ends in a catastrophe similar to the avalanche that killed Brand. In *Når vi døde vågner*, however, there is no voice of a *Deus Caritatis* (God of Love) at the conclusion, as there had been in *Brand*. The universe that Rubek leaves is a God-abandoned one. Ibsen had joined Friedrich Nietzsche in claiming that God is dead. The Christian "Pax vobiscum" (Peace be with you) the Catholic nurse utters blends with Maja's song of liberation. Maja survives the avalanche and ends up screaming repeatedly: "I am free!" But there is no paradise ahead for Maja or anyone else. This play was "The Epilogue" of Ibsen's writings.

Ibsen's authorship thus ended in 1899, the year that the Norwegian National Theater was rehoused in a grand new building. Outside, statues to Ibsen and Bjørnson were erected. Ibsen suffered his first stroke in 1900. He never fully recovered, and several smaller strokes forced him to give up his writing and his daily walks. He died on 23 May 1906. Suzannah died in 1914.

Henrik Ibsen is both a pathbreaking dramatist of supreme significance and his country's greatest literary artist. In addition to such poetic masterpieces as *Brand* and *Peer Gynt*, he authored the cycle of twelve plays, including *Et Dukkehjem*, *Vildanden*, and *Hedda Gabler*, that form the basis for his reputation in the English-speaking world, and, even more so, the foundation of modern European drama. Studied and performed on every continent and with far-flung artistic and social significance, Ibsen is a towering presence both in world literature and in the world of the theater.

Letters:

Tyve brev fra Henrik Ibsen, edited by Wilhelm Munthe (Oslo: Bibliofilklubben, 1932);

Samlede verker: Hundreårsutgave, volumes 16–18. edited by Didrik Arup Seip, Francis Bull, and Halvdan Koht (Oslo: Gyldendal, 1940–1949);

Brev 1845–1905, 2 volumes, edited by Øyvind Anker (Oslo: Universitetsforlaget, 1979–1981);

Brev 1844–1871, in *Henrik Ibsens skrifter*, volume 12, edited by Narve Fulsås (Oslo: University of Oslo/ Aschehoug, 2005).

Bibliography:

The International Ibsen Bibliography from the Centre for Ibsen Studies <http://www.nb.no/baser/ibsen/english.html> [accessed 10 September 2009].

Biographies:

Henrik Jæger, *Henrik Ibsen 1828–1888: A Critical Biography,* translated by William Morton Payne (Chicago: McClurg, 1890);

Georg Brandes, *Henrik Ibsen* (Copenhagen: Det Ny Aarhundrede, 1906);

Gerhard Gran, *Henrik Ibsen* (Christiania: Aschehoug, 1918);

Halvdan Koht, *The Life of Ibsen* (New York: Norton, 1931; London: Allen & Unwin, 1931);

Hans Heiberg, *Ibsen:–født til kunstner* (Oslo: Aschehoug, 1967);

Michael Meyer, *Ibsen* (New York: Doubleday, 1971);

Edvard Beyer, *Henrik Ibsen* (Oslo: Cappelen, 1978);

Robert Ferguson, *Henrik Ibsen: A New Biography* (London: Richard Cohen, 1996);

Ivo de Figueiredo, *Henrik Ibsen: Mennesket* (Oslo: Aschehoug, 2006).

References:

Asbjørn Aarseth, *Ibsens samtidsskuespill: En studie i glasskapets dramaturgi* (Oslo: Universitetsforlaget, 1999);

Louise von Bergen, *Nordisk teater i Montevideo: Kontextrelatered reception av Henrik Ibsen och August Strindberg,* Stockholm Studies in History of Literature, no. 51 (Stockholm: Almqvist & Wiksell International, 2006);

Birte Bernau, *Fontanes Ibsen-Rezeption: ein Beitrag zur poetologischen Standortbestimmung Fontanes* (Berlin: Pro Business, 2006);

Paul Binding, *With Wine-Leaves in His Hair: The Role of the Artist in Ibsen's Plays* (Norwich, U.K.: Norvik Press, 2006);

Pål Bjørby, Alvhild Dvergsdal, and Idar Stegane, eds., *Ibsen on the Cusp of the 21st Century: Critical Perspectives* (Laksevåg: Alvheim & Eide Akademisk Forlag, 2005);

Bjarne Buset, *Said about Ibsen–by Norwegian Writers* (Copenhagen: Gyldendal, 2006);

Martina Chmelarz-Moswitzer, *Mimesis und Auflösung der Form. Bildende Künstler und bildende Kunst in den Werden der skandinavischen Autoren Herman Bang, Henrik Ibsen und August Strindberg* (Vienna: Praesens, 2005);

Harold Clurman, *Ibsen* (New York: Macmillan, 1977);

Jacques De Decker, *Ibsen* (Paris: Gallimard, 2006);

Brian W. Downs, *Ibsen: The Intellectual Background* (New York: Octagon, 1969);

Jorge Dubatti, ed., *Henrik Ibsen y las estructuras del drama moderno* (Buenos Aires: Colihae, 2006);

Errol Durbach, *"Ibsen the Romantic": Analogues of Paradise in the Later Plays* (Athens: University of Georgia Press, 1982);

Hans Eitrem, *Ibsen og Grimstad* (Oslo: Aschehoug, 1940);

Jørgen Fafner, *Henrik Ibsens versdramatik* (Oslo: Aschehoug, 2007);

Armin Gebhardt, *Henrik Ibsen: Der grosse Gesellschaftsdramatiker* (Marburg: Tectum, 2005);

Michael Goldman, *Ibsen: The Dramaturgy of Fear* (New York: Columbia University Press, 1999);

Hans Herlof Grelland, *Tausheten og øyeblikket: Kierkegaard, Ibsen* (Kristiansand: Høyskoleforlaget, Norwegian Academic Press, 2007);

Stefano Bajma Griga, Gianna De Martino, and Ruth Anne Henderson, eds., *Ibsen–The Dark Side* (Turin: Carocci editore Universitá degli studi di Torino, 2005);

Einar Haugen, *Ibsen's Drama: Author to Audience* (Minneapolis: University of Minnesota Press, 1979);

Frode Helland, *Melankoliens spill: En studie i Henrik Ibsens siste dramaer* (Oslo: Universitetsforlaget, 2000);

Jørgen Dines Johansen, *Ind i natten: Seks kapitler om Ibsens sidste skuespil* (Odense: Syddansk Universitetsforlag, 2004);

Aldo Keel, *Ibsen für Eilige* (Berlin: Aufbau Taschenbuch Verlag, 2006);

Atle Kittang, *Ibsens heroisme* (Oslo: Gyldendal, 2002);

Naomi Lebowitz, *Ibsen and the Great World* (Baton Rouge: Louisiana State University Press, 1990);

Charles R. Lyons, *Henrik Ibsen: The Divided Consciousness* (Carbondale: Southern Illinois University Press, 1972);

Lyons, ed., *Critical Essays on Henrik Ibsen* (Boston: G. K. Hall, 1987);

James McFarlane, *Ibsen & Meaning: Studies, Essays & Prefaces 1953–87* (Norwich, U.K.: Norvik Press, 1989);

McFarlane, ed., *The Cambridge Companion to Ibsen* (New York: Cambridge University Press, 1994);

Toril Moe, *Henrik Ibsen and the Birth of Modernism: Art, Theater, Philosophy* (London: Oxford, 2006);

John Northam, *Ibsen: A Critical Study* (London: Cambridge University Press, 1973);

Northam, *Ibsen's Dramatic Method: A Study of the Prose Dramas* (Oslo: Universitetsforlaget, 1971);

Franco Perrelli, *Henrik Ibsen: Un profilo* (Bari: Edizioni di pagina, 2006);

Anne Marie Rekdal, *Frihetens dilemma: Ibsen lest med Lacan* (Oslo: Aschehoug, 2000);

Tore Rem, *Henry Gibsen/Henrik Ibsen: den provinsielle verdensdikteren: mottakelsen i Stor-britannia 1872–1906* (Oslo: Cappelen, 2006);

Michael Robinson, ed., *Turning the Century: Centennial Essays on Ibsen* (Norwich, U.K.: Norvik Press, 2006);

Helge Rønning, *Den umulige friheten: Henrik Ibsen og moderniteten* (Oslo: Gyldendal, 2006);

Astrid Sæther, *Suzannah: Fru Ibsen* (Oslo: Gyldendal, 2008);

Steven F. Sage, *Ibsen and Hitler: The Playwright, the Plagiarist, and the Plot for the Third Reich* (New York: Carroll & Graf, 2006);

Joan Templeton, *Ibsen's Women* (Cambridge: Cambridge University Press, 1997);

Templeton, *Munch's Ibsen: A Painter's Visions of a Playwright* (Seattle: University of Washington Press, 2008);

Theoharis Constantine Theoharis, *Ibsen's Drama: Right Action and Tragic Joy* (New York: St. Martin's Press, 1996);

Egil Törnqvist, *Ibsen-Byggmästaren*, Amsterdam Contributions to Scandinavian Studies, volume 2 (Amsterdam: Scandinavian Institute, University of Amsterdam, 2006);

Robin Young, *Time's Disinherited Children: Childhood, Regression and Sacrifice in the Plays of Henrik Ibsen* (Norwich, U.K.: Norvik Press, 1989);

Vigdis Ystad, *"–livets endeløse gåde": Ibsens dikt og drama* (Oslo: Aschehoug, 1996);

Farindokht Zahedi, *Henrik Ibsen and Iranian Modern Drama: Reception and Influence* (Oslo: University of Oslo, 2005).

Papers:

Most of Henrik Ibsen's original manuscripts and letters are found in the Manuscript Collection of the National Library (Nasjonalbiblioteket) in Oslo and in the Royal Library in Denmark.

Hans Jæger
(2 September 1854 – 8 February 1910)

Dean Krouk
University of California–Berkeley

BOOKS: *Kants fornuftskritik* (Christiania, 1878);
Olga (Christiania, 1883);
En intellektuelle forførelse (Christiania, 1884);
Fortale til Fra Kristiania-Bohêmen (Christiania: Huseby, 1885);
Fra Kristiania-Bohêmen (Christiania: H. Jæger, 1885);
Hans Jægers sidste ord i Bohemesagen eller, Den tale, som ikke blev holdt i Højesteret (Christiania: Huseby, 1886);
Min forsvarstale i Højesteret (Christiania: H. Jæger, 1886);
Kristiania-Billeder (Christiania: Eget, 1888);
Novelletter (Christiania: H. Jæger, 1889);
Syk Kjærlihet (Paris: A. Reiff, 1893);
Bekjendelser (Concarneau, 1902);
Fængsel og Fortvivlelse (Concarneau: H. Jæger, 1903);
Anarkiets Bibel (Copenhagen: Gyldendal, 1906);
Sosialismens ABC (Christiania, ca. 1910);
Syk Kjærlihet (Oslo: Pax, 1969).

Hans Jæger (portrait by Edvard Munch, 1889; Munch Museum, Oslo)

Critics and readers often find that the works of the bohemian and anarchist Hans Jæger are more significant as cultural and historical documents than as high-quality literature. Jæger himself was the first to admit that his ambition for a modern Norwegian novel surpassed his artistic talent. His historical importance results from his radical cultural and social criticism, and the scandalous literature he produced was both a vehicle for this critique and an expression of the bohemian lifestyle. As an extreme participant in the *sedelighetsdebatt* (debate about morality), which occupied Norwegian literature in the 1880s, Jæger advocated full sexual freedom and socialist revolution. He envisioned and attempted a type of documentary naturalism in the novel that would reveal the hypocrisy and destructiveness of the official Christian morality of the bourgeoisie, especially with regard to sexual matters. He attracted much public attention and infamy for his radical attacks on the moral and religious values of bourgeois society.

Jæger was at the center of a group of several dozen students, intellectuals, and radicals who comprised the bohemian population of Christiania (called Oslo since 1925). In 1885 the Norwegian government confiscated Jæger's novel *Fra Kristiania-Bohêmen* (From the Christiania Bohemia) immediately upon its publication. The work was censored, and the author was imprisoned for blasphemy and obscenity. After serving his brief time, Jæger spent many years in Paris and produced other works documenting the sexual lives of bohemians; many of these works were not available in Scandinavia until well into the twentieth century. Despite the censorship of his work, Jæger exerted a notable influence in young literary and artistic circles in Scandinavia in the late nineteenth century through his publicity and his relationships with other cultural figures, such as the young Edvard Munch.

Jæger's father, a police officer and the son of a Danish bailiff, met his mother in Arendal in southern Norway. Although Jæger was born on 2 September 1854 in Drammen, near Oslo in eastern Norway, he grew up in Bergen, where his family moved one year after his birth. By his early teenage years both of Jæger's parents had died. He went to live with his uncle in Arendal and eventually decided to become a sailor. He spent the years between 1867 and 1874 at sea; eventually, his life at sea led him to France, where he learned the language and began to read the works of Émile Zola. Zola's literary naturalism became a major influence on Jæger, particularly on his development of a theory and program for the modern Norwegian novel.

After many years at sea, Jæger followed his intellectual and philosophical interests to Christiania, where in 1875 he gained employment as a stenographer in the Norwegian Parliament. Jæger also began his studies of philosophy at this time, with a particular interest in Georg Wilhelm Friedrich Hegel, whose dialectical models often appear in Jæger's work. In the tightly autobiographical *Fra Kristiania-Bohêmen*, the narrator and author stand-in, Herman Eek, reminisces about his intense involvement with philosophical readings in the winter of 1877:

> Jeg sad alene på mit værelse henne i sofaen mellem de to vinduer. . . . Hegel lå opslåt på divanbordet foran mig. Jeg sad og stirred ud i luften med trætte miner . . . Kunde det nytte noget at bli ved med dette? To år af mit liv havde jeg nu vævet bort med Hegel, med Fichte, med Kant . . . uden at forstå det bitterste gran. . . . Var det ikke bedst at lægge det hele væk? Jeg var da ikke dum! . . . det kunde ikke være min skyld at jeg ikke forstod noget af det . . . ?

> (I sat alone in my room on the sofa between the two windows. . . . Hegel lay opened on the divan table in front of me. I sat and stared into the air with a tired expression. . . . Could it be of any use to continue with this? I had spent two years of my life with Hegel, with Fichte, with Kant . . . without understanding the slightest bit. . . . Wasn't it best to lay it all aside? I wasn't stupid! It couldn't be my fault that I didn't understand any of it . . . ?)

Jæger probably understood more about these German philosophers than his narrator did, because his first published work was about Immanuel Kant. Titled *Kants fornuftskritik* (1878, Kant's Critique of Reason), it was published with an unrelated short work by Gunnar Heiberg. In it, Jæger explains that Kant's critique of pure reason entails a rejection of both the immortality of the soul and of the necessity of a God or creator. The exposure to philosophical thought provided resources for Jæger's own developing criticism of society, whether he completely understood the philosophers he read or not. The thought of Kant, Hegel, and Johann Gottlieb Fichte remained influential in Jæger's intellectual development, particularly as inspiration for his ideals of anarchism, utopianism, and free love.

After this minor and rarely read philosophical work, Jæger did not produce any literature for several years, but he did continue to participate in social debates. Morality, women's emancipation, and sexual conduct were central concerns in Norwegian literature and public discourse in the 1880s. Henrik Ibsen's *Et dukkehjem* (1879, A Doll's House; translated as *Nora*, 1882) and Bjørnstjerne Bjørnsen's *En hanske* (1883, The Gauntlet) were central works in the public discussions of the rights of women and of sexual morality. The latter work brought up the issue of chastity before marriage for both men and women, indicating the injustice of the double standard licensed by official society, in which only men were forgiven for premarital sexual relationships. But Bjørnsen's solution, chastity for all, was nothing like the bohemian lifestyle of free love that Jæger came to depict and advocate in his literature.

An initial public indication of Jæger's views came in the winter of 1881–1882. Arbeidersamfundet (The Workers' Association) was hosting debates about Christiania's prostitution. An 1866 law legalized prostitution on the grounds that the conditions of indecency (*usedelighetsforholdene,* as they were called) needed to be monitored and ordered. The Workers' Association found that legalized prostitution, which was localized mostly in Christiania's Vika neighborhood, meant exploitation of the factory girls and working-class women who had little job security. Teachers and pastors joined the debates with objections to the morality of prostitution. Jæger's contribution began with a frank acknowledgment that sexuality could not be repressed. He shocked many present with his further assertion that prostitution was an effect of bourgeois marriage and that complete sexual freedom was the only possible solution.

Like many other significant events from Jæger's life in the 1880s, this speech was included in adapted form in *Fra Kristiania-Bohêmen.* Jæger's narrator, Herman Eek, sets the scene at the Workers' Association, where there is a discussion of the abolition of prostitution. Eek complains that the discussion was mostly a series of laments for the reigning immorality. Then Eek gives his own speech, which displays the argument Jæger had made against prostitution. Eek dismisses the earlier contributions to the discussion and commences his own account:

> Ondet består deri, at der i vort på ægteskabet baserede samfund også udenfor ægteskabet plejes legemlig omgang mellem kjønnene. Hvori har nu dette onde sin

rod? Jo. På den ene side deri, at vort samfund er basert på ægteskabet, uagtet denne institution viser sig ikke at være et udtryk for samfundsmedlemmernes kjønslige behov; og på den anden side deri, at fordelingen af det sociale arbejdes udbytte er sådan, at der i vort samfund gives en mængde kvinder, som dels yderst vanskelig og dels slet ikke kan leve af sit arbejde. Disse to ting er ondets rødder og disse rødder vil vi jo ikke rykke op, vi vil ikke socialisme, og vi vil ikke fri kjærlighet. Vi vil altså la disse rødder stå og dermed også beholde det onde som uundgåelig spirer frem af dem.

(The evil consists in that, in our marriage-based society, intimate relations between the sexes also occur outside of marriage. What is the root of this evil? Well, on one hand it is that our society is based on marriage, even though this institution does not show itself as an expression of the sexual needs of the members of society; on the other hand it is that the social division of labor is such, that there are a number of women in our society who can live off their work only with utmost difficulty or not at all. These two things are the roots of the problem, but we certainly wouldn't want to pull up these roots; we don't want socialism, and we don't want free love. So we want to let these roots remain and with them the evil that inevitably sprouts from them.)

In this literary adaptation of a speech he gave in 1882, Jæger sarcastically indicates two of the most important factors in his criticism of bourgeois society: his call for free love and for socialism. He discards any concerns for traditional morality and proposes that the reasonable, unembarrassed solution to the problem of prostitution is the abolishment of monogamous marriage and of the economic exploitation of women under capitalism. Free love would entail an open relationship between the sexes in which neither party was exploited or constrained in any way. Jæger notoriously suggested that under the rule of free love, a man could have an intimate relationship with twenty women, meaning that under monogamy he was robbed of nineteen-twentieths of his happiness. Jæger's speech, like Eek's version of it in the novel, was met with bitter indignation from the upholders of morality, and he was mocked and despised throughout Christiania.

This speech was the beginning of Jæger's radical public participation in the debates about morality. Jæger wrote about the works of Ibsen with approval, but he also wished that the author would go further in depicting "the children of the new age." In an article in *Dagbladet*, he praised Ibsen's 1881 *Gengangere* (translated as *Ghosts*, 1888) as a sign that a modern and free Norwegian literature was on its way. Still, he thought that Ibsen had not come to a complete enough awareness of the new reality and the new principles of freedom and happiness. Neither Ibsen nor Bjørnsen, thought Jæger, were new enough to record and portray truly the devel-

Title page for the published version of Jæger's argument (My Defense Speech in the Supreme Court) appealing the prison sentence he received after the government confiscated his novel Fra Kristiania-Bohêmen (1885, From the Christiania Bohemia) on grounds of blasphemy and obscenity (Widener Library, Harvard University)

oping modern life of the younger generation. In the following years, Jæger wrote his own dramas, *Olga* (1883, Olga) and *En intellektuelle forførelse* (1884, An Intellectual Seduction), vehicles for his ideas about morality and free love. The first play depicts a young woman's transformation, with the encouragement of Jæger's stand-in, Herman Eek, into a free-loving bohemian. The second play further portrays Olga's liberation as a conscious choice of freedom. These plays were failures, and he never tried to write drama again.

The event that really thrust Jæger into the center of the public debates was his publication of *Fra Kristiania-Bohêmen*. It remains the central and most significant work in Jæger's authorship, although it is more widely recognized for the scandal it caused than for its content. In November 1885, a month before the publication and confiscation of the work, Jæger published a crucial short document in preparation for the larger work's release. He called it *Fortale til Fra Kristiania-Bohêmen* (1885, Preface to *From the Christiania Bohemia*), and in it he concisely expressed his central artistic and social objectives. Jæger begins by admitting that *Fra Kristiania-Bohêmen* is "et monstrum af en bog–literært som socialt" (a monstrosity of a book–in both a literary and social sense). The work as a literary monstrosity, he explains, is a result of his having to undertake the task of introducing the modern Norwegian novel although he lacks literary originality and talent. The work's social monstrosity accompanies its literary naturalism, as Jæger specifies with his claim that "ethvert virkelig naturalistisk værk både ved sin form og ved sit indhold nødvendigvis må støde voldsomt an imod, hvad der nu for tiden ansees for god social tone" (every truly naturalistic work by virtue of both its form and content must by necessity strongly offend all that is at present regarded as a proper social tone).

Jæger continues by defining naturalism as "deterministic writing": it shows how an individual's actions inevitably result from the factual circumstances in which he finds himself. In such a view and in such literary representations, the individual has no moral responsibility for his actions. The type of individual Jæger aims to portray in his naturalistic art is one whose life has been impoverished by the constrictions of the herd's morality. When a determinist is a literary author, says Jæger, he will display this impoverishment of the individual:

> [Forfatteren tar] et rigtig forkrøblet exemplar af arten og lægger det frem for offentligheden; pege[r] på de spirer, som oprindelig fandtes, vise[r], hvordan de lidt efter lidt dræbtes under den moralske udvikling, og så stille[r] det frem i hele sin nøgne fattigdom, det ynkværdig forkrøblede liv, hvori denne kastreringsudvikling endte.
>
> ([The author takes] a really stunted specimen of the species and lays it out for the public; he points out the sprouts, that were originally found, shows how bit by bit they were destroyed during the process of moral development, and thus presents in all its naked poverty, the pitiably stunted life, to which this process of castration led.)

The deterministic naturalist sees the destructive or criminal actions of such a specimen in a nonmoral way, as the revenge of the stunted individual on a limiting and deforming society. The determinist shows sympathy for these "ulykkelige ofre" (unhappy sacrifices) of "den offentlige menings moralske tyranni" (the moral tyranny of public opinion). So the naturalistic author engages in journalistic activity by plunging into and recording the life of these sacrifices: the homeless, the suicides, the deserted, the impoverished and castrated "fremtidens fortidlig fødte børn" (too-early born children of the future).

Although Jæger begins his *Fortale* by describing the morally neutral observation of the deterministic and scientific naturalist, he ends by advocating a less impartial bohemian literature. He claims that the bohemians are growing in number because more and more individuals reject the security and falsity of bourgeois life with its concomitant Christianity, morality, and conception of rightness. The passive bohemian protest against bourgeois society–dropping out and seeking consolation in absinthe, intoxication, and women–must become active in the battle against the existing social conditions. To prepare for the society of the future, says Jæger, bohemian literature must be written, and his work is a provisional beginning. This belief accords with the first commandment of bohemian life: "du skal skrive ditt liv" (you shall write your life). Jæger ends the *Fortale* as it began, with a modest statement of his artistic insufficiency. In between these two self-deprecations comes a bombastic manifesto of social and artistic revolution.

The bohemian population of Christiania comprised students and intellectuals from a mostly bourgeois background rather than farmers or urban workers. The young men and women, inspired by new lifestyles and social philosophies, found themselves in a sharp generational conflict with the upholders of traditional values. They met in cafes, apartments, and at the Students' and the Workers' Associations to discuss critically and openly their new ideas of tolerance, complete expressive and artistic freedom, and free love. Jæger called the bohemians "mennesker for hvem det modern samfund er en øde, trøstesløs sandørk . . . fremtidens fortidlig fødte børn, mændene med de store behov, fremtidsbehovene, der først kan tilfredsstilles under friere, rigere, og skjønnere samfundsformer" (people for whom modern society is a desolate, unrelenting desert . . . the too-early born children of the future, men with great needs, the future's needs, that can only be satisfied under freer, richer, more beautiful social forms). Although they advocated earthly happiness and delight, the bohemians were often despairing and self-isolating, lost in homeless alienation from the existing bourgeois society they rejected. Jæger's works express this distressed aspect of the bohemian group in uneasy balance with descriptions of the supposedly blissful and vivacious life according to bohemian norms, the norms of the future. This potent hunger for life and existential enjoyment, when not satisfied, results in despair and thoughts of suicide. This polarity between the fruits of the earth and metaphysical despair is conspicuous in Jæger's literature.

Like most of Jæger's other works, *Fra Kristiania-Bohêmen* is barely fictional: it is a transparently veiled and mildly adapted document of autobiographical events. The main characters are the narrator, Herman Eek again, and his younger friend Jarmann. Eek is Jæger himself, and Jarmann is Jæger's friend Johan Seckmann Fleischer. The character of Jarmann is typical of the bohemian experience and development, encapsulating what life is like for a child of the future under the idiocy and tyranny of the present. At the opening of the novel, Jarmann visits the ill Eek and complains that he (Jarmann) is weary and deprived of energy to live. His frequent encounters with women have robbed him of his vitality, which reflects Jæger's belief, common at the time, that sexual abstinence could lead to serious illness, degeneration, and madness. Eek wonders how such a young man has been sapped as Jarmann is, and the story shifts to an account of Jarmann's arrival in Christiania as a dreamful fifteen-year-old.

A friend exposed Jarmann to the authors of the new Scandinavian literature—such as Ibsen, Bjørnsen, and Holger Drachmann—and even gave him a copy of Gunnar Heiberg's "En soirée dansante," the work with which Jæger's piece about Kant was published in 1878. Jarmann is eventually enticed into the *Vika* neighborhood, where, initially despite himself, he becomes a habitual customer of the prostitutes. After his beloved moves to Stockholm, Jarmann becomes despairing and rather predatory, still haunted by his loss.

By the time he takes his exams, Jarmann is an aimless wanderer of the streets of Christiania, obsessively following women, visiting the theater, thinking of suicide, and longing for lost purity. He realizes that he is anti-Christian while overhearing discussions of Charles Darwin and Christianity at the Workers' Association. He discovers that his despair is the fault of Christianity, with its oppressive restriction of earthly happiness, and he begins to understand that progress toward a freer, richer, and happier life rests on the abandonment of Christian beliefs about morality and the afterlife. At this point Eek and Jarmann meet and become freethinking friends, but eventually Jarmann proves too weak for the demands of freedom and shoots himself, a sacrifice to the limitations on life under the morality of bourgeois Christianity. In real life, Fleischer committed suicide as a twenty-four-year-old in 1884. The terrorism against the bourgeoisie that Jæger advanced in his plays involved driving their sons and daughters to despair and suicide in order to frighten society into change. This was one of the ethically questionable aspects of Jæger's program for a new society that led to censure from those who might otherwise have been sympathetic with his opinions and objectives.

Title page for Jæger's treatise (The Bible of Anarchy) advocating the abolition of government, money, and private property (New York Public Library)

Fra Kristiania-Bohêmen includes many accounts of Eek's erotic adventures and passages illustrating and criticizing the bounded conditions of life in contemporary society. The narrator imagines a new, modern life in which the individual's sexual self-expression is open and harmonious. Education toward this modernity is necessary, and Eek has plans for a girls' school where he would be the instructor in the new ways of free love and earthly happiness. This virtual harem of bourgeois girls needing instruction toward erotic freedom implies a view of women and near-pedophilia that is shocking to modern readers, although these ideas were not mentioned at the time the book was confiscated. Instead, the upholders of morality took issue with the work's frank depictions of visits to prostitutes and sex scenes, which are tame by later standards.

The authorities telegraphed announcements of the confiscation of *Fra Kristiania-Bohêmen* within hours of its publication on 11 December 1885, and Jæger was sentenced to eighty days' imprisonment in April of the following year. The censorship and trial were hotly controversial, occupying much public attention. The reactions of the press and literary circles in Norway were mixed. Of the major established Norwegian writers at the time, Jonas Lie and Arne Garborg spoke out most strongly in Jæger's defense. Lie appreciated the gravity of the work, calling it "et rop fra den dypeste og styggeste livets nød" (a cry from the deepest and ugliest distress of life), and he supported its open discussion of sexual issues as necessary in a democratic society concerned with the rights of the individual and of women. To suppress this discussion by punishing and censoring a single author, Lie thought, was equivalent to stopping the Gulf Stream with a cork. Garborg supported Jæger's right to freedom of speech but deprecated the work on purely literary grounds, saying it had to be rewritten. The newly formed organ of the workers' party, Vort Arbeide (Our Work), defended Jæger, and the Frisindede Studenterforening (Freethinking Students' Association) took a resolution decrying the restriction on free speech carried out by the government. The radical bohemian circle felt that the censorship was a betrayal by Johan Sverdrup's new liberal government.

Jæger himself spoke out in an impressive speech in his own defense, which resulted in his sentence being lessened to sixty days. In *Min forsvarstale i Højesteret* (1886, My Defense Speech in the Supreme Court) Jæger, greatly influenced by Zola, claimed that naturalistic literature was necessary for the enhancement and education of people in a democratic society. Both the liberal and conservative newspapers, however, supported the government's actions. Significantly, Ibsen, Bjørnsen, and Alexander Kielland, who might have been expected to support free discussion of social issues in the spirit of their own contemporary literary contributions, did not speak out for Jæger. He served the sentence in the winter of 1886–1887, after which he left for Paris. He had to return, though, to serve another sentence in the fall of 1888 for publishing *Fra Kristiania-Bohêmen* in Sweden under the deceptively innocent title *Julefortællinger af H. J.* (Christmas Tales by H. J.). Throughout the late 1880s, the newspapers continued to write about the threat of the Bohemian ideas and literature. *Fra Kristiania-Bohêmen* was not available in Scandinavia until 1950.

The naturalist painter and writer Christian Krohg gave a lecture during the height of the controversy. Krohg was Jæger's friend, author of the censored work *Albertine* (1886, Albertine), and later editor of a journal, *Impressionisten* (The Impressionist), to which Jæger frequently contributed. Krohg claimed that Jæger was not a naturalist, who would attempt to give an objective picture of reality, but rather an impressionist, whose personality and subjectivity informed the literary representation. Krohg praised Jæger as *"Nordens Manet"* (The Manet of the North). This title recalls Jæger's insistence on a nonobjective autobiographical literature. The Bohemian task of writing one's life has no pretense to a morally or politically neutral narrative position. Such writing is instead a subjective filter for all descriptions and representations of reality. As Jæger wrote in the journal, the impressionistic writer records "de tingene som gjør indtryk paa de menneskene man skriver om . . . i det øieblik de gjør indtryk" (the things that make an impression on the people one is writing about . . . at the moment the impression is made). A task of the journal *Impressionisten* was to present small impressions of the city, which Jæger contributed for the nine issues of the journal, spread over 1886–1887 and 1888 to 1890. In the eighth issue of *Impressionisten* the "Bohemian commandments" appeared, including "you shall write your own life" and "you shall take your own life" as the first and last. These statements are often attributed to Jæger, although he did not write them.

Jæger published some impressionistic pieces in *Kristiania-Billeder* (1888, Christiania-Pictures) and *Novelletter* (1889, Short Stories). *Novelletter* includes sketches of city life from Paris, where Jæger lived on and off for many years in the Montmartre district. He was there from 1890 until 1898, working on his erotic trilogy. The last two decades of Jæger's life were a time of incessant struggle to produce and publish his literary work. He spent his days in unrewarding employment at an American life insurance company in Paris. *Syk Kjærlihet* (Sick Love)–Jæger adopted his own idiosyncratic spelling; the correct spelling at the time was *kjærlighet*–was printed in Paris and immediately banned in 1893. The tragic love triangle presented in the work involves the syphilitic and impotent Jæger, his beloved bohemian princess, Vera, and her fiancé, Bjørck. It is another utterly autobiographical work consisting of letters to and from the three characters; Jæger predicted that it would be "det vidunderligste literaturverk som verden endnu har set" (the most wonderful literary work the world has yet seen). Instead, *Syk Kjærlihet* was banned all over Scandinavia, and none of the works in the trilogy was available there until 1969. Ibsen called it a book written by swine, about swine, and for swine ("en bok skrevet af svin, om svin, for svin"). Lie revealed some of the book's appeal when he said that he had to keep himself from beginning the copy Jæger had sent him, or he would not be able to stop reading.

The second volume of the trilogy, *Bekjendelser* (1902, Confessions), was printed in Brittany while Jæger was briefly residing in the coastal village of Concarneau. Jæger intended it as a continuation of *Syk Kjærlihet,* so it begins with chapter 24. The work is startlingly frank, presenting the author's sexual pathologies candidly. Instead of making the book available in shops, Jæger sold it himself, for ten crowns per copy. He did not sell many and wrote in letters from Concarneau that the book was a complete fiasco in an economic and literary sense. With characteristic self-judgment, he wrote that the work lacked the proper artistic expression to achieve its goals; yet, he was greatly relieved to be through with it. Jæger was able to sell even fewer copies–eleven–of the third volume, *Fængsel og Fortvivlelse* (1903, Prison and Despair). The unavailability of the erotic trilogy limited its significance and positive reception for a large portion of the twentieth century. Judgment of the literary quality of the trilogy became more favorable after the works were all available in the 1970s. Although repetitive, the works are at times passionately affecting, and some critics admire the intensity, honesty, and impressionistic narrative art of Jæger's accounts.

During his time in Paris in the 1890s Jæger also worked as a foreign correspondent for the Norwegian newspaper *Social-Demokraten*. He wrote about the Japanese-Chinese War in 1894–1895 and the Dreyfus affair in 1897–1898. By the turn of the century, Jæger had begun work on his large *Anarkiets Bibel* (The Bible of Anarchy), although it was not published until 1906. From the time of *Fra Kristiania-Bohêmen* to the new century, Jæger's main concern gradually shifted from sexual freedom to anarchism. An anticapitalist commitment was also present in his bohemian and erotic works, but the revolutionary political aspects of Jæger's thought and work acquired greater significance in the final decade of his life. He had a bitter hatred for authority and identified it with idiocy and injustice. As recorded in memoirs by his Danish friend J. J. Ipsen, Jæger sometimes expressed rather violent fantasies–for example, to demolish the capitalist center Paris with a canon or to murder each member of the Supreme Court in Norway. Ipsen also relates Jæger's pipe dreams: to win three million crowns gambling and use it to lead an anarchist revolt in Norway, and to establish an anarchist colony in Patagonia, coinhabited by Scandinavians and South American Indians. In a letter to Ipsen in 1908, Jæger expressed ambitions to build a plane and win huge sums at the premier flying competitions in France and England, where success would fund the implementation of his anarchist ideals.

Not all of Jæger's anarchist ambitions were so whimsical, though. In his conception, anarchy would overcome the idiocy and fraud of the existing social and economic order. Jæger advocated what he saw as the obviously rational reformation of society through the abolishment of money and private property. He pointed out the contradictions in capitalist society, and he thought that the causes of human constraint were all to be found in its idiotic economic organization. His ideal anarchist society, however naive and improbable, inspired the utopian *Anarkiets Bibel*. In the preface to the work, Jæger wrote:

> Gjennem mange tusen aar har ejendomsretten og pengene nu tvunget menneskeheden til omtrent kun at gjøre paa stedet marsch; gjennem mange tusen aar har disse idiotiske institutioner–lig to vældige blylodder, lænkede fast om menneskehedens ankler–gjort det snart sagt umuligt for menneskene at komme af flekken.
>
> (Through thousands of years, private property and money have forced mankind to merely run in place; through thousands of years these two idiotic institutions–like two heavy lead weights linked tightly around the ankles of mankind–have made it practically impossible for mankind to move from the spot.)

In the rest of the work, Jæger describes the development of capitalism in the nineteenth century as the progress of human idiocy. He mocks the optimism in the idea of cultural progress, claiming that man is alienated from himself under the existing conditions. Comprising ten books, the *Anarkiets Bibel* is long-winded and overbearing, and it has attracted few readers in its hundred years of existence. It is not a self-obsessed personal exposé but rather an agitation to revolt, and Jæger at times hoped that it could become a book with global significance. According to Ipsen, Jæger at other times lost faith in the work, felt isolated and ineffectual, and perceived the work as written by someone else.

In 1907 Jæger moved to Copenhagen, where he published an anarchist newspaper, *Korsaren* (The Corsair), with Ipsen. In articles in *Korsaren* he addressed issues such as the relationship between socialism and anarchism, the organization of work in an anarchist society, and the question of militarism. He thought that strict organization would be needed to achieve a socialist revolution and that the anarchist society, which would not force people to do any work they did not wish to do, would be achieved only after the initial revolution.

Despite Hans Jæger's ambitions for social revolt, his self-imposed dissociation from the farmers' and workers' movements in Norway prevented him from having much influence in the actual political and social movements of the day. He spent the last years of his life alone and sick in Oslo, where he died on 8 February 1910 after an operation for cancer.

References:

Halvor Fosli, *Kristianiabohemen* (Oslo: Det Norske Samlaget, 1994);

J. J. Ipsen, *Hans Jæger* (Copenhagen: Woel, 1926);

Olav Storstein, *Fra Jæger til Falk* (Oslo: Tiden Norsk Forlag, 1950).

Drude Krog Janson
(Judith Keller)
(18 October 1846 – 17 March 1934)

Ingrid K. Urberg
University of Alberta, Augustana Campus

BOOKS: *En ung pige* (Copenhagen: Gyldendal, 1887); republished as *En saloonkeepers datter* (Minneapolis & Chicago: Christian Rasmussen, 1889); translated by Gerald Thorson as *A Saloonkeeper's Daughter,* edited by Orm Øverland (Baltimore & London: Johns Hopkins University Press, 2002);

Tore: fortælling fra prærien (Christiania: Verdens Gang, 1894);

Mira: Et livsløb, as Judith Keller (Copenhagen: Gyldendal, 1897);

Helga Hvide, as Keller (Copenhagen: Gyldendal, 1908).

SELECTED PERIODICAL PUBLICATIONS–UNCOLLECTED: "Brev fra Amerika," *Nylænde,* 1 (1887): 39–42;

"En sjelden kvinde," *Nylænde,* 1 (1887): 81–87;

"Prestemod og presteforfølgelse," *Saamanden,* 1 (1888): 157–167, 174–180;

"En protest," *Nylænde,* 2 (1888): 52–56;

"Amerikanske kvindeslaver," *Nylænde,* 2 (1888): 209–212, 231–250, 273–282;

"Verdens martyrer," *Saamanden,* 5 (1892): 232–239;

"Stormen," as Judith Keller, *Nylænde,* 17 (1903–1904).

Drude Krog Janson was one of hundreds of mid- to late-nineteenth-century Norwegian immigrants who found the inspiration, confidence, and subject matter necessary to embark on a literary career after arriving in the United States. Unlike most of these authors, however, Janson was a social progressive who had been exposed to major Scandinavian and European literary trends, counting such Norwegian literary giants as Camilla Collett and Bjørnstjerne Bjørnson among her acquaintances and close friends. She was also atypical in that she successfully reached both Norwegian and Norwegian American audiences with her novels and essays, though the breakthrough qualities of her work have often been overlooked. Janson has been classified as a Norwegian, a Norwegian American, and an American author by different critics and literary scholars, but all agree that her American years (1882–1893) not only provided her with the impetus to write but also left an indelible mark on her later work.

Born on 18 October 1846 in Norderhov, Buskerud, to Ingeborg Christine Endresen and Hans Jensen Krog, a Lutheran minister and member of parliament, Drude Ulrike Petrea Krog learned to value reading and literature from a young age. Since formal educational opportunities for girls and women were limited in nineteenth-century Norway, she and her sisters received their education from private tutors at home, as was common for the upper middle class. At the age of twenty-one, Krog married Kristofer Nagel Janson, an aspiring poet and writer who held a theological degree. As Orm Øverland points out in his introduction to *A Saloonkeepers's Daughter* (2002), the English translation of *En ung pige* (1887, *A Young Girl*), Drude Krog Janson's first novel, this marriage was unconventional not only in Krog's choice to retain her maiden name but also in the determination of both parties to make the union a partnership. She used her husband's name, however, when she embarked on her literary career some twenty years later.

In 1867, shortly after their marriage, the couple moved to Gudbrandsdalen so that Janson could teach at the first *folkehøyskole* (folk high school) in Norway, run by the cleric Christopher Bruun. The folk-high-school movement started in Denmark and was led by bishop and poet N. F. S. Grundtvig. Grundtvig wanted to provide young people from rural areas with a holistic alternative to traditional educational models, a model in which communal activities and engagement in all aspects of the life of the high school were encouraged. Krog's twelve years at the folk high school were busy and intellectually stimulating. In addition to being the mother of seven young children, she attended classes, engaged in cultural debates and conversations, and met and developed relationships with major Scandinavian

Drude Krog Janson with her husband, Kristofer Janson, and their children, circa 1890 (Minnesota Historical Society)

cultural and literary figures. The author Bjørnson, the best-known Norwegian cultural figure of his day, and his wife, Karoline, lived near the school, and Krog and Janson developed a close friendship with this couple; the bond between Krog and Bjørnstjerne Bjørnson was particularly strong. Bjørnson and Danish literary and social critic Georg Brandes spoke highly of Krog's intellect and personality in their correspondence with each other, and she later served as the model for the strong female protagonist in Bjørnson's play *Geografi og Kærlighed* (1885, Geography and Love; translated as *Love and Geography,* 1914).

During the 1878–1879 school year Kristofer Janson was dismissed from Bruun's folk high school because of his radical theological leanings; this apparent misfortune led to travel opportunities for the Jansons that helped launch and shape Krog's writing career. Øverland notes that while Janson was on a speaking tour in the American Midwest, Krog traveled with the Bjørnsons and translated some of her husband's works from the Norwegian written norm, Landsmål, based on rural dialects, into the more conservative Dano-Norwegian Riksmål. In 1880, after Kristofer Janson's return, the couple traveled around Europe and spent time in Rome among a group of Norwegian intellectuals and artists. In Rome, Krog met and was inspired by playwright Henrik Ibsen and the pioneering feminist and author Collett. One of their sons fell ill and died in Norway while his parents were away. The theme of the loss of a child plays a prominent role in Krog's later works of fiction.

In 1882 Krog and her six children moved to Minneapolis to join her husband, who had emigrated the year before to serve as a Unitarian minister to the Norwegians. Krog was not a reluctant immigrant; in fact, she had encouraged her more reticent husband to make the move. In Minneapolis the couple continued to cultivate their literary interests. They organized and participated in social and cultural activities, and they kept in close touch with Scandinavian literary and cultural figures and trends, receiving visits from Bjørnson and the young Norwegian author Knut Hamsun, who worked as Kristofer Janson's secretary from 1883 to 1884.

In her correspondence to family and friends in Norway, Krog frequently expressed feelings of loneliness and alienation. Like her husband and her mentor

Cover for the English translation (2002) of Janson's first book, the novel En saloonkeepers datter (1889), originally published as En ung pige (A Young Girl) in 1887 (Thomas Cooper Library, University of South Carolina)

Bjørnson, she felt that the Lutheran clergy were largely responsible for promoting ignorance and intolerance among the immigrants. Conservative Norwegian Americans criticized Janson and Krog harshly for their religious and social views. At the same time Krog's American experience made her aware of the social malaise affecting Norwegian Americans in Minneapolis and introduced her to progressive political and social ideas and the American women's rights movement, all of which gave her material for essays and fiction and helped her launch her literary career.

In 1887 Krog, as Drude Krog Janson, wrote *En ung pige,* which was republished in 1889 in the United States under the title *En saloonkeepers datter.* In this bildungsroman Janson not only exposes such rampant societal problems as alcoholism, materialism, and the poor treatment of women among the Norwegian Americans, but she also discusses and debates these problems. Following the mandates and ideas of Brandes, Janson holds the American women's rights movement up as a model for social change as demonstrated in the life of the protagonist of the novel, Astrid Holm. Astrid emigrates from Norway to Minneapolis with her father and siblings. A conventional marriage within a Norwegian American community—marked by superficiality, hypocrisy, and close-mindedness—does not offer the fulfillment she will find as a Unitarian minister. After seeking advice from her hero, Bjørnstjerne Bjørnson, who is in the Midwest on a speaking tour, Astrid decides to break off her engagement and leave her father and oppressive home in order to pursue a degree in theology. The novel ends on a note of optimism as Astrid, who has decided to live out her life with a woman medical doctor, preaches to an American audience at her ordination. She hopes that one day the Norwegian Americans also will respond positively to her message.

The critical response to Janson's novel in Norway was mixed. While several critics praised the convincing psychological realism of the novel, an equal number were critical of the feminist theme in the book. Henrik Jæger failed to find any redeeming quality in the novel in his review in *Dagen* (18 November 1887). However, the encouragement and satisfaction Janson received from writing her first book apparently motivated her to continue writing. In a letter to her Norwegian friend Thea Seip on 30 July 1888, Janson noted that many readers understood and appreciated her message, also affirming her belief in the validity of her goal of spreading the truth about women's rights. Though the American edition of *En ung pige* received less critical attention than its Norwegian counterpart, it proved to be more popular, as evidenced by six printings in as many years.

Janson contributed essays to the Norwegian American journal *Saamanden* as well as to the Norwegian feminist journal *Nylænde* during her Minnesota years. Her topics included the appalling conditions of the American working poor, particularly female sweatshop workers, and the negative impact of materialism and unscrupulous businessmen on American society. In addition, Janson introduced her Norwegian readers to recent American publications and progressive leaders, such as antislavery Quaker activist Abby Kelley Foster, who fought for the right of women to speak in public. Janson also contributed to the morality debate raging in late-nineteenth-century Scandinavia. Janson's essays, which often include a missionary-like zeal, reveal that she was well read, aware of current cultural, social, and political debates in Norway and the United States, and that she was convinced the Scandinavian and American societies could learn from each other.

Though *En ung pige* was the only work of fiction that Janson published during her years in the United

States, evidence indicates she wrote at least two other pieces intended for publication, "Sorg" (Sorrow) and "Ensomhed" (Loneliness). Kristofer Janson, who served as his wife's literary confidant and adviser during this time, promoted these works by reading them aloud at Sunday evening gatherings in Minneapolis. Several of these unpublished works, as well as her second published novel, *Tore: fortælling fra prærien* (1894, Tore: A Tale from the Prairie), are set on the prairie and paint a dark picture of life in the new country. Though the critics saw redeeming qualities in these works, they also felt the tone was too dark for most readers, and they failed to appreciate the prairie setting. According to Sigrun Røssbø, the comments of "A. Vs.," a critic in the Norwegian American newspaper *Normanna* who reviewed Kristofer Janson's reading of *Ensomhed* (24 November 1888), are typical: *Ensomhed* was a stylistic improvement over *En ung pige*, but Janson, known for her intelligence and taste, should have written on city life and contributed to the "understanding of life in the upper classes in Norway, and in particular the mental life of young women and wives."

Janson could well have established a place for herself among the American progressives. In a letter to Bjørnson dated 22 May 1890 in which she discussed her belief in socialism, she indicated that she felt at home among this group. The breakup of her marriage, however, caused her to return to Europe in 1893 with four of her children. Literary histories and biographies have speculated a great deal regarding the role that Hamsun and/or Claude Madden, a young violinist who stayed with the Janson family in Minneapolis, played in this breakup, but Janson never commented publicly on this issue.

Janson continued to write upon returning to Europe, but a rather dark vision and a desire to help her family supplanted her desire to change and help society. *Tore: fortaelling fra prærien* was published in Norway the year after Janson returned. She may well have written it while she lived in the United States, and Røssbø argues that *Tore* is likely an expanded version of "Sorg," one of the dark prairie tales for which she was unable to find a publisher. This short novel is one of the few naturalistic novels in Norwegian American literature. With its rural setting, *Tore* provides a vivid depiction of the prairie thirty years before Ole E. Rølvaag's critically acclaimed *I de dage* (1924; translated as *Giants in the Earth*, 1927).

As in Rølvaag's work, the prairie in *Tore* is personified and plays such a prominent role that it attains character status. The prairie is part of a hostile environment where only the strongest survive, and Tore, the protagonist, is emotionally stronger than her husband, Siver: she is able to weather the blow of a prairie fire on their homestead in Minnesota while Siver, the weaker, succumbs and suffers a breakdown. Tore, who has emigrated from Norway with her husband, views the prairie as a negative force in her life; indeed, its storms, grasshoppers, and fires ultimately take everything from her: her crops and farm, the health of her husband, and the life of her favorite son. However, the prairie also has a positive impact on Tore's life, one she does not recognize. The prairie offers Tore economic opportunities and a chance to be independent, both of which were denied her in Norway, and it also provides a forum in which Tore can display her physical and emotional strength and develop them further. The freedom which Tore experiences on the prairie allows her, in fact, to attain a dignity and status that she would never have attained in the rigid social system in Norway. Despite its breakthrough qualities, *Tore* was, and continues to be, overlooked by critics.

Janson contributed a few book reviews to Scandinavian newspapers and journals after returning to Europe, but these did not provide her with the income she needed. Struggling with worry that she might not be able to provide for her children and herself, Janson wrote and published *Mira: Et livsløb* (1897, Mira: A Lifetime) under the pseudonym Judith Keller. She used this pseudonym for her fiction for the rest of her life. Though Janson wrote *Mira* to survive financially, she also felt compelled to reveal "the truth" to her readers. In a letter of 8 July 1898 to her friend Marthea Trøften, Janson wrote about *Mira*: "Og skulde jeg skrive, maatte jeg foran af alt skrive hvad livet havde lært mig" (And if I am going to write, I have to write above all else what life has taught me). The truth that Janson revealed in *Mira*—a thinly veiled autobiographical account of her marriage to and eventual estrangement from Kristofer Janson—was, in fact, too disturbing and vivid for many members of the Scandinavian literary establishment and led to a polarizing debate in the press. Hamsun's attack in *Dagbladet* (10 January 1898) was particularly harsh. Janson became deeply distraught after falling out with Bjørnson over this issue, and she was greatly relieved when the Norwegian writer Amalie Skram mediated a reconciliation.

The loss of a child and the ensuing grief are central themes in Janson's final two works of fiction: "Stormen" (1903–1904, The Storm), which was serialized in *Nylænde*, and *Helga Hvide* (1908), Janson's only work of fiction that is not set, at least partially, in the United States. The destructiveness of religious fanaticism is also addressed in *Helga Hvide*, and Sigrun Røssbø points out that the protagonist's husband, Sigurd, is clearly inspired by the fanatical minister in Ibsen's poetic drama *Brand* (1866; translated 1891). Bjørnson continued to be an influential figure in Janson's life, and her final novel, *Helga Hvide,* is dedicated to him. In her review of this work in *Nylænde* (December 1908) Gina Krog observed that *Helga Hvide* had not received the critical attention it deserved; Krog pointed out that many good works were overlooked in literary circles, *Helga Hvide* among them. Neither of Janson's final two works received more than mention from the critics, if that.

Janson moved around frequently in the years after she returned to Europe, spending time with friends and relatives in Germany, France, Denmark, and Norway, and she led a peripatetic lifestyle until her death in Copenhagen on 17 March 1934 at the age of eighty-eight. Her death received little notice in the mainstream Norwegian press.

Drude Krog Janson's literary production has never garnered widespread critical attention. However, Norwegian, Norwegian American, and, more recently, American critics who have encountered her work emphasize the contributions she made as a pioneering feminist writer in both Norway and the United States. Janson's correspondence reveals that depicting social and personal truths as well as general truths of the human condition were of utmost importance to her. She is remembered for boldly writing about these truths, and though this frankness resulted in some harsh criticism in her lifetime, it is now viewed in a more positive light.

References:

Nina Draxten, *Kristofer Janson in America* (Boston: Twayne, 1976);

Asbjørn Grønstad and Lene Johannesen, *To Become the Self One Is: A Critical Companion to Drude Krog Janson's* A Saloonkeeper's Daughter (Oslo: Novus, 2005);

Sigrun Røssbø, "Drude Krog Janson: Norwegian-American and Norwegian Author," thesis, University of Oslo, 1983;

Ingrid Urberg, "A Sense of Place: America through the Eyes of Norwegian-American Women Novelists," M.A. thesis, University of Wisconsin–Madison, 1996.

Papers:

Most of Drude Krog Janson's letters are housed in the Nasjonalbiblioteket (National Library) in Oslo. The Wisconsin State Historical Society in Madison and the Norwegian-American Historical Society Archives in Northfield, Minnesota, also hold selected letters.

Alexander L. Kielland
(18 February 1849 - 6 April 1906)

Hans H. Skei
University of Oslo

BOOKS: *Novelletter* (Copenhagen: Gyldendal, 1879);
Nye Novelletter (Copenhagen: Gyldendal, 1880);
For Scenen: tre Smaastykker (Copenhagen: Gyldendal, 1880);
Garman & Worse (Copenhagen: Gyldendal, 1880);
Arbeidsfolk (Copenhagen: Gyldendal, 1881);
Else: en Julefortælling (Copenhagen: Gyldendal, 1881); translated by Miles Menander Dawson as *Else: A Christmas Story* (Chicago: C. H. Kerr, 1894);
Skipper Worse (Copenhagen: Gyldendal, 1882);
To Novelletter fra Danmark (Copenhagen: Gyldendal, 1882);
Gift (Copenhagen: Gyldendal, 1883);
Fortuna (Copenhagen: Gyldendal, 1884);
Sne (Copenhagen: Gyldendal, 1886);
Tre Par: skuespill (Copenhagen: Gyldendal, 1886);
Bettys Formynder: skuespill (Copenhagen: Gyldendal, 1887);
Sankt Hans Fest (Copenhagen: Gyldendal, 1887);
Professoren: skuespill (Copenhagen: Gyldendal, 1888);
Jacob (Copenhagen: Gyldendal, 1891);
Mennesker og dyr (Copenhagen: Gyldendal, 1891);
Omkring Napoleon (Copenhagen & Christiania: Gyldendal, 1905).
Edition: *Samlede verker,* 4 volumes, edited by P. L. Stavnem and A. H. Winsnes (Copenhagen & Christiania: Gyldendal, 1919).

PLAY PRODUCTIONS: *Hans Majestæts Foged,* Christiania, Christiania Theater, December 1879;
Det hele er ingenting, Christiania, Christiania Theater, February 1880;
Tre Par, Copenhagen, Det Kongelige Teater, 18 November 1886;
Paa Hjemveien, Christiania, Christiania Theater, 29 April 1887;
Professoren, Christiania, Christiania Theater, 25 March 1889.

Alexander L. Kielland (from Edvard Beyer, ed., Norges Litteratur Historie, *volume 3 [Oslo: Cappelen, 1975]; University of Kansas Libraries)*

OTHER: *Agerhøns med Champagne: Opptegnelser til en selvbiografi,* edited by Øyvind Anker (Oslo: Gyldendal, 1983);

Artikler fra Stavanger Avis 1889, edited by E. O. Risa (Stavanger: Universitetsforlaget, 1983–1985);

Løvene i Fontainebleau: reise og novelletter fra Paris, edited by Owe Apeland (Oslo: Gyldendal, 1992).

Alexander L. Kielland is second only to Henrik Ibsen among Norwegian writers of the Modern Breakthrough. His best novels are of lasting value, despite that they are rooted in mid-nineteenth-century conflicts in a small Norwegian town. Kielland wrote about social change: he wrote in anger about religious hypocrisy, class conflicts, and the new class of businessmen who treated their employees badly and had few scruples about making money in business deals. In a few of his works Kielland depicted the decline and fall of a once prominent and wealthy trading house, clearly basing his novels on an established family concern that was sold before he became a writer.

Kielland was a major figure among Norwegian realist writers in the 1880s, those who followed the program of "putting issues up for debate," in the words of Danish literary critic and scholar Georg Brandes. Despite his background as a member of a wealthy family that offered him everything he could wish for as a child and young man, Kielland was driven by a strong indignation verging on rage against social inequities. Kielland's observations concerning injustice and hypocrisy were sharp; the literary method on which he often relied was satire. He always wrote, however, in a light, seemingly effortless, style. Kielland lived the life of an aristocrat; he dressed as a dandy; and his passion for a bounteous table led to obesity at an early age. He loved fly-fishing for trout and salmon; he was a competent musician; and for a period of nine years he enjoyed the love and respect of the workers at his brick factory. Living in high style, even when he could not afford it, and simultaneously writing in support of social justice and equality gave Kielland pangs of guilt. However, the many obvious conflicts and disharmonies of his life were also the basis for his most successful literary works. His essential works are comparably few, and he focused on only a few issues. Kielland's decision to become a writer led to a veritable flood of creativity; however, the period of his greatest activity lasted less than a decade.

Alexander Lange Kielland was born in Stavanger, on the southwestern coast of Norway, 18 February 1849. He was a patrician by birth as well as by attitude, born into a wealthy family of merchants. His great-great-grandfather, Jacob Kielland, established a trading house in the middle of the eighteenth century and became one the richest citizens in Stavanger. His son developed the company into shipbuilding and sea transportation, and the trading company was run by two more generations of rich and thrifty businessmen until the family sold it all in 1863, divided the profits, and lived on the interest. Alexander Kielland grew up as a rich man's son, number three among seven children, but the family fortune did not really last into his generation. Much in Kielland's adult life, both the choices he made and the decisions he avoided making as an established, popular writer and as a prominent civil servant connects to his tendency to spend more money than he made. Evidence of this habit can be found in hundreds of letters he wrote to his publisher, to writer friends, and to family members. He had four children, and he always complained that they cost him a great deal and seemed unfit for ordinary jobs. His letters to his publisher in Copenhagen were invariably about money or how to print books so they could be priced higher. Kielland could not afford the life he had been brought up to expect and enjoy. Writing and publishing books or working as a civil servant on a fixed salary did not provide him with such a life. After a fierce debate that actually split the ruling party, Venstre (The Left), into two factions, the Norwegian Parliament voted against granting him an honorary Artist's Grant. "The Kielland Case" still raises debate and discussion among political and literary historians; there is no other case quite like it in Norwegian history.

Kielland grew up in a house near a small lake in the heart of Stavanger, where his family had long been one of the richest, most prominent in the city. He adored his mother, Christiane Lange, and her death shortly before he turned thirteen was a great loss to him. His father remarried only a year later, but Alexander was never close to his stepmother. His father, Jens Zetlitz Kielland, was religious and conservative but had little talent for business. He was interested in music and painting, and, he did not oppose his son's plans to become a writer, even though as his father, Jens Kielland, might have had other plans for Alexander. Alexander went to the Cathedral School, where Latin was a major subject, and, from the fall of 1867 he studied law in Christiania (now Oslo). He graduated from law school without distinction and returned to Stavanger without having contributed to student life or making his mark in the capital city, a place he never really liked. Kielland began reading widely in his student years; Heinrich Heine and Søren Kierkegaard were among his favorite authors.

Kielland was secretly engaged to Beate Ramsland, whose parents belonged to a well-known religious sect in Norway, Haugianerne (The Haugians), a group Kielland depicted with great empathy for its positive values and also exposed for its greed and religious hypocrisy in his 1882 novel, *Skipper Worse*. Kielland and Ramsland were married in September 1871.

Kielland bought Malde Brickworks, just outside of Stavanger, and owned and ran it for nine years. He was interested in practical work and was remembered by his workers as a friendly and helpful employer. Beate bore him three children in the years between 1873 and 1876; their fourth child was born in 1882. Kielland's marriage was not a happy one, although there is no proof that Kielland pursued other women. In *Sannhetens pris: Alexander L. Kielland: en beretning* (1996, The Price of Truth: Alexander L. Kielland: An Account), however, Kielland's most recent biographer, Tor Obrestad, asserts that Kielland fathered an illegitimate child.

The 1870s and 1880s were years of turmoil and change, and new ideas and proposals slowly made their way to Denmark and Norway, in no small measure through the works of Brandes. Apparently, Kielland read avidly while running Malde Brickworks, spending more and more of his time on books by Bjørnstjerne Bjørnson and Jens Peter Jacobsen, and also reading works by Gustave Flaubert and other French writers. French literature became even more important to him in the spring of 1878 when he left Stavanger to spend about half a year in Paris. Kielland also read works by John Stuart Mill and Charles Darwin, and everything published by Brandes. In retrospect, Kielland appears to have gone about preparing himself for a writing career. Yet, he seems to have been ambivalent about his talent as a writer, while at the same time he was personally assertive and self-confident. He took the risk of leaving his wife and children behind and embarking on an unknown, uncertain path in order to write. He may have begun writing before he left Stavanger, but he had not published anything. In July 1878 Kielland published a play in one act, *Paa Hjemveien* (Homeward Bound), in *Nyt norsk Tidsskrift* (New Norwegian Magazine); this apprentice piece suggests many of the themes and dilemmas that came to occupy a central role in his oeuvre, but it does not reveal talent or promise unless considered as a precedent for what was to come. *Paa Hjemveien* made a mark and raised some attention, but mostly because of its harsh treatment of the clergy. About the same time, Kielland finished a couple of his short stories, called "novelletter," which really means "short, short story." In Paris, he read aloud from his texts and received praise from other writers. Kielland did not lack self-confidence at this time, although he might have felt some inner doubts about his future as a writer. In fact, on his way home from Paris, he called at the Copenhagen home of legendary editor Frederik Hegel at Dansk Gyldendal and showed Hegal his small collection of "novelletter." Kielland learned that Bjørnson had recommended him strongly to Hegel, and in the summer of 1879 Hegel published Kielland's first collection of short tales, titled simply *Novelletter*. The small

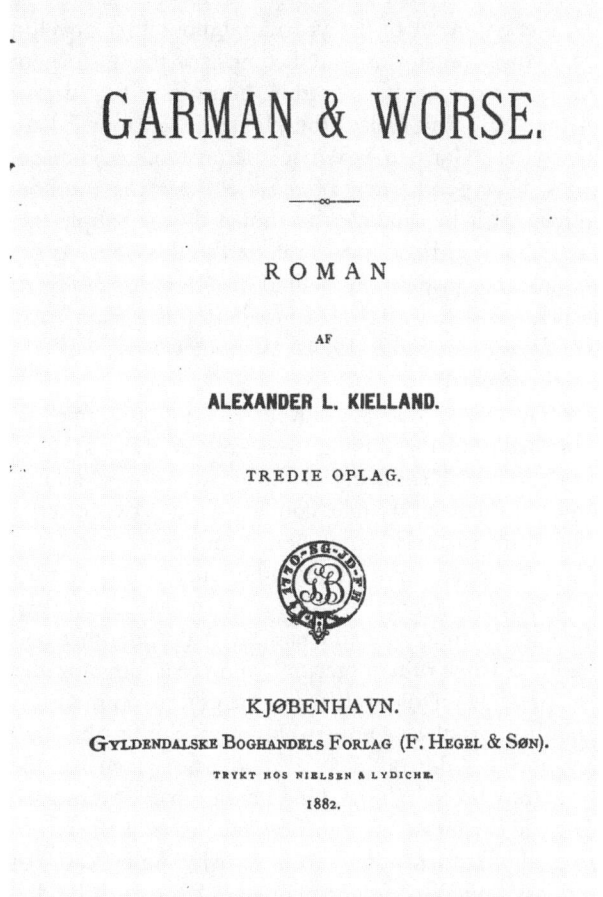

Title page for an edition of Kielland's first novel, originally published in 1880, about an old, renowned, and ethically managed company that is in decline during a difficult economic period (Harvard University Libraries)

book created a sensation all over Scandinavia. Not only was the genre something radically new, but also the style was light and pleasant. Humor and a sense of play and fun characterize many of the tales, even when they illustrate a social problem or point to wrongs that should be righted. Another collection of brief tales, *Nye Novelletter*, was published in 1880. This collection includes some of the most anthologized short stories in Norwegian literature.

Kielland probably knew that his indignation and his interest in the problems of contemporary society demanded the longer form, the novel. But he was hesitant and uncertain. He finally made up his mind to attempt writing a novel; Bjørnson as well as Edvard and Georg Brandes may be given credit for this decision. Kielland began work on his first novel in the summer of 1879, and after only five months the manuscript was dispatched to Hegel in Copenhagen. Hegel had no doubt as to the novel's merits, and in April 1880 *Gar-*

man & Worse reached the bookstores. Its publication was the literary event of the year, a fabulous first novel, a book that transforms and fictionalizes the history of Kielland's own family's trading house into the history of the "Rise and Fall of the House of Garman," later known as "Garman & Worse" because of its financial woes. How good a novel *Garman & Worse* was and how influential it became can be shown by the simple fact that Thomas Mann always referred to this novel as the model and inspiration behind his own *Buddenbrooks* (1901, translated by H. T. Lowe-Porter as *Buddenbrooks: The Decline of a Family*, 1924). Without *Garman & Worse*, no *Buddenbrooks!*

Garman & Worse is a novel about a group of people who make up the trading house of Garman. The old and renowned company is on its way down, and in times of financial trouble, conflicts arise between those who want to carry on as before and those with new ideas for a new time. The author makes this conflict even more poignant because it is also a conflict between the sexes: strong women characters fight prejudice and tradition while others succumb and break down under the pressure of old rules and prejudiced opinions. A mild irony is always present, but by and large the trading house is portrayed as a good place, even for the workers who toil all day long and are paid low wages. The old businessmen somehow take care of their people and offer them some sort of security. A new cadre of ruthless capitalist businessmen takes over, and the dignity and honesty of the old owners disappears. Kielland viciously and angrily attacks this new class of businessman in *Garman & Worse,* comparing their greed and ruthlessness to the dishonesty and deceit of civil servants and the clergy.

Garman & Worse is a realistic novel that posits questions and problems for discussion and action, shining a light on them, showing things for what they are and where they are, and calling out for people to listen. The social intentions of *Garman & Worse* are seldom expressed explicitly, however; instead, narrative, descriptions, individual characters, themes, symbols, and the different destinies of rich and poor carry his social message. Kielland chooses strong effects over a balanced view; he shows injustice and inequality boldly instead of carrying on discussions in measured tones. Kielland's "poetry of indignation" leads him to use his writing talents to light a fire in the social center, to draw people (readers, critics, and other writers) in so that they can be observed in the changing firelight. According to Kielland's "method," the author writes because he is angry, because his indignation—and his compassion—take command and compel him to do so. In a world of poverty, abuse, injustice, hypocrisy, and inequality, all within the limits of a small town, Kielland finds that the only healthy element is nature. In fact, nature is an active, integral part of all Kielland's novels. With wonderful descriptions of the ocean, the opening pages of *Garman & Worse* are but one example; the chapter on migratory birds that unexpectedly appears in the middle of *Arbeidsfolk* (1881, Working-Class People) is another, one that Kielland later described as his entrance pass to Paradise.

Kielland's first novel offers superb writing and a sense of compassion as well as an awareness of "the evils of the time" and a radical and oppositional view of society. Kielland enjoyed writing *Garman & Worse* and writing in general, comparing it with the feeling of having a salmon—or at least a trout—on one's fishing line. Later on, when his attacks on the evils of contemporary society became even more outspoken, he voiced regrets for being a coward when he wrote *Garman & Worse*. He felt that he should have gone further in depicting the rotten ruling class and the evil social system. None of Kielland's other books—and they are all competent, and some, quite good—however, can quite match the brilliance and easy mastery of his first novel.

In most of his novels Kielland targeted his own social class for criticism; he seemed to recognize and acknowledge all the lies, conceits, hypocrisy, and what he termed "patented heartlessness" of his own society. Kielland also wrote a few relatively uninteresting plays in between his novels. Shortly after the publication of *Garman & Worse,* he published *For Scenen* (1880, For the Stage), which included three plays: the formerly published *Paa Hjemveien, Hans Majestæts Foged,* and *Det hele er ingenting*. None of them was successful, on stage or as texts for reading. Seen from a more modern perspective, they are products of their time, written within a literary institution and in a culture in which most writers made attempts to write for the theater, despite the enormous shadow of Ibsen, who in 1881 shocked the nation with *Gengangere* (translated as *Ghosts*, 1906).

In November 1880 *Nye Novelletter* was published, and Kielland was hard at work on his next novel, *Arbeidsfolk,* which appeared in April 1881. The latter is without a doubt the most virulent attack Kielland ever made on a morally bankrupt bureaucracy, so vicious that even his closest allies thought he had gone too far. They may have been right in the sense that Kielland's vitriole diminished the novel as a literary work of art, but Kielland knew that all writing was political and that no one achieved anything by whispering to a sleeping people.

Kielland's father died in January 1881. Kielland sold his brickyard and left for Copenhagen. In the summer of 1881, his family joined him there, and they stayed in Copenhagen for two years. He had many close friends in the literary capital of Denmark and

Norway. Norwegian writers still published their books in Copenhagen, and Denmark was as important a book market for them as Norway. Kielland always enjoyed parties and long, rich dinners, and in Copenhagen he had plenty of opportunities to enjoy the good life. Yet, he also worked hard and diligently on new books: in less than three months during the summer of 1881, he wrote *Else: en Julefortælling* (1881, translated as *Else: A Christmas Story*, 1894).

Else: en Julefortælling and *Arbeidsfolk* were two of Kielland's most radically tendentious works; few books in Norwegian literature in this period or later could compete with them in vehemency. The split was enormous between the person Kielland appeared to be in real life–the affluent bon vivant who enjoyed fine food and wine, fancy attire, and an upper-class education– and the writer who advocated equality and justice. Yet, no one could be in doubt as to where Kielland stood in the ongoing political and moral debates: the radicals who wanted changes and improvements in Norwegian politics and society had a famous writer firmly on their side.

From May 1879 to late 1881 Kielland published two collections of short stories, a collection of three plays, and three novels. In July 1882 he published a novel, *Skipper Worse*. He had written the novel in three months, and although it may not be on a literary par with *Garman & Worse*, it has always been the most popular and the most widely read of all his novels. In addition to its criticism of members of a religious sect for their money-grubbing, shallow faith, and their interest in wealth instead of salvation, *Skipper Worse* also includes moving and convincing descriptions of the decent and well-meaning adherents to the same movement. *Skipper Worse* is set in the same locale as *Garman & Worse*, but the events in *Skipper Worse* take place a generation earlier, in the 1840s, in the years of the great herring fisheries. *Skipper Worse* deals with love and religion and with the conflicts that arise when they collide; it is also a book about trade and business deals, framed by descriptions of the sea, the herring industry, and the pace of life among industrious people in a small town. *Skipper Worse* was well received, not only by those who admired Kielland's bravery and his radical novels but also by reviewers and readers on the conservative side in politics.

To Novelletter fra Danmark (Two Short Stories from Denmark) was published in 1882. The short stories, "Trofast" (Loyal) and "Karen," have always been among the most popular of Kielland's short fictions. "Karen" is probably the most anthologized of all his short stories. The story makes use of satire and a certain hard edge in depicting the protagonist, Karen. Young Karen enjoys frequent trysts with the royal mail-

Title page for Kielland's novel about love, religion, and the herring industry (Harvard University Libraries)

man; she becomes pregnant but still works happily and to the satisfaction of all guests in the "Kro" (The Roadside Inn). When she finds out that her lover is already married, however, Karen commits suicide by drowning. "Karen" is told with ease and elegance, and although its narrative is shared by hundreds of sentimental popular songs from the same period, it still has a strong effect on the reader.

In 1883 Kielland published *Gift* (Poison), a novel that consistently attacks the double standards and hypocrisy of contemporary society, particularly of the educational system and the institution known as the "Latin School." *Gift* was Kielland's final book from Copenhagen; never again would he match the productivity of his years in the Danish capital. In this respect, Kielland follows the pattern of several other Norwegian writers who were more productive and wrote their best works abroad, away from Norwegian political strife and the issues that interfered with their writing. For Kielland and his contemporaries Bjørnson, Ibsen, and Jonas

Title page for Kielland's book about the French emperor (Harvard University Libraries)

Lie, voluntary exile from their homeland seems to have been a blessing.

Gift constitutes a harsh attack on the overemphasis upon and the general practice of teaching Latin in Norwegian schools and particularly on the methods used by teachers with absolutely no interest in their students, who just keep on teaching mechanically, as they have always done. "Little Marius," for example, finally gets his Latin right; but on the point of dying his last words are, ironically, "mensa rotunda" a phrase he says by rote. Apart from Kielland's criticism of the school system, *Gift* focuses on the question, how does a person live a life in accordance with his or her ideals and dreams instead of being forced to live a lie? The main characters, Abraham K. Løvdahl and his mother, Wenche, end up surrendering their ideals and adjust to a kind of life they oppose. Abraham is destroyed by an authoritarian upbringing at home, as well as by oppression at school. *Gift* proved provocative to many readers, not least to the authorities in church and school; and, it was perhaps no wonder that the Norwegian Parliament, after a heated debate and strong emotions on both sides, voted against giving Kielland an honorary salary as one of the nation's leading writers.

Gift had sequels in *Fortuna* (1884, Fortuna) and *Sankt Hans Fest* (1887, Midsummer's Eve). The trilogy focuses on the development–or rather the decline–of Abraham Løvdahl. Kielland may well have intended to create a self-portrait in the negative. He once claimed that Abraham was his double, an idea given credence by their sharing all three initials in their names. With luck and hard work Kielland managed to fare better than his fictional character. *Fortuna* voices well-known criticism of the new capitalists, while *Sankt Hans Fest* deals with the religious hypocrisy of a pastor who tries to stop an innocent Midsummer Day celebration. Kielland always had an eye for the wrongs in society. Even the simple but charming *Sne* (1886, Snow) takes on the dual evils of extreme political conservatism and misunderstood religious fervor.

In 1886 Kielland and his family moved to France and settled in the village of Cernay-la-Ville, just outside Paris, where his sister, Kitty, who was a painter, lived. They did not return to Norway until the summer of 1888. During this time, Kielland worked on several plays; one of them, *Tre Par* (1886, Three Couples) was by far the most successful, with its admixture of playfulness and serious discussion of love and marriage. *Tre Par* is probably the only Kielland play of interest today; the others, often one-act plays, are dated and clearly had little appeal to a contemporary audience and have none whatsoever today. *Bettys Formynder* (1887, Betty's Protector) and *Professoren* (1888, The Professor) are examples of Kielland's one-act plays.

When the Kielland family returned to Stavanger in 1888, Kielland set about establishing a newspaper, which he planned to edit. In January 1889 *Stavanger Avis* (Stavanger Newspaper) appeared, as an organ for the political Left on the western coast of Norway. Kielland was the contributing editor, and he managed to make many enemies during his tenure of a year or so as editor. The paper outlived his editorship and was published by his editorial assistant until 1907. Some of the newspaper articles in *Stavanger Avis* were later republished in *Mennesker og dyr* (1891, People and Animals). Recent Kielland biographers claim that Kielland was a better newspaper editor than earlier historians asserted.

In February 1889 Kielland celebrated his fortieth birthday; he did not receive a single congratulatory telegram. His readers as well as his political allies seemed to have forgotten him. He was in bad health, and his health deteriorated quickly in the years to come. Kielland also had serious financial problems. He had started the newspaper in the hope of making money, but he did not. His literary career had been impressive, resulting in many well-known works in the span of about ten years. But by 1890, Kielland was already an old, tired, unhealthy man; he was depressed, sleepless, overindulgent, and overweight. He still had a family to take care of, and he needed money, so he looked for well-paid work. In 1891 he was appointed mayor of Stavanger, and in 1902 he was named "amtmann" (the highest ranking civil servant) for the County of Romsdalen. At that point his writing had ceased. Kielland's almost magic decade of writing was what he had within him; he went on to give something back to the city in which he lived and to work with some of the same government and social officials he had criticized so roundly in his works.

The Kielland novels from Stavanger, *Garman & Worse* and *Skipper Worse* may be seen as the first and most successful effort to write a series of historical novels delineating Stavanger's development, its ups and downs, through much of the nineteenth century. This same story is also told in the trilogy about Abraham Løvdahl: *Gift, Fortuna*, and *Sankt Hans Fest*. The conclusion to the story rests with the novel *Jacob* (1891). This novel begins with a young man from the countryside who clerks in a store and steals a coin; Jacob's theft marks the beginning of his climb up the social scale; he becomes a powerful politician and businessman.

Jacob also concludes Kielland's career as a fiction writer. Clearly, the easy mastery of material and form, combined with real indignation and a strong social conscience, were no longer within his powers. He could refer to events, he could point to deficiencies, and he could imagine how things should be, but he could no longer create convincing characters and narratives for his readers. The next step in Kielland's career led him to what he often referred to as a degradation, to the office of mayor of Stavanger. Kielland proved to be an efficient and industrious civil servant, and he spent considerable time and energy appointing able people to important positions in the city. During a stay in Molde, a county town further north along the coast, a fierce fire destroyed most of the city of Ålesund. In spite of his many ailments and his obesity, Kielland oversaw rescue operations from a boat in the harbor, proving that he could direct others and serve as a competent administrator.

Kielland loved history and took a particular interest in Napoleon. In 1905, he published a book about the French emperor, simply titled *Omkring Napoleon* and dedicated to the Norwegian prime minister who led Norway's successful efforts to end its union with Sweden.

Kielland was hospitalized in Bergen several times and died there on 6 April 1906. The death certificate

Kielland in 1893 (painting by Eilif Peterssen; Store Norske Leksikon *<http://www.snl.no/.bilde/ Kielland%2C_Alexander_L._(malt_av_Petersen)>)*

lists "fat heart" as the cause of death. Alexander Lange Kielland had many admirers, especially early on in his career, but with books such as *Arbeidsfolk,* he also made many enemies: he was no longer the pleasant, entertaining storyteller with a style admired by colleagues as well as readers. But Kielland's realistic and critical books, dealing with social problems and questions of religion and morals, were rather quickly canonized, and literary historians soon established a lasting canonization of "The Four Great Writers" of the period: Bjørnson, Ibsen, Lie, and Kielland. The description "The Four Great Writers" is perhaps a deliberate effort to create an independent Norwegian literary history. Kielland was the youngest of these four writers, with the smallest production, so his reputation and later life in literary history and school anthologies were helped by his inclusion in the canon. Kielland's best books have stood the test of time, and they remain part of Norway's literary heritage. Interest in Kielland's writing has spiked whenever liberal or radical views are in vogue–for example, in the 1930s and 1970s.

Much has been written on Alexander L. Kielland and his books. In the early twentieth century the historical-biographical approach to Kielland prevailed. Studies of the relationship between Kielland's works and the culture and society of his day came only later. Scholars have either emphasized his criticism of a society on its way to "modernity" or focused on the style, narrative technique, and elegant and powerful structure of his best novels. A fairly large number of doctoral dissertations have been written on Kielland's work, both in and outside of Norway. Obrestad's biography of Kielland was published in 1996, and the 150th anniversary of Kielland's birth, celebrated in Stavanger in 1999, led to much interest and writing. Kielland's letters have also attracted attention; the first collection of such letters was published by his sons as early as in 1907. The standard collection of Kielland's letters in four volumes, *Brev 1869–1906,* appeared between 1978 and 1981. Kielland is considered one of the best and most interesting letter writers in Norwegian literature, and his wide correspondence includes his publisher and family members, as well as all the important Scandinavian writers of his time. New letters have even come to light since 2000.

Letters:

Breve fra Alexander L. Kielland: udgivne av hans Sønner, 2 volumes (Copenhagen: Gyldendal, 1907);

Breve til hans Datter (Christiania: Aschehoug, 1909);

Breve til hans Søn, Jens Zetlitz Kielland (Christiania: Gyldendal, 1910);

Brev, edited by Francis Bull (Oslo: Gyldendal, 1950);

Brev 1869–1906, 4 volumes, edited by Johannes Lunde (Oslo: Gyldendal, 1978–1981);

To par: Brevvekslingen mellom Alexander L. Kielland og Louise og Viggo Drewsen, edited by Tor Obrestad (Oslo: Cappelen, 1998);

Kielland privat: et brevportrett av ham selv, edited by Kjell Arild Pollestad (Oslo: Cappelen, 2006).

Biographies:

Mathilde Schjøtt, *Alexander Lange Kielland: liv og Værker. Et fem og tyve Aars Minde 1879–1904* (Christiania: Det norske Aktieforlaget, 1904);

Gerhard Gran, *Alexander Kielland og hans samtid* (Stavanger: Dreyer, 1922);

Baby Kielland, *Min far Alexander L. Kielland: belyst ved erindringer og breve* (Oslo: Gyldendal, 1929);

Francis Bull, *Omkring Alexander L. Kielland* (Oslo: Gyldendal, 1949);

Johan Riis, *Alexander L. Kielland: mennesket bak dikteren* (Oslo: Cappelen, 1973);

Martin Nag, *Nytt lys over Alexander L. Kielland* (Oslo: Solum, 1990);

Tor Obrestad, *Sannhetens pris: Alexander L. Kielland: en beretning* (Oslo: Cappelen, 1996).

References:

Owe Apeland, *Alexander L. Kiellands romaner: kunstnerisk stil og metode* (Oslo: Universitetsforlaget, 1971);

Nils Erik Bæhrendtz, *Alexander Kiellands litterära genombrott* (Uddevalla: Forum, 1952);

Willy Dahl, *Garman & Worse i nærlys* (Bergen: J. W. Eide, 1967);

Dahl, *Garman & Worse i nærlys og perspektiv* (Bergen: J. W. Eide, 1973);

Magne Drangseid, ed., *Kielland i Europa* (Bergen: Fagbokforlaget, 2008);

Bengt Hallgren, *Skitt eller kanel. Omkring Alexander L. Kielland. Åren 1878–1906* (Stockholm: Alba, 1987);

Johannes Lunde, *Alexander L. Kielland: Verdiarv og budskap. Garman & Worse. Skipper Worse* (Oslo: Gyldendal, 1970);

Lunde, *Handelshuset bak Garman & Worse: Jacob Kielland & Søn* (Oslo: Universitetsforlaget, 1963);

Lunde, *Liv og kunst i konflikt: Alexander L. Kielland 1883–1906* (Oslo: Gyldendal, 1975);

Tore Rem, *Forfatterens strategier: Alexander L. Kielland og hans krets* (Oslo: Universitetsforlaget, 2002);

Einar O. Risa, *Mannen i speilet: Alexander L. Kielland i Stavanger 1888–1902. En nedtur* (Oslo: Tiden, 1999);

Hans H. Skei, *Fragmenter til et Kielland-bilde* (Oslo: Det norske Videnskapsakademi, 2000);

Skei, ed., *Disharmoniens dikter: Alexander L. Kielland ved 150* (Oslo: Gyldendal, 1999);

Olav Storstein, *Kielland på ny: Alexander Kielland og hans diktning i lys av vår tid* (Oslo: Fabritius, 1936; revised, 1949).

Papers:

Collections of Alexander L. Kielland's papers are held in the National Library, Oslo; the Royal Library, Copenhagen; the State Archives, Stavanger; the Stavanger Museum; and the Stavanger Library.

Jens Kraft

(2 October 1720 – 18 March 1765)

Carl Henrik Koch
University of Copenhagen

BOOKS: *Explicationes in Is. Neutoni arithmeticam universalem, part I* (Copenhagen: Printed by A. Møller, 1741);

Theoria generalis, succincta construendi æquationes analyticas (Copenhagen: Printed by C. J. Møller, [1742?]);

Rigernes uskatteerlige Lyksalighed under den højpriselige Oldenborgske Stammes Regiering, bragt til den ønskeligste Fuldkommenhed under Vores Stormægtigste, Allenaadigste Monarch Friedrich den Femte (Copenhagen, 1749);

Logik eller Den Videnskab at tænke. Skrevet til Sorøe Ridder-Academies Nytte (Copenhagen: Sold by G. C. Rothe, 1751);

Ontologie, eller den første Deel af Metaphysik: Skrevet til Sorøe Ridder-Academies Nytte (Copenhagen: Privately printed, 1751);

Cosmologie, eller den anden Deel af Metaphysik: Skrevet til Sorøe Ridder-Academies Nytte (Copenhagen: Printed by Vaisenhuset, 1752);

Psychologie, eller den tredie Deel af Metaphysik: Skrevet til Sorøe Ridder-Academies Nytte (Copenhagen: Printed by Vaisenhuset, 1752);

Natur-Lærdommen om Gud, eller Den Naturlige Theologie: Skrevet til Sorøe Ridder-Academies Nytte (Copenhagen: Printed by det Kongel. Waysenhuus at the author's expense, 1753);

Kort Fortælning af de Vilde Folks fornemmeste Indretninger, Skikke og Meninger, til Oplysning af det menneskeliges Oprindelse og Fremgang i Almindelighed (Sorø: J. Lindgren, 1760);

Kritiske Breve til Videnskabernes Fremvext og Smagens Forbedring (Copenhagen: Privately printed, 1761);

Fortsættelse af de kritiske Breve til Videnskabernes Fremvext og Smagens Forbedring (Sorø: J. Lindgren, 1761);

Forelæsninger over Mekanik med hosføiede Tillæg (Sorø: J. Lindgren, 1763);

Forelæsninger over Statik og Hydrodynamik med Maskin-Væsenets Theorier (Sorø: J. Lindgren, 1764).

Edition: *Kort Fortælning af de vilde Folks fornemmeste Indretninger, Skikke og Meninger: til Oplysning af det menneskeliges Oprindelse og Fremgangi Almindelighed*, introduction by Ole Høiris (Højbjerg: Intervention Press, 1998).

Jens Kraft (from Gunnar Schrøder Kristiansen, Jens Kraft og opplysningen, *2001; <http://www.spartacus.no/index.php?ID=Bok&counter=50>)*

OTHER: "Systema Mundi . . . deductum ex principiis monadicis," in *Dissertation qui a remporté le prix proposé par L'Académie Royale des Sciences et Belles Lettres sur le Système des Monades avec les Pièces qui ont concouru* (Berlin, 1748);

"Tale til Erindring af Sorøe Ridderlige Akademies Stiftelses-Dag holden den 14 August 1764," in *Taler til Erindring af Sorøe Ridderlige Akademies Stiftelses-Dag holdne den 14 August 1764* (Sorø: Sorø Akademi, 1764), pp. 5–54.

SELECTED PERIODICAL PUBLICATIONS–
UNCOLLECTED: "Betænkninger over Neutons og Cartesii Systemata, tilligemed nye Anmærkninger

over Lyset," *Skrifter som udi Det Kiøbenhavnske Selskab af Lærdoms og Videnskabers Elskere Ere fremlagte og oplæste,* 3 (1747): 213–296;

"Afhandling om en Deel Contradictioner, Som findes i det sædvanlige Systema over Materien og de sammensatte Ting," *Skrifter som udi Det Kiøbenhavnske Selskab af Lærdoms og Videnskabers Elskere ere fremlagte og oplæste,* 6 (1754): 99–128;

"Om Sielens Udødelighed," *Skrifter som udi Det Kiøbenhavnske Selskab af Lærdoms og Videnskabers Elskere ere fremlagte og oplæste,* 6 (1754): 189–216.

Jens Kraft was the most prominent academic philosopher, mathematician, and physicist during the eighteenth-century Danish-Norwegian Dual Monarchy and one of the founders of scientific anthropology. He was born on 2 October 1720 in Frederiksstadn; his father, Anders Kraft, who died in 1725, was a lieutenant and later a captain in the Norwegian Infantry; his mother, Severine Ehrensfryd Scolt (or Schytt), died in 1722.

Kraft grew up as an orphan in Rostrupgaard Manor in Jutland, which was owned by his uncle, Major Jens Kraft. He matriculated in 1738 at the University of Copenhagen. As his mentor he chose astronomer, mathematician, and physicist Peder Nielsen Horrebow, who had once collaborated with well-known Danish astronomer Ole Rømer. This choice indicates that Kraft chose from the beginning to concentrate his attention on the mathematical disciplines.

Kraft obtained his bachelor's degree in 1739 and his master's degree in 1742. In 1740 he was awarded lodgings at Borch's Hall *(Collegium Meiceum),* which had been founded by chemist, physician, botanist, and philologist Ole Borch. As a resident, Kraft was obliged to publish and defend dissertations, and, accordingly, he wrote two mathematical papers. One of them is among the best mathematical papers from eighteenth-century Denmark. In *Explicationes in Is. Neutoni arithmeticam universalem, part I* (1741, Comments on Isaac Newton's *Arithmetica universalis,* part 1) he merely comments on the introductory parts of Isaac Newton's *Arithmetica universalis* (1707), but in *Theoria generalis, succincta construendi æquationes analyticas* (1742? A General Theory on Constructing Analytical Functions) he made some genuine contributions to mathematics.

In the spring of 1744 Kraft traveled abroad. His first stop was Halle, where he attended lectures by leading eighteenth-century academic philosopher Christian Wolff, a follower of Gottfried Wilhelm Leibniz, whose philosophy Wolff interpreted as partially Cartesian. As a cosmologist and physicist, Wolff accepted Leibniz's conception of body and force but rejected Newton's theory of gravitation. As a philosopher Kraft became a Wolffian, but as a physicist and cosmologist he later became a Newtonian.

From Halle, Kraft moved to Basel, where he met well-known mathematicians Johan Bernoulli and his son Daniel Bernoulli. The former was a follower of René Descartes; the latter, of Newton. Paris became the last stop on Kraft's "Grand European Tour," and there he met Newtonian Jean le Rond d'Alembert. French science, language, and culture made a deep and lasting impression on Kraft: whereas Ludvig Holberg, for example, used Latin words in his Danish prose, Kraft the Francophile used French words.

In 1746 Kraft was most probably back in Copenhagen. The same year the Society of Lovers of Science and Learning (later named the Royal Danish Academy of Science and Letters) published in its proceedings a physics paper by Kraft, "Betænkninger over Neutons og Cartesii Systemata, tilligemed nye Anmærkninger over Lyset" (Essay on Descartes's and Newton's Systems Together with Some New Remarks Concerning Light), in which he defended Newtonian cosmology against Cartesian criticism. Kraft's paper was the most outstanding Danish physics paper to be written in the eighteenth century, and it gained him admittance to the Society of Lovers of Science and Learning.

In 1747 Kraft was appointed professor of mathematics and philosophy at the Academy for Young Noblemen in the Danish provincial town of Sorø in Zealand. At the academy, which had been established that same year by the Danish king, Frederik V, young noblemen were instructed in theology, philosophy, rhetoric, history, foreign languages, jurisprudence, political science, and economics and also trained in dancing, fencing, and riding. The Academy for Young Noblemen was closed in 1793, but during the first twenty years of its existence it outshone the University of Copenhagen. In the same year as he was appointed professor, Kraft submitted an essay in Latin on the Leibnizian system of monads in response to a prize subject proposed by the Royal Academy of Science and Letters in Berlin. Kraft's prize essay, "Systema Mundi . . . deductum ex principiis monadicis" (The System of the World . . . Derived from the Principles of Monads), was published in *Dissertation qui a remporté le prix proposé par L'Académie Royale des Sciences et Belles Lettres sur le Système des Monades avec les Pièces qui ont concouru* (1748, The Dissertation that Won the Prize Proposed by the Royal Academy of Science and Letters on the System of Monads Together with the Competing Papers).

In his prize essay Kraft appears as a critical supporter of Wolffian philosophy. This philosophy dominated at the universities in Germany because of its pedagogical qualities and its encyclopedic incorporation of physics, cosmology, psychology, natural theology, and jurisprudence in a philosophical system based on logic and metaphysics and elaborated as an axiomatic, deductive system. For Wolff, mathematics was the ideal science, and he tried to apply the mathematical method to all other sciences. Without accepting Wolffianism in every detail, Kraft, too, acknowledged the mathematical method as universal.

As professor of philosophy, Kraft published five philosophical textbooks that together constitute a coherent Wolffian system. The first and biggest is his book on logic, *Logik eller Den Videnskab at tænke* (1751, Logic; or, The Science of Thinking). The eighteenth century was the century of logic, and the German book market abounded with books on logic written by Wolff's pupils. The Enlightenment held rational thinking as one of its tenets, and training in logic was considered a necessary part of the education of future civil servants and military leaders.

From 1751 to 1753 Kraft published the exposition of his metaphysical system in four textbooks: *Ontologie* (1751, Ontology), *Cosmologie* (1752, Cosmology), *Psychologie* (1752, Psychology), and *Natur-Lærdommen om Gud, eller Den Naturlige Theologie* (1753, Natural Knowledge of God; or, Natural Theology). In several respects Kraft's system deviated from Wolff's. For instance, Wolff held that psychology consists of two parts, rational psychology and empirical psychology; Kraft–anticipating Immanuel Kant's critique of rational psychology in *Kritik der reinen Vernunft* (1781; revised, 1787; translated as *Critique of Pure Reason*, 1855)–rejected the possibility of possessing rational or a priori knowledge of the soul. Therefore, psychology in his system was an empirical science, and he was perhaps the first in Denmark to advocate experimental psychology.

In 1760 Kraft published his most original work, *Kort Fortælning af de Vilde Folks fornemmeste Indretninger, Skikke og Meninger, til Oplysning af det menneskeliges Oprindelse og Fremgang i Almindelighed* (1760, A Short Account of the Most Important Institutions, Customs and Opinions of Savages for the Enlightenment of the Origin and Progress of Human Nature). Probably inspired by Montesquieu (Charles-Louis de Secondat, baron de La Brède et de Montesquieu), Kraft attempted in this work to argue for a naturalistic anthropology and a general political science. But possibly inspired by Jean-Jacques Rousseau, he also criticized contemporary culture and civilization. Like Rousseau, Kraft understood the right to own private property as a suspension of communal property and as a right created by the community itself. The right to private property created a dividing line between human beings and was responsible for the moral degeneration that characterized contemporary civilization, in glaring contrast to savage morality. Kraft also maintained that some human diseases were caused by the organization of contemporary civil society.

In his book Kraft wished to follow the development of "det menneskelige"–a Danish word best translated by the Ciceronian "Humanitas"–in order to show how social institutions and "self-created" opinions originate from human nature. Thus, he tried to explain "the human

Title page for Kraft's treatise on ontology, the first volume of his four-part exposition of his metaphysical system (from <http://www.formalontology.it/images/kraft-ontologie.jpg>)

being in terms of the human being"–that is, to explain human culture and civilization without presupposing divine intervention or intercultural influence. As a consistent naturalist, Kraft became one of the founders of scientific anthropology, and he knew that his approach to the study of human culture was innovative. In the introduction to his book he indicated that his account of the origin and character of primitive societies differed from what he had found in other books on savage societies. His account of the origins of "primitive" religions is also naturalistic. Like David Hume in *Natural History of Religion* (1757), Kraft rejected the monotheistic concept of God in natural theology as being the core of every religion, and he maintained that animism and polytheism preceded monotheism.

Although Kraft was a naturalist, he was certainly not a materialist. As a Wolffian and philosophical idealist,

Kraft attacked materialism in several papers— among others, in "Afhandling om en Deel Contradictioner, Som findes i det sædvanlige Systema over Materien og de sammensatte Ting" (1754, Essay on Some Contradictions to be Found in the Commonplace Systems Dealing with Matter and Compound Substances) and "Om Sielens Udødelighed" (1754, On the Immortality of the Soul). But in his "Tale til Erindring af Sorøe Ridderlige Akademies Stiftelses-Dag holden den 14 August 1764" (Speech Delivered on 14 August 1764 in order to Commemorate the Date of the Foundation of the Academy for Young Noblemen in Sorø) he launched an attack on French materialism from a biological rather than a philosophical point of view, an opinion that was especially aimed, it seems, at Julien Offray de La Mettrie and his *L'Homme machine* (1747, Man the Machine). In this speech he tried to prove that it is impossible, biologically, to account for the existence of human thoughts and sentiments. According to Kraft, the principles that explain the existence of life are utterly insufficient to explain the mental capacities of human beings.

In his *Logik eller Den Videnskab at tænke*, Kraft had said that art and fiction are for the sake of recreation and amusement and must not disturb serious and scientific studies. His vision was confined to the Enlightenment's concept of cultural education. Education was conceived as a development of man's ability for critical thinking, and the development of reason is what renders him a human being.

In 1761, in his journal *Den patriotiske Tilskuer* (The Patriotic Spectator), Jens Schielderup Sneedorff, professor of political science at the Academy for Young Noblemen in Sorø, defended art and belles lettres against the charge of having seduced people to abandon the accurate and thorough (that is, the mathematical) method. His target was Wolff and his Danish follower, Kraft. The mathematical method, Sneedorff says, is indispensable in the mathematical sciences, and to proceed methodically is always useful. But Man is not only a reasonable creature; he also has imagination, sentiments, and passions, and mathematics cannot describe the world in every detail. Thus, the use of the mathematical method is limited. In connection with aesthetic objects, not reason but taste provides the universal standards of judgment. Sneedorff's intention was not to attack mathematical science but to criticize the Wolffian tendency to use the mathematical method as a universal method of presentation.

In *Kritiske Breve til Videnskabernes Fremvext og Smagens Forbedring* (1761, Critical Letters to Assist the Growth of Science and the Improvement of Taste) and *Fortsættelse af de kritiske Breve til Videnskabernes Fremvext og Smagens Forbedring* (1761, Continuation of the Critical Letters to Assist the Growth of Science and the Improvement of Taste) Kraft launched a counterattack on Sneedorff in which he tried to prove that the mathematical sciences are more important and a greater advantage to human society and culture than are art and belles lettres. Taste and mathematical method are not incompatible, but a one-sided cultivation of taste may result in more energy being used to find the proper words than to find the truth. Moreover, sensual enjoyment, which Kraft considers to be the object of taste, may confuse and cloud the reason of man. The positive function of taste is simply pedagogical and designed to guide Man toward rational knowledge.

Kraft was married twice. His first wife was Bodil Cathrine Evertsen, with whom he had eight children; his second wife was Sophie Magdalena Langhorn, who bore him three children.

Jens Kraft published his scientific lectures as *Forelæsninger over Mekanik med hosføiede Tillæg* (1763, Letters on Mechanics with Appended Addenda) and *Forelæsninger over Statik og Hydrodynamik med Maskin-Væsenets Theorier* (1764, Lectures on Statics and Hydrodynamics Together with the Theories of Technology). For more than a half century these lectures were used as textbooks on the use of mathematics in natural science. Kraft died in Sorø on 18 March 1765. His lectures on fortification remain unpublished.

Biography:
O. Christensen, *Jens Kraft 1720–1765* (Lyngby: Dansk Historisk Håndbogsforlag, 1988).

References:
J. Düring Jørgensen, "Aufklärerische Gedanken über wilde Völker," *Kieler Studien Zur Deutschen Literaturgeschichte*, 16 (1983): 137–150;

C. H. Koch, *Dansk oplysningsfilosofi 1700–1800* (Copenhagen: Gyldendal, 2003), pp. 174–197;

Koch, *Jens Kraft som filosof*, The Royal Danish Academy of Science and Letters: Historisk-filosofiske Meddelelser, volume 64 (Copenhagen: Munksgaard, 1992);

Gunnar Schrøder Kristiansen, *Jens Kraft og opplysningen: filosofi og vitenskap i Danmark-Norge i det 18. århundre* (Oslo: Spartacus, 2001);

E. Reenberg Sand, "Jens Kraft–En dansk udviklingshistoriker fra 1700-tallet," *Chaos: Dansk-norsk tidsskrift for religionshistoriske studier*, 13 (1990): 28–47.

Vilhelm Krag
(24 December 1871 - 10 July 1933)

Henning Howlid Wærp
University of Tromsø

Translated by Lanae H. Isaacson

BOOKS: *Digte* (Bergen: John Grieg, 1891);

Nat: digte i prosa (Bergen: John Grieg, 1892);

Sange fra syden: reiseindtryk og stemninger (Bergen: John Grieg, 1893);

Vester i Blaafjeldet: eventyrdrama i 4 akter (Bergen: John Grieg, 1893);

Hjemve: første bog om familien Ravn (Bergen: John Grieg, 1895);

De gode gamle. To enaktere: De gamles juleaften og *Solnedgang* (Christiania: Aschehoug, 1895);

Den glade løitnant: lyrisk fortælling (Christiania: Aschehoug, 1896);

Den sidste dag: drama i tre akter (Christiania: Aschehoug, 1897);

Nye digte (Christiania: Aschehoug, 1897);

Fra de lave stuer (Christiania: Aschehoug, 1897);

Vestlandsviser (Christiania: Aschehoug, 1898);

Rachel Strømme (Christiania: Aschehoug, 1898);

Jul i skrivergaarden: novellecyclus (Christiania: Aschehoug, 1899);

Marianne (Copenhagen & Christiania: Det Nordiske Forlag, 1899);

Baldevins bryllup: idyl i tre akter (Christiania: Aschehoug, 1900);

Isaac Seehuusen (Christiania: Aschehoug, 1900; Minneapolis: C. Rasmussen, 1902);

Livet en leg: skuespil i fire akter (Christiania: Aschehoug, 1901);

Isaac Kapergast (Christiania: Aschehoug, 1901; Minneapolis: C. Rasmussen, 1903);

Lille Bodil (Christiania: Aschehoug, 1902);

Den gamle Garde (Christiania: Aschehoug, 1903);

Norge (Copenhagen: Det Nordiske Forlag, 1903);

Situationens herre: lystspil (Christiania: Aschehoug, 1903);

Thea Marie (Christiania: Aschehoug, 1904);

Holmerne de graa (Christiania: Aschehoug, 1905);

Vilhelm Krag (painting by Astri Welhaven Heiberg; Store Norske Leksikon <http://www.snl.no/.bilde/Krag%2C_Vilhelm_(maleri)>)

Jomfru Trofast: folkekomedie i 4 akter (Christiania: Aschehoug, 1906);

Major v. Knarren og hans Venner (Christiania: Aschehoug, 1906);

Vandringsmand (Christiania: Aschehoug 1907);

Sangen om Florens: drama paa Vers i fem Akter (Christiania: Aschehoug, 1907);

Fra det blaa Bryggerhus: af en Digters Optegnelser (Christiania: Aschehoug, 1911);

Hos Maarten og Silius (Christiania: Aschehoug, 1912);
Krøniken om Hr. Villum (Christiania: Aschehoug, 1913);
Stenansigtet (Christiania: Aschehoug, 1918);
Sange fra min Ø (Christiania: Aschehoug, 1918);
Viser og vers (Christiania: Aschehoug, 1919);
Verdensbarn (Christiania: Aschehoug, 1920);
Christiansand Sparebank 1824–1924: et jubilæumsskrift (Christiania: Aschehoug, 1924);
Baldevin. To idyller: Baldevins bryllup, Slangen i Paradis (Oslo: Aschehoug, 1925);
Min Barndoms Have: erindringer (Oslo: Aschehoug 1926);
Dengang vi var tyve år: erindringer (Oslo: Aschehoug, 1927);
Heirefjæren: Erindringer (Oslo: Aschehoug, 1928);
De skinnende hvide Seil: erindringer (Oslo: Aschehoug, 1931);
Denne taalmodigheda og andre betragninger (Oslo: Aschehoug, 1933).

Editions and Collections: *Sange: et Udvalg* (Christiania: Aschehoug, 1917);
Digte, edited and revised by Nils Collett Vogt (Oslo: Aschehoug, 1930);
Skrifter, 4 volumes (Oslo: Aschehoug 1930);
Stevnemøte: Vilhelm Krag i dikt og prosa, edited by Bjørn Hemmer and Kristen Jannike Larsen (Arendal: Kilden, 1991);
Vilhelm Krag skriver. Avis- og tidsskriftartikler av Vilhelm Krag, 3 volumes, edited by Jostein Andreassen (Søgne: Jostein Andreassen, 1992–1993);
Samlede dikt, 2 volumes, edited by Andreassen (Søgne: Jostein Andreassen, 1993, 1994).

PLAY PRODUCTIONS: *De gamles Juleaften,* Christiania, Christiania Theater, 5 February 1894;
Vanitas: en orientalsk akt, Christiania, Christiania Theater, 28 March 1894;
Baldevins bryllup, Christiania, Nationaltheateret, 21 November 1900;
Situationens herre, Christiania, Nationaltheateret, 3 November 1903;
Terje Vigen, based on Henrik Ibsen's poem, Christiania, Fahlstrøms Theater, 24 March 1905;
Jomfru Trofast, Christiania, Fahlstrøms Theater, 16 April 1906;
Sangen om Florens, Christiania, Nationaltheatret, 11 April 1907;
Slangen i Paradis, Christiania, Nationaltheateret, 1914;
Sommer i skjærene, music by Johan Halvorsen, Christiania, Den røde lykte, 9 April 1921.

SELECTED PERIODICAL PUBLICATIONS–UNCOLLECTED: "*Vanitas: en orientalsk akt,*" *Samtiden* (1894);

"Nordmænd," *Morgenbladet,* 16 March 1902, pp. 41–42;
"Amaldus Nielsen: Sørlandets maler," *Kunst og Kultur* (1912): 175–184;
'Vor "plads i solen,"' *Tidens Tegn,* 26 May 1917, pp. 6–7.

"The most unique figure in modern Nordic literature is . . . the singer Vilhelm Krag, whose strings the very Goddess of the Times has tuned." So wrote the critic Hjalmar Christensen in 1893. In the periodical *Samtiden* (Current Times) in 1898 the critic Erik Lie mentioned Krag under the heading "Om Fin-de-siècle digtningen" (On Fin-de-Siècle Poetry) and noted Krag's significance for the changes in Norwegian lyric: "In 1891, his 'Poems' appeared and precipitated uniform cries of enthusiasm in the Norwegian press and, among other events, led Herman Bang to present several public lectures in cities along the coast." The art historian Jens Thiis wrote about the reading of a poem by Krag at the Student Society in Christiania:

> Jeg vilde han skulle lese diktet selv, men det vilde han absolutt ikke. Han stod blek og slank, med sin eiendommelige skjønnhet i døråpningen, mens jeg leste så uttrykksfullt som jeg kunde i overbevisningen om diktets skjønnhet og verdi.
>
> Da diktet var ferdig, braket det løs et bifall, som jeg sjelden har hørt make til. En ungdommens dikter stod der i døråpningen og blev hyldet.
>
> (I wanted him to read the poem himself, but he definitely did not want to. He stood there in the doorway, pale and thin, with his own special beauty, while I read as expressively as I could in certain conviction of the beauty and value of the poem.
>
> When the poem ended, applause, the like of which I have seldom heard, broke out. A New Poet of the Young stood there in the threshold and received his recognition and honor.)

Krag was, however, only a star for a few years at the beginning of the 1890s. In the twenty-first century his work is of literary historical interest, with the exception of several single poems and a few merry stories and songs from the southern region of Norway. Yet, for Krag's hometown, Kristiansand, and the surrounding area, Krag is still important, not least because he gave two counties in Agder their name: Sørlandet (The Southland).

Krag was born on Christmas Eve 1871 in Kristiansand. As a seventeen-year-old he moved to Christiania to study law, but he never finished his studies. He continued living in the capital, although he still spent a great deal of time in Kristiansand and its environs, especially during the summers. Krag contributed articles to the newspapers *Dagbladet, Morgenbladet, Verdens Gang,* and *Tidens Tegn,* and wrote travel letters from his frequent extended stays abroad–especially from Paris, which he visited sixteen times, but also from Italy and Germany. In 1897 Krag married Alexander L. Kielland's daughter, Beate.

Krag took on the self-appointed role of "local correspondent for the Southland," and in countless newspaper columns he campaigned actively for the preservation of architecture and historical monuments to the culture of the south coast; he took the initiative to begin the State Archives in Kristiansand and the West-Agder County Museum, and he saved Christiansholm Fortress from virtual collapse by leading the demand for immediate restoration.

In addition to writing plays himself, from 1900 Krag served as a director for the Second Theatre in Christiania; he later worked as a director for Fahlstrøm's Theater and then at the National Theatre, where he served as chief director and principal from 1907 to 1911. Krag was chairman of the Norwegian Association of Writers from 1905 to 1908 and also editor of the periodicals *Juleaften* from 1901 to 1904 and *Kringsjaa* from 1907 to 1909. In 1911 Krag was appointed a Knight First Class of the Order of St. Olav. The same year, he became a chief consultant to Aschehoug Publishers, a position he held for life. The fact that Krag handled 2,400 of the publisher's 12,000 manuscripts during his tenure with Aschehoug says much about his great capacity for work.

Two of the poems for which Krag is best known, "Fandango" and "Landskab," are included in his debut collection, *Digte* (1891, Poems). "Fandango" begins:

> Ikke janitscharmusik!
> Stille, I marschtunge rythmer!
> Stille, for fan, musikanter!
>
> Tscherkesserinderne, tscherkesserinderne,
>   Lad dem blot komme!
> Ind skal de danse på spæde små fødder
>   Til dæmpet musik
>   fra fjerne guitarer.
> Surrende, kurrende, kjælende toner,
> Smilende, hvilende, hviskende toner,
>   Sanselig søde:
>   Fandango!

> (Not Janissary music!
> Silence, You march-laden Rhythms!
> Silence, by Satan, musicians!
>
> Mistresses of Tscherkesse, Mistresses of Tscherkesse,
>   Let them come on!
> In shall they dance on infant-small feet

Title page for Krag's verse drama (West in Blue Mountain), in which a Gypsy girl lures the hero to a mountain hut (Library of the University of Wisconsin–Madison)

>   To hushed music
>   From distant guitars.
> Whirring, stirring, enticing tones,
> Smiling, lolling, whispering tones,
>   Sensually sweet:
>   Fandango!)

The poem depicts a progression from the rejection of march-like rhythms in favor of softened guitar music and dance and back to a recall of the same march-like rhythms, after the slave girl Zerlina has directed the narrator's attention to autumn and vanity, decay and death, in the middle section:

> Zerlina, min terne, din hud er så blød,
>   Din mund er så frisk.
> Men–hvi bæver din mund, Zerlina?
>
> "Ak, herre, det lider mot høstens tid
>   og Persiens rose, de falder.
> Og duggen græder på nællikens mund,
>   Og løvet visner, o herre."

(Zerlina, my slave, your skin is so soft,
  Your mouth so fresh.
But—why does your mouth quiver, Zerlina?

"Ach, my lord, autumn is nearing
  and the roses of Persia, they are falling,
And the dew cries on the mouth of the carnation,
  And the leaves are withering away, oh lord.")

"Fandango" consists of two flight motions, two attempts to constitute a nonplace. The first "flight" is a turn away from the everyday, represented by the strict march music in section 1. The Orient, constructed in the rhythms of the language and the suggestive power of the words, becomes the new "place" for the speaker. The second "flight" is ultimately the denial of death in the last part of the poem, but in the meanwhile, it is a futile denial that leads to the experience of death that is also written into "the Orient of language." Even the first-person's power of imagination fails; time writes itself into language; and in the last two verse-lines of the poem, the speaker makes a final attempt to reach outside: "Musik musik, janitscharmusk / den store kinesiske tromme!" (Music, music, Janissary music / the great Chinese drum!). The recall of the Chinese drum can be compared to striking a gong, a wish to open a new scene, for the beginning of something new, started by a magic blow, or treading out of time. Such a movement is typical for Symbolism—not the longing for another place in the world but the acceptance of art as its own room for life. The speaker of the poem is a subject who does not wish to accept the world but to shape it himself.

Krag describes the creation of "Fandango" in his memoir *Dengang vi var tyve år* (1927, When We Were Twenty). In the spring of 1890 he had taken a Latin examination at the University of Christiania. He had done poorly and was

> i et afskyeligt Humør. Dertilmed sad jeg paa et afskyeligt Spisekvarter i samme afskyelige Hus hvor jeg bodde, og spiste afskyelig Mad. Jeg skulde op to Dage efter i Mathematik, som var det afskyeligste Fag, jeg vidste; jeg sad og spiste gammel Kalvesteg og puggede mathematiske Formler. . . . Pludselig reiser jeg mig fra Bordet og gaar. Jeg forlader Kalvestegen og Mathematikbogen og raver afsted som i Ørske. Inde paa mit Værelse sætter jeg mig ved mit Bord og skriver, skriver, og ved ikke selv hvad jeg skriver.
>
> (in an awful mood. To add to that, I was sitting in an awful dining room in the same awful house I lived in and eating awful food. In two days, I was scheduled to take the exam in Math, which was the most awful subject I knew of; I was sitting eating old veal roast and plugging away on math formulas. . . . Suddenly, I get up from the table and leave. I leave veal roast and math books and run off in a frenzy. In my room, I sit down at my table and write, write, and I don't know myself what I am writing.)

The mood in the poem is forced out as a counter-mood to a prosaic student room; the dormitory room is traded for a harem in Persia, and while student Krag is plagued by exam monitors and censors, the first-person *I* in the poem is himself, the lord over others. Persia moves to the fore as a negation of a prosaic place instead of a real place.

Significantly, the poem Krag wrote in 1890 in a pathetic dormitory room in Christiania is far more exotic and suggestive than some of the poems he wrote on his travels to Algeria and Tunisia in 1892, which were published in *Sange fra syden* (1893, Songs from the South). The poems in this final collection by Krag are virtual descriptions of journeys, while "Fandango" is a journey into fantasy and intertextual space with references to Hans Christian Andersen's tale "Nattergalen" (1844, The Nightingale)—the cry to the Chinese drum; to Wolfgang Amadeus Mozart's opera *Don Giovanni* (1787), in which Zerlina is the peasant girl Don Giovanni seduces; and to George Gordon, Lord Byron's *Don Juan* (1819–1824), in which the Mistresses of Tjerkesse appear. Forty composers wrote melodies for Krag's debut collection, but only a scant handful of composers found *Sange fra syden* of interest.

The poem "Der skreg en fugl" (A Bird Cried Out), also in *Digte,* consists of a single strophe:

> Der skreg en fugl over øde hav,
>   langt fra lande.
> Den skreg så sårt i den høstgrå dag,
> flaksed i brudte, afmægtige slag,
>   seiled på sorte vinger
> bortover hav. . . .
>
> (A bird cried out over the empty sea,
>   far from land.
> It cried so eerily in the autumn gray day,
> flapped with broken, weakened beats,
>   sailed on black wings
> away over the sea. . . .)

The poem is more of an expression of a melancholy mood than a description of nature. The vague, suggestive character of the poem is in line with the ideals of Symbolism and has inspired many musicians. In all, eleven composers have written melodies for the poem; among them are Christian Sinding, Edvard Grieg, Agathe Bacher Grøndal, and Johan Halvorsen.

The first line of "Der skreg en fugl" has a marked similarity to the first line of Johan Sebastian Welhaven's poem "Lokkende toner" (1860, Enchanting Tones):

"Der fløi en Fugl over Granehei" (A Bird Flew over the Forest). While the bird in Welhaven's poem leads the speaker into a hidden, harmonic nature, the landscape in Krag's poem offers more of an end-of-the-world feeling. One can also compare Krag's poem to a poem by Bjørnstjerne Bjørnson, "Over de høje Fjælde" (Over the High Mountains, 1870); Bjørnson's poem deals with an eagle who flies powerfully and triumphantly over the mountains. By contrast, the bird in Krag's poem scarcely has the power to lift off, something Thorolf Holmboe emphasized when he illustrated the poem in 1894. Holmboe's picture, a water-color, consists of a horizontal field with the sky covering the majority of the canvas and another field with the sea. The bird struggles low over the tops of the waves. Around this motif, Holmboe drew another bird, a stylized bird that spreads its wings around the picture. Krag's poem is written within the mantle of feathers. Nature is thereby written into art, a typical ideal for Symbolism.

In his memoir *Heirefjæren* (1928, Heron Feather) Krag wrote of experiencing the change from the era of Naturalism to that of Symbolism, of "the new time" for which he wanted to be an exponent:

> Naturalismen var den Mare, som red hele Verden; Poesien var erklæret for død. Selv en Versets Mester som Henrik Ibsen havde erklæret at Versets Tid var forbi.
>
> Men den Ungdom som voxte op i Slutten af Aarhundredet–fin de siècle–vi skulde vise, at Versets Tid tværtimod nu var oprunden; altfor længe havde Pegasus været spændt bag en Kjærre som en anden Mær for at trække Lasset for Politik, Moral, Religion eller Nation.
>
> Nu skulde Vingehesten befries og sprænge som en ung Hingst afsted udover Fantasiens blaanende Vidder. Kunsten for Kunsten!
>
> (Naturalism was the Nightmare that rode on the entire world. Poetry was declared dead. Even a verse master such as Henrik Ibsen declared that the time of poetry was over.
>
> But the young who grew up at the End of the Century–fin de siècle–we would show that the Time of Poetry had, on the contrary, now come to pass; for too long Pegasus had been harnessed to a carriage like another old nag in order to pull the load for Politics, Morality, Religion, or Nation.
>
> Now the Winged Horse is to be released and spring off as a young stallion, out over the azure expanses of Fantasy. Art for Art's Sake!)

The composite character of the literature of the 1890s, a literature in which one can find a harmonizing cultivation of beauty, certainly of a national nature, and an

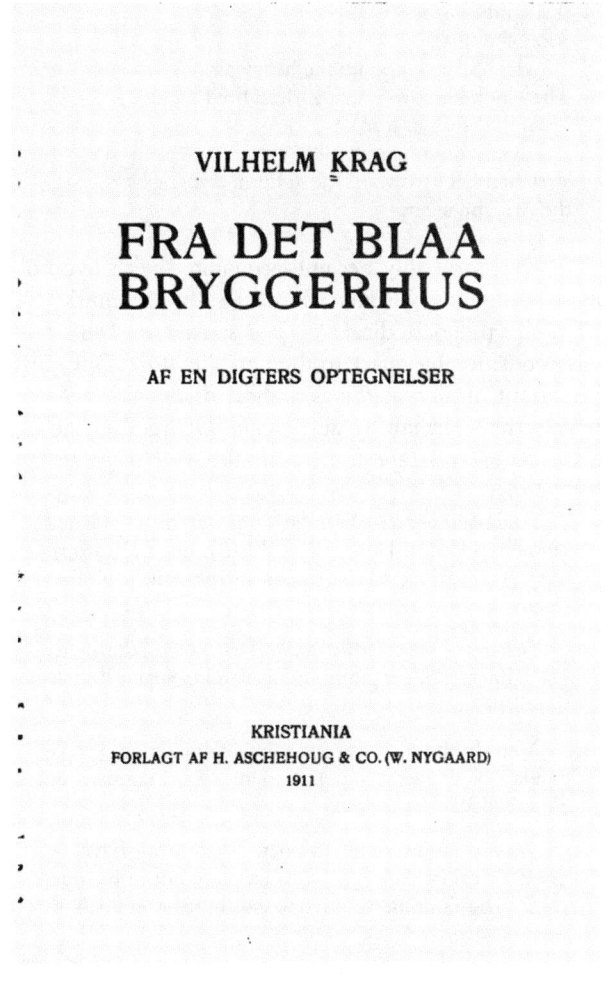

Title page for one of the collections of prose pieces (From the Blue Laundry) in which Krag depicts the nature and folklife of Sørlandet (The Southland), the name he coined for two counties in the Agder region of Norway (University of Michigan Libraries)

aesthetics of decadence that points on toward Modernism, also distinguishes Krag's writing. The poetic first-person is alternately a merry troubadour and a traveler on country roads. In the "Ouverture" to *Digte* Krag says: "Jeg har Alverdens Guld i min Taske / Mynt i min Lomme og Vin paa min Flaske" (I have all the gold in the world in my purse / coins in my pocket / and wine in my flask). In "Crepusculum" the speaker is a melancholy loner:

> Jeg sidder og ser på
>   to høie popler,
>   som strækker sig op i den tunge luft
> De ligner to bedende dødstrætte hænder
>   i angstens afsind.
>   stumt fortvivlede
> strakte vildt imod høstkveldens himmel
> den tusmørke, tause.

(I sit and look at
two tall poplars
    which stretch up into the heavy air.
They look like two praying, dead-tired hands
    in the craze of fear
        silently doubting
stretched wildly toward the autumn evening sky
the twilight, silent.)

Krag probably became acquainted with Symbolism through the Nordic periodicals. In Denmark, for example, the periodical *Ny Jord* started in 1888 and gave considerable space to the new literature. But most important of all was the periodical *Blätter für die Kunst*, which the German writer Stefan George started in 1892. Krag wrote about the periodical in *Heirefjæren*:

> I min allerførste Digtertid kom der hver Maaned ind af min Dør et Tidsskrift . . . Etsteds ude fra Europa. Og det kom ikke til andre end til mig i hele Norges Land.
>
> Det hed *Blätter für die Kunst*. Det havde ikke noget saa simpelt som Program; og der fandtes ingen Redaktionsartikler.
>
> Men Indholdet var en eneste flammende Propaganda: Ned med Nationalismen! Leve Poesien og Skjønheden!
>
> (In my earliest time as a poet, a periodical arrived at my door every month . . . from a place out in Europe. And it didn't come to anyone else but me in all Norway.
>
> It was called *Blätter für die Kunst*. It didn't have anything as prosaic as a program; and there were no editorial articles.
>
> But the contents were sheer incendiary propaganda: Down with Naturalism! Long live Poetry and Beauty!)

While Krag lived in Paris, he met Paul Verlaine, and he saw the premiere of Maurice Maeterlinck's *Pelléas et Mélisande* (1892), a play that made a great impression on him because of its break with the illusion of reality in realistic theater. Krag wrote in *Heirefjæren*:

> En Scene foregaar mellem to Elskende; det er om Vaaren; de mødes i en lys Lund en Morgen.
>
> Men ikke saa man Trærne i denne lyse Lund, ikke saa man Stammerne og Græsset. Tværsover Baggrund var der spændt et Tæppe; det var stiliserede Guldblomster og Guldblade hele Tæppet fra øverst til nederst.
>
> (A scene takes place between two lovers; it is Spring; they meet one morning in a light grove.
>
> But we don't see trees in the light grove, or trunks or grass. A carpet is stretched clear across the background; there are stylized gold flowers and gold leaves on the entire carpet from top to bottom.)

Krag's adventure drama *Vester i Blaafjeldet* (1893, West in Blue Mountain) includes examples of the primacy of both dreams and fantasies over reality and of a landscape consisting of gold and jewels, a nature that is not subject to the seasons and the life cycle of growth. In the play a Gypsy girl lures the protagonist, Jo Høg, to join her in a mountain hut that has been jolted out of nature and into artifice, into the order of luxury and ecstasy:

> Tatertøsen (med en krans av "Guldlyng" om håret):
> Nuvel da, Jo Høg, og mærk hvad jeg siger,
> Jeg selv er prinsesse i Blaafjeldets riger.
>   (Peger opad)
> Deroppe ser du det blaanende tag
> af fineste fløielsklæde,
> og prydet med smykker af alle slag
> og ildrøde fryndser dernede.
>   (Peger inover)
> Se inover hallen! Saa lavende fuld
> af stads og skinne stene,
> af gilde søjler og ildrødt guld
> hængt over stubber og grene.)
>
> (The Gypsy Girl [with a wreath of "Gold Heather" around her hair]:
> Now then, Jo Høg, and note what I say,
> I am the princess of the Realm of Blue Mountain.
>   [Points upward]
> Up there you see the azure roof
> of the finest velvet cloth,
> and decorated with jewels of all sorts
> and down below flaming red fringe.
>   [Points inward]
> See inside to the hall! See the full flush
> of glories and shining stones,
> of beauteous drapes and scarlet gold
> hung over the shrubs and branches.)

While the naturalists saw reality as a given, something close to the senses that one should re-create in works of art, the symbolists and their works of art did not refer to an earlier reality but instead created a new one. Art found itself in a different sphere from nature.

Krag was the first Scandinavian writer to publish a collection of prose poems, *Nat: digte i prosa* (1892, Night: Poems in Prose). With the title *Nat*, Krag wrote himself into the Romantic tradition of depicting dreams, a tradition in which night is the birthplace of the Romantic first-person *I* and the dream an expression for an intuitive form of art. The "joy" over the power of imagination that one finds in many Romantic poems is, however, missing from Krag's nightmarish prose poem:

> Jeg ligger og stirrer ud i mørket; og tilsidst forekommer det mig at være så underligt gult;–for mine øine former der sig så mange sære ting: store planter med tykke blade og opsvulmede frugter; men alt er i en uaf-

brudt strøm. Det driver stadig videre og videre over mig, og stadig kommer der nye planter forbi.

(I am lying and staring out into the darkness; and at last it seems to me that it is so wonderfully yellow;–before my eyes so many strange things are evolving: large plants with thick leaves and swollen fruits; but everything is in an uninterrupted stream that constantly moves on and on over me, and new plants constantly come by.)

The speaker in *Nat* challenges the experience of reality of "the everyday person," who in depicting an absinthe-buzz, suddenly bursts out:

Hvorfor sidder dere så stille og ser på mig med slige alvorlige øine? Er dere kanske rædde for at være med mig inat, når jeg skal ud i ørkenen–ud I den brændende ørken, hvor sciroccoen flyver igjennem luften som en hvid flamme. Ha, ha, du ser bekymret på mig og ryster dit brave hoved. Absalon du hædersmand; ja forresten, hvorledes skulde du kunne forstå det?

(Why are you sitting there so quietly and looking at me with such serious eyes? Are you perhaps scared of being with me tonight, when I shall be out in the desert–out in the burning desert, where scirocco fly through the air like a white flame. Ha, ha, you look at me so worried and shake your brave head, Absalon you man of honor–yes, by the way, how would you be able to understand it?)

The settings in which the speaker in *Nat* finds himself are vague and constantly changing, like a series of metamorphoses that, because of their instability, cannot provide a reference or definite point for a self-definition or for a benchmark in the surroundings. Every perception is uncertain, everything is simultaneously something else: "høit paa den svaiende stængel skjælver en valmues røde blomst;–men så er det ikke længer nogen blomst: det er blod der brænder, det er blod, der drypper i luende dråber og springer i stykker mod jorden i funklende gnister" (high on the swaying stem a poppy's red flower quivers;–but then it is no longer a flower: it is blood that burns, blood that drips in drooping drops and breaks into pieces, hitting the ground with twinkling sparks).

With the collections *Digte, Nat,* and *Nye digte* (1897, New Poems) Krag made his most important contribution to the renewal of the Norwegian lyric, even though they are uneven in quality. Not only was Krag in step with the literary trends of the time, but he himself was also an important part of the new Romantic movement. Sigbjørn Obstfelder, for example, described the effect that Krag's prose poetry had on him: "Jeg har atter læst 'Nat'–din sjels nat! Jeg iled ud over efterpå, måtte løbe over stok og sten, slå paraplyen mod veien, fordi det svinged så i mig" (I have reread "Nat"–your soul's

Title page for Krag's short-story collection (At Maarten and Silius's), in which he tries to create a stereotypical Southlander. The title characters are two old fishermen who live on the island of Steinsøya (University of Michigan Libraries).

night! Afterward, I rushed right out, I had to tear along, throwing my umbrella into the road, because I was swinging so much on the inside).

Krag's early poetry inspired artists of many kinds; for example, several of Harald Sohlberg's mermaid paintings from the 1890s were probably inspired by the mermaid Suleîma from *Nat*. Grieg, Grøndahl, and Sinding were among those who composed melodies to poems in *Digte*. In all, 119 melodies, 40 by Scandinavian composers, were written to poems in the collection.

In step with the life views of the first poetry collections are Krag's novels, *Hjemve* (1895, Homesickness) and *Den glade løitnant: lyrisk fortælling* (1896, The Merry Lieutenant: Lyrical Tale) with alternation between ecstatic affirmation of life and a paralyzing melancholy. The play *Vester i Blaafjeldet,* with a protagonist who resembles both Peer Gynt and Faust, is also typical of the adventure drama of symbolism (for example, the dramas of Maeterlinck and William Butler Yeats); the same is true of the dramatic fragment, *Vanitas: en orientalsk akt* (1894, Vanitas: An Asian One-Act). The play had its premiere at Christiania Theater on 28 March 1894, and the day after, a review appeared in *Dagbladet:* "Det var ikke sparet paa Knaldeffekten på Kristiania Theater igaaraftes.–Torden efter En ny Metode, veritabel elektrist Lynild, Pest, Død og Vanvid–det er i en kort Sum Det Væsentlige ved Aftenens Forestilling" (There was no limit to the thunderbolts at Christiania Theater last night–Thunder by a new means, real electric lightning strikes, disease, death and insanity–in short, that was the important thing about the evening's performance).

With *Vestlandsviser* (1898, Songs of Westland) a new diction entered Krag's oeuvre, a movement away from Symbolism and Exoticism and toward the folklore mood and humor of the homeland, with poems that borrow features from song tradition. This trend continues in *Sange fra min Ø* (1918, Songs from my Island) and *Viser og vers* (1919, Songs and Verses). Collections of poetry again piqued the interest of composers; in all, fifteen composers wrote melodies to the poems in these two collections. In 1903 *Norge* (Norway), a picture of Norway in verse with illustrations by Thorolf Holmboe, appeared.

Like his poetry from the same period, Krag's prose depictions from the 1890s take their subject matter from the nature and folklife of Sørlandet. Several of these prose collections–*Fra de lave stuer* (1897, From the Cottages), *Holmerne de graa* (1905, The Islets Gray), *Vandringsmand* (1907, Wanderer), and *Fra det blaa Bryggerhus* (1911, From the Blue Laundry)–are chatty. In the novels *Marianne* (1899), *Lille Bodil* (1902, Little Bodil), and *Thea Maria* (1904) and in the cycle of short studies *Jul i skrivergaarden* (1899, Christmas in the Court Recorder's House) the natural setting and folklife of the region are also the background for action. In the popular stories in *Hos Maarten og Silius* (1912, At Maarten and Silius's) Krag tried to create a stereotypical Southlander. The two old fishermen, Maarten and Silius on Steinsøya, are characterized by a disarming sense of peace and an unshakeable calm, but they also always have a quick retort hidden away. Their simple lives and common sense are uninfluenced by "city devils" and by Pietists.

A more farcical folk humor characterizes several of Krag's plays–among them *Baldevins bryllup* (1900, The Wedding of Baldevin), *Situationens herre* (1903, Lord of the Situation), *Jomfru Trofast* (1906, Miss True), and *Slangen i Paradis* (performed 1914, published 1925, Snake in Paradise). In the burlesque tales of *Major v. Knarren og hans Venner* (1906, Major v. Knarren and his Friends), the action is set in the time before 1814. The same is true in *Krøniken om Hr. Villum* (1913, Chronicle of Hr. Villum), but while the Knarren tales are in a completely humorous vein, the tale of Villum expresses more of a penchant for officer Romanticism–something that also runs through a novel such as *Den gamle Garde* (1903, The Old Guard). Precisely such a longing for the past or a search for places where time stands still–old manors, parks, and gardens–characterizes several of Krag's novels, among them *Rachel Strømme* (1898), in which Veheien's Old Vicarage is the starting point for the tale. *Isaac Seehusen* (1900) and *Isaac Kapergast* (1901), both of which take place before 1800, are set in Kjos Old Manor outside of Kristiansand. Even when a "modern" situation such as incest is discussed, as in the play *Den sidste dag* (1897, The Last Day), the action takes place in "an old manor in south Norway."

Drawing an absolute distinction between vague/exotic new Romantic writing and homeland poetry in terms of time frame in Krag's work is impossible; both the allegorical "medieval play" *Livet en leg* (1901, Life a Game) and the Renaissance drama *Sangen om Florens* (1907, Song of Florence) point in the direction of an earlier period in Krag's oeuvre. The same is true of the Symbolic novel *Stenansigtet* (1918, Stone Face), in which a formation in the mountains is personified and becomes a fast point of orientation for passing centuries, a frame for the comings and goings of people. From another angle, the sentimental play *De gode gamle* (1895, The Good Old Ones) with its dreamy presentation of old ideals points toward the later period in Krag's authorship. The same is true of the one-act play *Solnedgang* (1895, Sunset). A novel such as *Verdensbarn* (1920, Child of the World) does not point in the direction of either new Romanticism or homeland poetry: it is a modern urban novel with a hero who discards his roles, a tale similar to the later novels of Sigurd Hoel.

In any event, a change in Krag's works undoubtedly occurred toward the end of the 1890s. While Krag placed the action of the play *Vanitas* in the Far East, in the court of the king of Persia, the boundaries for *Baldevins bryllup,* for example, are an ordinary home in a little town in the south. The setting is now Krag's home district, and the gallery of characters no longer includes kings, dancers, and warriors, but instead, sea widows, servant girls, carpenters, and sailors. Instead of focusing on "strange moods" and/or setting the action in the Orient, Krag now found sources for inspiration in the home districts and their people. The subject matter was no simpler to deal with, however, for Krag had a greater purpose than that of writing down impressions from growing up in Kristiansand. What he intended was to undertake a literary mapping of the people and landscape in the southern part of Norway, a part of the country that in Krag's time was considered part of the Westland. Clearly, Krag saw this project as a breakthrough: in the autobiographical *Fra det blaa Bryggerhus,* he wrote: "Det er min Stolthed, at jeg er den første i

Pages from a 1925 letter in which Krag discusses his planning for his memoir Min Barndoms Have *(1926, My Childhood Garden) and the importance of the concept of Sørlandet (National Archives, Oslo)*

Verdenshistorien, som har elsket Lister og Mandals Amt og dyrket det med tilliggende Kystdistrikter" (I am proud to be the first in the history of the world who has loved Lister and Mandal Parishes and promoted them along with adjoining coastal districts).

In *Fra de lave stuer* Krag uses a certain delicate irony in depicting the experiences of travelers to the extreme south of Norway:

> Naar postbaaden gik ud fra den lille sjøby, stak den lige tilhavs. . . . For den, som intet herom vidste, saa det ud, som om skibet flygtede bort fra et landskab, der var mere end almindelig trist.
>
> De lave holmer var aldeles graaskaldede, og de hævede sig næsten jevnhøie indover saa langt en kunde se.
>
> Det lignede–helst I graaveir–en endeløs stenørken. Der var heller ikke meget liv mellem knatterne. Sort lav drog sig som stivt skind over de klippesider, som laa beskyttede for sjøspruten; enkelte steder bed etpar straa sig fast; men de var ganske gule og skjøre.
>
> Længere inde paa holmerne voxte lidt lyng, enkelte græstotter og nogle underlige, skjælagtige blomster uden duft. . . .–Restauratøren paa den store postbaad havde indrettet det saa listigt, at middagen netop serveredes, naar man gik fra den lille sjøby.

> "Det falder netop saa bekvemt der," sagde han, "thi der er intet interessant at se for passagererne paa denne strækning. Der er slet intet landskab, ved De."

(When the post boat departed from the little sea town, it headed directly out to sea. . . . For someone who did not know anything about it, it looked as though the ship was fleeing from a landscape that was more than commonly sad.

The low-lying islands were uniformly barren and gray, and they all rose to the very same height into the land as far as the eye could see.

It all looked like an endless desert of stones–especially in gray weather. In addition, there was hardly any life between the rocks. Black lichen stretched like stiff leather over the cliff sides where they lay protected from the sea spray; in a few places, a couple of straws were firmly holding on; but they were completely yellowed and withered.

Farther in on the island, a little heath, a few blades of grass, and some strange skeletal flowers without any fragrance at all grew. . . . The restaurant owner on the large post boat had arranged everything cleverly so that dinner would be served exactly as the boat was leaving the little sea village.

"It just works out so conveniently there," he said, "because there's nothing interesting for the passengers to see on that stretch. There's no landscape at all, you know.")

It was precisely that "lack of landscape" that Krag wanted to depict and address. He wanted to create a landscape of the Agder counties in the minds of people. At the time, the Agder Counties were a gray zone between East and West, a part of Norway that was not worth many lines in the travel guides of the time. Krag describes the situation in *Holmerne de graa:*

> Der er nogle Turister med ombord. De sidder nede og spiser Frokost eller de sidder i Flugtstole paa Promenadedækket og læser i sine Romaner.
>
> De bryder sig ikke om dette uinteressante Landskab. Baedecker omtaler ikke engang disse fattige Knauser. De skal videre iaften–østerpaa, vesterpaa, nordpaa.
>
> (There are some tourists onboard. They're sitting down and eating lunch or they're sitting in deck chairs on the Promenade Deck, reading their novels.
>
> They don't care about that uninteresting landscape at all. Baedecker does not even mention those pathetic outcroppings. They're off tonight–eastward, westward, north.)

In an article in the newspaper *Tidens Tegn* (26 May 1917) Krag gave the "standardized" tastes of tourists a blow: tourists have always sought "beautiful tracts elsewhere, places where nature has been easier to grasp for bourgeois tastes." How, then, to make this landscape visible? The Agder region was, of course, full of history and tradition, but to the aesthetic eye, the area had not yet arrived. "There are no scenic motifs in our districts." In *Min Barndoms Have* (1926, My Childhood Garden), his thirty-ninth book, his greatest success since his debut, he wrote: "Alle var enige om, at her var ret og slet stygt. Hvad var det for en Natur vi havde? Intet med Mæjestæt over, ingen kneisende Fjelde med Sne paa Toppen, ikke lidt Midnatssol engang. Bare Knaus og Knat og ingenting: ja lidt smaapent indimellem var det sagtens; men Motiver for en higende Kunstnersjæl? Ak, nei!" (All were in agreement that everything here was ugly pure and simple. What kind of Nature did we have? Nothing with Majesty about it, no towering peaks with snow on the top, not even the Midnight sun. Only rubble and stubble, and nothing; well, yes, there was something a tiny bit nice once in a while, but motifs for an aspiring artistic soul? Alas, no!).

Krag's first years as an author can be seen as a search for motifs elsewhere–in Paris, and on travels to the Mediterranean, to Algeria, and to Tunisia. By contrast, his later period as an author, from the end of the 1890s, focused on the project of transforming the Agder Counties into an artistic motif. In an article in *Kunst og Kultur* (1912) on the painter from Mandal, Amaldus Nielsen, who had consistently cultivated Agder motifs in his art and whom Krag saw as his foremost ally, Krag wrote:

> Det var jo ham, som havde malet det deilige Billedet fra Ny Hellesund i Nationalgalleriet. Og det Billede stansede jeg altid længe ved hver Søndag, naar jeg gik der. Og jeg følte altid en hemmelig Stolthed, naar fremmede Folk ogsaa stansede foran det og sagde, at de syntes det var vakkert. For vi sørfra var fra vor Barndom af ligefrem opdraget til at synes, at paa vore Kanter var det nærmest stygt.
>
> I Hardanger var der vakkert og østerpaa var der deiligt–men her? Her fandtes hverken de blaanende Fjelde fra "Brudeferden" eller de store brusende Granskoge som i Gudbrandsdalen og Valders.–Hist og her kunde det være "net" eller "smaapent"; det var det høieste. Men vakkert–for ikke at sige malerisk!–aa, Gudvelsigne Dem, er De gal?
>
> (He was the one who had painted that wonderful picture of Ny Hellesund in the National Gallery. And every Sunday I stood for a long time in front of that painting, whenever I went there. And I always felt a secret pride when foreigners also stood in front of it and said that they thought it was lovely. Because we Southlanders were brought up from our childhood to think that our region was on the verge of being ugly.
>
> It was lovely in Hardanger and it was lovely in the East–but here? Here, there were no blue mountains from "The Bridal Procession" or great roaring spruce forests as there were in Gudbrandsdalen and Valdres.–Here and there it could be "nice" or "a bit pretty;" that was the best. But lovely–not to say picturesque!–oh, God bless you, are you mad?)

Krag's efforts to give Sørlandet its own identity culminated in an article in *Morgenbladet* (16 March 1902) in which he publicly recommended calling the Agder Counties "Sørlandet." Only by granting the region its own name would its worth be affirmed:

> hvad der er noksaa paafaldende, er, at medens Folk i alle Landets øvrige Dele har faaet sit Navn, der baade betegner dem geografisk og sprogligt, mangler denne Landsdel ganske en saadan Betegnelse. Normændene bestaar som bekjendt af Østlændingerne, Vestlændingerne og Nordlændingerne; men vi her sørpaa,–vi er ingenting. Sprogligt seet staar vi jo nærmere de egentlige Vestlændinger end Østlændingen, og har derfor gjerne kaldt os Vestlændinger. Men denne Betegnelse er jo i Virkeligheden ganske falsk, i det Øieblik vi bor *sør*paa og ikke *vester*paa. Ogsaa sprogligt seet er Grænsen mellem disse Landsdele meget skarp. Men som sagt: hidindtil har vort Sprog manglet en Særbetegnelse for den sydlige Landsdel og dens Beboere.
>
> Det har naturligvis i Tidernes Løb været gjort Forsøg paa at rette paa denne Mangel, der, om ikke for andet, saa af rent praktiske Grunde ofte kan blive forvirrende. En vittig Bergenser foreslog engang, at vi skulde kalde

os Skagerakiere; thi han vilde ikke vide af, at vi kaldte os Væstlændinger,–en Betegnelse, der kun tilkom Folk fra Bergens Stift. Nogle unge Mennesker herfra har i den allersidste Tid forsøgt at kalde sig Sydlændinger;– men det Ord faar aldrig Hævd i Sproget, fordi det i Forveien betegner noget ganske andet: Folk fra det sydlige Europa. Men om de unge Mennesker kaldte sig *Sørlændinger?* Og om de kaldte sin Hjemstavn *Sørlandet?* Blev først Navnet brugt, og fik først Vanen slidt bort den uvante Smag, der altid hænger ved Ord, der laves og ikke laver sig selv, da vilde sikkerlig Navnet vise sig praktisk, og Sørlandet vilde ligesaalidt forvexles med Syden, som Østlandet nu forvexles med Østerland.

(what is noteworthy is that while people in all the other parts of the country have a name that designates them geographically and lingually, this part of the country is completely lacking in such a designation. As is known, Norwegians consist of Easterners, Westerners, and Northerners; but we in the South, we're nothing. With respect to language, we are surely closer to the Westerners than the Easterners, and so we have called ourselves Westerners. But in reality that designation is completely false, at the moment we say that we live in the South and not the West. In terms of language the border between these two parts of the country is very clear. But, as I said: until now our language has lacked a special designation for the southern part of the country and its inhabitants.

In the course of time there have been attempts made to correct that deficiency, but because of purely practical reasons, if nothing else, these attempts have often been confusing. A clever son of Bergen once recommended that we call ourselves "Skagerak-ers," because he did not want to hear about us calling ourselves Westerners, a term that only applied to people from Bergen Parish. Some of the younger people from around here have tried calling themselves Southerners but that term has never won a place in the language because it already represents something else entirely: People from Southern Europe.

But what if the young people called themselves *Southlanders?* And what if they called their home district *The Southland?* If the name was used and custom wore away the unusual aura that always accompanies words that are created and do not arise on their own, the name would be shown to be practical, and *Sørlandet* [South Land] would not be confused with Syden [The South], as Østland [East Land] is with Østerland [Eastern Land].)

Krag eventually succeeded in winning a place for that name. In *Illustrert Norsk Konversationsleksikon* from 1913, "Sørlandet" appeared as a reference word in a lexicon for the first time, and Krag was noted as the source for the word. On 28 May 1913 the Storting (Parliament) voted eighty-three "yeas" to forty "nays" to rename Vestlandsbanen (Westland Railroad)–that is, the stretch of track running from Oslo, Kongsberg, Kristiansand, to Stavanger–Sørlandsbanen (Southland Railroad), again with reference to Krag as the source of the name.

Krag traveled around as a literary anthropologist in the Agder Counties, settling in different places on the coast and inland for shorter or longer periods of time. He filled notebooks with words and expressions from the Agder dialects, and then he spiced his stories, such as *Fra det blaa Bryggerhus,* with such words:

Nu har en god og lærd Professor lært mig, at naar man skal samle norsk Folketradition, da er de første Betingelser to Ting: Skraatobak og Chokolade. Skraatobak til de gamle Mandfolk, Chokolade til Kjærringerne. Derfor reiser jeg aldrig uden Lommerne fulde af begge Dele.

(Now, a wise and learned professor has taught me that, when one collects Norwegian Folklore, there are two requisites to begin with: chewing tobacco and chocolate. Chewing tobacco for the old men folk, chocolate for the old women. Therefore, I never travel without my pockets full of both.)

Krag appears here as a collector, someone who came from outside the community and had to win the confidence of the people in order to succeed in approaching them more closely. Even though Krag was from Agder himself, he only felt himself halfway part of the "folk"; first, he had grown up in the largest city in the area, Kristiansand, and, second, he had gone on to study in the capital. Therefore, when he traveled around in the home district, he was always a bit of a "foreign fowl." In the story of Maarten and Silius in *Hos Maarten og Silius,* at the point when the protagonist lives with two old fishermen on the Kristiansand skerries, this duality appears quite clear:

"Haa driver naa Dere paa med nu for Tia," siger Silius, da Toddyen er bleven som den bør. . . . Ja saa maa jeg da ud med, at jeg driver paa med et Theater inde i Christiania. . . .

"Theater!" siger Maarten stille og forfærdet.

Haafernoe! siger Silius og reiser sig overende i Stolen. . . .

Jeg har aldrig før følt Haabløsheden ved at overbevise to Mennesker om Theatrets ethiske og æsthetiske Opgaver som her, ligeoverfor mine gamle kjære Venner Silius og Maarten.

("What are you working with just now, at the moment?" Silius asks, when the toddy is ready. . . . "Well, yes, I have to say, I'm working with a theater in Christiania. . . .

"Theater!" Maarten says quietly, aghast.

"What on earth!" Silius says, raising himself up in his chair. . . .

> Never before had I felt the hopelessness of convincing people of the ethical and aesthetic functions of the theater as I did here, in the company of my dear old friends Silius and Maarten.)

Clearly, the narrator in Krag's books is firmly and surely a foreigner in his home tracts. Sørlandet was not just a home district but also a new land for Krag, a land to be discovered. The element of the exotic is therefore apparently in his homeland poetry, even though it takes on a different character than it had earlier in his literary career.

In 1917 some of Krag's friends purchased a property on Helgøya Island in Ny-Hellesund as a gift for the twenty-fifth-anniversary celebration of his career as a poet. Krag settled on the island and in 1918 published his *Sange fra min Ø* in a limited edition of four thousand copies. The work received an enthusiastic reception. The opening poem, "Øen" (The Island), is significant because of its prelude and its length–233 lines. The poem is dedicated "to those who gave me the Island," and the first fifty-five lines deal with the situation before the gift, the sad state the poet lived in up to the time he received the gift: "Years passed by / like horrific nightmares / I don't even want to remember them." Only when he stopped wandering around and settled down on his island in the sea did he find peace–and renewed joy in living:

> Jeg eier udstrakte vidder, hvor lyngen staar og ringler
> med violette klokkespil
> i blanke augustdage.
>
> Jeg ved intet syn saa skjønt.
>
> Jeg eier skoge af pors
> der dufter mod himlen
> hedere end ambra,
> sødere end honning.
> I blanke augustdage
> driver duften tilhavs
> –Ingen derude aner,
> hvor den salige rus kommer fra.
>
> Jeg eier arkader af marehalm,
> som staar strunkne mellem rullesten
> lig spinkle søiler
> med fine kapitæler
> af usigelig graagrønt marmor.
> –Ingen ved, hvem færdes mellem arkaderne
> naar stilheden synker
> i sommernatten.
>
> (I own wide expanses, where the heather grows and chimes with violet bells
> on shining August days.
>
> I know of no sight so beautiful.
>
> I own a forest of bog myrtle
> Which sends its fragrance heavenward
> Warmer than ambra
> Sweeter than honey.
> In shining August days
> the fragrance drifts seaward.
> –No one out there suspects,
> where that blessed intoxicant comes from.
>
> I own arcades of seagrass,
> that stand erect between boulders
> like thin columns
> with fine capitals
> of unspeakably gray-green marble.
> –No one know who wanders between the arcades
> when the stillness falls
> in the summer night.)

Individualism and the mystique of nature are central components in "Øen." With its exultant quality, the poem resembles an ode, a praise poem that was used in the Romantic period to depict enthusiasm for nature and/or an approach to something mysterious. The primary feature of the ode is the address; such an address is found at the end of "Øen": "Aa venner" (Oh friends). The Romantic ode was often used in a situation in which the poet was in an artistic or existential crisis in order to reaffirm the power of the poetic voice. "Øen" functions in this way.

Krag wrote three memoirs: *Min Barndoms Have, Dengang vi var tyve år,* and *Heirefjæren. De skinnende hvide Seil* (1931, The Shining White Sails) can also be considered a memoir.

On his sixtieth birthday Vilhelm Krag was honored by the king; the prime minister, Gustav Vigeland; and Edvard Munch. For a long time he had been unhappy with the critics and the sales of his books, and he doubted his own ability as a poet. His works, with their combination of melancholy and idyllic tones, were increasingly out of touch with the time. His wife had left him in 1917; he never mentions her in any of his memoirs, even though they had four children. When Krag died of kidney failure at his summer home, Havbugta, in the vicinity of Kristiansand, on 10 July 1933, he seemed tired of life. His coffin was carried by boat with a great deal of ceremony to Oslo, where he was buried in Vår Frelsers Gravlund (Our Savior's Cemetery).

Biographies:
Herman Smitt Ingebretsen, *En dikter og en herre: Vilhelm Krags liv og diktning* (Oslo: Aschehoug, 1942);
Gunvald Opstad, *Fandango! En biografi om Vilhelm Krag* (Bergen: Vigmostad & Bjørke, 2002).

References:
L. Aas, "Vilhelm Krag: Det norske Sørlands Digter," *Gads danske Magasin* (1931): 178–185;

Jostein Andreassen, *Dikteren i Ny-Hellesund* (Søgne: Vilhelm Kragselskapet, 1997), pp. 5–18, 44–51;

Andreassen, "'Jeg er bleven rent indtagen i Flekkerø...': Flekkerøya og Vilhelm Krag," *Flekkerøy historielag: Årsskrift*, 3 (1993): 7–12;

Andreassen, *Sørlandet og Vilhelm Krag* (Søgne: Vilhelm Kragselskapet, 1996);

Andreassen, "Sørlandets samling er sørlandets fremgang," in *Blomstrende Sørland*, edited by Dagfinn Tveito (Oslo: Grøndahl Dreyer, 1994), pp. 20–23;

Andreassen, "Striden om *Skjærgaardshuset*," *Vest-Agder fylkesmuseums årbok* (1992): 7–49;

Andreassen, "Vilhelm Krag–en kort presentasjon," in *Festskrift til Sørlandets 100-årsdag, 16. mars 2002*, edited by Andreassen (Søgne: Krag-dagene, 2002), pp. 19–24;

Andreassen, "Vilhelm Krag som kulturprofet og politiker," in *P2-akademiet, L*, edited by Kulturredaksjonen, NRK P2 (Oslo: NRK P2, 1998), pp. 145–159;

Lars Thomas Braaten, "Disharmoni og diterisk forsoning; 1890-åra og noen hovedtrekk i Vilhelm Krag lyrikk," *Edda*, 6 (1975): 337–353;

Hjalmar Christensen, *Unge Nordmænd: et kritisk grundrids* (Christiania: Aschehoug, 1893), pp. 73–115;

Carl Fredrik Engelstad, *Fire norske diktere: Gunnar Heiberg, Nils Collett Vogt; Vilhelm Krag; Sigbjørn Obstfelder* (Oslo: AAS & WAHL, 1972);

Engelstad, "Vilhelm Krag," *Samtiden* (1971): 645–660;

Sturla Ertzeid, "Ny-Hellesund og Vilhelm Krag," in *Søgne før og nå*, volume 1, edited by Oddbjørn Eikestøl (Søgne: Søgne Kulturstyre, 1981), pp. 51–62;

Bjørn Hemmer, "Agder i diktningen," in *Bygd og by i Norge: Agder*, edited by Alv Kristiansen (Oslo: Gyldendal, 1977), pp. 188–196;

Andreas Jynge, "Vilhelm Krag," *Samtiden* (1933): 638–644;

Georg Møller, "Vilhelm Krag: litt fra hans forlagstid," in *En hilsen til Johan Grundt Tanum på femtiårsdagen 12. april 1941; i går, i dag, i morgen* (Oslo: Grøndahl, 1941);

Sigbjørn Obstfelder, "V. Krag.–*Nat*," in his *Samlede skrifter*, volume 1, edited by Solveig Tunold (Oslo: Gyldendal, 1950), pp. 236–247;

Elisabeth Oxfeldt, "Headless Women: Vilhelm Krag's and Jens August Schade's Neo-Romanticist and Surrealist Representations of Female Bodies," *Edda*, 2 (2006): 131–149;

Oxfeldt, *Nordic Orientalism: Paris and the Cosmopolitan Imagination 1800–1900* (Copenhagen: Museum Tusculanum Press, 2005), pp. 180–198;

Arnt Bryde Sundseth, *Vilhelm Krag: et bibliografisk forsøk* (Oslo: Damm, 1943);

Erling Heide Sørensen, *Sørlandsdikteren og tonekunsten: Vilhelm Krags diktning som inspirasjonskilde for norsk musikk* (Kristiansand: E. H. Sørensen, 1960);

Ingrid Terland, *Agder-forfattere gjennom tidene: en bibliografi. Del I: Skjønnlitterære forfattere født før 1900* (Kristiansand: Agder distriktshøgskole, 1988), pp. 108–118;

Jens Thiis, "Nittiårene og 'Samtiden,'" *Samtiden* (1940): 26–31;

"Vilhelm Krag og Birger Mörner," *Dagbladet*, 29 March 1894, p. 1;

Henning Howlid Wærp, "Da Krag diktet Sørlandet," in *Hvitt stakitt og fiberoptikk. Regionale myter–regional makt*, edited by Jon P. Knudsen and Hege Skjeie (Kristiansand: Høyskoleforlaget, 2002), pp. 71–84;

Wærp, *Diktet natur: Natur og landskap hos Andreas Munch, Vilhelm Krag og Hans Børli* (Oslo: Aschehoug 1997);

Wærp, "Vilhelm Krag: Fra Østerland til Sørlandet," *Ergo* (1995): 90–110;

H. Wiers-Jenssen, *Nationaltheatret gjennem 25 aar, 1899–1924* (Christiania: Gyldendal, 1924), pp. 210–245.

Magnus Brostrup Landstad
(7 October 1802 – 8 October 1880)

Lanae H. Isaacson

BOOKS: *Hjertesuk til hver Dag i Ugen, Morgen og Aften* (Christiania: Selskabet for Christelige Undervisnings- og Andagts-Bøgers Udgivelse, 1841; revised, 1846);

Neslands Kirke: et Digt (Fredrikshald: Christian Olsen, 1852);

Norske Folkeviser, by Landstad, Olea Crøger, and Ludvig Matthias Lindeman (Christiania: Tønsberg, 1853);

Jule-Salmer (Fredrikshald: Christian Olsen, 1856);

Kirke-Salmebog: et Udkast (Christiania: Fabritius, 1861);

Om Salmesagen: en Redegjørelse (Christiania: Dybwad, 1862);

Salmer og Sange (til Brug ved Missions-Møder og Missions-Feste) (Sandefjord: M. B. Landstad, 1863);

Kirkesalmebog efter offentlig Foranstaltning samlet og udarbeidet ved M.B. Landstad (Bergen: Giertsens Forlag, 1869?); revised as *Landstads reviderte salmebok* (Christiania: Salmebogforlaget, 1924);

Sange og Digte af forskjellige Slags, mest fra gamle Dage (Christiania: Dybwad, 1879);

Gamle Sagn om Hjartedølerne (Christiania: Dybwad, 1880);

Ættesagaer og Sagn fra Telemarken; efterladte optegnelser (Christiania: Dybwad, 1924);

Folkeviser fra Telemarken, edited by Knut Liestøl (Oslo: Aschehoug, 1925);

Mytiske Sagn fra Telemarken: Efterladte Optegnelser av M.B. Landstad (Oslo: Norsk Folkeminnelag, 1926);

Fra Telemarken: Skik og Sagn. Efterladte Optegnelser av M.B. Landstad (Oslo: Norsk Folkeminnelag, 1927);

Magnus Brostrup Landstads dagbok: 1825–1829, edited by Sigurd Kolsrud and Ingolf Kvamen (Oslo: Dybwad, 1950);

Skikker og sagn fra Telemark: etterlatte opptegnelser av M.B. Landstad, og er gitt en modern språkdrakt, edited by Truls R. Norby (Porsgrunn: Grenland, 1996).

Collections and Editions: *Salmebog for Lutherske Kristne i Amerika/M.B. Landstads salmebog* (Minneapolis: Den Forenede Kirkes Forlag, 1895);

Magnus Brostrup Landstad (Store Norske Leksikon <http://snl.no/.bilde/Landstad%2C_Magnus_Brostrup>)

Norske Folkeviser (Oslo: Norsk Folkeminnelag/Universitetsforlag, 1968);

Gamle Sagn om Hjartedølerne (Christiania: Notodden, 1985);

Mytiske Sagn fra Telemarken: Efterladte Optegnelser av M. B. Landstad (Porsgrunn: Grenland, 1995);

Telemarks blodige kjemper (Porsgrunn: Grenland, 1997);

Fra salmer til skjemteviser: en antologi av Otto Nes (Oslo: Cappelen, 1997).

OTHER: *Martin Luthers aandelige Sange, oversatte og med Anmærkninger ledsagede af M.B. Landstad udg med Foranstaltning af den kongelige norske Regjerings Departement for Kirke- og Undervisningsvæsenet,* translated by Landstad (Christiania: Fabritius, 1855); revised as *Samt 25 Salmer fra det 16. og 17. Aarhundrede* (Christiania: Fabritius, 1859);

Ludvig Matthias Lindeman, *Melodier til Landstads Salmebog,* edited by Landstad (Christiania: Cappelen, 1872).

The Telemark poet and pastor Magnus Brostrup Landstad compiled and edited two of the most important works of the nineteenth-century National Romantic Movement in Norway: *Norske Folkeviser* (1853, Norwegian Folk Ballads) and *Kirkesalmebog* (1869, Church Hymnal). A diligent collector of ballads, folk songs, legends, and tales, Landstad had a profound impact on the work of other folklorists and on the discipline of folklore itself. *Norske Folkeviser* and *Kirkesalmebog* were the products of great industry on the part of Landstad and his associates Olea Crøger and Ludvig Matthias Lindeman. *Norske Folkeviser* influenced subsequent ballad collections and also led to renewed interest in ballad singing in rural communities in Telemark. *Kirkesalmebog* was authorized for use in the Norwegian Church in 1869 and went through nearly annual printings before being significantly revised in 1924 as *Landstads reviderte salmebok* (Landstad's Revised Hymnal). Landstad's lack of academic credentials led some of his contemporaries to accuse him of embellishing the ballads and songs he collected from rural informants, but later reassessments of *Norske Folkeviser* suggest his fidelity to Telemark tradition.

Landstad was born on 7 October 1802 in Måsøy, Finnmark, the son of the minister Hans Landstad and Margrete Elisabeth Schnittler. When Landstad was two, the family moved to Øksnes in Vesterålen, where his father assumed leadership of the congregation. In 1811 Hans Landstad became the minister in Vinje, Telemark, and in 1819 he was appointed to the ministry in Seljord. Magnus Landstad received his early schooling from his mother, then from a house tutor, and, eventually, from his father. In 1822 he began his studies in theology at the University of Christiania. Landstad received his *cand. theol.* (Master of Theology) degree in 1827 and was sent to Gausdal as the resident chaplain. During his student days in Christiania he had met Wilhelmine (Mina) Margrethe Marie Lassen. They were married on 6 May 1829.

The couple moved to Kviteseid in Telemark when Landstad became minister at Kviteseid Church. On the death of his father in 1838, Landstad assumed the pastorship at Seljord and remained there until he became the minister of Fredrikshald Church in 1849.

Landstad served in Fredrikshald until 1859, when he assumed the position of ministry to Sandeherred in Vestfolden. The Landstads moved from parish to parish every ten years. They had several children, some of whom died, and the couple unsuccessfully tried to find a situation away from Telemark where their surviving children would have greater opportunities. A pastel of the Landstads drawn by Christian Olsen in 1851 depicts a serious couple whose earthly joys were few and far between.

Landstad's earliest poetry, written during his student days and his first years as a minister, took the form of hymns such as "Ser jeg mig i Verden Om" (If in the World I Look Around) and devotional songs. In 1841 he published his first collection of such poetry, *Hjertesuk til hver Dag i Ugen, Morgen og Aften* (Sighs of the Heart for Every Day of the Week, Morning and Evening). He also wrote and submitted occasional poems to journals such as *Skillings-Magazin* (Penny-Magazine). In "Trækfuglene" (The Migratory Birds), published in *Skillings-Magazin* in 1844, he compares an injured swallow to a human soul:

Der flygter Svalernes Skare!
Farvel, du mit Tagkammers Ven!
Din Rede jeg tage skal vare,
At du faar den urørt igjen.
Til Vaaren med Godveirsdage
du kommer igjen over Hav,
da flyver du maaske med Klage
henover din Gjenboers Grav.

Men der sidder En under Møne,
som vist ikke kan være med,
han synes at sukke og stønne.
Ak!–Vingen er vreden af Led!
Den Arme! han stirrer dem efter–
–nu ere de flugs ud af Syn.
O, kunde jeg give dig Kræfter
og sende dig bort som et Lyn!

O, kunde jeg give dig Foder
og pleie dig ømt i mit Bur!
Men ak, du vil finde din Broder
eller dø i den kolde Natur.–
Tilvisse, et lignende Noget
hvo har ikke smertelig følt?
I Verdens- og Mennesketoget
har mangen En vingeskuldt nølt,

og har dog ei villet modtage
sit Ly under Pleierens Haand,
men hellere endt sine Dage
derude for Vinterens Aand.
Gak ind kun med Tillid og Vilje,
kom, varm dig og slaa dig til Ro!
da maaske paa Tag og paa Tilje
en Vaardag du møder dem fro.

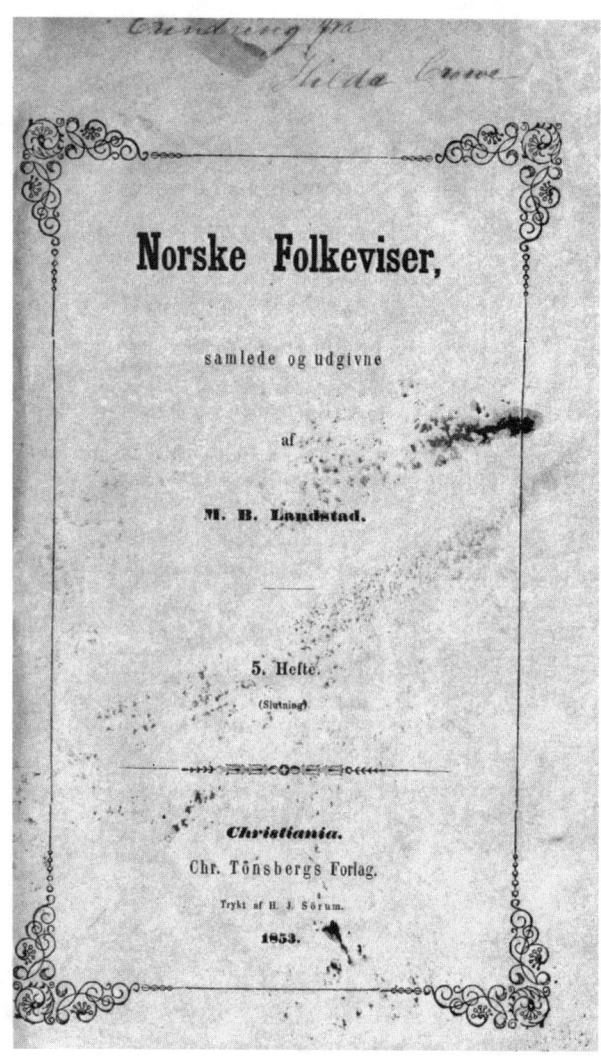

Title page for Landstad's collection of Norwegian folk ballads, on which he collaborated with Olea Crøger and Ludvig Matthias Lindeman (National Library of Scotland)

(There flies the band of swallows!
Farewell, you friend of my attic!
I'll guard your nest,
so that you reclaim it untouched.
Until on the good weather spring days
you come back over the sea,
then perhaps you'll fly with a lament
over the grave of your neighbor.

But one sits there under the sill,
one who cannot join the others,
he seems to sigh and groan.
Ach!–His wing is twisted from its joint!
The poor bird! he stares after them–
–now they're soon out of sight.
Oh, if only I could give you strength
and send you away quick as a lightning bolt!

Oh, if only I could give you food
and tenderly care for you in my home!
But alas, you want to find your brother
or die out in the cold.–
Surely, such pain
have we not all felt it?
In the course of our human strife
many have suffered such a shot,

and yet they have not wanted to take
their solace from the hand of the Savior,
but would rather end their days
out in the winter's fury.
Go on in now with trust and will,
come, warm yourself and rest in peace!
then perhaps on the roof and landing
you'll meet them in joy on a spring day.)

Landstad's 1852 collection *Neslands Kirke: et Digt* (Nesland Church: A Poem) is a cycle of twelve poems with a prose introduction. "Kvenne-Karis Vise" (Kari's Ballad), a pastiche of traditional ballad poetry, is part of the cycle, as is "Fra Neslands Kirke" (From Nesland Church), a poem that bears witness to generations of rural people and their religious gatherings, ceremonies, and observances. Landstad's work with the ballads of Telemark was a significant influence on all of his poetry from his first to his last collection.

Landstad's hymns and poems combine Lutheran concern for theological issues such as death, eternal life, sin, and God's mercy with his feelings for the community and the nation. To a great degree Landstad followed the practice of the Danish hymn writer Thomas Kingo in composing hymns and ordering the *Kirkesalmebog* according to the church calendar. His hymn "Fra Fjord og Fjære" (From Fjords and Mountain Cliffs) is at once a celebration of Christmas, a depiction of season and setting, an account of the Nativity, and an expression of hope for a future life:

Fra Fjord og Fjære,
fra Fjeld og dyben Dal
et: *Ære være!*
idag gjenlyde skal.
Fra Kirketaarne
i Fryds Basuner stød
for Guds Eenbaarne,
som er idag os fød:
vi var forlorne,
nu er vi frelst af Nød!
. . . .
Herude Kulde
er nu og dyben Sne,
Guds Himle fulde
af Stjerne dog at se;
for os optændes
en deilig Naadesol,

Guds Aasyn vendes
til os fra Himlens Stol,
naar alting endes,
vi der skal holde Jul.

(From fjords and mountain cliffs,
From hills and deep valleys
A single: *Glory be!*
shall echo today.
From church steeples
in joyous trombones resounding
for God's only begotten son,
born to us today;
we were bereft,
now we are saved from want!
. . . .
Out here it is so cold
and now the snow is deep,
Yet God's heaven is full
of stars we can see;
for us is lit
a beautiful sun of mercy,
God's countenance turns
to us from the throne of heaven,
when everything is ended,
we will hold Christmas there.)

The idea for *Norske Folkeviser* did not originate with Landstad but with Crøger, a pastor's daughter, a teacher, and a singer at Kviteseid Seminary. Crøger collected ballads and folk songs in Kviteseid and Seljord; but when she submitted her manuscript to the publisher P. T. Malling in 1842, she was evidently ignored because of her sex: her work vanished without her even receiving a response. The only traces left of her efforts are the records she shared with Landstad for *Norske Folkeviser* and those that the Norsk Folkeminnelag (Norwegian Folklore Society) published in 2004 as *Lilja bære blomster i enge folkeminneoppskrifter frå Telemark i 1840–50 åra* (Lily Flowers in the Meadows: Folklore Transcripts from Telemark from the Years 1840–50):

The Norwegian Folklore Society rights an historic wrong by letting Olea Styhr Crøger début as a writer. Crøger was born in 1801. During the 1840s, she tried to publish a manuscript that would have been the first significant collection of Norwegian folk ballads. She did not succeed in realizing the book project, mainly because she was a woman. Crøger's manuscript was lost, and the book she débuts with this year is compiled through a careful search of archives and collections.

Landstad pursued his own collecting efforts while serving as the minister of Kviteseid and Seljord churches from 1834 to 1848. In his foreword to *Norske Folkeviser,* he acknowledges that Crøger played "en vesentlig andel i denne samlings istandbringelse" (an important role in the preparation of this collection) and contributed *musikkbilagene* (musical notations and scores), one of the features that distinguishes the work from others of its kind. Landstad's foreword suggests multiple goals for the collection:

Folket elsker det gamle tilvante og har mistro til det nye, som derfor sent vinner fotfeste i fjellstuen. Hvor meget der enn i visse retninger kan være at utsette på denne folkets tilbakebliven i tidens strøm, så vil dog sprogforskeren, old- granskeren, poesiens og *nasjonalitetens venn,* når han får anledning til at gjøre seg bekjent med folket, finne meget, som for ham har verd, og han vil føle seg takknemlig for de ekte malme, som ennu kan brytes i deres fjell, og for det emningstre, han finner gjemt og oppspart i de mørke skove, hvor øksen ennu ikke har nået hen. Dørene til fjellstuen er imidlertid nu på mange måter oppladte, og den nyere tid med sine brogede, vekslende former trenger også herinn med en seirende makt. Det gamle må gå til grunne. . . . Under disse omstendigheter falt den tanke meg inn, at også jeg burde rekke min hånd til om mulig at redde et gammelt familiesmykke ut av det brennende hus.

(The people love the old things they're accustomed to and are suspicious of everything new, which is therefore slow to gain a foothold in the mountain abode. However much one finds fault with the reticence of people to join the flow of time in certain ways, yet will the linguist, the scholar of historical antiquities, the *friend of poetry and nationality* find much of worth when he has a chance to become acquainted with people, and he will feel grateful for the genuine ore that he is still able to break off from their mountains, and for the ancestral tree he finds hidden and protected in dark forests where the axe has still not found its way. The doors of the mountain cabin are now opening, and a newer time with its diverse, changing forms is treading on in with victorious power. The old way must pass. . . . Under these circumstances it occurred to me that I ought to extend my hand in order to save an old family jewel out of the burning house.)

Landstad organized the ballads and folk songs in *Norske Folkeviser* in nine sections: I. *Eventyrlige viser* (Ballads of Fantasy, Myth and Magic); II. *Draumekvæde* (The Dream Ballad); III. *Kæmpeviser* (Ballads of Warriors, Heroes and Giants); IV. *Ridderviser og Romancer* (Courtly Ballads and Romances); V. *Gamle Stev* (Old Single Strophes); VI. *Romancer* (Romances); VII. *Skjemtende Viser* (Ballads of Jest); VIII. *Nyere Viser af blandet Indhold* (Newer Ballads of Diverse Content); and IX. *Nyere Stev. Lege og Børnevers m.m. Tillæg* (Newer Single Strophes. Games and Children's Rhymes, etc. Additions). Variants of many of the ballads and narrative songs that Landstad collected in Telemark were also known in Denmark and Sweden. Svend Grundtvig's *Danmarks gamle Folkeviser* (1853, Danish Folk Ballads), for example, also includes Norwegian variants from Telemark sent in by the young scholar Sophus Bugge. *Draumkvædet,* however, seems to be a type of song unique to Norway.

Norske Folkeviser includes three distinct variants of *Draumkvædet,* the most extensive and well organized of which is one that Landstad compiled primarily from Maren Ramskeid of Kviteseid, with additional stanzas from other singers. In this *Draumkvædet* Olaf Ástason falls asleep on Christmas Eve and, in a trance or dream, wanders through heaven and hell. When he wakes up thirteen days later, he rides to the church and tells the pastor and congregation of his experiences.

In hell he encountered frightening creatures and the damned souls of unrepentant sinners. One horrific scene follows hard on another: "Eg hev gengid gjallarbrui hon er ekki god at gange, bikkja bit og ormen sting og stuten stend og stangar. Fer mánen skine, og veginne felle sa vide" (I have crossed Gjallar Bridge, that's not good to walk on, the she-wolf bites and the snake stings and the wild stud blocks the way. For the moon shines and the roads fall so wide).

Olaf then tells his listeners what rewards and blessings await merciful and loving souls in heaven: "Sæl er den i födesheimen fatike geve braud han tar inki ræddast i ann'heimen fer höyre pá hundegaul. Tunga talar–og sanning svarar pá dommedag" (Blessed is the one in the earthly home who gives the poor man bread, in the other world he need not fear the fierce snarls of dogs. Tongues speak–and the truth answers on the Day of Judgment).

Draumkvædet has been the subject of extensive research and discussion as well as an inspiration to new generations of ballad singers and poets. Much of the debate has focused on medieval visionary literature and the links between such literature and the Norwegian song. Ballad scholars have endeavored to trace the paths the ballad has followed, and some have stressed the Catholic elements in the poem. Whatever its sources, *Draumkvædet* is a symbol of Norway and one of the high points of its folk poetry.

Norske Folkeviser also includes ballads that Landstad describes as "meget udbredt over alle de nordiske Lande" (very spread out over all the Nordic countries). In "Olaf Liljukrands"–"Elverskud" in *Danmarks gamle Folkeviser*–Olaf encounters an *elveleik* (elf ring-dance) on the way to his wedding. Olaf repeatedly refuses to join the circle of elf maidens, and, in retaliation, they attack him, causing him to forget his bride and ride home to die. The final scene of the ballad brings more tragedy:

Drawing of Landstad's grave that appeared in the newspaper Verdens Gang *on 16 August 1884 (National Library of Norway)*

Og innan dagin den vart ljós,
med kvitari hand,
dá kom der tri lik af brúdrehus,
Sá mód kem Olaf af elvo.

Den eine var Olaf, den andre hans möy,
med kvitari hand,
og sá hans móder af sorgi laut döy,
Sá mód kem Olaf af elvo.

(And then before the day was light,
with a white hand,
there came three bodies out of the bridal house,
So sorrowful Olaf came from the elves.
The one was Olaf, the other his maid,
with a white hand,
and so his mother had died from sorrow,
So sorrowful Olaf came from the elves.)

Despite contemporary misgivings about Landstad and Crøger's scholarship, *Norske Folkeviser* served as an essential guide to Bugge in the preparation of his *Gamle norske Folkeviser* (1858, Old Norwegian Ballads).

Landstad's second major work, *Kirkesalmebog*, had a long genesis. He declined to take on the project when he was first approached to edit a new Norwegian church hymnal in 1848 but accepted when he was again asked four years later. The need for a new hymnal had long been keenly felt. In the 1830s and 1840s individual ministers had published hymnals for their own congregations. In *Antydning til et forbedret Psalmeverk for den Norske Kirke* (1840, Recommendations for an Improved Hymnal for the Norwegian Church), the poet Johan Sebastian Welhaven attacked the three hymnals then in use—Kingo's from 1699, O. Høegh Guldberg's from 1778, and the *Evangelisk-christelig Psalmebog* from 1798—and made an appeal for an entirely new work. Passions ran deep and strong.

In the middle of the furor, Wilhelm Andreas Wexels, the minister of Vår Frelsers Kirke (Our Savior's Church) in Christiania and a composer of hymns in his own right, proffered a new plan for a hymnal. Landstad severely criticized Wexel's proposal, claiming that the hymns he chose were not Norwegian enough, not national in language, and unpoetic. Such was the background for Landstad's agreement to edit a new, definitive Norwegian hymnal. Landstad submitted his *Kirke-Salmebog: et Udkast* (Church Hymnal: An Outline) in 1861, after years of collecting, editing, and translating hymns, as well as composing his own. His work was criticized for using too many uniquely Norwegian dialect words but won the support of the poet and leader of the cause of the Norwegian language, Ivar Aasen. Landstad's *Kirkesalmebog* managed to stave off the challenge of a hymnal proposed by Andreas Hauge, which was supported by conservatives, and secured authorization from the Norwegian Church in 1869.

Landstad drew on many sources for *Kirkesalmebog*. It included religious poetry by Petter Dass, Dorothe Engelbretsdatter, and Johan Nordahl Brun; hymns by Danish and German pastors and poets such as Kingo, Hans Adolph Brorson, and Martin Luther in Norwegian "gjendikting" (recomposition); and Landstad's own contributions, among them "Fra Fjord og Fjære," "Jeg løfter op til Gud min Sang" (I raise my Song to God), and the funereal "Jeg veed mig en Søvn i Jesu Navn" (I Know a Soul's Repose in Jesus' Name). Landstad considered hymns as the possession of the church and its congregation, as songs for religious use, and he revised them to increase their usefulness to worshipers. Of paramount importance to Landstad were clarity and intelligibility. After years of Danish hegemony in church and school—and attendant confusion among Norwegian churchgoers—Landstad spoke from the heart for Norwegian songs.

Anointed a Knight of St. Olav in 1870, Landstad in his later years suffered from poor health and moved to Christiania after a stroke in 1876, but he continued to collect and to write his own hymns and poems. His last personal collection, *Sange og Digte af forskjellige Slags, mest fra gamle Dage* (1879, Songs and Poems of Different Sorts, Mostly from Old Days), was published the year before his death. Landstad also left many collections of legends and folk narratives that were published after his death: *Gamle Sagn om Hjartedølerne* (1880, Old Legends of Hjartedølerne), *Ættesagaer og Sagn fra Telemarken* (1924, Family Sagas and Legends from Telemark), *Folkeviser fra Telemarken* (1925, Folk Ballads from Telemark), *Mytiske Sagn fra Telemarken* (1926, Mythic Legends from Telemark), *Fra Telemarken. Skik og Sagn* (1927, From Telemark. Customs and Legends), and *Skikker og sagn fra Telemark* (1996, Customs and Legends from Telemark). He died on 8 October 1880 and was buried in the Grove at Vår Frelsers Kirke (Domkirken).

Magnus Brostrup Landstad was a pivotal figure in the Norwegian National Romantic Movement of the nineteenth century. His work among ballad singers and storytellers in Telemark had a profound influence on the emerging sense of Norwegian identity and the national pride that went along with that identity. He inspired in Norwegians a feeling of pride in their past, and his career served as a catalyst for folklore studies throughout Scandinavia. His deep commitment to the tradition of Telemark is reflected in his impressive efforts to preserve the past and provide hope for an independent Norway in the future.

Letters:

H. T. Landstad, *M. B. Landstad på nært hold, belyst med familiebrev* (Seljord: Landstadsinstituttet, 1989 / Oslo: Landstadsinstituttet i Kommission hos Samlaget, 1989).

Bibliographies:

J. F. J. Schwabe, *Register over samtlige Vers i Landstads Salmebog* (Trondheim: J. F. J. Schwabe, 1880);

Hans Woll, *Salme-Konkordans til Landstads Salmebog: indeholdende Versenes Begyndelseslinjer i alfabetisk Orden, samtlige Koralmelodier* (Christiania: Dybwad, 1892);

M. E. Waldeland, *Alfabetisk Indholdsregister over alle Vers i Landstads Salmebog* (Minneapolis: Augsburg, 1921);

Christoph Heinrich Møller-Nielsen, *Salmekonkordans til Landstads reviderte salmebok* (Oslo: Den Norske Kirkes Presteforening, 1932).

References:

Ivar Bjørndal, *Magnus Brostrup Landstad: prest, dikter og borger i Fredrikshald 1849–1859* (Halden: Forum Bjørndal, 2002);

Egil Elseth, *Magnus Brostrup Landstad: pilegrimen og poeten* (Oslo: Verbum, 1986);

Elseth, *Magnus Brostrup Landstad: Kulturvilje og Kristentro* (Oslo: Luther Forlag, 1997);

Lanae H. Isaacson, "'Draumkvædet': The Structural Study of an Oral Variant," *Jahrbuch für Volksliedforschung*, 25 (1980): 51–66;

Gudrun Brauti Knutslid, *Diktarpresten Magnus Brostrup Landstad: halvdokumentarisk Roman* (Oslo: Ansgar, 1988);

Roar L. Tollnes, *Landstad og lokalmiljøet* (Sandefjord: Hovedkomitéen for Landstad-jubiléet, 2002);

K. Valkner, "Landstads og Hauges Salmebøker: Tilblivelseshistorie og hymnologisk Karakteristikk," *Norvegia Sacra* (1932): 1–129.

Jonas Lie
(6 November 1833 – 5 July 1908)

Milda Ostrauskaite
University of Wisconsin-Madison

BOOKS: *Digte* (Christiania: Dybwad, 1867);
Den Fremsynte, eller billeder fra Nordland (Copenhagen: Gyldendal, 1870); includes "Elias og Draugen" and "Capseilingen med Draugen," translated as "The Fisherman and the Draug" and "Tug of War," in *Weird Tales from Northern Seas,* edited and translated by R. Nisbet Bain (London: K. Paul, Trench, Trubner, 1893), pp. 1–20, 63–68; translated by Jessie Muir as *The Visionary, or Pictures from Nordland* (London: Hodder, 1894);
Fortællinger og skildringer fra Norge (Copenhagen: Gyldendal, 1872)–includes "Finneblod," translated by Bain as "Finn Blood," in *Weird Tales from Northern Seas,* pp. 135–158; and "Nordjordhesten: en liden Fortælling fra Skydskariolen," translated by Mrs. Arbuthnott as *Little Grey, the Pony of Norfjord; or, The Story of Gjermund and Sigrid* (Edinburgh: Thomas C. Jack / London: Hamilton, Adams & Ballantyne, 1873);
Tremasteren "Fremtiden," eller Liv Nordpaa: en Fortælling (Oslo & Copenhagen: Gyldendal, 1872); translated by Sara Chapman Thorp Bull as *The Barque Future; or, Life in the Far North* (Chicago: Griggs, 1879);
Lodsen og hans hustru (Copenhagen: Gyldendal, 1874); translated by Bull as *The Pilot and His Wife: A Norse Love Story* (Chicago: Griggs, 1876);
Faustina Strozzi (Copenhagen: Gyldendal, 1875);
Thomas Ross: fortælling (Copenhagen: Gyldendal, 1878);
Adam Schrader: fortælling (Copenhagen: Gyldendal, 1879);
Grabows Kat: skuespil i tre akter (Copenhagen: Gyldendal, 1880);
Rutland: fortælling (Copenhagen: Gyldendal, 1880);
"Gaa paa!": sjøfortælling (Copenhagen: Gyldendal, 1882);
Livsslaven (Copenhagen: Gyldendal, 1883); translated by Muir as *One of Life's Slaves* (London: Hodder, 1895);
Familjen paa Gilje: et interieur fra firtiaarene (Copenhagen: Gyldendal, 1883); translated by Samuel Coffin Eastman as *The Family at Gilje: A Domestic Story of

Jonas Lie (Store Norske Leksikon <http://snl.no/.bilde/Lie%2C_Jonas_(portrett)>)

the Forties* (New York: American-Scandinavian Foundation, 1920);
En Malstrøm: fortælling (Copenhagen: Gyldendal, 1884);
Otte fortællinger (Copenhagen: Gyldendal, 1885; Chicago: Skandinavens Boghandel, 1885)–includes "Jon Sunde," translated and adapted by H. B. Boyesen as *John Sunde* (New York: A. C. Armstrong, 1886);

Kommandørens Døtre: roman (Copenhagen: Gyldendal, 1886); translated by H. L. Brækstad and Gertrude Hughes as *The Commodore's Daughters* (London: Heinemann, 1892);

Et Samliv (Copenhagen: Gyldendal, 1887);

Maisa Jons (Copenhagen: Gyldendal, 1888);

Digte (Copenhagen: Gyldendal, 1889);

Onde Magter (Chicago: J. T. Relling, 1890);

Trold: en tylft eventyr (Copenhagen: Gyldendal, 1891)– includes "Jo i Sjøholmene," "Jorden drager," "Andværs-skarven," "Isak og Brønopræsten," "Vindtroldet," "Huldrefisken," "Vest i Blaafjledet," and "Det er mæ!" translated by Bain as "Jack of Sjöhölm and the Gan-Finn," "The Earth Draws," "The Cormorants of Andvær," "Isaac and the Parson of Brönö," "The Wind-Gnome," "The Huldrefish," "The Homestead Westward in the Blue Mountains," and "It's me!" in his *Weird Tales from Northern Seas;* and "Evina Feier," translated by G. Melby as "Evina, the Chimney Sweep's Daughter," in *Sturdy Folks and Other Stories by Norwegian Authors* (Minneapolis: K. C. Holter, n.d.);

Trold: en tylft eventyr. Ny samling (Copenhagen: Gyldendal, 1892);

Niobe: nutidsroman (Copenhagen: Gyldendal, 1893); translated by Brækstad as *Niobe* (London: Heinemann, 1897);

Lystige koner: skuespil i tre akter (Copenhagen: Gyldendal, 1894);

Naar Sol gaar ned: fortælling (Copenhagen: Gyldendal, 1895);

Dyre Rein: en historie fra oldefars hus (Copenhagen: Gyldendal, 1896);

Lindelin: eventyr-spil i fire akter (Copenhagen: Gyldendal, 1897);

Faste Forland (Copenhagen: Gyldendal, 1899);

Wulffie & Comp.: drama i tre akter (Copenhagen: Gyldendal, 1900);

Naar jernteppet falder: af livets komedie (Copenhagen: Gyldendal, 1901);

Fortællinger og skildringer (Copenhagen: Gyldendal, 1903; revised and enlarged edition, 1903);

Ulfvungerne: et blad af lidenskabernes bog (Copenhagen: Gyldendal, 1903);

Østenfor Sol, vestenfor Maane og bagom Babylons Taarn!: streif paa Jagtgebetet (Copenhagen: Gyldendal, 1905);

Eventyr (Copenhagen: Gyldendal, 1909);

Udmeldt af Klubben: lystspill i fire Akter (Oslo: Gyldendal, 1983).

Collection: *Samlede Digterværker,* edited by Paula Bergh, 10 volumes (Christiania: Gyldendal, 1920–1921).

PLAY PRODUCTIONS: *Grabows Kat,* Christiania, Christiania Theater, 24 September 1880;

Wulffie & Comp., Christiania, Christiania Theater, 10 April 1901;

Lindelin: eventyr-spil i fire akter, Christiania, Christiania Theater, 5 May 1902.

OTHER: *Sang ved Universitetsbibliothekar Paul Botten-Hansens Jordfæstelse den 10de Juli 1869* (Christiania, 1869), pp. 1–3;

Sang ved sexaen i Frimurerlogen den 30 november 1870 (Christiania, 1870), pp. 1–2;

Lie, Ferdinand Roll, and Anton Martin Schweigaard, *Minneord: professor Anton Martin Schweigaard* (N.p., 1870), pp. 1–13;

Lie, Henrik Ibsen, and A. Munch, *Sang Ved Tusendårs-Festen den 18de Juli 1872* (N.p., 1872);

Dikt til Ludvig M. Lindeman (N.p., ca. 1873), p. 1;

Lie and Fr. Gjertsen, *Sange ved afsløringen af Professor Schweigaards buste i Kristiania Handelstands-forening den 17de Mai kl. 12 middag* (Christiania: Kra, 1874);

Lie and Alexander Bull, *Ole Bulls Breve i Uddrag* (Copenhagen: Gyldendal, 1881);

Lie, "Löft dit hoved, du raske gut!" in *Fem Sange for Mandskor* (Christiania, Stockholm, Copenhagen & Leipzig: Warmuth Elkan & Schildknecht W. Hansen Breitkopf & Härtel, 1892);

Lie and Gunnar Wennerberg, *Ved Fædres Mindeskaal,* composed by Wennerberg (Christiania: Warmuth, 1894).

SELECTED PERIODICAL PUBLICATIONS– UNCOLLECTED: Lie and Kristofer Janson, "Gale Arne," *Illustreret Nyhedsblad,* 9 (1864): 1–6;

"Til 17 Mai 1864," *Illustreret Nyhedsblad,* 20 (1864): 1–2.

Along with Alexander L. Kielland, Henrik Ibsen, and Bjørnstjerne Bjørnson, Jonas Lie was one of the Great Four *(De fire store)* Norwegian writers of the nineteenth century. The Danish publishing house Gyldendal coined the term *De fire store* for marketing purposes, as a way of promoting works by their four greatest Norwegian writers. Later the term became a marker for the privileged status these four authors held in Norwegian literature. Lie is considered a pioneer of the modern Norwegian novel with respect to themes and a style that blends reality and fantasy, objective narration, psychological study, and impressionist sketches. Lie was the first author to write sea novels and the first writer after Petter Dass to introduce legends and fables from northern Norway into his works, particularly into his earliest novels, and later into the collections of tales *Trold: en tylft eventyr* (1891, Trolls: A Dozen Tales), *Trold: en tylft even-*

tyr. Ny samling (1892, Trolls: A Dozen Tales. New Collection), and the posthumous volume *Eventyr* (1909, Tales). Lie made use of elements and motifs from folklore to narrate stories whose imagination and originality can be compared to what the reader discovers in Hans Christian Andersen's tales. Lie's artistic ambitions can be summarized in the following quote from his story "Havets Fantasier" (Ocean's Fantasies), published in *Eventyr:* "Jo-o, det laa ganske rigtig i min Trang og Lidenskab med min Pens Magt at faa malt frem det hele Norge. Det var en Opgave–der laa mig i Blodet" (Well, yes, I had a true need and desire to paint all of Norway with the power of my pen. This task was in my blood).

During his lifetime Lie earned the title *hjemmenes dikter* (the poet of the homes) among the majority of Norwegian readers, who could identify with Lie's depiction of everyday family scenes in typical provincial bourgeois homes across the country. Within the framework of domestic life Lie's stories reflect the process of modernization in Norway, the stirring of industry and commerce, social conflicts, and the clash between the old and new views triggered by progress. Lie drew particular attention to the gap between social classes and to the status of women, winning support of the women's movement and women writers such as Amalie Skram. Despite Lie's popularity among ordinary readers, the title *hjemmenes dikter* had negative connotations among the critics and his fellow authors. Lie drew criticism for his narrow choice of themes–focusing on marriages, problematic relationships, and romantic tales–and for his failure to promote open social and political debates in his works. Lie's writing style differed significantly from the requirements of the Scandinavian Modern Breakthrough, a movement launched by Danish critic Georg Brandes in 1871, one year after Lie's own literary breakthrough. In a lecture series titled *Hovedstrømninger i det 19de Aarhundredes Litteratur* (1905, translated as *Main Currents in the Nineteenth Century Literature*), Brandes promoted the European trends of naturalism and realism and encouraged Scandinavian authors to bring up relevant political and social problems. From such a perspective, the indirect and subtle references to issues of modern life and the infusion of mysticism into his novels distinguished Lie from his contemporaries. Even though Lie occupied a respectful place as one of *De fire store,* his works were considered a little controversial and still are; this fact explains, perhaps, why Lie has attracted less attention from academe and publishers today than have his contemporaries Bjørnson, Ibsen, and Kielland.

Lie was born into a family of four children on 6 November 1833 in Hokksund, Eiker, southern Norway. He was baptized Jonas Idemil Lauritz Lie on 26 May 1834 in Eiker church. His first name rotated with the

Dust jacket for the 1983 first publication of Lie's play (Withdrawn from the Club), written in the early 1870s but considered unsuitable for performance (Wangsmo Antikvariat AS)

name Mons in the family tree, while his first middle name was a combination of his paternal grandmother's name, Ida, and Jean-Jacques Rousseau's *Émile* (1762). His second middle name honored his maternal grandfather, Lars Tiller, but was changed to Lauritz by his mother. The family was descended from Norwegian farmers living at Storli, south of Trondheim, in central Norway; but three generations before Lie was born, the family broke with the soil and became established in civil and judicial positions in various parts of Norway.

Lie's father, Mons Lie, continued the line of judicial officers. He was a successful attorney, a freethinker known for his meticulousness and diligence, and served as a prototype for the grandfather figure in Jonas Lie's novel *Naar Sol gaar ned* (1895, When the Sun Sets). Lie's mother, Pauline Christine Tiller, came from a family of men who operated small businesses, and after the death of her father she worked as a governess in Trondheim. She went on to secure a position in the home of a police officer, Mons Lie, Jonas Lie's great-grandfather, who was blind in his last days and needed assistance. In this home she met Jonas Lie's father, whom she married in 1829. Pauline Tiller Lie was dark-complexioned, and she always dressed in bright colors; these characteristics gave rise to the opinion that she had Gypsy or Sámi (people living in the northern parts of the Scandinavian countries) ancestors. Jonas Lie brought up the theme of mixed genetic makeup in several novels, particularly in his first novel, *Den Fremsynte, eller billeder fra Nordland* (1870; translated as *The Visionary, or Pictures from Nordland*, 1894) and in the short story "Finneblod" (translated as "Finn Blood," 1893) from the collection *Fortællinger og skildringer fra Norge* (1872, Stories and Pictures from Norway).

From his mother Lie inherited a love of books—literature, philosophy, and science. As a governess, Pauline was well educated and spoke English, German, and French fluently. Besides her interest in history and botany, Lie's mother was a passionate gardener. At the age of sixty she learned Latin, and in her seventies she was preoccupied with physics and mathematics. Jonas Lie grew up in a home with big family dinners and many guests. The last twenty years of her life Pauline was bedridden and spent her time reading world literature, including the works of Honoré de Balzac, George Sand, Immanuel Kant, and Norwegian philosopher and politician Niels Treschow. Pauline Lie's correspondence with the wife of Norwegian painter Erik Werenskjold reveals that she closely followed her son's development and fostered the artistic potential that she discovered before everyone else in the family did.

When Lie was five years old, the family moved to Tromsø, where his father was appointed town magistrate in 1838. Lie spent his childhood in Tromsø until he turned twelve. Located far up north, Tromsø was a bustling town of fishermen, sailors, and merchants. It was also a cosmopolitan city with many different ethnicities, including Sámi people and foreigners, particularly Russians. In Tromsø, Lie heard stories about trolls and ghosts, mostly from the servants in the house. These stories, the traditional lifestyle in the north, and the scenic polar landscape by the sea left lifelong impressions on Lie and inspired him to return to childhood memories in many of his novels, especially in the first three books, dedicated entirely to the northern region.

In 1846 Lie was sent to the Naval Academy in Fredriksvern to become an officer. The same year his father was appointed a district judge in Sunnhordland district, south of Bergen, on the west coast of Norway. The family bought Onereim, a farm in Kvindherred, where Lie and his brothers spent the weekends and holidays away from school. This farm was depicted in several of Lie's novels, including *Familjen paa Gilje: et interieur fra firtiaarene* (1883; translated as *The Family at Gilje: A Domestic Story of the Forties*, 1920).

After spending one year at the academy, Lie had to leave because of his nearsightedness. At the age of fifteen he joined his brothers at the Cathedral School in Bergen. While at this school, he wrote his first poem and became known as a skillful storyteller. In 1851 he moved to Heltberg and Reehorst's Latin School in Christiania (which became Oslo in 1925). The school prepared students for the entrance examinations to the university and was commonly referred to as "Heltberg's Student Factory." Among other talented young people who attended the school together with Lie were Ibsen, Bjørnson, and Aasmund Olavsson Vinje.

In the fall of 1851 Lie entered the University of Christiania and actively participated in student life. He visited literary student gatherings at Bjørnson's apartment, where Vinje was also a frequent guest. Both young writers, particularly Bjørnson, became good friends with Lie; the friendship lasted for many years. Bjørnson was not only Lie's friend but also his literary adviser and critic. Ibsen belonged to a different student circle than Lie did, but they often met at the literary café "Petri Kirke."

Lie also invited friends to his home for discussions about Norwegian literature and politics and for evenings of storytelling. He knew many friends who were skillful storytellers like himself, such as a medical student, Lindholm, from Sundmøre, whose story Lie retold in "Søndmørs-Ottringen" (Søndmør's Eight-Oar Boat), included in *Fortællinger og skildringer fra Norge*. At the time Lie began writing poems in the style of Henrik Wergeland, whom he greatly admired. A few of these poems, including "Solgud" (Sun God) and "Solveig," appeared in his first poetry collection, *Digte* (1867, Poems). According to Erik Lie, Jonas Lie was not happy with his earliest poems: "De var alle i den tåkete hasstemte ånd, som ødela så meget av den Wergelandske diktning" (They all were written in that opaque subdued mood that ruined so much of Wergelandian poetry).

In the spring of 1853 Lie became engaged to his cousin, Thomasine Henriette Lie. She was the daughter of Jonas's uncle, judicial lawyer Michael Strøm Lie. She had three sisters—Ida, Erika, and Birgitte—who were the prototypes for the daughters in *Familjen paa Gilje*. In the summer of the same year Lie passed his university examinations and had to choose his specialized studies. After considering theology and medicine, Lie decided on law. He graduated from the University of Christiania with a law degree in 1858 and found a position as a copier in the Revision Ministry. That year Lie published two poems, "Psalme" (Psalm) and "Emigrantenes

Længsel" (Emigrant's Longing), in the major Norwegian newspapers, *Morgenbladet* and *Illustreret Nyhedsblad*. Both poems show his ambiguous attitude toward religion and the strong influence of writer Wergeland in his choice of form and imagery.

Besides his first poetry publications, Lie began writing articles on foreign politics for the two newspapers. He commented on the Napoleonic Wars and the future of the German-speaking countries, and he outlined his vision of the European geopolitical map. The word "seer" was particularly stressed in his articles and later became an important motif in his literary works, especially in his breakthrough novel, *Den Fremsynte*. Lie's writing style was spontaneous and sensitive rather than analytical and reflective. Lie's articles were noticed in Norwegian political and cultural circles and served to identify him as a journalist for many years. Bjørnson, who was the theater director in Bergen and editor of the newspaper *Bergenposten,* recommended that Lie give up his career as a lawyer and devote his life to politics. In 1859 Lie received an offer to become an editor at *Christianiaposten,* but he rejected it to work as a legal assistant to his cousin Georg Henriksen in Kongsvinger, northeast of Christiania on the Swedish border. Lie lived close to Thomasine's family home at Svendborg and was a frequent guest in their house. In 1860 he married Thomasine and bought a spacious house at Sigridnæs, where their five children were born; two of Lie's children died. Lie held regular dinners for his Norwegian and Swedish guests, such as Vinje, Bjørnson, and Ole Bull. He became acquainted with his father-in-law's friend Adolf Bredo Stabel, a former editor of *Morgenbladet* and a director of the Norwegian Credit Bank. Stabel introduced Lie to many influential businessmen and helped him secure the profitable position of commissioner at Akers Savings Bank. Stabel also assured Lie that his work would be published in *Morgenbladet*. Lie wrote articles supporting the left-wing policies of Norwegian prime minister Jon Sverdrup, who advocated parliamentarism and defended farmers' and workers' rights. Lie met Sverdrup in person during his frequent business trips to Christiania; after a few years, he became Sverdrup's secretary.

By the early 1860s Lie was a wealthy businessman and passionate journalist who was able to purchase the newspaper *Illustreret Nyhedsblad*. Among the topics he discussed in his paper were the role of France in European politics, the political situation in Poland, and the Danish-German conflicts. Lie also wrote a series of articles about the political role of Norway in Europe. He promoted his vision of modern Norway with its strong and secure status in the international community. He argued for a Pan-Germanic Union consisting of Norway, Denmark, Sweden, and Germany;

Cover for Lie's dramatic poem (1875) about the Italian fight for freedom (Thorsens Antikvariat)

the union would still retain autonomous national governments. Lie's articles about Norway also appeared in the international press, in such newspapers as the *Frankfurter Journal,* the *New York Herald,* and *The Standard*. In addition to political articles, Lie published poems, biographies, and daily chronicles. Under his management, *Illustreret Nyhedsblad* became known as the newspaper advocating liberal and progressive ideas.

In 1867 Lie made his literary debut with *Digte* (Poems). The work includes his early poems written during the student years and new poems written in Kongsvinger, mostly for various occasions: birthdays, weddings, the memory and honor of his friends, including Bull, Vinje, and his business partner, Adolf Bredo Stabell. Other poems deal with political themes—such as the poem "Norgesbannerets drøm" (The Dream of the Norwegian Banner), dedicated to Lie's vision of a united Pan-Germania. The poems are sentimental, written in the tradition of Romanticism, with regular stanzas, meter, and rhyme. Lie's imitation of Wergeland's poetic style is visible throughout the collection. Probably one of the most successful poems is "Solveig." Norwegian composer Rikard Nordraak, who also wrote music for the Norwegian national anthem, composed the melody for Lie's poem. Lie's reputation as a passionate political journalist overshadowed his poetry debut, which did not receive much attention in Norwegian literary circles.

A year after publishing the poetry collection Lie went bankrupt and took on an enormous lifelong debt. After taking the position at the Akers Savings Bank, Lie became involved in lumber speculation and also made large investments in the stock market. When the wealthiest man in the district, John Collet Bredesen, who owned large tracts of forest and several farms, went bankrupt, many smaller businessmen, including Lie, also did. The merry years in Kongsvinger were over. The economic and psychological trauma Lie endured left a strong imprint on his writing; the bankruptcy motif runs like a red thread through his novels *En Malstrøm* (1884, A Whirlpool), *Et Samliv* (1887, Life Together), and *Faste Forland* (1899).

After considering immigration to America, Lie decided to stay and slowly pay off his debt from money he earned from writing. Lie's literary career became his major life project. His wife, Thomasine, supported his decision and helped him write almost all his works. Scholars today argue about how much she contributed to Lie's writing; many of them consider her his co-author. For the sixtieth-anniversary issue of the literary magazine *Samtiden* in 1893, Lie wrote an article in which he acknowledged Thomasine's contribution to his writing:

> Når jeg undtar Norfjordhesten, Slagter-Tobias og en del eventyr, vet jeg ikke den bok–og først og fremst romanene–hvor hun ikke har vært min avgjørende rettleder med hensyn til kunstformen og så å si min medarbeider gjennem hvert kapitel, strøket utskeielser fra emnet eller forlangt mere eller annnerledes diktet, i nødsfall selv lagt til. Det er gått gjennem hennes sikt og sil.
>
> (When I exclude Norfjordhesten, Slagter-Tobias and some tales, I do not know of any book–and, first and foremost, not the novels–where she has not been my critical advisor regarding the artistic form and so to speak my co-author throughout every chapter, striking out excesses in the material or requiring me to write more or in a different way, adding her own text if necessary. It has passed through her sieve and strainer.)

Lie sold all his property and moved back to Christiania in 1868. First, he tried to earn money by publishing articles and occasional poems; later he became a teacher at Heltberg's Student Factory. Lie maintained his interest in politics and served as Sverdrup's secretary. He also participated in the meetings of the Workers' and Students' Unions, where he was known not only as a poet but also as a talented orator.

Around 1870 Lie had a strong religious experience as a consequence of his recent economic crisis. In his letters to Bjørnson a couple of years later, Lie wrote about an all-forgiving God as a source of strength and meaning for his existence. The Christian faith, liberal and strongly influenced by Danish theologian N. F. S. Grundtvig, remained a foundation for Lie's life. Lie's religious views were not openly expressed in his works except for a few occasional poems. Nevertheless, tolerance and open Christian love for his fellow human beings are present in his writing as underlying elements in his portrayals of characters.

In 1870 Lie published his first novel, *Den Fremsynte*. Compared to Bjørnson and Ibsen, Lie entered the literary scene significantly later and described himself as "en senhøstens kar" (a man in his late fall). It was Bjørnson who, after hearing Lie read his manuscript, contacted director Frederik Hegel of the Gyldendal publishing company and made sure that Lie's manuscript was published as soon as possible, without Hegel's even reading the novel: "Kast den i trykkeriet straks, skynd på alle krefter, få den opp til Nordlandene før jul og over hele Skandinavien; den vil lyse som en hvit måke i den grå vinterluft" (Throw it in the printing office immediately, rush with all your might, get it out to the Nordic region before Christmas and across all of Scandinavia; it will shine as a white seagull in the grey winter sky). Indeed, as soon as *Den Fremsynte* appeared in bookstores, it became a great success in Norway and came out in three more editions in half a year.

As the title indicates, *Den Fremsynte* explores the presence of irrational and inexplicable forces in human life. It is the life story of David Holst and his extraordinary visionary gift, inherited from his mother who was publicly regarded as insane. Scared and confused, David attempts to fit into the merchants' and fishermen's society in a small town in northern Norway. Despite his efforts, David remains an outsider, understood by no one except his childhood sweetheart, Susanna, who believes that only love can bring David happiness and peace. She contradicts the local doctor's advice against marriage, and she cannot accept the scientific explanations that attribute visions to a mental ailment. However, Susanna and David are not destined to live together. In a vision David sees her dying, and he soon learns that she has drowned at sea during a storm. He spends the rest of his life as a lonely traveler and dies in his friend's home after telling his life story. He admits that Susanna taught him to love people and to appreciate life even though it is so full of inexplicable events and the secrets of human nature.

David's memories about the beauty of northern Norway and its people, his visions along with the local legends and myths told by his nanny, Sámi maid Anne

Cover for Lie's 1886 novel (translated as The Commodore's Daughters, 1892), which takes a pessimistic view of the possibility of female emancipation (from Edvard Beyer, ed., Norges Litteratur Historie, volume 3 [Oslo: Cappelen, 1975]; University of Kansas Libraries)

Kvæn, comprise the poetic and fantasy-filled semantic layer that occupies a significant place in *Den Fremsynte*. In this layer Lie recounts the legends he heard during his childhood years in Tromsø. Advised by Thomasine, Lie cut out significant parts of his work, including some of the tales, such as "Ved Enarsjøen" (By the Enar Lake), which was published later in the year in the magazine *For Idé og Virkelighed* and then included in Lie's *Otte fortællinger* (1885, Eight Stories).

Literary critics viewed *Den Fremsynte*, a work with considerable literary potential, as a romantic novel with overtly sentimental language and a banal story of love as a healing power. The other weakness in the book, also noted by critics of the time, was a lack of unifying structure. Moreover, Lie was the first author after Dass to write about northern Norway. His interest in the region, its folklore and traditions, can be seen as part of the National Romanticism program. After being a Danish province for more than five hundred years, Norway still remained an unexplored land at the end of the nineteenth century. Bad connections between isolated places made exploring Norway even more difficult. *Den Fremsynte* was a relevant book conforming to the goals of the Nationalist Movement in Norway.

Lie's breakthrough novel was written during the transition from Romanticism to realism in Scandinavian literature. Only a year after the publication of *Den Fremsynte*, Brandes announced his lecture series, *Hovedstrømninger*, and demanded that writers address social and political issues in their works and avoid idealization and unnecessary ornamentation. The ideology of the Modern Breakthrough affected Lie's writing form and his psychological portrayal of characters. For another decade, however, he remained an outsider to the literature of critical realism. In his letters from the 1870s, written to various cultural figures in Norway and Denmark, Lie emphasized the need for establishing the aesthetic foundation for a fledgling Norwegian National Literature: "I Norge staar vi i en Periode, som endnu holder paa med Skjønhedsmættelsen, og Sandhedsforklaringen har her mindre den første Rang, med mindre den tillige vil forklare sig i Skjønhed" (In Norway we live in a period which continues to satisfy the hunger for beauty, and the revelation of truth is less vital, unless it is accomplished with beauty).

Den Fremsynte is written in the tradition of late Romanticism; it focuses much more intensely on the conflict between the forces of life and death than on a harmonious universe. Lie's novel is built on countless contrasts of nature, people, and places as well as the personal conflict between fantasy and reality, and insanity and mental illness. This tension creates a mood of anxiety and restlessness in the novel and makes the story more dynamic. Lie maintains the same approach to the material in his later novels, only then he moves toward the aesthetics of modernism and the portrayal of a negative existence without hope of reconciliation with the worldview and aesthetics of Romanticism.

In 1871 Lie received a stipend for a research trip along the coast of Norway and to the north to study the character of the region's people, their lifestyle, and the natural surroundings. On this journey Lie collected material for his novel *Tremasteren "Fremtiden," eller Liv Nordpaa* (1872; translated as *The Barque Future; or, Life in the Far North*, 1879) and for his sea novel *Rutland* (1880). When Lie returned from his trip, he received more money and with his family left Norway for Rome. It was his first journey abroad, and it lasted about three years. During that period Lie and his family visited many European cities—among them, Amsterdam, Brussels, Paris, and Marseilles. Rome was the cultural center of Europe at the time; Lie met many Scandinavian artists and writers there: Bjørnson, who arrived there after Lie; sculptors Walter Runeberg, Christopher Borch, and Hans Børjesson; painters Johan Bøgh and Pietro Krohn; and writers Johannes Carsten Hauch and Meir Aron Goldschmidt. Lie visited galleries, museums, churches, and small local towns such as Pisa and Sienna. In the summertime he and his family went to a small mountain village, Rocca di Pappa, in the Albanese Mountains. Here, Lie wrote three books: *Fortællinger og skildringer fra Norge*; *Tremasteren "Fremtiden," eller Liv Nordpaa*; and *Lodsen og hans hustru* (1874; translated as *The Pilot and His Wife: A Norse Love Story*, 1876).

All three of Lie's works follow the romantic pattern of *Den Fremsynte*. Events take place in northern Norway; Lie provides descriptions of the contemporary life of the region and focuses on love relationships. *Fortællinger og skildringer fra Norge* is a collection of legends, tales, and romanticized childhood memories. Lie's second novel, *Tremasteren "Fremtiden," eller Liv Nordpaa*, combines material that he did not use in *Den Fremsynte* with the research he did in Tromsø on the Sámi people. The work focuses on the girl Marina, who survives a boat crash and is raised by the Sámi, Isak. Her love relationship and reunion with her uncle form the central narrative, with several side stories and descriptions of Sámi lands and traditions and the subtleties of the trading business in Bergen. The book suggests a religious undertone that stresses Christian forgiveness of sins and acceptance of one's destiny as the gift of God. There are no references to supernatural forces, and the story focuses entirely on contemporary life. *Tremasteren "Fremtiden"* is less sentimental than Lie's earlier work; however, the characters and plot are underdeveloped, and the dialogue is weak. The strength of the novel lies in its impressive description of local landscape.

Lodsen og hans hustru depicts the relationship of a married couple, with a romantic description of life at sea in the background. Lie emphasizes the emotional life of the pilot, Salve, and his jealous attacks on his wife, Elisabeth. After reading *Lodsen og hans hustru*, writer Camilla Collett observed that the theme of a man's jealousy and the portrayal of his feelings were rare in Norwegian literature. She found the book important for the women's movement because it also gave insight into the world of women, their sufferings at the hands of their husbands, and their total submissiveness and patience. The book implies inequality between the partners in marriage: when a woman silently acquiesces to her husband and his opinion, she loses self-respect and the possibility of personal development. Of the three books Lie wrote during his Rome period, *Lodsen og hans hustru* received the best reviews. The novel includes skillful descriptions of moods, complex psychological portraits of the characters, and lively dialogues.

In 1874 Lie returned to Christiania, where he stayed until 1877. The same year the Norwegian Parliament awarded him a lifelong artist's allowance, similar to those that Ibsen and Bjørnson had received. Lie also received the first Norwegian-Swedish King Oscar II Medal and the title of Olav's Knight. The king searched for supporters in literary and cultural circles, so Lie was frequently invited to the court and encouraged to write poetry in the king's honor. The king even offered to pay Lie's debt if he remained loyal, but Lie refused the offer because it threatened his artistic independence.

Despite the popularity of *Den Fremsynte* and a positive reception for his later books, Lie was still better known as a celebratory poet and a talented journalist. Because of his unwillingness to belong to any political party, he encountered difficulty finding acceptance in cultural circles. His refusal to contribute to Brandes's new magazine, *Det 19de Aarhundrede* (The Nineteenth Century), also made the foremost Danish critic turn away. Brandes was clearly offended and stopped reading Lie's books; not until the positive review of *Livsslaven* (1883; translated as *One of Life's Slaves,* 1895) did Brandes renew his friendship with Lie. The literary critics boycotted Lie, as did the political press. *Morgenbladet,* which represented the right wing and the narrow views of the aristocracy and well-off bourgeoisie in the capital, did not appreciate his literary talents. Lie's contributions to the newspaper suggested that he was a skillful article writer with great potential; yet, he was never taken seriously, since he lacked strongly held political persuasions.

During his stay in Christiania, Lie wrote two books, the dramatic poem *Faustina Strozzi* (1875), about the Italian fight for freedom, and a novel, *Thomas Ross* (1878), which did not draw much attention in Norwegian literary circles. Lie intended his poem for the stage, but the Royal Theater in Copenhagen and Christiania Theater rejected the script because of its lack of a strong conflict and its excessive descriptions of the Italian landscape. *Thomas Ross* tells a story of a young playwright and his relationship to two different types of women: the seductress and coquette, on the one hand, and the plain but virtuous young lady, on the other hand. The novel includes some autobiographical details, since its protagonist fails to write a successful play after returning from a stay in Italy, all of which is reminiscent of Lie's failure with *Faustina Strozzi*. In the novel, Lie focuses on a new theme of bourgeois city life, cultural dandyism, the admiration of foreign elegance, and style. Nevertheless, the plot of *Thomas Ross* is trivial, and the portrayal of the Christiania milieu is superficial. Lie's style, replete with long descriptions and addresses to the reader, suggests a loss of quality.

In the fall 1878 Lie left Norway and did not return for twenty-five years. The reason for his departure was debt; he managed to pay off the debt during his time away so he could return and buy property in his home country with a clear conscience. Lie moved to Germany, first to Stuttgart, then to Dresden, and he spent his summers in a little mountain town, Berchtesgaden, in the Salzburg Alps. A year after publishing *Thomas Ross,* Lie delivered a new novel, *Adam Schrader* (1879). The book provides an interesting psychological study but lacks originality and repeats the plot, the theme, and the imagery of *Thomas Ross*.

All Lie's works to this point fall outside the Modern Breakthrough. Lie avoided both the literary and the political polemics that increased in Norway during the late 1870s. He did not fully accept Brandes's emphasis on social concerns and the role of literature in setting problems under debate. In 1878 Lie wrote to Bjørnson: "Efter min Tro lader Norskhed og Folkelighed sig tusind Gange elskes ind i Folket end prygles ind i det; den usynbare Virkninger af en Digtning ere stærkere end de udvortes mer haandgribelige Slag i Politiken,–derom er jeg forvissset" (In my view, the Norwegian character and folk traditions reach the people one thousand times better with love than with the whip; the invisible effects of a literary text are stronger than the external and more tangible means in the politics–I am certain about that). Lie did agree with Brandes on the need to renew literary form and the requisite of an objective treatment of the text and its method of composition. In this case, Lie was particularly modern; starting with *Adam Schrader,* his writing style became more akin to the aesthetics of realism.

Lie's play *Grabows Kat: skuespil i tre akter* (Grabow's Cat: A Play in Three Acts), was staged at Christiania Theater on 24 September 1880. The play was performed seven times in Christiania, once at the National Stage in Bergen, and once at the Royal Theater in Stockholm. The drama concerns a young painter, Carl Witt, who produces his first masterpiece inspired by his love for his patron's daughter. The patron opposes the young man's relationship with his daughter. When Carl's masterpiece is finished, however, his patron not only admires the work but also destroys it in a jealous rage. The housekeeper's cat gets the blame for destroying the painting. The young couple wins approval for their marriage. Despite successful staging and a humorous tone, the play did not do well on the stage.

In the 1880s Lie became involved with political and cultural debates in Norway. He stated that he was a free artist, but he also held political views that did not coincide with those of either the left or the right wing. The critic Irgens Hansen provoked Lie into taking up journalism again by suggesting that Lie's play *Grabows Kat* devoted too much importance to the role of romantic love in creating the painter's masterpiece. In his literary articles Lie repeatedly defended his understanding of art as autonomous: "Kunsten er et noget for sig; der har sin egen Kjærlighet, egen Moral, egne Sorger og Glæde, kort–sit eget Liv" (Art is something for itself; it has its own love, its own moral, its own sorrows and joys, in short–it has its own life). The quote expresses an opinion that Lie maintained all his life. Moreover, Lie took a stand against naturalism and Émile Zola, whose scientific approach, in Lie's view, could not allow

Lie and his wife, Thomasine Henriette Lie, who was also his cousin, in 1903 (Store Norske Leksikon <http://www.snl.no/.bilde/Lie%2C_Jonas_(ekteparet%2C_foto)>)

the existence of irrational love and considered it an outdated element of Romanticism.

Lie clarified his literary position in the 1880 novel *Rutland*. The first part of *Rutland* concerns the sea voyage of the *Rutland*, a ship that plies the coastal route from Christiania to Trondheim. Lie provided detailed descriptions of the Norwegian coastline and a few sailors' tales about dragons. The central narrative deals with the love affair between Captain Kristian and one of the passengers, Lady Een. The couple marries in Trondheim and raises a son. The rest of the book deals with family life and the conflict between parents and son over the son's decision to become a sailor. This conflict also impacts the relationship between husband and wife, but all ends well when the son comes back home and marries his childhood sweetheart.

Rutland received great reviews in Norway; critic Francis Bull stated that the novel represented Lie's stylistic breakthrough, infused as it was with impressionistic elements and full of life, humor, and complex characters. Many critics praised Lie's portrait of the strong, practical Lady Een, who finds happiness in an equal partnership with the captain and self-realization as a businesswoman. In his novel Lie managed to demonstrate that a love relationship could be realistically portrayed without recourse to romantic sentimentality.

In 1882 Lie returned to Norway for the summer. He and his family stayed at Tromøy outside Arendal for four months, where he finished another sea novel *"Gaa paa!": sjøfortælling* (1882, "Aboard!": A Sea Novel). The novel caricatures the isolated, intolerant residents of a small town in Aafjorden. One of the townspeople, Rejer Jansen Juhl, breaks old habits, introducing modern economic life and a new tempo into the village; he tries to share the new knowledge that exists beyond the narrow confines of the village. The most important part of the book depicts Rejer's adventures at sea before coming home. Lie focuses on Reyjer's psychological development and the maturation of his character. The changes in Aafjorden point to the changes needed in all of Norway, especially the need for Norway to open up and accept progress in line with the times. The book reflects actual changes in the Norwegian economy and Lie's new social orientation. With its gallery of vivid characters, its impressionistic descriptions of the landscape and the interior, and its dynamic dialogue built on the language of the village people, *"Gaa paa!"* won the critics over and was highly regarded as Lie's best sea novel.

The work also demonstrated a major change from Dano-Norwegian to Norwegian.

After the vacation in Norway, Lie moved with his family to Paris, which became his second home until the last years of his life. Lie's apartment in Rue Canrot 4 (later in Avenue La Grande) was a meeting place for Scandinavian tourists and residents, principally Brandes, Collett, Edvard Grieg, Fridtjof Nansen, Arne Garborg, Sigbjørn Obstfelder, Hans E. Kinck, and Edvard Munch. Bjørnson lived ten minutes away from Lie, and they kept in close contact. Lie met with many Danish and Swedish authors as well, including Herman Bang, Victoria Benedictsson, and Oscar Levertin. Lie often stayed in his summer residence in Berchtesgaden, where he wrote the majority of his novels.

With *Livsslaven* in 1883, Lie earned his reputation as a member of the Modern Breakthrough. The novel portrays the working class and their squalid living conditions in Christiania. The readers follow the life of Nikolai from birth to imprisonment. Born a bastard, Nikolai grows up in suffering and fear in the home of an alcoholic, Holman. He apprentices with a blacksmith and saves his money in order to marry Silla, Holman's daughter. Despite his hard childhood, Nikolai becomes a kind, responsible boy with hopes for the future. Destructive forces shatter his dreams and turn him into a criminal. In a jealous rage, Nikolai kills his rival for Silla, a rich young man who insults Nikolai in public. (The theme of jealousy is more intensely portrayed in *Livsslaven* than in Lie's earlier works.) When Silla sees Nikolai in handcuffs, she jumps out of a window, killing herself. Nikolai is ordered to serve a life sentence for killing his rival.

When *Livsslaven* came out, critics considered it a naturalistic novel in which Lie came close to echoing Zola's ideas of determinism: that is, the corrupt environment into which Nikolai is born determines his destiny. Lie defended his novel, stating that it was much more involved than the sort of documentary, the *tranche de vie* (slice of life) that Zola would have written. According to Lie, *Livsslaven* had passion as well as an element of morality; only Nikolai's status as a bastard connects Lie's protagonist to the kind of natural determinism Zola had in mind. However, Nikolai's desire to escape from his environment and his willingness to take responsibility keep him from a downfall; he holds on to his moral values. The left-wing press, writers, and critics—such as Bang, Brandes, and Garborg—praised *Livsslaven*. Henrik Jæger pointed out that Lie had failed to give a realistic depiction of the poorest people in Christiania because he could not capture their spirit. Critics also found fault with Lie's colorless style.

Lie's next novel, *Familjen paa Gilje: et interieur fra fir-tiaarene,* has become a part of the Norwegian literary canon. It is an intimate domestic tale rich in humor and profound universal questions. The novel demonstrates a clash of old and modern worldviews, a conflict between love and financial security as well as a conflict between self-realization and adaptation to dominating social conventions. In the novel Gilje is an isolated residence of a Norwegian army officer and his family.

In an effort to save the family from financial disaster, the middle daughter, Inger-Johanna, leaves home for the capital and becomes engaged to her father's friend, Captain Rønnow. She spends four years in the city, only visiting Gilje one summer. After meeting the student Grip, however, Inger-Johanna decides to follow her heart; she breaks her engagement and returns home to Gilje. Her father never recovers from her breakup with Rønnow, and he forgives her only on his deathbed. Inger-Johanna's aunt Alette leaves her niece a decent inheritance so she can live independently. Grip, her sweetheart, becomes ill and dies in her arms; Inger-Johanna becomes a teacher and on Grip's behalf promotes progressive education and society inspired by Rousseau's philosophy. Besides the philosophical and social discussion, Lie also includes folk ballads that echo Inger-Johanna's destiny. Her story constitutes one of the primary narratives of the work, but Lie also interweaves stories of her sisters, Thinka and Thea, and her younger brother, Jørgen.

The other central narrative concerns the older generation at Gilje, Inger-Johanna's parents, Captain Jørgen and his wife, Ma. A horse trader, the Captain is head of the household, an egocentric, impulsive man given to drink. The captain is penny-wise, pound-foolish, constantly complaining over small household expenses while losing a lot of money trading horses. In spite of her dictatorial, petty husband, Ma holds the real reins of power in the household, quietly and imperceptibly. Preoccupied with the family's social status, Ma is also innovative and hardworking. By depicting the lives of four different women (Inger-Johanna, Thinka, Thea, and Ma), Lie delves into the issues of emancipation and the protests of women against the conservative nature of contemporary culture. The discussion of women's rights stands in an open dialogue with Collett's novel *Amtmandes døtre* (1854; translated as *The District Governor's Daughters,* 1992) and sheds a more optimistic light on the improvement of women's condition. Support for modern, progressive thought lies with the student Grip, who protests against the social backwardness and snobbish culture of the bourgeoisie.

On the one hand, *Familjen paa Gilje* addresses important changes of individual and family values in the contemporary Norwegian society, and on the other hand, it demonstrates innovative narrative techniques. Lie writes in an impressionistic style, focusing on the sensual and emotional description of the characters and their environment. Nature outside, interiors, and objects inside the house are linked to individual characters, reflecting their distinct personalities. The scenes in *Familjen paa Gilje* are not static but constantly move, submerged in vividly rapid action and shifting perspective from one character to another. Each episode in the narrative is essential to the story; episodes open in medias res and immediately catch the reader's attention. The characters are presented in the course of action and dramatic dialogues. By describing their interaction in rapidly changing situations, Lie manages to capture an impression, a moment during which the human soul becomes visible.

Familjen paa Gilje did not receive the enthusiastic reception accorded *Livsslaven*. Kielland described Lie's book as "en nydelig Roman om ingenting" (a beautiful novel about nothing), an assessment shared by the majority of literary critics, who decried Lie's lack of social criticism and political awareness. Once again, Lie had to defend himself for rejecting the straightforward style of critical realism. In Lie's opinion, there was no need to copy reality like a photograph; instead, one could create an impression of reality. Lie's aim was to influence the reader by depicting scenes from ordinary family life.

Familjen paa Gilje can be regarded as a step toward the perfection of Lie's writing style. In 1884 Lie published *En Malstrøm: fortælling* (Whirlpool: A Story), in which his impressionistic techniques unfolded entirely. Lie described his book as a painting:

> Bogen blev skrevet Scene paa Scene saa at sige al Fresco paa Væggen, som det steg frem for mit Syn. At fremstillingen under den Opgave i en kort Bog at nærværengjøre en hel Komplex af Distriktsfigurer er blevet etslags imressionistisk Maleri, er rigtig nok, og at det saa i adskilligt Omfang mere er blevet staaende ved Figurer end givet en videre Udførelse i Karakterer er ogsaa i visse Maader sandt.

> (The book was written scene by scene so to speak like a fresco on the wall, which emerged to my sight. It is quite true that the depiction, aimed to present an entire gallery of the region's figures in a short book, was a kind of impressionistic painting, and it is also true that in separate cases there is more focus on the figures than on the further development of their characters.)

Indeed, the novel consists of the dynamic scenes with expressive language filled with pauses and interruptions in the dialogues and the description of the characters and environment based on the visual and sensual apparatus:

> Det gamle, grønbrillede Öie havde skimtet unge Piger i hvide Kjoler, som bevægede sig i det fri under Bryluper og Fester i Sommertiden og dansede ovenfor paa Plænen, set Træerne om Kvælderne illuminerede med Begfakler og derunder allehaande ravende og lallende Skikkelser.

> (The old eye behind the green glasses had caught a glimpse of young girls in white dresses, who moved freely during weddings and celebrations in the summertime and danced on the lawn, had seen the trees in the evenings illuminated by torches and under them all sorts of tottering and babbling figures.)

Moreover, in *Malstrøm,* as the title implies, the various descriptions and images of water offer clues to interpreting the emotional states of the characters within the novel: the turgid carp pond near the family home represents stagnancy and immobility, emotional paralysis or stasis; the swirling waters of the mill and the sure and steady flow of water into Fossegaard mill represent constancy, progress, and stability; and the whirlpool of the title represents dramatic changes and tension within the family.

Similar to Lie's previous novel, *Malstrøm* is a realistic study of the decay of an old, respected firm in Fossegård. The financial downfall of the family recalls Lie's economic woes in Kongsvinger. The father, Mads Foss, egotistically forces his daughters, Antonia and Marianne, into marriage in order to liquidate his business debts. Throughout the book both sisters fight for their right to love and for financial independence. Antonia reveals her strong character in her attempts to create a loving family home and demonstrates her practical skills in running a successful soap factory, which saves her father's estate from bankruptcy. Marianne, on the other hand, ends up with lifelong guilt stemming from an extramarital affair that may have led to her husband's suicide. She finds peace, however, in devoting the rest of her life to poor children. The reviews of *Malstrøm* declared it a rather mediocre novel and did not acknowledge the originality of Lie's writing talent, which did deviate from the predominant realistic style.

A collection of short stories, *Otte fortællinger,* published a year later, demonstrates Lie's further artistic development of highly poetic and imagery-rich writing. The tales in the collection blend realism and fantasy in depicting human relationships. In the short story "Jon Sunde," Lie portrays an unhappy marriage between two people of different social backgrounds. "Susamel," on the other hand, depicts the destructive love of people who are overly possessive. Once again, Lie suggests that jealousy is a natural force that can be fought, but not defeated, by human powers. Susamel ends up strangling his wife, Nora, in his effort to own her completely. The emphasis on dark secrets of human desires and fantasy-rich storytelling recalls the use of the Gothic in Edgar Allan Poe's stories.

Lie returned to domestic interiors and women's emancipation in his next three novels: *Kommandørens Døtre* (1886, translated as *The Commodore's Daughters*, 1892), *Et Samliv,* and *Maisa Jons* (1888). All three works have similar plot development and focus on the conflict between individual aspirations and social roles, duties, and demands. While *Kommandørens Døtre* and *Maisa Jons* present pessimistic prospects on liberal social changes, particularly regarding women's lives, *Et Samliv* radiates a slight hope of finding inner peace and personal happiness through togetherness.

Lie's second collection of poetry, *Digte* (1889, Poems), comprised of occasional poems, provides a short break in his prose writing. Compared to his debut poetry, the poems in the second volume are well crafted and reflect the poet's dynamic, impressionistic style. A year later, Lie published another novel, *Onde Magter* (Evil Forces), which marks the beginning of a new literary cycle in his career. In contrast to his previous works, Lie turned away from depicting marriage in order to focus on the dark and destructive powers of the human psyche. *Onde Magter* tells the story of friendship, envy, and the struggle for power between two businessmen, Johnston and Bratt. Bratt is a simple man, obviously greedy for power and wealth, cruel to those who have wronged or slighted him but generous to a fault to friends. Johnston is the more complicated: the recipient of ill-gotten gains from insurance on a ship that has already foundered, Johnston suffers pangs of guilt and ends up committing suicide. Lie contrasts the human values of sympathy and understanding with the "onde magter" that lead individuals to seek power and wealth at the expense of others.

The two volumes of short stories and tales titled *Trold,* published in 1891 and 1892, present Lie's belief in the irrational side of human nature in the form of myths and legends. In these volumes Lie gives freedom to his own fantasy, using material from oral tradition as a background for his own stories, and he also retells legends and stories from Finnmark in northern Norway. Trolls in Lie's stories appear both as a present-day reality and as a remnant of the past. In the introduction to *Trold* 1, Lie wrote: [trold] ligger inde i Personligheden og binder den som urørligt Fjeldstykke, lunefuldt Hav og ustyrligt Vejr" ([trolls] dwell inside the personality and constrain it like an immobile rock, a treacherous sea and uncontrollable weather). In the preface to the first volume, Lie describes two kinds of trolls: temper, natural will, and explosive force; and angst and the fear of darkness and ghosts. With *Onde Magter* Lie's writing came to focus on the latter kind of troll. In all his stories Lie leaves out moralization and encourages the reader to ponder on their meaning. The poetic, ambiguous, and open-ended nature of his texts earn Lie an equal standing with other Scandinavian creators of modern literary tales, such as Andersen, Selma Lagerlöf, and Isaac Dinesen.

Lie continued developing the theme of trolls in his next novel, *Niobe* (1893), which he finished after his return to Norway for summer vacation in 1893. The novel presents a morbid tale of a dysfunctional family– Lie's tribute to decadent literature. Thekla Baard loathes her husband and betrays him with Doctor Stenvig. When her husband goes bankrupt and commits suicide, Thekla follows suit, killing herself and three of her children, whom she sees as hopeless and bereft of a future. The children actually represent three different kinds of lives: that of an artist, that of an entrepreneur, and that of a spiritual medium. Together, they do not amount to much; their lives are devoid of meaning. *Niobe* serves as an introduction to a cycle of works marked by pessimism and the victory of fatal forces.

Such is the play with an ironic title, *Lystige koner: skuespil i tre akter* (1894, Merry Wives: A Play in Three Acts), which portrays two unhappy marriages in which the wives pretend to be merry in order to hide their bitterness and dissatisfaction. Lie's next two novels, *Naar Sol gaar ned* (1895, When the Sun Sets) and *Dyre Rein: en historie fra oldefarens hus* (1896, Dyre Rein: a Story from the Great Grandfather's House), deal with judgment, death, and unfulfilled expectations. In *Naar Sol gaar ned,* a husband murders his wife because she openly cheats on him in front of their children and the grandfather. The craving for moral justice and punishment triggers the husband's actions and adds a religious undertone to the story.

In *Dyre Rein* an irrational, inexplicable death impulse controls the protagonist, whose name (Dyre Rein) means "wild beast." Like David in *Den Fremsynte,* Dyre Rein possesses the mystical powers of a visionary, only in *Dyre Rein,* love does not possess healing power, and the bride cannot protect her beloved from death. Driven by suicidal thoughts, Dyre Rein jumps into a waterfall on the eve of his wedding. The form and theme of the novel transcend critical realism, revealing modern angst, loneliness, and obscure laws of a fearful universe.

Lie's subsequent novel, *Faste Forland,* published in 1899, returns to a more realistic discourse. The novel focuses on the life of an aging writer, from his childhood to his successful literary debut. *Faste Forland* is Lie's most autobiographical work, one he called "Et stykke af min indre Livsroman" (A piece of my inner life's novel). It deals with artistic and religious searchings, love affairs, and the financial crisis that leads to the protagonist's literary calling.

Lie's next novel, *Naar jernteppet falder: af livets komedie* (1901, When the Iron Curtain Falls: From Life's Comedy), introduces an entirely new subject and a complex narrative with a large gallery of characters and intersecting life stories. The novel begins with an alarm caused by an insane passenger who on an eight-day voyage across the Atlantic informs his fellow passengers of an impending explosion aboard the ship. The first seven chapters of the book introduce half of the passengers in second class and give a glimpse of the chaotic, nameless crowd in steerage. Reactions of the other passengers vary from despair to cool self-control; they are as mysterious as the human psyche itself. The last chapter describes what happens on arrival in New York.

Lie's next novel, *Ulfvungerne: et blad af lidenskabernes bog* (1903, The Ulfvungs: A Page of the Passions' Book), returns to the depiction of a family; although it is skillfully designed, the book repeats the images, characters, and compositions of the previous domestic stories, such as *Familjen paa Gilje, Malstrøm,* and *Onde Magter.* The last work published before Lie's death was a novel, *Østenfor Sol, vestenfor Maane og bagom Babylons Taarn!: streif paa Jagtgebetet* (1905, East of the Sun, West of the Moon and behind Babylon's Tower!: A Strip on the Hunting Ground). The book combines magic, supernatural powers, and a realistic plot. Lie experimented with form, creating a mosaic of genres that vary from lyrical essays to animal fables, allegories, and myths. The novel tells the story of a researcher, Ole Stjernø, who dies with an unfulfilled dream of sacrificing himself for science because his envious, less talented colleague, William Adler, destroys his plans. However, William cannot penetrate Ole's most sacred space, his mind; therefore, Ole's inner world remains intact. The story returns to a dilemma present in Lie's previous works, the conflict between individual aspirations and social duties and responsibilities. With the power of fantasy, Ole escapes from his limited environment to an alternative free existence in the universe. *Østenfor Sol* has a pessimistic undertone and reveals a belief in unstoppable demonic forces that control the civilized world.

When Lie turned seventy in 1903, he and Thomasine decided to move back to Norway. They built a house, "Elisefryd," in Fredriksvern and moved into it in 1906. A year and a half later, Thomasine was diagnosed with cancer and underwent surgery. A few months afterward, she had a stroke; she died on 7 October 1907. Lie was almost blind and suffered from the sclerosis that was the cause of his own death on 5 July 1908 during a visit to his eldest son's home in Fleskum, Sandvika, a few miles west of Christiania. He is buried beside his wife in Fredriksvern.

In 1909 the collection of a poem, seven short stories, and a first chapter of a book Lie started were published under the title *Eventyr.* In 1983 the Norwegian language and literature club printed a newly found manuscript of Lie's play *Udmeldt af Klubben* (Withdrawn from the Club), written in the early 1870s. The play had been consigned to the archives of Christiania Theater as unsuitable for performance because of its lack of dramatic conflict and original ideas.

Although Jonas Lie started his career in his late thirties, he remained incredibly productive until the last years of his life, publishing poems, novels, plays, and short stories almost annually. His rich oeuvre shows the gradual development of his style from Romanticism to realism and impressionism, and in his last novel, *Østenfor Sol, vestenfor Maane og bagom Babylons Taarn!: streif paa Jagtgebetet,* he combined them all. Throughout his life Lie always defended free and independent artistic expression, and he did not identify himself with any particular ideology. He was passionately interested in political, cultural, and literary discussions, but he always maintained a neutral position, which was not an easy thing to do during the Modern Breakthrough or during heated debates about the union with Sweden. Lie was particularly careful to keep his writing and political views apart. However, in depicting everyday family life and the relationships of ordinary people, Lie addressed such social issues as the position of women in modern society, the institution of marriage, the education of children, and the conflicts between the working class and the more affluent classes in Norway. In the majority of his novels Lie focused on contemporary life and its realistic representation. He combined objective narration with sensual and emotional discourse, filling his texts with color, motion, sound, and scent. Realism did not provide a completely satisfactory model for Lie, so he created a parallel world occupied by trolls and dragons, magic and mystical irrational forces. In his later novels the symbolic and supernatural became dominant. Lie's description of the natural setting and interior space, his use of picturesque and dramatic scenes, his introduction of the vernacular in dialogue, and his blend of supernatural and realistic elements all significantly changed the aesthetics of the Norwegian novel.

Letters:

Jonas Lie og hans samtidige: breve i udvalg, edited by Carl Nærum (Christiania: Gyldendal, 1915).

Bibliography:

Kirsti Lome, *Jonas Lie: en bibliografi* (Oslo: Statens bibliotekskole, 1969).

Biographies:

Arne Garborg, *Jonas Lie: en udviklingshistorie* (Christiania: Aschehoug, 1893);

William H. Carpenter, *Jonas Lie* (Harrisburg, Pa.: Bookman, 1895);

The Late Jonas Lie (Harrisburg, Pa.: Bookman, 1908);

Erik Lie, *Oplevelser, med Breve, Illustrationer og Portrætter* (Christiania: Gyldendal, 1908);

Valborg Erichsen, *Jonas Lie som journalist* (Christiania: Malling, 1914);

Erik Lie, *Jonas Lie: en livskildring* (Oslo: Gyldendal, 1933);

Nils Lie, *Jonas Lie: fortalt for skoleungdom* (Oslo: Gyldendal, 1933);

Fredrik Ingerslev, *Jonas Lie: et persnoligheds- og typebillede* (Copenhagen: Gyldendal, 1939);

Johannes Skancke Martens, *Jonas Lie i Paris* (Oslo: Mortensen, 1967);

Willy Dahl, *Max Mauser—men Jonas Lie: studie i dikt og liv* (Bergen: Eide, 1990).

References:

Petter Aaslestad, *Dømt til Kunst: Jonas Lies romaner 1884–1905* (Oslo: Rådet for humanistisk forskning, 1992);

Per Adam, "Omkring hestesymbolet hos Jonas Lie," *Edda*, 71 (1971): 37–46;

Carl Olof Bergström, *Jonas Lies väg til Gilje* (Örebro: Nerikes Allehanda, 1949);

Alrik Gufstafson, "Jonas Lie," in his *Six Scandinavian Novelists* (Minneapolis: Minnesota University Press, 1940), pp. 25–72;

Ingard Hauge, *Jonas Lies diktning; tematikk og fortellekunst* (Oslo: Gyldendal, 1970);

Åse Hiorth Lervik, *Ideal og virkelighet: ekteskapet som motiv hos Jonas Lie* (Oslo: Universitetsforlaget, 1965);

Sverre Lyngstad, *Jonas Lie* (Boston: Twayne, 1977);

James Walter McFarlane, "Jonas Lie," in his *Ibsen and the Temper of Norwegian Literature* (London: Oxford University Press, 1960), pp. 97–103;

Per Mæleng, *Marginalia: femininiteten som undertekst. En litteraturvitenskapeligavhandling om Jonas Lies roman Familien paa Gilje. Et Interiør fra Firtiaarene* (Trondheim: Norges teknisk-naturvitenskapelige universitet, 2001);

Terje Stigen, "Jonas Lie," in *Forfatternes litteraturhistorie*, volume 1: *Fra Maurits Christopher Hansen til Arne Garborg*, edited by Kjell Heggelund, Simen Skensberg, and Helge Vold (Oslo: Gyldendal, 1980);

Harald-Bache Wiig, ed., *Sinn og samfunn: fem artikler om Jonas Lies forfatterskap* (Oslo: Gyldendal, 1983);

Erik Østerud, "Jonas Lies *Familien paa Gilje* inter artes," *Edda*, 3 (2002): 296–317.

Papers:

Most of Jonas Lie's manuscripts and other papers are in the Nasjonalbiblioteket (National Library) in Oslo.

Jørgen Moe
(22 April 1813 – 27 March 1882)

Aaron Schmitt
University of Wisconsin–Madison

BOOKS: *Samling af Sange, Folkeviser og Stev i norske Almuedialekter* (Christiania: Malling, 1840);

Norske Folkeeventyr, 2 volumes, by Moe and Peter Christian Asbjørnsen (Christiania: Johan Dahl, 1841, 1844; revised and enlarged, 1852); translated by George Webbe Dasent as *Popular Tales from the Norse* (Edinburgh: Edmonton & Douglas, 1859); revised Norwegian edition (Christiania: Dybwad, 1866; revised, 1868; revised, 1874);

Indberetning fra Cand. theol. Jørgen Moe om den af ham i Sommeren 1846 med offentl. Stipendium foretagne Reise til Hardanger (Christiania, 1847);

Indberetning "om en reise sommeren 1846 i Hardanger og om en reise 1847 i Setesdal og Telemark for å samle folkediktning" (Christiania, 1848);

Digte (Christiania: Feilburg & Landmark, 1849);

I Brønden og i Tjærnet: Smaahistorier for Børn (Christiania: Feilburg & Landmark, 1850);

At hænge paa Juletræet: nogle faa Digte (Christiania: Steensballe, 1855); republished as *En Liden Julegave: Gammelt og Nyt* (Christiania: Steensballe, 1859).

Collections: *Samlede Skrifte* (Christiania: Cammermeyer, 1877);

Dikt og Prosa (Bergen: J. W. Eide, 1968).

Editions in English: *Tales from the Fjeld: A Second Series of Popular Tales. From the Norse of P. Chr. Asbjørnsen,* translated by George Webbe Dasent (London: Chapman & Hall, 1874);

Northern Fairy Tales, translated by H. L. Brækstad (London: Sampson Low, Marston, Searle & Rivington, 1879);

Norwegian Fairy Tales by P. Chr. Asbjørnsen, translated by Brækstad (London: Sampson Low, Marston, Searle & Rivington, 1879);

Folk and Fairy Tales, translated by Brækstad (London: Sampson Low, Marston, Searle & Rivington, 1883);

Round the Yule Log: Norwegian Folk and Fairy Tales, translated by Brækstad (London: Sampson Low, Marston, Searle & Rivington, 1886);

Jørgen Moe (Store Norske Leksikon <http://snl.no/.bilde/Moe%2C_J%C3%B8rgen_(portrett-tegning)>

Norwegian Fairy Tales, translated by Abel Heywood (London: Routledge, 1895);

Norwegian Fairy Tales, from the Collection of Asbjørnsen and Moe, translated by John Gade (New York: American-Scandinavian Foundation, 1924);

East o' the Sun and West o' the Moon: With Other Norwegian Folktales, translated and retold by Gudrun

Thorne-Thompson (New York: Row, Peterson, 1946);

Norwegian Fairy Tales, edited and translated by Reidar Romskaug (London: University of London, 1961);

A Time for Trolls: Fairy Tales from Norway Told by P. C. Asbjørnsen and Jørgen Moe, translated by Joan Roll-Hansen (Oslo: Tanum, 1962);

Norwegian Folk Tales from the Collection of Peter Christian Asbjørnsen and Jørgen Moe, translated by Pat Shaw Iversen and Carl Norman (London: Allen & Unwin, 1963);

Folktales of Norway, translated by Iversen (Chicago: University of Chicago Press, 1968);

The Bumper Book of Norwegian Folktales, translated by Wenche Berger (Oslo: Aschehoug, 2001).

OTHER: *Tidskrift for litteratur og kritik, B.1.,* edited by Moe (København: Reitzel, 1841);

Maria Furuhjelm, *Nogle Ord til Nordens Mødre: en Bog for Folket,* translated into Norwegian by Martha Sanne, introduction by Moe (Christiania: Cammermeyer, 1877).

Jørgen Moe is best known for his work with Peter Christian Asbjørnsen on the seminal *Norske Folkeeventyr* (Norwegian Folktales; translated as *Popular Tales from the Norse,* 1859) which they began to publish in 1841 and revised throughout their careers. The work of the collaborators represented a major contribution to the resurgence and resurrection of Norwegian national, cultural, and linguistic identity in the middle decades of the nineteenth century. By collecting and editing folktales gathered from local informants throughout rural Norway, Asbjørnsen and Moe explored material that had been largely ignored by scholars. Their focus on folk literature not only highlighted sources of literary and cultural significance but also played into the debate about the need for an autonomous written Norwegian language, which had been replaced by written Danish centuries earlier, during the union with Denmark. With *Norske Folkeeventyr* Asbjørnsen and Moe contributed to the reclamation of this linguistic identity by retelling the tales in a manner closer to the spoken Norwegian of the day, incorporating many words, phrases, and syntactical structures common to Norwegian but utterly absent from written Danish. Their work is a significant part of the National Romantic Movement as Norwegians strove for a distinct cultural identity and state.

Moe's work on *Norske Folkeeventyr,* however, does not encompass the whole of his literary production. When *Norske Folkeeventyr* was published, Moe was twenty-eight and had just begun his career as a writer. He spent much of the 1840s working with Asbjørnsen on their collections of folktales, but in 1849 he came out with a work of his own, *Digte* (Poems), which signaled a shift in his life and career. Thereafter, he focused less on his work as a folklorist and more on his own writing. *Digte* and his other works from the 1850s have remained popular in Norway, appearing in updated editions, and many of his stories and poems are still used in Norwegian children's readers. Abroad, however, Moe's individual works have remained largely unread and untranslated. His primary contribution to the Norwegian and international literary canon remains *Norske Folkeeventyr,* which stands alongside the groundbreaking work of the brothers Jacob and Wilhelm Grimm and other well-known folklorists.

The fourth of eight children, Jørgen Engebretsen Moe was born on 22 April 1813 on the family estate in the Hole parish of the traditional district of Ringerike. The estate had been handed down to Moe's mother, Marthe Jørgensdatter, from her father; Moe's father, Engebret Olsen Moe, came from Vestre Vaker in Norderhov. Both parents were descended from long lines of landed farmers, and Moe's father was a prominent figure in the community and the nation, serving as a representative to the Storting (Parliament) and as mayor of Hole the year before his death. Moe's early life on the estate was crucial to his development as a folklorist and writer. According to an 1835 census, there were forty-one people living on the estate, including Moe's family, servants, farmhands, and free farmers. His father cultivated a strong working and spiritual fellowship among all members of his household, and Jørgen Moe came into intimate personal contact with all classes of people, making him aware from an early age of traditional folk life and culture. According to biographer Ørnulf Hodne in *Jørgen Moe: folkeminnesamler–dikter–prest* (1982, Jørgen Moe: Folklorist, Poet, Priest), Moe heard folktales and songs from such people as the milkmaid "Gamle Gunnhild" (Old Gunnhild), Ole Sagvolden, Engebret Askjem, and his sisters, Beate and Maren–all of whom either inspired his later work or even directly contributed to it.

In 1826 Moe left the family estate for the first time, to study for his college entrance exam with Chaplain Christian Støren at Norderhov Rectory. Here, Moe met and became fast friends with Asbjørnsen, who was one year older. As biographer Sonja Hagemann notes in *Jørgen Moe: barnas dikter* (1963, Jørgen Moe: Children's Poet), the young men shared a common interest in literature and the study of folklore. Despite the friendship of Asbjørnsen, Moe in 1829 suffered what was to become one of many personal crises throughout his life. He sank into a deep depression, but recovered enough to take his college entrance exams in Christiania (now Oslo) in January 1830.

Cover for Moe's first book, Samling af Sange, Folkeviser og Stev i norske Almuedialekter *(A Collection of Songs, Ballads, and Folk Verse in Popular Norwegian Dialects), published in 1840 (J. W. Cappelen Auction Catalogue 45, 14 December 2006)*

Moe's time at the University of Christiania was busy. Despite his father's wishes that he study law, Moe decided to study theology instead. He became actively involved in student life at the university. From 1832 to 1834 Moe belonged to *Studentersamfundet* (The Student Society) and participated in many of the contemporary cultural, political, and aesthetic debates concerning Norway and Europe. Moe's political and cultural leanings apparently drew him to the side of Johan Sebastian Welhaven in the disputes between Welhaven and Henrik Wergeland. Francis Bull reports that Moe declared in his personal papers that Wergeland was a "svin" (swine). Whatever the ramifications of his early alliances, Moe signed up as a contributor to the hand-written paper of *Studentersamfundet* and in fall 1833 became its editor. He wrote polemic and religious poetry and studied the works of the era's most influential authors, including Johann Wolfgang von Goethe, Adam Oehlenschläger, Christian Winther, Henrik Anker Bjerregaard, and Mauritz Hansen.

To support himself while studying at the university, Moe took the position of private home tutor for a merchant in Christiania. During this time he became engaged to a much younger woman but then fell in love with another woman, Catharina Daae, from western Norway, whom he felt was a kindred spirit. Because of the mores of the time he could not simply break his earlier engagement. Moe's internal conflict led to a serious bout with depression in the fall of 1834. He was so afflicted that he withdrew from the university and returned to the family estate. In 1835 his fiancée's father suggested that they break off the engagement.

The two years Moe spent battling depression at his family home proved vital to his early work as a folklorist. He corresponded frequently with Asbjørnsen, describing his plans for their work together and his struggles as a writer. In a letter of 31 October 1834 Moe wrote: "mit Liv, siger jeg, er saa tømt, saa ødt som Høstnaturen her, og denne trykkende Stilhed qvæler ethvert Forsøg paa selv at analysere den.... Jeg har forsøgt at drømme mig ind i min Barneverden igjen; hver Busk, hver Høi og Dal, ja hver Steen er jo et Symbol af den Tids lyse Leg; men uvilkaarlig paatrænger sig mig strax Sammeligningen mellem nu og da" (my life, I say, is as empty, as deserted as the nature of fall here, and this pressing silence strangles every attempt even to analyze it.... I have tried to dream myself back into my childhood world again; every bush, every height and valley, yes every stone is a symbol of that time's carefree play; but the comparison between then and now immediately imposes itself on me). Moe realized that in order to work and write, he needed to return to a world similar to that of his childhood. He needed to embrace a simpler life, closer to the natural world—such as he envisioned in his poetry—removed from the confusing struggles of his adult existence. Moe yearned for a simpler structure, a simpler discourse, and a move away from the literary traditions that had dominated.

While orienting himself to his new goals and literary objectives, Moe expanded his interests in folktale collections published in Norway, Denmark, and Germany. At this time he was probably familiar with Andreas Faye's *Norske Folkesagn* (1844, Norwegian Folk Legends) and the Grimm brothers' *Kinder- und Hausmärchen* (1812, 1815, Children's and Household Tales; translated as *German Popular Stories,* 1823, 1826), which had inspired Faye. Hodne suggests that Moe was less drawn to such works as achievements per se than as pioneering efforts that indicated a way forward for his own interests. The work of the Grimm brothers demonstrated that one could be faithful to the original sources while freely interpreting them. Moe was thus able to see that folklore research would provide an objective basis for his writing while enabling him to express his own artistic and literary aspirations.

In the spring of 1837 Moe and Asbjørnsen agreed to work on a collection of folktales and began their intense work, declaring they would perform their tasks "uden omdigtning, udsmykning eller digterisk behandling" (without rewriting, embellishment, or authorial manipulation). Moe let his scientific interest in the folktale take over in this respect, and he avoided allowing his own personal beliefs and artistic desires to influence his work. By the end of the year, Asbjørnsen had published a collection of five magic tales and three legends, *Nor: En Billedbog for den Norske Ungdom* (Mite: A Picture-Book for Norwegian Children), which included an anonymous foreword by Moe.

By 1838 Moe's literary ambitions were also beginning to bear fruit, as he published a fairytale-like poem, "Mus og Kat. Eventyr for Lullemand" (Mouse and Cat. A Tale for the Sandman), in the periodical *Billed-Magazin for Børn* (Picture Magazine for Children). Exemplifying many of the characteristics Moe sought to bring to his writing, the poem is childlike, without motives or moralization, like much of literature written for children at the time, and free of the abstractions common to literature of the age. Moe finally finished his university exam in theology in 1839.

Although Moe wanted to concentrate on his own work, he had to take various teaching positions in order to support himself—an difficult circumstance that would last thirteen years. His first job was that of private tutor at Hasselberg in Norderhov, in the Ringerike district, and he later assisted in the establishment of the Ringerike Middelskole (Ringerike Middle School). Following this assignment, he taught at private schools and homes in Christiania, and in 1845 he secured a position at Krigsskolen (The Military Academy) that would last until 1853.

Even though Moe was frustrated by the conflict between his teaching and work, he was productive as a folklore researcher and a writer during these years. In 1840 Moe on his own published *Samling af Sange, Folkeviser og Stev i norske Almuedialekter* (A Collection of Songs, Ballads, and Folk Verse in Popular Norwegian Dialects). While most of the songs are the work of various rural poets, with only a few truly traditional songs, the collection is nevertheless the first volume of folksongs printed in Norway. Moe's foreword to the book set forth his beliefs about the importance of folklore for a national literature and for a new Norwegian written language. In that same year Moe and Asbjørnsen finally found a publisher for their folklore and released an advertisement for subscriptions to the book with the preliminary title *Norske Folke og Barneeventyr* (Norwegian Folk and Children's Tales).

In 1841 the publisher Johan Dahl brought out an untitled ninety-eight-page pamphlet of Moe and Asbjørnsen's work; in 1844 three more pamphlets were collected as the second volume of the first edition of *Norske Folkeeventyr*. In the foreword to their first volume Moe and Asbjørnsen wrote that they hoped to reconstruct the tales "med Troskab—uden Forskjønnelse af nogen Omstændighed eller forandring af nogen Begivenhed" (with fidelity—without embellishment by any means or the change of any event). Moe and Asbjørnsen had to work, however, largely with notes and from what they remembered of their contact with their informants. In Moe's notes from the time, he wrote about the tale "Herreperr":

En Mand og en Kone—3 sønner—langt borte i en Skov boede de—de døde—efter dem: en Gryde, en Takke, en Katte—den Ældste Gryden—Mellemste Takken—Yngste Katten.—Ældste: naar jeg laaner bort Gryden, saa faaer jeg skrabe den.—Mellemste: Naar jeg laaner bort Takken, saa faaer jeg Lefse.—Den Yngste: Om jeg laaner bort Katten saa faaer jeg ikke noget; faaer Katten lidt Melk saa vil hun ha'e den selv.

(A man and a woman—3 sons—they lived far away in a forest—they left: a kettle, an iron griddle, a cat—the oldest the kettle—the middle son the iron griddle—the youngest the cat.—The oldest: When I lend out the kettle, I'll get to scrape it.—The middle son: When I lend out the griddle, I'll get lefse [soft flatbread].—The youngest: If I lend out the cat, I'll get nothing; if the cat gets a little milk, it'll get to have it itself.)

The work of Moe and Asbjørnsen was, therefore, not an exact reconstruction but a retelling of what they heard on their journeys throughout Norway. Their process created a distance between the stories they were told and the texts they delivered in their collections. Moe conscientiously attempted to retain the discourse of the folktales to make up for this problem, preserving as much of the oral tradition as he could. The written texts of the tales often included much of the popularly used Norwegian vocabulary, Norwegian syntax, and idiomatic usage, essentially building a kind of new "Norwegianized" version of the written Danish with which they had to work.

While Moe considered the original rhetoric as an important element of his work, Asbjørnsen was not always in complete agreement with Moe about his preservation of certain structures. In their correspondence he sometimes reproached Moe for using too many dialect constructions. In a letter he went so far as to call them "childish plebeianism." Asbjørnsen eventually backed away from this position, and, like Moe, he tried to model his style on the oral variants they both heard and collected. The overall design of their tales represented a compromise between some use of dialect and spoken Norwegian and a careful retouching of the tales

Cover for the 1844 edition of Moe and Peter Christen Asbjørnsen's seminal collection (Norwegian Folktales; translated as Popular Tales from the Norse, 1854), which originally appeared as four pamphlets in 1841 and 1844 (from a facsimile edition [Oslo: Damms Antikvariat, 1993]; Damms Antikvariat)

to make them more readable. The tales have lost some of their spoken quality with the addition of smaller details not present in Moe and Asbjørnsen's notes, but the changes the two researchers made did not create new tales, simply tales that were clearer to follow in a literary context.

In addition to working with Asbjørnsen in the early 1840s, Moe continued to publish versions of folktales, research, and his own poetry independently. In the second edition of *H. E. Fearnley: Smaadigte til Udenadlæsning* (1842, H. E. Fearnley: Short Poems to be Read Aloud) Moe contributed the poem "Gjerterudsfuglen" (The Black Woodpecker) that he had learned from Gamle Gunnhild, the milkmaid of the Moe estate from his youth. The poem is based on the legend of the creation of the black woodpecker, a tale which Moe declared to be "Ægtenorsk" (truly Norwegian) because of its description of the origins of a portion of the Norwegian landscape. Hagemann notes that the tale is contained within a Christian myth.

During the summers of 1846 and 1847 Moe went on two journeys to collect folktales, for which he received a stipend from the University of Christiania. Moe centered his travels on the areas of Hardanger, Telemark, and Setesdalen in southeastern and south-central Norway. These journeys not only provided material for Moe's folkloric and literary interests but also allowed him to leave the city of Christiania, which he felt was oppressive. Moe saw these journeys as a method of cleansing himself and as a source of inspiration for his spiritual and intellectual life. Following each journey, Moe delivered reports to the University of Christiania. Most important for Moe, these trips gave him the strength he needed to begin work on his own writing.

On 28 November 1848 Moe applied for another stipend to continue his research into folk traditions and was awarded a one-year post at the University of Christiania. In his application he made it clear that he intended to continue his journeys to collect more material. Fearful that his stipend would not be renewed in 1849, Moe wrote to Jacob Grimm in Berlin asking for advice and assistance. Despite Grimm's reassurance, Moe's fears proved justified. He was granted only a half-year's stipend for 1850, with reduced wages and expiration on 1 July 1850.

As Moe's research opportunities vanished, he began to spend more time working on his literary aspirations. In 1849 he published his collection *Digte*. Many of the poems from *Digte* are still read in Norway, particularly by schoolchildren, including "Slædefart" (Sledding), "Blomster-Ole" (Flower-Ole), and "En Søndagsmorgen" (A Sunday Morning). While Moe did not intend these poems for children specifically, they were based in large part on the tales he heard as a child, and he often tried to achieve a childlike perspective. In a letter to Asbjørnsen, Moe mentioned that he realized that young readers could enjoy the poems. The unpretentious introduction to *Digte* was characteristic of Moe's collection as a whole. In his poems Moe made use of a first-person narrator, as in "Sætergjentens Søndag" (The Chalet Girl's Sunday), in which the speaker longs for a beloved and for membership in a community. While Moe is distanced from the speaker, he is able to bring to her plight his own emotion, realizing in the poem his depression and angst over his life and work.

In 1850 Moe published *I Brønden og i Tjærnet: Smaahistorier for Børn* (In the Well and in the Pond: Short Stories for Children). This collection is still read in Norway, and has remained unchanged since its publication, apart from minor normalizations in spelling and grammar to fit the modern written language. Moe's text represents the world from a child's point of view, writing from the perspective of two young siblings, Beate and Viggo. The world in which Beate lives is filled with objects that come to life–especially her doll Lille-Beate (Little Beate), who gives Beate advice and guides her through her childhood. Many of the stories are inspired by a central Romantic motif, under which Moe invokes the atmosphere of the folktale by bringing the fantastic in contact with the realistic.

In February 1850 Moe returned to the family estate. In a 17 August 1852 letter to Camilla Collett he wrote: "Jeg længes nu netop efter at komme bort herfra for Alvor, op i en grøn Fjelddal, med Birkeløvsduft og friske naturlige Døler for at prøve hvad jeg med Herrens Hjælp og i hans Tjeneste, om end med svake Kræfter, formaaer" (I long at this very moment to come away from here in earnest, up in a green mountain valley, with the scent of birch leaves and refreshing, unaffected rural people to try what I can with the help of God and in his service, what one with weak strength can manage). In 1853 Moe was ordained a minister and married twenty-year-old Johanne Frederikke Sophie. Moe and his wife moved from Christiania to Krødsherad, a small rural district to the northwest of the city where Moe had his first position as a minister.

In 1855 Moe published his final work, *At hænge paa Juletræet: nogle faa Digte* (Decorating the Christmas Tree: A Few Poems); it was republished in 1859 as *En Liden Julegave: Gammelt og Nyt* (A Small Christmas Gift: Old and New). The collection centers on religious themes, and its style is in keeping with Moe's work as a minister. He uses a simple, conversational tone and reveals a longing for an unphilosophical, spontaneous life free from pride. "Alle skapningen sukker tilsammen i smerte" (All Creation Sighs Together in Sorrow) is among the poems in the collection that have been included in Norwegian hymnbooks.

Moe spent the rest of his life as a minister in the parishes of Krødsherad and Sigdal and in Bragernes and Vestre Aker. Because of the large amount of work involved in his ministry, he had little time for the folklore on which he had worked so eagerly earlier in life. In 1865 he turned over all of his collected notes on folktales to Asbjørnsen and Sophus Bugge, essentially ending his career as a folklorist. In 1875 he became bishop of Christiansand. He died on 27 March 1882.

Jørgen Moe is best remembered for his contributions to *Norske Folkeeventyr*, a work that has been published in Norway many times and been translated both wholly or in part into English and other languages. It is read all over the world, with new editions and translations still being published in the twenty-first century.

Letters:
Fra det nationale gjennembruds tid: breve fra Jøgen Moe til P. Chr. Asbjørnsen og andre, edited by Andres Krogvig (Christiania: Aschehoug, 1915).

Biographies:
Moltke Moe, *P. Chr. Asbjørnsen, Jørgen Moe, Ivar Aasen* (Christiania: Malling, 1915);

Christen L. Dahler, *Jørgen Moe: et digterliv* (Christiania: Sarheim, 1916);

Finn Grimnes, *Dikteren Jørgen Moe* (Oslo: Malling, 1929);

Sonja Hagemann, *Jørgen Moe: barnas dikter* (Oslo: Aschehoug, 1963);

Ørnulf Hodne, *Jørgen Moe: folkeminnesamler–dikter–prest* (Oslo: Universitetsforlaget, 1982).

References:
Sigurd Aa. Aarnes, "Predikanten Jørgen Moe," *Kirke og Kultur* (1966): 131–145;

Hallvard Bakken, "Jørgen Moe som sagnforteller," *Edda: Nordisk Tidsskrift for Litteraturforskning* (1935): 476–479;

Francis Bull, "Samlere og diktere: Asbjørnsen, Moe Landstad og andre," in *Norsk Litteratur Historie,* volume 3, edited by Bull and others (Oslo: Aschehoug, 1959), pp. 465–504;

Ørnulf Hodne, *Jørgen Moe og folkeeventyrene: en studie i nasjonalromantisk folkloristikk* (Oslo: Universitetsforlaget, 1979);

Anders Krogvig, *Bøker og Mennesker* (Christiania: Aschehoug, 1919);

Knut Liestøl, "Jørgen Moe som eventyrforteljar," *Syn og Segn* (1932): 145–156;

Egil Sundland, *"Det var en gang–et menneske": tolkninger av Asbjørnsen og Moes undereventyr som allegorier på menneskelig innsikt og erkjennelse* (Oslo: Cappelen, 1995);

Knud Wentzel, *Eventyr-studier* (Odense: Odense Universitetsforlaget, 1998).

Papers:
Most of Jørgen Engebretsen Moe's papers, letters, and other effects are at the Nasjonalbiblioteket (National Library) in Oslo.

Andreas Munch
(19 October 1811 – 27 June 1884)

Henning Howlid Wærp
University of Tromsø

Translated by Lanae H. Isaacson

BOOKS: *Ephemerer: dikt* (Christiania: Johan Dahl, 1836);

Sangerinden: et Digt (Christiania: Johan Dahl, 1837);

Kong Sverres Ungdom: Drama i 3 Acter (Christiania: Johan Dahl, 1837);

Donna Clara: en Natscene (Christiania: Johan Dahl, 1840);

Den Eensomme: en Sjælehistorie (Christiania: Johan Dahl, 1846);

Digte, gamle og nye (Christiania: Johan Dahl, 1848);

Billeder fra Nord og Syd (Christiania: Wulfsberg, 1849);

Nye Digte (Christiania: Tønsberg, 1850);

Sorg og Trøst: Nogle Digte (Christiania: Feilberg & Landmark, 1852);

Salomon de Caus: Dramatisk Digtning (Christiania: Tønsberg, 1854); translated by John Chapman as *Salomon de Caus: A Lyric Drama* (London, 1855);

Digte og fortællinger, ældre og nyere (Christiania: Tønsberg, 1855);

En Aften paa Giske, historisk Skuespil i een Akt (Christiania: Tønsberg, 1855);

Lord William Russell: Historisk Tragødie i fem Akter (Christiania: Tønsberg, 1857); translated by John Heyliger Burt as *William and Rachel Russell: A Tragedy in Five Acts* (London, 1862);

Kongehallen i Bergen: Festspil med Sang i 1 Akt (Christiania, 1860);

Nyeste Digte (Christiania: Tønsberg, 1861);

Pigen fra Norge: historisk-romantisk fortælling (Christiania: Tønsberg, 1861); translated by Mrs. Robert Birkbeck as *The Maid of Norway: An Historical Romance* (London: Chatto & Windus, 1878);

Nye Digte: Andet forøgede Oplag (Christiania: Tønsberg, 1862);

Hertug Skule: Tragoedie i fem Akter (Copenhagen: Gad, 1864);

Jesu Billede: Digtkrands efter en romersk Legende (Christiania: Cappelen, 1865);

Reiseminder (Christiania: Tønsberg, 1865);

Andreas Munch (Norwegian Folk Museum)

Eftersommer: Ny Digtsammling (Copenhagen: Forlagsbureauet, 1867);

Moder og Søn: Drama i tre akter (Copenhagen: Gad, 1871);

Udvalgte Digte (Copenhagen: Forlagsbureauet, 1873);

Barndoms- og Ungdoms-Minder (Christiania: Aschehoug, 1874);

Fjældsøen: Eventyr-Drama i fire Akter (Copenhagen: Gad, 1875);

Fangen paa Munkholm: Dramatisk Billede (Christiania: Den norske Forlagsforening, 1875);

Mindedigte over norske og danske Mænd og Kvinder fra 1834 til 1877 (Christiania: Malling, 1877);

Pave og reformator: Historisk Digtning (Copenhagen: Gad, 1880);

I Finnmarken: digte (Copenhagen: Gad, 1882);

Samlede Skrifter, 4 volumes, edited by M. J. Monrad and Hartvig Lassen (Copenhagen: Gad, 1887–1890).

Editions: *Kongedatterens Brudefart: digte* (Christiania: Tønsberg, 1861);

Pigen fra Norge: historisk-romantisk fortælling (Copenhagen: Gad, 1890).

PLAY PRODUCTIONS: *Kong Sverres Ungdom,* Christiania, Christiania Theater, 4 October 1837;

Donna Clara: en Natscene, Christiania, Christiania Theater, 22 November 1840;

Salomon de Caus, Christiania, Christiania Theater, 3 September 1854;

En Aften paa Giske, Christiania, Christiania Theater, 26 April 1855;

Lord William Russell, Christiania, Christiania Theater, 13 December 1857;

Kongehallen i Bergen, Christiania, Christiania Theater, 22 August 1860;

Hertug Skule, Christiania, Christiania Theater, 5 March 1865;

En Frokost paa Slottet Schwarzenburg, Christiania, Christiania Theater, 11 December 1868;

Fjældsøen, Copenhagen, 25 May 1875.

TRANSLATIONS: Alfred Tennyson, *Enoch Arden: Digt* (Copenhagen: Forlagsbureauet, 1866);

Sir Walter Scott, *Pigen ved Søen: Romantisk Digt i sex Sange* (Copenhagen: Forlagsbureauet, 1871);

Tennyson, *Idyller om Kong Arthur* (Copenhagen: Forlagsbureauet 1876);

Nicolaus Lenau, *Faust: et Digt af Nicolai Lenau* (Copenhagen: Forlagsbureauet, 1883).

OTHER: "Tre Nætter paa Havet," in *Hjemmet og Vandringen: en Aarbog for 1847* (Christiania: Fabritius, 1847), pp. 77–88;

Poems, in *Norwegisches Bauernleben* (Düsseldorf: Eduard Schulte, 1852);

"De tre Kilders Dal. Reisebillede," in *Ved Løvfaldstid* (Christiania: Tønsberg, 1867), pp. 59–78.

SELECTED PERIODICAL PUBLICATIONS—UNCOLLECTED: "Fart paa en Jernbane," *Ny Hermoder: et æsthetisk Ugeskrift,* 1, no. 13 (1841): 290–293;

"Norsk Litteratur," *Norsk Tidsskrift for Videnskab og Litteratur* (1848): 125–132;

"Anmeldelse av nye Skrifter," *Nordisk Universitets-Tidsskrift,* no. 1 (1856): 188–191;

"Noget fra Verdensudstillingen i Paris," *Illustreret Nyhedsblad,* no. 1 (1856): 1–2; no. 2 (1856): 6–8;

"Nye Udgravninger i Rom," *Norden: Et Maanedsskrift,* no. 2 (1866): 295–307.

In the 1850s, the decade between the eclipse of Johan Sebastian Welhaven and Henrik Wergeland and the ascendancy of Henrik Ibsen and Bjørnstjerne Bjørnson, Andreas Munch was considered to be Norway's greatest writer. Munch's historical plays were performed on Norwegian and Danish stages, and several of his dramas were also translated and produced in Germany and England. His collection *Sorg og Trøst: Nogle Digte* (1852, Sorrow and Solace: Some Poems) appeared in seven editions before 1891. A gifted critic of art and literary works who was known for his accounts of travel, Munch was the editor of *Den Constitutionelle* in the 1840s. During the 1860s, Munch's house in Homansbyen, Christiania (now Oslo), was the gathering place for many of the artists and writers of the day, among them Bjørnson, Magdalene Thoresen, Camilla Collett, M. J. Monrad, A. M. Schweigaard, Edvard Grieg, and Fritz Thaulow. When Munch moved to Copenhagen, he hosted similar gatherings with Hans Christian Andersen, Christian Winter, M. A. Goldschmidt, F. Paludan-Müller, Johannes Ewald, and others in attendance. An indication of Munch's prominence in literary and artistic circles is that in 1879 the young Knut Hamsun brought his manuscript to Munch for his opinion.

The greatest testament to the esteem in which his contemporaries held Munch was perhaps the unanimous decision by Parliament to grant Munch a Writer's Wage in recognition of his literary accomplishments and the uncontested place he held in Norwegian, Nordic, and European literature. He was the first Norwegian to receive such an honor. Monrad, the philosopher and tone-setting literary critic, wrote consistently favorable reviews of Munch's books, and as late as 1887 he referred to Munch, Wergeland, and Welhaven as the three-leaf clover of great poetic spirits in Norway. But with its emphasis on *forsoning* (reconciliation) and *skjønnhet* (beauty), Munch's late Romantic writing became increasingly out of step with the times. He also consistently opposed the growing emphasis on realism in literature.

In the twenty-first century Munch has been nearly completely forgotten, not only among members of the reading public but also among literary historians: no monograph deals with his oeuvre; no biography treats his life. Yet, because it is so much a product of a particular time and place, Munch's oeuvre is all

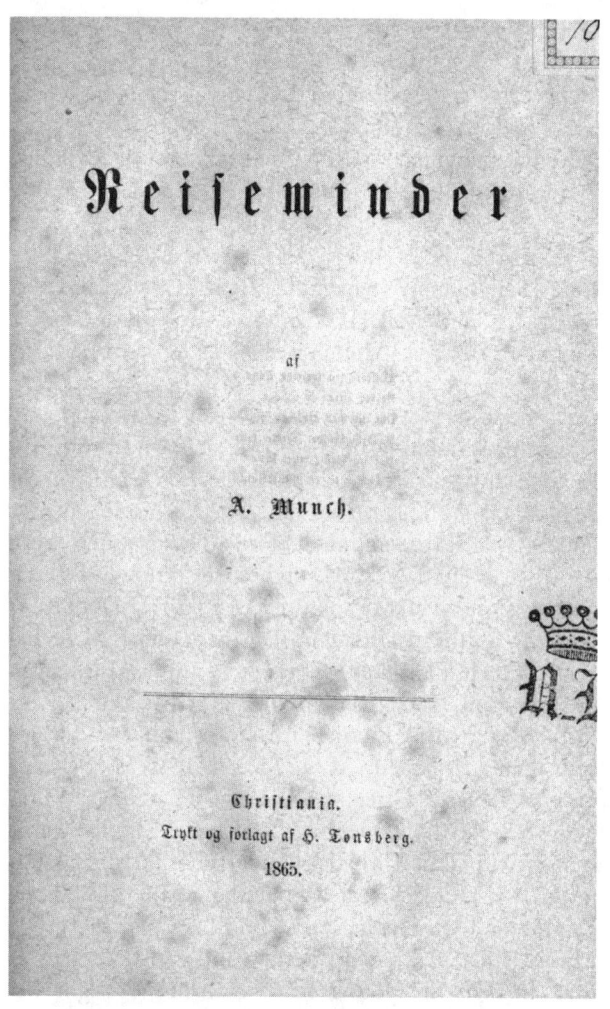

Title page for Munch's book (Travel Memories) that includes an account of the 1862 World Exhibition in London (Robarts Library, University of Toronto)

the more revealing of its cultural moment. For all of his interest in *fortidens landskap* (the landscape of the past) with its typical enthusiasms for ruins, antiquities, and historical traces in nature, he also was fascinated with *fremtidens landskap* (the landscape of the future) with its steamships and train travel. Not only did the construction of rail lines alter the landscape physically; the actual experience of the landscape took on color from the new means of transportation. While poets of the Romantic era sought to expand their horizons and awareness through works of art, the power of steam and industry created an external parallel to those efforts: "Together flow South and North / There are no longer any Boundaries / With Industry's Magic Words / We see the World Open," Munch wrote in "Over Brenner-Alp," a poem about a train trip through the Alps (1873, *Udvalgte Digte*).

The son of the writer and religious leader Johan Storm Munch and Else Munch, Andreas Munch was born on 19 October 1811 in Sande, Vestfold. He lived in Sande and Christiania until his father was appointed bishop of Kristiansand in 1823. He received his *examen artium* (Exam Degree in Arts) in 1830 and then studied philosophy and law. From 1831 to 1845 he earned a living as a copywriter in the Department of Finance.

Munch made his literary debut in 1836 with *Ephemerer* (Ephemera), a collection of poetry that holds a special place in his oeuvre. While Munch's works include sensitive, empathetic descriptions, a touch of sentimentality, and an abiding melancholy as hallmarks, the poems in *Ephemerer* express ebullient enthusiasm for the ideas of the French Revolution; sing the praises of Napoleon, Greek freedom fighters, and George Gordon, Lord Byron; and sternly criticize the paragraph of the Norwegian Constitution barring Jews from Norway. Fervent patriotism and criticism of the union with Sweden are also evident in the *Ephemerer* poems. In later collections such criticism was absent, as Munch wrote many poems honoring the Swedish monarchy.

Ephemerer was reviewed in *Den Constitutionelle* by Schweigaard, who praised Munch's independence and maturity as a writer. Schweigaard's piece was an early example of a modern literary review, for it was directed to the book-buying public. Furthermore, the review was the first criticism of poetry published in *Den Constitutionelle,* a newspaper that served as an important forum for literary criticism in the 1830s and 1840s.

Munch's next book, *Sangerinden* (1837, The Songstress), consists of a long, epic poem that fills thirty pages. The action in the poem takes place in "Italien, du mine Drømmers Land" (Italy, You, the Land of my Dreams), introducing his frequently recurring motifs—love of Italy and travel. Munch followed *Sangerinden* with the saga drama *Kong Sverres Ungdom* (1837, King Sverre's Youth), which won the prize of 100 Specidaler for the best Norwegian play written in celebration of the opening of Christiania Theater—beating out Wergeland's entry, *Campbellerne* (The Campbells). Munch's next play, *Donna Clara* (1840), was set in Spain during the Middle Ages, an era of special interest to Munch, and was translated into German and Swedish. In 1841 Munch became the editor of *Den Constitutionelle,* a post he held until 1846. "The literary activity of *Den Constitutionelle* was crucial and epochal in the history of the press," writes the press historian Gunnar Christie Wasberg. "*Den Constitutionelle* raised the level of debate from the constant stream of curses and insinuations that were characteristic of the Norwegian press until then."

With his marriage in 1844 to Charlotte Amalie Juul, a merchant's daughter with whom he had two sons, Munch became financially independent. In 1846 he and his family embarked on a two-year study tour of France, Italy, Switzerland, and Germany, providing material for many of his later poems. Also in 1846 he published the story *Den Eensomme* (The Lonely One), which captures the essential melancholy of his writings. *Den Eensomme* depicts the hermit-like existence of a house tutor in an isolated Norwegian mountain valley. In his diary the lonely one reflects on the connection between people and nature, constantly searching for a more meaningful experience in his life but never finding it. In the end, the lonely one dies alone in a small cabin on the mountain. In 1848 Munch published *Digte, gamle og nye* (Poems, Old and New), a varied collection of poems that he had written in the twelve years following his debut. Occasional poems—celebratory songs and eulogies—comprise a special section in *Digte, gamle og nye* and in Munch's other collections.

In the story "Den sidste Biskop i Hamar" (The Last Bishop of Hamar) in the collection *Billeder fra Nord og Syd* (1849, Pictures from North and South) Munch recounts an episode from the time of the Reformation. Although Munch was a Lutheran, he was fascinated by the Catholic religious life of the Middle Ages, and he describes Catholicism with remarkable insight in the story.

Munch followed *Billeder fra Nord og Syd* with *Nye Digte* (1850, New Poems). *Nye Digte* consists of independent poems such as the tableau poem "Brudefærden" (Wedding Procession), written to complement Adolph Tidemand and Hans Gude's painting *Brudefærd i Hardanger* (Wedding Procession in Hardanger), and a cycle of romances, "Kongedatterens Brudefart: et Digt i tolv Romanzer" (Bridal Procession of the Princess: A Poem in Twelve Romances). The cycle deals with Håkon Håkonsson's daughter Kristina, who was sent to Spain to marry a Spanish prince. In this poem Munch writes of two of his favorite subject areas: the Middle Ages and the meeting of the cultures of northern and southern Europe.

In 1850 Munch's wife and one of his sons died. Their deaths increased the melancholy in Munch's poetry and also led to constant, restless travel. Although Munch believed his poetry collections of 1848 and 1850 to be his best works, the public of his day preferred the 1852 volume *Sorg og Trøst,* a series of poems he wrote to lament the death of his wife. One of his best poems, "Paa Biblioteket" (At the Library), appears in *Sorg og Trøst;* it was written after he had secured an appointment as an amanuensis at the University Library. It is one of the few Munch poems that appear in modern anthologies:

Munch's second wife, the former Amalie Raben, in 1896. They were married in 1865 (painting by Anna E. Munch; from the Norwegian Nurses Association's online magazine, Sykepleiens <http://www.sykepleien.no/ikbViewer/page/sykepleien/vis/artikkel-nyhet?p_document_id=264307>).

Vær hilsede
I stille Haller!
Stille og fredede som Klosterets,
Men ikke dumpe, ikke lukkede
Som disse!
Netop da Verden
Med dens Lyst og dens Farver
Havde lukket sig for mig—
Da Sorgens Dække var faldet
Mellem mig og de Levendes Land—
Stille Haller! Da aabnede I
Eders Porte for den Udstødte

(Hail
You still Halls!
Still and peaceful as the Cloisters,
But not hollow, not closed
Like those!
Just when the World
With its Joys and Colors
Had closed for me—
When the Veil over of Sorrow had fallen
Between me and the Land of the Living—
Still Halls! Then You opened
Your Portals for the One cast away)

Often brought out in new editions, *Sorg og Trøst* was also translated into German and set to music by the Swedish composer Per Ulrik Stenhammar as *Sorg och Tröst, satta i musik för röst med piano* (1865, Sorrow and Solace, Set to Music for Voice and Piano). After the success of *Sorg og Trøst,* Munch's publisher, Christian Tønsberg, offered to republish *Ephemerer,* which had long been unavailable, but Munch decided instead to publish a collection of what he thought to be his best work, *Digte og fortællinger, ældre og nyere* (1855, Poems and Stories, Old and New).

Munch's historical drama *Salomon de Caus* (1854; translated, 1855), deals with the French engineer de Caus, who laid the groundwork for construction of the steam engine. According to the literary historian Hans Olaf Hansen, the play drew "great attention, not only in the poet's homeland but also abroad, and especially in Germany." Munch's next play, *En Aften paa Giske* (1855, An Evening at Giske), was set in the High Middle Ages in Norway.

Munch enjoyed even greater success and acclaim with his dramatic tragedy set in England in the 1600s, *Lord William Russell* (1857; translated as *William and Rachel Russell,* 1862). The play was performed thirty times at Christiania Theater and eleven times at the Royal Theater in Copenhagen; Ibsen wrote a favorable review of it in the 20 December 1857 issue of *Illustreret Nyhedsblad. Lord William Russell* was attacked and praised by critics from the opposing idealistic and realistic camps. An advocate of realism, Georg Brandes criticized *Lord William Russell* in an 1869 issue of *Illustreret Tidende* as "one of the last possible examples" of what he characterized as the school and manner of the early nineteenth-century Danish playwright Adam Oehlenschläger:

> A student of Oehlenschläger would rather praise the magnificence of *[Lord William Russell]* than delve into it and break it down in order to understand, he would praise rather than characterize. The intent of the follower of Oehlenschläger is to move and excite, not to analyze and examine; his method is a lyrical rhetoric that does not lead the playgoer to introspection but to a glance upward, out into the blue.

Diametrically opposed to the view of Brandes, Monrad championed the play in his long essay *Fragmentariske Studier over A. Munchs Tragødie:* Lord William Russell (1858, Fragmentary Studies of A. Munch's Tragedy: *Lord William Russell*), calling it a first-class example of the tragedy genre:

> The tragic hero is strong and direct; he is led by an unswerving, easily understood purpose and controlled by a strong, clear, complete pathos which he announces or rather declaims in strong, clear, full tones; he walks with an open visor and erect head, without precondition or ulterior motive, and, when he falls, he falls clearly, directly, with no hesitation, he falls, if we dare use such a vapid expression, to his full length, an undeniable, complete, resounding fall.

Munch's drama was scarcely meant to be psychological or realistic. His approach in the play was suggested by his enthusiastic description of the English artist Sir George Hayler's historical painting *Lord William Russell before His Judges* in "Noget fra Verdensudstillingen i Paris" (Something from the World Exposition in Paris), a travel letter he published in *Illustreret Nyhedsblad* in 1856:

> On one side, the judges selected and appointed by the Court, they wear red cloaks and their faces are merry or vacant, one can see that the Blood Judgment has fallen. On the other side, Lord Russell, his wife, in all their love and pristine nobility.

Like the painting, the play idealizes the defendant and can be read as an attempt to realize the "ideal conflict" Hayler's painting reveals. In his play Munch uses the trial in the Old Bailey as the central scene. Clearly, Munch would not have felt at all undone by Brandes's criticism of the drama according to the tenets of realism. "Let us compare the piece with history for a moment," Brandes wrote. "Lady Russell spent fourteen years in a joyless marriage to another man, and therefore she was hardly the Seraphine that the fifteen-year-old Juliet [was]." Munch could certainly have responded that *Lord William Russell* was not a character study of an individual but an analysis of how Russell resigned himself to dying as a spokesman for higher truth and how love proved a highly effective power in human life. The play was translated into German and into English.

In 1861 Munch published *Pigen fra Norge* (translated as *The Maid of Norway,* 1878), a romantic historical novel influenced by the writing of B. S. Ingemann and Sir Walter Scott. His *Nyeste Digte* (1861, Newest Poems) included "Hilsen til de unge Studenter" (Greetings to the Young Students), a song that was sung at matriculation for new students at the University of Oslo until 1969:

> Helligt er Studentens Kald!
> Vær så hilset, Brødre unge,
> Her I Aandens Tempelhal!
> Hør vor glade Velkomst runge!
>
> (Holy is the Student's Call!
> Be greeted, Young Brothers,
> Here in the Hall of the Temple of the Spirit!
> Hear our glad Welcome resound!)

The poetry garland "Fra Throndhjems-Reisen" (From Trondheim Travels) comprises a separate section in *Nyeste Digte* in which Munch describes his travels to Trondheim to attend the coronation of Karl V. He had been assigned the task of writing a cantata for the coronation in Nidaros Cathedral in the city on 5 August 1860.

In 1864 Munch published the drama *Hertug Skule* (Lord Skule), which was produced in 1865 after Ibsen's *Kongsemnerene* (The Royal Pretenders). Both plays deal with the battle between Håkon Håkonsson and Lord Skule for the Norwegian throne in the 1200s. In 1865 Munch published another poetry garland, *Jesu Billede* (Picture of Christ); it is based on the medieval legend of Veronica, the woman who gave Christ her scarf to wipe the sweat from his brow and ease his suffering during the Crucifixion; when the scarf was returned to her, it bore the imprint of Christ's face. *Jesu Billede* was well received and often republished and translated. Also that year Munch married a Danish woman, Amalie Raben.

The collection *Eftersommer* (1867, Late Summer) includes a series of poems about Italy, a land with which Munch had a long association. He had lived in Italy with his first wife for two years in the 1840s and had returned with his surviving son in 1858, after having received a state travel grant for the study of art and literary history abroad. The second stay in Italy had ended with the death of his son in 1859. Munch returned to Italy for a third time in 1865 on a honeymoon with his second wife. Biographical details from Munch's life are woven into several of the poems from Italy. "Gjensyn" (Meeting Again) is a good example:

Tre Gang førte mig Skjæbnen til dig, du herlige Roma,
Mægtig endnu i dit Fald, Mindernes fredede Stad!
To Gang fyldte du mig Livsbægret med funklende Guldviin,
En Gang med bitter Malurt, tung, som din evige Sorg.
Førstegang bragte jeg dig min Ungdoms Drøm og min Elskov–
Med Poesiens Daab rigt du indviede dem.
Andengang bragte jeg dig mit Savn og min nagende Uro–
Ak–selv dit rislende Væld ei kunde bortskylle dem.
Flygte jeg maatte fra dig midt i dit Foraars Violduft.

(Three times Fate has brought me to you, glorious Rome,
Still mighty in your Decline, the hallowed City of Memory
Two times you filled the Chalice of my Life with sparkling Gold Wine,
One time, with bitter Herbs, heavy as your eternal Sorrow.

Title page for the first volume of Munch's collected writings (New York Public Library)

The first Time I brought you my youthful Dreams and my Love–
You richly blessed them, christening them with Poetry.
The second Time I brought you my Loss and my nagging Unease–
Ach–even your rustling Stream could not wash them away.
I had to flee from you in the Middle of your eternal Fragrance of Violet.)

Additional autobiographical details are included in *Reiseminder* (1865, Travel Memories) and in *Barndoms-og Ungdoms-Minder* (1874, Memories of Childhood and Youth), along with much cultural historical material. In *Reiseminder* Munch includes a description from the World Exhibition in London in 1862 that presents a horrific crowd scene, a portrait of "the mass" of panic-stricken people. The scene captures a new time: the age of urbanism. While the throngs, the masses, were previously connected to disturbances, revolutions or wars, they now appeared as part and parcel of the modern city. Munch was an early artist in describing the new phenomenon of mundane city life.

Although no record has been found of the publication of Munch's play *En Frokost paa Slottet Schwarzenburg* (Repast at Castle Schwarzenburg), it was apparently performed at the Christiania Theater in 1868. Based on a historical play by Friedrich Schiller, *En Frokost paa Slottet Schwarzenburg* takes place in 1547 and focuses on the struggle between Lutherans and the papacy. The play was performed five times at Christiania Theater.

Munch attained some success with his play *Moder og Søn: Drama i tre akter* (Mother and Son: Drama in Three Acts), which was performed fourteen times at the Royal Theater in Copenhagen in 1871. On the other hand, his *Fjældsøen: Eventyr-Drama i fire Akter* (1875, Mountain Lake: An Adventure-Drama in Four Acts) was only performed three times at the same theater. The action in another play published in 1875, *Fangen paa Munkholm: Dramatisk Billede* (The Prisoner of Munkholm: Dramatic Picture), takes place on a small island near Trondheim. The play deals with the Danish politician Peder Griffenfeld, who was found guilty of treason in 1676 and was imprisoned at Munkholm Fortress from 1680 to 1698.

Mindedigte over norske og danske Mænd og Kvinder fra 1834 til 1877 (1877, Eulogies for Norwegian and Danish Men and Women, from 1834 to 1877) shows Munch's impressive gift for versification and his talent for writing public poetry. The fact that eulogies, celebratory songs, prologues, and cantatas for official occasions constitute an important part of Munch's lyrical production and occupy such a central and accepted place in his collections must be understood within the context of the contemporary reaction to that type of poetry. As opposed to the modern understanding of the lyric as a personal expression, such poetry was considered a a noteworthy branch of lyric poetry in Munch's era. The poetry cycle *Pave og reformator* (1880, Pope and Reformer), Munch's last great work, deals with Adrian of Utretcht, who was elected pope in 1521 and took the name Hadrian VI. His last book, *I Finnmarken* (1882, In Finnmark), is a poem of twenty-one stanzas that depicted a violent storm and the lives of a fishing family in Finnmark.

During his last years Munch played host to a wide circle of guests at his summer house in Denmark, "Villa Marina." He was member of Det kongelige Videnskabernes Selskab in Trondheim from 1858, Videnselskabet in Christiania from 1862, and Vetenskaps- och Vitterhets-Samhället in Gothenburg from 1866, and he received several decorations from the Swedish-Norwegian king. He died in Denmark on 27 June 1884 and was brought back to Norway to be buried at Vor Frelsers Gravlund, next to his first wife. On the one-year anniversary of his death a memorial was unveiled by his second wife.

On Munch's death, Collett praised his writing:

> Andreas Munch represents an element in our Norwegian social life that we miss most deeply, perhaps without realizing it: the element of the heart, the emotions, the element that we identify with the female in contrast to the ferocity of the battleground and the unwillingness to compromise and make amends that seem to be the exclusive domain of the other half of "Christian humanity" . . . It is in such societies that poets such as A. Munch step forth as intermediaries, and perhaps that is why we classify him as a poet for women . . . And yet—the stronger sex is now in charge and sets contemporary trends and customs; that is why voices such as Andreas Munch's have greater difficulty reaching us and why he has not been as valued as he fully deserved.

According to Collett, Munch suffered the same fate as contemporary women writers who received little respect from male writers and critics.

For the modern reader, the works of Andreas Munch are particularly interesting for the author's response to technology and the process of modernization. His travel letters and reports from exhibitions and presentations at home and abroad are especially notable. Some pieces, such as "Fart paa en Jernbane" (1841, Journey on a Railroad), and his reports on the 1865 World Exhibition in Paris that were published in *Illustreret Nyhedsblad* were not included in his books and appear only in his *Samlede Skrifter* (Collected Writings). His writings provide a good illustration of a writer with a Romantic sensibility beginning to confront modern urban life and industrialization.

References:

Sigurd Aa. Aarnes, *"Æstetisk Lutheraner" og andre studier i norsk senromantikk* (Bergen: Universitetsforlaget, 1968);

Aarnes, "Inn og ut av kanon—Andreas Munch som eksempel," *Nordica Bergensia*, 17 (1998): 168-187;

Edvard Beyer and Morten Moi, *Norsk litteraturkritikks historie*, volume 1 (Oslo: Universitetsforlaget, 1990), pp. 139-176;

Georg Brandes, "Lord William Russell," *Illustreret Tidende*, 519 (1869): 423-424;

Camilla Collett, "Et mindesmerke over A. Munch," in her *Samlede Verker,* volume 3 (Christiania: Gyldendal, 1913), pp. 395–396;

Hans Olaf Hansen, *Den norske Literatur fra 1814 indtil vore Dage* (Copenhagen: Fr. Wøldike, 1862), pp. 109–127;

Søren Kjørup, "Tekstens billede–Om Andreas Munchs digt 'Brudefærden,'" in *Beiträge zur nordischen Pholologie 19: Nordische Romantik, Aktender XVIII. Studienkonferenz der IASS 1988,* edited by Oskar Bandle and others (Basel: Helbing & Lichtenhahn, 1991), pp. 121–128;

Arild Linneberg, *Norsk litteraturkritikks historie,* volume 2 (Oslo: Universitetsforlaget, 1992), pp. 92–149;

M. J. Monrad, "En Aften paa Giske," *Norsk Tidsskrift for Videnskap og Litteratur* (1854–1855): 355–366;

Monrad, *Fragmentariske Studier over A. Munchs Tragødie: Lord William Russell* (Christiania: Tønsberg, 1858);

Monrad, *Literaturen og dens Dele: En Indledning til Literaturstudium* (Christiania: Fabritius, 1876), p. 28;

Monrad, "Salomon de Caus," *Norsk Tidsskrift for Videnskap og Litteratur* (1854–1855): 144–150;

Henning Howlid Wærp, *Diktet natur: Natur og landskap hos Andreas Munch, Vilhelm Krag og Hans Børli* (Oslo: Aschehoug, 1997);

Gunnar Christie Wasberg, *Norsk presse i hundre år, 1820–1920* (Oslo: Gyldendal, 1969).

Johan Storm Munch
(31 August 1778 – 26 January 1832)

Lanae H. Isaacson

BOOKS: *Sang paa en værdig Moders Fødselsdag, den 25de Februar 1801* (Copenhagen: K. H. Seidelin, 1801);
Mindetale over Christian August: holden paa Fredrikshald den 10de August 1810 (Christiania: Wulfsberg, 1810);
Norges Farvel til Hans Kongelige Høihed Christian August, Svearigets Kronprinds udg. af Johan Storm Munch (Christiania: Wulfsberg, 1810);
Skaaler: den 28de Januar 1810 (Christiania, 1810);
Fjeldblomster (Christiania: Jacob Lehmann, 1813);
Prolog bestemt til at fremsiges paa Hans Høihed Prinds Christian Frederiks Fødselsdag, Den 18de September 1813, og det Dramatiske Selskabs første Forestilling i Theater–Halv-aaret (Christiania: Jacob Lehmann, 1813);
Nordens Forening (Christiania: Jacob Lehmann, 1814);
Saga: et Fjerdingsaars-Skrift, 3 volumes (Christiania: Nørron litteratur, 1816–1820);
Stormen: Prolog ved det Dramatiske Selskabs Forestilling paa Hans Majestæt Kongens høie Fødselsdag den 26de Januar (Christian: Jacob Lehmann, 1819);
Tale i det Norske Bibelselskabs høitidelige Møde i Christiania den 21de October 1820 (Christiania: Printed at the Wulfsbergske Press by Rasmus Hviid, 1820);
Farvel til Aggershuus-Slots og Aggers Menigheder (Christiania: Grøndahl, 1823);
Præsten i Hallingdal, eller Hævnen (Christiansand: Printed for O. P. Moe by S. A. Steen, 1825);
Nogle betimelige Ord om Nødvendigheden af at indskrænke Brændevinets Misbrug og den ved Lov af 1ste Juli 1816 tilladte Brændevinsbrænden i Fædrelandet: tilegnede Kongeriget Norges Femte ordentlige Storthing (Kristiansand: Printed by O. P. Moe for S. A. Steen, 1827);
I kveld er eg glad: folkevise bearb. Av Knut Nystedt: tekst av J. St. Munch (Oslo: Norsk musikforlaget, n.d.).

TRANSLATIONS: Virgil, *Forsøg til en metrisk Oversettelse af Virgil's Æneide, Anden Sang* (Copenhagen: K. H. Seidelin, 1804);
Gjenlyd af Swea's Sorg over Nordens store Tab (Christiania: Wulfsberg, 1810);

Johan Storm Munch (from <http://www.agderkultur.no/Bispene/side_3.htm>)

Friedrich Schiller, *Don Karlos, Infant af Spanien* (Christiania, 1812);
Jean Racine, *Athalia: Sørgespil med Chor* (Christiania: Jacob Lehmann, 1818).

The literary career of Johan Storm Munch—encompassing the Treaty of Kiel in 1814 and the transfer of Norway from the unified monarchy with Denmark to the Swedish crown—represents something of a critical crossroads in Nordic history and literature. Munch's solid support for the union with Sweden secured him the role of the favorite of the new regime, while his acquaintance with the poet Adam Oehlenschläger made Munch a witness to the flowering of Romantic poetry. His works show a growing awareness of Norwegian regional language and culture and the links between Old Norse and Norwegian rural dialects, particularly that of Gudbrandsdal, as well as the influence of Renaissance literary lions such as William Shakespeare and contemporary authors in Denmark and Germany such as Oehlenschläger and Friedrich Schiller. As Ivar Havnevik observes, "It is therefore a question of judgment as to whether Munch's lyric is the end-point for Danish-Norwegian common literature or the first evidence of Norway's new, independent literary history. Lack of independence (and imitation of other writers) point back in time, the value of innovation to the future." Munch translated Old Norse sagas, and wrote occasional poetry, such as patriotic songs and celebratory and funeral verses for members of the royal family.

The son of the parson Peter Munch of Vaage Parish and Christine Sophie Storm, Munch was born in Vaage, Oppland, on 31 August 1778. The poet Edvard Storm was his maternal uncle. He received his initial education from his father and finished his preparatory studies in 1796. He received his theology degree from the University of Copenhagen in 1799. From 1800 to 1805 he served as the house tutor to the Løvenskiold family at their estate on Sjælland. This post put him in contact with the leading families in Denmark and Norway, and in 1805 he was called by Marcus Rosenkrantz to serve as resident chaplain at Skjeberg. He went on to serve Prince Christian August as field chaplain until the prince returned to Sweden in 1810. Munch then served as an instructor at the Prince Christian August Memorial Foundation and followed that appointment with several years as a teacher and lecturer in Christiania. On 9 March 1810 he married Else Petronelle Hofgaard. The following year she gave birth to their son Andreas, who became a major writer. In 1813 Munch was named to serve the parish of Sande, and in 1817 he received the prestigious appointment of parson in Aker and chaplain to the castle of Akershus. Munch reached the pinnacle of his climb in the church with an appointment as bishop of the Kristiansand Diocese in 1823. He and his wife had a second son, Johan Storm, in 1827.

Munch began his literary career with translations such as *Forsøg til en metrisk Oversettelse af Virgil's Æneide, Anden Sang* (1804, Attempt at a Metrical Translation of Virgil's *Aeneid,* Second Song). Ever the loyal subject of the Swedish monarch and the royal family, Munch also contributed various essays after the death of Prince Christian August in the prince's honor: *Mindetale over Christian August: holden paa Fredrikshald den 10de August 1810* (1810, Eulogy for Christian August: Held at Fredrikshald the 10 August 1810), and *Norges Farvel til Hans Kongelige Høihed Christian August, Svearigets Kronprinds* (1810, Norway's Farewell to His Royal Highness Christian August, Sweden's Crown Prince). It seemed to the Swedish king that Munch was the bishop Norway needed during its time of transition for he was learned, literary, and patriotic while also being politically compliant. Munch's subsequent translations of works by Schiller and Jean Racine, though admired, have not stood the test of time.

During his ministry Munch wrote eulogies, memorials, and prologues, as was customary for a man of the cloth. He also wrote patriotic songs that became standard fare in various poetry collections and anthologies: "Norges Løve" (Norway's Lions) recalls Esaias Tegnér's "Det gamla Göta lejon" (The Old Lion of Gotland), while "De tre Høie Ord" (The Three Holiest Words) suggests Schiller's "Die Worte des Glaubens" (The Words of Belief). In neither case did Munch find his own independent expression. His patriotic poetry was generally conventional in mood and expression. An exception to this assessment is perhaps "Nordmandssang" (Song of the Norwegian), a more personal work included in his collection of poetry, which ends with the stirring line "For gamle Norge kan vi dø! For Norge vil vi leve!" (For Old Norway we can die! For Norway we will live!).

Munch's sole collection of poems is *Fjeldblomster* (1813, Mountain Flowers). The poems suggest Munch's industrious study of such contemporary writers as Schiller and Johann Wolfgang von Goethe and the influence of the Danish dramatist and poet–Munch's Copenhagen acquaintance and inspiration–Oehlenschläger. Munch clearly gained a good deal of insight and ideas for poetry and verse-making from the Danish master. "The light, flowing versification that distinguishes his poems in general, the short, bouncy verse forms he uses with a certain predilection," write Henrik Jæger and Otto Anderssen, "are apparently due to the study of Oehlenschläger." In a cycle of poems in *Fjeldblomster,* "Sommerreise i Norge 1812" (Summer Voyage in Norway 1812), Munch paints a picture of his experiences in his homeland and includes a tribute to Oehlenschläger:

O, ædle Skjald, som midt i Mulm og Nat
Paa Nordens Himmel straalte frem saa brat
Og spreder nu din skjønne Morgenrøde!
Ei værdigen kan tolke dig min Sang,
Hvor tidt mig kvæget har din Harpes Klang,
Men høit mit Hjerte banker dig imøde.

O gavned dig mit Norges Granelund!
O varst du her i denne Aftenstund,

Du skulde dig mit varme Haandtryk tyde:
Modtag mit Hjertes Tak indtil min Grav
For alt det herlige, som du os gav,
Og længe end din gyldne Harpe lyde!

(Oh, Noble Skald, who in the mire and night
In the Northern sky shone so suddenly
And spread your beautiful Red-Dawn!
My song can not do you justice,
How often has your harp soothed me,
But my heart beats wildly to greet you.

And the Fir Grove of my Norway would embrace you!
And were you here this Even Hour,
Then, you would feel my warm handshake:
Accept the Thanks of my heart until my grave
For all the Glory you gave us,
And long may your golden Harp sound!)

Although Munch intended to publish a second volume of *Fjeldblomster*, the first did not generate enough interest or income, and he gave up his plan.

From 1816 to 1820 Munch edited the review *Saga*. In the essays and studies he published in *Saga*, Munch and like-minded researchers and scholars pursued a keen interest in the Old Norse sagas. Much of their writing for *Saga* focused on translating the Icelandic sagas from Latin into modern Danish. Munch and his colleagues also shared an abiding interest in the dialects, particularly in the dialect of Gudbrandsdalen, Munch's home district. Munch compiled vocabulary lists that showed the connections between Old Norse and the contemporary dialects. He was one of the first to make connections between individual words from the old language and from spoken Norwegian. Munch's efforts to draw such direct parallels caused much debate and consternation, and he was often criticized for trying to make Norwegian rural language into Norwegian written language. Munch did much to advance the study of both Old Norse and the rural dialects. As Jæger and Anderssen point out, he was "one of the first who struck out on the road that later developments in the study of language would follow."

Twelve years after the publication of his collection of poems Munch published the play *Præsten i Hallingdal* (1825, The Pastor of Hallingdal). Munch held up the strict, unswerving, uncompromising ministers of seventeenth- and eighteenth-century Norway as models for the protagonist of his play, the minister of Hallingdal. The play was never performed, but a monologue in *Præsten i Hallingdal* suggests what Munch could have accomplished if there had been more interest and support for the poems he wrote. The passage is spoken by the pastor in the midst of summer beauty:

Aandens udspring, Skaber, Evighøie!
I dit lyse Tempel staar jeg her!
See til Støvet med dit Faderøie!
O, jeg føler, at Du est mig nær;
Dig fornemmer jeg i Bladets Susen,
Dig i Morgen-Aftenrødens Glands;
Dig jeg hører udi Stormens Brusen,
Dig Jeg ser i Nattens Stjernekrands.

I min Barm jeg hører klart din Stemme;
Dig jeg skuer i dit Sandheds Ord;
Udi Bønnen kan jeg grant fornemme,
At din Himmel stiger ned til Jord.–
O, jeg føler dybt udi mit Hjerte,
At Du elsker Støvets svage Søn,
Huldt ham fører gjennem Fryd og Smerte
Til en bedre Verden evig, skjøn.

(The Source of the Spirit, Creator, Ever High!
I stand here in your light Temple!
See down to the dust with your fatherly Eye!
O, I feel that You are near me;
I sense you in the Whisper of the Leaves,
In the Rose Dawn's Glow;
I hear you in the Roar of the Storm,
I see You in the Night's Wreath of Stars.

In my Breast I clearly hear your Voice;
I see You in your Words of Truth;
In Prayer I can sense,
That Your Heaven bows down to Earth.–
Oh, I feel deep in my Heart,
That You love the Frail Son of the dust,
Always lead him through Joy and Pain
To a better World eternal and beautiful.)

As a high church official, Munch was authoritarian, strict, and critical of those who exercised leniency with minor men of the cloth and parishioners. The ministers of the Enlightenment in Norway had given some latitude concerning the liturgy, certain offices, and priestly attire; Munch sought to bring back a degree of uniformity and enforce church regulations. Particular targets for Munch's ire were lay preachers and ministers who sympathized with lay missionaries and the Hernnhutern Movement. At the same time, Munch sought to simplify church ritual so that it would be more intelligible to ordinary members of rural congregations, but his efforts were shelved by church officials. Because Munch sought to follow church dictates closely, he made enemies as well as friends as he advanced in his religious appointments. Munch carried on a running conflict with Pastor Gabriel Kielland of Finnøy over church policies and procedures. Munch was especially critical of the misuse of alcohol in rural districts, and one of his final essays concerned laws enacted to curb alcoholism in Norway, *Nogle betimelige Ord om Nødvendigheden af at indskrænke Brændevinets Misbrug og den ved Lov af 1ste Juli*

1816 tilladte Brændevinsbrænden i Fædrelandet (1827, Some Timely Words on the Necessity of Preventing the Misuse of Brandy and the Law of First July 1816 Allowing the Distilling of Brandy in the Fatherland). For his efforts on behalf of the Norwegian religious community, Munch received a Gold Medallion as an Honorary Citizen in 1821; he became a member of Det Kongelige Norske Videnskabers Selskab (The Royal Norwegian Academy of Sciences) in 1823. A member of the Swedish Nordstjärneorden (Order of the North Star) since 1819, Munch was awarded the Cross of Commander of the same order two days before his death in Kristiansand on 26 January 1832.

Johan Storm Munch was a minor lyric poet at a crucial time in Norway's history. His fame was much eclipsed by that of his illustrious son Andreas, with whom he shared a talent for melodic verse and a lively interest in Norwegian historical sources. Munch may be seen as a man in the middle, a poet who not only looked to the past in his oeuvre but also reflected the spirit of the present. His son was the future.

References:

Ivar Havnevik, *Dikt i Norge: Lyrikkhistorie 200–2000* (Oslo: Pax, 2000), pp. 173–174;

Henrik Jæger and Otto Anderssen, *Illustreret norsk literaturhistorie,* volume 2, part 1 (Christiania: Bigler, 1896), pp. 18–27.

Sigbjørn Obstfelder

(21 November 1866 - 29 July 1900)

Jan Sjåvik
University of Washington, Seattle

BOOKS: *Digte* (Bergen: Grieg, 1893)–includes "Jeg ser," "Kval," "Nocturne," and "Barcarole"; translated by Charles Wharton Stork as "I Look," "Torture," "Nocturne," and "Barcarole," in *Anthology of Norwegian Lyrics* (Princeton: Princeton University Press, 1942);

To noveletter (Bergen: Grieg, 1895);

Korset (Copenhagen: Gyldendal, 1896);

De røde dråber (Copenhagen: Gyldendal, 1897);

En Præsts Dagbog (Copenhagen: Gyldendal, 1900); translated by James McFarlane as *A Priest's Diary* (Norwich, U.K.: Norvik Press, 1987);

Efterladte Arbeider (Copenhagen: Gyldendal, 1903)–includes "Roser," translated by Stork as "The Rose," in *Anthology of Norwegian Lyrics* (Princeton: Princeton University Press, 1942), p. 120;

Brokker og stubber: En etterlatt samling dikt og lyriske fragmenter (Oslo: Gyldendal, 1995).

Editions and Collections: *Skrifter*, 2 volumes (Christiania: Gyldendal, 1917);

Samlede skrifter, 2 volumes (Oslo: Gyldendal, 1930);

Samlede skrifter, 2 volumes (Oslo: Gyldendal, 1943);

Samlede skrifter, 3 volumes (Oslo: Gyldendal, 1950);

Dikt i samling–prosa i utvalg (Oslo: Gyldendal, 1993);

Dikt i samling, 3 volumes (Oslo: Gyldendal, 2000);

Verden er ny: Dikt, reiseskildringer, kritikk (Oslo: Den norske lyrikklubben, 2000);

Samlede dikt (Oslo: Gyldendal, 2001).

Sigbjørn Obstfelder (from Dagbladet *<http://www.dagbladet.no/kultur/2007/02/19/492495.html>)*

A symbolist writer with a Scandinavian reputation, Sigbjørn Obstfelder was one of the most important poets of the period, not only in Norwegian literature but also in Scandinavian literature. Known for his treatment of such themes as alienation, insanity, and fear of female eroticism, he profoundly influenced other Norwegian writers during the 1890s, his one brief decade of literary production. While his impact on European literature has been minor–an exception is that he may have served as the model for the protagonist in Rainer Maria Rilke's novel *Die Aufzeichnungen des Malte Laurids Brigge* (1910; translated as *The Notebooks of Malte Laurids Brigge*, 1949)–he remains popular in his native Norway, where his collected works have appeared in many editions.

Obstfelder was born in the city of Stavanger in southwestern Norway to Herman Frederik Obstfelder, a baker by trade, and his wife Serina, née Egelandsdal. The eighth of sixteen children, of whom only six reached adulthood, Obstfelder spent his childhood in an oppressive fundamentalist religious environment where every inclination toward having fun or feeling joy was considered anathema. His life became even bleaker after his mother's death in 1880, and there is reason to believe that he was still an unusually insecure young man at the time of his graduation from high school in 1884. Two years later, Obstfelder entered the University of Christiania (now Oslo) to study philology, but in 1888 he switched to the study of engineering at Christiania Technical College. His younger brother, Herman, had immigrated to the United States, settling in Milwaukee, Wisconsin, and Obstfelder hoped to follow suit. At the time of his engineering examinations in 1890, however, Obstfelder suffered a nervous breakdown—it appears that several members of his family suffered from a tendency toward mental problems—and left without completing his course of studies.

Starting in the fall of 1890 Obstfelder spent an unhappy year in the United States, constantly fighting his mental condition. After his return to Norway in the fall of 1891, the illness worsened to the point that he had to be hospitalized. He was released toward the end of the year. The hallucinations that he experienced during this period profoundly affected his writing.

Obstfelder had written his first literary exercises many years earlier, and he became increasingly serious about his artistic work during his second year at the technical school, writing several of the poems included in his first collection. After recovering from his breakdown, he resumed writing, and some of his finest poems were written during a journey through France and Belgium in the fall of 1892. *Digte* (Poems) was published a year later.

One of the central poems of *Digte*, "Jeg ser" (I Look), expresses the poet's fundamental inability to feel at home in the world. The speaker looks at the world around him:

Jeg ser på den hvide himmel,
jeg ser på de gråblå skyer,
jeg ser på den blodige sol.
Dette er altså verden.
Dette er altså klodernes hjem.
En regndråbe!

Jeg ser på de høie huse,
jeg ser på de tusende vinduer,
jeg ser på det fjerne kirketårn.
Dette er altså jorden.
Dette er altså menneskenes hjem.
De gråblå skyer samler sig. Solen blev borte.
Jeg ser på de velklædte herrer,
jeg ser på de smilende damer,
jeg ser på de ludende heste.
Hvor de gråblå skyer blir tunge.
Jeg ser, jeg ser . . .
Jeg er vist kommet på en feil klode!
Her er så underligt. . . .

(I look at the white sky,
I look at the grayish blue clouds,
I look at the bloody sun.
So this is the world.
So this is the home of planets.
A drop of rain!

I look at the tall houses,
I look at the thousand windows,
I look at the distant church tower.
So this is the earth.
So this is the home of human beings.
The grayish blue clouds gather. The sun disappeared.
I look at the well dressed gentlemen,
I look at the smiling ladies,
I look at the bent down horses.
How heavy the grayish blue clouds are getting.
I look, I look . . .
I think I have gotten to the wrong planet!
It is so strange here. . . .)

The speaker's alienation is not from such universally feared aspects of human life as suffering, pain, or evil; rather, the poet feels like a stranger to good and ample nutrition, happiness, and contentment as expressed by the smiles of the ladies, and industry and commerce as signified by the tired horses. It is the manifestations of normal human life that cause the speaker to conclude that he has ended up on the wrong planet. The natural world as found on that same planet also seems alienated, however, or at least out of harmony with the human beings who are sustained by it, for the clouds are dark and heavy; the sun is bloody; and the single animal in the poem, a representative of those beasts on whose backs human civilization may be said to rest, is weary. "Jeg ser" can be read not only as a conventional and general expression of alienation but also perhaps as a specific indictment of the lack of harmony between humanity and the natural world that accompanies the advances of modern technological and commercial civilization.

"Jeg ser" may be considered an expression of both a personal and a social problematic. "Kan speilet tale?" (Can the Mirror Speak?), on the other hand, deals with a profoundly personal question:

"Kan speilet tale?
Speilet kan tale!
Speilet skal se på dig hver morgen,
forskende,
se på dig med det dybe, kloge øie,
—dit eget!
hilse dig med det varme, det mørkeblå øie:
Er du ren?
Er du tro?"

("Can the mirror speak?
The mirror can speak!
The mirror shall look at you each morning,
searchingly,
look at you with the deep, wise eye,

–your own!
greet you with the warm dark blue eye:
Are you pure?
Are you faithful?")

The purity and faithfulness in question refer to the speaker's ambivalent attitude toward the opposite sex and express Obstfelder's fear of the female erotic, one of the major themes of his work. Scandinavian literature of the 1890s is replete with instances of this ambivalence, as woman, in the figure of the Madonna, is celebrated for her purity while reviled for her sexual nature. The ocular imagery gestures at the self-observation and self-reflection common to both Obstfelder's work and Norwegian literature in general at the time, in which there was a marked turning away from social concerns toward a focus on the individual psyche. The warm dark-blue eye in the mirror becomes a secular substitute for the all-seeing eye of God, and the mind of the individual–here represented by that of the poet–achieves almost cosmic status. Coupled with the theme of alienation from society as a whole expressed in "Jeg ser," the speaker's ambivalence toward female eroticism and the strong focus on self-reflection in "Kan speilet tale?" result in the kind of solipsism that characterizes much mental illness.

The painful nature of the relationship between man and woman is also the subject of the poem "Brudens blege ansigt" (The Bride's Pale Face), in which sexual love is depicted as both illusory and necessary for the continuation of life:

Brudens blege ansigt
ser jeg foran flokken–
kirkens dør står åben,
salmens toner bruser.
Klædt i hvide klæder,
bleg som selve døden
går hun ind til livet,
fryden,
gråden.

(The pale face of the bride
I see in front of the crowd–
the door of the church is open,
the tone of the hymn swells.
Dressed in white clothes,
pale as death itself
she walks in to life,
the joy,
the weeping.)

The bride has joy in store for her but also weeping; she is characterized by the pallor of death, and her white dress symbolizes not purity but the death that awaits her. Simultaneously, her sacrifice of her life is at one with all living things–"Vår går, vår dør . . . / liv smiler, liv iler / død imøde" (Spring passes, spring dies . . . / life smiles, life hurries / to meet death), Obstfelder states later in the poem–for death is the destiny of all living things in order that life itself may go on:

Ja, alt på jorden må blegne,
hver blussende drøm dø,
men blussende liv skal spire
af din brudenats frydsvangre ve!

(Yes, everything on the earth must grow pale,
every glowing dream must die.
but glowing life shall germinate
from the pain of your bridal night, teeming with joy!)

Obstfelder's general sense of alienation is thus tempered by a vitalism akin to that of the early works of the later Norwegian poet and novelist Tarjei Vesaas, in which life and death are also viewed as two sides of the same phenomenon.

The poem "Genre" (Genre Painting) expresses the hope that marriage and family life may hold some promise of joy in spite of the pathos of human life. The speaker comes home and observes his wife and child asleep:

De sover.
Begge sover.
Den lille deilige i vuggen.
Den *store* deilige i sengen.

(They are asleep.
Both of them are asleep.
The little lovely one in the cradle.
The *big* lovely one in the bed.)

There is also a night-light in Obstfelder's word picture, as well as a gas lamp that can be seen outside the window because the curtain is not completely closed. The speaker senses that this gas lamp "strækker hals og glor på min kones skulder" (stretches its neck and ogles my wife's shoulder), which fills him with jealousy, after which he states that he is going to bed:

Jeg vil trykke to kys på dine smilehuller,
–som smiler i søvne,–
og på dine fingre,
og på trolovelsesringen,
og på sølvkorset om halsen.
Jeg vil liste mig stilfærdig op til dig,
og bli varm hos dig.
Og glemme,
at vi sommetider ikke er, som vi burde være,
mod hinanden.

(I will press two kisses against your dimples,
–which smile in your sleep–
and onto your fingers,

and onto the engagement ring,
and onto the silver cross around your neck.
I will sneak quietly up to you,
and become warm with you.
And forget,
that at times we do not treat each other,
the way we ought to.)

This scene is perhaps as close as it is possible to get to an idyll in Obstfelder's universe, but the reader is left with the question of what kind of man is capable of jealousy toward a streetlight. Like many other poems in Obstfelder's *Digte,* "Genre" takes as its theme the inability of human beings to get along with each other and with their world.

Obstfelder showed early on that he loved the prose poem—a favorite genre of the Symbolists—and experimented with prose pieces of varying length. In 1895 he published *To noveletter* (Two Novelettes), a slender volume consisting of the stories "Liv" (a woman's name, the meaning of which is "life") and "Sletten" (the Plain). "Liv," which was written in 1893, expresses the same moods that are found in *Digte.* Its narrator is a Norwegian man living in Paris; from the beginning of the text he does not seem mentally robust. He is extremely withdrawn, is sensitive to loud noises and other sensory stimuli, and spends much of his time in a basement café. With a tendency toward paranoia he wonders why people look at him the way they do, as he gradually withdraws from what little human contact he has left.

At his lodgings he can hear the steps of a woman who lives directly above him, and in his self-imposed sensory deprivation he begins to fantasize about her. When he finally contacts her, he discovers that she has been sick in bed for the past five days, suffering from tuberculosis. Her name is Liv, and she is an Icelandic orphan who has no friends in Paris. As the narrator cares for her as best he can, he becomes deeply attached to her, for her illness means that she is not an erotic threat to him. When Liv dies in his arms, having shared her fears and futile hopes with him, he feels even lonelier than before and completely alienated from normal human life:

> Boulevardene gjør mig syg. De bugnende bryster, de hævede hoder, dragterne, som gynger på lækre , smidige hofter, smilene, – alt dette, som skriger: kys, lev, nyd, – damer, løftet på kjælne herrehænder ind i lokkende mørke vogne, lyd av kys bag portièrer, lyd av dusdrikken i dårlig vin, saftige håndtryk af logrende venner – – å det blir så kvalmt! En taus forstenet gråt snører mig struben, over at menneskeglæden er en skjøge, som fylder hele atmosfæren med sin billige parfumes stank.

Lithograph of Obstfelder by Edvard Munch (from Mary Kay Norseng, Sigbjørn Obstfelder, *1982; Thomas Cooper Library, University of South Carolina)*

(The boulevards make me sick. The bulging breasts, the lifted heads, the clothes, which rock on luscious, supple hips, the smiles, – all this, that cries out: kiss, live, enjoy, – ladies lifted by caressing gentlemen's hands into enticing dark wagons, the sound of kisses behind drapes, the sound of friendships being sealed by the drinking of cheap wine, juicy handshakes by friends wagging their tails – – oh, it is so nauseating! Silent petrified crying knots my throat over the fact that human joy is a harlot who fills the air with the stench of her cheap perfume.)

The narrator's alienation is reminiscent of that of the speaker in the poem "Jeg ser," and his mental state at the end of "Liv" suggests an impending breakdown.

"Sletten" was written in 1895 while Obstfelder lived in Stockholm, Copenhagen, and Berlin. It tells about the relationship between the narrator and a woman named Naomi. In contrast to the relationship in "Liv," Naomi is a healthy young woman who meets the narrator on many occasions, and who finally moves in with him. While the narrator in "Sletten" is similar to the protagonist in "Liv" in that both of them are poets who find adjusting to living in a world of human beings difficult, Naomi saves the protagonist in "Sletten" from loneliness and perhaps also from mental illness. He, in turn, worships her. As he comes home one evening, five months after the two of them have started living together, he imagines her asleep in their home: "Jeg blev næsten angst, det var som om Gud selv var derinde" (I became almost afraid; it was as if God himself was in there). The protagonist in "Sletten" has successfully managed to integrate woman as Madonna with woman as lover.

Like the stories in *To noveletter,* the novella *Korset* (1896, The Cross) is also a love story, but in contrast to "Sletten," it ends tragically. A first-person narrative, it details the relationship between the narrator and a woman named Rebekka; only toward the end of the narrative does the reader realize that Rebekka has committed suicide. The narrator tries to absolve himself from guilt, but apparently, he, a writer, has been difficult to deal with, and he has more or less driven Rebekka to her death. *Korset* is not a remarkable narrative, but it includes Obstfelder's most incisive critique of the literary artist.

Obstfelder also tried his hand at writing plays. In his longest and most significant drama, *De røde dråber* (1897, The Red Drops), the protagonist is an alchemist named Odd Berg, who is in search of the beginning of life. Like other Obstfelder protagonists, Berg vacillates between participation in life, embodied by his fiancée Borghild, and his dream of gaining hidden knowledge, symbolized by his assistant Lili. Torn between the options represented by the two women, Odd finds himself thoroughly alienated in the end, unable to respond to Borghild's love.

At his death on 29 July 1900 Obstfelder left unfinished what is commonly regarded as his major work, the novel *En Præsts Dagbog* (1900, A Priest's Journal). Based on Obstfelder's own illness, it is a profound treatment of the theme of alienation and, like "Liv," a meditation on the possibility of peace through death. The minister protagonist is desperately searching for meaning in life, and in his attempt to see God he experiences several hallucinations. He gains no permanent sense of life's meaning, however, and the unfinished nature of the work may be read as gesturing at the futility of man's search for spiritual knowledge, meaning, and mental equilibrium.

A master of the prose poem, Obstfelder left behind many poems, and sixteen were included in the posthumous *Efterladte Arbeider* (1903, Posthumous Works). Determining exactly what should properly be regarded as a prose poem in Obstfelder's oeuvre, and what should be considered just a short piece of prose, presents some difficulty. Obstfelder's best-known prose poem, "Roser" (Roses), written in 1886 and reworked in 1892, is not among the sixteen published in 1903 but is an excellent representative of the genre.

"Roser" reads like a dream in which the dreamer finds himself covered with rose petals. With the musical structure of a fugue and with such notations as *piano, pianissimo, furioso,* and *morendo* appended, its main theme is the presence of roses, while the theme is expressed through such different contrapuntal voices as the wish to die in the arms of a rose mother-figure and the desire to be united with a rose lover whose heart beats in unison with that of the speaker:

> Der er *to*. Der er *to*.
> p.Det slår. – Det slår.
> Der er *to*. Der er *to*.
> pp.Det slår. – Det slår.
> ....
> Der er ét.
>
> (There are *two*. There are *two*.
> p.It beats. – It beats.
> There are *two*. There are *two*.
> pp.It beats. – It beats.
> ....
> There is one.)

At the end of the poem the dreamer dies:

> Hjertet slappes. Hjertet blir en – rose – som visner. Og saften tørrer. Og bladene krymper sammen.
>
> Vildt ud mot horizonten, roser, vildt stirrer han, vildt, roser, roser, roseblade (furioso), rosekopper :|: rosebægre :|: roseduft, rosegråt, rose – rosefarver, – (mor.) roser.
>
> ....
>
> Vildt stirrer han ud mod horizonten, ud mod – roser.
>
> Og dør.
>
> (His heart weakens. The heart becomes a – rose – that wilts. And the juice dries. And the petals shrink.
>
> Wildly he stares out toward the horizon, wildly, roses, roses, rose petals (furioso), rosebuds :|: rose cups :|: rose fragrance, rose cries, rose – rose colors, – (mor.) roses.
>
> ....
>
> Wildly he stares out toward the horizon, out toward – roses.
>
> And dies.)

As in both Obstfelder's poetry and longer prose works, the contradictions of existence can only be resolved through death.

Sigbjørn Obstfelder's influence in the English-speaking world may have been negligible, but in Scandinavia he is regarded as one of the most important precursors of Modernism. In his native Norway he is viewed as one of the most significant poets of the second half of the nineteenth century, and such poems as "Jeg ser" and "Roser" hold an honored place in the literary canon, appreciated by readers and critics alike.

Letters:

Breve til hans bror, edited by Solveig Tunold (Stavanger: Stabenfeldt, 1949);

Brev fra Sigbjørn Obstfelder, edited by Arne Hannevik (Oslo: Gyldendal, 1966);

Sjalusi! Brev til Ingeborg (45 brev 1897–1900), edited by Martin Nag (Stavanger: Kvekerforlaget, 1998).

Biographies:

Johan Faltin Bjørnsen, Sigbjørn Obstfelder: Mennesket, poeten og grubleren (Oslo: Gyldendal, 1959);

Martin Nag, Sigbjørn Obstfelder: Uro og skaperkraft (Oslo: Solum, 1996).

References:

Asbjørn Aarnes, ed., Obstfelder: Fjorten essays (Oslo: Aschehoug, 1997);

Sverre Arestad, "Sigbjørn Obstfelder and America," Norwegian-American Studies, 29 (1983): 253–292;

Christian Claussen, Sigbjørn Obstfelder i hans digtning og breve: En psykologisk studie (Christiania: Gyldendal, 1924);

Trygve Greiff, Sigbjørn Obstfelder (Oslo: Cammermeyer, 1944);

Arne Hannevik, Obstfelder og mystikken (Oslo: Gyldendal, 1960);

Brit Holgersen, –på en feil klode: Sigbjørn Obstfelder–mennesket og dikteren (Stavanger: Dreyer, 1997);

Andreas G. Lombnæs, "Obstfelders modernitet," Edda: Nordisk Tidsskrift for Litteraturforskning, 103 (2003): 4–19;

Johan A. Mortensen, Sigbjørn Obstfelder: Hans forhold til kvinden og erotiken (Copenhagen: Munksgaard, 1940);

Mary Kay Norseng, Sigbjørn Obstfelder (Boston: Twayne, 1982);

George C. Schoolfield, "Sigbjørn Obstfelder: A Study in Idealism," Edda: Nordisk Tidsskrift for Litteraturforskning, 57 (1957): 193–223;

Paul Thompson, "In Search of Faith and Fixing Points: Strindberg, Obstfelder and the Age of Post-Naturalism," Scandinavica: An International Journal of Scandinavian Studies, 28 (May 1989): 55–73.

Papers:

Most of Sigbjørn Obstfelder's papers are in the National Library (Nasjonalbiblioteket) in Oslo; some are at the Munch Museum, Oslo.

Alvilde Prydz
(5 August 1846 – 5 September 1922)

John Eason
University of Wisconsin–Madison

BOOKS: *Agn og Agnar* (Christiania: Cammermeyer, 1880);
I Moll: Noveller og Skitser (Christiania: Cammermeyer, 1885);
Undervejs: Noveller og Skitser (Christiania: Omtvedt, 1889);
Lykke (Christiania: Omtvedt, 1890);
Paa Fuglvik (Christiania: Cammermeyer, 1891);
Arnak (Copenhagen: Schubothe, 1892);
Mennesker (Christiania: Aschehoug, 1892);
Drøm (Christiania: Aschehoug, 1893);
Bellis (Christiania: Cammermeyer, 1895);
Gunvor Thorsdatter til Hærø (Christiania: Cammermeyer, 1896);
Blade (Christiania: Cammermeyer, 1898);
Sylvia (Copenhagen: Det Nordiske Forlag, 1898);
Aino (Copenhagen: Det Nordiske Forlag, 1900);
Det lovede Land (Copenhagen: Det Nordiske Forlag, 1902);
Undine, et Interieur (Christiania: Gyldendal, 1904);
Akkorder (Christiania: Cammermeyer, 1905);
Barnene paa Hærø Gaard (Christiania: Gyldendal, 1906);
I Ulvedalen (Christiania: Gyldendal, 1909);
Mens det var sommer (Christiania: Gyldendal, 1911);
To Enaktere: Han kommer; I fortrolighet (Christiania: Gyldendal, 1911);
Torbjørn Vik (Christiania: Gyldendal, 1913);
Paa Granem Gaard (Copenhagen: Gyldendal, 1915);
Digte (Copenhagen: Gyldendal, 1916);
To Mennesker (Copenhagen: Gyldendal, 1918);
De dage og de aar (Copenhagen: Gyldendal, 1919).

PLAY PRODUCTION: *Aino,* Christiania, Nationaltheatret, 13 February 1901.

Alvilde Prydz (from Project Gutenberg <http://www.gutenberg.org/files/17114/17114-h/images/tieni15.jpg>)

Alvilde Prydz was one of the most prolific Norwegian writers of the nineteenth-century Modern Breakthrough. She succeeded in dispelling the myth that men wrote and published more than women. But, like most other women writers of her day, Prydz was rejected by the literary establishment despite her significant literary contributions; she quickly disappeared from the literary scene and record. The melancholy and loneliness so prevalent in Prydz's oeuvre probably resulted from the harsh treatment she received from critics who refused to believe that a woman could write creatively or have anything worthwhile to say. The lack of support or recognition by critics not only contributed to Prydz's waning self-confidence as a writer but also thwarted her efforts to secure a comfortable standard of living. The intellectual establishment consistently refused to award her the endowments she applied for year after year. The consequent lack of funding made it impossible for her to receive proper medical care for the chronic physical ailments she endured for most of her life. Only her own drive and determination to make her voice heard enabled Prydz to create meaningful works.

Prydz was born at Tosterød Estate in Berg, Østfold, on 5 August 1846. Her father, Paul Fredrik Birkenbusch Prydz, was from an old German family that had eventually migrated to Norway. At the time of Alvilde's birth, Paul Prydz worked as both a merchant and a farmer. Andersine Nicoline ("Signe") Lund, Alvilde Prydz's mother, was from an artistic family of Danish origin. She and her husband had thirteen children, two of whom died at birth. Alvilde attended elementary school in Halden, which was known as Fredrikshald at that time. In 1862 Paul Prydz sold the Tosterød Estate because of poor finances and moved to Ørje in Østfold to take a job as a customs inspector. His wife and children, Alvilde among them, relocated to Christiania (now Oslo). The prospects of an education for Alvilde were better in the city, but she was unhappy and longed to return to the countryside around Østfold. Her love of nature eventually led Alvilde Prydz to create vivid descriptions of nature, one of her hallmarks as a writer. At seventeen she moved to Telemark to work as a governess for the children of E. H. Fridrichsen, a pastor at Mo Vicarage.

After two years in Telemark, Prydz returned to Christiania to take a course for governesses during the winter of 1866–1867. On completion of the course, she moved back to the home of the Fridrichsens, who had relocated to Hitra. She remained with the family for three years, working as a governess during the day and writing at night. The rigorous lifestyle in Hitra took its toll on her physically, and because she was already unwell, she returned to her mother's home in Christiania and assisted in running the household. These were difficult, grueling times for Prydz, but she was on her way to becoming one of the most exceptional and underappreciated writers of the Modern Breakthrough.

Like many other writers of the Modern Breakthrough, male and female, Prydz sought social change, particularly with respect to the role of women and the relationships between the sexes. Unlike Henrik Ibsen and August Strindberg, who spoke with the male voice of authority, Alvilde spoke as a woman writer and wrote for the "women's movement." She frequently wrote about the oppression of women, which she regarded as the most important social issue. Most of her stories deal with men and women, both married and unmarried couples, who face a myriad of challenges because of the inability of women to reach their full potential in love or life. Prydz's works deal with oppression in ways that male writers could only attempt to emulate.

Stylistically, Prydz's authorship may best be described as paradoxical, for like other women writers of the Modern Breakthrough, she embraced both Romanticism and realism in order to depict the two-sided existence of women in society, an existence that trapped them between romantic and realistic modes of living. Though Prydz was often realistic in her depictions of family life, which parallel the "greater" social concerns of the day, the melancholy tone that prevailed in her works underscored her main concern, the unrealized potential of women. Prydz is generally classified as a neo-Romantic because of her penchant for symbols, her frequent use of imagery from nature, her lyrical prose, and her philosophical and spiritual concerns.

Prydz's first published work, *Agn og Agnar* (1880, Agn and Agnar), was also the first work to deal with the complex and fragmented existence of many women. This short romantic novel was written during the winter of 1879–1880 while Prydz was visiting a childhood friend, Judith Hansen, and her husband, Andreas, in Jostedal. *Agn og Agnar* takes place in a remote, impoverished corner of Norway and deals with a young, intensely emotional girl whose love for another is thwarted. She succeeds in relinquishing that love. *Agn og Agnar* was regarded as too romantic and old-fashioned by the critics and by Prydz herself; however, the novel makes effective use of irony and treats the themes that Prydz explored in later works, namely the experience of longing, love, and loss of love.

I Moll (1885, In a Minor Key) was Prydz's first short-story collection. Most of the short stories in *I Moll* deal with the inability of women to meet expectations in love and life; in each story this theme plays out differently. While critics often asserted that Prydz's male characters were all too flat and lifeless, in the short story "Resultater" (Results) she introduced much more multidimensional male characters, who are in some respects every bit as much victims of society as women. "Musik i hemmet" (Music at Home), from the same collection, also has a male protagonist, but men in "Musik i hemmet," unlike those in "Resultater," are depicted as cold and calculating. The voice of the female character speaks more openly and freely when she is finally able to reveal her true feelings. Other stories from *I Moll*– "Valsen" (The Waltz), "Småstel" (Small Tools), and "Forventninger" (Expectations)–all feature female protagonists who are forced to deal with oppression and hardship. The stories share a concern for the conflicts that occur in married life and the problems women generally encounter. A lack of financial security for women

Cover for Prydz's novel (Gunvor Thorsdatter of Hærø), about a woman who gives up the opportunity for love and marriage to work for the good of her island community (Thorsens Antikvariat)

exacerbates the situations they already face. Prydz also focused on the inability of men and women to communicate effectively with each other. "Valsen" tells the story of a young woman who dies of heartbreak after a failed relationship; the foundation of the young woman's life crumbles, and despair over her fate pushes her over the edge. "Forventninger" introduces Helene Ørn, whose expectations of love are dashed; a domineering, controlling husband prevents her from reaching her full potential. "Småstel" breaks Prydz's pattern of portraying bourgeois leading ladies to depict women of the lower class. The main character in "Småstel" is a small-town schoolteacher. In this story Prydz takes on the confining environment in which the female protagonist is forced to live. Prydz makes clear that marriage is a necessity for women to survive and that love, present or absent, does not matter at all. After the publication of *I Moll* in 1885, Prydz received a government stipend and traveled in Denmark, Germany, Switzerland, and Italy.

Undervejs (Underway) followed *I Moll* in 1889, and, thematically and stylistically, it shares much in common with the previous work. With this work, as with *I Moll*, Prydz depicted self-reliant, courageous female characters. Rather than dazzling the reader with elaborate descriptions, Prydz focused on life's "greater problems," particularly on the struggle of women to win honor and dignity in a patriarchal society. Included in *Undervejs* are the short stories "For tung paa Haanden" (Too Heavy in Your Hand), a tale of unrequited love between two young people, and "Ved Fjorden" (At the Fjord), a look at the "tanteproblem," the overabundance of single women in nineteenth-century urban locales. "Inger Sypige" (Inger the Seamstress) is a compelling story about a young lower-class seamstress whose mother becomes the victim of exploitation during the period of industrialization in Norway. Like many other poor women of the working class, Inger's mother earns too little money by sewing alone to survive. "En Fejltagelse" (A Mistake) tells the story of yet another unhappy girl who suffers from heartbreak and lost love but finds the strength to survive.

Prydz's next two novels were *Lykke* (1890, Fortune) and its sequel, *Paa Fuglvik* (1891, At Fuglvik). In *Lykke* a fanatical, young doctor, Gerhard Juell, travels to rural communities in order to preach modern theories of welfare to farmers. He hopes his preaching will shape ordinary people into exceptional individuals. Juell is an idealist whose charity exists only in theory; he lacks the desire or will to initiate reform. In *Paa Fuglvik* the once proud, idealistic doctor is now exhausted, in shambles. None of his dreams have been realized, and he now leads the life of a rumpled and neglected married man.

In 1892 Prydz published her third short-story collection, *Arnak,* which includes descriptions of her stay in Paris. The theme of the unhappy destiny of women occurs once again, but in one of the stories, "Kjærlighedens Højsant" (Love's Highest), Prydz pays homage to a love that conquers everything, even death, as the heroine chooses a career that offers a secure financial future over her former goal of living the more uncertain life of an artist.

The novel *Mennesker* (1892, People) and its sequel, *Drøm* (1893, Dream), portray marriage in a much more realistic way than previously seen. In terms of structure, *Drøm* is often regarded as the strongest and most consistent work in Prydz's entire oeuvre. The battle of the sexes is the general subject of both works. The main character in *Mennesker* and *Drøm* is Helene Ørn, a woman with a great need for independence and a great deal of erotic consciousness. Ominous signs in the story foreshadow an unhappy relationship between Helene and her husband, the insidious Knud Grip. The problematic, dysfunctional tenor of their marriage leads to dire consequences culminating in the tragic death of Helene and Knud's child. In *Mennesker* and *Drøm* Prydz probed the psyche of her characters, offering sharp and revealing depictions of family life and revealing the powerful contrast between the busy external world of men and the more confined existence of women. Men demand absolute subordination and consideration without giving any, and they also have recourse to life away from home; women are unable to voice their own frustrations and needs; they have limited contact with each other; and they are effectively locked away within the home. *Drøm* and *Mennekser* delve deeply into the conflict between the sexes within the context of marriage; they share this focus with other works of the Modern Breakthrough.

The short-story collection *Bellis*, published in 1895, consists of two parts: the first part takes place in Italy; the second, in Norway. The style in *Bellis* is much more lyrical than in previous works; and poetic descriptions of nature abound–particularly nature in southern climes, where joie de vivre prevails. In contrast to the descriptions of love and warmth in the south, the north is portrayed with less attention to milieu and atmosphere.

The novel *Gunvor Thorsdatter til Hærø* (1896, Gunvor Thorsdatter of Hærø) was inspired by a trip Prydz took to Nordland in 1895. Prydz included many descriptions of nature in the work and employed a style that may be described as lyrical prose. Many literary historians and critics regard *Gunvor Thorsdatter til Hærø* as the work with which Prydz made the greatest impression. The text is full of mystical and symbolic elements of nature and divinity, and the theme of the battle of the sexes–undoubtedly one of the most important in Prydz's oeuvre–takes center stage. In this novel Prydz focuses on the double standard and its impact on the lives of men and women. Gunvor, the heroine of the novel, makes the difficult decision to break off her engagement and give up erotic love in order to work for the common good of her island community. Gunvor's longings and desires are placed in a more positive light than in most of Prydz's other stories, as she is not only able to achieve independence but also to determine her own destiny. Gunvor is a remarkable, vital, intelligent, and independent woman, in many ways superior to men. Gunvor becomes a goddess figure who delineates the powers of fate and nature. After her death, Gunvor becomes the patron saint of the island community. Gunvor's persona is best linked to the ideals and hopes of the "women's movement" of the time.

Prydz's short novel *Sylvia* (1898) presents a sharp contrast to the optimistic tone in *Gunvor Thorsdattter til Hærø*. *Sylvia* is a melancholy work about a woman's longing and false hopes. In this work Prydz criticizes the traditional upbringing that keeps girls from obtaining the same sort of education as boys. Because of its lyrical language, symbolism, and descriptions of natural settings, *Sylvia* is much more akin to Prydz's short-story collections *Bellis* and *Blade,* the latter collection appearing the same year as *Sylvia*. In contrast to the rest of the novel, the ending of *Sylvia* is somewhat more optimistic: the heroine rejects convention and leaves romantic daydreaming behind.

The play *Aino* (published 1900), which opened at the Nationaltheatret on 13 February 1901, is regarded as Prydz's dramatic breakthrough. *Aino,* a three-act drama, played a total of eight times and received much praise for its stance on children's rights, a cause Prydz championed openly, as was well-known at the time. In contrast to most other women characters in Prydz's works, the female protagonist Aino is so self-absorbed that she selfishly chooses to get rid of her child in order to secure the freedom necessary to pursue her own indulgences.

Prydz also dealt with motherhood, albeit in a completely different way, in *Det lovede Land* (1902, The Promised Land). The novel is deeply melancholy, filled with depictions of pain and suffering, but it also includes undercurrents of optimism. The most important issues Prydz raises in *Det lovede Land* concern the rights of mothers to private life and to love in old age. The answers she provides confirm that women do indeed have such rights.

Undine, et Interieur (Undine, an Interior), which was never performed on stage, was published in 1904. As in the social dramas of the 1890s, *Undine* features "la femme fatale," a dangerously seductive woman who awakens erotic passions in a man only to annihilate him. Prydz chose not to overplay eroticism in her work but rather to focus on such negative human qualities as laziness, arrogance, and social antipathy toward women that harms both men and women.

Prydz further explores the efforts of women to secure acceptance and appreciation in her short-story collection *Akkorder* (1905, Accords). Another novel, *Barnene paa Hærø Gaard* (The Children at Hærø Farm), followed in 1906. This novel takes the reader back to the same small island community that served as the setting for Prydz's 1896 novel, *Gunvor Thorsdatter til Hærø*. *Barnene paa Hærø Gaard* takes on a lyrical style and includes many scenes from nature; the novel suggests a utopian society in which women and men are equal. Gunvor's symbolic death realizes the ideal. The social and spiritual powers stemming from Gunvor's love have an enormous impact on the men of the island community and help them change into more responsible, more loving partners. Many critics regard *Barnene paa Hærø Gaard* as Prydz's best novel from the earliest years of the twentieth century.

I Ulvedalen (1909, In Ulvedalen) also includes many depictions of natural surroundings, but in this novel the images are much more foreboding. Jon Ulvson, a young, revolutionary priest, is removed from his position for preaching radical socialism; his controversial stance ultimately destroys his own family. *I Ulvedalen* does, however, include some humor, as does the previous short-story collection, *Bellis,* and the novel *De dage og de aar* (1919, Those Days and Years). Prydz included a lighter side to her narrative, a humor that counterbalanced tragic endings. *Mens det var sommer* (1911, While It Was Summer) presents many of the same sorts of scenes from nature as those found in *I Ulvedalen.* The main difference between the two novels lies in the greater optimism of the later novel. In *Mens det var sommer* nature lifts burdens and buoys the spirits of unhappy, suffering individuals.

After finishing *Mens det var sommer,* Prydz slowed the pace of her writing somewhat; her next novel, *Torbjørn Vik,* was not published until 1913. The male protagonist, Torbjørn Vik, recalls the central character in "Resultater" in *I Moll.* Vik possesses special gifts; his tragic death, however, prevents him from using and enhancing any of these gifts. *Paa Granem Gaard* (1915, At Granem Farm) is essentially a dramatization of the 1909 novel *Mens det var sommer,* though it was not performed. As in *Mens det var sommer,* evil is dispelled, and the woman who represents goodness resurfaces and resolves all central conflicts. However, her existence is one of loneliness, as she calls the forest home.

In 1911 Prydz published *To Enaktere: Han kommer; I fortrolighet* (Two One-Act Plays: He Is Coming; In Confidence). In *Han kommer,* which is generally regarded as the better of the two plays, Reidar returns to his hometown after having been away for many years and is forced to contend with a small-town mentality that seems frozen in time. *Han kommer* has been read as an attack on the conservative small-town bourgeois environment as well as a critique of the double standard that allows men to travel the world while confining women to waiting patiently at home. As in other social dramas of the 1890s, Gundell, like many other female protagonists, breaks off her engagement when she discovers her fiancé's infidelity; she decides that there must be something better in store for her.

To Mennesker (1918, Two People) included two previous novels—*Mennesker* and *Drøm*—neither of which was changed from the original. A collection of poetry titled simply *Digte* (1916, Poems) and *De dage og de aar* were Prydz's last published works. The central male character of *De dage og de aar,* a poor boy who fails to win over the girl he sets his heart on, follows a popular narrative pattern. However, the protagonist in this novel seems to have little if any connection to reality, a situation he struggles to comprehend and come to terms with throughout the story.

Alvilde Prydz's final work was not finished when she died on 5 September 1922. Though a relatively long one, Prydz's life was laden with adversity. Despite her bouts with depression, failing physical health, intense loneliness, and above all, her bitter struggle to win acceptance from the prominent critics who dismissed her works and denied her the funding she so desperately needed to live, Prydz was one of Norway's most prolific writers of the Modern Breakthrough. Her published works, which consisted of more than two dozen pieces, ranged from novels and plays to poetry and short-story collections. While her individual works are generally classified as either Romantic or realistic, Prydz's oeuvre often embraces aspects of both. Many critics viewed this oscillation between, for example, the lyrical language of Romanticism and the much more "realistic" portrayals of everyday life as a sign of weakness in form. What such critics failed to see was that Prydz more than made up for structural flaws in her works by adding new layers of complexity and intensity. These characteristics made—and still make—her works exciting and worthwhile to read.

Biography:

Lilly Heber, *Kvindeskikkelseri norsk aandslivs historie, 2: Alvilde Prydz* (Oslo: Olaf Norlis, 1925).

References:

Irene Engelstad, "Mellom Melankoli og Heroisme," in *Norsk kvinnelitteraturhistorie,* volume 1: *1600–1900,* edited by Engelstad and others (Oslo: Pax, 1988), pp. 212–218;

Anne Mari Harper, "Alvilde Prydz–feminist i antifeministisk tid," *Hovedoppgave i norsk høsten* (Olso: Universitetet i Oslo, 1977), pp. 19–43;

Åse Hiorth Lervik, "Alvilde Prydz–en nedvurdert forfatter," *Kronikktjeneste,* 1 (1991): 49–54.

Dagny Juel Przybyszewska
(8 June 1867 – 5 June 1901)

Lanae H. Isaacson

BOOKS: *Kiedy slonce zachodzi* (Warsaw: Jan Fiszer, 1901?);

Krucze gniazdo: dramat w 3 aktach (Warsaw: Jan Fiszer, 1902);

Synden og to andre skuespill (Lysaker: Solum, 1978)—comprises *Synden, Når solen går ned,* and *Ravnegård;*

Kongsvinger-kvinne og verdensborger: Dagny Juel som dikter og kulturarbeider (Kongsvinger: Solør-Odal og Kongsvinger Museum, 1987).

Collection: *Samlede tekster,* edited by Kari Sommerseth Jacobsen, Roar Lishaugen, Terje Tønnesen (Kongsvinger: Kulturforlaget BRAK/Kongsvinger Museum, 1996).

PLAY PRODUCTIONS: *Hrich (Synden),* Prague, Intimní Voiné Jeviste, 1 May 1898;

Osoby (Ravnegård), Cracow, Cracow Theater, December 1902.

TRANSLATIONS: Sigbjørn Obstfelder, "Liv," *Pan,* September–November 1895;

Stanisław Przybyszewski, *Underveis* (Christiania & Copenhagen: Cammermeyer, 1895).

SELECTED PERIODICAL PUBLICATIONS–UNCOLLECTED: *Den sterkere, Samtiden,* 7 (1896): 449–459;

Synden, Moderní Revue, 9 (1898): 129–138;

"Sing mir das Lied vom Leben und vom Tode," translated by Stanisław Przybyszewski, *Samtiden,* 11 (1900): 289–297;

"Rediviva," *Dagbladet,* 22 January 1977, p. 2; reprinted in *Kongsvinger-kvinne og verdensborger, Dagny Juel som dikter og kulturarbeider* (Kongsvinger: Solør-Odal og Kongsvinger Museum, 1987).

In the center of the circle of Northern European writers and artists, bohemians who routinely gathered at Zum schwarzen Ferkel (At the Black Piglet), Julius Türke's tavern in Berlin, was the beautiful and gifted Dagny Juel. Juel fell in with the painters, writers, play-

Dagny Juel Przybyszewska (National Library of Poland, Warsaw; from Mary Kay Norseng, Dagny: Dagny Juel Przybyszewska, the Woman and the Myth, *1991; Thomas Cooper Library, University of South Carolina)*

wrights, and poets who made Zum schwarzen Ferkel their home away from home—such pivotal figures in Nordic art and literature as Sigbjørn Obstfelder, Gustav Vigeland, Ola Hansson, Christian Krohg and Oda Krohg, Holger Drachmann, and Strindberg. Juel experimented with writing prose and poetry and created a new kind of drama that broke with realism and led the way to expressionism. She was a controversial figure in her day, admired by some for her intelligence, artistry, and creativity, hated and scandalized by others as a femme fatale among the bohemians of Zum schwarzen Ferkel.

The second of four daughters, Juel was born Dagny Juell in Jonas Lie-Gården, Kongsvinger, Hedmark, on 8 June 1867. Her parents were a highly respected doctor, Hans Lemmich Juell, and Minda Blehr, also the daughter of a doctor. Dagny's sisters were Gudrun, Astrid, and Ragnhild; Dagny was closest to the youngest, Ragnhild. In 1873, Hans Juell moved his family to a large estate house, Rolighed (Serenity), which became the center for the Juell family, even for the adult married daughters and their families: all the married daughters routinely returned home, and Astrid never left. The family members were generally supportive and sympathetic toward each other; Hans Juell and his wife encouraged each daughter to pursue individual interests and goals, and Rolighed always welcomed the families and friends of all four daughters.

At seven, Juell entered Anna Stang's Girls' School in Kongsvinger; she left after six years and was confirmed in Vinger Church on 1 October 1882. After her confirmation, Juell was sent to a private school in Erfurt, Germany, where she studied an additional two years. Juell did not reveal much interest in further academic study. From 1885 to 1886 she studied piano privately with Erika Nissen and Westye Waalev in Christiania (today Oslo).

In the fall of 1888 Juell was invited to serve as a governess for the children of her uncle and aunt, Pastor Otto and Randi Blehr, who served a congregation northeast of Bergen in the small community of Førde. Juell frequently visited Bergen, acquiring a wide circle of friends in the process: according to her biographer Mary Kay Norseng, her days were filled with "dances and operas and people" and with the piano. She grew fond of her young charges and remained their governess until the fall of 1889 when her father came to accompany her return to Kongsvinger and then more piano study in Christiania.

In February 1892 Juell went to Berlin to continue her piano study. She remained in Berlin for the spring and summer months. In the fall of 1892, she returned to Kongsvinger via Lund, where she spent a month with her older married sister Gudrun and her family. In the early 1890s Juell began experimenting with changes in her maiden name; she alternated dropping the final *l* in Juell and retaining it. By the time she married she used the single *l* version. In February 1893 she returned to Berlin to study at Holländer's Conservatory of Music. Led by the Norwegian painter Edvard Munch, she joined the trendsetting, avant-garde artists and authors who met at Zum schwarzen Ferkel. Her motivation to join the bohemians was both personal and a sign of the times.

Juell was talented, freethinking, and determined to live by her musical art and by her own myth of the assertive modern woman. By March 1893 she had fallen in love with the Polish writer Stanisław Przybyszewski, one of the bohemians who frequented Zum schwarzen Ferkel and kept it going. Juell and Przybyszewski married on 18 August 1893 in Berlin, and Dagny Juell became Dagny Juel Przybyszewska. Together, the couple provided the bohemians with an artistic center; they held the group together despite Strindberg's assertions that Przybyszewska drove a wedge between the members of the circle. The Przybyszewskis were also the motivating force behind *Pan* (1895), the most progressive European art journal of the decade.

In addition to her work on *Pan* and her promotion of Scandinavian writers and artists, Przybyszewska began writing poems and shorter prose. She wrote her short story "Rediviva" in Berlin, four months after her marriage to Przybyszewski, and as Norseng points out, "Rediviva" foreshadowed what occurred with Przybyszewski's mistress, Marta Foerder, who already had two children with Przybyszewski before his marriage. "Rediviva" remained in manuscript form until it was published in the Norwegian periodical *Dagbladet* in 1977.

"Rediviva" is the story of dangerous passion run amok and of the dire consequences of such passion. The story is brief and concentrated, and this concentrated form makes the first-person narrative more frightening. The plot in "Rediviva" moves quickly with an almost explosive burst of passion, a feeling of "livsens lykke" (the joy of life) that sweeps in and sweeps everything–and everyone–aside. The passion of the lovers is a living being and a dangerous one. The immediate casualty of the game is the woman standing between the two lovers, who has to die to serve their passions. Her suicide assures the victory of passion, but it also leads to her ominous return and constant presence; she never leaves the side of her rival, even during lovemaking.

Even more tragically, the constant presence of the displaced woman returned to life is not shared between the lovers; the new female lover alone suffers the torment; the man sees and feels nothing. The heat of the moment runs cold in the omnipresence of "Rediviva." In this short story, Przybyszewska moves far from concrete realism, the depiction of social life and political situations and what is actually going on between individuals within communities, to the feelings of an individual, an exploration of what effects uncontrollable, generally malevolent inner passions have on the individual and others. She also moves far from the traditional literary depiction of the woman as an innocent victim of male exploitation and sexual gratification; she creates a picture of an active, dynamic, passion-driven individual who wreaks as much havoc as any man. Joy and reckless abandon are rapidly replaced by nagging guilt and terror; then devil-may-care defiance flashes; and finally, resignation and hot passion turned cold complete and conclude the tale. The fate of the assertive, engaged female lover becomes a kind of living death—and all these changes, according to Norseng, occur in short order and in the mind of the narrator.

From 1893 to 1898 the Przybyszewskis remained in Berlin, where they lived always on the brink of abject poverty and often crossed the brink. Artistically, they may well have been soul mates and co-artists, but their married life was constantly marred by Przybyszewski's alcoholism, obsessions with satanism, and infidelity. (He continued a liaison with Marta Foerder until her suicide by poison on 9 June 1896.) The Przybyszewskis made frequent trips to Rolighed, where they stayed for lack of funds needed to secure life on their own. Przybyszewska wavered between longing for home when abroad and an equally strong drive to pursue her artistic life beyond the narrow confines of Kongsvinger. She tried to combine both roles, although they were mutually exclusive. She could not play the role of traditional wife and mother and simultaneously live the role of creative performing artist and free spirit. Her solution, to alternate roles and settings for her roles, to create a dichotomy within her life, ultimately proved unworkable. The Przybyszewskis' two children were both born at Rolighed: their son, Zenon, on 28 September 1895, and their daughter, Iwa, on 5 September 1897. Much of Przybyszewska's married life was spent apart from her husband and at Rolighed; she also left her children with her mother, sisters, or family friends for extended periods in order to follow Przybyszewski to Berlin, Paris, and Spain.

In 1895 Przybyszewska wrote her first play, *Den sterkere* (1896, The Stronger), the only play published in Norway during her lifetime. Like the short story "Rediviva," *Den sterkere* deals with destructive passions; the brevity of the play only increases the horror at unchecked passion, the power of conjoined love and hate to destroy those in its wake. In *Den sterkere*, all feelings seem on edge, at fever pitch. The setting for the action in *Den sterkere* is incongruously a garden room or terrace and a peaceful summer garden in the evening. The scene begins in medias res, initially somewhat confusing: Dr. Knut Tonder and his wife Siri are discussing a "nightmare" from Siri's past, her affair with another man:

Siri: Er det virkelig umuligt for dig at glemme det? Skal vi hele vort liv knuges af denne mare?

Przybyszewska's husband, Stanisław Przybyszewski, in 1895 (portrait by Edvard Munch; Munch Museum, Oslo; from Mary Kay Norseng, Dagny: Dagny Juel Przybyszewska, the Woman and the Myth, *1991; Thomas Cooper Library, University of South Carolina)*

Knut: Hvordan kan man vel glemme noget, som graver i en evig og altid? Jeg har engang læst om en mand, som altid fulgtes af sit eget skelet. Tror du, han nogensinde glemte det?

Siri: Dit skelet begynder at gjøre mig mørkræd. Jeg ser det stirre ud af øinene dine. Jeg tør ikke tale til dig, jeg . . .

Knut: Men forstaar du da ikke, at din taushed piner mig? Det er, som om du gjemmer dig bort for mig. Du blir mig saa fremmed og fjern . . .

Siri: Men taler jeg om det, saa piner det dig dobbelt. Tror du ikke, jeg ser, hvordan du lider? Tror du, jeg er saa blind?

Knut: Nei, nei, du misforstaar mig. Det hjælper mig netop at tale om det. Det beroliger mig. Jeg ønsker ofte, du vilde fortælle mig lidt nærmere om det. Sig mig . . . hvor er han nu? Han reiste langt bort, ikke sandt?

Siri: Ja, han reiste langt bort. Hvorhen ved jeg ikke.

(Siri: Is it really impossible for you to forget it? Shall we be tormented by that nightmare our whole life?

The Przybyszewskis in 1895 (from Mary Kay Norseng, Dagny: Dagny Juel Przybyszewska, the Woman and the Myth, *1991; Thomas Cooper Library, University of South Carolina)*

Knut: How can someone forget something that burrows in him forever and ever? I once read of a man who was always followed by his skeleton. Do you believe he ever forgot it?

Siri: Your skeleton is beginning to make me afraid of the dark. I see it staring out of your eyes. I don't dare talk to you, I . . .

Knut: But don't you understand that your silence torments me? It's as though you're hiding yourself away from me. You are becoming so strange and foreign to me . . .

Siri: But if I speak of it, it will only torment you doubly. Don't you believe that I see how you suffer? Do you think I'm blind?

Knut: No, no, you misunderstand me. It helps me to talk about it. It calms me down. I often wish that you would tell me a little more about it. Tell me . . . where is he now? He went away, didn't he?

Siri: Yes, he went far away. I don't know where.)

In the scene the emotions (words) of the couple bounce from one to the other, they form cue responses, generally of fear that borders on hate and loathing—or love. Love and hate are not distant or divided but follow hard on each other. Each character feels love and hate toward his or her partner, not in succession or intermittently but simultaneously. The dialogue covers all emotional stances with no pauses; passions run the gamut, colliding on their way.

Siri's former lover, Tor Rabbe, comes into this emotional turmoil seeking to reclaim Siri, to "make a play" for his former lover. The painful past between the two breaks through to the surface, along with Tor's vow to retake Siri, to force her to leave just as Knut feared and foresaw.

In the second act the conversation between Knut and Siri quickly settles on Tor and, again, Knut and Siri rehash the past, this time with ever-quickening responses. The audience learns that Tor and Siri were engaged when Knut entered the scene. Again, expressions of intense passion flow. The end for Knut and Siri lies in the possibility that the grand passion was just an illusion. At the end of the play, the audience is left with the question "Who was the stronger? Tor or Knut?" Conceivably, Siri could claim the role of the stronger, as her "evil soul" enables her to play at love and hate for Knut and Tor, to make both men miserable. However, the stronger may well have been all the collective emotions and passions within all three characters, the unseen forces that motivate Knut, Siri, and Tor, throwing them all into a whirlpool in which love and hate, guilt and the memory of the past, combine to destroy all three.

In many ways *Den sterkere* sets the course for Przybyszewska's other plays: *Synden* (1898, The Sin), *Når solen går ned* (written 1899, published 1978; When the Sun Sets), and *Ravnegård* (1902). Performed at the Free Intime Scene in Prague in 1898, *Synden* describes the falling of the child-woman Hadasa for a guest, Leon, and her betrayal and murder of her husband, Miriam. Leon, initially considered a harmless enough guest and no threat to the supposedly secure marriage of Hadasa and Miriam, proves himself to be a pernicious, persistent seducer, and Hadasa falls for his charms. Her subsequent denials that anything has changed or transpired are belied by the farce she plays for Miriam. In *Synden*, love, even love denied, brings out the evil (the sin) that lurks beneath the calmest scene, the seemingly placid surface. Once Hadasa's passion is awakened or rekindled by Leon, she is only a step or two away from murder.

In *Når solen går ned* Fin's love for Ivi has driven his wife to suicide by drowning. But Fin's wife does not go quietly to her grave; her ghost returns nightly to torment and crush her rival and to destroy the love of Fin and Ivi. Ivi has chosen her passion for Fin, she has defied convention and old-style propriety to love and hate of her own free will. Her choice has not brought her happiness or joy or peace but instead has guaranteed her ambivalence and an authentic self that is not the prosaic "good girl" self, the dutiful innocent, but a self who answers her own conflicting and conflicted passions to the death. Similarly in *Ravnegård*, Gudrun's evil, long-standing passion for her younger sister Sigrid's new husband, Thor, reignited and reciprocated when Sigrid and Thor return home for a visit, leads to Sigrid's death and to a condemnation of love.

The scenes and settings of Przybyszewska's plays are as surreal as the plays themselves. In *Den sterkere* the peaceful terrace and the quiet summer garden in evening contrast markedly with the constant wrangling, the declarations of love and expressions of hate and defiance of the dialogue. The setting for *Når solen går ned* is a dark room made even darker by Gobelin tapestries and heavy rugs. A table with a lit candelabra occupies the foreground while, in the background, Ivi, dressed in a long, white gown, reclines on a large bed. In the beginning of *Ravnegård*, Gudrun, the "evil sister," is tending an ominous fire in a massive fireplace; flames leap up and threaten. On a table in the middle of the room are the strange giant flowers that Gudrun tends and keeps in mysterious vases, something that suggests death more than life. All the settings of Przybyszewska's plays are foreboding, strange, incongruous; they suggest a weird world where evil passions hold sway, threatening to destroy all who enter and encounter each other.

Like her plays, Przybyszewska's poetry represents a new direction—the avant-garde that she sought among the bohemians in Berlin, Cracow, and Warsaw. Much of Przybyszewska's poetry has a surreal nightmare quality, an ominous, threatening side to it, something seen in the settings and dialogue of her plays. Her poetic oeuvre also reflects the influence and inspiration of the French poet, Paul Verlaine, who prized music above all else, a sentiment that struck a responsive chord with the

Paperback cover for a collection of Przybyszewska's dramatic works (The Sin and Two Other Plays), published in 1978 (Widener Library, Harvard University)

pianist/poet Przybyszewska. The poems are generally undated, written during the hardscrabble days in Berlin, Cracow, and Warsaw. Her prose poem cycle "Sing mir das Lied vom Leben und vom Tode," appeared in *Samtiden* in 1900; her other poems *(digte)* were published in *Samtiden* in 1975 and in the editions and collections of her work that appeared in the 1990s, as her status as a poet and dramatist received more critical attention.

The poem "Til Astrid!" suggests the ominous, dark quality in Przybyszewska's poetry and her emphasis on nightmares and dreams, on the eternal song of storm and lightning:

Evigheden snor sig bleg langs himmelrunden.
En stemme lyder fra skyen.
En stemme lyder fra grunden:
Evighedens brøn er stormene, som synger,
Synger en sang om skyen,

Synger en sang om grunden,
Synger en sang om evigheden, der flammer langs himmelrunden,
Evigheden skummer hvid om klippeskrænten,
Hæver sine arme,
Og dens stemme lyder:
Lyn og storm, I synger mine sange,
I er født i smerte,
I er født I harme!
. . . .
Du kjære nattemare!
Du er mit hjertes smertensbarn:
I dine sorte vingers garn
Du fanger altid mine drømmes skare.

Du stirrer ind i hjernens tomme hule,
Imens vi begge skjeler op mod solen,
Der flindsende gyder sin gyldne flod
Over strømmens blod.

(Pale Eternity winds along the celestial arc.
A voice sounds from the clouds above.
A voice sounds from the depths below:
The wells of Eternity are the storms that sing,
Sing a song about the clouds above,
Sing a song about the depths below,
Sing a song about Eternity that burns along the heavenly arc,
Eternity foams white on the edge of the cliff,
Raises its arms,
And its voice calls out:
Lightning and storms, you sing my songs,
You are born in pain,
You are born in peril!
. . . .
You dear nightmare!
You are my heart's child of pain:
In the yarn of your black wings
You always capture the flashing light of my dreams.

You stare into the brain's empty recesses,
While we both squint up at the sun,
That shining pours its golden river
Over the stream's blood.)

The world that Przybyszewska creates in her poetry is an ominous one, filled with images of stars and storms, songs and suns, seas and rivers that run red with blood and mean to do the poet or her dreams harm. Unlike dreams that are part and parcel of the past and are recollected wistfully or even pleasantly, the poet's nightmares are living beings who accompany the poet on her terrifying journeys, who capture the light from her dreams in their snares and traps.

One of the most remarkable poems by this remarkable poet describes the act of singing, of sending a song and soul out into the world, of transcending time and space, only to be brought back to earth by one who has not shared the experience in the same way, one who has listened but has not joined the song's journey or answered the song's eternal call. Prefaced by the title or comment *Et la tristesse de tout cela, oh, mon âme* (And the sadness of all that, oh, my soul), the poem depicts what happens when a singer and her soul soar on wings of song, when an artist gives her all or even transcends what she is capable of but fails to take another with her. Przybyszewska captures both the transcendent moment and the tragedy and *tristesse* when it all ends.

In 1898 the Przybyszewskis left Berlin and moved to Cracow, where they lived until 1899, when they were again in dire straits. The play *Synden* was translated into Czech and performed in Prague; it was published in the Czech capital in 1899, by which time Przybyszewska and her children were living in Zakopane, Poland, for extended periods. In January 1900 the Przybyszewskis separated; their son Zenon returned to Rolighed; their daughter, Iwa, was sent to the Polish painter Aniela Pajakowna. Przybyszewska returned to Rolighed in June 1900 and remained there until December. In the spring of 1901 she moved to Warsaw. On 26 April 1901 Przybyszewska, Zenon, and a friend of the family, Wladyslaw Emeryk, traveled to Tbilisi, Georgia. Przybyszewska died on 5 June 1901 when a deranged and suicidal Emeryk, distressed by the end of the Przybyszewskis' marriage, shot her and then himself in the presence of Zenon. She was buried in Tbilisi amid scandal and shame to her family.

For nearly ninety-five years the literary accomplishments of Dagny Juel Przybyszewska were buried by scandal and the tragedy of her death. Her fame as a femme fatale, the muse of the Nordic bohemians at Zum schwarzen Ferkel, overwhelmed her literary talents and the innovation she brought to drama and poetry. Przybyszewska also had her admirers, those who recognized her talents and her efforts to portray women as dynamic individuals who could act assertively and independently. Obscured by rumors, the fictions that Strindberg had created, and the scandalmongers, however, Przybyszewska became a mystery and a myth. Then in the 1990s, editions and collections of her works began to appear, and literary critics recognized her achievements. The editors of Przybyszewska's *Samlede tekster* (1996, Collected Works) offer an assessment of her talent in their introduction: they say that her

> produksjon er temmelig beskjeden, men likevel såvidt omfattende–ikke minst med hensyn til sjangerutvalg– at man kan få et innblikk i både skrivemåter og–ferdigheter. Tekstene etterlater liten tvil om at vi her har å gjøre med en skribent både med usedvanlig god litterær teft og et blikk for uttrykks-måter som plasserer henne ved siden av sine mannlige samtidige forfattere.

(production is quite modest but in any case sufficiently extensive—not the least with respect to choice of genre—that we can get an insight into both her way of writing and her expertise. The texts leave little doubt that we are dealing with a writer with both uncommonly good literary skill and an insight into modes of expression that place her alongside her male contemporaries.)

Biographies:

Ewa K. Kossak, *Dagny Przybyszewska: zblakana gwiazda* (Warsaw: Panstwowy Instutut Wydawniczy, 1973, 1975);

Juel Stubberud, *Dagny Juell* (Kongsvinger: Kino og teaternemnda, 1977);

Mary Kay Norseng, *Dagny: Dagny Juel Przybyszewska, the Woman and the Myth* (Seattle: University of Washington Press, 1991).

References:

Sonja Hagemann, "Brev som sannhets bevis," *Dagbladet,* 5 February 1963, p. 5;

Roar Lishaugen, *Dagny Juel: den moderne damen* (Kongsvinger: Kvinnemuseet, 2001);

Lishaugen, *Dagny Juel: tro, håp og undergang* (Oslo: Andresen & Butenschen, 2002);

Lishaugen, *Dagny Juels liv og verk* (Kongsvinger: Kivnnemuseet på Rolighed);

I. M. Lunde, "Dagny—modernismens første dame," in *Norsk dramatisk årbok* (Oslo: Norske dramatikeres forbund, 1999), pp. 74–79;

Martin Nag, *Dagny Juel: skjebne som et Ibsen-drama: Artikler* (Oslo: Bokvennen, 1997);

Nag, *Kongsvinger-kvinne og verdensborger Dagny Juel som dikter og kultur-arbeider* (Kongsvinger: Solør-Odal Historielag/Kongsvinger Museum, 1987);

Aleksandra Sawicka, *Dagny Juel Przybyszewska: fakty i legendy* (Gdansk: Slowo/Obraz Terytoria, 2006);

Kristin Valla, *Skuddene I Tbilisi: I fotsporene til bohemen Dagny Juel* (Oslo: Kagge, 2006).

Papers:

Dagny Juel Przybyszewska's letters are found in various private family collections and in the archives of the University of Oslo; the Royal Library, Stockholm; the Munch Museum, Oslo; the Muzeum im Jana Kasprowicza, Inowrochow; the Muzeum Adama Mickiewicza, Warsaw; the Royal Archive, Oslo; and the Solør-Odal og Kongsvinger Museum in Kongsvinger.

Per Sivle
(6 April 1857 – 6 September 1904)

Eirik Helleve
Nynorsk kultursentrum

BOOKS: *En digters drøm: Tidsaanden tilegnet,* as Simon de Vita (Christiania, 1878);

Digte, as Peder Sivle (Bergen: Lavik, 1879);

Sogor: Ein Bundel (Christiania: Cammermeyer, 1887);

Vossa-Stubba (Christiania: Det Norske Samlaget, 1887; enlarged edition, Bergen: Mons Litleré, 1892);

Streik (Christiania: Cammermeyer, 1891);

Blandet Selskab (Høvik: Bibliothek for de tusen hjem, 1891);

Noreg: Nationale digte (Christiania: Norli, 1894);

Nye Vossa-Stubbar (Christiania: Hydle, 1894);

Bersøglis- og andre Viser (Christiania: Hydle, 1895);

Sivle-Stubbar (Sandnes: Ingvald Dahle, 1895);

Skaldemaal (Bergen: Litleré, 1896);

Nationalt Selvmord (Christiania, 1897);

En Fyrstikke og andre Viser (Christiania: Det Norske Aktieforlag, 1898);

Folk og fæ (Christiania: John Fredrikson, 1898);

Olavs-Kvæde (Oslo: Bogvennen, 1901).

Collections: *Skrifter,* 3 volumes, edited by Severin Eskeland (Christiania: Gyldendal, 1909–1910);

Skrifter, edited by Bjarte Birkeland (Oslo: Gyldendal, 1957);

Dikt i samling, edited by Knut Johansen (Oslo: Per Sivle Forlag, 1978);

Per Sivles beste, edited by Birkeland (Oslo: Det Norske Samlaget, 1992).

Per Sivle (Store Norske Leksikon <http://www.snl.no/.bilde/ Sivle%2C_Per_(portrett)>)

Per Sivle's works are not widely read today, but in the second half of the ninteenth century he was one of the most prominent Norwegian poets. Sivle's poetry focuses on two central issues: his personal search for peace of mind and his desire for the dissolution of the union between Norway and Sweden. Sivle did not live long enough to resolve these issues. Throughout his life he sought stability and harmony, but he did not find either. He never settled in a house of his own, and he was constantly on the move, staying with friends and family. His dire finances, irregular life, poor health, and the diminishing quality of his poems eventually became too much, and Sivle died by his own hand at the age of forty-seven.

Sivle was born on 6 April 1857 in the parish of Flåm, in western Norway. He was given the name Peder, the Danish equivalent of Per, the name he used later in life. His parents, who did not marry until after Sivle was born, settled in the vicinity of the farm where his father, Eirik Sivle, grew up, at Stalheim in Vossestrand. His father traded horses, which brought the family a healthy income but led him to spend many months away from the family home each year. Sivle's mother, Susanna Ryum, died in the fall of 1859, having given birth to her third set of twin boys in only two and a half years. Five of the six babies were stillborn; only Per survived. Because of his mother's early death and his father's absence for work, Sivle spent his early childhood with various relatives, finally settling with Bottolv and Brytteva Brekke at age six.

Eirik Sivle brought back knowledge of all kinds from his travels, and he bought his son many books. Among these were Norwegian folktales and Snorre's sagas, books that gave Sivle much joy. He sought more education, and at the age of fifteen he left for Sogndal, where he enrolled in the *folkehøgskule,* a kind of school that sought to give its pupils a sound general education. Sivle spent two years in Sogndal, where he befriended Henrik Krohn, a prominent figure in the movement to promote the use of Landsmål, a written language based on all of the Norwegian dialects and created by Ivar Aasen. (In 1929 this language became known as Nynorsk.)

In 1875 Sivle moved to Christiania (now Oslo). His ambition was to become a minister, but he had to abandon those studies because of an illness his doctor ascribed to his reading too much. Sivle then decided to try his luck as a writer. He had already seen some of his work in print–his first publication was an account of a legend from Aurland, which had been published in the 2 March 1872 issue of the newspaper *Vossingen.* Sivle's earliest poems were written in Dano-Norwegian, but he really found his poetic voice when he started using Landsmål. His first Landsmål poem, "Den fyrste songen" (The First Song), was published in the Oslo newspaper *Fedraheimen* on 24 November 1877. In its original form, it has two stanzas. In the first, the speaker thinks back to his earliest memories as a newborn boy: "The first song I ever heard / was my mother singing by my cradle." He continues by thinking of how his mother's singing would soothe his troubles and make him dream of a better world. In the second stanza, the speaker seems older and the reader senses that his troubles are of a different kind. Still, by imagining the voice of his now dead mother, the speaker is able to return to his childhood and the calming effect his mother would have upon him. The phrasing is excellent throughout the poem, and it never approaches the sentimentality into which a less skillful writer would have been drawn. When it was printed in *Fedraheimen,* the poem was signed only by an "S," and Sivle never included the poem in any of his books. Lars Søraas the elder composed a melody for the poem, and when it was included in songbooks, the author was listed as unknown. Sivle was not officially revealed to be the author until Anders Hovden published *Per Sivle: Ei livssogu* (1905, Per Sivle: A Life). To this day, the frequently sung piece remains his best-known and most popular poem.

Sivle was fluent in both Landsmål and Dano-Norwegian, and throughout his life he used both languages. Dano-Norwegian seemed to suit him best when he was writing newspaper articles. When he used Landsmål his writings became more lively and less clichéd. His poems written in Landsmål were far better than those in Dano-Norwegian.

Sivle's first book, the slim volume *En digters drøm* (A Poet's Dream), was published in 1878 under the pen name Simon de Vita. The only poem in the book, "En digters drøm," is an epic poem that deals with the struggles of a young author. The central figure is an ordinary student. Early in the poem he suddenly gets an idea for a play, which he finishes on Christmas eve. When he falls asleep, he dreams of going to see his own play, three hundred years after it was written. The audience is made up entirely of skeletons, representing those who have been corrupted by the student's poetry. The skeletons recognize him, and throw him into a burning hole. In the conclusion the student awakes, throws his play away, and returns to his father. *En digters drøm* was ignored by most newspapers, but those who reviewed it found it to be promising, even though it was clearly the work of a young poet. In later years Sivle called the poem "pure madness."

In early 1879 Sivle returned to his home area. At first he lodged with the Brekke family, but he soon moved on to stay with his cousin Anders Hylland at Dyrdal, a small farm by the Nærøy Fjord. He remained there until the fall, working on the farm. His health was precarious, as he still suffered from the illness that had halted his studies. He frequently broke into tears, seemingly for no reason at all. He kept writing, still in Dano-Norwegian, and in fall 1879 he published a second volume of poetry, simply titled *Digte* (Poems), using his given name, Peder Sivle. *Digte* is a collection of religious poems, most of them probably written during his years in Christiania. Many of these poems deal with man's struggle with religion and how he is torn between doubt and belief, and between sin and grace. The epic poem "Gutten med blomsten" (The Boy with the Flower) stands out from the others. Slightly reminiscent of "Den fyrste songen," the poem tells of a young, happy boy who loses his mother at a young age and eventually moves to a city. Unable to regain his happiness there, he eventually travels to the mountains, where he falls asleep in the snow. He dreams of his dead mother, who tries to comfort him. He never wakes up.

Sivle returned to Christiania in the fall of 1879 with the intention of curing all his ills. In a 29 January

Cover for Sivle's only novel (1891, Strike), based on a labor dispute in the timber industry that had taken place in 1881 (Library of the University of California, Berkeley)

letter to his own parents, Sivle's friend Johan Fleischer described Sivle as "both sad and ill" and predicted, "he will certainly not live for long." The poet did survive, but it was obvious that he could not return to his studies. In early 1881 he moved to Langum, outside Drammen, where his father had bought a farm. He worked on the farm without much success. He also spent a lot of time pondering what to do with his life. When Sivle met his Christiania friends half a year later, they all described him as a new person. One of the biggest changes he had undergone was a break with religion. Sivle no longer harbored any thoughts of becoming a minister; he now saw himself as a poet. He had also become more politically aware and active: he voiced his views more openly and gradually became the center of attention in various social gatherings both in Drammen and Christiania.

In Drammen, Sivle wrote frequently for the newspaper *Buskerud Amtstidende* (Busterud County News), contributing mainly political articles but also some poems. Prior to the governmental elections in 1882 he appealed to the voters to support selected candidates under the heading "Enhver Splittelse vil bringe Fordærv" (All Divisions Create Destruction). That headline coincides with one of his strongest political views, that a nation should cooperate and stay together in order to prosper. In September 1883 Sivle became the editor of *Buskerud Amtstidende,* a position he held for a little more than a year. As a political journalist he made use of his extensive knowledge of history, but he lacked the independent mind that characterizes the best political commentators. Sivle faithfully supported Johan Sverdrup and the other leaders of Venstre (The Left).

In late 1884 Sivle left for Copenhagen. Even if he still had doubts about his abilities as a writer, his confidence was rising after his successful stint as a newspaper editor. He finished his story "Berre ein hund" (Just a Dog), which was published in *Nyt Tidsskrift* (New Magazine) the same year. The story takes place in the area where he grew up and is told through the perspective of a young boy. When an English mountaineer tries to reach a cave halfway up a steep mountainside, he loses his footing and falls to his death. The boy takes care of the mountaineer's dog, but his father dislikes the animal and orders one of his farmhands to shoot it. For the first time, Sivle uses his own language: a Landsmål heavily inflected by his own dialect. The story, an artistic breakthrough that made Sivle's name famous, remains one of his best-known stories.

In Copenhagen, Sivle mixed socially with people from the Faroe Islands. He viewed them as distant relatives, and was happy to discover that the Faroese and he could understand each other, even when they all spoke their native languages. Sivle heard many Faroese poems, and he was always intrigued by how such poetry celebrated the history of the Faroes. His readers were soon treated to his own accounts of the old Norse kings and heroes. His poem "Thord Folesson" was printed in the Christiania newspaper *Fedraheimen* on 8 April 1885. The poem deals with Thord Folesson, the flag bearer of King Olav during the battle at Stiklestad in 1030. Although Folesson is mortally wounded in the battle, he manages to ram the flag into the ground before he dies. In all his later books of poetry, but mainly in *Noreg: Nationale digte* (1894, Norway: National Poems), *Skaldemaal* (1896, The Voice of the Poets), and *Olavs-Kvæde* (1901, Olav Poems), Sivle often wrote about important persons and events in Norwegian history.

In the summer of 1885 Sivle traveled westward to Jutland and eventually ended up at Askov Højskole, where he enrolled as a student in the fall. His days in Denmark had done wonders for his mental health, and the poems he wrote at Askov were clearly the work of a poet at ease with himself. Sivle got on well with his fellow students and began to spend time with Wenche Nilsen, a woman who was the same age as Sivle but whose background could hardly be more different. Nilsen came from a wealthy family in Bergen, and she actively sought adventure and travel. Prior to her stay at Askov she had lived in France and Germany, where she studied arts and language and took a strong interest in literature. At the end of the school year Nilsen returned to Bergen by boat. Sivle accompanied her to Copenhagen, the departure point for her boat, and they became engaged there on 18 May 1886.

Sivle returned to Askov to spend the summer writing, and he finished two books, *Sogor* (Stories) and *Vossa-Stubba* (Stories from Voss). Both were published in 1887 and received high praise from the critics. The main differences between these collections are the language used and the seriousness of the stories. *Sogor* uses the same dialect-colored Landsmål of "Berre ein hund," which is included. All five stories in *Sogor* are rather serious, while the stories of *Vossa-Stubba* are written in his pure local dialect and are more humorous in tone. Some of the stories in *Vossa-Stubba,* which Sivle embellished and polished, were based on stories told by a local storyteller.

In 1887 Sivle, in addition to publishing his story collections, became the editor of *Kristianiaposten,* a Venstre newspaper. His main reason for accepting this position was that he needed a regular income to marry his fiancée. They married in August 1887, and the following year their only child, Susanna, was born.

Although his first years of marriage brought him joy, Sivle's four years as editor slowly turned into a nightmare. At the time Venstre was splitting in two factions, and those close to the government sorely needed a supportive paper. To those living in Norway and especially those in the press, it was obvious that supporters of the government had gotten rid of the previous editor because he criticized the government too much. Sivle, who had spent the last two years in Denmark, had a harder time seeing what was going on. He was out of touch with Norwegian politics and still followed Sverdrup blindly, even though Sverdrup was losing his influence and was no longer a central figure in Venstre. Sivle's continuous support for Sverdrup meant that his old friends in Christiania came to view him differently, and he was heavily criticized, not only in other papers. In Arne Garborg's drama *Uforsonlige* (1888, The Unforgiving) one of the characters, the weak and powerless editor Henning, is clearly based on Sivle.

Sverdrup's government fell in 1889. As a result, Sivle did not get the position for which he had applied in the National Archives in Trondheim. Instead, he remained the editor of *Kristianiaposten* for another two years, finally taking a leave in 1891 to spend more time on his own writing. For the rest of his life he never held a regular job.

Sivle's first book after resuming his career as a full-time author was his only novel, *Streik* (1891, Strike). The book was based on a real conflict that took place in Drammen a decade earlier. In 1881 the timber industry had suffered a minor downfall. Workers on several sawmills went on strike, and the conflicts remained tense until soldiers from the army opened fire on the masses, leaving one man dead. The following day the strikes ended. The theme of the novel was valid, and Sivle clearly supported the workers in their strike. Still, the critics asked why he had waited ten years before addressing this issue. Most critics also felt that he wrote better short stories and poems.

In 1891 Sivle received an author's grant from the government. The money had to be used abroad, and in early 1892 he left for Denmark, where he had spent a productive time just half a decade earlier. This time, however, he started work on what he intended to become his second novel, a family saga from the area where he grew up, but got nowhere. Also, he was struggling financially. The grant was soon spent, and he had to borrow both winter clothing and money. Sivle returned to Christiania after four months in Denmark, unhappy and with growing health problems. He had recurring headaches, which made it even harder to write.

Sivle got another government grant in 1892. A new and extended edition of *Vossa-Stubba* was published that year, including six new stories. Only one of the new stories, "Kjikartn" (The Binoculars), was previously unpublished—the remaining new stories had been printed in various magazines and newspapers. Sivle was embarking on a pattern he subsequently followed, first selling poems or stories to newspapers and then collecting them into books.

Sivle's next grant—the last he received for several years—was spent traveling in Great Britain, where he especially enjoyed his trips to Scotland. In the relations between Scotland and England he saw a parallel with the situation in Norway and Denmark. After three months in Great Britain he returned home to the financial struggles that had become habitual. His wife moved back to her parents' home in Bergen, where she got a job as a teacher. Sivle himself moved in with his father and borrowed even more money. His debts kept rising, and he received yet another advance on the novel he intended to write, but he still got nowhere with it. In his desperation Sivle started to drink more heavily. Staying away from alcohol was another struggle Sivle failed to win. In 1880 Sivle had feared becoming addicted to morphine; his doctor at the time suggested the unusual remedy of drinking alcohol as a substitute for the painkiller.

Sivle returned to a Norway at a time when the main political issue was the union with Sweden. The two countries had been united since 1814, with Sweden as the more powerful of the pair. Norway had its own government but no foreign policy under the Swedish crown. In Norway there was a strong opposition against the union. Many of the loudest and most influential voices of the opposition belonged to the Landsmål movement, including writers such as Garborg and the editor of *Den 17de Mai* (The 17th of May), Rasmus Steinsvik. Sivle's poems from this decade, starting with the collection *Noreg* in 1894, are concerned with this theme. Sivle was one of the few Norwegian authors who discussed the union in their writings, and in *Noreg,* a slim volume of poetry, all the poems can be read as arguments for a break with Sweden. In the opening poem, "Noreg," he calls for Norwegians to give their lives for their country. In other poems he writes about historical figures such as Harald Hårfagre, the first king to rule over all of Norway, or about major historical events such as the battle at Svolder in the year 1000.

In his search for stability Sivle spent almost a year with his friend Hovden in Lista in the south of Norway. There he was able to write *Nye Vossa-Stubbar* (New Stories from Voss), published in fall 1894, and a new book of poetry, *Bersøglis- og andre Viser* (Plainspoken Poems and Other Poems), published in spring 1895, both of which received general praise. In summer 1895 Hovden's wife caught an illness that proved fatal, and Sivle traveled westward along the coast, settling briefly in Sandnes outside Stavanger, where he was reunited with his family for the first time in two years. He ventured on a lecture tour, in which he gave listeners a mixture of politics and poetry, with the main message being his advocacy for the dissolution of the union. His lecture, *Nationalt Selvmord* (A National Suicide), was published in 1897. In a time when public speakers had as much influence as newspapers did, his spoken and written words helped shape public opinion. In 1896 Sivle returned to Christiania. He kept writing, and his 1896 book *Skaldemaal* received praise from the critics. His later works, *En Fyrstikke og andre Viser* (1898, A Match and Other Songs), *Folk og fæ* (1898, People and Cattle), and *Olavs-Kvæde,* were largely ignored by the press.

When Sivle's father died in fall 1898, Sivle inherited the farm and some money; he also got a government grant again in 1898. All this meant that he was finally able to support his own family. They all settled on the farm, and for a while it seemed as if his childhood dream had come true. He lived the quiet life of a poet, with a small farm of his own. But it turned out that Sivle was not suited for such a life. His wife, with her background from the city of Bergen, had to do most of the farm work, while Sivle drank heavily. The couple struggled to find harmony. They sold the farm in 1900, after having spent money from yet another grant in Germany and Denmark, and settled in Drammen.

Sivle realized that he would not get any more grants as long as he did not publish anything, and *Olavs-Kvæde,* his final book of poetry, appeared in 1901. The few reviewers who mentioned it criticized the lack of new poems. Sivle felt he had failed in the only field in which he had experienced success. After a lot of public discussion, Sivle received a final governmental grant in 1902. The next year saw Høgre (The Right) win the election, and the amount given to support authors was cut in half. In the discussions concerning which authors should receive government support, Sivle's name was hardly mentioned. He felt like a forgotten man.

In June 1904 Sivle entered the offices of *Buskerud Amtstidende* with a poem called "Eit Testament" (A Will). When the paper printed it, the editors changed the title to "Eit Ord" (A Word). It is one of Sivle's finest and also one of his most autobiographical poems. It opens with the speaker saying goodbye to his country; he goes on to tell the story of his life. In the final stanza he again says goodbye to his country; the poem ends:

Men eg vil Noreg
so indarleg væl,
at hugheilt so gav eg det
Hjarta og Sjæl.

(But I want nothing
but the best for my country,
which is why I've given it
my heart and soul.)

Sivle read the poem publicly on various occasions that summer, and his friends asked him how seriously they should take it: did he intend to move to another country, or was he talking about suicide? He openly confirmed that he had lost the will to live. Still, he had not lost his ability to be entertaining, and at his final public event in Drammen on 21 August 1904 he read his funniest stories before changing the mood completely by reading "Eit Ord."

Hovden met Sivle in Christiania in late August and tried to talk him out of the suicide set forth in "Eit Testament." Hovden's wife, Wenche, did the same, speaking to him on the morning of 6 September 1904, but it was too late. Around noon that same day Sivle was found dead in a public bath in Christiania, a gun by his side.

Per Sivle's books are rarely read today. The 1970s saw a brief revival of some of his writings, including the novel *Streik,* but with the exception of his most popular poems and stories his body of work remains unknown to most. Still, he was an important figure at the end of the nineteenth century, and his finest works deserve the reader's attention and a long life.

Biographies:

Anders Hovden, *Per Sivle: Ei livssogu* (Christiania: Norigs Ungdomslag og Student-Maallaget, 1905);

Bjarte Birkeland, *Per Sivle* (Oslo: Det Norske Samlaget, 1961);

Alfred Fidjestøl, *Eit halvt liv: ein biografi om Per Sivle* (Oslo: Det Norske Samlaget, 2007).

Reference:

Bjarte Birkeland, ed., *Sivle frå Voss* (Oslo: Det Norske Samlaget, 1974).

Amalie Skram
(22 August 1846 – 15 March 1905)

Katherine Hanson
University of Washington

and

Judith Messick
Northwestern University

BOOKS: *Constance Ring* (Christiania: Huseby, 1885); translated by Judith Messick and Katherine Hanson as *Constance Ring* (Seattle: Seal Press, 1988);

Sjur Gabriel (Copenhagen: Salmonsen, 1887);

To Venner (Copenhagen: Salmonsen, 1887);

Om Albertine: pamflett (Christiania: Huseby, 1887);

Lucie (Copenhagen: Schubothe, 1888); translated by Hanson and Messick as *Lucie* (Norwich, U.K.: Norvik Press, 2001);

Fjældmennesker: lystspill i fire akter, by Skram and Erik Skram (Copenhagen: Schubothe, 1889);

S. G. Myre (Copenhagen: Schubothe, 1890);

Børnefortællinger (Copenhagen: Schubothe, 1890);

Kjærlighed i nord og syd: noveller (Copenhagen: Schubothe, 1891)–includes "Bøn og anfægtelse," "Knut Tandberg," and *Fru Inés;*

Forrådt (Copenhagen: Schubothe, 1892); translated by Aileen Hennes as *Betrayed* (London & New York: Pandora, 1986);

Agnete: drama i tre akter (Copenhagen: Schubothe, 1893); translated by Verne Moberg as *Agnete,* in *Slaves of Love and Other Stories,* edited by James McFarlane (Oxford: Oxford University Press, 1982);

Professor Hieronimus (Copenhagen: Gyldendal, 1895); translated by Alice Stronach and G. B. Jacoby as *Professor Hieronimus* (London: John Lane, 1899);

På Sct. Jørgen (Copenhagen: Gyldendal, 1895); translated by Hanson and Messick as "St. Jørgen's," in *Under Observation* (Seattle: Women in Translation, 1992);

Afkom (Copenhagen: Gyldendal, 1898);

Sommer: sma fortællinger (Copenhagen: Gyldendal, 1899)–includes "Sommer," "Memento Mori," "Glæde," "Post festum," "Den røde gardin," and "En Rose";

Julehelg (Copenhagen: Gyldendal, 1900);

Amalie Skram (Store Norske Leksikon <http://snl.no/.bilde/Skram%2C_Amalie_(portrett)>)

Landsforrædere (Copenhagen: Gyldendal, 1901);

Mennesker: ufuldendt roman (Copenhagen: Gyldendal, 1905);

Udvalgte fortællinger (Copenhagen: Gyldendal, 1909)–includes "Madam Høiers lejfolk," translated by Anders Orbeck as "Madame Høyer's Tenants," in

Norway's Best Stories, edited by Hanna Astrup Larsen (New York: American-Scandinavian Foundation, 1927), pp. 557–570; also includes "Karen's Jul," translated by Janet Garton as "Karen's Christmas," in *Slaves of Love and Other Stories;*

"Optimistisk Læsemaade": Amalie Skrams litteraturkritikk, edited by Irene Englestad (Oslo: Gyldendal, 1987);

Fortellinger (Oslo: Pax, 1993)–includes "Byråsjef Krogh's."

Edition and Collection: *Fru Inés* (Oslo: Gyldendal, 1925);

Samlede værker, 9 volumes (Copenhagen: Gyldendal, 1905–1993).

Edition in English: *Under Observation,* translated by Katherine Hanson and Judith Messick (Seattle: Women in Translation, 1992)–includes "Professor Hieronymous" and "St. Jørgen's."

PLAY PRODUCTIONS: *Fjældmennesker: lystspill i fire akter,* Copenhagen, Dagmarteatret, 1892;

Agnete: drama i tre akter, Copenhagen, Dagmarteatret, 21 March 1893.

TRANSLATION: Arne Garborg, *Den fortabte Fader,* translated into Danish by Skram (Copenhagen: Gyldendal, 1901).

Amalie Skram began her writing career during a period of literary and social ferment in Scandinavia. During the 1870s and 1880s traditional values in the spheres of religion, politics, and art were under attack. The most prominent voices in these controversies were men like Henrik Ibsen, Bjørnstjerne Bjørnson, and Georg Brandes; few women were bold enough to speak out in the public debate. In *Amtmandens Døttre* (The District Governor's Daughters), published in 1855–1856, the novelist Camilla Collett had claimed a woman's right to make her own decisions about marriage. But Skram was the first Norwegian woman who openly attacked the double standard of sexual morality, the hypocrisies of the church, and the inequities in the class system. Like her male colleagues, Skram believed in the social value of literature–that books and plays had an obligation to tell the truth, however ugly and shocking. Her writing was driven by compassion for the downtrodden and by sincere indignation toward institutions that oppressed and deformed human relationships. Then as now Skram's art caused a stir. Throughout the decade of Skram's greatest productivity, during which she published at least a major work a year, her novels were savagely condemned by conservative elements of her society. Yet, her books have endured, finding new audiences that appreciate her fearless honesty and her willingness to explore the darker realities of human experience.

Skram's literary reputation has undergone change during the past century. Her reputation was originally based on her powerful four-volume cycle, *Hellemyrsfolket* (The People of Hellemyr), published from 1887 to 1898. Generally regarded as her masterwork, the tetralogy traces the fortunes of an impoverished Bergen family through successive generations of poverty, alcoholism, and crime. Her vivid and unsentimental portrayal of Norwegian society, both rural and urban, earned Skram the reputation of being Norway's greatest naturalistic writer. Since the 1970s critical attention has shifted to her novels about marriage and her two asylum novels, *Professor Hieronimus* (1895; translated as *Professor Hieronimus,* 1899) and *På Sct. Jørgen* (1895, translated as "St. Jørgen's," 1992). The four marriage novels–*Constance Ring* (1885; translated as *Constance Ring,* 1988); *Lucie* (1888; translated as *Lucie,* 2001); *Fru Inés* (Mrs. Inés), originally published in the 1891 collection *Kjærlighed i nord og syd* (Love in North and South); and *Forrådt* (1892; translated as *Betrayed,* 1986)–share a profoundly pessimistic view of the possibility of lasting happiness between the sexes. Skram's marriage novels, like her two asylum novels, were deeply influenced by her own experiences. Marriage and the problematic relations between men and women were issues that occupied her throughout her writing career.

In life as well as art, Skram challenged conventional ideas of female behavior. She was born Amalie Alver in Bergen on 22 August 1846, the daughter of Mons Monson Alver, a shopkeeper, and Lovise Sivertsen Alver, a former housemaid. She was one of nine children, only five of whom survived until adulthood. In spite of their modest background, the parents were ambitious for their children and sent Amalie and her four brothers to the city's best schools. Even as a child, Amalie's exceptional beauty and intelligence made her the center of attention, although later in her life she came to believe that her beauty was a curse that deformed her relationships with other people. In an 1896 letter to Gerhard Gran, her brother Ludvig described two opposing aspects of her personality: a cheerful, energetic participation in daily life combined with a darker, withdrawn, idealistic awareness of sin and suffering. Throughout her life she pondered religious questions; her faith waxed and waned, but she retained a deep conviction of the world's pains and sorrows. Her life was marked by abrupt changes in circumstance. Between her Bergen childhood and her years as a celebrated author in Copenhagen she experienced poverty and economic security, marriage and divorce, sickness and health, obscurity and public acclaim.

Title page for Skram's first novel (translated, 1988), about a young woman trapped in a marriage to a man she does not love (University of Michigan Libraries)

In 1863 Alver's father suddenly went bankrupt and fled to America, leaving the family in desperate straits. Seven months later, in October 1864, she made an advantageous marriage to a prosperous Bergen sea captain nine years her senior, Bernt Ulrik August Müller. Although the two had little in common, the marriage provided financial security, higher social status, and an unusual breadth of experience for a nineteenth-century woman. During the following decade Amalie Müller spent extended periods at sea with her husband, sailing around the world. Having studied French and German at school, she learned English and used the time at sea to read contemporary novels in all three languages. By the time she was twenty-two, she had two sons—Jacob Worm Müller was born in 1866 and Ludvig August Müller in 1868. In 1869 she sailed with her husband and children on a two-year voyage to Australia. The ship paid extended visits to ports in Peru, Spain, and Constantinople, experiences that she drew on in her later fiction.

In 1876 Bernt Müller retired from the sea, and the family settled on the island of Ask, outside Bergen. Pressures on the marriage increased, and in the fall of 1877 Amalie tried to get a divorce. Faced with a wall of opposition from family and friends, she had a mental breakdown and entered Gaustad Mental Hospital in Christiania (now Oslo), where she spent nearly two months under the benign care of Dr. Ole Rømer Sandberg. Released in February 1878 she left Bergen for good, taking her children to live with her brothers in eastern Norway. In the fall of 1878 she received an uncontested three-year separation. The unsuccessful marriage to Müller had a great impact on her view of life and the fiction she later wrote.

Amalie Müller's first publications were articles and reviews of contemporary literature. Even before the separation, she had been drawn into the circle of young leftist writers surrounding *Bergens Tidende*, the city's major newspaper. She took part in amateur theatricals and cultivated her interest in literature, particularly the naturalistic literature that represented a new trend in Scandinavian letters. Her first published work, a favorable review of the Danish author J. P. Jacobsen's debut novel, *Fru Marie Grubbe* (1877), appeared in *Bergens Tidende* on 17 February 1877, unsigned. Between 1877 and 1883 she wrote for *Smaalenenes Amtstidende* and *Dagbladet* under the signature "i.e." Writing anonymously or pseudonymously because she feared losing custody of her children, she reviewed works by many of the important writers of the day—plays by Ibsen and Bjørnson, novels by Alexander L. Kielland and Arne Garborg, and short stories by Jonas Lie, Leo Tolstoy, and George Eliot. Notable among her articles is a long review of Ibsen's *Et Dukkehjem* (1879, A Doll's House, translated as *Nora*, 1882) and of Collett's *Mod Strømmen* (1879, Against the Current). Her articles are often lengthy and perceptive analyses in which she defends the naturalistic insistence that truth be revealed, no matter how ugly or unpleasant, and offers criticism when characters lack psychological development and depth. She was particularly receptive to works that examined the position of women in society and called for reform in the relations between the sexes. Writing literary criticism proved to be an invaluable apprenticeship that let her immerse herself in contemporary literary currents, hone her writing skills, and develop her views on the function and aesthetics of literature. Her reviews and articles are marked by unusual self-assurance and independence, qualities remarkable for a young woman with limited formal education and no obvious credentials within the Norwegian literary milieu.

From the beginning the young writer had a strategic sense of how to build a professional career. She cultivated the acquaintance of the writers and politicians of the Left and embraced their new ideas about literature and art. Within weeks after her release from Gaustad in 1877 Müller wrote to Bjørnson, enclosing a flattering analysis of his recent play *Kongen* (translated as *The King*, 1914) with the request that he read it before she sent it to a publisher. The letter, from an unknown and anonymous "Hr. M." to one of the most famous literary figures of the day, piqued Bjørnson's interest and launched a correspondence and friendship that lasted many years. The letter to Bjørnson began a practice of reaching out to influential literary figures for validation and support, a practice she followed for the rest of her life. The identity of "i.e." was soon an open secret, and her bold articles drew praise from the radical authors she admired. Bjørnson provided an entrée to the literary elite of first Norway, and later Denmark.

As a beautiful, divorced writer with radical male friends, Müller felt increasingly conspicuous in Fredrikshald, and in 1881 she moved with her children to the more permissive environment of Christiania, where they lived with her brother Wilhelm. Her circle in Christiania included artists and writers such as Garborg, Christian Krogh, and Frits Thaulow. She also became acquainted with educated, progressive women such as Vilhelmine Ullmann, Margrethe Vullum, and Mathilde Schjøtt, whose company may have encouraged her to begin writing fiction. In 1882 her first short story, "Madam Høiers lejfolk" (translated as "Madame Høyer's Tenants," 1927), appeared anonymously in *Nyt Tidskrift*. It portrays a family living in abject poverty and a callous landlady who evicts them when they cannot pay the rent: the mother's newborn babies die, and the desperate woman is taken to prison. The detailed and starkly realistic descriptions of people and locations in "Madam Høiers lejfolk" became the hallmark of all of Amalie Skram's future writing. Predictably, its focus on the destructive effects of poverty created shock and controversy among the Norwegian public, the first of many controversies that her fiction provoked during her literary career. Many of the prominent writers who admired her bold reviews did not enthusiastically support her move onto their artistic terrain. Even among her admirers, her controversial themes and blunt writing style caused consternation and alarm. Stung by the controversy that the story provoked, she wrote to a friend that she did not care if people liked what she wrote; she only wanted them to react and not be indifferent. In spite of her brave words, for a time she considered moving to America.

In August 1882, at a celebration of Bjørnson's twenty-fifth anniversary as a poet, Müller met the Danish writer Erik Skram, who opened for her a new world of happiness and passionate literary collaboration. Taught by experience to fear emotional entanglements, she at first resisted getting involved with him. During the two years of their courtship they wrote long letters to each other several times a week, exchanging gossip, discussing literature, theater, and politics. Raised in different countries, with different emotional and sexual histories, they explored their different positions in the current social debate about sexual morality. Erik Skram argued from the point of view of a man who not only enjoyed sex but also believed that love was the highest, most fulfilling experience a man and woman could share. Müller, whose previous sexual experience had been unhappy, felt that a person became a whole human being through suffering, not love. Extending her sympathies to other women, she rejected the exploitation and injustice implicit in the double standard. Skram's arguments prevailed, and in April 1884 they married and settled in Copenhagen. Her later letters to Erik describe her joyous transformation as a result of their marriage. But the issues they debated during their courtship remained a central concern in her life and art. For both parties, the marriage was an intellectual and emotional union, a loving and turbulent partnership with many separations caused by their individual pursuits of professional careers. Their decision to marry was also a joint commitment to earning their living as writers, an agreement to share the economic burden of the household. Recognizing that his wife's talent surpassed his own, Erik read and critiqued her manuscripts. He provided emotional and editorial support and encouraged her to write from her own experience.

Amalie Skram's first novel, *Constance Ring*, was published in the summer of 1885. Its young heroine, married to an older man she does not love, seeks a divorce when she discovers his sexual liaison with their housemaid. Fearful of scandal, her friends and family try to block the divorce. Even Constance's minister urges her to turn the other cheek, to accept her husband's behavior as normal and to maintain the marriage at all costs. Constance yields to the pressure and remains in a marriage that is repugnant to her. But when she is freed by a providential storm in which her husband drowns at sea, she discovers not happiness but depression and the recognition that her education and background have provided no options for an independent life. With no way to support herself she agrees to marry Lorck, a young doctor who has long pursued her. The marriage brings a sexual awakening for Constance, but it is short lived, collapsing when she discovers that her husband still supports a child that he fathered with a young servant girl, Kristine, before their marriage. Horrified and jealous, Constance thinks not

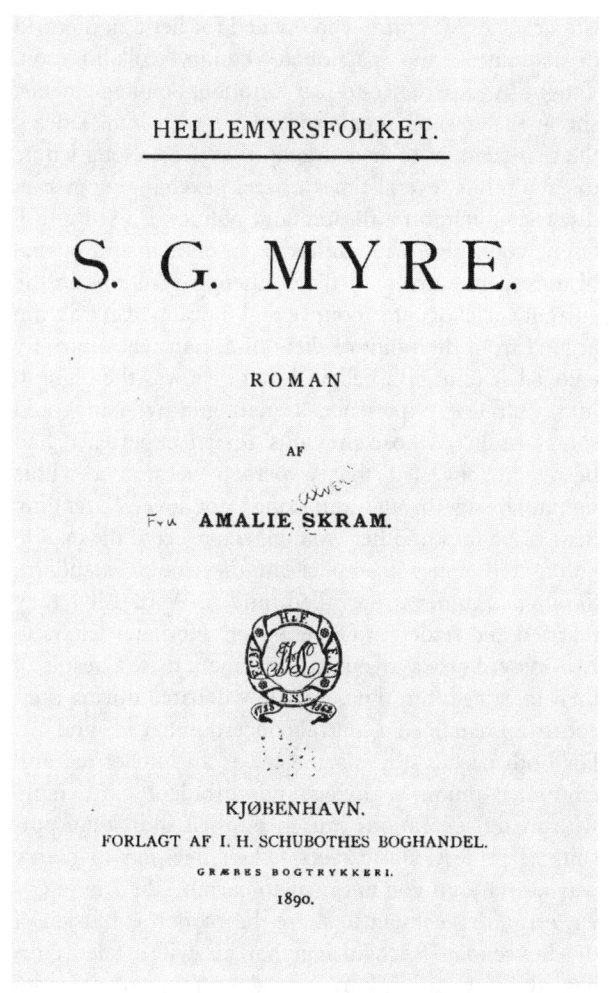

Title page for the third novel in Skram's Hellemyrsfolket *(The People of Hellemyr)* tetralogy (University of Michigan Libraries)

only about her own loss but also about the hypocritical and exploitive social system that allows men to seduce poor young women with impunity. She withdraws from her husband, and during the months of cold estrangement that follow, she is courted by Meier, a cynical young artist. This relationship also ends in shock and disgust after Constance spends a night with him and discovers that her seamstress, Emma, is his mistress. Convinced of the unbridgeable moral gulf between men and women, Constance repudiates a society that condones the double standard and the exploitation of lower-class women. Contaminated by her own action, unable to live in a world of lies and deceit, she commits suicide.

Skram's unsparing examination of marital misery and sexual double standards in the novel created shockwaves. *Constance Ring* became part of the great Scandinavian debate about sexual morality. Newspaper articles attacked the morality and artistry of the novel. Bjørnson wrote to say that he was disappointed and angered by her decision to write a novel. Another critic disparagingly compared Skram to Émile Zola and his novel *Nana* (1880): Constance was "Nana under northern skies." The novel was attacked for its style, its rough, abrupt prose, and its heavy-handed criticism of male behavior. Then as now, critics faulted the passages in which characters function mainly as political and cultural exemplars. Yet, to modern readers *Constance Ring* remains one of Skram's most impressive novels. Its enduring power lies in its moving psychological portraits, its truthful examination of dysfunctional relationships between the sexes, and its exploration of the gulfs of incomprehension between men and women.

The frankness of Skram's writing did not endear her to potential publishers. She had to struggle to get *Constance Ring* into print. Frederik V. Hegel of the prestigious Gyldendal firm in Copenhagen had agreed to publish the novel; but when he read the page proofs, he withdrew his offer. He correctly anticipated the public reaction and left the young author to find a publisher for herself. Although Skram protested the decision in several vigorous letters to Hegel, he remained unmoved. After Hegel's rejection, no Danish publisher was willing to risk the notoriety and possible financial loss involved in publishing *Constance Ring,* so Skram was forced into the humiliating position of publishing the book on a commission basis with the Norwegian bookseller Olaf Huseby. During the next decade, a period of astonishing literary productivity, during which she wrote nine novels, a play, and several collections of short stories, her difficulties finding publishers continued. *Sjur Gabriel* (1887) and *To Venner* (1887, Two Friends), the first two volumes of the *Hellemyrsfolket* tetralogy, were published on a profit-sharing basis with the Salmonsen Company. Not until 1888, when she was looking for a publisher for *Lucie,* did she find in Paul Langhoff of Schubothe a publisher willing to support her work financially. With Schubothe she published *S. G. Myre,* the third volume of *Hellemyrsfolket,* in 1890, and two other novels about women in loveless marriages, *Fru Inés* in 1891 and *Forrådt* in 1892. Finally, in 1895, a decade after Hegel had rejected *Constance Ring,* she persuaded Gyldendal, then under the more liberal editorship of Jacob Hegel, to publish her books. She remained with Gyldendal, advised and supported by her gifted editor, Peter Nansen, for the remainder of her writing career.

In the months that followed *Constance Ring* Skram published two novellas in the journal *Tilskueren* (The Spectators): "Bøn og Anfægtelse" (Prayer and Remorse) in May and "Knut Tandberg" in the November–December issue of 1886. Skram later included them in *Kjærlighed i nord og syd.* Both stories are set in contemporary Christiania and depict a marriage strained by infidelity, but here the similarity ends. The author explores how different class backgrounds, religious beliefs, and emotional temperaments can influence the way couples cope with marital difficulties.

Skram's long-standing concern with the sexual exploitation of lower-class women flared up during a campaign against prostitution in Christiania in 1886. In December, Krogh published his novel *Albertine,* which excoriated the police for their harsh treatment of a young prostitute while ignoring the men who paid for her. Krogh's book caused an uproar and was confiscated by the Norwegian authorities. In September 1887 Skram entered the fray with her pamphlet *Om Albertine* (About Albertine), protesting against different standards for men and women and arguing the injustice of penalizing women for behavior they were driven to by economic need.

In fall 1887 Skram began her ambitious *Hellemyrsfolket* project tracing one family through four generations of social change with the publication of *Sjur Gabriel* and *To Venner. Sjur Gabriel* begins in the 1830s on a small, hardscrabble farm called Hellemyr, a few miles north of Bergen. The farm's owner, Sjur Gabriel, and his wife, Oline, unable to feed their family on farming alone, supplement their income by fishing and selling their catch at the wharf in Bergen. The meager landscape, the farm buildings, the city with its narrow streets and wooden buildings are described in vivid detail. Skram's naturalistic depiction of rural life marked a departure from the way the Norwegian peasant had previously been portrayed—in Bjørnson's *bondefortellinger* (peasant tales). While Bjørnson's tales are realistic, the reality is bathed in sunlight. Skram portrays another reality: hard work, harsh conditions, and little hope of improving one's lot. Some of her characters seek solace in religion with its promise of a better life after death; others, like Oline, take refuge in alcohol.

Much of the distinctiveness of Skram's characters derives from their dialogue. They speak in a dialect called *strilemål,* a bold decision on Skram's part because it challenged literary convention and because Norwegian dialects had as yet no official written form. While modern critics recognize her innovative use of dialect, her contemporaries in Norway and in Denmark complained that the passages written in dialect were unintelligible. Conservative critics were also offended by the coarse manners of the characters and their primitive living conditions. A childbirth scene, in particular, was condemned for its vulgarity. When Oline's labor starts in the middle of the night, Sjur Gabriel has no choice but to call on a hideous old woman, whom he fears and detests, to help his wife deliver the baby. Skram's graphic depiction of childbirth in rural, primitive conditions was a first in Norwegian literature.

Vesle-Gabriel, the newborn, survives his infancy despite his mother's bouts with illness and drunkenness. Sjur Gabriel cares for his son with a mother's tenderness, and for six years the boy is the one bright spot in his life. But when the boy falls gravely ill and dies, both parents interpret their son's death as God's punishment for their sinful lives. Their remorse is exceeded only by their sense of defeat and hopelessness, and the novel ends with these words: "Fra den dag av drakk både mannen og konen på Hellemyren" (From that day on both husband and wife drank at Hellemyr).

To Venner, published less than two months after *Sjur Gabriel,* picks up the story of the family in the early 1850s. The children have moved away from the farm and have found work in Bergen. Their parents, Oline especially, are even more debased: she is often seen in town, always drunk, a laughingstock for school children, a burning shame for her children and grandchildren. For Oline's grandson Sivert the shame is so acute that he seeks escape by enlisting as a cabin boy on the bark *To Venner.* Sivert goes to sea in chapter three, and the remainder of the novel is an account of his first journey. Writing with the authority of her years at sea, Skram depicts life aboard a sailing ship in all its rawness and brutality.

A novice at the bottom of the social hierarchy, Sivert is subjected to ridicule and humiliation. He learns the ropes quickly and wins acceptance among the crew, but falls short on tests of his character. A letter home is more false than true, an exaggeration of his accomplishments and bravery. Another letter, this one from home to the mean-spirited ship's cook, reveals that Sivert's grandmother is *Småfylla,* the town drunk. Crushed by the revelation, Sivert starts to think of his grandparents as a curse he cannot escape. He fights back, but so viciously he nearly kills the cook. Card playing leads to petty theft, which he denies when confronted. Whether through luck or deception, Sivert always manages to avoid the consequences of his missteps. The novel ends with a masterful description of a storm at sea in which *To Venner* suffers irreparable damage, but before it goes down, the crew is rescued.

In letters to Lie and Garborg, Skram explained how she came to write the Hellemyr novels. Growing up in Bergen she had heard about a young man who had committed suicide. She soon realized that before she could tell his story she had to write about his grandparents and parents. The influences of heredity and environment were generations deep, and Skram believed that by showing these influences she could bring her readers to view human shortcomings with understanding and compassion. At the time of its publi-

Title page for Skram's collection (Love in North and South), which includes two short stories and the novel Fru Inés (Mrs. Inés), which was published separately in 1925 (University of Michigan Libraries)

cation, *To Venner* found few compassionate readers, however. Once again, Skram's use of dialect was an obstacle, and the realistic depiction of lusty sailors carousing and whoring while in foreign ports was viewed as offensive. Skram's insistence on telling the truth was turning her into a pariah.

In 1888 Skram began the third volume of *Hellemyrsfolket, S. G. Myre;* but the work went slowly, and she had to spend periods away from home to find conditions in which she could write. She laid the unfinished novel aside and started a new book: *Lucie,* the second of her marriage novels. Skram wrote to a friend that she felt compelled to write this novel—that the subject would not release her until she put pen to paper. With sociological precision, she faithfully re-created the streets, apartments, and tenements of Christiania. Conversations and scenes captured many of the passionate political and social controversies occurring in her society. But personal concerns also figure in the novel. Skram's marriage had been going badly, and the couple may have been considering a separation.

The theme of jealousy looms large in the marriage between Lucie, a beautiful young Tivoli dancer, and Gerner, a wealthy, older man of a higher class. In *Constance Ring,* lower-class women exist only in the background of the central plot: men use Kristine and Emma as sexual surrogates for women like Constance. In *Lucie,* Skram moves the lower-class girl to the foreground. The novel depicts what happens within a marriage and society if the wife has had a sexually liberated past. Both parties have come to the relationship with sexual experience, but for Gerner the liaison with the uninhibited Lucie has been a sexual awakening. In the grip of his passion for Lucie, Gerner tries to erase the social and cultural gap between them and make her into a bourgeois wife. The novel anatomizes the destructive effects of Gerner's educational project. At first Lucie is eager to be his student—she wants to be made new, to walk the streets of Christiania as a respectable lady with a prosperous husband. But Gerner's efforts to create a new identity for Lucie gradually strip her of the characteristics he loved in the first place. Lucie's warmth and spontaneity become sources of embarrassment instead of pleasure. Tormented by jealousy of her past, filled with self-doubt, Gerner is outraged because Lucie refuses to be "ydmyk og angrende, en botferdig Magdalena i sinn og miner" (humble and repentant, a penitential Magdalene in mind and deportment). Increasingly at cross purposes, the two slide into a baffled fury, astonished and horrified by each other's demands.

In Skram's portrayal there are two victims in this marriage: both are presented with all their contradictions. Skram mercilessly depicts Gerner's arrogance and pride, but she also shows his suffering. Poisoned by jealousy, he has driven his wife away, fully recognizing the folly of his actions. Yet, in spite of his frustration and misery, his love for his wife endures. Gerner tenderly cares for Lucie during her pregnancy and accepts her abuse without recrimination. In this strange and lurid novel, in which horror piles upon horror, Skram shines a truthful light on the complexities of human relationships. As in *Constance Ring,* the view is pessimistic about the possibilities of lasting happiness between men and women divided by differences in power, class, and social attitudes.

Lucie was published in the autumn of 1888, and to Skram's surprise the work sold well. But as with her other novels, *Lucie* aroused both praise and savage criticism. Her topics—domestic misery, hypocrisy, frigidity, prostitution, crime, drunkenness, mental illness—

revealed the underside of her society, and conservative elements in her society did not forgive her.

In January 1889 Skram published a short story, "Bobler" (Bubbles), in the magazine *Ny Jord* (New Earth), and in February she and Erik collaborated on a four-act comedy, *Fjældmennesker.* (Mountain Folk), intending it for performance at a student society. In April she traveled to Norway to apply for a state stipend as an artist. Always entrepreneurial, she solicited letters of endorsement from literary men such as Lie, Brandes, and Sophus Schandorph. In spite of her efforts in Christiania, Skram's application for state support was rejected by Norwegian authorities. One member of the committee that denied her application said he could not support the author of *Lucie.* (Not until 1901, in a more liberal Denmark, did Skram finally receive a small government stipend recognizing her artistic work.)

After she left Christiania, Skram spent several months with her brother Ludvig in Kongsberg, breathing Norwegian air and returning to her work on *S. G. Myre*. She wrote lively letters to Erik about the walks she took and the people she observed. In one letter, she mentioned visits to a midwife. In Kongsberg, she discovered she was pregnant with her third child. Her daughter, Johanne, was born on 9 October 1889, when Skram was forty-three. The child became the center of her parents' life and provided a common commitment in a marriage that was increasingly strained by the absences and economic pressures involved in maintaining separate writing careers.

Work on *S. G. Myre* progressed slowly during the winter after her daughter's birth. In May 1890 Skram spent several weeks away from home, struggling to complete the book. Published that fall, the novel is both fiction and cultural history. It is panoramic in scope, with several subplots, a large cast of characters, and a focus on the city of Bergen. The action advances into the late 1850s, years Skram could bring to life from her own memories of her Bergen childhood. As in her earlier Hellemyr novels, Skram delineates class background with detailed descriptions of homes and social rituals: parties, prayer meetings, even funerals. Her keen ear for dialect and speech patterns contributes yet another layer of authenticity.

The pulse of the novel is in the characters' struggle to secure a living and to satisfy their longing for love. Sivert Jensen is back in Bergen, determined to find work and make a living in town. An erotic undercurrent runs through the narrative sparking relationships that cross the boundaries of social class: Sivert responds impetuously to the flirtations of Lydia, the daughter of his employer; Petra willingly accepts the caresses of the master of the house where she is a domestic servant; and her sister Andrea, who cannot resist the excitement of the town's nightlife, shirks her duties at home. Everyone wants to mate, it seems, but more often than not lovemaking leads to feelings of guilt, shame and regret.

Religion is another important influence governing the lives of Skram's characters regardless of class. The wealthiest may not attend prayer meetings or recite hymns; yet, they too judge themselves and their actions according to biblical law. When his wife dies, Consul Smith is beset by nagging doubts that the venereal disease he contracted on a business trip may have caused his wife's illness, and his thoughts echo Sjur Gabriel's after the death of his son, Vesle-Gabriel: "Syndens straff var dog forferdelig. En eneste times lettsindighet og hele livet lagt øde" (The punishment of sin was terrible. A single hour's recklessness and an entire life laid to ruin). The theme of retribution does not weigh as heavily in this book, however, as in the earlier volumes of *Hellemyrsfolket;* though the characters are at times overcome with feelings of guilt and shame, in *S. G. Myre* their instinct to survive is strong enough to pull them back on course.

Sivert's recklessness costs him his job on the wharf, but before long he finds work as a shop clerk. The general store where Sivert works is one of the focal points in the narrative. Located on the busiest street in Bergen's business district, the store is a meeting place for all segments of society. The store is where Petra and Sivert meet, where Sivert sees Lydia again years after his banishment, where members of Sivert's family can find him to ask for money. The store is also where Sivert becomes a petty thief, "borrowing" from the till to maintain his expensive habits.

Sivert's grandparents, Sjur Gabriel and Oline, live out their lives in drunkenness and squalor. The shadow they cast on him is accentuated by their deaths, both of which he witnesses. Sjur Gabriel dies of natural causes, but Oline accidently dies at Sivert's hands. Because no one saw the accident Sivert rationalizes that he need not confess. He accepts Consul Smith's proposal that he assume ownership of the store under a changed name (Sivert Jensen becomes S. G. Myre), on the condition he settle down and marry. Two marriages end the novel: Sivert takes Petra for his wife, and Smith marries Lydia.

Exhausted by her efforts to complete *S. G. Myre,* Skram laid aside the Hellemyr cycle for several years. The birth of her daughter created economic pressure for her to produce books quickly, and shorter works became her preferred mode. In late 1890 she published *Børnefortællinger* (Children's Stories). In January 1891 she proposed a new collection of stories to Schubothe, many of which had been published before. *Kjærlighed i nord og syd* included "Bøn og anfægtelse" and "Knut Tandberg" along with a new novella, *Fru Inés*. Set in Constantinople, the plot of *Fru Inés* draws on Skram's

Title page for Skram's play (translated, 1982) about a woman who obtains money by illegal means but believes her action to be justified (University of Michigan Libraries)

memories of a visit twelve years earlier on her voyage around the world with Müller. The following year she published another short novel: *Forrådt*. Both *Fru Inés* and *Forrådt* look unflinchingly at personalities and marital relationships in crisis. As in Skram's earlier marriage novels, relationships founder because of differences of class, sexual experience, and morality. The male and female characters cannot help inflicting grievous psychic wounds on each other. Love and death are linked in these novels as they are in *Lucie* and *Constance Ring*.

In March 1893 Skram's play *Agnete* (translated, 1982) was performed in Copenhagen. Parallels between *Agnete* and Ibsen's *Et Dukkehjem* have been noted by theater and literary critics. The heroines of both works, Nora and Agnete, obtain money by illegal means and feel their actions are justified, but neither of the men in whom they confide share their vision of a love that is all-forgiving and accepting. Unlike Ibsen's heroine, Agnete is a divorced woman, and Skram's play invites the audience to speculate on Nora's life after she leaves her "Doll's House." Performances of *Agnete* were well received in Danish and Norwegian theaters and continue to be popular in Norway. *Agnete* was translated and performed in Germany in 1895.

Later in the spring of 1893 Skram began work on the last volume of the Hellemyr cycle. From the beginning the writing did not go well. As with *S. G. Myre*, the demands of a panoramic novel required her to leave home. She spent the summer in Bergen soaking up the atmosphere in which her characters lived and breathed, listening to the language they spoke. She wrote to Brandes about her troubles. In Copenhagen there were too many disturbances; she needed to be completely alone, preferably in an unfamiliar room with an unfamiliar table where nobody paid any attention to her. She believed that if she could only get the beginning right and the rest mapped out, she could continue at home. Letters from Bergen to Erik reflect increasing anxiety about the book, her daughter's health, and the state of their marriage. She reviewed their history together and the problems that persisted between them. Unable to write, she worried about her failure to earn money and her fears that Erik was seeing another woman. In September she wrote to tell Erik that she had had a miscarriage. Work on the novel became increasingly impossible.

In February 1894, exhausted by the efforts to reconcile the demands of marriage, motherhood, and her writing career, Skram had a second mental breakdown. Encouraged by her husband and her family doctor, she admitted herself to the psychiatric ward of the Copenhagen City Hospital, under the care of Dr. Knud Pontoppidan, one of the most celebrated psychiatrists in Scandinavia. Although she had entered Ward Six voluntarily, she and Dr. Pontoppidan were soon at odds, and after a few fruitless months, he declared her insane and transferred her, against her will, to St. Hans mental asylum for a period of a year. Detained there for two months before she could convince the new superintendent that she was sane and should be released, she emerged from her experience with one goal: to tell the world about the treatment she had received. Her two asylum novels: *Professor Hieronimus* and *På Sct. Jørgen,* the first books she published with Gyldendal, were published in 1895. They are blistering attacks on an aggressive and dehumanizing system of medical authority empowered to hold people against their will, strip them of adult prerogatives, and label them indelibly.

Skram's heroine, Else Kant, is a painter torn between the demands of marriage and motherhood and the demands of art. Frustrated and distraught, she can no longer function in either domain. When her husband and family doctor suggest a rest cure at the City Hospital under the care of the famous Professor Hieronimus, Else reluctantly agrees. Instead of the restful environment Else envisions, she encounters patients who scream and pound and invade her room. Shocked and horrified by the noise and routines of Ward Six, Else realizes that she is imprisoned and subject to the absolute authority of Professor Hieronimus. Everyone on the ward defers to him: the nurses, the younger doctors, and the women patients. A battle of wills ensues in which Else demands minimal rights and tries to convince him that she is sane and should be released. To the professor, all powerful in the institution, Else's rebellions against his will are proofs of insanity. In his view, her desire for self-expression is the illness. For Else, self-expression is at the core of her identity. She struggles to control her anger and fear and convert it into arguments that will sway the professor. Unmoved, he decides to transfer her against her will to an insane asylum for an indefinite period.

During her struggles to maintain her sanity amid the clamor and coercions of Ward Six, Else finds solace in the nurses, who provide loving care. She begins to see the other patients as victims of dominating men: exhausted by childbearing, rejected for promiscuity, cast off for their inability to conform to social conventions. On the eve of her transfer to St. Jørgen's, Else writes a letter to the professor, vowing that she will hold him accountable for the intolerable conditions of their confinement. When she gets out, she will be the voice of all the other oppressed and imprisoned women.

På Sct. Jørgen, the companion volume, appeared several months later in November 1895. As in *Professor Hieronimus,* Skram demonstrates her characteristic concern with the oppressed and downtrodden. At first glance, the novel seems to follow the same pattern as *Professor Hieronimus*: Else again struggles to prove her sanity and to free herself from a coercive medical establishment. Some critics have viewed the novel as repetitive, driven mainly by Skram's need to tell the complete story of her breakdown. Yet, many of the issues in *Professor Hieronimus* are expanded and developed in *På Sct. Jørgen.* The physical journey from Ward Six to St. Jørgen's prefigures the emotional and cognitive journey Else experiences there. Authority wears a benevolent mask at St. Jørgen's. The superintendent allows Else to have a private room and write to her husband, but the superintendent's bond with Hieronimus remains intact. He too wants to educate Else into the proper female role. He wants to change her style of communication, to sweeten her discourse and make it less individualistic. To an extent he succeeds. Else's perspective widens during her stay in the hospital. Increasingly, anger and fear are replaced by sympathy and fellow feeling toward the women who share her confinement. During her stay at St. Jørgens, Else struggles to find some meaning in her experience as a mental patient. She tries to understand what "insanity" means to her physicians, to question their power to label and incarcerate. After a month she finally convinces the superintendent of her sanity and wins her release. Else leaves St. Jørgen's with a new understanding of herself and a determination not to forget Hieronimus.

For Skram, writing about the experience was a crucial part of her recovery. Shortly after her release in the spring of 1894 she wrote to Bjørnson:

Selv om ikke forbitrelsen over den uhørte mishandling jeg har måttet lide, drev mig til at skrive, så vilde muligheden for at redde, om det så kun var *ét éneste* medmennske (I samme kasus som jeg selv var)– fra at falde i Pontoppidans *forfærdelige* hænder, være nok til at gjøre det.

(It's more than bitterness at the unheard of mistreatment I suffered that drives me to write: the possibility of saving *just one* fellow human being [in the same state I was myself] from falling into Pontoppidan's *dreadful* hands would be enough to justify it.)

Skram's two asylum novels had a powerful effect. The public was alarmed by her vivid, naturalistic descriptions of the suicidal and demented patients housed together on Ward Six. *Professor Hierinimus* and *På Sct. Jørgen* fueled a public debate about the rights of mental patients in Denmark. Although Dr. Pontoppidan issued a public defense, the debate led to several needed reforms in patient care. In 1897, his reputation damaged by Skram's books and lawsuits by former patients, Pontoppidan resigned his position at the Copenhagen City Hospital. For Skram the experience had lasting consequences. She blamed her husband and family physician for not extricating her from a situation that was clearly intolerable. After her release she spent some weeks in St. Joseph's hospital to regain her strength. She then went abroad, first to Russia and Finland, and later in 1895 to Paris for several months with her friends Hulda and Arne Garborg. The Skrams reconciled, but irreparable damage had been done, and they continued to spend long periods apart.

Skram's years following the completion of the asylum novels were marked by poor health, personal loss, and marital discord. Increasingly, she turned to friends for comfort and support. In December 1896 she began a correspondence with the prominent politician and writer Viggo Hørup, an intense epistolary relationship in which she sought his counsel for problems in her life and marriage. In August 1897 she learned that

Title page for one of Skram's two novels that depict conditions in insane asylums. They were based on her own experiences and led to a public debate about the rights of mental patients in Denmark (University of Michigan Libraries).

her beloved brother Ludvig had died of tuberculosis. A year later, she learned of the deaths of her first husband and her father in America.

Throughout these trials, Skram continued to work sporadically; some of her writing difficulties had apparently been eased by the publication of the asylum novels. Several of her short stories appeared in the journal *Tilskueren* between 1895 and 1897. These are unlike her earlier short prose pieces—plot and character development are more spare—and are instead like meditations on the themes of marriage, love, and death. The mood is somber, of loss and regret over love that has been squandered and cannot be retrieved.

Finally completed and published in the fall of 1898, *Afkom* (Descendants), the last volume of the *Hellemyrsfolket* series, picks up the lives of the two couples—Sivert and Petra Frimann Myre and Consul and Lydia Munthe Smith—some fifteen years after their marriages, announced at the end of *S. G. Myre*. The eldest of the couples' offspring are on the cusp of adulthood, and their lives are intertwined, despite social and economic differences, even as their parents' lives were entangled. Skram claimed that she had to write a saga about several generations in order to explain a young man's crime and subsequent suicide. The young man is Sivert Myre's son, Severin, who in desperation steals money from his best friend, Henrik Smith. Severin's actions are depicted in terms of heredity (Severin has inherited his father's cowardice and dishonesty) and environment (poverty has brought the family to the verge of starvation).

Skram took advantage of her large cast of characters to explore other themes as well, preoccupations that had engaged her throughout her career. Five marriages, both harmonious and disharmonious, are depicted, and at the end of the novel the Myres' daughter marries out of economic necessity while the Smiths' daughter weds out of boredom. Most of the women are defined by their roles as mothers as well as wives. Lydia Smith has long conversations about motherhood with her sister-in-law Milla and confesses to a greater affection for her youngest child than for her husband; Petra's sister, Andrea Ravn, neglects her only child; and Petra is undoubtedly the most hateful and tyrannical mother in all Norwegian literature. Love is another of the central themes. The Smiths' children Lina and Henrik speak of the love and devotion between sister and brother. Lina believes she will never love anyone more than her brother, while Henrik's infatuation for his Aunt Milla turns into melancholic longing after her death. Fie Myre is caught up in an affair with an upper-class man she knows will never marry her; yet, she is filled with gratitude for the love that has shown her "meningen med tilværelsen" (the meaning of existence) and inspires her to acts of kindness. Sivert Myre experiences the transformative power of love at the end of his life in a prison cell through God's mercy and forgiveness. The god of his parents and grandparents, a punishing god who exacts retribution through many generations, has given way to a mild and compassionate god.

In response to a letter from Professor Harald Høffding praising *Afkom*, Skram stated that she was compelled to write about life's dark side not out of anger and indignation, as she once had, but out of compassion "fordi jeg lærte at forstå, at være medlidende. En inderlig medlidenhed med alle, alle, mest med de elendigste og usleste, fylder, ja overfylder mit hjærte" (because I learned to understand, to be compassionate. A fervent compassion with everyone, everyone, mostly the most miserable and wretched, fills, indeed, overflows my heart). Skram's letters to friends and colleagues often mention that the writing process left her emotionally drained. She claimed she suffered along with her characters, shedding tears while she wrote; in later years especially, she fell prey to self-doubt, worrying that what she had written did not measure up to her own high standards.

When the final page proofs of *Afkom* had been sent to the publisher, Skram was mentally and physically exhausted, and in December 1898 she retreated to a sanatorium in Norway for a few weeks. In early March 1899 she wrote to her editor, Peter Nansen, about a new book, a collection of short stories to include those that had recently appeared in *Tilskueren*. *Sommer* (Summer) was published later that spring and comprised, in addition to the new story "Sommer," "Memento Mori" (1895), "Glæde" (1896, Joy), "Post Festum" (1896, After the Party), "Den røde Gardin" (1897, The Red Curtain), and "En Rose" (1897, A Rose).

In October 1899 Skram wrote to friends that she could no longer live with the belief that her husband was unfaithful and was filing for divorce. Her religious ideals combined with the painful experiences of her first marriage made her view infidelity as an unendurable betrayal. For both parties the divorce was a source of grief and regret. Mutual admiration and shared literary goals could not overcome the problems of their differences in temperament and attitudes toward sexual morality.

The Skrams were divorced in January 1900. Once again, Amalie Skram had to face the stigma of being a divorced woman and a single mother. At a time when she no longer had the health or energy to work at full capacity, she had to assume the financial burden of maintaining a home for herself and her daughter. She knew she had to write and publish in order to earn money, but she no longer had Erik's editorial assistance and encouragement. For a period of about two years she did manage to reinvent herself, calling on friends and colleagues such as Edvard Brandes for support and advice, preparing books and articles for publication and handling her own finances.

During the spring of 1900 Skram worked fitfully on a book she described as "Afkoms afkom" (The Descendents' Descendents) but then abruptly laid it aside to start a new novel, *Julehelg* (Christmas), reputedly based on her brother Ludvig's diary. *Julehelg* appeared just before Christmas 1900 and was a critical and popular success. The protagonist, Arne Hoff, is a young teacher who finally experiences acceptance and love during a temporary assignment in an idyllic mountain town when he boards with a charming couple and their young children. In the atmosphere of a supportive and happy home, so different from the one he shares with his mother, he truly blossoms. Despite a sad ending, the story carries an affirmative message of love's transformative power. Within weeks of publication the book entered a second printing. Seizing the opportunity, Skram sent copies to the influential men who would review her application for a Danish author's stipend. This time her efforts to receive state support were successful. The Danish government awarded her an annual stipend in the spring of 1901. The award reinforced Skram's bittersweet recognition that Denmark put more value on her work than her native country, a slight she never forgot.

Skram's resentment about the reception of her work in Norway and the personal attacks she had endured in the Norwegian press was evident in *Landsforrædere* (Traitors), a thirty-page booklet published in April 1901. The title refers to the term reserved for Norwegian authors who took their books to Danish publishing houses. Skram had always written for a Norwegian audience, as her Norwegian settings and characters reveal. But it was Denmark, not Norway, that had provided her with an artistic home. Being labeled a traitor infuriated her, and she proudly claimed her identity as a Danish writer: "Norsk er og blir jeg til min dødsdag. Men norsk forfatter er jeg ikke" (I am Norwegian and will be until my dying day. But I am not a Norwegian author).

Skram's anger was not meant for all of her countrymen, of course. Over the years she had received praise as well as blame in Norway. A Norwegian whose friendship she particularly valued was Arne Garborg. She greatly respected him as an author and in spring 1901 told him she wished to translate his novel *Den burtkomne Faderen* (1899, The Lost Father), into Danish. Skram negotiated with Gyldendal to publish the translation along with her foreword, and by the end of July had sent a first draft to Garborg. Progress on the book came to a halt in August when Skram suffered a serious flare-up of phlebitis that confined her to bed for several weeks. She published the translation later that year.

Skram's chronic health problems worsened and restricted her activities in the years after 1901, though she managed to keep up her correspondence with her many friends. She made vigorous efforts to seek treatment for phlebitis and her other illnesses, spending increasing amounts of time in clinics and hospitals. In late 1904 phlebitis forced her to move from Klasensgade to a new apartment where she did not have to cope with stairs. Financial anxiety added to her other burdens. If she could not write, she could not earn money to support herself and her daughter. Letters to Nansen at Gyldendal revealed her distress at not being able to make progress on her new book *Mennesker* (People), which she had begun in 1902. Gyldendal agreed to

Statue of Skram in Bergen (Britannica Online Encyclopaedia)

publish the novel in installments, but meeting the monthly quota for pages became a burden. She was only able to manage three installments before her death at age fifty-eight on 15 March 1905. The work was published as *Mennesker: ufuldendt roman* (1905, People: Unfinished Novel).

A view of Skram's career as a writer would not be complete without special recognition of her letters. More than a thousand have been preserved, saved by more than one hundred people with whom she corresponded. From the early 1860s she wrote to her favorite schoolmaster and to childhood friends in Bergen. When she began to write stories and novels, she wrote to contemporary authors and enclosed her books. She wrote to her publishers, editors, and translators, carefully monitoring the editing and publication of her work. Her relationship with Hegel and Nansen of Gyldendal show the fluid boundaries between her business and personal relationships. Her publishers provided artistic support, and they provided the money she needed to support her family. As her business letters show, she was always entrepreneurial, looking for ways to reissue, translate, and sell her work. Skram's business letters provide a vivid glimpse of a woman managing a professional career at the turn of the century.

The letters also bound Skram to friends and family. She had many women friends, notably Hulda Garborg and Anne Cathrine Achen, with whom she conducted a lengthy correspondence. The more than six hundred letters between Amalie and Erik Skram trace the sad trajectory of their relationship from their meeting in 1882 to their divorce in 1899. As she became increasingly estranged from Erik, she relied on male correspondents such as Viggo Hørup and Valdemar Irminger for advice and emotional support. *Mellom slagene* (Between Battles), a chronological selection of Skram's letters by Eugenia Kielland, was published in 1955. Other volumes of her letters have been published since, most notably Skram's exchanges with Bjørnson, Hørup, and other Danish writers. Janet Garton's edition of the complete correspondence between Amalie and Erik Skram (2002) provides an intimate view of their relationship and the literary circles in which they moved.

Skram scholarship has enjoyed a renaissance in Norway since the 1970s when the women's movement focused attention on feminist authors. Literary scholar Irene Engelstad contributed groundbreaking studies of Skram's marriage and asylum novels. In 1994 a committee made up of scholars and enthusiasts established an Amalie Skram Society (Amalie Skram-Selskapet) in Bergen. The society organizes an annual program in August to commemorate Skram's birthday, as well as scholarly conferences, including one in August 2005 to mark the centenary of her death. Most important, perhaps, the society's yearly publication of articles encourages and promotes new scholarship on Skram's life and work.

Amalie Skram's success can be seen today in the continuing popular attention to her life and work. In 1981 Torunn Ystaas produced a play based on her letters, *Ut med deg, skitne madam! Amalie Skram—sett gjennom hennes brev* (Get Out, You Miserable Woman! A view of Amalie Skram through her letters). Since 1990 the novels have been republished and translated into English, Dutch, and German, evoking great interest in feminist circles in Scandinavia and abroad. Several have been turned into plays, television movies, and feature films. In 1992 a highly acclaimed production, *Hellemyrsfolket,* was staged at Bergen's National Theater in Gunnar Staalesen's dramatization, and during that period the tetralogy was on the city's best-seller list. In 1996 Amalie Skram's life and work were accorded an extraordinary public honor when the city of Bergen celebrated the sesquicentennial of her birth in several days of civic events, including a library exhibit of her novels, public readings of her letters, and the staging of a play based on *Professor Hieronimus*. Such celebrations show that Skram's work still has the power to speak to modern women and men.

Letters:

Mellom slagene: Brev, edited by Eugenia Kielland (Oslo: Aschehoug, 1955);

"Brevveksling med Amalie Skram 1896-1897," in *Hørup i brev og digte: breve digte og litterære prosastykker til belysning af Viggo Hørup og hans kreds,* edited by Karsten Thorborg (Copenhagen: Akademisk forlag, 1981), pp. 304-338, 342-353;

"Og nu vil jeg tale ud"–"Men nu vil jeg også tale ud": Brevvekslingen mellom Bjørnstjerne Bjørnson og Amalie Skram, edited by Øyvind Anker and Edvard Beyer (Oslo: Gyldendal, 1982);

Elskede Amalie: Brevvekslingen mellom Amalie og Erik Skram, 3 volumes, edited by Janet Garton (Oslo: Gyldendal, 2002);

Caught in the Enchanters's Net: Amalie and Erik Skram's Letters, edited and translated by Garton (Norwich, U.K.: Norvik Press, 2003);

Amalie Skram: Brevveksling med andre nordiske forfattere, edited by Garton (Copenhagen: C. A. Reitzel, 2005).

Bibliography:

Liv Glasser, "Amalie Skram bibliografi," in *Amalie: Silkestrilen sin datter,* edited by Elisabeth Aasen (Oslo & Bergen: Pax Amalie Skram-selskapet, 1996), pp. 151-204.

Biographies:

Antonie Tiberg, *Amalie Skram som kunstner og menneske* (Christiania: Aschehoug, 1910);

Liv Køltzow, *Den unge Amalie Skram: Et portrett fra det nittende århundre* (Oslo: Gyldendal, 1992).

References:

Elisabeth Aasen, ed., *Amalie: "Silkestrilen sin datter"* (Oslo & Bergen: Pax Amalie Skram-selskapet, 1996);

Aasen, Elisabeth Armand, Yngvild Bøe, and Gunnar Staalesen, eds., *Amalie Skram Selskapet Årbok,* 12 volumes (Bergen: Amalie Skram Selskapet, 1994-2005);

Ragni Bjerkelund, *Amalie Skram: Dansk borger, norsk forfatter* (Oslo: Aschehoug, 1988);

Aasen and Pål Bjørby, eds., *Amalie Skram–150 år: Nye perspektiver på Amalie Skram forskningen,* series 10 (Bergen: Senter for humanistisk kvinneforskning, University of Bergen, 1997);

Aasen and Elisabeth Haavet, eds., *Amalie Skram: Dikterliv i brytningstid,* series 6 (Bergen: Senter for humanistisk kvinneforskning, University of Bergen, 1993);

Anne-Lise Amadou, "Madame Bovary i *Constance Ring*," in *Fransk i Norge* (Oslo: Aschehoug, 1975), pp. 87-105;

Mai Bente Bonnevie, "Den gifte kvinnen i det borgerlige ekteskap. Belyst ved fire ekteskapsromaner av Amalie Skram," in *Et annet språk: analyser av norsk kvinnelitteratur,* edited by Bonnevie and others (Oslo: Pax, 1977), pp. 40-68;

Lise Busk-Jensen, "Psykiske strukturer i Amalie Skrams romaner," *Edda: Nordisk Tidsskrift for Litteraturforskning,* 5 (1984): 15-44;

Pil Dahlerup, "Den kvindelige naturalist," *Vinduet,* 2 (1975): 30-37;

Dahlerup, "Amalie Skram," in *Kønsrolle i litteraturen,* edited by Hans Hertel (Copenhagen: Gyldendal, 1976), pp. 49-58;

Gun Edberg-Caldwell, "The Voyage Out: Amalie Skram's *Professor Hieronimus* and Charlotte Perkins Gilman's 'The Yellow Wallpaper,'" *Nora,* 5 (1997): 95-104;

Irene Engelstad, *Amalie Skram om seg selv* (Oslo: Den Norske Bokklubben, 1981);

Engelstad, *Kjærlighet og kvinneundertrykking* (Oslo: Pax, 1978);

Engelstad, *Sammenbrudd og gjennombrudd: Amalie Skrams romaner om ekteskap og sinnssyknom* (Oslo: Pax, 1984);

Engelstad and Janneken Øverland, "En radical kritikkav det borgerlige ekteskapet," in *Frihet til å skrive* (Oslo: Pax, 1981), pp. 15-23;

Engelstad, Liv Køltzow, and Gunnar Staalesen, *Amalie Skrams Verden* (Oslo: Gyldendal, 1996);

Janet Garton, "Amalie Skram's Many Masks: Fragments of an Epistolary Autobiography," *Scandinavica,* 44 (May 2005): 5-27;

Garton, "Language and Gender in the Correspondence of Amalie and Erik Skram," in *Ästhetik der skandinavischen Moderne,* edited by Annegret Heitmann and Karin Hoff (Frankfurt am Main & New York: Peter Lang, 1998);

Garton, "'Why do Norwegians hate Denmark so much?': National Consciousness in Amalie and Erik Skram's Correspondence," in *Nordic Letters 1870-1910,* edited by Garton and Michael Robinson (Norwich, U.K.: Norvik Press, 1999), pp. 264-280;

Inger Alver Gløersen, *Min faster Amalie Skram* (Oslo: Gyldendal, 1965);

Christine Hamm, *Medlidenhet og melodrama: Amalie Skrams romaner om ekteskap* (Oslo: Unipub, 2006);

Katherine Hanson, "Amalie Skram and Her Publishers," in *Nordic Letters 1870-1910,* pp. 264-280;

Hanson and Judith Messick, "Skrams kamp for å skaffe seg forlag," in *Bokhistorie,* edited by Tore Rem (Oslo: Gyldendal, 2003), pp. 144–165;

Borghild Krane, *Amalie Skram og kvinnens problem* (Oslo: Gyldendal, 1951);

Krane, *Amalie Skrams diktning: Tema og variasjoner* (Oslo: Gyldendal, 1961);

Finn Frederik Krarup, "Stil, krop, og psyke: Tendenser in Amalie Skram's forfatterskab," *Synsvinkler,* 6, no. 17 (1997): 51–66;

Unni Langaas, "The Struggle for the Body: Hysteria and Rebellion in Amalie Skram's Novel *Professor Hironimous*," *Scandinavian Studies,* 75, no. 1 (2003): 55–88;

Judith Messick, "Amalie Skram's Talking Cure Revisited," in *Nordic Letters 1870–1910,* pp. 281–305;

Messick, "*Constance Ring* and the Tradition of the Female Quixote," *Scandinavian Literature in a Transcultural Context,* edited by Sven Rossel (Seattle: University of Washington Press, 1986), pp. 52–56;

Janet Rasmussen, "Amalie Skram as Literary Critic," *Edda: Nordisk Tidsskrift for Litteraturforskning,* 1 (1984): 1–11;

Anne Birgitte Rønning, "'Kvinnelig vanvidd og mannlig rasjonalitet': En analyse av Amalie Skram, *Professor Hieroimus* og *På St. Jørgen*," *Edda: Nordisk Tidsskrift for Litteraturforskning,* 5 (1984): 275–288;

Aflene Tybjærg Schacke, "Edvard Brandes og Amalie Skram: Til belysning af 'gennembrudsmændenes' vurdering af kvindelige forfatteskaber," *Edda: Nordisk Tidsskrift for Litteraturforskning,* 5 (1984): 257–273;

Turid Sverre, "The Barrenness of Silence: The Difficult Heritage of Mothers and Daughters in Norwegian Women's Literature," *Edda: Nordisk Tidsskrift for Litteraturforskning,* 4 (1983): 329–338;

Sivert Ødegaard, "Livsbehov og destruksjon som litterære tema: Et bidrag til forståelse av Amalie Skram's roman *Forrådt*," *Edda: Nordisk Tidsskrift for Litteraturforskning,* 5 (1996): 151–161;

Ødegaard, "'Min længsel går mod andre kloder': Tvedtidig seksualitet i Amalie Skram's liv og diktning," *Norsk Litterære Årbok* (1998): 72–96.

Papers:

Amalie Skram's unpublished letters are in the manuscript divisions of the Royal Library and Royal Archives in Copenhagen, the National Library in Oslo, and the University Library in Bergen.

Mattis Størssøn

(ca. 1500 – 28 May 1569)

Lanae H. Isaacson

BOOK: *Norske Kongers Krønicke oc bedrifft, indtil unge Kong Haagens tid, som døde Anno Domini 1263. Udset aff gammel Norske paa Danske, trolig i 1540-årene* (Copenhagen: J. Mortensen, 1594).

Edition: *Den norske krønike*, edited by Mikjel Sørlie (Oslo: Universitetsforlag, 1962).

SELECTED PERIODICAL PUBLICATION–UNCOLLECTED: "Kort Beretning om Kiøbmændene ved Bryggen og deres første Indkommelse i Bergen," *Norske Magasin*, 1 (1858): 41–63.

Mattis Størssøn was at the center of learning and cultural and civic leadership in sixteenth-century Bergen. Recognized as one of a small contingent of learned scholars who set the intellectual trends in Bergen, Størssøn helped foster humanism in the western city well in advance of its appearance and development in the rest of Norway. Størssøn was encouraged in his study and translations of Old Norse sagas by Christoffer Valkendorf, Erik Munk, and Erik Rosenkrantz, the regents of Bergenhus, the center of regal power in the city, and the official representatives of the Danish crown. Along with Geble Pederssøn and Absalon Pederssøn Beyer, Størssøn moved Bergen to the cultural and literary forefront. He is remembered today for writing the first published history of Norway, *Norske Kongers Krønicke oc bedrifft, indtil unge Kong Haagens tid, som døde Anno Domini 1263. Udset aff gammel Norske paa Danske, trolig i 1540-årene* (1594, The Norwegian Royal Chronicle and Accomplishments until the Time of King Haagen, Who Died in A.D. 1263. Translated from Old Norwegian to Danish, Probably in the 1540s). For his chronicle Størssøn drew on his own translations of the *kongesagaer* (royal sagas) from Old Norse to Danish, and it reflects his critical acumen and his sense of style.

Mattis (Mats) Størssøn was born around 1500 in the county of Agder or, possibly, Sunnhorland. Nothing is known of his parents or his early years, but his expertise in Old Norse and Latin suggests a strong foundation of studies in languages and literature. According to his will, a document witnessed by his son Stør in 1567, Størssøn was married twice; Stør and his other children were the offspring of his first wife, of whom nothing else—including her name—is known. His second wife was Lucia Hansdatter.

Størssøn's scholarly accomplishments attracted the attention of administrative and civic leaders, and in 1538 or 1539 he was appointed *lagmann* (chief administrator and commissioner) for Agder. Along with Pederssøn, Størssøn served as a delegate to the commission held to establish and codify new Lutheran Church regulations and teaching standards in Oslo and Hamar Parish in 1539. In 1540 he was named to the even more important post of *lagmann* for Bergen; he held this office for the rest of his life. He accompanied Munk on a military campaign to win Steinvikholm and settle disputes and conflicts in the area in 1564; later in the 1560s he served on a royal warship that plied the coastal waters to northern Norway to secure the region for the Danish crown.

With support and encouragement from the humanists who ran Bergen, Størssøn began writing his chronicle of Norwegian history around 1540. *Norske Kongers Krønicke* is not simply a translation of the Old Norse sagas that Størssøn knew better than anyone else in Bergen; it is also a reformulation of them for the use of the learned men who were in charge of the city. Two influential groups competed for the upper hand in sixteenth-century Bergen: the humanist scholars and regents of the Danish crown who ran the government, the Church, and the schools—including Pederssøn's Bergen Latin Cathedral School—from Bergenhus; and the Hanseatic League, the German traders and entrepreneurs headquartered in Lübeck who operated Bryggen (The Wharf) and controlled the goods and money that flowed in and out of the city. Størssøn's work played an important role on the side of Bergenhus: it reasserted the rights of the Bergen citizenry and reconfirmed the legitimacy of the Danish crown in Bergen and the rest of Norway.

Norske Kongers Krønicke begins expansively with a survey of world geography, topography, and history that includes legends and myths common to the Nordic region. Størssøn then narrows the focus to the north and the emergence of an omnipotent leader,

> ein høffding som hed *Otthin*. Hand vor ein blodmand, thet ær, han slachtett folch og fæ och offred till affguder. . . . Otthinus vor ein duelig krigsmand, oc foer viide om land och vanth mange land vnder sig. Hand haffde stor lycke, saa at hand vant huad hand slo paa. Der aff trode alle at naar som Otthin lagde sin hand paa dem hand vdsende till strids, da vor seiieruindingen vist ij handen, och naar dhe vore ij nød, tha kalled the paa Otthins naffn, thet hialp thennom.

> (a chieftain who was called *Otthin*. He was a blood-man, that is, he killed people and animals and sacrificed to the pagan gods. . . . Otthinus was an able warrior, and he went far about the land and conquered many lands. He had great fortune in that he won what he battled for. That is why everyone believed that when Otthin laid his hand on those he sent out into battle, victory was assured, and when they were in need, they called on Otthin's name, that helped them.)

From Otthin (Oden) Størssøn turns to the kings of Norway and the other Nordic lands. *Norske Kongers Krønicke* is not simply a list of royal names; it is the humanist Størssøn's effort to bring to life the monarchs of the past and to legitimize the sixteenth-century monarchy. The older kings emerge from the misty legends and become individuals with unique attributes. Størssøn offers detailed portraits of past kings as a way of securing the idea of "the once and future king" against the possible intervention of foreign interlopers in the halls of political power.

The institution of the monarchy progresses in Størssøn's account from regional to national in scope. His account of Haralldr haarfager (Harald Fair-Hair) marks the transition from the era of petty regional kings who were little more than "the first among many" to a monarch whose realm coincides with the borders of Norway. It is also an early example of biography. The humanists in Bergen focused their attention on the lives of important individuals, both those in their community, such as Pedersøn, for example, and on the kings who had ruled Norway. Beyer wrote the first record of daily life in Bergen, *Liber Capituli Bergensis: Absalon Pedersøn Beyers Dagbog over Begivenheder, især i Bergen, 1552–1572* (1860, Book of the Bergen Chapter: Absalon Pedersøn Beyer's Diary of Events, Particularly in Bergen, 1552–1572), and the first Norwegian biography, *Oration om Mester Geble, 1571* (1963, Oration on Master Geble, 1571).

Størssøn's account begins with the ten-year-old Harald inheriting his father's regional kingship and quickly expanding it through warfare to include additional provinces and regions. His decision to pursue the goal of national kingship is inspired by a woman:

> Ther konning Haralldr kom nogitt till alders, da sende hand bud till kongens dotter aff Hordeland wid Bergen som hedt Gødhe, och wilde haffue hende till sin frille. Den tiid hun forstod theris ærinde, tha suarde hun saa: Ingen lunde will ieg saa spille min jom-frudom, att tage then konning till mand som icke haffuer mere land eller rige, wden ett fylche eller to. . . . Jeg will vel vere hans echte hustru om han vill giøre thett for min skyld, att tuinge vnder sig alt Norriges rige, raade och regere thett liige som koning Gorm ij Danmarch och konning Erich i Suerrige, tha ber han icke forgeffuis kongen nafn. . . . Koning Haralldr suarid: Jeg tacker henne for suaren, hun haffuer nu giffuit meg thett wdi sinde som ieg aldrig før kunde tencke. Therfore loffuer ieg gud som alting raader, at ieg huercken skal lade klippe mitt haar eller rage mitt scheg før end ieg faar alt Norrigs rige wndher meg mett schatt, schylder, och all vnderdanighedt, eller ieg skal dø ther føre.

> (When King Harald got older, he sent a message to the daughter of the king of Hordeland in Bergen; she was named Gødhe, and [Harald] wanted her for his consort. When she understood his errand, she answered with this: Never will I waste my virginity by taking for my husband a king who does not own more lands or realms than a county or two. . . . I will be his true wife if he will do this for my sake: conquer all of Norway's realms and rule and govern just as King Gorm in Denmark and King Erich in Sweden, then he will not bear the name of king in vain. . . . King Harald answered: I thank her for the answer she has given which has made me think of something I never thought of before. Therefore I promise God who rules all things that I will neither cut my hair or shave my beard before I have all of Norway under me with all taxes, duties and all liege men, or I shall die for that cause.)

Størssøn concludes his story of Harald Fair-Hair with a poetic reference to a mother's dream that has come true and with an effort to link Harald to all subsequent Norwegian kings and to their legitimate regal descendants in Copenhagen:

> Saa ær sagt fraa koning Haralldr haarfager att hand war then deligste, største och sterkiste mand som tha fanst ij Norrige, rund och venligh modt sine wndersotte. Da wor fulkommen den drøm som hans moder drømde then tiid hun vor medt hannom. Hende drømde att hun tog ein torne aff sin barm, och ther bleff aff eitt stort tre, och rodfestis ij jorden och opvoxte saa høygt att hende syntis thett schyggede offuer alt Norrige. . . . Quisterne aff træet betegnit hans affkom som spreddis

offuer allt Norrige, och haffuer alltiid weridt konger ij Norrige aff hans slecht siden.

(So it is said of Harald Fair-Hair that he was the most wonderful, strongest and grandest man in all Norway, evenhanded and friendly to all his liege men. The dream his mother had dreamt when she bore him had come to fruition. She dreamed that she took a thorn from her bosom, and it became a great tree, and set its roots in the earth and grew so tall that it seemed to her that it shadowed all Norway. . . . The branches of the tree designated his offspring who spread all over Norway, and since then, kings of Norway have always been of his descent.)

Norske Kongers Krønicke is a record of the Norwegian monarchy, king by king and era by era. It would be an error to regard the work as an early blow for the kind of nationalism that prevailed in nineteenth-century Norway and led to Norwegian independence in 1905. Instead, *Norske Kongers Krønicke* is a stylish, sometimes poetic, historical account and a shortened rendition of *kongesagaer* written by a scholarly humanist on behalf of his fellow Bergen humanists, who pursued knowledge of the regal past on its own merits. Thoughts of Norwegian independence from Denmark were nonexistent among the Bergen humanists, who owed their intellectual attainments and influence to academics of the University of Copenhagen.

On a first reading, Størssøn's other preserved work, "Kort Beretning om Kiømændene ved Bryggen og deres første Indkommelse i Bergen" (Short Account of the Merchants at The Wharf and Their First Appearance in Bergen), probably written between 1550 and 1560, also strikes one as advocating Norwegian independence; its publication in *Norsk Magasin* in 1858 may have been an attempt to use it to advance the kind of nationalism that did lead to independence. But this purpose was not Størssøn's. In the middle of the sixteenth century the power and money struggle between Bergenhus and Bryggen had grown intense. The Bergen citizenry chafed under the economic domination of the Germans and were only too willing to support the Danish monarchy—their monarchy—in what was regarded as a play for power between foreigners and locals. In this context Størssøn's "Kort Beretning" was first and foremost a political document that took aim at the growing power of the Hanseatic League and asserted the primacy of the Danish crown and its representatives such as Valkendorf, Munk, and Rosenkrantz. Coincidentally, "Kort Beretning" also served the interests of the Bergen locals who feared the growing economic power of the Hansas and felt threatened by the tug-of-war between Bergenhus and Bryggen. Størssøn died on 28 May 1569.

Mattis Størssøn was one of the trendsetting Bergen humanists who were at the forefront of scholarly, civic, religious, and intellectual pursuits in the city. Because of his scholarship, his solid grounding in Latin and Old Norse, and his intellectual pursuits, he held the lamp of learning high in sixteenth-century Bergen and shone its light on his country's past.

Reference:

Jon Gunnar Jørgensen, "Sagaoversettelser i Norge på 1500-tallet," *Collegium medievale,* 2 (1993): 169–198.

Papers:

The manuscript for Mattis Størssøn's *Norske Kongers Krønicke* is in the Arnamagnæanske Samling (Collection) at the University of Copenhagen. Manuscripts for "Kort Beretning" are in the Arnamagnæanske Samlingand in the Ny Kongelig Samling of Det Kongelige Bibliotek (The Royal Library) in Copenhagen.

Magdalene Thoresen

(3 June 1819 – 28 March 1903)

Lorna Selley
University of Wisconsin–Madison

BOOKS: *Digte af en Dame* (Bergen: Giertsen, 1860);

Fortællinger (Copenhagen: Gyldendal, 1863);

Studenten (Copenhagen: Gyldendal, 1863);

Signes historie: en Fortælling (Copenhagen: Gyldendal, 1864);

Min bedstemors Fortælling (Copenhagen: Gyldendal, 1866);

Den Lystige Fætter: Indeholdende humoristiske Fortællinger (Tønsberg: Gyldendal, 1868);

Solen i Siljedalen: en Fortælling (Copenhagen: Gyldendal, 1868);

Drøm og Liv (Copenhagen: Gyldendal, 1869);

Fra Lille Bælt (Copenhagen: Gyldendal, 1869);

Et rigt Parti: Skuespil i to Akter (Copenhagen: Gyldendal, 1870);

Billeder fra Vestkysten af Norge (Copenhagen: Gyldendal, 1872);

Nyere Fortællinger (Copenhagen: Gyldendal, 1873);

Livsbilleder (Copenhagen: Gyldendal, 1877);

Inden Døre: Skuespil i tre Handlinger (Copenhagen: Gyldendal, 1877);

Kristoffer Valkendorf og Hanseaterne: historisk Skuespil i 5 Handlinger (Copenhagen: Gyldendal, 1878);

Herluf Nordal: en Fortælling fra det forrige Aarhundrede (Copenhagen: Gyldendal, 1879);

En opgaaende Sol: Skuespil i fire Handlinger (Copenhagen: Gyldendal, 1881);

Søløven (Copenhagen: Schubothe, 1884);

Billeder fra Midnatsolens Land, 2 volumes (Copenhagen: Gyldendal, 1884, 1886);

Digte (Copenhagen: Gyldendal, 1887);

Mindre Fortællinger (Copenhagen: Gyldendal, 1891);

Elvedrag og andre Fortællinger (Copenhagen: Gyldendal, 1893);

Livsluft: Fortællinger (Copenhagen: Gyldendal, 1895);

En Udflytning: Skuespil i 3 Handlinger (Copenhagen: Gyldendal, 1897);

Udenom Afgrunden: Fortællinger (Copenhagen: Gyldendal, 1897);

Skæbner og Viljer: Fortællinger (Copenhagen: Gyldendal, 1899);

Udvalgte Fortællinger (Copenhagen: Gyldendal, 1903);

Magdalene Thoresen (Den Store Danske <http://www.denstoredanske.dk/@api/deki/files/67170/=Anne_Magdalene_Thoresen_1819-1903.jpg>)

Romaner og Fortællinger, 5 volumes (Copenhagen: Gyldendal, 1904–1905);

Helhesten: en Julefortælling paa Vers (Copenhagen: Gyldendal, 1909).

Collection: *Magdalene Thoresen i utvalg* (Oslo: Eide, 1994).

PLAY PRODUCTIONS: *Et Vidne,* Drammen, Udenlandsk Teater, 19 December 1852;

Kongedatterens Bøn, Drammen, Udenlandsk Teater, 15 April 1853;

Dramatisk Diktning i 1 Akt, Drammen, Udenlandsk Teater, 15 April 1853;

Lys og Skygge, Drammen, Udenlandsk Teater, 1 February 1860;

Et rigt Parti: Skuespil i to Akter, Copenhagen, Det Kongelige Teater, 27 April 1870;

Inden Døre: Skuespil i tre Handlinger, Oslo, Christiania Theater, 4 May 1877;

Kristoffer Valkendorf og Hanseaterne: historisk Skuespil i 5 Handlinger, Copenhagen, Det Kongelige Teater, 27 April 1878;

Udflytning: Skuespil i 3 Handlinger, Copenhagen, Det Kongelige Teater, 2 October 1878;

En opgaaende Sol: Skuespil i fire Handlinger, Copenhagen, Det Kongelige Teater, 1 September 1882.

OTHER: "Fredericia," in *Festskrift i Anledning af Fredericia-Slagets Halvtredsaarsdag,* edited by Wilhelm Larsen (Århus: Jydsk Forlags-Forretning, 1899).

Magdalene Thoresen's works are seldom read today, and her authorship has received little interest from twentieth-century European and North American scholarship. However, Thoresen received considerable recognition for her poetry, prose, and drama from critics and the reading public in Scandinavia and Germany during the mid and late nineteenth century. Her personal history, however, is well documented because of her association with the playwright Henrik Ibsen, as well as her longstanding friendship with the poet and playwright Bjørnsterne Bjørnson. During her lifetime Thoresen was connected to Norway's national literary movement, but much of her work is now overshadowed by that of Ibsen's and Bjørnson's.

Thoresen was born in Denmark and spent most of her life there; her works were published there. However, she was outspoken in expressing a closer affinity for the Norwegian people and the rugged natural landscape of Norway than of Denmark. She has been described as having a bold, sharp, but sympathetic temperament; her poetry, prose, and plays are equally bold and emotionally charged. Thoresen's works have generally been classified within the National Romantic tradition since she focused on the Norwegian landscape, the ordinary people, and the national character of Norwegians. However, Thoresen also dared to depict female eroticism, a clear departure from National Romanticism. Many of her works are autobiographical.

Anne Magdalene Kragh was born on 3 June 1819 in the small fishing town of Fredericia in Jutland, Denmark. Her childhood was not a particularly happy one, as her family faced daily struggles because of poverty and limited resources. Her father was the captain of a fishing boat in Fredericia, where he also licensed buildings for seamen, and her mother, Anne Kirstine, was the daughter of a servant. Magdalene was the second eldest of five siblings. She lived with her paternal grandmother for fourteen years, and the two developed a close relationship. Her grandmother instilled in her a strong Lutheran faith that was later a dominant element in her writing and a source of comfort through considerable emotional turmoil. As a child Kragh felt excluded and distanced from the local community because of her emotional sensitivity and her desire to develop creatively. When her grandmother died suddenly on the day of her confirmation, Kragh returned to her parents. Her life at home was unhappy and tumultuous. At the age of twenty she was sent away to study. Kragh received financial support from a local wealthy well-wisher for her studies in Copenhagen. She initially struggled with her studies; her last two years of studying were more successful and enjoyable. Kragh was inspired by German authors such as Johann Wolfgang von Goethe, Friedrich Schiller, and Orla Lahmann. She considered herself revolutionary in her thinking and outlook and found the literary world stimulating. Her studies included thorough instruction in the Danish classics, including works by Adam Oehlenschläger, Johan Ludvig Heiberg, and Frederik Paludan-Müller.

Kragh was productive and successful in Copenhagen with respect to her studies, but her personal life proved turbulent and stressful. She fell in love with an Icelandic student, Grímur Thomsen, who later went on to achieve considerable literary success. She had a son by Thomsen, but concealed the fact from her friends and family, and the child was put into a home in Copenhagen. Kragh then moved to the remote town of Herøy, on the west coast of Norway, where she became governess to the children of the pastor Hans Conrad Thoresen. The pastor was a widower, nineteen years her senior, who had five children; the eldest was thirteen, the youngest, two. The setting of Herøy was Kragh's first experience with the striking Norwegian landscape. The wild, rugged surroundings later provided inspiration for her writing.

Kragh's new position as governess in the pastor's house was the beginning of happier times. She soon developed a close friendship with the pastor. She took well to caring for the pastor's children, despite her initial nervousness, and living in the pastor's home further solidified her religious faith. Hans Conrad Thoresen soon realized that Kragh had strong religious convictions and a good measure of creativity; he was encouraging and supportive of her pursuit of a literary career. Thoresen instructed her in Latin and the classics and

Title page for Thoresen's novel (The Sun in Silje Valley), which includes pictures of the Norwegian landscape (Oxford University Libraries)

encouraged her other educational pursuits. In the autumn of 1844 Thoresen and his governess were married. Before they were married, Kragh, according to her letters, told Thoresen of her earlier love affair with Thomsen.

In order to promote his wife's literary talents, Thoresen encouraged and paid for his wife to travel. Magdalene Thoresen embarked on several European trips alone, traveling to Germany, Switzerland, and France. Her husband also believed that his wife would be more successful as a writer if the family moved to Bergen. In 1844 he was awarded the position of Vicar of Korskirken in Bergen. The couple soon became involved in the development of a new theater there, Det Norske Teatret (The Norwegian Theatre), which opened in 1850. Along with Bjørnson, Ibsen, and others, Thoresen contributed to a new surge of Norwegian national awareness in literary and theatrical circles in Bergen and elsewhere. During the theater's first four years, Magdalene Thoresen submitted four plays anonymously: *Et Vidne* (1852, Witness), *Kongedatterens Bøn* (1853, The Prayer of the Princess), *Dramatisk Diktning i 1 Akt* (1853, Dramatic Poetry in One Act), and *Lys og Skygge* (1860, Light and Shadow).

None of the plays were published or produced at the time, but three were later staged by Ibsen at Det Norske Teatret. While Norway's budding national literary movement was unfolding, Thoresen met Bjørnson. The two became close friends, both writers describing the friendship as "a spiritual marriage." Thoresen later described him as her "spiritual father" through whom she became a writer. During these early years in Bergen, Thoresen coached several young writers and encouraged them to become formally educated. One of them was Ivar Aasen, who later formulated Nynorsk into a written Norwegian language.

In June 1858 Hans Conrad Thoresen died, leaving his wife to raise his children. Initially, Thoresen was determined to stay in Norway, her newfound home, and she tried to establish herself as a writer in Bergen; she received little formal recognition and later moved with her stepchildren to Denmark to develop her career as a writer in her homeland. Before she moved, she anonymously submitted her poetry collection, *Digte af en Dame* (1860, Poems by a Lady), which was edited and published by Bjørnson. This collection of poems was notable because of their direct discussion of female sexuality. The collection was also dark and somber in tone. The poems were praised by Elin Page for their well-crafted composition: "The finesse with which the poems are crafted bears witness to genius and to true artistic application."

In 1861 Thoresen returned to Copenhagen, after having burned most of her manuscripts in a feeling of despair. She felt deeply disappointed by the lack of recognition she had received in Norway. On her arrival in Denmark, Thoresen initially felt homesick for Norway, which she considered her adopted homeland and the place that let her fully develop her literary style and her artistic talents. Thoresen was determined to provide for her five stepchildren by pursuing a literary career in Copenhagen. She became part of the literary scene, and she befriended Danish literary critic and leader of the Modern Breakthrough, Georg Brandes. Although she wrote in the spirit of the National Romantics, she wanted her works to be read and appreciated by everyday people.

In 1863 Thoresen published her first full-length novel, *Studenten* (The Student). It has been compared to Arne Garborg's *Bondestudentar* (1883, Peasant Students). Thoresen's protagonist, Brune, is sent to Copenhagen to study medicine when he is twenty. He struggles with his studies and falls in love with a Norwegian girl, but she dies in a leprosy epidemic. Brune is depicted as a native son of the rugged Norwegian west coast who cannot adjust to the cultural life of the city.

The next year, Thoresen published her first successful work, *Signes historie: en Fortælling* (1864, Signe's Story: A Tale). As in *Studenten,* Thoresen's protagonist, Signe, is closely tied to the Norwegian landscape, much like Thoresen herself. After a love affair with another student, Signe becomes pregnant; the hostile community rejects her. The novel was well received by the public, although critics accused her of imitating Bjørnson's *bondefortællinger* (peasant tales). In 1863 Ibsen, reviewing her novel, claimed that the difference, and not the similarity with the *bondefortællinger* deserved comparison. Thoresen's descriptions are landscape studies with figures in the foreground. Bjørnson's stories are portrait paintings with a landscape background.

In 1866 Thoresen returned to Norway. She settled in Christiania and tried to establish herself there. She frequently met Bjørnson, who was flattered by her admiration of him but responded to her intense affection with mixed signals. The friendship between these two writers broke in 1866 when Thoresen's novel *Min bedstemors Fortælling* (1866, My Grandmother's Tale) was published. Bjørnson accused Thoresen of repeating their conversations in her book, word for word. Thoresen denied that her protagonist was even based on Bjørnson.

Thoresen's desire for recognition and literary success in Norway went unrealized. In 1869 the Norwegian government refused to give her a writer's grant. She interpreted this as a rejection from Norway and a signal that she was no longer welcome. After another brief period of traveling in Europe, she returned to Copenhagen. Thoresen tried to publish several of her works in Copenhagen–at first without success. Her situation improved when her short story "En Aften i Bergen" (An Evening in Bergen) was published in the Danish literary magazine *Illustreret Tid*. This was a breakthrough for Thoresen, as the short story was well received by the Danish reading public. After the success of "En Aften i Bergen," Hegel became Thoresen's publisher and in 1868 published her novel *Solen i Siljedalen* (The Sun in Silje Valley), a work that included pictures of the Norwegian landscape. This novel, like her later works, *Billeder fra Vestkysten af Norge* (1872, Pictures from the West Coast of Norway) and *Billeder fra Midnatsolens Land* (1884, 1886, Pictures from the Land of the Midnight Sun), features fictional tales with factual accounts of the topography and history of various places in Norway. In the past, these works were deemed her finest because of her close affinity to the Norwegian landscape and because of her ability to depict people and environments sympathetically. Thoresen went on to publish two novels, *Drøm og Liv* (1869, Dream and Life) and *Fra Lille Bælt* (1869, From Little Belt), which included characters who closely resembled her father. In 1872 Thoresen moved to the coastal town of Frederiksværk, Sjælland, because her youngest stepson wished to study at the polytechnic college in town. At this location, Thoresen republished a collection of stories as *Nyere Fortællinger* (1873, New Tales). She spent some time in 1873 and 1874 traveling around Sweden and Norway, where she gave a series of public readings from her works. In November 1874 she returned to Denmark to help her stepson Thomas, who had fallen ill; he died a short while later.

Thoresen moved with her youngest stepson to Zurich, where he planned to study for his technical degree. During her three years in Zurich she collected several of her earlier short stories under the title *Livsbilleder* (Pictures from Life) in 1877. She also wrote a series of plays, including *Inden Døre* (1877, Indoors), *Kristoffer Valkendorf og Hanseaterne* (1878, Kristoffer Valkendorf and the Hansas), and *En opgaaende sol* (published 1881, produced 1882, A Rising Sun), all of which received less recognition than her previous works of prose. Nonetheless, the plays were successful when performed in theaters in Denmark, Norway, and Sweden. *Inden Døre* depicted the urban lives of merchants in Copenhagen, signaling a departure from her earlier prose focus on rural and peasant life in Norway. Initially, the play was well received and did fairly well at Det Kongelige Teater in Copenhagen, at least for one season. *Inden Døre* was later performed at Dagmarteatret. Thoresen's plays were also staged and performed in Christiania and Stockholm. Theater critics of the time described these plays as well composed but displaying flaws in character development and composition.

In 1879 Thoresen published *Herluf Nordahl: en Fortælling fra det forrige Aarhundrede* (Herluf Nordahl: a Tale from the former Century). Her personal experience is reflected in the novel's sexual charge. According to Page, "In her letters, Magdalene comments on the constant conflict within herself between 'Eros,' her own passionate sexual nature, and her equally strong sense of morality." While Bjørnson frequently defended Thoresen's works, the sexual element in her writing became objectionable to him. He described her as being "forever in bridal attire." In the 1880s Thoresen published more prose, with more success. Her *Billeder fra Midnatsolens Land* was especially well received. She also published *Digte* (1887, Poems). Her later prose received less acclaim. In 1891 *Mindre Fortællinger* (Smaller Tales) was published, followed by *Elvedrag og andre Fortællinger* (Elf-Draught and Other Tales) in 1893 and by *Livsluft* (Life's Breath) in 1895. Toward the end of her career, translations of her works became more popular, including her collected works, which were translated into German.

On Magdalene Thoresen's eightieth birthday a public party and a private party were held for her by the city of Copenhagen. During these celebrations, she received a medal of honor from the Danish king, Christian IX. Thoresen spent the rest of her life in Copenhagen, where she died on 28 March 1903.

Letters:

Breve fra Magdalene Thoresen 1855–1901, edited by Julius Clausen and P. Fr. Rist (Copenhagen: Gyldendal, 1919);

"Fem selvbiografiske brev fra Magdalene Thoresen," *Edda: Nordisk Tidsskrift for Litteraturforskning,* 53 (1954): 392–400;

Magdalene Thoresen og Georg Brandes: en brevveksling 1865–1872, edited by Jorunn Hareide (Oslo: Emilia, 2002).

References:

Elin Page, "Magdalene Thoresen," *New Comparison: A Journal of Comparative and General Literary Studies,* 4 (1987): 72–91;

Page, *The Real Lady from the Sea: A Study in the Authorship of Magdalene Thoresen (1819–1903)* (Bergen: Alvheim & Eide, 2002).

Christian Braunmann Tullin

(6 September 1728 – 21 January 1765)

Lanae H. Isaacson

BOOKS: *Et par Ord til de Skiøne i Anledning af et Bröllup i Christiania* (Christiania, 1752);

En Maji-Dag: den 6te Maji da velædle og høyfornæmme Kiøbmand Morten Leuch (Copenhagen, 1758);

Et Indlæg til Fornuftens Ret fra Qvindekiönnet: af Dato 5 December 1758 da Højædle og Velbyrdige Herr Morten Leuch Eliesen . . . sin Ægteskabsforening med Velædle og Højfornæmme Jomfru Dorthe Mogensen (Christiania: Schwach, 1758);

Afbrudte Tanker ved en döende Sösters Seng (Copenhagen, 1760);

Södhed i Bitterhed, Livet i Döden (Copenhagen, 1760);

Sørge-Tanker over Dödens Magt mod Dyden (Copenhagen: Svare, 1760);

Taarefuld Erindring af en höytelsket Söster nu salig i Himmelen, Birgitte Marie Tullin (Copenhagen: Svare, 1760);

Tanker om det Tilkommende (Copenhagen: Svare, 1760);

Søefarten dens oprindelse og virkninger (Copenhagen: Selskabet for de skiønne og nyttige Videnskaber, Skrifter, 1761);

Skabningens ypperlighed i henseende til de skabte tings orden og sammenhæng (Copenhagen: Selskabet for de skiønne og nyttige Videnskaber, Skrifter, 1764);

Raadmand Christian Braunmann Tullins samtlige Skrifter, 3 volumes (Copenhagen: Nicolaus Møller, 1770–1773).

Editions and Collections: *Christ. Brauman [sic] Tullins Udvalgte Digte*, foreword by K. L. Rahbek (Copenhagen: Seidelin, 1799);

Christian Brauman Tullin's udvalgte Skrivter (Copenhagen: C. Steen, 1833);

Christian Braunmann [sic] Tullins samtlige skrifter, 3 volumes, edited by Harald Noreng (Oslo: Glyldendal, 1972–1976).

Christian Braunmann Tullin (oil painting by an unknown artist in the portrait collection of Frederiksborg Castle; from Edvard Beyer, ed., Norges Litteratur Historie, *volume 1 [Oslo: Cappelen, 1974]; Library of Congress)*

Christian Braunmann Tullin, the premier Danish-Norwegian poet of his generation, was known for writing just the right poem for the right occasion. Tullin was able to capture the divine beauty and glory of nature for an appreciative Christiania aristocracy. Through his poetry, Tullin created the idea of an Arcadia beyond the borders of the city and its commerce and culture. Tullin was known in his day for his delightful Danish poetry and for poetic and personal gifts that carried him far in society and into the upper echelon of the civic sphere as an important public official. Modern readers remember Tullin for his remarkable *leilighetsdigte* (occasional poems), especially *En Maji-Dag* (1758, A May-Day), a tribute to the natural world that caught the imagination of readers and poetry lovers in Christiania and throughout Europe, resulting in its translation into many European languages.

Tullin was born in Christiania (now Oslo) on 6 September 1728 to Gulbrand Hansen Tullin and Ragnild Hansdatter Dehli Tullin. His father was of humble origins, having been born on a farm called Tull-lien in Ringebu. Gulbrand Tullin had worked his way up the cultural and social ladder from his start as a servant to city commissioner in Kristiansand. In 1724 he had moved to Christiania, where he carved out a modest niche as a merchandise dealer and in time became a wealthy, influential merchant with a thriving business.

Tullin was sent to Christiania Cathedral School, the premier school of the day. He completed his studies and entered the University of Copenhagen in 1745. In 1748 he received an honors degree in theology and delivered his first sermon at Trinitas Kirke (Trinity Church). Tullin returned to Christiania, but no callings were open to someone so young. He abandoned plans to become a pastor and dabbled in literary and legal studies. Barely twenty, Tullin already had considerable talents of kinds that were appreciated among the Christiania bourgeoisie. A gifted musician and dancer, Tullin also painted portraits of himself and of socially prominent people. He could speak English, French, and German fluently, and he was in constant demand as a witty speaker and conversationalist as well as a poet for religious, social, and civic occasions.

His father having died in 1742, and his mother having remarried, Tullin was assisted in finding a position by his stepfather, Claus Therkelsen Koefoed, an official with the Tariff and Toll Commission in Christiania. Initially employed at a factory in Fåbro, Lysaker, Tullin soon became the manager of the business. He then joined the Tariff and Toll Commission, rising from toll inspector in 1757 to director of the commission in 1764. During these years Tullin also held civic positions. In 1760 he was named vice commissioner for the city of Christiania and three years latter was appointed head commissioner by the king. Tullin's climb up the social ladder—a climb higher than his father had ever managed—was aided by his marriage in 1760 to Mette Kruckow, the daughter of Pastor Peter Kruckow and the well-connected Magdalena Feddersen Kruckow. Everything—natural talent and personality, a society that appreciated the kind of poetry that was Tullin's forte, and the most useful family, business, and civic connections—combined to make Tullin preeminently successful. His death on 21 January 1765 cut short this remarkable career.

In Tullin's day the city of Christiania came into its own culturally. Although not the equal of Copenhagen, with its royal court, Christiania was a wealthy city of commerce and trade. Together, merchants and civic leaders formed a new aristocracy, one that set a premium on the accoutrements of wealth and prestige. Without Copenhagen's focus on the royal court, the Christiania aristocracy created a society known for its banquets, balls, and excursions to the country and its landed estates. Musical and literary accomplishments were prized. This upper-echelon milieu provided the setting, scene, and clientele for Tullin's *leilighetsdigte*. He composed poems to celebrate debuts, birthdays, and weddings—everything from birth and baptism to death and burial. Early on, his occasional poetry had a religious tinge, but as Tullin matured as a poet he honed his skills at writing *hyrdepoesi* (shepherd poetry), a refined, elegant expression of joy over the glories of nature and the sublime role of the individual as a simple shepherd in Arcadia, the divinely created Paradise on Earth. Of course, "nature" to the Christiania aristocrats did not refer to the wild, untamed, unknown regions of the wide world; their definition of "getting back to nature" meant a peaceful retreat to their fully staffed rural estates, where they played the roles of ladies and lords of leisure and luxury, all within the bounds of safety, sensual pleasure, and apparent respectability.

Tullin's best-known work, *En Maji-Dag* is an elaborate poem written in celebration of a wedding held on 6 May 1758. Indeed, the poem is itself nearly as florid, expansive, and grand as the spring season it celebrates. Readers wander with the poet through many scenes in nature before finally settling down to the glorious nuptials of the bride and groom, the culminating episode of the poem. *En Maji-Dag* is addressed to a Muse who is woven in and out of the poem, almost forgotten in a few scenes, then reappearing as the poem's messenger to the happy couple.

In the initial scene of *En Maji-Dag* the poet calls on his Muse, his companion on the journey, and depicts a civilized world he would leave to its perfidy:

> Min Muse kom og lad os flye
> Fra dette melancholske Fængsel,
> Hvor Ønsker daglig døe i Trængsel,
> Og fødes for at døe paa ny.
> Hvor Kunst og Vid kun pønser paa
> Den bedste Plan til nye Sorger,
> Hvor Rigdom sulter for at faae
> Det Støv den for sin Arving borger.
>
> (My Muse come and let us fly
> From this melancholy Prison,
> Where Wishes daily die in Stress,
> And are born to die anew.

Where Art and Learning only ponder
The best Plan for new Sorrows,
Where Wealth hungers in order to acquire
The very Dust saved for its own Heir.)

In the world of the city everything is turned topsy-turvy, lies pass for the truth, fools as wise and devils and miscreants rule the day: "Hvor Sindets Roe sin Afsked tog, Da Nøjsomhed blev gjort landflygtig" (Where Peace of Mind has taken its Leave, When Propriety was made to flee). The despairing poet beseeches his Muse to accompany him in fleeing and searching for a place where one can live in peace.

The poet recalls a day in May, and, on the basis of that recollection, he revisits Nature and rediscovers its wonders. The scene shifts to a world of wonder and pure delight, a world akin to the blissful pastoral described in "Thyrsis til Melikrona." The ominous, artificial, upside-down world of the city—the world of commerce and culture—has been replaced by a May day with its untainted, fresh, direct appeal to the senses. The poet is surrounded by nature, and, like Jean-Jacques Rousseau, he glories in its beauty. Awakening the poet's senses, Nature is the artist of a wondrous landscape, the architect of the poet's renewal.

All around the poet are sights and scenes of well-being, of growth, of bounty. The natural world is "en Blomstersal" (a Room of Flowers). Entering into this world are birds of every kind, who add melodies of indescribable beauty, of "yndig Harmonie" (delightful harmony). The song of a single lark touches the poet deeply:

Her flød i dette Øjeblik
En Tonestrøm i Luft og Øre,
Saa alt hvad Sjelen kunne røre
Jeg her i denne Solo fik . . .

(Here in that Moment flowed
A Stream of Tones in the Air and Ear,
So whatever could touch the Soul
I received in that Solo . . .)

In that moment, the poet ponders the mysterious origins of such beauty:

Al Kunst og Ferdighed forsvandt,
Saa snart jeg hørte denne lille:
Ja hvilken Mester torde spille
Mod denne fødde Musicant?
"*O lille søde Fløjtenist!*
"*Hvo gav dig disse Egenskaber?*
Saa raabte jeg mod Bjerget hist,
Og Echo svarede:—*en Skaber.*

(All Art and Craft vanished,
As soon as I heard that little one:
Yes, what Master dared play
Against that born Musician?
"*Oh sweet little Flautist!*
"*Who gave your these Gifts?*
Thus I cried to the Mountain over there,
And Echo answered:—*a Creator.*)

The "Navnløse Væsen . . . *Store Du!*" (Nameless Being . . . *Great Thee!*) then becomes the focus of the poet's energies and admiration. The perfection and beauty of nature and the reason of the poet demand "*en Skaber . . . Hvis Fodspor vises allevegne*" (a Creator . . . Whose Footsteps are seen everywhere). The poet directs his praise, his wonder, his awe to the God of Reason, which he understands to be the creative spark in Nature and in the soul of man. Could man deny the power of God? the poet wonders—and trembles at the mere thought.

The poet then hears "en Stemme som fra Skoven kom" (a Voice which comes from the Forest)—the voice of Menalcas, who sings an aria to Spring and to his love for Melicinda, his bride:

Velkommen yndig Vaar!
Just nu min Lykke gaaer
Iført med Pomp og Pragt
I al sin Maji Dragt.
O hvad for Liv og Lyst
Opfylder her mit Bryst!
Om alting nu forsvandt,
Jeg Savn og Sorg ei fandt:
Min Roe seer alt sin Havn
I Melicindas Favn.

(Welcome glorious Spring!
Just now my Happiness goes about
Clad in Pomp and Glory
In all its May Apparel.
Oh, what Life and Joy
Now Fill my Breast!
If everything should now disappear,
I would not find Loss and Sorrow:
My Peace sees all its Safe-Harbor
In Melicinda's Embrace.)

From this point onward the poet turns his attention—and address—to the jubilant, fortunate bridegroom and the lovely bride. *En Maji-Dag* becomes a song of rejoicing and praise for the union of the happy couple:

Nu saae jeg Himlen smiled',
Jeg saae at Lykken selv fra Skjebnens Arme iled',
Og af en talrig Flok
Velsingelser omringet,
Just I det store Øjeblik,

Da Ja mod Ja i møde gik,
Sig ned til Dig og Din Mage svinged'.

(Now I saw Heaven smiling,
I saw Joy itself rush from the Arms of Fortune,
And surrounded by a great
Flock Of Blessings,
Precisely in the great Moment,
When Yes met Yes,
It encircled You and Your Mate.)

In *En Maji-Dag* Tullin describes a poetic journey from the everyday world of conflict and contrivance to the natural world of peace and beauty created by God for the pleasure and wonder of human beings. The poet and his partner, the Muse, find their true, unfettered selves in nature—an ideal created in the mind and memory of the poet, not the nature of wild expanses and uncontrollable events. Tullin's nature is that of a grand manor, a villa on the outskirts of Christiania.

Tullin's *hyrdepoesi* was enthusiastically received by the cultured Christiania aristocracy. His "Thyrsis til Melikrona" (Thyrsis to Melikrona), written in 1758–1759 is representative of the genre: the poem begins with the shepherd Thyrsis driving his flock out "till Dorimons Græsgang" (to Dorimon's Grassy Plain), where shepherdesses and nymphs are frolicking, lolling about, and entwining floral wreaths. Thyrsis describes his fellow shepherds—one in particular:

Den Byrde
En Hyrde
Om Dagen har, ved Solens Glød
At svede
Af Hede
Gjør denne Aftenlye saa sød:
Helst naar han saaer Hvile i en Hyrdindes Skjød.

(That Burden
A Herd
Has in Daytime, by the Warmth of the Sun
To sweat
From Heat
Makes the Evening Ease ever sweet:
Especially when he sees Rest in a Shepherdess's Bosom.)

In a pastoral setting, amid passive sheep and a peaceful nature falling to rest, the shepherd also rests and—as the poet implies in veiled, resplendent language—perhaps does more than rest. Thyrsis also seeks "et Blund . . . Et sødere Leie" (a Rest . . . A sweeter Bed), beside his beloved Melikrona. His gratitude for what Tullin describes as rest at eventide fills the last strophe of this suggestive pastoral:

Men søde Hyrdinde, hvis nogen vil fortryde paa
At Thyrsis den gang paa saa kostbar Pude laae,
Hvor glad skal han blive, ifald du vil da svare den:
Sligt under jeg Thyrsis fordi han er min Ven!
Den Ære
At bære
Det navn af Melikronas Ven,
Troe dette
Vil sette
Ham i en bundløs Gjeld igjen;
Fortæl kun hvorledes han skal betale den.

(But sweet Shepherdess, if anyone will disparage
That Thyrsis that once lay on so precious a pillow,
How glad he shall be, if you answer him:
Such I granted Thyrsis because he is my Friend!
That honor
Of bearing
The name of Melikrona's Friend,
Believe that
Will set
Him in a boundless Debt once again;
Only tell him how he shall repay it.)

Tullin added to his contemporary reputation with two prizewinning poems for competitions sponsored by Selskabet for de skiønne og nyttige Videnskaber (The Society for Beautiful and Useful Sciences). In *Søefarten dens oprindelse og virkninger* (1761, Oceanic Transport, Its Origin and Effects), Tullin suggests that while the developments and improvements in sea transport may have deleterious effects on others in foreign lands, God—omnipotent and omnipresent—decides what will be. In *Skabningens ypperlighed i henseende til de skabte tings orden og sammenhæng* (1764, The Creation's Primacy with Respect to the Order and Connections of Things Created) he argues that everything has its place in a harmoniously built world that witnesses the wisdom and omnipotence of the Creator. During his brief life Tullin also wrote a series of more than 160 essays and lectures on political, civic, and literary topics; the series was published after his death as "Afbrudte Tanker om adskillige Materier, i alphabetisk Orden" (Interrupted Thoughts on Several Matters, in Alphabetical Order), in his *samtlige Skrifter* (1770–1773, Collected Works).

Christian Braunmann Tullin's poetic star shone brightly for a fleeting moment in time. Always in poor health, he took on too many duties and led an intensely active social life that included a great deal of drinking. The premier poet of his day in Denmark as well as in Norway, he is an important representative of the tastes and trends of his native Christiania in the mid eighteenth century.

Letters:

Bøllingske Breve: til I.A. Cramer (Christiania, ca. 1760);
Utrykte breve fra Christian Braunmann Tullin (Christiania, 1861).

Biography:

Harald Noreng, *Chr. Braunmann Tullin: Kultur og natur i en norsk klassikers verk* (Oslo: Gyldendal, 1951).

References:

Edvard Beyer, *Utsyn over norsk litteratur* (Oslo: Cappelen, 1983), pp. 44–45;

Finn Gaunaa, *En analyse af Christian Braunmann Tullins Prisskriftet om Søefartens Oprindelse og Virkninger* (Roskilde: Roskilde Universitetscenter, 1984);

Harald Noreng, "Majdagens litterære kilder," *Edda: Nordisk Tidsskrift for Litteraturforskning,* 67 (1967): 81–89;

Jan Inge Sørbø, "Tullins 'Majdagen' et originalt dikt," in his *Essay om teologi og litteratur* (Oslo: Det Norske Samlaget, 1994), pp. 75–87;

Anette Walmann, "Sjelens adel: en studie av elitens selvforståelse med utgangspunkt i Christian Braunmann Tullins diktning," thesis, University of Oslo, 2002;

Solveig Øye, *Fortolkning og sentimentalitet: landskap og betrakter i dikt af Christian Braunmann Tullin, Peder Christopher Stenersen, Claus Frimann og Peder Harboe Frimann* (Oslo: University of Oslo, 1998).

Johan Vibe

(10 September 1748 – 9 February 1782)

Lanae H. Isaacson

BOOK: *De nysgerrige Mandfolk: Comoedie i tre Acter* (Copenhagen, 1783).

OTHER: Ludvig Harboe and Ove Høegh Guldberg, eds., *Psalme-Bog, eller En Samling af gamle og nye Psalmer til Guds Ære og Hans Meeninghed Opbyggelse: efter Kongelig allernaadigst Befaling udgivet, tilligemed Collecter, Epistler og Evangelier, Lidelses Historien, Kirke-samt andre Bønner,* contributions by Vibe (Copenhagen: Printed by det Kongelig Waysenhuuses Bogtrykkerie, 1778);

W. P. Sommerfeldt, ed., *Norske Selskabs Vers-Protokol utgitt i anledning av 150-årsdagen for Johan Herman Wessels død,* contributions by Vibe (Oslo: Det Norske Selskab, 1935);

"En Sang," in *Norske tekster: Lyrikk,* edited by Idar Stegane, Eiliv Vinje, and Asbjørn Aarseth (Oslo: Cappelen, 1998), pp. 202–203.

PLAY PRODUCTION: *De nysgerrige Mandfolk: Comoedie i tre Acter,* Copenhagen, Det kongelige Teater, 14 December 1778.

Johan Vibe served as the first secretary of Det Norske Selskab (The Norwegian Society), a formal organization of scholars, students, and literati who met at Wessels Kro (Wessel's Inn), the tavern and club rooms operated by Anna Cathrine Juel at Sværtegade 7 in Copenhagen. Det Norske Selskab had begun in Juel's café on Læderstræde as an informal literary club led by Owe Gierløv Meyer. The society followed the pattern of literary and cultural societies springing to life in many Danish and Norwegian cities and towns. The main purpose of the society was to provide a place where each member could meet with friends and drive away boredom. Det Norske Selskab became the focal point for such literary figures as Vibe, Johan Herman Wessel, Niels Krog Bredal, Johan Nordahl Brun, Søren Monrad, and Claus Fasting.

As one of the central founding members and officers of Det Norske Selskab, Vibe composed many of the social and drinking songs that formed the society's repertoire. Although his poetic oeuvre and literary contributions may seem scant in comparison with those of his contemporary and coleader in the society, Wessel, Vibe apparently won recognition through the strength and magnetism of his personality.

The drinking songs in the eighteenth century reveal the essence of the Norwegian society. Many songs were didactic, teaching people to accept their own failings and the many flaws of the world. In many of them the theme that involved the Enlightenment more than any other was raised: What makes a person happy?

Vibe's drinking songs expressed the values and rationale underlying Det Norske Selskab. In these songs he gave vent to the joys in living of the individual members of the group; he also touched on the fleeting pleasures afforded by wine, women, and song. For Vibe, the beauty, merriment, and pleasures of the flesh, life, and the moment were all too closely akin to and intertwined with death, which was always lurking nearby.

One of two brothers active in Det Norske Selskab, Vibe was born in the Bragernes area of the city of Drammen on 10 September 1748 to Major Johan Christian Vibe and Anne Cathrine Pihl. His younger brother, Joachim Christian, a Latin scholar in Det Norske Selskab, later became a civic leader and official in western Iceland. Johan Vibe completed his education at Christiania Katedralskole in 1766; he went on to serve as a teacher for the children of Pastor, later Bishop, Ole Irgens of Fåberg Parish, Gudbrandsdal. Vibe quickly became embroiled in a love affair with the pastor's wife, who was twenty years younger than her husband and had been only seventeen when, following tradition, she was forced to marry him. Vibe left Fåberg and entered the University of Copenhagen to study Greek, particularly the poems extolling wine and women by Anacreon (circa 500 B.C.), with whom Vibe felt spiritual kinship. Like his contemporary in Det Norske Selskab, Wessel, Vibe left the university without receiving a degree. He moved on to work as an assistant to the surveyor of Fyn, Denmark, Caspar Wessel, brother of the poet.

Vibe did not remain in Fyn long; he returned to Copenhagen, where Det Norske Selskab and the friends he knew there became the center of his life.

A tragic love affair with the actress and singer Caroline Walter seems to lie at the heart of Vibe's actual experience with love. For a time, Vibe and Walter lived together. However, Walter was apparently forced out of artistic circles and performances in Copenhagen by jealous rivals and moved to Sweden, where she met and married musician C. F. Müller. For a while, Vibe apparently worked as a secretary for the prime minister, Ove Høegh Guldberg, then as a cabinet secretary for commerce for Crown Prince Frederik.

Vibe's *drikkeviser og selskabssange* (drinking and society songs) represent both the *Gullalder* (Golden Age) of Det Norske Selskab, when Wessel and Vibe set the tone, and friendship. "En Sang" in *Norske tekster: Lyrikk* (1998, Norwegian Works: Lyric Poetry) expresses Vibe's joy in living while blending melancholy in the face of death:

> Den, Skaberen skiænkte en oplyst Forstand,
> Han elsker og drikker, imedens han kan;
> Thi naar man først Foden hos Charon har sat,
> Saa siges al Elskov og Viinen god Nat.
> Lad Viin da og Elskov opvarme dit Bryst;
> Snart røver dig Døden al sværmende Lyst.
> Og blev du end gammel, saa bliver du dog,
> Hvad endnu er værre, saa bliver du klog.
> Lyksalighed, Maalet for Jordiske Fliid,
> Lær den ej af Viise, du spilder din Tid;
> Kun Saften af pressede Druer, min Ven!
> Og Pigernes Kysse kan give dig den.
> Hos Viinen og Elskov boer lærdom og Vid,
> Jeg kiender ej Stierner, jeg veed dog min Tid;
> Thi naar jeg ej Piger og Viinen har kiær,
> Saa veed jeg tilvisse, min Ende er nær.
> I strænge Theologi! Hindrer mig ej
> At vandre bekrandset den lystige Vey,
> Jeg frygter kun lidet at blive fortabt
> Af den, som har Piger og Vindruer skabt.
> Al Skabningens Herre er naadig og god;
> Til Trøst for de skabte hans Viisdom tillod
> I Druen at finde en Lindring mod Harm
> Og Forsmag paa Himlen i Pigernes Arm.
> Mit høyeste Gode skal ønskes min Ven:
> At drikke og elske og elskes igien:
> Naar Døden da Ende paa Vellyster giør,
> Saa har du dog levet, forinden du døer.

> (He, who the Creator has granted an enlightened Mind,
> He loves and drinks while he can;
> For when one first sets his foot in Charon's death-ship,
> Then all love and wine are bid good Night.
> Let wine then and love warm your breast;
> Soon Death will steal all keen passion from you.
> And if you do not get old, you'll become yet,
> What's worst yet, you'll become wise.
> Pleasure, the goal of all earthly toil,
> Do not learn it from the wise, you'll be wasting your time;
> Only juice from pressed grapes, my friend!
> And the kisses of young girls can give it to you.
> In wine and love are learning and wisdom,
> I do not know stars but I know my time;
> For when I no longer love girls and wine,
> Then I'll know for sure that my end is near.
> You strict theology! Don't hinder me
> In wandering adorned with wreaths on my merry way,
> I hardly fear being led astray
> By the one who has created girls and wine grapes.
> The Lord of all Creation is gracious and good;
> As a comfort for his creations his wisdom has decreed
> That a solace against harm be found in grapes
> And a foretaste of heaven in the arms of young girls.
> I wish my friend my highest good:
> To drink and love and be loved in return:
> When Death brings an end to pure pleasures,
> Then you have lived before you die.)

Vibe's "Afskeeds-Viise" (Song of Farewell) gives a good sense of what Det Norske Selskab meant for the poet and other members of the Norwegian society in Copenhagen. The poem also provides some clues to Vibe's everyday life away from Det Norske Selskab. Initially, Vibe's farewell seems to return to his prosaic surveying job on Fyn; in the opening stanzas of "Afskeeds-Viise," Vibe and his good friend Caspar say goodbye to those gathered at Wessels Kro and strike out for everyday work:

> Farvel, Norske Selskab og Brødre saa bliid,
> Jeg maae mig nu recommendere.
> Alting, siger Salomon, haver sin Tid,
> Det maae jeg nu sande med meere.
> Vor Herre Jer frie
> Fra Popelsie,
> I, som her i Byen restere!
> Jeg er en Landmaaler af den Profession,
> Som man Assistant monne kalde;
> I liflige Fyen der er min Station,
> Saa underlig Lodden mon falde!
> Jeg reyser derhen
> Med Caspar min Ven;
> Men I miste tvende Udvalde.

> (Farewell, Norwegian Society and Brothers so mild,
> I must now recommend myself.
> Everything, says Solomon, has its Time,
> I must affirm that many times over.
> May our Lord free you
> From all Pedantry,
> You who are staying here in town!
> I'm a surveyor by profession,
> Someone they call an assistant;
> My station is in lively Fyn,
> So strange falls the plumb-weight of my fate!
> I'm going there
> With Caspar my friend;
> But you're losing two select men!)

The song of farewell quickly changes from a hearty goodbye from a worker to an appeal to the founder of Det Norske Selskab, Owe Gierløw Meyer, to preserve the integrity and mission of the society and to encourage the "posies" (poems) of its literary garden while weeding out those who do not belong. The poet quickly moves to a final farewell, not just a leave-taking for work but a parting from life. The poem works on two levels: the prosaic work a day level and the poetic (transcendent) one of brief beauty. What the poet requests is entry in the records of the society, notice in the logbook of poetic life as—first and last—a son of Norway who loved and rejoiced in life with his fellows. The stirring of pride in his native land echoes through the poet's farewell, which finally becomes a eulogy delivered by another devoted member and the director of Det Norske Selskab:

> I Vers-Protocollen sligt Minde mig skriv
> Personen var fød udi Norge,
> Særdeles genegen til syndefuldt Liv,
> Var heller ej fri for at borge.
> Paa andre han drak,
> Hans Stads var en Frak
> Hans Roes: han var fød udi Norge.
>
> (In the Verse-Protocol write such a remembrance of me:
> The person was born in Norway,
> Especially inclined to a sinful life,
> Not someone to vouch for either.
> He drank on the tabs of others,
> His finery a cloak
> To his laud: He was born in Norway.)

Touchingly, Vibe passes on his position as secretary to Wessel, who will continue where Vibe left off and lead on until his own end. Mention of the "circle" points both to the surveyor's tools and trade and to the cycle of life that leads from the dying Vibe to his brother-poet Wessel. The conclusion of the stanza points to Wessel as following the path that Vibe is taking.

"Afskeeds-Viise" ends as an expression of gratitude for every patron and friend, for all the brothers and colleagues who kept the drinks coming and the poet's glass filled to the brim. The poet's farewell to Det Norske Selskab and life becomes an expression of thanksgiving for those who helped and guided a poet on his path through life.

In his drinking and society songs, Vibe constantly intertwined feelings of love, earthly pleasure, jubilation, and loyal brotherhood with the constant specter of death. The result is a poetry of optimism and high spirit with an undercurrent of poignancy.

As Liv Bliksrud notes, the Golden Age of Det Norske Selskab was intense but short, just as Vibe's life proved to be. The glory days of the society barely extended to more than ten years, from 1772 to Guldberg's ministry in 1784. Wessel's death a year later also marked the end of the society's greatest time. For Vibe, life on the edge, overindulging in wine and sexual escapades, shortened his days, and he fell gravely ill. He was cared for during his final illness by Madame Juel and loyal members of Det Norske Selskab, the only family he had. Vibe died on 9 February 1782. The Müllers composed and performed the *Sørge-Cantate i anledning af Johan Vibes død: opført i Christiania ved Madame Müller den 28 Februarii 1782* (1782; Funeral Cantata on the Occasion of the Death of Johan Vibe: Performed in Christiania by Madame Müller on 28 February 1782).

Det Norske Selskab had stirred feelings of national identity among the Norwegians, many of whom still remained loyal to the monarchy and union with Denmark, some of whom foresaw a new independent path for Norway. With the establishment of the University of Christiania (today Oslo), the archives of Det Norske Selskab were sent to Norway to become part of the new university library and archives. But the ship carrying the records—including Vibe's manuscripts—sank at sea, and everything was lost. Some of Vibe's poetry had been recorded, however, in *Norske Selskabs Vers-Protokol* (Norwegian Society's Verse-Protocol), published for members of Det Norske Selskab on the 150th anniversary of Wessel's death in 1935. Hardly religious in the traditional sense, Vibe contributed a couple of hymns celebrating life, temporal joys, and nature to the hymnal edited by Ludvig Harboe and ultrareligious minister Ove Høegh Guldberg, *Psalme-Bog, eller En Samling af gamle og nye Psalmer til Guds Ære og Hans Meenigheds Opbyggelse* (1778, Hymnal; or, A Collection of Old and New Hymns to God's Glory and the Elucidation of His Congregation). Vibe's comedy, *De nysgerrige Mandfolk* (The Curious Men), his only play, was published in 1783 and performed at the Royal Theatre in Copenhagen on 14 December 1778.

Together with Wessel and the literary lions of Wessels Kro, Johan Vibe led Det Norske Selskab in its ascendancy and through its remarkable—and brief—golden age. Vibe's society and drinking songs were the key to the raison d'être of the society as well as an expression of Vibe's attitude toward life.

References:

Liv Bliksrud, *Den smilende makten: Norske Selskab i København og Johan Herman Wessel* (Oslo: Aschehoug, 1999);

Francis Bull, *Norske Selskab i København 1772–1812: Tre kåserier av Francis Bull* (Oslo: Det Norske Selskab, 1972), pp. 34–39;

Ivar Havnevik, *Dikt i Norge: Lyrikkhistorie 200–2000* (Oslo: Pax, 2002), p. 151;

A. H. Winsnes, *Det norske Selskab 1772–1812* (Christiania: Aschehoug, 1924).

A. O. Vinje
(6 April 1818 – 30 July 1870)

Jan Sjåvik
University of Washington

BOOKS: *Ferdaminni fraa Sumaren 1860*, 2 volumes (Christiania: A. O. Vinje, 1861);
A Norseman's Views of Britain and the British (Edinburgh: W. P. Nimmo, 1863); translated into Nynorsk by Vinje and H. A. Halvorsen as *Bretland og Britane* (Christiania: Det Norske Samlaget, 1873);
Diktsamling (Christiania: Cappelen, 1864);
Storegut (Christiania: A. O. Vinje, 1866; enlarged edition, Christiania: Det Norske Samlaget, 1868);
Blandkorn (Christiania: Cammermeyer, 1867);
Vaar Politik (Christiania: A. E. Rolstad, 1870);
Om Schweigaard (Christiania: H. E. Larsen, 1870);
Olaf Digre (Oslo: Cappelen, 1927).

Editions and Collections: *Skrifter i Utval*, 6 volumes (Christiania: Det Norske Samlaget, 1883–1890);
Dikt og prosaskrifter i utval, edited by Halvdan Koht (Christiania: Aschehoug, 1903);
Skrifter i Samling, 5 volumes (Christiania: Cappelen, 1916–1921);
Skrifter i samling: Folkeutgåve, 5 volumes, edited by Olav Midttun (Oslo: Cappelen, 1942–1948);
Fjøllstaven min og andre ferdaskildringar, edited by Midttun (Oslo: Det Norske Samlaget, 1967);
Dølen: Eit vikublad. 1858–1870, 3 volumes, edited by Reidar Djupedal (Oslo: Noregs Boklag, 1970–1973);
Att vera døl, edited by Djupedal (Oslo: Det Norske Samlaget, 1972);
A. O. Vinjes beste, edited by Halldis Moren Vesaas (Oslo: Det Norske Samlaget, 1991);
Skrifter i samling, 6 volumes (Oslo: Det Norske Samlaget, 1993).

A. O. Vinje (portrait by Johan Nordhagen; Store Norske Leksikon <http://snl.no/.bilde/Vinje%2C_Aasmund_(portrett)>)

A poet, journalist, and essayist, A. O. Vinje is one of the founding fathers of the Nynorsk variant of written Norwegian, a form of the language initially established by Ivar Aasen in the 1840s and 1850s as an alternative to the Danish-influenced written norm used by educated Norwegians of his day. Vinje came from the county of Telemark—the dialects of which were used extensively by Aasen in his work—and was one of the first significant Norwegian men of letters in modern times whose origins lay in the lower-class rural population. The son of a *husmann* (cotter), Vinje transcended both the class divide and the social and cultural gap between rural and urban nineteenth-century Norway.

Aasmund Olavsson Vinje was born on 6 April 1818 to Olav Aasmundsson and Torbjørg Gjermundsdotter of Vinje parish. Olav Aasmundsson rented a *husmannsplass* (cottager's farm) belonging to the farm Vinje, which he cultivated with great skill and from which the family derived a reasonably comfortable living. Olav Aasmundsson was well regarded in the community for his hard work and known for his way with words and brilliant mind, and his son considered him his most influential teacher.

Vinje read widely as a child and young man and also received deep impressions from the Telemark countryside, particularly during long days as a herding boy. After he was confirmed in the fall of 1834, the local State Church minister recruited him as an itinerant schoolmaster; this post gave him the opportunity to participate in a basic course for teachers. Vinje attended the Asker Normal School for two years, beginning in 1841, after which he taught school in the town of Mandal for five years. During this time his reading became increasingly disciplined as he aimed to qualify for matriculation at Norway's single university, which was in the capital city, Christiania (now Oslo). He lost his teaching position when the school in Mandal was reorganized in 1848, and he moved to the capital.

In Christiania, Vinje eked out a living writing for the newspaper *Morgenbladet* (The Morning Post) while continuing his preparations for university matriculation by attending H. A. S. Heltberg's crammer for mature students; Henrik Ibsen, Bjørnstjerne Bjørnson, and Jonas Lie attended the same school at various times. Vinje was dismissed from the 1849 matriculation examinations for attempting to help a fellow student. He qualified for matriculation the following year but without distinguishing himself. Vinje completed his university studies by taking a law degree in 1856.

Vinje was a highly talented conversationalist whose humor, irony, and satirical wit attracted some people and repulsed others. After alienating the editor of *Morgenbladet* in 1850, he started a satirical weekly magazine, named *Andhrimner* for a cook in Nordic mythology, with the dramatist Ibsen and the editor and librarian Paul Botten Hansen. Vinje had responsibility for the political content. Most of his income, however, came from the daily paper *Drammens Tidende* (Drammen News), for which he wrote twice-weekly columns in Dano-Norwegian from 1851 to 1859. These columns—approximately seven hundred in all—allowed him to pursue his interests in politics, economics, higher education, and Norway's cultural life. His practical sense and his background as a farm boy show up in his columns about such pedestrian topics as fertilizer and breeds of cattle. He also wrote occasional poetry that was published in various periodicals.

Vinje started his own weekly magazine, *Dølen* (The Dalesman), in 1858; the first issue was dated 10 October. *Dølen* was written almost entirely in Landsmål (later known as Nynorsk), for Vinje believed that it was essential to the progress of Norway as a nation that it distinguish itself linguistically and culturally from Denmark, which had ruled Norway for four hundred years—up to the end of the Napoleonic Wars in 1814. Vinje wrote most of the content of *Dølen* himself, although there were a few contributions from others such as the language reformer Aasen. The subjects discussed were as varied as the content of Vinje's columns in *Drammens Tidende*, for which he stopped writing on 19 February 1859 with a solemn declaration that he would never again pollute his Norwegian spirit by writing in Danish. The first issue of *Dølen* included a verse:

Vort Folk i Trældom længe gjekk
Med Sorg forutan Sæli.
Men som det att' si Frihet fekk,
So maa det faa sit Mæli.–

(Our people were long kept in slavery
with grief devoid of joy.
But just as it got its freedom back,
So must it get its language.–)

There were breaks in the publication of *Dølen* when Vinje went on trips, which he did rather frequently. During the summer of 1860 he traveled from Christiania to Trondheim to attend the crowning of the king of Norway, Karl IV—also known as King Karl XV Bernadotte of Sweden—in the Nidaros Cathedral. In lieu of the skipped issues of *Dølen*, Vinje promised his subscribers equivalent material drawn from his experiences during the journey. He kept his promise with his first, longest, and most important book, *Ferdaminni fraa Sumaren 1860* (Travel Memories from the Summer of 1860), which was published in two parts in January and July 1861.

Ferdaminni fraa Sumaren 1860 is a mixture of travelogue, essays, and poetry. Vinje travels by train, on foot, and by ship. He tells about individuals he met, social conditions, and the landscape and makes excursions into history, mythology, and politics. In a section titled "Huldra" (The Wood Nymph) he weaves together his impressions of a beautiful farm girl named Anne with folk beliefs about Roveguro (Gudrun with the tail) but tempers his romantic story with a realistic account of the betrayal and death of Anne's older sister, Ragnhild, who had died a year earlier in the bed in which Vinje spends the night. Although he is taken with Anne's beauty, he views female beauty and dress with humor in a stanza included in the section "Dansen" (The Dance):

Ja, kvinna er vel staut og snill
og gjæv å høyra og å sjå.
Men før ho rett kan verta gild,
som fuglen må ho fjører få.

(Yes, woman is both excellent and kind
and good to listen to and look at.
But before she can become truly splendid,
like a bird she must get feathers.)

The seventy-five-year-old Malene from Folldalen is a favorite traveling companion, and the long section about her shows off Vinje's skill as a conversationalist. There is a sharp ironic contrast in the section "Dei to grannar i Odalen" (The Two Neighbors at Odalen), about two men who can agree on nothing but the fact that they hate each other. One is reasonable and loves life; by using modern farming techniques he achieves such a degree of prosperity that he is able to build a church. The other subscribes to a dark and pietistic religiosity, according to which the earth is nothing but a vale of tears. Constantly dwelling on this negative religious vision diverts his energies, and he ends up living in utter misery—thus creating a self-fulfilling prophecy. In "Grauten på Grut" (The Porridge at Grut) Vinje satirizes farm life by describing how he is fed porridge full of hulls: "Eg fekk god mjølk og åt og åt, og det skura ned gjennom halsen, liksom når grantoppen vert slipa og dregen ned igjennom omnspipa" (I was given good milk and ate and ate, and it ground down my throat, just like when a chimney is being cleaned by having the tip of a fir tree pulled down through it). "Garden med alle dei føderåd" (The Farm with All the Retired Farmers) uses irony and hyperbole to critique the traditional retirement system for farmers, in which a new farmer is expected to provide the previous owner with a certain amount of farm products such as milk, meat, and produce for the rest of the latter's life. Vinje describes a situation in which the present farmer is providing for two retirees, with the result that none of them has enough to live on.

Vinje referred to his form of irony as "tvisyn" (double vision) and used it to expose laziness, folly, and corruption. A utilitarian as well as a rationalist, he spoke in favor of practical solutions to the problems at hand. Constantly drawing on his knowledge of domestic animals as a source of imagery, he extolled the goat—the nanny rather than the billy—as an example worthy of human emulation. The goats find creative solutions to whatever problems they face without undue reliance on principle, and their lack of consistency is their strength. Vinje's ideal goat sounds like a pragmatist.

Like the rest of Vinje's oeuvre, *Ferdaminni fraa Sumaren 1860* abounds with descriptions of nature. These passages are often both lyrical and reflective, as in the poem "Ved Rondane" (At the Ronde Mountains), also known as "No ser eg atter slike fjell og dalar" (Again I See Such Mountains and Valleys). Set to music by Edvard Grieg, it is one of Norway's best-known art songs. It appears in *Ferdaminni fraa Sumaren 1860* when Vinje has reached the high mountain plateau of central Norway and is reminded of the valleys and mountains he knew as a youth in his native Telemark. Reflecting on how his life experience has changed him, he realizes that he is still the same person

Title page for Vinje's A Norseman's Views of Britain and the British *(1873), originally published in English and translated into Nynorsk by the author and H. A. Halvorsen (Widener Library, Harvard University)*

that he was as a young man: "Forsona koma atter gamle tankar: / Det same hjarta er som eldre banker" (Old thoughts returned reconciled: / The same heart beats, but older). As he considers the passing of time from his youth to middle age, he is at peace with the fact that his life will eventually come to an end: "Og inn i siste svevn meg ein gong huggar / dei gamle minne og dei gamle skuggar" (And some time old memories and old shadows / will comfort me into my last sleep). Human beings are inextricably linked to nature, and their lot is the same as that of all other living things: death. The Vinje scholar Olav Midttun has estimated that the first edition of *Ferdaminni fraa Sumaren 1860* was printed in one thousand copies and did not make much money for the author.

Cobbling together several small travel grants, Vinje left for England and Scotland in June 1862; he spent most of his time in Edinburgh, where he recorded his impressions in a book that took the form of sixteen letters to Johan Sebastian Welhaven, a professor of philosophy at the University of Christiania who was also a major poet. *A Norseman's Views of Britain and the British* was published in Edinburgh in June 1863 and was well received in Scotland, although less so in England. It is both a travelogue and a serious attempt at a sociological analysis of British life and society, which Vinje criticizes for its materialism and its abuse of the poor. He returned to Christiania in July 1863. He translated about half of the book into Nynorsk; the translation was finished by H. A. Halvorsen and published after Vinje's death as *Bretland og Britane* (1873, Britain and the British).

Since his youth Vinje had written both occasional and lyrical poetry. His earliest poems were in Dano-Norwegian, but with the start of *Dølen* his poetic production was in Nynorsk. In the fall of 1864 Vinje published *Diktsamling* (Poetry Collection); of its 125 poems, only 37 are in Dano-Norwegian. An outstanding example of Vinje's poetry is "Tytebæret" (The Lingonberry), which displays both the utmost simplicity of theme and formal perfection:

Tytebæret uppå tuva
voks utav ei liti von.
Skogen med si grøne huva
fostrar mang ein raudleitt son.
Ein gong seint om hausten lagde
liten svein til bær-skogs ut:
"Raudt eg lyser," bæret sagde,
"kom åt meg, du vesle-gut.
Her ifrå du må meg taka:
Moge bær er utan ro.
Mal meg sundt at du kan smaka
svaledrykken av mitt blod!
Mognar du, so vil du beda
just den same bøn som eg.
Mogen mann det mest må gleda
burt for folk å gjeva seg."

(The lingonberry on the tussock
grew from such a tiny hope.
The forest with its green cap
fosters many a ruddy son.
Late in the fall a little boy
went to gather berries:
"I'm shining red," said the berry,
"come to me, you little boy.
You must take me away from here:
a ripe berry has no peace.
Crush me so that you may taste
the quenching drink of my blood!
When you ripen, you will pray
just the same prayer as I.
The greatest joy for a mature man
is to give himself away for others.")

With imagery anchored in the quotidian reality of the archetypal Norwegian—few outdoor activities are more common in Norway than gathering wild berries—"Tytebæret" expresses both Vinje's own yearning for an opportunity to use his gifts in the service of his country and a common human desire to be of use to one's social group. Spoken by the berry itself, this desire appears to be utterly natural, while the reference to drinking its blood places a common human desire in the Christian context of Communion. The lingonberry's need for self-sacrifice thus resonates with both the natural world and a transcendental reality that was widely accepted by Vinje's contemporaries. The simple *abab* rhyme scheme and the alternation between feminine and masculine endings combine with the trochaic meter to produce an undulating rhythm that reflects the inevitability and universality of the cycles found in the natural world.

Long a controversial figure in Norwegian public life, Vinje strengthened his reputation as a serious literary artist with the publication of *Diktsamling*. In 1865 he was given a job in the Ministry of Justice; while it was not quite a sinecure position, there was an understanding that Vinje should be given the necessary time off to continue his literary activities. *Dølen* began appearing regularly again, and Vinje worked on a poetry cycle, *Storegut* (1866, Big Boy), that drew on legendary material from Telemark. Combining narrative and lyrical poetry, *Storegut* is about an old man, Olav, and his big, strong son, Storegut. Storegut is ambushed and brutally murdered by his enemy, Gunnstein Grytebekk. Vinje's purpose in the cycle is to give an overview of rural life in Telemark during the closing years of the 1700s, and Olav and Storegut are placed in accurate historical and cultural contexts. Vinje describes farm life, religious beliefs and practices, dealings with the supernatural, and the suffering that common people had to endure at the hands of government officials, particularly while serving in the military. *Storegut* was well received and was republished in an enlarged edition two years later.

Vinje's *Blandkorn* (1867, Mixed Grain) comprises texts reprinted from *Dølen* as well as additional poems. One of the latter is "Lenda frå Land" (Lenda from Land), a long narrative poem about a horse who swims with her colt across a lake and gets stuck in a tiny meadow because she lacks the sense to turn around. The colt starves to death, and Lenda almost dies. Vinje refers to this mind-set as "hestenatur" (the nature of a horse) and sums up the attitude of people who have it:

Han gjenger seg fast, og han aldri kan snu.
Og motgang hans tanke ei mognar.
Han skifter ei meining som folk skulde tru.
Han brester, men aldri han bognar.

(He gets stuck and can never turn around.
Adversity does not cause his ideas to mature.
He does not change his opinion as one would think.
He breaks, but he never bends.)

People who are like the horse Lenda may be long on principle but short on prudence; it is safe to assume that Vinje did not consider himself to be one of them.

Vinje showed little good judgment in one of his next writing projects, however. A satirical narrative titled "Elsk og Giftarmaal" (Love and Marriage) was serialized in *Dølen* in 1867; it recounted barely fictionalized scandals that Vinje knew of from his time in Mandal and was embarrassing to living individuals in Christiania. After receiving a warning from his employer, he abandoned the project. He had also alienated a group of friends—the so-called *Døleringen* (Circle of Dalesmen)—with whom he had begun a new periodical, *Vort Land* (Our Country), in which *Dølen* had been incorporated as the *kjeller* (basement) at the foot of each page.

There was greater promise in the poetic cycle "Ståle," the beginning of which appeared in *Dølen*, but Vinje was unable to complete it. The title character is a young man from a mountain community who leaves home because of his thirst for knowledge, much like Vinje himself had done.

In early 1868 Vinje was fired from the Ministry of Justice. The conservative government was in favor of the union with Sweden, to which Vinje had voiced strong opposition in *Dølen*. The firing was clearly an attempt at silencing him by depriving him of the income that, at least in part, made his literary and journalistic work possible. Angered, Vinje only intensified his attacks on the government in *Dølen*.

On 20 June 1869 Vinje married Rosa Kjeldseth. His last significant series of articles in *Dølen* examined the life and times of the conservative politician Anton Martin Schweigaard. As a professor of law and political economy, as well as a member of parliament from 1842 to 1869, Schweigaard was Norway's foremost public figure. The series began immediately after Schweigaard's death in 1870 and constituted both a reevaluation of the man and a critical survey of Norwegian history and culture since the 1820s.

Vinje's wife died in childbirth on 12 April 1870. Vinje died of stomach cancer on 30 July, a few days after the final issue of *Dølen* appeared. His articles criticizing the government and his articles on Schweigaard were collected and posthumously published in 1870 as *Vaar Politik* (Our Politics) and *Om Schweigaard* (On Schweigaard).

A. O. Vinje has not had much influence outside of Norway. To several generations of Norwegians, however, he has been one of the country's most visible poets, especially because some of his poems have been set to music and become part of Norway's national heritage. Critics regard him as an outstanding essayist and one of Norway's pioneering journalists. His most significant contribution, however, may be to the development of Nynorsk as a written form of Norwegian. His talent as a writer, combined with his use of Nynorsk as his primary medium of expression, demonstrated that a credible alternative to Dano-Norwegian existed and helped to make it attractive to other Norwegian men and women of letters.

Letters:

Halvhundrad Brev, edited by Halvdan Koht (Oslo: Det Norske Samlaget, 1915);

Brev, edited by Olav Midttun (Oslo: Det Norske Samlaget, 1969).

Biographies:

Halvdan Koht, *A. O. Vinje: Stutt Livsskildring* (Christiania: Aschehoug, 1909);

Olav Midttun, *A. O. Vinje* (Oslo: Det Norske Samlaget, 1960);

Olav Vesaas, *A. O. Vinje: Ein tankens hærmann* (Oslo: Cappelen, 2001).

References:

Arne Bergsgård, *Aasmund Vinje: Norsk nasjonal konservatisme* (Oslo: Aschehoug, 1940);

Olav Bø, "'Storegut': Tradisjonen og diktverk," *Norveg,* 31 (1988): 143–156;

Reidar Djupedal, "Aasmund Vinje, mannen som grunnla moderne norsk presse," *Nordisk Tidskrift,* 45 (1969): 1–8;

Eli Glomnes, Øyvind T. Gulliksen, and Olav Solberg, eds., *"At Føle Paa Nationens Puls": Åtte artiklar om Aasmund O. Vinje* (Oslo: Novus, 1992);

Jon Haarberg, *Vinje på vrangen: Momenter til revurdering av en nasjonal klassiker* (Oslo: Universitetsforlaget, 1985);

Idar Handagaard, *Aasmund Vinje i Staale-Diktet* (Oslo: Norli, 1909);

Sigmund Skaard, *A. O. Vinje og antikken* (Oslo: Dybwad, 1938);

Erik Østerud, "To tett og to vrang: Vinje gjennomstrikket," *Edda: Nordisk Tidsskrift for Litteraturforskning,* 3 (1987): 253–266.

Papers:

A. O. Vinje's papers are in the Nasjonalbiblioteket (National Library) in Oslo.

Nils Collett Vogt

(24 September 1864 – 23 December 1937)

Hans H. Skei
University of Oslo

BOOKS: *Digte* (Copenhagen: Philipsen, 1887);
Familiens sorg (Copenhagen: Philipsen, 1889);
Fra Vaar til Høst (Christiania: Olaf Norli, 1894);
Musikk og Vaar (Christiania: Olaf Norli, 1896);
Det dyre brød (Christiania: Olaf Norli, 1900);
Harriet Blich (Christiania: Aschehoug, 1902);
Mennesker (Christiania: Aschehoug, 1903);
Fra Kristiania (Christiania: Aschehoug, 1904);
Septemberbrand (Christiania: Aschehoug, 1907);
Paa reise (Christiania: Aschehoug, 1907);
Digte i utvalg (Christiania: Aschehoug, 1908; revised, 1919; revised again, 1923);
Naar musikken dør: Skuespil i fire akter (Christiania: Aschehoug, 1909);
Spændte sind (Christiania: Aschehoug, 1910)–includes *Ingrid*;
Moren (Christiania: Aschehoug, 1913);
Therese (Christiania: Aschehoug, 1914);
De skadeskudte: skuespil i tre akter (Christiania: Aschehoug, 1916);
Hjemkomst (Christiania: Aschehoug, 1917);
Smaa breve fra Finnmarken (Christiania: Aschehoug, 1918);
Karneval (Christiania: Aschehoug, 1920);
Levende og døde (Christiania: Aschehoug, 1922);
Ned fra bjerget (Oslo: Aschehoug, 1924);
Vind og bølge (Oslo: Aschehoug, 1927);
Forbi er forbi (Oslo: Aschehoug, 1929);
Et liv i dikt (Oslo: Aschehoug, 1930; revised, 1937);
Fra gutt til mann (Oslo: Aschehoug, 1932);
Oplevelser (Oslo: Aschehoug, 1934).

PLAY PRODUCTION: *De skadeskudte,* Oslo, Nationaltheatret, Spring 1913.

Nils Collett Vogt's collected poems, published in 1930, was called *Et liv i dikt* (A Life in Poetry). Whatever he did and wherever he went, he was first and foremost a poet. He started out in a time when literary realism dominated and writers were urged to discuss social problems in their books. He made his poetic debut in 1887 and

Nils Collett Vogt (Store Norske Leksikon <http://snl.no/.bilde/Vogt%2C_Nils_Collett_(portrettfoto_i_profil)>

became a forerunner of sentiments and attitudes that came to dominate the 1890s in Norwegian letters, a period often called "New Romanticism" and a decade in which poetry was again written, read, and appreciated. All through his life he remained a product of the 1880s, with its political conflicts and the new thoughts and ideas that threatened to overthrow the stable, religious, and conservative class into which he was born. He was opposed to ideas and values that he met at home and in school; he made friends with the most radical and decadent of authors in the 1890s, but he never joined any movement. He was a loner.

Vogt worked as a literary critic and a journalist; he made many attempts to write for the theater; he also wrote a novel early in his career. Time and again he tried to write sequels to that novel, but he never succeeded. Late in his life, after he had published many collections of poetry, dozens of prologues, and occasional poems, he wrote one of the best memoirs in Norwegian literature.

Vogt's life was one of illness and despair; he was hardly ever satisfied with his work and its critical reception, even when the latter was laudatory. He always spoke of being afflicted with some kind of nervous disorder, and he spent much time in sanatoriums all over Europe. Yet, he also did valuable work for the Union of Norwegian Authors. His voice was distinctive in a time of political turbulence and changing literary ideals, although he was eventually left behind by a new generation of poets that included Olaf Bull, Arnulf Øverland, and Herman Wildenvey. His sense of isolation and loneliness, of being an exile at home and abroad, also makes his work strangely modern, although his poetry remained within the tradition of the 1880s.

Vogt was born in Christiania (today Oslo) on 24 September 1864. He was the first son of Jens and Johanne Christiane Collett Vogt. The Vogt family had served the nation with several high-ranking and industrious civil servants; the Colletts were even more illustrious, having politicians, including a government minister, civil servants, and creative artists among them, and having important links to the rich classes in Denmark. Vogt's father developed and ran the new horse-drawn tram cars in the Norwegian capital, and his mother read poetry and wrote at least one book of cultural and historical interest. Nils went to the best schools, but because of radical ideas that went against the conservative views of teachers at the Cathedral School in Christiania, he had to finish high school in the city of Hamar, where he did fairly well.

Early on, Vogt knew that he could not live on what he earned by writing for newspapers and from poems published now and then in magazines. He found a job as a teacher at an estate in the county of Värmland in Sweden, but he spent only one summer there. Back in Christiania, he went to socialist meetings and was pleased with the changes that had taken place in Norwegian politics: Parliamentarism had been established, and Venstre (the party in opposition to Høire, the conservative party) had come to power. He passed one of the entrance exams to the University of Christiania—*examen philosophicum*—and planned to go to law school. This career choice, however, did not suit him.

Vogt had been a correspondent for many small newspapers in which he anonymously published radical texts, and a few of his poems were published in established journals when he was quite young. He met Carl Nærup, perhaps the first professional literary critic in Norway, clearly a decisive influence behind Vogt's first attempt at collecting and publishing his youthful poetry. Vogt went to Copenhagen, where almost all Norwegian literature of the time was published, and his *Digte* appeared in 1887. Vogt was then twenty-three years old, and although few people bought the slight volume of poems, and the reviews were few and rather negative, some critics saw a new talent in these poems. In the broader context of Norwegian literary history, the book is deemed important because a new poet made his voice heard among all the novels and plays and the total domination of the book market by Henrik Ibsen, Bjørnstjerne Bjørnson, Alexander L. Kielland, and Jonas Lie and later by Amalie Skram and Arne Garborg. Only one poem from the first collection survives in his collected poems, but it is one of the most anthologized of all Norwegian poems: "Var jeg blot en gran i skogen" (Were I But a Spruce in the Forest), in which concrete pictures of natural forces express mind and soul. The storms may scatter all leaves from other trees, but the spruce just bends a little and stands tall, green, and strong. The poet knows he is not of such strength, but perhaps a mildly ironic twist is that the trees that scatter their leaves receive new leaves the next summer. No doubt Vogt's poetry is rooted in his personal contradictions, and his poems are confessional; they mirror his situation and emotions. In his best poetry, though, his personal experience is lifted onto a new level.

Vogt lived in Copenhagen for some time before and after the publication of *Digte*. He spent much time with Christian Krogh, who influenced him to follow the dictum of the literary bohemia of the day and "write his own life." Vogt's first novel, *Familiens sorg* (1889, The Sorrow of the Family), was based on his own youth and the conflicts he experienced at home with the expectations of two families and his youthful opposition to most of the ideas they cherished. In *Familiens sorg*, a young man believes in the new and radical ideas of his time—shown in events set in 1883–1884, when the political unrest was at its height—and comes to oppose his father, a judge. The young man sees a bright future for his country and his people and finds inspiration in great writers and public figures such as Bjørnson and Henrik Wergeland. But he cannot win, and he gives up his fight, although he still doubts the wisdom of the older generation. The book did not sell well, but the reviews in Norway were favorable, and the autobiographical elements of the novel did not initially draw comments.

Early in 1890 Vogt returned to Christiania, but he did not receive the warm reception he expected. His mother was proud of him for having written the novel, but a journalist attacked the author viciously in *Morgenbladet* for having sacrificed decent people to make a name for himself. The Vogt family trusted the conservative *Morgenbladet* as if it were the Bible, and although most misunderstandings and disagreements were sorted out later, Vogt felt that he had no home in Josefinegaten, a prestigious residential area of Christiania. He left for good, but when he wrote his memoirs forty years later, nostalgia and sadness over the conflict with his family filled the pages. The dispute with his father, who died in 1892, was never settled. Despite all the sadness involved, Vogt also knew that he had followed his conscience.

Vogt moved frequently in the following years. After his father's death, his mother gave him one thousand kroner, a considerable sum at the time, and told him to "travel and become something." He did travel, and he wrote poems constantly. He collected the poems he had written during the difficult years in the beginning of the 1890s. *Fra Vaar til Høst* (From Spring to Autumn) was published in 1894, and new collections of poetry, *Musikk og Vaar* (Music and Spring) and *Det dyre brød* (Dear Bread), followed in 1896 and 1900, respectively. While his first two books had been published in Copenhagen, these three books were published in Christiania by a small publisher who took care of his authors. The poems were written in Rome, Capri, Copenhagen, and Christiania. From 1892 to 1893 Vogt spent most of the time in Italy. In Capri he met a Swedish woman who was ten years his senior. Siri Maria Thyselius was the daughter of a former Swedish prime minister, and the family had a considerable estate at Finnåker in the county of Västmanland. He was thirty and she forty when they married. Their daughter, Johanne, known as Lillan, was born in 1896; their son, John, was born in 1898, but he died at three. Vogt was never fully accepted by his wife's distinguished Swedish family, and he had a problematic relationship to the Finnåker property—which badly needed repair and in which Siri owned only a share.

Vogt was never a practical man: he was not physically strong, and from the early 1890s he often referred to a nervous condition that made it difficult for him to work. Finnåker became a place to which he could retire for relaxation. He traveled frequently to foreign countries—France, Italy, and Switzerland—but he also spent time in different places in Norway. In 1902 he published his second novel, *Harriet Blich*. *Harriet Blich* sold well, and a year later a collection of short stories, *Mennesker* (People), was so well received that its author might have considered becoming a novelist and short-story writer instead of remaining a poet. Poetry remained Vogt's favorite genre, however, even when he worked as a literary critic, wrote reviews for journals, and published correspondence from journeys he undertook. He made serious attempts to write plays and rounded off his career as a writer with memoirs; yet, he wanted to be and remained a poet all his life and lives on in literary history primarily as a poet.

Two collections of poetry were published in 1904 and 1907, respectively: *Fra Kristiania* (From Christiania) and *Septemberbrand* (September Fire). Vogt's poetry was received with enthusiasm by reviewers in Norway as well as in Denmark, although dissenting voices could be heard, and the author often listened more to those than to the positive ones. In 1907 he published a collection of short fiction and critical essays. *Paa reise* (Travels) shows Vogt at his best and worst as a fiction writer, and is an uneven book. He wrote from the places where he lived in Norway and elsewhere in 1905. At the time he felt that he had to flee Sweden because of the conflict with Norway over the union. Vogt loved Swedish culture and literature but hated Swedish politics and feared what the Swedes might do when the Norwegian Parliament broke with Sweden in June 1905. Years later, he still feared that the Swedes might attack Norway, and he was ill at ease even at Finnåker. Only after World War I was he fairly confident that all conflicts between the neighboring countries were settled. Vogt's fears were greatly exaggerated, but they suggest a mind in conflict with itself, creating literature of uneven quality on the basis of such conflicts.

Vogt had written a one-act play in 1904, which was staged at the Nationaltheatret but was only performed for two nights. Beginning in 1910 he wrote other plays, among them *Spændte sind* (1910, Anxious Minds) and *Therese* (1914). A play called *Naar musikken dør* (1909, When the Music Dies) was revised into *Ingrid* (included in the book, *Spændte sind*), only to be further reworked into *De skadeskudte* (published 1916, Those Shot), which was staged at the Nationaltheatret in the spring of 1913 and brought Vogt one of his greatest successes. Some of Vogt's plays were reworked and achieved moderate success in Norway and Denmark. Vogt's plays were of minor importance, hardly mentioned even in literary histories and never played after their brief runs on the stage.

Vogt was not only, as he claimed himself, a child of his time; the combination of the radicalism of the 1880s and the Romanticism of the 1890s that inform so much of his writing clearly proved to be without lasting value. Only a few of his poems have lived on in the collective memory of the nation from which he fled so often and to which he returned time and again and that he praised in poems of original power and strange and persuasive impact. In 1917 he published *Hjemkomst* (Homecoming); the collection includes the much celebrated and anthologized poem "Norsk sang" (Norwegian Song). In 1914 the prologue to "Hjemkomst" was chosen as the celebratory poem for the centennial of the Norwegian Constitution. Vogt's love of Norway is expressed in many poems, among them a couple of poems in memory of Wergeland, one of Norway's greatest poets.

From 1912 on Vogt lived in Norway most of the time, although he still had a home and family in Sweden. He still traveled to various health resorts and often stayed for prolonged periods at sanatoriums. Living in Norway meant that he could participate in the literary life of the nation. He reviewed books on a regular basis for *Dagbladet*, and he served the Norwegian Writers' Union as chairman from 1916 to 1919 and as a member of the literary council between 1921 and 1927. He was made an honorary member of the Union in 1929, and he was awarded a lifelong Artist's Grant from the government in 1923.

A trip to Finnmarken in northernmost Norway resulted in the book *Smaa breve fra Finnmarken* (Short Letters from Finnmarken) in 1918. A collection of articles and essays from *Dagbladet*, *Levende og døde* (The Living and the Dead), was published in 1922. Vogt decided to stop reading and reviewing books in 1925 in order to spend more time on his own work. In the same year he visited the United States, where he read poems and gave speeches to commemorate one hundred years of Norwegian immigration to the United States. He spent Norwegian Independence Day, 17 May, in New York and enjoyed it thoroughly. All in all, the early 1920s were good years in Vogt's life and career. No one doubted his talent as a poet, but he had also proved that he could contribute to the Writers' Union and work on a regular basis for a newspaper as book critic and correspondent. He seems to have had a good relationship with his wife and daughter, although they spent little time together. When he published a collection of poetry with the biblical title *Ned fra bjerget* (Down from the Mountain) in 1924, he took on the mantle of the old sage who could only look backward, seeing everything in retrospect.

Vogt finally came to terms with the bitterness and anger of his younger years in an atonement colored by resignation. He saw shadows and approaching darkness everywhere. *Ned fra bjerget* is Vogt's most comprehensive collection, and in poem after poem he found poetic form for experiences he had not had the courage to touch on before: a young sister who died at an early age; the three-year-old son who died; even servants and farmhands at Finnåker.

Vogt spent much time abroad in the latter half of the 1920s. He left Norway and claimed that he would never return. He had become an old man, and he had begun to doubt his talent and whether he could write poems again. In 1927 he traveled to many cities in Germany, Italy, and Austria, hoping to restore some of his health or at least to suffer less from his many ailments (diabetes being one of them). He returned to Finnåker but shortly thereafter was at a health resort for a long period. During the long months that followed, he wrote short and less significant poems, but they all combined to make up his last collection, *Vind og bølge* (1927, Wind and Wave). Later, he wrote to a friend that he was ashamed of having published such a collection; the reception to *Vind og bølge* was mixed. The only other late collection was *Et liv i dikt*. In the meantime, with the publication of four brief dramas in *Forbi er forbi* (1929, Past is Past), Vogt achieved success as a playwright. A couple of plays even had success as early radio dramas in the Nordic countries; the plays served to contradict his assertion that everything was finished and part of the past. Vogt's plays suggest that the past is an integral part of the present.

For a few years Vogt worked on a memoir to explain where things went wrong and to defend why he acted as he did. *Fra gutt til mann* (1932, From Boy to Man) is a major work in Norwegian memoir literature and a personal victory for an aging man. Shorter texts, fragments, sketches, stories that might have been worked into a second volume, but never reached completion, were published in *Oplevelser* (1934, Experiences).

In the mid 1930s both Vogt and his wife became seriously ill. Siri died at Finnåker in 1936. Vogt was hospitalized for a year in Stockholm, but the Norwegian Writers' Union, then led by Sigrid Undset, took the initiative to bring him to Lillehammer and place him in a Red Cross clinic. Writer friends came to visit, among them Undset and Nini Roll Anker. He died in the hospital on 23 December 1937. His daughter, Lillan, took the urn with his ashes from Norway and placed it in the private chapel at Finnåker, where it remains.

Nils Collett Vogt described himself as half a stranger in his society, never having a sense of belonging anywhere. He regarded this feeling as a small tragedy. He felt that he had the potential for greatness, but he never felt totally confident. A 2004 biography, by Jo Ørjasæter, has established the bare facts of his life. A few of Vogt's poems remain standard in anthologies of Norwegian poetry.

Letters:
Brev fra Nils Collett Vogt til Nini Roll Anker, edited by Eugenia Kielland (Oslo: Aschehoug, 1947).

Biography:
Jo Ørjasæter, *Nils Collett Vogt: Dikter, opprører, kulturpersonlighet* (Oslo: Aschehoug, 2004).

Papers:
Letters, manuscripts, and other papers of Nils Collett Vogt are in the manuscript collection of the National Library in Oslo.

Johan Sebastian Welhaven
(22 December 1807 – 21 October 1873)

Jan Sjåvik
University of Washington

BOOKS: *Henr. Wergelands Digtekunst og Polemik ved Aktstykker oplyste* (Christiania: HoJohanppes Forlag, 1832);

Norges Dæmring: Et polemisk Digt (Christiania: Johan Dahl, 1834);

Digte (Christiania: Johan Dahl, 1839);

Antydning til et forbedret Psalmeverk for den norske kirke (Christiania: Johan Dahl, 1840);

Nyere Digte (Christiania: Johan Dahl, 1845);

Halvhundrede Digte (Copenhagen: Reitzel, 1848);

Reisebilleder og Digte (Christiania: Tønsberg, 1851);

Om Ludvig Holberg (Christiania: Tønsberg, 1854);

Skildringer (Christiania: Johan Dahl, 1860);

En Digtsamling (Christiania: Johan Dahl, 1860);

Ewald og de norske Digtere: fire literairhistoriske Fremstillinger (Christiania: Malling, 1863);

Samlede Skrifter, 8 volumes (Copenhagen: Gyldendal, 1867–1868).

Editions and Collections: *Udvalgte Digte*, edited by Arne Løchen (Christiania: Aschehoug, 1896);

Samlede Digterverker, 4 volumes, edited by Løchen (Christiania: Gyldendal, 1906–1907);

Samlede Digterverker, 4 volumes, edited by Løchen (Christiania: Gyldendal, 1921);

Digte i udvalg (Oslo: Gyldendal, 1927);

Samlede Digterverker, 3 volumes (Oslo: Gyldendal, 1943);

Skrifter, 2 volumes, edited by Bjarne Gran (Bergen: Grieg, 1943);

Norges demring og andre dikt (Oslo: Blix, 1944);

Norges Dæmring, edited by Knut Johansen (Bergen: Eide, 1972);

Samlede verker, 5 volumes, edited by Ingard Hauge (Oslo: Universitetsforlaget, 1990–1992);

Blomster og torner: dikt og prosa i utvalg, edited by Willy Dahl (Bergen: Vigmostad & Bjerke, 2007).

Edition in English: "The Soul of Poetry," "Ganymede," "Like an April Day," "The Lotus," "The Nixie," "Bird-Notes," "Norway's Highlands," "Afternoon on the Water," "The Cup Reversed," "Night Thoughts," "My Saint," and "A Singer's Prayer," in *Anthology of Norwegian Lyrics*,

Johan Sebastian Welhaven (section of a drawing by J. V. Gertner, 1843; Store Norske Leksikon <http://snl.no/.bilde/Welhaven%2C_Johan_Sebastian_(portrettegning%2C_utsnitt)>*)*

translated by Charles Wharton Stork (Princeton: Princeton University Press, 1942), pp. 3–22.

The poet Johan Sebastian Welhaven came to the forefront of Norwegian literary and cultural life in the turbulent 1830s, when he was one of the country's chief exponents of a form of nationalism that emphasized the continuity of the cultural connections between Norway and Denmark and, through Denmark, with Germany and the rest of continental Europe. He became the rallying point for those who wanted to preserve such traditional aesthetic values as clarity and harmony. Their opponents, the so-called *patrioter* (patriots), held that Norway should emphasize the cultural traditions represented by its indigenous farmers to the exclusion of maintaining both the historical connections to Denmark and the political ties to Sweden. The leading light in this group was the poet Henrik Wergeland. While both less flamboyant and less talented than Wergeland, Welhaven wrote with great skill, sensitivity, and intellectual engagement, as well as fidelity to the aesthetic theories of Scandinavia's leading critic at the time, the poet and dramatist Johan Ludvig Heiberg. A Hegelian who believed that the literature of the time ought to be a synthesis of Enlightenment rationality and Romantic sensibility, Heiberg provided Welhaven with powerful arguments against those who, in their opinion, erred either on the side of excessive rationality or on that of overabundant emotion. Welhaven was the second cousin of the critic on his mother's side, which meant that he had more than abstract theoretical reasons for subscribing to Heiberg's ideas about literature. A stanza written to accompany a copy of his *Norges Dæmring: Et polemisk Digt* (1834, Norway's Dawn: A Polemical Poem) that Welhaven sent to Heiberg expresses the significance that he found in their family connection:

Min Mo'r er Datter af en Cammermeyer,
og han var gift med Deres Faders Tante,
og tro mig, blandt Kognaterne, jeg eier
er denne Dame mig den mest pikante.
Jeg venter, at De Tankegangen gjætter:
hun gjør Dem efter Kjødet til min Fætter.
O, gid De fandt, naar her De burger Sonden,
blot nogle Glimt af Fætterskab i Aanden!

(My mother is the daughter of a Cammermeyer,
and he was married to your father's aunt,
and believe me, among my mother's relatives
this lady is the one that I find to be the spiciest one.
I expect that you are catching my drift:
She makes you my cousin in the flesh.
Oh, might you find, when here you probe,
at least a few glimpses of that cousin quality of spirit!)

Johan Sebastian Cammermeyer Welhaven was born in Bergen on 22 December 1807 to Johan Ernst Welhaven, the Lutheran State Church priest at St. Jørgen Leper Hospital, and Else Margrethe Welhaven, née Cammermeyer. He began attending Latin school in 1817; in 1825 he received his matriculation certificate with lackluster marks and became a student at the University of Christiania (now Oslo). His father wanted him to study theology, but the subject did not interest Welhaven. After his father died in 1828, he had to contribute to the support of his family through tutoring and other work; he never got his degree.

One of Wergeland's strengths as a poet lay in his ability to create powerfully striking and unconventional images; Heiberg's and Welhaven's ideals of clarity and harmony are often glaringly absent from Wergeland's poems. Welhaven, who in the preface to his collected works (1867–1868) admitted that in his youth he had shown "megen Kamp-Iver" (much eagerness to fight), was unable to remain silent after Wergeland published the long narrative poem *Skabelsen, Mennesket og Messias* (Creation, Man, and the Messiah) in 1830. Welhaven's first salvo against Wergeland was the poem "Til Henrik Wergeland!" (To Henrik Wergeland!), published in the paper *Morgenbladet* (The Morning Post) on 15 August 1830. In the first stanza Welhaven asks:

Hvorlænge vil Du rase mod Fornuften?
Hvorlænge svinge Donquixotisk Spær?
Seer Du da ei, din Sværmenom i Luften,
er kun en Dalen mod et bundløst Kjær?
For Sol Du tager Sumpens Metheorer,
en Øgle er den Pegasus Du sporer.

(How long will you rage against reason?
How long swing a spear like Don Quixote?
Do you not see that your hovering in the air
is nothing but falling into a bottomless pond?
You believe that the meteors of the muck are the sun,
And the Pegasus you spur is a lizard.)

The seven stanzas that follow continue in a similar vein, concluding that "Din Rang du sikkred Dig med tusind Stemmer: / Rang blandt Parnassets Daarekistelemmer" (You secured your rank with a thousand votes: / A rank among the inmates of the insanity asylum of the Parnassus). Welhaven and Heiberg's aesthetics held that in the binary opposites reason and passion, human and animal, land and air, and reality and appearance, the former member of each pair was privileged; Welhaven believed that Wergeland's poetry gave more place to the "wrong" term in each pair. He particularly objected to the passion displayed in Wergeland's poem.

After trading epigrammatic insults with Wergeland in the handwritten paper of the local student society, Welhaven published *Henr. Wergelands Digtekunst og Polemik ved Aktstykker oplyste* (1832, Henrik Wergeland's Literary Art and Polemics, Illuminated with Documents), in which he denied that Wergeland's poetry and ideas had any merit whatsoever. While claiming not to "forvexle Personen med dens Frembringelser" (confuse the person with his products), Welhaven asserted that he had come to loathe Wergeland's character "i samme Grad, som hans Muse" (to the same

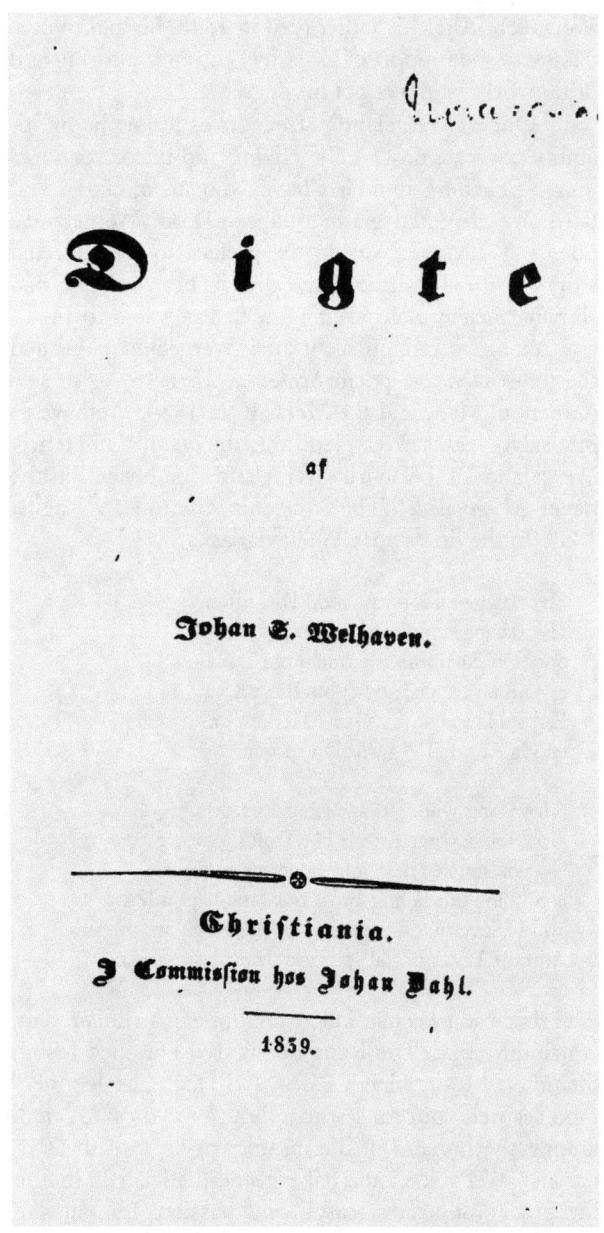

Title page for Welhaven's first poetry collection (Poems). It includes "Nøkken" (translated as "The Nixie," 1942), his first poem drawn from Norwegian folklore (Oxford University Library).

illa Collett, became one of Norway's most important prose writers.)

Welhaven's first significant long poetic work was *Norges Dæmring*. To emphasize his belief in the necessity of cultural continuity with Denmark, he published it on 14 November 1834–the birthday of the Danish Romantic poet Adam Oehlenschläger. It consists of seventy-six sonnets, a form that was attractive to Welhaven because of its balance and harmony. His prologue warns the reader to expect needling by the poet's "literaire Landser" (literary lances), and contemporary society–particularly Welhaven's own social class–is indeed castigated in *Norges Dæmring*, while the poet pays homage to Norwegian nature and the nation's past. Bergen, Welhaven's hometown, is characterized as "et lidet Eden" (a little Eden), while Kristiansand is "En halvdød Hval, der gisper mat paa Land" (a half-dead whale, which feebly gasps on land). The sonneteer also offers advice on poetry, telling an unnamed adversary not to seek freedom "i den ydre Norm" (in the outer norm)–referring to nontraditional verse forms–or "hos en taaget Skare" (from a foggy crowd), presumably Wergeland's supporters. In sonnet 31 he characterizes such supporters as "Hoben" (the mob) which "fletter løvet omkring Narrestaven" (braids the foliage around his fool's rod)–a reference to Proverbs 14:3, "In the fool's mouth is a rod of pride; but the lips of the wise shall preserve them." Welhaven acknowledged in the preface to his collected works that he was not "rigtig vaabenklædt" (properly armed) when he wrote *Norges Dæmring* and therefore was far too heavy-handed at times.

Welhaven's critique of the mores of his own social group continue in the essay "Christianias Vinter- og Sommer-Dvale" (Christiania's Winter and Summer Torpor), which was published in two parts in 1834 in the periodical *Vidar*, named for an Old Norse god. He criticizes the lack of refined social life in Christiania and suggests that increased attention to art would meet the social needs of the educated classes and have an uplifting effect on the common people, who will otherwise be inclined to seek vulgar entertainment. (In *Norges Dæmring* people in the capital were said to relieve their boredom by various "Stimulantser . . . man drikker Punsch, forlover sig og dandser" [stimulants . . . one drinks punch, gets engaged, and dances].)

Welhaven visited France in 1836 and wrote a series of "Skizzer fra Frankrig" (Sketches from France) that were published in the Christiania newspaper *Den Constitutionelle* (For the Constitution) during the summer of that year. The pieces are straightforwardly descriptive and informative. Welhaven's essay on the Paris morgue combines realism and a limited use of emotion: it is truly a synthesis of Enlightenment rationalism and Romantic sentiment.

degree as his muse). These statements were so strong and the wounds so deep that there was little prospect of reconciliation. Welhaven and Wergeland's sister Camilla were in love, and she sympathized with the views of Welhaven and his circle; but since Welhaven was hated by both her brother and her father, the relationship was doomed. After several years of limited association, Welhaven broke off all contact with her when he secretly became engaged to Ida Kjerulf in 1837. (Camilla Wergeland married Peter Jonas Collett in 1841 and, as Cam-

Welhaven's first collection of poetry, *Digte* (1839, Poems), includes "Vildt og Tamt" (Wild and Tame), in which he bitterly satirizes the lives of young women in Christiania by showing that the difference between them and young women in New Guinea is just a matter of degree: the New Guineans choose fish bones and rusty nails for their ornaments, while the Norwegians, "Modeverdnens Tryllerinder" (Enchantresses of the World of Fashion), "snøre Livet ind og Ryggen / danne Midjen efter Myggen" (draw together their bodices and backs / fashion their waists like that of a mosquito) and "plyndre Paafugl, Struds og Ræve" (plunder peacocks, ostriches and foxes) to decorate themselves. "Efter Soiréen" (After the Ball), on the other hand, shows that Welhaven understands the tragedy of young women whose parents compel them to marry men they do not love.

Digte also includes "Nøkken" (translated as "The Nixie," 1942), Welhaven's first poem based in Norwegian folklore. The nixie, or water sprite, is traditionally a dangerous being who lures people to their deaths; but Welhaven transmutes him into a singer of a *Vemodskvad* (melancholy ballad), which is more in line with Heiberg's aesthetics. In "Nøkken" a nixie plays the harp because he suffers the pains of unrequited love:

> Jeg døver min Sorrig i Suus og Larm;
> men ak, min Barm
> vil aldrig dit Billed miste.
>
> (I deaden my sorrow in roaring and noise;
> but oh, my breast
> will never lose your image.)

One might read "Nøkken" as an expression of Welhaven's love for Kjerulf, whose mother forbade her to be publicly engaged to him.

"Søfuglen" (The Sea-Bird) is, perhaps, the poem in *Digte* that has had the greatest impact on Norwegian literature. The simple story of a wild duck that is hunted and wounded and dives to the bottom of a lake to die, it is generally acknowledged as the inspiration for Henrik Ibsen's drama *Vildanden* (1884; translated as *The Wild Duck*, 1890). The poems "Sisyphos" (Sisyphus) and "Glaukos" (Glaucus) take their subjects from classical antiquity, while "Goliath" and "Nehemias" (Nehemiah) have Old Testament motifs. Welhaven sometimes used such poems to refer to his own role as a major participant in the culture wars. Sisyphus, for example, only appears to be laboring in vain as he forever rolls his stone uphill:

> Han har en Trøst, han kæmper ei forgjæves:
> Naar Stenen styrter i den steile Bakke,
> og naar den atter gjennem Uren Hæves,
> den knuser stedse dog en Øgles Nakke.
>
> (He has one comfort, he is not fighting in vain:
> When the stone rolls down the steep slope,
> and when it again is lifted up through the rockfall,
> it often crushes a lizard's neck.)

Welhaven also identifies with Nehemiah, who went back to Jerusalem to rebuild the Temple: "Der staaer en Skræk af byggende Mænd, / some vælge at mure med Sværd ved Lænd" (Fear radiates from building men / who choose to do masonry work with a sword at their loins). The implication is that Welhaven's "sword" may be a pen, but he, too, is fighting a heroic battle against adversaries who ought to stand in awe of him.

In November 1840 Welhaven was appointed to the lectureship in philosophy at the University of Christiania for which he had applied the previous year. The appointment process took unusually long because Welhaven was a controversial figure and because he had not taken a degree beyond his *Examen Philosophicum*, which indicated only that he had completed a certain level of general education and could be admitted to the study of a particular field.

Shortly after Welhaven received the appointment, Kjerulf died. Her death figures prominently in his next collection, *Nyere Digte* (1845, Newer Poems). *Nyere Digte* includes "Digtets Aand" (translated as "The Spirit of Poetry," 1942), in which Welhaven presents his "intentional" theory of poetry. He argues that something is present in the poet's soul that is higher than language but can, nevertheless, be transmitted to the poet's audience through a linguistic work of art. This something is the poet's intention: a "frigjort Tanke" (idea made free) that "boede i Sjælen / før Strophens Liv blev til" (lived in the soul / before the life of the stanza came into being). This "tankefunk" (spark of an idea) runs through the poem, "En Gjennemgang til Livet / i Læserens Bryst" (a passage to the life / in the reader's breast), where it will

> . . . næres og bevæges
> og blive lig den Ild,
> der laa i Digtersjælen,
> før Strophens Liv blev til.
>
> (. . . be nourished and moved
> and become like the fire,
> which lay in the poet's soul,
> before the life of the stanza came into being.)

The successful transmission of his "Tankebilled" (idea image) is the supreme accomplishment for which the poet hopes; it is more important than even his reputation:

> Lad kun hans Rygte hæves
> mod sky af Døgnets Vind,

det er dog ei den sande
Kvegelse for hans Sind.

(Just let his reputation
be lifted to the sky by the wind of the day,
still it is not the true
refreshment for his mind.)

The poet's desire, "med eller uden Ry" (with or without reputation), is for his work to be reborn in a succession of readers and thereby achieve immortality: "dermed er der lovet / hans Verk et evigt Liv" (therewith has been promised / his work eternal life). The reader's experience of the work should duplicate the poet's intention, and the poem fails if the reader derives something else from it than the poet—consciously or unconsciously—has put into it. A good reading, from the author's point of view, entails the re-creation of the authorial intention in the reader's mind.

Another poem in the collection, "Det tornede Træ" (The Thorny Tree), can be read both as an expression of Welhaven's experience of adversity in general and as a statement about his loss of Kjerulf in particular:

Ynder du Træet, da maa du ei hade
den hvasse Torn mellem Blomster og Blade;
da Træet var ungt med den blødeste Hud,
blev den et standset, forkommet skud:
en Torn er en Kvist, der har taget Skade.
Tænk hvad et spirende Liv maa lide
hvor Mørket ruger og Taagerne skride!
Ja, see dig om paa den fattige Plet,
hvor Træet leed og blev torneklædt,
og bar dog Blomster, duftende, blide.
Blandt al den Glæde, en Vaar udfolder,
er Tornen et Savn, som Planten beholder.
Den siger i Væxternes stumme Sprog:
"Jeg saarer, men ak, jeg gjemmer dog
en større Smerte end jeg forvolder."

(If you love the tree, you must not hate
the sharp thorn among flowers and leaves;
when the tree was young with the softest skin,
it became an arrested and ruined shoot:
a thorn is a twig that has been damaged.
Imagine how a sprouting life must suffer
where darkness broods and the fog moves!
Yes, look around at that poor spot,
where the tree suffered and was clothed with thorns,
and still bore fragrant and gentle flowers.
Among all the joy unfolded by spring,
the thorn is a lack that the plant keeps.
It says in the silent language of plants:
"I hurt, but oh, I still hide
a greater pain than I cause.")

In "Birken" (The Birch Tree) the birch is a silent witness to the speaker's joy and loss:

Jeg veed et Sted i Dalen
hvor Elven bag Hækken gaar;
der tømte jeg Frydspokalen
engang i de lyse Aar.
. . . .
Den saa min fagre Glæde,
der nu er lagt i Støv;
over mit Blomstersæde
bæved dens unge Løv.

(I know a place in the valley
where the river runs behind the hedge;
there I emptied the goblet of joy
once in the light years.
. . . .
It saw my beautiful joy,
which has now become dust;
above my seat of flowers
its young foliage trembled.)

While *Digte* included a single poem—"Nøkken"—that drew on Norwegian folk belief and legend, folklore motifs are common in *Nyere Digte*. Fairies, wood nymphs, and other beings from the unseen world provide Welhaven with a wealth of imagery, and several poems draw heavily on specific legends and popular beliefs. In "Huldren" (The Wood Nymph) human emotions have a supernatural counterpart in those of the nymph. During the spring and summer she expresses her joy throughout the natural world as she "udslaaer . . . naar Jonsok kommer / Tapeter og Høitidsfaner / væv'de af Løv og Blommer" (unfolds . . . when Saint John's Eve comes / wall coverings and celebration banners / woven from foliage and flowers). But when fall arrives, she has to move into the mountain for the winter "med tunge Sukke" (with heavy sighs). At that time she becomes dangerous to humans, as she can "dit Sind forandre" (alter your mind):

Paa Folkets Munde
boer Sagnet om Spillemanden,
der kom fra visne Lunde
med Kummersky paa Panden.
Han rørte siden
sit Spil over Blomsterenge;
men Suk fra Løvfaldstiden
bævede paa hans Strænge.

(In the mouths of the people
lives the legend about the fiddler,
who came from withered groves
with a cloud of affliction on his brow.
He later touched
his instrument on flower meadows;
but the sighs from fall
trembled on his strings.)

One of the finest poems inspired by the death of Kjerulf is the long ballad "Det omvendte Bæger" (translated as "The Cup Reversed," 1942), about the recently widowed "Hr. Gilbert af Billingskov, / som ei kunde Sorgen glemme" (Sir Gilbert of Billingskov, / who could not forget his sorrow). He "grublet og vaaget / og sørger endnu den lange Nat" (brooded and stayed awake / and still grieves all night long); "hans Blik er af Kummer taaget" (his eyes are clouded by suffering); and his "Hest og Hunde har glemt hans Stemme" (horse and dogs have forgotten his voice). He has sought solace in listening to "Munkenes Litani" (the litany of the monks) and "Bønner og Psalmer / om Gravens Fred og om Himlens Palmer" (prayers and hymns / about the peace of the grave and the palms of Heaven), to no avail. Activities such as "larmende Jagt med Falk og med Hunde" (loud hunting with falcon and dogs) actually deepened his sorrow, for "Sorgen fulgte i Vildtets Spor / og lagde i Horn og Buesnor / et Suk, der aabned hans Vunde" (the grief followed in the tracks of the game / and laid in horn and bowstring / a sigh that opened his wound). As Gilbert sits in his castle "i den dybe, rugende Sorg, / som Taaren ei har formildet" (in the deep and brooding grief / which the tear has not yet alleviated), he hears singing outside. The grove of the elves will be opened to him, the song says; he is to empty the singer's "funklende Bæger" (shining cup), "og, som de lette, svindende Drømme, / skal Mindernes blege Hær forgaae" (and, like the light, departing dreams / shall the host of pale memories disappear). Gilbert goes out into the moonlit night:

> Da saae han Kredsen paa Blomstergrunden
> og da var Alfernes Bolig funden.
> Som Elven i Dalen gik hans Blod,
> og med sit Bankende Bryst han stod
> ved Runestenen i Lunden.
> Hvad hæver sig her fra Kildevover,
> hvad kalder ham her, hvor Vaaren sover?
> Det er den deilige Kildens Fee
> med Kinder og Barm, der ligne Snee,
> som Daggryet skinner over.
>
> Sin blændende Arm hun mildt bevæger
> og hæver det funklende, fulde Bæger,
> og siger med lifligt klingende Røst:
> "Paa Glemselen følger nyskabt Lyst,
> som ganske din Smerte læger."

(Then he saw the circle on the flowery ground
and then was the dwelling of the elves found.
His blood rushed like the river in the valley,
and with his pounding chest he stood
by the rune stone in the grove.
What lifts itself up from the waves of the spring,
what calls him here, where springtime sleeps?
It is the lovely fairy of the spring
with cheeks and breast that look like snow,
with dawn shining on.

She kindly moves her brilliant arm
and lifts the sparkling, full cup,
and says with a pleasantly sounding voice:
"After the forgetting comes a newly created desire,
that will completely heal your pain.")

The cup is a metaphor for the erotic invitation from the fairy; although Norwegian folklore has an ambiguous view of sexual intercourse between humans and supernatural creatures, Welhaven presents the fairy maiden as a temptress who is trying to turn Gilbert into a faithless knight and deprive him of his strength. Gilbert resists the temptation, as "et elsket Navn . . . klang i hans Sjæl" (a beloved name . . . sounded in his soul). Not wanting to lose the memory of his dead wife, he flings the cup away, and the fairy's spell is broken; he "havde sin Troskab prøvet" (had tested his faithfulness). Memories flood into his mind, together with "Taaren, der kom i Sukkenes Følge" (the tear that followed his sighs), and the memories create "et slør som ved Dag og ved Nat . . . kunde hans Afgrund dølge" (a veil which by day and by night . . . was able to hide his abyss). Full of vigor, he returns to his usual activities, and, as a symbol of his transformation, he has the image of an upturned cup painted on his shield.

The best known of the poems in *Nyere Digte* with sources in folklore is "Asgaardsreien" (The Host of the Dead), which uses beliefs about the *oskorei*–the vagrant host of the restless dead. It begins by describing the *oskorei* as "et Tog paa skummende sorte Heste" (a host riding foamy black horses) through the air; they are led by the Norse god Thor, who strikes his shield and causes red flames to burst forth. The company of spirits screams and inspires fear, and "Folket lytter / med stigende Angst i de dirrende Hytter" (people listen / with growing dread in the trembling cottages). Christmas, when the restless dead celebrate "hos Trolde og Jetter" (with trolls and giants), is a favorite time for outings of the *oskorei*. They are particularly attracted by drunkenness and fighting. A wedding feast is being held on three successive days during Christmas at the farm Øvre-Flage. On the third day the company is preparing for a solemn toast to the bride when a jilted suitor and his brother force their way into the house. The brothers–appropriately named Grim (Ugly) and Ulv (Wolf)–cast aside the drunken and sleepy men and the women who are trying to protect the groom. They seize him and pull him out into the yard to be slaughtered, but he draws his knife and, "af Vinterens Luftning styrket" (invigorated by the winter air), kills Grim. Ulv forces the groom to the ground and has his knife to his rival's throat when the *oskorei* arrive: "Ulv holdt inde og stod bedøvet, / og skjælved og bæved som Aspeløvet" (Ulv stopped and stood as if in a trance, / and trembled and shook like an aspen leaf). The spectral host grab Ulv by the hair and carry him off; the groom, although severely wounded, has recovered by spring. In the final stanza Welhaven reveals that the source of the story is the groom, now an old man, who has entertained his family with the tale for years:

> Nu sidder han bøiet og høit bedaget,
> og kan sin Æt omkring Arnen samle,
> nu sidder han ofte med Sagn i Laget
> og korter Tiden for Unge og Gamle.
> Saa var det seneste Julekveld,
> da Ungdommen raabte: "Fortæl, fortæl!"
> Da flammed hans Blik, da saa han tilbage,
> da maned han frem sine Bryllupsdage.
>
> (Now he sits bent over with advanced age,
> and can gather his posterity around the fire,
> now he often sits telling stories in the gathering
> and shortens the time for young and old.
> Thus it was last Christmas Eve,
> when the youth shouted: "Tell, tell!"
> Then his eye flamed, then he looked back,
> then he conjured up his wedding days.)

The ending is a masterful rhetorical move: it allows Welhaven, a city dweller and representative of the educated classes, to justify his knowledge of the story by placing it in the mouth of its sole surviving central character, a representative of the rural folk. Also, by telling the narrative in Dano-Norwegian he establishes a link between a story of the people and the language of his own cultural group.

The ballad "Jutulsbjerget" (The Giant's Mountain) is based on a legend of a mountain in the northern part of Gudbrandsdalen that was believed to be inhabited by trolls. When Hr. (Sir) Havard Staur forces a dwarf to let him into the mountain, he sees the beautiful daughter of the king of the giants and immediately falls in love with her. Havard strikes his fire steel against a rock to produce a fire over the woman and thereby brings her into the human world. But as a result, she becomes unspeakably ugly. Havard flees and is never able to fall in love again.

In "En Vise om Hellig Olaf" (A Ballad about St. Olaf) Olaf and his men are struggling to complete construction of a church in time for it to be consecrated at Whitsuntide when the dwarves on a nearby mountain begin tossing down stones and logs in an effort to destroy the building. Olaf responds with Christian magic: he "kyssed Hjalted paa sin Klinge, / og han holdt det høit mod Dværgehallens Væg, / og han korsede sin Bringe" (kissed the hilt of his sword, / and he held it up high against the wall of the dwarves' hall, / and he crossed his chest). Miraculously, the stones fit into the wall, the logs come to rest as beams, and an unusually large rectangular stone ends up exactly where the altar should be. Welhaven concludes the ballad by connecting the legend with contemporary folklife: although the walls of Olaf's church have long since disappeared, the altar stone is still in place, and the young men of the valley meet their sweethearts there. The memory of Olaf lives on with the stone, "og hans Saga gaaer, / gjennem Norges Vaar, / sødt som Fuglesang i Lunde" (and his Saga persists / through Norway's Spring / sweetly like Birdsong in a Grove).

In addition to poetry, Welhaven also wrote essays on literature, art, and politics. Many were published in *Den Constitutionelle*. An important contribution was a series of articles titled "Om norske Presse-Anliggender" (1838, About Conditions in the Norwegian Press) that provide insights into his thinking about both politics and aesthetics. His pamphlet *Antydning til et forbedret Psalmeverk for den norske kirke* (1840, Suggestions for an Improved Hymnal for the Church of Norway) received a good deal of criticism. "Billeder fra Bergenskysten" (Pictures from the Bergen Coast) resulted from a journey to Bergen and its environs and was serialized in *Den Constitutionelle* in 1842.

In 1845 Welhaven married Josephine Bidoulac, a Danish woman. He was promoted to professor of philosophy at the University of Christiania in 1846.

Welhaven's next collection, *Halvhundrede Digte* (1848, Fifty Poems), includes the ballad "Dyre Vaa." The title character is a large, strong man whose neighbors tease him by suggesting that he is big enough to fight trolls in the manner of the ancient god Thor. Dyre agrees but insists that the fight must take place in the dark so that he will not be frightened by the appearance of the trolls. One Christmas, when "Øllet gik rundt og Natten faldt paa" (the beer was passed around and it was dark"), Dyre and his friends hear the bellowing of a troll on the other side of Lake Totak. Dyre rows across the lake and ferries the troll, who has shrunk himself to fit in the boat, to his destination. As payment the troll leaves behind the thumb of his mitten so that Dyre can get an idea of his actual size. The thumb measures four bushels.

The collection also includes Welhaven's finest poem inspired by the death of Kjerulf, "Den Salige" (The Blessed One; translated as "My Saint," 1942). Perhaps the most personally revealing poem in Welhaven's oeuvre, "Den Salige" is a good example of his mature work. In the first of the three stanzas the speaker greets the spirit of his deceased beloved. In the second stanza he describes how he was able to come to terms with her death:

Alt er følt, fuldkommet og erindret,
Alt fornyes evig i mit Sind;
mildt og ømt har Sorgen, der er lindret,
spredet Mindets Fred om mine Trin.
Sorgen vaaged hvor din Aske blunder,
og den vandred gjennem Ørkner hen,
og tilsidst, ved Kjerlighedens Under,
fik jeg dig du Salige igjen.

(Everything is felt, perfected and recollected,
everything is eternally renewed in my mind;
mildly and gently has the soothed grief
spread memory's peace around my steps.
Grief stayed awake where your ashes slumber,
and it wandered through deserts,
and finally, through the miracle of love
I got you blessed one back.)

The final stanza relates how the return of her gentle spirit has illuminated the speaker's long night of sorrow. It concludes with the vow that she gives him: "og jeg hører atter hvad du lover, / at vi aldrig mer skal skilles ad" (and again I hear what you are promising, / that we will never again become separated). The poem cannot be seen as a successful work according to the theory of poetry set forth in "Digtets Aand," for the "Tankebilled" it presents is as open to a bitterly ironic reading of the speaker as deluded as it is to a more straightforward interpretation of him as blessed.

In 1850 Welhaven and some friends traveled extensively in rural southern Norway. The journey gave him material for the prose narrative "Vasdrag og Skovmarker" (Waterways and Forests), in which he describes nature scenes, recounts legends and folk beliefs, and offers portraits of his informants. His model was the work of the folklore collector Peter Christen Asbjørnsen, whose findings were often presented in highly fictionalized frame stories. "Vasdrag og Skovmarker" was published with "Billeder fra Bergenskysten" and sixteen poems as *Reisebilleder og Digte* (1851, Travel Pictures and Poems).

Many of the poems in *Reisebilleder og Digte* draw on Norwegian nature and folklife. An example is "Møllergutten" (The Miller Boy), about the real-life Telemark master fiddler Torgeir Augundsson. Augundsson was brought to the capital by the famed violinist Ole Bull, who shared the concert stage with him. In Welhaven's poem Augundsson learns to play by listening to the sound of a waterfall inhabited by a water sprite skilled at fiddling.

In the ballad "Raad for Uraad" (A Remedy for an Extremity) the ugly and disagreeable Knud Labeit uses his wealth to secure the beautiful Ingeborg Fagerliden for his bride, even though she loves the strong and healthy Gudmund Thordsen Storebingen. To get to the church for the wedding ceremony Knud, Ingeborg, and

Print of a painting of Welhaven by Mathias Calmeyer (from Arne Løchen, Johan Sebastian Welhaven: Liv og Skrifter, *1900; Robarts Library, University of Toronto)*

their guests must cross a river, but the bridge has been washed out. Knut offers his best ox as payment to anyone who will carry him and his bride across the flooded river. Gudmund springs out of the bushes, seizes Ingeborg, and carries her across. No one has the courage to follow them. This display of strength, courage, and initiative shows the community that the marriage of Knud and Ingeborg is a mismatch. They persuade Knud to relinquish his claim so that Ingeborg can marry Gudmund.

During his final years Welhaven made several valuable contributions to Norwegian literary history. *Om Ludvig Holberg* (About Ludvig Holberg) was originally an article in a collection of portrait plates; it was published separately in 1854. "Digteren fra Alstadhoug, Peder Dass" (The Poet of Alstadhoug, Petter Dass) is a substantial scholarly article that was published in the *Nordisk Universitets-Tidsskrift* (Nordic University Periodical) in 1856.

In 1856 Welhaven wrote a not particularly successful story, "En Sjel i Vildmarken" (A Soul in the Wilderness), which was published in a Christiania newspaper. It was collected with "Vasdrag og Skovmarker" and "Billeder fra Bergenskysten," both reprinted from *Reisebilleder og Digte*, as *Skildringer* (1860, Depictions).

Also in 1860 Welhaven published *En Digtsamling* (A Poetry Collection). Many of the poems in the volume express a strong religious longing, and thoughts about death are prevalent. In "En Sangers Bøn" (translated as "A Singer's Prayer," 1942) the speaker asks for the grace of God when faced with "den store Livets Gaade" (the great riddle of life). "Lokkende Toner" (Enticing Notes; translated as "Bird-Notes," 1942) unites a general Romantic longing with a more specifically religious desire for that which is beyond the visible world; but it also places the speaker in a Norwegian nature setting:

> Jeg stod i Birkenes høie Sal,
> mens Midsommerdagen helded;
> der tindrede Dug i dyben Dal,
> det skinned som Guld af Fjeldet.
> Da bæved Lunden, da lød det nær
> som af en susende Vinge,
> og grant jeg hørte fra Fjeld og Træ'r
> de lokkende Toner klinge:
> Tilirlil Tove,
> langt, langt bort i Skove!
>
> (I stood in the high hall of the birches,
> while the midsummer day came to an end;
> dew sparkled in the deep valley,
> the mountain shone like gold.
> Then the grove trembled, it sounded nearby
> like a rustling wing,
> and clearly I heard from mountain and trees
> the enticing notes sound:
> Tirilil Tove,
> far, far away in the forest!)

En Digtsamling was Welhaven's final poetry collection. In 1863 he published *Ewald og de norske Digtere: fire literairhistoriske Fremstillinger* (Ewald and the Norwegian Poets: Four Literary Historical Presentations), in which he discusses the relationship between Danish and Norwegian writers in the period before 1814. Failing health forced him to retire from his professorship in 1867; by then his career as a writer had also come to an end.

Johan Sebastian Welhaven's significance for Norwegian literature during his lifetime cannot be overestimated. Along with his rival Wergeland, he was one of the two most important poets in Norway during the decades following the establishment of the constitution in 1814. To later generations of Norwegian critics and readers he has been overshadowed, albeit not entirely eclipsed, by Wergeland. Nevertheless, he retains a central place in Norwegian literary history.

Letters:

Welhavens kjærlighetsbrever til Ida Kjerulf, edited by Otto Louis Mohr (Oslo: Aschehoug, 1945).

Biographies:

Arne Løchen, *J. S. Welhaven: Liv og Skrifter* (Christiania: Aschehoug, 1900);

Reidar Andersen-Næss, *J. S. Welhaven: Mennesket og dikteren* (Oslo: Universitetsforlaget, 1959);

Tore Vassdal, *Bastian: Johan Sebastian Cammermeyer Welhaven som bergenser og vestlending* (Bergen: Sigma, 2006).

References:

Asbjørn Aarnes, "Über 'Das Unsagbare,'" *Orbis Litterarum: International Review of Literary Studies,* 40, no. 4 (1985): 285–299;

Aarnes and Paul Grøtved, eds., *Demringens tolker: En essaysamling om Johan Sebastian Welhaven* (Oslo: Aventura, 1990);

Gerhard Gran, *Norges Dæmring: En litteraturhistorisk Indledning* (Bergen: Grieg, 1899);

Gregor Gumpert, *Johan Sebastian Welhavens Ästhetik und Dichtungstheorie* (Münster: Kleinheinrich, 1990);

Ingard Hauge, *Tanker og tro i Welhavens poesi* (Oslo: Gyldendal, 1955);

Unni Langås, "'I dette Brev skal jeg lægge al min Kunst og mit Hjerte': Welhavens kjærlighetsbrev til Ida Kjerulf," *Norsk Litteraturvitenskapelig Tidsskrift,* 3, no. 2 (2000): 106–121;

Per Saugstad, *J. S. Welhaven: En idealenes vokter* (Oslo: Gyldendal, 1967);

Jan Sjåvik, "Presence and Absence in J. S. Welhaven, 'Den Salige,'" *Scandinavian Studies,* 65, no. 2 (1993): 196–206;

Paulus Svendsen, "Schiller–Welhaven–Kierkegaard," *Nerthus: Nordisch-deutsche Beitrage,* 3 (1972): 7–18;

Tore Vassdal, *Bastian: Johan Sebastian Cammermeyer Welhaven som bergenser og vestlending* (Bergen: Sigma, 2006).

Papers:

Most of Johan Sebastian Welhaven's papers are in the Nasjonalbiblioteket (National Library) in Oslo.

Henrik Wergeland

(17 June 1808 – 12 July 1845)

Ann Schmiesing
University of Colorado at Boulder

BOOKS: *"Ah!"* as Siful Sifadda (Christiania, 1827);
Irreparabile Tempus (Christiania, 1828);
Sinclars Død (Christiania: Trykt paa Forfatterens Forlag hos Gundersen, 1828);
Digte: Første Ring (Christiania: Jacob Lehmanns Enke, 1829);
Phantasmer (Christiania: Jacob Lehmanns Enke, 1829);
Harlequin Virtuos (Christiania, 1830);
Skabelsen, Mennesket og Messias (Christiania: Johannesen, 1830);
For Almuen, 1 (Christiania: Jacob Lehmanns Enke, 1830);
For Almuen, 2 (Christiania: Steen, 1830);
Den norske Bondes nyttige Kundskab om de Læge-, Farve-, Garve-, samt Gift-Planter der vore paa hans Jord (Christiania, 1831);
Opium: skuespil i tre acter (Christiania, 1831);
Levnets- og Velfærds-Viisdom (Christiania: Forfatternes Forlag, 1831);
Om Smag og Behag man ikke disputere (Christiania, 1832);
Digte: Anden Ring (Christiania: Jacob Lehmanns Enke, 1833);
Cæsaris: et Digt, 1831 (Christiania: Steen, 1833);
Spaniolen (Christiania, 1833);
Norges Historie (Christiania: Hoppe, 1834);
Den indiske Cholera (Christiania, 1835);
De sidste Kloge (Christiania, 1835);
Barnemordersken (Christiania, 1835);
Papegøien (Christiania: Johan Dahl, 1835);
Nogle Ord fra Prækestolen (Christiania: Johan Krohn, 1836);
Norge i 1800 og 1836 (Christiania: Carl L. Roshauw, 1836);
Udtog af Norges Historie: Til Brug i Borger- og Almueskoler (Christiania: Winther, 1836);
Campbellerne, eller Den hjemkomne Søn (Christiania: R. Hviids Enke, 1837);
Kong Carl Johans Historie: Hvad Tidsrummet fra hans Valg til svensk Thronfølger betræffer (Christiania: Malling, 1837);

Henrik Wergeland (lithograph by an unknown artist, 1830s; Store Norske Leksikon <http://snl.no/Henrik_Wergeland>)

Hytten, eller Kristian Ildens Afreise fra Norge (Christiania, 1837);
Stockholmsfareren (Christiania, 1837);
Stockholmsfareren No. 2 (Christiania: Johan Krohn, 1837);
Selskabet "Kringla" eller "Norske Almacks" (Christiania: Risum, 1839);
Den Konstitutionelle (Christiania, 1839);
Jan van Huysums Blomsterstykke (Christiania, 1840);
"Verden tilhører os Jurister!" (Christiania, 1840);

Indlæg i Jødesagen: Til Understøttelse for Forslaget om Ophævelse af Norges Grundlovs §2, sidste Passus (Christiania: Malling, 1841);

Vinægers Fjeldeventyr (Christiania, 1841);

Engelsk Salt (Christiania: Mallings Officin, 1841);

Svalen: et Skjærsommermorgens-Eventyr for Mødre, som have mistet Barn (Christiania, 1841);

Norges Konstitutions Historie, 4 volumes (Christiania: Guldberg & Dzwonkowski, 1841–1843);

Storthingsmanden, Gudbrandsdølen Ole Haagenstag (Christiania, 1842);

Jødesagen i det norske Storthing (Christiania: Johan Dahl, 1842);

Langeleiken: En krands af Digtninger i Dølemaal (Christiania: Winther, 1842);

Jøden: ni blomstrende Tørneqviste (Christiania, 1842);

Venetianerne, eller Venskab og Kjærlighed (Christiania: Lehmannske, 1843);

Ole Bull, efter Opgivelser af ham selv biografisk skildrete af Henrik Wergeland (Christiania: Guldberg & Dzwonkowski, 1843);

Jødinden: elleve blomstrende Tornekviste (Christiania: Fabritius, 1844);

Den engelske Lods (Christiania, 1844);

Farbrors 474 Skaaler: Samlede og udgivne af Ola Nordmand, Studiosus. Med et Brev fra Henrik Wergeland som Fortale (Christiania, 1844);

Mennesket: et Digt (Christiania, 1845);

Hasselnødder, med og uden Kjerne, dog til Tidsfordriv, plukkede af min henvisende Livs-Busk (Christiania: Tønsberg, 1845);

Fjeldstuen: skuespil med Sang i tre Akter. Henrik wergelands sidste Værk (Christiania: Fabritius, 1848).

Collections: *Henrik Wergelands Samlede Skrifter*, 9 volumes, edited by Hartvig Lassen (Christiania, 1852–1857);

Udvalgte Skrifter af Henrik Wergeland, edited by Lassen, third edition (Copenhagen: Gad, 1876);

Skrifter i Udvalg, 7 volumes, introduction by Carl Nærup (Christiania: Huseby, 1896–1897);

Digte i udvalg, 2 volumes (Christiania: Aschehoug, 1897, 1898);

Samlede skrifter, trykt og utrykt, 23 volumes, edited by Herman Jæger and Didrik Arup Seip (Christiania / Oslo: Steen, 1918–1940);

Wergeland for hvermann: Lyrikk og prosa, edited by Harald Beyer (Oslo: Gyldendal, 1947);

Henrik Wergelands samlede barnediktning, edited by Sonja Hagemann (Oslo: Aschehoug, 1976);

Den første gang: Henrik Wergelands dikt i utvalg (Oslo: Gyldendal, 1995).

Editions in English: *Henrik Wergeland, the Norwegian Poet*, translated by Illit Grøndahl (Newcastle-on-Tyne: Fenwick & Wade, 1920);

Eagle Wings: Poetry by Bjørnson, Ibsen, and Wergeland in an English Version, translated by Axel Gerhard Dehly (Auburndale, Me.: Maydell, 1943);

Poems, translated by G. M. Gathorne-Hardy, Jethro Bithell, and Illit Grøndahl, preface by Francis Bull (Westport, Conn.: Greenwood Press, 1970);

The Army of Truth: Selected Poems in the Historic Fight to Obtain Equal Rights for Jews in Nineteenth-Century Norway, edited by Ragnhild Galtung, translated by Gathorne-Hardy, Grøndahl, and Anne Born (Madison: University of Wisconsin Press, 2003).

PLAY PRODUCTIONS: *Campbellerne*, Christiania, Christiania Theater, 24 January 1838;

Venetianerne, Christiania, Christiania Theater, 27 January 1841;

Efterspil til Fjeldeventyret, Christiania, Christiania Theater, Spring 1844;

Søkadetterne iland, Christiania, Christiania Theater, 9 April 1855.

Henrik Wergeland was a poet, patriot, dramatist, historian, and social activist whose short life shaped Norway in the first half of the nineteenth century; one might justifiably refer to this period of Norwegian history as the age of Wergeland. What is surprising is that Wergeland merits this distinction even though only about one-fifth of his voluminous writings are of enduring literary value. As the Norwegian literary scholar Francis Bull acknowledges in the preface to a 1970 edition of Wergeland's poems in English translation, the bulk of Wergeland's work is of interest only to scholars of Norwegian history or to Wergeland specialists. Wergeland's dramas and farces tend to be second-rate at best, and his detractors regarded many of his poetic works as so fanciful and unrestrained that they constitute mere bombast. He was not a faithful recorder of everyday experience or a poet accustomed to the calm beauty of the classical aesthetic; nor did he aspire to be. But what Wergeland was, as a writer and a cultural figure, far outweighs what he was not. Wergeland's poetic genius lay in his originality, spontaneity, and wit, as well as in the brilliance and dynamism of his imagery. Nils Collett Vogt wrote in a poem in 1914 that Wergeland's strength as a poet and human being was like the life-affirming rays of the sun. His poetry is active rather than meditative and reflective, a quality that is mirrored in his life and deeds. Among the many causes for which he is remembered are his efforts to overturn the clause in the Norwegian constitution barring entry to Jews, his campaign against what he viewed as Denmark's cultural hegemony over Norway, and his dedication to improving the lives of the common people.

Painting of cavalry troops breaking up a student demonstration on Norway's Constitution Day (17 May) in 1829. Wergeland's farce Phantasmer *(1828, Phantasms) was inspired by the incident, in which Wergeland was struck with the side of a saber (National Archives of Norway).*

Henrik Arnold Wergeland was born on 17 June 1808 in Kristiansand in southern Norway to Nicolai Wergeland, a politically engaged writer and critic who taught at the Latin school, and Alette Dorothea Wergeland, née Thaulow, the daughter of a civil servant. Both parents were artistic: Nicolai Wergeland was an amateur painter and enthusiastic about music, and his wife had acted in her youth. Henrik had four siblings: Augusta, born in 1810; Harald Titus Alexis, born in 1811; Camilla, born in 1813; and Joseph Frantz Oscar, born in 1815. (Under her married name, Camilla Collett, Camilla distinguished herself as one of Norway's most important prose writers of the nineteenth century.) In 1814 Nicolai Wergeland traveled to Eidsvoll, a town north of Christiania (today Oslo), to serve as a representative to the assembly that wrote and ratified the Norwegian Constitution in the wake of the Treaty of Kiel, which ended Norway's centuries-long union with Denmark and ceded Norway to Sweden. Though many representatives argued that Denmark could terminate the union but had no right to cede Norway to another country without consulting the Norwegians, Nicolai Wergeland was in favor of the union with Sweden.

In 1817 Nicolai Wergeland became the parish pastor at Eidsvoll. Henrik Wergeland was influenced by the spirit of patriotism and liberalism that his father embodied and that pervaded the historic town. During his first two years in Eidsvoll, Wergeland was taught at home by a tutor, after which he was sent to school in Christiania. He composed satirical verses about his teachers and drew caricatures, and during school holidays he wrote comedies. His first published work, a novella titled "Blodstenen" (The Bloodstone), appeared in the Christiania newspaper *Morgenbladet* in 1821. Despite these early signs of interest in a literary career, Wergeland's teachers and peers did not consider him particularly talented.

Wergeland matriculated as a theology student at the University of Christiania in 1825. In the autumn of 1826 he was named editor of the student paper *Samfundsbladet* but was removed from the post after only a month. He returned as editor in the autumn of 1827.

On 4 November 1827 Wergeland was present at the Christiania Theater during a protest against a play by the Swedish director Johan Peter Strömberg. The play, *Fredsfesten* (The Celebration of Peace)–also known as *Unionen* (The Union)–commemorated the election on 4 November 1814 of Sweden's King Carl XIII as king of Norway in accordance with the Treaty of Kiel. Many Norwegians in the audience did not share Strömberg's celebratory mood. Wergeland insisted to the authorities who investigated the protest that he had not taken part in it.

A far more serious controversy has its origins in a July 1828 argument between Wergeland and the procurator (township lawyer) J. O. Praëm, during which Wergeland alleged within earshot of several bystanders that Praëm was exploiting the peasants in and around Eidsvoll. Praëm later served as lawyer for Petty Officer Ole Andersen Lie, the defendant in what became known as "Gardermo-saken" (the Gardermoen case). The case stemmed from an altercation between Wergeland and officers at a military parade on 20 September 1828 in Gardermoen. Wergeland and two friends had stopped in Gardermoen on their way back to Eidsvoll after a visit to Christiania. In response to Wergeland's allegedly disrespectful conduct and refusal to get out of the way, Lie struck Wergeland with the flat edge of his saber. Wergeland believed that his honor had been insulted and his liberty violated, and what might have been a rather insignificant affair resulted in a drawn-out legal entanglement that ended in 1832 with Wergeland being fined 120 kroner and made to pay court costs. In the meantime, the relationship between Wergeland and Praëm had grown ever more acrimonious. Viewing it as his moral duty to expose Praëm's unjust treatment of the common people, Wergeland sought to thwart Praëm's political ambitions by parodying Praëm in his farces. He also carried on his dispute with Praëm in the pages of the newspaper *Morgenbladet*. In an article on 15 April 1831 he branded Praëm a criminal against Norway and against humanity. Praëm accused Wergeland of besmirching his name, and protracted litigation ensued. The feud lasted until 1844. Praëm once noted, accurately, that at times Wergeland became so uncontrollably agitated that one who did not know him would think that he was drunk.

During his student years Wergeland was a prolific writer of lyric poetry, romances, and plays. His poetry far outshone his dramatic work. In his first play, *Ah!* (1827), several characters squabble over who will become precentor after the ailing incumbent, Filebom, dies. Certain that Filebom is in his death throes, the disputants utter a collective "ah!" in disappointment when he walks into the room as the curtain falls. *Ah!* was the first of many works that Wergeland wrote under the pseudonym Siful Sifadda, a name probably inspired by the war stallion Sulin Sifadda in the Ossian legends. Siful Sifadda became not only a pseudonym but also a sort of alter ego for Wergeland, who referred to Sifadda as his half brother. The true identity of Siful Sifadda was never a secret. Though many of the farces Wergeland wrote under the pseudonym are relatively weak, they constitute, as Rolf Nyboe Nettum has observed, the most original dramatic work in Norwegian literature between the achievements of the Norwegian-born writers Ludvig Holberg and Johan Herman Wessel and those of Henrik Ibsen and Bjørnstjerne Bjørnson. Although he modeled his style in part on those of comic dramatists such as Aristophanes and Ludwig Tieck, Wergeland's farces for the most part can be considered dramatic only in a formal sense; although some were performed by university students, most were not intended to be produced on the stage.

Like *Ah!*, the short farce *Deus ex Machina, eller væk I usle Comedianter! Væk!* (1828, Deus ex Machina; or, Away, You Wretched Comedians! Away!) has merited little attention in Wergeland scholarship. Its overtly political subject matter, however, points the way toward many of Wergeland's later farces. Europe is personified in the play; its principal lament is that a leader is attempting to slip absolutism into liberalism. (Wergeland did not publish the play, and it has not been produced. It appears in his *Samlede Skrifter, trykt og utrykt* [1918–1940, Collected Works, Published and Unpublished], in which the chronological register notes that it was written before April 1828. Nettum, however, states that the year in which Wergeland wrote the play is unknown.) *Irreparabile Tempus* (1828, Irreparable Time), in which a group of superficial young women suddenly find that the character Faster Tid (Aunt Time) has aged them considerably, is more serious in tone than Wergeland's other early farces. The tragedy *Sinclars Død* (1828, Sinclair's Death) is an immature work notable principally for its effusive dedicatory poem in which Wergeland portrays the Swedish king, Carl Johan, as a pan-Scandinavianist and freedom-bearer. Although Wergeland was an ardent promoter of liberty and of Norwegians' right to celebrate their own culture, in particular their Constitution Day on 17 May, he was branded a traitor by many in Norway because of reverence for Carl Johan. In contrast to his admiration of the Swedish king, Wergeland was violently opposed to the Danish influence on Norwegian culture. When a toast to the Danish actors at the theater in Christiania was proposed at a student banquet, he smashed his glass against the heating stove. He campaigned against Danish cultural influence in many of his later works.

Wergeland submitted *Opium* (1831), written in the fall of 1828, to the Christianias offentlige Theater (Christiania Public Theater), but it was rejected. Ha, Ho, and Hu, gentlemen-in-waiting to the king, falsely claim to have won the hand of Sylvia. When the king decrees that any of the three who is lying must die, Sylvia makes them fall into a deathlike sleep by giving them opium. The king not only learns of her trick but also wins her hand for himself. Wergeland's portrayal of the military in the piece was influenced by the September 1828 incident in Gardermoen.

Like *Opium*, the farce *Phantasmer* (1829, Phantasms) was inspired by an actual event. The student association to which Wergeland belonged had decided in January of that year to celebrate Constitution Day, but students loyal to the Swedish king had opposed this decision and sought to overturn it. The cavalry was mobilized to quell the demonstration, and Wergeland received another saber rap on his green student uniform. *Phantasmer* voices Wergeland's indignation at such attempts to curb Norwegians' freedom of expression.

In 1829 Wergeland received his divinity degree and returned to Eidsvoll. That same year he published *Digte: Første Ring* (Poems: First Cycle). Although uneven in quality and at times eccentric, the collection demonstrates the dynamism and quick improvisational spirit of his poetic talent. Despite its flaws, many commentators prefer *Digte, Første Ring* to Wergeland's more mature work on the grounds that it best demonstrates what makes him so striking in the history of Norwegian poetry. In contrast to the emphasis on traditional forms in Norwegian poetry before Wergeland, many of the poems in the collection are not stanzaic and are unrhymed. Wergeland's detractors viewed his originality of form as formlessness, while his admirers countered that his poems exhibited an exciting fluidity of form that, like his rich imagery, prevented them from becoming static and stodgy. The "Stella" poems in the book represent Wergeland's version of the eternal feminine; they were inspired by several women with whom he was infatuated during his student years, not by an actual Stella. *Digte, Første Ring* also includes many poems with an emphasis on liberty. In the "Hymne til Friheden" (Hymn to Liberty) Wergeland celebrates America's founding fathers and laments that France "unfastened / Liberty's belt, broke her crown in two like a wedding ring, / Alas! before she was the nation's bride" (translated by Jethro Bithell). Turning to Norway, he describes the Norwegian mountains as "arched to a temple, / A home for Freedom the exile; / The waterfall's rainbow is the smoke of Liberty's hearthstone" (translated by Bithell).

Liberty is also a prominent theme in the unwieldy 720-page epic poem *Skabelsen, Mennesket og Messias* (1830, Creation, Man and Messiah), which Wergeland began in 1827 but did not complete until the spring of 1830. The work begins in the ethereal realms while the earth is still chaos, proceeds in the second part to humankind from the creation to Christ, and in the third examines Christ's redemption of humanity. Throughout the work Wergeland argues against superstition and tyranny, holds freedom and love as the highest principles that should guide human nature, and displays an optimism that denies the existence of absolute evil. A Danish critic described the work as an overture to the July Revolution in France that overthrew King Charles X.

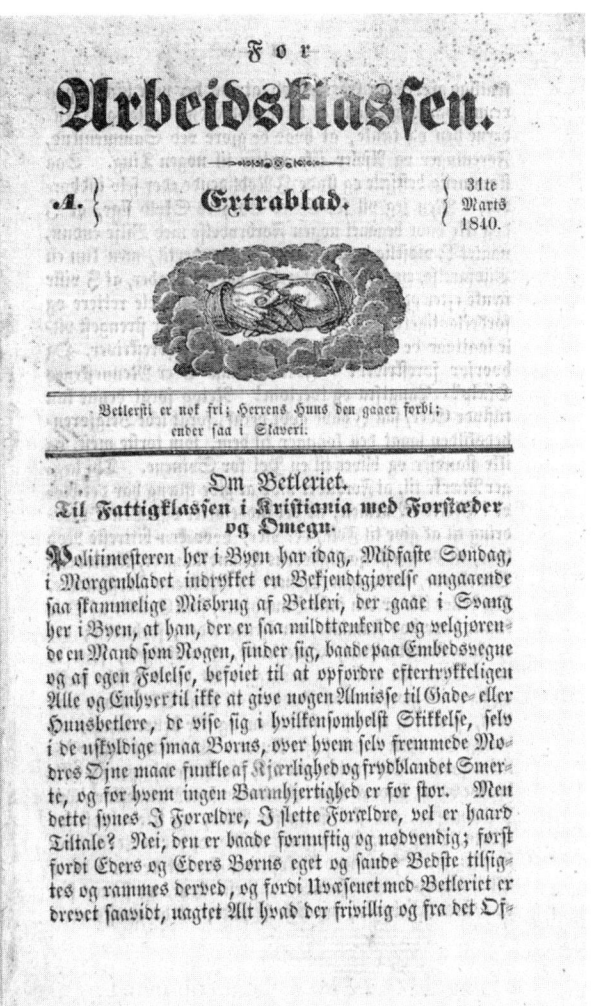

Front page of the first issue of Wergeland's paper (For the Working Classes), which was published from 1840 to 1845 (National Archives of Norway)

The cultural debate of the 1830s between Wergeland and the poet Johan Sebastian Welhaven was launched by the publication of *Skabelsen, Mennesket og Messias*. Wergeland regarded the poem as a model for other Norwegian writers to follow–a view that was most decidedly not shared by Welhaven, who had designed the frontispiece for the work before reading it. Welhaven was appalled by what he regarded as the turgid language and uncontrolled nature of the poem. He made his opinion known in his first published poem, "Til Henrik Wergeland!" (To Henrik Wergeland!), which appeared anonymously in *Morgenbladet* on 15 August 1830. Welhaven insists in the poem that Wergeland's frenzied flights of fancy in *Skabelsen, Mennesket og Messias* made even the heavens seem ridiculous and that when reading the poem one began to think that even the seraphs should don fool's caps. While others had compared Wergeland to William Shakespeare or

Friedrich Gottlieb Klopstock, Welhaven countered that Wergeland's poetry included only platitudes. In a response to Welhaven's criticisms published in *Morgenbladet* on 16 August, Wergeland referred to *Skabelsen, Mennesket og Messias* as "Menneskehedens Epos og Republikanernes Bibel" (an epic of mankind and the Bible of the Republicans).

Wergeland continued to promote the education of the common people in works such as *For Almuen* (For the Common People), which appeared in two parts in 1830. He also continued to make his political sentiments known in his farces. In *Harlequin Virtuos* (1830, Harlequin Virtuoso) a Norwegian who regards his taste as superior to that of his countrymen, in part because his mother was a Dane, promises two foreign musicians who are visiting Christiania that whoever performs best will win the hand of his adopted daughter, Alvilde. Erling, the Norwegian Alvilde loves, triumphs by appearing in the guise of Harlequin and claiming that he has come all the way from Sicily and is thus more "foreign" than the visiting musicians. The work is an effective diatribe against those who idolized Danish culture.

Wergeland accompanied his father to Sweden in 1830, visited England and France in 1831, and traveled with an English friend to western Norway in 1832. He continued to champion liberty in poems such as *Spaniolen* (The Spaniard) and *Cæsaris* (Caesar), both published in 1833, in which he denounced the tyranny of Sweden's allies Spain and Russia.

During this time Wergeland continued to experience discord with Welhaven. The two writers possessed quite different views concerning the foundations and future of Norwegian culture. These differences led each to harbor a deep antipathy toward the other, which was exacerbated for a time by the mutual affection between Welhaven and Wergeland's sister, Camilla. The differences in their respective positions concerning Norwegian culture were, nevertheless, more nuanced than is commonly assumed. Wergeland is often simply depicted as rejecting Danish culture and promoting Norwegianness, and Welhaven as doing the opposite. Whereas Wergeland's enemies proclaimed that his patriotic platform would lead to cultural isolation, he possessed a deep appreciation for foreign interaction and the universal attributes of humanity. These universal attributes, he believed, found unique expression in the cultures of individual nations. He objected not to cultural interaction among nations but to the cultural hegemony he identified in the pervasive Danish influence on Norwegian culture. As for Welhaven, his detractors portrayed him as a traitor to Norwegian native traditions who blindly consumed Danish culture, but in reality his disgust was reserved mainly for what he regarded as the naive boastfulness of the nationalists. In his view the nationalists failed to realize that a Norwegian intellectual, artistic, and literary community could not be formed with the snap of a finger, and they also seemed at times to suggest that the Danish cultural influence on Norwegian culture could or should be thoroughly expunged–a notion with which he disagreed.

The controversy between Welhaven and Wergeland yields insights into the divide in nineteenth-century Norway between the *embetsstand* (bureaucracy) and the *bønder* (farmers). Clergymen, civil servants, and members of academia and other professions were included in the *embetsstand;* the term *bønder* was applied primarily to the landowning peasant farmers, although also in a general sense to farmhands and other rural laborers. Wergeland's efforts to improve the lot of the lower classes made him a natural champion of the *bønder*. He strove to be a model Norwegian patriot in word and deed. In addition to championing various Norwegian causes in his writings, he ate typical Norwegian food and dressed in homespun. In Christiania he was allied with Norskhedspartiet (the Norwegianness Party). Wergeland and the members of Norskhedspartiet were referred to–sometimes sarcastically–as *patrioter* (patriots). On the other hand, Welhaven and his adherents were referred to as Intelligentspartiet (the Party of the Intelligentsia) and frequently derided as *Danomaner* (Danomaniacs). In 1832 they founded Studenterforbundet (The Students' Alliance) after withdrawing from the Students' Union.

In the poem "Theatret" (The Theater), which appeared anonymously in *Morgenbladet* on 13 January 1832, Welhaven addressed what he considered the deplorable state of Norwegian theater, which at the time was dominated by Danish acting and directing and had a repertoire composed largely of foreign pieces. Describing Norwegian drama as depraved, he singled out Wergeland's farces as "Poesiens frækkeste Halunker" (Poetry's most shameless Scoundrels). Wergeland responded to Welhaven's charges in *Morgenbladet* on 24 January. Anyone who attempted to defend the hiring of Danish actors at the theater in Christiania on the grounds of a lack of talented Norwegian actors, he insisted, should instead work to foster Norwegian acting. Moreover, he noted that the theater management's antipathy to Norwegian literature made Norwegian authors reluctant to write dramas.

Wergeland continued his refutation in his farce *Om Smag og Behag man ikke disputere* (1832, One Does Not Argue over Taste and Pleasure), published on 8 February, in which he depicts Norway as Mecklenburg and Denmark as Oldenburg. Both settings are fictional, but they recall the Danish Oldenburg dynasty, which had ruled Norway during its centuries-long union with Denmark, and also bring to mind Welhaven's Mecklenburg ancestry. Wergeland portrays Mecklenburg as under the cultural domination of Oldenburg. Mecklenburg citizens gather to attend a dramatic performance by Oldenburg actors. Their adulation of Oldenburg and denigration of their own culture parodies the Danomania of Welhaven and his followers. They are aghast when a harlequin from Mecklenburg, instead of an Oldenburger, gives the prologue to the performance. Unable to understand the harlequin's comments about satire and drama, they heckle him and call to have him replaced on stage by an exhibit of Oldenburg livestock. In a further display of their self-hatred they claim that Oldenburg farm animals are more refined than their Mecklenburg counterparts: the squeals of Oldenburg pigs reveal great linguistic sophistication, they say, but Mecklenburg pigs can only grunt. They further claim that Mecklenburgers could learn the proper pronunciation of vowels from Oldenburg swine and consonants from Oldenburg oxen. In this manner Wergeland seeks to ridicule what he viewed as the Danomaniacs' snobbish associations of Danish pronunciation with refinement and Norwegian pronunciation with coarseness. Finally resigned to the spectators' rejection of Mecklenburg culture, Wergeland's exasperated harlequin can respond to their accusations only with various versions of the statement "om Smag og Behag man ikke disputere."

Wergeland insisted that *Om Smag og Behag man ikke disputere* was directed not against Danes but against "norskfødte unorske Daarer" (Norwegian-born un-Norwegian fools). He also claimed that the Danomaniacs' adulation of all things Danish had done nothing to improve the allegedly depraved aesthetic that Welhaven criticized in writings such as "Theatret." Instead of enabling Norwegians to discriminate between high and low culture and to prefer the former to the latter, the cultural snobbery of Welhaven and others had merely shamed Norwegian audiences into believing that Danish culture—even Danish low culture—was inherently superior to anything that Norway could produce.

Welhaven published *Henrik Wergelands Digtekunst og Polemik* (Henrik Wergeland's Poetry and Polemics) four months after *Om Smag og Behag man ikke disputere* appeared. He criticizes what he perceives as the bombast of Wergeland's writings, as well as Wergeland's failure to respect established poetic norms. He also scoffs at Wergeland's insistence that such norms hinder the poet's ability to write sublime poetry and tap into his creative genius. According to Welhaven, Wergeland's violation of aesthetic principles is not only an embarrassment in itself but, first and foremost, an

Cover for Wergeland's 1844 poetry volume (The English Pilot), one of his best-loved works (Staatsbibliotek zu Berlin)

embarrassment to Norwegian culture. Welhaven furthered his view that Norway should emerge from its insularity and interact with other cultures in his sonnet cycle *Norges Dæmring* (1834, Norway's Dawn).

Wergeland caricatured Welhaven and the Danomaniacs in *Papegøien* (1835, The Parrot), a farce in which Welhaven appears as "Polemikkel Poetikkel." Polemikkel Poetikkel's chief characteristic is his exaggerated reverence for the Danish writer Adam Oehlenschläger, referred to as "Prometheus," while Siful Sifadda, Wergeland's alter ego, is ridiculed by Polemikkel Poetikkel and his cronies for his lack of embarrassment over being a Norwegian. In contrast to *Om Smag og Behag man ikke disputere, Papegøien* condemns not only the Danomaniacs but also the Danes—or, at least, the Danish bookseller Zacharias Güldenthal. When Güldenthal's talking parrot reminds him that he has always said that there are dumb people in Norway, Güldenthal agrees to send the bird to sell books in Norway. Güldenthal's only concern is that the Norwegians might suspect that their bookseller is really a bird; but another character convinces him that it will matter little to the Norwegians as long as the parrot is of Danish nationality. As in the menagerie scene in *Om Smag og*

Behag man ikke disputere, Wergeland voices his disgust in *Papegøien* over the Danomaniacs' association of Norwegianness with lack of refinement. Güldenthal sends the parrot to Norway with the instruction to "overdynge Landet med danske Sager, men hemmeligen undertrykke alt indenlandsk" (cover the land with Danish things, but secretly suppress everything native).

As in *Om Smag og Behag man ikke disputere* and *Papegøien,* Wergeland's hopes and fears for Norway are on public display in *Norge i 1800 og 1836* (Norway in 1800 and 1836), which he wrote in 1836 and labeled a "Syttende Mai-Farce" (Constitution Day Farce). In the first act, set in 1800, a character laments that Christiania is a capital city without a university, bank, or stock market and with little in the way of a library, bookstore, publisher, or newspaper. *Stockholmsfareren* (1837, The Stockholm Traveler) was also written to commemorate Constitution Day and was followed by a sequel, *Stockholmsfareren No. 2.* These works, like his early farces and dramas, were composed for performance by university students and were not produced by the theater in Christiania. Wergeland wrote several dramatic works in the 1830s but never achieved any significant success in the genre. The characters in his farces are for the most part embodiments of the political views he wished to advance or ridicule. Whether in his farces or in his more serious plays, Wergeland's characters were too one-dimensional to be effective on the stage.

One of the few plays by Wergeland that was produced at the Christiania Theater was *Campbellerne, eller Den hjemkomne Søn* (published 1837, produced 1838, The Campbells; or, The Son Returned). The play is best known for the protest, known as the *Campbellerslag* (Campbells' Battle), that it spurred. Wergeland had received second prize for the play in a competition held to mark the opening of a new theater in Christiania. The old theater had burned down in November 1835, and the new theater, built in Bankplassen (Bank Square), opened on 4 October 1837. Andreas Munch took first prize in the competition with *Kong Sverres Ungdom* (King Sverre's Youth). In a meeting at the office of Johan Dahl, who had published Wergeland's *Papegøien* and Welhaven's *Norges Dæmring,* Welhaven's supporters agreed to disrupt performances of *Campbellerne* by whistling. They insisted that their rejection of Wergeland's play was not a rejection of Norwegian nationalism; they claimed that they were protesting against the play on the grounds that its aesthetic deficiencies made it an embarrassment to the Norwegian people.

Wergeland scholars have tended to agree that the play is among Wergeland's weakest dramatic works. The first act, which takes place in the East Indies, conveys the homesickness and love of William, a captain and member of the Scottish Campbell clan, for his native Scotland—and thus, given Wergeland's affinity for that country, perhaps underscores his own feelings of patriotism for Norway. After a disjointed series of events, William rescues a young lady from a snake and discovers that she is the niece and foster daughter of Lord Campbell. Their shared clan affiliation enables the pair to marry in Scotland in the second act. The nationalist tone of the work is heightened at the end, when clansmen appear in tartan kilts to the tune "The Campbells Are Coming."

Welhaven's supporters—though not Welhaven himself—held *pipekonserter* (whistle concerts) during performances of *Campbellerne*. Some merchants refused to sell whistles to the protesters, and there was little support for their objectives. The precise number of whistlers is unknown; reports range from twenty to sixty at the first performance, depending on whether the reporter was a supporter of Wergeland or of Welhaven. During the second performance of *Campbellerne* on 28 January 1838 protesters circulated a letter asking spectators to whistle. After disrupting the beginning of the play with their whistling, the protesters began whistling again after the first act and reportedly continued for an hour. Some whistlers were sent to the loges, and two were dispatched to Wergeland's seat.

Wergeland requested that the orchestra play the national song, in the hope that it would drown out the whistling. The protest subsided only when an actor appealed to the spectators to allow the troupe to finish the piece, although toward the end the whistling began with renewed vigor. A melee ensued in the theater, with coins, roasted apples, and balls made out of the newspaper *Den Constitutionelle* used as projectiles. The police proved incapable of ending the fracas, which continued outside with fistfights.

Although the protests were an embarrassment to Wergeland, they also won him great sympathy; in the court of public opinion he was regarded as the victor. He regarded the Campbells' Battle as his proudest moment, stating in his autobiographical sketch *Hasselnødder* (1845, Hazelnuts) that it ended with "mine Fienders morderske Nederlag" (my enemies' murderous defeat). Welhaven's followers alleged that Wergeland had bought one hundred tickets for *Campbellerne* for his acquaintances, hoping to inspire generous applause for the piece. Welhaven and Wergeland continued to criticize each other in the following years, though their feud had largely ended before Wergeland's death.

The cultural debate with Welhaven coincided with a difficult period in Wergeland's professional life. In part because of his legal difficulties stemming from the Gardermoen case and his dispute with Praëm,

Wergeland on his deathbed (drawing by A. Tidemann; Store Norske Leksikon <http://snl.no/Henrik_Wergeland>)

Wergeland had been unable to obtain a position as a parish minister. Seeking another career path, he had begun in 1834 to study medicine, though he did not take examinations. Much of his energy in the mid 1830s was devoted to journalistic endeavors, such as editing the weekly paper *Statsborgeren,* which advocated causes of interest to Norway's *bønder.* In 1836 he became a research assistant at the University Library in Christiania.

The Campbells' Battle was not only a public victory for Wergeland but also led the way to a greater measure of personal happiness. With his earnings from *Campbellerne,* he was able to purchase a small house in Grønlia on the outskirts of Christiania. Because of the home's location, it was faster to row across the fjord than to walk around it; so Wergeland also purchased a boat and, to avoid having the boat stolen while he was in town, he stored the oars at the home of Peder Svendsen Bekkevold, a former sailor who owned a grocery near the docks. Wergeland soon fell in love with one of Bekkevold's daughters, Amalie Sophie, who was eleven years his junior. They were married in Eidsvoll on 27 April 1839.

In December 1838 Wergeland wrote the poem "Kongens Ankomst" (The King's Arrival) in celebration of Carl Johan's visit to Christiania. The poem, published in *Morgenbladet* in January 1839 and read to the king in French translation, pleased Carl Johan immensely. But on 12 February 1839 Wergeland and some Germans stopped by the palace on their way home from a restaurant to visit a friend who was on duty with the royal guard. The friend admitted them into the guardroom, where they drank punch and smoked pipes. The head of the watch, one of Wergeland's many adversaries, ordered the guests to leave, but they were still there when he returned a few minutes later. The matter was reported to the king, who was deeply disappointed by Wergeland's involvement, and Wergeland's friend was punished. Wergeland feared that the incident would be a blow to his career and wrote the well-known poem "Smukke Skyer" (1839, Beautiful Clouds), in which he consoles his wife for his lack of material success by telling her that their home is in the beautiful clouds at sunset.

Although Wergeland's prospects looked dim, Carl Johan offered him a yearly stipend. Wergeland accepted it with the stipulation that it be given to him as payment for his continued promotion of public education. His paper *For Arbeidsklassen* (For the Working Classes), published from 1840 to 1845, included many popular songs for children; it enhanced his status among the common people, and peasants came from far away to visit him. But his acceptance of the stipend led his adversaries to brand him a court pensioner who had betrayed his principles.

Such accusations increased when Wergeland was named Norway's chief archivist in 1840; he officially assumed the position in early 1841. His friend Ludvig Kristensen Daa was among those who claimed that Wergeland was selling himself to the king, and Daa criticized him publicly in the press. The rift inspired Wergeland to write the farce *Engelsk Salt* (1841, English Salt), whose motto, taken from Johan Nordahl Brun, reads: "Det Land, som vil have Patrioter, maa taale, at de ere Mennesker" (That land that will have patriots must tolerate that they are human beings). Wergeland's conciliatory tone also surfaces in the final verse of the concluding song of the farce, where he calls out to "norske Brødre" (Norwegian brothers) to unite in their patriotism for Norway. The controversy with Daa grew, and when an editorial in *Morgenbladet* accused Wergeland of being in an angry mood, he responded with the poem "Mig selv" (Myself). Although it is undeniable that Wergeland's temper was quickly aroused, in view of his ever active mind and the exquisite images in his nature poetry, he seems hardly to exaggerate when he writes, "Jeg, som læser Henrykkelser paa hvert af Centifoliens, den Vaargaves, hundrede Blade– / *mig* skulde en slet Avis bringe til at kvæle en Sekund med Ærgrelse?" (I who read rapture in each petal of the hundred-leaved rose, that gift of spring– / *Me* should a wretched rag cause to quench one second with vexation?). In a penetrating assessment of his life, he further asks, "Har jeg ikke en Himmel, fordi den er fuld af drivende Skyer, / Solens Eventyrlande?" (Have I no heaven because it is full of drifting clouds, / fairylands of the sun? [translated by Illit Grøndahl]). He would hate an eternally cloudless sky, he notes, as much as he hates eyes that stupidly stare.

As during previous times of difficulty in his life, Wergeland's literary output continued unabated despite the controversies that dogged him in the early 1840s. Among his published works from this time is *Jan van Huysums Blomsterstykke* (1840, Jan van Huysum's Flower-Piece), which scholars have praised as among his finest poetry. The work depicts a Dutch family whose members are transformed into flowers, and then into the flowers on a painting, after the family members are massacred by Spanish soldiers. In addition, he published a four-volume history of the Norwegian Constitution (1841–1843), a work facilitated by his role as Norway's official archivist.

Perhaps the most significant cause to which Wergeland devoted himself in the early 1840s was his campaign to overturn clause 2 of Norway's Constitution. This clause denied entry into Norway by Jews and was, as Wergeland tirelessly pointed out, incompatible with the spirit of liberalism with which the Constitution had been written. His work to persuade the *Storting* (Parliament) to extend rights of residence to Jews began in 1841. As he related in *Hasselnødder,* however, he had actually first been inspired to take up the Jewish cause ten years earlier, after being deeply moved by the religiosity of two Moroccan Jews he met while traveling in Paris in 1831. In addition to writing polemical pieces against clause 2, Wergeland wrote the poetry collections *Jøden: ni blomstrende Torneqviste* (1842, The Jew: Nine Blossoming Briar Shoots) and *Jødinden: Elleve blomstrende Torneqviste* (1844, The Jewish Woman: Eleven Blossoming Briar Shoots), which emphasize his belief that every religion has brotherly love at its core. In "Følg Kaldet!" (Follow the Call!), one of the best-known poems in *Jødinden,* he also speaks of the difficulties involved in trying to effect social change. He is, he observes, a poet from a small nation with a language largely confined to the nation's borders:

> Kongeørn, med Lænke spændt
> om sit Been og Vingen brudt,
> som i over tyve Aar,
> siden den blev halvdød skudt,
> har for simpel Gaardhund tjent
> paa en ensom Bondegaard,
> lider dog
> ei den arme Digters Vaande
> som i lidet Folk er født,
> hen i Verdens Hjørne stødt,
> med et Sprog,
> som ei rækker fra sin Krog
> længer end dets Læbers Aande.
>
> (Royal eagle, captive made
> Broken-winged, with fettered limb,
> He that twenty years and more,
> Since the shot that crippled him,
> Plies the humble watch-dog's trade
> By a lonely cottage door,
> Cannot know
> All the wretched poet's woe
> Of a little nation born,
> In a spot remote, forlorn,
> With a speech,
> Which can never further reach
> Than the uttered breath may go [translated by G. M. Gathorne-Hardy].)

But Wergeland's sense that he must, despite these and other hindrances, follow the path of truth prevails, as he proceeds to write in "Følg Kaldet!":

> Skulde Skjaldens Ord, den skjære
> Dugg af Lysets Funker, varm
> som om Blod sprang af hans Barm,
> Eneste i Verden være,
> som foruden Spor og Minde
> kan forspildes og forsvinde?
> Op! hvis Herrens egen Røst
> fylder med en Storm dit Bryst!
> Ud den bruse i det Øde!
> Bedre Tiders Morgenrøde
> vil den frem af Mulmet støde.
>
> (Must the poet's word, the pure
> Dew of light's own sparks, that start
> Warm as blood from out his heart,
> Here, where all things else endure,
> Unremembered and untraced
> Disappear and run to waste?

Up! If God's own voice invest
With a storm thy heaving breast!
Cry aloud in desert ways!
And the dawn of better days
From the dark thy word shall raise [translated by Gathorne-Hardy].)

In the last year of his life Wergeland's commitment to "follow the call" and continue to work for the extension of rights to Jews is particularly remarkable when one considers that he had to deal not only with Norwegians' prejudices against the Jews but, on a personal level, with his steadily declining health as well. Beyond this, he had growing financial worries as a result of the years of litigation with Praëm. The poem "Auktion over 'Grotten'" (1844, The Grotto at Auction) relates his fears that he will have to sell "Grotten" (the Grotto), the house near the royal park he had bought in 1841. Reflecting in the poem on the origins of the litigation, Wergeland writes of his soul:

Men engang i min Ungdom gik
Det kanske lidt for fort.
Af Bondens Ryg
en Igle styg
jeg vilde rive altfor snyg;
men selv jeg fik et giftigt Stik,
et Ar saa dybt og sort.

(Yet once it stepped, when I was young
Perchance too fast and far.
I strove to hack
A horse-leech black
Too brusquely from the peasant's back;
But 'twas myself, alas! was stung,
Festering and deep the scar [translated by Gathorne-Hardy].)

Wergeland sent "Auktion over 'Grotten'" to a friend, whose intervention led to an arrangement whereby the Grotto was indeed sold, but with the option to purchase it again in two years. In April 1844 he moved into smaller quarters. In May, he began to suffer from the lung illness that took his life.

He continued his literary output during the fourteen months of his illness. In addition to writing *Jødinden,* he commenced work on the play *Fjeldstuen* (1848, The Mountain Cabin), also known as *Amerikafarerne* (The Travelers to America), in which he opposes immigration to America. The poetry cycle *Den engelske Lods* (1844, The English Pilot) has a melodramatic plot but also poetry of striking beauty, as in "Længsel efter Land" (Longing for Land):

O, Kaptain, hvorhen, hvorhen
gaar Seiladsen uden Ende?
Nye Horizonter spænde

Statue of Wergeland in downtown Oslo, erected in 1881 (photograph by Rolf Øhman; from AftenPosten *<http://www.aftenposten.no/english/local/article2488573.ece>)*

sig omkring mig ud igjen.
Briggen alt i rastløs Fart
susende igjennemlænste
Hundreder af samme Art,
kun af Syner ombegrænste.

(Captain, whither, whither—tell me!—
Goes the voyage without ending,
Coiled horizons as to quell me
Ever new about me bending?
While the brig in restless haste
Rushing sailed through many a hundred
By the selfsame mirage paced,—
While I wondered
Whether distance were defeated,
Visioned shores by waves were sundered
And into the air deleted . . . [translated by Grøndahl].)

In 1845 Wergeland published a revision of *Skabelsen, Mennesket og Messias* under the title *Mennesket* (The Human Being). In the opening scene, where the spirits Ohebiel and Phun-Abiriel converse, he presents his optimistic message that each individual can attain something of God's greatness if he or she merely follows his call:

> Det være nok, at Alt om os er godt,
> at, som til Overflod, det Godes
> Farve og Form er Skjønhed, at, saalangt vi see,
> Guds Storhed voxer. Vi har Deel i denne,
> til Odelarv, saavidt vi kan den fatte.
>
> (Be it enough that all around is good,
> That, even to superfluity, the good
> Is fair in hue and form, that, out of sight,
> God's greatness grows. In this we have a share,
> As heirs by birth, so far as we can grasp it [translated by Gathorne-Hardy].)

An optimism of a different sort runs through Wergeland's humorous autobiographical work *Hasselnødder,* which was published a week after his death. He chose this name, he explained, because he intended that the reader would enjoy the various anecdotes and events he recounts in the work as entertainment, just as one might enjoy a handful of hazelnuts or other snack food in a leisure hour. In addition to looking back on many episodes in his life, he looks forward to his impending death in *Hasselnødder*. His positive view of death is also present in many of the other works he wrote on his sickbed. In "Paa Sygeleiet" (1844, On the Sickbed), the prefatory poem to *Jødinden,* he does not care whether Death views his feverishness and shivering as a triumph, for to him they are the storms of early spring that herald what in death will be heaven's summer.

Wergeland died on 12 July 1845. His funeral on 17 July was attended by well-known Norwegians as well as by the lower classes. After his death, his reputation in Norway as a patriot and poet continued to grow, with prominent Norwegians such as Bjørnson styling their own efforts on behalf of the Norwegian nation on Wergeland's. Not only Wergeland's poetry and patriotism have become almost legendary in Norway, but also his humanity. Danish-Jewish writer Meir Goldschmidt wrote in a letter that reached Wergeland just days before his death, "Naar jeg tenker paa Dem, Wergeland, er jeg stolt af at være Menneske" (When I think of you, Wergeland, I am proud to be a human being).

Letters:

Breve fra Henrik Wergeland, edited by Hartvig Lassen (Christiania: Malling, 1867);

Brev til Henrik Wergeland 1827–1845, edited by Leiv Amundsen (Oslo: Cappelen / Det norske språk og litteraturselskap, 1956);

Henrik Wergeland: Brevene til Amalie, med andre supplementer til Wergelands samlede skrifter vesentlig fra Jonas Skougaards samlinger, edited by Amundsen (Oslo: Cappelen, 1974).

Biographies:

Hartvig Lassen, *Henrik Wergeland og hans samtid,* second edition (Christiania: Malling, 1877);

Herluf Møller, *Henrik Wergeland* (Copenhagen: Gad, 1915);

Harald Beyer, *Henrik Wergeland* (Oslo: Aschehoug, 1946);

Reidar Myhre, *Henrik Wergeland* (Oslo: Ansgar, 1950);

Hans Heiberg, *Så stort et hjerte: Henrik Wergeland* (Oslo: Aschehoug, 1972);

Yngvar Ustvedt, *Henrik Wergeland* (Oslo: Tiden, 1975);

Odd Arvid Storsveen, *Mig selv: En biografi on Henrik Wergeland* (Oslo: Cappelen Damm, 2008).

References:

Sigurd Aage Aasen, *Og nevner vi Henrik Wergelands navn: Wergelands kultusen som nasjonsbyggende faktor* (Oslo: Universitetsforlaget, 1991);

Kristen Austarheim, *Henrik Wergeland: En psykiatrisk studie,* 2 volumes (Bergen: Universitetsforlaget, 1966);

Liv Bliksrud, "Wergelands Don Juan-drama: En tolkning av Barnemordersken," *Edda: Nordisk Tidsskrift for Litteraturforskning,* 2 (1989): 118–126;

Jostein Greibokk, "'Den hedeste Flamme i Nordmandens Indre . . . ': Forskyvning i Henrik Wergelands tankeunivers?" *Edda: Nordisk Tidsskrift for Litteraturforskning,* no. 3 (1996): 201–211;

Sonja Hagemann, *Hjertets geni: Henrik Wergelands diktning for barn* (Oslo: Aschehoug, 1964);

Jon Haarberg, "Henrik Wergelands Hassel-Nødder: Sujett for kildegranskere," *Edda: Nordisk Tidsskrift for Litteraturforskning,* 5 (1983): 283–297;

Frode Helland, *Voldens blomster? Henrik Wergelands Blomsterstykke i estetikkhistorisk lys* (Oslo: Universitetsforlag, 2003);

Anne Jorunn Kydland, Dagne Groven Myhren, and Vigdis Ystad, *Henrik Wergeland: såmannen* (Oslo: Aschehoug, 2008);

Unni Langås, "Romantikkens kropp: Henrik Wergeland i et kjønnperspektiv," *Edda: Nordisk Tidsskrift for Litteraturforskning,* 2 (2003): 12–80;

Örjan Lindberger, *Wergeland och Sverige* (Stockholm: Kooperativa förbundets bokförlag, 1947);

Odd Martin Mæland, *Eros og Mytos: En studie i Henrik Wergelands ungdomslyrikk* (Bergen: Universitetsforlaget, 1969);

Aslaug Groven Michaelsen, *En undersøkelse av Henrik Wergelands farsediktning,* 2 volumes (Tangen: Krystalline, 1987, 1988);

Dagne Groven Myhren, *Blomsten og stjernen: En kritisk imøtegåelse av Eros og mytos: En studie av Henrik Wergelands ungdomslyrikk av Odd Martin Mæland* (Oslo: Universitetsforlaget, 1974);

Myhren, *Kjærlighet og logos: En undersøkelse og en sammenlikning av Henrik Wergelands verdensdikt Skabelsen, mennesket og Messias (1830) og Mennesket (1845)* (Oslo: Solum, 1991);

Rolf Nyboe Nettum, *Fantasiens regnbuebro: Siful Sifaddas farser og andre essays om Henrik Wergeland* (Oslo: Aschehoug, 1992);

Nettum, "Siful Sifaddas farser–og romantikken," *Edda: Nordisk Tidsskrift for Litteraturforskning,* no. 2 (1989): 127–140;

Kristian Ottosen, Britt Ormaasen, Oskar Kvasnes, and Ann Sass, eds., *Jewish Life and Culture in Norway: Wergeland's Legacy* (New York: Abel Abrahamsen, 2003);

Per Saugstad, *Skjulte lengsler: En studie i Henrik Wergelands lyrikk* (Oslo: E. G. Mortensen, 1946);

Ann Schmiesing, *Norway's Christiania Theatre, 1827–1867: From Danish Showhouse to National Stage* (Teaneck, N.J.: Fairleigh Dickinson University Press, 2006);

Didrik Arup Seip, *Norskhet i sproget hos Wergeland og hans samtid* (Christiania: Aschehoug, 1914);

Bjarte Sindre, "Henrik Wergeland og dæmringsfeiden," *Edda: Nordisk Tidsskrift for Litteraturforskning,* no. 2 (1969): 106–129;

Odd Arvid Storsveen, *Henrik Wergelands norske historie: Et bidrag til nasjonalhistoriens mythos* (Oslo: Norges forskningsråd, 1997).

Papers:
The University Library in Trondheim holds the largest collection of Henrik Wergeland's manuscripts and papers, though some original materials can also be found at the University of Bergen and the National Library in Oslo.

Books for Further Reading

Aarnes, Sigurd Aa., ed. *"Laserne": studier i den dansk-norske felleslitteratur etter 1814.* Oslo: Aschehoug, 1994.

Aarnes, ed. *Norsk litteratur gjennom øyenvitner: en litteraturhistorisk kildesamling 1830–1970.* Bergen: Universitetsforlaget, 1979.

Aarnes, ed. *Norsk litteraturkritikk: fra Tullin til A. H. Winsnes. En antologi,* U-bøkene, volume 116. Bergen: Universitetsforlag, 1970.

Andersen, Per Thomas. *Norsk litteraturhistorie.* Oslo: Universitetsforlaget, 2001.

Arntzen, Jon Gunnar, ed. *Norsk biografisk leksikon,* 10 volumes. Oslo: Kunnskapsforlaget, 1999–2005.

Bache-Wiig, Harald, and Astrid Sæther, eds. *100 år etter: —om det litterære livet i Norge i 1890-åra.* Oslo: Aschehoug, 1993.

Beyer, Edvard. *Utsyn over norsk litteratur.* Lund: Gleerup, 1966.

Beyer, ed. *Norges litteraturhistorie,* 6 volumes. Oslo: Cappelen, 1974–1975; revised edition, Oslo: Bokklubben Nye Bøker, 1982–1984.

Beyer, Arild Linneberg, and Morten Moi, eds. *Norsk litteraturkritikks historie: 1770–1940,* 2 volumes. Oslo: Universitetsforlag, 1990, 1992.

Beyer, Harald. *Norsk litteraturhistorie.* Oslo: Aschehoug, 1952, translated and edited by Einar Haugen as *A History of Norwegian Literature.* New York: New York University, 1956.

Bull, Francis, Fredrik Paasche, A. H. Wisnes, and Philip Houm. *Norsk litteraturhistorie,* 7 volumes. Oslo: Aschehoug, 1955–1963.

Dahl, Willy. *Norges litteratur,* 3 volumes. Oslo: Aschehoug, 1981–1989.

Derry, Thomas Kingston. *A Short History of Norway,* second edition. London: Allen & Unwin, 1968.

Downs, Brian Westerdale. *Modern Norwegian Literature, 1860–1918.* Cambridge: Cambridge University Press, 1966.

Engelstad, Irene, and others, eds. *Norsk kvinnelitteraturhistorie,* 3 volumes. Oslo: Pax, 1988–1990.

Falnes, Oscar Julius. *National Romanticism in Norway.* New York: Columbia University Press / London: P. S. King & Son, 1933.

Fidjestøl, Bjarne, and others, eds. *Norsk litteratur i tusen år: teksthistoriske linjer.* Oslo: LNU/Cappelen, 1994.

Garton, Janet. *Norwegian Women's Writing, 1850–1990.* Women in Context, volume 1. London: Athlone Press, 1993.

Gjerset, Knut. *History of the Norwegian People,* 2 volumes. New York: Macmillan, 1915.

Books for Further Reading

Havnevik, Ivar. *Dikt i Norge: Lyrikkhistorie 200–2000.* Oslo: Pax, 2002.

Heggelund, Kjell, Simen Skjønsberg, and Helge Vold, eds. *Forfatternes litteraturhistorie,* 4 volumes. Oslo: Gyldendal, 1980.

Jensson, Liv. *Biografisk skuespillerleksikon: norske, danske og svenske skuespillere på norske scener særlig på 1800-tallet.* Oslo: Universitetsforlag, 1981.

Johansen, Jørgen Dines. *Litteratur og begær: ti studier i dansk og norsk 1800-tals litteratur.* University of Southern Denmark Studies in Scandinavian Language and Literature, volume 55. Odense: Syddansk Universitetsforlag, 2003.

Kronen, Torleiv. *De store årene: fransk innflytelse på norsk åndsliv 1880–1900.* Oslo: Dreyer, 1982.

Larsen, Karen. *A History of Norway.* Princeton: Published for the American-Scandinavian Foundation by Princeton University Press, 1948.

Lyche, Lise. *Norges teaterhistorie.* Asker: Tell, 1991.

Michaelsen, Aslaug Groven. *Den gyldne lenke: norsk litteraturutvikling og det harmoniske imperativ.* Oslo: Dreyer, 1977.

Mortensen, Klaus Peter. *Spejlinger: litteratur og refleksion.* Hellerup: Spring, 2000.

Næss, Harald S., ed. *A History of Norwegian Literature.* Lincoln: University of Nebraska Press, 1993.

Parmann, Øistein, ed. *Norge sett med kunstnerøyne.* Oslo: Dreyer, 1983.

Rem, Tore, ed. *Bokhistorie.* Oslo: Gyldendal, 2003.

Rian, Øystein. *For Norge, Kjempers Fødeland: 12 Portrett frå Dansketida.* Oslo: Det Norske Samlaget, 2007.

Robinson, Michael, and Janet Garton, eds. *Nordic letters 1870–1910.* Norwich, U.K.: Norvik Press, 1999.

Ruge, Herman. *Litteraturhistoriske billeder: 1550–1830.* Oslo: Cappelen, 1928.

Zuck, Virpi, ed. *Dictionary of Scandinavian Literature.* New York: Greenwood Press, 1990.

Contributors

Laila Akslen
John Eason . . . . *University of Wisconsin–Madison*
Katherine Hanson . . . . *University of Washington*
Eirik Helleve . . . . *Nynorsk kultursentrum*
Torild Homstad . . . . *St. Olaf College*
Lanae H. Isaacson
Carl Henrik Koch . . . . *University of Copenhagen*
Dean Krouk. . . . . *University of California–Berkeley*
Judith Messick. . . . . *Northwestern University*
Milda Ostrauskaite . . . . *University of Wisconsin–Madison*
Astrid Sæther. . . . . *University of Oslo*
Ann Schmiesing. . . . . *University of Colorado at Boulder*
Aaron Schmitt . . . . *University of Wisconsin–Madison*
Lorna Selley . . . . *University of Wisconsin–Madison*
Jan Sjåvik. . . . . *University of Washington*
Hans H. Skei . . . . *University of Oslo*
Donna H. Stockton . . . . *University of Colorado at Boulder*
Tanya Thresher. . . . . *University of Wisconsin–Madison*
Bjørn Tysdahl . . . . *University of Oslo*
Ingrid K. Urberg. . . . . *University of Alberta, Augustana Campus*
Henning Howlid Wærp. . . . . *University of Tromsø*

Cumulative Index

Dictionary of Literary Biography, Volumes 1-354
Dictionary of Literary Biography Yearbook, 1980-2002
Dictionary of Literary Biography Documentary Series, Volumes 1-19
Concise Dictionary of American Literary Biography, Volumes 1-7
Concise Dictionary of British Literary Biography, Volumes 1-8
Concise Dictionary of World Literary Biography, Volumes 1-4

Cumulative Index

DLB before number: *Dictionary of Literary Biography,* Volumes 1-354
Y before number: *Dictionary of Literary Biography Yearbook,* 1980-2002
DS before number: *Dictionary of Literary Biography Documentary Series,* Volumes 1-19
CDALB before number: *Concise Dictionary of American Literary Biography,* Volumes 1-7
CDBLB before number: *Concise Dictionary of British Literary Biography,* Volumes 1-8
CDWLB before number: *Concise Dictionary of World Literary Biography,* Volumes 1-4

A

An A.B.C. of British Scenario Writers: Rowan Atkinson, Ronnie Barker, John Cleese....DLB-352

Aakjær, Jeppe 1866-1930....DLB-214

Aarestrup, Emil 1800-1856....DLB-300

Aasen, Ivar 1813-1896....DLB-354

Abani, Chris 1966-....DLB-347

Abbey, Edward 1927-1989....DLB-256, 275

Abbey, Edwin Austin 1852-1911....DLB-188

Abbey, Maj. J. R. 1894-1969....DLB-201

Abbey Press....DLB-49

The Abbey Theatre and Irish Drama, 1900-1945....DLB-10

Abbot, Willis J. 1863-1934....DLB-29

Abbott, Edwin A. 1838-1926....DLB-178

Abbott, Jacob 1803-1879....DLB-1, 42, 243

Abbott, Lee K. 1947-....DLB-130

Abbott, Leonard 1878-1953....DLB-345

Abbott, Lyman 1835-1922....DLB-79

Abbott, Robert S. 1868-1940....DLB-29, 91

'Abd al-Hamid al-Katib circa 689-750....DLB-311

'Abduh, Muhammad 1849-1905....DLB-346

à Beckett, Gilbert Abbott 1811-1856....DLB-344

Abe Kōbō 1924-1993....DLB-182

Abelaira, Augusto 1926-....DLB-287

Abelard, Peter circa 1079-1142?....DLB-115, 208

Abelard-Schuman....DLB-46

Abell, Arunah S. 1806-1888....DLB-43

Abell, Kjeld 1901-1961....DLB-214

Abercrombie, Lascelles 1881-1938....DLB-19

The Friends of the Dymock Poets....Y-00

Aberdeen University Press Limited....DLB-106

Abish, Walter 1931-....DLB-130, 227

Ablesimov, Aleksandr Onisimovich 1742-1783....DLB-150

Aboubakr, Mas'udah 1954-....DLB-346

Abraham à Sancta Clara 1644-1709....DLB-168

Abrahams, Doris Caroline (see Brahms, Caryl)

Abrahams, Peter 1919-....DLB-117, 225; CDWLB-3

Abramov, Fedor Aleksandrovich 1920-1983....DLB-302

Abrams, M. H. 1912-....DLB-67

Abramson, Jesse 1904-1979....DLB-241

Abrogans circa 790-800....DLB-148

Abschatz, Hans Aßmann von 1646-1699....DLB-168

Abse, Dannie 1923-....DLB-27, 245

Abu al-'Atahiyah 748-825?....DLB-311

Abu Nuwas circa 757-814 or 815....DLB-311

Abu Tammam circa 805-845....DLB-311

Abutsu-ni 1221-1283....DLB-203

Academy Chicago Publishers....DLB-46

Accius circa 170 B.C.-circa 80 B.C.....DLB-211

"An account of the death of the Chevalier de La Barre," Voltaire....DLB-314

Accrocca, Elio Filippo 1923-1996....DLB-128

Ace Books....DLB-46

Achebe, Chinua 1930-....DLB-117; CDWLB-3

Achillini, Claudio 1574-1640....DLB-339

Achtenberg, Herbert 1938-....DLB-124

Ackerley, J. R. 1896–1967....DLB-352

Ackerman, Diane 1948-....DLB-120

Ackroyd, Peter 1949-....DLB-155, 231

Acorn, Milton 1923-1986....DLB-53

Acosta, José de 1540-1600....DLB-318

Acosta, Oscar Zeta 1935?-1974?....DLB-82

Acosta Torres, José 1925-....DLB-209

Actors Theatre of Louisville....DLB-7

Adair, Gilbert 1944-....DLB-194

Adair, James 1709?-1783?....DLB-30

Aðalsteinn Kristmundsson (see Steinn Steinarr)

Adam, Graeme Mercer 1839-1912....DLB-99

Adam, Robert Borthwick, II 1863-1940....DLB-187

Adame, Leonard 1947-....DLB-82

Adameșteanu, Gabriel 1942-....DLB-232

Adamic, Louis 1898-1951....DLB-9

Adamov, Arthur Surenovitch 1908-1970....DLB-321

Adamovich, Georgii 1894-1972....DLB-317

Adams, Abigail 1744-1818....DLB-183, 200

Adams, Alice 1926-1999....DLB-234; Y-86

Adams, Bertha Leith (Mrs. Leith Adams, Mrs. R. S. de Courcy Laffan) 1837?-1912....DLB-240

Adams, Brooks 1848-1927....DLB-47

Adams, Charles Francis, Jr. 1835-1915....DLB-47

Adams, Douglas 1952-2001....DLB-261; Y-83

Adams, Franklin P. 1881-1960....DLB-29

Adams, Glenda 1939-....DLB-325

Adams, Hannah 1755-1832....DLB-200

Adams, Henry 1838-1918....DLB-12, 47, 189

Adams, Herbert Baxter 1850-1901....DLB-47

Adams, James Truslow 1878-1949....DLB-17; DS-17

Adams, John 1735-1826....DLB-31, 183

Adams, John Quincy 1767-1848....DLB-37

Adams, Léonie 1899-1988....DLB-48

Adams, Levi 1802-1832....DLB-99

Adams, Richard 1920-....DLB-261

Adams, Samuel 1722-1803....DLB-31, 43

Adams, Sarah Fuller Flower 1805-1848....DLB-199

Adams, Thomas 1582/1583-1652....DLB-151

Adams, William Taylor 1822-1897....DLB-42

J. S. and C. Adams [publishing house]....DLB-49

Adamson, Harold 1906-1980....DLB-265

Adamson, Sir John 1867-1950....DLB-98

Adamson, Robert 1943-....DLB-289

Adcock, Arthur St. John 1864-1930....DLB-135

Adcock, Betty 1938-....DLB-105

"Certain Gifts"....DLB-105

Tribute to James Dickey....Y-97

Adcock, Fleur 1934-....DLB-40

Cumulative Index DLB 354

Addams, Jane 1860-1935 .... DLB-303
Addison, Joseph 1672-1719 ... DLB-101; CDBLB-2
Ade, George 1866-1944 .... DLB-11, 25
Adebayo, Diran 1968- DLB-347
Adeler, Max (see Clark, Charles Heber)
Adlard, Mark 1932- DLB-261
Adler, Richard 1921- DLB-265
Adonias Filho
   (Adonias Aguiar Filho)
   1915-1990................ DLB-145, 307
Adorno, Theodor W. 1903-1969 .... DLB-242
Adoum, Jorge Enrique 1926- DLB-283
Advance Publishing Company DLB-49
Adventures of Huckleberry Finn (Documentary)
   .... DLB-343
Ady, Endre 1877-1919...... DLB-215; CDWLB-4
AE 1867-1935 .... DLB-19; CDBLB-5
Ælfric circa 955-circa 1010 .... DLB-146
Aeschines circa 390 B.C.-circa 320 B.C. DLB-176
Aeschylus 525-524 B.C.-456-455 B.C.
   ....DLB-176; CDWLB-1
Aesthetic Papers DLB-1
Aesthetics
   Eighteenth-Century Aesthetic
     Theories DLB-31
African Literature
   Letter from Khartoum............. Y-90
African American
   Afro-American Literary Critics:
     An Introduction................ DLB-33
   The Black Aesthetic: Background DS-8
   The Black Arts Movement,
     by Larry Neal DLB-38
   Black Theaters and Theater Organizations
     in America, 1961-1982:
     A Research List DLB-38
   Black Theatre: A Forum [excerpts] ... DLB-38
   Callaloo [journal]..................... Y-87
   Community and Commentators:
     Black Theatre and Its Critics..... CDBLB-38
   The Emergence of Black
     Women Writers...............DS-8
   The Hatch-Billops Collection........ DLB-76
   A Look at the Contemporary Black
     Theatre Movement DLB-38
   The Moorland-Spingarn Research
     Center DLB-76
   "The Negro as a Writer," by
     G. M. McClellan.............. DLB-50
   "Negro Poets and Their Poetry," by
     Wallace Thurman DLB-50
   Olaudah Equiano and Unfinished Journeys:
     The Slave-Narrative Tradition and
     Twentieth-Century Continuities, by
     Paul Edwards and Pauline T.
     Wangman DLB-117
   PHYLON (Fourth Quarter, 1950),
     The Negro in Literature:
     The Current Scene DLB-76
   The Schomburg Center for Research
     in Black Culture DLB-76

Three Documents [poets], by John
   Edward Bruce DLB-50
After Dinner Opera Company Y-92
Agard, John 1949- DLB-347
Agassiz, Elizabeth Cary 1822-1907...... DLB-189
Agassiz, Louis 1807-1873 .... DLB-1, 235
Agbabi, Patience 1965- DLB-347
Agbenugba, Gbenga (see Opesan, Ola)
Agee, James
   1909-1955 .... DLB-2, 26, 152; CDALB-1
   The Agee Legacy: A Conference at
     the University of Tennessee
     at Knoxville.................... Y-89
Agnon, Shmuel Yosef 1887-1970........ DLB-329
Agopian, Ștefan 1947- DLB-353
Aguilera Malta, Demetrio 1909-1981.... DLB-145
Aguirre, Isidora 1919- DLB-305
Agustini, Delmira 1886-1914 .... DLB-290
Ahlin, Lars 1915-1997 .... DLB-257
Ai 1947- DLB-120
Ai Wu 1904-1992 .... DLB-328
Aichinger, Ilse 1921- DLB-85, 299
Aickman, Robert 1914-1981........... DLB-261
Aidoo, Ama Ata 1942- DLB-117; CDWLB-3
Aiken, Conrad
   1889-1973......... DLB-9, 45, 102; CDALB-5
Aiken, Joan 1924-2004 .... DLB-161
Aikin, John 1747-1822................. DLB-336
Aikin, Lucy 1781-1864 .... DLB-144, 163
Ainsworth, William Harrison
   1805-1882 .... DLB-21
Aïssé, Charlotte-Elizabeth 1694?-1733 ... DLB-313
Aistis, Jonas 1904-1973 ..... DLB-220; CDWLB-4
Aitken, Adam 1960- DLB-325
Aitken, George A. 1860-1917 .... DLB-149
Robert Aitken [publishing house]........ DLB-49
Aitmatov, Chingiz 1928- DLB-302
Ajvaz, Michal 1949- DLB-353
Akatdamkoeng Raphiphat, M.C.
   1905-1932 .... DLB-348
Akenside, Mark 1721-1770 .... DLB-109
Akhmatova, Anna Andreevna
   1889-1966 .... DLB-295
Akins, Zoë 1886-1958............... DLB-26
Aksakov, Ivan Sergeevich 1823-1826 .....DLB-277
Aksakov, Sergei Timofeevich
   1791-1859..................... DLB-198
Aksyonov, Vassily 1932-2009 .... DLB-302
Akunin, Boris (Grigorii Shalvovich Chkhartishvili)
   1956- DLB-285
Akutagawa Ryūnosuke 1892-1927 ...... DLB-180
Alabaster, William 1568-1640........ DLB-132
Alain de Lille circa 1116-1202/1203 ..... DLB-208
Alain-Fournier 1886-1914............. DLB-65

Alanus de Insulis (see Alain de Lille)
Alarcón, Francisco X. 1954- DLB-122
Alarcón, Justo S. 1930- DLB-209
Alba, Nanina 1915-1968............... DLB-41
Albahari, David 1948- DLB-353
Albee, Edward 1928- DLB-7, 266; CDALB-1
Albert, Octavia 1853-ca. 1889 .... DLB-221
Albert the Great circa 1200-1280 .... DLB-115
Alberti, Rafael 1902-1999............. DLB-108
Albertinus, Aegidius circa 1560-1620.... DLB-164
Alcaeus born circa 620 B.C. DLB-176
Alcoforado, Mariana, the Portuguese Nun
   1640-1723..................... DLB-287
Alcott, Amos Bronson
   1799-1888............ DLB-1, 223; DS-5
Alcott, Louisa May 1832-1888
   ...DLB-1, 42, 79, 223, 239; DS-14; CDALB-3
Alcott, William Andrus 1798-1859.... DLB-1, 243
Alcuin circa 732-804................. DLB-148
Aldana, Francisco de 1537-1578 .... DLB-318
Aldanov, Mark (Mark Landau)
   1886-1957 ....DLB-317
Alden, Henry Mills 1836-1919.......... DLB-79
Alden, Isabella 1841-1930 .... DLB-42
John B. Alden [publishing house]........ DLB-49
Alden, Beardsley, and Company DLB-49
Aldington, Richard
   1892-1962 ....DLB-20, 36, 100, 149
Aldis, Dorothy 1896-1966 .... DLB-22
Aldis, H. G. 1863-1919................ DLB-184
Aldiss, Brian W. 1925- DLB-14, 261, 271
Aldrich, Thomas Bailey
   1836-1907 ....DLB-42, 71, 74, 79
Alegría, Ciro 1909-1967 .... DLB-113
Alegría, Claribel 1924- DLB-145, 283
Aleixandre, Vicente 1898-1984...... DLB-108, 329
Aleksandravičius, Jonas (see Aistis, Jonas)
Aleksandrov, Aleksandr Andreevich
   (see Durova, Nadezhda Andreevna)
Alekseeva, Marina Anatol'evna
   (see Marinina, Aleksandra)
d'Alembert, Jean Le Rond 1717-1783 .... DLB-313
Alencar, José de 1829-1877............ DLB-307
Aleramo, Sibilla (Rena Pierangeli Faccio)
   1876-1960 .... DLB-114, 264
Aleshkovsky, Petr Markovich 1957- ... DLB-285
Aleshkovsky, Yuz 1929- DLB-317
Alexander, Cecil Frances 1818-1895..... DLB-199
Alexander, Charles 1868-1923 .... DLB-91
Charles Wesley Alexander
   [publishing house] DLB-49
Alexander, James 1691-1756.......... DLB-24
Alexander, Lloyd 1924- DLB-52
Alexander, Meena 1951- DLB-323

322

Alexander, Sir William, Earl of Stirling 1577?-1640 . . . . DLB-121	Allston, Washington 1779-1843 . . . . DLB-1, 235	American Sunday-School Union DLB-49
Alexie, Sherman 1966- DLB-175, 206, 278	Almeida, Manuel Antônio de 1831-1861 . . . . DLB-307	American Temperance Union DLB-49
Alexis, Willibald 1798-1871 . . . . DLB-133	John Almon [publishing house] DLB-154	American Tract Society. DLB-49
Alf laylah wa laylah ninth century onward DLB-311	Alonzo, Dámaso 1898-1990. . . . . DLB-108	The American Trust for the British Library . . . Y-96
Alfonso X 1221-1284. . . . . DLB-337	Alsop, George 1636-post 1673 . . . . DLB-24	American Writers' Congress 25-27 April 1935 . . . . DLB-303
Alfonsine Legal Codes. DLB-337	Alsop, Richard 1761-1815 . . . . DLB-37	American Writers Congress
Alfred, King 849-899 . . . . DLB-146	Henry Altemus and Company. DLB-49	The American Writers Congress (9-12 October 1981) Y-81
Alger, Horatio, Jr. 1832-1899 . . . . DLB-42	Altenberg, Peter 1885-1919 . . . . DLB-81	The American Writers Congress: A Report on Continuing Business Y-81
Algonquin Books of Chapel Hill DLB-46	Althusser, Louis 1918-1990 . . . . DLB-242	Ames, Fisher 1758-1808. . . . . DLB-37
Algren, Nelson 1909-1981 . . . . DLB-9; Y-81, 82; CDALB-1	Altolaguirre, Manuel 1905-1959 . . . . DLB-108	Ames, Mary Clemmer 1831-1884 . . . . DLB-23
Nelson Algren: An International Symposium Y-00	Aluko, T. M. 1918- DLB-117	Ames, William 1576-1633 . . . . DLB-281
Ali, Agha Shahid 1949-2001 . . . . DLB-323	Alurista 1947- DLB-82	Amfiteatrov, Aleksandr 1862-1938 . . . . . . DLB-317
Ali, Ahmed 1908-1994. . . . . DLB-323	Alvarez, A. 1929- DLB-14, 40	Amiel, Henri-Frédéric 1821-1881 . . . . DLB-217
Ali, Monica 1967- DLB-323	Alvarez, Julia 1950- DLB-282	Amini, Johari M. 1935- DLB-41
'Ali ibn Abi Talib circa 600-661 . . . . DLB-311	Alvaro, Corrado 1895-1956. . . . . DLB-264	Amis, Kingsley 1922-1995. . . . . DLB-15, 27, 100, 139, 326, 352; Y-96; CDBLB-7
Alinsky, Saul 1909-1972. . . . . DLB-345	Alver, Betti 1906-1989 . . . . . DLB-220; CDWLB-4	Amis, Martin 1949- DLB-14, 194
Aljamiado Literature DLB-286	Alvi, Moniza 1954- DLB-347	Ammianus Marcellinus circa A.D. 330-A.D. 395 . . . . DLB-211
Allan, Andrew 1907-1974. . . . . DLB-88	Amadi, Elechi 1934- DLB-117	Ammons, A. R. 1926-2001 . . . . . . DLB-5, 165, 342
Allan, Ted 1916-1995. . . . . DLB-68	Amado, Jorge 1912-2001 . . . . DLB-113	Amory, Thomas 1691?-1788 . . . . DLB-39
Allbeury, Ted 1917-2005 . . . . DLB-87	Amalrik, Andrei 1938-1980 . . . . DLB-302	Amsterdam, 1998 Booker Prize winner, Ian McEwan DLB-326
Alldritt, Keith 1935- DLB-14	Ambler, Eric 1909-1998. . . . . DLB-77	Amyot, Jacques 1513-1593. . . . . DLB-327
Allen, Dick 1939- DLB-282	The Library of America. DLB-46	Anand, Mulk Raj 1905-2004 . . . . DLB-323
Allen, Ethan 1738-1789 . . . . DLB-31	The Library of America: An Assessment After Two Decades Y-02	Anania, Michael 1939- DLB-193
Allen, Frederick Lewis 1890-1954 . . . . DLB-137	America: or, A Poem on the Settlement of the British Colonies, by Timothy Dwight DLB-37	Anaya, Rudolfo A. 1937- DLB-82, 206, 278
Allen, Gay Wilson 1903-1995 . . . . . DLB-103; Y-95		Ancrene Riwle circa 1200-1225 . . . . DLB-146
Allen, George 1808-1876 . . . . DLB-59	American Bible Society Department of Library, Archives, and Institutional Research Y-97	Andersch, Alfred 1914-1980 . . . . DLB-69
Allen, Grant 1848-1899 . . . . DLB-70, 92, 178		Andersen, Benny 1929- DLB-214
Allen, Henry W. 1912-1991. . . . . Y-85	American Conservatory Theatre DLB-7	Andersen, Hans Christian 1805-1875 . . . . DLB-300
Allen, Hervey 1889-1949. . . . . DLB-9, 45, 316	American Culture American Proletarian Culture: The Twenties and Thirties DS-11	Anderson, Alexander 1775-1870 . . . . DLB-188
Allen, James 1739-1808 . . . . DLB-31		Anderson, David 1929- DLB-241
Allen, James Lane 1849-1925. . . . . DLB-71	Studies in American Jewish Literature Y-02	Anderson, Frederick Irving 1877-1947. . . . . DLB-202
Allen, Jay Presson 1922- DLB-26	The American Library in Paris Y-93	
John Allen and Company DLB-49	American Literature The Literary Scene and Situation and . . . (Who Besides Oprah) Really Runs American Literature? Y-99	Anderson, Jessica 1916- DLB-325
Allen, Paula Gunn 1939- DLB-175		Anderson, Margaret 1886-1973 . . . . DLB-4, 91
Allen, Samuel W. 1917- DLB-41		Anderson, Maxwell 1888-1959 . . . . DLB-7, 228
Allen, Woody 1935- DLB-44	Who Owns American Literature, by Henry Taylor Y-94	Anderson, Patrick 1915-1979 . . . . DLB-68
George Allen [publishing house] DLB-106		Anderson, Paul Y. 1893-1938 . . . . DLB-29
George Allen and Unwin Limited DLB-112	Who Runs American Literature? Y-94	Anderson, Poul 1926-2001 . . . . DLB-8
Allende, Isabel 1942- DLB-145; CDWLB-3	American News Company. DLB-49	Tribute to Isaac Asimov Y-92
Alline, Henry 1748-1784 . . . . DLB-99	A Century of Poetry, a Lifetime of Collecting: J. M. Edelstein's Collection of Twentieth- Century American Poetry Y-02	Anderson, Robert 1750-1830 . . . . DLB-142
Allingham, Margery 1904-1966. . . . . DLB-77		Anderson, Robert 1917- DLB-7
The Margery Allingham Society Y-98	The American Poets' Corner: The First Three Years (1983-1986) Y-86	Anderson, Sherwood 1876-1941 . . . . DLB-4, 9, 86; DS-1; CDALB-4
Allingham, William 1824-1889 . . . . DLB-35		
Allison, Dorothy 1949- DLB-350	American Publishing Company DLB-49	Andrade, Jorge (Aluísio Jorge Andrade Franco) 1922-1984 . . . . DLB-307
W. L. Allison [publishing house] DLB-49	American Spectator [Editorial] Rationale From the Initial Issue of the American Spectator (November 1932). DLB-137	
The Alliterative Morte Arthure and the Stanzaic Morte Arthur circa 1350-1400 . . . . DLB-146		Andrade, Mario de 1893-1945. . . . . DLB-307
	American Stationers' Company DLB-49	Andrade, Oswald de (José Oswald de Sousa Andrade) 1890-1954 . . . . DLB-307
Allott, Kenneth 1912-1973 . . . . DLB-20	The American Studies Association of Norway Y-00	

Andreae, Johann Valentin 1586-1654 .... DLB-164
Andreas Capellanus fl. circa 1185....... DLB-208
Andreas-Salomé, Lou 1861-1937 .... DLB-66
Andreev, Leonid Nikolaevich
   1871-1919..................... DLB-295
Andreevski, Petre M. 1934-2006........ DLB-353
Andres, Stefan 1906-1970 .... DLB-69
Andresen, Sophia de Mello Breyner
   1919-2004..................... DLB-287
Andreu, Blanca 1959- DLB-134
Andrewes, Lancelot 1555-1626......DLB-151, 172
Andrews, Charles M. 1863-1943 .... DLB-17
Andrews, Miles Peter ?-1814 .... DLB-89
Andrews, Stephen Pearl 1812-1886 ..... DLB-250
Andrian, Leopold von 1875-1951........ DLB-81
Andrić, Ivo
   1892-1975.........DLB-147, 329; CDWLB-4
Andreini, Francesco
   before 1548?-1624 .... DLB-339
Andreini, Giovan Battista 1576-1654 .... DLB-339
Andreini, Isabella 1562-1604 .... DLB-339
Andrieux, Louis (see Aragon, Louis)
Andrus, Silas, and Son DLB-49
Andrzejewski, Jerzy 1909-1983......... DLB-215
Angell, James Burrill 1829-1916 .... DLB-64
Angell, Roger 1920- DLB-171, 185
Angelou, Maya 1928- DLB-38; CDALB-7
   Tribute to Julian Mayfield Y-84
Anger, Jane fl. 1589.................. DLB-136
Angers, Félicité (see Conan, Laure)
The Anglo-Saxon Chronicle
   circa 890-1154 .... DLB-146
Angus and Robertson (UK) Limited DLB-112
Anhalt, Edward 1914-2000............. DLB-26
Anim-Addo, Jean 1948- DLB-347
Anissimov, Myriam 1943- DLB-299
Anker, Nini Roll 1873-1942 .... DLB-297
Annenkov, Pavel Vasil'evich
   1813?-1887.....................DLB-277
Annensky, Innokentii Fedorovich
   1855-1909 .... DLB-295
Henry F. Anners [publishing house]...... DLB-49
Annolied between 1077 and 1081 .... DLB-148
Anouilh, Jean 1910-1987............. DLB-321
Ansay, A. Manette 1964- DLB-350
Anscombe, G. E. M. 1919-2001 .... DLB-262
Anselm of Canterbury 1033-1109....... DLB-115
Ansky, S. (Sh. An-Ski; Solomon Zainwil [Shloyme-
   Zanvl] Rapoport) 1863-1920 .... DLB-333
Anstey, F. 1856-1934 ....DLB-141, 178
Anstruther, Joyce (see Struther, Jan)
'Antarah ('Antar ibn Shaddad al-'Absi)
   ?-early seventh century?........... DLB-311

Anthologizing New Formalism DLB-282
Anthony, Michael 1932- DLB-125
Anthony, Piers 1934- DLB-8
Anthony, Susanna 1726-1791 .... DLB-200
Antin, David 1932- DLB-169
Antin, Mary 1881-1949 ....DLB-221; Y-84
Anton Ulrich, Duke of Brunswick-Lüneburg
   1633-1714..................... DLB-168
Antrim, Donald 1958- DLB-350
Antrobus, John 1933- DLB-352
Antschel, Paul (see Celan, Paul)
Antunes, António Lobo 1942- DLB-287
Anyidoho, Kofi 1947- DLB-157
Anzaldúa, Gloria 1942- DLB-122
Anzengruber, Ludwig 1839-1889 ...... DLB-129
Apess, William 1798-1839 ....DLB-175, 243
Apodaca, Rudy S. 1939- DLB-82
Apollinaire, Guillaume
   1880-1918 ....DLB-258, 321
Apollonius Rhodius third century B.C.....DLB-176
Appeal to Reason, The 1895-1922 .... DLB-345
Appelfeld, Aharon 1932- DLB-299
Apple, Max 1941- DLB-130
D. Appleton and Company DLB-49
Appleton-Century-Crofts DLB-46
Applewhite, James 1935- DLB-105
   Tribute to James Dickey............... Y-97
Apple-wood Books DLB-46
April, Jean-Pierre 1948- DLB-251
Apukhtin, Aleksei Nikolaevich
   1840-1893 ....DLB-277
Apuleius circa A.D. 125-post A.D. 164
   .... DLB-211; CDWLB-1
Aquin, Hubert 1929-1977............. DLB-53
Aquinas, Thomas 1224/1225-1274...... DLB-115
Aragon, Louis 1897-1982 .... DLB-72, 258
Aragon, Vernacular Translations in the
   Crowns of Castile and 1352-1515 ... DLB-286
Aralica, Ivan 1930- DLB-181
Aratus of Soli
   circa 315 B.C.-circa 239 B.C. DLB-176
Arbasino, Alberto 1930- DLB-196
Arbor House Publishing Company DLB-46
Arbuthnot, John 1667-1735........... DLB-101
Arcadia House DLB-46
Arce, Julio G. (see Ulica, Jorge)
Archer, William 1856-1924............ DLB-10
Archilochhus
   mid seventh century B.C.E..........DLB-176
The Archpoet circa 1130?-? DLB-148
Archpriest Avvakum (Petrovich)
   1620?-1682.................... DLB-150
Arden, John 1930- DLB-13, 245

Arden of Faversham DLB-62
Ardis Publishers Y-89
Ardizzone, Edward 1900-1979 .... DLB-160
Arellano, Juan Estevan 1947- DLB-122
The Arena Publishing Company DLB-49
Arena Stage........................ DLB-7
Arenas, Reinaldo 1943-1990........... DLB-145
Arendt, Hannah 1906-1975 .... DLB-242
Arensberg, Ann 1937- Y-82
Arghezi, Tudor 1880-1967 ... DLB-220; CDWLB-4
Arguedas, José María 1911-1969 .... DLB-113
Argüelles, Hugo 1932-2003 .... DLB-305
Argueta, Manlio 1936- DLB-145
'Arib al-Ma'muniyah 797-890 .... DLB-311
Arias, Ron 1941- DLB-82
Arishima Takeo 1878-1923............ DLB-180
Aristophanes circa 446 B.C.-circa 386 B.C.
   ....DLB-176; CDWLB-1
Aristotle 384 B.C.-322 B.C.
   ....DLB-176; CDWLB-1
Ariyoshi Sawako 1931-1984........... DLB-182
Arkoun, Mohammed 1928- DLB-346
Arland, Marcel 1899-1986 .... DLB-72
Arlen, Michael 1895-1956 ....DLB-36, 77, 162
Arlt, Roberto 1900-1942.............. DLB-305
Armah, Ayi Kwei 1939-   ...DLB-117; CDWLB-3
Armantrout, Rae 1947- DLB-193
Der arme Hartmann ?-after 1150 .... DLB-148
Armed Services Editions............... DLB-46
Armitage, G. E. (Robert Edric)
   1956- DLB-267
Armstrong, Jeanette 1948- DLB-334
Armstrong, Martin Donisthorp
   1882-1974.....................DLB-197
Armstrong, Richard 1903-1986 .... DLB-160
Armstrong, Terence Ian Fytton (see Gawsworth, John)
Arnauld, Antoine 1612-1694 ....DLB-268
Arndt, Ernst Moritz 1769-1860.......... DLB-90
Arnim, Achim von 1781-1831 .... DLB-90
Arnim, Bettina von 1785-1859 .... DLB-90
Arnim, Elizabeth von (Countess Mary Annette
   Beauchamp Russell) 1866-1941 .....DLB-197
Arno Press DLB-46
Arnold, Edwin 1832-1904 .... DLB-35
Arnold, Edwin L. 1857-1935 ....DLB-178
Arnold, Matthew
   1822-1888 .... DLB-32, 57; CDBLB-4
   Preface to *Poems* (1853)............. DLB-32
Arnold, Thomas 1795-1842 .... DLB-55
Edward Arnold [publishing house]...... DLB-112
Arnott, Peter 1962- DLB-233
Arnow, Harriette Simpson 1908-1986 ..... DLB-6

Arp, Bill (see Smith, Charles Henry)

Arpino, Giovanni 1927-1987 . . . . DLB-177

Arrabal, Fernando 1932- DLB-321

Arrebo, Anders 1587-1637 . . . . DLB-300

Arreola, Juan José 1918-2001 . . . . DLB-113

Arrian circa 89-circa 155 . . . . DLB-176

J. W. Arrowsmith [publishing house] DLB-106

Arrufat, Antón 1935- DLB-305

Art
    John Dos Passos: Artist Y-99
    The First Post-Impressionist
        Exhibition DS-5
    The Omega Workshops DS-10
    The Second Post-Impressionist
        Exhibition DS-5

Artale, Giuseppi 1628-1679 . . . . DLB-339

Artaud, Antonin 1896-1948 . . . . DLB-258, 321

Artel, Jorge 1909-1994 . . . . DLB-283

Arthur, Timothy Shay
    1809-1885 . . . . DLB-3, 42, 79, 250; DS-13

Artmann, H. C. 1921-2000 . . . . DLB-85

Artsybashev, Mikhail Petrovich
    1878-1927 . . . . DLB-295

Arvin, Newton 1900-1963 . . . . DLB-103

Asbjørnsen, Peter Christen 1812-1885 . . . . DLB-354

Asch, Nathan 1902-1964 . . . . DLB-4, 28

    Nathan Asch Remembers Ford Madox
    Ford, Sam Roth, and Hart Crane Y-02

Asch, Sholem 1880-1957 . . . . DLB-333

Ascham, Roger 1515/1516-1568 . . . . DLB-236

Aseev, Nikolai Nikolaevich
    1889-1963 . . . . DLB-295

Ash, John 1948- DLB-40

Ashbery, John 1927- DLB-5, 165; Y-81

Ashbridge, Elizabeth 1713-1755 . . . . DLB-200

Ashburnham, Bertram Lord
    1797-1878 . . . . DLB-184

Ashendene Press DLB-112

Asher, Sandy 1942- Y-83

Ashton, Winifred (see Dane, Clemence)

Asimov, Isaac 1920-1992 . . . . DLB-8; Y-92
    Tribute to John Ciardi Y-86

Askew, Anne circa 1521-1546 . . . . DLB-136

Aspazija 1865-1943 . . . . DLB-220; CDWLB-4

Asselin, Olivar 1874-1937 . . . . DLB-92

The Association of American Publishers Y-99

The Association for Documentary Editing Y-00

The Association for the Study of
    Literature and Environment (ASLE) Y-99

Astell, Mary 1666-1731 . . . . DLB-252, 336

Astley, Thea 1925- DLB-289

Astley, William (see Warung, Price)

Asturias, Miguel Ángel 1899-1974
    . . . . DLB-113, 290, 329; CDWLB-3

Atava, S. (see Terpigorev, Sergei Nikolaevich)

Atheneum Publishers DLB-46

Atherton, Gertrude 1857-1948 . . . . . DLB-9, 78, 186

Athlone Press DLB-112

Atkins, Josiah circa 1755-1781 . . . . DLB-31

Atkins, Russell 1926- DLB-41

Atkinson, Kate 1951- DLB-267

Atkinson, Louisa 1834-1872 . . . . DLB-230

Atkinson, Rowan 1956– (see An A.B.C. of British
    Scenario Writers)

The Atlantic Monthly Press DLB-46

Attaway, William 1911-1986 . . . . DLB-76

Atwood, Margaret 1939- DLB-53, 251, 326

Aubert, Alvin 1930- DLB-41

Aub, Max 1903-1972 . . . . DLB-322

Aubert de Gaspé, Phillipe-Ignace-François
    1814-1841 . . . . DLB-99

Aubert de Gaspé, Phillipe-Joseph
    1786-1871 . . . . DLB-99

Aubigné, Théodore Agrippa d'
    1552-1630 . . . . DLB-327

Aubin, Napoléon 1812-1890 . . . . DLB-99

Aubin, Penelope 1685-circa 1731 . . . . DLB-39
    Preface to *The Life of Charlotta
    du Pont* (1723) DLB-39

Aubrey-Fletcher, Henry Lancelot (see Wade, Henry)

Auchincloss, Louis 1917- DLB-2, 244; Y-80

Auden, W. H. 1907-1973 . . . DLB-10, 20; CDBLB-6

Audiberti, Jacques 1899-1965 . . . . DLB-321

Audio Art in America: A Personal Memoir Y-85

Audubon, John James 1785-1851 . . . . DLB-248

Audubon, John Woodhouse
    1812-1862 . . . . DLB-183

Auerbach, Berthold 1812-1882 . . . . DLB-133

Auernheimer, Raoul 1876-1948 . . . . DLB-81

Augier, Emile 1820-1889 . . . . DLB-192

Augustine 354-430 . . . . DLB-115

Aulnoy, Marie-Catherine Le Jumel
    de Barneville, comtesse d'
    1650/1651-1705 . . . . DLB-268

Aulus Gellius
    circa A.D. 125-circa A.D. 180? DLB-211

Austen, Jane 1775-1817 . . . . . . DLB-116; CDBLB-3

Auster, Paul 1947- DLB-227

Austin, Alfred 1835-1913 . . . . DLB-35

Austin, J. L. 1911-1960 . . . . DLB-262

Austin, Jane Goodwin 1831-1894 . . . . DLB-202

Austin, John 1790-1859 . . . . DLB-262

Austin, Mary Hunter
    1868-1934 . . . . DLB-9, 78, 206, 221, 275

Austin, William 1778-1841 . . . . DLB-74

Australie (Emily Manning)
    1845-1890 . . . . DLB-230

Authors and Newspapers Association DLB-46

Authors' Publishing Company DLB-49

Avallone, Michael 1924-1999 . . . . . DLB-306; Y-99
    Tribute to John D. MacDonald Y-86
    Tribute to Kenneth Millar Y-83
    Tribute to Raymond Chandler Y-88

Avalon Books DLB-46

Avancini, Nicolaus 1611-1686 . . . . DLB-164

Avendaño, Fausto 1941- DLB-82

Averroës 1126-1198 . . . . DLB-115

Avery, Gillian 1926- DLB-161

Avicenna 980-1037 . . . . DLB-115

Ávila Jiménez, Antonio 1898-1965 . . . . DLB-283

Avison, Margaret 1918-1987 . . . . DLB-53

Avon Books DLB-46

Avyžius, Jonas 1922-1999 . . . . DLB-220

Awdry, Wilbert Vere 1911-1997 . . . . DLB-160

Awoonor, Kofi 1935- DLB-117

Ayala, Francisco 1906- DLB-322

Ayckbourn, Alan 1939- DLB-13, 245

Ayer, A. J. 1910-1989 . . . . DLB-262

Aymé, Marcel 1902-1967 . . . . DLB-72

Aytoun, Sir Robert 1570-1638 . . . . DLB-121

Aytoun, William Edmondstoune
    1813-1865 . . . . DLB-32, 159

Azevedo, Aluísio 1857-1913 . . . . DLB-307

Azevedo, Manuel Antônio Álvares de
    1831-1852 . . . . DLB-307

al-Azm, Sadik Jalal 1934- DLB-346

Azorín (José Martínez Ruiz)
    1873-1967 . . . . DLB-322

B

B.V. (see Thomson, James)

Ba Jin 1904-2005 . . . . DLB-328

Babbitt, Irving 1865-1933 . . . . DLB-63

Babbitt, Natalie 1932- DLB-52

John Babcock [publishing house] DLB-49

Babel, Isaak Emmanuilovich
    1894-1940 . . . . DLB-272

Babits, Mihály 1883-1941 . . . DLB-215; CDWLB-4

Babrius circa 150-200 . . . . DLB-176

Babson, Marian 1929- DLB-276

Baca, Jimmy Santiago 1952- DLB-122

Bacchelli, Riccardo 1891-1985 . . . . DLB-264

Bache, Benjamin Franklin 1769-1798 . . . . . DLB-43

Bachelard, Gaston 1884-1962 . . . . DLB-296

Bacheller, Irving 1859-1950 . . . . DLB-202

Bachman, Richard (see King, Stephen)

Bachmann, Ingeborg 1926-1973 . . . . DLB-85

Bačinskaitė-Bučienė, Salomėja (see Nėris, Salomėja)

Bacon, Delia 1811-1859 . . . . DLB-1, 243

Bacon, Francis 1561-1626 .... DLB-151, 236, 252; CDBLB-1

Bacon, Sir Nicholas circa 1510-1579 ..... DLB-132

Bacon, Roger circa 1214/1220-1292 ..... DLB-115

Bacon, Thomas circa 1700-1768 .... DLB-31

Bacovia, George 1881-1957 .... DLB-220; CDWLB-4

Richard G. Badger and Company DLB-49

Badr, Liana 1952- DLB-346

Bagaduce Music Lending Library Y-00

Bage, Robert 1728-1801 .... DLB-39

Bagehot, Walter 1826-1877 .... DLB-55

Baggesen, Jens 1764-1826 .... DLB-300

Bagley, Desmond 1923-1983 .... DLB-87

Bagley, Sarah G. 1806-1848? DLB-239

Bagnold, Enid 1889-1981 .... DLB-13, 160, 191, 245

Bagryana, Elisaveta 1893-1991 .... DLB-147; CDWLB-4

Bahr, Hermann 1863-1934 .... DLB-81, 118

Baïf, Jean-Antoine de 1532-1589 .... DLB-327

Bail, Murray 1941- DLB-325

Bailey, Abigail Abbot 1746-1815 .... DLB-200

Bailey, Alfred Goldsworthy 1905-1997 .... DLB-68

Bailey, H. C. 1878-1961 .... DLB-77

Bailey, Jacob 1731-1808 .... DLB-99

Bailey, Paul 1937- DLB-14, 271

Bailey, Philip James 1816-1902 .... DLB-32

Francis Bailey [publishing house] DLB-49

Baillargeon, Pierre 1916-1967 .... DLB-88

Baillie, Hugh 1890-1966 .... DLB-29

Baillie, Joanna 1762-1851 .... DLB-93, 344

Bailyn, Bernard 1922- DLB-17

Bain, Alexander
English Composition and Rhetoric (1866) [excerpt] DLB-57

Bainbridge, Beryl 1933- DLB-14, 231

Baird, Irene 1901-1981 .... DLB-68

Baker, Alison 1953- DLB-335

Baker, Augustine 1575-1641 .... DLB-151

Baker, Carlos 1909-1987 .... DLB-103

Baker, David 1954- DLB-120

Baker, George Pierce 1866-1935 .... DLB-266

Baker, Herschel C. 1914-1990 .... DLB-111

Baker, Houston A., Jr. 1943- DLB-67

Baker, Howard
Tribute to Caroline Gordon Y-81
Tribute to Katherine Anne Porter Y-80

Baker, Kevin 1958- DLB-350

Baker, Nicholson 1957- DLB-227; Y-00

Review of Nicholson Baker's *Double Fold: Libraries and the Assault on Paper* Y-00

Baker, Ray Stannard (David Grayson) 1870-1946 .... DLB-345

Baker, Samuel White 1821-1893 .... DLB-166

Baker, Thomas 1656-1740 .... DLB-213

Walter H. Baker Company ("Baker's Plays") DLB-49

The Baker and Taylor Company DLB-49

Bakhtin, Mikhail Mikhailovich 1895-1975 .... DLB-242

Bakunin, Mikhail Aleksandrovich 1814-1876 .... DLB-277

Balabán, Jan 1961- DLB-353

Balaban, John 1943- DLB-120

Balasubramanyam, Rajeev 1974- DLB-347

Bald, Wambly 1902-1990 .... DLB-4

Balde, Jacob 1604-1668 .... DLB-164

Balderston, John 1889-1954 .... DLB-26

Baldwin, James 1924-1987
...... DLB-2, 7, 33, 249, 278; Y-87; CDALB-1

Baldwin, Joseph Glover 1815-1864 .... DLB-3, 11, 248

Baldwin, Louisa (Mrs. Alfred Baldwin) 1845-1925 .... DLB-240

Baldwin, Roger 1884-1981 .... DLB-345

Baldwin, William circa 1515-1563 ..... DLB-132

Richard and Anne Baldwin [publishing house] DLB-170

Bale, John 1495-1563 .... DLB-132

Balestrini, Nanni 1935- DLB-128, 196

Balfour, Sir Andrew 1630-1694 .... DLB-213

Balfour, Arthur James 1848-1930 .... DLB-190

Balfour, Sir James 1600-1657 .... DLB-213

Ballantine Books DLB-46

Ballantyne, R. M. 1825-1894 .... DLB-163

Ballard, J. G. 1930-2009 .... DLB-14, 207, 261, 319

Ballard, Martha Moore 1735-1812 ..... DLB-200

Ballerini, Luigi 1940- DLB-128

Ballou, Maturin Murray (Lieutenant Murray) 1820-1895 .... DLB-79, 189

Robert O. Ballou [publishing house] DLB-46

Bal'mont, Konstantin Dmitrievich 1867-1942 .... DLB-295

Balzac, Guez de 1597?-1654 .... DLB-268

Balzac, Honoré de 1799-1855 .... DLB-119

Bambara, Toni Cade 1939-1995 .... DLB-38, 218; CDALB-7

Bamford, Samuel 1788-1872 .... DLB-190

A. L. Bancroft and Company DLB-49

Bancroft, George 1800-1891 ... DLB-1, 30, 59, 243

Bancroft, Hubert Howe 1832-1918 .... DLB-47, 140

Bandeira, Manuel 1886-1968 .... DLB-307

Bandele, Biyi 1967- DLB-347

Bandelier, Adolph F. 1840-1914 .... DLB-186

Bang, Herman 1857-1912 .... DLB-300

Bangs, John Kendrick 1862-1922 ..... DLB-11, 79

Banim, John 1798-1842 .... DLB-116, 158, 159

Banim, Michael 1796-1874 .... DLB-158, 159

Banks, Iain (M.) 1954- DLB-194, 261

Banks, John circa 1653-1706 .... DLB-80

Banks, Russell 1940- DLB-130, 278

Bannerman, Helen 1862-1946 .... DLB-141

Bantam Books DLB-46

Banti, Anna 1895-1985 .... DLB-177

Banville, John 1945- DLB-14, 271, 326

Banville, Théodore de 1823-1891 .... DLB-217

Bao Tianxiao 1876-1973 .... DLB-328

Baraka, Amiri 1934- DLB-5, 7, 16, 38; DS-8; CDALB-1

Barakat, Halim 1936- DLB-346

Barańczak, Stanisław 1946- DLB-232

Baranskaia, Natal'ia Vladimirovna 1908- DLB-302

Baratham, Gopal 1935-2002 .... DLB-348

Baratynsky, Evgenii Abramovich 1800-1844 .... DLB-205

Barba-Jacob, Porfirio 1883-1942 .... DLB-283

Barbauld, Anna Laetitia 1743-1825 .... DLB-107, 109, 142, 158, 336

Barbeau, Marius 1883-1969 .... DLB-92

Barber, John Warner 1798-1885 .... DLB-30

Bàrberi Squarotti, Giorgio 1929- DLB-128

Barbey d'Aurevilly, Jules-Amédée 1808-1889 .... DLB-119

Barbier, Auguste 1805-1882 .... DLB-217

Barbieri, Nicolò 1576-1641 .... DLB-339

Barbilian, Dan (see Barbu, Ion)

Barbour, Douglas 1940- DLB-334

Barbour, John circa 1316-1395 .... DLB-146

Barbour, Ralph Henry 1870-1944 .... DLB-22

Barbu, Ion 1895-1961 ...... DLB-220; CDWLB-4

Barbusse, Henri 1873-1935 .... DLB-65

Barclay, Alexander circa 1475-1552 ..... DLB-132

E. E. Barclay and Company DLB-49

C. W. Bardeen [publishing house] DLB-49

Barham, Richard Harris 1788-1845 ..... DLB-159

Barich, Bill 1943- DLB-185

Baring, Maurice 1874-1945 .... DLB-34

Baring-Gould, Sabine 1834-1924 ... DLB-156, 190

Barker, A. L. 1918-2002 .... DLB-14, 139

Barker, Clive 1952- DLB-261

Barker, Dudley (see Black, Lionel)

Barker, George 1913-1991 .... DLB-20

Barker, Harley Granville 1877-1946 ...... DLB-10

Barker, Howard 1946- DLB-13, 233

Barker, James Nelson 1784-1858 .... DLB-37

Barker, Jane 1652-1727 .... DLB-39, 131

Barker, Lady Mary Anne 1831-1911 .... DLB-166

Barker, Pat 1943- DLB-271, 326

Barker, Ronnie 1929-2005 (see An A.B.C. of British Scenario Writers)

Barker, William circa 1520-after 1576....DLB-132

Arthur Barker Limited................DLB-112

Barkov, Ivan Semenovich 1732-1768.....DLB-150

Barks, Coleman 1937- DLB-5

Barlach, Ernst 1870-1938..........DLB-56, 118

Barlow, Joel 1754-1812................DLB-37

   The Prospect of Peace (1778)............DLB-37

Barnard, John 1681-1770...............DLB-24

Barnard, Marjorie (M. Barnard Eldershaw) 1897-1987....................DLB-260

Barnard, Robert 1936- DLB-276

Barne, Kitty (Mary Catherine Barne) 1883-1957....................DLB-160

Barnes, Barnabe 1571-1609............DLB-132

Barnes, Djuna 1892-1982.....DLB-4, 9, 45; DS-15

Barnes, Jim 1933- DLB-175

Barnes, Julian 1946- DLB-194; Y-93

   Notes for a Checklist of Publications......Y-01

Barnes, Margaret Ayer 1886-1967.........DLB-9

Barnes, Peter 1931-..............DLB-13, 233

Barnes, William 1801-1886...............DLB-32

A. S. Barnes and Company..............DLB-49

Barnes and Noble Books..............DLB-46

Barnet, Miguel 1940-................DLB-145

Barney, Natalie 1876-1972.........DLB-4; DS-15

Barnfield, Richard 1574-1627...........DLB-172

Baroja, Pío 1872-1956................DLB-322

Richard W. Baron [publishing house].....DLB-46

Barr, Amelia Edith Huddleston 1831-1919...................DLB-202, 221

Barr, Robert 1850-1912.............DLB-70, 92

Barral, Carlos 1928-1989..............DLB-134

Barrax, Gerald William 1933- DLB-41, 120

Barreno, Maria Isabel (see The Three Marias: A Landmark Case in Portuguese Literary History)

Barrès, Maurice 1862-1923...........DLB-123

Barrett, Andrea 1954- DLB-335

Barrett, Eaton Stannard 1786-1820......DLB-116

Barrie, J. M. (Sir James Matthew, Baronet Barrie) 1860-1937 ..DLB-10, 141, 156, 352; CDBLB-5

Barrie and Jenkins....................DLB-112

Barrio, Raymond 1921- DLB-82

Barrios, Gregg 1945- DLB-122

Barry, Philip 1896-1949............DLB-7, 228

Barry, Robertine (see Françoise)

Barry, Sebastian 1955- DLB-245

Barse and Hopkins....................DLB-46

Barstow, Stan 1928- DLB-14, 139, 207

   Tribute to John Braine................Y-86

Barth, John 1930- DLB-2, 227

Barthelme, Donald 1931-1989.............DLB-2, 234; Y-80, 89

Barthelme, Frederick 1943-.....DLB-244; Y-85

Barthes, Roland 1915-1980............DLB-296

Bartholomew, Frank 1898-1985.........DLB-127

Bartlett, John 1820-1905............DLB-1, 235

Bartol, Cyrus Augustus 1813-1900....DLB-1, 235

Barton, Bernard 1784-1849.............DLB-96

Barton, John ca. 1610-1675 ....DLB-236

Barton, Thomas Pennant 1803-1869.....DLB-140

Bartram, John 1699-1777...............DLB-31

Bartram, William 1739-1823............DLB-37

Barykova, Anna Pavlovna 1839-1893....DLB-277

Bashshar ibn Burd circa 714-circa 784....DLB-311

Basic Books........................DLB-46

Basille, Theodore (see Becon, Thomas)

Bass, Rick 1958- DLB-212, 275

Bass, T. J. 1932- Y-81

Bassani, Giorgio 1916-2000....DLB-128, 177, 299

Basse, William circa 1583-1653.........DLB-121

Bassett, John Spencer 1867-1928.........DLB-17

Bassler, Thomas Joseph (see Bass, T. J.)

Bate, Walter Jackson 1918-1999 .....DLB-67, 103

Bateman, Stephen circa 1510-1584......DLB-136

Christopher Bateman [publishing house]................ DLB-170

Bates, H. E. 1905-1974.............DLB-162, 191

Bates, Katharine Lee 1859-1929.........DLB-71

Batiushkov, Konstantin Nikolaevich 1787-1855.....................DLB-205

B. T. Batsford [publishing house].......DLB-106

Batteux, Charles 1713-1780 ....DLB-313

Battiscombe, Georgina 1905-2006.......DLB-155

The Battle of Maldon circa 1000 ....DLB-146

Baudelaire, Charles 1821-1867 ....DLB-217

Baudrillard, Jean 1929- DLB-296

Bauer, Bruno 1809-1882 ....DLB-133

Bauer, Wolfgang 1941- DLB-124

Baum, L. Frank 1856-1919 ....DLB-22

Baum, Vicki 1888-1960.................DLB-85

Baumbach, Jonathan 1933- Y-80

Bausch, Richard 1945- DLB-130

   Tribute to James Dickey Y-97

   Tribute to Peter Taylor Y-94

Bausch, Robert 1945- DLB-218

Bautista, Lualhati 1946- DLB-348

Bawden, Nina 1925- DLB-14, 161, 207

Bax, Clifford 1886-1962 ....DLB-10, 100

Baxter, Charles 1947- DLB-130

Bayer, Eleanor (see Perry, Eleanor)

Bayer, Konrad 1932-1964 ....DLB-85

Bayle, Pierre 1647-1706............DLB-268, 313

Bayley, Barrington J. 1937- DLB-261

Bayly, Thomas Haynes (Q. in the Corner) 1797-1839......................DLB-344

Baynes, Pauline 1922- DLB-160

Baynton, Barbara 1857-1929...........DLB-230

Bazin, Hervé (Jean Pierre Marie Hervé-Bazin) 1911-1996.......................DLB-83

Bazzani Cavazzoni, Virginia 1669-1720?....................DLB-339

The BBC Four Samuel Johnson Prize for Non-fiction.......................Y-02

Beach, Sylvia 1887-1962...........DLB-4; DS-15

Beacon Press........................DLB-49

Beadle and Adams...................DLB-49

Beagle, Peter S. 1939- Y-80

Beal, M. F. 1937-......................Y-81

Beale, Howard K. 1899-1959............DLB-17

Beard, Charles A. 1874-1948............DLB-17

Beat Generation (Beats)
   As I See It, by Carolyn Cassady......DLB-16

   A Beat Chronology: The First Twenty-five Years, 1944-1969................DLB-16

   The Commercialization of the Image of Revolt, by Kenneth Rexroth....DLB-16

   Four Essays on the Beat Generation...DLB-16

   in New York City................DLB-237

   in the West.....................DLB-237

   Outlaw Days....................DLB-16

   Periodicals of....................DLB-16

Beattie, Ann 1947- DLB-218, 278; Y-82

Beattie, James 1735-1803.............DLB-109

Beatty, Chester 1875-1968............DLB-201

Beauchemin, Nérée 1850-1931..........DLB-92

Beauchemin, Yves 1941- DLB-60

Beaugrand, Honoré 1848-1906..........DLB-99

Beaulieu, Victor-Lévy 1945- DLB-53

Beaumarchais, Pierre-Augustin Caron de 1732-1799......................DLB-313

Beaumer, Mme de ?-1766...............DLB-313

Beaumont, Francis circa 1584-1616 and Fletcher, John 1579-1625 ....DLB-58; CDBLB-1

Beaumont, Sir John 1583?-1627.........DLB-121

Beaumont, Joseph 1616-1699 ....DLB-126

Beauvoir, Simone de 1908-1986.....DLB-72; Y-86

   Personal Tribute to Simone de Beauvoir....Y-86

Beaver, Bruce 1928-..................DLB-289

Bechdel, Alison 1960- DLB-345

Becher, Ulrich 1910-1990 ....DLB-69

Beck, Warren 1896-1986 ....DLB-335

Becker, Carl 1873-1945 ....DLB-17

Becker, Jurek 1937-1997............DLB-75, 299

Becker, Jurgen 1932- DLB-75

Beckett, Mary 1926- DLB-319
Beckett, Samuel 1906-1989.....................
 DLB-13, 15, 233, 319, 321, 329; Y-90; CDBLB-7
Beckford, William 1760-1844 .... DLB-39, 213
Beckham, Barry 1944- DLB-33
Bećković, Matija 1939- DLB-181
Becon, Thomas circa 1512-1567........ DLB-136
Becque, Henry 1837-1899................ DLB-192
Beddoes, Thomas 1760-1808 .... DLB-158
Beddoes, Thomas Lovell 1803-1849...... DLB-96
Bede circa 673-735 .... DLB-146
Bedford-Jones, H. 1887-1949 .... DLB-251
Bedregal, Yolanda 1913-1999 .... DLB-283
Beebe, William 1877-1962............DLB-275
Beecher, Catharine Esther
 1800-1878................... DLB-1, 243
Beecher, Henry Ward 1813-1887 .... DLB-3, 43, 250
Beer, George L. 1872-1920 .... DLB-47
Beer, Johann 1655-1700 .... DLB-168
Beer, Patricia 1919-1999 .... DLB-40
Beerbohm, Max 1872-1956......... DLB-34, 100
Beer-Hofmann, Richard 1866-1945 ...... DLB-81
Beers, Henry A. 1847-1926............. DLB-71
S. O. Beeton [publishing house] DLB-106
Begley, Louis 1933- DLB-299
Bégon, Elisabeth 1696-1755 .... DLB-99
Behan, Brendan
 1923-1964 .... DLB-13, 233; CDBLB-7
Behn, Aphra 1640?-1689 .... DLB-39, 80, 131
Behn, Harry 1898-1973 .... DLB-61
Behrman, S. N. 1893-1973 ....DLB-7, 44
Beklemishev, Iurii Solomonvich
 (see Krymov, Iurii Solomonovich)
Belaney, Archibald Stansfeld (see Grey Owl)
Belasco, David 1853-1931 .... DLB-7
Clarke Belford and Company........... DLB-49
Belgian Luxembourg American Studies
 Association..................... Y-01
Belinsky, Vissarion Grigor'evich
 1811-1848..................... DLB-198
Belitt, Ben 1911-2003 .... DLB-5
Belknap, Jeremy 1744-1798 .... DLB-30, 37
Bell, Adrian 1901-1980................ DLB-191
Bell, Clive 1881-1964 ....DS-10
Bell, Daniel 1919- DLB-246
Bell, Gertrude Margaret Lowthian
 1868-1926 ....DLB-174
Bell, James Madison 1826-1902 .... DLB-50
Bell, Madison Smartt 1957- DLB-218, 278
 Tribute to Andrew Nelson Lytle Y-95
 Tribute to Peter Taylor............... Y-94
Bell, Marvin 1937- DLB-5
Bell, Millicent 1919- DLB-111

Bell, Quentin 1910-1996............... DLB-155
Bell, Vanessa 1879-1961 ....DS-10
George Bell and Sons DLB-106
Robert Bell [publishing house] DLB-49
Bellamy, Edward 1850-1898............ DLB-12
Bellamy, Joseph 1719-1790 .... DLB-31
John Bellamy [publishing house]........DLB-170
La Belle Assemblée 1806-1837 .... DLB-110
Bellezza, Dario 1944-1996 .... DLB-128
Belli, Carlos Germán 1927- DLB-290
Belli, Gioconda 1948- DLB-290
Belloc, Hilaire 1870-1953 ....DLB-19, 100, 141, 174
Belloc, Madame (see Parkes, Bessie Rayner)
Bellonci, Maria 1902-1986 .... DLB-196
Bellow, Saul 1915-2005
 .... DLB-2, 28, 299, 329; Y-82;
 DS-3; CDALB-1
 Tribute to Isaac Bashevis Singer......... Y-91
Belmont Productions DLB-46
Belov, Vasilii Ivanovich 1932- DLB-302
Bels, Alberts 1938- DLB-232
Belševica, Vizma 1931- ... DLB-232; CDWLB-4
Bely, Andrei 1880-1934 .... DLB-295
Bemelmans, Ludwig 1898-1962 .... DLB-22
Bemis, Samuel Flagg 1891-1973 .... DLB-17
William Bemrose [publishing house] DLB-106
Ben no Naishi 1228?-1271?............. DLB-203
Benavente, Jacinto 1866-1954.......... DLB-329
Benchley, Robert 1889-1945........... DLB-11
Bencúr, Matej (see Kukučín, Martin)
Benedetti, Mario 1920-2009 .... DLB-113
Benedict, Pinckney 1964- DLB-244
Benedict, Ruth 1887-1948............. DLB-246
Benedictus, David 1938- DLB-14
Benedikt Gröndal 1826-1907 .... DLB-293
Benedikt, Michael 1935- DLB-5
Benediktov, Vladimir Grigor'evich
 1807-1873 .... DLB-205
Beneš Jan (see Hakl, Emil)
Benét, Stephen Vincent
 1898-1943 ....DLB-4, 48, 102, 249
 Stephen Vincent Benét Centenary Y-97
Benét, William Rose 1886-1950 .... DLB-45
Benford, Gregory 1941- Y-82
Benítez, Sandra 1941- DLB-292
Benjamin, Park 1809-1864 .....DLB-3, 59, 73, 250
Benjamin, Peter (see Cunningham, Peter)
Benjamin, S. G. W. 1837-1914 .... DLB-189
Benjamin, Walter 1892-1940 .... DLB-242
Benlowes, Edward 1602-1676 .... DLB-126
Benn, Gottfried 1886-1956............. DLB-56

Benn Brothers Limited DLB-106
Bennett, Alan 1934- DLB-310
Bennett, Arnold
 1867-1931.... DLB-10, 34, 98, 135; CDBLB-5
 The Arnold Bennett Society........... Y-98
Bennett, Charles 1899-1995 .... DLB-44
Bennett, Emerson 1822-1905 .... DLB-202
Bennett, Gwendolyn 1902-1981 .... DLB-51
Bennett, Hal 1930- DLB-33
Bennett, James Gordon 1795-1872 .... DLB-43
Bennett, James Gordon, Jr. 1841-1918 .... DLB-23
Bennett, John 1865-1956 .... DLB-42
Bennett, Louise 1919-2006...DLB-117; CDWLB-3
Benni, Stefano 1947- DLB-196
Benoist, Françoise-Albine Puzin de
 La Martinière 1731-1809 .... DLB-313
Benoit, Jacques 1941- DLB-60
Benrimo, J. Harry 1874-1942 .... DLB-341
Benson, A. C. 1862-1925 .... DLB-98
Benson, E. F. 1867-1940 .... DLB-135, 153
 The E. F. Benson Society............. Y-98
 The Tilling Society.................. Y-98
Benson, Jackson J. 1930- DLB-111
Benson, Robert Hugh 1871-1914 .... DLB-153
Benson, Stella 1892-1933 .... DLB-36, 162
Bent, James Theodore 1852-1897........DLB-174
Bent, Mabel Virginia Anna ?-? DLB-174
Bentham, Jeremy 1748-1832.... DLB-107, 158, 252
Bentley, E. C. 1875-1956 .... DLB-70
Bentley, Phyllis 1894-1977 .... DLB-191
Bentley, Richard 1662-1742 .... DLB-252
Richard Bentley [publishing house] DLB-106
Benton, Robert 1932- DLB-44
Benziger Brothers DLB-49
Beowulf circa 900-1000 or 790-825
 .... DLB-146; CDBLB-1
Berberova, Nina 1901-1993 ....DLB-317
Berent, Wacław 1873-1940............ DLB-215
Beresford, Anne 1929- DLB-40
Beresford, John Davys
 1873-1947..............DLB-162, 178, 197
 "Experiment in the Novel" (1929)
 [excerpt]...................... DLB-36
Beresford-Howe, Constance 1922- DLB-88
R. G. Berford Company................ DLB-49
Berg, Elizabeth 1948- DLB-292
Berg, Stephen 1934- DLB-5
Bergelson, David (Dovid Bergelson)
 1884-1952 .... DLB-333
Bergengruen, Werner 1892-1964 .... DLB-56
Berger, John 1926- DLB-14, 207, 319, 326
Berger, Meyer 1898-1959 .... DLB-29

Berger, Thomas 1924- DLB-2; Y-80
   A Statement by Thomas Berger Y-80
Bergman, Hjalmar 1883-1931 .... DLB-259
Bergman, Ingmar 1918-2007 .... DLB-257
Bergson, Henri 1859-1941 .... DLB-329
Berkeley, Anthony 1893-1971 .... DLB-77
Berkeley, George 1685-1753 ..... DLB-31, 101, 252
The Berkley Publishing Corporation DLB-46
Berkman, Alexander 1870-1936 .... DLB-303
Berlin, Irving 1888-1989 .... DLB-265
Berlin, Lucia 1936- DLB-130
Berman, Marshall 1940- DLB-246
Berman, Sabina 1955- DLB-305
Bernal, Vicente J. 1888-1915 .... DLB-82
Bernanos, Georges 1888-1948 .... DLB-72
Bernard, Catherine 1663?-1712 .... DLB-268
Bernard, Harry 1898-1979 .... DLB-92
Bernard, John 1756-1828 .... DLB-37
Bernard of Chartres circa 1060-1124? DLB-115
Bernard of Clairvaux 1090-1153 .... DLB-208
Bernard, Richard 1568-1641/1642 .... DLB-281
Bernard Silvestris
   fl. circa 1130-1160 .... DLB-208
Bernardin de Saint-Pierre 1737-1814 ...... DLB-313
Bernari, Carlo 1909-1992 .... DLB-177
Bernhard, Thomas
   1931-1989 .... DLB-85, 124; CDWLB-2
Berniéres, Louis de 1954- DLB-271
Bernstein, Charles 1950- DLB-169
Béroalde de Verville, François
   1556-1626 .... DLB-327
Berriault, Gina 1926-1999 .... DLB-130
Berrigan, Daniel 1921- DLB-5
Berrigan, Ted 1934-1983 .... DLB-5, 169
Berry, James 1924- DLB-347
Berry, Wendell 1934- ... DLB-5, 6, 234, 275, 342
Berryman, John 1914-1972 .... DLB-48; CDALB-1
Bersianik, Louky 1930- DLB-60
Berssenbrugge, Mei-mei 1947- DLB-312
Thomas Berthelet [publishing house] DLB-170
Berto, Giuseppe 1914-1978 .... DLB-177
Bertocci, Peter Anthony 1910-1989 ..... DLB-279
Bertolucci, Attilio 1911-2000 .... DLB-128
Berton, Pierre 1920-2004 .... DLB-68
Bertrand, Louis "Aloysius" 1807-1841 .... DLB-217
Besant, Sir Walter 1836-1901 .... DLB-135, 190
Bessa-Luís, Agustina 1922- DLB-287
Bessette, Gerard 1920-2005 .... DLB-53
Bessie, Alvah 1904-1985 .... DLB-26
Bester, Alfred 1913-1987 .... DLB-8
Besterman, Theodore 1904-1976 .... DLB-201

Beston, Henry (Henry Beston Sheahan)
   1888-1968 .... DLB-275
Best-Seller Lists
   An Assessment Y-84
   What's Really Wrong With
      Bestseller Lists Y-84
Bestuzhev, Aleksandr Aleksandrovich
   (Marlinsky) 1797-1837 .... DLB-198
Bestuzhev, Nikolai Aleksandrovich
   1791-1855 .... DLB-198
Betham-Edwards, Matilda Barbara
   (see Edwards, Matilda Barbara Betham-)
Bethune, Mary McLeod 1875-1955 ...... DLB-345
Betjeman, John
   1906-1984 .... DLB-20; Y-84; CDBLB-7
Betocchi, Carlo 1899-1986 .... DLB-128
Bettarini, Mariella 1942- DLB-128
Betts, Doris 1932- DLB-218; Y-82
Beveridge, Albert J. 1862-1927 .... DLB-17
Beveridge, Judith 1956- DLB-325
Beverley, Robert circa 1673-1722 .... DLB-24, 30
Bevilacqua, Alberto 1934- DLB-196
Bevington, Louisa Sarah 1845-1895 ..... DLB-199
Beyer, Absalon Pederssøn 1528?-1575 .... DLB-354
Beyle, Marie-Henri (see Stendhal)
Bèze, Théodore de (Theodore Beza)
   1519-1605 .... DLB-327
Bhatt, Sujata 1956- DLB-323
Białoszewski, Miron 1922-1983 .... DLB-232
Bianco, Margery Williams 1881-1944 .... DLB-160
Bibaud, Adèle 1854-1941 .... DLB-92
Bibaud, Michel 1782-1857 .... DLB-99
Bibliography
   Bibliographical and Textual Scholarship
      Since World War II Y-89
   Center for Bibliographical Studies and
      Research at the University of
      California, Riverside Y-91
   The Great Bibliographers Series Y-93
   Primary Bibliography: A Retrospective Y-95
Bichsel, Peter 1935- DLB-75
Bickerstaff, Isaac John 1733-circa 1808 .... DLB-89
Drexel Biddle [publishing house] DLB-49
Bidermann, Jacob
   1577 or 1578-1639 .... DLB-164
Bidwell, Walter Hilliard 1798-1881 .... DLB-79
Biehl, Charlotta Dorothea 1731-1788 ..... DLB-300
Bienek, Horst 1930-1990 .... DLB-75
Bierbaum, Otto Julius 1865-1910 .... DLB-66
Bierce, Ambrose 1842-1914?
   ..... DLB-11, 12, 23, 71, 74, 186; CDALB-3
Bigelow, William F. 1879-1966 .... DLB-91
Biggers, Earl Derr 1884-1933 .... DLB-306
Biggle, Lloyd, Jr. 1923-2002 .... DLB-8
Bigiaretti, Libero 1905-1993 .... DLB-177
Bigland, Eileen 1898-1970 .... DLB-195

Biglow, Hosea (see Lowell, James Russell)
Bigongiari, Piero 1914-1997 .... DLB-128
Bilac, Olavo 1865-1918 .... DLB-307
Bilenchi, Romano 1909-1989 .... DLB-264
Billinger, Richard 1890-1965 .... DLB-124
Billings, Hammatt 1818-1874 .... DLB-188
Billings, John Shaw 1898-1975 .... DLB-137
Billings, Josh (see Shaw, Henry Wheeler)
Binchy, Maeve 1940- DLB-319
Binding, Rudolf G. 1867-1938 .... DLB-66
Bing Xin 1900-1999 .... DLB-328
Bingay, Malcolm 1884-1953 .... DLB-241
Bingham, Caleb 1757-1817 .... DLB-42
Bingham, George Barry 1906-1988 ..... DLB-127
Bingham, Sallie 1937- DLB-234
William Bingley [publishing house] DLB-154
Binyon, Laurence 1869-1943 .... DLB-19
Biographia Brittanica DLB-142
Biography
   Biographical Documents Y-84, 85
   A Celebration of Literary Biography Y-98
   Conference on Modern Biography Y-85
   The Cult of Biography
      Excerpts from the Second Folio Debate:
      "Biographies are generally a disease of
      English Literature" Y-86
   New Approaches to Biography: Challenges
      from Critical Theory, USC Conference
      on Literary Studies, 1990 .... Y-90
   "The New Biography," by Virginia Woolf,
      New York Herald Tribune,
      30 October 1927 .... DLB-149
   "The Practice of Biography," in *The English
      Sense of Humour and Other Essays*, by
      Harold Nicolson DLB-149
   "Principles of Biography," in *Elizabethan
      and Other Essays*, by Sidney Lee ... DLB-149
   Remarks at the Opening of "The Biographical
      Part of Literature" Exhibition, by
      William R. Cagle Y-98
   Survey of Literary Biographies Y-00
   A Transit of Poets and Others: American
      Biography in 1982 .... Y-82
   The Year in Literary
      Biography Y-83–01
Biography, The Practice of:
   An Interview with B. L. Reid Y-83
   An Interview with David Herbert Donald ... Y-87
   An Interview with Humphrey Carpenter Y-84
   An Interview with Joan Mellen Y-94
   An Interview with John Caldwell Guilds Y-92
   An Interview with William Manchester ... Y-85
John Bioren [publishing house] DLB-49
Bioy Casares, Adolfo 1914-1999 .... DLB-113
Birch, Thomas 1705-1766 .... DLB-336
Bird, Isabella Lucy 1831-1904 .... DLB-166
Bird, Robert Montgomery 1806-1854 .... DLB-202

Bird, William 1888-1963 . . . . DLB-4; DS-15
    The Cost of the *Cantos:* William Bird
      to Ezra Pound Y-01

Birdsell, Sandra 1942- DLB-334

Birken, Sigmund von 1626-1681 . . . . DLB-164

Birney, Earle 1904-1995 . . . . DLB-88

Birrell, Augustine 1850-1933 . . . . DLB-98

Bisher, Furman 1918- DLB-171

Bishop, Elizabeth
    1911-1979 . . . . DLB-5, 169; CDALB-6
    The Elizabeth Bishop Society Y-01

Bishop, John Peale 1892-1944 . . . . DLB-4, 9, 45

Bismarck, Otto von 1815-1898 . . . . DLB-129

Bisset, Robert 1759-1805 . . . . DLB-142

Bissett, Bill 1939- DLB-53

Bitov, Andrei Georgievich 1937- DLB-302

Bittel, Adriana 1946- DLB-353

Bitzius, Albert (see Gotthelf, Jeremias)

Bjørnboe, Jens 1920-1976 . . . . DLB-297

Bjørnson, Bjørnstjerne 1832-1910 . . . DLB-329, 354

Bjørnvig, Thorkild 1918-2004 . . . . DLB-214

Black, David (D. M.) 1941- DLB-40

Black, Gavin (Oswald Morris Wynd)
    1913-1998 . . . . DLB-276

Black, Lionel (Dudley Barker)
    1910-1980 . . . . DLB-276

Black, Winifred 1863-1936 . . . . DLB-25

Walter J. Black [publishing house] DLB-46

Blackamore, Arthur 1679-? DLB-24, 39

Blackburn, Alexander L. 1929- Y-85

Blackburn, John 1923-1993 . . . . DLB-261

Blackburn, Paul 1926-1971 . . . . DLB-16; Y-81

Blackburn, Thomas 1916-1977 . . . . DLB-27

Blacker, Terence 1948- DLB-271

Blackman, Malorie 1962- DLB-347

Blackmore, R. D. 1825-1900 . . . . DLB-18

Blackmore, Sir Richard 1654-1729 . . . . . . DLB-131

Blackmur, R. P. 1904-1965 . . . . DLB-63

Blackwell, Alice Stone 1857-1950 . . . . DLB-303

Basil Blackwell, Publisher DLB-106

Blackstone, William 1723-1780 . . . . DLB-336

Blackwood, Algernon Henry
    1869-1951 . . . . DLB-153, 156, 178

Blackwood, Caroline 1931-1996 . . . . . DLB-14, 207

William Blackwood and Sons, Ltd. DLB-154

Blackwood's Edinburgh Magazine
    1817-1980 . . . . DLB-110

Blades, William 1824-1890 . . . . DLB-184

Blaga, Lucian 1895-1961 . . . . DLB-220

Blagden, Isabella 1817?-1873 . . . . DLB-199

Blair, Eric Arthur (see Orwell, George)

Blair, Francis Preston 1791-1876 . . . . DLB-43

Blair, Hugh
    Lectures on Rhetoric and Belles Lettres (1783),
    [excerpts] DLB-31

Blair, James circa 1655-1743 . . . . DLB-24

Blair, John Durburrow 1759-1823 . . . . DLB-37

Blais, Marie-Claire 1939- DLB-53

Blaise, Clark 1940- DLB-53

Blake, George 1893-1961 . . . . DLB-191

Blake, James Carlos 1947- DLB-350

Blake, Lillie Devereux 1833-1913 . . . . DLB-202, 221

Blake, Nicholas (C. Day Lewis)
    1904-1972 . . . . DLB-77

Blake, William
    1757-1827 . . . . . DLB-93, 154, 163; CDBLB-3

The Blakiston Company DLB-49

Blanchard, Stephen 1950- DLB-267

Blanchot, Maurice 1907-2003 . . . . . . DLB-72, 296

Blanckenburg, Christian Friedrich von
    1744-1796 . . . . DLB-94

Blandiana, Ana 1942- DLB-232; CDWLB-4

Blanshard, Brand 1892-1987 . . . . DLB-279

Blasco Ibáñez, Vicente 1867-1928 . . . . DLB-322

Blaser, Robin 1925- DLB-165

Blaumanis, Rudolfs 1863-1908 . . . . DLB-220

Bleasdale, Alan 1946- DLB-245

Bledsoe, Albert Taylor
    1809-1877 . . . . DLB-3, 79, 248

Bleecker, Ann Eliza 1752-1783 . . . . DLB-200

Blelock and Company DLB-49

Blennerhassett, Margaret Agnew
    1773-1842 . . . . DLB-99

Geoffrey Bles [publishing house] DLB-112

Blessington, Marguerite, Countess of
    1789-1849 . . . . DLB-166

Blew, Mary Clearman 1939- DLB-256

Blicher, Steen Steensen 1782-1848 . . . . . . DLB-300

The Blickling Homilies circa 971 . . . . . . DLB-146

Blind, Mathilde 1841-1896 . . . . DLB-199

The Blind Assassin, 2000 Booker Prize winner,
    Margaret Atwood DLB-326

Blish, James 1921-1975 . . . . DLB-8

E. Bliss and E. White
    [publishing house] DLB-49

Bliven, Bruce 1889-1977 . . . . DLB-137

Blixen, Karen 1885-1962 . . . . DLB-214

Bloch, Ernst 1885-1977 . . . . DLB-296

Bloch, Robert 1917-1994 . . . . DLB-44
    Tribute to John D. MacDonald Y-86

Block, Lawrence 1938- DLB-226

Block, Rudolph (see Lessing, Bruno)

Blok, Aleksandr Aleksandrovich
    1880-1921 . . . . DLB-295

Blondal, Patricia 1926-1959 . . . . DLB-88

Bloom, Harold 1930- DLB-67

Bloom, Valerie 1956- DLB-347

Bloomer, Amelia 1818-1894 . . . . DLB-79

Bloomfield, Robert 1766-1823 . . . . DLB-93

Bloomsbury Group DS-10
    The *Dreannought* Hoax DS-10

Bloor, Ella Reeve 1862-1951 . . . . DLB-303

Blotner, Joseph 1923- DLB-111

Blount, Thomas 1618?-1679 . . . . DLB-236

Bloy, Léon 1846-1917 . . . . DLB-123

Blože, Vytautas P. 1930- DLB-353

Blue Cloud, Peter (Aroniawenrate)
    1933- DLB-342

Blume, Judy 1938- DLB-52
    Tribute to Theodor Seuss Geisel Y-91

Blunck, Hans Friedrich 1888-1961 . . . . . . DLB-66

Blunden, Edmund 1896-1974 . . . . DLB-20, 100, 155

Blundeville, Thomas 1522?-1606 . . . . DLB-236

Blunt, Lady Anne Isabella Noel
    1837-1917 . . . . DLB-174

Blunt, Wilfrid Scawen 1840-1922 . . . . . DLB-19, 174

Bly, Carol 1930- DLB-335

Bly, Nellie (see Cochrane, Elizabeth)

Bly, Robert 1926- DLB-5, 342

Blyton, Enid 1897-1968 . . . . DLB-160

Boaden, James 1762-1839 . . . . DLB-89

Boal, Augusto 1931- DLB-307

Boas, Frederick S. 1862-1957 . . . . DLB-149

The Bobbs-Merrill Company DLB-46, 291

The Bobbs-Merrill Archive at the
    Lilly Library, Indiana University Y-90

Boborykin, Petr Dmitrievich
    1836-1921 . . . . DLB-238

Bobrov, Semen Sergeevich
    1763?-1810 . . . . DLB-150

Bobrowski, Johannes 1917-1965 . . . . DLB-75

Bocage, Manuel Maria Barbosa du
    1765-1805 . . . . DLB-287

Bodenheim, Maxwell 1892-1954 . . . . . . DLB-9, 45

Bodenstedt, Friedrich von 1819-1892 . . . . DLB-129

Bodini, Vittorio 1914-1970 . . . . DLB-128

Bodkin, M. McDonnell 1850-1933 . . . . . . DLB-70

Bodley, Sir Thomas 1545-1613 . . . . DLB-213

Bodley Head DLB-112

Bodmer, Johann Jakob 1698-1783 . . . . DLB-97

Bodmershof, Imma von 1895-1982 . . . . . . DLB-85

Bodor, Ádám 1936- DLB-353

Bodsworth, Fred 1918- DLB-68

Böðvar Guðmundsson 1939- DLB-293

Boehm, Sydney 1908-1990 . . . . DLB-44

Boer, Charles 1939- DLB-5

Boethius circa 480-circa 524 . . . . DLB-115

Boethius of Dacia circa 1240-? DLB-115

Bogan, Louise 1897-1970 . . . . .DLB-45, 169

Bogarde, Dirk 1921-1999. . . . . .DLB-14

Bogdanov, Aleksandr Aleksandrovich
1873-1928 . . . . .DLB-295

Bogdanovich, Ippolit Fedorovich
circa 1743-1803 . . . . .DLB-150

Bogosian, Eric 1953- DLB-341

David Bogue [publishing house] DLB-106

Bohjalian, Chris 1960- DLB-292

Böhme, Jakob 1575-1624 . . . . .DLB-164

H. G. Bohn [publishing house] DLB-106

Bohse, August 1661-1742. . . . . .DLB-168

Boie, Heinrich Christian 1744-1806. . . . . . .DLB-94

Boileau-Despréaux, Nicolas 1636-1711. . . .DLB-268

Bojunga, Lygia 1932- DLB-307

Bok, Edward W. 1863-1930. . . . . . .DLB-91; DS-16

Boland, Eavan 1944- DLB-40

Boldrewood, Rolf (Thomas Alexander Browne)
1826?-1915 .DLB-230

Bolingbroke, Henry St. John, Viscount
1678-1751 . . . . .DLB-101, 336

Böll, Heinrich
1917-1985 . . . . DLB-69, 329; Y-85; CDWLB-2

Bolling, Robert 1738-1775 . . . . .DLB-31

Bolotov, Andrei Timofeevich
1738-1833 . . . . .DLB-150

Bolt, Carol 1941- DLB-60

Bolt, Robert 1924-1995 . . . . .DLB-13, 233

Bolton, Herbert E. 1870-1953 . . . . .DLB-17

Bonarelli, Guidubaldo 1563-1608 . . . . . . .DLB-339

Bonaventura. DLB-90

Bonaventure circa 1217-1274 . . . . .DLB-115

Bonaviri, Giuseppe 1924- DLB-177

Bond, Edward 1934- DLB-13, 310

Bond, Michael 1926- DLB-161

Bondarev, Iurii Vasil'evich 1924- DLB-302

The Bone People, 1985 Booker Prize winner,
Keri Hulme DLB-326

Albert and Charles Boni
[publishing house] DLB-46

Boni and Liveright. DLB-46

Bonnefoy, Yves 1923- DLB-258

Bonner, Marita 1899-1971 . . . . .DLB-228

Bonner, Paul Hyde 1893-1968. . . . . DS-17

Bonner, Sherwood (see McDowell, Katharine
Sherwood Bonner)

Robert Bonner's Sons DLB-49

Bonnin, Gertrude Simmons (see Zitkala-Ša)

Bonsanti, Alessandro 1904-1984 . . . . .DLB-177

Bontempelli, Massimo 1878-1960 . . . . . . .DLB-264

Bontemps, Arna 1902-1973 . . . . .DLB-48, 51

The Book Buyer (1867-1880, 1884-1918,
1935-1938 . . . . DS-13

The Book League of America DLB-46

Book Reviewing
The American Book Review: A Sketch. . . .Y-92
Book Reviewing and the
Literary Scene. Y-96, 97
Book Reviewing in America Y-87–94
Book Reviewing in America and the
Literary Scene. Y-95
Book Reviewing in Texas Y-94
Book Reviews in Glossy Magazines Y-95
Do They or Don't They?
Writers Reading Book Reviews Y-01
The Most Powerful Book Review
in America [*New York Times
Book Review*]. Y-82
Some Surprises and Universal Truths. Y-92
The Year in Book Reviewing and the
Literary Situation Y-98

Book Supply Company DLB-49

The Book Trade History Group Y-93

Bookchin, Murray 1921-2006 . . . . .DLB-345

The Booker Prize. Y-96–98
Address by Anthony Thwaite,
Chairman of the Booker Prize Judges
Comments from Former Booker
Prize Winners Y-86

Boorde, Andrew circa 1490-1549. . . . . . . .DLB-136

Boorstin, Daniel J. 1914-2004 . . . . .DLB-17
Tribute to Archibald MacLeish Y-82
Tribute to Charles Scribner Jr.. . . . . .Y-95

Booth, Franklin 1874-1948. . . . . .DLB-188

Booth, Mary L. 1831-1889 . . . . .DLB-79

Booth, Philip 1925-2007. . . . . .Y-82

Booth, Wayne C. 1921-2005 . . . . .DLB-67

Booth, William 1829-1912. . . . . .DLB-190

Bor, Josef 1906-1979. . . . . .DLB-299

Borchardt, Rudolf 1877-1945 . . . . .DLB-66

Borchert, Wolfgang 1921-1947 . . . . . .DLB-69, 124

Bording, Anders 1619-1677 . . . . .DLB-300

Borel, Pétrus 1809-1859. . . . . .DLB-119

Borgen, Johan 1902-1979 . . . . .DLB-297

Borges, Jorge Luis
1899-1986 . . . DLB-113, 283; Y-86; CDWLB-3
The Poetry of Jorge Luis Borges Y-86
A Personal Tribute Y-86

Borgese, Giuseppe Antonio 1882-1952 . . .DLB-264

Börne, Ludwig 1786-1837 . . . . .DLB-90

Bornstein, Miriam 1950- DLB-209

Borowski, Tadeusz
1922-1951 . . . . .DLB-215; CDWLB-4

Borrow, George 1803-1881 . . . . . .DLB-21, 55, 166

Bosanquet, Bernard 1848-1923 . . . . .DLB-262

Boscán, Juan circa 1490-1542 . . . . .DLB-318

Bosch, Juan 1909-2001 . . . . .DLB-145

Bosco, Henri 1888-1976. . . . . .DLB-72

Bosco, Monique 1927- DLB-53

Bosman, Herman Charles 1905-1951 . . . .DLB-225

Bossuet, Jacques-Bénigne 1627-1704 . . . . . .DLB-268

Bostic, Joe 1908-1988. . . . . .DLB-241

Boston, Lucy M. 1892-1990 . . . . .DLB-161

Boston Quarterly Review. DLB-1

Boston University
Editorial Institute at Boston University. . . .Y-00
Special Collections at Boston University. . .Y-99

Boswell, James
1740-1795 . . . . .DLB-104, 142; CDBLB-2

Boswell, Robert 1953- DLB-234

Bosworth, David Y-82
Excerpt from "Excerpts from a Report
of the Commission," in *The Death
of Descartes* Y-82

Bote, Hermann circa 1460-circa 1520. . . .DLB-179

Botev, Khristo 1847-1876 . . . . .DLB-147

Botkin, Vasilii Petrovich 1811-1869 . . . . . .DLB-277

Botta, Anne C. Lynch 1815-1891 . . . . .DLB-3, 250

Botto, Ján (see Krasko, Ivan)

Bottome, Phyllis 1882-1963 . . . . .DLB-197

Bottomley, Gordon 1874-1948. . . . . .DLB-10

Bottoms, David 1949- DLB-120; Y-83
Tribute to James Dickey Y-97

Bottrall, Ronald 1906-1959 . . . . .DLB-20

Bouchardy, Joseph 1810-1870 . . . . .DLB-192

Boucher, Anthony 1911-1968 . . . . .DLB-8

Boucher, Jonathan 1738-1804 . . . . .DLB-31

Boucher de Boucherville, Georges
1814-1894 . . . . .DLB-99

Boucicault, Dion (Dionysius Boursiquot, Dion
Bourcicault, Lee Moreton)
1820-1890 . . . . DLB -344

Boudreau, Daniel (see Coste, Donat)

Bouhours, Dominique 1628-1702 . . . . . . .DLB-268

Boudjedra, Rachid 1941- DLB-346

Boujah, Slaheddine 1956- DLB-346

Bourassa, Napoléon 1827-1916 . . . . .DLB-99

Bourget, Paul 1852-1935 . . . . .DLB-123

Bourinot, John George 1837-1902 . . . . . . .DLB-99

Bourjaily, Vance 1922- DLB-2, 143

Bourne, Edward Gaylord 1860-1908. . . . . .DLB-47

Bourne, Randolph 1886-1918 . . . . .DLB-63

Bousoño, Carlos 1923- DLB-108

Bousquet, Joë 1897-1950 . . . . .DLB-72

Bova, Ben 1932- Y-81

Bovard, Oliver K. 1872-1945 . . . . .DLB-25

Bove, Emmanuel 1898-1945 . . . . .DLB-72

Bowen, Elizabeth
1899-1973 . . . . .DLB-15, 162; CDBLB-7

Bowen, Francis 1811-1890. . . . . . . .DLB-1, 59, 235

Bowen, John 1924- DLB-13

Bowen, Marjorie 1886-1952 . . . . .DLB-153

Bowen-Merrill Company DLB-49

Bowering, George 1935- DLB-53

Bowering, Marilyn 1949- DLB-334

Bowers, Bathsheba 1671-1718........... DLB-200

Bowers, Claude G. 1878-1958 .... DLB-17

Bowers, Edgar 1924-2000................ DLB-5

Bowers, Fredson Thayer
   1905-1991 .... DLB-140; Y- 91

   The Editorial Style of Fredson Bowers.... Y-91

   Fredson Bowers and
      Studies in Bibliography .... Y- 91

   Fredson Bowers and the Cambridge
      Beaumont and Fletcher .... Y- 91

   Fredson Bowers as Critic of Renaissance
      Dramatic Literature.............. Y- 91

   Fredson Bowers as Music Critic......... Y-91

   Fredson Bowers, Master Teacher........Y- 91

   An Interview [on Nabokov] Y-80

   Working with Fredson Bowers......... Y-91

Bowles, Paul 1910-1999 ...... DLB-5, 6, 218; Y-99

Bowles, Samuel, III 1826-1878 .... DLB-43

Bowles, William Lisle 1762-1850 .... DLB-93

Bowling, Tim 1964- DLB-334

Bowman, Louise Morey 1882-1944 ..... DLB-68

Bowne, Borden Parker 1847-1919........DLB-270

Boyd, James 1888-1944........... DLB-9; DS-16

Boyd, John 1912-2002 .... DLB-310

Boyd, John 1919- DLB-8

Boyd, Martin 1893-1972 .... DLB-260

Boyd, Thomas 1898-1935..... DLB-9, 316; DS-16

Boyd, William 1952- DLB-231

Boye, Karin 1900-1941 .... DLB-259

Boyesen, Hjalmar Hjorth
   1848-1895 ....DLB-12, 71; DS-13

Boylan, Clare 1948- DLB-267

Boyle, Kay 1902-1992
   .... DLB-4, 9, 48, 86; DS-15; Y-93

Boyle, Roger, Earl of Orrery 1621-1679 ... DLB-80

Boyle, T. Coraghessan
   1948- DLB-218, 278; Y-86

Božić, Mirko 1919- DLB-181

Bracciolini, Francesco 1566-1645 ...... DLB-339

Brackenbury, Alison 1953- DLB-40

Brackenridge, Hugh Henry
   1748-1816.................. DLB-11, 37

   The Rising Glory of America....... DLB-37

Brackett, Charles 1892-1969........... DLB-26

Brackett, Leigh 1915-1978 .... DLB-8, 26

John Bradburn [publishing house] DLB-49

Bradbury, Malcolm 1932-2000...... DLB-14, 207

Bradbury, Ray 1920- DLB-2, 8; CDALB-6

Bradbury and Evans................ DLB-106

Braddon, Mary Elizabeth
   1835-1915..................DLB-18, 70, 156

Bradford, Andrew 1686-1742 .... DLB-43, 73

Bradford, Gamaliel 1863-1932 .... DLB-17

Bradford, John 1749-1830.............. DLB-43

Bradford, Roark 1896-1948 .... DLB-86

Bradford, William 1590-1657 .... DLB-24, 30

Bradford, William, III 1719-1791 ..... DLB-43, 73

Bradlaugh, Charles 1833-1891 .... DLB-57

Bradley, David 1950- DLB-33

Bradley, F. H. 1846-1924 .... DLB-262

Bradley, Katherine Harris (see Field, Michael)

Bradley, Marion Zimmer 1930-1999 ...... DLB-8

Bradley, William Aspenwall 1878-1939 .... DLB-4

Ira Bradley and Company DLB-49

J. W. Bradley and Company........... DLB-49

Bradshaw, Henry 1831-1886 .... DLB-184

Bradstreet, Anne
   1612 or 1613-1672 .... DLB-24; CDALB-2

Bradūnas, Kazys 1917- DLB-220

Bradwardine, Thomas circa 1295-1349 .. DLB-115

Brady, Frank 1924-1986 .... DLB-111

Frederic A. Brady [publishing house] DLB-49

Braga, Rubem 1913-1990............. DLB-307

Bragg, Melvyn 1939- DLB-14, 271

Brahe, Tycho 1546-1601............. DLB-300

Brahms, Caryl 1901-1982............ DLB-352

Charles H. Brainard [publishing house] ... DLB-49

Braine, John 1922-1986 ..DLB-15; Y-86; CDBLB-7

Braithwait, Richard 1588-1673 .... DLB-151

Braithwaite, William Stanley
   1878-1962................... DLB-50, 54

Bräker, Ulrich 1735-1798 .... DLB-94

Bramah, Ernest 1868-1942............. DLB-70

Branagan, Thomas 1774-1843 .... DLB-37

Brancati, Vitaliano 1907-1954......... DLB-264

Branch, William Blackwell 1927- DLB-76

Brand, Christianna 1907-1988 ....DLB-276

Brand, Dionne 1953- DLB-334

Brand, Max (see Faust, Frederick Schiller)

Brandão, Raul 1867-1930 .... DLB-287

Branden Press...................... DLB-46

Brandes, Georg 1842-1927 .... DLB-300

Branner, H.C. 1903-1966 .... DLB-214

Brant, Sebastian 1457-1521............DLB-179

Brantôme (Pierre de Bourdeille)
   1540?-1614................... DLB-327

Brassey, Lady Annie (Allnutt)
   1839-1887..................... DLB-166

Brathwaite, Edward Kamau
   1930- DLB-125; CDWLB-3

Brault, Jacques 1933- DLB-53

Braun, Matt 1932- DLB-212

Braun, Volker 1939- DLB-75, 124

Brautigan, Richard
   1935-1984 ....DLB-2, 5, 206; Y-80, 84

Braverman, Kate 1950- DLB-335

Braxton, Joanne M. 1950- DLB-41

Bray, Anne Eliza 1790-1883 .... DLB-116

Bray, Thomas 1656-1730 .... DLB-24

Brazdžionis, Bernardas 1907-2002 ...... DLB-220

George Braziller [publishing house] DLB-46

The Bread Loaf Writers' Conference 1983 ... Y-84

Breasted, James Henry 1865-1935 .... DLB-47

Brecht, Bertolt
   1898-1956 ....DLB-56, 124; CDWLB-2

Bredal, Niels Krog 1732-1778 .... DLB-354

Bredel, Willi 1901-1964 .... DLB-56

Breeze, Jean "Binta" 1956- DLB-347

Bregendahl, Marie 1867-1940 .... DLB-214

Breitinger, Johann Jakob 1701-1776....... DLB-97

Brekke, Paal 1923-1993 .... DLB-297

Bremser, Bonnie 1939- DLB-16

Bremser, Ray 1934-1998............. DLB-16

Brennan, Christopher 1870-1932 .... DLB-230

Brentano, Bernard von 1901-1964 .... DLB-56

Brentano, Clemens 1778-1842 .... DLB-90

Brentano, Franz 1838-1917 .... DLB-296

Brentano's........................ DLB-49

Brenton, Howard 1942- DLB-13

Breslin, Jimmy 1929-1996............. DLB-185

Breton, André 1896-1966......... DLB-65, 258

Breton, Nicholas circa 1555-circa 1626... DLB-136

The Breton Lays
   1300-early fifteenth century....... DLB-146

Brett, Lily 1946- DLB-325

Brett, Simon 1945- DLB-276

Brewer, Gil 1922-1983 .... DLB-306

Brewer, Luther A. 1858-1933 ....DLB-187

Brewer, Warren and Putnam DLB-46

Brewster, Elizabeth 1922- DLB-60

Breytenbach, Breyten 1939- DLB-225

Bridge, Ann (Lady Mary Dolling Sanders O'Malley)
   1889-1974..................... DLB-191

Bridge, Horatio 1806-1893............ DLB-183

Bridgers, Sue Ellen 1942- DLB-52

Bridges, Robert
   1844-1930 .... DLB-19, 98; CDBLB-5

The Bridgewater Library DLB-213

Bridie, James 1888-1951................ DLB-10

Brieux, Eugene 1858-1932 .... DLB-192

Brigadere, Anna 1861-1933 . DLB-220; CDWLB-4

Briggs, Charles Frederick
   1804-1877.................... DLB-3, 250

Brighouse, Harold 1882-1958.......... DLB-10

Bright, Mary Chavelita Dunne
   (see Egerton, George)

Brightman, Edgar Sheffield 1884-1953 ... DLB-270

B. J. Brimmer Company DLB-46

Brines, Francisco 1932- DLB-134

Brink, André 1935- DLB-225

Brinley, George, Jr. 1817-1875 .... DLB-140

Brinnin, John Malcolm 1916-1998 .... DLB-48

Brisbane, Albert 1809-1890 .... DLB-3, 250

Brisbane, Arthur 1864-1936 .... DLB-25

British Academy DLB-112

The British Critic 1793-1843 .... DLB-110

British Library
   The American Trust for the
     British Library Y-96
   The British Library and the Regular
     Readers' Group Y-91
   Building the New British Library
     at St Pancras Y-94

British Literary Prizes DLB-207; Y-98

British Literature
   The "Angry Young Men" DLB-15
   Author-Printers, 1476-1599 .... DLB-167
   The Comic Tradition Continued DLB-15
   Documents on Sixteenth-Century
     Literature DLB-167, 172
   Eikon Basilike 1649 .... DLB-151
   Letter from London Y-96
   A Mirror for Magistrates DLB-167
   "Modern English Prose" (1876),
     by George Saintsbury DLB-57
   Sex, Class, Politics, and Religion [in the
     British Novel, 1930-1959] DLB-15
   Victorians on Rhetoric and Prose
     Style DLB-57
   The Year in British Fiction Y-99–01
   "You've Never Had It So Good," Gusted
     by "Winds of Change": British
     Fiction in the 1950s, 1960s,
     and After DLB-14

British Literature, Old and Middle English
   Anglo-Norman Literature in the
     Development of Middle English
     Literature DLB-146
   The *Alliterative Morte Arthure and the
     Stanzaic Morte Arthur*
     circa 1350-1400 .... DLB-146
   Ancrene Riwle circa 1200-1225 .... DLB-146
   The *Anglo-Saxon Chronicle* circa
     890-1154 .... DLB-146
   The *Battle of Maldon* circa 1000 .... DLB-146
   Beowulf circa 900-1000 or
     790-825 .... DLB-146; CDBLB-1
   The Blickling Homilies circa 971 ..... DLB-146
   The Breton Lays
     1300-early fifteenth century DLB-146
   The *Castle of Perseverance*
     circa 1400-1425 .... DLB-146
   The Celtic Background to Medieval
     English Literature DLB-146
   The Chester Plays circa 1505-1532;
     revisions until 1575 .... DLB-146
   Cursor Mundi circa 1300 .... DLB-146

The English Language: 410
   to 1500 .... DLB-146

The Germanic Epic and Old English
   Heroic Poetry: *Widsith, Waldere*,
   and *The Fight at Finnsburg* DLB-146

Judith circa 930 .... DLB-146

The Matter of England 1240-1400 ... DLB-146

The Matter of Rome early twelfth to
   late fifteenth centuries DLB-146

Middle English Literature:
   An Introduction DLB-146

The Middle English Lyric DLB-146

Morality Plays: *Mankind* circa 1450-1500
   and *Everyman* circa 1500 .... DLB-146

N-Town Plays circa 1468 to early
   sixteenth century DLB-146

Old English Literature:
   An Introduction DLB-146

Old English Riddles
   eighth to tenth centuries DLB-146

The Owl and the Nightingale
   circa 1189-1199 .... DLB-146

The Paston Letters 1422-1509 .... DLB-146

The Seafarer circa 970 .... DLB-146

The *South English Legendary* circa
   thirteenth to fifteenth centuries DLB-146

*The British Review and London Critical
   Journal* 1811-1825 .... DLB-110

Brito, Aristeo 1942- DLB-122

Brittain, Vera 1893-1970 .... DLB-191

Briusov, Valerii Iakovlevich
   1873-1924 .... DLB-295

Brizeux, Auguste 1803-1858 .... DLB-217

Broadway Publishing Company DLB-46

Broch, Hermann
   1886-1951 .... DLB-85, 124; CDWLB-2

Brochu, André 1942- DLB-53

Brock, Edwin 1927-1997 .... DLB-40

Brockes, Barthold Heinrich
   1680-1747 .... DLB-168

Brod, Max 1884-1968 .... DLB-81

Brodber, Erna 1940- DLB-157

Brodhead, John R. 1814-1873 .... DLB-30

Brodkey, Harold 1930-1996 .... DLB-130

Brodsky, Joseph (Iosif Aleksandrovich Brodsky)
   1940-1996 .... DLB-285, 329; Y-87
   Nobel Lecture 1987 .... Y-87

Brodsky, Michael 1948- DLB-244

Broeg, Bob 1918-2005 .... DLB-171

Brøgger, Suzanne 1944- DLB-214

Brome, Richard circa 1590-1652 .... DLB-58

Brome, Vincent 1910-2004 .... DLB-155

Bromfield, Louis 1896-1956 .... DLB-4, 9, 86

Bromige, David 1933- DLB-193

Broner, E. M. 1930- DLB-28
   Tribute to Bernard Malamud Y-86

Bronk, William 1918-1999 .... DLB-165

Bronnen, Arnolt 1895-1959 .... DLB-124

Brontë, Anne 1820-1849 .... DLB-21, 199, 340

Brontë, Branwell 1817-1848 .... DLB-340

Brontë, Charlotte 1816-1855
   .... DLB-21, 159, 199, 340; CDBLB-4

Brontë, Emily 1818-1848
   .... DLB-21, 32, 199, 340; CDBLB-4

The Brontë Society Y-98

Brook, Stephen 1947- DLB-204

Brook Farm 1841-1847 .... DLB-1; 223; DS-5

Brooke, Frances 1724-1789 .... DLB-39, 99

Brooke, Henry 1703?-1783 .... DLB-39

Brooke, L. Leslie 1862-1940 .... DLB-141

Brooke, Margaret, Ranee of Sarawak
   1849-1936 .... DLB-174

Brooke, Rupert
   1887-1915 .... DLB-19, 216; CDBLB-6
   The Friends of the Dymock Poets Y-00

Brooker, Bertram 1888-1955 .... DLB-88

Brooke-Rose, Christine 1923- DLB-14, 231

Brookner, Anita 1928- DLB-194, 326; Y-87

Brooks, Charles Timothy 1813-1883 ... DLB-1, 243

Brooks, Cleanth 1906-1994 .... DLB-63; Y-94
   Tribute to Katherine Anne Porter Y-80
   Tribute to Walker Percy Y-90

Brooks, Gwendolyn
   1917-2000 .... DLB-5, 76, 165; CDALB-1
   Tribute to Julian Mayfield Y-84

Brooks, Jeremy 1926-1994 .... DLB-14

Brooks, Mel 1926- DLB-26

Brooks, Noah 1830-1903 .... DLB-42; DS-13

Brooks, Richard 1912-1992 .... DLB-44

Brooks, Van Wyck 1886-1963 .... DLB-45, 63, 103

Brophy, Brigid 1929-1995 .... DLB-14, 70, 271

Brophy, John 1899-1965 .... DLB-191

Brorson, Hans Adolph 1694-1764 .... DLB-300

Brossard, Chandler 1922-1993 .... DLB-16

Brossard, Nicole 1943- DLB-53

Broster, Dorothy Kathleen 1877-1950 .... DLB-160

Brother Antoninus (see Everson, William)

Brotherton, Lord 1856-1930 .... DLB-184

Brougham, John 1810-1880 .... DLB-11

Brougham and Vaux, Henry Peter
   Brougham, Baron 1778-1868 .... DLB-110, 158

Broughton, James 1913-1999 .... DLB-5

Broughton, Rhoda 1840-1920 .... DLB-18

Broun, Heywood 1888-1939 .... DLB-29, 171

Browder, Earl 1891-1973 .... DLB-303

Brown, Alice 1856-1948 .... DLB-78

Brown, Bob 1886-1959 .... DLB-4, 45; DS-15

Brown, Cecil 1943- DLB-33

Brown, Charles Brockden 1771-1810
   .... DLB-37, 59, 73; CDALB-2

Cumulative Index

Brown, Christy 1932-1981 .... DLB-14

Brown, Dee 1908-2002 .... Y-80

Brown, Frank London 1927-1962 .... DLB-76

Brown, Fredric 1906-1972 .... DLB-8

Brown, George Mackay
1921-1996 .... DLB-14, 27, 139, 271

Brown, Harry 1917-1986 .... DLB-26

Brown, Ian 1945- DLB-310

Brown, Larry 1951- DLB-234, 292

Brown, Lew 1893-1958 .... DLB-265

Brown, Marcia 1918- DLB-61

Brown, Margaret Wise 1910-1952 ...... DLB-22

Brown, Morna Doris (see Ferrars, Elizabeth)

Brown, Oliver Madox 1855-1874 .... DLB-21

Brown, Sterling 1901-1989 ...... DLB-48, 51, 63

Brown, T. E. 1830-1897 .... DLB-35

Brown, Thomas Alexander (see Boldrewood, Rolf)

Brown, Warren 1894-1978 .... DLB-241

Brown, William Hill 1765-1793 .... DLB-37

Brown, William Wells
1815-1884 .... DLB-3, 50, 183, 248

Brown University
The Festival of Vanguard Narrative Y-93

Browne, Charles Farrar 1834-1867 ..... DLB-11

Browne, Frances 1816-1879 .... DLB-199

Browne, Francis Fisher 1843-1913 .... DLB-79

Browne, Howard 1908-1999 .... DLB-226

Browne, J. Ross 1821-1875 .... DLB-202

Browne, Michael Dennis 1940- DLB-40

Browne, Sir Thomas 1605-1682 .... DLB-151

Browne, William, of Tavistock
1590-1645 .... DLB-121

Browne, Wynyard 1911-1964 ...... DLB-13, 233

Browne and Nolan DLB-106

Brownell, W. C. 1851-1928 .... DLB-71

Browning, Elizabeth Barrett
1806-1861 .... DLB-32, 199; CDBLB-4

Browning, Robert
1812-1889 .... DLB-32, 163; CDBLB-4

Essay on Chatterton DLB-32

Introductory Essay: *Letters of Percy Bysshe Shelley* (1852) DLB-32

"The Novel in [Robert Browning's] 'The Ring and the Book'" (1912), by Henry James DLB-32

Brownjohn, Allan 1931- DLB-40

Tribute to John Betjeman Y-84

Brownson, Orestes Augustus
1803-1876 .... DLB-1, 59, 73, 243; DS-5

Bruccoli, Matthew J. 1931-2008 ...... DLB-103

Joseph [Heller] and George [V. Higgins] ... Y-99

Response [to Busch on Fitzgerald] Y-96

Tribute to Albert Erskine Y-93

Tribute to Charles E. Feinberg Y-88

Working with Fredson Bowers Y-91

Bruce, Charles 1906-1971 .... DLB-68

Bruce, John Edward 1856-1924

Three Documents [African American poets] DLB-50

Bruce, Leo 1903-1979 .... DLB-77

Bruce, Mary Grant 1878-1958 .... DLB-230

Bruce, Philip Alexander 1856-1933 .... DLB-47

Bruce-Novoa, Juan 1944- DLB-82

Bruchac, Joseph 1942- DLB-342

Bruckman, Clyde 1894-1955 .... DLB-26

Bruckner, Ferdinand 1891-1958 .... DLB-118

Brun, Johan Nordahl 1745-1816 .... DLB-354

Brundage, John Herbert (see Herbert, John)

Brunner, John 1934-1995 .... DLB-261

Tribute to Theodore Sturgeon Y-85

Brutus, Dennis
1924- DLB-117, 225; CDWLB-3

Bryan, C. D. B. 1936- DLB-185

Bryan, Judith 1964- DLB-347

Bryan, William Jennings 1860-1925 .... DLB-303

Bryant, Arthur 1899-1985 .... DLB-149

Bryant, William Cullen 1794-1878
.... DLB-3, 43, 59, 189, 250; CDALB-2

Bryce, James 1838-1922 .... DLB-166, 190

Bryce Echenique, Alfredo
1939- DLB-145; CDWLB-3

Bryden, Bill 1942- DLB-233

Brydges, Sir Samuel Egerton
1762-1837 .... DLB-107, 142

Bryskett, Lodowick 1546?-1612 .... DLB-167

Buchan, John 1875-1940 .... DLB-34, 70, 156

Buchanan, George 1506-1582 .... DLB-132

Buchanan, Robert 1841-1901 .... DLB-18, 35

"The Fleshly School of Poetry and Other Phenomena of the Day" (1872) DLB-35

"The Fleshly School of Poetry: Mr. D. G. Rossetti" (1871), by Thomas Maitland DLB-35

Buchler, Justus 1914-1991 .... DLB-279

Buchman, Sidney 1902-1975 .... DLB-26

Buchner, Augustus 1591-1661 .... DLB-164

Büchner, Georg
1813-1837 .... DLB-133; CDWLB-2

Bucholtz, Andreas Heinrich 1607-1671 ... DLB-168

Buck, Pearl S.
1892-1973 ...... DLB-9, 102, 329; CDALB-7

Bucke, Charles 1781-1846 .... DLB-110

Bucke, Richard Maurice 1837-1902 .... DLB-99

Buckingham, Edwin 1810-1833 .... DLB-73

Buckingham, Joseph Tinker 1779-1861 ... DLB-73

Buckler, Ernest 1908-1984 .... DLB-68

Buckley, Vincent 1925-1988 .... DLB-289

Buckley, William F., Jr.
1925-2008 .... DLB-137; Y-80

Publisher's Statement From the Initial Issue of *National Review* (19 November 1955) DLB-137

Buckminster, Joseph Stevens
1784-1812 .... DLB-37

Buckner, Robert 1906-1989 .... DLB-26

Buckstone, John Baldwin 1802-1879 .... DLB-344

Budd, Thomas ?-1698 .... DLB-24

Budé, Guillaume 1468-1540 .... DLB-327

Budrys, A. J. 1931- DLB-8

Buechner, Frederick 1926- Y-80

Buell, John 1927- DLB-53

Buenaventura, Enrique 1925-2003 ..... DLB-305

Bufalino, Gesualdo 1920-1996 .... DLB-196

Buffon, Georges-Louis Leclerc de
1707-1788 .... DLB-313

"Le Discours sur le style" DLB-314

Job Buffum [publishing house] DLB-49

Bugge, Sophus 1833-1907 .... DLB-354

Bugnet, Georges 1879-1981 .... DLB-92

al-Buhturi 821-897 .... DLB-311

Buies, Arthur 1840-1901 .... DLB-99

Bukiet, Melvin Jules 1953- DLB-299

Bukowski, Charles 1920-1994 .... DLB-5, 130, 169

Bulatović, Miodrag
1930-1991 .... DLB-181; CDWLB-4

Bulgakov, Mikhail Afanas'evich
1891-1940 .... DLB-272

Bulgarin, Faddei Venediktovich
1789-1859 .... DLB-198

Bulger, Bozeman 1877-1932 .... DLB-171

Bull, Olaf 1883-1933 .... DLB-297

Bullein, William
between 1520 and 1530-1576 .... DLB-167

Bullins, Ed 1935- DLB-7, 38, 249

Bulosan, Carlos 1911-1956 .... DLB-312

Bulwer, John 1606-1656 .... DLB-236

Bulwer-Lytton, Edward (also Edward Bulwer) 1803-1873 .... DLB-21

"On Art in Fiction" (1838) DLB-21

Bumpus, Jerry 1937- Y-81

Bunce and Brother DLB-49

Bunin, Ivan 1870-1953 .... DLB-317, 329

Bunner, H. C. 1855-1896 .... DLB-78, 79

Bunthanong Somsaiphon 1953- DLB-348

Bunting, Basil 1900-1985 .... DLB-20

Buntline, Ned (Edward Zane Carroll Judson) 1821-1886 .... DLB-186

Bunyan, John 1628-1688 .... DLB-39; CDBLB-2

The Author's Apology for His Book DLB-39

Buonarroti *il Giovane*, Michelangelo
1568-1646 .... DLB-339

Burch, Robert 1925- DLB-52

Burciaga, José Antonio 1940- DLB-82

Burdekin, Katharine (Murray Constantine)
1896-1963 ....DLB-255

Bürger, Gottfried August 1747-1794 ....DLB-94

Burgess, Anthony (John Anthony Burgess Wilson)
1917-1993 ......DLB-14, 194, 261; CDBLB-8

    The Anthony Burgess Archive at
the Harry Ransom Humanities
Research Center Y-98

    Anthony Burgess's *99 Novels:*
An Opinion Poll Y-84

Burgess, Gelett 1866-1951 ....DLB-11

Burgess, John W. 1844-1931 ....DLB-47

Burgess, Thornton W. 1874-1965 ....DLB-22

Burgess, Stringer and Company DLB-49

Burgos, Julia de 1914-1953 ....DLB-290

Burick, Si 1909-1986 ....DLB-171

Burk, John Daly circa 1772-1808 ....DLB-37

Burk, Ronnie 1955- DLB-209

Burke, Edmund 1729?-1797 ....DLB-104, 252, 336

Burke, James Lee 1936- DLB-226, 350

Burke, Johnny 1908-1964 ....DLB-265

Burke, Kenneth 1897-1993..........DLB-45, 63

Burke, Thomas 1886-1945 ....DLB-197

Burley, Dan 1907-1962..................DLB-241

Burley, W. J. 1914-2002 ....DLB-276

Burlingame, Edward Livermore
1848-1922 ....DLB-79

Burliuk, David 1882-1967 ....DLB-317

Burman, Carina 1960- DLB-257

Burnard, Bonnie 1945- DLB-334

Burnet, Gilbert 1643-1715 ....DLB-101

Burnett, Frances Hodgson
1849-1924 ....DLB-42, 141; DS-13, 14

Burnett, W. R. 1899-1982 ....DLB-9, 226

Burnett, Whit 1899-1973 ....DLB-137

Burney, Charles 1726-1814 ....DLB-336

Burney, Fanny 1752-1840................DLB-39

    Dedication, *The Wanderer* (1814) DLB-39

    Preface to *Evelina* (1778)...............DLB-39

Burns, Alan 1929- DLB-14, 194

Burns, Joanne 1945- DLB-289

Burns, John Horne 1916-1953.............Y-85

Burns, Robert 1759-1796 .....DLB-109; CDBLB-3

Burns and Oates DLB-106

Burnshaw, Stanley 1906-2005 ...... DLB-48; Y-97

    James Dickey and Stanley Burnshaw
Correspondence Y-02

    Review of Stanley Burnshaw: The
Collected Poems and Selected
Prose.........................Y-02

    Tribute to Robert Penn Warren Y-89

Burr, C. Chauncey 1815?-1883 ....DLB-79

Burr, Esther Edwards 1732-1758 ....DLB-200

Burroughs, Edgar Rice 1875-1950.........DLB-8

    The Burroughs Bibliophiles Y-98

Burroughs, John 1837-1921 .... DLB-64, 275

Burroughs, Margaret T. G. 1917- DLB-41

Burroughs, William S., Jr. 1947-1981 .....DLB-16

Burroughs, William Seward 1914-1997
............DLB-2, 8, 16, 152, 237; Y-81, 97

Burroway, Janet 1936- DLB-6

Burt, Maxwell Struthers
1882-1954 ....DLB-86; DS-16

A. L. Burt and Company................DLB-49

Burton, Hester 1913-2000 ....DLB-161

Burton, Isabel Arundell 1831-1896 ......DLB-166

Burton, Miles (see Rhode, John)

Burton, Richard Francis
1821-1890 ....DLB-55, 166, 184

Burton, Robert 1577-1640 ....DLB-151

Burton, Virginia Lee 1909-1968 ....DLB-22

Burton, William Evans 1804-1860........DLB-73

Burwell, Adam Hood 1790-1849 ....DLB-99

Bury, Lady Charlotte 1775-1861 ....DLB-116

Busch, Charles 1954- DLB-341

Busch, Frederick 1941-2006..........DLB-6, 218

    Excerpts from Frederick Busch's USC
Remarks [on F. Scott Fitzgerald] Y-96

    Tribute to James Laughlin.............Y-97

    Tribute to Raymond Carver Y-88

Busch, Niven 1903-1991 ....DLB-44

Busenello, Gian Francesco 1598-1659....DLB-339

Bushnell, Horace 1802-1876 ....DS-13

Business & Literature
    The Claims of Business and Literature:
An Undergraduate Essay by
Maxwell Perkins Y-01

Bussières, Arthur de 1877-1913 ....DLB-92

Butler, Charles circa 1560-1647 ....DLB-236

Butler, Guy 1918-2001................DLB-225

Butler, Joseph 1692-1752 ....DLB-252

Butler, Josephine Elizabeth 1828-1906....DLB-190

Butler, Juan 1942-1981................DLB-53

Butler, Judith 1956- DLB-246

Butler, Octavia E. 1947-2006 ....DLB-33

Butler, Pierce 1884-1953 ....DLB-187

Butler, Robert Olen 1945- DLB-173, 335

Butler, Samuel 1613-1680 ....DLB-101, 126

Butler, Samuel
1835-1902 ....DLB-18, 57, 174; CDBLB-5

Butler, William Francis 1838-1910.......DLB-166

E. H. Butler and Company DLB-49

Butor, Michel 1926- DLB-83

Nathaniel Butter
[publishing house] DLB-170

Butterworth, Hezekiah 1839-1905........DLB-42

Buttitta, Ignazio 1899-1997 ....DLB-114

Butts, Mary 1890-1937 ....DLB-240

Buzo, Alex 1944- DLB-289

Buzzati, Dino 1906-1972 ....DLB-177

Byars, Betsy 1928- DLB-52

Byatt, A. S. 1936- DLB-14, 194, 319, 326

Byles, Mather 1707-1788.................DLB-24

Henry Bynneman
[publishing house]................ DLB-170

Bynner, Witter 1881-1968 ....DLB-54

Byrd, William circa 1543-1623 .... DLB-172

Byrd, William, II 1674-1744......... DLB-24, 140

Byrne, John Keyes (see Leonard, Hugh)

Byron, George Gordon, Lord
1788-1824 ....DLB-96, 110; CDBLB-3

    The Byron Society of America Y-00

Byron, Henry J. 1834-1884 ....DLB-344

Byron, Robert 1905-1941 ....DLB-195

Byzantine Novel, The Spanish..........DLB-318

C

Caballero Bonald, José Manuel
1926- DLB-108

Cabañero, Eladio 1930-2000 ....DLB-134

Cabell, James Branch 1879-1958 ....DLB-9, 78

Cabeza de Baca, Manuel 1853-1915 .....DLB-122

Cabeza de Baca Gilbert, Fabiola
1898-1993 ....DLB-122

Cable, George Washington
1844-1925 .... DLB-12, 74; DS-13

Cable, Mildred 1878-1952 ....DLB-195

Cabral, Manuel del 1907-1999.........DLB-283

Cabral de Melo Neto, João
1920-1999 ....DLB-307

Cabrera, Lydia 1900-1991 ....DLB-145

Cabrera Infante, Guillermo
1929- DLB-113; CDWLB-3

Cabrujas, José Ignacio 1937-1995........DLB-305

Cadell [publishing house]...............DLB-154

Cady, Edwin H. 1917- DLB-103

Caedmon fl. 658-680.................DLB-146

Caedmon School circa 660-899 ....DLB-146

Caesar, Irving 1895-1996...............DLB-265

Cafés, Brasseries, and Bistros DS-15

Cage, John 1912-1992.................DLB-193

Cahan, Abraham 1860-1951 .... DLB-9, 25, 28

Cahn, Sammy 1913-1993 ....DLB-265

Cain, George 1943- DLB-33

Cain, James M. 1892-1977 ....DLB-226

Cain, Paul (Peter Ruric, George Sims)
1902-1966 ....DLB-306

Caird, Edward 1835-1908 ....DLB-262

Caird, Mona 1854-1932...............DLB-197

Čaklais, Māris 1940-2003 . . . . DLB-353
Čaks, Aleksandrs
   1901-1950 . . . . DLB-220; CDWLB-4
Caldecott, Randolph 1846-1886 . . . . DLB-163
John Calder Limited
   [Publishing house] DLB-112
Calderón de la Barca, Fanny
   1804-1882 . . . . DLB-183
Caldwell, Ben 1937- DLB-38
Caldwell, Erskine 1903-1987 . . . . DLB-9, 86
H. M. Caldwell Company DLB-49
Caldwell, Taylor 1900-1985 . . . . DS-17
Calhoun, John C. 1782-1850 . . . . DLB-3, 248
Călinescu, George 1899-1965 . . . . DLB-220
Calisher, Hortense 1911-2009 . . . . DLB-2, 218
Calkins, Mary Whiton 1863-1930 . . . . DLB-270
Callaghan, Mary Rose 1944- DLB-207
Callaghan, Morley 1903-1990 . . . . DLB-68; DS-15
Callahan, S. Alice 1868-1894 . . . . DLB-175, 221
Callaloo [journal] Y-87
Callimachus circa 305 B.C.-240 B.C. DLB-176
Calmer, Edgar 1907-1986 . . . . DLB-4
Calverley, C. S. 1831-1884 . . . . DLB-35
Calvert, George Henry
   1803-1889 . . . . DLB-1, 64, 248
Calverton, V. F. (George Goetz)
   1900-1940 . . . . DLB-303
Calvin, Jean 1509-1564 . . . . DLB-327
Calvino, Italo 1923-1985 . . . . DLB-196
Cambridge, Ada 1844-1926 . . . . DLB-230
Cambridge Press DLB-49
Cambridge Songs (Carmina Cantabrigensia)
   circa 1050 . . . . DLB-148
Cambridge University
   Cambridge and the Apostles DS-5
Cambridge University Press DLB-170
Camden, William 1551-1623 . . . . DLB-172
Camden House: An Interview with
   James Hardin Y-92
Cameron, Eleanor 1912-2000 . . . . DLB-52
Cameron, George Frederick
   1854-1885 . . . . DLB-99
Cameron, Lucy Lyttelton 1781-1858 . . . . DLB-163
Cameron, John (see Macdonell, A. G.)
Cameron, Peter 1959- DLB-234
Cameron, William Bleasdell 1862-1951 . . . DLB-99
Camm, John 1718-1778 . . . . DLB-31
Camões, Luís de 1524-1580 . . . . DLB-287
Camon, Ferdinando 1935- DLB-196
Camp, Walter 1859-1925 . . . . DLB-241
Campana, Dino 1885-1932 . . . . DLB-114
Campbell, Bebe Moore 1950-2006 . . . . . DLB-227
Campbell, David 1915-1979 . . . . DLB-260

Campbell, Gabrielle Margaret Vere
   (see Shearing, Joseph, and Bowen, Marjorie)
Campbell, James Dykes 1838-1895 . . . . . DLB-144
Campbell, James Edwin 1867-1896 . . . . . . DLB-50
Campbell, John 1653-1728 . . . . DLB-43
Campbell, John W., Jr. 1910-1971 . . . . DLB-8
Campbell, Ramsey 1946- DLB-261
Campbell, Robert 1927-2000 . . . . DLB-306
Campbell, Roy 1901-1957 . . . . DLB-20, 225
Campbell, Thomas 1777-1844 . . . . . . DLB-93, 144
Campbell, William Edward (see March, William)
Campbell, William Wilfred 1858-1918 . . . . DLB-92
Campion, Edmund 1539-1581 . . . . DLB-167
Campion, Thomas
   1567-1620 . . . . DLB-58, 172; CDBLB-1
Campo, Rafael 1964- DLB-282
Campton, David 1924-2006 . . . . DLB-245
Camus, Albert 1913-1960 . . . . . . DLB-72, 321, 329
Camus, Jean-Pierre 1584-1652 . . . . DLB-268
The Canadian Publishers' Records Database . . Y-96
Canby, Henry Seidel 1878-1961 . . . . DLB-91
Cancioneros DLB-286
Candelaria, Cordelia 1943- DLB-82
Candelaria, Nash 1928- DLB-82
Candide, Voltaire DLB-314
Canetti, Elias
   1905-1994 . . . . . DLB-85, 124, 329; CDWLB-2
Canham, Erwin Dain 1904-1982 . . . . DLB-127
Canin, Ethan 1960- DLB-335, 350
Canitz, Friedrich Rudolph Ludwig von
   1654-1699 . . . . DLB-168
Cankar, Ivan 1876-1918 . . . . . DLB-147; CDWLB-4
Cannan, Gilbert 1884-1955 . . . . DLB-10, 197
Cannan, Joanna 1896-1961 . . . . DLB-191
Cannell, Kathleen 1891-1974 . . . . DLB-4
Cannell, Skipwith 1887-1957 . . . . DLB-45
Canning, George 1770-1827 . . . . DLB-158
Cannon, Jimmy 1910-1973 . . . . DLB-171
Cano, Daniel 1947- DLB-209
   Old Dogs / New Tricks? New
   Technologies, the Canon, and the
   Structure of the Profession Y-02
Cantar de mio Cid circa 1200 . . . . DLB-337
Cantigas in the Galician-Portuguese
   Cancioneiros DLB-337
Cantú, Norma Elia 1947- DLB-209
Cantwell, Robert 1908-1978 . . . . DLB-9
Jonathan Cape and Harrison Smith
   [publishing house] DLB-46
Jonathan Cape Limited DLB-112
Čapek, Karel 1890-1938 . . . . DLB-215; CDWLB-4
Capen, Joseph 1658-1725 . . . . DLB-24
Capes, Bernard 1854-1918 . . . . DLB-156

Caponegro, Mary 1956- DLB-335
Capote, Truman 1924-1984
   . . . . DLB-2, 185, 227; Y-80, 84; CDALB-1
Capps, Benjamin 1922- DLB-256
Caproni, Giorgio 1912-1990 . . . . DLB-128
Caragiale, Mateiu Ioan 1885-1936 . . . . . . DLB-220
Carballido, Emilio 1925- DLB-305
Cardarelli, Vincenzo 1887-1959 . . . . DLB-114
Cardenal, Ernesto 1925- DLB-290
Cárdenas, Reyes 1948- DLB-122
Cardinal, Marie 1929-2001 . . . . DLB-83
Cardoso, Luís 1958- DLB-348
Cardoza y Aragón, Luis 1901-1992 . . . . . DLB-290
Carducci, Giosuè 1835-1907 . . . . DLB-329
Carew, Jan 1920- DLB-157
Carew, Thomas 1594 or 1595-1640 . . . . . DLB-126
Carey, Henry circa 1687-1689-1743 . . . . . . DLB-84
Carey, Mathew 1760-1839 . . . . DLB-37, 73
M. Carey and Company DLB-49
Carey, Peter 1943- DLB-289, 326
Carey and Hart DLB-49
Carlell, Lodowick 1602-1675 . . . . DLB-58
Carleton, William 1794-1869 . . . . DLB-159
G. W. Carleton [publishing house] DLB-49
Carlile, Richard 1790-1843 . . . . DLB-110, 158
Carlson, Ron 1947- DLB-244
Carlyle, Jane Welsh 1801-1866 . . . . DLB-55
Carlyle, Thomas
   1795-1881 . . . . . . DLB-55, 144, 338; CDBLB-3
   "The Hero as Man of Letters:
   Johnson, Rousseau, Burns"
   (1841) [excerpt] DLB-57
   The Hero as Poet. Dante; Shakspeare
   (1841) DLB-32
Carman, Bliss 1861-1929 . . . . DLB-92
Carmina Burana circa 1230 . . . . DLB-138
Carnap, Rudolf 1891-1970 . . . . DLB-270
Carnero, Guillermo 1947- DLB-108
Carossa, Hans 1878-1956 . . . . DLB-66
Carpenter, Humphrey
   1946-2005 . . . . DLB-155; Y-84, 99
Carpenter, Stephen Cullen ?-1820? DLB-73
Carpentier, Alejo
   1904-1980 . . . . DLB-113; CDWLB-3
Carr, Caleb 1955- DLB-350
Carr, Emily 1871-1945 . . . . DLB-68
Carr, John Dickson 1906-1977 . . . . DLB-306
Carr, Marina 1964- DLB-245
Carr, Virginia Spencer 1929- DLB-111; Y-00
Carrera Andrade, Jorge 1903-1978 . . . . . . DLB-283
Carrier, Roch 1937- DLB-53
Carrillo, Adolfo 1855-1926 . . . . DLB-122
Carroll, Gladys Hasty 1904-1999 . . . . DLB-9

Carroll, John 1735-1815................DLB-37
Carroll, John 1809-1884 ....DLB-99
Carroll, Lewis
    1832-1898......DLB-18, 163, 178; CDBLB-4
    The Lewis Carroll Centenary...........Y-98
    The Lewis Carroll Society
        of North America.................Y-00
Carroll, Paul 1927-1996................DLB-16
Carroll, Paul Vincent 1900-1968.........DLB-10
Carroll and Graf Publishers............DLB-46
Carruth, Hayden 1921-..........DLB-5, 165
    Tribute to James Dickey...............Y-97
    Tribute to Raymond Carver............Y-88
Carryl, Charles E. 1841-1920...........DLB-42
Carson, Anne 1950-................DLB-193
Carson, Rachel 1907-1964..............DLB-275
Carswell, Catherine 1879-1946..........DLB-36
Cartagena, Alfonso de circa 1384-1456...DLB-286
Cartagena, Teresa de 1425?-?.........DLB-286
Cărtărescu, Mirea 1956-..............DLB-232
Carte, Thomas 1686-1754..............DLB-336
Carter, Angela 1940-1992..DLB-14, 207, 261, 319
Carter, Elizabeth 1717-1806...........DLB-109
Carter, Henry (see Leslie, Frank)
Carter, Hodding, Jr. 1907-1972..........DLB-127
Carter, Jared 1939-.................DLB-282
Carter, John 1905-1975...............DLB-201
Carter, Landon 1710-1778..............DLB-31
Carter, Lin 1930-1988....................Y-81
Carter, Martin 1927-1997....DLB-117; CDWLB-3
Carter, Robert, and Brothers............DLB-49
Carter and Hendee....................DLB-49
Cartwright, Jim 1958-................DLB-245
Cartwright, John 1740-1824............DLB-158
Cartwright, William circa 1611-1643.....DLB-126
Caruthers, William Alexander
    1802-1846....................DLB-3, 248
Carver, Jonathan 1710-1780.............DLB-31
Carver, Raymond 1938-1988....DLB-130; Y-83,88
    First Strauss "Livings" Awarded to Cynthia
        Ozick and Raymond Carver
        An Interview with Raymond Carver...Y-83
Carvic, Heron 1917?-1980.............DLB-276
Cary, Alice 1820-1871................DLB-202
Cary, Joyce 1888-1957....DLB-15, 100; CDBLB-6
Cary, Patrick 1623?-1657.............DLB-131
Casal, Julián del 1863-1893............DLB-283
Case, John 1540-1600.................DLB-281
Casey, Gavin 1907-1964...............DLB-260
Casey, Juanita 1925-.................DLB-14
Casey, Michael 1947-...................DLB-5
Cassady, Carolyn 1923-...............DLB-16

"As I See It".........................DLB-16
Cassady, Neal 1926-1968...........DLB-16, 237
Cassell and Company..................DLB-106
Cassell Publishing Company............DLB-49
Cassill, R. V. 1919-2002.........DLB-6, 218; Y-02
    Tribute to James Dickey..............Y-97
Cassity, Turner 1929-...........DLB-105; Y-02
Cassius Dio circa 155/164-post 229......DLB-176
Cassola, Carlo 1917-1987..............DLB-177
Castellano, Olivia 1944-..............DLB-122
Castellanos, Rosario
    1925-1974........DLB-113, 290; CDWLB-3
Castelo Branco, Camilo 1825-1890......DLB-287
Castile, Protest Poetry in..............DLB-286
Castile and Aragon, Vernacular Translations
    in Crowns of 1352-1515...........DLB-286
Castillejo, Cristóbal de 1490?-1550......DLB-318
Castillo, Ana 1953-.............DLB-122, 227
Castillo, Rafael C. 1950-.............DLB-209
The Castle of Perserverance
    circa 1400-1425..................DLB-146
Castlemon, Harry (see Fosdick, Charles Austin)
Castro, Brian 1950-.................DLB-325
Castro, Consuelo de 1946-............DLB-307
Castro Alves, Antônio de 1847-1871.....DLB-307
Čašule, Kole 1921-..................DLB-181
Caswall, Edward 1814-1878..............DLB-32
Catacalos, Rosemary 1944-............DLB-122
Cather, Willa 1873-1947
    ....DLB-9, 54, 78, 256; DS-1; CDALB-3
    The Willa Cather Pioneer Memorial
        and Education Foundation........Y-00
Catherine II (Ekaterina Alekseevna), "The Great,"
    Empress of Russia 1729-1796.......DLB-150
Catherwood, Mary Hartwell 1847-1902...DLB-78
Catledge, Turner 1901-1983............DLB-127
Catlin, George 1796-1872..........DLB-186, 189
Cato the Elder 234 B.C.-149 B.C..........DLB-211
Cattafi, Bartolo 1922-1979............DLB-128
Catton, Bruce 1899-1978...............DLB-17
Catullus circa 84 B.C.-54 B.C.
    ....DLB-211; CDWLB-1
Causley, Charles 1917-2003.............DLB-27
Caute, David 1936-..............DLB-14, 231
Cavendish, Duchess of Newcastle,
    Margaret Lucas
    1623?-1673..........DLB-131, 252, 281
Cawein, Madison 1865-1914.............DLB-54
William Caxton [publishing house]......DLB-170
The Caxton Printers, Limited...........DLB-46
Caylor, O. P. 1849-1897...............DLB-241
Caylus, Marthe-Marguerite de
    1671-1729......................DLB-313
Cayrol, Jean 1911-2005................DLB-83

Cecil, Henry 1902-1976................DLB-352
Cecil, Lord David 1902-1986...........DLB-155
Cela, Camilo José
    1916-2002............DLB-322, 329; Y-89
    Nobel Lecture 1989..................Y-89
Celan, Paul 1920-1970.......DLB-69; CDWLB-2
Celati, Gianni 1937-.................DLB-196
Celaya, Gabriel 1911-1991.............DLB-108
Céline, Louis-Ferdinand 1894-1961........DLB-72
Celtis, Conrad 1459-1508..............DLB-179
Cendrars, Blaise 1887-1961............DLB-258
The Steinbeck Centennial.................Y-02
Censorship
    The Island Trees Case: A Symposium on
        School Library Censorship........Y-82
Center for Bibliographical Studies and
    Research at the University of
    California, Riverside.................Y-91
Center for Book Research................Y-84
The Center for the Book in the Library
    of Congress.........................Y-93
    A New Voice: The Center for the
        Book's First Five Years..........Y-83
Centlivre, Susanna 1669?-1723..........DLB-84
The Centre for Writing, Publishing and
    Printing History at the University
    of Reading..........................Y-00
The Century Company..................DLB-49
A Century of Poetry, a Lifetime of Collecting:
    J. M. Edelstein's Collection of
    Twentieth-Century American Poetry.....Y-02
Cernuda, Luis 1902-1963...............DLB-134
Cerruto, Oscar 1912-1981..............DLB-283
Cervantes, Lorna Dee 1954-............DLB-82
Césaire, Aimé 1913-.................DLB-321
de Céspedes, Alba 1911-1997...........DLB-264
Cetina, Gutierre de 1514-17?-1556......DLB-318
Ch., T. (see Marchenko, Anastasiia Iakovlevna)
Cha, Theresa Hak Kyung 1951-1982.....DLB-312
Chaadaev, Petr Iakovlevich
    1794-1856.......................DLB-198
Chabon, Michael 1963-...............DLB-278
Chacel, Rosa 1898-1994...........DLB-134, 322
Chacón, Eusebio 1869-1948.............DLB-82
Chacón, Felipe Maximiliano 1873-?......DLB-82
Chadwick, Henry 1824-1908............DLB-241
Chadwyck-Healey's Full-Text Literary Databases:
    Editing Commercial Databases of
    Primary Literary Texts...............Y-95
Challans, Eileen Mary (see Renault, Mary)
Chalmers, George 1742-1825............DLB-30
Chaloner, Sir Thomas 1520-1565.......DLB-167
Chamberlain, Samuel S. 1851-1916.......DLB-25
Chamberland, Paul 1939-..............DLB-60
Chamberlin, William Henry 1897-1969....DLB-29

Chambers, Charles Haddon 1860-1921 . . . DLB-10

Chambers, María Cristina (see Mena, María Cristina)

Chambers, Robert W. 1865-1933 . . . . DLB-202

W. and R. Chambers
[publishing house] DLB-106

Chambers, Whittaker 1901-1961 . . . . DLB-303

Chamfort, Sébastien-Roch Nicolas de
1740?-1794 . . . . DLB-313

Chamisso, Adelbert von 1781-1838 . . . . . . DLB-90

Champfleury 1821-1889 . . . . DLB-119

Champier, Symphorien 1472?-1539? DLB-327

Chan, Jeffery Paul 1942- DLB-312

Chandler, Harry 1864-1944 . . . . DLB-29

Chandler, Norman 1899-1973 . . . . DLB-127

Chandler, Otis 1927-2006 . . . . DLB-127

Chandler, Raymond
1888-1959 . . . DLB-226, 253; DS-6; CDALB-5

Raymond Chandler Centenary Y-88

Chang, Diana 1934- DLB-312

Channing, Edward 1856-1931 . . . . DLB-17

Channing, Edward Tyrrell
1790-1856 . . . . DLB-1, 59, 235

Channing, William Ellery
1780-1842 . . . . DLB-1, 59, 235

Channing, William Ellery, II
1817-1901 . . . . DLB-1, 223

Channing, William Henry
1810-1884 . . . . DLB-1, 59, 243

Chapelain, Jean 1595-1674 . . . . DLB-268

Chaplin, Charlie 1889-1977 . . . . DLB-44

Chaplin, Ralph 1887-1961 . . . . DLB-345

Chapman, George
1559 or 1560-1634 . . . . DLB-62, 121

Chapman, Olive Murray 1892-1977 . . . . . DLB-195

Chapman, R. W. 1881-1960 . . . . DLB-201

Chapman, William 1850-1917 . . . . DLB-99

John Chapman [publishing house] DLB-106

Chapman and Hall [publishing house] . . . DLB-106

Chappell, Fred 1936- DLB-6, 105

"A Detail in a Poem" DLB-105

Tribute to Peter Taylor Y-94

Chappell, William 1582-1649 . . . . DLB-236

Char, René 1907-1988 . . . . DLB-258

Charbonneau, Jean 1875-1960 . . . . DLB-92

Charbonneau, Robert 1911-1967 . . . . DLB-68

Charles, Gerda 1914-1996 . . . . DLB-14

William Charles [publishing house] DLB-49

Charles d'Orléans 1394-1465 . . . . DLB-208

Charley (see Mann, Charles)

Charrière, Isabelle de 1740-1805 . . . . DLB-313

Charskaia, Lidiia 1875-1937 . . . . DLB-295

Chart Korbjitti 1954- DLB-348

Charteris, Leslie 1907-1993 . . . . DLB-77

Chartier, Alain circa 1385-1430 . . . . DLB-208

Charyn, Jerome 1937- Y-83

Chase, Borden 1900-1971 . . . . DLB-26

Chase, Edna Woolman 1877-1957 . . . . . . DLB-91

Chase, James Hadley (René Raymond)
1906-1985 . . . . DLB-276

Chase, Mary Coyle 1907-1981 . . . . DLB-228

Chase-Riboud, Barbara 1936- DLB-33

Chateaubriand, François-René de
1768-1848 . . . . DLB-119

Châtelet, Gabrielle-Emilie Du
1706-1749 . . . . DLB-313

Chatterjee, Debjani 1952- DLB-347

Chatterjee, Upamanyu 1959- DLB-323

Chatterton, Thomas 1752-1770 . . . . DLB-109

Essay on Chatterton (1842), by
Robert Browning DLB-32

Chatto and Windus DLB-106

Chatwin, Bruce 1940-1989 . . . . DLB-194, 204

Chaucer, Geoffrey
1340?-1400 . . . . DLB-146; CDBLB-1

New Chaucer Society Y-00

Chaudhuri, Amit 1962- DLB-267, 323

Chaudhuri, Nirad C. 1897-1999 . . . . DLB-323

Chauncy, Charles 1705-1787 . . . . DLB-24

Chauveau, Pierre-Joseph-Olivier
1820-1890 . . . . DLB-99

Chávez, Denise 1948- DLB-122

Chávez, Fray Angélico 1910-1996 . . . . . . DLB-82

Chayefsky, Paddy 1923-1981 . . . . . DLB-7, 44; Y-81

Cheesman, Evelyn 1881-1969 . . . . DLB-195

Cheever, Ezekiel 1615-1708 . . . . DLB-24

Cheever, George Barrell 1807-1890 . . . . . . DLB-59

Cheever, John 1912-1982
. . . . DLB-2, 102, 227; Y-80, 82; CDALB-1

Cheever, Susan 1943- Y-82

Cheke, Sir John 1514-1557 . . . . DLB-132

Chekhov, Anton Pavlovich 1860-1904 . . . . DLB-277

Chelsea House DLB-46

Chênedollé, Charles de 1769-1833 . . . . . . DLB-217

Cheney, Brainard
Tribute to Caroline Gordon Y-81

Cheney, Ednah Dow 1824-1904 . . . . . . DLB-1, 223

Cheney, Harriet Vaughan 1796-1889 . . . . . DLB-99

Chénier, Marie-Joseph 1764-1811 . . . . . . DLB-192

Cheng Xiaoqing 1893-1976 . . . . DLB-328

Cherny, Sasha 1880-1932 . . . . DLB-317

Chernyshevsky, Nikolai Gavrilovich
1828-1889 . . . . DLB-238

Cherry, Kelly 1940- DLB-335; Y-83

Cherryh, C. J. 1942- DLB-335; Y-80

Chesebro', Caroline 1825-1873 . . . . DLB-202

Chesney, Sir George Tomkyns
1830-1895 . . . . DLB-190

Chesnut, Mary Boykin 1823-1886 . . . . . . DLB-239

Chesnutt, Charles Waddell
1858-1932 . . . . DLB-12, 50, 78

Chesson, Mrs. Nora (see Hopper, Nora)

Chester, Alfred 1928-1971 . . . . DLB-130

Chester, George Randolph 1869-1924 . . . DLB-78

The Chester Plays circa 1505-1532;
revisions until 1575 . . . . DLB-146

Chesterfield, Philip Dormer Stanhope,
Fourth Earl of 1694-1773 . . . . DLB-104

Chesterton, G. K. 1874-1936
. . . DLB-10, 19, 34, 70, 98, 149, 178; CDBLB-6

"The Ethics of Elfland" (1908) DLB-178

Chettle, Henry circa 1560-circa 1607 . . . . DLB-136

Cheuse, Alan 1940- DLB-244

Chew, Ada Nield 1870-1945 . . . . DLB-135

Cheyney, Edward P. 1861-1947 . . . . DLB-47

Chiabrera, Gabriello 1552-1638 . . . . DLB-339

Chiang Yee 1903-1977 . . . . DLB-312

Chiara, Piero 1913-1986 . . . . DLB-177

Chicanos
Chicano History DLB-82

Chicano Language DLB-82

Chicano Literature: A Bibliography . . . DLB-209

A Contemporary Flourescence of Chicano
Literature Y-84

Literatura Chicanesca: The View From
Without DLB-82

Child, Francis James 1825-1896 . . . DLB-1, 64, 235

Child, Lydia Maria 1802-1880 . . . . . DLB-1, 74, 243

Child, Philip 1898-1978 . . . . DLB-68

Childers, Erskine 1870-1922 . . . . DLB-70

Children's Literature
Afterword: Propaganda, Namby-Pamby,
and Some Books of Distinction . . . DLB-52

Children's Book Awards and Prizes . . . DLB-61

Children's Book Illustration in the
Twentieth Century DLB-61

Children's Illustrators, 1800-1880 . . . DLB-163

The Harry Potter Phenomenon Y-99

Pony Stories, Omnibus
Essay on DLB-160

The Reality of One Woman's Dream:
The de Grummond Children's
Literature Collection Y-99

School Stories, 1914-1960 . . . . DLB-160

The Year in Children's Books . . Y-92–96, 98–01

The Year in Children's Literature Y-97

Childress, Alice 1916-1994 . . . . DLB-7, 38, 249

Childress, Mark 1957- DLB-292

Childs, George W. 1829-1894 . . . . DLB-23

Chilton Book Company DLB-46

Chin, Frank 1940- DLB-206, 312

Chin, Justin 1969- DLB-312

Chin, Marilyn 1955- DLB-312

Chinweizu 1943- DLB-157

Chinnov, Igor' 1909-1996 . . . . DLB-317

Chitham, Edward 1932- DLB-155

Chittenden, Hiram Martin 1858-1917 . . . . . DLB-47

Chivers, Thomas Holley 1809-1858 . . . DLB-3, 248

Chkhartishvili, Grigorii Shalvovich
(see Akunin, Boris)

Chocano, José Santos 1875-1934 . . . . DLB-290

Cholmondeley, Mary 1859-1925 . . . . DLB-197

Chomsky, Noam 1928- DLB-246

Chopin, Kate 1850-1904 . . . DLB-12, 78; CDALB-3

Chopin, René 1885-1953 . . . . DLB-92

Choquette, Adrienne 1915-1973 . . . . DLB-68

Choquette, Robert 1905-1991 . . . . DLB-68

Choyce, Lesley 1951- DLB-251

Chrétien de Troyes
circa 1140-circa 1190 . . . . DLB-208

Christensen, Inger 1935-2009 . . . . DLB-214

Christensen, Lars Saabye 1953- DLB-297

The Christian Examiner DLB-1

The Christian Publishing Company DLB-49

Christie, Agatha
1890-1976 . . . . DLB-13, 77, 245; CDBLB-6

Christine de Pizan
circa 1365-circa 1431 . . . . DLB-208

Christopher, John (Sam Youd) 1922- . . . DLB-255

Christus und die Samariterin circa 950 . . . . . . DLB-148

Christy, Howard Chandler 1873-1952 . . . . DLB-188

Chu, Louis 1915-1970 . . . . DLB-312

Chukovskaia, Lidiia 1907-1996 . . . . DLB-302

Chulkov, Mikhail Dmitrievich
1743?-1792 . . . . DLB-150

Church, Benjamin 1734-1778 . . . . DLB-31

Church, Francis Pharcellus 1839-1906 . . . . . DLB-79

Church, Peggy Pond 1903-1986 . . . . DLB-212

Church, Richard 1893-1972 . . . . DLB-191

Church, William Conant 1836-1917 . . . . . . DLB-79

Churchill, Caryl 1938- DLB-13, 310

Churchill, Charles 1731-1764 . . . . DLB-109

Churchill, Winston 1871-1947 . . . . DLB-202

Churchill, Sir Winston
1874-1965 . . . DLB-100, 329; DS-16; CDBLB-5

Churchyard, Thomas 1520?-1604 . . . . DLB-132

E. Churton and Company DLB-106

Chute, Carolyn 1947- DLB-350

Chute, Marchette 1909-1994 . . . . DLB-103

Chwin, Stefan 1949- DLB-353

Ciampoli, Giovanni Battista
1590-1643 . . . . DLB-339

Ciardi, John 1916-1986 . . . . DLB-5; Y-86

Cibber, Colley 1671-1757 . . . . DLB-84

Cicero 106 B.C.-43 B.C. DLB-211, CDWLB-1

Cicognini, Giacinto Andrea
1606-1649 . . . . DLB-339

Cima, Annalisa 1941- DLB-128

Čingo, Živko 1935-1987 . . . . DLB-181

Cioran, E. M. 1911-1995 . . . . DLB-220

Čipkus, Alfonsas (see Nyka-Niliūnas, Alfonsas)

Cirese, Eugenio 1884-1955 . . . . DLB-114

Cīrulis, Jānis (see Bels, Alberts)

Cisneros, Antonio 1942- DLB-290

Cisneros, Sandra 1954- DLB-122, 152

City Lights Books DLB-46

Civil War (1861–1865)
Battles and Leaders of the Civil War DLB-47
Official Records of the Rebellion DLB-47
Recording the Civil War DLB-47

Cixous, Hélène 1937- DLB-83, 242

Claire d'Albe, Sophie Cottin DLB-314

Clampitt, Amy 1920-1994 . . . . DLB-105

Tribute to Alfred A. Knopf Y-84

Clancy, Tom 1947- DLB-227

Clapper, Raymond 1892-1944 . . . . DLB-29

Clare, John 1793-1864 . . . . DLB-55, 96

Clarendon, Edward Hyde, Earl of
1609-1674 . . . . DLB-101

Clark, Alfred Alexander Gordon (see Hare, Cyril)

Clark, Ann Nolan 1896-1995 . . . . DLB-52

Clark, C. E. Frazer, Jr. 1925-2001 . . DLB-187; Y-01

C. E. Frazer Clark Jr. and
Hawthorne Bibliography DLB-269

The Publications of C. E. Frazer
Clark Jr. DLB-269

Clark, Catherine Anthony 1892-1977 . . . . . DLB-68

Clark, Charles Heber 1841-1915 . . . . DLB-11

Clark, Davis Wasgatt 1812-1871 . . . . DLB-79

Clark, Douglas 1919-1993 . . . . DLB-276

Clark, Eleanor 1913-1996 . . . . DLB-6

Clark, J. P. 1935- DLB-117; CDWLB-3

Clark, Lewis Gaylord
1808-1873 . . . . DLB-3, 64, 73, 250

Clark, Mary Higgins 1929- DLB-306

Clark, Walter Van Tilburg
1909-1971 . . . . DLB-9, 206

Clark, William 1770-1838 . . . . DLB-183, 186

Clark, William Andrews, Jr.
1877-1934 . . . . DLB-187

C. M. Clark Publishing Company DLB-46

Clarke, Sir Arthur C. 1917-2008 . . . . DLB-261

Tribute to Theodore Sturgeon Y-85

Clarke, Austin 1896-1974 . . . . DLB-10, 20

Clarke, Austin C. 1934- DLB-53, 125

Clarke, George Elliott 1960- DLB-334

Clarke, Gillian 1937- DLB-40

Clarke, James Freeman
1810-1888 . . . . DLB-1, 59, 235; DS-5

Clarke, John circa 1596-1658 . . . . DLB-281

Clarke, Lindsay 1939- DLB-231

Clarke, Marcus 1846-1881 . . . . DLB-230

Clarke, Pauline 1921- DLB-161

Clarke, Rebecca Sophia 1833-1906 . . . . DLB-42

Clarke, Samuel 1675-1729 . . . . DLB-252

Robert Clarke and Company DLB-49

Clarkson, Thomas 1760-1846 . . . . DLB-158

Claudel, Paul 1868-1955 . . . . . . DLB-192, 258, 321

Claudius, Matthias 1740-1815 . . . . DLB-97

Clausen, Andy 1943- DLB-16

Claussen, Sophus 1865-1931 . . . . DLB-300

Clawson, John L. 1865-1933 . . . . DLB-187

Claxton, Remsen and Haffelfinger DLB-49

Clay, Cassius Marcellus 1810-1903 . . . . DLB-43

Clayton, Richard (see Haggard, William)

Cleage, Pearl 1948- DLB-228

Cleary, Beverly 1916- DLB-52

Cleary, Kate McPhelim 1863-1905 . . . . . . DLB-221

Cleaver, Vera 1919-1992 and
Cleaver, Bill 1920-1981 . . . . DLB-52

Cleese, John 1939- (see An A.B.C. of British
Scenario Writers)

Cleeve, Brian 1921-2003 . . . . DLB-276

Cleland, John 1710-1789 . . . . DLB-39

Clemens, Samuel Langhorne (Mark Twain)
1835-1910 . . . . DLB-11, 12, 23, 64, 74,
186, 189; CDALB-3

Comments From Authors and Scholars on
their First Reading of *Huck Finn* Y-85

Huck at 100: How Old Is
Huckleberry Finn? Y-85

Mark Twain on Perpetual Copyright Y-92

A New Edition of *Huck Finn* Y-85

Mark Twain's *Adventures of Huckleberry Finn*
(Documentary) DLB-343

Clement, Hal 1922-2003 . . . . DLB-8

Clemo, Jack 1916-1994 . . . . DLB-27

Clephane, Elizabeth Cecilia 1830-1869 . . . DLB-199

Cleveland, John 1613-1658 . . . . DLB-126

Cliff, Michelle 1946- DLB-157; CDWLB-3

Clifford, Lady Anne 1590-1676 . . . . DLB-151

Clifford, James L. 1901-1978 . . . . DLB-103

Clifford, Lucy 1853?-1929 . . . . . DLB-135, 141, 197

Clift, Charmian 1923-1969 . . . . DLB-260

Clifton, Lucille 1936- DLB-5, 41

Clines, Francis X. 1938- DLB-185

Clive, Caroline (V) 1801-1873 . . . . DLB-199

Edward J. Clode [publishing house] DLB-46

Clough, Arthur Hugh 1819-1861 . . . . DLB-32

Cloutier, Cécile 1930- DLB-60

Clouts, Sidney 1926-1982 . . . . DLB-225

Clutton-Brock, Arthur 1868-1924 . . . . DLB-98

Coates, Robert M. 1897-1973 .... DLB-4, 9, 102; DS-15

Coatsworth, Elizabeth 1893-1986 .... DLB-22

Cobb, Charles E., Jr. 1943- DLB-41

Cobb, Frank I. 1869-1923 .... DLB-25

Cobb, Irvin S. 1876-1944 .... DLB-11, 25, 86

Cobbe, Frances Power 1822-1904 .... DLB-190

Cobbett, William 1763-1835 ..... DLB-43, 107, 158

Cobbledick, Gordon 1898-1969 .... DLB-171

Cochran, Thomas C. 1902-1999 .... DLB-17

Cochrane, Elizabeth 1867-1922 ..... DLB-25, 189

Cockerell, Sir Sydney 1867-1962 .... DLB-201

Cockerill, John A. 1845-1896 .... DLB-23

Cocteau, Jean 1889-1963 ...... DLB-65, 258, 321

Coderre, Emile (see Jean Narrache)

Cody, Liza 1944- DLB-276

Coe, Jonathan 1961- DLB-231

Coetzee, J. M. 1940- DLB-225, 326, 329

Coffee, Lenore J. 1900?-1984 .... DLB-44

Coffin, Robert P. Tristram 1892-1955 .... DLB-45

Coghill, Mrs. Harry (see Walker, Anna Louisa)

Cogswell, Fred 1917-2004 .... DLB-60

Cogswell, Mason Fitch 1761-1830 .... DLB-37

Cohan, George M. 1878-1942 .... DLB-249

Cohen, Arthur A. 1928-1986 .... DLB-28

Cohen, Leonard 1934- DLB-53

Cohen, Matt 1942- DLB-53

Cohen, Morris Raphael 1880-1947 ...... DLB-270

Colasanti, Marina 1937- DLB-307

Colbeck, Norman 1903-1987 .... DLB-201

Colden, Cadwallader 1688-1776 ... DLB-24, 30, 270

Colden, Jane 1724-1766 .... DLB-200

Cole, Barry 1936- DLB-14

Cole, George Watson 1850-1939 .... DLB-140

Colegate, Isabel 1931- DLB-14, 231

Coleman, Emily Holmes 1899-1974 .... DLB-4

Coleman, Wanda 1946- DLB-130

Coleridge, Hartley 1796-1849 .... DLB-96

Coleridge, Mary 1861-1907 .... DLB-19, 98

Coleridge, Samuel Taylor 1772-1834 .... DLB-93, 107; CDBLB-3

Coleridge, Sara 1802-1852 .... DLB-199

Colet, John 1467-1519 .... DLB-132

Colette 1873-1954 .... DLB-65

Colette, Sidonie Gabrielle (see Colette)

Colinas, Antonio 1946- DLB-134

Coll, Joseph Clement 1881-1921 .... DLB-188

A Century of Poetry, a Lifetime of Collecting: J. M. Edelstein's Collection of Twentieth-Century American Poetry Y-02

Collett, Camilla 1813-1895 .... DLB-354

Collier, John 1901-1980 .... DLB-77, 255

Collier, John Payne 1789-1883 .... DLB-184

Collier, Mary 1690-1762 .... DLB-95

Collier, Robert J. 1876-1918 .... DLB-91

P. F. Collier [publishing house] DLB-49

Collin and Small DLB-49

Collingwood, R. G. 1889-1943 .... DLB-262

Collingwood, W. G. 1854-1932 .... DLB-149

Collins, An floruit circa 1653 .... DLB-131

Collins, Anthony 1676-1729 .... DLB-252, 336

Collins, Arthur 1681?-1762 .... DLB-336

Collins, Martha 1940- DLB-342

Collins, Merle 1950- DLB-157

Collins, Michael 1964- DLB-267

Collins, Michael (see Lynds, Dennis)

Collins, Mortimer 1827-1876 .... DLB-21, 35

Collins, Tom (see Furphy, Joseph)

Collins, Wilkie 1824-1889 ...... DLB-18, 70, 159; CDBLB-4

"The Unknown Public" (1858) [excerpt] DLB-57

The Wilkie Collins Society Y-98

Collins, William 1721-1759 .... DLB-109

Isaac Collins [publishing house] DLB-49

William Collins, Sons and Company DLB-154

Collis, Maurice 1889-1973 .... DLB-195

Collom, Jack 1931- DLB-342

Collyer, Mary 1716?-1763? DLB-39

Colman, Benjamin 1673-1747 .... DLB-24

Colman, George, the Elder 1732-1794 .... DLB-89

Colman, George, the Younger 1762-1836 .... DLB-89

S. Colman [publishing house] DLB-49

Colombo, John Robert 1936- DLB-53

Colonial Literature DLB-307

Colquhoun, Patrick 1745-1820 .... DLB-158

Colter, Cyrus 1910-2002 .... DLB-33

Colum, Padraic 1881-1972 .... DLB-19

The Columbia History of the American Novel A Symposium on Y-92

Columbus, Christopher 1451-1506 ..... DLB-318

Columella fl. first century A.D. DLB-211

Colvin, Sir Sidney 1845-1927 .... DLB-149

Colwin, Laurie 1944-1992 .... DLB-218; Y-80

Comden, Betty 1915- and Green, Adolph 1918-2002 ..... DLB-44, 265

Comi, Girolamo 1890-1968 .... DLB-114

Comisso, Giovanni 1895-1969 .... DLB-264

Commager, Henry Steele 1902-1998 ..... DLB-17

Commynes, Philippe de circa 1447-1511 .... DLB-208

Compton, D. G. 1930- DLB-261

Compton-Burnett, Ivy 1884?-1969 ...... DLB-36

Conan, Laure (Félicité Angers) 1845-1924 .... DLB-99

Concord, Massachusetts
Concord History and Life DLB-223

Concord: Literary History of a Town DLB-223

The Old Manse, by Hawthorne DLB-223

The Thoreauvian Pilgrimage: The Structure of an American Cult .. DLB-223

Concrete Poetry DLB-307

Conde, Carmen 1901-1996 .... DLB-108

Condillac, Etienne Bonnot de 1714-1780 .... DLB-313

Condorcet, Marie-Jean-Antoine-Nicolas Caritat, marquis de 1743-1794 .... DLB-313

"The Tenth Stage" DLB-314

Congreve, William 1670-1729 .... DLB-39, 84; CDBLB-2

Preface to *Incognita* (1692) DLB-39

W. B. Conkey Company DLB-49

Conlon, Evelyn 1952- DLB-319

Conn, Stewart 1936- DLB-233

Connell, Evan S., Jr. 1924- DLB-2, 335; Y-81

Connelly, Marc 1890-1980 .... DLB-7; Y-80

Connolly, Cyril 1903-1974 .... DLB-98

Connolly, James B. 1868-1957 .... DLB-78

Connor, Ralph (Charles William Gordon) 1860-1937 .... DLB-92

Connor, Tony 1930- DLB-40

Conquest, Robert 1917- DLB-27

Conrad, Joseph 1857-1924 .... DLB-10, 34, 98, 156; CDBLB-5

John Conrad and Company DLB-49

Conroy, Jack 1899-1990 .... Y-81

A Tribute [to Nelson Algren] Y-81

Conroy, Pat 1945- DLB-6

The Conservationist, 1974 Booker Prize winner, Nadine Gordimer DLB-326

Considine, Bob 1906-1975 .... DLB-241

Consolo, Vincenzo 1933- DLB-196

Constable, Henry 1562-1613 .... DLB-136

Archibald Constable and Company DLB-154

Constable and Company Limited DLB-112

Constant, Benjamin 1767-1830 .... DLB-119

Constant de Rebecque, Henri-Benjamin de (see Constant, Benjamin)

Constantine, David 1944- DLB-40

Constantine, Murray (see Burdekin, Katharine)

Constantin-Weyer, Maurice 1881-1964 .... DLB-92

Contempo (magazine)
Contempo Caravan: Kites in a Windstorm Y-85

The Continental Publishing Company DLB-49

A Conversation between William Riggan and Janette Turner Hospital Y-02

Conversations with Editors Y-95

Conway, Anne 1631-1679 . . . . .DLB-252

Conway, Moncure Daniel 1832-1907. . .DLB-1, 223

Cook, Ebenezer circa 1667-circa 1732 . . . . .DLB-24

Cook, Edward Tyas 1857-1919 . . . . .DLB-149

Cook, Eliza 1818-1889. . . . . .DLB-199

Cook, George Cram 1873-1924. . . . . .DLB-266

Cook, Michael 1933-1994 . . . . .DLB-53

David C. Cook Publishing Company DLB-49

Cooke, George Willis 1848-1923. . . . . .DLB-71

Cooke, John Esten 1830-1886 . . . . .DLB-3, 248

Cooke, Philip Pendleton
    1816-1850 . . . . .DLB-3, 59, 248

Cooke, Rose Terry 1827-1892 . . . . .DLB-12, 74

Increase Cooke and Company. DLB-49

Cook-Lynn, Elizabeth 1930- DLB-175

Coolbrith, Ina 1841-1928. . . . . .DLB-54, 186

Cooley, Dennis 1944- DLB-334

Cooley, Peter 1940- DLB-105

"Into the Mirror". DLB-105

Coolidge, Clark 1939- DLB-193

Coolidge, Susan (see Woolsey, Sarah Chauncy)

George Coolidge [publishing house] DLB-49

Coomaraswamy, Ananda 1877-1947 . . . . .DLB-323

Cooper, Anna Julia 1858-1964. . . . . .DLB-221

Cooper, Edith Emma (see Field, Michael)

Cooper, Giles 1918-1966 . . . . .DLB-13

Cooper, J. California 19??- DLB-212

Cooper, James Fenimore
    1789-1851 . . . . . . .DLB-3, 183, 250; CDALB-2

The Bicentennial of James Fenimore Cooper:
An International Celebration Y-89

The James Fenimore Cooper Society Y-01

Cooper, Kent 1880-1965 . . . . .DLB-29

Cooper, Susan 1935- DLB-161, 261

Cooper, Susan Fenimore 1813-1894. . . . . .DLB-239

William Cooper [publishing house] DLB-170

J. Coote [publishing house] DLB-154

Coover, Robert 1932- DLB-2, 227; Y-81

Tribute to Donald Barthelme Y-89

Tribute to Theodor Seuss Geisel. Y-91

Copeland and Day. DLB-49

Ćopić, Branko 1915-1984 . . . . .DLB-181

Copland, Robert 1470?-1548 . . . . .DLB-136

Coppard, A. E. 1878-1957 . . . . .DLB-162

Coppée, François 1842-1908 . . . . .DLB-217

Coppel, Alfred 1921-2004 . . . . .Y-83

Tribute to Jessamyn West Y-84

Coppola, Francis Ford 1939- DLB-44

Copway, George (Kah-ge-ga-gah-bowh)
    1818-1869 . . . . .DLB-175, 183

Copyright

The Development of the Author's
    Copyright in Britain DLB-154

The Digital Millennium Copyright Act:
Expanding Copyright Protection in
Cyberspace and Beyond. Y-98

Editorial: The Extension of Copyright Y-02

Mark Twain on Perpetual Copyright Y-92

Public Domain and the Violation
    of Texts. Y-97

The Question of American Copyright
    in the Nineteenth Century
Preface, by George Haven Putnam
The Evolution of Copyright, by
    Brander Matthews
Summary of Copyright Legislation in
    the United States, by R. R. Bowker
Analysis of the Provisions of the
    Copyright Law of 1891, by
    George Haven Putnam
The Contest for International Copyright,
    by George Haven Putnam
Cheap Books and Good Books,
    by Brander Matthews DLB-49

Writers and Their Copyright Holders:
    the WATCH Project. Y-94

Corazzini, Sergio 1886-1907 . . . . .DLB-114

Corbett, Richard 1582-1635 . . . . .DLB-121

Corbière, Tristan 1845-1875 . . . . .DLB-217

Corcoran, Barbara 1911- DLB-52

Cordelli, Franco 1943- DLB-196

Corelli, Marie 1855-1924. . . . . .DLB-34, 156

Corle, Edwin 1906-1956 . . . . .Y-85

Corman, Cid 1924-2004 . . . . .DLB-5, 193

Cormier, Robert 1925-2000. . . .DLB-52; CDALB-6

Tribute to Theodor Seuss Geisel. Y-91

Corn, Alfred 1943- DLB-120, 282; Y-80

Corneille, Pierre 1606-1684 . . . . .DLB-268

Cornford, Frances 1886-1960 . . . . .DLB-240

Cornish, Sam 1935- DLB-41

Cornish, William
    circa 1465-circa 1524. . . . . .DLB-132

Cornwall, Barry (see Procter, Bryan Waller)

Cornwallis, Sir William, the Younger
    circa 1579-1614 . . . . .DLB-151

Cornwell, David John Moore (see le Carré, John)

Cornwell, Patricia 1956- DLB-306

Coronel Urtecho, José 1906-1994 . . . . . . .DLB-290

Corpi, Lucha 1945- DLB-82

Corrington, John William
    1932-1988 . . . . .DLB-6, 244

Corriveau, Monique 1927-1976 . . . . .DLB-251

Corrothers, James D. 1869-1917 . . . . .DLB-50

Corso, Gregory 1930-2001 . . . . . .DLB-5, 16, 237

Cortázar, Julio 1914-1984 . . . DLB-113; CDWLB-3

Cortese, Giulio Cesare circa
    1570-1626? .DLB-339

Cortéz, Carlos 1923-2005 . . . . .DLB-209

Cortez, Jayne 1936- DLB-41

Corvinus, Gottlieb Siegmund 1677-1746 . . . .DLB-168

Corvo, Baron (see Rolfe, Frederick William)

Cory, Annie Sophie (see Cross, Victoria)

Cory, Desmond (Shaun Lloyd McCarthy)
    1928-2001 .DLB-276

Cory, William Johnson 1823-1892 . . . . . . .DLB-35

Coryate, Thomas 1577?-1617 . . . . . .DLB-151, 172

Ćosić, Dobrica 1921- DLB-181; CDWLB-4

Cosin, John 1595-1672. . . . . .DLB-151, 213

Cosmopolitan Book Corporation DLB-46

Cossa, Roberto 1934- DLB-305

Costa, Margherita 1600/1610?-1657 . . . . .DLB-339

Costa, Maria Velho da (see The Three Marias:
    A Landmark Case in Portuguese
    Literary History)

Costain, Thomas B. 1885-1965. . . . . .DLB-9

Coste, Donat (Daniel Boudreau)
    1912-1957 . . . . .DLB-88

Costello, Louisa Stuart 1799-1870 . . . . . . .DLB-166

Cota-Cárdenas, Margarita 1941- DLB-122

Côté, Denis 1954- DLB-251

Cotten, Bruce 1873-1954. . . . . .DLB-187

Cotter, Joseph Seamon, Jr. 1895-1919 . . . . .DLB-50

Cotter, Joseph Seamon, Sr. 1861-1949. . . . .DLB-50

Cottin, Sophie 1770-1807 . . . . .DLB-313

Claire d'Albe DLB-314

Joseph Cottle [publishing house] DLB-154

Cotton, Charles 1630-1687 . . . . .DLB-131

Cotton, John 1584-1652 . . . . .DLB-24

Cotton, Sir Robert Bruce 1571-1631 . . . . .DLB-213

Couani, Anna 1948- DLB-325

Coulter, John 1888-1980 . . . . .DLB-68

Coupland, Douglas 1961- DLB-334

Cournos, John 1881-1966 . . . . .DLB-54

Courteline, Georges 1858-1929 . . . . .DLB-192

Cousins, Margaret 1905-1996 . . . . .DLB-137

Cousins, Norman 1915-1990. . . . . .DLB-137

Couvreur, Jessie (see Tasma)

Coventry, Francis 1725-1754 . . . . .DLB-39

Dedication, *The History of Pompey
    the Little* (1751). DLB-39

Coverdale, Miles 1487 or 1488-1569. . . . .DLB-167

N. Coverly [publishing house] DLB-49

Covici-Friede DLB-46

Cowan, Peter 1914-2002 . . . . .DLB-260

Coward, Noel 1899-1973 . . .DLB-10, 245; CDBLB-6

Coward, McCann and Geoghegan DLB-46

Cowles, Gardner 1861-1946 . . . . .DLB-29

Cowles, Gardner "Mike", Jr.
    1903-1985 . . . . .DLB-127, 137

Cowley, Abraham 1618-1667 . . . . . .DLB-131, 151

Cowley, Hannah 1743-1809. . . . . .DLB-89

Cowley, Malcolm
    1898-1989 . . . . DLB-4, 48; DS-15; Y-81, 89

Cowper, Richard (John Middleton Murry Jr.)
   1926-2002 .... DLB-261
Cowper, William 1731-1800 ...... DLB-104, 109
Cox, A. B. (see Berkeley, Anthony)
Cox, James McMahon 1903-1974 ...... DLB-127
Cox, James Middleton 1870-1957 ...... DLB-127
Cox, Leonard circa 1495-circa 1550 ..... DLB-281
Cox, Palmer 1840-1924 .... DLB-42
Coxe, Louis 1918-1993 .... DLB-5
Coxe, Tench 1755-1824 .... DLB-37
Coyne, Joseph Stirling 1803-1868 ...... DLB-344
Cozzens, Frederick S. 1818-1869 ...... DLB-202
Cozzens, James Gould 1903-1978 ....
   .... DLB-9, 294; Y-84; DS-2; CDALB-1
   Cozzens's *Michael Scarlett* Y-97
   Ernest Hemingway's Reaction to
      James Gould Cozzens Y-98
   James Gould Cozzens—A View
      from Afar Y-97
   James Gould Cozzens: How to
      Read Him Y-97
   James Gould Cozzens Symposium and
      Exhibition at the University of
      South Carolina, Columbia Y-00
   Mens Rea (or Something) Y-97
   Novels for Grown-Ups Y-97
Crabbe, George 1754-1832 .... DLB-93
Crace, Jim 1946- DLB-231
Crackanthorpe, Hubert 1870-1896 ...... DLB-135
Craddock, Charles Egbert (see Murfree, Mary N.)
Cradock, Thomas 1718-1770 .... DLB-31
Craig, Daniel H. 1811-1895 .... DLB-43
Craik, Dinah Maria 1826-1887 ...... DLB-35, 163
Cramer, Richard Ben 1950- DLB-185
Cranch, Christopher Pearse
   1813-1892 .... DLB-1, 42, 243; DS-5
Crane, Hart 1899-1932 ..... DLB-4, 48; CDALB-4
   Nathan Asch Remembers Ford Madox
      Ford, Sam Roth, and Hart Crane Y-02
Crane, R. S. 1886-1967 .... DLB-63
Crane, Stephen
   1871-1900 .... DLB-12, 54, 78; CDALB-3
   Stephen Crane: A Revaluation, Virginia
      Tech Conference, 1989 .... Y-89
   The Stephen Crane Society Y-98, 01
Crane, Walter 1845-1915 .... DLB-163
Cranmer, Thomas 1489-1556 ...... DLB-132, 213
Crapsey, Adelaide 1878-1914 .... DLB-54
Crashaw, Richard 1612/1613-1649 ...... DLB-126
Crate, Joan 1953- DLB-334
Craven, Avery 1885-1980 .... DLB-17
Crawford, Charles 1752-circa 1815 ...... DLB-31
Crawford, F. Marion 1854-1909 .... DLB-71
Crawford, Isabel Valancy 1850-1887 ..... DLB-92
Crawley, Alan 1887-1975 .... DLB-68

Crayon, Geoffrey (see Irving, Washington)
Crayon, Porte (see Strother, David Hunter)
Creamer, Robert W. 1922- DLB-171
Creasey, John 1908-1973 .... DLB-77
Creative Age Press DLB-46
Creative Nonfiction Y-02
Crébillon, Claude-Prosper Jolyot de *fils*
   1707-1777 .... DLB-313
Crébillon, Claude-Prosper Jolyot de *père*
   1674-1762 .... DLB-313
William Creech [publishing house] DLB-154
Thomas Creede [publishing house] DLB-170
Creel, George 1876-1953 .... DLB-25
Creeley, Robert 1926-2005
   .... DLB-5, 16, 169; DS-17
Creelman, James
   1859-1915 .... DLB-23
Cregan, David 1931- DLB-13
Creighton, Donald 1902-1979 .... DLB-88
Crémazie, Octave 1827-1879 .... DLB-99
Crémer, Victoriano 1909?- DLB-108
Crenne, Hélisenne de (Marguerite de Briet)
   1510?-1560? DLB-327
Crescas, Hasdai circa 1340-1412? DLB-115
Crespo, Angel 1926-1995 .... DLB-134
Cresset Press DLB-112
Cresswell, Helen 1934- DLB-161
Crèvecoeur, Michel Guillaume Jean de
   1735-1813 .... DLB-37
Crewe, Candida 1964- DLB-207
Crews, Harry 1935- DLB-6, 143, 185
Crichton, Michael (John Lange, Jeffrey Hudson,
   Michael Douglas) 1942-2008 ..DLB-292; Y-81
Crispin, Edmund (Robert Bruce Montgomery)
   1921-1978 .... DLB-87
Cristofer, Michael 1946- DLB-7
Criticism
   Afro-American Literary Critics:
      An Introduction DLB-33
   The Consolidation of Opinion: Critical
      Responses to the Modernists DLB-36
   "Criticism in Relation to Novels"
      (1863), by G. H. Lewes DLB-21
   The Limits of Pluralism DLB-67
   Modern Critical Terms, Schools, and
      Movements DLB-67
   "Panic Among the Philistines":
      A Postscript, An Interview
      with Bryan Griffin Y-81
   The Recovery of Literature: Criticism
      in the 1990s: A Symposium Y-91
   The Stealthy School of Criticism (1871),
      by Dante Gabriel Rossetti DLB-35
Crnjanski, Miloš
   1893-1977 .... DLB-147; CDWLB-4
Crocker, Hannah Mather 1752-1829 .... DLB-200
Crockett, David (Davy)
   1786-1836 .... DLB-3, 11, 183, 248

Croft-Cooke, Rupert (see Bruce, Leo)
Crofts, Freeman Wills 1879-1957 .... DLB-77
Croker, John Wilson 1780-1857 .... DLB-110
Croly, George 1780-1860 .... DLB-159
Croly, Herbert 1869-1930 .... DLB-91
Croly, Jane Cunningham 1829-1901 ..... DLB-23
Crompton, Richmal 1890-1969 .... DLB-160
Cronin, A. J. 1896-1981 .... DLB-191
Cros, Charles 1842-1888 .... DLB-217
Crosby, Caresse 1892-1970 and
   Crosby, Harry 1898-1929 and .. DLB-4; DS-15
Crosby, Harry 1898-1929 .... DLB-48
Crosland, Camilla Toulmin (Mrs. Newton
   Crosland) 1812-1895 .... DLB-240
Cross, Amanda (Carolyn G. Heilbrun)
   1926-2003 .... DLB-306
Cross, Gillian 1945- DLB-161
Cross, Victoria 1868-1952 .... DLB-135, 197
Crossley-Holland, Kevin 1941- DLB-40, 161
Crothers, Rachel 1870-1958 .... DLB-7, 266
Thomas Y. Crowell Company DLB-49
Crowley, John 1942- Y-82
Crowley, Mart 1935- DLB-7, 266
Crown Publishers DLB-46
Crowne, John 1641-1712 .... DLB-80
Crowninshield, Edward Augustus
   1817-1859 .... DLB-140
Crowninshield, Frank 1872-1947 .... DLB-91
Croy, Homer 1883-1965 .... DLB-4
Crumley, James 1939-2008 .... DLB-226; Y-84
Cruse, Mary Anne 1825?-1910 .... DLB-239
Cruz, Migdalia 1958- DLB-249
Cruz, Sor Juana Inés de la 1651-1695 .... DLB-305
Cruz, Victor Hernández 1949- DLB-41
Cruz e Sousa, João 1861-1898 .... DLB-307
Csokor, Franz Theodor 1885-1969 ...... DLB-81
Csoóri, Sándor 1930- DLB-232; CDWLB-4
Cuadra, Pablo Antonio 1912-2002 ..... DLB-290
Cuala Press DLB-112
Cudworth, Ralph 1617-1688 .... DLB-252
Cueva, Juan de la 1543-1612 .... DLB-318
Cugoano, Quobna Ottabah 1797-? Y-02
Cullen, Countee
   1903-1946 .... DLB-4, 48, 51; CDALB-4
Culler, Jonathan D. 1944- DLB-67, 246
Cullinan, Elizabeth 1933- DLB-234
Culverwel, Nathaniel 1619?-1651? DLB-252
Cumberland, Richard 1732-1811 .... DLB-89
Cummings, Constance Gordon
   1837-1924 .... DLB-174
Cummings, E. E.
   1894-1962 .... DLB-4, 48; CDALB-5
   The E. E. Cummings Society Y-01

Cummings, Ray 1887-1957 . . . . .DLB-8

Cummings and Hilliard DLB-49

Cummins, Maria Susanna 1827-1866 . . . . .DLB-42

Cumpián, Carlos 1953- DLB-209

Cunard, Nancy 1896-1965. . . . . .DLB-240

Joseph Cundall [publishing house]. DLB-106

Cuney, Waring 1906-1976 . . . . .DLB-51

Cuney-Hare, Maude 1874-1936. . . . . .DLB-52

Cunha, Euclides da 1866-1909 . . . . .DLB-307

Cunningham, Allan 1784-1842 . . . . .DLB-116, 144

Cunningham, J. V. 1911-1985 . . . . .DLB-5

Cunningham, Michael 1952- DLB-292

Cunningham, Peter (Peter Lauder, Peter
  Benjamin) 1947- DLB-267

Peter F. Cunningham [publishing house]. . .DLB-49

Cunqueiro, Alvaro 1911-1981 . . . . .DLB-134

Cuomo, George 1929- Y-80

Cupples, Upham and Company DLB-49

Cupples and Leon DLB-46

Cuppy, Will 1884-1949 . . . . .DLB-11

Curiel, Barbara Brinson 1956- DLB-209

Curley, Daniel 1918-1988 . . . . .DLB-335

Edmund Curll [publishing house] DLB-154

Currie, James 1756-1805 . . . . .DLB-142

Currie, Mary Montgomerie Lamb Singleton,
  Lady Currie (see Fane, Violet)

Currie, Sheldon 1934- DLB-334

Cursor Mundi circa 1300 . . . . .DLB-146

Curti, Merle E. 1897-1996 . . . . .DLB-17

Curtis, Anthony 1926- DLB-155

Curtis, Cyrus H. K. 1850-1933 . . . . .DLB-91

Curtis, George William
  1824-1892 . . . . .DLB-1, 43, 223

Curzon, Robert 1810-1873. . . . . .DLB-166

Curzon, Sarah Anne 1833-1898. . . . . .DLB-99

Cusack, Dymphna 1902-1981 . . . . .DLB-260

Cushing, Eliza Lanesford 1794-1886 . . . . .DLB-99

Cushing, Harvey 1869-1939 . . . . .DLB-187

Custance, Olive (Lady Alfred Douglas)
  1874-1944 .DLB-240

Cynewulf circa 770-840 . . . . .DLB-146

Cyrano de Bergerac, Savinien de
  1619-1655 . . . . .DLB-268

Czepko, Daniel 1605-1660. . . . . .DLB-164

Czerniawski, Adam 1934- DLB-232

D

Dabit, Eugène 1898-1936. . . . . .DLB-65

Daborne, Robert circa 1580-1628 . . . . . . .DLB-58

Dąbrowska, Maria
  1889-1965 . . . . .DLB-215; CDWLB-4

Dabydeen, David 1955- DLB-347

Dacey, Philip 1939- DLB-105

"Eyes Across Centuries:
  Contemporary Poetry and 'That
  Vision Thing,'" DLB-105

Dach, Simon 1605-1659. . . . . .DLB-164

Dacier, Anne Le Fèvre 1647-1720. . . . . . .DLB-313

Dagerman, Stig 1923-1954. . . . . .DLB-259

Daggett, Rollin M. 1831-1901 . . . . .DLB-79

D'Aguiar, Fred 1960- DLB-157

Dahl, Roald 1916-1990 . . . . .DLB-139, 255

Tribute to Alfred A. Knopf Y-84

Dahlberg, Edward 1900-1977 . . . . .DLB-48

Dahn, Felix 1834-1912. . . . . .DLB-129

The Daily Worker DLB-303

Dal', Vladimir Ivanovich (Kazak Vladimir
  Lugansky) 1801-1872 . . . . .DLB-198

Dale, Peter 1938- DLB-40

Daley, Arthur 1904-1974 . . . . DLB-171

Dall, Caroline Healey 1822-1912. . . . .DLB-1, 235

Dallas, E. S. 1828-1879 . . . . .DLB-55

The Gay Science [excerpt](1866). DLB-21

The Dallas Theater Center DLB-7

D'Alton, Louis 1900-1951 . . . . .DLB-10

Dalton, Roque 1935-1975 . . . . .DLB-283

Daly, Carroll John 1889-1958 . . . . .DLB-226

Daly, T. A. 1871-1948 . . . . .DLB-11

Damon, S. Foster 1893-1971 . . . . .DLB-45

William S. Damrell [publishing house]. DLB-49

Dana, Charles A. 1819-1897 . . . . . .DLB-3, 23, 250

Dana, Richard Henry, Jr.
  1815-1882 . . . . .DLB-1, 183, 235

Danarto 1940- DLB-348

Dandridge, Ray Garfield 1882-1930 . . . . . .DLB-51

Dane, Clemence 1887-1965 . . . . .DLB-10, 197

Danforth, John 1660-1730 . . . . .DLB-24

Danforth, Samuel, I 1626-1674 . . . . .DLB-24

Danforth, Samuel, II 1666-1727. . . . . .DLB-24

Dangerous Acquaintances, Pierre-Ambroise-François
  Choderlos de Laclos DLB-314

Daniel, John M. 1825-1865 . . . . .DLB-43

Daniel, Samuel 1562 or 1563-1619 . . . . . . .DLB-62

Daniel Press DLB-106

Daniel', Iulii 1925-1988 . . . . .DLB-302

Daniells, Roy 1902-1979 . . . . .DLB-68

Daniels, Jim 1956- DLB-120

Daniels, Jonathan 1902-1981 . . . . .DLB-127

Daniels, Josephus 1862-1948 . . . . .DLB-29

Daniels, Sarah 1957- DLB-245

Danilevsky, Grigorii Petrovich
  1829-1890 . . . . .DLB-238

Dannay, Frederic 1905-1982 . . . . .DLB-137

Danner, Margaret Esse 1915-1984. . . . . . .DLB-41

Danojlić, Milovan 1937- DLB-353

John Danter [publishing house] DLB-170

Danticat, Edwidge 1969- DLB-350

Dantin, Louis (Eugene Seers)
  1865-1945 . . . . .DLB-92

Danto, Arthur C. 1924- DLB-279

Danzig, Allison 1898-1987. . . . . .DLB-171

D'Arcy, Ella circa 1857-1937. . . . . .DLB-135

Darío, Rubén 1867-1916 . . . . .DLB-290

Dark, Eleanor 1901-1985. . . . . .DLB-260

Darke, Nick 1948- DLB-233

Darley, Felix Octavious Carr
  1822-1888 . . . . .DLB-188

Darley, George 1795-1846 . . . . .DLB-96

Darmesteter, Madame James
  (see Robinson, A. Mary F.)

Darrow, Clarence 1857-1938 . . . . .DLB-303

Darwin, Charles 1809-1882. . . . . DLB-57, 166

Darwin, Erasmus 1731-1802 . . . . .DLB-93

Daryush, Elizabeth 1887-1977 . . . . .DLB-20

Das, Kamala 1934-2009. . . . . .DLB-323

Dashkova, Ekaterina Romanovna
  (née Vorontsova) 1743-1810 . . . . .DLB-150

Dashwood, Edmée Elizabeth Monica de la Pasture
  (see Delafield, E. M.)

Dass, Petter 1647-1707 . . . . .DLB-354

Dattani, Mahesh 1958- DLB-323

Daudet, Alphonse 1840-1897. . . . . .DLB-123

d'Aulaire, Edgar Parin 1898-1986 and
  d'Aulaire, Ingri 1904-1980. . . . . .DLB-22

Davenant, Sir William 1606-1668 . . . .DLB-58, 126

Davenport, Guy 1927-2005 . . . . .DLB-130

Tribute to John Gardner Y-82

Davenport, Marcia 1903-1996. . . . . DS-17

Davenport, Robert circa 17th century DLB-58

Daves, Delmer 1904-1977 . . . . .DLB-26

Davey, Frank 1940- DLB-53

Davidson, Avram 1923-1993 . . . . .DLB-8

Davidson, Donald 1893-1968 . . . . .DLB-45

Davidson, Donald 1917-2003. . . . . .DLB-279

Davidson, John 1857-1909 . . . . .DLB-19

Davidson, Lionel 1922- DLB-14, 276

Davidson, Robyn 1950- DLB-204

Davidson, Sara 1943- DLB-185

Davíð Stefánsson frá Fagraskógi
  1895-1964 . . . . .DLB-293

Davie, Donald 1922-1995 . . . . .DLB-27

Davie, Elspeth 1919-1995 . . . . .DLB-139

Davies, Sir John 1569-1626 . . . . .DLB-172

Davies, John, of Hereford 1565?-1618. . . .DLB-121

Davies, Rhys 1901-1978. . . . . .DLB-139, 191

Davies, Robertson 1913-1995 . . . . .DLB-68

Davies, Samuel 1723-1761 . . . . DLB-31

Davies, Thomas 1712?-1785 . . . . DLB-142, 154

Davies, W. H. 1871-1940 . . . . DLB-19, 174

Peter Davies Limited DLB-112

Davin, Nicholas Flood 1840?-1901 . . . . . . DLB-99

Daviot, Gordon 1896?-1952 . . . . DLB-10
(see also Tey, Josephine)

Davis, Arthur Hoey (see Rudd, Steele)

Davis, Benjamin J. 1903-1964 . . . . DLB-303

Davis, Charles A. (Major J. Downing)
1795-1867 . . . . DLB-11

Davis, Clyde Brion 1894-1962 . . . . DLB-9

Davis, Dick 1945- DLB-40, 282

Davis, Frank Marshall 1905-1987 . . . . DLB-51

Davis, H. L. 1894-1960 . . . . DLB-9, 206

Davis, Jack 1917-2000 . . . . DLB-325

Davis, John 1774-1854 . . . . DLB-37

Davis, Lydia 1947- DLB-130

Davis, Margaret Thomson 1926- DLB-14

Davis, Ossie 1917-2005 . . . . DLB-7, 38, 249

Davis, Owen 1874-1956 . . . . DLB-249

Davis, Paxton 1925-1994 . . . . Y-89

Davis, Rebecca Harding
1831-1910 . . . . DLB-74, 239

Davis, Richard Harding 1864-1916
. . . . DLB-12, 23, 78, 79, 189; DS-13

Davis, Samuel Cole 1764-1809 . . . . DLB-37

Davis, Samuel Post 1850-1918 . . . . DLB-202

Davison, Frank Dalby 1893-1970 . . . . DLB-260

Davison, Peter 1928- DLB-5

Davydov, Denis Vasil'evich
1784-1839 . . . . DLB-205

Davys, Mary 1674-1732 . . . . DLB-39

Preface to *The Works of Mrs. Davys*
(1725) DLB-39

DAW Books DLB-46

Dawe, Bruce 1930- DLB-289

Dawson, Ernest 1882-1947 . . . . DLB-140; Y-02

Dawson, Fielding 1930-2002 . . . . DLB-130

Dawson, Sarah Morgan 1842-1909 . . . . . DLB-239

Dawson, William 1704-1752 . . . . DLB-31

Day, Angel fl. 1583-1599 . . . . DLB-167, 236

Day, Benjamin Henry 1810-1889 . . . . DLB-43

Day, Clarence 1874-1935 . . . . DLB-11

Day, Dorothy 1897-1980 . . . . DLB-29

Day, Frank Parker 1881-1950 . . . . DLB-92

Day, John circa 1574-circa 1640 . . . . DLB-62

Day, Marele 1947- DLB-325

Day, Thomas 1748-1789 . . . . DLB-39

John Day [publishing house] DLB-170

The John Day Company DLB-46

Mahlon Day [publishing house] DLB-49

Day Lewis, C. (see Blake, Nicholas)

Dazai Osamu 1909-1948 . . . . DLB-182

Deacon, William Arthur 1890-1977 . . . . . . DLB-68

Deal, Borden 1922-1985 . . . . DLB-6

de Angeli, Marguerite 1889-1987 . . . . DLB-22

De Angelis, Milo 1951- DLB-128

Debord, Guy 1931-1994 . . . . DLB-296

De Bow, J. D. B. 1820-1867 . . . . DLB-3, 79, 248

Debs, Eugene V. 1855-1926 . . . . DLB-303

de Bruyn, Günter 1926- DLB-75

de Camp, L. Sprague 1907-2000 . . . . DLB-8

De Carlo, Andrea 1952- DLB-196

De Casas, Celso A. 1944- DLB-209

Dechert, Robert 1895-1975 . . . . DLB-187

Declaration of the Rights of Man and of
the Citizen DLB-314

Declaration of the Rights of Woman, Olympe
de Gouges DLB-314

de Cleyre, Voltairine 1866-1912 . . . . DLB-345

Dedications, Inscriptions, and
Annotations Y-01–02

De' Dottori, Carlo 1618-1686 . . . . DLB-339

Dee, John 1527-1608 or 1609 . . . . . DLB-136, 213

Deeping, George Warwick 1877-1950 . . . . DLB-153

Deffand, Marie de Vichy-Chamrond,
marquise Du 1696-1780 . . . . DLB-313

Defoe, Daniel
1660-1731 . . . DLB-39, 95, 101, 336; CDBLB-2

Preface to *Colonel Jack* (1722) DLB-39

Preface to *The Farther Adventures of
Robinson Crusoe* (1719) DLB-39

Preface to *Moll Flanders* (1722) DLB-39

Preface to *Robinson Crusoe* (1719) DLB-39

Preface to *Roxana* (1724) DLB-39

de Fontaine, Felix Gregory 1834-1896 . . . . DLB-43

De Forest, John William
1826-1906 . . . . DLB-12, 189

DeFrees, Madeline 1919- DLB-105

"The Poet's Kaleidoscope: The
Element of Surprise in the
Making of the Poem" DLB-105

DeGolyer, Everette Lee 1886-1956 . . . . . . DLB-187

de Graff, Robert 1895-1981 . . . . Y-81

de Graft, Joe 1924-1978 . . . . DLB-117

De Groen, Alma 1941- DLB-325

De Heinrico circa 980? DLB-148

Deighton, Len 1929- DLB-87; CDBLB-8

DeJong, Meindert 1906-1991 . . . . DLB-52

Dekker, Thomas
circa 1572-1632 . . . . . DLB-62, 172; CDBLB-1

Delacorte, George T., Jr. 1894-1991 . . . . . DLB-91

Delafield, E. M. 1890-1943 . . . . DLB-34

Delahaye, Guy (Guillaume Lahaise)
1888-1969 . . . . DLB-92

de la Mare, Walter 1873-1956
. . . . DLB-19, 153, 162, 255; CDBLB 6

Deland, Margaret 1857-1945 . . . . DLB-78

Delaney, Shelagh 1939- DLB-13; CDBLB-8

Delano, Amasa 1763-1823 . . . . DLB-183

Delany, Martin Robinson 1812-1885 . . . . . DLB-50

Delany, Samuel R. 1942- DLB-8, 33

de la Roche, Mazo 1879-1961 . . . . DLB-68

Delavigne, Jean François Casimir
1793-1843 . . . . DLB-192

Delbanco, Nicholas 1942- DLB-6, 234

Delblanc, Sven 1931-1992 . . . . DLB-257

Del Castillo, Ramón 1949- DLB-209

Deledda, Grazia 1871-1936 . . . . DLB-264, 329

De Lemene, Francesco 1634-1704 . . . . . . DLB-339

De Leon, Daniel 1852-1914 . . . . DLB-345

De León, Nephtal 1945- DLB-82

Deleuze, Gilles 1925-1995 . . . . DLB-296

Delfini, Antonio 1907-1963 . . . . DLB-264

Delfino, Giovanni 1617-1699 . . . . DLB-339

Delgado, Abelardo Barrientos
1931-2004 . . . . DLB-82

Del Giudice, Daniele 1949- DLB-196

De Libero, Libero 1906-1981 . . . . DLB-114

Delibes, Miguel 1920- DLB-322

Delicado, Francisco
circa 1475-circa 1540? DLB-318

DeLillo, Don 1936- DLB-6, 173

de Lint, Charles 1951- DLB-251

de Lisser H. G. 1878-1944 . . . . DLB-117

Dell, Floyd 1887-1969 . . . . DLB-9

Dell Publishing Company DLB-46

Della Valle, Federico circa 1560-1628 . . . . DLB-339

delle Grazie, Marie Eugene 1864-1931 . . . . DLB-81

Deloney, Thomas died 1600 . . . . DLB-167

Deloria, Ella C. 1889-1971 . . . . DLB-175

Deloria, Vine, Jr. 1933-2005 . . . . DLB-175

del Rey, Lester 1915-1993 . . . . DLB-8

Del Vecchio, John M. 1947- DS-9

Del'vig, Anton Antonovich 1798-1831 . . . DLB-205

de Man, Paul 1919-1983 . . . . DLB-67

DeMarinis, Rick 1934- DLB-218

Demby, William 1922- DLB-33

De Mille, James 1833-1880 . . . . DLB-99, 251

de Mille, William 1878-1955 . . . . DLB-266

Deming, Alison Hawthorne 1946- DLB-342

Deming, Barbara 1917-1984 . . . . DLB-345

Deming, Philander 1829-1915 . . . . DLB-74

Deml, Jakub 1878-1961 . . . . DLB-215

Demorest, William Jennings 1822-1895 . . . DLB-79

De Morgan, William 1839-1917 . . . . DLB-153

Demosthenes 384 B.C.-322 B.C. DLB-176

Henry Denham [publishing house] DLB-170

Denham, Sir John 1615-1669. . . . . . . .DLB-58, 126

Denison, Merrill 1893-1975 . . . . .DLB-92

T. S. Denison and Company DLB-49

Dennery, Adolphe Philippe
 1811-1899 . . . . .DLB-192

Dennie, Joseph 1768-1812 . . . . . DLB-37, 43, 59, 73

Dennis, C. J. 1876-1938 . . . . .DLB-260

Dennis, John 1658-1734. . . . . .DLB-101

Dennis, Nigel 1912-1989 . . . . .DLB-13, 15, 233

Denslow, W. W. 1856-1915 . . . . .DLB-188

Dent, J. M., and Sons. DLB-112

Dent, Lester 1904-1959 . . . . .DLB-306

Dent, Tom 1932-1998 . . . . .DLB-38

Denton, Daniel circa 1626-1703. . . . . .DLB-24

DePaola, Tomie 1934- DLB-61

De Quille, Dan 1829-1898. . . . . .DLB-186

De Quincey, Thomas
 1785-1859 . . . . .DLB-110, 144; CDBLB-3

 "Rhetoric" (1828; revised, 1859)
  [excerpt] .DLB-57

 "Style" (1840; revised, 1859)
  [excerpt] .DLB-57

Derby, George Horatio 1823-1861. . . . . . . .DLB-11

J. C. Derby and Company. DLB-49

Derby and Miller .DLB-49

De Ricci, Seymour 1881-1942 . . . . .DLB-201

Derleth, August 1909-1971 . . . . .DLB-9; DS-17

Derrida, Jacques 1930-2004 . . . . .DLB-242

The Derrydale Press DLB-46

Derzhavin, Gavriil Romanovich
 1743-1816 .DLB-150

Desai, Anita 1937- DLB-271, 323

Desani, G. V. 1909-2000 . . . . .DLB-323

Desaulniers, Gonzalve 1863-1934 . . . . .DLB-92

Desbordes-Valmore, Marceline
 1786-1859 .DLB-217

Descartes, René 1596-1650 . . . . .DLB-268

Deschamps, Emile 1791-1871 . . . . .DLB-217

Deschamps, Eustache 1340?-1404 . . . . . . .DLB-208

Desbiens, Jean-Paul 1927- DLB-53

des Forêts, Louis-Rene 1918-2001 . . . . .DLB-83

Deshpande, Shashi 1938- DLB-323

Desiato, Luca 1941- DLB-196

Desjardins, Marie-Catherine
 (see Villedieu, Madame de)

Desnica, Vladan 1905-1967 . . . . .DLB-181

Desnos, Robert 1900-1945. . . . . .DLB-258

Des Périers, Bonaventure
 1510?-1543? DLB-327

Desportes, Philippe 1546-1606. . . . . .DLB-327

DesRochers, Alfred 1901-1978. . . . . .DLB-68

Des Roches, Madeleine 1520?-1587? and
 Catherine des Roches 1542-1587?. DLB-327

Des Roches, Madeleine
 1520?-1587? DLB-327

Desrosiers, Léo-Paul 1896-1967. . . . . .DLB-68

Dessaulles, Louis-Antoine 1819-1895 . . . . .DLB-99

Dessì, Giuseppe 1909-1977 . . . . .DLB-177

Destouches, Louis-Ferdinand
 (see Céline, Louis-Ferdinand)

Desvignes, Lucette 1926- DLB-321

DeSylva, Buddy 1895-1950 . . . . .DLB-265

De Tabley, Lord 1835-1895 . . . . .DLB-35

Deutsch, Babette 1895-1982 . . . . .DLB-45

Deutsch, Niklaus Manuel
 (see Manuel, Niklaus)

André Deutsch Limited DLB-112

Devanny, Jean 1894-1962 . . . . .DLB-260

Deveaux, Alexis 1948- DLB-38

De Vere, Aubrey 1814-1902. . . . . .DLB-35

Devereux, second Earl of Essex, Robert
 1565-1601 .DLB-136

The Devin-Adair Company. DLB-46

De Vinne, Theodore Low 1828-1914 . . . .DLB-187

Devlin, Anne 1951- DLB-245

DeVoto, Bernard 1897-1955. . . . . .DLB-9, 256

De Vries, Peter 1910-1993 . . . . .DLB-6; Y-82

 Tribute to Albert Erskine Y-93

Dewart, Edward Hartley 1828-1903 . . . . . .DLB-99

Dewdney, Christopher 1951- DLB-60

Dewdney, Selwyn 1909-1979 . . . . .DLB-68

Dewey, John 1859-1952. . . . . .DLB-246, 270

Dewey, Orville 1794-1882 . . . . .DLB-243

Dewey, Thomas B. 1915-1981. . . . . .DLB-226

DeWitt, Robert M., Publisher DLB-49

DeWolfe, Fiske and Company. DLB-49

Dexter, Colin 1930- DLB-87

de Young, M. H. 1849-1925. . . . . .DLB-25

Dhlomo, H. I. E. 1903-1956 . . . . . . .DLB-157, 225

Dhu al-Rummah (Abu al-Harith Ghaylan ibn 'Uqbah)
 circa 696-circa 735. . . . . .DLB-311

Dhuoda circa 803-after 843 . . . . .DLB-148

The Dial 1840-1844 . . . . .DLB-223

The Dial Press DLB-46

"Dialogue entre un prêtre et un moribond,"
 Marquis de Sade DLB-314

Diamond, I. A. L. 1920-1988. . . . . .DLB-26

Dias Gomes, Alfredo 1922-1999 . . . . .DLB-307

Díaz del Castillo, Bernal
 circa 1496-1584. . . . . .DLB-318

Dibble, L. Grace 1902-1998. . . . . .DLB-204

Dibdin, Charles the Younger
 1768-1833 .DLB-344

Dibdin, Thomas 1771-1841 . . . . .DLB-344

Dibdin, Thomas Frognall 1776-1847 . . . . .DLB-184

Di Cicco, Pier Giorgio 1949- DLB-60

Dick, Philip K. 1928-1982 . . . . .DLB-8

Dick and Fitzgerald DLB-49

Dickens, Charles 1812-1870
 . . .DLB-21, 55, 70, 159, 166; DS-5; CDBLB-4

Dickey, Eric Jerome 1961- DLB-292

Dickey, James 1923-1997. . . . . . . DLB-5, 193, 342;
 Y-82, 93, 96, 97; DS-7, 19; CDALB-6

 James Dickey and Stanley Burnshaw
  Correspondence Y-02

 James Dickey at Seventy–A Tribute Y-93

 James Dickey, American Poet Y-96

 The James Dickey Society. Y-99

 The Life of James Dickey: A Lecture to
  the Friends of the Emory Libraries,
  by Henry Hart Y-98

 Tribute to Archibald MacLeish Y-82

 Tribute to Malcolm Cowley Y-89

 Tribute to Truman Capote Y-84

 Tributes [to Dickey]. Y-97

Dickey, William 1928-1994 . . . . .DLB-5

Dickinson, Emily
 1830-1886 . . . . .DLB-1, 243; CDALB-3

Dickinson, John 1732-1808 . . . . .DLB-31

Dickinson, Jonathan 1688-1747 . . . . .DLB-24

Dickinson, Patric 1914-1994 . . . . .DLB-27

Dickinson, Peter 1927- DLB-87, 161, 276

John Dicks [publishing house] DLB-106

Dickson, Gordon R. 1923-2001. . . . . .DLB-8

Dictionary of Literary Biography
 Annual Awards for *Dictionary of
 Literary Biography* Editors and
 Contributors. Y-98–02

*Dictionary of Literary Biography
 Yearbook* Awards Y-92–93, 97–02

The Dictionary of National Biography DLB-144

Diderot, Denis 1713-1784. . . . . .DLB-313

 "The Encyclopedia" DLB-314

Didion, Joan 1934-
 . . . . DLB-2, 173, 185; Y-81, 86; CDALB-6

Di Donato, Pietro 1911-1992. . . . . .DLB-9

Die Fürstliche Bibliothek Corvey Y-96

Diego, Gerardo 1896-1987. . . . . .DLB-134

Dietz, Howard 1896-1983 . . . . .DLB-265

Díez, Luis Mateo 1942- DLB-322

Digby, Everard 1550?-1605 . . . . .DLB-281

Digges, Thomas circa 1546-1595. . . . . . . .DLB-136

The Digital Millennium Copyright Act:
 Expanding Copyright Protection in
 Cyberspace and Beyond Y-98

Diktonius, Elmer 1896-1961 . . . . .DLB-259

Dillard, Annie 1945- DLB-275, 278; Y-80

Dillard, R. H. W. 1937- DLB-5, 244

Charles T. Dillingham Company. DLB-49

G. W. Dillingham Company. DLB-49

Cumulative Index

Edward and Charles Dilly
   [publishing house] DLB-154
Dilthey, Wilhelm 1833-1911 .... DLB-129
Dimić, Moma 1944-2008 .... DLB-353
Dimitrova, Blaga 1922- ... DLB-181; CDWLB-4
Dimov, Dimitr 1909-1966 .... DLB-181
Dimsdale, Thomas J. 1831?-1866 ...... DLB-186
Dinescu, Mircea 1950- DLB-232
Dinesen, Isak (see Blixen, Karen)
Ding Ling 1904-1986 .... DLB-328
Dingelstedt, Franz von 1814-1881 ...... DLB-133
Dini, Nh. 1936- DLB-348
Dinis, Júlio (Joaquim Guilherme
   Gomes Coelho) 1839-1871 .... DLB-287
Dintenfass, Mark 1941- Y-84
Diogenes, Jr. (see Brougham, John)
Diogenes Laertius circa 200 .... DLB-176
DiPrima, Diane 1934- DLB-5, 16
Disch, Thomas M. 1940-2008 ...... DLB-8, 282
"Le Discours sur le style," Georges-Louis Leclerc
   de Buffon DLB-314
Disgrace, 1999 Booker Prize winner,
   J. M. Coetzee DLB-326
Diski, Jenny 1947- DLB-271
Disney, Walt 1901-1966 .... DLB-22
Disraeli, Benjamin 1804-1881 .... DLB-21, 55
D'Israeli, Isaac 1766-1848 .... DLB-107
DLB Award for Distinguished
   Literary Criticism Y-02
Ditlevsen, Tove 1917-1976 .... DLB-214
Ditzen, Rudolf (see Fallada, Hans)
Divakaruni, Chitra Banerjee 1956- DLB-323
Dix, Dorothea Lynde 1802-1887 ..... DLB-1, 235
Dix, Dorothy (see Gilmer, Elizabeth Meriwether)
Dix, Edwards and Company DLB-49
Dix, Gertrude circa 1874-? DLB-197
Dixie, Florence Douglas 1857-1905 ..... DLB-174
Dixon, Ella Hepworth
   1855 or 1857-1932 .... DLB-197
Dixon, Paige (see Corcoran, Barbara)
Dixon, Richard Watson 1833-1900 ..... DLB-19
Dixon, Stephen 1936- DLB-130
Djebar, Assia (Fatima-Zohra Imalayène)
   1936- DLB-346
DLB Award for Distinguished
   Literary Criticism Y-02
Dmitriev, Andrei Viktorovich 1956- DLB-285
Dmitriev, Ivan Ivanovich 1760-1837 ..... DLB-150
Dobell, Bertram 1842-1914 .... DLB-184
Dobell, Sydney 1824-1874 .... DLB-32
Dobie, J. Frank 1888-1964 .... DLB-212
Dobles Yzaguirre, Julieta 1943- DLB-283
Döblin, Alfred 1878-1957 ..... DLB-66; CDWLB-2

Dobroliubov, Nikolai Aleksandrovich
   1836-1861 .... DLB-277
Dobson, Austin 1840-1921 .... DLB-35, 144
Dobson, Rosemary 1920- DLB-260
Doctorow, E. L.
   1931- DLB-2, 28, 173; Y-80; CDALB-6
Dodd, Susan M. 1946- DLB-244
Dodd, William E. 1869-1940 .... DLB-17
Anne Dodd [publishing house] DLB-154
Dodd, Mead and Company DLB-49
Doderer, Heimito von 1896-1966 .... DLB-85
B. W. Dodge and Company DLB-46
Dodge, Mary Abigail 1833-1896 ...... DLB-221
Dodge, Mary Mapes
   1831?-1905 .... DLB-42, 79; DS-13
Dodge Publishing Company DLB-49
Dodgson, Charles Lutwidge (see Carroll, Lewis)
Dodsley, Robert 1703-1764 .... DLB-95
R. Dodsley [publishing house] DLB-154
Dodson, Owen 1914-1983 .... DLB-76
Dodwell, Christina 1951- DLB-204
Doesticks, Q. K. Philander, P. B.
   (see Thomson, Mortimer)
Doheny, Carrie Estelle 1875-1958 ...... DLB-140
Doherty, John 1798?-1854 .... DLB-190
Doig, Ivan 1939- DLB-206
Doinaş, Ştefan Augustin 1922- DLB-232
Dokmai Sot 1905-1963 .... DLB-348
Dolet, Etienne 1509-1546 .... DLB-327
Domínguez, Sylvia Maida 1935- DLB-122
Donaghy, Michael 1954- DLB-282
Patrick Donahoe [publishing house] DLB-49
Donald, David H. 1920- DLB-17; Y-87
Donaldson, Scott 1928- DLB-111
La doncella Theodor late-thirteenth or fourteenth
   century DLB-337
Doni, Rodolfo 1919- DLB-177
Donleavy, J. P. 1926- DLB-6, 173
Donnadieu, Marguerite (see Duras, Marguerite)
Donne, John
   1572-1631 .... DLB-121, 151; CDBLB-1
Donnelly, Ignatius 1831-1901 .... DLB-12
R. R. Donnelley and Sons Company DLB-49
Donoghue, Emma 1969- DLB-267
Donohue and Henneberry DLB-49
Donoso, José 1924-1996 ..... DLB-113; CDWLB-3
M. Doolady [publishing house] DLB-49
Dooley, Ebon (see Ebon)
Doolittle, Hilda 1886-1961 ..... DLB-4, 45; DS-15
Doplicher, Fabio 1938- DLB-128
Dor, Milo 1923-2005 .... DLB-85
George H. Doran Company DLB-46

Dorat, Jean 1508-1588 .... DLB-327
Dorcey, Mary 1950- DLB-319
Dorgelès, Roland 1886-1973 .... DLB-65
Dorn, Edward 1929-1999 .... DLB-5
Dorr, Rheta Childe 1866-1948 .... DLB-25
Dorris, Michael 1945-1997 .... DLB-175
Dorset and Middlesex, Charles Sackville,
   Lord Buckhurst, Earl of 1643-1706 ... DLB-131
Dorsey, Candas Jane 1952- DLB-251
Dorst, Tankred 1925- DLB-75, 124
Dos Passos, John 1896-1970
   .... DLB-4, 9, 316; DS-1, 15; CDALB-5
   John Dos Passos: A Centennial
      Commemoration Y-96
   John Dos Passos: Artist Y-99
   John Dos Passos Newsletter Y-00
   U.S.A. (Documentary) DLB-274
Dostoevsky, Fyodor 1821-1881 .... DLB-238
Doubiago, Sharon 1946- DLB-342
Doubleday and Company DLB-49
Doubrovsky, Serge 1928- DLB-299
Dougall, Lily 1858-1923 .... DLB-92
Doughty, Charles M. 1843-1926 .. DLB-19, 57, 174
Douglas, Lady Alfred (see Custance, Olive)
Douglas, Ellen (Josephine Ayres Haxton)
   1921- DLB-292
Douglas, Gavin 1476-1522 .... DLB-132
Douglas, Keith 1920-1944 .... DLB-27
Douglas, Norman 1868-1952 ...... DLB-34, 195
Douglass, Frederick 1817-1895
   .... DLB-1, 43, 50, 79, 243; CDALB-2
   Frederick Douglass Creative Arts Center. Y-01
Douglass, William circa 1691-1752 ..... DLB-24
Dourado, Autran 1926- DLB-145, 307
Dove, Arthur G. 1880-1946 .... DLB-188
Dove, Rita 1952- DLB-120; CDALB-7
Dover Publications DLB-46
Doves Press DLB-112
Dovlatov, Sergei Donatovich
   1941-1990 .... DLB-285
Dowden, Edward 1843-1913 .... DLB-35, 149
Dowell, Coleman 1925-1985 .... DLB-130
Dowland, John 1563-1626 .... DLB-172
Downes, Gwladys 1915- DLB-88
Downing, J., Major (see Davis, Charles A.)
Downing, Major Jack (see Smith, Seba)
Dowriche, Anne
   before 1560-after 1613 .... DLB-172
Dowson, Ernest 1867-1900 .... DLB-19, 135
William Doxey [publishing house] DLB-49
Doyle, Sir Arthur Conan
   1859-1930 ... DLB-18, 70, 156, 178; CDBLB-5
   The Priory Scholars of New York Y-99

Doyle, Kirby 1932-2003 . . . . DLB-16

Doyle, Roddy 1958- DLB-194, 326

Drabble, Margaret
    1939- DLB-14, 155, 231; CDBLB-8

    Tribute to Graham Greene Y-91

Drach, Albert 1902-1995 . . . . .DLB-85

Drachmann, Holger 1846-1908 . . . . .DLB-300

Dracula (Documentary) DLB-304

Dragojević, Danijel 1934- DLB-181

Dragún, Osvaldo 1929-1999 . . . . .DLB-305

Drake, Samuel Gardner 1798-1875 . . . . . .DLB-187

Drakulić, Slavenka 1949- DLB-353

Drama (*See* Theater)

The Dramatic Publishing Company DLB-49

Dramatists Play Service DLB-46

Drant, Thomas early 1540s?-1578 . . . . . .DLB-167

Draper, John W. 1811-1882 . . . . .DLB-30

Draper, Lyman C. 1815-1891 . . . . .DLB-30

Drayton, Michael 1563-1631 . . . . .DLB-121

Dreiser, Theodore 1871-1945
    . . . . DLB-9, 12, 102, 137; DS-1; CDALB-3

    The International Theodore Dreiser
        Society Y-01

    Notes from the Underground
        of *Sister Carrie* Y-01

Dresser, Davis 1904-1977 . . . . .DLB-226

Drew, Elizabeth A.
    "A Note on Technique" [excerpt]
    (1926) DLB-36

Drewe, Robert 1943- DLB-325

Drewitz, Ingeborg 1923-1986 . . . . .DLB-75

Drieu La Rochelle, Pierre 1893-1945 . . . . .DLB-72

Drinker, Elizabeth 1735-1807 . . . . .DLB-200

Drinkwater, John 1882-1937 . . . . . DLB-10, 19, 149

    The Friends of the Dymock Poets Y-00

Dropkin, Celia (Tsilye Dropkin)
    1887-1956 . . . . .DLB-333

Droste-Hülshoff, Annette von
    1797-1848 . . . . DLB-133; CDWLB-2

The Drue Heinz Literature Prize
    Excerpt from "Excerpts from a Report
    of the Commission," in David
    Bosworth's *The Death of Descartes*
    An Interview with David Bosworth Y-82

Drummond, William, of Hawthornden
    1585-1649 . . . . .DLB-121, 213

Drummond, William Henry 1854-1907 . . . .DLB-92

Drummond de Andrade, Carlos
    1902-1987 . . . . .DLB-307

Druzhinin, Aleksandr Vasil'evich
    1824-1864 . . . . .DLB-238

Druzhnikov, Yuri 1933- DLB-317

Dryden, Charles 1860?-1931 . . . . .DLB-171

Dryden, John
    1631-1700 . . . . . .DLB-80, 101, 131; CDBLB-2

Držić, Marin
    circa 1508-1567 . . . . .DLB-147; CDWLB-4

Duane, William 1760-1835 . . . . .DLB-43

Du Bartas, Guillaume 1544-1590 . . . . . . .DLB-327

Dubé, Marcel 1930- DLB-53

Dubé, Rodolphe (see Hertel, François)

Du Bellay, Joachim 1522?-1560 . . . . .DLB-327

Dubie, Norman 1945- DLB-120

Dubin, Al 1891-1945 . . . . .DLB-265

Du Boccage, Anne-Marie 1710-1802 . . . . .DLB-313

Dubois, Silvia 1788 or 1789?-1889 . . . . . . .DLB-239

Du Bois, W. E. B.
    1868-1963 . . . . DLB-47, 50, 91, 246; CDALB-3

Du Bois, William Pène 1916-1993 . . . . . . .DLB-61

Dubrovina, Ekaterina Oskarovna
    1846-1913 . . . . .DLB-238

Dubus, Andre 1936-1999 . . . . .DLB-130

    Tribute to Michael M. Rea Y-97

Dubus, Andre, III 1959- DLB-292

Ducange, Victor 1783-1833 . . . . .DLB-192

Du Chaillu, Paul Belloni 1831?-1903 . . . . .DLB-189

Ducharme, Réjean 1941- DLB-60

Dučić, Jovan 1871-1943 . . . . . DLB-147; CDWLB-4

Duck, Stephen 1705?-1756 . . . . .DLB-95

Gerald Duckworth and Company
    Limited DLB-112

Duclaux, Madame Mary (see Robinson, A. Mary F.)

Dudek, Louis 1918-2001 . . . . .DLB-88

Dudintsev, Vladimir Dmitrievich
    1918-1998 . . . . .DLB-302

Dudley-Smith, Trevor (see Hall, Adam)

Duell, Sloan and Pearce DLB-46

Duerer, Albrecht 1471-1528 . . . . .DLB-179

Duff Gordon, Lucie 1821-1869 . . . . .DLB-166

Dufferin, Helen Lady, Countess of Gifford
    1807-1867 . . . . .DLB-199

Duffield and Green DLB-46

Duffy, Maureen 1933- DLB-14, 310

Dufief, Nicholas Gouin 1776-1834 . . . . . .DLB-187

Dufresne, John 1948- DLB-292

Dugan, Alan 1923-2003 . . . . .DLB-5

Dugard, William 1606-1662 . . . . . . DLB-170, 281

William Dugard [publishing house] DLB-170

Dugas, Marcel 1883-1947 . . . . .DLB-92

William Dugdale [publishing house] DLB-106

Du Guillet, Pernette 1520?-1545 . . . . .DLB-327

Duhamel, Georges 1884-1966 . . . . .DLB-65

Dujardin, Edouard 1861-1949 . . . . .DLB-123

Dukes, Ashley 1885-1959 . . . . .DLB-10

Dumas, Alexandre *fils* 1824-1895 . . . . . . .DLB-192

Dumas, Alexandre *père* 1802-1870 . . . . .DLB-119, 192

Dumas, Henry 1934-1968 . . . . .DLB-41

du Maurier, Daphne 1907-1989 . . . . .DLB-191

Du Maurier, George 1834-1896 . . . . .DLB-153, 178

Dummett, Michael 1925- DLB-262

Dunbar, Paul Laurence
    1872-1906 . . . . .DLB-50, 54, 78; CDALB-3

    Introduction to *Lyrics of Lowly Life* (1896),
        by William Dean Howells DLB-50

Dunbar, William
    circa 1460-circa 1522 . . . . .DLB-132, 146

Duncan, Dave 1933- DLB-251

Duncan, David James 1952- DLB-256

Duncan, Norman 1871-1916 . . . . .DLB-92

Duncan, Quince 1940- DLB-145

Duncan, Robert 1919-1988 . . . . DLB-5, 16, 193

Duncan, Ronald 1914-1982 . . . . .DLB-13

Duncan, Sara Jeannette 1861-1922 . . . . . . .DLB-92

Dunigan, Edward, and Brother DLB-49

Dunlap, John 1747-1812 . . . . .DLB-43

Dunlap, William 1766-1839 . . . . DLB-30, 37, 59

Dunlop, William "Tiger" 1792-1848 . . . . . .DLB-99

Dunmore, Helen 1952- DLB-267

Dunn, Douglas 1942- DLB-40

Dunn, Harvey Thomas 1884-1952 . . . . . .DLB-188

Dunn, Mary (Dunn, Olive Mary)
    1899-1958 . . . . .DLB-352

Dunn, Stephen 1939- DLB-105

    "The Good, The Not So Good" DLB-105

Dunne, Dominick 1925-2009 . . . . .DLB-306

Dunne, Finley Peter 1867-1936 . . . . . .DLB-11, 23

Dunne, John Gregory 1932- Y-80

Dunne, Philip 1908-1992 . . . . .DLB-26

Dunning, Ralph Cheever 1878-1930 . . . . . .DLB-4

Dunning, William A. 1857-1922 . . . . .DLB-17

Duns Scotus, John circa 1266-1308 . . . . . .DLB-115

Dunsany, Lord (Edward John Moreton
    Drax Plunkett, Baron Dunsany)
    1878-1957 . . . . DLB-10, 77, 153, 156, 255

Dunton, W. Herbert 1878-1936 . . . . .DLB-188

John Dunton [publishing house] DLB-170

Duong Thu Huong 1947- DLB-348

Dupin, Amantine-Aurore-Lucile (see Sand, George)

Du Pont de Nemours, Pierre Samuel
    1739-1817 . . . . .DLB-313

Dupuy, Eliza Ann 1814-1880 . . . . .DLB-248

Durack, Mary 1913-1994 . . . . .DLB-260

Durand, Lucile (see Bersianik, Louky)

Duranti, Francesca 1935- DLB-196

Duranty, Walter 1884-1957 . . . . .DLB-29

Duras, Marguerite (Marguerite Donnadieu)
    1914-1996 . . . . .DLB-83, 321

Durfey, Thomas 1653-1723 . . . . .DLB-80

Durova, Nadezhda Andreevna
    (Aleksandr Andreevich Aleksandrov)
    1783-1866 . . . . .DLB-198

Durrell, Lawrence 1912-1990
    . . . . DLB-15, 27, 204; Y-90; CDBLB-7

William Durrell [publishing house]....... DLB-49

Dürrenmatt, Friedrich
   1921-1990 .... DLB-69, 124; CDWLB-2

Duston, Hannah 1657-1737............. DLB-200

Dutt, Toru 1856-1877 .... DLB-240

E. P. Dutton and Company DLB-49

Duun, Olav 1876-1939 .... DLB-297

Duvoisin, Roger 1904-1980 .... DLB-61

Duyckinck, Evert Augustus
   1816-1878 .... DLB-3, 64, 250

Duyckinck, George L. 1823-1863 ..... DLB-3, 250

Duyckinck and Company DLB-49

Dvoryanova, Emiliya 1958- DLB-353

Dwight, John Sullivan 1813-1893 ..... DLB-1, 235

Dwight, Timothy 1752-1817 .... DLB-37

   America: or, A Poem on the Settlement
   of the British Colonies, by
   Timothy Dwight DLB-37

Dybek, Stuart 1942- DLB-130

   Tribute to Michael M. Rea............. Y-97

Dyer, Charles 1928- DLB-13

Dyer, Sir Edward 1543-1607............ DLB-136

Dyer, George 1755-1841 .... DLB-93

Dyer, John 1699-1757 .... DLB-95

Dyk, Viktor 1877-1931 .... DLB-215

Dylan, Bob 1941- DLB-16

E

Eager, Edward 1911-1964............. DLB-22

Eagleton, Terry 1943- DLB-242

Eames, Wilberforce
   1855-1937...................... DLB-140

Earle, Alice Morse
   1853-1911...................... DLB-221

Earle, John 1600 or 1601-1665......... DLB-151

James H. Earle and Company DLB-49

Early Medieval Spanish Theater DLB-337

East Europe
   Independence and Destruction,
   1918-1941 .... DLB-220

   Social Theory and Ethnography:
   Language and Ethnicity in
   Western versus Eastern Man.... DLB-220

Eastlake, William 1917-1997 .... DLB-6, 206

Eastman, Carol ?- DLB-44

Eastman, Charles A. (Ohiyesa)
   1858-1939 ....DLB-175

Eastman, Crystal 1881-1928........... DLB-345

Eastman, Max 1883-1969.............. DLB-91

Eaton, Daniel Isaac 1753-1814 .... DLB-158

Eaton, Edith Maude 1865-1914 .... DLB-221, 312

Eaton, Winnifred 1875-1954........ DLB-221, 312

Eberhart, Richard
   1904-2005 .... DLB-48; CDALB-1

   Tribute to Robert Penn Warren Y-89

Ebner, Jeannie 1918-2004 .... DLB-85

Ebner-Eschenbach, Marie von
   1830-1916 .... DLB-81

Ebon 1942- DLB-41

E-Books' Second Act in Libraries Y-02

Ecbasis Captivi circa 1045 .... DLB-148

Ecco Press....................... DLB-46

Echard, Laurence 1670?-1730 .... DLB-336

Echegaray, José 1832-1916 .... DLB-329

Eckhart, Meister circa 1260-circa 1328... DLB-115

The Eclectic Review 1805-1868.......... DLB-110

Eco, Umberto 1932- DLB-196, 242

Eddison, E. R. 1882-1945 .... DLB-255

Edel, Leon 1907-1997 .... DLB-103

Edelfeldt, Inger 1956- DLB-257

J. M. Edelstein's Collection of Twentieth-
   Century American Poetry (A Century of Poetry,
   a Lifetime of Collecting).............. Y-02

Edes, Benjamin 1732-1803 .... DLB-43

Edgar, David 1948- DLB-13, 233

   Viewpoint: Politics and
   Performance DLB-13

Edgerton, Clyde 1944- DLB-278

Edgeworth, Maria
   1768-1849...............DLB-116, 159, 163

The Edinburgh Review 1802-1929 .... DLB-110

Edinburgh University Press DLB-112

Editing
   Conversations with Editors Y-95

   Editorial Statements.............. DLB-137

   The Editorial Style of Fredson Bowers ... Y-91

   Editorial: The Extension of Copyright ... Y-02

   We See the Editor at Work............ Y-97

   Whose *Ulysses?* The Function of Editing .. Y-97

The Editor Publishing Company DLB-49

Editorial Institute at Boston University Y-00

Edmonds, Helen Woods Ferguson
   (see Kavan, Anna)

Edmonds, Randolph 1900-1983......... DLB-51

Edmonds, Walter D. 1903-1998 .... DLB-9

Edric, Robert (see Armitage, G. E.)

Edschmid, Kasimir 1890-1966 .... DLB-56

Edson, Margaret 1961- DLB-266

Edson, Russell 1935- DLB-244

Edwards, Amelia Anne Blandford
   1831-1892 ....DLB-174

Edwards, Dic 1953- DLB-245

Edwards, Edward 1812-1886 .... DLB-184

Edwards, Jonathan 1703-1758........DLB-24, 270

Edwards, Jonathan, Jr. 1745-1801 .... DLB-37

Edwards, Junius 1929- DLB-33

Edwards, Matilda Barbara Betham
   1836-1919 ....DLB-174

Edwards, Richard 1524-1566 .... DLB-62

Edwards, Sarah Pierpont 1710-1758 ..... DLB-200

James Edwards [publishing house] DLB-154

Effinger, George Alec 1947- DLB-8

Egede, Hans 1686-1758 .... DLB-354

Egerton, George 1859-1945 .... DLB-135

Eggleston, Edward 1837-1902.......... DLB-12

Eggleston, Wilfred 1901-1986 .... DLB-92

Eglītis, Anšlavs 1906-1993 .... DLB-220

Eguren, José María 1874-1942 .... DLB-290

Ehrenreich, Barbara 1941- DLB-246

Ehrenstein, Albert 1886-1950........... DLB-81

Ehrhart, W. D. 1948- DS-9

Ehrlich, Gretel 1946- DLB-212, 275

Eich, Günter 1907-1972 .... DLB-69, 124

Eichelberger, Ethyl 1945-1990 .... DLB-341

Eichendorff, Joseph Freiherr von
   1788-1857...................... DLB-90

Eifukumon'in 1271-1342 .... DLB-203

Eigner, Larry 1926-1996............ DLB-5, 193

Eikon Basilike 1649................... DLB-151

Eilhart von Oberge
   circa 1140-circa 1195 .... DLB-148

Einar Benediktsson 1864-1940......... DLB-293

Einar Kárason 1955- DLB-293

Einar Már Guðmundsson 1954- DLB-293

Einhard circa 770-840................. DLB-148

Eiseley, Loren 1907-1977.........DLB-275, DS-17

Eisenberg, Deborah 1945- DLB-244

Eisenreich, Herbert 1925-1986.......... DLB-85

Eisner, Kurt 1867-1919 .... DLB-66

Ekelöf, Gunnar 1907-1968 .... DLB-259

Eklund, Gordon 1945- Y-83

Ekman, Kerstin 1933- DLB-257

Ekwensi, Cyprian
   1921-2007 ....DLB-117; CDWLB-3

Elaw, Zilpha circa 1790-? DLB-239

George Eld [publishing house] DLB-170

Elder, Lonne, III 1931- DLB-7, 38, 44

Paul Elder and Company DLB-49

Eldershaw, Flora (M. Barnard Eldershaw)
   1897-1956 .... DLB-260

Eldershaw, M. Barnard (see Barnard, Marjorie and
   Eldershaw, Flora)

The Elected Member, 1970 Booker Prize winner,
   Bernice Rubens DLB-326

The Electronic Text Center and the Electronic
   Archive of Early American Fiction at the
   University of Virginia Library.......... Y-98

Eliade, Mircea 1907-1986 ... DLB-220; CDWLB-4

Elie, Robert 1915-1973................. DLB-88

Elin Pelin 1877-1949 ....DLB-147; CDWLB-4

Eliot, George
   1819-1880 .... DLB-21, 35, 55; CDBLB-4

The George Eliot Fellowship Y-99

Eliot, John 1604-1690 . . . . DLB-24

Eliot, T. S. 1888-1965
. . . . . . DLB-7, 10, 45, 63, 245, 329; CDALB-5

T. S. Eliot Centennial: The Return
of the Old Possum Y-88

The T. S. Eliot Society: Celebration and
Scholarship, 1980-1999 . . . . Y-99

Eliot's Court Press DLB-170

Elizabeth I 1533-1603 . . . . DLB-136

Elizabeth von Nassau-Saarbrücken
after 1393-1456 . . . . DLB-179

Elizondo, Salvador 1932- DLB-145

Elizondo, Sergio 1930- DLB-82

Elkin, Stanley
1930-1995 . . . . DLB-2, 28, 218, 278; Y-80

Elles, Dora Amy (see Wentworth, Patricia)

Ellet, Elizabeth F. 1818?-1877 . . . . DLB-30

Ellin, Stanley 1916-1986 . . . . DLB-306, 335

Elliot, Ebenezer 1781-1849 . . . . DLB-96, 190

Elliot, Frances Minto (Dickinson)
1820-1898 . . . . DLB-166

Elliott, Charlotte 1789-1871 . . . . DLB-199

Elliott, George 1923- DLB-68

Elliott, George P. 1918-1980 . . . . DLB-244

Elliott, Janice 1931-1995 . . . . DLB-14

Elliott, Sarah Barnwell 1848-1928 . . . . . . DLB-221

Elliott, Sumner Locke 1917-1991 . . . . DLB-289

Elliott, Thomes and Talbot DLB-49

Elliott, William, III 1788-1863 . . . . DLB-3, 248

Ellis, Alice Thomas (Anna Margaret Haycraft)
1932- DLB-194

Ellis, Bret Easton 1964- DLB-292

Ellis, Edward S. 1840-1916 . . . . DLB-42

Frederick Staridge Ellis
[publishing house] DLB-106

Ellis, George E.
"The New Controversy Concerning
Miracles DS-5

The George H. Ellis Company DLB-49

Ellis, Havelock 1859-1939 . . . . DLB-190

Ellison, Harlan 1934- DLB-8, 335

Tribute to Isaac Asimov Y-92

Ellison, Ralph
1914-1994 . . . DLB-2, 76, 227; Y-94; CDALB-1

Ellmann, Richard 1918-1987 . . . . . . DLB-103; Y-87

Ellroy, James 1948- DLB-226; Y-91

Tribute to John D. MacDonald Y-86

Tribute to Raymond Chandler Y-88

Elster, Kristian 1841-1881 . . . . DLB-354

Eluard, Paul 1895-1952 . . . . DLB-258

Elyot, Thomas 1490?-1546 . . . . DLB-136

Elytis, Odysseus 1911-1996 . . . . DLB-329

Emanuel, James Andrew 1921- DLB-41

Emecheta, Buchi 1944- DLB-117; CDWLB-3

Emerson, Ralph Waldo 1803-1882
. . . . DLB-1, 59, 73, 183, 223, 270, 351;
DS-5; CDALB-2

Ralph Waldo Emerson in 1982 . . . . Y-82

The Ralph Waldo Emerson Society Y-99

Emerson, William 1769-1811 . . . . DLB-37

Emerson, William R. 1923-1997 . . . . Y-97

Emin, Fedor Aleksandrovich
circa 1735-1770 . . . . DLB-150

Emmanuel, Pierre 1916-1984 . . . . DLB-258

Empedocles fifth century B.C. DLB-176

Empson, William 1906-1984 . . . . DLB-20

Enchi Fumiko 1905-1986 . . . . DLB-182

"The Encyclopedia," Denis Diderot DLB-314

Ende, Michael 1929-1995 . . . . DLB-75

Endō Shūsaku 1923-1996 . . . . DLB-182

Engel, Marian 1933-1985 . . . . DLB-53

Engelbretsdatter, Dorothe 1634-1716 . . . . DLB-354

Engel'gardt, Sof'ia Vladimirovna
1828-1894 . . . . DLB-277

Engels, Friedrich 1820-1895 . . . . DLB-129

Engels, John 1931- DLB-342

Engle, Paul 1908-1991 . . . . DLB-48

Tribute to Robert Penn Warren Y-89

English, Thomas Dunn 1819-1902 . . . . . . DLB-202

The English Patient, 1992 Booker Prize winner,
Michael Ondaatje DLB-326

Ennius 239 B.C.-169 B.C. DLB-211

Enquist, Per Olov 1934- DLB-257

Enright, Anne 1962- DLB-267

Enright, D. J. 1920-2002 . . . . DLB-27

Enright, Elizabeth 1909-1968 . . . . . . DLB-22, 335

Enright, Nick 1950-2003 . . . . DLB-325

Enslin, Theodore 1925- DLB-342

Epic, The Sixteenth-Century Spanish DLB-318

Epictetus circa 55-circa 125-130 . . . . DLB-176

Epicurus 342/341 B.C.-271/270 B.C. DLB-176

d'Epinay, Louise (Louise-Florence-Pétronille Tardieu
d'Esclavelles, marquise d'Epinay)
1726-1783 . . . . DLB-313

Epps, Bernard 1936- DLB-53

Epshtein, Mikhail Naumovich 1950- . . . DLB-285

Epstein, Julius 1909-2000 and
Epstein, Philip 1909-1952 . . . . DLB-26

Epstein, Leslie 1938- DLB-299

Editors, Conversations with Y-95

Equiano, Olaudah
circa 1745-1797 . . . . . . DLB-37, 50; CDWLB-3

Olaudah Equiano and Unfinished
Journeys: The Slave-Narrative
Tradition and Twentieth-Century
Continuities DLB-117

Eragny Press DLB-112

Erasmus, Desiderius 1467-1536 . . . . DLB-136

Erba, Luciano 1922- DLB-128

Erdman, Nikolai Robertovich
1900-1970 . . . . DLB-272

Erdrich, Louise
1954- DLB-152, 175, 206; CDALB-7

Erenburg, Il'ia Grigor'evich 1891-1967 . . . DLB-272

Erichsen-Brown, Gwethalyn Graham
(see Graham, Gwethalyn)

Eriugena, John Scottus circa 810-877 . . . . . DLB-115

Ernst, Paul 1866-1933 . . . . DLB-66, 118

Erofeev, Venedikt Vasil'evich
1938-1990 . . . . DLB-285

Erofeev, Viktor Vladimirovich
1947- DLB-285

Ershov, Petr Pavlovich 1815-1869 . . . . DLB-205

Erskine, Albert 1911-1993 . . . . Y-93

At Home with Albert Erskine Y-00

Erskine, John 1879-1951 . . . . DLB-9, 102

Erskine, Mrs. Steuart ?-1948 . . . . DLB-195

Ertel', Aleksandr Ivanovich
1855-1908 . . . . DLB-238

Ervine, St. John Greer 1883-1971 . . . . DLB-10

Eschenburg, Johann Joachim
1743-1820 . . . . DLB-97

Escofet, Cristina 1945- DLB-305

Escoto, Julio 1944- DLB-145

Esdaile, Arundell 1880-1956 . . . . DLB-201

Esenin, Sergei Aleksandrovich
1895-1925 . . . . DLB-295

Eshleman, Clayton 1935- DLB-5

Espaillat, Rhina P. 1932- DLB-282

Espanca, Florbela 1894-1930 . . . . DLB-287

Espriu, Salvador 1913-1985 . . . . DLB-134

Ess Ess Publishing Company DLB-49

Essex House Press DLB-112

Esson, Louis 1878-1943 . . . . DLB-260

Essop, Ahmed 1931- DLB-225

Esterházy, Péter 1950- DLB-232; CDWLB-4

Estes, Eleanor 1906-1988 . . . . DLB-22

Estes and Lauriat DLB-49

Estienne, Henri II (Henricus Stephanus)
1531-1597 . . . . DLB-327

Estleman, Loren D. 1952- DLB-226

Eszterhas, Joe 1944- DLB-185

Etherege, George 1636-circa 1692 . . . . DLB-80

Ethridge, Mark, Sr. 1896-1981 . . . . DLB-127

Ets, Marie Hall 1893-1984 . . . . DLB-22

Etter, David 1928- DLB-105

Ettner, Johann Christoph 1654-1724 . . . . . DLB-168

Etzioni, Amitai 1929- DLB-345

Eucken, Rudolf 1846-1926 . . . . DLB-329

Eudora Welty Remembered in
Two Exhibits Y-02

Eugene Gant's Projected Works Y-01

Eugenides, Jeffrey 1960- DLB-350

Cumulative Index

Eupolemius fl. circa 1095 . . . . DLB-148

Euripides circa 484 B.C.-407/406 B.C.
. . . . DLB-176; CDWLB-1

Evans, Augusta Jane 1835-1909 . . . . DLB-239

Evans, Caradoc 1878-1945 . . . . DLB-162

Evans, Charles 1850-1935 . . . . DLB-187

Evans, Donald 1884-1921. . . . . DLB-54

Evans, George Henry 1805-1856 . . . . DLB-43

Evans, Hubert 1892-1986. . . . . DLB-92

Evans, Mari 1923- DLB-41

Evans, Mary Ann (see Eliot, George)

Evans, Nathaniel 1742-1767 . . . . DLB-31

Evans, Sebastian 1830-1909 . . . . DLB-35

Evans, Ray 1915-2007 . . . . DLB-265

M. Evans and Company. DLB-46

Evaristi, Marcella 1953- DLB-233

Evaristo, Bernardine 1959- DLB-347

Evenson, Brian 1966- DLB-335

Everett, Alexander Hill 1790-1847 . . . . . . DLB-59

Everett, Edward 1794-1865. . . . . . . DLB-1, 59, 235

Everett, Percival 1956- DLB-350

Everson, R. G. 1903- DLB-88

Everson, William 1912-1994. . . . DLB-5, 16, 212

Evreinov, Nikolai 1879-1953. . . . . DLB-317

Ewald, Johannes 1743-1781. . . . . DLB-300

Ewart, Gavin 1916-1995. . . . . DLB-40

Ewing, Juliana Horatia 1841-1885 . . . DLB-21, 163

The Examiner 1808-1881 . . . . DLB-110

Exley, Frederick 1929-1992 . . . . . . DLB-143; Y-81

Editorial: The Extension of Copyright. Y-02

von Eyb, Albrecht 1420-1475 . . . . .DLB-179

Eyre and Spottiswoode DLB-106

Ezekiel, Nissim 1924-2004 . . . . DLB-323

Ezera, Regīna 1930- DLB-232

Ezzo ?-after 1065. . . . . DLB-148

F

Faber, Frederick William 1814-1863. . . . . . DLB-32

Faber and Faber Limited. DLB-112

Fabrio, Nedjeljko 1937- DLB-353

Faccio, Rena (see Aleramo, Sibilla)

Facsimiles
  The Uses of Facsimile: A Symposium Y-90

Fadeev, Aleksandr Aleksandrovich
  1901-1956 . . . . DLB-272

Fagundo, Ana María 1938- DLB-134

Fainzil'berg, Il'ia Arnol'dovich
  (see Il'f, Il'ia and Petrov, Evgenii)

Fair, Ronald L. 1932- DLB-33

Fairfax, Beatrice (see Manning, Marie)

Fairlie, Gerard 1899-1983 . . . . DLB-77

Faldbakken, Knut 1941- DLB-297

Falkberget, Johan (Johan Petter Lillebakken)
  1879-1967. DLB-297

Fallada, Hans 1893-1947. . . . . DLB-56

The Famished Road, 1991 Booker Prize winner,
  Ben Okri DLB-326

Fancher, Betsy 1928- Y-83

Fane, Violet 1843-1905. . . . . DLB-35

Fanfrolico Press. DLB-112

Fanning, Katherine 1927-2000 . . . . DLB-127

Fanon, Frantz 1925-1961 . . . . DLB-296

Fanshawe, Sir Richard 1608-1666. . . . . . DLB-126

Fantasy Press Publishers. DLB-46

Fante, John 1909-1983 . . . . DLB-130; Y-83

Al-Farabi circa 870-950 . . . . DLB-115

Farabough, Laura 1949- DLB-228

Farah, Nuruddin 1945- . . . DLB-125; CDWLB-3

Farber, Norma 1909-1984. . . . . DLB-61

A Farewell to Arms (Documentary) DLB-308

Fargue, Léon-Paul 1876-1947 . . . . DLB-258

Farigoule, Louis (see Romains, Jules)

Farjeon, Eleanor 1881-1965 . . . . DLB-160

Farley, Harriet 1812-1907 . . . . DLB-239

Farley, Walter 1920-1989 . . . . DLB-22

Farmborough, Florence 1887-1978 . . . . . DLB-204

Farmer, Beverley 1941- DLB-325

Farmer, Penelope 1939- DLB-161

Farmer, Philip José 1918-2009 . . . . DLB-8

Farnaby, Thomas 1575?-1647 . . . . DLB-236

Farnese, Isabella (Suor Francesca di Gesù Maria)
  1593-1651 . . . . DLB-339

Farningham, Marianne (see Hearn, Mary Anne)

Farquhar, George circa 1677-1707 . . . . DLB-84

Farquharson, Martha (see Finley, Martha)

Farrar, Frederic William 1831-1903 . . . . . DLB-163

Farrar, Straus and Giroux. DLB-46

Farrar and Rinehart DLB-46

Farrell, J. G. 1935-1979 . . . . .DLB-14, 271, 326

Farrell, James T. 1904-1979. . . . DLB-4, 9, 86; DS-2

Fast, Howard 1914-2003. . . . . DLB-9

Fasting, Claus 1746-1791. . . . . DLB-354

Faulkner, William 1897-1962
  . . . . . DLB-9, 11, 44, 102, 316, 330; DS-2; Y-86;
                                                 CDALB-5

  Faulkner and Yoknapatawpha
    Conference, Oxford, Mississippi Y-97

  Faulkner Centennial Addresses Y-97

  "Faulkner 100—Celebrating the Work,"
    University of South Carolina,
    Columbia. Y-97

  Impressions of William Faulkner Y-97

  William Faulkner and the People-to-People
    Program. Y-86

  William Faulkner Centenary
    Celebrations Y-97

  The William Faulkner Society Y-99

George Faulkner [publishing house]. DLB-154

Faulks, Sebastian 1953- DLB-207

Fauset, Jessie Redmon 1882-1961. . . . . . . DLB-51

Faust, Frederick Schiller (Max Brand)
  1892-1944 . . . . DLB-256

Faust, Irvin
  1924- DLB-2, 28, 218, 278; Y-80, 00

  I Wake Up Screaming [Response to
    Ken Auletta] Y-97

  Tribute to Bernard Malamud. Y-86

  Tribute to Isaac Bashevis Singer. Y-91

  Tribute to Meyer Levin Y-81

Fawcett, Edgar 1847-1904. . . . . DLB-202

Fawcett, Millicent Garrett 1847-1929 . . . . DLB-190

Fawcett Books. DLB-46

Fay, Theodore Sedgwick 1807-1898 . . . . . DLB-202

Fearing, Kenneth 1902-1961 . . . . DLB-9

Federal Writers' Project DLB-46

Federman, Raymond 1928-2009. . . . . Y-80

Fedin, Konstantin Aleksandrovich
  1892-1977. .DLB-272

Fedorov, Innokentii Vasil'evich
  (see Omulevsky, Innokentii Vasil'evich)

Fefer, Itzik (Itsik Fefer) 1900-1952. . . . . . DLB-333

Feiffer, Jules 1929- DLB-7, 44

Feinberg, Charles E. 1899-1988 . . . . DLB-187; Y-88

Feind, Barthold 1678-1721 . . . . DLB-168

Feinstein, Elaine 1930- DLB-14, 40

Feirstein, Frederick 1940- DLB-282

Feiss, Paul Louis 1875-1952 . . . . .DLB-187

Feldman, Irving 1928- DLB-169

Felipe, Carlos 1911-1975. . . . . DLB-305

Felipe, Léon 1884-1968. . . . . DLB-108

Fell, Frederick, Publishers. DLB-46

Fellowship of Southern Writers Y-98

Felltham, Owen 1602?-1668. . . . . . . DLB-126, 151

Felman, Shoshana 1942- DLB-246

Fels, Ludwig 1946- DLB-75

Felton, Cornelius Conway
  1807-1862. . . . . DLB-1, 235

Fel'zen, Iurii (Nikolai Berngardovich Freidenshtein)
  1894?-1943. .DLB-317

Mothe-Fénelon, François de Salignac de la
  1651-1715 .DLB-268

Fenn, Harry 1837-1911. . . . . DLB-188

Fennario, David 1947- DLB-60

Fenner, Dudley 1558?-1587? DLB-236

Fenno, Jenny 1765?-1803 . . . . DLB-200

Fenno, John 1751-1798 . . . . DLB-43

R. F. Fenno and Company DLB-49

Fenoglio, Beppe 1922-1963. . . . . .DLB-177

Fenton, Geoffrey 1539?-1608 . . . . DLB-136

Fenton, James 1949- DLB-40

    The Hemingway/Fenton
    Correspondence Y-02

Ferber, Edna 1885-1968.......DLB-9, 28, 86, 266

Ferdinand, Vallery, III (see Salaam, Kalamu ya)

Ferguson, Adam 1723-1816............DLB-336

Ferguson, Sir Samuel 1810-1886.........DLB-32

Ferguson, William Scott 1875-1954.......DLB-47

Fergusson, Robert 1750-1774...........DLB-109

Ferland, Albert 1872-1943..............DLB-92

Ferlinghetti, Lawrence
    1919- DLB-5, 16; CDALB-1

    Tribute to Kenneth Rexroth Y-82

Fermor, Patrick Leigh 1915- DLB-204

Fern, Fanny (see Parton, Sara Payson Willis)

Fernández de Heredia, Juan
    circa 1310-1396...................DLB-337

Fernando, Lloyd 1926-2008............DLB-348

Ferrars, Elizabeth (Morna Doris Brown)
    1907-1995.......................DLB-87

Ferré, Rosario 1942- DLB-145

Ferreira, Vergílio 1916-1996............DLB-287

E. Ferret and Company DLB-49

Ferrier, Susan 1782-1854 ....DLB-116

Ferril, Thomas Hornsby 1896-1988......DLB-206

Ferrini, Vincent 1913-2007..............DLB-48

Ferron, Jacques 1921-1985..............DLB-60

Ferron, Madeleine 1922- DLB-53

Ferrucci, Franco 1936- DLB-196

Fet, Afanasii Afanas'evich
    1820?-1892.....................DLB-277

Fetridge and Company DLB-49

Feuchtersleben, Ernst Freiherr von
    1806-1849.....................DLB-133

Feuchtwanger, Lion 1884-1958..........DLB-66

Feuerbach, Ludwig 1804-1872..........DLB-133

Feuillet, Octave 1821-1890.............DLB-192

Feydeau, Georges 1862-1921...........DLB-192

Fibiger, Mathilde 1830-1872............DLB-300

Fichte, Johann Gottlieb 1762-1814.......DLB-90

Ficke, Arthur Davison 1883-1945........DLB-54

Fiction
    American Fiction and the 1930s DLB-9

    Fiction Best-Sellers, 1910-1945 ....DLB-9

    Postmodern Holocaust Fiction DLB-299

    The Year in Fiction Y-84, 86, 89, 94–99

    The Year in Fiction: A Biased View Y-83

    The Year in U.S. Fiction Y-00, 01

    The Year's Work in Fiction: A Survey.....Y-82

Fiedler, Leslie A. 1917-2003 ....DLB-28, 67

    Tribute to Bernard Malamud Y-86

    Tribute to James Dickey Y-97

Field, Barron 1789-1846................DLB-230

Field, Edward 1924- DLB-105

Field, Eugene
    1850-1895 ....DLB-23, 42, 140; DS-13

Field, John 1545?-1588 ....DLB-167

Field, Joseph M. 1810-1856 ....DLB-248

Field, Marshall, III 1893-1956..........DLB-127

Field, Marshall, IV 1916-1965..........DLB-127

Field, Marshall, V 1941- DLB-127

Field, Michael (Katherine Harris Bradley)
    1846-1914 and (Edith Emma Cooper)
    1862-1913 ....DLB-240, 344

"The Poetry File" DLB-105

Field, Nathan 1587-1619 or 1620.........DLB-58

Field, Rachel 1894-1942...............DLB-9, 22

Fielding, Helen 1958- DLB-231

Fielding, Henry
    1707-1754........DLB-39, 84, 101; CDBLB-2

    "Defense of *Amelia*" (1752)...........DLB-39

    The History of the Adventures of Joseph Andrews
    [excerpt] (1742)..................DLB-39

    Letter to [Samuel] Richardson on *Clarissa*
    (1748) DLB-39

    Preface to *Joseph Andrews* (1742).......DLB-39

    Preface to Sarah Fielding's *Familiar
    Letters* (1747) [excerpt] DLB-39

    Preface to Sarah Fielding's *The
    Adventures of David Simple* (1744) ...DLB-39

    Review of *Clarissa* (1748) DLB-39

    Tom Jones (1749) [excerpt] DLB-39

Fielding, Sarah 1710-1768...............DLB-39

    Preface to *The Cry* (1754) DLB-39

Fields, Annie Adams 1834-1915 ....DLB-221

Fields, Dorothy 1905-1974.............DLB-265

Fields, James T. 1817-1881..........DLB-1, 235

Fields, Julia 1938- DLB-41

Fields, Osgood and Company DLB-49

Fields, W. C. 1880-1946...............DLB-44

Fierstein, Harvey 1954-................DLB-266

Figes, Eva 1932- DLB-14, 271

Figuera, Angela 1902-1984 ....DLB-108

Filicaia, Vincenzo de 1642-1707 ....DLB-339

Filmer, Sir Robert 1586-1653..........DLB-151

Filson, John circa 1753-1788............DLB-37

Finch, Anne, Countess of Winchilsea
    1661-1720 ....DLB-95

Finch, Annie 1956- DLB-282

Finch, Robert 1900- DLB-88

Findley, Timothy 1930-2002 ....DLB-53

Finlay, Ian Hamilton 1925- DLB-40

Finley, Martha 1828-1909 ....DLB-42

Finn, Elizabeth Anne (McCaul)
    1825-1921......................DLB-166

Finnegan, Seamus 1949- DLB-245

Finney, Jack 1911-1995 ....DLB-8

Finney, Walter Braden (see Finney, Jack)

Fiorillo, Silvio 1560 or 1565?-1634? DLB-339

Firbank, Ronald 1886-1926.............DLB-36

Firmin, Giles 1615-1697...............DLB-24

First Edition Library/Collectors'
    Reprints, Inc........................Y-91

Fischart, Johann
    1546 or 1547-1590 or 1591.........DLB-179

Fischer, Karoline Auguste Fernandine
    1764-1842......................DLB-94

Fischer, Tibor 1959- DLB-231

Fish, Stanley 1938- DLB-67

Fishacre, Richard 1205-1248...........DLB-115

Fisher, Clay (see Allen, Henry W.)

Fisher, Dorothy Canfield
    1879-1958 ....DLB-9, 102

Fisher, Leonard Everett 1924- DLB-61

Fisher, Roy 1930- DLB-40

Fisher, Rudolph 1897-1934 ....DLB-51, 102

Fisher, Steve 1913-1980 ....DLB-226

Fisher, Sydney George 1856-1927........DLB-47

Fisher, Vardis 1895-1968 ....DLB-9, 206

Fiske, John 1608-1677 ....DLB-24

Fiske, John 1842-1901 ....DLB-47, 64

Fitch, Thomas circa 1700-1774..........DLB-31

Fitch, William Clyde 1865-1909 ....DLB-7

Fitzball, Edward 1792-1873 ....DLB-344

FitzGerald, Edward 1809-1883 ....DLB-32

Fitzgerald, F. Scott 1896-1940
    ....DLB-4, 9, 86; Y-81, 92;
    DS-1, 15, 16; CDALB-4

    F. Scott Fitzgerald: A Descriptive
    Bibliography, Supplement (2001) Y-01

    F. Scott Fitzgerald Centenary
    Celebrations Y-96

    F. Scott Fitzgerald Inducted into the
    American Poets' Corner at St. John
    the Divine; Ezra Pound Banned......Y-99

    "F. Scott Fitzgerald: St. Paul's Native Son
    and Distinguished American Writer":
    University of Minnesota Conference,
    29-31 October 1982 ....Y-82

    First International F. Scott Fitzgerald
    Conference.....................Y-92

    The Great Gatsby (Documentary) DLB-219

    Tender Is the Night (Documentary) DLB-273

Fitzgerald, Penelope
    1916-2000 ....DLB-14, 194, 326

Fitzgerald, Robert 1910-1985...............Y-80

FitzGerald, Robert D. 1902-1987........DLB-260

Fitzgerald, Thomas 1819-1891...........DLB-23

Fitzgerald, Zelda Sayre 1900-1948..........Y-84

Fitzhugh, Louise 1928-1974.............DLB-52

Fitzhugh, William circa 1651-1701........DLB-24

Flagg, James Montgomery 1877-1960 ....DLB-188

Flamand, Dinu 1947- DLB-353

Flanagan, Thomas 1923-2002 ....Y-80

Flanner, Hildegarde 1899-1987 ....DLB-48

Flanner, Janet 1892-1978 ....DLB-4; DS-15

Flannery, Peter 1951- DLB-233

Flashman, Harry Paget
    (see Fraser, George MacDonald)

Cumulative Index

Flaubert, Gustave 1821-1880 . . . . . . DLB-119, 301

Flavin, Martin 1883-1967 . . . . DLB-9

Fleck, Konrad (fl. circa 1220) DLB-138

Flecker, James Elroy 1884-1915 . . . . . . DLB-10, 19

Fleeson, Doris 1901-1970 . . . . DLB-29

Fleißer, Marieluise 1901-1974 . . . . . . DLB-56, 124

Fleischer, Nat 1887-1972 . . . . DLB-241

Fleming, Abraham 1552?-1607 . . . . DLB-236

Fleming, Ian 1908-1964 . . DLB-87, 201; CDBLB-7

Fleming, Joan 1908-1980 . . . . DLB-276

Fleming, May Agnes 1840-1880 . . . . DLB-99

Fleming, Paul 1609-1640 . . . . DLB-164

Fleming, Peter 1907-1971 . . . . DLB-195

Fletcher, Andrew 1653-1716 . . . . DLB-336

Fletcher, Giles, the Elder 1546-1611 . . . . . DLB-136

Fletcher, Giles, the Younger
   1585 or 1586-1623 . . . . DLB-121

Fletcher, J. S. 1863-1935 . . . . DLB-70

Fletcher, John 1579-1625 . . . . DLB-58

Fletcher, John Gould 1886-1950 . . . . DLB-4, 45

Fletcher, Phineas 1582-1650 . . . . DLB-121

Flieg, Helmut (see Heym, Stefan)

Flint, F. S. 1885-1960 . . . . DLB-19

Flint, Timothy 1780-1840 . . . . DLB-73, 186

Fløgstad, Kjartan 1944- DLB-297

Florensky, Pavel Aleksandrovich
   1882-1937 . . . . DLB-295

Flores, Juan de fl. 1470-1500 . . . . DLB-286

Flores y Blancaflor circa 1375-1400 . . . . DLB-337

Flores-Williams, Jason 1969- DLB-209

Florio, John 1553?-1625 . . . . DLB-172

Flower, Benjamin Orange 1859-1918 . . . . DLB-345

Fludd, Robert 1574-1637 . . . . DLB-281

Flynn, Elizabeth Gurley 1890-1964 . . . . . DLB-303

Fo, Dario 1926- DLB-330; Y-97

   Nobel Lecture 1997: Contra Jogulatores
      Obloquentes Y-97

Foden, Giles 1967- DLB-267

Fofanov, Konstantin Mikhailovich
   1862-1911 . . . . DLB-277

Foix, J. V. 1893-1987 . . . . DLB-134

Foley, Martha 1897-1977 . . . . DLB-137

Folger, Henry Clay 1857-1930 . . . . DLB-140

Folio Society DLB-112

Follain, Jean 1903-1971 . . . . DLB-258

Follen, Charles 1796-1840 . . . . DLB-235

Follen, Eliza Lee (Cabot) 1787-1860 . . . DLB-1, 235

Follett, Ken 1949- DLB-87; Y-81

Follett Publishing Company DLB-46

John West Folsom [publishing house] DLB-49

Folz, Hans
   between 1435 and 1440-1513 . . . . DLB-179

Fonseca, Manuel da 1911-1993 . . . . DLB-287

Fonseca, Rubem 1925- DLB-307

Fontane, Theodor
   1819-1898 . . . . DLB-129; CDWLB-2

Fontenelle, Bernard Le Bovier de
   1657-1757 . . . . DLB-268, 313

Fontes, Montserrat 1940- DLB-209

Fonvisin, Denis Ivanovich
   1744 or 1745-1792 . . . . DLB-150

Foote, Horton 1916-2009 . . . . DLB-26, 266

Foote, Mary Hallock
   1847-1938 . . . . DLB-186, 188, 202, 221

Foote, Samuel 1721-1777 . . . . DLB-89

Foote, Shelby 1916-2005 . . . . DLB-2, 17

Forbes, Calvin 1945- DLB-41

Forbes, Ester 1891-1967 . . . . DLB-22

Forbes, John 1950-1998 . . . . DLB-325

Forbes, Rosita 1893?-1967 . . . . DLB-195

Forbes and Company DLB-49

Force, Peter 1790-1868 . . . . DLB-30

Forché, Carolyn 1950- DLB-5, 193

Ford, Charles Henri 1913-2002 . . . . DLB-4, 48

Ford, Corey 1902-1969 . . . . DLB-11

Ford, Ford Madox
   1873-1939 . . . . DLB-34, 98, 162; CDBLB-6

   Nathan Asch Remembers Ford Madox
     Ford, Sam Roth, and Hart Crane Y-02

J. B. Ford and Company DLB-49

Ford, Jesse Hill 1928-1996 . . . . DLB-6

Ford, John 1586-? DLB-58; CDBLB-1

Ford, R. A. D. 1915-1998 . . . . DLB-88

Ford, Richard 1944- DLB-227

Ford, Worthington C. 1858-1941 . . . . DLB-47

Fords, Howard, and Hulbert DLB-49

Foreman, Carl 1914-1984 . . . . DLB-26

Forester, C. S. 1899-1966 . . . . DLB-191

   The C. S. Forester Society Y-00

Forester, Frank (see Herbert, Henry William)

Formalism, New

   Anthologizing New Formalism DLB-282

   The Little Magazines of the
     New Formalism DLB-282

   The New Narrative Poetry DLB-282

   Presses of the New Formalism and
     the New Narrative DLB-282

   The Prosody of the New Formalism . DLB-282

   Younger Women Poets of the
     New Formalism DLB-282

Forman, Harry Buxton 1842-1917 . . . . . . DLB-184

Fornés, María Irene 1930- DLB-7, 341

Forrest, Leon 1937-1997 . . . . DLB-33

Forsh, Ol'ga Dmitrievna 1873-1961 . . . . . DLB-272

Forster, E. M. 1879-1970
  . . DLB-34, 98, 162, 178, 195; DS-10; CDBLB-6

"Fantasy," from *Aspects of the Novel*
   (1927) DLB-178

Forster, Georg 1754-1794 . . . . DLB-94

Forster, John 1812-1876 . . . . DLB-144

Forster, Margaret 1938- DLB-155, 271

Forsyth, Frederick 1938- DLB-87

Forsyth, William
   "Literary Style" (1857) [excerpt] DLB-57

Forten, Charlotte L. 1837-1914 . . . . . . DLB-50, 239

   Pages from Her Diary DLB-50

Fortini, Franco 1917-1994 . . . . DLB-128

Fortune, Mary ca. 1833-ca. 1910 . . . . DLB-230

Fortune, T. Thomas 1856-1928 . . . . DLB-23

Fosdick, Charles Austin 1842-1915 . . . . . . DLB-42

Fosse, Jon 1959- DLB-297

Foster, David 1944- DLB-289

Foster, Genevieve 1893-1979 . . . . DLB-61

Foster, Hannah Webster
   1758-1840 . . . . DLB-37, 200

Foster, John 1648-1681 . . . . DLB-24

Foster, Michael 1904-1956 . . . . DLB-9

Foster, Myles Birket 1825-1899 . . . . DLB-184

Foster, William Z. 1881-1961 . . . . DLB-303

Foucault, Michel 1926-1984 . . . . DLB-242

Robert and Andrew Foulis
   [publishing house] DLB-154

Fouqué, Caroline de la Motte 1774-1831 . . . DLB-90

Fouqué, Friedrich de la Motte
   1777-1843 . . . . DLB-90

Four Seas Company DLB-46

Four Winds Press DLB-46

Fournier, Henri Alban (see Alain-Fournier)

Fowler, Christopher 1953- DLB-267

Fowler, Connie May 1958- DLB-292

Fowler and Wells Company DLB-49

Fowles, John
   1926-2005 . . . . . DLB-14, 139, 207; CDBLB-8

Fox, John 1939- DLB-245

Fox, John, Jr. 1862 or 1863-1919 . . . DLB-9; DS-13

Fox, Paula 1923- DLB-52

Fox, Richard Kyle 1846-1922 . . . . DLB-79

Fox, William Price 1926- DLB-2; Y-81

   Remembering Joe Heller Y-99

Richard K. Fox [publishing house] DLB-49

Foxe, John 1517-1587 . . . . DLB-132

Fraenkel, Michael 1896-1957 . . . . DLB-4

Frame, Ronald 1953- DLB-319

France, Anatole 1844-1924 . . . . DLB-123, 330

France, Richard 1938- DLB-7

Francis, Convers 1795-1863 . . . . DLB-1, 235

Francis, Dick 1920- DLB-87; CDBLB-8

Francis, Sir Frank 1901-1988 . . . . DLB-201

Francis, H. E. 1924- DLB-335

Francis, Jeffrey, Lord 1773-1850.........DLB-107

C. S. Francis [publishing house].........DLB-49

Franck, Sebastian 1499-1542 ....DLB-179

Francke, Kuno 1855-1930 ....DLB-71

Françoise (Robertine Barry) 1863-1910....DLB-92

François, Louise von 1817-1893.........DLB-129

Frank, Bruno 1887-1945...............DLB-118

Frank, Leonhard 1882-1961 ....DLB-56, 118

Frank, Melvin 1913-1988..............DLB-26

Frank, Waldo 1889-1967 ....DLB-9, 63

Franken, Rose 1895?-1988 ...... DLB-228, Y-84

Franklin, Benjamin
 1706-1790.....DLB-24, 43, 73, 183; CDALB-2

Franklin, James 1697-1735 ....DLB-43

Franklin, John 1786-1847 ....DLB-99

Franklin, Miles 1879-1954 ....DLB-230

Franklin Library....................DLB-46

Frantz, Ralph Jules 1902-1979 ....DLB-4

Franzos, Karl Emil 1848-1904 ....DLB-129

Fraser, Antonia 1932- DLB-276

Fraser, G. S. 1915-1980 ....DLB-27

Fraser, George MacDonald
 1925-2008 ....DLB-352

Fraser, Kathleen 1935- DLB-169

Frattini, Alberto 1922- DLB-128

Frau Ava ?-1127....................DLB-148

Fraunce, Abraham 1558?-1592 or 1593...DLB-236

Frayn, Michael 1933- DLB-13, 14, 194, 245

Frazier, Charles 1950- DLB-292

Fréchette, Louis-Honoré 1839-1908.......DLB-99

Frederic, Harold 1856-1898....DLB-12, 23; DS-13

Freed, Arthur 1894-1973 ....DLB-265

Freeling, Nicolas 1927-2003 ....DLB-87

 Tribute to Georges Simenon Y-89

Freeman, Douglas Southall
 1886-1953 ....DLB-17; DS-17

Freeman, Joseph 1897-1965 ....DLB-303

Freeman, Judith 1946- DLB-256

Freeman, Legh Richmond 1842-1915 .....DLB-23

Freeman, Mary E. Wilkins
 1852-1930 ....DLB-12, 78, 221

Freeman, R. Austin 1862-1943 ....DLB-70

Freidank circa 1170-circa 1233..........DLB-138

Freiligrath, Ferdinand 1810-1876 ....DLB-133

Fremlin, Celia 1914- DLB-276

Frémont, Jessie Benton 1834-1902.......DLB-183

Frémont, John Charles
 1813-1890 ....DLB-183, 186

French, Alice 1850-1934 ....DLB-74; DS-13

French, David 1939- DLB-53

French, Evangeline 1869-1960 ....DLB-195

French, Francesca 1871-1960 ....DLB-195

James French [publishing house] DLB-49

Samuel French [publishing house] DLB-49

Samuel French, Limited...............DLB-106

French Literature
 Georges-Louis Leclerc de Buffon, "Le Discours sur le style"..................DLB-314
 Marie-Jean-Antoine-Nicolas Caritat, marquis de Condorcet, "The Tenth Stage"...DLB-314
 Sophie Cottin, *Claire d'Albe* DLB-314
 Declaration of the Rights of Man and of the Citizen DLB-314
 Denis Diderot, "The Encyclopedia" ..DLB-314
 Epic and Beast Epic................DLB-208
 French Arthurian Literature DLB-208
 Olympe de Gouges, *Declaration of the Rights of Woman* DLB-314
 Françoise d'Issembourg de Graffigny, *Letters from a Peruvian Woman* DLB-314
 Claude-Adrien Helvétius, *The Spirit of Laws* DLB-314
 Paul Henri Thiry, baron d'Holbach (writing as Jean-Baptiste de Mirabaud), *The System of Nature*.....................DLB-314
 Pierre-Ambroise-François Choderlos de Laclos, *Dangerous Acquaintances*..........DLB-314
 Lyric Poetry DLB-268
 Louis-Sébastien Mercier, *Le Tableau de Paris*..................DLB-314
 Charles-Louis de Secondat, baron de Montesquieu, *The Spirit of Laws*...DLB-314
 Other Poets DLB-217
 Poetry in Nineteenth-Century France: Cultural Background and Critical Commentary DLB-217
 Roman de la Rose: Guillaume de Lorris 1200 to 1205-circa 1230, Jean de Meun 1235/1240-circa 1305 .....DLB-208
 Jean-Jacques Rousseau, *The Social Contract* DLB-314
 Marquis de Sade, "Dialogue entre un prêtre et un moribond"................DLB-314
 Saints' Lives DLB-208
 Troubadours, *Trobairitz,* and Trouvères DLB-208
 Anne-Robert-Jacques Turgot, baron de l'Aulne, "Memorandum on Local Government" DLB-314
 Voltaire, "An account of the death of the chevalier de La Barre"..............DLB-314
 Voltaire, *Candide*..................DLB-314
 Voltaire, *Philosophical Dictionary*......DLB-314

French Theater
 Medieval French Drama DLB-208
 Parisian Theater, Fall 1984: Toward a New Baroque..................Y-85

Freneau, Philip 1752-1832 ....DLB-37, 43

 The Rising Glory of America DLB-37

Freni, Melo 1934- DLB-128

Fréron, Elie Catherine 1718-1776 ....DLB-313

Freshfield, Douglas W. 1845-1934 ......DLB-174

Freud, Sigmund 1856-1939 ....DLB-296

Freytag, Gustav 1816-1895 ....DLB-129

Fríða Á. Sigurðardóttir 1940- DLB-293

Fridegård, Jan 1897-1968..............DLB-259

Fried, Erich 1921-1988 ....DLB-85

Friedan, Betty 1921-2006..............DLB-246

Friedman, Bruce Jay 1930- DLB-2, 28, 244

Friedman, Carl 1952- DLB-299

Friedman, Kinky 1944- DLB-292

Friedrich von Hausen circa 1171-1190....DLB-138

Friel, Brian 1929- DLB-13, 319

Friend, Krebs 1895?-1967? DLB-4

Fries, Fritz Rudolf 1935- DLB-75

Frisch, Max 1911-1991 .. DLB-69, 124; CDWLB-2

Frischlin, Nicodemus 1547-1590 ....DLB-179

Frischmuth, Barbara 1941- DLB-85

Fritz, Jean 1915- DLB-52

Froissart, Jean circa 1337-circa 1404......DLB-208

Fromm, Erich 1900-1980..............DLB-296

Fromentin, Eugene 1820-1876 ....DLB-123

Frontinus circa A.D. 35-A.D. 103/104 .....DLB-211

Frost, A. B. 1851-1928.........DLB-188; DS-13

Frost, Carol 1948- DLB-342

Frost, Robert
 1874-1963 .....DLB-54, 342; DS-7; CDALB-4

 The Friends of the Dymock Poets........Y-00

Frostenson, Katarina 1953- DLB-257

Frothingham, Octavius Brooks
 1822-1895 ....DLB-1, 243

Froude, James Anthony
 1818-1894 ....DLB-18, 57, 144

Fruitlands 1843-1844..........DLB-1, 223; DS-5

Fry, Christopher 1907-2005 ....DLB-13

 Tribute to John Betjeman Y-84

Fry, Roger 1866-1934 .... DS-10

Fry, Stephen 1957- DLB-207

Frye, Northrop 1912-1991....... DLB-67, 68, 246

Fuchs, Daniel 1909-1993 ..... DLB-9, 26, 28; Y-93

 Tribute to Isaac Bashevis Singer Y-91

Fuentes, Carlos 1928- DLB-113; CDWLB-3

Fuertes, Gloria 1918-1998 ....DLB-108

Fugard, Athol 1932- DLB-225

The Fugitives and the Agrarians:
 The First Exhibition Y-85

Fujiwara no Shunzei 1114-1204.........DLB-203

Fujiwara no Tameaki 1230s?-1290s?.....DLB-203

Fujiwara no Tameie 1198-1275 ....DLB-203

Fujiwara no Teika 1162-1241...........DLB-203

Fuks, Ladislav 1923-1994 ....DLB-299

Fulbecke, William 1560-1603?..........DLB-172

Fuller, Charles 1939- DLB-38, 266

Fuller, Henry Blake 1857-1929..........DLB-12

Fuller, John 1937- DLB-40

Fuller, Margaret (see Fuller, Sarah)

Fuller, Roy 1912-1991............... DLB-15, 20

    Tribute to Christopher Isherwood Y-86

Fuller, Samuel 1912-1997 .... DLB-26

Fuller, Sarah 1810-1850 .... DLB-1, 59, 73, 183, 223, 239; DS-5; CDALB-2

Fuller, Thomas 1608-1661 .... DLB-151

Fullerton, Hugh 1873-1945............. DLB-171

Fullwood, William fl. 1568............. DLB-236

Fulton, Alice 1952- DLB-193

Fulton, Len 1934- Y-86

Fulton, Robin 1937- DLB-40

Funkhouser, Erica 1949- DLB-342

Furbank, P. N. 1920- DLB-155

Furetière, Antoine 1619-1688 .... DLB-268

Furman, Laura 1945- Y-86

Furmanov, Dmitrii Andreevich 1891-1926 .... DLB-272

Furness, Horace Howard 1833-1912 ..... DLB-64

Furness, William Henry 1802-1896 .... DLB-1, 235

Furnivall, Frederick James 1825-1910.... DLB-184

Furphy, Joseph (Tom Collins) 1843-1912.................... DLB-230

Furst, Alan 1941- DLB-350

Furthman, Jules 1888-1966............. DLB-26

    Shakespeare and Montaigne: A Symposium by Jules Furthman Y-02

Furui Yoshikichi 1937- DLB-182

Fushimi, Emperor 1265-1317 .... DLB-203

Futabatei Shimei (Hasegawa Tatsunosuke) 1864-1909 .... DLB-180

Fyleman, Rose 1877-1957 .... DLB-160

G

G., 1972 Booker Prize winner, John Berger DLB-326

Gaarder, Jostein 1952- DLB-297

Gadallah, Leslie 1939- DLB-251

Gadamer, Hans-Georg 1900-2002 ...... DLB-296

Gadda, Carlo Emilio 1893-1973......... DLB-177

Gaddis, William 1922-1998 .... DLB-2, 278

    William Gaddis: A Tribute............ Y-99

Gág, Wanda 1893-1946 .... DLB-22

Gagarin, Ivan Sergeevich 1814-1882 .... DLB-198

Gage, Matilda Joslyn 1826-1898........ DLB-345

Gagnon, Madeleine 1938- DLB-60

Gaiman, Neil 1960- DLB-261

Gaine, Hugh 1726-1807 .... DLB-43

Hugh Gaine [publishing house] DLB-49

Gaines, Ernest J. 1933- DLB-2, 33, 152; Y-80; CDALB-6

Gaiser, Gerd 1908-1976 .... DLB-69

Gaitskill, Mary 1954- DLB-244

Galarza, Ernesto 1905-1984 .... DLB-122

Galaxy Science Fiction Novels DLB-46

Galbraith, Robert (or Caubraith) circa 1483-1544 .... DLB-281

Gale, Zona 1874-1938............DLB-9, 228, 78

Galen of Pergamon 129-after 210 ....DLB-176

Gales, Winifred Marshall 1761-1839 .... DLB-200

Galich, Aleksandr 1918-1977 .... DLB-317

Medieval Galician-Portuguese Poetry.... DLB-287

Gall, Louise von 1815-1855 .... DLB-133

Gallagher, Tess 1943- DLB-120, 212, 244

Gallagher, Wes 1911-1997 .... DLB-127

Gallagher, William Davis 1808-1894 ..... DLB-73

Gallant, Mavis 1922- DLB-53

Gallegos, María Magdalena 1935- DLB-209

Gallico, Paul 1897-1976...............DLB-9, 171

Gallop, Jane 1952- DLB-246

Galloway, Grace Growden 1727-1782.... DLB-200

Galloway, Janice 1956- DLB-319

Gallup, Donald 1913-2000 .... DLB-187

Galsworthy, John 1867-1933.................
    DLB-10, 34, 98, 162, 330; DS-16; CDBLB-5

Galt, John 1779-1839 ....DLB-99, 116, 159

Galton, Sir Francis 1822-1911 .... DLB-166

Galvin, Brendan 1938- DLB-5

Gambaro, Griselda 1928- DLB-305

Gambit..................... DLB-46

Gamboa, Reymundo 1948- DLB-122

Gammer Gurton's Needle................ DLB-62

Gan, Elena Andreevna (Zeneida R-va) 1814-1842 .... DLB-198

Gander, Forrest 1956- DLB-342

Gandhi, Mohandas Karamchand 1869-1948 .... DLB-323

Gandlevsky, Sergei Markovich 1952- DLB-285

Gannett, Frank E. 1876-1957 .... DLB-29

Gant, Eugene: Projected Works Y-01

Gao Xingjian 1940- DLB-330; Y-00

    Nobel Lecture 2000: "The Case for Literature".................... Y-00

Gaos, Vicente 1919-1980 .... DLB-134

Garborg, Arne 1851-1924 .... DLB-354

Garborg, Hulda 1862-1934 .... DLB-354

García, Andrew 1854?-1943 .... DLB-209

García, Cristina 1958- DLB-292

García, Lionel G. 1935- DLB-82

García, Richard 1941- DLB-209

García, Santiago 1928- DLB-305

García Márquez, Gabriel 1927- DLB-113, 330; Y-82; CDWLB-3

The Magical World of Macondo Y-82

Nobel Lecture 1982: The Solitude of Latin America Y-82

A Tribute to Gabriel García Márquez Y-82

García Marruz, Fina 1923- DLB-283

García-Camarillo, Cecilio 1943- DLB-209

Garcilaso de la Vega circa 1503-1536 .... DLB-318

Garcilaso de la Vega, Inca 1539-1616.... DLB-318

Gardam, Jane 1928- DLB-14, 161, 231

Gardell, Jonas 1963- DLB-257

Garden, Alexander circa 1685-1756 ...... DLB-31

Gardiner, John Rolfe 1936- DLB-244

Gardiner, Margaret Power Farmer (see Blessington, Marguerite, Countess of)

Gardner, John 1933-1982....DLB-2; Y-82; CDALB-7

Garfield, Leon 1921-1996............ DLB-161

Garis, Howard R. 1873-1962 .... DLB-22

Garland, Hamlin 1860-1940...DLB-12, 71, 78, 186

    The Hamlin Garland Society........... Y-01

Garneau, François-Xavier 1809-1866..... DLB-99

Garneau, Hector de Saint-Denys 1912-1943 .... DLB-88

Garneau, Michel 1939- DLB-53

Garner, Alan 1934- DLB-161, 261

Garner, Helen 1942- DLB-325

Garner, Hugh 1913-1979 .... DLB-68

Garnett, David 1892-1981 .... DLB-34

Garnett, Eve 1900-1991 .... DLB-160

Garnett, Richard 1835-1906............ DLB-184

Garnier, Robert 1545?-1590............. DLB-327

Garrard, Lewis H. 1829-1887 .... DLB-186

Garraty, John A. 1920-2007 ....DLB-17

Garrett, Almeida (João Baptista da Silva Leitão de Almeida Garrett) 1799-1854..................... DLB-287

Garrett, George 1929-2008 .... DLB-2, 5, 130, 152; Y-83

Literary Prizes Y-00

My Summer Reading Orgy: Reading for Fun and Games: One Reader's Report on the Summer of 2001...... Y-01

A Summing Up at Century's End Y-99

Tribute to James Dickey............... Y-97

Tribute to Michael M. Rea............ Y-97

Tribute to Paxton Davis............. Y-94

Tribute to Peter Taylor............. Y-94

Tribute to William Goyen Y-83

A Writer Talking: A Collage Y-00

Garrett, John Work 1872-1942 .... DLB-187

Garrick, David 1717-1779 .... DLB-84, 213

Garrison, William Lloyd 1805-1879........ DLB-1, 43, 235; CDALB-2

Garro, Elena 1920-1998 .... DLB-145

Garshin, Vsevolod Mikhailovich 1855-1888 .... DLB-277

Garth, Samuel 1661-1719...............DLB-95
Garve, Andrew 1908-2001..............DLB-87
Garvey, Marcus 1887-1940............DLB-345
Gary, Romain 1914-1980..........DLB-83, 299
Gascoigne, George 1539?-1577.........DLB-136
Gascoyne, David 1916-2001 ....DLB-20
Gash, Jonathan (John Grant) 1933- DLB-276
Gaskell, Elizabeth Cleghorn
    1810-1865......DLB-21, 144, 159; CDBLB-4
    The Gaskell Society....................Y-98
Gaskell, Jane 1941- DLB-261
Gaspey, Thomas 1788-1871.............DLB-116
Gass, William H. 1924- DLB-2, 227
Gates, Doris 1901-1987 ....DLB-22
Gates, Henry Louis, Jr. 1950- DLB-67
Gates, Lewis E. 1860-1924..............DLB-71
Gatto, Alfonso 1909-1976 ....DLB-114
Gault, William Campbell 1910-1995.....DLB-226
    Tribute to Kenneth Millar..............Y-83
Gaunt, Mary 1861-1942 ....DLB-174, 230
Gautier, Théophile 1811-1872..........DLB-119
Gautreaux, Tim 1947- DLB-292
Gauvreau, Claude 1925-1971............DLB-88
Gavelis, Ričardas 1950-2002 ....DLB-353
The Gawain-Poet
    fl. circa 1350-1400.................DLB-146
Gawsworth, John (Terence Ian Fytton
    Armstrong) 1912-1970.............DLB-255
Gay, Ebenezer 1696-1787...............DLB-24
Gay, John 1685-1732 ....DLB-84, 95
Gayarré, Charles E. A. 1805-1895........DLB-30
Charles Gaylord [publishing house]......DLB-49
Gaylord, Edward King 1873-1974 ....DLB-127
Gaylord, Edward Lewis 1919-2003 ......DLB-127
Gazdanov, Gaito 1903-1971............DLB-317
Gébler, Carlo 1954- DLB-271
Geda, Sigitas 1943-....................DLB-232
Geddes, Gary 1940-....................DLB-60
Geddes, Virgil 1897-1989................DLB-4
Gedeon (Georgii Andreevich Krinovsky)
    circa 1730-1763....................DLB-150
Gee, Maggie 1948- DLB-207
Gee, Shirley 1932- DLB-245
Geibel, Emanuel 1815-1884.............DLB-129
Geiogamah, Hanay 1945- DLB-175
Geis, Bernard, Associates...............DLB-46
Geisel, Theodor Seuss 1904-1991 ...DLB-61; Y-91
Gelb, Arthur 1924- DLB-103
Gelb, Barbara 1926- DLB-103
Gelber, Jack 1932- DLB-7, 228
Gélinas, Gratien 1909-1999 ....DLB-88

Gellert, Christian Fürchtegott
    1715-1769......................DLB-97
Gellhorn, Martha 1908-1998............Y-82, 98
Gems, Pam 1925- DLB-13
Genet, Jean 1910-1986........ DLB-72, 321; Y-86
Genette, Gérard 1930- DLB-242
Genevoix, Maurice 1890-1980...........DLB-65
Genis, Aleksandr Aleksandrovich
    1953- DLB-285
Genlis, Stéphanie-Félicité Ducrest, comtesse de
    1746-1830 ....DLB-313
Genovese, Eugene D. 1930- DLB-17
Gent, Peter 1942- Y-82
Geoffrey of Monmouth
    circa 1100-1155...................DLB-146
George, Elizabeth 1949- DLB-306
George, Henry 1839-1897..............DLB-23
George, Jean Craighead 1919- DLB-52
George, W. L. 1882-1926...............DLB-197
George III, King of Great Britain
    and Ireland 1738-1820 ....DLB-213
Georgslied 896?......................DLB-148
Gerber, Merrill Joan 1938- DLB-218
Gerhardie, William 1895-1977...........DLB-36
Gerhardt, Paul 1607-1676..............DLB-164
Gérin, Winifred 1901-1981 ....DLB-155
Gérin-Lajoie, Antoine 1824-1882.........DLB-99
German Literature
    A Call to Letters and an Invitation
        to the Electric Chair DLB-75
    The Conversion of an Unpolitical
        Man DLB-66
    The German Radio Play DLB-124
    The German Transformation from the
        Baroque to the Enlightenment DLB-97
    Germanophilism DLB-66
    A Letter from a New Germany..........Y-90
    The Making of a People DLB-66
    The Novel of Impressionism...........DLB-66
    Pattern and Paradigm: History as
        Design........................DLB-75
    Premisses.......................DLB-66
    The 'Twenties and Berlin DLB-66
    Wolfram von Eschenbach's Parzival:
        Prologue and Book 3 ....DLB-138
    Writers and Politics: 1871-1918.......DLB-66
German Literature, Middle Ages
    Abrogans circa 790-800............DLB-148
    Annolied between 1077 and 1081 .....DLB-148
    The Arthurian Tradition and
        Its European Context DLB-138
    Cambridge Songs (Carmina Cantabrigensia)
        circa 1050.....................DLB-148
    Christus und die Samariterin circa 950 ...DLB-148
    De Heinrico circa 980?...............DLB-148
    Ecbasis Captivi circa 1045 ....DLB-148
    Georgslied 896?.....................DLB-148

German Literature and Culture from
    Charlemagne to the Early Courtly
    Period DLB-148; CDWLB-2
The Germanic Epic and Old English
    Heroic Poetry: Widsith, Waldere,
    and The Fight at Finnsburg DLB-146
Graf Rudolf between circa
    1170 and circa 1185 ....DLB-148
Heliand circa 850 ....DLB-148
Das Hildebrandslied
    circa 820..........DLB-148; CDWLB-2
Kaiserchronik circa 1147.............DLB-148
The Legends of the Saints and a
    Medieval Christian
    Worldview DLB-148
Ludus de Antichristo circa 1160........DLB-148
Ludwigslied 881 or 882.............DLB-148
Muspilli circa 790-circa 850 ....DLB-148
Old German Genesis and Old German
    Exodus circa 1050-circa 1130 .....DLB-148
Old High German Charms
    and Blessings DLB-148; CDWLB-2
The Old High German Isidor
    circa 790-800...................DLB-148
Petruslied circa 854?.................DLB-148
Physiologus circa 1070-circa 1150......DLB-148
Ruodlieb circa 1050-1075............DLB-148
"Spielmannsepen" (circa 1152
    circa 1500) DLB-148
The Strasbourg Oaths 842 ....DLB-148
Tatian circa 830 ....DLB-148
Waltharius circa 825 ....DLB-148
Wessobrunner Gebet circa 787-815 ......DLB-148
German Theater
    German Drama 800-1280 ....DLB-138
    German Drama from Naturalism
        to Fascism: 1889-1933 ....DLB-118
Gernsback, Hugo 1884-1967.........DLB-8, 137
Gerould, Katharine Fullerton
    1879-1944 ....DLB-78
Samuel Gerrish [publishing house] DLB-49
Gerrold, David 1944- DLB-8
Gersão, Teolinda 1940- DLB-287
Gershon, Karen 1923-1993 ....DLB-299
Gershwin, Ira 1896-1983...............DLB-265
    The Ira Gershwin Centenary Y-96
Gerson, Jean 1363-1429...............DLB-208
Gersonides 1288-1344................DLB-115
Gerstäcker, Friedrich 1816-1872 ....DLB-129
Gertsen, Aleksandr Ivanovich
    (see Herzen, Alexander)
Gerstenberg, Heinrich Wilhelm von
    1737-1823 ....DLB-97
Gervinus, Georg Gottfried
    1805-1871 ....DLB-133
Gery, John 1953- DLB-282
Geßner, Solomon 1730-1788...........DLB-97
Geston, Mark S. 1946- DLB-8
Al-Ghazali 1058-1111 ....DLB-115

Ghelderode, Michel de (Adolphe-Adhémar Martens) 1898-1962 .... DLB-321
al-Ghitani, Gamal 1945- DLB-346
Ghiu, Bogdan 1958- DLB-353
Ghose, Zulfikar 1935- DLB-323
Ghosh, Amitav 1956- DLB-323
The Ghost Road, 1995 Booker Prize winner, Pat Barker DLB-326
Gibbings, Robert 1889-1958........... DLB-195
Gibbon, Edward 1737-1794........ DLB-104, 336
Gibbon, John Murray 1875-1952 .... DLB-92
Gibbon, Lewis Grassic (see Mitchell, James Leslie)
Gibbons, Floyd 1887-1939 .... DLB-25
Gibbons, Kaye 1960- DLB-292
Gibbons, Reginald 1947- DLB-120
Gibbons, Stella 1902-1989 .... DLB-352
Gibbons, William eighteenth century..... DLB-73
Gibran, Kahlil 1883-1931 .... DLB-346
Gibson, Charles Dana 1867-1944................ DLB-188; DS-13
Gibson, Graeme 1934- DLB-53
Gibson, Margaret 1944- DLB-120
Gibson, Margaret Dunlop 1843-1920..... DLB-174
Gibson, Wilfrid 1878-1962 .... DLB-19
    The Friends of the Dymock Poets Y-00
Gibson, William 1914-2008 .... DLB-7
Gibson, William 1948- DLB-251
Gide, André 1869-1951 .... DLB-65, 321, 330
Giguère, Diane 1937- DLB-53
Giguère, Roland 1929-2003 .... DLB-60
Gil de Biedma, Jaime 1929-1990........ DLB-108
Gil-Albert, Juan 1906-1994............ DLB-134
Gilbert, Anthony 1899-1973 .... DLB-77
Gilbert, Elizabeth 1969- DLB-292
Gilbert, Sir Humphrey 1537-1583....... DLB-136
Gilbert, Michael 1912-2006 .... DLB-87
Gilbert, Sandra M. 1936- DLB-120, 246
Gilbert, W. S. 1836-1911 .... DLB-344
Gilchrist, Alexander 1828-1861 .... DLB-144
Gilchrist, Ellen 1935- DLB-130
Gilder, Jeannette L. 1849-1916 .... DLB-79
Gilder, Richard Watson 1844-1909.... DLB-64, 79
Gildersleeve, Basil 1831-1924.......... DLB-71
Giles, Henry 1809-1882 .... DLB-64
Giles of Rome circa 1243-1316 .... DLB-115
Gilfillan, George 1813-1878 .... DLB-144
Gilfillan, Merrill 1945- DLB-342
Gill, Eric 1882-1940 .... DLB-98
Gill, Sarah Prince 1728-1771 .... DLB-200
William F. Gill Company DLB-49
Gillespie, A. Lincoln, Jr. 1895-1950 .... DLB-4

Gillespie, Haven 1883-1975 .... DLB-265
Gilliam, Florence fl. twentieth century DLB-4
Gilliatt, Penelope 1932-1993........... DLB-14
Gillott, Jacky 1939-1980............... DLB-14
Gilman, Caroline H. 1794-1888 .... DLB-3, 73
Gilman, Charlotte Perkins 1860-1935 ... DLB-221
    The Charlotte Perkins Gilman Society.... Y-99
W. and J. Gilman [publishing house] DLB-49
Gilmer, Elizabeth Meriwether 1861-1951 .... DLB-29
Gilmer, Francis Walker 1790-1826 .... DLB-37
Gilmore, Mary 1865-1962 .... DLB-260
Gilroy, Frank D. 1925- DLB-7
Gimferrer, Pere (Pedro) 1945- DLB-134
Ginger, Aleksandr S. 1897-1965 .... DLB-317
Gingrich, Arnold 1903-1976............ DLB-137
    Prospectus From the Initial Issue of *Esquire* (Autumn 1933)......... DLB-137
    "With the Editorial Ken," Prospectus From the Initial Issue of *Ken* (7 April 1938) DLB-137
Ginibi, Ruby Langford 1934- DLB-325
Ginsberg, Allen 1926-1997.... DLB-5, 16, 169, 237; CDALB-1
Ginzburg, Evgeniian1904-1977......... DLB-302
Ginzburg, Lidiia Iakovlevna 1902-1990 .. DLB-302
Ginzburg, Natalia 1916-1991 .... DLB-177
Ginzkey, Franz Karl 1871-1963.......... DLB-81
Gioia, Dana 1950- DLB-120, 282
Giono, Jean 1895-1970 .... DLB-72, 321
Giotti, Virgilio 1885-1957............. DLB-114
Giovanni, Nikki 1943- ... DLB-5, 41; CDALB-7
Giovannitti, Arturo 1884-1959 .... DLB-303
Gipson, Lawrence Henry 1880-1971 ..... DLB-17
Girard, Rodolphe 1879-1956 .... DLB-92
Giraudoux, Jean 1882-1944 .... DLB-65, 321
Girondo, Oliverio 1891-1967 .... DLB-283
Gissing, George 1857-1903 ...... DLB-18, 135, 184
    The Place of Realism in Fiction (1895)... DLB-18
Giudici, Giovanni 1924- DLB-128
Giuliani, Alfredo 1924- DLB-128
Gjellerup, Karl 1857-1919 .... DLB-300, 330
Glackens, William J. 1870-1938 .... DLB-188
Gladilin, Anatolii Tikhonovich 1935- .. DLB-302
Gladkov, Fedor Vasil'evich 1883-1958 ....DLB-272
Gladstone, William Ewart 1809-1898 ....DLB-57, 184
Glaeser, Ernst 1902-1963 .... DLB-69
Glancy, Diane 1941- DLB-175
Glanvill, Joseph 1636-1680........... DLB-252
Glanville, Brian 1931- DLB-15, 139
Glapthorne, Henry 1610-1643? DLB-58

Glasgow, Ellen 1873-1945............ DLB-9, 12
    The Ellen Glasgow Society Y-01
Glasier, Katharine Bruce 1867-1950 ..... DLB-190
Glaspell, Susan 1876-1948 ...... DLB-7, 9, 78, 228
Glass, Julia 1956- DLB-350
Glass, Montague 1877-1934 .... DLB-11
Glassco, John 1909-1981 .... DLB-68
Glatstein, Jacob (Yankev Glatshteyn) 1896-1971..................... DLB-333
Glauser, Friedrich 1896-1938 .... DLB-56
Glavin, Anthony 1946- DLB-319
F. Gleason's Publishing Hall............ DLB-49
Gleim, Johann Wilhelm Ludwig 1719-1803..................... DLB-97
Glendinning, Robin 1938- DLB-310
Glendinning, Victoria 1937- DLB-155
Glidden, Frederick Dilley (Luke Short) 1908-1975..................... DLB-256
Glinka, Fedor Nikolaevich 1786-1880.... DLB-205
Glover, Keith 1966- DLB-249
Glover, Richard 1712-1785 .... DLB-95
Glover, Sue 1943- DLB-310
Glück, Louise 1943- DLB-5
Glyn, Elinor 1864-1943 .... DLB-153
Glynn, Martin 1957- DLB-347
Gnedich, Nikolai Ivanovich 1784-1833... DLB-205
Gobineau, Joseph-Arthur de 1816-1882 .... DLB-123
The God of Small Things, 1997 Booker Prize winner, Arundhati Roy................ DLB-326
Godber, John 1956- DLB-233
Godbout, Jacques 1933- DLB-53
Goddard, Morrill 1865-1937 .... DLB-25
Goddard, William 1740-1817 .... DLB-43
Godden, Rumer 1907-1998............ DLB-161
Godey, Louis A. 1804-1878 .... DLB-73
Godey and McMichael................ DLB-49
Godfrey, Dave 1938- DLB-60
Godfrey, Thomas 1736-1763............ DLB-31
Godine, David R., Publisher............ DLB-46
Godkin, E. L. 1831-1902 .... DLB-79
Godolphin, Sidney 1610-1643 .... DLB-126
Godwin, Gail 1937- DLB-6, 234, 350
M. J. Godwin and Company DLB-154
Godwin, Mary Jane Clairmont 1766-1841...................... DLB-163
Godwin, Parke 1816-1904 .... DLB-3, 64, 250
Godwin, William 1756-1836 ...... DLB-39, 104, 142, 158, 163, 262, 336; CDBLB-3
    Preface to *St. Leon* (1799) DLB-39
Goering, Reinhard 1887-1936 .... DLB-118
Goes, Albrecht 1908- DLB-69

Goethe, Johann Wolfgang von
  1749-1832 . . . . DLB-94; CDWLB-2
Goetz, Curt 1888-1960 . . . . DLB-124
Goffe, Thomas circa 1592-1629. . . . . .DLB-58
Goffstein, M. B. 1940- DLB-61
Gogarty, Oliver St. John 1878-1957 . . . .DLB-15, 19
Gogol, Nikolai Vasil'evich 1809-1852 . . . .DLB-198
Goh Poh Seng 1936- DLB-348
Goines, Donald 1937-1974 . . . . .DLB-33
Gold, Herbert 1924- DLB-2; Y-81
  Tribute to William Saroyan. Y-81
Gold, Michael 1893-1967. . . . . .DLB-9, 28
Goldbarth, Albert 1948- DLB-120
Goldberg, Dick 1947- DLB-7
Golden Cockerel Press. DLB-112
Goldfaden, Abraham (Avrom Goldfadn)
  1840-1908 . . . . .DLB-333
Golding, Arthur 1536-1606 . . . . DLB-136
Golding, Louis 1895-1958 . . . . DLB-195
Golding, William 1911-1993 . . . .
  . DLB-15, 100, 255, 326, 330; Y-83; CDBLB-7
  Nobel Lecture 1993. . . . . .Y-83
  The Stature of William Golding Y-83
Goldman, Emma 1869-1940 . . . . .DLB-221
Goldman, William 1931- DLB-44
Goldring, Douglas 1887-1960 . . . . DLB-197
Goldschmidt, Meïr Aron 1819-1887 . . . . .DLB-300
Goldsmith, Oliver 1730?-1774
  . . .DLB-39, 89, 104, 109, 142, 336; CDBLB-2
Goldsmith, Oliver 1794-1861. . . . . .DLB-99
Goldsmith Publishing Company DLB-46
Goldstein, Richard 1944- DLB-185
Goldsworthy, Peter 1951- DLB-325
Gollancz, Sir Israel 1864-1930 . . . . DLB-201
Victor Gollancz Limited. DLB-112
Gomberville, Marin Le Roy, sieur de
  1600?-1674 . . . . DLB-268
Gombrowicz, Witold
  1904-1969 . . . . DLB-215; CDWLB-4
Gomez, Madeleine-Angélique Poisson de
  1684-1770 . . . . .DLB-313
Gómez de Ciudad Real, Alvar (Alvar Gómez
  de Guadalajara) 1488-1538 . . . . DLB-318
Gómez-Quiñones, Juan 1942- DLB-122
Laurence James Gomme
  [publishing house] DLB-46
Gompers, Samuel 1850-1924 . . . . .DLB-303
Gonçalves Dias, Antônio 1823-1864 . . . . .DLB-307
Goncharov, Ivan Aleksandrovich
  1812-1891 . . . . .DLB-238
Goncourt, Edmond de 1822-1896 . . . . . . DLB-123
Goncourt, Jules de 1830-1870 . . . . DLB-123
Gonzales, Rodolfo "Corky" 1928- DLB-122
Gonzales-Berry, Erlinda 1942- DLB-209

"Chicano Language". DLB-82
González, Angel 1925- DLB-108
Gonzalez, Genaro 1949- DLB-122
Gonzalez, N. V. M. 1915-1999. . . . . .DLB-312, 348
González, Otto-Raúl 1921- DLB-290
Gonzalez, Ray 1952- DLB-122
González de Mireles, Jovita
  1899-1983 . . . . .DLB-122
González Martínez, Enrique
  1871-1952 . . . . .DLB-290
González-T., César A. 1931- DLB-82
Gonzalo de Berceo
  circa 1195-circa 1264 . . . . DLB-337
Goodis, David 1917-1967 . . . . .DLB-226
Goodison, Lorna 1947- DLB-157
Goodman, Allegra 1967- DLB-244, 350
Goodman, Nelson 1906-1998 . . . . .DLB-279
Goodman, Paul 1911-1972. . . . . DLB-130, 246
The Goodman Theatre DLB-7
Goodrich, Frances 1891-1984 and
  Hackett, Albert 1900-1995 . . . . .DLB-26
Goodrich, Samuel Griswold
  1793-1860 . . . . DLB-1, 42, 73, 243
S. G. Goodrich [publishing house] DLB-49
C. E. Goodspeed and Company DLB-49
Goodwin, Stephen 1943- Y-82
Googe, Barnabe 1540-1594 . . . . DLB-132
Gookin, Daniel 1612-1687 . . . . .DLB-24
Gopegui, Belén 1963- DLB-322
Goran, Lester 1928- DLB-244
Gordimer, Nadine
  1923- DLB-225, 326, 330; Y-91
  Nobel Lecture 1991. . . . . .Y-91
Gordin, Jacob (Yankev Gordin)
  1853-1909 . . . . .DLB-333
Gordon, Adam Lindsay 1833-1870 . . . . . .DLB-230
Gordon, Caroline
  1895-1981 . . . . DLB-4, 9, 102; DS-17; Y-81
Gordon, Charles F. (see OyamO)
Gordon, Charles William (see Connor, Ralph)
Gordon, Giles 1940- DLB-14, 139, 207
Gordon, Helen Cameron, Lady Russell
  1867-1949 . . . . .DLB-195
Gordon, Lyndall 1941- DLB-155
Gordon, Mack 1904-1959 . . . . DLB-265
Gordon, Mary 1949- DLB-6; Y-81
Gordon, Neil (see Macdonell, A. G.)
Gordon, Richard 1921- DLB-352
Gordon, Thomas ca. 1692-1750. . . . . .DLB-336
Gordone, Charles 1925-1995. . . . . .DLB-7
Gore, Catherine
  1799 or 1800-1861. . . . . DLB-116, 344
Gore-Booth, Eva 1870-1926 . . . . .DLB-240
Gores, Joe 1931- DLB-226; Y-02

Tribute to Kenneth Millar Y-83
Tribute to Raymond Chandler Y-88
Gorey, Edward 1925-2000. . . . . DLB-61
Gorgias of Leontini
  circa 485 B.C.-376 B.C. DLB-176
Gor'ky, Maksim 1868-1936. . . . . .DLB-295
Gorodetsky, Sergei Mitrofanovich
  1884-1967 . . . . .DLB-295
Gorostiza, José 1901-1979 . . . . .DLB-290
Görres, Joseph 1776-1848 . . . . .DLB-90
Gospodinov, Georgi 1968- DLB-353
Gosse, Edmund 1849-1928 . . . . . DLB-57, 144, 184
Gosson, Stephen 1554-1624. . . . . DLB-172
  The Schoole of Abuse (1579) DLB-172
Gotanda, Philip Kan 1951- DLB-266
Gotlieb, Phyllis 1926- DLB-88, 251
Go-Toba 1180-1239 . . . . .DLB-203
Gottfried von Straßburg
  died before 1230 . . . . . . .DLB-138; CDWLB-2
Gotthelf, Jeremias 1797-1854 . . . . .DLB-133
Gottschalk circa 804/808-869. . . . . .DLB-148
Gottsched, Johann Christoph
  1700-1766 . . . . .DLB-97
Götz, Johann Nikolaus 1721-1781 . . . . . . .DLB-97
Goudge, Elizabeth 1900-1984 . . . . DLB-191
Gouges, Olympe de 1748-1793 . . . . DLB-313
  Declaration of the Rights of Woman DLB-314
Gough, John B. 1817-1886. . . . . .DLB-243
Gough, Richard 1735-1809 . . . . DLB-336
Gould, Wallace 1882-1940. . . . . .DLB-54
Gournay, Marie de 1565-1645. . . . . .DLB-327
Govoni, Corrado 1884-1965 . . . . DLB-114
Govrin, Michal 1950- DLB-299
Gower, John circa 1330-1408 . . . . .DLB-146
Goyen, William 1915-1983 . . . . . DLB-2, 218; Y-83
Goytisolo, José Augustín 1928- DLB-134
Goytisolo, Juan 1931- DLB-322
Goytisolo, Luis 1935- DLB-322
Gozzano, Guido 1883-1916. . . . . .DLB-114
Grabbe, Christian Dietrich 1801-1836. . . . .DLB-133
Gracq, Julien (Louis Poirier) 1910-2007. . . .DLB-83
Grade, Chaim (Khayim Grade)
  1910-1982 . . . . .DLB-333
Grady, Henry W. 1850-1889 . . . . DLB-23
Graf, Oskar Maria 1894-1967 . . . . .DLB-56
Graf Rudolf between circa 1170 and
  circa 1185 . . . . .DLB-148
Graff, Gerald 1937- DLB-246
Graffigny, Françoise d'Issembourg de
  1695-1758 . . . . .DLB-313
  Letters from a Peruvian Woman DLB-314
Richard Grafton [publishing house] DLB-170
Grafton, Sue 1940- DLB-226

Graham, Frank 1893-1965 .... DLB-241

Graham, George Rex 1813-1894 .... DLB-73

Graham, Gwethalyn (Gwethalyn Graham
  Erichsen-Brown) 1913-1965 .... DLB-88

Graham, Jorie 1951- DLB-120

Graham, Joyce Maxtone (see Struther, Jan)

Graham, Katharine 1917-2001 .... DLB-127

Graham, Lorenz 1902-1989 .... DLB-76

Graham, Philip 1915-1963 .... DLB-127

Graham, R. B. Cunninghame
  1852-1936 .... DLB-98, 135, 174

Graham, Shirley 1896-1977 .... DLB-76

Graham, Stephen 1884-1975 .... DLB-195

Graham, W. S. 1918-1986 .... DLB-20

William H. Graham [publishing house] ... DLB-49

Graham, Winston 1910-2003 .... DLB-77

Grahame, Kenneth 1859-1932 ... DLB-34, 141, 178

Grainger, Martin Allerdale 1874-1941 .... DLB-92

Gramatky, Hardie 1907-1979 .... DLB-22

Gramcko, Ida 1924-1994 .... DLB-290

Gramsci, Antonio 1891-1937 .... DLB-296

La gran conquista de Ultramar
  thirteenth century................ DLB 337

Granada, Fray Luis de 1504-1588 ..... DLB-318

Grand, Sarah 1854-1943.......... DLB-135, 197

Grandbois, Alain 1900-1975 .... DLB-92

Grandson, Oton de circa 1345-1397 .... DLB-208

Grange, John circa 1556-?........... DLB-136

Granger, Thomas 1578-1627........... DLB-281

Granich, Irwin (see Gold, Michael)

Granin, Daniil 1918- DLB-302

Granovsky, Timofei Nikolaevich
  1813-1855...................... DLB-198

Grant, Anne MacVicar 1755-1838 ..... DLB-200

Grant, Duncan 1885-1978................DS-10

Grant, George 1918-1988 .... DLB-88

Grant, George Monro 1835-1902......... DLB-99

Grant, Harry J. 1881-1963 .... DLB-29

Grant, James Edward 1905-1966 .... DLB-26

Grant, John (see Gash, Jonathan)

War of the Words (and Pictures): The Creation
  of a Graphic Novel Y-02

Grass, Günter 1927- DLB-75, 124, 330; CDWLB-2

  Nobel Lecture 1999:
    "To Be Continued . . ." Y-99

  Tribute to Helen Wolff................ Y-94

Grasty, Charles H. 1863-1924 .... DLB-25

Grau, Shirley Ann 1929- DLB-2, 218

Graves, John 1920- Y-83

Graves, Richard 1715-1804............. DLB-39

Graves, Robert 1895-1985
  ....DLB-20, 100, 191; DS-18; Y-85; CDBLB-6

The St. John's College
  Robert Graves Trust Y-96

Gray, Alasdair 1934- DLB-194, 261, 319

Gray, Asa 1810-1888 .... DLB-1, 235

Gray, David 1838-1861............... DLB-32

Gray, Simon 1936-2008 .... DLB-13

Gray, Robert 1945- DLB-325

Gray, Thomas 1716-1771 .... DLB-109; CDBLB-2

Grayson, Richard 1951- DLB-234

Grayson, William J. 1788-1863.... DLB-3, 64, 248

The Great Bibliographers Series............ Y-93

The Great Gatsby (Documentary) DLB-219

"The Greatness of Southern Literature":
  League of the South Institute for the
  Study of Southern Culture and History
  .... Y-02

Grech, Nikolai Ivanovich 1787-1867 ..... DLB-198

Greeley, Horace 1811-1872... DLB-3, 43, 189, 250

Green, Adolph 1915-2002 .... DLB-44, 265

Green, Anna Katharine
  1846-1935 .... DLB-202, 221

Green, Duff 1791-1875 .... DLB-43

Green, Elizabeth Shippen 1871-1954 .... DLB-188

Green, Gerald 1922-2006 .... DLB-28

Green, Henry 1905-1973 .... DLB-15

Green, Jonas 1712-1767................ DLB-31

Green, Joseph 1706-1780............... DLB-31

Green, Julien 1900-1998 .... DLB-4, 72

Green, Paul 1894-1981 .... DLB-7, 9, 249; Y-81

Green, T. H. 1836-1882 .... DLB-190, 262

Green, Terence M. 1947- DLB-251

T. and S. Green [publishing house]....... DLB-49

Green Tiger Press.................... DLB-46

Timothy Green [publishing house]....... DLB-49

Greenaway, Kate 1846-1901........... DLB-141

Greenberg, Joanne 1932- DLB-335

Greenberg: Publisher DLB-46

Greene, Asa 1789-1838................ DLB-11

Greene, Belle da Costa 1883-1950 ...... DLB-187

Greene, Graham 1904-1991
  ....DLB-13, 15, 77, 100, 162, 201, 204;
                         Y-85, 91; CDBLB-7

  Tribute to Christopher Isherwood Y-86

Greene, Robert 1558-1592 .... DLB-62, 167

Greene, Robert Bernard (Bob), Jr.
  1947- DLB-185

Benjamin H Greene [publishing house] ... DLB-49

Greenfield, George 1917-2000.......... Y-91, 00

  Derek Robinson's Review of George
    Greenfield's *Rich Dust*............. Y-02

Greenhow, Robert 1800-1854........... DLB-30

Greenlee, William B. 1872-1953 .... DLB-187

Greenough, Horatio 1805-1852 ..... DLB-1, 235

Greenwell, Dora 1821-1882 .... DLB-35, 199

Greenwillow Books................... DLB-46

Greenwood, Grace
  (see Lippincott, Sara Jane Clarke)

Greenwood, Walter 1903-1974........DLB-10, 191

Greer, Ben 1948- DLB-6

Greflinger, Georg 1620?-1677.......... DLB-164

Greg, W. R. 1809-1881............... DLB-55

Greg, W. W. 1875-1959 .... DLB-201

Gregg, Josiah 1806-1850.......... DLB-183, 186

Gregg Press..................... DLB-46

Gregory, Horace 1898-1982 .... DLB-48

Gregory, Isabella Augusta Persse, Lady
  1852-1932 .... DLB-10

Gregory of Rimini circa 1300-1358 ..... DLB-115

Gregynog Press.................... DLB-112

Greiff, León de 1895-1976 .... DLB-283

Greiffenberg, Catharina Regina von
  1633-1694 .... DLB-168

Greig, Noël 1944- DLB-245

Grekova, Irina (Elena Sergeevna Venttsel')
  1907-2002...................... DLB-302

Grendel, Lajos 1948- DLB-353

Grenfell, Wilfred Thomason
  1865-1940...................... DLB-92

Grenier, Robert 1941- DLB-342

Grenville, Kate 1950- DLB-325

Gress, Elsa 1919-1988 .... DLB-214

Gretkowska, Manuela 1964- DLB-353

Greve, Felix Paul (see Grove, Frederick Philip)

Greville, Fulke, First Lord Brooke
  1554-1628 .... DLB-62, 172

Grey, Sir George, K.C.B. 1812-1898 .... DLB-184

Grey, Lady Jane 1537-1554 .... DLB-132

Grey, Zane 1872-1939.............. DLB-9, 212

  Zane Grey's West Society............. Y-00

Grey Owl (Archibald Stansfeld Belaney)
  1888-1938 ....DLB-92; DS-17

Grey Walls Press.................... DLB-112

Griboedov, Aleksandr Sergeevich
  1795?-1829..................... DLB-205

Grice, Paul 1913-1988 ....DLB-279

Grier, Eldon 1917- DLB-88

Grieve, C. M. (see MacDiarmid, Hugh)

Griffin, Bartholomew fl. 1596...........DLB-172

Griffin, Bryan

  "Panic Among the Philistines":
    A Postscript, An Interview
    with Bryan Griffin................ Y-81

Griffin, Gerald 1803-1840 .... DLB-159

The Griffin Poetry Prize................. Y-00

Griffith, Elizabeth 1727?-1793........ DLB-39, 89

  Preface to *The Delicate Distress* (1769)... DLB-39

Griffith, George 1857-1906............DLB-178

Ralph Griffiths [publishing house] DLB-154

Griffiths, Trevor 1935- DLB-13, 245

S. C. Griggs and Company DLB-49

Griggs, Sutton Elbert 1872-1930 .... DLB-50

Grignon, Claude-Henri 1894-1976....... DLB-68

Grigor'ev, Apollon Aleksandrovich
1822-1864 .... DLB-277

Grigorovich, Dmitrii Vasil'evich
1822-1899 .... DLB-238

Grigson, Geoffrey 1905-1985........... DLB-27

Grillparzer, Franz
1791-1872 .... DLB-133; CDWLB-2

Grimald, Nicholas
circa 1519-circa 1562 .... DLB-136

Grimké, Angelina Weld 1880-1958 .... DLB-50, 54

Grimké, Sarah Moore 1792-1873 .... DLB-239

Grimm, Frédéric Melchior 1723-1807 .... DLB-313

Grimm, Hans 1875-1959 .... DLB-66

Grimm, Jacob 1785-1863 .... DLB-90

Grimm, Wilhelm
1786-1859 .... DLB-90; CDWLB-2

Grimmelshausen, Johann Jacob Christoffel von
1621 or 1622-1676 ...... DLB-168; CDWLB-2

Grimshaw, Beatrice Ethel 1871-1953 ..... DLB-174

Grímur Thomsen 1820-1896 .... DLB-293

Grin, Aleksandr Stepanovich
1880-1932 .... DLB-272

Grindal, Edmund 1519 or 1520-1583 .... DLB-132

Gripe, Maria (Kristina) 1923-2007 .... DLB-257

Griswold, Rufus Wilmot
1815-1857 .... DLB-3, 59, 250

Gronlund, Laurence 1846-1899 .... DLB-303

Grosart, Alexander Balloch 1827-1899.... DLB-184

Grosholz, Emily 1950- DLB-282

Gross, Milt 1895-1953 .... DLB-11

Grosset and Dunlap DLB-49

Grosseteste, Robert circa 1160-1253 ..... DLB-115

Grossman, Allen 1932- DLB-193

Grossman, David 1954- DLB-299

Grossman, Vasilii Semenovich
1905-1964 .... DLB-272

Grossman Publishers DLB-46

Grosvenor, Gilbert H. 1875-1966........ DLB-91

Groth, Klaus 1819-1899............... DLB-129

Groulx, Lionel 1878-1967 .... DLB-68

Grove, Frederick Philip (Felix Paul Greve)
1879-1948 .... DLB-92

Grove Press DLB-46

Groys, Boris Efimovich 1947- DLB-285

Grubb, Davis 1919-1980 .... DLB-6

Gruelle, Johnny 1880-1938 .... DLB-22

von Grumbach, Argula
1492-after 1563? DLB-179

Grundtvig, N. F. S. 1783-1872 .... DLB-300

Grundy, Sydney 1848-1914 .... DLB-344

Grymeston, Elizabeth
before 1563-before 1604 .... DLB-136

Grynberg, Henryk 1936- DLB-299

Gryphius, Andreas
1616-1664 .... DLB-164; CDWLB-2

Gryphius, Christian 1649-1706 .... DLB-168

Guare, John 1938- DLB-7, 249

Guarini, Battista 1538-1612 .... DLB-339

Guarnieri, Gianfrancesco 1934- DLB-307

Guberman, Igor Mironovich 1936- DLB-285

Gubbins, Nathaniel (Gubbins, Norman Hector L.)
1893-1976 .... DLB-352

Guðbergur Bergsson 1932- DLB-293

Guðmundur Böðvarsson 1904-1974 .... DLB-293

Guðmundur Gíslason Hagalín
1898-1985 .... DLB-293

Guðmundur Magnússon (see Jón Trausti)

Guerra, Tonino 1920- DLB-128

Guest, Barbara 1920- DLB-5, 193

Guevara, Fray Antonio de 1480?-1545 ... DLB-318

Guèvremont, Germaine 1893-1968 .... DLB-68

Guglielminetti, Amalia 1881-1941 ...... DLB-264

Guidacci, Margherita 1921-1992 .... DLB-128

Guillén, Jorge 1893-1984 .... DLB-108

Guillén, Nicolás 1902-1989 .... DLB-283

Guilloux, Louis 1899-1980 .... DLB-72

Guilpin, Everard
circa 1572-after 1608? DLB-136

Guiney, Louise Imogen 1861-1920 ..... DLB-54

Guiterman, Arthur 1871-1943 .... DLB-11

Gul', Roman 1896-1986............... DLB-317

Gumilev, Nikolai Stepanovich
1886-1921 .... DLB-295

Günderrode, Caroline von
1780-1806 .... DLB-90

Gundulić, Ivan 1589-1638 ... DLB-147; CDWLB-4

Gunesekera, Romesh 1954- DLB-267, 323

Gunn, Bill 1934-1989.................. DLB-38

Gunn, James E. 1923- DLB-8

Gunn, Neil M. 1891-1973 .... DLB-15

Gunn, Thom 1929- DLB-27; CDBLB-8

Gunnar Gunnarsson 1889-1975 .... DLB-293

Gunnars, Kristjana 1948- DLB-60

Günther, Johann Christian 1695-1723 .... DLB-168

Gupta, Sunetra 1965- DLB-323

Gurganus, Allan 1947- DLB-350

Gurik, Robert 1932- DLB-60

Gurney, A. R. 1930- DLB-266

Gurney, Ivor 1890-1937................. Y-02

The Ivor Gurney Society Y-98

Guro, Elena Genrikhovna 1877-1913..... DLB-295

Gustafson, Ralph 1909-1995 .... DLB-88

Gustafsson, Lars 1936- DLB-257

Gütersloh, Albert Paris 1887-1973 .... DLB-81

Guterson, David 1956- DLB-292

Guthrie, A. B., Jr. 1901-1991 .... DLB-6, 212

Guthrie, Ramon 1896-1973 .... DLB-4

Guthrie, Thomas Anstey (see Anstey, FC)

Guthrie, Woody 1912-1967 .... DLB-303

The Guthrie Theater DLB-7

Gutiérrez Nájera, Manuel 1859-1895..... DLB-290

Guttormur J. Guttormsson 1878-1966.... DLB-293

Gutzkow, Karl 1811-1878............... DLB-133

Guy, Ray 1939- DLB-60

Guy, Rosa 1925- DLB-33

Guyot, Arnold 1807-1884 .... DS-13

Gwynn, R. S. 1948- DLB-282

Gwynne, Erskine 1898-1948 .... DLB-4

Gyles, John 1680-1755................. DLB-99

Gyllembourg, Thomasine 1773-1856..... DLB-300

Gyllensten, Lars 1921- DLB-257

Gyrðir Elíasson 1961- DLB-293

Gysin, Brion 1916-1986................. DLB-16

H

H.D. (see Doolittle, Hilda)

Habiby, Emile 1922-1996.............. DLB-346

Habermas, Jürgen 1929- DLB-242

Habington, William 1605-1654 .... DLB-126

Hacker, Marilyn 1942- DLB-120, 282

Hackett, Albert 1900-1995............. DLB-26

Hacks, Peter 1928- DLB-124

Hadas, Rachel 1948- DLB-120, 282

Hadden, Briton 1898-1929 .... DLB-91

Hagedorn, Friedrich von 1708-1754...... DLB-168

Hagedorn, Jessica Tarahata 1949- DLB-312

Hagelstange, Rudolf 1912-1984......... DLB-69

Hagerup, Inger 1905-1985............. DLB-297

Haggard, H. Rider
1856-1925 .... DLB-70, 156, 174, 178

Haggard, William (Richard Clayton)
1907-1993 .... DLB-276; Y-93

Hagy, Alyson 1960- DLB-244

Hahn-Hahn, Ida Gräfin von 1805-1880 .. DLB-133

Haig-Brown, Roderick 1908-1976 .... DLB-88

Haight, Gordon S. 1901-1985 .... DLB-103

Hailey, Arthur 1920-2004 .... DLB-88; Y-82

Haines, John 1924- DLB-5, 212

Hake, Edward fl. 1566-1604 .... DLB-136

Hake, Thomas Gordon 1809-1895 .... DLB-32

Hakl, Emil (Jan Beneš) 1958- DLB-353

Hakluyt, Richard 1552?-1616 .... DLB-136

Halas, František 1901-1949 .... DLB-215

Halbe, Max 1865-1944 .... DLB-118

Halberstam, David 1934-2007 .... DLB-241
Haldane, Charlotte 1894-1969 .... DLB-191
Haldane, J. B. S. 1892-1964 .... DLB-160
Haldeman, Joe 1943- DLB-8
Haldeman-Julius Company............ DLB-46
Hale, E. J., and Son.................. DLB-49
Hale, Edward Everett
    1822-1909 .... DLB-1, 42, 74, 235
Hale, Janet Campbell 1946- DLB-175
Hale, Kathleen 1898-2000 .... DLB-160
Hale, Leo Thomas (see Ebon)
Hale, Lucretia Peabody 1820-1900....... DLB-42
Hale, Nancy 1908-1988 . . DLB-86; DS-17; Y-80, 88
Hale, Sarah Josepha (Buell)
    1788-1879 .... DLB-1, 42, 73, 243
Hale, Susan 1833-1910 .... DLB-221
Hales, John 1584-1656 .... DLB-151
Halévy, Ludovic 1834-1908 .... DLB-192
Haley, Alex 1921-1992 .... DLB-38; CDALB-7
Haliburton, Thomas Chandler
    1796-1865................... DLB-11, 99
Hall, Adam (Trevor Dudley-Smith)
    1920-1995 .... DLB-276
Hall, Anna Maria 1800-1881 .... DLB-159
Hall, Donald 1928- DLB-5, 342
Hall, Edward 1497-1547 .... DLB-132
Hall, Halsey 1898-1977............... DLB-241
Hall, James 1793-1868 .... DLB-73, 74
Hall, James B. 1918- DLB-335
Hall, Joseph 1574-1656 .... DLB-121, 151
Hall, Radclyffe 1880-1943 .... DLB-191
Hall, Rodney 1935- DLB-289
Hall, Sarah Ewing 1761-1830 .... DLB-200
Hall, Stuart 1932- DLB-242
Samuel Hall [publishing house] DLB-49
al-Hallaj 857-922 .... DLB-311
Hallam, Arthur Henry 1811-1833 .... DLB-32
    On Some of the Characteristics of
    Modern Poetry and On the
    Lyrical Poems of Alfred
    Tennyson (1831) DLB-32
Halldór Laxness (Halldór Guðjónsson)
    1902-1998 .... DLB-293, 331
Halleck, Fitz-Greene 1790-1867 ...... DLB-3, 250
Haller, Albrecht von 1708-1777........ DLB-168
Halliday, Brett (see Dresser, Davis)
Halligan, Marion 1940- DLB-325
Halliwell-Phillipps, James Orchard
    1820-1889 .... DLB-184
Hallmann, Johann Christian
    1640-1704 or 1716? DLB-168
Hallmark Editions DLB-46
Halper, Albert 1904-1984 .... DLB-9
Halperin, John William 1941- DLB-111

Halpern, Moshe Leib (Moyshe Leyb Halpern)
    1886-1932 .... DLB-333
Halstead, Murat 1829-1908 .... DLB-23
Hamann, Johann Georg 1730-1788....... DLB-97
Hamburger, Michael 1924- DLB-27
Hamilton, Alexander 1712-1756 .... DLB-31
Hamilton, Alexander 1755?-1804........ DLB-37
Hamilton, Charles (see Richards, Frank)
Hamilton, Cicely 1872-1952......... DLB-10, 197
Hamilton, Edmond 1904-1977 .... DLB-8
Hamilton, Elizabeth 1758-1816..... DLB-116, 158
Hamilton, Gail (see Corcoran, Barbara)
Hamilton, Gail (see Dodge, Mary Abigail)
Hamish Hamilton Limited DLB-112
Hamilton, Hugo 1953- DLB-267
Hamilton, Ian 1938-2001 .... DLB-40, 155
Hamilton, Jane 1957- DLB-350
Hamilton, Janet 1795-1873 .... DLB-199
Hamilton, Mary Agnes 1884-1962...... DLB-197
Hamilton, Patrick 1904-1962 ...... DLB-10, 191
Hamilton, Virginia 1936-2002 ...DLB-33, 52; Y-01
Hamilton, Sir William 1788-1856....... DLB-262
Hamilton-Paterson, James 1941- DLB-267
Hammerstein, Oscar, 2nd 1895-1960 .... DLB-265
Hammett, Dashiell
    1894-1961 .... DLB-226; DS-6; CDALB-5
    An Appeal in TAC Y-91
    The Glass Key and Other Dashiell
        Hammett Mysteries............... Y-96
    Knopf to Hammett: The Editoral
        Correspondence Y-00
    The Maltese Falcon (Documentary).... DLB-280
Hammon, Jupiter 1711-died between
    1790 and 1806 .... DLB-31, 50
Hammond, John ?-1663 .... DLB-24
Hamner, Earl 1923- DLB-6
Hampson, John 1901-1955 .... DLB-191
Hampton, Christopher 1946- DLB-13
Hamsun, Knut 1859-1952 ....DLB-297, 330
Handel-Mazzetti, Enrica von 1871-1955 ... DLB-81
Handke, Peter 1942- DLB-85, 124
Handlin, Oscar 1915- DLB-17
Hankin, St. John 1869-1909 .... DLB-10
Hanley, Clifford 1922- DLB-14
Hanley, James 1901-1985 .... DLB-191
Hannah, Barry 1942- DLB-6, 234
Hannay, James 1827-1873 .... DLB-21
Hannes Hafstein 1861-1922 .... DLB-293
Hano, Arnold 1922- DLB-241
Hanrahan, Barbara 1939-1991 .... DLB-289
Hansberry, Lorraine
    1930-1965 .... DLB-7, 38; CDALB-1

Hansen, Joseph 1923-2004............ DLB-226
Hansen, Martin A. 1909-1955 .... DLB-214
Hansen, Maurits
    1794-1842...................... DLB-354
Hansen, Thorkild 1927-1989 .... DLB-214
Hanson, Elizabeth 1684-1737 .... DLB-200
Hapgood, Norman 1868-1937 .... DLB-91
Happel, Eberhard Werner 1647-1690.... DLB-168
Haq, Kaiser 1950- DLB-323
Harbach, Otto 1873-1963............. DLB-265
The Harbinger 1845-1849............ DLB-1, 223
Harburg, E. Y. "Yip" 1896-1981........ DLB-265
Harcourt Brace Jovanovich............ DLB-46
Hardenberg, Friedrich von (see Novalis)
Harding, Walter 1917-1996 .... DLB-111
Hardwick, Elizabeth 1916-2007 .... DLB-6
Hardy, Alexandre 1572?-1632 ....DLB-268
Hardy, Frank 1917-1994 .... DLB-260
Hardy, Thomas
    1840-1928 ...... DLB-18, 19, 135; CDBLB-5
    "Candour in English Fiction" (1890) ... DLB-18
Hare, Cyril 1900-1958 .... DLB-77
Hare, David 1947- DLB-13, 310
Hare, R. M. 1919-2002................ DLB-262
Hargrove, Marion 1919-2003.......... DLB-11
Häring, Georg Wilhelm Heinrich
    (see Alexis, Willibald)
Harington, Donald 1935- DLB-152
Harington, Sir John 1560-1612......... DLB-136
Harjo, Joy 1951- DLB-120, 175, 342
Harkness, Margaret (John Law)
    1854-1923 ....DLB-197
Harley, Edward, second Earl of Oxford
    1689-1741..................... DLB-213
Harley, Robert, first Earl of Oxford
    1661-1724..................... DLB-213
Harlow, Robert 1923- DLB-60
Harman, Moses 1830-1910............. DLB-345
Harman, Thomas fl. 1566-1573 .... DLB-136
Harness, Charles L. 1915-2005 .... DLB-8
Harnett, Cynthia 1893-1981........... DLB-161
Harnick, Sheldon 1924- DLB-265
    Tribute to Ira Gershwin Y-96
    Tribute to Lorenz Hart................ Y-95
Harper, Edith Alice Mary (see Wickham, Anna)
Harper, Fletcher 1806-1877............. DLB-79
Harper, Frances Ellen Watkins
    1825-1911 .... DLB-50, 221
Harper, Michael S. 1938- DLB-41
Harper and Brothers.................. DLB-49
Harpur, Charles 1813-1868 .... DLB-230
Harraden, Beatrice 1864-1943 .... DLB-153

George G. Harrap and Company
  Limited DLB-112
Harriot, Thomas 1560-1621 .... DLB-136
Harris, Alexander 1805-1874 .... DLB-230
Harris, Benjamin ?-circa 1720 ...... DLB-42, 43
Harris, Christie 1907-2002 .... DLB-88
Harris, Claire 1937- DLB-334
Harris, Errol E. 1908- DLB-279
Harris, Frank 1856-1931 .... DLB-156, 197
Harris, George Washington
  1814-1869 .... DLB-3, 11, 248
Harris, Joanne 1964- DLB-271
Harris, Joel Chandler
  1848-1908 .... DLB-11, 23, 42, 78, 91
  The Joel Chandler Harris Association Y-99
Harris, Mark 1922-2007 .... DLB-2; Y-80
  Tribute to Frederick A. Pottle Y-87
Harris, William 1720-1770 .... DLB-336
Harris, William Torrey 1835-1909 ...... DLB-270
Harris, Wilson 1921- DLB-117; CDWLB-3
Harrison, Mrs. Burton
  (see Harrison, Constance Cary)
Harrison, Charles Yale 1898-1954 .... DLB-68
Harrison, Constance Cary 1843-1920 .... DLB-221
Harrison, Frederic 1831-1923 .... DLB-57, 190
  "On Style in English Prose" (1898) DLB-57
Harrison, Harry 1925- DLB-8
James P. Harrison Company DLB-49
Harrison, Jim 1937- Y-82
Harrison, M. John 1945- DLB-261
Harrison, Mary St. Leger Kingsley (see Malet, Lucas)
Harrison, Paul Carter 1936- DLB-38
Harrison, Susan Frances 1859-1935 ...... DLB-99
Harrison, Tony 1937- DLB-40, 245
Harrison, William 1535-1593 .... DLB-136
Harrison, William 1933- DLB-234
Harrisse, Henry 1829-1910 .... DLB-47
Harry, J. S. 1939- DLB-325
The Harry Ransom Humanities Research Center
  at the University of Texas at Austin Y-00
Harryman, Carla 1952- DLB-193
Harsdörffer, Georg Philipp 1607-1658 .... DLB-164
Harsent, David 1942- DLB-40
Hart, Albert Bushnell 1854-1943 .... DLB-17
Hart, Anne 1768-1834 .... DLB-200
Hart, Elizabeth 1771-1833 .... DLB-200
Hart, Jonathan Locke 1956- DLB-334
Hart, Julia Catherine 1796-1867 .... DLB-99
Hart, Kevin 1954- DLB-325
Hart, Lorenz 1895-1943 .... DLB-265
  Larry Hart: Still an Influence Y-95
  Lorenz Hart: An American Lyricist Y-95

The Lorenz Hart Centenary Y-95
Hart, Moss 1904-1961 .... DLB-7, 266
Hart, Oliver 1723-1795 .... DLB-31
Rupert Hart-Davis Limited DLB-112
Harte, Bret 1836-1902
  .... DLB-12, 64, 74, 79, 186; CDALB-3
Harte, Edward Holmead 1922- DLB-127
Harte, Houston Harriman 1927- DLB-127
Harte, Jack 1944- DLB-319
Hartlaub, Felix 1913-1945 .... DLB-56
Hartlebon, Otto Erich 1864-1905 .... DLB-118
Hartley, David 1705-1757 .... DLB-252
Hartley, L. P. 1895-1972 .... DLB-15, 139
Hartley, Marsden 1877-1943 .... DLB-54
Hartling, Peter 1933- DLB-75
Hartman, Geoffrey H. 1929- DLB-67
Hartmann, Sadakichi 1867-1944 .... DLB-54
Hartmann von Aue
  circa 1160-circa 1205 .... DLB-138; CDWLB-2
Hartshorne, Charles 1897-2000 .... DLB-270
Haruf, Kent 1943- DLB-292
Harvey, Gabriel 1550?-1631 ... DLB-167, 213, 281
Harvey, Jack (see Rankin, Ian)
Harvey, Jean-Charles 1891-1967 .... DLB-88
Harvill Press Limited DLB-112
Harwood, Gwen 1920-1995 .... DLB-289
Harwood, Lee 1939- DLB-40
Harwood, Ronald 1934- DLB-13
al-Hasan al-Basri 642-728 .... DLB-311
Hašek, Jaroslav 1883-1923 ... DLB-215; CDWLB-4
Hásek, Jiří (see Krchovský, J. H.)
Haskins, Charles Homer 1870-1937 ...... DLB-47
Haskins, Lola 1943- DLB-342
Haslam, Gerald 1937- DLB-212
Hass, Robert 1941- DLB-105, 206
Hasselstrom, Linda M. 1943- DLB-256
Hastings, Michael 1938- DLB-233
Hatar, Győző 1914-2006 .... DLB-215
The Hatch-Billops Collection DLB-76
Hathaway, William 1944- DLB-120
Hatherly, Ana 1929- DLB-287
Hauch, Carsten 1790-1872 .... DLB-300
Hauff, Wilhelm 1802-1827 .... DLB-90
Hauge, Olav H. 1908-1994 .... DLB-297
Haugen, Paal-Helge 1945- DLB-297
Haugwitz, August Adolph von
  1647-1706 .... DLB-168
Hauptmann, Carl 1858-1921 .... DLB-66, 118
Hauptmann, Gerhart
  1862-1946 ..... DLB-66, 118, 330; CDWLB-2
Hauser, Marianne 1910-2006 .... Y-83

Havel, Václav 1936- DLB-232; CDWLB-4
Haven, Alice B. Neal 1827-1863 .... DLB-250
Havergal, Frances Ridley 1836-1879 ..... DLB-199
Hawes, Stephen 1475?-before 1529 ...... DLB-132
Hawker, Robert Stephen 1803-1875 ...... DLB-32
Hawkes, John
  1925-1998 .... DLB-2, 7, 227; Y-80, Y-98
  John Hawkes: A Tribute Y-98
  Tribute to Donald Barthelme Y-89
Hawkesworth, John 1720-1773 .... DLB-142
Hawkins, Sir Anthony Hope (see Hope, Anthony)
Hawkins, Sir John 1719-1789 ... DLB-104, 142, 336
Hawkins, Walter Everette 1883-? DLB-50
Hawthorne, Nathaniel 1804-1864
  .. DLB-1, 74, 183, 223, 269; DS-5; CDALB-2
  The Nathaniel Hawthorne Society Y-00
  The Old Manse DLB-223
Hawthorne, Sophia Peabody
  1809-1871 .... DLB-183, 239
Hay, John 1835-1905 .... DLB-12, 47, 189
Hay, John 1915- DLB-275
Hayashi Fumiko 1903-1951 .... DLB-180
Haycox, Ernest 1899-1950 .... DLB-206
Haycraft, Anna Margaret (see Ellis, Alice Thomas)
Hayden, Robert
  1913-1980 .... DLB-5, 76; CDALB-1
Haydon, Benjamin Robert 1786-1846 .... DLB-110
Hayes, John Michael 1919- DLB-26
Hayley, William 1745-1820 .... DLB-93, 142
Haym, Rudolf 1821-1901 .... DLB-129
Hayman, Robert 1575-1629 .... DLB-99
Hayman, Ronald 1932- DLB-155
Hayne, Paul Hamilton
  1830-1886 .... DLB-3, 64, 79, 248
Hays, Mary 1760-1843 .... DLB-142, 158
Hayslip, Le Ly 1949- DLB-312
Hayward, John 1905-1965 .... DLB-201
Haywood, Eliza 1693?-1756 .... DLB-39
  Dedication of Lasselia [excerpt]
    (1723) DLB-39
  Preface to The Disguis'd Prince
    [excerpt] (1723) DLB-39
  The Tea-Table [excerpt] DLB-39
Haywood, William D. 1869-1928 .... DLB-303
Willis P. Hazard [publishing house] DLB-49
Hazelton, George C., Jr. 1868-1921 ...... DLB-341
Hazlewood, C. H. 1819-1875 .... DLB-344
Hazlitt, William 1778-1830 .... DLB-110, 158
Hazzard, Shirley 1931- DLB-289; Y-82
Head, Bessie
  1937-1986 .... DLB-117, 225; CDWLB-3
Headley, Joel T. 1813-1897 ... DLB-30, 183; DS-13
Headley, Victor 1959- DLB-347

Cumulative Index   DLB 354

Heaney, Seamus 1939- DLB-40, 330; Y-95; CDBLB-8

    Nobel Lecture 1994: Crediting Poetry Y-95

Heard, Nathan C. 1936- DLB-33

Hearn, Lafcadio 1850-1904 ...... DLB-12, 78, 189

Hearn, Mary Anne (Marianne Farningham, Eva Hope) 1834-1909 .... DLB-240

Hearne, John 1926- DLB-117

Hearne, Samuel 1745-1792 .... DLB-99

Hearne, Thomas 1678?-1735 ...... DLB-213, 336

Hearst, William Randolph 1863-1951 .... DLB-25

Hearst, William Randolph, Jr. 1908-1993 .... DLB-127

Heartman, Charles Frederick 1883-1953 .... DLB-187

Heat and Dust, 1975 Booker Prize winner, Ruth Prawer Jhabvala............. DLB-326

Heath, Catherine 1924-1991............. DLB-14

Heath, James Ewell 1792-1862 .... DLB-248

Heath, Roy A. K. 1926- DLB-117

Heath-Stubbs, John 1918- DLB-27

Heavysege, Charles 1816-1876.......... DLB-99

Hebbel, Friedrich 1813-1863............ DLB-129; CDWLB-2

Hebel, Johann Peter 1760-1826.......... DLB-90

Heber, Richard 1774-1833 .... DLB-184

Hébert, Anne 1916-2000 .... DLB-68

Hébert, Jacques 1923-2007 .... DLB-53

Hebreo, León circa 1460-1520 .... DLB-318

Hecht, Anthony 1923-2004 .... DLB-5, 169

Hecht, Ben 1894-1964 ....DLB-7, 9, 25, 26, 28, 86

Hecker, Isaac Thomas 1819-1888..... DLB-1, 243

Hedge, Frederic Henry 1805-1890 .... DLB-1, 59, 243; DS-5

Hefner, Hugh M. 1926- DLB-137

Hegel, Georg Wilhelm Friedrich 1770-1831..................... DLB-90

Heiberg, Gunnar 1857-1929 .... DLB-354

Heiberg, Johan Ludvig 1791-1860 ...... DLB-300

Heiberg, Johanne Luise 1812-1890..... DLB-300

Heide, Robert 1939- DLB-249

Heidegger, Martin 1889-1976 .... DLB-296

Heidenstam, Verner von 1859-1940..... DLB-330

Heidish, Marcy 1947- Y-82

Heißenbüttel, Helmut 1921-1996....... DLB-75

Heike monogatari................. DLB-203

Hein, Christoph 1944- ... DLB-124; CDWLB-2

Hein, Piet 1905-1996 .... DLB-214

Heine, Heinrich 1797-1856 ... DLB-90; CDWLB-2

Heinemann, Larry 1944- DS-9

William Heinemann Limited DLB-112

Heinesen, William 1900-1991......... DLB-214

Heinlein, Robert A. 1907-1988.......... DLB-8

Heinrich, Willi 1920-2005 .... DLB-75

Heinrich Julius of Brunswick| 1564-1613 .... DLB-164

Heinrich von dem Türlin fl. circa 1230................... DLB-138

Heinrich von Melk fl. after 1160................... DLB-148

Heinrich von Veldeke circa 1145-circa 1190 .... DLB-138

Heinse, Wilhelm 1746-1803 .... DLB-94

Heinz, W. C. 1915-2008.............DLB-171

Heiskell, John 1872-1972.......... DLB-127

Hejinian, Lyn 1941- DLB-165

Helder, Herberto 1930- DLB-287

Heliand circa 850.................. DLB-148

Heller, Joseph 1923-1999 ...... DLB-2, 28, 227; Y-80, 99, 02

    Excerpts from Joseph Heller's USC Address, "The Literature of Despair" Y-96

    Remembering Joe Heller, by William Price Fox Y-99

    A Tribute to Joseph Heller............ Y-99

Heller, Michael 1937- DLB-165

Hellman, Lillian 1906-1984 ..... DLB-7, 228; Y-84

Hellwig, Johann 1609-1674............. DLB-164

Helprin, Mark 1947- ..DLB-335; Y-85; CDALB-7

Helvétius, Claude-Adrien 1715-1771..... DLB-313

    The Spirit of Laws.................. DLB-314

Helwig, David 1938- DLB-60

Hemans, Felicia 1793-1835 .... DLB-96

Hemenway, Abby Maria 1828-1890..... DLB-243

Hemingway, Ernest 1899-1961 ....DLB-4, 9, 102, 210, 316, 330; Y-81, 87, 99; DS-1, 15, 16; CDALB-4

    A Centennial Celebration Y-99

    Come to Papa Y-99

    The Ernest Hemingway Collection at the John F. Kennedy Library........ Y-99

    Ernest Hemingway Declines to Introduce *War and Peace* Y-01

    Ernest Hemingway's Reaction to James Gould Cozzens Y-98

    Ernest Hemingway's Toronto Journalism Revisited: With Three Previously Unrecorded Stories Y-92

    Falsifying Hemingway Y-96

    A Farewell to Arms (Documentary).... DLB-308

    Hemingway Centenary Celebration at the JFK Library............... Y-99

    The Hemingway/Fenton Correspondence Y-02

    Hemingway in the JFK Y-99

    The Hemingway Letters Project Finds an Editor Y-02

    Hemingway Salesmen's Dummies Y-00

    Hemingway: Twenty-Five Years Later Y-85

    A Literary Archaeologist Digs On: A Brief Interview with Michael Reynolds Y-99

    Not Immediately Discernible . . . but Eventually Quite Clear: The *First Light* and *Final Years* of Hemingway's Centenary Y-99

    Packaging Papa: *The Garden of Eden* Y-86

    Second International Hemingway Colloquium: Cuba Y-98

Hémon, Louis 1880-1913............. DLB-92

Hempel, Amy 1951- DLB-218

Hempel, Carl G. 1905-1997 ....DLB-279

Hemphill, Paul 1936-2009 .... Y-87

Hénault, Gilles 1920-1996 .... DLB-88

Henchman, Daniel 1689-1761 .... DLB-24

Henderson, Alice Corbin 1881-1949 ..... DLB-54

Henderson, Archibald 1877-1963 .... DLB-103

Henderson, David 1942- DLB-41

Henderson, George Wylie 1904-1965 .... DLB-51

Henderson, Zenna 1917-1983............. DLB-8

Henighan, Tom 1934- DLB-251

Henisch, Peter 1943- DLB-85

Henkin, Joshua 1964- DLB-350

Henley, Beth 1952- Y-86

Henley, William Ernest 1849-1903....... DLB-19

Henniker, Florence 1855-1923 .... DLB-135

Henning, Rachel 1826-1914 .... DLB-230

Henningsen, Agnes 1868-1962......... DLB-214

Henry, Alexander 1739-1824 .... DLB-99

Henry, Buck 1930- DLB-26

Henry, Marguerite 1902-1997 .... DLB-22

Henry, O. (see Porter, William Sydney)

Henry, Robert Selph 1889-1970 ....DLB-17

Henry, Will (see Allen, Henry W.)

Henry VIII of England 1491-1547...... DLB-132

Henry of Ghent circa 1217-1229 - 1293 .... DLB-115

Henryson, Robert 1420s or 1430s-circa 1505 .... DLB-146

Henschke, Alfred (see Klabund)

Hensher, Philip 1965- DLB-267

Hensley, Sophie Almon 1866-1946....... DLB-99

Henson, Lance 1944- DLB-175

Hentoff, Nat 1925- DLB-345

Hess, Karl 1923-1994................ DLB-345

Henty, G. A. 1832-1902 .... DLB-18, 141

    The Henty Society.................... Y-98

Hentz, Caroline Lee 1800-1856 ...... DLB-3, 248

Heraclitus fl. circa 500 B.C..........DLB-176

Herbert, Agnes circa 1880-1960........DLB-174

Herbert, Alan Patrick 1890-1971 .....DLB-10, 191

Herbert, Edward, Lord, of Cherbury 1582-1648 ....DLB-121, 151, 252

Herbert, Frank 1920-1986 ..... DLB-8; CDALB-7

Herbert, George 1593-1633 .. DLB-126; CDBLB-1

Herbert, Henry William 1807-1858 . . . . . DLB-3, 73
Herbert, John 1926-2001 . . . . DLB-53
Herbert, Mary Sidney, Countess of Pembroke
  (see Sidney, Mary)
Herbert, Xavier 1901-1984 . . . . DLB-260
Herbert, Zbigniew
  1924-1998 . . . . DLB-232; CDWLB-4
Herbst, Josephine 1892-1969 . . . . DLB-9
Herburger, Gunter 1932- DLB-75, 124
Herculano, Alexandre 1810-1877 . . . . DLB-287
Hercules, Frank E. M. 1917-1996 . . . . DLB-33
Herder, Johann Gottfried 1744-1803 . . . . . . DLB-97
B. Herder Book Company DLB-49
Heredia, José-María de 1842-1905 . . . . DLB-217
Herford, Charles Harold 1853-1931 . . . . . DLB-149
Hergesheimer, Joseph 1880-1954 . . . . . . DLB-9, 102
Heritage Press DLB-46
Hermann the Lame 1013-1054 . . . . DLB-148
Hermes, Johann Timotheu 1738-1821 . . . . . DLB-97
Hermlin, Stephan 1915-1997 . . . . DLB-69
Hernández, Alfonso C. 1938- DLB-122
Hernandez, Amado V. 1903-1970 . . . . DLB-348
Hernández, Inés 1947- DLB-122
Hernández, Miguel 1910-1942 . . . . DLB-134
Hernton, Calvin C. 1932- DLB-38
Herodotus circa 484 B.C.-circa 420 B.C.
  . . . . DLB-176; CDWLB-1
Héroët, Antoine 1490?-1567? DLB-327
Heron, Robert 1764-1807 . . . . DLB-142
Herr, Michael 1940- DLB-185
Herrera, Darío 1870-1914 . . . . DLB-290
Herrera, Fernando de 1534?-1597 . . . . DLB-318
Herrera, Juan Felipe 1948- DLB-122
E. R. Herrick and Company DLB-49
Herrick, Robert 1591-1674 . . . . DLB-126
Herrick, Robert 1868-1938 . . . . DLB-9, 12, 78
Herrick, William 1915-2004 . . . . Y-83
Herrmann, John 1900-1959 . . . . DLB-4
Hersey, John
  1914-1993 . . . DLB-6, 185, 278, 299; CDALB-7
Hertel, François 1905-1985 . . . . DLB-68
Hervé-Bazin, Jean Pierre Marie (see Bazin, Hervé)
Hervey, John, Lord 1696-1743 . . . . DLB-101
Herwig, Georg 1817-1875 . . . . DLB-133
Herzen, Alexander (Aleksandr Ivanovich
  Gersten) 1812-1870 . . . . DLB-277
Herzog, Emile Salomon Wilhelm
  (see Maurois, André)
Hesiod eighth century B.C. DLB-176
Hess, Karl 1923-1994 . . . . DLB-345
Hesse, Hermann
  1877-1962 . . . . DLB-66, 330; CDWLB-2

Hessus, Eobanus 1488-1540 . . . . DLB-179
Heureka! (see Kertész, Imre and Nobel Prize
  in Literature: 2002) Y-02
Hewat, Alexander circa 1743-circa 1824 . . . DLB-30
Hewett, Dorothy 1923-2002 . . . . DLB-289
Hewitt, John 1907-1987 . . . . DLB-27
Hewlett, Maurice 1861-1923 . . . . DLB-34, 156
Heyen, William 1940- DLB-5
Heyer, Georgette 1902-1974 . . . . DLB-77, 191
Heym, Stefan 1913-2001 . . . . DLB-69
Heyse, Paul 1830-1914 . . . . DLB-129, 330
Heytesbury, William
  circa 1310-1372 or 1373 . . . . DLB-115
Heyward, Dorothy 1890-1961 . . . . DLB-7, 249
Heyward, DuBose 1885-1940 . . . DLB-7, 9, 45, 249
Heywood, John 1497?-1580? DLB-136
Heywood, Thomas 1573 or 1574-1641 . . . . DLB-62
Hiaasen, Carl 1953- DLB-292
Hibberd, Jack 1940- DLB-289
Hibbs, Ben 1901-1975 . . . . DLB-137
  "The Saturday Evening Post reaffirms
  a policy," Ben Hibb's Statement
  in *The Saturday Evening Post*
  (16 May 1942) DLB-137
Hichens, Robert S. 1864-1950 . . . . DLB-153
Hickey, Emily 1845-1924 . . . . DLB-199
Hickman, William Albert 1877-1957 . . . . . DLB-92
Hicks, Granville 1901-1982 . . . . DLB-246
Hidalgo, José Luis 1919-1947 . . . . DLB-108
Hiebert, Paul 1892-1987 . . . . DLB-68
Hieng, Andrej 1925- DLB-181
Hierro, José 1922-2002 . . . . DLB-108
Higgins, Aidan 1927- DLB-14
Higgins, Colin 1941-1988 . . . . DLB-26
Higgins, George V.
  1939-1999 . . . . DLB-2; Y-81, 98–99
  Afterword [in response to Cozzen's
    Mens Rea (or Something)] Y-97
  At End of Day: The Last George V.
    Higgins Novel Y-99
  The Books of George V. Higgins:
    A Checklist of Editions
    and Printings Y-00
  George V. Higgins in Class Y-02
  Tribute to Alfred A. Knopf Y-84
  Tributes to George V. Higgins Y-99
  "What You Lose on the Swings You Make
    Up on the Merry-Go-Round" Y-99
Higginson, Thomas Wentworth
  1823-1911 . . . . DLB-1, 64, 243
Highsmith, Patricia 1921-1995 . . . . DLB-306
Highwater, Jamake 1942?- DLB-52; Y-85
Highway, Tomson 1951- DLB-334
Hijuelos, Oscar 1951- DLB-145
Hildegard von Bingen 1098-1179 . . . . DLB-148

Das Hildesbrandslied
  circa 820 . . . . DLB-148; CDWLB-2
Hildesheimer, Wolfgang 1916-1991 . . . DLB-69, 124
Hildreth, Richard 1807-1865 . . . DLB-1, 30, 59, 235
Hill, Aaron 1685-1750 . . . . DLB-84
Hill, Geoffrey 1932- DLB-40; CDBLB-8
George M. Hill Company DLB-49
Hill, "Sir" John 1714?-1775 . . . . DLB-39
Lawrence Hill and Company,
  Publishers DLB-46
Hill, Joe 1879-1915 . . . . DLB-303
Hill, Leslie 1880-1960 . . . . DLB-51
Hill, Reginald 1936- DLB-276
Hill, Susan 1942- DLB-14, 139
Hill, Walter 1942- DLB-44
Hill and Wang DLB-46
Hillberry, Conrad 1928- DLB-120
Hillerman, Tony 1925-2008 . . . . DLB-206, 306
Hilliard, Gray and Company DLB-49
Hills, Lee 1906-2000 . . . . DLB-127
Hillyer, Robert 1895-1961 . . . . DLB-54
Hilsenrath, Edgar 1926- DLB-299
Hilton, James 1900-1954 . . . . DLB-34, 77
Hilton, Walter died 1396 . . . . DLB-146
Hilton and Company DLB-49
Himes, Chester 1909-1984 . . . DLB-2, 76, 143, 226
Joseph Hindmarsh [publishing house] DLB-170
Hine, Daryl 1936- DLB-60
Hingley, Ronald 1920- DLB-155
Hinojosa-Smith, Rolando 1929- DLB-82
Hinton, S. E. 1948- CDALB-7
Hippel, Theodor Gottlieb von
  1741-1796 . . . . DLB-97
Hippius, Zinaida Nikolaevna
  1869-1945 . . . . DLB-295
Hippocrates of Cos fl. circa
  425 B.C. DLB-176; CDWLB-1
Hirabayashi Taiko 1905-1972 . . . . DLB-180
Hirsch, E. D., Jr. 1928- DLB-67
Hirsch, Edward 1950- DLB-120
Hirschbein, Peretz (Perets Hirshbeyn)
  1880-1948 . . . . DLB-333
Hirshfield, Jane 1953- DLB-342
"Historical Novel," The Holocaust DLB-299
Ho Anh Thai 1960- DLB-348
Hoagland, Edward 1932- DLB-6
Hoagland, Everett H., III 1942- DLB-41
Hoban, Russell 1925- DLB-52; Y-90
Hobbes, Thomas 1588-1679 . . . DLB-151, 252, 281
Hobby, Oveta 1905-1995 . . . . DLB-127
Hobby, William 1878-1964 . . . . DLB-127
Hobsbaum, Philip 1932- DLB-40

Cumulative Index

Hobsbawm, Eric (Francis Newton) 1917- DLB-296
Hobson, Laura Z. 1900-1986 .... DLB-28
Hobson, Sarah 1947- DLB-204
Hoby, Thomas 1530-1566 .... DLB-132
Hoccleve, Thomas circa 1368-circa 1437 .... DLB-146
Hoch, Edward D. 1930- DLB-306
Hochhuth, Rolf 1931- DLB-124
Hochman, Sandra 1936- DLB-5
Hocken, Thomas Morland 1836-1910 ... DLB-184
Hocking, William Ernest 1873-1966 ..... DLB-270
Hodder and Stoughton, Limited DLB-106
Hodgins, Jack 1938- DLB-60
Hodgman, Helen 1945- DLB-14
Hodgskin, Thomas 1787-1869 .... DLB-158
Hodgson, Ralph 1871-1962 .... DLB-19
Hodgson, William Hope 1877-1918 .... DLB-70, 153, 156, 178
Hodrová, Daniela 1946- DLB-353
Hoe, Robert, III 1839-1909 .... DLB-187
Hoeg, Peter 1957- DLB-214
Hoel, Sigurd 1890-1960 .... DLB-297
Hoem, Edvard 1949- DLB-297
Hoffenstein, Samuel 1890-1947 .... DLB-11
Hoffman, Alice 1952- DLB-292
Hoffman, Charles Fenno 1806-1884 .... DLB-3, 250
Hoffman, Daniel 1923- DLB-5
    Tribute to Robert Graves Y-85
Hoffmann, E. T. A. 1776-1822 .... DLB-90; CDWLB-2
Hoffman, Frank B. 1888-1958 .... DLB-188
Hoffman, William 1925- DLB-234
    Tribute to Paxton Davis Y-94
Hoffmanswaldau, Christian Hoffman von 1616-1679 .... DLB-168
Hofmann, Michael 1957- DLB-40
Hofmannsthal, Hugo von 1874-1929 .... DLB-81, 118; CDWLB-2
Hofmo, Gunvor 1921-1995 .... DLB-297
Hofstadter, Richard 1916-1970 ..... DLB-17, 246
Hofstein, David (Dovid Hofshteyn) 1889-1952 .... DLB-333
Hogan, Desmond 1950- DLB-14, 319
Hogan, Linda 1947- DLB-175
Hogan and Thompson DLB-49
Hogarth Press DLB-112; DS-10
Hogg, James 1770-1835 .... DLB-93, 116, 159
Hohberg, Wolfgang Helmhard Freiherr von 1612-1688 .... DLB-168
von Hohenheim, Philippus Aureolus Theophrastus Bombastus (see Paracelsus)
Hohl, Ludwig 1904-1980 .... DLB-56

Højholt, Per 1928- DLB-214
Holan, Vladimir 1905-1980 .... DLB-215
d'Holbach, Paul Henri Thiry, baron 1723-1789 .... DLB-313
    The System of Nature (as Jean-Baptiste de Mirabaud) DLB-314
Holberg, Ludvig 1684-1754 .... DLB-300
Holbrook, David 1923- DLB-14, 40
Holcroft, Thomas 1745-1809 .... DLB-39, 89, 158
    Preface to *Alwyn* (1780) DLB-39
Holden, Jonathan 1941- DLB-105
    "Contemporary Verse Story-telling" ... DLB-105
Holden, Molly 1927-1981 .... DLB-40
Hölderlin, Friedrich 1770-1843 .... DLB-90; CDWLB-2
Holdstock, Robert 1948- DLB-261
Holiday, 1974 Booker Prize winner, Stanley Middleton DLB-326
Holiday House DLB-46
Holinshed, Raphael died 1580 .... DLB-167
Holland, J. G. 1819-1881 .... DS-13
Holland, Norman N. 1927- DLB-67
Hollander, John 1929- DLB-5
Holley, Marietta 1836-1926 .... DLB-11
Hollinghurst, Alan 1954- DLB-207, 326
Hollingshead, Greg 1947- DLB-334
Hollingsworth, Margaret 1940- DLB-60
Hollo, Anselm 1934- DLB-40
Holloway, Emory 1885-1977 .... DLB-103
Holloway, John 1920- DLB-27
Holloway House Publishing Company ... DLB-46
Holman-Hunt, Diana 1913-1993 ...... DLB-352
Holme, Constance 1880-1955 .... DLB-34
Holmes, Abraham S. 1821?-1908 .... DLB-99
Holmes, John Clellon 1926-1988 ..... DLB-16, 237
    "Four Essays on the Beat Generation" DLB-16
Holmes, Mary Jane 1825-1907 ..... DLB-202, 221
Holmes, Oliver Wendell 1809-1894 ...... DLB-1, 189, 235; CDALB-2
Holmes, Richard 1945- DLB-155
Holmes, Thomas James 1874-1959 ...... DLB-187
The Holocaust "Historical Novel" DLB-299
Holocaust Fiction, Postmodern DLB-299
Holocaust Novel, The "Second-Generation" DLB-299
Holroyd, Michael 1935- DLB-155; Y-99
Holst, Hermann E. von 1841-1904 ..... DLB-47
Holt, John 1721-1784 .... DLB-43
Henry Holt and Company DLB-49, 284
Holt, Rinehart and Winston DLB-46
Holtby, Winifred 1898-1935 .... DLB-191
Holthusen, Hans Egon 1913-1997 ..... DLB-69

Hölty, Ludwig Christoph Heinrich 1748-1776 .... DLB-94
Holub, Miroslav 1923-1998 .... DLB-232; CDWLB-4
Holz, Arno 1863-1929 .... DLB-118
Home, Henry, Lord Kames (see Kames, Henry Home, Lord)
Home, John 1722-1808 .... DLB-84, 336
Home, William Douglas 1912-1992 ..... DLB-13
Home Publishing Company DLB-49
Homer circa eighth-seventh centuries B.C. DLB-176; CDWLB-1
Homer, Winslow 1836-1910 .... DLB-188
Homes, Geoffrey (see Mainwaring, Daniel)
Honan, Park 1928- DLB-111
Hone, William 1780-1842 .... DLB-110, 158
Hongo, Garrett Kaoru 1951- DLB-120, 312
Honig, Edwin 1919- DLB-5
Hood, Hugh 1928-2000 .... DLB-53
Hood, Mary 1946- DLB-234
Hood, Thomas 1799-1845 .... DLB-96
Hook, Sidney 1902-1989 .... DLB-279
Hook, Theodore 1788-1841 .... DLB-116
Hooke, Nathaniel 1685?-1763 .... DLB-336
Hooker, Jeremy 1941- DLB-40
Hooker, Richard 1554-1600 .... DLB-132
Hooker, Thomas 1586-1647 .... DLB-24
hooks, bell 1952- DLB-246
Hooper, Johnson Jones 1815-1862 .... DLB-3, 11, 248
Hope, A. D. 1907-2000 .... DLB-289
Hope, Anthony 1863-1933 .... DLB-153, 156
Hope, Christopher 1944- DLB-225
Hope, Eva (see Hearn, Mary Anne)
Hope, Laurence (Adela Florence Cory Nicolson) 1865-1904 .... DLB-240
Hopkins, Ellice 1836-1904 .... DLB-190
Hopkins, Gerard Manley 1844-1889 .... DLB-35, 57; CDBLB-5
Hopkins, John ?-1570 .... DLB-132
Hopkins, John H., and Son DLB-46
Hopkins, Lemuel 1750-1801 .... DLB-37
Hopkins, Pauline Elizabeth 1859-1930 .... DLB-50
Hopkins, Samuel 1721-1803 .... DLB-31
Hopkinson, Francis 1737-1791 .... DLB-31
Hopkinson, Nalo 1960- DLB-251
Hopper, Nora (Mrs. Nora Chesson) 1871-1906 .... DLB-240
Hoppin, Augustus 1828-1896 .... DLB-188
Hora, Josef 1891-1945 .... DLB-215; CDWLB-4
Horace 65 B.C.-8 B.C. DLB-211; CDWLB-1
Horgan, Paul 1903-1995 .... DLB-102, 212; Y-85
    Tribute to Alfred A. Knopf Y-84

Horizon Press..........................DLB-46

Horkheimer, Max 1895-1973...........DLB-296

Hornby, C. H. St. John 1867-1946.......DLB-201

Hornby, Nick 1957- DLB-207, 352

Horne, Frank 1899-1974 ....DLB-51

Horne, Richard Henry (Hengist)
    1802 or 1803-1884 ....DLB-32

Horne, Thomas 1608-1654 ....DLB-281

Horney, Karen 1885-1952 ....DLB-246

Hornung, E. W. 1866-1921 ....DLB-70

Horovitz, Israel 1939- DLB-7, 341

Horta, Maria Teresa (see The Three Marias:
    A Landmark Case in Portuguese
    Literary History)

Horton, George Moses 1797?-1883? DLB-50

    George Moses Horton Society Y-99

Horváth, Ödön von 1901-1938.....DLB-85, 124

Horwood, Harold 1923- DLB-60

E. and E. Hosford [publishing house] DLB-49

Hoskens, Jane Fenn 1693-1770?.........DLB-200

Hoskyns, John circa 1566-1638.....DLB-121, 281

Hosokawa Yūsai 1535-1610............DLB-203

Hospers, John 1918- DLB-279

Hospital, Janette Turner 1942- DLB-325

Hostovský, Egon 1908-1973............DLB-215

Hotchkiss and Company DLB-49

Hotel du Lac, 1984 Booker Prize winner,
    Anita Brookner DLB-326

Hough, Emerson 1857-1923..........DLB-9, 212

Houghton, Stanley 1881-1913 ....DLB-10

Houghton Mifflin Company DLB-49

Hours at Home DS-13

Household, Geoffrey 1900-1988 ....DLB-87

Housman, A. E. 1859-1936 ... DLB-19; CDBLB-5

Housman, Laurence 1865-1959..........DLB-10

Houston, Pam 1962- DLB-244

Houwald, Ernst von 1778-1845 ....DLB-90

Hovey, Richard 1864-1900 ....DLB-54

How Late It Was, How Late, 1994 Booker Prize winner,
    James Kelman DLB-326

Howard, Donald R. 1927-1987 ....DLB-111

Howard, Maureen 1930- Y-83

Howard, Richard 1929- DLB-5

Howard, Roy W. 1883-1964 ....DLB-29

Howard, Sidney 1891-1939 .... DLB-7, 26, 249

Howard, Thomas, second Earl of Arundel
    1585-1646 ....DLB-213

Howe, E. W. 1853-1937..............DLB-12, 25

Howe, Henry 1816-1893 ....DLB-30

Howe, Irving 1920-1993................DLB-67

Howe, Joseph 1804-1873 ....DLB-99

Howe, Julia Ward 1819-1910.....DLB-1, 189, 235

Howe, Percival Presland 1886-1944......DLB-149

Howe, Susan 1937- DLB-120

Howe, Tina 1937- DLB-341

Howell, Clark, Sr. 1863-1936............DLB-25

Howell, Evan P. 1839-1905 ....DLB-23

Howell, James 1594?-1666..............DLB-151

Howell, Soskin and Company DLB-46

Howell, Warren Richardson 1912-1984.....DLB-140

Howells, William Dean 1837-1920
    .... DLB-12, 64, 74, 79, 189; CDALB-3

    Introduction to Paul Laurence
        Dunbar's *Lyrics of Lowly Life*
        (1896) DLB-50

    The William Dean Howells Society Y-01

Howitt, Mary 1799-1888 .... DLB-110, 199

Howitt, William 1792-1879 ....DLB-110

Hoyem, Andrew 1935- DLB-5

Hoyers, Anna Ovena 1584-1655 ....DLB-164

Hoyle, Fred 1915-2001 ....DLB-261

Hoyos, Angela de 1940- DLB-82

Henry Hoyt [publishing house] DLB-49

Hoyt, Palmer 1897-1979...............DLB-127

Hrabal, Bohumil 1914-1997............DLB-232

Hrabanus Maurus 776?-856............DLB-148

Hronský, Josef Cíger 1896-1960 ....DLB-215

Hrotsvit of Gandersheim
    circa 935-circa 1000................DLB-148

Hubbard, Elbert 1856-1915.............DLB-91

Hubbard, Kin 1868-1930...............DLB-11

Hubbard, William circa 1621-1704 ....DLB-24

Huber, Therese 1764-1829..............DLB-90

Huch, Friedrich 1873-1913 ....DLB-66

Huch, Ricarda 1864-1947 ....DLB-66

Huddle, David 1942- DLB-130

Hudgins, Andrew 1951- DLB-120, 282

Hudson, Henry Norman 1814-1886 ......DLB-64

Hudson, Stephen 1868?-1944 ....DLB-197

Hudson, W. H. 1841-1922...... DLB-98, 153, 174

Hudson and Goodwin.................DLB-49

Huebsch, B. W., oral history Y-99

B. W. Huebsch [publishing house]........DLB-46

Hueffer, Oliver Madox 1876-1931.......DLB-197

Huelle, Paweł 1957- DLB-353

Huet, Pierre Daniel
    Preface to *The History of Romances*
        (1715) DLB-39

Hugh of St. Victor circa 1096-1141 ......DLB-208

Hughes, David 1930- DLB-14

Hughes, Dusty 1947- DLB-233

Hughes, Hatcher 1881-1945 ....DLB-249

Hughes, John 1677-1720...............DLB-84

Hughes, Langston 1902-1967 ....DLB-4, 7, 48,
    51, 86, 228, 315; DS-15; CDALB-5

Hughes, Richard 1900-1976.........DLB-15, 161

Hughes, Ted 1930-1998.............DLB-40, 161

Hughes, Thomas 1822-1896 ....DLB-18, 163

Hugo, Richard 1923-1982 ....DLB-5, 206

Hugo, Victor 1802-1885 ...... DLB-119, 192, 217

Hugo Awards and Nebula Awards DLB-8

Huidobro, Vicente 1893-1948 ....DLB-283

Hull, Richard 1896-1973 ....DLB-77

Hulda (Unnur Benediktsdóttir Bjarklind)
    1881-1946.....................DLB-293

Hulme, Keri 1947- DLB-326

Hulme, T. E. 1883-1917................DLB-19

Hulton, Anne ?-1779?.................DLB-200

Humanism, Sixteenth-Century
    Spanish DLB-318

Humboldt, Alexander von 1769-1859 .....DLB-90

Humboldt, Wilhelm von 1767-1835.......DLB-90

Hume, David 1711-1776....... DLB-104, 252, 336

Hume, Fergus 1859-1932...............DLB-70

Hume, Sophia 1702-1774 ....DLB-200

Hume-Rothery, Mary Catherine
    1824-1885 ....DLB-240

Humishuma
    (see Mourning Dove)

Hummer, T. R. 1950- DLB-120

Humor
    American Humor: A Historical
        Survey DLB-11

    American Humor Studies Association Y-99

    The Comic Tradition Continued
        [in the British Novel]...........DLB-15

    Humorous Book Illustration DLB-11

    International Society for Humor Studies... Y-99

    Newspaper Syndication of American
        Humor DLB-11

    Selected Humorous Magazines
        (1820-1950) DLB-11

Bruce Humphries [publishing house] DLB-46

Humphrey, Duke of Gloucester
    1391-1447 ....DLB-213

Humphrey, William
    1924-1997 .... DLB-6, 212, 234, 278

Humphreys, David 1752-1818...........DLB-37

Humphreys, Emyr 1919- DLB-15

Humphreys, Josephine 1945- DLB-292

Humphries, Barry 1934- DLB-352

Hunayn ibn Ishaq 809-873 or 877 ....DLB-311

Huncke, Herbert 1915-1996 ....DLB-16

Huneker, James Gibbons
    1857-1921 ....DLB-71

Hunold, Christian Friedrich
    1681-1721 ....DLB-168

Hunt, Irene 1907- DLB-52

Hunt, Leigh 1784-1859 .... DLB-96, 110, 144

Hunt, Violet 1862-1942..........DLB-162, 197

Cumulative Index

Hunt, William Gibbes 1791-1833 .... DLB-73
Hunter, Evan (Ed McBain)
   1926-2005 .... DLB-306; Y-82
    Tribute to John D. MacDonald Y-86
Hunter, Jim 1939- DLB-14
Hunter, Kristin 1931- DLB-33
    Tribute to Julian Mayfield Y-84
Hunter, Mollie 1922- DLB-161
Hunter, N. C. 1908-1971 .... DLB-10
Hunter-Duvar, John 1821-1899 .... DLB-99
Huntington, Henry E.
   1850-1927..................... DLB-140
    The Henry E. Huntington Library Y-92
Huntington, Susan Mansfield
   1791-1823..................... DLB-200
Hurd and Houghton................. DLB-49
Hurst, Fannie 1889-1968 .... DLB-86
Hurst and Blackett DLB-106
Hurst and Company................. DLB-49
Hurston, Zora Neale
   1901?-1960......... DLB-51, 86; CDALB-7
Husserl, Edmund 1859-1938 .... DLB-296
Husson, Jules-François-Félix
   (see Champfleury)
Huston, John 1906-1987 .... DLB-26
Hutcheson, Francis 1694-1746 ..... DLB-31, 252
Hutchinson, Ron 1947- DLB-245
Hutchinson, R. C. 1907-1975 .... DLB-191
Hutchinson, Thomas 1711-1780 ..... DLB-30, 31
Hutchinson and Company
   (Publishers) Limited............. DLB-112
Huth, Angela 1938- DLB-271
Hutton, Richard Holt 1826-1897 ...... DLB-57
von Hutten, Ulrich 1488-1523 ....DLB-179
Huxley, Aldous 1894-1963
   ..... DLB-36, 100, 162, 195, 255; CDBLB-6
Huxley, Elspeth Josceline
   1907-1997...................DLB-77, 204
Huxley, T. H. 1825-1895 .... DLB-57
Huyghue, Douglas Smith
   1816-1891.................... DLB-99
Huysmans, Joris-Karl 1848-1907 .... DLB-123
Hwang, David Henry
   1957- DLB-212, 228, 312
Hyde, Donald 1909-1966 .... DLB-187
Hyde, Mary 1912-2003............... DLB-187
Hyman, Trina Schart 1939- DLB-61

I

Iavorsky, Stefan 1658-1722 .... DLB-150
Iazykov, Nikolai Mikhailovich
   1803-1846 .... DLB-205
Ibáñez, Armando P. 1949- DLB-209
Ibáñez, Sara de 1909-1971 .... DLB-290

Ibarbourou, Juana de 1892-1979........ DLB-290
Ibn Abi Tahir Tayfur 820-893 .... DLB-311
Ibn Bajja circa 1077-1138............. DLB-115
Ibn Gabirol, Solomon
   circa 1021-circa 1058 .... DLB-115
Ibn al-Muqaffa' circa 723-759 .... DLB-311
Ibn al-Mu'tazz 861-908............... DLB-311
Ibn Qutaybah 828-889 .... DLB-311
Ibn al-Rumi 836-896................. DLB-311
Ibn Sa'd 784-845..................... DLB-311
Ibrahim al-Mawsili
   742 or 743-803 or 804 .... DLB-311
Ibrahim, Sonallah 1937- DLB-346
Ibsen, Henrik 1828-1906 .... DLB-354
Ibuse Masuji 1898-1993 .... DLB-180
Ichijō Kanera
   (see Ichijō Kaneyoshi)
Ichijō Kaneyoshi (Ichijō Kanera)
   1402-1481 .... DLB-203
Idle, Eric 1943- DLB-352
Idris, Yusuf 1927-1991................ DLB-346
Idrus 1921-1979 .... DLB-348
Iffland, August Wilhelm
   1759-1814...................... DLB-94
Iggulden, John 1917- DLB-289
Ignatieff, Michael 1947- DLB-267
Ignatow, David 1914-1997 .... DLB-5
Ike, Chukwuemeka 1931- DLB-157
Ikkyū Sōjun 1394-1481................ DLB-203
Iles, Francis (see Berkeley, Anthony)
Il'f, Il'ia (Il'ia Arnol'dovich Fainzil'berg)
   1897-1937.....................DLB-272
Ilkov, Ani 1957- DLB-353
Illich, Ivan 1926-2002................ DLB-242
Illustration
   Children's Book Illustration in the
     Twentieth Century DLB-61
   Children's Illustrators, 1800-1880 ... DLB-163
   Early American Book Illustration DLB-49
   The Iconography of Science-Fiction
     Art........................ DLB-8
   The Illustration of Early German
     Literary Manuscripts, circa
     1150-circa 1300 .... DLB-148
   Minor Illustrators, 1880-1914 ...... DLB-141
Illyés, Gyula 1902-1983 .... DLB-215; CDWLB-4
Imalayène, Fatima-Zohra (see Djebar, Assia)
Imbs, Bravig 1904-1946 .... DLB-4; DS-15
Imbuga, Francis D. 1947- DLB-157
Immermann, Karl 1796-1840 .... DLB-133
Imru' al-Qays circa 526-circa 565 ...... DLB-311
In a Free State, 1971 Booker Prize winner,
   V. S. Naipaul DLB-326
Inchbald, Elizabeth 1753-1821 ...... DLB-39, 89
Indiana University Press.............. Y-02

Industrial Workers of the World (IWW)
   1905- DLB-345
Ingamells, Rex 1913-1955 .... DLB-260
Inge, William 1913-1973.... DLB-7, 249; CDALB-1
Ingelow, Jean 1820-1897 .... DLB-35, 163
Ingemann, B. S. 1789-1862............ DLB-300
Ingersoll, Ralph 1900-1985..............DLB-127
Ingersoll, Robert G. 1833-1899 .... DLB-345
The Ingersoll Prizes Y-84
Ingoldsby, Thomas (see Barham, Richard Harris)
Ingraham, Joseph Holt 1809-1860 .... DLB-3, 248
Inman, John 1805-1850 .... DLB-73
Innerhofer, Franz 1944- DLB-85
Innes, Michael (J. I. M. Stewart)
   1906-1994 ....DLB-276
Innis, Harold Adams 1894-1952......... DLB-88
Innis, Mary Quayle 1899-1972.......... DLB-88
Inō Sōgi 1421-1502.................. DLB-203
Inoue Yasushi 1907-1991 .... DLB-182
"The Greatness of Southern Literature":
   League of the South Institute for the
   Study of Southern Culture and History
   .... Y-02
International Publishers Company DLB-46
Internet (publishing and commerce)
   Author Websites..................... Y-97
   The Book Trade and the Internet Y-00
   E-Books Turn the Corner Y-98
   The E-Researcher: Possibilities
     and Pitfalls.................. Y-00
   Interviews on E-publishing............ Y-00
   John Updike on the Internet Y-97
   LitCheck Website.................... Y-01
   Virtual Books and Enemies of Books..... Y-00
Interviews
   Adoff, Arnold...................... Y-01
   Aldridge, John W. Y-91
   Anastas, Benjamin Y-98
   Baker, Nicholson Y-00
   Bank, Melissa Y-98
   Bass, T. J........................ Y-80
   Bernstein, Harriet................... Y-82
   Betts, Doris Y-82
   Bosworth, David Y-82
   Bottoms, David Y-83
   Bowers, Fredson..................... Y-80
   Burnshaw, Stanley Y-97
   Carpenter, Humphrey Y-84, 99
   Carr, Virginia Spencer Y-00
   Carver, Raymond Y-83
   Cherry, Kelly Y-83
   Conroy, Jack Y-81
   Coppel, Alfred Y-83
   Cowley, Malcolm Y-81
   Davis, Paxton...................... Y-89

Devito, Carlo Y-94	Penzler, Otto Y-96	An Interview with Judith Krug
De Vries, Peter Y-82	Plimpton, George Y-99	An Interview with Phyllis Schlafly
Dickey, James Y-82	Potok, Chaim Y-84	An Interview with Edward B. Jenkinson
Donald, David Herbert Y-87	Powell, Padgett Y-01	An Interview with Lamarr Mooneyham
Editors, Conversations with Y-95	Prescott, Peter S. .Y-86	An Interview with Harriet Bernstein Y-82
Ellroy, James. Y-91	Rabe, David Y-91	Islas, Arturo 1938-1991 . . . . .DLB-122
Fancher, Betsy Y-83	Rechy, John. Y-82	Isma'il, Isma'il Fahd 1940- DLB-346
Faust, Irvin Y-00	Reid, B. L. Y-83	Issit, Debbie 1966- DLB-233
Fulton, Len Y-86	Reynolds, Michael. Y-95, 99	Ivanauskaitė, Jurga 1961-2007 . . . . .DLB-353
Furst, Alan. Y-01	Robinson, Derek .Y-02	Ivanišević, Drago 1907-1981 . . . . .DLB-181
Garrett, George Y-83	Rollyson, Carl. Y-97	Ivanov, Georgii 1894-1954. . . . . .DLB-317
Gelfman, Jane Y-93	Rosset, Barney Y-02	Ivanov, Viacheslav Ivanovich
Goldwater, Walter Y-93	Schlafly, Phyllis Y-82	1866-1949. . . . . .DLB-295
Gores, Joe Y-02	Schroeder, Patricia. Y-99	Ivanov, Vsevolod Viacheslavovich
Greenfield, George Y-91	Schulberg, Budd Y-81, 01	1895-1963 . . . . .DLB-272
Griffin, Bryan Y-81	Scribner, Charles, III. Y-94	Ivask, Yuri 1907-1986. . . . . .DLB-317
Groom, Winston .Y-01	Sipper, Ralph. Y-94	Ivaska, Astrīde 1926- DLB-232
Guilds, John Caldwell Y-92	Smith, Cork. Y-95	M. J. Ivers and Company. DLB-49
Hamilton, Virginia Y-01	Staley, Thomas F. Y-00	Iwaniuk, Wacław 1915-2001 . . . . .DLB-215
Hardin, James Y-92	Styron, William. .Y-80	Iwano Hōmei 1873-1920 . . . . .DLB-180
Harris, Mark Y-80	Talese, Nan Y-94	Iwaszkiewicz, Jarosław
Harrison, Jim. Y-82	Thornton, John. .Y-94	1894-1980 . . . . .DLB-215
Hazzard, Shirley .Y-82	Toth, Susan Allen Y-86	Iyayi, Festus 1947- DLB-157
Herrick, William .Y-01	Tyler, Anne Y-82	Izumi Kyōka
Higgins, George V. Y-98	Vaughan, Samuel. Y-97	1873-1939 . . . . .DLB-180
Hoban, Russell Y-90	Von Ogtrop, Kristin Y-92	
Holroyd, Michael Y-99	Wallenstein, Barry. Y-92	# J
Horowitz, Glen Y-90	Weintraub, Stanley Y-82	
Iggulden, John. Y-01	Williams, J. Chamberlain Y-84	Jabra, Jabra Ibrahim 1920-1994 . . . . .DLB-346
Jakes, John. Y-83	Into the Past: William Jovanovich's Reflections in Publishing Y-02	al-Jabri, Mohammed 'Abed 1935- DLB-346
Jenkinson, Edward B. Y-82	Ionesco, Eugène 1909-1994 . . . . .DLB-321	Jackmon, Marvin E. (see Marvin X)
Jenks, Tom. Y-86	Ireland, David 1927- DLB-289	Jacks, L. P. 1860-1955 . . . . .DLB-135
Kaplan, Justin Y-86	The National Library of Ireland's New James Joyce Manuscripts. Y-02	Jackson, Angela 1951- DLB-41
King, Florence Y-85		Jackson, Charles 1903-1968. . . . . .DLB-234
Klopfer, Donald S. Y-97	Irigaray, Luce 1930- DLB-296	Jackson, Helen Hunt 1830-1885 . . . . .DLB-42, 47, 186, 189
Krug, Judith. Y-82	Irving, John 1942- DLB-6, 278; Y-82	
Lamm, Donald Y-95	Irving, Washington 1783-1859 . . . . .DLB-3, 11, 30, 59, 73, 74, 183, 186, 250; CDALB-2	Jackson, Holbrook 1874-1948 . . . . .DLB-98
Laughlin, James .Y-96		Jackson, Laura Riding 1901-1991 . . . . .DLB-48
Lawrence, Starling. Y-95		Jackson, Shirley 1916-1965 . . . . .DLB-6, 234; CDALB-1
Lindsay, Jack Y-84	Irwin, Grace 1907- DLB-68	
Mailer, Norman. .Y-97	Irwin, Will 1873-1948 . . . . .DLB-25	Jacob, Max 1876-1944 . . . . .DLB-258
Manchester, William Y-85	Isaksson, Ulla 1916-2000 . . . . .DLB-257	Jacob, Naomi 1884?-1964 . . . . .DLB-191
Max, D. T. Y-94	Iser, Wolfgang 1926-2007 . . . . .DLB-242	Jacob, Piers Anthony Dillingham (see Anthony, Piers)
McCormack, Thomas. Y-98	Isherwood, Christopher 1904-1986 . . . . .DLB-15, 195; Y-86	
McNamara, Katherine. Y-97		Jacob, Violet 1863-1946. . . . . .DLB-240
Mellen, Joan Y-94	The Christopher Isherwood Archive, The Huntington Library Y-99	Jacobi, Friedrich Heinrich 1743-1819 . . . . . .DLB-94
Menaker, Daniel .Y-97		Jacobi, Johann Georg 1740-1841 . . . . .DLB-97
Mooneyham, Lamarr Y-82	Ishiguro, Kazuo 1954- DLB-194, 326	George W. Jacobs and Company. DLB-49
Murray, Les. Y-01	Ishikawa Jun 1899-1987. . . . . .DLB-182	Jacobs, Harriet 1813-1897 . . . . .DLB-239
Nosworth, David. Y-82	Iskander, Fazil' Abdulevich 1929- DLB-302	Jacobs, Joseph 1854-1916. . . . . .DLB-141
O'Connor, Patrick. Y-84, 99		Jacobs, W. W. 1863-1943. . . . . .DLB-135
Ozick, Cynthia Y-83		The W. W. Jacobs Appreciation Society . . .Y-98
Penner, Jonathan Y-83	The Island Trees Case: A Symposium on School Library Censorship	
Pennington, Lee. .Y-82		Jacobsen, J. P. 1847-1885 . . . . .DLB-300

Cumulative Index

Jacobsen, Jørgen-Frantz 1900-1938 ...... DLB-214
Jacobsen, Josephine 1908- DLB-244
Jacobsen, Rolf 1907-1994 .... DLB-297
Jacobson, Dan 1929- DLB-14, 207, 225, 319
Jacobson, Howard 1942- DLB-207
Jacques de Vitry circa 1160/1170-1240 ... DLB-208
Jæger, Frank 1926-1977 .... DLB-214
Jæger, Hans 1854-1910 .... DLB-354
Ja'far al-Sadiq circa 702-765 .... DLB-311
William Jaggard [publishing house] DLB-170
Jahier, Piero 1884-1966........... DLB-114, 264
al-Jahiz circa 776-868 or 869 .... DLB-311
Jahnn, Hans Henny 1894-1959 ..... DLB-56, 124
Jaimes, Freyre, Ricardo 1866?-1933 ..... DLB-283
Jakes, John 1932- DLB-278; Y-83
   Tribute to John Gardner Y-82
   Tribute to John D. MacDonald Y-86
Jakobína Johnson (Jakobína Sigurbjarnardóttir)
   1883-1977..................... DLB-293
Jakobson, Roman 1896-1982 .... DLB-242
James, Alice 1848-1892............... DLB-221
James, C. L. R. 1901-1989 .... DLB-125
James, Clive 1939- DLB-325
James, George P. R. 1801-1860 .... DLB-116
James, Henry 1843-1916
   .... DLB-12, 71, 74, 189; DS-13; CDALB-3
   "The Future of the Novel" (1899) DLB-18
   "The Novel in [Robert Browning's]
   'The Ring and the Book'"
   (1912) DLB-32
James, John circa 1633-1729 .... DLB-24
James, M. R. 1862-1936 .... DLB-156, 201
James, Naomi 1949- DLB-204
James, P. D. (Phyllis Dorothy James White)
   1920- DLB-87, 276; DS-17; CDBLB-8
   Tribute to Charles Scribner Jr. Y-95
James, Thomas 1572?-1629 .... DLB-213
U. P. James [publishing house] DLB-49
James, Will 1892-1942 .... DS-16
James, William 1842-1910 ....DLB-270
James VI of Scotland, I of England
   1566-1625 ....DLB-151, 172
   *Ane Schort Treatise Conteining Some Revlis
   and Cautelis to Be Obseruit and
   Eschewit in Scottis Poesi* (1584)......DLB-172
Jameson, Anna 1794-1860.......... DLB-99, 166
Jameson, Fredric 1934- DLB-67
Jameson, J. Franklin 1859-1937 .... DLB-17
Jameson, Storm 1891-1986.............. DLB-36
Jančar, Drago 1948- DLB-181
Janés, Clara 1940- DLB-134
Janevski, Slavko
   1920-2000.......... DLB-181; CDWLB-4
Janowitz, Tama 1957- DLB-292

Janson, Drude Krog (Judith Keller)
   1846-1934 .... DLB-354
Jansson, Tove 1914 2001 .... DLB-257
Janvier, Thomas 1849-1913 .... DLB-202
Japan
   "The Development of Meiji Japan" .. DLB-180
   "Encounter with the West" DLB-180
Japanese Literature
   Letter from Japan................. Y-94, 98
   Medieval Travel Diaries........... DLB-203
   Surveys: 1987-1995 .... DLB-182
Jaramillo, Cleofas M. 1878-1956........ DLB-122
Jaramillo Levi, Enrique 1944- DLB-290
Jarir after 650-circa 730................ DLB-311
Jarman, Mark 1952- DLB-120, 282
Jarrell, Randall
   1914-1965 .... DLB-48, 52; CDALB-1
Jarrold and Sons DLB-106
Jarry, Alfred 1873-1907 .... DLB-192, 258
Jarves, James Jackson 1818-1888 .... DLB-189
Jasim, 'Aziz al-Sayyid 1941-1991?....... DLB-346
Jasmin, Claude 1930- DLB-60
Jaunsudrabiņš, Jānis 1877-1962 .... DLB-220
Javellana, Stevan 1918-1977 .... DLB-348
Jay, John 1745-1829.................. DLB-31
Jean de Garlande (see John of Garland)
Jefferies, Richard 1848-1887 .... DLB-98, 141
   The Richard Jefferies Society........... Y-98
Jeffers, Lance 1919-1985................ DLB-41
Jeffers, Robinson
   1887-1962...... DLB-45, 212, 342; CDALB-4
Jefferson, Thomas
   1743-1826......... DLB-31, 183; CDALB-2
Jégé 1866-1940 .... DLB-215
Jelinek, Elfriede 1946- DLB-85, 330
Jellicoe, Ann 1927- DLB-13, 233
Jemison, Mary circa 1742-1833......... DLB-239
Jen, Gish 1955- DLB-312
Jenkins, Dan 1929- DLB-241
Jenkins, Elizabeth 1905- DLB-155
Jenkins, Robin 1912-2005..........DLB-14, 271
Jenkins, William Fitzgerald (see Leinster, Murray)
Herbert Jenkins Limited.............. DLB-112
Jennings, Elizabeth 1926-2001 .... DLB-27
Jennings, Paul 1943- DLB-352
Jens, Walter 1923- DLB-69
Jensen, Axel 1932-2003 .... DLB-297
Jensen, Johannes V. 1873-1950..... DLB-214, 330
Jensen, Merrill 1905-1980............. DLB-17
Jensen, Thit 1876-1957 .... DLB-214
Jephson, Robert 1736-1803............ DLB-89
Jerome, Jerome K. 1859-1927 .....DLB-10, 34, 135
   The Jerome K. Jerome Society.......... Y-98

Jerome, Judson 1927-1991............. DLB-105
   "Reflections: After a Tornado"...... DLB-105
Jerrold, Douglas 1803-1857 ....DLB-158, 159, 344
Jersild, Per Christian 1935- DLB-257
Jesih, Milan 1950- DLB-353
Jesse, F. Tennyson 1888-1958........... DLB-77
Jewel, John 1522-1571................ DLB-236
John P. Jewett and Company DLB-49
Jewett, Sarah Orne 1849-1909 ....DLB-12, 74, 221
Studies in American Jewish Literature Y-02
Jewish Literature of Medieval Spain..... DLB-337
The Jewish Publication Society.......... DLB-49
Jewitt, John Rodgers 1783-1821 .... DLB-99
Jewsbury, Geraldine 1812-1880 .... DLB-21
Jewsbury, Maria Jane 1800-1833 .... DLB-199
Jeyaretnam, Philip 1964- DLB-348
Jhabvala, Ruth Prawer
   1927- DLB-139, 194, 323, 326
Jiang Guangci 1901-1931 .... DLB-328
Jiménez, Juan Ramón 1881-1958 ... DLB-134, 330
Jiménez de Rada, Rodrigo
   after 1170-1247................. DLB-337
Jin, Ha 1956- DLB-244, 292
Joans, Ted 1928-2003............. DLB-16, 41
Joaquin, Nick 1917-2004.............. DLB-348
Jodelle, Estienne 1532?-1573........... DLB-327
Jōha 1525-1602..................... DLB-203
Jóhann Sigurjónsson 1880-1919 .... DLB-293
Jóhannes úr Kötlum 1899-1972 .... DLB-293
Johannis de Garlandia (see John of Garland)
John, Errol 1924-1988 .... DLB-233
John, Eugenie (see Marlitt, E.)
John of Dumbleton
   circa 1310-circa 1349 .... DLB-115
John of Garland (Jean de Garlande,
   Johannis de Garlandia)
   circa 1195-circa 1272 .... DLB-208
The John Reed Clubs................. DLB-303
Johns, Captain W. E. 1893-1968 .... DLB-160
Johnson, Mrs. A. E. ca. 1858-1922...... DLB-221
Johnson, Amelia (see Johnson, Mrs. A. E.)
Johnson, Amryl 1944-2001............ DLB-347
Johnson, B. S. 1933-1973 .... DLB-14, 40
Johnson, Charles 1679-1748 .... DLB-84
Johnson, Charles 1948- DLB-33, 278
Johnson, Charles S. 1893-1956....... DLB-51, 91
Johnson, Colin (Mudrooroo) 1938- ... DLB-289
Johnson, Denis 1949- DLB-120
Johnson, Diane 1934- ....DLB 350; Y-80
Johnson, Dorothy M. 1905–1984........ DLB-206
Johnson, E. Pauline (Tekahionwake)
   1861-1913 ....DLB-175

Johnson, Edgar 1901-1995 . . . . .DLB-103

Johnson, Edward 1598-1672 . . . . .DLB-24

Johnson, Eyvind 1900-1976 . . . . .DLB-259, 330

Johnson, Fenton 1888-1958 . . . . .DLB-45, 50

Johnson, Georgia Douglas
1877?-1966 . . . . .DLB-51, 249

Johnson, Gerald W. 1890-1980 . . . . .DLB-29

Johnson, Greg 1953- DLB-234

Johnson, Helene 1907-1995 . . . . .DLB-51

Jacob Johnson and Company DLB-49

Johnson, James Weldon
1871-1938 . . . . .DLB-51; CDALB-4

Johnson, John H. 1918-2005 . . . . .DLB-137

"Backstage," Statement From the
Initial Issue of *Ebony*
(November 1945 . . . . .DLB-137

Johnson, Joseph [publishing house] DLB-154

Johnson, Linton Kwesi 1952- DLB-157

Johnson, Lionel 1867-1902 . . . . .DLB-19

Johnson, Nunnally 1897-1977 . . . . .DLB-26

Johnson, Owen 1878-1952 . . . . .Y-87

Johnson, Pamela Hansford 1912-1981 . . . . .DLB-15

Johnson, Pauline 1861-1913 . . . . .DLB-92

Johnson, Ronald 1935-1998 . . . . .DLB-169

Johnson, Samuel 1696-1772 . . . DLB-24; CDBLB-2

Johnson, Samuel
1709-1784 . . . . DLB-39, 95, 104, 142, 213

Rambler, no. 4 (1750) [excerpt] DLB-39

The BBC Four Samuel Johnson Prize
for Non-fiction Y-02

Johnson, Samuel 1822-1882 . . . . .DLB-1, 243

Johnson, Susanna 1730-1810 . . . . .DLB-200

Johnson, Terry 1955- DLB-233

Johnson, Uwe 1934-1984 . . . . . DLB-75; CDWLB-2

Benjamin Johnson [publishing house] DLB-49

Benjamin, Jacob, and Robert Johnson
[publishing house] DLB-49

Johnston, Annie Fellows 1863-1931 . . . . . . .DLB-42

Johnston, Basil H. 1929- DLB-60

Johnston, David Claypole 1798?-1865 . . . .DLB-188

Johnston, Denis 1901-1984 . . . . .DLB-10

Johnston, Ellen 1835-1873 . . . . .DLB-199

Johnston, George 1912-1970 . . . . .DLB-260

Johnston, George 1913-1970 . . . . .DLB-88

Johnston, Sir Harry 1858-1927 . . . . .DLB-174

Johnston, Jennifer 1930- DLB-14

Johnston, Mary 1870-1936 . . . . .DLB-9

Johnston, Richard Malcolm 1822-1898 . . . .DLB-74

Johnston, Wayne 1958- DLB-334

Johnstone, Charles 1719?-1800? DLB-39

Johst, Hanns 1890-1978 . . . . .DLB-124

Jökull Jakobsson 1933-1978 . . . . .DLB-293

Jolas, Eugene 1894-1952 . . . . .DLB-4, 45

Jolley, Elizabeth 1923-2007 . . . . .DLB-325

Jón Stefán Sveinsson or Svensson (see Nonni)

Jón Trausti (Guðmundur Magnússon)
1873-1918 . . . . .DLB-293

Jón úr Vör (Jón Jónsson) 1917-2000 . . . . .DLB-293

Jónas Hallgrímsson 1807-1845 . . . . .DLB-293

Jones, Alice C. 1853-1933 . . . . .DLB-92

Jones, Charles C., Jr. 1831-1893 . . . . .DLB-30

Jones, D. G. 1929- DLB-53

Jones, David 1895-1974 . . .DLB-20, 100; CDBLB-7

Jones, Diana Wynne 1934- DLB-161

Jones, Ebenezer 1820-1860 . . . . .DLB-32

Jones, Ernest 1819-1868 . . . . .DLB-32

Jones, Gayl 1949- DLB-33, 278

Jones, George 1800-1870 . . . . .DLB-183

Jones, Glyn 1905-1995 . . . . .DLB-15

Jones, Gwyn 1907-1999 . . . . .DLB-15, 139

Jones, Henry Arthur 1851-1929 . . . . .DLB-10, 344

Jones, Hugh circa 1692-1760 . . . . .DLB-24

Jones, James 1921-1977 . . . . . . .DLB-2, 143; DS-17

James Jones Papers in the Handy
Writers' Colony Collection at
the University of Illinois at
Springfield Y-98

The James Jones Society Y-92

Jones, Jenkin Lloyd 1911-2004 . . . . .DLB-127

Jones, John Beauchamp 1810-1866 . . . . . .DLB-202

Jones, Joseph, Major
(see Thompson, William Tappan)

Jones, LeRoi (see Baraka, Amiri)

Jones, Lewis 1897-1939 . . . . .DLB-15

Jones, Madison 1925- DLB-152

Jones, Marie 1951- DLB-233

Jones, Preston 1936-1979 . . . . .DLB-7

Jones, Rodney 1950- DLB-120

Jones, Thom 1945- DLB-244

Jones, Sir William 1746-1794 . . . . .DLB-109

Jones, William Alfred 1817-1900 . . . . .DLB-59

Jones's Publishing House DLB-49

Jong, Erica 1942- DLB-2, 5, 28, 152

Jonke, Gert F. 1946-2009 . . . . .DLB-85

Jonson, Ben
1572?-1637 . . . . .DLB-62, 121; CDBLB-1

Jonsson, Tor 1916-1951 . . . . .DLB-297

Jordan, June 1936- DLB-38

Jorgensen, Johannes 1866-1956 . . . . .DLB-300

José, F. Sionil 1924- DLB-348

Jose, Nicholas 1952- DLB-325

Joseph, Anthony 1966- DLB-347

Joseph, Jenny 1932- DLB-40

Joseph and George Y-99

Michael Joseph Limited DLB-112

Josephson, Matthew 1899-1978 . . . . .DLB-4

Josephus, Flavius 37-100 . . . . .DLB-176

Josephy, Alvin M., Jr.
Tribute to Alfred A. Knopf Y-84

Josiah Allen's Wife (see Holley, Marietta)

Josipovici, Gabriel 1940- DLB-14, 319

Josselyn, John ?-1675 . . . . .DLB-24

Joudry, Patricia 1921-2000 . . . . .DLB-88

Jouve, Pierre Jean 1887-1976 . . . . .DLB-258

Jovanovich, William 1920-2001 . . . . .Y-01

Into the Past: William Jovanovich's
Reflections on Publishing Y-02

[Response to Ken Auletta] Y-97

The Temper of the West: William
Jovanovich Y-02

Tribute to Charles Scribner Jr. Y-95

Jovine, Francesco 1902-1950 . . . . .DLB-264

Jovine, Giuseppe 1922-1998 . . . . .DLB-128

Joyaux, Philippe (see Sollers, Philippe)

Joyce, Adrien (see Eastman, Carol)

Joyce, James 1882-1941
. . . . .DLB-10, 19, 36, 162, 247; CDBLB-6

Danis Rose and the Rendering of *Ulysses* Y-97

James Joyce Centenary: Dublin, 1982 . . . .Y-82

James Joyce Conference Y-85

A Joyce (Con)Text: Danis Rose and the
Remaking of *Ulysses* Y-97

The National Library of Ireland's
New James Joyce Manuscripts Y-02

The New *Ulysses* Y-84

Public Domain and the Violation of
Texts Y-97

The Quinn Draft of James Joyce's
Circe Manuscript Y-00

Stephen Joyce's Letter to the Editor of
The Irish Times Y-97

Ulysses, Reader's Edition: First Reactions . . .Y-97

We See the Editor at Work Y-97

Whose *Ulysses*? The Function of Editing . . .Y-97

Jozsef, Attila 1905-1937 . . . . . DLB-215; CDWLB-4

San Juan de la Cruz 1542-1591 . . . . .DLB-318

Juan Manuel 1282-1348 . . . . .DLB-337

Juarroz, Roberto 1925-1995 . . . . .DLB-283

Orange Judd Publishing Company DLB-49

Judd, Sylvester 1813-1853 . . . . .DLB-1, 243

Judith circa 930 .DLB-146

Juel-Hansen, Erna 1845-1922 . . . . .DLB-300

Julian of Norwich 1342-circa 1420 . . . . . .DLB-1146

Julius Caesar
100 B.C.-44 B.C. DLB-211; CDWLB-1

June, Jennie
(see Croly, Jane Cunningham)

Jung, Carl Gustav 1875-1961 . . . . .DLB-296

Jung, Franz 1888-1963 . . . . .DLB-118

Jünger, Ernst 1895-1998 . . . . . .DLB-56; CDWLB-2

Cumulative Index

Der jüngere Titurel circa 1275 . . . . DLB-138

Jung-Stilling, Johann Heinrich
   1740-1817 . . . . DLB-94

Junqueiro, Abílio Manuel Guerra
   1850-1923 . . . . DLB-287

Just, Ward (Ward S. Just) 1935- DLB-335

Justice, Donald 1925-2004 . . . . Y-83

Juvenal circa A.D. 60-circa A.D. 130
   . . . . DLB-211; CDWLB-1

The Juvenile Library
   (see M. J. Godwin and Company)

K

Kadare, Ismail 1936- DLB-353

Kacew, Romain (see Gary, Romain)

Kafka, Franz 1883-1924 . . . . . DLB-81; CDWLB-2

Kahn, Gus 1886-1941 . . . . DLB-265

Kahn, Roger 1927- DLB-171

Kaikō Takeshi 1939-1989 . . . . DLB-182

Káinn (Kristján Níels Jónsson/Kristjan
   Niels Julius) 1860-1936 . . . . DLB-293

Kaiser, Georg 1878-1945 . . . . DLB-124; CDWLB-2

Kaiserchronik circa 1147 . . . . DLB-148

Kaleb, Vjekoslav 1905-1996 . . . . DLB-181

Kalechofsky, Roberta 1931- DLB-28

Kaler, James Otis 1848-1912 . . . . DLB-12, 42

Kalmar, Bert 1884-1947 . . . . DLB-265

Kalu, Peter (Carl Peters) 1962- DLB-347

Kamensky, Vasilii Vasil'evich
   1884-1961 . . . . DLB-295

Kames, Henry Home, Lord
   1696-1782 . . . . DLB-31, 104

Kamo no Chōmei (Kamo no Nagaakira)
   1153 or 1155-1216 . . . . DLB-203

Kamo no Nagaakira (see Kamo no Chōmei)

Kampmann, Christian 1939-1988 . . . . . . DLB-214

Kanafani, Ghassan 1936-1972 . . . . DLB-346

Kandel, Lenore 1932- DLB-16

Kane, Sarah 1971-1999 . . . . DLB-310

Kaneko, Lonny 1939- DLB-312

Kang, Younghill 1903-1972 . . . . DLB-312

Kanin, Garson 1912-1999 . . . . DLB-7

   A Tribute (to Marc Connelly) Y-80

Kaniuk, Yoram 1930- DLB-299

Kant, Hermann 1926- DLB-75

Kant, Immanuel 1724-1804 . . . . DLB-94

Kantemir, Antiokh Dmitrievich
   1708-1744 . . . . DLB-150

Kantor, MacKinlay 1904-1977 . . . . DLB-9, 102

Kányádi, Sándor 1929- DLB-353

Kanze Kōjirō Nobumitsu 1435-1516 . . . . DLB-203

Kanze Motokiyo (see Zeimi)

Kaplan, Fred 1937- DLB-111

Kaplan, Johanna 1942- DLB-28

Kaplan, Justin 1925- DLB-111; Y-86

Kaplinski, Jaan 1941- DLB-232

Kapnist, Vasilii Vasilevich 1758?-1823 . . . DLB-150

Kapuściński, Ryszard 1932-2007 . . . . DLB-353

Karadžić, Vuk Stefanović
   1787-1864 . . . . DLB-147; CDWLB-4

Karamzin, Nikolai Mikhailovich
   1766-1826 . . . . DLB-150

Karinthy, Frigyes 1887-1938 . . . . DLB-215

Karlfeldt, Erik Axel 1864-1931 . . . . DLB-330

Karmel, Ilona 1925-2000 . . . . DLB-299

Karnad, Girish 1938- DLB-323

Karsch, Anna Louisa 1722-1791 . . . . DLB-97

Kasack, Hermann 1896-1966 . . . . DLB-69

Kasai Zenzō 1887-1927 . . . . DLB-180

Kaschnitz, Marie Luise 1901-1974 . . . . . . DLB-69

Kassák, Lajos 1887-1967 . . . . DLB-215

Kaštelan, Jure 1919-1990 . . . . DLB-147

Kästner, Erich 1899-1974 . . . . DLB-56

Kataev, Evgenii Petrovich
   (see Il'f, Il'ia and Petrov, Evgenii)

Kataev, Valentin Petrovich 1897-1986 . . . DLB-272

Katenin, Pavel Aleksandrovich
   1792-1853 . . . . DLB-205

Kattan, Naim 1928- DLB-53

Katz, Steve 1935- Y-83

Ka-Tzetnik 135633 (Yehiel Dinur)
   1909-2001 . . . . DLB-299

Kauffman, Janet 1945- DLB-218; Y-86

Kauffmann, Samuel 1898-1971 . . . . DLB-127

Kaufman, Bob 1925-1986 . . . . DLB-16, 41

Kaufman, George S. 1889-1961 . . . . DLB-7

Kaufmann, Walter 1921-1980 . . . . DLB-279

Kavan, Anna (Helen Woods Ferguson
   Edmonds) 1901-1968 . . . . DLB-255

Kavanagh, P. J. 1931- DLB-40

Kavanagh, Patrick 1904-1967 . . . . DLB-15, 20

Kaverin, Veniamin Aleksandrovich
   (Veniamin Aleksandrovich Zil'ber)
   1902-1989 . . . . DLB-272

Kawabata Yasunari 1899-1972 . . . . . DLB-180, 330

Kay, Guy Gavriel 1954- DLB-251

Kay, Jackie 1961- DLB-347

Kaye-Smith, Sheila 1887-1956 . . . . DLB-36

Kazakov, Iurii Pavlovich 1927-1982 . . . . . DLB-302

Kazin, Alfred 1915-1998 . . . . DLB-67

Keane, John B. 1928-2002 . . . . DLB-13

Keary, Annie 1825-1879 . . . . DLB-163

Keary, Eliza 1827-1918 . . . . DLB-240

Keating, H. R. F. 1926- DLB-87

Keatley, Charlotte 1960- DLB-245

Keats, Ezra Jack 1916-1983 . . . . DLB-61

Keats, John 1795-1821 . . . DLB-96, 110; CDBLB-3

Keble, John 1792-1866 . . . . DLB-32, 55

Keckley, Elizabeth 1818?-1907 . . . . DLB-239

Keeble, John 1944- Y-83

Keeffe, Barrie 1945- DLB-13, 245

Keeley, James 1867-1934 . . . . DLB-25

W. B. Keen, Cooke and Company DLB-49

The Mystery of Carolyn Keene Y-02

Kefala, Antigone 1935- DLB-289

Keillor, Garrison 1942- Y-87

Keith, Marian (Mary Esther MacGregor)
   1874?-1961 . . . . DLB-92

Keller, Gary D. 1943- DLB-82

Keller, Gottfried
   1819-1890 . . . . DLB-129; CDWLB-2

Keller, Helen 1880-1968 . . . . DLB-303

Keller, Judith (see Janson, Drude Krog)

Kelley, Edith Summers 1884-1956 . . . . DLB-9

Kelley, Emma Dunham ?-? DLB-221

Kelley, Florence 1859-1932 . . . . DLB-303

Kelley, William Melvin 1937- DLB-33

Kellogg, Ansel Nash 1832-1886 . . . . DLB-23

Kellogg, Steven 1941- DLB-61

Kelly, George E. 1887-1974 . . . . DLB-7, 249

Kelly, Hugh 1739-1777 . . . . DLB-89

Kelly, Piet and Company DLB-49

Kelly, Robert 1935- DLB-5, 130, 165

Kelman, James 1946- DLB-194, 319, 326

Kelmscott Press DLB-112

Kelton, Elmer 1926- DLB-256

Kemble, Charles 1775-1854 . . . . DLB-344

Kemble, E. W. 1861-1933 . . . . DLB-188

Kemble, Fanny 1809-1893 . . . . DLB-32

Kemelman, Harry 1908-1996 . . . . DLB-28

Kempe, Margery circa 1373-1438 . . . . . . DLB-146

Kempinski, Tom 1938- DLB-310

Kempner, Friederike 1836-1904 . . . . DLB-129

Kempowski, Walter 1929-2007 . . . . DLB-75

Kenan, Randall 1963- DLB-292

Claude Kendall [publishing company] DLB-46

Kendall, Henry 1839-1882 . . . . DLB-230

Kendall, May 1861-1943 . . . . DLB-240

Kendell, George 1809-1867 . . . . DLB-43

Keneally, Thomas 1935- DLB-289, 299, 326

Kenedy, P. J., and Sons DLB-49

Kenkō circa 1283-circa 1352 . . . . DLB-203

Kenna, Peter 1930-1987 . . . . DLB-289

Kennan, George 1845-1924 . . . . DLB-189

Kennedy, A. L. 1965- DLB-271

Kennedy, Adrienne 1931- DLB-38, 341

Kennedy, John Pendleton 1795-1870 . . . DLB-3, 248

Kennedy, Leo 1907-2000 . . . . DLB-88

Kennedy, Margaret 1896-1967 . . . . .DLB-36

Kennedy, Patrick 1801-1873 . . . . .DLB-159

Kennedy, Richard S. 1920-2002 . . . . DLB-111; Y-02

Kennedy, William 1928- DLB-143; Y-85

Kennedy, X. J. 1929- DLB-5

    Tribute to John Ciardi Y-86

Kennelly, Brendan 1936- DLB-40

Kenner, Hugh 1923-2003 . . . . .DLB-67

    Tribute to Cleanth Brooks Y-80

Mitchell Kennerley [publishing house] DLB-46

Kennett, White 1660-1728 . . . . .DLB-336

Kenney, James 1780?-1849 . . . . .DLB-344

Kenny, Maurice 1929- DLB-175

Kent, Frank R. 1877-1958 . . . . .DLB-29

Kentfield, Calvin 1924-1975 . . . . .DLB-335

Kenyon, Jane 1947-1995 . . . . .DLB-120

Kenzheev, Bakhyt Shkurullaevich
    1950- DLB-285

Keough, Hugh Edmund 1864-1912 . . . . . .DLB-171

Keppler and Schwartzmann DLB-49

Ker, John, third Duke of Roxburghe
    1740-1804 . . . . .DLB-213

Ker, N. R. 1908-1982 . . . . .DLB-201

Keralio-Robert, Louise-Félicité de
    1758-1822 . . . . .DLB-313

Keris Mas 1922-1992 . . . . .DLB-348

Kerlan, Irvin 1912-1963 . . . . .DLB-187

Kermode, Frank 1919- DLB-242

Kern, Jerome 1885-1945 . . . . .DLB-187

Kernaghan, Eileen 1939- DLB-251

Kerner, Justinus 1786-1862 . . . . .DLB-90

Kerouac, Jack
    1922-1969 . . . DLB-2, 16, 237; DS-3; CDALB-1

    Auction of Jack Kerouac's
        On the Road Scroll Y-01

    The Jack Kerouac Revival Y-95

    "Re-meeting of Old Friends":
        The Jack Kerouac Conference Y-82

    Statement of Correction to "The Jack
        Kerouac Revival" Y-96

Kerouac, Jan 1952-1996 . . . . .DLB-16

Charles H. Kerr and Company DLB-49

Kerr, Orpheus C. (see Newell, Robert Henry)

Kersh, Gerald 1911-1968 . . . . .DLB-255

Kertész, Imre DLB-299, 330, 353; Y-02

Kesey, Ken 1935-2001 . . DLB-2, 16, 206; CDALB-6

Kessel, Joseph 1898-1979 . . . . .DLB-72

Kessel, Martin 1901-1990 . . . . .DLB-56

Kesten, Hermann 1900-1996 . . . . .DLB-56

Keun, Irmgard 1905-1982 . . . . .DLB-69

Key, Ellen 1849-1926 . . . . .DLB-259

Key and Biddle .DLB-49

Keynes, Sir Geoffrey 1887-1982 . . . . .DLB-201

Keynes, John Maynard 1883-1946 . . . . DS-10

Keyserling, Eduard von 1855-1918 . . . . . . .DLB-66

Khalifeh, Sahar 1941- DLB-346

al-Khalil ibn Ahmad circa 718-791 . . . . . . .DLB-311

Khalvati, Mimi 1944- DLB-347

Khamsing Srinawk 1930- DLB-348

Khan, Adib 1949- DLB-323

Khan, Ismith 1925-2002 . . . . .DLB-125

Khan-Din, Ayub 1961- DLB-347

al-Khansa' fl. late sixth-mid
    seventh centuries DLB-311

Kharik, Izi 1898-1937 . . . . .DLB-333

Kharitonov, Evgenii Vladimirovich
    1941-1981 . . . . .DLB-285

Kharitonov, Mark Sergeevich 1937- DLB-285

Kharjas, The DLB-337

Khaytov, Nikolay 1919- DLB-181

Khemnitser, Ivan Ivanovich
    1745-1784 . . . . .DLB-150

Kheraskov, Mikhail Matveevich
    1733-1807 . . . . .DLB-150

Khin Hnin Yu 1925-2003 . . . . .DLB-348

Khlebnikov, Velimir 1885-1922 . . . . .DLB-295

Khodasevich, Vladislav 1886-1939 . . . . . . .DLB-317

Khomiakov, Aleksei Stepanovich
    1804-1860 . . . . .DLB-205

Khristov, Boris 1945- DLB-181

Khukrit Pramoj, M.R. 1911-1995 . . . . . . .DLB-348

Khuri, Raif 1913-1967 . . . . .DLB-346

Khvoshchinskaia, Nadezhda Dmitrievna
    1824-1889 . . . . .DLB-238

Khvostov, Dmitrii Ivanovich
    1757-1835 . . . . .DLB-150

Kibirov, Timur Iur'evich (Timur
    Iur'evich Zapoev) 1955- DLB-285

Kidd, Adam 1802?-1831 . . . . .DLB-99

William Kidd [publishing house] DLB-106

Kidde, Harald 1878-1918 . . . . .DLB-300

Kidder, Tracy 1945- DLB-185

Kielland, Alexander L. 1849-1906 . . . . . . .DLB-354

Kiely, Benedict 1919-2007 . . . . .DLB-15, 319

Kieran, John 1892-1981 . . . . .DLB-171

Kierkegaard, Søren 1813-1855 . . . . .DLB-300

Kies, Marietta 1853-1899 . . . . .DLB-270

Kiggins and Kellogg DLB-49

Kiley, Jed 1889-1962 . . . . .DLB-4

Kilgore, Bernard 1908-1967 . . . . .DLB-127

Kilian, Crawford 1941- DLB-251

Killens, John Oliver 1916-1987 . . . . .DLB-33

    Tribute to Julian Mayfield Y-84

Killigrew, Anne 1660-1685 . . . . .DLB-131

Killigrew, Thomas 1612-1683 . . . . .DLB-58

Kilmer, Joyce 1886-1918 . . . . .DLB-45

Kilroy, Thomas 1934- DLB-233

Kilwardby, Robert circa 1215-1279 . . . . . .DLB-115

Kilworth, Garry 1941- DLB-261

Kim, Anatolii Andreevich 1939- DLB-285

Kimball, Richard Burleigh 1816-1892 . . . .DLB-202

Kincaid, Jamaica 1949-
    . . . . DLB-157, 227; CDALB-7; CDWLB-3

Kinck, Hans Ernst 1865-1926 . . . . .DLB-297

King, Charles 1844-1933 . . . . .DLB-186

King, Clarence 1842-1901 . . . . .DLB-12

King, Florence 1936- Y-85

King, Francis 1923- DLB-15, 139

King, Grace 1852-1932 . . . . .DLB-12, 78

King, Harriet Hamilton 1840-1920 . . . . . .DLB-199

King, Henry 1592-1669 . . . . .DLB-126

Solomon King [publishing house] DLB-49

King, Stephen 1947- DLB-143, 350; Y-80

King, Susan Petigru 1824-1875 . . . . .DLB-239

King, Thomas 1943- DLB-175, 334

King, Woodie, Jr. 1937- DLB-38

Kinglake, Alexander William
    1809-1891 . . . . .DLB-55, 166

Kingo, Thomas 1634-1703 . . . . .DLB-300

Kingsbury, Donald 1929- DLB-251

Kingsley, Charles
    1819-1875 . . . . DLB-21, 32, 163, 178, 190

Kingsley, Henry 1830-1876 . . . . .DLB-21, 230

Kingsley, Mary Henrietta 1862-1900 . . . . .DLB-174

Kingsley, Sidney 1906-1995 . . . . .DLB-7

Kingsmill, Hugh 1889-1949 . . . . .DLB-149

Kingsolver, Barbara
    1955- DLB-206; CDALB-7

Kingston, Maxine Hong
    1940- . . DLB-173, 212, 312; Y-80; CDALB-7

Kingston, William Henry Giles
    1814-1880 . . . . .DLB-163

Kinnan, Mary Lewis 1763-1848 . . . . .DLB-200

Kinnell, Galway 1927- DLB-5, 342; Y-87

Kinsella, John 1963- DLB-325

Kinsella, Thomas 1928- DLB-27

Kipling, Rudyard 1865-1936
    . . . . DLB-19, 34, 141, 156, 330; CDBLB-5

Kipphardt, Heinar 1922-1982 . . . . .DLB-124

Kirby, William 1817-1906 . . . . .DLB-99

Kircher, Athanasius 1602-1680 . . . . .DLB-164

Kireevsky, Ivan Vasil'evich 1806-1856 . . . .DLB-198

Kireevsky, Petr Vasil'evich 1808-1856 . . . .DLB-205

Kirk, Hans 1898-1962 . . . . .DLB-214

Kirk, John Foster 1824-1904 . . . . .DLB-79

Kirkconnell, Watson 1895-1977 . . . . .DLB-68

Kirkland, Caroline M.
    1801-1864 . . . . .DLB-3, 73, 74, 250; DS-13

Kirkland, Joseph 1830-1893 . . . . .DLB-12

Francis Kirkman [publishing house]......DLB-170
Kirkpatrick, Clayton 1915-2004........DLB-127
Kirkup, James 1918-2009..............DLB-27
Kirouac, Conrad (see Marie-Victorin, Frère)
Kirsch, Sarah 1935-..................DLB-75
Kirst, Hans Hellmut 1914-1989........DLB-69
Kiš, Danilo 1935-1989.....DLB-181; CDWLB-4
Kita Morio 1927-....................DLB-182
Kitcat, Mabel Greenhow 1859-1922.....DLB-135
Kitchin, C. H. B. 1895-1967...........DLB-77
Kittredge, William 1932-........DLB-212, 244
Kiukhel'beker, Vil'gel'm Karlovich
  1797-1846........................DLB-205
Kizer, Carolyn 1925-..............DLB-5, 169
Kjaerstad, Jan 1953-.................DLB-297
Klabund 1890-1928....................DLB-66
Klaj, Johann 1616-1656..............DLB-164
Klappert, Peter 1942-.................DLB-5
Klass, Philip (see Tenn, William)
Klein, A. M. 1909-1972................DLB-68
Kleist, Ewald von 1715-1759...........DLB-97
Kleist, Heinrich von
  1777-1811..............DLB-90; CDWLB-2
Klíma, Ivan 1931-.......DLB-232; CDWLB-4
Klimentev, Andrei Platonovic
  (see Platonov, Andrei Platonovich)
Klinger, Friedrich Maximilian
  1752-1831.........................DLB-94
Kliuev, Nikolai Alekseevich 1884-1937...DLB-295
Kliushnikov, Viktor Petrovich
  1841-1892.........................DLB-238
Klopfer, Donald S.
  Impressions of William Faulkner........Y-97
  Oral History Interview with Donald
    S. Klopfer.........................Y-97
  Tribute to Alfred A. Knopf............Y-84
Klopstock, Friedrich Gottlieb
  1724-1803.........................DLB-97
Klopstock, Meta 1728-1758.............DLB-97
Kluge, Alexander 1932-................DLB-75
Kluge, P. F. 1942-.....................Y-02
Knapp, Joseph Palmer 1864-1951........DLB-91
Knapp, Samuel Lorenzo 1783-1838......DLB-59
J. J. and P. Knapton [publishing house]..DLB-154
Kniazhnin, Iakov Borisovich
  1740-1791.........................DLB-150
Knickerbocker, Diedrich (see Irving, Washington)
Knigge, Adolph Franz Friedrich Ludwig,
  Freiherr von 1752-1796.............DLB-94
Charles Knight and Company..........DLB-106
Knight, Damon 1922-2002...............DLB-8
Knight, Etheridge 1931-1992...........DLB-41
Knight, John S. 1894-1981.............DLB-29
Knight, Sarah Kemble 1666-1727....DLB-24, 200

Knight-Bruce, G. W. H. 1852-1896......DLB-174
Knister, Raymond 1899-1932............DLB-68
Knoblock, Edward 1874-1945............DLB-10
Knopf, Alfred A. 1892-1984..............Y-84
  Knopf to Hammett: The Editoral
    Correspondence......................Y-00
Alfred A. Knopf [publishing house]......DLB-46
Knorr von Rosenroth, Christian
  1636-1689.........................DLB-168
Knowles, James Sheridan 1784-1862.....DLB-344
Knowles, John 1926-2001......DLB-6; CDALB-6
Knox, Frank 1874-1944.................DLB-29
Knox, John circa 1514-1572...........DLB-132
Knox, John Armoy 1850-1906...........DLB-23
Knox, Lucy 1845-1884.................DLB-240
Knox, Ronald Arbuthnott 1888-1957.....DLB-77
Knox, Thomas Wallace 1835-1896.......DLB-189
Knudsen, Jakob 1858-1917.............DLB-300
Knut, Dovid 1900-1955................DLB-317
Ko Surangkhanang 1911-1999..........DLB-348
Kobayashi Takiji 1903-1933...........DLB-180
Kober, Arthur 1900-1975...............DLB-11
Kobiakova, Aleksandra Petrovna
  1823-1892.........................DLB-238
Kocbek, Edvard 1904-1981...DLB-147; CDWLB-4
Koch, C. J. 1932-....................DLB-289
Koch, Howard 1902-1995................DLB-26
Koch, Kenneth 1925-2002................DLB-5
Kōda Rohan 1867-1947.................DLB-180
Koehler, Ted 1894-1973...............DLB-265
Koenigsberg, Moses 1879-1945..........DLB-25
Koeppen, Wolfgang 1906-1996...........DLB-69
Koertge, Ronald 1940-................DLB-105
Koestler, Arthur 1905-1983.......Y-83; CDBLB-7
Kogawa, Joy 1935-...................DLB-334
Kohn, John S. Van E. 1906-1976.......DLB-187
Kokhanovskaia
  (see Sokhanskaia, Nadezhda Stepanova)
Kokoschka, Oskar 1886-1980...........DLB-124
Kolatkar, Arun 1932-2004.............DLB-323
Kolb, Annette 1870-1967...............DLB-66
Kolbenheyer, Erwin Guido
  1878-1962......................DLB-66, 124
Kolleritsch, Alfred 1931-..............DLB-85
Kolodny, Annette 1941-................DLB-67
Koltès, Bernard-Marie 1948-1989.......DLB-321
Kol'tsov, Aleksei Vasil'evich
  1809-1842........................DLB-205
Komarov, Matvei circa 1730-1812.......DLB-150
Komroff, Manuel 1890-1974..............DLB-4
Komunyakaa, Yusef 1947-..............DLB-120
Kondoleon, Harry 1955-1994...........DLB-266

Koneski, Blaže 1921-1993....DLB-181; CDWLB-4
Kong Boun Chhoeun 1939-............DLB-348
Konigsburg, E. L. 1930-...............DLB-52
Konparu Zenchiku 1405-1468?.........DLB-203
Konrád, György 1933-.....DLB-232; CDWLB-4
Konrad von Würzburg
  circa 1230-1287...................DLB-138
Konstantinov, Aleko 1863-1897........DLB-147
Konwicki, Tadeusz 1926-..............DLB-232
Koontz, Dean 1945-..................DLB-292
Kooser, Ted 1939-...................DLB-105
Kopit, Arthur 1937-....................DLB-7
Kops, Bernard 1926?-..................DLB-13
Korn, Rachel (Rokhl Korn)
  1898-1982........................DLB-333
Kornbluth, C. M. 1923-1958.............DLB-8
Körner, Theodor 1791-1813.............DLB-90
Kornfeld, Paul 1889-1942.............DLB-118
Korolenko, Vladimir Galaktionovich
  1853-1921........................DLB-277
Kosinski, Jerzy 1933-1991.......DLB-2, 299; Y-82
Kosmač, Ciril 1910-1980..............DLB-181
Kosovel, Srečko 1904-1926............DLB-147
Kostrov, Ermil Ivanovich 1755-1796....DLB-150
Kotzebue, August von 1761-1819........DLB-94
Kotzwinkle, William 1938-............DLB-173
Kovačević, Dušan 1948-...............DLB-353
Kovačić, Ante 1854-1889..............DLB-147
Kovalevskaia, Sof'ia Vasil'evna
  1850-1891........................DLB-277
Kovič, Kajetan 1931-.................DLB-181
Kozlov, Ivan Ivanovich 1779-1840.....DLB-205
Kracauer, Siegfried 1889-1966........DLB-296
Kraf, Elaine 1946-.....................Y-81
Kraft, Jens 1720-1765................DLB-354
Krag, Vilhelm 1871-1933..............DLB-354
Kramer, Jane 1938-...................DLB-185
Kramer, Larry 1935-..................DLB-249
Kramer, Mark 1944-...................DLB-185
Kranjčević, Silvije Strahimir 1865-1908...DLB-147
Krasko, Ivan 1876-1958...............DLB-215
Krasna, Norman 1909-1984..............DLB-26
Kraus, Hans Peter 1907-1988..........DLB-187
Kraus, Karl 1874-1936................DLB-118
Krause, Herbert 1905-1976............DLB-256
Krauss, Ruth 1911-1993................DLB-52
Krauth, Nigel 1949-..................DLB-325
Krchovský, J. H. (Jiří Hásek) 1960-...DLB-353
Kreisel, Henry 1922-1991..............DLB-88
Krestovsky V.
  (see Khvoshchinskaia, Nadezhda Dmitrievna)

Krestovsky, Vsevolod Vladimirovich
  1839-1895 . . . . DLB-238
Kreuder, Ernst 1903-1972 . . . . DLB-69
Krėvė-Mickevičius, Vincas 1882-1954 . . . . DLB-220
Kreymborg, Alfred 1883-1966 . . . . DLB-4, 54
Krieger, Murray 1923-2000 . . . . DLB-67
Krim, Seymour 1922-1989 . . . . DLB-16
Kripke, Saul 1940- DLB-279
Kristensen, Tom 1893-1974 . . . . DLB-214
Kristeva, Julia 1941- DLB-242
Kristján Níels Jónsson/Kristjan Niels Julius
  (see Káinn)
Kritzer, Hyman W. 1918-2002 . . . . Y-02
Krivulin, Viktor Borisovich 1944-2001 . . . DLB-285
Krleža, Miroslav
  1893-1981 . . . . DLB-147; CDWLB-4
Krock, Arthur 1886-1974 . . . . DLB-29
Kroetsch, Robert 1927- DLB-53
Kropotkin, Petr Alekseevich 1842-1921 . . . DLB-277
Kross, Jaan 1920-2007 . . . . DLB-232
Kruchenykh, Aleksei Eliseevich
  1886-1968 . . . . DLB-295
Krúdy, Gyula 1878-1933 . . . . DLB-215
Krutch, Joseph Wood
  1893-1970 . . . . DLB-63, 206, 275
Krylov, Ivan Andreevich 1769-1844 . . . . . . DLB-150
Krymov, Iurii Solomonovich
  (Iurii Solomonovich Beklemishev)
  1908-1941 . . . . DLB-272
Kubin, Alfred 1877-1959 . . . . DLB-81
Kubrick, Stanley 1928-1999 . . . . DLB-26
Kudrun circa 1230-1240 . . . . DLB-138
Kuffstein, Hans Ludwig von 1582-1656 . . DLB-164
Kuhlmann, Quirinus 1651-1689 . . . . DLB-168
Kuhn, Thomas S. 1922-1996 . . . . DLB-279
Kuhnau, Johann 1660-1722 . . . . DLB-168
Kukol'nik, Nestor Vasil'evich
  1809-1868 . . . . DLB-205
Kukučín, Martin
  1860-1928 . . . . DLB-215; CDWLB-4
Kulbak, Moyshe 1896-1937 . . . . DLB-333
Kumin, Maxine 1925- DLB-5
Kuncewicz, Maria 1895-1989 . . . . DLB-215
Kundera, Milan 1929- DLB-232; CDWLB-4
Kunene, Mazisi 1930- DLB-117
al-Kuni, Ibrahim 1948- DLB-346
Kunikida Doppo 1869-1908 . . . . DLB-180
Kunitz, Stanley 1905-2006 . . . . DLB-48
Kunjufu, Johari M. (see Amini, Johari M.)
Kunnert, Gunter 1929- DLB-75
Kunze, Reiner 1933- DLB-75
Kuo, Helena 1911-1999 . . . . DLB-312
Kupferberg, Tuli 1923- DLB-16

Kuprin, Aleksandr Ivanovich
  1870-1938 . . . . DLB-295
Kuraev, Mikhail Nikolaevich 1939- DLB-285
Kurahashi Yumiko 1935- DLB-182
Kureishi, Hanif 1954- DLB-194, 245, 352
Kürnberger, Ferdinand 1821-1879 . . . . DLB-129
Kurz, Isolde 1853-1944 . . . . DLB-66
Kusenberg, Kurt 1904-1983 . . . . DLB-69
Kushchevsky, Ivan Afanas'evich
  1847-1876 . . . . DLB-238
Kushner, Tony 1956- DLB-228
Kuttner, Henry 1915-1958 . . . . DLB-8
Kuzmin, Mikhail Alekseevich
  1872-1936 . . . . DLB-295
Kuznetsov, Anatoli 1929-1979 . . . . . . DLB-299, 302
Kvitko, Leib (Leyb Kvitko)
  1890-1952 . . . . DLB-333
Kyd, Thomas 1558-1594 . . . . DLB-62
Kyffin, Maurice circa 1560?-1598 . . . . DLB-136
Kyger, Joanne 1934- DLB-16
Kyne, Peter B. 1880-1957 . . . . DLB-78
Kyōgoku Tamekane 1254-1332 . . . . DLB-203
Kyrklund, Willy 1921- DLB-257

L

L.E.L. (see Landon, Letitia Elizabeth)
Labé, Louise 1520?-1566 . . . . DLB-327
Laberge, Albert 1871-1960 . . . . DLB-68
Laberge, Marie 1950- DLB-60
Labiche, Eugène 1815-1888 . . . . DLB-192
Labrunie, Gerard (see Nerval, Gerard de)
La Bruyère, Jean de 1645-1696 . . . . DLB-268
La Calprenède 1609?-1663 . . . . DLB-268
Lacan, Jacques 1901-1981 . . . . DLB-296
La Capria, Raffaele 1922- DLB-196
La Ceppède, Jean de 1550?-1623 . . . . DLB-327
La Chaussée, Pierre-Claude Nivelle de
  1692-1754 . . . . DLB-313
Laclos, Pierre-Ambroise-François Choderlos de
  1741-1803 . . . . DLB-313
  Dangerous Acquaintances DLB-314
Lacombe, Patrice
  (see Trullier-Lacombe, Joseph Patrice)
Lacretelle, Jacques de 1888-1985 . . . . DLB-65
Lacy, Ed 1911-1968 . . . . DLB-226
Lacy, Sam 1903-2003 . . . . DLB-171
Ladd, Joseph Brown 1764-1786 . . . . DLB-37
La Farge, Oliver 1901-1963 . . . . DLB-9
Lafayette, Marie-Madeleine, comtesse de
  1634-1693 . . . . DLB-268
Laferrière, Dany 1953- DLB-334
Laffan, Mrs. R. S. de Courcy
  (see Adams, Bertha Leith)
Lafferty, R. A. 1914-2002 . . . . DLB-8

La Flesche, Francis 1857-1932 . . . . DLB-175
La Fontaine, Jean de 1621-1695 . . . . DLB-268
Laforet, Carmen 1921-2004 . . . . DLB-322
Laforge, Jules 1860-1887 . . . . DLB-217
Lagerkvist, Pär 1891-1974 . . . . DLB-259, 331
Lagerlöf, Selma 1858-1940 . . . . DLB-259, 331
Lagorio, Gina 1922- DLB-196
La Guma, Alex
  1925-1985 . . . . DLB-117, 225; CDWLB-3
Lahaise, Guillaume (see Delahaye, Guy)
La Harpe, Jean-François de 1739-1803 . . . . DLB-313
Lahiri, Jhumpa 1967- DLB-323
Lahontan, Louis-Armand de Lom d'Arce,
  Baron de 1666-1715? DLB-99
Lai He 1894-1943 . . . . DLB-328
Laing, Kojo 1946- DLB-157
Laird, Carobeth 1895-1983 . . . . Y-82
Laird and Lee DLB-49
Lake, Paul 1951- DLB-282
Lalić, Ivan V. 1931-1996 . . . . DLB-181
Lalić, Mihailo 1914-1992 . . . . DLB-181
Lalonde, Michèle 1937- DLB-60
Lamantia, Philip 1927-2005 . . . . DLB-16
Lamartine, Alphonse de
  1790-1869 . . . . DLB-217
Lamb, Lady Caroline 1785-1828 . . . . DLB-116
Lamb, Charles
  1775-1834 . . . . DLB-93, 107, 163; CDBLB-3
Lamb, Mary 1764-1874 . . . . DLB-163
Lambert, Angela 1940- DLB-271
Lambert, Anne-Thérèse de (Anne-Thérèse de
  Marguenat de Courcelles, marquise de Lambert)
  1647-1733 . . . . DLB-313
Lambert, Betty 1933-1983 . . . . DLB-60
La Mettrie, Julien Offroy de
  1709-1751 . . . . DLB-313
Lamm, Donald
  Goodbye, Gutenberg? A Lecture at
    the New York Public Library,
    18 April 1995 . . . . Y-95
Lamming, George 1927- . . . DLB-125; CDWLB-3
La Mothe Le Vayer, François de
  1588-1672 . . . . DLB-268
L'Amour, Louis 1908-1988 . . . . DLB-206; Y-80
Lampman, Archibald 1861-1899 . . . . DLB-92
Lamson, Wolffe and Company DLB-49
Lancer Books DLB-46
Lanchester, John 1962- DLB-267
Lander, Peter (see Cunningham, Peter)
Landesman, Jay 1919- and
  Landesman, Fran 1927- DLB-16
Landolfi, Tommaso 1908-1979 . . . . DLB-177
Landon, Letitia Elizabeth 1802-1838 . . . . . . DLB-96
Landor, Walter Savage 1775-1864 . . . . DLB-93, 107
Landry, Napoléon-P. 1884-1956 . . . . DLB-92
Landstad, Magnus Brostrup 1802-1880 . . . DLB-354

Landvik, Lorna 1954- DLB-292

Lane, Charles 1800-1870 ...... DLB-1, 223; DS-5

Lane, F. C. 1885-1984 .... DLB-241

Lane, Laurence W. 1890-1967 .... DLB-91

Lane, M. Travis 1934- DLB-60

Lane, Patrick 1939- DLB-53

Lane, Pinkie Gordon 1923- DLB-41

John Lane Company................. DLB-49

Laney, Al 1896-1988................DLB-4, 171

Lang, Andrew 1844-1912...... DLB-98, 141, 184

Langer, Susanne K. 1895-1985 ....DLB-270

Langevin, André 1927- DLB-60

Langford, David 1953- DLB-261

Langgässer, Elisabeth 1899-1950 .... DLB-69

Langhorne, John 1735-1779 .... DLB-109

Langland, William
  circa 1330-circa 1400 .... DLB-146

Langton, Anna 1804-1893 .... DLB-99

Lanham, Edwin 1904-1979.............. DLB-4

Lanier, Sidney 1842-1881 .... DLB-64; DS-13

Lanyer, Aemilia 1569-1645 .... DLB-121

Lao She 1899-1966................... DLB-328

Lapine, James 1949- DLB-341

Lapointe, Gatien 1931-1983 .... DLB-88

Lapointe, Paul-Marie 1929- DLB-88

La Ramée, Pierre de (Petrus Ramus, Peter Ramus)
  1515-1572..................... DLB-327

Larcom, Lucy 1824-1893 .... DLB-221, 243

Lardner, John 1912-1960 ....DLB-171

Lardner, Ring 1885-1933
  ......DLB-11, 25, 86, 171; DS-16; CDALB-4

  Lardner 100: Ring Lardner
    Centennial Symposium Y-85

Lardner, Ring, Jr. 1915-2000........DLB-26, Y-00

Larivey, Pierre de 1541-1619 .... DLB-327

Larkin, Philip 1922-1985 ..... DLB-27; CDBLB-8

  The Philip Larkin Society Y-99

La Roche, Sophie von 1730-1807 .... DLB-94

La Rochefoucauld, François duc de
  1613-1680..................... DLB-268

La Rocque, Gilbert 1943-1984 .... DLB-60

Laroque de Roquebrune, Robert
  (see Roquebrune, Robert de)

Laroui, Abdallah 1933- DLB-346

Larrick, Nancy 1910-2004 .... DLB-61

Lars, Claudia 1899-1974................ DLB-283

Larsen, Nella 1893-1964............... DLB-51

Larsen, Thøger 1875-1928 .... DLB-300

Larson, Clinton F. 1919-1994.......... DLB-256

La Sale, Antoine de
  circa 1386-1460/1467 .... DLB-208

Las Casas, Fray Bartolomé de
  1474-1566..................... DLB-318

Lasch, Christopher 1932-1994 .... DLB-246

Lasdun, James 1958- DLB-319

Lasker-Schüler, Else 1869-1945 ..... DLB-66, 124

Lasnier, Rina 1915-1997 .... DLB-88

Lassalle, Ferdinand 1825-1864 .... DLB-129

Last Orders, 1996 Booker Prize winner,
  Graham Swift................... DLB-326

La Taille, Jean de 1534?-1611?......... DLB-327

Lat, U 1866-1921 .... DLB-348

Late-Medieval Castilian Theater DLB-286

Latham, Robert 1912-1995............ DLB-201

Lathan, Emma (Mary Jane Latsis [1927-1997] and
  Martha Henissart [1929-   ]) DLB-306

Lathrop, Dorothy P. 1891-1980 .... DLB-22

Lathrop, George Parsons 1851-1898 ..... DLB-71

Lathrop, John, Jr. 1772-1820........... DLB-37

Latimer, Hugh 1492?-1555............ DLB-136

Latimore, Jewel Christine McLawler
  (see Amini, Johari M.)

Latin Histories and Chronicles of
  Medieval Spain.................. DLB-337

Latin Literature, The Uniqueness of DLB-211

La Tour du Pin, Patrice de 1911-1975.... DLB-258

Latymer, William 1498-1583 .... DLB-132

Laube, Heinrich 1806-1884 .... DLB-133

Laud, William 1573-1645 .... DLB-213

Laughlin, James 1914-1997......DLB-48; Y-96, 97

  A Tribute [to Henry Miller] Y-80

  Tribute to Albert Erskine............. Y-93

  Tribute to Kenneth Rexroth........... Y-82

  Tribute to Malcolm Cowley............ Y-89

Laumer, Keith 1925-1993 .... DLB-8

Lauremberg, Johann 1590-1658........ DLB-164

Laurence, Margaret 1926-1987.......... DLB-53

Laurentius von Schnüffis 1633-1702..... DLB-168

Laurents, Arthur 1917- DLB-26, 341

Laurie, Annie (see Black, Winifred)

Laut, Agnes Christiana 1871-1936 ...... DLB-92

Lauterbach, Ann 1942- DLB-193

Lautréamont, Isidore Lucien Ducasse,
  Comte de 1846-1870 .... DLB-217

Lavater, Johann Kaspar 1741-1801 ...... DLB-97

Lavin, Mary 1912-1996 .... DLB-15, 319

Law, John (see Harkness, Margaret)

Lawes, Henry 1596-1662 .... DLB-126

Lawler, Ray 1922- DLB-289

Lawless, Anthony (see MacDonald, Philip)

Lawless, Emily (The Hon. Emily Lawless)
  1845-1913 .... DLB-240

Lawless, Gary 1951- DLB-342

Lawrence, D. H. 1885-1930
  ..... DLB-10, 19, 36, 98, 162, 195; CDBLB-6

The D. H. Lawrence Society of
  North America Y-00

Lawrence, David 1888-1973............ DLB-29

Lawrence, Jerome 1915-2004 .... DLB-228

Lawrence, Seymour 1926-1994 .... Y-94

  Tribute to Richard Yates Y-92

Lawrence, T. E. 1888-1935............. DLB-195

  The T. E. Lawrence Society............ Y-98

Lawson, George 1598-1678 .... DLB-213

Lawson, Henry 1867-1922 .... DLB-230

Lawson, John ?-1711................. DLB-24

Lawson, John Howard 1894-1977 ...... DLB-228

Lawson, Louisa Albury 1848-1920....... DLB-230

Lawson, Robert 1892-1957............. DLB-22

Lawson, Victor F. 1850-1925 .... DLB-25

Layard, Austen Henry 1817-1894....... DLB-166

Layton, Irving 1912-2006 .... DLB-88

LaZamon fl. circa 1200............... DLB-146

Lazarević, Laza K. 1851-1890..........DLB-147

Lazarus, George 1904-1997 .... DLB-201

Lazhechnikov, Ivan Ivanovich
  1792-1869..................... DLB-198

Lazić, Radmila 1949- DLB-353

Le Minh Khue 1949- DLB-348

Lea, Henry Charles 1825-1909 .... DLB-47

Lea, Sydney 1942- DLB-120, 282

Lea, Tom 1907-2001 .... DLB-6

Leacock, John 1729-1802 .... DLB-31

Leacock, Stephen 1869-1944 .... DLB-92

Lead, Jane Ward 1623-1704 .... DLB-131

Leadenhall Press.................... DLB-106

"The Greatness of Southern Literature":
  League of the South Institute for the
  Study of Southern Culture and History
  .... Y-02

Leakey, Caroline Woolmer 1827-1881 .... DLB-230

Leapor, Mary 1722-1746............. DLB-109

Lear, Edward 1812-1888 ....DLB-32, 163, 166

Leary, Timothy 1920-1996 .... DLB-16

W. A. Leary and Company DLB-49

Léautaud, Paul 1872-1956 .... DLB-65

Leavis, F. R. 1895-1978................ DLB-242

Leavitt, David 1961- DLB-130, 350

Leavitt and Allen DLB-49

Le Blond, Mrs. Aubrey 1861-1934.......DLB-174

le Carré, John (David John Moore Cornwell)
  1931- DLB-87; CDBLB-8

  Tribute to Graham Greene............ Y-91

  Tribute to George Greenfield.......... Y-00

Lécavelé, Roland (see Dorgeles, Roland)

Lechlitner, Ruth 1901-1989 .... DLB-48

Leclerc, Félix 1914-1988.............. DLB-60

Le Clézio, J. M. G. 1940- DLB-83

Leder, Rudolf (see Hermlin, Stephan)

Lederer, Charles 1910-1976 . . . . DLB-26

Ledwidge, Francis 1887-1917 . . . . DLB-20

Lee, Chang-rae 1965- DLB-312

Lee, Cherylene 1953- DLB-312

Lee, Dennis 1939- DLB-53

Lee, Don L. (see Madhubuti, Haki R.)

Lee, George W. 1894-1976 . . . . DLB-51

Lee, Gus 1946- DLB-312

Lee, Harper 1926- DLB-6; CDALB-1

Lee, Harriet 1757-1851 and
    Lee, Sophia 1750-1824 . . . . DLB-39

Lee, Laurie 1914-1997 . . . . DLB-27

Lee, Leslie 1935- DLB-266

Lee, Li-Young 1957- DLB-165, 312

Lee, Manfred B. 1905-1971 . . . . DLB-137

Lee, Nathaniel circa 1645-1692 . . . . DLB-80

Lee, Robert E. 1918-1994 . . . . DLB-228

Lee, Sir Sidney 1859-1926 . . . . DLB-149, 184

    "Principles of Biography," in
    Elizabethan and Other Essays DLB-149

Lee, Tanith 1947- DLB-261

Lee, Vernon
    1856-1935 . . . . DLB-57, 153, 156, 174, 178

Lee and Shepard DLB-49

Le Fanu, Joseph Sheridan
    1814-1873 . . . . DLB-21, 70, 159, 178

Lefèvre d'Etaples, Jacques
    1460?-1536 . . . . DLB-327

Leffland, Ella 1931- Y-84

le Fort, Gertrud von 1876-1971 . . . . DLB-66

Le Gallienne, Richard 1866-1947 . . . . DLB-4

Legaré, Hugh Swinton
    1797-1843 . . . . DLB-3, 59, 73, 248

Legaré, James Mathewes 1823-1859 . . . . DLB-3, 248

Léger, Antoine-J. 1880-1950 . . . . DLB-88

Leggett, William 1801-1839 . . . . DLB-250

Le Guin, Ursula K.
    1929- DLB-8, 52, 256, 275; CDALB-6

Lehman, Ernest 1915-2005 . . . . DLB-44

Lehmann, John 1907-1989 . . . . DLB-27, 100

John Lehmann Limited DLB-112

Lehmann, Rosamond 1901-1990 . . . . DLB-15

Lehmann, Wilhelm 1882-1968 . . . . DLB-56

Leiber, Fritz 1910-1992 . . . . DLB-8

Leibniz, Gottfried Wilhelm 1646-1716 . . . . DLB-168

Leicester University Press DLB-112

Leigh, Carolyn 1926-1983 . . . . DLB-265

Leigh, W. R. 1866-1955 . . . . DLB-188

Leinster, Murray 1896-1975 . . . . DLB-8

Leiser, Bill 1898-1965 . . . . DLB-241

Leisewitz, Johann Anton 1752-1806 . . . . DLB-94

Leitch, Maurice 1933- DLB-14

Leithauser, Brad 1943- DLB-120, 282

Leivick, H[alper] (H. Leyvik)
    1888-1962 . . . . DLB-333

Leland, Charles G. 1824-1903 . . . . DLB-11

Leland, John 1503?-1552 . . . . DLB-136

Leland, Thomas 1722-1785 . . . . DLB-336

Lemaire de Belges, Jean 1473-? DLB-327

Lemay, Pamphile 1837-1918 . . . . DLB-99

Lemelin, Roger 1919-1992 . . . . DLB-88

Lemercier, Louis-Jean-Népomucène
    1771-1840 . . . . DLB-192

Le Moine, James MacPherson 1825-1912 . . DLB-99

Lemon, Mark 1809-1870 . . . . DLB-163

Le Moyne, Jean 1913-1996 . . . . DLB-88

Lemperly, Paul 1858-1939 . . . . DLB-187

Leñero, Vicente 1933- DLB-305

L'Engle, Madeleine 1918-2007 . . . . DLB-52

Lennart, Isobel 1915-1971 . . . . DLB-44

Lennox, Charlotte 1729 or 1730-1804 . . . . . DLB-39

Lenox, James 1800-1880 . . . . DLB-140

Lenski, Lois 1893-1974 . . . . DLB-22

Lentricchia, Frank 1940- DLB-246

Lenz, Hermann 1913-1998 . . . . DLB-69

Lenz, J. M. R. 1751-1792 . . . . DLB-94

Lenz, Siegfried 1926- DLB-75

León, Fray Luis de 1527-1591 . . . . DLB-318

Leon, Henry Cecil (see Cecil, Henry)

Leonard, Elmore 1925- DLB-173, 226

Leonard, Hugh 1926- DLB-13

Leonard, William Ellery 1876-1944 . . . . DLB-54

Leong, Russell C. 1950- DLB-312

Leonov, Leonid Maksimovich
    1899-1994 . . . . DLB-272

Leonowens, Anna 1834-1914 . . . . DLB-99, 166

Leont'ev, Konstantin Nikolaevich
    1831-1891 . . . . DLB-277

Leopold, Aldo 1887-1948 . . . . DLB-275

LePan, Douglas 1914-1998 . . . . DLB-88

Lepik, Kalju 1920-1999 . . . . DLB-232

Leprohon, Rosanna Eleanor 1829-1879 . . . . DLB-99

Le Queux, William 1864-1927 . . . . DLB-70

Lermontov, Mikhail Iur'evich
    1814-1841 . . . . DLB-205

Lerner, Alan Jay 1918-1986 . . . . DLB-265

Lerner, Max 1902-1992 . . . . DLB-29

Lernet-Holenia, Alexander 1897-1976 . . . . . DLB-85

Le Rossignol, James 1866-1969 . . . . DLB-92

Lesage, Alain-René 1668-1747 . . . . DLB-313

Lescarbot, Marc circa 1570-1642 . . . . DLB-99

LeSeur, William Dawson 1840-1917 . . . . . . DLB-92

LeSieg, Theo. (see Geisel, Theodor Seuss)

Leskov, Nikolai Semenovich
    1831-1895 . . . . DLB-238

Leslie, Doris before 1902-1982 . . . . DLB-191

Leslie, Eliza 1787-1858 . . . . DLB-202

Leslie, Frank (Henry Carter)
    1821-1880 . . . . DLB-43, 79

Frank Leslie [publishing house] DLB-49

Leśmian, Bolesław 1878-1937 . . . . DLB-215

Lesperance, John 1835?-1891 . . . . DLB-99

Lespinasse, Julie de 1732-1776 . . . . DLB-313

Lessing, Bruno 1870-1940 . . . . DLB-28

Lessing, Doris
    1919- DLB-15, 139; Y-85; CDBLB-8

Lessing, Gotthold Ephraim
    1729-1781 . . . . DLB-97; CDWLB-2

    The Lessing Society Y-00

L'Estoile, Pierre de 1546-1611 . . . . DLB-327

Le Sueur, Meridel 1900-1996 . . . . DLB-303

Lettau, Reinhard 1929-1996 . . . . DLB-75

Letters from a Peruvian Woman, Françoise d'Issembourg
    de Graffigny DLB-314

The Hemingway Letters Project Finds
    an Editor Y-02

Lever, Charles 1806-1872 . . . . DLB-21

Lever, Ralph ca. 1527-1585 . . . . DLB-236

Leverson, Ada 1862-1933 . . . . DLB-153

Levertov, Denise
    1923-1997 . . . . DLB-5, 165, 342; CDALB-7

Levi, Peter 1931-2000 . . . . DLB-40

Levi, Primo 1919-1987 . . . . DLB-177, 299

Levien, Sonya 1888-1960 . . . . DLB-44

Levin, Meyer 1905-1981 . . . . DLB-9, 28; Y-81

Levin, Phillis 1954- DLB-282

Lévinas, Emmanuel 1906-1995 . . . . DLB-296

Levine, Norman 1923- DLB-88

Levine, Philip 1928- DLB-5

Levis, Larry 1946- DLB-120

Lévi-Strauss, Claude 1908- DLB-242

Levitov, Aleksandr Ivanovich
    1835?-1877 . . . . DLB-277

Levy, Andrea 1956- DLB-347

Levy, Amy 1861-1889 . . . . DLB-156, 240

Levy, Benn Wolfe 1900-1973 . . . . DLB-13; Y-81

Levy, Deborah 1959- DLB-310

Lewald, Fanny 1811-1889 . . . . DLB-129

Lewes, George Henry 1817-1878 . . . . . DLB-55, 144

    "Criticism in Relation to Novels"
    (1863) DLB-21

    The Principles of Success in Literature
    (1865) [excerpt] DLB-57

Lewis, Agnes Smith 1843-1926 . . . . DLB-174

Lewis, Alfred H. 1857-1914 . . . . DLB-25, 186

Lewis, Alun 1915-1944 . . . . DLB-20, 162

Lewis, C. Day (see Day Lewis, C.)

Lewis, C. I. 1883-1964 ....DLB-270

Lewis, C. S. 1898-1963
..........DLB-15, 100, 160, 255; CDBLB-7

    The New York C. S. Lewis Society Y-99

Lewis, Charles B. 1842-1924 ....DLB-11

Lewis, David 1941-2001................DLB-279

Lewis, Henry Clay 1825-1850 ....DLB-3, 248

Lewis, Janet 1899-1999..................Y-87

    Tribute to Katherine Anne Porter Y-80

Lewis, Matthew Gregory
1775-1818................DLB-39, 158, 178

Lewis, Meriwether 1774-1809......DLB-183, 186

Lewis, Norman 1908-2003............DLB-204

Lewis, R. W. B. 1917-2002............DLB-111

Lewis, Richard circa 1700-1734.........DLB-24

Lewis, Saunders 1893-1985 ....DLB-310

Lewis, Sinclair 1885-1951
..........DLB-9, 102, 331; DS-1; CDALB-4

    Sinclair Lewis Centennial Conference Y-85

    The Sinclair Lewis Society.............Y-99

Lewis, Wilmarth Sheldon 1895-1979 ....DLB-140

Lewis, Wyndham 1882-1957 ....DLB-15

Time and Western Man
[excerpt] (1927) DLB-36

Lewisohn, Ludwig 1882-1955 ..DLB-4, 9, 28, 102

Leyendecker, J. C. 1874-1951 ....DLB-188

Leyner, Mark 1956- DLB-292

Lezama Lima, José 1910-1976......DLB-113, 283

Lézardière, Marie-Charlotte-Pauline Robert de
1754-1835.....................DLB-313

L'Heureux, John 1934- DLB-244

Libbey, Laura Jean 1862-1924 ....DLB-221

Libedinsky, Iurii Nikolaevich
1898-1959 ....DLB-272

The Liberator........................DLB-303

Library History Group..................Y-01

E-Books' Second Act in Libraries Y-02

The Library of America DLB-46

The Library of America: An Assessment
After Two Decades..................Y-02

Libro de Alexandre
(early thirteenth century) DLB-337

Libro de Apolonio (late thirteenth century)..DLB-337

Libro del Caballero Zifar
(circa 1300-1325) DLB-337

Libro de miserio d'omne (circa 1300-1340)...DLB-337

Licensing Act of 1737 ....DLB-84

Leonard Lichfield I [publishing house]....DLB-170

Lichtenberg, Georg Christoph
1742-1799.....................DLB-94

The Liddle Collection..................Y-97

Lidman, Sara 1923-2004................DLB-257

Lie, Jonas 1833-1908 ....DLB-354

Lieb, Fred 1888-1980 ....DLB-171

Liebling, A. J. 1904-1963 ....DLB-4, 171

Lieutenant Murray (see Ballou, Maturin Murray)

Life and Times of Michael K, 1983 Booker Prize winner,
J. M. Coetzee DLB-326

Life of Pi, 2002 Booker Prize winner,
Yann Martel DLB-326

Lighthall, William Douw 1857-1954......DLB-92

Lihn, Enrique 1929-1988 ....DLB-283

Lilar, Françoise (see Mallet-Joris, Françoise)

Lili'uokalani, Queen 1838-1917 ....DLB-221

Lillo, George 1691-1739 ....DLB-84

Lilly, J. K., Jr. 1893-1966...............DLB-140

Lilly, Wait and Company DLB-49

Lily, William circa 1468-1522..........DLB-132

Lim, Catherine 1942- DLB-348

Lim, Shirley Geok-lin 1944- DLB-312, 348

Lim, Suchen Christine 1948- DLB-348

Lima, Jorge de 1893-1953..............DLB-307

Lima Barreto, Afonso Henriques de
1881-1922 ....DLB-307

Limited Editions Club DLB-46

Limón, Graciela 1938- DLB-209

Limonov, Eduard 1943- DLB-317

Lincoln and Edmands..................DLB-49

Lind, Jakov 1927-2007 ....DLB-299

Linda Vilhjálmsdóttir 1958- DLB-293

Linden, Colin (see Brahms, Caryl)

Lindesay, Ethel Forence
(see Richardson, Henry Handel)

Lindgren, Astrid 1907-2002 ....DLB-257

Lindgren, Torgny 1938- DLB-257

Lindsay, Alexander William, Twenty-fifth
Earl of Crawford 1812-1880 ....DLB-184

Lindsay, Sir David circa 1485-1555 .....DLB-132

Lindsay, David 1878-1945 ....DLB-255

Lindsay, Jack 1900-1990.................Y-84

Lindsay, Lady (Caroline Blanche
Elizabeth Fitzroy Lindsay)
1844-1912 ....DLB-199

Lindsay, Norman 1879-1969..........DLB-260

Lindsay, Vachel
1879-1931.............DLB-54; CDALB-3

The Line of Beauty, 2004 Booker Prize winner,
Alan Hollinghurst DLB-326

Linebarger, Paul Myron Anthony
(see Smith, Cordwainer)

Ling Shuhua 1900-1990 ....DLB-328

Link, Arthur S. 1920-1998 ....DLB-17

Linn, Ed 1922-2000 ....DLB-241

Linn, John Blair 1777-1804 ....DLB-37

Lins, Osman 1924-1978 ....DLB-145, 307

Linton, Eliza Lynn 1822-1898 ....DLB-18

Linton, William James 1812-1897........DLB-32

Barnaby Bernard Lintot
[publishing house] DLB-170

Lion Books........................DLB-46

Lionni, Leo 1910-1999 ....DLB-61

Lippard, George 1822-1854 ....DLB-202

Lippincott, Sara Jane Clarke
1823-1904 ....DLB-43

J. B. Lippincott Company...............DLB-49

Lippmann, Walter 1889-1974 ....DLB-29

Lipska, Ewa 1945- DLB-353

Lipton, Lawrence 1898-1975 ....DLB-16

Lisboa, Irene 1892-1958...............DLB-287

Liscow, Christian Ludwig
1701-1760 ....DLB-97

Lish, Gordon 1934- DLB-130

    Tribute to Donald Barthelme...........Y-89

    Tribute to James Dickey...............Y-97

Lisle, Charles-Marie-René Leconte de
1818-1894 ....DLB-217

Lispector, Clarice
1925?-1977........DLB-113, 307; CDWLB-3

LitCheck Website Y-01

Literary Awards and Honors Y-81–02

    Booker Prize..................Y-86, 96–98

    The Drue Heinz Literature Prize Y-82

    The Elmer Holmes Bobst Awards
in Arts and Letters................Y-87

    The Griffin Poetry Prize................Y-00

    Literary Prizes [British] DLB-15, 207

    National Book Critics Circle
Awards Y-00–01

    The National Jewish
Book Awards....................Y-85

    Nobel Prize Y-80–02

    Winning an Edgar Y-98

The Literary Chronicle and Weekly Review
1819-1828 ....DLB-110

Literary Periodicals:

    Callaloo Y-87

    Expatriates in Paris DS-15

    New Literary Periodicals:
A Report for 1987.................Y-87

    A Report for 1988 ....Y-88

    A Report for 1989 ....Y-89

    A Report for 1990 ....Y-90

    A Report for 1991 ....Y-91

    A Report for 1992 ....Y-92

    A Report for 1993 ....Y-93

    Literary Research Archives
The Anthony Burgess Archive at
the Harry Ransom Humanities
Research Center Y-98

    Archives of Charles Scribner's Sons.....DS-17

    Berg Collection of English and
American Literature of the
New York Public Library..........Y-83

    The Bobbs-Merrill Archive at the
Lilly Library, Indiana University.....Y-90

    Die Fürstliche Bibliothek Corvey........Y-96

Guide to the Archives of Publishers,
  Journals, and Literary Agents in
  North American Libraries............Y-93

The Henry E. Huntington Library.......Y-92

The Humanities Research Center,
  University of Texas................Y-82

The John Carter Brown Library........Y-85

Kent State Special Collections........Y-86

The Lilly Library....................Y-84

The Modern Literary Manuscripts
  Collection in the Special
  Collections of the Washington
  University Libraries..............Y-87

A Publisher's Archives: G. P. Putnam.....Y-92

Special Collections at Boston
  University........................Y-99

The University of Virginia Libraries......Y-91

The William Charvat American Fiction
  Collection at the Ohio State
  University Libraries..............Y-92

Literary Societies....................Y-98–02

  The Margery Allingham Society........Y-98

  The American Studies Association
    of Norway........................Y-00

  The Arnold Bennett Society..........Y-98

  The Association for the Study of
    Literature and Environment
    (ASLE)..........................Y-99

  Belgian Luxembourg American Studies
    Association.....................Y-01

  The E. F. Benson Society............Y-98

  The Elizabeth Bishop Society.........Y-01

  The [Edgar Rice] Burroughs
    Bibliophiles....................Y-98

  The Byron Society of America........Y-00

  The Lewis Carroll Society
    of North America.................Y-00

  The Willa Cather Pioneer Memorial
    and Education Foundation..........Y-00

  New Chaucer Society.................Y-00

  The Wilkie Collins Society..........Y-98

  The James Fenimore Cooper Society.....Y-01

  The Stephen Crane Society..........Y-98, 01

  The E. E. Cummings Society..........Y-01

  The James Dickey Society............Y-99

  John Dos Passos Newsletter..........Y-00

  The Priory Scholars [Sir Arthur Conan
    Doyle] of New York...............Y-99

  The International Theodore Dreiser
    Society.........................Y-01

  The Friends of the Dymock Poets......Y-00

  The George Eliot Fellowship.........Y-99

  The T. S. Eliot Society: Celebration and
    Scholarship, 1980-1999...........Y-99

  The Ralph Waldo Emerson Society......Y-99

  The William Faulkner Society........Y-99

  The C. S. Forester Society..........Y-00

  The Hamlin Garland Society..........Y-01

  The [Elizabeth] Gaskell Society......Y-98

  The Charlotte Perkins Gilman Society....Y-99

  The Ellen Glasgow Society...........Y-01

  Zane Grey's West Society............Y-00

  The Ivor Gurney Society.............Y-98

  The Joel Chandler Harris Association....Y-99

  The Nathaniel Hawthorne Society......Y-00

  The [George Alfred] Henty Society....Y-98

  George Moses Horton Society.........Y-99

  The William Dean Howells Society.....Y-01

  WW2 HMSO Paperbacks Society........Y-98

  American Humor Studies Association....Y-99

  International Society for Humor Studies....Y-99

  The W. W. Jacobs Appreciation Society...Y-98

  The Richard Jefferies Society.......Y-98

  The Jerome K. Jerome Society........Y-98

  The D. H. Lawrence Society of
    North America....................Y-00

  The T. E. Lawrence Society..........Y-98

  The [Gotthold] Lessing Society......Y-00

  The New York C. S. Lewis Society.....Y-99

  The Sinclair Lewis Society..........Y-99

  The Jack London Research Center.....Y-00

  The Jack London Society.............Y-99

  The Cormac McCarthy Society........Y-99

  The Melville Society................Y-01

  The Arthur Miller Society...........Y-01

  The Milton Society of America.......Y-00

  International Marianne Moore Society....Y-98

  International Nabokov Society.......Y-99

  The Vladimir Nabokov Society........Y-01

  The Flannery O'Connor Society.......Y-99

  The Wilfred Owen Association........Y-98

  Penguin Collectors' Society.........Y-98

  The [E. A.] Poe Studies Association....Y-99

  The Katherine Anne Porter Society....Y-01

  The Beatrix Potter Society..........Y-98

  The Ezra Pound Society..............Y-01

  The Powys Society...................Y-98

  Proust Society of America...........Y-00

  The Dorothy L. Sayers Society........Y-98

  The Bernard Shaw Society............Y-99

  The Society for the Study of
    Southern Literature..............Y-00

  The Wallace Stevens Society.........Y-99

  The Harriet Beecher Stowe Center.....Y-00

  The R. S. Surtees Society...........Y-98

  The Thoreau Society.................Y-99

  The Tilling [E. F. Benson] Society....Y-98

  The Trollope Societies..............Y-00

  H. G. Wells Society.................Y-98

  The Western Literature Association...Y-99

  The William Carlos Williams Society...Y-99

  The Henry Williamson Society........Y-98

  The [Nero] Wolfe Pack...............Y-99

  The Thomas Wolfe Society............Y-99

  Worldwide Wodehouse Societies.......Y-98

  The W. B. Yeats Society of N.Y.......Y-99

  The Charlotte M. Yonge Fellowship....Y-98

Literary Theory
  The Year in Literary Theory........Y-92–Y-93

Literature at Nurse, or Circulating Morals (1885),
  by George Moore...................DLB-18

Litt, Toby 1968-....................DLB-267, 319

Littell, Eliakim 1797-1870............DLB-79

Littell, Robert S. 1831-1896..........DLB-79

Little, Brown and Company............DLB-49

Little Magazines and Newspapers.......DS-15

  Selected English-Language Little
    Magazines and Newspapers
    [France, 1920-1939].............DLB-4

The Little Magazines of the
  New Formalism....................DLB-282

The Little Review 1914-1929.........DS-15

Littlewood, Joan 1914-2002...........DLB-13

Liu, Aimee E. 1953-..................DLB-312

Liu E 1857-1909......................DLB-328

Lively, Penelope 1933-...DLB-14, 161, 207, 326

Liverpool University Press...........DLB-112

The Lives of the Poets (1753).......DLB-142

Livesay, Dorothy 1909-1996...........DLB-68

Livesay, Florence Randal 1874-1953....DLB-92

Livings, Henry 1929-1998.............DLB-13

Livingston, Anne Home 1763-1841...DLB-37, 200

Livingston, Jay 1915-2001............DLB-265

Livingston, Myra Cohn 1926-1996......DLB-61

Livingston, William 1723-1790........DLB-31

Livingstone, David 1813-1873.........DLB-166

Livingstone, Douglas 1932-1996.......DLB-225

Livshits, Benedikt Konstantinovich
  1886-1938 or 1939................DLB-295

Livy 59 B.C.-A.D. 17.........DLB-211; CDWLB-1

Liyong, Taban lo (see Taban lo Liyong)

Lizárraga, Sylvia S. 1925-...........DLB-82

Llamazares, Julio 1955-..............DLB-322

Lleshanaku, Luljeta 1968-............DLB-353

Llewellyn, Kate 1936-................DLB-325

Llewellyn, Richard 1906-1983.........DLB-15

Lloréns Torres, Luis 1876-1944.......DLB-290

Edward Lloyd [publishing house]......DLB-106

Llull, Ramon (1232?-1316?)...........DLB-337

Lobato, José Bento Monteiro
  1882-1948........................DLB-307

Lobel, Arnold 1933-..................DLB-61

Lochhead, Liz 1947-..................DLB-310

Lochridge, Betsy Hopkins (see Fancher, Betsy)

Locke, Alain 1886-1954...............DLB-51

Locke, David Ross 1833-1888........DLB-11, 23

Locke, John 1632-1704....DLB-31, 101, 213, 252

Locke, Richard Adams 1800-1871.......DLB-43

Locker-Lampson, Frederick
1821-1895 . . . . DLB-35, 184

Lockhart, John Gibson
1794-1854 . . . . DLB-110, 116 144

Locklin, Gerald 1941- DLB-335

Lockridge, Francis 1896-1963 . . . . DLB-306

Lockridge, Richard 1898-1982 . . . . DLB-306

Lockridge, Ross, Jr. 1914-1948 . . . . . DLB-143; Y-80

Locrine and Selimus DLB-62

Lodge, David 1935- DLB-14, 194

Lodge, George Cabot 1873-1909 . . . . DLB-54

Lodge, Henry Cabot 1850-1924 . . . . DLB-47

Lodge, Thomas 1558-1625 . . . . DLB-172

  Defence of Poetry (1579) [excerpt] DLB-172

Loeb, Harold 1891-1974 . . . . DLB-4; DS-15

Loeb, William 1905-1981 . . . . DLB-127

Loesser, Frank 1910-1969 . . . . DLB-265

Lofting, Hugh 1886-1947 . . . . DLB-160

Logan, Deborah Norris 1761-1839 . . . . DLB-200

Logan, James 1674-1751 . . . . DLB-24, 140

Logan, John 1923-1987 . . . . DLB-5

Logan, Martha Daniell 1704?-1779 . . . . . . DLB-200

Logan, William 1950- DLB-120

Logau, Friedrich von 1605-1655 . . . . DLB-164

Logue, Christopher 1926- DLB-27

Lohenstein, Daniel Casper von
1635-1683 . . . . DLB-168

Lohrey, Amanda 1947- DLB-325

Lo-Johansson, Ivar 1901-1990 . . . . DLB-259

Lokert, George (or Lockhart)
circa 1485-1547 . . . . DLB-281

Lomonosov, Mikhail Vasil'evich
1711-1765 . . . . DLB-150

London, Jack
1876-1916 . . . . . DLB-8, 12, 78, 212; CDALB-3

  The Jack London Research Center Y-00

  The Jack London Society Y-99

The London Magazine 1820-1829 . . . . DLB-110

Long, David 1948- DLB-244

Long, H., and Brother DLB-49

Long, Haniel 1888-1956 . . . . DLB-45

Long, Ray 1878-1935 . . . . DLB-137

Longfellow, Henry Wadsworth
1807-1882 . . . . DLB-1, 59, 235; CDALB-2

Longfellow, Samuel 1819-1892 . . . . DLB-1

Longford, Elizabeth 1906-2002 . . . . DLB-155

  Tribute to Alfred A. Knopf Y-84

Longinus circa first century DLB-176

Longley, Michael 1939- DLB-40

T. Longman [publishing house] DLB-154

Longmans, Green and Company DLB-49

Longmore, George 1793?-1867 . . . . DLB-99

Longstreet, Augustus Baldwin
1790-1870 . . . . DLB-3, 11, 74, 248

D. Longworth [publishing house] . . . . DLB 49

Lønn, Øystein 1936- DLB-297

Lonsdale, Frederick 1881-1954 . . . . DLB-10

Loos, Anita 1893-1981 . . . . . DLB-11, 26, 228; Y-81

Lopate, Phillip 1943- Y-80

Lope de Rueda 1510?-1565? DLB-318

Lopes, Fernão 1380/1390?-1460? DLB-287

Lopez, Barry 1945- DLB-256, 275, 335

López, Diana (see Isabella, Ríos)

López, Josefina 1969- DLB-209

López de Ayala, Pero (1332-1407) DLB-337

López de Córdoba, Leonor (1362 or
1363-1412?/1430? DLB-337

López de Mendoza, Íñigo
(see Santillana, Marqués de)

López Velarde, Ramón 1888-1921 . . . . . . DLB-290

Loranger, Jean-Aubert 1896-1942 . . . . DLB-92

Lorca, Federico García 1898-1936 . . . . . . DLB-108

Lord, John Keast 1818-1872 . . . . DLB-99

Lorde, Audre 1934-1992 . . . . DLB-41

Lorimer, George Horace 1867-1937 . . . . . . DLB-91

A. K. Loring [publishing house] DLB-49

Loring and Mussey DLB-46

Lorris, Guillaume de (see *Roman de la Rose*)

Lossing, Benson J. 1813-1891 . . . . DLB-30

Lothar, Ernst 1890-1974 . . . . DLB-81

D. Lothrop and Company DLB-49

Lothrop, Harriet M. 1844-1924 . . . . DLB-42

Loti, Pierre 1850-1923 . . . . DLB-123

Lotichius Secundus, Petrus 1528-1560 . . . . DLB-179

Lott, Emmeline fl. nineteenth century . . . DLB-166

Louisiana State University Press Y-97

Lounsbury, Thomas R. 1838-1915 . . . . DLB-71

Louÿs, Pierre 1870-1925 . . . . DLB-123

Løveid, Cecile 1951- DLB-297

Lovejoy, Arthur O. 1873-1962 . . . . DLB-270

Lovelace, Earl 1935- DLB-125; CDWLB-3

Lovelace, Richard 1618-1657 . . . . DLB-131

John W. Lovell Company DLB-49

Lovell, Coryell and Company DLB-49

Lover, Samuel 1797-1868 . . . . DLB-159, 190

Lovesey, Peter 1936- DLB-87

  Tribute to Georges Simenon Y-89

Lovinescu, Eugen
1881-1943 . . . . DLB-220; CDWLB-4

Lovingood, Sut
(see Harris, George Washington)

Low, Samuel 1765-? DLB-37

Lowell, Amy 1874-1925 . . . . DLB-54, 140

Lowell, James Russell 1819-1891
. . . . DLB-1, 11, 64, 79, 189, 235; CDALB-2

Lowell, Robert
1917-1977 . . . . DLB-5, 169; CDALB-7

Lowenfels, Walter 1897-1976 . . . . DLB-4

Lowndes, Marie Belloc 1868-1947 . . . . DLB-70

Lowndes, William Thomas
1798-1843 . . . . DLB-184

Humphrey Lownes [publishing house] DLB-170

Lowry, Lois 1937- DLB-52

Lowry, Malcolm 1909-1957 . . . DLB-15; CDBLB-7

Lowry, Robert 1919-1994 . . . . DLB-335

Lowther, Pat 1935-1975 . . . . DLB-53

Loy, Mina 1882-1966 . . . . DLB-4, 54

Loynaz, Dulce María 1902-1997 . . . . DLB-283

Lozeau, Albert 1878-1924 . . . . DLB-92

Lu Ling 1923-1994 . . . . DLB-328

Lu Xun 1881-1936 . . . . DLB-328

Lu Yin 1898?-1934 . . . . DLB-328

Lubbock, Percy 1879-1965 . . . . DLB-149

Lubis, Mochtar 1922-2004 . . . . DLB-348

Lubrano, Giacomo
1619-1692 or 1693 . . . . DLB-339

Lucan A.D. 39-A.D. 65 . . . . DLB-211

Lucas, E. V. 1868-1938 . . . . DLB-98, 149, 153

Fielding Lucas Jr. [publishing house] DLB-49

Luce, Clare Booth 1903-1987 . . . . DLB-228

Luce, Henry R. 1898-1967 . . . . DLB-91

John W. Luce and Company DLB-46

Lucena, Juan de ca. 1430-1501 . . . . DLB-286

Lucian circa 120-180 . . . . DLB-176

Lucie-Smith, Edward 1933- DLB-40

Lucilius circa 180 B.C.-102/101 B.C. DLB-211

Lucini, Gian Pietro 1867-1914 . . . . DLB-114

Luco Cruchaga, Germán 1894-1936 . . . . . DLB-305

Lucretius circa 94 B.C.-circa 49 B.C.
. . . . DLB-211; CDWLB-1

Luder, Peter circa 1415-1472 . . . . DLB-179

Ludlam, Charles 1943-1987 . . . . DLB-266

Ludlum, Robert 1927-2001 . . . . Y-82

Ludus de Antichristo circa 1160 . . . . DLB-148

Ludvigson, Susan 1942- DLB-120

Ludwig, Jack 1922- DLB-60

Ludwig, Otto 1813-1865 . . . . DLB-129

Ludwigslied 881 or 882 . . . . DLB-148

Luera, Yolanda 1953- DLB-122

Luft, Lya 1938- DLB-145

Lugansky, Kazak Vladimir
(see Dal', Vladimir Ivanovich)

Lugn, Kristina 1948- DLB-257

Lugones, Leopoldo 1874-1938 . . . . DLB-283

Luhan, Mabel Dodge 1879-1962 . . . . DLB-303

Lukács, Georg (see Lukács, György)

Lukács, György
1885-1971 . . . . DLB-215, 242; CDWLB-4

Luke, Peter 1919-1995. . . . . .DLB-13

Lummis, Charles F. 1859-1928 . . . . .DLB-186

Lundkvist, Artur 1906-1991 . . . . .DLB-259

Lunts, Lev Natanovich
1901-1924 . . . . .DLB-272

F. M. Lupton Company. DLB-49

Lupus of Ferrières
circa 805-circa 862. . . . . .DLB-148

Lurie, Alison 1926- DLB-2, 350

Lussu, Emilio 1890-1975 . . . . .DLB-264

Lustig, Arnošt 1926- DLB-232, 299

Luther, Martin
1483-1546 . . . . DLB-179; CDWLB-2

Luzi, Mario 1914-2005. . . . . .DLB-128

L'vov, Nikolai Aleksandrovich
1751-1803 . . . . .DLB-150

Lyall, Gavin 1932-2003 . . . . .DLB-87

Lydgate, John circa 1370-1450 . . . . .DLB-146

Lyly, John circa 1554-1606 . . . . .DLB-62, 167

Lynch, Martin 1950- DLB-310

Lynch, Patricia 1898-1972 . . . . .DLB-160

Lynch, Richard fl. 1596-1601 . . . . .DLB-172

Lynd, Robert 1879-1949 . . . . .DLB-98

Lynds, Dennis (Michael Collins)
1924-2005 . . . . .DLB-306

Tribute to John D. MacDonald Y-86

Tribute to Kenneth Millar Y-83

Why I Write Mysteries: Night and Day . . .Y-85

Lynes, Jeanette 1956- DLB-334

Lyon, Matthew 1749-1822. . . . . .DLB-43

Lyotard, Jean-François
1924-1998 . . . . .DLB-242

Lyricists
Additional Lyricists: 1920-1960 . . . . .DLB-265

Lysias circa 459 B.C.-circa 380 B.C. DLB-176

Lytle, Andrew 1902-1995 . . . . .DLB-6; Y-95

Tribute to Caroline Gordon Y-81

Tribute to Katherine Anne Porter Y-80

Lytton, Edward
(see Bulwer-Lytton, Edward)

Lytton, Edward Robert Bulwer
1831-1891 . . . . .DLB-32

M

Ma Ma Lay, Gya-ne-gyaw 1917-1982. . . . .DLB-348

Ma Sanda 1947- DLB-348

Maalouf, Amin 1949- DLB-346

Maass, Joachim 1901-1972. . . . . .DLB-69

Mabie, Hamilton Wright 1845-1916 . . . . . .DLB-71

Mac A'Ghobhainn, Iain (see Smith, Iain Crichton)

MacArthur, Charles 1895-1956 . . . . .DLB-7, 25, 44

Macaulay, Catherine 1731-1791 . . . . .DLB-104, 336

Macaulay, David 1945- DLB-61

Macaulay, Rose 1881-1958 . . . . .DLB-36

Macaulay, Thomas Babington
1800-1859 . . . . .DLB-32, 55; CDBLB-4

Macaulay Company. DLB-46

MacBeth, George 1932-1992. . . . . .DLB-40

Macbeth, Madge 1880-1965 . . . . .DLB-92

MacCaig, Norman 1910-1996 . . . . .DLB-27

MacDiarmid, Hugh
1892-1978 . . . . DLB-20; CDBLB-7

MacDonald, Ann-Marie 1958- DLB-334

MacDonald, Cynthia 1928- DLB-105

MacDonald, George 1824-1905. . . . DLB-18, 163, 178

MacDonald, John D.
1916-1986 . . . . DLB-8, 306; Y-86

MacDonald, Philip 1899?-1980 . . . . .DLB-77

Macdonald, Ross (see Millar, Kenneth)

Macdonald, Sharman 1951- DLB-245

MacDonald, Wilson 1880-1967. . . . . .DLB-92

Macdonald and Company (Publishers) . . .DLB-112

Macdonell, A. G. 1895-1941 . . . . .DLB-352

MacEwen, Gwendolyn 1941-1987. . . .DLB-53, 251

Macfadden, Bernarr 1868-1955. . . . . . .DLB-25, 91

MacGregor, John 1825-1892 . . . . .DLB-166

MacGregor, Mary Esther (see Keith, Marian)

Macherey, Pierre 1938- DLB-296

Machado, Antonio 1875-1939 . . . . .DLB-108

Machado, Manuel 1874-1947. . . . . .DLB-108

Machado de Assis, Joaquim Maria
1839-1908 . . . . .DLB-307

Machar, Agnes Maule 1837-1927 . . . . .DLB-92

Machaut, Guillaume de
circa 1300-1377 . . . . .DLB-208

Machen, Arthur Llewelyn Jones
1863-1947 . . . . DLB-36, 156, 178

MacIlmaine, Roland fl. 1574 . . . . .DLB-281

MacInnes, Colin 1914-1976. . . . . .DLB-14

MacInnes, Helen 1907-1985. . . . . .DLB-87

Mac Intyre, Tom 1931- DLB-245

Mačiulis, Jonas (see Maironis, Jonas)

MacIvor, Daniel 1962- DLB-334

Mack, Maynard 1909-2001 . . . . .DLB-111

Mackall, Leonard L. 1879-1937 . . . . .DLB-140

MacKay, Isabel Ecclestone 1875-1928 . . . . .DLB-92

Mackay, Shena 1944- DLB-231, 319

MacKaye, Percy 1875-1956 . . . . .DLB-54

Macken, Walter 1915-1967 . . . . .DLB-13

MacKenna, John 1952- DLB-319

Mackenzie, Alexander 1763-1820 . . . . .DLB-99

Mackenzie, Alexander Slidell
1803-1848 . . . . .DLB-183

Mackenzie, Compton 1883-1972 . . . .DLB-34, 100

Mackenzie, Henry 1745-1831 . . . . .DLB-39

The Lounger, no. 20 (1785) DLB-39

Mackenzie, Kenneth (Seaforth Mackenzie)
1913-1955 . . . . .DLB-260

Mackenzie, William 1758-1828 . . . . .DLB-187

Mackey, Nathaniel 1947- DLB-169

Mackey, William Wellington 1937- DLB-38

Mackintosh, Elizabeth (see Tey, Josephine)

Mackintosh, Sir James 1765-1832 . . . . . . .DLB-158

Macklin, Charles 1699-1797. . . . . .DLB-89

Maclaren, Ian (see Watson, John)

Maclaren-Ross, Julian 1912-1964. . . . . . . .DLB-319

MacLaverty, Bernard 1942- DLB-267

MacLean, Alistair 1922-1987 . . . . .DLB-276

MacLean, Katherine Anne 1925- DLB-8

Maclean, Norman 1902-1990 . . . . .DLB-206

MacLeish, Archibald 1892-1982
. . . . DLB-4, 7, 45; Y-82; DS-15; CDALB-7

MacLennan, Hugh 1907-1990 . . . . .DLB-68

MacLeod, Alistair 1936- DLB-60

Macleod, Fiona (see Sharp, William)

Macleod, Norman 1906-1985 . . . . .DLB-4

Mac Low, Jackson 1922-2004 . . . . .DLB-193

MacMahon, Bryan 1909-1998 . . . . .DLB-319

Macmillan and Company DLB-106

The Macmillan Company DLB-49

Macmillan's English Men of Letters,
First Series (1878-1892) DLB-144

MacNamara, Brinsley 1890-1963 . . . . .DLB-10

MacNeice, Louis 1907-1963. . . . . .DLB-10, 20

Macphail, Andrew 1864-1938 . . . . .DLB-92

Macpherson, James 1736-1796. . . . . .DLB-109, 336

Macpherson, Jay 1931- DLB-53

Macpherson, Jeanie 1884-1946 . . . . .DLB-44

Macrae Smith Company DLB-46

MacRaye, Lucy Betty (see Webling, Lucy)

John Macrone [publishing house] DLB-106

MacShane, Frank 1927-1999 . . . . .DLB-111

Macy-Masius DLB-46

Madden, David 1933- DLB-6

Madden, Sir Frederic 1801-1873 . . . . .DLB-184

Maddow, Ben 1909-1992 . . . . .DLB-44

Maddux, Rachel 1912-1983 . . . . . . .DLB-234; Y-93

Madgett, Naomi Long 1923- DLB-76

Madhubuti, Haki R. 1942- DLB-5, 41; DS-8

Madison, James 1751-1836 . . . . .DLB-37

Madsen, Svend Åge 1939- DLB-214

Madrigal, Alfonso Fernández de (El Tostado)
ca. 1405-1455 . . . . .DLB-286

Maeterlinck, Maurice 1862-1949 . . . .DLB-192, 331

The Little Magazines of the
New Formalism. DLB-282

Magee, David 1905-1977 .... DLB-187

Maginn, William 1794-1842 .... DLB-110, 159

Maggi, Carlo Maria 1630-1699 .... DLB-339

Magoffin, Susan Shelby 1827-1855 ...... DLB-239

Mahan, Alfred Thayer 1840-1914 .... DLB-47

Mahapatra, Jayanta 1928- DLB-323

Maheux-Forcier, Louise 1929- DLB-60

Mahfouz, Naguib (Najīb Mahfūz)
1911-2006. . . . . .DLB-331, 346; Y-88

    Nobel Lecture 1988 .... Y-88

Mahin, John Lee 1902-1984 .... DLB-44

Mahon, Derek 1941- DLB-40

Maiakovsky, Vladimir Vladimirovich
1893-1930 .... DLB-295

Maikov, Apollon Nikolaevich
1821-1897..................... DLB-277

Maikov, Vasilii Ivanovich 1728-1778 ..... DLB-150

Mailer, Norman 1923-2007
........DLB-2, 16, 28, 185, 278; Y-80, 83, 97;
DS-3; CDALB-6

    Tribute to Isaac Bashevis Singer......... Y-91

    Tribute to Meyer Levin Y-81

Maillart, Ella 1903-1997 .... DLB-195

Maillet, Adrienne 1885-1963 .... DLB-68

Maillet, Antonine 1929- DLB-60

Maillu, David G. 1939- DLB-157

Maimonides, Moses 1138-1204 .... DLB-115

Main Selections of the Book-of-the-Month
Club, 1926-1945................... DLB-9

Mainwaring, Daniel 1902-1977.......... DLB-44

Mair, Charles 1838-1927................ DLB-99

Mair, John circa 1467-1550 .... DLB-281

Maironis, Jonas 1862-1932 . . DLB-220; CDWLB-4

Mais, Roger 1905-1955..... DLB-125; CDWLB-3

Maitland, Sara 1950- DLB-271

Major, Andre 1942- DLB-60

Major, Charles 1856-1913 .... DLB-202

Major, Clarence 1936- DLB-33

Major, Kevin 1949- DLB-60

Major Books....................... DLB-46

Makanin, Vladimir Semenovich
1937- DLB-285

Makarovič, Svetlana 1939 - DLB-353

Makarenko, Anton Semenovich
1888-1939 .... DLB-272

Makemie, Francis circa 1658-1708 .... DLB-24

The Making of Americans Contract............ Y-98

Makovsky, Sergei 1877-1962........... DLB-317

Maksimov, Vladimir Emel'ianovich
1930-1995 .... DLB-302

Maksimović, Desanka
1898-1993 ....DLB-147; CDWLB-4

Malamud, Bernard 1914-1986
........DLB-2, 28, 152; Y-80, 86; CDALB-1

Bernard Malamud Archive at the
Harry Ransom Humanities
Research Center Y-00

Mălăncioiu, Ileana 1940- DLB-232

Malaparte, Curzio
(Kurt Erich Suckert) 1898-1957 ..... DLB-264

Malerba, Luigi 1927- DLB-196

Malet, Lucas 1852-1931 .... DLB-153

Malherbe, François de 1555-1628. . . . . . . DLB-327

Mallarmé, Stéphane 1842-1898 .... DLB-217

Malleson, Lucy Beatrice (see Gilbert, Anthony)

Mallet-Joris, Françoise (Françoise Lilar)
1930- DLB-83

Mallock, W. H. 1849-1923 ....DLB-18, 57

    "Every Man His Own Poet; or,
    The Inspired Singer's Recipe
    Book" (1877) DLB-35

    "Le Style c'est l'homme" (1892)...... DLB-57

    Memoirs of Life and Literature (1920),
    [excerpt]................. DLB-57

Mallon, Thomas 1951- DLB-350

Malone, Dumas 1892-1986 .... DLB-17

Malone, Edmond 1741-1812........... DLB-142

Malory, Sir Thomas
circa 1400-1410 - 1471 ... DLB-146; CDBLB-1

Malouf, David 1934- DLB-289

Malpede, Karen 1945- DLB-249

Malraux, André 1901-1976............ DLB-72

The Maltese Falcon (Documentary) DLB-280

Malthus, Thomas Robert
1766-1834.................DLB-107, 158

Maltz, Albert 1908-1985.............. DLB-102

Malzberg, Barry N. 1939- DLB-8

Mamet, David 1947- DLB-7

Mamin, Dmitrii Narkisovich
1852-1912 .... DLB-238

Manaka, Matsemela 1956- DLB-157

Mañas, José Ángel 1971- DLB-322

Manchester University Press DLB-112

Mandel, Eli 1922-1992............... DLB-53

Mandel'shtam, Nadezhda Iakovlevna
1899-1980 .... DLB-302

Mandel'shtam, Osip Emil'evich
1891-1938 .... DLB-295

Mandeville, Bernard 1670-1733 .... DLB-101

Mandeville, Sir John
mid fourteenth century DLB-146

Mandiargues, André Pieyre de
1909-1991 .... DLB-83

Manea, Norman 1936- DLB-232

Manfred, Frederick 1912-1994 ....DLB-6, 212, 227

Manfredi, Gianfranco 1948- DLB-196

Mangan, Sherry 1904-1961 .... DLB-4

Manganelli, Giorgio 1922-1990 .... DLB-196

Manger, Itzik (Itsik Manger)
1901-1969 .... DLB-333

Mani Leib (Mani Leyb Brahinsky)
1883-1953 .... DLB-333

Maniam, K. S. 1942- DLB-348

Manilius fl. first century A.D. DLB-211

Mankiewicz, Herman 1897-1953 .... DLB-26

Mankiewicz, Joseph L. 1909-1993 .... DLB-44

Mankowitz, Wolf 1924-1998 .... DLB-15

Manley, Delarivière 1672?-1724 ...... DLB-39, 80

    Preface to *The Secret History, of Queen
    Zarah, and the Zarazians* (1705) DLB-39

Mann, Abby 1927- DLB-44

Mann, Charles 1929-1998 .... Y-98

Mann, Emily 1952- DLB-266

Mann, Heinrich 1871-1950......... DLB-66, 118

Mann, Horace 1796-1859.......... DLB-1, 235

Mann, Klaus 1906-1949 .... DLB-56

Mann, Mary Peabody 1806-1887....... DLB-239

Mann, Thomas
1875-1955.........DLB-66, 331; CDWLB-2

Mann, William D'Alton 1839-1920 ......DLB-137

Mannin, Ethel 1900-1984......... DLB-191, 195

Manning, Emily (see Australie)

Manning, Frederic 1882-1935.......... DLB-260

Manning, Laurence 1899-1972......... DLB-251

Manning, Marie 1873?-1945............ DLB-29

Manning and Loring DLB-49

Mannyng, Robert fl.
1303-1338 .... DLB-146

Mano, D. Keith 1942- DLB-6

Manor Books...................... DLB-46

Manrique, Gómez 1412?-1490 .... DLB-286

Manrique, Jorge ca. 1440-1479 .... DLB-286

Mansfield, Katherine 1888-1923........ DLB-162

Mantel, Hilary 1952- DLB-271

Manuel, Niklaus circa 1484-1530........DLB-179

Manzini, Gianna 1896-1974 ....DLB-177

Mao Dun 1896-1981 .... DLB-328

Mapanje, Jack 1944- DLB-157

Maraini, Dacia 1936- DLB-196

Maraise, Marie-Catherine-Renée Darcel de
1737-1822 .... DLB-314

Maramzin, Vladimir Rafailovich
1934- DLB-302

March, William (William Edward Campbell)
1893-1954 .... DLB-9, 86, 316

Marchand, Leslie A. 1900-1999 .... DLB-103

Marchant, Bessie 1862-1941............ DLB-160

Marchant, Tony 1959- DLB-245

Marchenko, Anastasiia Iakovlevna
1830-1880 .... DLB-238

Marchessault, Jovette 1938- DLB-60

Marcinkevičius, Justinas 1930- DLB-232

Marcos, Plínio (Plínio Marcos de Barros)
  1935-1999 .... DLB-307
Marcus, Frank 1928- DLB-13
Marcuse, Herbert 1898-1979 .... DLB-242
Marden, Orison Swett 1850-1924 ..... DLB-137
Marechera, Dambudzo 1952-1987 ...... DLB-157
Marcy, Mary E. 1877-1922 .... DLB-345
Marek, Richard, Books DLB-46
Mares, E. A. 1938- DLB-122
Margolin, Anna (Rosa Lebensbaum [Roza
  Lebensboym]) 1887-1952]) DLB-333
Margoshes, Dave 1941- DLB-334
Marguerite de Navarre 1492-1549 .... DLB-327
Margulies, Donald 1954- DLB-228
Mariana, Juan de 1535 or 1536-1624 .... DLB-318
Mariani, Paul 1940- DLB-111
Marías, Javier 1951- DLB-322
Marie de France fl. 1160-1178 ..... DLB-208
Marie-Victorin, Frère (Conrad Kirouac)
  1885-1944 .... DLB-92
Marin, Biagio 1891-1985 .... DLB-128
Marinella, Lucrezia 1571?-1653 .... DLB-339
Marinetti, Filippo Tommaso
  1876-1944 .... DLB-114, 264
Marinina, Aleksandra (Marina Anatol'evna
  Alekseeva) 1957- DLB-285
Marinković, Ranko
  1913-2001 .... DLB-147; CDWLB-4
Marino, Giambattista 1569-1625 .... DLB-339
Marion, Frances 1886-1973 .... DLB-44
Marius, Richard C. 1933-1999 .... Y-85
Marivaux, Pierre Carlet de Chamblain de
  1688-1763 .... DLB-314
Markandaya, Kamala 1924-2004 ...... DLB-323
Markevich, Boleslav Mikhailovich
  1822-1884 .... DLB-238
Markfield, Wallace 1926-2002 ...... DLB-2, 28
Markham, E. A. 1939- DLB-319
Markham, Edwin 1852-1940 .... DLB-54, 186
Markish, David 1938- DLB-317
Markish, Peretz (Perets Markish)
  1895-1952 .... DLB-333
Markle, Fletcher 1921-1991 .... DLB-68; Y-91
Marlatt, Daphne 1942- DLB-60
Marlitt, E. 1825-1887 .... DLB-129
Marlowe, Christopher
  1564-1593 .... DLB-62; CDBLB-1
Marlyn, John 1912-1985 .... DLB-88
Marmion, Shakerley 1603-1639 ...... DLB-58
Marmontel, Jean-François 1723-1799 .... DLB-314
Der Marner before 1230-circa 1287 .... DLB-138
Marnham, Patrick 1943- DLB-204
Marot, Clément 1496-1544 .... DLB-327
The Marprelate Tracts 1588-1589 ... DLB-132

Marquand, John P. 1893-1960 .... DLB-9, 102
Marques, Helena 1935- DLB-287
Marqués, René 1919-1979 .... DLB-113, 305
Marquis, Don 1878-1937 .... DLB-11, 25
Marriott, Anne 1913-1997 .... DLB-68
Marryat, Frederick 1792-1848 ...... DLB-21, 163
Marsé, Juan 1933- DLB-322
Marsh, Capen, Lyon and Webb DLB-49
Marsh, George Perkins
  1801-1882 .... DLB-1, 64, 243
Marsh, James 1794-1842 .... DLB-1, 59
Marsh, Narcissus 1638-1713 .... DLB-213
Marsh, Ngaio 1899-1982 .... DLB-77
Marshall, Alan 1902-1984 .... DLB-260
Marshall, Arthur 1910-1989 .... DLB-352
Marshall, Edison 1894-1967 .... DLB-102
Marshall, Edward 1932- DLB-16
Marshall, Emma 1828-1899 .... DLB-163
Marshall, James 1942-1992 .... DLB-61
Marshall, Joyce 1913- DLB-88
Marshall, Paule 1929- DLB-33, 157, 227
Marshall, Tom 1938-1993 .... DLB-60
Marsilius of Padua
  circa 1275-circa 1342 .... DLB-115
Mars-Jones, Adam 1954- DLB-207, 319
Marson, Una 1905-1965 .... DLB-157
Marston, John 1576-1634 .... DLB-58, 172
Marston, Philip Bourke 1850-1887 .... DLB-35
Marston, Westland 1819-1890 .... DLB-344
Martel, Yann 1963- DLB-326, 334
Martens, Kurt 1870-1945 .... DLB-66
Martí, José 1853-1895 .... DLB-290
Martial circa A.D. 40-circa A.D. 103
  .... DLB-211; CDWLB-1
William S. Martien [publishing house] DLB-49
Martin, Abe (see Hubbard, Kin)
Martin, Catherine ca. 1847-1937 ... DLB-230
Martin, Charles 1942- DLB-120, 282
Martin, Claire 1914- DLB-60
Martin, David 1915-1997 .... DLB-260
Martin, Jay 1935- DLB-111
Martin, Johann (see Laurentius von Schnüffis)
Martin, S. I. 1961- DLB-347
Martin, Thomas 1696-1771 .... DLB-213
Martin, Violet Florence (see Ross, Martin)
Martin du Gard, Roger 1881-1958 ... DLB-65, 331
Martineau, Harriet
  1802-1876 .... DLB-21, 55, 159, 163, 166, 190
Martínez, Demetria 1960- DLB-209
Martínez de Toledo, Alfonso
  1398?-1468 .... DLB-286
Martínez, Eliud 1935- DLB-122

Martínez, Max 1943- DLB-82
Martínez, Rubén 1962- DLB-209
Martín Gaite, Carmen 1925-2000 .... DLB-322
Martín-Santos, Luis 1924-1964 ..... DLB-322
Martinson, Harry 1904-1978 .... DLB-259, 331
Martinson, Moa 1890-1964 .... DLB-259
Martone, Michael 1955- DLB-218
Martyn, Edward 1859-1923 .... DLB-10
Marvell, Andrew
  1621-1678 .... DLB-131; CDBLB-2
Marvin X 1944- DLB-38
Marx, Karl 1818-1883 .... DLB-129
Marzials, Theo 1850-1920 .... DLB-35
Masefield, John 1878-1967
  .... DLB-10, 19, 153, 160; CDBLB-5
Masham, Damaris Cudworth, Lady
  1659-1708 .... DLB-252
Masino, Paola 1908-1989 .... DLB-264
Mason, A. E. W. 1865-1948 .... DLB-70
Mason, Bobbie Ann
  1940- DLB-173; Y-87; CDALB-7
Mason, F. van Wyck (Geoffrey Coffin, Frank W.
  Mason, Ward Weaver) 1901-1978 .... DLB-306
Mason, William 1725-1797 .... DLB-142
Mason Brothers DLB-49
The Massachusetts Quarterly Review
  1847-1850 .... DLB-1
The Masses DLB-303
Massey, Gerald 1828-1907 .... DLB-32
Massey, Linton R. 1900-1974 .... DLB-187
Massie, Allan 1938- DLB-271
Massinger, Philip 1583-1640 .... DLB-58
Masson, David 1822-1907 .... DLB-144
Masters, Edgar Lee
  1868-1950 .... DLB-54; CDALB-3
Masters, Hilary 1928- DLB-244
Masters, Olga 1919-1986 .... DLB-325
Mastronardi, Lucio 1930-1979 ...... DLB-177
Mat' Maria (Elizaveta Kuz'mina-Karavdeva
  Skobtsova, née Pilenko) 1891-1945 .... DLB-317
Matevski, Mateja 1929- DLB-181; CDWLB-4
Mather, Cotton
  1663-1728 .... DLB-24, 30, 140; CDALB-2
Mather, Increase 1639-1723 .... DLB-24
Mather, Richard 1596-1669 .... DLB-24
Matheson, Annie 1853-1924 .... DLB-240
Matheson, Richard 1926- DLB-8, 44
Matheus, John F. 1887-1986 .... DLB-51
Mathews, Aidan 1956- DLB-319
Mathews, Cornelius 1817?-1889 .... DLB-3, 64, 250
Elkin Mathews [publishing house] .. DLB-112
Mathews, John Joseph 1894-1979 .... DLB-175
Mathias, Roland 1915-2007 .... DLB-27

Mathis, June 1892-1927 . . . . DLB-44	Mayhew, Jonathan 1720-1766 . . . . DLB-31	McCoy, Horace 1897-1955 . . . . DLB-9
Mathis, Sharon Bell 1937- DLB-33	Mayne, Ethel Colburn 1865-1941 . . . . . DLB-197	McCrae, Hugh 1876-1958 . . . . DLB-260
Matković, Marijan 1915-1985. . . . . DLB-181	Mayne, Jasper 1604-1672 . . . . DLB-126	McCrae, John 1872-1918 . . . . DLB-92
Matoš, Antun Gustav 1873-1914 . . . . DLB-147	Mayne, Seymour 1944- DLB-60	McCrumb, Sharyn 1948- DLB-306
Matos Paoli, Francisco 1915-2000 . . . . . . DLB-290	Mayor, Flora Macdonald 1872-1932. . . . . . DLB-36	McCullagh, Joseph B. 1842-1896. . . . . DLB-23
Matsumoto Seichō 1909-1992 . . . . DLB-182	Mayröcker, Friederike 1924- DLB-85	McCullers, Carson 1917-1967 . . . . . . DLB-2, 7, 173, 228; CDALB-1
The Matter of England 1240-1400 . . . . . . DLB-146	Mayr, Suzette 1967- DLB-334	McCulloch, Thomas 1776-1843 . . . . DLB-99
The Matter of Rome early twelfth to late fifteenth century DLB-146	Mazrui, Ali A. 1933- DLB-125	McCunn, Ruthanne Lum 1946- DLB-312
Matthew of Vendôme circa 1130-circa 1200 . . . . DLB-208	Mažuranić, Ivan 1814-1890 . . . . DLB-147	McDermott, Alice 1953- DLB-292
	Mazursky, Paul 1930- DLB-44	McDonald, Forrest 1927- DLB-17
Matthews, Brander 1852-1929 . . . . .DLB-71, 78; DS-13	McAlmon, Robert 1896-1956. . . DLB-4, 45; DS-15	McDonald, Walter 1934- DLB-105, DS-9
Matthews, Brian 1936- DLB-325	"A Night at Bricktop's" Y-01	"Getting Started: Accepting the Regions You Own—or Which Own You" DLB-105
Matthews, Jack 1925- DLB-6	McArthur, Peter 1866-1924 . . . . DLB-92	
Matthews, Victoria Earle 1861-1907. . . . . DLB-221	McAuley, James 1917-1976 . . . . DLB-260	Tribute to James Dickey. Y-97
Matthews, William 1942-1997 . . . . DLB-5	Robert M. McBride and Company DLB-46	McDougall, Colin 1917-1984 . . . . DLB-68
Matthías Jochumsson 1835-1920 . . . . DLB-293	McCabe, Patrick 1955- DLB-194	McDowell, Katharine Sherwood Bonner 1849-1883 . . . . DLB-202, 239
Matthías Johannessen 1930- DLB-293	McCafferty, Owen 1961- DLB-310	
Matthiessen, F. O. 1902-1950. . . . . DLB-63	McCaffrey, Anne 1926- DLB-8	Obolensky McDowell [publishing house] DLB-46
Matthiessen, Peter 1927- DLB-6, 173, 275	McCaffrey, Steve 1947- DLB-334	
Maturin, Charles Robert 1780-1824 . . . . .DLB-178	McCann, Colum 1965- DLB-267	McEwan, Ian 1948- DLB-14, 194, 319, 326
Matute, Ana María 1926- DLB-322	McCarthy, Cormac 1933- DLB-6, 143, 256	McFadden, David 1940- DLB-60
Maugham, W. Somerset 1874-1965 . . . . . DLB-10, 36, 77, 100, 162, 195; CDBLB-6	The Cormac McCarthy Society Y-99	McFall, Frances Elizabeth Clarke (see Grand, Sarah)
	McCarthy, Karen 1966- DLB-347	
Maupassant, Guy de 1850-1893 . . . . DLB-123	McCarthy, Mary 1912-1989. . . . . . . .DLB-2; Y-81	McFarland, Ron 1942- DLB-256
Maupertuis, Pierre-Louis Moreau de 1698-1759. DLB-314	McCarthy, Shaun Lloyd (see Cory, Desmond)	McFarlane, Leslie 1902-1977 . . . . DLB-88
	McCay, Winsor 1871-1934 . . . . DLB-22	McFee, William 1881-1966. . . . . DLB-153
Maupin, Armistead 1944- DLB-278	McClane, Albert Jules 1922-1991. . . . . . .DLB-171	McGahan, Andrew 1966- DLB-325
Mauriac, Claude 1914-1996 . . . . DLB-83	McClatchy, C. K. 1858-1936 . . . . DLB-25	McGahern, John 1934- DLB-14, 231, 319
Mauriac, François 1885-1970 . . . . . . DLB-65, 331	McClellan, George Marion 1860-1934. . . . DLB-50	McGee, Thomas D'Arcy 1825-1868. . . . . . DLB-99
Maurice, Frederick Denison 1805-1872 . . . DLB-55	"The Negro as a Writer" DLB-50	McGeehan, W. O. 1879-1933. . . . . . . .DLB-25, 171
Maurois, André 1885-1967. . . . . DLB-65	McCloskey, Robert 1914-2003 . . . . DLB-22	McGill, Ralph 1898-1969 . . . . DLB-29
Maury, James 1718-1769 . . . . DLB-31	McCloy, Helen 1904-1992 . . . . DLB-306	McGinley, Phyllis 1905-1978 . . . . DLB-11, 48
Mavor, Elizabeth 1927- DLB-14	McClung, Nellie Letitia 1873-1951. . . . . . . DLB-92	McGinniss, Joe 1942- DLB-185
Mavor, Osborne Henry (see Bridie, James)	McClure, James 1939-2006. . . . . .DLB-276	McGirt, James E. 1874-1930. . . . . DLB-50
Maxwell, Gavin 1914-1969. . . . . DLB-204	McClure, Joanna 1930- DLB-16	McGlashan and Gill DLB-106
Maxwell, William 1908-2000. . . . . DLB-218, 278; Y-80	McClure, Michael 1932- DLB-16	McGough, Roger 1937- DLB-40
	McClure, Phillips and Company DLB-46	McGrath, John 1935- DLB-233
Tribute to Nancy Hale Y-88	McClure, S. S. 1857-1949 . . . . DLB-91	McGrath, Patrick 1950- DLB-231
H. Maxwell [publishing house]. DLB-49	A. C. McClurg and Company DLB-49	McGraw, Erin 1957- DLB-335
John Maxwell [publishing house] DLB-106	McCluskey, John A., Jr. 1944- DLB-33	McGraw-Hill DLB-46
May, Elaine 1932- DLB-44	McCollum, Michael A. 1946- Y-87	McGuane, Thomas 1939- DLB-2, 212; Y-80
May, Karl 1842-1912 . . . . DLB-129	McConnell, William C. 1917- DLB-88	Tribute to Seymour Lawrence Y-94
May, Thomas 1595/1596-1650 . . . . DLB-58	McCord, David 1897-1997 . . . . DLB-61	McGuckian, Medbh 1950- DLB-40
Mayer, Bernadette 1945- DLB-165	McCord, Louisa S. 1810-1879 . . . . DLB-248	McGuffey, William Holmes 1800-1873 . . . DLB-42
Mayer, Mercer 1943- DLB-61	McCorkle, Jill 1958- DLB-234; Y-87	McGuinness, Frank 1953- DLB-245
Mayer, O. B. 1818-1891 . . . . DLB-3, 248	McCorkle, Samuel Eusebius 1746-1811 . . . DLB-37	McHenry, James 1785-1845 . . . . DLB-202
Mayes, Herbert R. 1900-1987. . . . . DLB-137	McCormick, Anne O'Hare 1880-1954. . . . DLB-29	McIlvanney, William 1936- DLB-14, 207
Mayes, Wendell 1919-1992. . . . . DLB-26	McCormick, Kenneth Dale 1906-1997 . . . . . . Y-97	McIlwraith, Jean Newton 1859-1938 . . . . . DLB-92
Mayfield, Julian 1928-1984. . . . . . . .DLB-33; Y-84	McCormick, Robert R. 1880-1955. . . . . . . DLB-29	McInerney, Jay 1955- DLB-292
Mayhew, Henry 1812-1887. . . . . . DLB-18, 55, 190	McCourt, Edward 1907-1972 . . . . DLB-88	McInerny, Ralph 1929- DLB-306

McIntosh, Maria Jane 1803-1878....DLB-239, 248

McIntyre, James 1827-1906............DLB-99

McIntyre, O. O. 1884-1938............DLB-25

McKay, Claude 1889-1948.....DLB-4, 45, 51, 117

The David McKay Company..........DLB-49

McKay, Don 1942-................DLB-334

McKean, William V. 1820-1903.........DLB-23

McKenna, Stephen 1888-1967.........DLB-197

The McKenzie Trust....................Y-96

McKerrow, R. B. 1872-1940............DLB-201

McKinley, Robin 1952-..............DLB-52

McKinnon, K. C. (see Pelletier, Cathie)

McKnight, Reginald 1956-...........DLB-234

McLachlan, Alexander 1818-1896........DLB-99

McLaren, Floris Clark 1904-1978........DLB-68

McLaverty, Michael 1907-1992.........DLB-15

McLean, Duncan 1964-..............DLB-267

McLean, John R. 1848-1916............DLB-23

McLean, William L. 1852-1931..........DLB-25

McLennan, William 1856-1904..........DLB-92

McLoughlin Brothers.................DLB-49

McLuhan, Marshall 1911-1980..........DLB-88

McMaster, John Bach 1852-1932........DLB-47

McMillan, Terry 1951-..............DLB-292

McMurtry, Larry 1936-
.......DLB-2, 143, 256; Y-80, 87; CDALB-6

McNally, Terrence 1939-.........DLB-7, 249

McNeil, Florence 1937-..............DLB-60

McNeile, Herman Cyril 1888-1937.......DLB-77

McNickle, D'Arcy 1904-1977.....DLB-175, 212

McPhee, John 1931-............DLB-185, 275

McPherson, James Alan 1943-.....DLB-38, 244

McPherson, Sandra 1943-..............Y-86

McTaggart, J. M. E. 1866-1925.........DLB-262

McWhirter, George 1939-.............DLB-60

McWilliam, Candia 1955-............DLB-267

McWilliams, Carey 1905-1980.........DLB-137

"*The Nation's* Future," Carey
McWilliams's Editorial Policy
in *Nation*...................DLB-137

Mda, Zakes 1948-................DLB-225

Mead, George Herbert 1863-1931.......DLB-270

Mead, L. T. 1844-1914...............DLB-141

Mead, Matthew 1924-...............DLB-40

Mead, Taylor circa 1931-.............DLB-16

Meany, Tom 1903-1964...............DLB-171

Mears, Gillian 1964-................DLB-325

Mechthild von Magdeburg
circa 1207-circa 1282..............DLB-138

Medieval Galician-Portuguese Poetry....DLB-287

Medieval Spanish Debate Liberature.....DLB-337

Medieval Spanish Epics...............DLB-337

Medieval Spanish Exempla Literature....DLB-337

Medieval Spanish Spiritual Literature....DLB-337

Medill, Joseph 1823-1899..............DLB-43

Medoff, Mark 1940-..................DLB-7

Meek, Alexander Beaufort
1814-1865.................DLB-3, 248

Meeke, Mary ?-1816.................DLB-116

Mehta, Ved 1934-..................DLB-323

Mei, Lev Aleksandrovich 1822-1862.....DLB-277

Meinke, Peter 1932-..................DLB-5

Meireles, Cecília 1901-1964............DLB-307

Mejía, Pedro 1497-1551...............DLB-318

Mejia Vallejo, Manuel 1923-...........DLB-113

Melanchthon, Philipp 1497-1560........DLB-179

Melançon, Robert 1947-..............DLB-60

Melfi, Leonard 1935-2001.............DLB-341

Mell, Max 1882-1971..............DLB-81, 124

Mellow, James R. 1926-1997..........DLB-111

Mel'nikov, Pavel Ivanovich
1818-1883.....................DLB-238

Meltzer, David 1937-................DLB-16

Meltzer, Milton 1915-...............DLB-61

Melville, Elizabeth, Lady Culross
circa 1585-1640................DLB-172

Melville, Herman
1819-1891....DLB-3, 74, 250, 349; CDALB-2

The Melville Society.................Y-01

Melville, James
(Roy Peter Martin) 1931-........DLB-276

"Memorandum on Local Government," Anne-
Robert-Jacques Turgot, bacon de
l'Aulne........................DLB-314

Mena, Juan de 1411-1456.............DLB-286

Mena, María Cristina 1893-1965....DLB-209, 221

Menaker, Daniel 1941-..............DLB-335

Menander 342-341 B.C.-circa 292-291 B.C.
....................DLB-176; CDWLB-1

Menantes (see Hunold, Christian Friedrich)

Mencke, Johann Burckhard 1674-1732...DLB-168

Mencken, H. L. 1880-1956
........DLB-11, 29, 63, 137, 222; CDALB-4

"Berlin, February, 1917".............Y-00

From the Initial Issue of *American Mercury*
(January 1924)..................DLB-137

Mencken and Nietzsche: An
Unpublished Excerpt from H. L.
Mencken's *My Life as Author and
Editor*..........................Y-93

Mendele Moyhker Sforim (Solomon Jacob
Abramowitz [Sholem Yankev Abramovitsch])
1836-1917.....................DLB-333

Mendelssohn, Moses 1729-1786.........DLB-97

Mendes, Catulle 1841-1909............DLB-217

Méndez M., Miguel 1930-.............DLB-82

Mendoza, Diego Hurtado de
1504-1575....................DLB-318

Mendoza, Eduardo 1943-............DLB-322

Menzini, Benedetto 1646-1704.........DLB-339

The Mercantile Library of New York........Y-96

Mercer, Cecil William (see Yates, Dornford)

Mercer, David 1928-1980..........DLB-13, 310

Mercer, John 1704-1768...............DLB-31

Mercer, Johnny 1909-1976............DLB-265

Mercier, Louis-Sébastien 1740-1814......DLB-314

Le Tableau de Paris..................DLB-314

Meredith, George
1828-1909....DLB-18, 35, 57, 159; CDBLB-4

Meredith, Louisa Anne 1812-1895..DLB-166, 230

Meredith, Owen
(see Lytton, Edward Robert Bulwer)

Meredith, William 1919-...............DLB-5

Meres, Francis
Palladis Tamia, Wits Treasurie (1598)
[excerpt]................DLB-172

Merezhkovsky, Dmitrii Sergeevich
1865-1941....................DLB-295

Mergerle, Johann Ulrich
(see Abraham ä Sancta Clara)

Mérimée, Prosper 1803-1870.......DLB-119, 192

Merino, José María 1941-.............DLB-322

Merivale, John Herman 1779-1844.......DLB-96

Meriwether, Louise 1923-.............DLB-33

Merleau-Ponty, Maurice 1908-1961......DLB-296

Merlin Press........................DLB-112

Mernissi, Fatima 1940-...............DLB-346

Merriam, Eve 1916-1992...............DLB-61

The Merriam Company................DLB-49

Merril, Judith 1923-1997.............DLB-251

Tribute to Theodore Sturgeon..........Y-85

Merrill, Christopher 1957-...........DLB-342

Merrill, James 1926-1995........DLB-5, 165; Y-85

Merrill and Baker....................DLB-49

The Mershon Company................DLB-49

Merton, Thomas 1915-1968.......DLB-48; Y-81

Merwin, W. S. 1927-.........DLB-5, 169, 342

Julian Messner [publishing house]........DLB-46

Mészöly, Miklós 1921-2001............DLB-232

J. Metcalf [publishing house]...........DLB-49

Metcalf, John 1938-.................DLB-60

The Methodist Book Concern..........DLB-49

Methuen and Company...............DLB-112

Meun, Jean de (see *Roman de la Rose*)

Mew, Charlotte 1869-1928.........DLB-19, 135

Mewshaw, Michael 1943-..............Y-80

Tribute to Albert Erskine.............Y-93

Meyer, Conrad Ferdinand 1825-1898....DLB-129

Meyer, E. Y. 1946-..................DLB-75

Cumulative Index   DLB 354

Meyer, Eugene 1875-1959 . . . . DLB-29

Meyer, Michael 1921-2000 . . . . DLB-155

Meyers, Jeffrey 1939- DLB-111

Meynell, Alice 1847-1922 . . . . DLB-19, 98

Meynell, Viola 1885-1956 . . . . DLB-153

Meyrink, Gustav 1868-1932 . . . . DLB-81

Mézières, Philipe de circa 1327-1405 . . . . . DLB-208

Michael, Ib 1945- DLB-214

Michael, Livi 1960- DLB-267

Michaëlis, Karen 1872-1950 . . . . DLB-214

Michaels, Anne 1958- DLB-299

Michaels, Leonard 1933-2003 . . . . DLB-130

Michaux, Henri 1899-1984 . . . . DLB-258

Micheaux, Oscar 1884-1951 . . . . DLB-50

Michel of Northgate, Dan
 circa 1265-circa 1340 . . . . DLB-146

Micheline, Jack 1929-1998 . . . . DLB-16

Michener, James A. 1907?-1997 . . . . DLB-6

Micklejohn, George circa 1717-1818 . . . . . . DLB-31

Middle Hill Press DLB-106

Middleton, Christopher 1926- DLB-40

Middleton, Conyers 1683-1750 . . . . DLB-336

Middleton, Richard 1882-1911 . . . . DLB-156

Middleton, Stanley 1919- DLB-14, 326

Middleton, Thomas 1580-1627 . . . . DLB-58

Midnight's Children, 1981 Booker Prize winner,
 Salman Rushdie DLB-326

Miegel, Agnes 1879-1964 . . . . DLB-56

Mieželaitis, Eduardas 1919-1997 . . . . DLB-220

Miguéis, José Rodrigues 1901-1980 . . . . . DLB-287

Mihailović, Dragoslav 1930- DLB-181

Mihalić, Slavko 1928- DLB-181

Mikhailov, A.
 (see Sheller, Aleksandr Konstantinovich)

Mikhailov, Mikhail Larionovich
 1829-1865 . . . . DLB-238

Mikhailovsky, Nikolai Konstantinovich
 1842-1904 . . . . DLB-277

Miliauskaitė, Nijolė 1950-2002 . . . . DLB-353

Miles, Josephine 1911-1985 . . . . DLB-48

Miles, Susan (Ursula Wyllie Roberts)
 1888-1975 . . . . DLB-240

Miliković, Branko 1934-1961 . . . . DLB-181

Milius, John 1944- DLB-44

Mill, James 1773-1836 . . . . DLB-107, 158, 262

Mill, John Stuart
 1806-1873 . . . . . DLB-55, 190, 262; CDBLB-4

 Thoughts on Poetry and Its Varieties
  (1833) DLB-32

Andrew Millar [publishing house] DLB-154

Millar, John 1735-1801 . . . . DLB-336

Millar, Kenneth
 1915-1983 . . . . DLB-2, 226; Y-83; DS-6

Millás, Juan José 1946- DLB-322

Millay, Edna St. Vincent
 1892-1950 . . . . DLB-45, 249; CDALB-4

Millen, Sarah Gertrude 1888-1968 . . . . . . DLB-225

Miller, Andrew 1960- DLB-267

Miller, Arthur 1915-2005 . . DLB-7, 266; CDALB-1

 The Arthur Miller Society Y-01

Miller, Caroline 1903-1992 . . . . DLB-9

Miller, Eugene Ethelbert 1950- DLB-41

 Tribute to Julian Mayfield Y-84

Miller, Heather Ross 1939- DLB-120

Miller, Henry
 1891-1980 . . . . DLB-4, 9; Y-80; CDALB-5

Miller, Hugh 1802-1856 . . . . DLB-190

Miller, J. Hillis 1928- DLB-67

Miller, Jane 1949- DLB-342

Miller, Jason 1939- DLB-7

Miller, Joaquin 1839-1913 . . . . DLB-186

Miller, May 1899-1995 . . . . DLB-41

Miller, Paul 1906-1991 . . . . DLB-127

Miller, Perry 1905-1963 . . . . DLB-17, 63

Miller, Sue 1943- DLB-143

Miller, Vassar 1924-1998 . . . . DLB-105

Miller, Walter M., Jr. 1923-1996 . . . . DLB-8

Miller, Webb 1892-1940 . . . . DLB-29

James Miller [publishing house] DLB-49

Millett, Kate 1934- DLB-246

Millhauser, Steven 1943- DLB-2, 350

Millican, Arthenia J. Bates 1920- DLB-38

Milligan, Alice 1866-1953 . . . . DLB-240

Milligan, Spike 1918-2002 . . . . DLB-352

Mills, Magnus 1954- DLB-267

Mills and Boon DLB-112

Milman, Henry Hart 1796-1868 . . . . DLB-96

Milne, A. A. (Alan Alexander Milne)
 1882-1956 . . . . DLB-10, 77, 100, 160, 352

Milner, Ron 1938- DLB-38

William Milner [publishing house] DLB-106

Milnes, Richard Monckton (Lord Houghton)
 1809-1885 . . . . DLB-32, 184

Milton, John
 1608-1674 . . . . . DLB-131, 151, 281; CDBLB-2

 The Milton Society of America Y-00

Miłosz, Czesław
 1911-2004 . . . . DLB-215, 331; CDWLB-4

Minakami Tsutomu 1919-2004 . . . . DLB-182

Minamoto no Sanetomo 1192-1219 . . . . . DLB-203

Minco, Marga 1920- DLB-299

The Minerva Press DLB-154

Mina, Hanna 1924- DLB-346

Minnesang circa 1150-1280 . . . . DLB-138

 The Music of *Minnesang* DLB-138

Minns, Susan 1839-1938 . . . . DLB-140

Minsky, Nikolai 1855-1937 . . . . DLB-317

Minton, Balch and Company DLB-46

Minyana, Philippe 1946- DLB-321

Mirbeau, Octave 1848-1917 . . . . . . DLB-123, 192

Mirikitani, Janice 1941- DLB-312

Mirk, John died after 1414? DLB-146

Miró, Gabriel 1879-1930 . . . . DLB-322

Miró, Ricardo 1883-1940 . . . . DLB-290

Miron, Gaston 1928-1996 . . . . DLB-60

A Mirror for Magistrates DLB-167

Mirsky, D. S. 1890-1939 . . . . DLB-317

Mishima Yukio 1925-1970 . . . . DLB-182

Mistral, Frédéric 1830-1914 . . . . DLB-331

Mistral, Gabriela 1889-1957 . . . . DLB-283, 331

Mistry, Rohinton 1952- DLB-334

Mitchel, Jonathan 1624-1668 . . . . DLB-24

Mitchell, Adrian 1932- DLB-40

Mitchell, Donald Grant
 1822-1908 . . . . DLB-1, 243; DS-13

Mitchell, Gladys 1901-1983 . . . . DLB-77

Mitchell, H. L. 1906-1989 . . . . DLB-345

Mitchell, James Leslie 1901-1935 . . . . DLB-15

Mitchell, John (see Slater, Patrick)

Mitchell, John Ames 1845-1918 . . . . DLB-79

Mitchell, Joseph 1908-1996 . . . . DLB-185; Y-96

Mitchell, Julian 1935- DLB-14

Mitchell, Ken 1940- DLB-60

Mitchell, Langdon 1862-1935 . . . . DLB-7

Mitchell, Loften 1919-2001 . . . . DLB-38

Mitchell, Margaret 1900-1949 . . DLB-9; CDALB-7

Mitchell, S. Weir 1829-1914 . . . . DLB-202

Mitchell, W. J. T. 1942- DLB-246

Mitchell, W. O. 1914-1998 . . . . DLB-88

Mitchison, Naomi Margaret (Haldane)
 1897-1999 . . . . DLB-160, 191, 255, 319

Mitford, Jessica 1917-1996 . . . . DLB-352

Mitford, Mary Russell 1787-1855 . . . . DLB-110, 116

Mitford, Nancy 1904-1973 . . . . DLB-191

Mitford, William 1744-1827 . . . . DLB-336

Mittelholzer, Edgar
 1909-1965 . . . . DLB-117; CDWLB-3

Mitterer, Erika 1906-2001 . . . . DLB-85

Mitterer, Felix 1948- DLB-124

Mitternacht, Johann Sebastian
 1613-1679 . . . . DLB-168

Miyamoto Yuriko 1899-1951 . . . . DLB-180

Mizener, Arthur 1907-1988 . . . . DLB-103

Mo, Timothy 1950- DLB-194

Moberg, Vilhelm 1898-1973 . . . . DLB-259

Las Mocedades de Rodrigo (circa 1300) DLB-337

Modern Age Books DLB-46

Modern Language Association of America
The Modern Language Association of
America Celebrates Its Centennial . . . Y-84

The Modern Library DLB-46

Modern School Movement, The DLB-345

Modiano, Patrick 1945- DLB-83, 299

Modjeska, Drusilla 1946- DLB-325

Moe, Jørgen 1813-1882 . . . . DLB-354

Moffat, Yard and Company DLB-46

Moffet, Thomas 1553-1604 . . . . DLB-136

Mofolo, Thomas 1876-1948 . . . . DLB-225

Mohr, Nicholasa 1938- DLB-145

Moix, Ana María 1947- DLB-134

Molesworth, Louisa 1839-1921 . . . . DLB-135

Molière (Jean-Baptiste Poquelin)
1622-1673 . . . . DLB-268

Møller, Poul Martin 1794-1838 . . . . DLB-300

Möllhausen, Balduin 1825-1905 . . . . DLB-129

Molnár, Ferenc 1878-1952 . . . DLB-215; CDWLB-4

Molnár, Miklós (see Mészöly, Miklós)

Molodowsky, Kadya (Kadye Molodovski)
1894-1975 . . . . DLB-333

Momaday, N. Scott
1934- DLB-143, 175, 256; CDALB-7

Mommsen, Theodor 1817-1903 . . . . DLB-331

Moncrieff, W. T. (William Thomas Thomas)
1794-1857 . . . . DLB-344

Monin, P. 1883-1940 . . . . DLB-348

Monkhouse, Allan 1858-1936 . . . . DLB-10

Monette, Paul 1945-1995 . . . . DLB-350

Monro, Harold 1879-1932 . . . . DLB-19

Monroe, Harriet 1860-1936 . . . . DLB-54, 91

Monsarrat, Nicholas 1910-1979 . . . . DLB-15

Montagu, Lady Mary Wortley
1689-1762 . . . . DLB-95, 101

Montague, C. E. 1867-1928 . . . . DLB-197

Montague, John 1929- DLB-40

Montaigne, Michel de 1533-1592 . . . . DLB-327

Montale, Eugenio 1896-1981 . . . . . . DLB-114, 331

Montalvo, Garci Rodríguez de
ca. 1450?-before 1505 . . . . DLB-286

Montalvo, José 1946-1994 . . . . DLB-209

Montemayor, Jorge de 1521?-1561? DLB-318

Montero, Rosa 1951- DLB-322

Monterroso, Augusto 1921-2003 . . . . DLB-145

Montesquieu, Charles-Louis de Secondat, baron de
1689-1755 . . . . DLB-314

The Spirit of Laws DLB-314

Montesquiou, Robert de 1855-1921 . . . . . . DLB-217

Montgomerie, Alexander
circa 1550?-1598 . . . . DLB-167

Montgomery, James 1771-1854 . . . . . DLB-93, 158

Montgomery, John 1919- DLB-16

Montgomery, Lucy Maud
1874-1942 . . . . DLB-92; DS-14

Montgomery, Marion 1925- DLB-6

Montgomery, Robert Bruce (see Crispin, Edmund)

Montherlant, Henry de 1896-1972 . . . DLB-72, 321

The Monthly Review 1749-1844 . . . . DLB-110

Monti, Ricardo 1944- DLB-305

Montigny, Louvigny de 1876-1955 . . . . . . DLB-92

Montoya, José 1932- DLB-122

Moodie, John Wedderburn Dunbar
1797-1869 . . . . DLB-99

Moodie, Susanna 1803-1885 . . . . DLB-99

Moody, Joshua circa 1633-1697 . . . . DLB-24

Moody, William Vaughn 1869-1910 . . . . DLB-7, 54

Moon Tiger, 1987 Booker Prize winner,
Penelope Lively DLB-326

Moorcock, Michael
1939- DLB-14, 231, 261, 319

Moore, Alan 1953- DLB-261

Moore, Brian 1921-1999 . . . . DLB-251

Moore, Catherine L. 1911-1987 . . . . DLB-8

Moore, Clement Clarke 1779-1863 . . . . DLB-42

Moore, Dora Mavor 1888-1979 . . . . DLB-92

Moore, G. E. 1873-1958 . . . . DLB-262

Moore, George 1852-1933 . . . . DLB-10, 18, 57, 135

Literature at Nurse, or Circulating Morals
(1885) DLB-18

Moore, J. Howard 1862-1916 . . . . DLB-345

Moore, Lorrie 1957- DLB-234

Moore, Marianne
1887-1972 . . . . DLB-45; DS-7; CDALB-5

International Marianne Moore Society Y-98

Moore, Mavor 1919- DLB-88

Moore, Richard 1927- DLB-105

"The No Self, the Little Self, and
the Poets" DLB-105

Moore, T. Sturge 1870-1944 . . . . DLB-19

Moore, Thomas 1779-1852 . . . . DLB-96, 144

Moore, Ward 1903-1978 . . . . DLB-8

Moore, Wilstach, Keys and Company DLB-49

Moorehead, Alan 1901-1983 . . . . DLB-204

Moorhouse, Frank 1938- DLB-289

Moorhouse, Geoffrey 1931- DLB-204

Moorish Novel of the Sixteenth
Century, The DLB-318

The Moorland-Spingarn Research
Center DLB-76

Moorman, Mary C. 1905-1994 . . . . DLB-155

Mora, Pat 1942- DLB-209

Moraes, Dom 1938-2004 . . . . DLB-323

Moraes, Vinicius de 1913-1980 . . . . DLB-307

Moraga, Cherríe 1952- DLB-82, 249

Morales, Alejandro 1944- DLB-82

Morales, Mario Roberto 1947- DLB-145

Morales, Rafael 1919- DLB-108

Morality Plays: Mankind circa 1450-1500
and Everyman circa 1500 . . . . DLB-146

Morand, Paul 1888-1976 . . . . DLB-65

Morante, Elsa 1912-1985 . . . . DLB-177

Morata, Olympia Fulvia 1526-1555 . . . . . . DLB-179

Moravia, Alberto 1907-1990 . . . . DLB-177

Mordaunt, Elinor 1872-1942 . . . . DLB-174

Mordovtsev, Daniil Lukich 1830-1905 . . . DLB-238

More, Hannah
1745-1833 . . . . DLB-107, 109, 116, 158

More, Henry 1614-1687 . . . . DLB-126, 252

More, Sir Thomas
1477/1478-1535 . . . . DLB-136, 281

Morejón, Nancy 1944- DLB-283

Morellet, André 1727-1819 . . . . DLB-314

Morency, Pierre 1942- DLB-60

Moreno, Dorinda 1939- DLB-122

Moretti, Marino 1885-1979 . . . . DLB-114, 264

Morgan, Berry 1919-2002 . . . . DLB-6

Morgan, Charles 1894-1958 . . . . DLB-34, 100

Morgan, Edmund S. 1916- DLB-17

Morgan, Edwin 1920- DLB-27

Morgan, John Pierpont 1837-1913 . . . . DLB-140

Morgan, John Pierpont, Jr. 1867-1943 . . . . DLB-140

Morgan, Robert 1944- DLB-120, 292

Morgan, Sally 1951- DLB-325

Morgan, Sydney Owenson, Lady
1776?-1859 . . . . DLB-116, 158

Morgner, Irmtraud 1933-1990 . . . . DLB-75

Morhof, Daniel Georg 1639-1691 . . . . DLB-164

Mori, Kyoko 1957- DLB-312

Mori Ōgai 1862-1922 . . . . DLB-180

Mori, Toshio 1910-1980 . . . . DLB-312

Móricz, Zsigmond 1879-1942 . . . . DLB-215

Morier, James Justinian
1782 or 1783?-1849 . . . . DLB-116

Mörike, Eduard 1804-1875 . . . . DLB-133

Morin, Paul 1889-1963 . . . . DLB-92

Morison, Richard 1514?-1556 . . . . DLB-136

Morison, Samuel Eliot 1887-1976 . . . . DLB-17

Morison, Stanley 1889-1967 . . . . DLB-201

Moritz, Karl Philipp 1756-1793 . . . . DLB-94

Moriz von Craûn circa 1220-1230 . . . . DLB-138

Morley, Christopher 1890-1957 . . . . DLB-9

Morley, John 1838-1923 . . . . . . DLB-57, 144, 190

Moro, César 1903-1956 . . . . DLB-290

Morris, George Pope 1802-1864 . . . . DLB-73

Morris, James Humphrey (see Morris, Jan)

Morris, Jan 1926- DLB-204

Morris, Lewis 1833-1907 . . . . DLB-35

Morris, Margaret 1737-1816 . . . . DLB-200

Morris, Mary McGarry 1943- DLB-292

Morris, Richard B. 1904-1989 .... DLB-17

Morris, William 1834-1896
..... DLB-18, 35, 57, 156, 178, 184; CDBLB-4

Morris, Willie 1934-1999 .... Y-80

 Tribute to Irwin Shaw Y-84

 Tribute to James Dickey.............. Y-97

Morris, Wright
1910-1998........... DLB-2, 206, 218; Y-81

Morrison, Arthur 1863-1945 .... DLB-70, 135, 197

Morrison, Charles Clayton 1874-1966 .... DLB-91

Morrison, John 1904-1998 .... DLB-260

Morrison, Toni 1931-
..... DLB-6, 33, 143, 331; Y-81, 93; CDALB-6

 Nobel Lecture 1993 .... Y-93

Morrissy, Mary 1957- DLB-267

William Morrow and Company......... DLB-46

Morse, James Herbert 1841-1923......... DLB-71

Morse, Jedidiah 1761-1826 .... DLB-37

Morse, John T., Jr. 1840-1937.......... DLB-47

Morselli, Guido 1912-1973 .... DLB-177

Morte Arthure, the *Alliterative* and the
 Stanzaic circa 1350-1400 .... DLB-146

Mortimer, Favell Lee 1802-1878 .... DLB-163

Mortimer, John
1923-2009 ..... DLB-13, 245, 271; CDBLB-8

Morton, Carlos 1942- DLB-122

Morton, H. V. 1892-1979 .... DLB-195

Morton, John Maddison 1811-1891 ..... DLB-344

John P. Morton and Company DLB-49

Morton, Nathaniel 1613-1685 .... DLB-24

Morton, Sarah Wentworth 1759-1846 .... DLB-37

Morton, Thomas circa 1579-circa 1647.... DLB-24

Moscherosch, Johann Michael
1601-1669 .... DLB-164

Humphrey Moseley
[publishing house] DLB-170

Möser, Justus 1720-1794 .... DLB-97

Moses, Daniel David 1952- DLB-334

Mosley, Nicholas 1923- DLB-14, 207

Mosley, Walter 1952- DLB-306

Moss, Arthur 1889-1969................ DLB-4

Moss, Howard 1922-1987............... DLB-5

Moss, Thylias 1954- DLB-120

Mother Earth 1906-1918................ DLB-345

Motion, Andrew 1952- DLB-40

Motley, John Lothrop
1814-1877............. DLB-1, 30, 59, 235

Motley, Willard 1909-1965......... DLB-76, 143

Mott, Lucretia 1793-1880 .... DLB-239

Benjamin Motte Jr.
[publishing house] DLB-154

Motteux, Peter Anthony 1663-1718 ...... DLB-80

Mottram, R. H. 1883-1971 .... DLB-36

Mount, Ferdinand 1939- DLB-231

Mouré, Erin 1955- DLB-60

Mourning Dove (Humishuma) between
 1882 and 1888?-1936.........DLB-175, 221

Movies
 Fiction into Film, 1928-1975: A List
 of Movies Based on the Works
 of Authors in British Novelists,
 1930-1959 .... DLB-15

 Movies from Books, 1920-1974 .... DLB-9

Mowat, Farley 1921- DLB-68

A. R. Mowbray and Company,
 Limited..................... DLB-106

Mowrer, Edgar Ansel 1892-1977 .... DLB-29

Mowrer, Paul Scott 1887-1971.......... DLB-29

Edward Moxon [publishing house]...... DLB-106

Joseph Moxon [publishing house].......DLB-170

Moyes, Patricia 1923-2000 ....DLB-276

Mphahlele, Es'kia (Ezekiel)
 1919-2008 ....DLB-125, 225; CDWLB-3

Mrożek, Sławomir 1930- ... DLB-232; CDWLB-4

Mtshali, Oswald Mbuyiseni
 1940- DLB-125, 225

Mu Shiying 1912-1940 .... DLB-328

al-Mubarrad 826-898 or 899 .... DLB-311

Mucedorus......................... DLB-62

Mudford, William 1782-1848 .... DLB-159

Mudrooroo (see Johnson, Colin)

Mueller, Lisel 1924- DLB-105

Muhajir, El (see Marvin X)

Muhajir, Nazzam Al Fitnah (see Marvin X)

Muhammad the Prophet circa 570-632... DLB-311

Mühlbach, Luise 1814-1873 .... DLB-133

Muir, Edwin 1887-1959 ....DLB-20, 100, 191

Muir, Helen 1937- DLB-14

Muir, John 1838-1914..............DLB-186, 275

Muir, Percy 1894-1979 .... DLB-201

Mujū Ichien 1226-1312................ DLB-203

Mukherjee, Bharati 1940- DLB-60, 218, 323

Mulcaster, Richard 1531 or 1532-1611... DLB-167

Muldoon, Paul 1951- DLB-40

Mulisch, Harry 1927- DLB-299

Mulkerns, Val 1925- DLB-319

Müller, Friedrich (see Müller, Maler)

Müller, Heiner 1929-1995............. DLB-124

Müller, Maler 1749-1825.............. DLB-94

Muller, Marcia 1944- DLB-226

Müller, Wilhelm 1794-1827............. DLB-90

Mumford, Lewis 1895-1990 .... DLB-63

Munby, A. N. L. 1913-1974 .... DLB-201

Munby, Arthur Joseph 1828-1910 .... DLB-35

Munch, Andreas 1811-1884 .... DLB-354

Munch, Johan Storm 1778-1832 .... DLB-354

Munday, Anthony 1560-1633.........DLB-62, 172

Mundt, Clara (see Mühlbach, Luise)

Mundt, Theodore 1808-1861 .... DLB-133

Munford, Robert circa 1737-1783 .... DLB-31

Mungoshi, Charles 1947- DLB-157

Munif, Abdelrahman 1933-2004 .... DLB-346

Munk, Kaj 1898-1944................ DLB-214

Munonye, John 1929- DLB-117

Muñoz Molina, Antonio 1956- DLB-322

Munro, Alice 1931- DLB-53

George Munro [publishing house] DLB-49

Munro, H. H.
 1870-1916.......... DLB-34, 162; CDBLB-5

Munro, Neil 1864-1930 .... DLB-156

Norman L. Munro [publishing house] DLB-49

Munroe, Kirk 1850-1930 .... DLB-42

Munroe and Francis DLB-49

James Munroe and Company........... DLB-49

Joel Munsell [publishing house] DLB-49

Munsey, Frank A. 1854-1925 .... DLB-25, 91

Frank A. Munsey and Company DLB-49

Mura, David 1952- DLB-312

Murakami Haruki 1949- DLB-182

Muratov, Pavel 1881-1950 ....DLB-317

Murayama, Milton 1923- DLB-312

Murav'ev, Mikhail Nikitich 1757-1807 ... DLB-150

Murdoch, Iris 1919-1999
 .... DLB-14, 194, 233, 326; CDBLB-8

Murdock, James
 From *Sketches of Modern Philosophy* DS-5

Murdoch, Rupert 1931- DLB-127

Murfree, Mary N. 1850-1922 ....DLB-12, 74

Murger, Henry 1822-1861 .... DLB-119

Murger, Louis-Henri (see Murger, Henry)

Murnane, Gerald 1939- DLB-289

Murner, Thomas 1475-1537 ....DLB-179

Muro, Amado 1915-1971 .... DLB-82

Murphy, Arthur 1727-1805.........DLB-89, 142

Murphy, Beatrice M. 1908-1992......... DLB-76

Murphy, Dervla 1931- DLB-204

Murphy, Emily 1868-1933 .... DLB-99

Murphy, Jack 1923-1980 .... DLB-241

John Murphy and Company DLB-49

Murphy, John H., III 1916- DLB-127

Murphy, Richard 1927-1993 .... DLB-40

Murphy, Tom 1935- DLB-310

Murray, Albert L. 1916- DLB-38

Murray, Gilbert 1866-1957 .... DLB-10

Murray, Jim 1919-1998................ DLB-241

John Murray [publishing house]........ DLB-154

Murray, Judith Sargent 1751-1820 .... DLB-37, 200

Murray, Les 1938- DLB-289

Murray, Pauli 1910-1985 .... DLB-41

Murry, John Middleton 1889-1957 ...... DLB-149

"The Break-Up of the Novel" (1922) DLB-36

Murry, John Middleton, Jr. (see Cowper, Richard)

Musäus, Johann Karl August 1735-1787 .... DLB-97

al-Musawi, Muhsin 1945- DLB-346

Muschg, Adolf 1934- DLB-75

Musil, Robert 1880-1942 .... DLB-81, 124; CDWLB-2

Muslim Burmat 1943- DLB-348

Muspilli circa 790-circa 850 .... DLB-148

Musset, Alfred de 1810-1857 .... DLB-192, 217

Benjamin B. Mussey and Company DLB-49

Muste, A. J. 1885-1967 .... DLB-303

Mutafchieva, Vera 1929- DLB-181

Mutis, Alvaro 1923- DLB-283

Mwangi, Meja 1948- DLB-125

Mya Than Tint 1929-1998 .... DLB-348

Myers, Frederic W. H. 1843-1901 .... DLB-190

Myers, Gustavus 1872-1942 .... DLB-47

Myers, L. H. 1881-1944 .... DLB-15

Myers, Walter Dean 1937- DLB-33

Myerson, Julie 1960- DLB-267

Mykle, Agnar 1915-1994 .... DLB-297

Mykolaitis-Putinas, Vincas 1893-1967 .... DLB-220

Myles, Eileen 1949- DLB-193

Myrdal, Jan 1927- DLB-257

Mystery
1985: The Year of the Mystery: A Symposium Y-85

Comments from Other Writers Y-85

The Second Annual New York Festival of Mystery Y-00

Why I Read Mysteries Y-85

Why I Write Mysteries: Night and Day, by Michael Collins Y-85

N

Na Prous Boneta circa 1296-1328 .... DLB-208

Nabl, Franz 1883-1974 .... DLB-81

Nabokov, Véra 1902-1991 .... Y-91

Nabokov, Vladimir 1899-1977 ...... DLB-2, 244, 278, 317; Y-80, 91; DS-3; CDALB-1
International Nabokov Society Y-99

An Interview [On Nabokov], by Fredson Bowers Y-80

Nabokov Festival at Cornell Y-83

The Vladimir Nabokov Archive in the Berg Collection of the New York Public Library: An Overview Y-91

The Vladimir Nabokov Society Y-01

Nádas, Péter 1942- DLB-353

Nádaši, Ladislav (see Jégé)

Naden, Constance 1858-1889 .... DLB-199

Nader, Ralph 1934- DLB-345

Nadezhdin, Nikolai Ivanovich 1804-1856 .... DLB-198

Nadir, Moshe (Moyshe Nadir; Isaac Reis [Yitskhok Reyz]) 1885-1943 .... DLB-333

Nadson, Semen Iakovlevich 1862-1887 ... DLB-277

Naevius circa 265 B.C.-201 B.C. DLB-211

Nafis and Cornish DLB-49

Nagai Kafū 1879-1959 .... DLB-180

Nagel, Ernest 1901-1985 .... DLB-279

Nagibin, Iurii Markovich 1920-1994 ..... DLB-302

Nagrodskaia, Evdokiia Apollonovna 1866-1930 .... DLB-295

Nahman of Bratslav (Nakhmen Bratslaver) 1772-1810 .... DLB-333

Naidus, Leib (Leyb Naydus) 1890-1918 .... DLB-333

Naipaul, Shiva 1945-1985 .... DLB-157; Y-85

Naipaul, V. S. 1932- DLB-125, 204, 207, 326, 331; Y-85, 01; CDBLB-8; CDWLB-3
Nobel Lecture 2001: "Two Worlds" Y-01

Nakagami Kenji 1946-1992 .... DLB-182

Nakano-in Masatada no Musume (see Nijō, Lady)

Nałkowska, Zofia 1884-1954 .... DLB-215

Namora, Fernando 1919-1989 .... DLB-287

Joseph Nancrede [publishing house] DLB-49

Naranjo, Carmen 1930- DLB-145

Narayan, R. K. 1906-2001 .... DLB-323

Narbikova, Valeriia Spartakovna 1958- DLB-285

Narezhny, Vasilii Trofimovich 1780-1825 .... DLB-198

Narrache, Jean (Emile Coderre) 1893-1970 .... DLB-92

Nasby, Petroleum Vesuvius (see Locke, David Ross)

Eveleigh Nash [publishing house] DLB-112

Nash, Ogden 1902-1971 .... DLB-11

Nashe, Thomas 1567-1601? DLB-167

Nason, Jerry 1910-1986 .... DLB-241

Nasr, Seyyed Hossein 1933- DLB-279

Nasrallah, Emily 1931- DLB-346

Nast, Condé 1873-1942 .... DLB-91

Nast, Thomas 1840-1902 .... DLB-188

Nastasijević, Momčilo 1894-1938 ...... DLB-147

Nathan, George Jean 1882-1958 .... DLB-137

Nathan, Leonard 1924- DLB-342

Nathan, Robert 1894-1985 .... DLB-9

Nation, Carry A. 1846-1911 .... DLB-303

National Book Critics Circle Awards Y-00–01

The National Jewish Book Awards Y-85

Natsume Sōseki 1867-1916 .... DLB-180

Naughton, Bill 1910-1992 .... DLB-13

Nava, Michael 1954- DLB-306

Navarro, Joe 1953- DLB-209

Naylor, Gloria 1950- DLB-173

Nazor, Vladimir 1876-1949 .... DLB-147

Ndebele, Njabulo 1948- DLB-157, 225

Neagoe, Peter 1881-1960 .... DLB-4

Neal, John 1793-1876 .... DLB-1, 59, 243

Neal, Joseph C. 1807-1847 .... DLB-11

Neal, Larry 1937-1981 .... DLB-38

The Neale Publishing Company DLB-49

Nearing, Scott 1883-1983 .... DLB-303

Nebel, Frederick 1903-1967 .... DLB-226

Nebrija, Antonio de 1442 or 1444-1522 .. DLB-286

Nedreaas, Torborg 1906-1987 .... DLB-297

F. Tennyson Neely [publishing house] DLB-49

Negoițescu, Ion 1921-1993 .... DLB-220

Negri, Ada 1870-1945 .... DLB-114

Nehru, Pandit Jawaharlal 1889-1964 ..... DLB-323

Neihardt, John G. 1881-1973 ...... DLB-9, 54, 256

Neidhart von Reuental circa 1185-circa 1240 .... DLB-138

Neilson, John Shaw 1872-1942 .... DLB-230

Nekrasov, Nikolai Alekseevich 1821-1877 .... DLB-277

Nekrasov, Viktor Platonovich 1911-1987 .... DLB-302

Neledinsky-Meletsky, Iurii Aleksandrovich 1752-1828 .... DLB-150

Nelligan, Emile 1879-1941 .... DLB-92

Nelson, Alice Moore Dunbar 1875-1935 ... DLB-50

Nelson, Antonya 1961- DLB-244

Nelson, Kent 1943- DLB-234

Nelson, Richard 1950- DLB-341

Nelson, Richard K. 1941- DLB-275

Nelson, Thomas, and Sons [U.K.] DLB-106

Nelson, Thomas, and Sons [U.S.] DLB-49

Nelson, William 1908-1978 .... DLB-103

Nelson, William Rockhill 1841-1915 ...... DLB-23

Nemerov, Howard 1920-1991 ..... DLB-5, 6; Y-83

Németh, László 1901-1975 .... DLB-215

Nepos circa 100 B.C.-post 27 B.C. DLB-211

Nèris, Salomėja 1904-1945 .. DLB-220; CDWLB-4

Neruda, Pablo 1904-1973 .... DLB-283, 331

Nerval, Gérard de 1808-1855 .... DLB-217

Nervo, Amado 1870-1919 .... DLB-290

Nesbit, E. 1858-1924 .... DLB-141, 153, 178

Cumulative Index

Ness, Evaline 1911-1986 .... DLB-61
Nestroy, Johann 1801-1862 .... DLB-133
Nettleship, R. L. 1846-1892 .... DLB-262
Neugeboren, Jay 1938- DLB-28, 335
Neukirch, Benjamin 1655-1729 .... DLB-168
Neumann, Alfred 1895-1952 .... DLB-56
Neumann, Ferenc (see Molnár, Ferenc)
Neumark, Georg 1621-1681 .... DLB-164
Neumeister, Erdmann 1671-1756 .... DLB-168
Nevins, Allan 1890-1971 .... DLB-17; DS-17
Nevinson, Henry Woodd 1856-1941 .... DLB-135
The New American Library DLB-46
New Directions Publishing Corporation ... DLB-46
The New Monthly Magazine 1814-1884 ..... DLB-110
New York Times Book Review Y-82
John Newbery [publishing house] DLB-154
Newbolt, Henry 1862-1938 .... DLB-19
Newbound, Bernard Slade (see Slade, Bernard)
Newby, Eric 1919-2006 .... DLB-204
Newby, P. H. 1918-1997 .... DLB-15, 326
Thomas Cautley Newby
  [publishing house] DLB-106
Newcomb, Charles King 1820-1894 ... DLB-1, 223
Newell, Peter 1862-1924 .... DLB-42
Newell, Robert Henry 1836-1901 .... DLB-11
Newhouse, Edward 1911-2002 .... DLB-335
Newhouse, Samuel I. 1895-1979 .... DLB-127
Newland, Courttia 1973- DLB-347
Newman, Cecil Earl 1903-1976 .... DLB-127
Newman, David 1937- DLB-44
Newman, Frances 1883-1928 .... Y-80
Newman, Francis William 1805-1897 .... DLB-190
Newman, G. F. 1946- DLB-310
Newman, John Henry
  1801-1890 .... DLB-18, 32, 55
Mark Newman [publishing house] DLB-49
Newmarch, Rosa Harriet 1857-1940 ..... DLB-240
George Newnes Limited DLB-112
Newsome, Effie Lee 1885-1979 .... DLB-76
Newton, A. Edward 1864-1940 .... DLB-140
Newton, Sir Isaac 1642-1727 .... DLB-252
Nexø, Martin Andersen 1869-1954 ..... DLB-214
Nezval, Vítěslav
  1900-1958 .... DLB-215; CDWLB-4
Ngugi wa Thiong'o
  1938- DLB-125; CDWLB-3
Nguyen Huy Thiep 1950- DLB-348
Nguyen Minh Chau 1930-1989 .... DLB-348
Niatum, Duane 1938- DLB-175
The *Nibelungenlied* and the *Klage*
  circa 1200 .... DLB-138
Nichol, B. P. 1944-1988 .... DLB-53

Nicholas of Cusa 1401-1464 .... DLB-115
Nichols, Ann 1891?-1966 .... DLB-249
Nichols, Beverly 1898-1983 .... DLB-191
Nichols, Dudley 1895-1960 .... DLB-26
Nichols, Grace 1950- DLB-157
Nichols, John 1940- Y-82
Nichols, Mary Sargeant (Neal) Gove
  1810-1884 .... DLB-1, 243
Nichols, Peter 1927- DLB-13, 245
Nichols, Roy F. 1896-1973 .... DLB-17
Nichols, Ruth 1948- DLB-60
Nicholson, Edward Williams Byron
  1849-1912 .... DLB-184
Nicholson, Geoff 1953- DLB-271
Nicholson, Norman 1914-1987 .... DLB-27
Nicholson, William 1872-1949 .... DLB-141
Ní Chuilleanáin, Eiléan 1942- DLB-40
Nicol, Eric 1919- DLB-68
Nicolai, Friedrich 1733-1811 .... DLB-97
Nicolas de Clamanges circa 1363-1437 ... DLB-208
Nicolay, John G. 1832-1901 and
  Hay, John 1838-1905 .... DLB-47
Nicole, Pierre 1625-1695 .... DLB-268
Nicolson, Adela Florence Cory (see Hope, Laurence)
Nicolson, Harold 1886-1968 ....DLB-100, 149
  "The Practice of Biography," in
    *The English Sense of Humour and
    Other Essays* DLB-149
Nicolson, Nigel 1917-2004 .... DLB-155
Ní Dhuibhne, Éilís 1954- DLB-319
Niebuhr, Reinhold 1892-1971 ......DLB-17; DS-17
Niedecker, Lorine 1903-1970 .... DLB-48
Nieman, Lucius W. 1857-1935 .... DLB-25
Nietzsche, Friedrich
  1844-1900 .... DLB-129; CDWLB-2
  Mencken and Nietzsche: An Unpublished
    Excerpt from H. L. Mencken's *My Life
    as Author and Editor* Y-93
Nievo, Stanislao 1928- DLB-196
Niggli, Josefina 1910-1983 .... Y-80
Nightingale, Florence 1820-1910 .... DLB-166
Nigov, Anton (see Õnnepalu, Tõnu)
Nijō, Lady (Nakano-in Masatada no Musume)
  1258-after 1306 .... DLB-203
Nijō Yoshimoto 1320-1388 .... DLB-203
Nikitin, Ivan Savvich 1824-1861 ....DLB-277
Nikitin, Nikolai Nikolaevich 1895-1963 ...DLB-272
Nikolev, Nikolai Petrovich 1758-1815.... DLB-150
Niles, Hezekiah 1777-1839 .... DLB-43
Nimitmongkol Navarat, M.R.
  1908-1948 .... DLB-348
Nims, John Frederick 1913-1999 .... DLB-5
  Tribute to Nancy Hale Y-88
Nin, Anaïs 1903-1977 .... DLB-2, 4, 152

Nína Björk Árnadóttir 1941-2000 .... DLB-293
Niño, Raúl 1961- DLB-209
Nissenson, Hugh 1933- DLB-28, 335
Der Nister (Pinchas Kahanovitch [Pinkhes
  Kahanovitsh]) 1884-1950 .... DLB-333
Niven, Frederick John 1878-1944 .... DLB-92
Niven, Larry 1938- DLB-8
Nixon, Howard M. 1909-1983 .... DLB-201
Nizan, Paul 1905-1940 .... DLB-72
Njegoš, Petar II Petrović
  1813-1851 ....DLB-147; CDWLB-4
Nkosi, Lewis 1936- DLB-157, 225
Noah, Mordecai M. 1785-1851 .... DLB-250
Noailles, Anna de 1876-1933 .... DLB-258
Nobel Peace Prize
  The Nobel Prize and Literary Politics Y-88
  Elie Wiesel Y-86
Nobel Prize in Literature
  Shmuel Yosef Agnon DLB-329
  Vicente Aleixandre DLB-108, 329
  Ivo Andrić DLB-147, 329; CDWLB-4
  Miguel Ángel Asturias DLB-113, 290,
                              329; CDWLB-3
  Samuel Beckett DLB-13, 15, 233, 319,
                         321, 329; Y-90; CDBLB-7
  Saul Bellow DLB-2, 28, 299, 329;
                              Y-82; DS-3; CDALB-1
  Jacinto Benavente DLB-329
  Henri Bergson DLB-329
  Bjørnstjerne Bjørnson DLB-329
  Heinrich Böll ...DLB-69, 329; Y-85; CDWLB-2
  Joseph Brodsky DLB-285, 329; Y-87
  Pearl S. Buck DLB-9, 102, 329; CDALB-7
  Ivan Bunin DLB-317, 329
  Albert Camus DLB-72, 321, 329
  Elias Canetti DLB-85, 124, 329; CDWLB-2
  Giosuè Carducci DLB-329
  Camilo José Cela DLB-322, 329; Y-89
  Sir Winston Churchill DLB-100, 329;
                                  DS-16; CDBLB-5
  J. M. Coetzee DLB-225, 326, 329
  Grazia Deledda DLB-264, 329
  Jose Echegaray DLB-329
  T. S. Eliot DLB-7, 10, 45, 63, 245, 329;
                                   Y-88, 99; CDALB-5
  Odysseus Elytis DLB-329
  Rudolf Eucken DLB-329
  William Faulkner DLB-9, 11, 44, 102, 316,
                              330; DS-2; Y-86; CDALB-5
  Dario Fo DLB-330; Y-97
  Anatole France DLB-123, 330
  John Galsworthy DLB-10, 34, 98, 162,
                              330; DS-16; CDBLB-5
  Gao Xingjian DLB-330; Y-00
  Gabriel García Márquez DLB-13,
                              330; Y-82; CDWLB-3
  André Gide DLB-65, 321, 330

388

Karl Gjellerup DLB-300, 330
William Golding DLB-15, 100, 255, 326, 330; Y-83; CDBLB-7
Nadine Gordimer DLB-225, 326, 330; Y-91
Günter Grass DLB-75, 124, 330; Y-99
Halldór Laxness DLB-293, 331
Knut Hamsun DLB-297, 330
Gerhart Hauptmann DLB-66, 118, 330; CDWLB-2
Seamus Heaney DLB-40, 330; Y-95; CDBLB-8
Verner von Heidenstam DLB-330
Ernest Hemingway DLB-4, 9, 102, 210, 316, 330; Y-81, 87, 99; DS-1, 15, 16; CDALB-4
Hermann Hesse DLB-66, 330; CDWLB-2
Paul Heyse DLB-129, 330
Elfriede Jelinek DLB-85, 330
Johannes V. Jensen DLB-214, 330
Juan Ramón Jiménez DLB-134, 330
Eyvind Johnson DLB-259, 330
Erik Axel Karlfeldt DLB-330
Yasunari Kawabata DLB-180, 330
Imre Kertész DLB-299, 330; Y-02
Rudyard Kipling DLB-19, 34, 141, 156, 330; CDBLB-5
Pär Lagerkvist DLB-259, 331
Selma Lagerlöf DLB-259, 331
Sinclair Lewis
. . . . . . .DLB-9, 102, 331; DS-1; CDALB-4
Maurice Maeterlinck DLB-192, 331
Najīb Mahfūz Y-88, 331; Y-88
Thomas Mann DLB-66, 331; CDWLB-2
Roger Martin du Gard DLB-65, 331
Harry Martinson DLB-259, 331
François Mauriac DLB-65, 331
Czesław Miłosz DLB-215, 331; CDWLB-4
Frédéric Mistral . . . . DLB-215, 331; D
Gabriela Mistral DLB-283, 331
Theodor Mommsen DLB-331
Eugenio Montale DLB-114, 331
Toni Morrison
. .DLB-6, 33, 143, 331; Y-81, 93; CDALB-6
V. S. Naipaul
. . . . DLB-125, 204, 207, 326, 331; Y-85, 01; CDBLB-8; CDWLB-3
Pablo Neruda DLB-283, 331
Kenzaburō Ōe DLB-182, 331; Y-94
Eugene O'Neill DLB-7, 331; CDALB-5
Boris Pasternak DLB-302, 331
Octavio Paz DLB-290, 331; Y-90, 98
Saint-John Perse DLB-258, 331
Harold Pinter . . .DLB-13, 310, 331; CDBLB-8
Luigi Pirandello DLB-264, 331
Henrik Pontoppidan DLB-300, 331
Salvatore Quasimodo DLB-114, 332
Władysław Stanisław Reymont DLB-332

Romain Rolland DLB-65, 332
Bertrand Russell DLB-100, 262, 332
Nelly Sachs DLB-332
José Saramago DLB-287, 332; Y-98
Jean-Paul Sartre DLB-72, 296, 321, 332
George Seferis DLB-332
Jaroslav Seifert
. . . . DLB-215, 332; Y-84; CDBLB-4
George Bernard Shaw
. . . . DLB-10, 57, 190, 332; CDBLB-6
Mikhail Aleksandrovich Sholokov
. . . . .DLB-272, 332
Henryk Sienkiewicz DLB-332
Frans Eemil Sillanpää DLB-332
Claude Simon DLB-83, 332; Y-85
Isaac Bashevis Singer
. . . .DLB-6, 28, 52, 278, 332; Y-91; CDALB-1
Aleksandr Solzhenitsyn DLB-302, 332
Wole Soyinka
. . . . . DLB-125, 332; Y-86, 87; CDWLB-3
Carl Spitteler DLB-129, 332
John Steinbeck
. . . . . DLB-7, 9, 212, 275, 309, 332; DS-2; CDALB-5
Sully Prudhomme DLB-332
Wisława Szymborska DLB-232, 332; Y-96; CDWLB-4
Rabindranath Tagore DLB-323, 332
Sigrid Undset DLB-297, 332
Derek Walcott
. . . . . DLB-117, 332; Y-81, 92; CDWLB-3
Patrick White DLB-260, 332
William Butler Yeats
. . . . . DLB-10, 19, 98, 156, 332; CDBLB-5
Nobre, António 1867-1900 . . . . .DLB-287
Nodier, Charles 1780-1844 . . . . .DLB-119
Noël, Marie (Marie Mélanie Rouget)
1883-1967 . . . . .DLB-258
Noel, Roden 1834-1894 . . . . .DLB-35
Nogami Yaeko 1885-1985 . . . . .DLB-180
Nogo, Rajko Petrov 1945- DLB-181
Nolan, William F. 1928- DLB-8
    Tribute to Raymond Chandler Y-88
Noland, C. F. M. 1810?-1858 . . . . .DLB-11
Noma Hiroshi 1915-1991 . . . . .DLB-182
Nonesuch Press DLB-112
Creative Nonfiction Y-02
Nonni (Jón Stefán Sveinsson or Svensson)
1857-1944 . . . . .DLB-293
Noon, Jeff 1957- DLB-267
Noonan, Robert Phillipe (see Tressell, Robert)
Noonday Press DLB-46
Noone, John 1936- DLB-14
Nora, Eugenio de 1923- DLB-134
Nordan, Lewis 1939- DLB-234, 350
Nordbrandt, Henrik 1945- DLB-214

Nordhoff, Charles 1887-1947 . . . . .DLB-9
Norén, Lars 1944- DLB-257
Norfolk, Lawrence 1963- DLB-267
Norman, Charles 1904-1996 . . . . .DLB-111
Norman, Marsha 1947- DLB-266; Y-84
Norris, Charles G. 1881-1945 . . . . .DLB-9
Norris, Frank
  1870-1902 . . . . . . .DLB-12, 71, 186; CDALB-3
Norris, Helen 1916- DLB-292
Norris, John 1657-1712 . . . . .DLB-252
Norris, Leslie 1921-2006 . . . . DLB-27, 256
Norse, Harold 1916-2009 . . . . .DLB-16
Norte, Marisela 1955- DLB-209
North, Marianne 1830-1890 . . . . .DLB-174
North, Roger 1651-1734 . . . . .DLB-336
North Point Press DLB-46
NorthSun, Nila 1951- DLB-342
Nortje, Arthur 1942-1970 . . . . .DLB-125, 225
Norton, Alice Mary (see Norton, Andre)
Norton, Andre 1912-2005 . . . . .DLB-8, 52
Norton, Andrews
  1786-1853 . . . . .DLB-1, 235; DS-5
Norton, Caroline
  1808-1877 . . . . .DLB-21, 159, 199
Norton, Charles Eliot
  1827-1908 . . . . .DLB-1, 64, 235
Norton, John 1606-1663 . . . . .DLB-24
Norton, Mary 1903-1992 . . . . .DLB-160
Norton, Thomas 1532-1584 . . . . .DLB-62
W. W. Norton and Company DLB-46
Norwood, Robert 1874-1932 . . . . .DLB-92
Nosaka Akiyuki 1930- DLB-182
Nossack, Hans Erich
  1901-1977 . . . . .DLB-69
Notker Balbulus circa 840-912 . . . . .DLB-148
Notker III of Saint Gall
  circa 950-1022 . . . . .DLB-148
Notker von Zweifalten ?-1095 . . . . .DLB-148
Nou Hach 1916-1975? DLB-348
Nourse, Alan E. 1928-1992 . . . . .DLB-8
Novak, Slobodan 1924- DLB-181
Novak, Vjenceslav 1859-1905 . . . . .DLB-147
Novakovich, Josip 1956- DLB-244
Novalis 1772-1801 . . . . DLB-90; CDWLB-2
Novaro, Mario 1868-1944 . . . . .DLB-114
Novás Calvo, Lino 1903-1983 . . . . .DLB-145
Novelists
  Library Journal Statements and
    Questionnaires from First Novelists Y-87
Novels
  The Columbia History of the American Novel
    A Symposium on Y-92
  The Great Modern Library Scam Y-98
  Novels for Grown-Ups Y-97

The Proletarian Novel DLB-9
Novel, The "Second-Generation" Holocaust
. . . . DLB-299
The Year in the Novel Y-87–88, Y-90–93
Novels, British
"The Break-Up of the Novel" (1922),
by John Middleton Murry DLB-36
The Consolidation of Opinion: Critical
Responses to the Modernists DLB-36
"Criticism in Relation to Novels"
(1863), by G. H. Lewes DLB-21
"Experiment in the Novel" (1929)
[excerpt], by John D. Beresford . . . DLB-36
"The Future of the Novel" (1899), by
Henry James DLB-18
The Gay Science (1866), by E. S. Dallas
[excerpt] DLB-21
A Haughty and Proud Generation
(1922), by Ford Madox Hueffer . . DLB-36
Literary Effects of World War II DLB-15
"Modern Novelists –Great and Small"
(1855), by Margaret Oliphant DLB-21
The Modernists (1932),
by Joseph Warren Beach DLB-36
A Note on Technique (1926), by
Elizabeth A. Drew [excerpts] DLB-36
Novel-Reading: *The Works of Charles
Dickens; The Works of W. Makepeace
Thackeray* (1879),
by Anthony Trollope DLB-21
Novels with a Purpose (1864), by
Justin M'Carthy DLB-21
"On Art in Fiction" (1838),
by Edward Bulwer. DLB-21
The Present State of the English Novel
(1892), by George Saintsbury DLB-18
Representative Men and Women:
A Historical Perspective on
the British Novel, 1930-1960 . . . . . DLB-15
"The Revolt" (1937), by Mary Colum
[excerpts] DLB-36
"Sensation Novels" (1863), by
H. L. Manse DLB-21
Sex, Class, Politics, and Religion [in
the British Novel, 1930-1959] DLB-15
Time and Western Man (1927),
by Wyndham Lewis [excerpts] . . . DLB-36
Noventa, Giacomo
1898-1960 . . . . DLB-114
Novikov, Nikolai Ivanovich
1744-1818 . . . . DLB-150
Novomeský, Laco 1904-1976 . . . . DLB-215
Nowlan, Alden 1933-1983 . . . . DLB-53
Nowra, Louis 1950- DLB-325
Noyes, Alfred 1880-1958 . . . . DLB-20
Noyes, Crosby S. 1825-1908 . . . . DLB-23
Noyes, Nicholas 1647-1717 . . . . DLB-24
Noyes, Theodore W. 1858-1946 . . . . DLB-29
Nozick, Robert 1938-2002 . . . . DLB-279
N-Town Plays circa 1468 to early
sixteenth century DLB-146
Nugent, Frank 1908-1965 . . . . DLB-44

Nunez, Sigrid 1951- DLB-312
Nušić, Branislav
1864-1938 . . . . DLB-147; CDWLB-4
David Nutt [publishing house] DLB-106
Nwapa, Flora
1931-1993 . . . . DLB-125; CDWLB-3
Nye, Edgar Wilson (Bill)
1850-1896 . . . . DLB-11, 23, 186
Nye, Naomi Shihab 1952- DLB-120
Nye, Robert 1939- DLB-14, 271
Nyka-Niliūnas, Alfonsas 1919- DLB-220

O

Oakes, Urian circa 1631-1681 . . . . DLB-24
Oakes Smith, Elizabeth
1806-1893 . . . . DLB-1, 239, 243
Oakley, Violet 1874-1961 . . . . DLB-188
Oates, Joyce Carol 1938-
. . . . DLB-2, 5, 130; Y-81; CDALB-6
Tribute to Michael M. Rea. Y-97
Ōba Minako 1930- DLB-182
Ober, Frederick Albion 1849-1913 . . . . . DLB-189
Ober, William 1920-1993 . . . . Y-93
Oberholtzer, Ellis Paxson 1868-1936 . . . . . DLB-47
The Obituary as Literary Form Y-02
Obradović, Dositej 1740?-1811 . . . . DLB-147
Obstfelder, Sigbjørn 1866-1900 . . . . DLB-354
O'Brien, Charlotte Grace 1845-1909 . . . . DLB-240
O'Brien, Edna
1932- DLB-14, 231, 319; CDBLB-8
O'Brien, Fitz-James 1828-1862 . . . . DLB-74
O'Brien, Flann (see O'Nolan, Brian)
O'Brien, Kate 1897-1974 . . . . DLB-15
O'Brien, Tim
1946- DLB-152; Y-80; DS-9; CDALB-7
Ó Cadhain, Máirtín 1905-1970 . . . . DLB-319
O'Casey, Sean 1880-1964 . . . . . DLB-10; CDBLB-6
Occom, Samson 1723-1792 . . . . DLB-175
Occomy, Marita Bonner 1899-1971 . . . . . DLB-51
Ochs, Adolph S. 1858-1935 . . . . DLB-25
Ochs-Oakes, George Washington
1861-1931 . . . . DLB-137
Ockley, Simon 1678-1720 . . . . DLB-336
O'Connor, Flannery 1925-1964
. . . . DLB-2, 152; Y-80; DS-12; CDALB-1
The Flannery O'Connor Society Y-99
O'Connor, Frank 1903-1966 . . . . DLB-162
O'Connor, Joseph 1963- DLB-267
O'Conor, Charles, of Belanagare
1709/1710-1791 . . . . DLB-336
Octopus Publishing Group DLB-112
Oda Sakunosuke 1913-1947 . . . . DLB-182
Odell, Jonathan 1737-1818 . . . . DLB-31, 99
O'Dell, Scott 1903-1989 . . . . DLB-52

Odets, Clifford 1906-1963 . . . . DLB-7, 26
Odhams Press Limited DLB-112
Odio, Eunice 1922-1974 . . . . DLB-283
Odoevsky, Aleksandr Ivanovich
1802-1839 . . . . DLB-205
Odoevsky, Vladimir Fedorovich
1804 or 1803-1869 . . . . DLB-198
Odoevtseva, Irina 1895-1990 . . . . DLB-317
O'Donnell, Peter 1920- DLB-87
O'Donovan, Michael (see O'Connor, Frank)
O'Dowd, Bernard 1866-1953 . . . . DLB-230
Ōe, Kenzaburō 1935- DLB-182, 331; Y-94
Nobel Lecture 1994: Japan, the
Ambiguous, and Myself Y-94
Oehlenschläger, Adam 1779-1850 . . . . . . DLB-300
O'Faolain, Julia 1932- DLB-14, 231, 319
O'Faolain, Sean 1900-1991 . . . . DLB-15, 162
Off-Loop Theatres DLB-7
Offord, Carl Ruthven 1910-1990 . . . . DLB-76
Offshore, 1979 Booker Prize winner,
Penelope Fitzgerald DLB-326
Offutt, Chris 1958- DLB-335
O'Flaherty, Liam 1896-1984 . . . . DLB-36, 162; Y-84
Ogarev, Nikolai Platonovich 1813-1877 . . . DLB-277
J. S. Ogilvie and Company DLB-49
Ogilvy, Eliza 1822-1912 . . . . DLB-199
Ogot, Grace 1930- DLB-125
O'Grady, Desmond 1935- DLB-40
Ogunyemi, Wale 1939- DLB-157
O'Hagan, Howard 1902-1982 . . . . DLB-68
O'Halloran, Sylvester 1728-1807 . . . . DLB-336
O'Hara, Frank 1926-1966 . . . . DLB-5, 16, 193
O'Hara, John
1905-1970 . . . DLB-9, 86, 324; DS-2; CDALB-5
John O'Hara's Pottsville Journalism Y-88
O'Hare, Kate Richards 1876-1948 . . . . . . DLB-303
O'Hegarty, P. S. 1879-1955. . . . . DLB-201
Ohio State University
The William Charvat American Fiction
Collection at the Ohio State
University Libraries Y-92
Okada, John 1923-1971 . . . . DLB-312
Okara, Gabriel 1921- DLB-125; CDWLB-3
O'Keeffe, John 1747-1833 . . . . DLB-89
Nicholas Okes [publishing house] DLB-170
Okigbo, Christopher
1930-1967 . . . . DLB-125; CDWLB-3
Okot p'Bitek 1931-1982 . . . . . DLB-125; CDWLB-3
Okpewho, Isidore 1941- DLB-157
Okri, Ben 1959- DLB-157, 231, 319, 326
Ólafur Jóhann Sigurðsson 1918-1988 . . . . DLB-293
The Old Devils, 1986 Booker Prize winner,
Kingsley Amis DLB-326

Old Dogs / New Tricks? New Technologies, the Canon, and the Structure of the Profession Y-02

Old Franklin Publishing House DLB-49

Old German Genesis and *Old German Exodus* circa 1050-circa 1130. . . . . .DLB-148

The *Old High German Isidor* circa 790-800 . . . . DLB-148

Older, Fremont 1856-1935. . . . . .DLB-25

Oldham, John 1653-1683. . . . . DLB-131

Oldman, C. B. 1894-1969 . . . . DLB-201

Oldmixon, John 1673?-1742. . . . . DLB-336

Olds, Bruce 1951- DLB-350

Olds, Sharon 1942- DLB-120

Olearius, Adam 1599-1671 . . . . DLB-164

O'Leary, Ellen 1831-1889 . . . . .DLB-240

O'Leary, Juan E. 1879-1969 . . . . DLB-290

Olesha, Iurii Karlovich 1899-1960. . . . . . . DLB-272

Oliphant, Laurence 1829?-1888. . . . . . DLB-18, 166

Oliphant, Margaret 1828-1897. . . DLB-18, 159, 190

"Modern Novelists–Great and Small" (1855) DLB-21

Oliveira, Carlos de 1921-1981 . . . . .DLB-287

Oliver, Chad 1928-1993. . . . . DLB-8

Oliver, Mary 1935- DLB-5, 193, 342

Ollier, Claude 1922- DLB-83

Olsen, Tillie 1912/1913-2007 . . . . DLB-28, 206; Y-80; CDALB-7

Olson, Charles 1910-1970 . . . . DLB-5, 16, 193

Olson, Elder 1909-1992. . . . . DLB-48, 63

Olson, Sigurd F. 1899-1982 . . . . DLB-275

The Omega Workshops. DS-10

Omotoso, Kole 1943- DLB-125

Omulevsky, Innokentii Vasil'evich 1836 [or 1837]-1883 . . . . DLB-238

Ondaatje, Michael 1943- DLB-60, 323, 326

O'Neill, Eugene 1888-1953 . . . . DLB-7, 331; CDALB-5

Eugene O'Neill Memorial Theater Center. DLB-7

Eugene O'Neill's Letters: A Review Y-88

Onetti, Juan Carlos 1909-1994 . . . . DLB-113; CDWLB-3

Onions, George Oliver 1872-1961 . . . . DLB-153

Õnnepalu, Tõnu (Emil Tode, Anton Nigov) 1962- DLB-353

Onofri, Arturo 1885-1928 . . . . .DLB-114

O'Nolan, Brian 1911-1966. . . . . DLB-231

Oodgeroo of the Tribe Noonuccal (Kath Walker) 1920-1993 . . . . .DLB-289

Opesan, Ola (Gbenga Agbenugba) 1966- DLB-347

Opie, Amelia 1769-1853. . . . . DLB-116, 159

Opitz, Martin 1597-1639 . . . . DLB-164

Oppen, George 1908-1984. . . . . .DLB-5, 165

Oppenheim, E. Phillips 1866-1946 . . . . . . .DLB-70

Oppenheim, James 1882-1932. . . . . .DLB-28

Oppenheimer, Joel 1930-1988 . . . . . . .DLB-5, 193

Optic, Oliver (see Adams, William Taylor)

Orczy, Emma, Baroness 1865-1947 . . . . . . .DLB-70

Oregon Shakespeare Festival Y-00

Origo, Iris 1902-1988. . . . . DLB-155

O'Riordan, Kate 1960- DLB-267

Orlovitz, Gil 1918-1973 . . . . .DLB-2, 5

Orlovsky, Peter 1933- DLB-16

Ormond, John 1923-1990 . . . . .DLB-27

Ornitz, Samuel 1890-1957 . . . . DLB-28, 44

O'Rourke, P. J. 1947- DLB-185

Orozco, Olga 1920-1999 . . . . .DLB-283

Orten, Jiří 1919-1941 . . . . DLB-215

Ortese, Anna Maria 1914-1998 . . . . DLB-177

Ortiz, Lourdes 1943- DLB-322

Ortiz, Simon J. 1941- . . . DLB-120, 175, 256, 342

Ortnit and *Wolfdietrich* circa 1225-1250. . . . . DLB-138

Orton, Joe 1933-1967. . . . . DLB-13, 310; CDBLB-8

Orwell, George (Eric Arthur Blair) 1903-1950 . . . DLB-15, 98, 195, 255; CDBLB-7

The Orwell Year Y-84

(Re-)Publishing Orwell Y-86

Ory, Carlos Edmundo de 1923- DLB-134

Osbey, Brenda Marie 1957- DLB-120

Osbon, B. S. 1827-1912 . . . . DLB-43

Osborn, Sarah 1714-1796. . . . . DLB-200

Osborne, John 1929-1994 . . . . . DLB-13; CDBLB-7

Oscar and Lucinda, 1988 Booker Prize winner, Peter Carey DLB-326

Osgood, Frances Sargent 1811-1850 . . . . . DLB-250

Osgood, Herbert L. 1855-1918 . . . . DLB-47

James R. Osgood and Company DLB-49

Osgood, McIlvaine and Company. DLB-112

O'Shaughnessy, Arthur 1844-1881 . . . . DLB-35

Patrick O'Shea [publishing house] DLB-49

Osipov, Nikolai Petrovich 1751-1799 . . . . .DLB-150

Oskison, John Milton 1879-1947 . . . . DLB-175

Osler, Sir William 1849-1919. . . . . DLB-184

Osofisan, Femi 1946- DLB-125; CDWLB-3

Ostenso, Martha 1900-1963. . . . . .DLB-92

Ostlere, Gordon Stanley (see Gordon, Richard)

Ostrauskas, Kostas 1926- DLB-232

Ostriker, Alicia 1937- DLB-120

Ostrovsky, Aleksandr Nikolaevich 1823-1886 . . . . DLB-277

Ostrovsky, Nikolai Alekseevich 1904-1936 . . . . DLB-272

Osundare, Niyi 1947- DLB-157; CDWLB-3

Oswald, Eleazer 1755-1795 . . . . DLB-43

Oswald von Wolkenstein 1376 or 1377-1445 . . . . DLB-179

Otero, Blas de 1916-1979. . . . . .DLB-134

Otero, Miguel Antonio 1859-1944. . . . . . . .DLB-82

Otero, Nina 1881-1965 . . . . .DLB-209

Otero Silva, Miguel 1908-1985 . . . . .DLB-145

Otfried von Weißenburg circa 800-circa 875? DLB-148

Otis, Broaders and Company DLB-49

Otis, James (see Kaler, James Otis)

Otis, James, Jr. 1725-1783. . . . . DLB-31

Otsup, Nikolai 1894-1958 . . . . DLB-317

Ottaway, James 1911-2000. . . . . DLB-127

Ottendorfer, Oswald 1826-1900 . . . . .DLB-23

Ottieri, Ottiero 1924-2002 . . . . DLB-177

Otto-Peters, Louise 1819-1895. . . . . .DLB-129

Otway, Thomas 1652-1685 . . . . DLB-80

Ouellette, Fernand 1930- DLB-60

Ouida 1839-1908. . . . . DLB-18, 156

Outing Publishing Company DLB-46

Overbury, Sir Thomas circa 1581-1613 . . . . DLB-151

The Overlook Press. DLB-46

Ovid 43 B.C.-A.D. 17 . . . . DLB-211; CDWLB-1

Oviedo, Gonzalo Fernández de 1478-1557 . . . . DLB-318

Owen, Guy 1925-1981 . . . . .DLB-5

Owen, John 1564-1622 . . . . DLB-121

John Owen [publishing house]. DLB-49

Peter Owen Limited. DLB-112

Owen, Robert 1771-1858 . . . . DLB-107, 158

Owen, Wilfred 1893-1918 . . . . .DLB-20; DS-18; CDBLB-6

A Centenary Celebration Y-93

The Wilfred Owen Association. Y-98

The Owl and the Nightingale circa 1189-1199 . . . . DLB-146

Owsley, Frank L. 1890-1956 . . . . DLB-17

Oxenford, John 1812-1877. . . . . .DLB-344

Oxford, Seventeenth Earl of, Edward de Vere 1550-1604 . . . . DLB-172

OyamO (Charles F. Gordon) 1943- DLB-266

Ozerov, Vladislav Aleksandrovich 1769-1816 . . . . DLB-150

Ozick, Cynthia 1928- DLB-28, 152, 299; Y-82

First Strauss "Livings" Awarded to Cynthia Ozick and Raymond Carver An Interview with Cynthia Ozick. Y-83

Tribute to Michael M. Rea Y-97

P

Pace, Richard 1482?-1536 . . . . DLB-167

Pacey, Desmond 1917-1975............. DLB-88
Pacheco, José Emilio 1939-........ DLB-290
Pack, Robert 1929-................. DLB-5
Paddy Clarke Ha Ha Ha, 1993 Booker Prize winner, Roddy Doyle.................. DLB-326
Padell Publishing Company........... DLB-46
Padgett, Ron 1942-................. DLB-5
Padilla, Ernesto Chávez 1944-...... DLB-122
L. C. Page and Company............. DLB-49
Page, Louise 1955-................. DLB-233
Page, P. K. 1916-.................. DLB-68
Page, Thomas Nelson 1853-1922...............DLB-12, 78; DS-13
Page, Walter Hines 1855-1918....... DLB-71, 91
Paget, Francis Edward 1806-1882...... DLB-163
Paget, Violet (see Lee, Vernon)
Pagliarani, Elio 1927-............. DLB-128
Pagnol, Marcel 1895-1974........... DLB-321
Pain, Barry 1864-1928..............DLB-135, 197
Pain, Philip ?-circa 1666.......... DLB-24
Paine, Robert Treat, Jr. 1773-1811....... DLB-37
Paine, Thomas 1737-1809.... DLB-31, 43, 73, 158; CDALB-2
Painter, George D. 1914-2005......... DLB-155
Painter, William 1540?-1594.......... DLB-136
Palazzeschi, Aldo 1885-1974....... DLB-114, 264
Palei, Marina Anatol'evna 1955-..... DLB-285
Palencia, Alfonso de 1424-1492..... DLB-286
Palés Matos, Luis 1898-1959....... DLB-290
Paley, Grace 1922-2007............ DLB-28, 218
Paley, William 1743-1805........... DLB-252
Palfrey, John Gorham 1796-1881.................. DLB-1, 30, 235
Palgrave, Francis Turner 1824-1897...... DLB-35
Palin, Michael 1943-............... DLB-352
Palissy, Bernard 1510?-1590?......... DLB-327
Palmer, Joe H. 1904-1952............DLB-171
Palmer, Michael 1943-.............. DLB-169
Palmer, Nettie 1885-1964........... DLB-260
Palmer, Vance 1885-1959............ DLB-260
Paltock, Robert 1697-1767.......... DLB-39
Paludan, Jacob 1896-1975........... DLB-214
Paludin-Müller, Frederik 1809-1876...... DLB-300
Pan Books Limited................. DLB-112
Panaev, Ivan Ivanovich 1812-1862..... DLB-198
Panaeva, Avdot'ia Iakovlevna 1820-1893................. DLB-238
Panama, Norman 1914-2003 and Frank, Melvin 1913-1988.......... DLB-26
Pancake, Breece D'J 1952-1979...... DLB-130
Panduro, Leif 1923-1977............ DLB-214
Pane, Armijn 1908-1970............. DLB-348

Panero, Leopoldo 1909-1962......... DLB-108
Pangborn, Edgar 1909-1976.......... DLB-8
Panizzi, Sir Anthony 1797-1879........ DLB-184
Panneton, Philippe (see Ringuet)
Panova, Vera Fedorovna 1905-1973..... DLB-302
Panshin, Alexei 1940-.............. DLB-8
Pansy (see Alden, Isabella)
Pantheon Books.................... DLB-46
Papadat-Bengescu, Hortensia 1876-1955..................... DLB-220
Papantonio, Michael 1907-1976........ DLB-187
Paperback Library................. DLB-46
Paperback Science Fiction.............. DLB-8
Papini, Giovanni 1881-1956........... DLB-264
Paquet, Alfons 1881-1944............. DLB-66
Paracelsus 1493-1541...............DLB-179
Paradis, Suzanne 1936-............. DLB-53
Páral, Vladimír, 1932-............. DLB-232
Pardoe, Julia 1804-1862............. DLB-166
Paré, Ambroise 1510 or 1517?-1590..... DLB-327
Paredes, Américo 1915-1999......... DLB-209
Pareja Diezcanseco, Alfredo 1908-1993.. DLB-145
Parents' Magazine Press............. DLB-46
Paretsky, Sara 1947-............... DLB-306
Parfit, Derek 1942-................ DLB-262
Parise, Goffredo 1929-1986.............DLB-177
Parish, Mitchell 1900-1993........... DLB-265
Parizeau, Alice 1930-1990.......... DLB-60
Park, Ruth 1923?-.................. DLB-260
Parke, John 1754-1789.............. DLB-31
Parker, Dan 1893-1967.............. DLB-241
Parker, Dorothy 1893-1967...... DLB-11, 45, 86
Parker, Gilbert 1860-1932........... DLB-99
Parker, James 1714-1770............. DLB-43
Parker, John [publishing house]........ DLB-106
Parker, Matthew 1504-1575........... DLB-213
Parker, Robert B. 1932-............ DLB-306
Parker, Stewart 1941-1988........... DLB-245
Parker, Theodore 1810-1860 ... DLB-1, 235; DS-5
Parker, William Riley 1906-1968..... DLB-103
J. H. Parker [publishing house]........ DLB-106
Parkes, Bessie Rayner (Madame Belloc) 1829-1925..................... DLB-240
Parkman, Francis 1823-1893.........DLB-1, 30, 183, 186, 235
Parks, Gordon 1912-2006............. DLB-33
Parks, Suzan-Lori 1964-........... DLB-341
Parks, Tim 1954-................... DLB-231
Parks, William 1698-1750........... DLB-43
William Parks [publishing house]........ DLB-49
Parley, Peter (see Goodrich, Samuel Griswold)

Parmenides late sixth-fifth century B.C. DLB-176
Parnell, Thomas 1679-1718........... DLB-95
Parnicki, Teodor 1908-1988.......... DLB-215
Parnok, Sofiia Iakovlevna (Parnokh) 1885-1933................. DLB-295
Parr, Catherine 1513?-1548........... DLB-136
Parra, Nicanor 1914-............... DLB-283
Parrington, Vernon L. 1871-1929...... DLB-17, 63
Parrish, Maxfield 1870-1966........ DLB-188
Parronchi, Alessandro 1914-........ DLB-128
Parshchikov, Aleksei Maksimovich (Raiderman) 1954-............. DLB-285
Parsons, Albert R. 1848-1887......... DLB-345
Parsons, Lucy E. 1853?-1942......... DLB-345
Partisan Review................... DLB-303
Parton, James 1822-1891............ DLB-30
Parton, Sara Payson Willis 1811-1872................DLB-43, 74, 239
S. W. Partridge and Company......... DLB-106
Parun, Vesna 1922- DLB-181; CDWLB-4
Pascal, Blaise 1623-1662.............DLB-268
Pasinetti, Pier Maria 1913-2006.........DLB-177
  Tribute to Albert Erskine............. Y-93
Pasolini, Pier Paolo 1922-1975......DLB-128, 177
Pastan, Linda 1932-................ DLB-5
Pasternak, Boris 1890-1960.................. DLB-302, 331
Paston, George (Emily Morse Symonds) 1860-1936.................DLB-149, 197
The Paston Letters 1422-1509.......... DLB-146
Pastoral Novel of the Sixteenth Century, The........................... DLB-318
Pastorius, Francis Daniel 1651-circa 1720.................. DLB-24
Patchen, Kenneth 1911-1972......... DLB-16, 48
Patchett, Ann 1963-............... DLB-350
Pater, Walter 1839-1894...DLB-57, 156; CDBLB-4
  Aesthetic Poetry (1873)............. DLB-35
  "Style" (1888) [excerpt]............ DLB-57
Paterson, A. B. "Banjo" 1864-1941...... DLB-230
Paterson, Katherine 1932-........... DLB-52
Patmore, Coventry 1823-1896....... DLB-35, 98
Paton, Alan 1903-1988..........DLB-225; DS-17
Paton, Joseph Noel 1821-1901......... DLB-35
Paton Walsh, Jill 1937-............. DLB-161
Patrick, Edwin Hill ("Ted") 1901-1964....DLB-137
Patrick, John 1906-1995............. DLB-7
Patrick, Robert 1937-.............. DLB-341
Pattee, Fred Lewis 1863-1950......... DLB-71
Patterson, Alicia 1906-1963..........DLB-127
Patterson, Eleanor Medill 1881-1948..... DLB-29
Patterson, Eugene 1923-............DLB-127
Patterson, Joseph Medill 1879-1946...... DLB-29

Pattillo, Henry 1726-1801 . . . . DLB-37

Paul, Elliot 1891-1958 . . . . DLB-4; DS-15

Paul, Jean (see Richter, Johann Paul Friedrich)

Paul, Kegan, Trench, Trubner and
    Company Limited DLB-106

Peter Paul Book Company DLB-49

Stanley Paul and Company Limited DLB-112

Paulding, James Kirke
    1778-1860 . . . . DLB-3, 59, 74, 250

Paulin, Tom 1949- DLB-40

Pauper, Peter, Press DLB-46

Paustovsky, Konstantin Georgievich
    1892-1968 . . . . DLB-272

Pavese, Cesare 1908-1950 . . . . DLB-128, 177

Pavić, Milorad 1929- DLB-181; CDWLB-4

Pavlov, Konstantin 1933- DLB-181

Pavlov, Nikolai Filippovich 1803-1864 . . . . . DLB-198

Pavlova, Karolina Karlovna 1807-1893 . . . . . DLB-205

Pavlović, Miodrag
    1928- DLB-181; CDWLB-4

Pavlovsky, Eduardo 1933- DLB-305

Paxton, John 1911-1985 . . . . DLB-44

Payn, James 1830-1898 . . . . DLB-18

Payne, John 1842-1916 . . . . DLB-35

Payne, John Howard 1791-1852 . . . . DLB-37

Payson and Clarke DLB-46

Paz, Octavio 1914-1998 . . . DLB-290, 331; Y-90, 98

    Nobel Lecture 1990 . . . . Y-90

Pazzi, Roberto 1946- DLB-196

Pea, Enrico 1881-1958 . . . . DLB-264

Peabody, Elizabeth Palmer
    1804-1894 . . . . DLB-1, 223

    Preface to *Record of a School:
    Exemplifying the General Principles
    of Spiritual Culture* DS-5

Elizabeth Palmer Peabody
    [publishing house] DLB-49

Peabody, Josephine Preston 1874-1922 . . . DLB-249

Peabody, Oliver William Bourn
    1799-1848 . . . . DLB-59

Peace, Roger 1899-1968 . . . . DLB-127

Peacham, Henry 1578-1644? DLB-151

Peacham, Henry, the Elder
    1547-1634 . . . . DLB-172, 236

Peachtree Publishers, Limited DLB-46

Peacock, Molly 1947- DLB-120

Peacock, Thomas Love 1785-1866 . . . . DLB-96, 116

Pead, Deuel ?-1727 . . . . DLB-24

Peake, Mervyn 1911-1968 . . . . . . DLB-15, 160, 255

Peake, Richard Brinsley 1792-1847 . . . . . . DLB-344

Peale, Rembrandt 1778-1860 . . . . DLB-183

Pear Tree Press DLB-112

Pearce, Donn 1928- DLB-350

Pearce, Philippa 1920-2006 . . . . DLB-161

H. B. Pearson [publishing house] DLB-49

Pearson, Hesketh 1887-1964 . . . . DLB-149

Peattie, Donald Culross 1898-1964 . . . . . . DLB-275

Pechersky, Andrei (see Mel'nikov, Pavel Ivanovich)

Peck, George W. 1840-1916 . . . . DLB-23, 42

H. C. Peck and Theo. Bliss
    [publishing house] DLB-49

Peck, Harry Thurston 1856-1914 . . . . . DLB-71, 91

Peden, William 1913-1999 . . . . DLB-234

    Tribute to William Goyen Y-83

Peele, George 1556-1596 . . . . DLB-62, 167

Pegler, Westbrook 1894-1969 . . . . DLB-171

Péguy, Charles 1873-1914 . . . . DLB-258

Peirce, Charles Sanders 1839-1914 . . . . . . DLB-270

Pekić, Borislav 1930-1992 . . . DLB-181; CDWLB-4

Pelecanos, George P. 1957- DLB-306

Peletier du Mans, Jacques 1517-1582 . . . . . DLB-327

Pelevin, Viktor Olegovich 1962- DLB-285

Pellegrini and Cudahy DLB-46

Pelletier, Aimé (see Vac, Bertrand)

Pelletier, Cathie 1953- DLB-350

Pelletier, Francine 1959- DLB-251

Pellicer, Carlos 1897?-1977 . . . . DLB-290

Pemberton, Sir Max 1863-1950 . . . . DLB-70

de la Peña, Terri 1947- DLB-209

Penfield, Edward 1866-1925 . . . . DLB-188

Penguin Books [U.K.] DLB-112

    Fifty Penguin Years Y-85

    Penguin Collectors' Society Y-98

Penguin Books [U.S.] DLB-46

Penn, William 1644-1718 . . . . DLB-24

Penn Publishing Company DLB-49

Penna, Sandro 1906-1977 . . . . DLB-114

Pennell, Joseph 1857-1926 . . . . DLB-188

Penner, Jonathan 1940- Y-83

Pennington, Lee 1939- Y-82

Penton, Brian 1904-1951 . . . . DLB-260

Pepper, Stephen C. 1891-1972 . . . . DLB-270

Pepys, Samuel
    1633-1703 . . . . DLB-101, 213; CDBLB-2

Percy, Thomas 1729-1811 . . . . DLB-104

Percy, Walker 1916-1990 . . . . DLB-2; Y-80, 90

    Tribute to Caroline Gordon Y-81

Percy, William 1575-1648 . . . . DLB-172

Perec, Georges 1936-1982 . . . . DLB-83, 299

Perelman, Bob 1947- DLB-193

Perelman, S. J. 1904-1979 . . . . DLB-11, 44

Peretz, Isaac Leib (Yitskhok Leybush Perets)
    1852-1915 . . . . DLB-333

Perez, Raymundo "Tigre" 1946- DLB-122

Pérez de Ayala, Ramón 1880-1962 . . . . . . DLB-322

Pérez de Guzmán, Fernán
    ca. 1377-ca. 1460 . . . . DLB-286

Pérez-Reverte, Arturo 1951- DLB-322

Peri Rossi, Cristina 1941- DLB-145, 290

Perkins, Eugene 1932- DLB-41

Perkins, Maxwell
    The Claims of Business and Literature:
    An Undergraduate Essay Y-01

Perkins, William 1558-1602 . . . . DLB-281

Perkoff, Stuart Z. 1930-1974 . . . . DLB-16

Perley, Moses Henry 1804-1862 . . . . DLB-99

Permabooks DLB-46

Perovsky, Aleksei Alekseevich
    (Antonii Pogorel'sky) 1787-1836 . . . . . DLB-198

Perrault, Charles 1628-1703 . . . . DLB-268

Perri, Henry 1561-1617 . . . . DLB-236

Perrin, Alice 1867-1934 . . . . DLB-156

Perruchi, Andrea 1651-1704 . . . . DLB-339

Perry, Anne 1938- DLB-276

Perry, Bliss 1860-1954 . . . . DLB-71

Perry, Eleanor 1915-1981 . . . . DLB-44

Perry, Henry (see Perri, Henry)

Perry, Matthew 1794-1858 . . . . DLB-183

Perry, Sampson 1747-1823 . . . . DLB-158

Pers, Ciro di 1599-1663 . . . . DLB-339

Perse, Saint-John 1887-1975 . . . . DLB-258, 331

Persius A.D. 34-A.D. 62 . . . . DLB-211

Perutz, Leo 1882-1957 . . . . DLB-81

Pesetsky, Bette 1932- DLB-130

Pessanha, Camilo 1867-1926 . . . . DLB-287

Pessoa, Fernando 1888-1935 . . . . DLB-287

Pestalozzi, Johann Heinrich 1746-1827 . . . . DLB-94

Peter, Laurence J. 1919-1990 . . . . DLB-53

Peter of Spain circa 1205-1277 . . . . DLB-115

Peterkin, Julia 1880-1961 . . . . DLB-9

Peters, Carl (see Kalu, Peter)

Peters, Ellis (Edith Pargeter)
    1913-1995 . . . . DLB-276

Peters, Lenrie 1932- DLB-117

Peters, Robert 1924- DLB-105

    "Foreword to *Ludwig of Baviria*" DLB-105

Petersham, Maud 1889-1971 and
    Petersham, Miska 1888-1960 . . . . DLB-22

Peterson, Charles Jacobs 1819-1887 . . . . . . DLB-79

Peterson, Len 1917-2008 . . . . DLB-88

Peterson, Levi S. 1933- DLB-206

Peterson, Louis 1922-1998 . . . . DLB-76

Peterson, T. B., and Brothers DLB-49

Petitclair, Pierre 1813-1860 . . . . DLB-99

Petrescu, Camil 1894-1957 . . . . DLB-220

Petronius circa A.D. 20-A.D. 66
    . . . . DLB-211; CDWLB-1

Petrov, Aleksandar 1938- DLB-181

Cumulative Index DLB 354

Petrov, Evgenii (Evgenii Petrovich Kataev)
1903-1942 .... DLB-272

Petrov, Gavriil 1730-1801 .... DLB-150

Petrov, Valeri 1920- DLB-181

Petrov, Vasilii Petrovich 1736-1799 ...... DLB-150

Petrović, Rastko
1898-1949 .... DLB-147; CDWLB-4

Petrus Alfonsi (Pedro Alfonso, Pierre Alphonse)
fl. 1106-circa 1125 .... DLB-337

Petrushevskaia, Liudmila Stefanovna
1938- DLB-285

Petruslied circa 854? DLB-148

Petry, Ann 1908-1997 .... DLB-76

Pettie, George circa 1548-1589 .... DLB-136

Pétur Gunnarsson 1947- DLB-293

Peyton, K. M. 1929- DLB-161

Pfaffe Konrad fl. circa 1172 .... DLB-148

Pfaffe Lamprecht fl. circa 1150 .... DLB-148

Pfeiffer, Emily 1827-1890 .... DLB-199

Pforzheimer, Carl H. 1879-1957 .... DLB-140

Phaedrus circa 18 B.C.-circa A.D. 50 ..... DLB-211

Phaer, Thomas 1510?-1560 .... DLB-167

Phaidon Press Limited DLB-112

Pham Thi Hoai 1960- DLB-348

Pharr, Robert Deane 1916-1992 .... DLB-33

Phelps, Elizabeth Stuart 1815-1852 ..... DLB-202

Phelps, Elizabeth Stuart 1844-1911 ... DLB-74, 221

Philander von der Linde
(see Mencke, Johann Burckhard)

Philby, H. St. John B. 1885-1960 ...... DLB-195

Philip, Marlene Nourbese 1947- ...DLB-157, 334

Philippe, Charles-Louis 1874-1909 ...... DLB-65

Philips, John 1676-1708 .... DLB-95

Philips, Katherine 1632-1664 .... DLB-131

Phillipps, Sir Thomas 1792-1872 ...... DLB-184

Phillips, Caryl 1958- DLB-157

Phillips, David Graham
1867-1911 .... DLB-9, 12, 303

Phillips, Jayne Anne 1952- DLB-292; Y-80

Tribute to Seymour Lawrence Y-94

Phillips, Mike 1941- DLB-347

Phillips, Robert 1938- DLB-105

"Finding, Losing, Reclaiming: A Note
on My Poems" DLB-105

Tribute to William Goyen Y-83

Phillips, Stephen 1864-1915 .... DLB-10

Phillips, Ulrich B. 1877-1934 .... DLB-17

Phillips, Wendell 1811-1884 .... DLB-235

Phillips, Willard 1784-1873 .... DLB-59

Phillips, William 1907-2002 .... DLB-137

Phillips, Sampson and Company DLB-49

Phillpotts, Adelaide Eden (Adelaide Ross)
1896-1993 .... DLB-191

Phillpotts, Eden 1862-1960...DLB-10, 70, 135, 153

Philo circa 20-15 B.C.-circa A.D. 50 .... DLB-176

Philosophical Dictionary, Voltaire......... DLB-314

Philosophical Library DLB-46

Philosophy
Eighteenth-Century Philosophical
Background................. DLB-31
Philosophic Thought in Boston DLB-235
Translators of the Twelfth Century:
Literary Issues Raised and
Impact Created DLB-115

Elihu Phinney [publishing house]........ DLB-49

Phoenix, John (see Derby, George Horatio)

PHYLON (Fourth Quarter, 1950),
The Negro in Literature:
The Current Scene................. DLB-76

Physiologus circa 1070-circa 1150......... DLB-148

П.O. (Pi O, Peter Oustabasides)
1951- DLB-325

Piccolo, Lucio 1903-1969 .... DLB-114

Pichette, Henri 1924-2000 .... DLB-321

Pickard, Tom 1946- DLB-40

William Pickering [publishing house].... DLB-106

Pickthall, Marjorie 1883-1922........... DLB-92

Picoult, Jodi 1966- DLB-292

Pictorial Printing Company DLB-49

Piel, Gerard 1915-2004................ DLB-137

"An Announcement to Our Readers,"
Gerard Piel's Statement in *Scientific
American* (April 1948) DLB-137

Pielmeier, John 1949- DLB-266

Piercy, Marge 1936- DLB-120, 227

Pierre, DBC 1961- DLB-326

Pierro, Albino 1916-1995 .... DLB-128

Pignotti, Lamberto 1926- DLB-128

Pike, Albert 1809-1891................ DLB-74

Pike, Zebulon Montgomery 1779-1813... DLB-183

Pillat, Ion 1891-1945................. DLB-220

Pil'niak, Boris Andreevich (Boris Andreevich
Vogau) 1894-1938 ....DLB-272

Pilon, Jean-Guy 1930- DLB-60

Pinar, Florencia fl. ca. late
fifteenth century.................. DLB-286

Pinckney, Eliza Lucas 1722-1793......... DLB-200

Pinckney, Josephine 1895-1957........... DLB-6

Pindar circa 518 B.C.-circa 438 B.C.
.....................DLB-176; CDWLB-1

Pindar, Peter (see Wolcot, John)

Pineda, Cecile 1942- DLB-209

Pinero, Arthur Wing 1855-1934..... DLB-10, 344

Piñero, Miguel 1946-1988............. DLB-266

Pinget, Robert 1919-1997 .... DLB-83

Pinkerton, John 1758-1825 .... DLB-336

Pinkney, Edward Coote
1802-1828 .... DLB-248

Pinnacle Books DLB-46

Piñon, Nélida 1935- DLB-145, 307

Pinski, David (Dovid Pinski)
1872-1959................. DLB-333

Pinsky, Robert 1940- Y-82
Reappointed Poet Laureate Y-98

Pinter, Harold 1930-2008
.... DLB-13, 310, 331; CDBLB-8
Writing for the Theatre DLB-13

Pinto, Fernão Mendes 1509/1511?-1583.. DLB-287

Piontek, Heinz 1925- DLB-75

Piozzi, Hester Lynch [Thrale]
1741-1821.................DLB-104, 142

Piper, H. Beam 1904-1964 .... DLB-8

Piper, Watty DLB-22

Pirandello, Luigi 1867-1936 .... DLB-264, 331

Pirckheimer, Caritas 1467-1532 ......DLB-179

Pirckheimer, Willibald 1470-1530........DLB-179

Pires, José Cardoso 1925-1998 .... DLB-287

Pisar, Samuel 1929- Y-83

Pisarev, Dmitrii Ivanovich 1840-1868.....DLB-277

Pisemsky, Aleksei Feofilaktovich
1821-1881 .... DLB-238

Pišťanek, Peter 1960- DLB-353

Pitkin, Timothy 1766-1847 .... DLB-30

Pitt, George Dibdin 1795-1855......... DLB-344

Pitter, Ruth 1897-1992 .... DLB-20

Pix, Mary 1666-1709 .... DLB-80

Pixerécourt, René Charles Guilbert de
1773-1844..................... DLB-192

Pizarnik, Alejandra 1936-1972 .... DLB-283

Plá, Josefina 1909-1999............. DLB-290

Plaatje, Sol T. 1876-1932.......... DLB-125, 225

Placzek, Joyce Maxtone Graham (see Struther, Jan)

Planchon, Roger 1931- DLB-321

Plante, David 1940- Y-83

Plantinga, Alvin 1932- DLB-279

Platen, August von 1796-1835 .... DLB-90

Plath, Sylvia
1932-1963 .... DLB-5, 6, 152; CDALB-1

Plato circa 428 B.C.-348-347 B.C.
.....................DLB-176; CDWLB-1

Plato, Ann 1824-?................. DLB-239

Platon 1737-1812.................... DLB-150

Platonov, Andrei Platonovich (Andrei
Platonovich Klimentev)
1899-1951 ....DLB-272

Platt, Charles 1945- DLB-261

Platt and Munk Company DLB-46

Plautus circa 254 B.C.-184 B.C.
.....................DLB-211; CDWLB-1

Playboy Press DLB-46

John Playford [publishing house] DLB-170

Der Pleier fl. circa 1250 .... DLB-138

Pleijel, Agneta 1940- DLB-257

Plenzdorf, Ulrich 1934- DLB-75

Pleshcheev, Aleksei Nikolaevich
   1825?-1893 . . . . DLB-277

Plessen, Elizabeth 1944- DLB-75

Pletnev, Petr Aleksandrovich
   1792-1865 . . . . DLB-205

Pliekšāne, Elza Rozenberga (see Aspazija)

Pliekšāns, Jānis (see Rainis, Jānis)

Plievier, Theodor 1892-1955 . . . . DLB-69

Plimpton, George 1927-2003 . . DLB-185, 241; Y-99

Pliny the Elder A.D. 23/24-A.D. 79 . . . . DLB-211

Pliny the Younger
   circa A.D. 61-A.D. 112 . . . . DLB-211

Plomer, William
   1903-1973 . . . . DLB-20, 162, 191, 225

Plotinus 204-270. . . . . DLB-176; CDWLB-1

Plowright, Teresa 1952- DLB-251

Plume, Thomas 1630-1704 . . . . DLB-213

Plumly, Stanley 1939- DLB-5, 193

Plumpp, Sterling D. 1940- DLB-41

Plunkett, James 1920-2003. . . . . DLB-14

Plutarch
   circa 46-circa 120. . . . . . . DLB-176; CDWLB-1

Plymell, Charles 1935- DLB-16

Pocket Books DLB-46

Pocock, Isaac 1782-1835. . . . . DLB-344

Podestá, José J. 1858-1937 . . . . DLB-305

Poe, Edgar Allan 1809-1849
   . . . . DLB-3, 59, 73, 74, 248; CDALB-2

   The Poe Studies Association Y-99

Poe, James 1921-1980 . . . . DLB-44

Poema de Alfonso XI (1348). DLB-337

Poema de Fernán González
   (between 1251 and 1258) DLB-337

The Poet Laureate of the United States Y-86

   Statements from Former Consultants
     in Poetry. Y-86

Poetry
   Aesthetic Poetry (1873) DLB-35

   A Century of Poetry, a Lifetime of
     Collecting: J. M. Edelstein's
     Collection of Twentieth-
     Century American Poetry. Y-02

   "Certain Gifts," by Betty Adcock DLB-105

   Concrete Poetry. DLB-307

   Contempo Caravan: Kites in a
     Windstorm Y-85

   "Contemporary Verse Story-telling,"
     by Jonathan Holden DLB-105

   "A Detail in a Poem," by Fred
     Chappell DLB-105

   "The English Renaissance of Art"
     (1908), by Oscar Wilde. DLB-35

   "Every Man His Own Poet; or,
     The Inspired Singer's Recipe
     Book" (1877), by
     H. W. Mallock DLB-35

   "Eyes Across Centuries: Contemporary
     Poetry and 'That Vision Thing,'"
     by Philip Dacey. DLB-105

   A Field Guide to Recent Schools
     of American Poetry. Y-86

   "Finding, Losing, Reclaiming:
     A Note on My Poems,
     by Robert Phillips" DLB-105

   "The Fleshly School of Poetry and Other
     Phenomena of the Day" (1872). . . . DLB-35

   "The Fleshly School of Poetry:
     Mr. D. G. Rossetti" (1871) DLB-35

   The G. Ross Roy Scottish Poetry Collection
     at the University of South Carolina . . . Y-89

   "Getting Started: Accepting the Regions
     You Own–or Which Own You,"
     by Walter McDonald DLB-105

   "The Good, The Not So Good," by
     Stephen Dunn. DLB-105

   The Griffin Poetry Prize Y-00

   The Hero as Poet. Dante; Shakspeare
     (1841), by Thomas Carlyle. DLB-32

   "Images and 'Images,'" by Charles
     Simic. DLB-105

   "Into the Mirror," by Peter Cooley . . . DLB-105

   "Knots into Webs: Some Autobiographical
     Sources," by Dabney Stuart DLB-105

   "L'Envoi" (1882), by Oscar Wilde DLB-35

   "Living in Ruin," by Gerald Stern. . . . DLB-105

   Looking for the Golden Mountain:
     Poetry Reviewing Y-89

   Lyric Poetry (French). DLB-268

   Medieval Galician-Portuguese
     Poetry. DLB-287

   "The No Self, the Little Self, and the
     Poets," by Richard Moore. DLB-105

   On Some of the Characteristics of Modern
     Poetry and On the Lyrical Poems of
     Alfred Tennyson (1831) DLB-32

   The Pitt Poetry Series: Poetry Publishing
     Today Y-85

   "The Poetry File," by Edward
     Field DLB-105

   Poetry in Nineteenth-Century France:
     Cultural Background and Critical
     Commentary DLB-217

   The Poetry of Jorge Luis Borges Y-86

   "The Poet's Kaleidoscope: The Element
     of Surprise in the Making of the
     Poem" by Madeline DeFrees. DLB-105

   The Pre-Raphaelite Controversy. DLB-35

   Protest Poetry in Castile DLB-286

   "Reflections: After a Tornado,"
     by Judson Jerome DLB-105

   Statements from Former Consultants
     in Poetry. Y-86

   Statements on the Art of Poetry DLB-54

   The Study of Poetry (1880), by
     Matthew Arnold. DLB-35

   A Survey of Poetry Anthologies,
     1879-1960 . . . . DLB-54

   Thoughts on Poetry and Its Varieties
     (1833), by John Stuart Mill DLB-32

   Under the Microscope (1872), by
     A. C. Swinburne. DLB-35

   The Unterberg Poetry Center of the
     92nd Street Y Y-98

   Victorian Poetry: Five CriticalViews . . DLBV-35

   Year in Poetry Y-83–92, 94–01

   Year's Work in American Poetry. Y-82

Poets
   The Lives of the Poets (1753) DLB-142

   Minor Poets of the Earlier
     Seventeenth Century DLB-121

   Other British Poets Who Fell
     in the Great War. DLB-216

   Other Poets [French] DLB-217

   Second-Generation Minor Poets of
     the Seventeenth Century DLB-126

   Third-Generation Minor Poets of
     the Seventeenth Century DLB-131

Pogodin, Mikhail Petrovich 1800-1875. . . . DLB-198

Pogorel'sky, Antonii
   (see Perovsky, Aleksei Alekseevich)

Pohl, Frederik 1919- DLB-8

   Tribute to Isaac Asimov Y-92

   Tribute to Theodore Sturgeon Y-85

Poirier, Louis (see Gracq, Julien)

Poláček, Karel 1892-1945 . . . DLB-215; CDWLB-4

Polanyi, Michael 1891-1976 . . . . DLB-100

Pole, Reginald 1500-1558 . . . . DLB-132

Polevoi, Nikolai Alekseevich 1796-1846. . . DLB-198

Polezhaev, Aleksandr Ivanovich
   1804-1838 . . . . DLB-205

Poliakoff, Stephen 1952- DLB-13

Polidori, John William 1795-1821 . . . . . . DLB-116

Polite, Carlene Hatcher 1932- DLB-33

Pollard, Alfred W. 1859-1944 . . . . DLB-201

Pollard, Edward A. 1832-1872. . . . . DLB-30

Pollard, Graham 1903-1976 . . . . DLB-201

Pollard, Percival 1869-1911 . . . . DLB-71

Pollard and Moss DLB-49

Pollock, Sharon 1936- DLB-60

Polonsky, Abraham 1910-1999 . . . . DLB-26

Polonsky, Iakov Petrovich 1819-1898 . . . . DLB-277

Polotsky, Simeon 1629-1680 . . . . DLB-150

Polybius circa 200 B.C.-118 B.C.. . . . . DLB-176

Pomialovsky, Nikolai Gerasimovich
   1835-1863 . . . . DLB-238

Pomilio, Mario 1921-1990 . . . . DLB-177

Pompéia, Raul (Raul d'Avila Pompéia)
   1863-1895 . . . . DLB-307

Ponce, Mary Helen 1938- DLB-122

Ponce-Montoya, Juanita 1949- DLB-122

Ponet, John 1516?-1556. . . . . DLB-132

Ponge, Francis 1899-1988 . . . . DLB-258; Y-02

Poniatowska, Elena
   1933- DLB-113; CDWLB-3

Ponsard, François 1814-1867 . . . . DLB-192
William Ponsonby [publishing house]. DLB-170
Pontiggia, Giuseppe 1934- DLB-196
Pontoppidan, Henrik 1857-1943 . . . . DLB-300, 331
Pony Stories, Omnibus Essay on DLB-160
Poole, Ernest 1880-1950. . . . . DLB-9
Poole, Sophia 1804-1891. . . . . DLB-166
Poore, Benjamin Perley 1820-1887 . . . . DLB-23
Popa, Vasko 1922-1991. . . . . DLB-181; CDWLB-4
Pope, Abbie Hanscom 1858-1894. . . . . . . DLB-140
Pope, Alexander
   1688-1744. . . . . . DLB-95, 101, 213; CDBLB-2
Poplavsky, Boris 1903-1935 . . . . DLB-317
Popov, Aleksandr Serafimovich
   (see Serafimovich, Aleksandr Serafimovich)
Popov, Evgenii Anatol'evich 1946- DLB-285
Popov, Mikhail Ivanovich
   1742-circa 1790. . . . . DLB-150
Popović, Aleksandar 1929-1996 . . . . DLB-181
Popper, Karl 1902-1994 . . . . DLB-262
Popular Culture Association/
   American Culture Association Y-99
Popular Library DLB-46
Poquelin, Jean-Baptiste (see Molière)
Porete, Marguerite ?-1310. . . . . DLB-208
Porlock, Martin (see MacDonald, Philip)
Porpoise Press. DLB-112
Porta, Antonio 1935-1989. . . . . DLB-128
Porter, Anna Maria 1780-1832 . . . . . DLB-116, 159
Porter, Cole 1891-1964. . . . . DLB-265
Porter, David 1780-1843 . . . . DLB-183
Porter, Dorothy 1954-2008. . . . . DLB-325
Porter, Eleanor H. 1868-1920 . . . . DLB-9
Porter, Gene Stratton (see Stratton-Porter, Gene)
Porter, Hal 1911-1984. . . . . DLB-260
Porter, Henry circa sixteenth century DLB-62
Porter, Jane 1776-1850. . . . . DLB-116, 159
Porter, Katherine Anne 1890-1980
   . . . . . . .DLB-4, 9, 102; Y-80; DS-12; CDALB-7
   The Katherine Anne Porter Society Y-01
Porter, Peter 1929- DLB-40, 289
Porter, William Sydney (O. Henry)
   1862-1910. . . . . . . DLB-12, 78, 79; CDALB-3
Porter, William T. 1809-1858 . . . . . DLB-3, 43, 250
Porter and Coates. DLB-49
Portillo Trambley, Estela 1927-1998 . . . . . DLB-209
Portis, Charles 1933- DLB-6
Medieval Galician-Portuguese Poetry DLB-287
Posey, Alexander 1873-1908 . . . . .DLB-175
Possession, 1990 Booker Prize winner,
   A. S. Byatt DLB-326
Postans, Marianne circa 1810-1865. . . . . . DLB-166
Postgate, Raymond 1896-1971 . . . . .DLB-276

Postl, Carl (see Sealsfield, Carl)
Postmodern Holocaust Fiction DLB-299
Poston, Ted 1906-1974 . . . . DLB-51
Potekhin, Aleksei Antipovich
   1829-1908 . . . . DLB-238
Potok, Chaim 1929-2002 . . . . DLB-28, 152
   A Conversation with Chaim Potok Y-84
   Tribute to Bernard Malamud. Y-86
Potter, Beatrix 1866-1943 . . . . DLB-141
   The Beatrix Potter Society Y-98
Potter, David M. 1910-1971 . . . . DLB-17
Potter, Dennis 1935-1994 . . . . DLB-233
Potter, Stephen 1900-1969 . . . . DLB-352
John E. Potter and Company DLB-49
Pottle, Frederick A. 1897-1987 . . . . . DLB-103; Y-87
Poulin, Jacques 1937- DLB-60
Pound, Ezra 1885-1972
   . . . . DLB-4, 45, 63; DS-15; CDALB-4
   The Cost of the *Cantos:* William Bird
      to Ezra Pound Y-01
   The Ezra Pound Society. Y-01
Poverman, C. E. 1944- DLB-234
Povey, Meic 1950- DLB-310
Povich, Shirley 1905-1998 . . . . .DLB-171
Powderly, Terence V. 1849-1924. . . . . DLB-345
Powell, Anthony 1905-2000 . . . DLB-15; CDBLB-7
   The Anthony Powell Society: Powell and
      the First Biennial Conference Y-01
Powell, Dawn 1897-1965
   Dawn Powell, Where Have You Been
      All Our Lives?. Y-97
Powell, Adam Clayton, Jr. 1908-1973 . . . . DLB-345
Powell, John Wesley 1834-1902 . . . . DLB-186
Powell, Padgett 1952- DLB-234
Powers, J. F. 1917-1999. . . . . DLB-130
Powers, Jimmy 1903-1995 . . . . DLB-241
Powers, Richard 1957- DLB-350
Pownall, David 1938- DLB-14
Powys, John Cowper 1872-1963. . . . . DLB-15, 255
Powys, Llewelyn 1884-1939 . . . . DLB-98
Powys, T. F. 1875-1953. . . . . DLB-36, 162
   The Powys Society. Y-98
Poynter, Nelson 1903-1978 . . . . DLB-127
Prada, Juan Manuel de 1970- DLB-322
Prado, Adélia 1935- DLB-307
Prado, Pedro 1886-1952 . . . . DLB-283
Prados, Emilio 1899-1962. . . . . DLB-134
Praed, Mrs. Caroline (see Praed, Rosa)
Praed, Rosa (Mrs. Caroline Praed)
   1851-1935 . . . . DLB-230
Praed, Winthrop Mackworth 1802-1839 . . DLB-96
Praeger Publishers DLB-46
Praetorius, Johannes 1630-1680 . . . . DLB-168

Pratolini, Vasco 1913-1991 . . . . .DLB-177
Pratt, E. J. 1882-1964 . . . . DLB-92
Pratt, Samuel Jackson 1749-1814 . . . . DLB-39
Preciado Martin, Patricia 1939- DLB-209
Préfontaine, Yves 1937- DLB-53
Prelutsky, Jack 1940- DLB-61
Prentice, George D. 1802-1870. . . . . DLB-43
Prentice-Hall. DLB-46
Prescott, Orville 1906-1996 . . . . Y-96
Prescott, William Hickling
   1796-1859. . . . . DLB-1, 30, 59, 235
Prešeren, France
   1800-1849 . . . . DLB-147; CDWLB-4
Presses (*See also* Publishing)
   Small Presses in Great Britain and
      Ireland, 1960-1985 . . . . DLB-40
   Small Presses I: Jargon Society. Y-84
   Small Presses II: The Spirit That Moves
      Us Press. Y-85
   Small Presses III: Pushcart Press Y-87
Preston, Margaret Junkin
   1820-1897 . . . . DLB-239, 248
Preston, May Wilson 1873-1949. . . . . DLB-188
Preston, Thomas 1537-1598 . . . . DLB-62
Preti, Girolamo 1582-1626 . . . . DLB-339
Prévert, Jacques 1900-1977 . . . . DLB-258
Prévost d'Exiles, Antoine François
   1697-1763 . . . . DLB-314
Price, Anthony 1928- DLB-276
Price, Reynolds 1933- DLB-2, 218, 278
Price, Richard 1723-1791 . . . . DLB-158
Price, Richard 1949- Y-81
Prichard, Katharine Susannah
   1883-1969 . . . . DLB-260
Prideaux, John 1578-1650. . . . . DLB-236
Priest, Christopher 1943- DLB-14, 207, 261
Priestley, J. B. 1894-1984
   . . . . DLB-10, 34, 77, 100, 139; Y-84; CDBLB-6
Priestley, Joseph 1733-1804. . . . . DLB-252, 336
Prigov, Dmitrii Aleksandrovich 1940- . . DLB-285
Prime, Benjamin Young 1733-1791 . . . . . . DLB-31
Primrose, Diana floruit circa 1630 . . . . . . DLB-126
Prince, F. T. 1912-2003. . . . . DLB-20
Prince, Nancy Gardner
   1799-circa 1856 . . . . DLB-239
Prince, Thomas 1687-1758 . . . . DLB-24, 140
Pringle, Thomas 1789-1834 . . . . DLB-225
Printz, Wolfgang Casper 1641-1717 . . . . . DLB-168
Prior, Matthew 1664-1721 . . . . DLB-95
Prisco, Michele 1920-2003 . . . . .DLB-177
Prishvin, Mikhail Mikhailovich
   1873-1954 .DLB-272
Pritchard, William H. 1932- DLB-111
Pritchett, V. S. 1900-1997 . . . . DLB-15, 139

Private Eye 1961- DLB-352

Probyn, May 1856 or 1857-1909 ....DLB-199

Procter, Adelaide Anne 1825-1864....DLB-32, 199

Procter, Bryan Waller 1787-1874......DLB-96, 144

Proctor, Robert 1868-1903............DLB-184

Prokopovich, Feofan 1681?-1736 ....DLB-150

Prokosch, Frederic 1906-1989 ....DLB-48

Pronzini, Bill 1943- DLB-226

Propertius circa 50 B.C.-post 16 B.C.
...................DLB-211; CDWLB-1

Propper, Dan 1937- DLB-16

Prose, Francine 1947- DLB-234

Protagoras circa 490 B.C.-420 B.C. DLB-176

Protest Poetry in Castile
ca. 1445-ca. 1506..................DLB-286

Proud, Robert 1728-1813...............DLB-30

Proulx, Annie 1935- DLB-335, 350

Proust, Marcel 1871-1922................DLB-65

    Marcel Proust at 129 and the Proust
    Society of America Y-00

    Marcel Proust's *Remembrance of Things Past*:
    The Rediscovered Galley Proofs......Y-00

Prutkov, Koz'ma Petrovich
1803-1863 ....DLB-277

Prydz, Alvilde 1846-1922..............DLB-354

Prynne, J. H. 1936- DLB-40

Pryzbyszewska, Dagny Juel 1867-1901....DLB-354

Przybyszewski, Stanislaw 1868-1927 ......DLB-66

Pseudo-Dionysius the Areopagite floruit
circa 500 ....DLB-115

Public Lending Right in America
PLR and the Meaning of Literary
Property Y-83

    Statement by Sen. Charles
    McC. Mathias, Jr. PLR..............Y-83

    Statements on PLR by American Writers ...Y-83

Public Lending Right in the United Kingdom
The First Year in the United Kingdom Y-83

Publishers [listed by individual names]
Publishers, Conversations with:
An Interview with Charles Scribner III ...Y-94

    An Interview with Donald Lamm........Y-95

    An Interview with James Laughlin Y-96

    An Interview with Patrick O'Connor Y-84

Publishing
The Art and Mystery of Publishing:
Interviews......................Y-97

    Book Publishing Accounting: Some Basic
    Concepts........................Y-98

    1873 Publishers' Catalogues DLB-49

    The Literary Scene 2002: Publishing, Book
    Reviewing, and Literary Journalism...Y-02

    Main Trends in Twentieth-Century
    Book Clubs....................DLB-46

    Overview of U.S. Book Publishing,
    1910-1945.....................DLB-9

    The Pitt Poetry Series: Poetry Publishing
    Today Y-85

Publishing Fiction at LSU Press Y-87

The Publishing Industry in 1998:
Sturm-und-drang.com Y-98

The Publishing Industry in 1999 ....Y-99

Publishers and Agents: The Columbia
Connection....................Y-87

Responses to Ken Auletta Y-97

Southern Writers Between the Wars....DLB-9

The State of Publishing...............Y-97

Trends in Twentieth-Century
Mass Market Publishing.........DLB-46

The Year in Book Publishing..........Y-86

Pückler-Muskau, Hermann von
1785-1871......................DLB-133

Puértolas, Soledad 1947- DLB-322

Pufendorf, Samuel von 1632-1694........DLB-168

Pugh, Edwin William 1874-1930 ....DLB-135

Pugin, A. Welby 1812-1852.............DLB-55

Puig, Manuel 1932-1990 ....DLB-113; CDWLB-3

Puisieux, Madeleine d'Arsant de
1720-1798 ....DLB-314

Pulgar, Hernando del (Fernando del Pulgar)
ca. 1436-ca. 1492..................DLB-286

Pulitzer, Joseph 1847-1911 ....DLB-23

Pulitzer, Joseph, Jr. 1885-1955 ....DLB-29

Pulitzer Prizes for the Novel, 1917-1945.....DLB-9

Pulliam, Eugene 1889-1975 ....DLB-127

Punch, or, The London Charivari
1841-2002 ....DLB-352

Purcell, Deirdre 1945- DLB-267

Purchas, Samuel 1577?-1626 ....DLB-151

Purdy, Al 1918-2000 ....DLB-88

Purdy, James 1923-2009.............DLB-2, 218

Purdy, Ken W. 1913-1972 ....DLB-137

Pusey, Edward Bouverie 1800-1882 ......DLB-55

Pushkin, Aleksandr Sergeevich
1799-1837 ....DLB-205

Pushkin, Vasilii L'vovich
1766-1830 ....DLB-205

Putu Wijaya 1944- DLB-348

Putnam, George Palmer
1814-1872 ....DLB-3, 79, 250, 254

G. P. Putnam [publishing house] DLB-254

G. P. Putnam's Sons [U.K.] DLB-106

G. P. Putnam's Sons [U.S.]..............DLB-49

    A Publisher's Archives: G. P. Putnam.....Y-92

Putnam, Hilary 1926- DLB-279

Putnam, Samuel 1892-1950 ....DLB-4; DS-15

Putniņš, Pauls 1937- DLB-353

Puttenham, George 1529?-1590.........DLB-281

Puzo, Mario 1920-1999 ....DLB-6

Pyle, Ernie 1900-1945 ....DLB-29

Pyle, Howard
1853-1911 ....DLB-42, 188; DS-13

Pyle, Robert Michael 1947- DLB-275

Pym, Barbara 1913-1980...... DLB-14, 207; Y-87

Pynchon, Thomas 1937- DLB-2, 173

Pyramid Books DLB-46

Pyrnelle, Louise-Clarke 1850-1907 ....DLB-42

Pythagoras circa 570 B.C.-? DLB-176

Q

Qasim, 'Abd al-Hakim 1935-1990 ....DLB-346

Qays ibn al-Mulawwah circa 680-710 ....DLB-311

Qian Zhongshu 1910-1998 ....DLB-328

Quad, M. (see Lewis, Charles B.)

Quaritch, Bernard 1819-1899 ....DLB-184

Quarles, Francis 1592-1644 ....DLB-126

The Quarterly Review 1809-1967.........DLB-110

Quasimodo, Salvatore 1901-1968 ...DLB-114, 332

Queen, Ellery (see Dannay, Frederic, and
Manfred B. Lee)

Queen, Frank 1822-1882..............DLB-241

The Queen City Publishing House DLB-49

Queirós, Eça de 1845-1900 ....DLB-287

Queneau, Raymond 1903-1976 ......DLB-72, 258

Quennell, Peter 1905-1993 ....DLB-155, 195

Quental, Antero de
1842-1891 ....DLB-287

Quesada, José Luis 1948- DLB-290

Quesnel, Joseph 1746-1809 ....DLB-99

Quiller-Couch, Sir Arthur Thomas
1863-1944 ....DLB-135, 153, 190

Quin, Ann 1936-1973 ....DLB-14, 231

Quinault, Philippe 1635-1688...........DLB-268

Quincy, Samuel, of Georgia
fl. eighteenth century................DLB-31

Quincy, Samuel, of Massachusetts
1734-1789 ....DLB-31

Quindlen, Anna 1952- DLB-292

Quine, W. V. 1908-2000 ....DLB-279

Quinn, Anthony 1915-2001............DLB-122

Quinn, John 1870-1924 ....DLB-187

Quiñónez, Naomi 1951- DLB-209

Quintana, Leroy V. 1944- DLB-82

Quintana, Miguel de 1671-1748
A Forerunner of Chicano
Literature DLB-122

Quintilian circa A.D. 40-circa A.D. 96.....DLB-211

Quintus Curtius Rufus fl. A.D. 35 ....DLB-211

Harlin Quist Books DLB-46

Quoirez, Françoise (see Sagan, Françoise)

Qutb, Sayyid 1906-1966 ....DLB-346

R

Raabe, Wilhelm 1831-1910 ....DLB-129

Raban, Jonathan 1942- DLB-204

Rabe, David 1940- DLB-7, 228; Y-91
Rabelais, François 1494?-1593 .... DLB-327
Rabi'ah al-'Adawiyyah circa 720-801 .... DLB-311
Raboni, Giovanni 1932- DLB-128
Rachilde 1860-1953 .... DLB-123, 192
Racin, Kočo 1908-1943............. DLB-147
Racine, Jean 1639-1699 .... DLB-268
Rackham, Arthur 1867-1939........... DLB-141
Raczymow, Henri 1948- DLB-299
Radauskas, Henrikas
  1910-1970........... DLB-220; CDWLB-4
Radcliffe, Ann 1764-1823 ....DLB-39, 178
Raddall, Thomas 1903-1994 .... DLB-68
Radford, Dollie 1858-1920 .... DLB-240
Radichkov, Yordan 1929-2004 .... DLB-181
Radiguet, Raymond 1903-1923 .... DLB-65
Radishchev, Aleksandr Nikolaevich
  1749-1802..................... DLB-150
Radnóti, Miklós 1909-1944 . DLB-215; CDWLB-4
Radrigán, Juan 1937- DLB-305
Radulović, Jovan 1951- DLB-353
Radványi, Netty Reiling (see Seghers, Anna)
Rafat, Taufiq 1927-1998 .... DLB-323
Rahv, Philip 1908-1973............. DLB-137
Raich, Semen Egorovich 1792-1855 ..... DLB-205
Raičković, Stevan 1928- DLB-181
Raiderman (see Parshchikov, Aleksei Maksimovich)
Raimund, Ferdinand Jakob 1790-1836 .... DLB-90
Raine, Craig 1944- DLB-40
Raine, Kathleen 1908-2003............. DLB-20
Rainis, Jānis 1865-1929..... DLB-220; CDWLB-4
Rainolde, Richard
  circa 1530-1606 .... DLB-136, 236
Rainolds, John 1549-1607............. DLB-281
Rakić, Milan 1876-1938 .....DLB-147; CDWLB-4
Rakosi, Carl 1903-2004 .... DLB-193
Rakovszky, Zsuzsa 1950- DLB-353
Ralegh, Sir Walter
  1554?-1618............. DLB-172; CDBLB-1
Raleigh, Walter
  Style (1897) [excerpt]................ DLB-57
Ralin, Radoy 1923-2004.............. DLB-181
Ralph, Julian 1853-1903 .... DLB-23
Ramanujan, A. K. 1929-1993 .... DLB-323
Ramat, Silvio 1939- DLB-128
Ramée, Marie Louise de la (see Ouida)
Ramírez, Sergio 1942- DLB-145
Ramke, Bin 1947- DLB-120
Ramler, Karl Wilhelm 1725-1798 .... DLB-97
Ramon Ribeyro, Julio 1929-1994 ...... DLB-145
Ramos, Graciliano 1892-1953 .... DLB-307
Ramos, Manuel 1948- DLB-209

Ramos Sucre, José Antonio 1890-1930... DLB-290
Ramous, Mario 1924- DLB-128
Rampersad, Arnold 1941- DLB-111
Ramsay, Allan 1684 or 1685-1758 .... DLB-95
Ramsay, David 1749-1815 .... DLB-30
Ramsay, Martha Laurens 1759-1811..... DLB-200
Ramsey, Frank P. 1903-1930 .... DLB-262
Ranch, Hieronimus Justesen
  1539-1607.................... DLB-300
Ranck, Katherine Quintana 1942- DLB-122
Rand, Avery and Company DLB-49
Rand, Ayn 1905-1982 ...DLB-227, 279; CDALB-7
Rand McNally and Company DLB-49
Randall, David Anton 1905-1975 .... DLB-140
Randall, Dudley 1914-2000 .... DLB-41
Randall, Henry S. 1811-1876 .... DLB-30
Randall, James G. 1881-1953 .... DLB-17
The Randall Jarrell Symposium: A Small
  Collection of Randall Jarrells........ Y-86
Excerpts From Papers Delivered at the
  Randall Jarrel Symposium.......... Y-86
Randall, John Herman, Jr. 1899-1980.....DLB-279
Randhawa, Ravinder 1952- DLB-347
Randolph, A. Philip 1889-1979.......... DLB-91
Anson D. F. Randolph
  [publishing house] DLB-49
Randolph, Thomas 1605-1635...... DLB-58, 126
Random House DLB-46
Rankin, Ian (Jack Harvey) 1960- DLB-267
Henry Ranlet [publishing house] DLB-49
Ransom, Harry 1908-1976 .... DLB-187
Ransom, John Crowe
  1888-1974.......... DLB-45, 63; CDALB-7
Ransome, Arthur 1884-1967 .... DLB-160
Rao, Raja 1908-2006 .... DLB-323
Raphael, Frederic 1931- DLB-14, 319
Raphaelson, Samson 1896-1983......... DLB-44
Rare Book Dealers
  Bertram Rota and His Bookshop........ Y-91
  An Interview with Glenn Horowitz Y-90
  An Interview with Otto Penzler Y-96
  An Interview with Ralph Sipper........ Y-94
  New York City Bookshops in the
    1930s and 1940s: The Recollections
    of Walter Goldwater Y-93
Rare Books
  Research in the American Antiquarian
    Book Trade Y-97
  Two Hundred Years of Rare Books and
    Literary Collections at the
    University of South Carolina Y-00
Rascón Banda, Víctor Hugo 1948- DLB-305
Rashi circa 1040-1105................. DLB-208
Raskin, Ellen 1928-1984............. DLB-52
Rasputin, Valentin Grigor'evich
  1937- DLB-302

Rastell, John 1475?-1536...........DLB-136, 170
Rattigan, Terence
  1911-1977............. DLB-13; CDBLB-7
Raven, Simon 1927-2001 ....DLB-271
Ravenhill, Mark 1966- DLB-310
Ravnkilde, Adda 1862-1883........... DLB-300
Rawicz, Piotr 1919-1982.............. DLB-299
Rawlings, Marjorie Kinnan 1896-1953
  ....DLB-9, 22, 102; DS-17; CDALB-7
Rawlins, C. L. 1949- DLB-342
Rawlinson, Richard 1690-1755......... DLB-213
Rawlinson, Thomas 1681-1725 .... DLB-213
Rawls, John 1921-2002................DLB-279
Raworth, Tom 1938- DLB-40
Ray, David 1932- DLB-5
Ray, Gordon Norton 1915-1986.....DLB-103, 140
Ray, Henrietta Cordelia 1849-1916 ...... DLB-50
Raymond, Ernest 1888-1974........... DLB-191
Raymond, Henry J. 1820-1869........DLB-43, 79
Raymond, René (see Chase, James Hadley)
Razaf, Andy 1895-1973 .... DLB-265
al-Razi 865?-925? DLB-311
Razón de amor con los denuestos del agua y el vino
  (1230-1250) DLB-337
Rea, Michael 1927-1996 .... Y-97
Michael M. Rea and the Rea Award for
  the Short Story Y-97
Reach, Angus 1821-1856 .... DLB-70
Read, Herbert 1893-1968.......... DLB-20, 149
Read, Martha Meredith
  fl. nineteenth century DLB-200
Read, Opie 1852-1939 .... DLB-23
Read, Piers Paul 1941- DLB-14
Reade, Charles 1814-1884 .... DLB-21
Reader's Digest Condensed Books....... DLB-46
Readers Ulysses Symposium................ Y-97
Reading, Peter 1946- DLB-40
Reading Series in New York City Y-96
Reaney, James 1926- DLB-68
Rebhun, Paul 1500?-1546.............DLB-179
Rèbora, Clemente 1885-1957 .... DLB-114
Rebreanu, Liviu 1885-1944 .... DLB-220
Rechy, John 1934- DLB-122, 278; Y-82
Redding, J. Saunders 1906-1988.......DLB-63, 76
Rede, William Leman 1802-1847....... DLB-344
J. S. Redfield [publishing house]......... DLB-49
Redgrove, Peter 1932-2003............. DLB-40
Redmon, Anne 1943- Y-86
Redmond, Eugene B. 1937- DLB-41
Redol, Alves 1911-1969 .... DLB-287
James Redpath [publishing house] DLB-49

Reed, Henry 1808-1854................DLB-59

Reed, Henry 1914-1986................DLB-27

Reed, Ishmael
    1938- DLB-2, 5, 33, 169, 227; DS-8

Reed, Rex 1938- DLB-185

Reed, Sampson 1800-1880..........DLB-1, 235

Reed, Talbot Baines 1852-1893........DLB-141

Reedy, William Marion 1862-1920.......DLB-91

Reese, Lizette Woodworth 1856-1935....DLB-54

Reese, Thomas 1742-1796..............DLB-37

Reeve, Clara 1729-1807...............DLB-39

    Preface to *The Old English Baron*
        (1778)........................DLB-39

    The Progress of Romance (1785)
        [excerpt].....................DLB-39

Reeves, James 1909-1978.............DLB-161

Reeves, John 1926- DLB-88

Reeves-Stevens, Garfield 1953- DLB-251

Régio, José (José Maria dos Reis Pereira)
    1901-1969........................DLB-287

Henry Regnery Company................DLB-46

Rêgo, José Lins do 1901-1957.........DLB-307

Rehberg, Hans 1901-1963.............DLB-124

Rehfisch, Hans José 1891-1960........DLB-124

Reich, Ebbe Kløvedal 1940- DLB-214

Reid, Alastair 1926- DLB-27

Reid, B. L. 1918-1990................DLB-111

Reid, Christopher 1949- DLB-40

Reid, Forrest 1875-1947..............DLB-153

Reid, Helen Rogers 1882-1970.........DLB-29

Reid, James fl. eighteenth century DLB-31

Reid, Mayne 1818-1883.............DLB-21, 163

Reid, Thomas 1710-1796...........DLB-31, 252

Reid, V. S. (Vic) 1913-1987...........DLB-125

Reid, Whitelaw 1837-1912.............DLB-23

Reilly and Lee Publishing Company......DLB-46

Reimann, Brigitte 1933-1973..........DLB-75

Reinmar der Alte circa 1165-circa 1205...DLB-138

Reinmar von Zweter
    circa 1200-circa 1250..............DLB-138

Reisch, Walter 1903-1983..............DLB-44

Reizei Family........................DLB-203

Religion
    A Crisis of Culture: The Changing
        Role of Religion in the
        New Republic..................DLB-37

The Remains of the Day, 1989 Booker Prize winner,
    Kazuo Ishiguro..................DLB-326

Remarque, Erich Maria
    1898-1970.............DLB-56; CDWLB-2

Remington, Frederic
    1861-1909..............DLB-12, 186, 188

Remizov, Aleksei Mikhailovich
    1877-1957......................DLB-295

Renaud, Jacques 1943- DLB-60

Renault, Mary 1905-1983 ....Y-83

Rendell, Ruth (Barbara Vine)
    1930- DLB-87, 276

Rensselaer, Maria van Cortlandt van
    1645-1689......................DLB-200

Repplier, Agnes 1855-1950............DLB-221

Repše, Gundega 1960- DLB-353

Reshetnikov, Fedor Mikhailovich
    1841-1871......................DLB-238

Restif (Rétif) de La Bretonne, Nicolas-Edme
    1734-1806......................DLB-314

Rettenbacher, Simon 1634-1706........DLB-168

Retz, Jean-François-Paul de Gondi,
    cardinal de 1613-1679.............DLB-268

Reuchlin, Johannes 1455-1522.........DLB-179

Reuter, Christian 1665-after 1712.......DLB-168

Fleming H. Revell Company............DLB-49

Reverdy, Pierre 1889-1960............DLB-258

Reuter, Fritz 1810-1874 ....DLB-129

Reuter, Gabriele 1859-1941............DLB-66

Reventlow, Franziska Gräfin zu
    1871-1918.......................DLB-66

Review of Reviews Office.............DLB-112

Rexroth, Kenneth 1905-1982
    ...... DLB-16, 48, 165, 212; Y-82; CDALB-1

    The Commercialization of the Image
        of Revolt.....................DLB-16

Rey, H. A. 1898-1977.................DLB-22

Reyes, Carlos José 1941- DLB-305

Reymont, Władysław Stanisław
    1867-1925......................DLB-332

Reynal and Hitchcock.................DLB-46

Reynolds, G. W. M. 1814-1879.........DLB-21

Reynolds, John Hamilton
    1794-1852.......................DLB-96

Reynolds, Sir Joshua 1723-1792........DLB-104

Reynolds, Mack 1917-1983..............DLB-8

Reza, Yazmina 1959- DLB-321

Reznikoff, Charles 1894-1976........DLB-28, 45

Rhetoric
    Continental European Rhetoricians,
        1400-1600, and Their Influence
        in Reaissance England..........DLB-236

    A Finding Guide to Key Works on
        Microfilm DLB-236

    Glossary of Terms and Definitions of
        Rhetoic and Logic.............DLB-236

Rhett, Robert Barnwell 1800-1876........DLB-43

Rhode, John 1884-1964................DLB-77

Rhodes, Eugene Manlove 1869-1934....DLB-256

Rhodes, James Ford 1848-1927.........DLB-47

Rhodes, Richard 1937- DLB-185

Rhys, Jean 1890-1979
    .... DLB-36, 117, 162; CDBLB-7; CDWLB-3

Ribeiro, Bernadim
    fl. ca. 1475/1482-1526/1544.........DLB-287

Ricardo, David 1772-1823......... DLB-107, 158

Ricardou, Jean 1932- DLB-83

Riccoboni, Marie-Jeanne (Marie-Jeanne de
    Heurles Laboras de Mézières Riccoboni)
    1713-1792......................DLB-314

Rice, Anne (A. N. Roquelare, Anne Rampling)
    1941- DLB-292

Rice, Christopher 1978- DLB-292

Rice, Elmer 1892-1967................DLB-4, 7

Rice, Grantland 1880-1954......... DLB-29, 171

Rich, Adrienne 1929- DLB-5, 67; CDALB-7

Richard, Mark 1955- DLB-234

Richard de Fournival
    1201-1259 or 1260................DLB-208

Richards, David Adams 1950- DLB-53

Richards, Frank 1876-1961...........DLB-352

Richards, George circa 1760-1814........DLB-37

Richards, I. A. 1893-1979..............DLB-27

Richards, Laura E. 1850-1943..........DLB-42

Richards, William Carey 1818-1892.....DLB-73

Grant Richards [publishing house]......DLB-112

Richardson, Charles F. 1851-1913........DLB-71

Richardson, Dorothy M. 1873-1957.....DLB-36

    The Novels of Dorothy Richardson
        (1918), by May Sinclair..........DLB-36

Richardson, Henry Handel
    (Ethel Florence Lindesay Robertson)
    1870-1946 .... DLB-197, 230

Richardson, Jack 1935- DLB-7

Richardson, John 1796-1852...........DLB-99

Richardson, Samuel
    1689-1761..........DLB-39, 154; CDBLB-2

    Introductory Letters from the Second
        Edition of *Pamela* (1741).........DLB-39

    Postscript to [the Third Edition of]
        Clarissa (1751)................DLB-39

    Preface to the First Edition of
        Pamela (1740).................DLB-39

    Preface to the Third Edition of
        Clarissa (1751) [excerpt].........DLB-39

    Preface to Volume 1 of *Clarissa*
        (1747).......................DLB-39

    Preface to Volume 3 of *Clarissa*
        (1748).......................DLB-39

Richardson, Willis 1889-1977..........DLB-51

Riche, Barnabe 1542-1617.............DLB-136

Richepin, Jean 1849-1926.............DLB-192

Richler, Mordecai 1931-2001...........DLB-53

Richter, Conrad 1890-1968..........DLB-9, 212

Richter, Hans Werner 1908-1993........DLB-69

Richter, Johann Paul Friedrich
    1763-1825...............DLB-94; CDWLB-2

Joseph Rickerby [publishing house]......DLB-106

Rickword, Edgell 1898-1982............DLB-20

Riddell, Charlotte 1832-1906...........DLB-156

Riddell, John (see Ford, Corey)

Ridge, John Rollin 1827-1867 . . . . .DLB-175

Ridge, Lola 1873-1941 . . . . DLB-54

Ridge, William Pett 1859-1930 . . . . DLB-135

Riding, Laura (see Jackson, Laura Riding)

Ridler, Anne 1912-2001 . . . . DLB-27

Ridruego, Dionisio 1912-1975 . . . . DLB-108

Riel, Louis 1844-1885 . . . . DLB-99

Riemer, Johannes 1648-1714 . . . . DLB-168

Riera, Carme 1948- DLB-322

Rifbjerg, Klaus 1931- DLB-214

Riffaterre, Michael 1924-2006 . . . . DLB-67

Rifkin, Jeremy 1945- DLB-345

A Conversation between William Riggan
  and Janette Turner Hospital Y-02

Riggs, Lynn 1899-1954 . . . . .DLB-175

Riis, Jacob 1849-1914 . . . . DLB-23

John C. Riker [publishing house] DLB-49

Riley, James 1777-1840 . . . . DLB-183

Riley, Joan 1958- DLB-347

Riley, John 1938-1978 . . . . DLB-40

Rilke, Rainer Maria
  1875-1926 . . . . DLB-81; CDWLB-2

Rim Kin 1911-1959 . . . . DLB-348

Rimanelli, Giose 1926- DLB-177

Rimbaud, Jean-Nicolas-Arthur
  1854-1891 . . . . DLB-217

Rinehart and Company DLB-46

Ringuet 1895-1960 . . . . DLB-68

Ringwood, Gwen Pharis 1910-1984 . . . . . . DLB-88

Rinser, Luise 1911-2002 . . . . DLB-69

Rinuccini, Ottavio 1562-1621 . . . . DLB-339

Ríos, Alberto 1952- DLB-122

Ríos, Isabella 1948- DLB-82

Ripley, Arthur 1895-1961 . . . . DLB-44

Ripley, George 1802-1880 . . . . DLB-1, 64, 73, 235

The Rising Glory of America:
  Three Poems DLB-37

The Rising Glory of America: Written in 1771
  (1786), by Hugh Henry Brackenridge
  and Philip Freneau DLB-37

Riskin, Robert 1897-1955 . . . . DLB-26

Risse, Heinz 1898-1989 . . . . DLB-69

Rist, Johann 1607-1667 . . . . DLB-164

Ristikivi, Karl 1912-1977 . . . . DLB-220

Ritchie, Anna Mowatt 1819-1870 . . . . . DLB-3, 250

Ritchie, Anne Thackeray 1837-1919 . . . . . . DLB-18

Ritchie, Thomas 1778-1854 . . . . DLB-43

Rites of Passage, 1980 Booker Prize winner,
  William Golding DLB-326

The Ritz Paris Hemingway Award Y-85

  Mario Varga Llosa's Acceptance Speech . . Y-85

Rivard, Adjutor 1868-1945 . . . . DLB-92

Rive, Richard 1931-1989 . . . . DLB-125, 225

Rivera, José 1955- DLB-249

Rivera, Marina 1942- DLB-122

Rivera, Tomás 1935-1984 . . . . DLB-82

Rivers, Conrad Kent 1933-1968 . . . . DLB-41

Riverside Press DLB-49

Rivington, James circa 1724-1802 . . . . DLB-43

Charles Rivington [publishing house] DLB-154

Rivkin, Allen 1903-1990 . . . . DLB-26

Rizal, José 1861-1896 . . . . DLB-348

Rno, Sung J. 1967- DLB-341

Roa Bastos, Augusto 1917-2005 . . . . DLB-113

Robbe-Grillet, Alain 1922-2008 . . . . DLB-83

Robbins, Tom 1936- Y-80

Roberts, Charles G. D. 1860-1943 . . . . DLB-92

Roberts, Dorothy 1906-1993 . . . . DLB-88

Roberts, Elizabeth Madox
  1881-1941 . . . . DLB-9, 54, 102

Roberts, John (see Swynnerton, Thomas)

Roberts, Kate 1891-1985 . . . . DLB-319

Roberts, Keith 1935-2000 . . . . DLB-261

Roberts, Kenneth 1885-1957 . . . . DLB-9

Roberts, Michèle 1949- DLB-231

Roberts, Theodore Goodridge
  1877-1953 . . . . DLB-92

Roberts, Ursula Wyllie (see Miles, Susan)

Roberts, William 1767-1849 . . . . DLB-142

James Roberts [publishing house] DLB-154

Roberts Brothers DLB-49

A. M. Robertson and Company DLB-49

Robertson, Ethel Florence Lindesay
  (see Richardson, Henry Handel)

Robertson, T. W. 1829-1871 . . . . DLB-344

Robertson, William 1721-1793 . . . . . DLB-104, 336

Robin, Leo 1895-1984 . . . . DLB-265

Robins, Elizabeth 1862-1952 . . . . DLB-197

Robinson, A. Mary F. (Madame James
  Darmesteter, Madame Mary
  Duclaux) 1857-1944 . . . . DLB-240

Robinson, Casey 1903-1979 . . . . DLB-44

Robinson, Derek 1932- Y-02

Robinson, Edwin Arlington
  1869-1935 . . . . DLB-54; CDALB-3

  Review by Derek Robinson of George
    Greenfield's Rich Dust Y-02

Robinson, Henry Crabb 1775-1867 . . . . . .DLB-107

Robinson, James Harvey 1863-1936 . . . . . DLB-47

Robinson, Lennox 1886-1958 . . . . DLB-10

Robinson, Mabel Louise 1874-1962 . . . . . . DLB-22

Robinson, Marilynne 1943- DLB-206, 350

Robinson, Mary 1758-1800 . . . . DLB-158

Robinson, Richard circa 1545-1607 . . . . . DLB-167

Robinson, Therese 1797-1870 . . . . . . DLB-59, 133

Robison, Mary 1949- DLB-130

Roblès, Emmanuel 1914-1995 . . . . DLB-83

Roccatagliata Ceccardi, Ceccardo
  1871-1919 . . . . DLB-114

Rocha, Adolfo Correira da (see Torga, Miguel)

Roche, Billy 1949- DLB-233

Rochester, John Wilmot, Earl of
  1647-1680 . . . . DLB-131

Rochon, Esther 1948- DLB-251

Rock, Howard 1911-1976 . . . . .DLB-127

Rockwell, Norman Perceval 1894-1978 . . DLB-188

Rodgers, Carolyn M. 1945- DLB-41

Rodgers, W. R. 1909-1969 . . . . DLB-20

Rodney, Lester 1911- DLB-241

Rodoreda, Mercé 1908-1983 . . . . DLB-322

Rodrigues, Nelson 1912-1980 . . . . DLB-307

Rodríguez, Claudio 1934-1999 . . . . DLB-134

Rodríguez, Joe D. 1943- DLB-209

Rodriguez, Judith 1936- DLB-325

Rodríguez, Luis J. 1954- DLB-209

Rodriguez, Richard 1944- DLB-82, 256

Rodríguez Julia, Edgardo 1946- DLB-145

Roe, E. P. 1838-1888 . . . . DLB-202

Roethke, Theodore
  1908-1963 . . . . DLB-5, 206; CDALB-1

Rogers, Jane 1952- DLB-194

Rogers, Pattiann 1940- DLB-105

Rogers, Samuel 1763-1855 . . . . DLB-93

Rogers, Will 1879-1935 . . . . DLB-11

Rohmer, Sax 1883-1959 . . . . DLB-70

Roig, Montserrat 1946-1991 . . . . DLB-322

Roiphe, Anne 1935- Y-80

Rojas, Arnold R. 1896-1988 . . . . DLB-82

Rojas, Fernando de ca. 1475-1541 . . . . . . DLB-286

Roland de la Platière, Marie-Jeanne
  (Madame Roland) 1754-1793 . . . . . . DLB-314

Rolfe, Edwin (Solomon Fishman)
  1909-1954 . . . . DLB-303

Rolfe, Frederick William
  1860-1913 . . . . DLB-34, 156

Rolland, Romain 1866-1944 . . . . DLB-65, 332

Rolle, Richard circa 1290-1300 - 1349 . . . DLB-146

Rölvaag, O. E. 1876-1931 . . . . DLB-9, 212

Romains, Jules 1885-1972 . . . . DLB-65, 321

A. Roman and Company DLB-49

Roman de la Rose: Guillaume de Lorris
  1200/1205-circa 1230, Jean de
  Meun 1235-1240-circa 1305 . . . . DLB-208

Romano, Lalla 1906-2001 . . . . .DLB-177

Romano, Octavio 1923-2005 . . . . DLB-122

Rome, Harold 1908-1993 . . . . DLB-265

Romero, Leo 1950- DLB-122

Romero, Lin 1947- DLB-122

Romero, Orlando 1945- DLB-82	Rossner, Judith 1935- DLB-6	Richard Royston [publishing house] DLB-170
Ronsard, Pierre de 1524-1585 ....DLB-327	Rostand, Edmond 1868-1918 ....DLB-192	Rozanov, Vasilii Vasil'evich 1856-1919 ....DLB-295
Rook, Clarence 1863-1915...........DLB-135	Rosten, Leo 1908-1997 ....DLB-11	Różewicz, Tadeusz 1921- DLB-232
Roosevelt, Theodore 1858-1919 .... DLB-47, 186, 275	Rostenberg, Leona 1908-2005.........DLB-140	Ruark, Gibbons 1941- DLB-120
Root, Waverley 1903-1982 ....DLB-4	Rostopchina, Evdokiia Petrovna 1811-1858 ....DLB-205	Ruban, Vasilii Grigorevich 1742-1795 ....DLB-150
Root, William Pitt 1941- DLB-120	Rostovsky, Dimitrii 1651-1709.........DLB-150	Rubens, Bernice 1928-2004..... DLB-14, 207, 326
Roquebrune, Robert de 1889-1978 ....DLB-68	Rota, Bertram 1903-1966..............DLB-201	Rubião, Murilo 1916-1991.............DLB-307
Rorty, Richard 1931-2007 .... DLB-246, 279	Bertram Rota and His Bookshop Y-91	Rubina, Dina Il'inichna 1953- DLB-285
Rosa, João Guimarães 1908-1967... DLB-113, 307	Roth, Gerhard 1942- DLB-85, 124	Rubinshtein, Lev Semenovich 1947- ...DLB-285
Rosales, Luis 1910-1992 ....DLB-134	Roth, Henry 1906?-1995..............DLB-28	Rudd and Carleton DLB-49
Roscoe, William 1753-1831 ....DLB-163	Roth, Joseph 1894-1939................DLB-85	Rudd, Steele (Arthur Hoey Davis) DLB-230
Rose, Dilys 1954- DLB-319	Roth, Philip 1933- DLB-2, 28, 173; Y-82; CDALB-6	Rudkin, David 1936- DLB-13
Rose, Ernestine 1810-1892..............DLB-345	Rothenberg, Jerome 1931- DLB-5, 193	Rudnick, Paul 1957- DLB-266
Rose, Reginald 1920-2002..............DLB-26	Rothschild Family DLB-184	Rudnicki, Adolf 1909-1990 ....DLB-299
Rose, Wendy 1948- DLB-175	Rotimi, Ola 1938-2000 ....DLB-125	Rudolf von Ems circa 1200-circa 1254 ...DLB-138
Rosegger, Peter 1843-1918 ....DLB-129	Rotrou, Jean 1609-1650 ....DLB-268	Ruffhead, Owen 1723-1769 ....DLB-336
Rosei, Peter 1946- DLB-85	Rousseau, Jean-Jacques 1712-1778 ....DLB-314	Ruffin, Josephine St. Pierre 1842-1924 ....DLB-79
Rosen, Norma 1925- DLB-28	*The Social Contract*..................DLB-314	Rufo, Juan Gutiérrez 1547?-1620?.......DLB-318
Rosenbach, A. S. W. 1876-1952........DLB-140	Routhier, Adolphe-Basile 1839-1920 .....DLB-99	Ruganda, John 1941- DLB-157
Rosenbaum, Ron 1946- DLB-185	Routier, Simone 1901-1987 ....DLB-88	Ruggles, Henry Joseph 1813-1906........DLB-64
Rosenbaum, Thane 1960- DLB-299	George Routledge and Sons...........DLB-106	Ruiz, Juan, Arcipreste de Hita 1330-1343 ....DLB-337
Rosenberg, Isaac 1890-1918 ....DLB-20, 216	Roversi, Roberto 1923- DLB-128	Ruiz de Burton, María Amparo 1832-1895 ....DLB-209, 221
Rosenfarb, Chava (Khave Roznfarb) 1923- DLB-333	Rowe, Elizabeth Singer 1674-1737 ....DLB-39, 95	Rukeyser, Muriel 1913-1980 ....DLB-48
Rosenfeld, Isaac 1918-1956 ....DLB-28	Rowe, Nicholas 1674-1718 ....DLB-84	Rule, Jane 1931-2007.................DLB-60
Rosenfeld, Morris (Moris Roznfeld) 1862-1923 ....DLB-333	Rowlands, Ian 1964- DLB-310	Rulfo, Juan 1918-1986...... DLB-113; CDWLB-3
Rosenthal, Harold 1914-1999 ....DLB-241	Rowlands, Samuel circa 1570-1630 .....DLB-121	Rumaker, Michael 1932- DLB-16, 335
Jimmy, Red, and Others: Harold Rosenthal Remembers the Stars of the Press Box Y-01	Rowlandson, Mary circa 1637-circa 1711 ....DLB-24, 200	Rumens, Carol 1944- DLB-40
	Rowley, William circa 1585-1626 ....DLB-58	Rummo, Paul-Eerik 1942- DLB-232
Rosenthal, M. L. 1917-1996............DLB-5	Rowling, J. K. The Harry Potter Phenomenon Y-99	Runnel, Hando 1938- DLB-353
Rosenwald, Lessing J. 1891-1979 ....DLB-187		Runyon, Damon 1880-1946 ..... DLB-11, 86, 171
Rospigliosi, Giulio (Pope Clement IX) 1600-1669 ....DLB-339	Rowse, A. L. 1903-1997...............DLB-155	*Ruodlieb* circa 1050-1075 ....DLB-148
Ross, Alexander 1591-1654...........DLB-151	Rowson, Susanna Haswell circa 1762-1824 .... DLB-37, 200	Rush, Benjamin 1746-1813 ....DLB-37
Ross, Harold 1892-1951 ....DLB-137	Roy, Arundhati 1961- DLB-323, 326	Rush, Rebecca 1779-? DLB-200
Ross, Jerry 1926-1955 ....DLB-265	Roy, Camille 1870-1943...............DLB-92	Rushdie, Salman 1947- DLB-194, 323, 326
Ross, Leonard Q. (see Rosten, Leo)	The G. Ross Roy Scottish Poetry Collection at the University of South Carolina Y-89	Rusk, Ralph L. 1888-1962.............DLB-103
Ross, Leone 1969- DLB-347		Ruskin, John 1819-1900 ......DLB-55, 163, 190; CDBLB-4
Ross, Lillian 1927- DLB-185	Roy, Gabrielle 1909-1983 ....DLB-68	
Ross, Martin 1862-1915..............DLB-135	Roy, Jules 1907-2000 ....DLB-83	Russ, Joanna 1937- DLB-8
Ross, Sinclair 1908-1996 ....DLB-88	The Royal Court Theatre and the English Stage Company..................DLB-13	Russell, Benjamin 1761-1845 ....DLB-43
Ross, W. W. E. 1894-1966.............DLB-88		Russell, Bertrand 1872-1970.... DLB-100, 262, 332
Rosselli, Amelia 1930-1996 ....DLB-128	The Royal Court Theatre and the New Drama......................DLB-10	Russell, Charles Edward 1860-1941 ......DLB-25
Rossen, Robert 1908-1966 ....DLB-26		Russell, Charles M. 1864-1926 ....DLB-188
Rosset, Barney 1922- Y-02	The Royal Shakespeare Company at the Swan Y-88	Russell, Eric Frank 1905-1978 ....DLB-255
Rossetti, Christina 1830-1894 ... DLB-35, 163, 240		Russell, Fred 1906-2003...............DLB-241
Rossetti, Dante Gabriel 1828-1882 .... DLB-35; CDBLB-4	Royall, Anne Newport 1769-1854 ....DLB-43, 248	Russell, George William (see AE)
	Royce, Josiah 1855-1916 .... DLB-270	Russell, Countess Mary Annette Beauchamp (see Arnim, Elizabeth von)
The Stealthy School of Criticism (1871) DLB-35	The Roycroft Printing Shop............DLB-49	
	Royde-Smith, Naomi 1875-1964 ....DLB-191	Russell, Willy 1947- DLB-233
	Royster, Vermont 1914-1996 ....DLB-127	B. B. Russell and Company............DLB-49

R. H. Russell and Son. DLB-49

Rutebeuf fl.1249-1277. . . . . DLB-208

Rutherford, Mark 1831-1913 . . . . DLB-18

Ruxton, George Frederick
   1821-1848 . . . . DLB-186

R-va, Zeneida
   (see Gan, Elena Andreevna)

Ryan, Gig 1956- DLB-325

Ryan, James 1952- DLB-267

Ryan, Michael 1946- Y-82

Ryan, Oscar 1904-1988 . . . . DLB-68

Rybakov, Anatolii Naumovich
   1911-1994. . . . . DLB-302

Ryder, Jack 1871-1936 . . . . DLB-241

Ryga, George 1932-1987 . . . . DLB-60

Rylands, Enriqueta Augustina Tennant
   1843-1908 . . . . DLB-184

Rylands, John 1801-1888 . . . . DLB-184

Ryle, Gilbert 1900-1976 . . . . DLB-262

Ryleev, Kondratii Fedorovich 1795-1826 . DLB-205

Rymer, Thomas 1643?-1713 . . . . DLB-101, 336

Ryskind, Morrie 1895-1985 . . . . DLB-26

Rzhevsky, Aleksei Andreevich
   1737-1804 . . . . DLB-150

S

El Saadawi, Nawal 1931- DLB-346

The Saalfield Publishing Company DLB-46

Saba, Umberto 1883-1957 . . . . DLB-114

Sábato, Ernesto 1911- DLB-145; CDWLB-3

Saberhagen, Fred 1930-2007. . . . . DLB-8

Sabin, Joseph 1821-1881. . . . . DLB-187

Sabino, Fernando (Fernando Tavares Sabino)
   1923-2004 . . . . DLB-307

Sacer, Gottfried Wilhelm 1635-1699. . . . . DLB-168

Sachs, Hans 1494-1576 . . . . . . DLB-179; CDWLB-2

Sachs, Nelly 1891-1970. . . . . DLB-332

Sá-Carneiro, Mário de 1890-1916. . . . . . . DLB-287

Sack, John 1930-2004 . . . . DLB-185

Sackler, Howard 1929-1982 . . . . DLB-7

Sackville, Lady Margaret 1881-1963 . . . . DLB-240

Sackville, Thomas 1536-1608 and
   Norton, Thomas 1532-1584. . . . . DLB-62

Sackville, Thomas 1536-1608 . . . . DLB-132

Sackville-West, Edward 1901-1965 . . . . . DLB-191

Sackville-West, Vita 1892-1962 . . . . . DLB-34, 195

Sacred Hunger, 1992 Booker Prize winner,
   Barry Unsworth. DLB-326

Sá de Miranda, Francisco de
   1481-1588?. DLB-287

Sade, Marquis de (Donatien-Alphonse-François,
   comte de Sade) 1740-1814 . . . . DLB-314

   "Dialogue entre un prêtre et un
      moribond" DLB-314

Sadlier, Mary Anne 1820-1903 . . . . DLB-99

D. and J. Sadlier and Company DLB-49

Sadoff, Ira 1945- DLB-120

Sadoveanu, Mihail 1880-1961 . . . . DLB-220

al-Sadr, Muhammad Baqir 1935-1980 . . . DLB-346

Sadur, Nina Nikolaevna 1950- DLB-285

Sáenz, Benjamin Alire 1954- DLB-209

Saenz, Jaime 1921-1986 . . . . DLB-145, 283

Saffin, John circa 1626-1710 . . . . DLB-24

Sagan, Françoise 1935-2004 . . . . DLB-83

Sage, Robert 1899-1962 . . . . DLB-4

Sagel, Jim 1947- DLB-82

Sagendorph, Robb Hansell 1900-1970 . . . DLB-137

Sahagún, Carlos 1938- DLB-108

Sahgal, Nayantara 1927- DLB-323

Sahkomaapii, Piitai (see Highwater, Jamake)

Sahl, Hans 1902-1993 . . . . DLB-69

Said, Edward W. 1935-2003 . . . . DLB-67, 346

Saigyō 1118-1190 . . . . DLB-203

Saijo, Albert 1926- DLB-312

Saiko, George 1892-1962 . . . . DLB-85

Sainte-Beuve, Charles-Augustin
   1804-1869 . . . . DLB-217

Saint-Exupéry, Antoine de 1900-1944 . . . . DLB-72

Saint-Gelais, Mellin de 1490?-1558 . . . . . DLB-327

St. John, J. Allen 1872-1957. . . . . DLB-188

St John, Madeleine 1942- DLB-267

St. Johns, Adela Rogers 1894-1988 . . . . . . DLB-29

St. Omer, Garth 1931- DLB-117

Saint Pierre, Michel de 1916-1987 . . . . . . DLB-83

Saintsbury, George 1845-1933 . . . . . . DLB-57, 149

   "Modern English Prose" (1876) DLB-57

   The Present State of the English
     Novel (1892),. DLB-18

Saint-Simon, Louis de Rouvroy, duc de
   1675-1755 . . . . DLB-314

St. Dominic's Press DLB-112

The St. John's College Robert Graves Trust . . Y-96

St. Martin's Press DLB-46

St. Nicholas 1873-1881 . . . . DS-13

Saiokuken Sōchō 1448-1532. . . . . DLB-203

Saki (see Munro, H. H.)

Salaam, Kalamu ya 1947- DLB-38

Salacrou, Armand 1899-1989 . . . . DLB-321

Šalamun, Tomaž 1941- . . . DLB-181; CDWLB-4

Salas, Floyd 1931- DLB-82

Sálaz-Marquez, Rubén 1935- DLB-122

Salcedo, Hugo 1964- DLB-305

Salemson, Harold J. 1910-1988. . . . . DLB-4

Salesbury, William 1520?-1584?. DLB-281

Salih, Tayeb 1929- DLB-346

Salinas, Luis Omar 1937- DLB-82

Salinas, Pedro 1891-1951 . . . . DLB-134

Salinger, J. D.
   1919- DLB-2, 102, 173; CDALB-1

Salkey, Andrew 1928-1995 . . . . DLB-125

Sallust circa 86 B.C.-35 B.C.
   . . . . DLB-211; CDWLB-1

Salt, Waldo 1914-1987 . . . . DLB-44

Salter, James 1925- DLB-130

Salter, Mary Jo 1954- DLB-120

Saltus, Edgar 1855-1921. . . . . DLB-202

Saltykov, Mikhail Evgrafovich
   1826-1889 . . . . DLB-238

Salustri, Carlo Alberto (see Trilussa)

Salverson, Laura Goodman 1890-1970. . . . DLB-92

Samain, Albert 1858-1900 . . . . DLB-217

Sampson, Richard Henry (see Hull, Richard)

Samuels, Ernest 1903-1996. . . . . DLB-111

Sanborn, Franklin Benjamin
   1831-1917. . . . . DLB-1, 223

Sánchez, Florencio 1875-1910 . . . . DLB-305

Sánchez, Luis Rafael 1936- DLB-145, 305

Sánchez, Philomeno "Phil" 1917- DLB-122

Sánchez, Ricardo 1941-1995. . . . . DLB-82

Sánchez, Saúl 1943- DLB-209

Sanchez, Sonia 1934- DLB-41; DS-8

Sánchez de Arévalo, Rodrigo
   1404-1470. . . . . DLB-286

Sánchez de Badajoz, Diego ?-1552? DLB-318

Sánchez Ferlosio, Rafael 1927- DLB-322

Sand, George 1804-1876 . . . . DLB-119, 192

Sandburg, Carl
   1878-1967. . . . . DLB-17, 54; CDALB-3

Sandel, Cora (Sara Fabricius)
   1880-1974. . . . . DLB-297

Sandemose, Aksel 1899-1965 . . . . DLB-297

Sanders, Edward 1939- DLB-16, 244

Sanderson, Robert 1587-1663 . . . . DLB-281

Sandoz, Mari 1896-1966. . . . . DLB-9, 212

Sandwell, B. K. 1876-1954 . . . . DLB-92

Sandy, Stephen 1934- DLB-165

Sandys, George 1578-1644 . . . . DLB-24, 121

Sanger, Margaret 1878-1933 . . . . DLB-345

Sangster, Charles 1822-1893. . . . . DLB-99

Sanguineti, Edoardo 1930- DLB-128

Sanjōnishi Sanetaka 1455-1537 . . . . DLB-203

San Pedro, Diego de fl. ca. 1492 . . . . DLB-286

Sansay, Leonora ?-after 1823 . . . . DLB-200

Sansom, William 1912-1976 . . . . DLB-139

Santa Maria Egipçiaca thirteenth-fourteenth
   centuries. DLB-337

Sant'Anna, Affonso Romano de
   1937- DLB-307

Santayana, George
  1863-1952 . . . . . . DLB-54, 71, 246, 270; DS-13

Santiago, Danny 1911-1988 . . . . DLB-122

Santillana, Marqués de (Íñigo López de Mendoza)
  1398-1458 . . . . DLB-286

Santmyer, Helen Hooven 1895-1986 . . . . Y-84

Santos, Bienvenido N. 1911-1996 . . . DLB-312, 348

Santos, Lope K. 1879-1963 . . . . DLB-348

Sanvitale, Francesca 1928- DLB-196

Sapidus, Joannes 1490-1561 . . . . DLB-179

Sapir, Edward 1884-1939 . . . . DLB-92

Sapper (see McNeile, Herman Cyril)

Sappho circa 620 B.C.-circa 550 B.C.
  . . . . DLB-176; CDWLB-1

Saramago, José 1922- DLB-287, 332; Y-98

  Nobel Lecture 1998: How Characters
  Became the Masters and the Author
  Their Apprentice Y-98

Sarban (John W. Wall) 1910-1989 . . . . DLB-255

Sardou, Victorien 1831-1908 . . . . DLB-192

Sarduy, Severo 1937-1993 . . . . DLB-113

Sargent, Pamela 1948- DLB-8

Saro-Wiwa, Ken 1941- DLB-157

Saroyan, Aram
  Rites of Passage [on William Saroyan] Y-83

Saroyan, William
  1908-1981 . . . . . DLB-7, 9, 86; Y-81; CDALB-7

Sarraute, Nathalie 1900-1999 . . . . DLB-83, 321

Sarrazin, Albertine 1937-1967 . . . . DLB-83

Sarris, Greg 1952- DLB-175

Sarrocchi, Margherita 1560-1617 . . . . DLB-339

Sarton, May 1912-1995 . . . . DLB-48; Y-81

Sartre, Jean-Paul
  1905-1980 . . . . DLB-72, 296, 321, 332

Sassoon, Siegfried
  1886-1967 . . . . DLB-20, 191; DS-18

  A Centenary Essay Y-86

  Tributes from Vivien F. Clarke and
  Michael Thorpe Y-86

Sata Ineko 1904-1998 . . . . DLB-180

Saturday Review Press DLB-46

Saunders, George W. 1958- DLB-335

Saunders, James 1925-2004 . . . . DLB-13

Saunders, John Monk 1897-1940 . . . . DLB-26

Saunders, Margaret Marshall
  1861-1947 . . . . DLB-92

Saunders and Otley DLB-106

Saussure, Ferdinand de 1857-1913 . . . . DLB-242

Savage, James 1784-1873 . . . . DLB-30

Savage, Marmion W. 1803?-1872 . . . . DLB-21

Savage, Richard 1697?-1743 . . . . DLB-95

Savard, Félix-Antoine 1896-1982 . . . . DLB-68

Savery, Henry 1791-1842 . . . . DLB-230

Savić, Milisav 1945- DLB-353

Saville, (Leonard) Malcolm 1901-1982 . . . DLB-160

Saville, 1976 Booker Prize winner,
  David Storey DLB-326

Savinio, Alberto 1891-1952 . . . . DLB-264

Sawyer, Robert J. 1960- DLB-251

Sawyer, Ruth 1880-1970 . . . . DLB-22

Sayer, Mandy 1963- DLB-325

Sayers, Dorothy L.
  1893-1957 . . . . DLB-10, 36, 77, 100; CDBLB-6

  The Dorothy L. Sayers Society Y-98

Sayle, Charles Edward 1864-1924 . . . . DLB-184

Sayles, John Thomas 1950- DLB-44

Sbarbaro, Camillo 1888-1967 . . . . DLB-114

Scala, Flaminio (Flavio) 1552-1624 . . . . . . DLB-339

Scalapino, Leslie 1947- DLB-193

Scannell, Vernon 1922-2007 . . . . DLB-27

Scarry, Richard 1919-1994 . . . . DLB-61

Scève, Maurice circa 1502-circa 1564 . . . . . DLB-327

Schack, Hans Egede 1820-1859 . . . . DLB-300

Schaefer, Jack 1907-1991 . . . . DLB-212

Schaeffer, Albrecht 1885-1950 . . . . DLB-66

Schaeffer, Susan Fromberg 1941- . . . DLB-28, 299

Schaff, Philip 1819-1893 . . . . DS-13

Schaper, Edzard 1908-1984 . . . . DLB-69

Scharf, J. Thomas 1843-1898 . . . . DLB-47

Schede, Paul Melissus 1539-1602 . . . . DLB-179

Scheffel, Joseph Viktor von 1826-1886 . . . DLB-129

Scheffler, Johann 1624-1677 . . . . DLB-164

Schéhadé, Georges 1905-1999 . . . . DLB-321

Schelling, Andrew 1953- DLB-342

Schelling, Friedrich Wilhelm Joseph von
  1775-1854 . . . . DLB-90

Scherer, Wilhelm 1841-1886 . . . . DLB-129

Schenkkan, Robert 1953- DLB-341

Scherfig, Hans 1905-1979 . . . . DLB-214

Schickele, René 1883-1940 . . . . DLB-66

Schiff, Dorothy 1903-1989 . . . . DLB-127

Schiller, Friedrich
  1759-1805 . . . . DLB-94; CDWLB-2

Schindler's Ark, 1982 Booker Prize winner,
  Thomas Keneally DLB-326

Schirmer, David 1623-1687 . . . . DLB-164

Schlaf, Johannes 1862-1941 . . . . DLB-118

Schlegel, August Wilhelm 1767-1845 . . . . . . DLB-94

Schlegel, Dorothea 1763-1839 . . . . DLB-90

Schlegel, Friedrich 1772-1829 . . . . DLB-90

Schleiermacher, Friedrich 1768-1834 . . . . . . DLB-90

Schlesinger, Arthur M., Jr. 1917-2007 . . . . . . DLB-17

Schlumberger, Jean 1877-1968 . . . . DLB-65

Schmid, Eduard Hermann Wilhelm
  (see Edschmid, Kasimir)

Schmidt, Arno 1914-1979 . . . . DLB-69

Schmidt, Johann Kaspar (see Stirner, Max)

Schmidt, Michael 1947- DLB-40

Schmidtbonn, Wilhelm August
  1876-1952 . . . . DLB-118

Schmitz, Aron Hector (see Svevo, Italo)

Schmitz, James H. 1911-1981 . . . . DLB-8

Schnabel, Johann Gottfried 1692-1760 . . . . DLB-168

Schnackenberg, Gjertrud 1953- DLB-120

Schnitzler, Arthur
  1862-1931 . . . . DLB-81, 118; CDWLB-2

Schnurre, Wolfdietrich 1920-1989 . . . . DLB-69

Schocken Books DLB-46

Scholartis Press DLB-112

Scholderer, Victor 1880-1971 . . . . DLB-201

The Schomburg Center for Research
  in Black Culture DLB-76

Schönbeck, Virgilio (see Giotti, Virgilio)

Schönherr, Karl 1867-1943 . . . . DLB-118

Schoolcraft, Jane Johnston 1800-1841 . . . . DLB-175

School Stories, 1914-1960 . . . . DLB-160

Schopenhauer, Arthur 1788-1860 . . . . DLB-90

Schopenhauer, Johanna 1766-1838 . . . . DLB-90

Schorer, Mark 1908-1977 . . . . DLB-103

Schottelius, Justus Georg 1612-1676 . . . . . DLB-164

Schouler, James 1839-1920 . . . . DLB-47

Schoultz, Solveig von 1907-1996 . . . . DLB-259

Schrader, Paul 1946- DLB-44

Schreiner, Olive
  1855-1920 . . . . DLB-18, 156, 190, 225

Schroeder, Andreas 1946- DLB-53

Schubart, Christian Friedrich Daniel
  1739-1791 . . . . DLB-97

Schubert, Gotthilf Heinrich 1780-1860 . . . . DLB-90

Schücking, Levin 1814-1883 . . . . DLB-133

Schulberg, Budd 1914-2009 . . . DLB-6, 26, 28; Y-81

  Excerpts from USC Presentation
  [on F. Scott Fitzgerald] Y-96

F. J. Schulte and Company DLB-49

Schulz, Bruno 1892-1942 . . . . DLB-215; CDWLB-4

Schulze, Hans (see Praetorius, Johannes)

Schupp, Johann Balthasar 1610-1661 . . . . . DLB-164

Schurz, Carl 1829-1906 . . . . DLB-23

Schuyler, George S. 1895-1977 . . . . DLB-29, 51

Schuyler, James 1923-1991 . . . . DLB-5, 169

Schwartz, Delmore 1913-1966 . . . . DLB-28, 48

Schwartz, Jonathan 1938- Y-82

Schwartz, Lynne Sharon 1939- DLB-218

Schwarz, Sibylle 1621-1638 . . . . DLB-164

Schwarz-Bart, Andre 1928-2006 . . . . DLB-299

Schwerner, Armand 1927-1999 . . . . DLB-165

Schwob, Marcel 1867-1905 . . . . DLB-123

Sciascia, Leonardo 1921-1989 . . . . DLB-177

Science Fiction and Fantasy
   Documents in British Fantasy and
      Science Fiction DLB-178

   Hugo Awards and Nebula Awards DLB-8

   The Iconography of Science-Fiction
      Art DLB-8

   The New Wave DLB-8

   Paperback Science Fiction DLB-8

   Science Fantasy DLB-8

   Science-Fiction Fandom and
      Conventions DLB-8

   Science-Fiction Fanzines: The Time
      Binders DLB-8

   Science-Fiction Films DLB-8

   Science Fiction Writers of America
      and the Nebula Award DLB-8

   Selected Science-Fiction Magazines and
      Anthologies DLB-8

   A World Chronology of Important Science
      Fiction Works (1818-1979) DLB-8

   The Year in Science Fiction
      and Fantasy Y-00, 01

Scot, Reginald circa 1538-1599. . . . . DLB-136

Scotellaro, Rocco 1923-1953. . . . . DLB-128

Scott, Alicia Anne (Lady John Scott)
   1810-1900. . . . . DLB-240

Scott, Catharine Amy Dawson
   1865-1934 . . . . DLB-240

Scott, Dennis 1939-1991. . . . . DLB-125

Scott, Dixon 1881-1915 . . . . DLB-98

Scott, Duncan Campbell 1862-1947 . . . . . DLB-92

Scott, Evelyn 1893-1963 . . . . DLB-9, 48

Scott, F. R. 1899-1985. . . . . DLB-88

Scott, Frederick George 1861-1944. . . . . . DLB-92

Scott, Geoffrey 1884-1929 . . . . DLB-149

Scott, Harvey W. 1838-1910. . . . . DLB-23

Scott, John 1948- DLB-325

Scott, Lady Jane (see Scott, Alicia Anne)

Scott, Paul 1920-1978 . . . . DLB-14, 207, 326

Scott, Sarah 1723-1795 . . . . DLB-39

Scott, Tom 1918-1995. . . . . DLB-27

Scott, Sir Walter 1771-1832
   . . . . . . DLB-93, 107, 116, 144, 159; CDBLB-3

Scott, William Bell 1811-1890. . . . . DLB-32

Walter Scott Publishing Company
   Limited. DLB-112

William R. Scott [publishing house] DLB-46

Scott-Heron, Gil 1949- DLB-41

Scribe, Eugène 1791-1861 . . . . DLB-192

Scribner, Arthur Hawley 1859-1932 . . . . DS-13, 16

Scribner, Charles 1854-1930 . . . . DS-13, 16

Scribner, Charles, Jr. 1921-1995 . . . . Y-95

   Reminiscences DS-17

Charles Scribner's Sons DLB-49; DS-13, 16, 17

   Archives of Charles Scribner's Sons DS-17

Scribner's Magazine DS-13

Scribner's Monthly DS-13

Scripps, E. W. 1854-1926 . . . . DLB-25

Scudder, Horace Elisha 1838-1902 . . . . DLB-42, 71

Scudder, Vida Dutton 1861-1954 . . . . DLB-71

Scudéry, Madeleine de 1607-1701 . . . . . . DLB-268

Scupham, Peter 1933- DLB-40

The Sea, 2005 Booker Prize winner,
   John Banville DLB-326

The Sea, The Sea, 1978 Booker Prize winner,
   Iris Murdoch DLB-326

Seabrook, William 1886-1945. . . . . DLB-4

Seabury, Samuel 1729-1796. . . . . DLB-31

Seacole, Mary Jane Grant 1805-1881 . . . . DLB-166

The Seafarer circa 970 . . . . DLB-146

Sealsfield, Charles (Carl Postl)
   1793-1864. . . . . DLB-133, 186

Searle, John R. 1932- DLB-279

Sears, Edward I. 1819?-1876. . . . . DLB-79

Sears Publishing Company DLB-46

Seaton, George 1911-1979 . . . . DLB-44

Seaton, William Winston 1785-1866. . . . . DLB-43

Sebillet, Thomas 1512-1589 . . . . DLB-327

Martin Secker [publishing house] DLB-112

Martin Secker, and Warburg Limited DLB-112

Secombe, Harry Donald 1921-2001 . . . . . DLB-352

The "Second Generation" Holocaust
   Novel DLB-299

Sedgwick, Arthur George 1844-1915 . . . . DLB-64

Sedgwick, Catharine Maria
   1789-1867 . . . . DLB-1, 74, 183, 239, 243

Sedgwick, Ellery 1872-1960 . . . . DLB-91

Sedgwick, Eve Kosofsky 1950- DLB-246

Sedley, Sir Charles 1639-1701 . . . . DLB-131

Seeberg, Peter 1925-1999 . . . . DLB-214

Seeger, Alan 1888-1916. . . . . DLB-45

Seers, Eugene (see Dantin, Louis)

Seferis, George 1900-1971. . . . . DLB-332

Segal, Erich 1937- Y-86

Segal, Lore 1928- DLB-299

Šegedin, Petar 1909-1998 . . . . DLB-181

Seghers, Anna 1900-1983 . . . . DLB-69; CDWLB-2

Seid, Ruth (see Sinclair, Jo)

Seidel, Frederick Lewis 1936- Y-84

Seidel, Ina 1885-1974 . . . . DLB-56

Seifert, Jaroslav
   1901-1986 . . . DLB-215, 332; Y-84; CDWLB-4

   Jaroslav Seifert Through the Eyes of
      the English-Speaking Reader Y-84

   Three Poems by Jaroslav Seifert Y-84

Seifullina, Lidiia Nikolaevna 1889-1954 . . . DLB-272

Seigenthaler, John 1927- DLB-127

Sein Tin 1899-1942. . . . . DLB-348

Seizin Press DLB-112

Séjour, Victor 1817-1874 . . . . DLB-50

Séjour Marcou et Ferrand, Juan Victor
   (see Séjour, Victor)

Sekowski, Józef-Julian, Baron Brambeus
   (see Senkovsky, Osip Ivanovich)

Selby, Bettina 1934- DLB-204

Selby, Hubert Jr. 1928-2004 . . . . DLB-2, 227

Selden, George 1929-1989 . . . . DLB-52

Selden, John 1584-1654 . . . . DLB-213

Selenić, Slobodan 1933-1995 . . . . DLB-181

Self, Edwin F. 1920- DLB-137

Self, Will 1961- DLB-207

Seligman, Edwin R. A. 1861-1939 . . . . . . DLB-47

Selimović, Meša
   1910-1982 . . . . DLB-181; CDWLB-4

Sellars, Wilfrid 1912-1989 . . . . DLB-279

Sellings, Arthur (Arthur Gordon Ley)
   1911-1968 . . . . DLB-261

Selous, Frederick Courteney 1851-1917 . . . DLB-174

Seltzer, Chester E. (see Muro, Amado)

Thomas Seltzer [publishing house] DLB-46

Selvadurai, Shyam 1965- DLB-323

Selvon, Sam 1923-1994 . . . . DLB-125; CDWLB-3

Semel, Nava 1954- DLB-299

Semmes, Raphael 1809-1877 . . . . DLB-189

Senancour, Etienne de 1770-1846 . . . . . . DLB-119

Sena, Jorge de 1919-1978 . . . . DLB-287

Sendak, Maurice 1928- DLB-61

Sender, Ramón J. 1901-1982 . . . . DLB-322

Seneca the Elder
   circa 54 B.C.-circa A.D. 40 . . . . DLB-211

Seneca the Younger
   circa 1 B.C.-A.D. 65 . . . . . DLB-211; CDWLB-1

Senécal, Eva 1905-1988 . . . . DLB-92

Sengstacke, John 1912-1997 . . . . DLB-127

Seni Saowaphong 1918- DLB-348

Senior, Olive 1941- DLB-157

Senkovsky, Osip Ivanovich
   (Józef-Julian Sekowski, Baron Brambeus)
   1800-1858 . . . . DLB-198

Seno Gumira Ajidarma 1958- DLB-348

Šenoa, August 1838-1881 . . . . DLB-147; CDWLB-4

Sentimental Fiction of the Sixteenth
   Century DLB-318

Sepamla, Sipho 1932-2007 . . . . DLB-157, 225

Serafimovich, Aleksandr Serafimovich
   (Aleksandr Serafimovich Popov)
   1863-1949 . . . . DLB-272

Serao, Matilde 1856-1927 . . . . DLB-264

Seredy, Kate 1899-1975 . . . . DLB-22

Sereni, Vittorio 1913-1983 . . . . DLB-128

William Seres [publishing house] DLB-170

Sergeev-Tsensky, Sergei Nikolaevich (Sergei
   Nikolaevich Sergeev) 1875-1958 . . . . . DLB-272

Serling, Rod 1924-1975 ....DLB-26
Sernine, Daniel 1955- DLB-251
Serote, Mongane Wally 1944- DLB-125, 225
Serraillier, Ian 1912-1994...............DLB-161
Serrano, Nina 1934- DLB-122
Service, Robert 1874-1958..............DLB-92
Sessler, Charles 1854-1935.............DLB-187
Seth, Vikram 1952- DLB-120, 271, 323
Seton, Elizabeth Ann 1774-1821.........DLB-200
Seton, Ernest Thompson
    1860-1942 ....DLB-92; DS-13
Seton, John circa 1509-1567...........DLB-281
Setouchi Harumi 1922- DLB-182
Settle, Mary Lee 1918-2005...............DLB-6
Seume, Johann Gottfried 1763-1810.......DLB-94
Seuse, Heinrich 1295?-1366............DLB-179
Seuss, Dr. (see Geisel, Theodor Seuss)
Severianin, Igor' 1887-1941...........DLB-295
Severin, Timothy 1940- DLB-204
Sévigné, Marie de Rabutin Chantal,
    Madame de 1626-1696 ....DLB-268
Sewall, Joseph 1688-1769................DLB-24
Sewall, Richard B. 1908-2003..........DLB-111
Sewall, Samuel 1652-1730...............DLB-24
Sewell, Anna 1820-1878.................DLB-163
Sewell, Stephen 1953- DLB-325
Sexton, Anne 1928-1974 ...DLB-5, 169; CDALB-1
Seymour-Smith, Martin 1928-1998 .....DLB-155
Sgorlon, Carlo 1930- DLB-196
Shaara, Michael 1929-1988 ....Y-83
Shabel'skaia, Aleksandra Stanislavovna
    1845-1921 ....DLB-238
Shadwell, Thomas 1641?-1692 ....DLB-80
Shaffer, Anthony 1926-2001 ....DLB-13
Shaffer, Peter 1926- DLB-13, 233; CDBLB-8
Muhammad ibn Idris al-Shafi'i 767-820 ...DLB-311
Shaftesbury, Anthony Ashley Cooper,
    Third Earl of 1671-1713 ....DLB-101, 336
Shaginian, Marietta Sergeevna
    1888-1982 ....DLB-272
Shahnan Ahmad 1933- DLB-348
Shairp, Mordaunt 1887-1939 ....DLB-10
Shakespeare, Nicholas 1957- DLB-231
Shakespeare, William
    1564-1616 ......DLB-62, 172, 263; CDBLB-1
    The New Variorum Shakespeare.........Y-85
    Shakespeare and Montaigne: A Symposium
        by Jules Furthman.................Y-02
    $6,166,000 for a *Book!* Observations on
        *The Shakespeare First Folio: The History
        of the Book* Y-01
    Taylor-Made Shakespeare? Or Is
        "Shall I Die?" the Long-Lost Text
        of Bottom's Dream? Y-85

The Shakespeare Globe Trust Y-93
Shakespeare Head Press................DLB-112
Shakhova, Elisaveta Nikitichna
    1822-1899 ....DLB-277
Shakhovskoi, Aleksandr Aleksandrovich
    1777-1846......................DLB-150
Shalamov, Varlam Tikhonovich
    1907-1982 ....DLB-302
Shammas, Anton 1950- DLB-346
al-Shanfara fl. sixth century DLB-311
Shange, Ntozake 1948- DLB-38, 249
Shanley, John Patrick 1950- DLB-341
Shapcott, Thomas W. 1935- DLB-289
Shapir, Ol'ga Andreevna 1850-1916 .....DLB-295
Shapiro, Gerald 1950- DLB-335
Shapiro, Karl 1913-2000 ....DLB-48
Sharon Publications....................DLB-46
Sharov, Vladimir Aleksandrovich
    1952- DLB-285
Sharp, Margery 1905-1991 ....DLB-161
Sharp, William 1855-1905 ....DLB-156
Sharpe, Tom 1928- DLB-14, 231
Shaw, Albert 1857-1947 ....DLB-91
Shaw, George Bernard
    1856-1950 ...DLB-10, 57, 190, 332; CDBLB-6
    The Bernard Shaw Society Y-99
    "Stage Censorship: The Rejected
        Statement" (1911) [excerpts].....DLB-10
Shaw, Henry Wheeler 1818-1885 ....DLB-11
Shaw, Irwin
    1913-1984 ......DLB-6, 102; Y-84; CDALB-1
Shaw, Joseph T. 1874-1952..............DLB-137
    "As I Was Saying," Joseph T. Shaw's
        Editorial Rationale in *Black Mask*
        (January 1927)................DLB-137
Shaw, Mary 1854-1929 ....DLB-228
Shaw, Robert 1927-1978............DLB-13, 14
Shaw, Robert B. 1947- DLB-120
Shawn, Wallace 1943- DLB-266
Shawn, William 1907-1992..............DLB-137
Frank Shay [publishing house]..........DLB-46
al-Shaykh, Hanan 1945- DLB-346
Shchedrin, N. (see Saltykov, Mikhail Evgrafovich)
Shcherbakova, Galina Nikolaevna
    1932- DLB-285
Shcherbina, Nikolai Fedorovich
    1821-1869 ....DLB-277
Shea, John Gilmary 1824-1892 ....DLB-30
Sheaffer, Louis 1912-1993 ....DLB-103
Sheahan, Henry Beston (see Beston, Henry)
Shearing, Joseph 1886-1952.............DLB-70
Shebbeare, John 1709-1788 ....DLB-39
Sheckley, Robert 1928-2005 ....DLB-8
Shedd, William G. T. 1820-1894 ....DLB-64

Sheed, Wilfrid 1930- DLB-6
Sheed and Ward [U.S.] DLB-46
Sheed and Ward Limited [U.K.] DLB-112
Sheldon, Alice B. (see Tiptree, James, Jr.)
Sheldon, Edward 1886-1946 ....DLB-7
Sheldon and Company DLB-49
Sheller, Aleksandr Konstantinovich
    1838-1900 ....DLB-238
Shelley, Mary Wollstonecraft 1797-1851
    ....DLB-110, 116, 159, 178; CDBLB-3
    Preface to *Frankenstein; or, The
        Modern Prometheus* (1818) DLB-178
Shelley, Percy Bysshe
    1792-1822 ......DLB-96, 110, 158; CDBLB-3
Shelnutt, Eve 1941- DLB-130
Shelton, Richard 1933- DLB-342
Shem Tov de Carrión (Isaac Ibn Ardutiel)
    fl. circa 1350-1360................DLB-337
Shen Congwen 1902-1988.............DLB-328
Shenshin (see Fet, Afanasii Afanas'evich)
Shenstone, William 1714-1763 ....DLB-95
Shepard, Clark and Brown DLB-49
Shepard, Ernest Howard 1879-1976.....DLB-160
Shepard, Sam 1943- DLB-7, 212, 341
Shepard, Thomas, I, 1604 or 1605-1649 ...DLB-24
Shepard, Thomas, II, 1635-1677 ....DLB-24
Shepherd, Luke fl. 1547-1554...........DLB-136
Sherburne, Edward 1616-1702..........DLB-131
Sheridan, Frances 1724-1766 ....DLB-39, 84
Sheridan, Richard Brinsley
    1751-1816 ....DLB-89; CDBLB-2
Sherman, Francis 1871-1926 ....DLB-92
Sherman, Martin 1938- DLB-228
Sherriff, R. C. 1896-1975.......DLB-10, 191, 233
Sherrod, Blackie 1919- DLB-241
Sherry, Norman 1935- DLB-155
    Tribute to Graham Greene Y-91
Sherry, Richard 1506-1551 or 1555......DLB-236
Sherwood, Mary Martha 1775-1851 .....DLB-163
Sherwood, Robert E. 1896-1955 ...DLB-7, 26, 249
Shevyrev, Stepan Petrovich
    1806-1864 ....DLB-205
Shi Tuo (Lu Fen) 1910-1988 ....DLB-328
Shiel, M. P. 1865-1947................DLB-153
Shields, Carol 1935-2003..........DLB-334, 350
Shiels, George 1886-1949 ....DLB-10
Shiga Naoya 1883-1971 ....DLB-180
Shiina Rinzō 1911-1973 ....DLB-182
Shikishi Naishinnō 1153?-1201 ....DLB-203
Shillaber, Benjamin Penhallow
    1814-1890 ....DLB-1, 11, 235
Shimao Toshio 1917-1986 ....DLB-182
Shimazaki Tōson 1872-1943 ....DLB-180

Cumulative Index

Shimose, Pedro 1940- DLB-283

Shine, Ted 1931- DLB-38

Shinkei 1406-1475................. DLB-203

Ship, Reuben 1915-1975............. DLB-88

Shirer, William L. 1904-1993 .... DLB-4

Shirinsky-Shikhmatov, Sergii Aleksandrovich
   1783-1837..................... DLB-150

Shirley, James 1596-1666 .... DLB-58

Shishkov, Aleksandr Semenovich
   1753-1841.................... DLB-150

Shmelev, I. S. 1873-1950.............. DLB-317

Shockley, Ann Allen 1927- DLB-33

Sholem Aleichem (Sholem Aleykhem; Sholem Yakov Rabinowitz [Sholem Yankev Rabinovitsch]) 1859-1916..................... DLB-333

Sholokhov, Mikhail Aleksandrovich
   1905-1984 ....DLB-272, 332

Shōno Junzō 1921- DLB-182

Shore, Arabella 1820?-1901 .... DLB-199

Shore, Louisa 1824-1895 .... DLB-199

Short, Luke (see Glidden, Frederick Dilley)

Peter Short [publishing house] DLB-170

Shorter, Dora Sigerson 1866-1918 ...... DLB-240

Shorthouse, Joseph Henry 1834-1903 .... DLB-18

Short Stories
   Michael M. Rea and the Rea Award
     for the Short Story................ Y-97
   The Year in Short Stories Y-87
   The Year in the Short Story Y-88, 90–93

Shōtetsu 1381-1459................... DLB-203

Showalter, Elaine 1941- DLB-67

Shreve, Anita 1946- DLB-292

Shteiger, Anatolii 1907-1944 .... DLB-317

Shukshin, Vasilii Makarovich
   1929-1974..................... DLB-302

Shulevitz, Uri 1935- DLB-61

Shulman, Max 1919-1988............. DLB-11

Shute, Henry A. 1856-1943 .... DLB-9

Shute, Nevil (Nevil Shute Norway)
   1899-1960 .... DLB-255

Shuttle, Penelope 1947- DLB-14, 40

Shvarts, Evgenii L'vovich 1896-1958 ..... DLB-272

Sibawayhi circa 750-circa 795 .... DLB-311

Sibbes, Richard 1577-1635 .... DLB-151

Sibiriak, D. (see Mamin, Dmitrii Narkisovich)

Siburapha 1905-1974 .... DLB-348

Sidaoru'ang 1943- DLB-348

Siddal, Elizabeth Eleanor 1829-1862 .... DLB-199

Sidgwick, Ethel 1877-1970............. DLB-197

Sidgwick, Henry 1838-1900 .... DLB-262

Sidgwick and Jackson Limited DLB-112

Sidhwa, Bapsi 1939- DLB-323

Sidney, Margaret (see Lothrop, Harriet M.)

Sidney, Mary 1561-1621.............. DLB-167

Sidney, Sir Philip
   1554-1586 .... DLB-167; CDBLB-1

   An Apologie for Poetrie (the Olney edition,
     1595, of *Defence of Poesie*)........ DLB-167

Sidney's Press DLB-49

The Siege of Krishnapur, 1973 Booker Prize winner,
   J. G. Farrell.................... DLB-326

Sienkiewicz, Henryk 1846-1916 .... DLB-332

Sierra, Rubén 1946- DLB-122

Sierra Club Books.................... DLB-49

Siger of Brabant circa 1240-circa 1284 ... DLB-115

Sigourney, Lydia Huntley
   1791-1865.......DLB-1, 42, 73, 183, 239, 243

Silkin, Jon 1930-1997 .... DLB-27

Silko, Leslie Marmon
   1948- DLB-143, 175, 256, 275

Sillanpää, Frans Eemil 1888-1964....... DLB-332

Silliman, Benjamin 1779-1864......... DLB-183

Silliman, Ron 1946- DLB-169

Silliphant, Stirling 1918-1996 .... DLB-26

Sillitoe, Alan 1928- DLB-14, 139; CDBLB-8

   Tribute to J. B. Priestly................ Y-84

Silman, Roberta 1934- DLB-28

Silone, Ignazio (Secondino Tranquilli)
   1900-1978..................... DLB-264

Silva, Beverly 1930- DLB-122

Silva, Clara 1905-1976 .... DLB-290

Silva, José Asunció 1865-1896 .... DLB-283

Silverberg, Robert 1935- DLB-8

Silverman, Kaja 1947- DLB-246

Silverman, Kenneth 1936- DLB-111

Simak, Clifford D. 1904-1988........... DLB-8

Simcoe, Elizabeth 1762-1850........... DLB-99

Simcox, Edith Jemima 1844-1901 ...... DLB-190

Simcox, George Augustus 1841-1905..... DLB-35

Sime, Jessie Georgina 1868-1958 .... DLB-92

Simenon, Georges 1903-1989.......DLB-72; Y-89

Simic, Charles 1938- DLB-105

   "Images and 'Images'"............ DLB-105

Simionescu, Mircea Horia 1928- DLB-232

Simmel, Georg 1858-1918 .... DLB-296

Simmel, Johannes Mario 1924-2009...... DLB-69

Valentine Simmes [publishing house] DLB-170

Simmons, Ernest J. 1903-1972 .... DLB-103

Simmons, Herbert Alfred 1930- DLB-33

Simmons, James 1933- DLB-40

Simms, William Gilmore
   1806-1870...........DLB-3, 30, 59, 73, 248

Simms and M'Intyre................. DLB-106

Simon, Claude 1913-2005 .....DLB-83, 332; Y-85

   Nobel Lecture Y-85

Simon, Neil 1927- DLB-7, 266

Simon, S. J. 1904-1948 .... DLB-352

Simon and Schuster DLB-46

Simonov, Konstantin Mikhailovich
   1915-1979..................... DLB-302

Simons, Katherine Drayton Mayrant
   1890-1969 .... Y-83

Simović, Ljubomir 1935- DLB-181

Simpkin and Marshall
   [publishing house] DLB-154

Simple, Peter (see Welch, James Colin Ross and
   Wharton, Michael Bernard)

Simpson, Helen 1897-1940 .... DLB-77

Simpson, John Palgrave 1807-1887...... DLB-344

Simpson, Louis 1923- DLB-5

Simpson, N. F. 1919- DLB-13

Sims, George 1923-1999.......... DLB-87; Y-99

Sims, George Robert 1847-1922 ..DLB-35, 70, 135

Sinán, Rogelio 1902-1994......... DLB-145, 290

Sinclair, Andrew 1935- DLB-14

Sinclair, Bertrand William 1881-1972..... DLB-92

Sinclair, Catherine 1800-1864.......... DLB-163

Sinclair, Clive 1948- DLB-319

Sinclair, Jo 1913-1995................ DLB-28

Sinclair, Lister 1921-2006 .... DLB-88

Sinclair, May 1863-1946 .... DLB-36, 135

   The Novels of Dorothy Richardson
     (1918) DLB-36

Sinclair, Upton 1878-1968...... DLB-9; CDALB-5

Upton Sinclair [publishing house]........ DLB-46

Singer, Isaac Bashevis 1904-1991
   .. DLB-6, 28, 52, 278, 332, 333; Y-91; CDALB-1

Singer, Israel Joshua (Yisroel-Yehoyshue Zinger)
   1893-1944 .... DLB-333

Singer, Mark 1950- DLB-185

Singh, Khushwant 1915- DLB-323

Singmaster, Elsie 1879-1958 .... DLB-9

Siniavsky, Andrei (Abram Tertz)
   1925-1997 .... DLB-302

Sinisgalli, Leonardo 1908-1981......... DLB-114

Siodmak, Curt 1902-2000.............. DLB-44

Sîrbu, Ion D. 1919-1989 .... DLB-232

Siringo, Charles A. 1855-1928 .... DLB-186

Sissay, Lemn 1967- DLB-347

Sissman, L. E. 1928-1976 .... DLB-5

Sisson, C. H. 1914-2003 .... DLB-27

Sitwell, Edith 1887-1964 ...... DLB-20; CDBLB-7

Sitwell, Osbert 1892-1969............DLB-100, 195

Sivanandan, Ambalavaner 1923- DLB-323

Sivle, Per 1857-1904 .... DLB-354

Sixteenth-Century Spanish Epic, The.... DLB-318

Skácel, Jan 1922-1989................ DLB-232

Skalbe, Kārlis 1879-1945 .... DLB-220

Skármeta, Antonio
   1940- DLB-145; CDWLB-3

Skavronsky, A. (see Danilevsky, Grigorii Petrovich)

Skeat, Walter W. 1835-1912............DLB-184

William Skeffington [publishing house]...DLB-106

Skelton, John 1463-1529 ....DLB-136

Skelton, Robin 1925-1997 ....DLB-27, 53

Škėma, Antanas 1910-1961 ....DLB-220

Skidelsky, Secha Jascha (see Simon, S. J.)

Skinner, Constance Lindsay
  1877-1939 ....DLB-92

Skinner, John Stuart 1788-1851 ....DLB-73

Skipsey, Joseph 1832-1903..............DLB-35

Skou-Hansen, Tage 1925- DLB-214

Skram, Amalie 1846-1905 ....DLB-354

Skrzynecki, Peter 1945- DLB-289

Skujiņš, Zigmunds 1926- DLB-353

Škvorecký, Josef 1924- DLB-232; CDWLB-4

Slade, Bernard 1930- DLB-53

Slamnig, Ivan 1930- DLB-181

Slančeková, Božena (see Timrava)

Slataper, Scipio 1888-1915 ....DLB-264

Slater, Patrick 1880-1951 ....DLB-68

Slaveykov, Pencho 1866-1912 ....DLB-147

Slaviček, Milivoj 1929- DLB-181

Slavitt, David 1935- DLB-5, 6

Sleigh, Burrows Willcocks Arthur
  1821-1869 ....DLB-99

Sleptsov, Vasilii Alekseevich 1836-1878 ...DLB-277

Slesinger, Tess 1905-1945............DLB-102

Slessor, Kenneth 1901-1971 ....DLB-260

Slick, Sam (see Haliburton, Thomas Chandler)

Sloan, John 1871-1951 ....DLB-188

Sloane, William, Associates DLB-46

Słobodzianek, Tadeusz 1955- DLB-353

Slonimsky, Mikhail Leonidovich
  1897-1972......................DLB-272

Sluchevsky, Konstantin Konstantinovich
  1837-1904 ....DLB-277

Small, Maynard and Company DLB-49

Smart, Christopher 1722-1771 ....DLB-109

Smart, David A. 1892-1957 ....DLB-137

Smart, Elizabeth 1913-1986 ....DLB-88

Smart, J. J. C. 1920- DLB-262

Smartt, Dorothea 1963- DLB-347

Smedley, Menella Bute 1820?-1877 .....DLB-199

William Smellie [publishing house] DLB-154

Smiles, Samuel 1812-1904 ....DLB-55

Smiley, Jane 1949- DLB-227, 234

Smith, A. J. M. 1902-1980 ....DLB-88

Smith, Adam 1723-1790 ....DLB-104, 252, 336

Smith, Adam (George Jerome Waldo
  Goodman) 1930- DLB-185

Smith, Alexander 1829-1867 ....DLB-32, 55

"On the Writing of Essays" (1862) DLB-57

Smith, Amanda 1837-1915 ....DLB-221

Smith, Anna Deavere 1950- DLB-341

Smith, Betty 1896-1972 ....Y-82

Smith, Carol Sturm 1938- Y-81

Smith, Charles Henry 1826-1903 ....DLB-11

Smith, Charlotte 1749-1806.........DLB-39, 109

Smith, Chet 1899-1973................DLB-171

Smith, Cordwainer 1913-1966...........DLB-8

Smith, Dave 1942- DLB-5

  Tribute to James Dickey Y-97

  Tribute to John Gardner Y-82

Smith, Dodie 1896-1990 ....DLB-10

Smith, Doris Buchanan 1934-2002 ....DLB-52

Smith, E. E. 1890-1965 ....DLB-8

Smith, Elihu Hubbard 1771-1798.........DLB-37

Smith, Elizabeth Oakes (Prince)
  (see Oakes Smith, Elizabeth)

Smith, Eunice 1757-1823 ....DLB-200

Smith, F. Hopkinson 1838-1915 .... DS-13

Smith, George D. 1870-1920 ....DLB-140

Smith, George O. 1911-1981 ....DLB-8

Smith, Goldwin 1823-1910 ....DLB-99

Smith, H. Allen 1907-1976 ....DLB-11, 29

Smith, Harry B. 1860-1936 ....DLB-187

Smith, Hazel Brannon 1914-1994 ....DLB-127

Smith, Henry circa 1560-circa 1591......DLB-136

Smith, Horatio (Horace)
  1779-1849 ....DLB-96, 116

Smith, Iain Crichton (Iain Mac a'Ghobhainn)
  1928-1998 ....DLB-40, 139, 319, 352

Smith, J. Allen 1860-1924 ....DLB-47

Smith, James 1775-1839 ....DLB-96

Smith, Jessie Willcox 1863-1935 ....DLB-188

Smith, John 1580-1631................DLB-24, 30

Smith, John 1618-1652................DLB-252

Smith, Josiah 1704-1781 ....DLB-24

Smith, Ken 1938- DLB-40

Smith, Lee 1944- DLB-143; Y-83

Smith, Logan Pearsall 1865-1946........DLB-98

Smith, Margaret Bayard 1778-1844 .....DLB-248

Smith, Mark 1935- Y-82

Smith, Michael 1698-circa 1771 ....DLB-31

Smith, Pauline 1882-1959 ....DLB-225

Smith, Red 1905-1982 .... DLB-29, 171

Smith, Roswell 1829-1892 ....DLB-79

Smith, Samuel Harrison 1772-1845 ....DLB-43

Smith, Samuel Stanhope 1751-1819 ....DLB-37

Smith, Sarah (see Stretton, Hesba)

Smith, Sarah Pogson 1774-1870 ....DLB-200

Smith, Seba 1792-1868...........DLB-1, 11, 243

Smith, Stevie 1902-1971................DLB-20

Smith, Sydney 1771-1845 ....DLB-107

Smith, Sydney Goodsir 1915-1975........DLB-27

Smith, Sir Thomas 1513-1577 ....DLB-132

Smith, Vivian 1933- DLB-325

Smith, W. Gordon 1928-1996 ....DLB-310

Smith, Wendell 1914-1972 ....DLB-171

Smith, William fl. 1595-1597 ....DLB-136

Smith, William 1727-1803 ....DLB-31

  A General Idea of the College of Mirania
    (1753) [excerpts] DLB-31

Smith, William 1728-1793 ....DLB-30

Smith, William Gardner 1927-1974 ....DLB-76

Smith, William Henry 1808-1872 ....DLB-159

Smith, William Jay 1918- DLB-5

Smith, Winchell 1871-1933 ....DLB-341

Smith, Elder and Company DLB-154

Harrison Smith and Robert Haas
  [publishing house] DLB-46

J. Stilman Smith and Company DLB-49

W. B. Smith and Company DLB-49

W. H. Smith and Son.................DLB-106

Smith, Zadie 1975- DLB-347

Leonard Smithers [publishing house].....DLB-112

Smollett, Tobias
  1721-1771...........DLB-39, 104; CDBLB-2

  Dedication to *Ferdinand Count Fathom*
    (1753) DLB-39

  Preface to *Ferdinand Count Fathom*
    (1753) DLB-39

  Preface to *Roderick Random* (1748) DLB-39

Smythe, Francis Sydney 1900-1949 ......DLB-195

Snelling, William Joseph 1804-1848 .....DLB-202

Snellings, Rolland (see Touré, Askia Muhammad)

Snodgrass, W. D. 1926-2009 ....DLB-5

Snoj, Jože 1934- DLB-353

Snorri Hjartarson 1906-1986..........DLB-293

Snow, C. P.
  1905-1980 .....DLB-15, 77; DS-17; CDBLB-7

Snyder, Gary
  1930- DLB-5, 16, 165, 212, 237, 275, 342

Sobiloff, Hy 1912-1970................DLB-48

The Social Contract, Jean-Jacques
  Rousseau......................DLB-314

The Society for Textual Scholarship and
  TEXT Y-87

The Society for the History of Authorship,
  Reading and Publishing Y-92

Söderberg, Hjalmar 1869-1941 ....DLB-259

Södergran, Edith 1892-1923 ....DLB-259

Soffici, Ardengo 1879-1964 ....DLB-114, 264

Sofola, 'Zulu 1938- DLB-157

Sokhanskaia, Nadezhda Stepanovna
  (Kokhanovskaia) 1823?-1884 ....DLB-277

Sokolov, Sasha (Aleksandr Vsevolodovich Sokolov) 1943- DLB-285

Solano, Solita 1888-1975 .... DLB-4

Soldati, Mario 1906-1999 .... DLB-177

Soledad (see Zamudio, Adela)

Šoljan, Antun 1932-1993 .... DLB-181

Sollers, Philippe (Philippe Joyaux) 1936- DLB-83

Sollogub, Vladimir Aleksandrovich 1813-1882. .... DLB-198

Sollors, Werner 1943- DBL-246

Solmi, Sergio 1899-1981 .... DLB-114

Sologub, Fedor 1863-1927 .... DLB-295

Solomon, Carl 1928- DLB-16

Solórzano, Carlos 1922- DLB-305

Souloukhin, Vladimir Alekseevich 1924-1997. .... DLB-302

Solov'ev, Sergei Mikhailovich 1885-1942 .... DLB-295

Solov'ev, Vladimir Sergeevich 1853-1900. .... DLB-295

Solstad, Dag 1941- DLB-297

Solway, David 1941- DLB-53

Solzhenitsyn, Aleksandr 1918-2008. .... DLB-302, 332
 Solzhenitsyn and America Y-85

Some Basic Notes on Three Modern Genres: Interview, Blurb, and Obituary Y-02

Somerville, Edith Œnone 1858-1949 .... DLB-135

Something to Answer For, 1969 Booker Prize winner, P. H. Newby. DLB-326

Somov, Orest Mikhailovich 1793-1833 ... DLB-198

Sønderby, Knud 1909-1966 .... DLB-214

Sone, Monica 1919- DLB-312

Song, Cathy 1955- DLB-169, 312

Sonnevi, Göran 1939- DLB-257

Sono Ayako 1931- DLB-182

Sontag, Susan 1933-2004 .... DLB-2, 67

Sophocles 497/496 B.C.-406/405 B.C. DLB-176; CDWLB-1

Šopov, Aco 1923-1982 .... DLB-181

Sorel, Charles ca.1600-1674. .... DLB-268

Sørensen, Villy 1929-2001 .... DLB-214

Sorensen, Virginia 1912-1991 .... DLB-206

Sorge, Reinhard Johannes 1892-1916.... DLB-118

Sorokin, Vladimir Georgievich 1955- DLB-285

Sorrentino, Gilbert 1929-2006 ... DLB-5, 173; Y-80

Sosa, Roberto 1930- DLB-290

Sotheby, James 1682-1742. .... DLB-213

Sotheby, John 1740-1807. .... DLB-213

Sotheby, Samuel 1771-1842. .... DLB-213

Sotheby, Samuel Leigh 1805-1861 ..... DLB-213

Sotheby, William 1757-1833 .... DLB-93, 213

Soto, Gary 1952- DLB-82

Soueif, Ahdaf 1950- DLB-267

Souster, Raymond 1921- DLB-88

The *South English Legendary* circa thirteenth-fifteenth centuries........ DLB-146

Southerland, Ellease 1943- DLB-33

Southern, Terry 1924-1995............. DLB-2

Southern Illinois University Press.......... Y-95

Southern Literature
 Fellowship of Southern Writers Y-98
 The Fugitives and the Agrarians: The First Exhibition Y-85
 "The Greatness of Southern Literature": League of the South Institute for the Study of Southern Culture and History Y-02
 The Society for the Study of Southern Literature.............. Y-00
 Southern Writers Between the Wars ... DLB-9

Southerne, Thomas 1659-1746 .... DLB-80

Southey, Caroline Anne Bowles 1786-1854. .... DLB-116

Southey, Robert 1774-1843 ...... DLB-93, 107, 142

Southwell, Robert 1561?-1595 .... DLB-167

Southworth, E. D. E. N. 1819-1899 ...... DLB-239

Sowande, Bode 1948- DLB-157

Tace Sowle [publishing house] DLB-170

Soyfer, Jura 1912-1939 .... DLB-124

Soyinka, Wole 1934-
 .... DLB-125, 332; Y-86, 87; CDWLB-3
 Nobel Lecture 1986: This Past Must Address Its Present Y-86

Spacks, Barry 1931- DLB-105

Spalding, Frances 1950- DLB-155

Spanish Byzantine Novel, The DLB-318

Spanish Travel Writers of the Late Middle Ages................ DLB-286

Spark, Muriel 1918-2006 .... DLB-15, 139; CDBLB-7

Michael Sparke [publishing house] DLB-170

Sparks, Jared 1789-1866 .... DLB-1, 30, 235

Sparshott, Francis 1926- DLB-60

Späth, Gerold 1939- DLB-75

Spatola, Adriano 1941-1988 .... DLB-128

Spaziani, Maria Luisa 1924- DLB-128

Specimens of Foreign Standard Literature 1838-1842 .... DLB-1

The *Spectator* 1828- DLB-110

Spedding, James 1808-1881 .... DLB-144

Spee von Langenfeld, Friedrich 1591-1635 .... DLB-164

Speght, Rachel 1597-after 1630......... DLB-126

Speke, John Hanning 1827-1864........ DLB-166

Spellman, A. B. 1935- DLB-41

Spence, Catherine Helen 1825-1910..... DLB-230

Spence, Thomas 1750-1814 .... DLB-158

Spencer, Anne 1882-1975 .... DLB-51, 54

Spencer, Charles, third Earl of Sunderland 1674-1722..................... DLB-213

Spencer, Elizabeth 1921- DLB-6, 218

Spencer, George John, Second Earl Spencer 1758-1834..................... DLB-184

Spencer, Herbert 1820-1903.........DLB-57, 262
 "The Philosophy of Style" (1852) DLB-57

Spencer, Scott 1945- Y-86

Spender, J. A. 1862-1942 .... DLB-98

Spender, Stephen 1909-1995... DLB-20; CDBLB-7

Spener, Philipp Jakob 1635-1705........ DLB-164

Spenser, Edmund circa 1552-1599 .... DLB-167; CDBLB-1
 Envoy from *The Shepheardes Calender* DLB-167
 "The Generall Argument of the Whole Booke," from *The Shepheardes Calender* DLB-167
 "A Letter of the Authors Expounding His Whole Intention in the Course of this Worke: Which for that It Giueth Great Light to the Reader, for the Better Vnderstanding Is Hereunto Annexed," from *The Faerie Queene* (1590).... DLB-167
 "To His Booke," from *The Shepheardes Calender* (1579)... DLB-167
 "To the Most Excellent and Learned Both Orator and Poete, Mayster Gabriell Haruey, His Verie Special and Singular Good Frend E. K. Commendeth the Good Lyking of This His Labour, and the Patronage of the New Poete," from *The Shepheardes Calender* DLB-167

Sperr, Martin 1944- DLB-124

Spewack, Bella Cowen 1899-1990 ...... DLB-266

Spewack, Samuel 1899-1971........... DLB-266

Spicer, Jack 1925-1965 ....DLB-5, 16, 193

Spiegelman, Art 1948- DLB-299

Spielberg, Peter 1929- Y-81

Spielhagen, Friedrich 1829-1911........ DLB-129

"Spielmannsepen" (circa 1152-circa 1500) .. DLB-148

Spier, Peter 1927- DLB-61

Spillane, Mickey 1918-2006 .... DLB-226

Spink, J. G. Taylor 1888-1962 .... DLB-241

Spinrad, Norman 1940- DLB-8
 Tribute to Isaac Asimov............. Y-92

Spires, Elizabeth 1952- DLB-120

The Spirit of Laws, Claude-Adrien Helvétius DLB-314

The Spirit of Laws, Charles-Louis de Secondat, baron de Montesquieu DLB-314

Spitteler, Carl 1845-1924 .... DLB-129, 332

Spivak, Lawrence E. 1900-1994 ....DLB-137

Spofford, Harriet Prescott 1835-1921 ....DLB-74, 221

Sponde, Jean de 1557-1595 .... DLB-327

Sports

Jimmy, Red, and Others: Harold
  Rosenthal Remembers the Stars
  of the Press Box Y-01

The Literature of Boxing in England
  through Arthur Conan Doyle Y-01

Notable Twentieth-Century Books
  about Sports DLB-241

Sprigge, Timothy L. S. 1932- DLB-262

Spring, Howard 1889-1965 .... DLB-191

Springs, Elliott White 1896-1959 .... DLB-316

Sproxton, Birk 1943-2007 .... DLB-334

Squibob (see Derby, George Horatio)

Squier, E. G. 1821-1888 .... DLB-189

Staal-Delaunay, Marguerite-Jeanne Cordier de
  1684-1750 .... DLB-314

Stableford, Brian 1948- DLB-261

Stacpoole, H. de Vere 1863-1951 .... DLB-153

Staël, Germaine de 1766-1817 ...... DLB-119, 192

Staël-Holstein, Anne-Louise Germaine de
  (see Staël, Germaine de)

Staffeldt, Schack 1769-1826 .... DLB-300

Stafford, Jean 1915-1979 .... DLB-2, 173

Stafford, William 1914-1993 .... DLB-5, 206

Stallings, Laurence 1894-1968 ..... DLB-7, 44, 316

Stallworthy, Jon 1935- DLB-40

Stampp, Kenneth M. 1912- DLB-17

Stănescu, Nichita 1933-1983 .... DLB-232

Stanev, Emiliyan 1907-1979 .... DLB-181

Stanford, Ann 1916-1987 .... DLB-5

Stangerup, Henrik 1937-1998 .... DLB-214

Stanihurst, Richard 1547-1618 .... DLB-281

Stanitsky, N. (see Panaeva, Avdot'ia Iakovlevna)

Stankevich, Nikolai Vladimirovich
  1813-1840 .... DLB-198

Stanković, Borisav ("Bora")
  1876-1927 .... DLB-147; CDWLB-4

Stanley, Henry M. 1841-1904 .... DLB-189; DS-13

Stanley, Thomas 1625-1678 .... DLB-131

Stannard, Martin 1947- DLB-155

William Stansby [publishing house] DLB-170

Stanton, Elizabeth Cady 1815-1902 .... DLB-79

Stanton, Frank L. 1857-1927 .... DLB-25

Stanton, Maura 1946- DLB-120

Stapledon, Olaf 1886-1950 .... DLB-15, 255

Star Spangled Banner Office DLB-49

Stark, Freya 1893-1993 .... DLB-195

Starkey, Thomas circa 1499-1538 .... DLB-132

Starkie, Walter 1894-1976 .... DLB-195

Starkweather, David 1935- DLB-7

Starrett, Vincent 1886-1974 .... DLB-187

Stasiuk, Andrzej 1960- DLB-353

Stationers' Company of London, The DLB-170

Statius circa A.D. 45-A.D. 96 .... DLB-211

Stavis, Barrie 1906-2007 .... DLB-341

Staying On, 1977 Booker Prize winner,
  Paul Scott DLB-326

Stead, Christina 1902-1983 .... DLB-260

Stead, Robert J. C. 1880-1959 .... DLB-92

Steadman, Mark 1930- DLB-6

Stearns, Harold E. 1891-1943 ...... DLB-4; DS-15

Stebnitsky, M. (see Leskov, Nikolai Semenovich)

Stedman, Edmund Clarence 1833-1908 ... DLB-64

Steegmuller, Francis 1906-1994 .... DLB-111

Steel, Flora Annie 1847-1929 ...... DLB-153, 156

Steele, Max 1922-2005 .... Y-80

Steele, Richard
  1672-1729 .... DLB-84, 101; CDBLB-2

Steele, Timothy 1948- DLB-120

Steele, Wilbur Daniel 1886-1970 .... DLB-86

Wallace Markfield's "Steeplechase" Y-02

Steere, Richard circa 1643-1721 .... DLB-24

Stefán frá Hvítadal (Stefán Sigurðsson)
  1887-1933 .... DLB-293

Stefán Guðmundsson (see Stephan G. Stephansson)

Stefán Hörður Grímsson
  1919 or 1920-2002 .... DLB-293

Steffens, Lincoln 1866-1936 .... DLB-303

Stefanovski, Goran 1952- DLB-181

Stegner, Wallace
  1909-1993 .... DLB-9, 206, 275; Y-93

Stehr, Hermann 1864-1940 .... DLB-66

Steig, William 1907-2003 .... DLB-61

Stein, Gertrude 1874-1946
  .... DLB-4, 54, 86, 228; DS-15; CDALB-4

Stein, Leo 1872-1947 .... DLB-4

Stein and Day Publishers DLB-46

Steinbarg, Eliezer (Eliezer Shtaynbarg)
  1880-1932 .... DLB-333

Steinbeck, John 1902-1968 ....
  DLB-7, 9, 212, 275, 309, 332; DS-2; CDALB-5

  John Steinbeck Research Center,
    San Jose State University Y-85

  The Steinbeck Centennial Y-02

Steinem, Gloria 1934- DLB-246

Steiner, George 1929- DLB-67, 299

Steinhoewel, Heinrich 1411/1412-1479 ... DLB-179

Steinn Steinarr (Aðalsteinn Kristmundsson)
  1908-1958 .... DLB-293

Steinunn Sigurðardóttir 1950- DLB-293

Steloff, Ida Frances 1887-1989 .... DLB-187

Stendhal 1783-1842 .... DLB-119

Stephan G. Stephansson (Stefán Guðmundsson)
  1853-1927 .... DLB-293

Stephen, Leslie 1832-1904 ...... DLB-57, 144, 190

Stephen Family (Bloomsbury Group) DS-10

Stephens, A. G. 1865-1933 .... DLB-230

Stephens, Alexander H. 1812-1883 .... DLB-47

Stephens, Alice Barber 1858-1932 .... DLB-188

Stephens, Ann 1810-1886 .... DLB-3, 73, 250

Stephens, Charles Asbury 1844?-1931 .... DLB-42

Stephens, James 1882?-1950 .... DLB-19, 153, 162

Stephens, John Lloyd 1805-1852 .... DLB-183, 250

Stephens, Michael 1946- DLB-234

Stephensen, P. R. 1901-1965 .... DLB-260

Sterling, George 1869-1926 .... DLB-54

Sterling, James 1701-1763 .... DLB-24

Sterling, John 1806-1844 .... DLB-116

Stern, Gerald 1925- DLB-105

"Living in Ruin" DLB-105

Stern, Gladys B. 1890-1973 .... DLB-197

Stern, Madeleine B. 1912-2007 ..... DLB-111, 140

Stern, Richard 1928- DLB-218; Y-87

Stern, Stewart 1922- DLB-26

Sterne, Laurence 1713-1768 .... DLB-39; CDBLB-2

Sternheim, Carl 1878-1942 .... DLB-56, 118

Sternhold, Thomas ?-1549 .... DLB-132

Steuart, David 1747-1824 .... DLB-213

Stevens, Henry 1819-1886 .... DLB-140

Stevens, Wallace 1879-1955
  .... DLB-54, 342; CDALB-5

  The Wallace Stevens Society Y-99

Stevenson, Anne 1933- DLB-40

Stevenson, D. E. 1892-1973 .... DLB-191

Stevenson, Lionel 1902-1973 .... DLB-155

Stevenson, Robert Louis
  1850-1894 ...... DLB-18, 57, 141, 156, 174;
                                DS-13; CDBLB-5

  "On Style in Literature:
    Its Technical Elements" (1885) DLB-57

Stewart, Donald Ogden
  1894-1980 .... DLB-4, 11, 26; DS-15

Stewart, Douglas 1913-1985 .... DLB-260

Stewart, Dugald 1753-1828 .... DLB-31

Stewart, George, Jr. 1848-1906 .... DLB-99

Stewart, George R. 1895-1980 .... DLB-8

Stewart, Harold 1916-1995 .... DLB-260

Stewart, J. I. M. (see Innes, Michael)

Stewart, Maria W. 1803?-1879 .... DLB-239

Stewart, Randall 1896-1964 .... DLB-103

Stewart, Sean 1965- DLB-251

Stewart and Kidd Company DLB-46

Sthen, Hans Christensen 1544-1610 ..... DLB-300

Stickney, Trumbull 1874-1904 .... DLB-54

Stieler, Caspar 1632-1707 .... DLB-164

Stifter, Adalbert 1805-1868 .. DLB-133; CDWLB-2

Stiles, Ezra 1727-1795 .... DLB-31

Still, James 1906-2001 .... DLB-9; Y-01

Stirling, S. M. 1953- DLB-251

Stirner, Max 1806-1856 .... DLB-129

Stith, William 1707-1755 . . . . DLB-31

Stivens, Dal 1911-1997 . . . . DLB-260

Elliot Stock [publishing house] DLB-106

Stockton, Annis Boudinot 1736-1801 . . . . DLB-200

Stockton, Frank R. 1834-1902 . DLB-42, 74; DS-13

Stockton, J. Roy 1892-1972. . . . . DLB-241

Ashbel Stoddard [publishing house] DLB-49

Stoddard, Charles Warren 1843-1909 . . . DLB-186

Stoddard, Elizabeth 1823-1902. . . . . DLB-202

Stoddard, Richard Henry
   1825-1903 . . . . DLB-3, 64, 250; DS-13

Stoddard, Solomon 1643-1729 . . . . DLB-24

Stoker, Bram
   1847-1912 . . . . .DLB-36, 70, 178; CDBLB-5

   On Writing *Dracula,* from the
     Introduction to *Dracula* (1897) DLB-178

   Dracula (Documentary). DLB-304

Frederick A. Stokes Company DLB-49

Stokes, Rose Pastor 1879-1933 . . . . DLB-345

Stokes, Thomas L. 1898-1958 . . . . DLB-29

Stokesbury, Leon 1945- DLB-120

Stolberg, Christian Graf zu 1748-1821 . . . . DLB-94

Stolberg, Friedrich Leopold Graf zu
   1750-1819. DLB-94

Stone, Lucy 1818-1893. . . . . DLB-79, 239

Stone, Melville 1848-1929 . . . . DLB-25

Stone, Robert 1937- DLB-152

Stone, Ruth 1915- DLB-105

Stone, Samuel 1602-1663 . . . . DLB-24

Stone, William Leete 1792-1844 . . . . DLB-202

Herbert S. Stone and Company DLB-49

Stone and Kimball DLB-49

Stoppard, Tom
   1937- DLB-13, 233; Y-85; CDBLB-8

   Playwrights and Professors. DLB-13

Storey, Anthony 1928- DLB-14

Storey, David 1933- . . .DLB-13, 14, 207, 245, 326

Storm, Theodor
   1817-1888. . . . . DLB-129; CDWLB-2

Storni, Alfonsina 1892-1938 . . . . DLB-283

Størssøn, Mattis ca. 1500-1569 . . . . DLB-354

Story, Thomas circa 1670-1742 . . . . DLB-31

Story, William Wetmore 1819-1895 . . . DLB-1, 235

Storytelling: A Contemporary Renaissance . . . Y-84

Stoughton, William 1631-1701 . . . . DLB-24

Stout, Rex 1886-1975 . . . . DLB-306

Stow, John 1525-1605 . . . . DLB-132

Stow, Randolph 1935- DLB-260

Stowe, Harriet Beecher 1811-1896 . . . . . DLB-1,12,
             42, 74, 189, 239, 243; CDALB-3

   The Harriet Beecher Stowe Center Y-00

Stowe, Leland 1899-1994 . . . . DLB-29

Stoyanov, Dimitr Ivanov (see Elin Pelin)

Strabo 64/63 B.C.-circa A.D. 25 . . . . .DLB-176

Strachey, Lytton 1880-1932 . . . . . DLB-149; DS-10

   Preface to *Eminent Victorians*. DLB-149

William Strahan [publishing house] DLB-154

Strahan and Company DLB-106

Strand, Mark 1934- DLB-5

The Strasbourg Oaths 842 . . . . DLB-148

Stratemeyer, Edward 1862-1930. . . . . DLB-42

Strati, Saverio 1924- DLB-177

Stratton and Barnard DLB-49

Stratton-Porter, Gene 1863-1924. . DLB-221; DS-14

Straub, Peter 1943- Y-84

Strauß, Botho 1944- DLB-124

Strauß, David Friedrich 1808-1874. . . . . . DLB-133

Strauss, Jennifer 1933- DLB-325

The Strawberry Hill Press DLB-154

Strawson, P. F. 1919-2006. . . . . DLB-262

Streatfeild, Noel 1895-1986. . . . . DLB-160

Street, Cecil John Charles (see Rhode, John)

Street, G. S. 1867-1936 . . . . DLB-135

Street and Smith DLB-49

Streeter, Edward 1891-1976 . . . . DLB-11

Streeter, Thomas Winthrop 1883-1965 . . DLB-140

Stretton, Hesba 1832-1911 . . . . DLB-163, 190

Stribling, T. S. 1881-1965 . . . . DLB-9

Der Stricker circa 1190-circa 1250 . . . . . . DLB-138

Strickland, Samuel 1804-1867. . . . . DLB-99

Strindberg, August 1849-1912 . . . . DLB-259

Stringer, Arthur 1874-1950 . . . . DLB-92

Stringer and Townsend. DLB-49

Strittmatter, Erwin 1912-1994. . . . . DLB-69

Strniša, Gregor 1930-1987 . . . . DLB-181

Strode, William 1630-1645 . . . . DLB-126

Strong, L. A. G. 1896-1958. . . . . DLB-191

Strother, David Hunter (Porte Crayon)
   1816-1888 . . . . DLB-3, 248

Strouse, Jean 1945- DLB-111

Strugatsky, Arkadii Natanovich
   1925- DLB-302

Strugatsky, Boris Natanovich 1933- . . . DLB-302

Struther, Jan 1901-1953 . . . . DLB-352

Strype, John 1643-1737 . . . . DLB-336

Stuart, Dabney 1937- DLB-105

   "Knots into Webs: Some
     Autobiographical Sources" DLB-105

Stuart, Gilbert 1743-1786 . . . . DLB-336

Stuart, Jesse 1906-1984. . . . . . DLB-9, 48, 102; Y-84

Lyle Stuart [publishing house] DLB-46

Stuart, Ruth McEnery 1849?-1917 . . . . . DLB-202

Stub, Ambrosius 1705-1758. . . . . DLB-300

Stubbs, Harry Clement (see Clement, Hal)

Stubenberg, Johann Wilhelm von
   1619-1663 . . . . DLB-164

Stuckenberg, Viggo 1763-1905 . . . . DLB-300

Studebaker, William V. 1947- DLB-256

Studies in American Jewish Literature Y-02

Studio DLB-112

Stukeley, William 1687-1765 . . . . DLB-336

Stump, Al 1916-1995 . . . . DLB-241

Sturgeon, Theodore 1918-1985. . . . . .DLB-8; Y-85

Sturges, Preston 1898-1959 . . . . DLB-26

Styron, William 1925-2006
   . . . . DLB-2, 143, 299; Y-80; CDALB-6

   Tribute to James Dickey. Y-97

SuAndi 1951- DLB-347

Suard, Jean-Baptiste-Antoine
   1732-1817. . . . . DLB-314

Suárez, Clementina 1902-1991 . . . . DLB-290

Suárez, Mario 1925- DLB-82

Suassuna, Ariano 1927- DLB-307

Such, Peter 1939- DLB-60

Suchart, Sawatsi 1945- DLB-348

Suckling, Sir John 1609-1641? DLB-58, 126

Suckow, Ruth 1892-1960 . . . . DLB-9, 102

Sudermann, Hermann 1857-1928. . . . . . . DLB-118

Sue, Eugène 1804-1857. . . . . DLB-119

Sue, Marie-Joseph (see Sue, Eugène)

Suetonius circa A.D. 69-post A.D. 122 . . . . DLB-211

Suggs, Simon (see Hooper, Johnson Jones)

Sui Sin Far (see Eaton, Edith Maude)

Suits, Gustav 1883-1956. . . . . DLB-220; CDWLB-4

Sukenick, Ronald 1932-2004 . . . . . . DLB-173; Y-81

   An Author's Response Y-82

Sukhovo-Kobylin, Aleksandr Vasil'evich
   1817-1903. . . . . .DLB-277

Suknaski, Andrew 1942- DLB-53

Sullam, Sara Copio circa 1592-1641 . . . . . DLB-339

Sullivan, Alan 1868-1947 . . . . DLB-92

Sullivan, C. Gardner 1886-1965 . . . . DLB-26

Sullivan, Frank 1892-1976 . . . . DLB-11

Sully Prudhomme (René François-Armand
   Prudhomme) 1839-1907 . . . . DLB-332

Sulte, Benjamin 1841-1923 . . . . DLB-99

Sulter, Maud 1960-2008 . . . . DLB-347

Sulzberger, Arthur Hays 1891-1968 . . . . . .DLB-127

Sulzberger, Arthur Ochs 1926- DLB-127

Sulzer, Johann Georg 1720-1779 . . . . DLB-97

Sumarokov, Aleksandr Petrovich
   1717-1777 . . . . DLB-150

Summers, Hollis 1916-1987 . . . . DLB-6

Sumner, Charles 1811-1874 . . . . DLB-235

Sumner, William Graham 1840-1910. . . . .DLB-270

Henry A. Sumner
   [publishing house] DLB-49

Sundman, Per Olof 1922-1992.........DLB-257

Supervielle, Jules 1884-1960..........DLB-258

Surtees, Robert Smith 1803-1864.......DLB-21

The R. S. Surtees Society............Y-98

Sutcliffe, Matthew 1550?-1629..........DLB-281

Sutcliffe, William 1971-............DLB-271

Sutherland, Efua Theodora 1924-1996...DLB-117

Sutherland, John 1919-1956...........DLB-68

Sutro, Alfred 1863-1933..............DLB-10

Sutzkever, Abraham (Avrom Sutzkever) 1913-..................DLB-333

Svava Jakobsdóttir 1930-............DLB-293

Svendsen, Hanne Marie 1933-........DLB-214

Svevo, Italo (Ettore Schmitz) 1861-1928..................DLB-264

Swados, Harvey 1920-1972...........DLB-2, 335

Swain, Charles 1801-1874............DLB-32

Swallow Press......................DLB-46

Swan Sonnenschein Limited..........DLB-106

Swanberg, W. A. 1907-1992..........DLB-103

Swedish Literature
The Literature of the Modern Breakthrough..............DLB-259

Swenson, May 1919-1989.............DLB-5

Swerling, Jo 1897-1964..............DLB-44

Swift, Graham 1949-............DLB-194, 326

Swift, Jonathan 1667-1745........DLB-39, 95, 101; CDBLB-2

Swinburne, A. C. 1837-1909..........DLB-35, 57; CDBLB-4

Under the Microscope (1872)........DLB-35

Swineshead, Richard floruit circa 1350...DLB-115

Swinnerton, Frank 1884-1982.........DLB-34

Swisshelm, Jane Grey 1815-1884......DLB-43

Swope, Herbert Bayard 1882-1958.....DLB-25

Swords, James ?-1844................DLB-73

Swords, Thomas 1763-1843...........DLB-73

T. and J. Swords and Company.......DLB-49

Swynnerton, Thomas (John Roberts) circa 1500-1554................DLB-281

Syal, Meera 1961-..................DLB-347

Sykes, Ella C. ?-1939...............DLB-174

Sylvester, Josuah 1562 or 1563-1618....DLB-121

Symonds, Emily Morse (see Paston, George)

Symonds, John Addington 1840-1893..................DLB-57, 144

"Personal Style" (1890).............DLB-57

Symons, A. J. A. 1900-1941..........DLB-149

Symons, Arthur 1865-1945......DLB-19, 57, 149

Symons, Julian 1912-1994.....DLB-87, 155; Y-92

Julian Symons at Eighty.............Y-92

Symons, Scott 1933-................DLB-53

Synge, John Millington 1871-1909.........DLB-10, 19; CDBLB-5

Synge Summer School: J. M. Synge and the Irish Theater, Rathdrum, County Wiclow, Ireland............Y-93

Syrett, Netta 1865-1943..........DLB-135, 197

The System of Nature, Paul Henri Thiry, baron d'Holbach (as Jean-Baptiste de Mirabaud)..................DLB-314

Szabó, Lőrinc 1900-1957.............DLB-215

Szabó, Magda 1917-2007.............DLB-215

Sze, Arthur 1950-..................DLB-342

Szymborska, Wisława 1923-.......DLB-232, 332; Y-96; CDWLB-4

Nobel Lecture 1996: The Poet and the World..........Y-96

T

Taban lo Liyong 1939?-.............DLB-125

al-Tabari 839-923...................DLB-311

Tablada, José Juan 1871-1945........DLB-290

Le Tableau de Paris, Louis-Sébastien Mercier......................DLB-314

Tabori, George 1914-2007............DLB-245

Tabucchi, Antonio 1943-.............DLB-196

Taché, Joseph-Charles 1820-1894......DLB-99

Tachihara Masaaki 1926-1980........DLB-182

Tacitus circa A.D. 55-circa A.D. 117 ....DLB-211; CDWLB-1

Tadijanović, Dragutin 1905-2007......DLB-181

Tafdrup, Pia 1952-.................DLB-214

Tafolla, Carmen 1951-..............DLB-82

Taggard, Genevieve 1894-1948.......DLB-45

Taggart, John 1942-................DLB-193

Tagger, Theodor (see Bruckner, Ferdinand)

Tagore, Rabindranath 1861-1941...DLB-323, 332

Taher, Bahaa' 1935-................DLB-346

Taiheiki late fourteenth century........DLB-203

Tait, J. Selwin, and Sons.............DLB-49

Tait's Edinburgh Magazine 1832-1861......DLB-110

The Takarazaka Revue Company..........Y-91

al-Takarli, Fuad 1927-2008............DLB-346

Talander (see Bohse, August)

Talese, Gay 1932-..................DLB-185

Tribute to Irwin Shaw..............Y-84

Talev, Dimitr 1898-1966.............DLB-181

Taliaferro, H. E. 1811-1875...........DLB-202

Tallent, Elizabeth 1954-..............DLB-130

TallMountain, Mary 1918-1994........DLB-193

Talvj 1797-1870....................DLB-59, 133

Tamási, Áron 1897-1966.............DLB-215

Tamer, Zakaria 1931-...............DLB-346

Tammsaare, A. H. 1878-1940................DLB-220; CDWLB-4

Tan, Amy 1952-.......DLB-173, 312; CDALB-7

Tandori, Dezső 1938-...............DLB-232

Tan, Hwee Hwee 1974-.............DLB-348

Tanner, Thomas 1673/1674-1735.......DLB-213

Tanizaki Jun'ichirō 1886-1965........DLB-180

Tapahonso, Luci 1953-..............DLB-175

The Mark Taper Forum..............DLB-7

Taradash, Daniel 1913-2003..........DLB-44

Tarasov-Rodionov, Aleksandr Ignat'evich 1885-1938..................DLB-272

Tarbell, Ida M. 1857-1944............DLB-47

Tardieu, Jean 1903-1995.............DLB-321

Tardivel, Jules-Paul 1851-1905........DLB-99

Targan, Barry 1932-................DLB-130

Tribute to John Gardner.............Y-82

Tarkington, Booth 1869-1946.......DLB-9, 102

Tashlin, Frank 1913-1972............DLB-44

Tasma (Jessie Couvreur) 1848-1897.....DLB-230

Tassoni, Alessandro 1565-1635........DLB-339

Tate, Allen 1899-1979......DLB-4, 45, 63; DS-17

Tate, James 1943-.................DLB-5, 169

Tate, Nahum circa 1652-1715.........DLB-80

Tatian circa 830....................DLB-148

Taufer, Veno 1933-.................DLB-181

Tauler, Johannes circa 1300-1361........DLB-179

Tavares, Salette 1922-1994............DLB-287

Tavčar, Ivan 1851-1923..............DLB-147

Taverner, Richard ca. 1505-1575........DLB-236

Tay, Simon S. C. 1961-..............DLB-348

Taylor, Ann 1782-1866...............DLB-163

Taylor, Bayard 1825-1878......DLB-3, 189, 250

Taylor, Bert Leston 1866-1921..........DLB-25

Taylor, Charles H. 1846-1921..........DLB-25

Taylor, Edward circa 1642-1729........DLB-24

Taylor, Elizabeth 1912-1975..........DLB-139

Taylor, Sir Henry 1800-1886..........DLB-32

Taylor, Henry 1942-.................DLB-5

Who Owns American Literature........Y-94

Taylor, Jane 1783-1824..............DLB-163

Taylor, Jeremy circa 1613-1667........DLB-151

Taylor, John 1577 or 1578 - 1653........DLB-121

Taylor, Mildred D. 1943-.............DLB-52

Taylor, Peter 1917-1994....DLB-218, 278; Y-81, 94

Taylor, Susie King 1848-1912..........DLB-221

Taylor, Tom 1817-1880..............DLB-344

Taylor, William Howland 1901-1966.....DLB-241

William Taylor and Company..........DLB-49

Teale, Edwin Way 1899-1980.........DLB-275

Teasdale, Sara 1884-1933.............DLB-45

Teffi, Nadezhda 1872-1952............DLB-317

Teillier, Jorge 1935-1996.............DLB-283

Telles, Lygia Fagundes 1924-......DLB-113, 307

The Temper of the West: William Jovanovich Y-02

Temple, Sir William 1555?-1627........ DLB-281

Temple, Sir William 1628-1699 .... DLB-101

Temple, William F. 1914-1989 .... DLB-255

Temrizov, A. (see Marchenko, Anastasia Iakovlevna)

Tench, Watkin ca. 1758-1833 .... DLB-230

Tencin, Alexandrine-Claude Guérin de
   1682-1749...................... DLB-314

Tender Is the Night (Documentary)....... DLB-273

Tendriakov, Vladimir Fedorovich
   1923-1984 .... DLB-302

Tenn, William 1919- DLB-8

Tennant, Emma 1937- DLB-14

Tenney, Tabitha Gilman 1762-1837 ...DLB-37, 200

Tennyson, Alfred 1809-1892... DLB-32; CDBLB-4

   On Some of the Characteristics of
     Modern Poetry and On the Lyrical
     Poems of Alfred Tennyson
     (1831) DLB-32

Tennyson, Frederick 1807-1898 .... DLB-32

Tenorio, Arthur 1924- DLB-209

Teofilov, Ivan 1931- DLB-353

"The Tenth Stage," Marie-Jean-Antoine-Nicolas
   Caritat, marquis de Condorcet...... DLB-314

Tepl, Johannes von
   circa 1350-1414/1415..............DLB-179

Tepliakov, Viktor Grigor'evich
   1804-1842 .... DLB-205

Terence circa 184 B.C.-159 B.C. or after
   .... DLB-211; CDWLB-1

St. Teresa of Ávila 1515-1582 .... DLB-318

Terhune, Albert Payson 1872-1942........ DLB-9

Terhune, Mary Virginia 1830-1922 ......DS-13

Terpigorev, Sergei Nikolaevich (S. Atava)
   1841-1895 ....DLB-277

Terry, Megan 1932- DLB-7, 249

Terson, Peter 1932- DLB-13

Tesich, Steve 1943-1996 .... Y-83

Tessa, Delio 1886-1939................. DLB-114

Testi, Fulvio 1593-1646................. DLB-339

Testori, Giovanni 1923-1993
   ....DLB-128, 177

Texas
   The Year in Texas Literature Y-98

Tey, Josephine 1896?-1952 .... DLB-77

Thacher, James 1754-1844 .... DLB-37

Thacher, John Boyd 1847-1909......... DLB-187

Thackeray, William Makepeace
   1811-1863... DLB-21, 55, 159, 163; CDBLB-4

Tham, Claire 1967- DLB-348

Thames and Hudson Limited.......... DLB-112

Thanet, Octave (see French, Alice)

Thaxter, Celia Laighton
   1835-1894 .... DLB-239

Thayer, Caroline Matilda Warren
   1785-1844.................... DLB-200

Thayer, Douglas H. 1929- DLB-256

Theater
   Black Theatre: A Forum [excerpts] ... DLB-38
   Community and Commentators:
     Black Theatre and Its Critics..... DLB-38
   German Drama from Naturalism
     to Fascism: 1889-1933......... DLB-118
   A Look at the Contemporary Black
     Theatre Movement DLB-38
   The Lord Chamberlain's Office and
     Stage Censorship in England..... DLB-10
   New Forces at Work in the American
     Theatre: 1915-1925 .... DLB-7
   Off Broadway and Off-Off Broadway .. DLB-7
   Oregon Shakespeare Festival Y-00
   Plays, Playwrights, and Playgoers DLB-84
   Playwrights on the Theater DLB-80
   Playwrights and Professors DLB-13
   Producing *Dear Bunny, Dear Volodya:*
     The Friendship and the Feud.......... Y-97
   Viewpoint: Politics and Performance,
     by David Edgar............... DLB-13
   Writing for the Theatre,
     by Harold Pinter DLB-13
   The Year in Drama Y-82–85, 87–98
   The Year in U.S. Drama Y-00

Theater, English and Irish
   Anti-Theatrical Tracts............. DLB-263
   The Chester Plays circa 1505-1532;
     revisions until 1575 .... DLB-146
   Dangerous Years: London Theater,
     1939-1945 .... DLB-10
   A Defense of Actors............. DLB-263
   The Development of Lighting in the
     Staging of Drama, 1900-1945 .... DLB-10
   Education..................... DLB-263
   The End of English Stage Censorship,
     1945-1968 .... DLB-13
   Epigrams and Satires DLB-263
   Eyewitnesses and Historians DLB-263
   Fringe and Alternative Theater in
     Great Britain DLB-13
   The Great War and the Theater,
     1914-1918 [Great Britain] DLB-10
   Licensing Act of 1737 .... DLB-84
   Morality Plays: *Mankind* circa 1450-1500
     and *Everyman* circa 1500........ DLB-146
   The New Variorum Shakespeare Y-85
   N-Town Plays circa 1468 to early
     sixteenth century DLB-146
   Politics and the Theater DLB-263
   Practical Matters DLB-263
   Prologues, Epilogues, Epistles to Readers,
     and Excerpts from Plays DLB-263
   The Publication of English
     Renaissance Plays DLB-62
   Regulations for the Theater........ DLB-263
   Sources for the Study of Tudor and
     Stuart Drama................ DLB-62
   Stage Censorship: "The Rejected Statement"
     (1911), by Bernard Shaw
     [excerpts].................... DLB-10
   Synge Summer School: J. M. Synge and
     the Irish Theater, Rathdrum,
     County Wiclow, Ireland Y-93
   The Theater in Shakespeare's Time .. DLB-62
   The Theatre Guild................. DLB-7
   The Townely Plays fifteenth and
     sixteenth centuries........... DLB-146
   The Year in British Drama......... Y-99–01
   The Year in Drama: London Y-90
   The Year in London Theatre.......... Y-92
   A Yorkshire Tragedy................. DLB-58

Theaters
   The Abbey Theatre and Irish Drama,
     1900-1945 .... DLB-10
   Actors Theatre of Louisville DLB-7
   American Conservatory Theatre...... DLB-7
   Arena Stage DLB-7
   Black Theaters and Theater
     Organizations in America,
     1961-1982: A Research List DLB-38
   The Dallas Theater Center DLB-7
   Eugene O'Neill Memorial Theater
     Center DLB-7
   The Goodman Theatre DLB-7
   The Guthrie Theater DLB-7
   The Mark Taper Forum............. DLB-7
   The National Theatre and the Royal
     Shakespeare Company: The
     National Companies DLB-13
   Off-Loop Theatres................. DLB-7
   The Royal Court Theatre and the
     English Stage Company DLB-13
   The Royal Court Theatre and the
     New Drama DLB-10
   The Takarazaka Revue Company Y-91

Thegan and the Astronomer
   fl. circa 850..................... DLB-148

Thein Pe Myint 1914-1978............. DLB-348

Thelwall, John 1764-1834.......... DLB-93, 158

Theocritus circa 300 B.C.-260 B.C........DLB-176

Theodorescu, Ion N. (see Arghezi, Tudor)

Theodulf circa 760-circa 821 .... DLB-148

Theophrastus circa 371 B.C.-287 B.C......DLB-176

Thériault, Yves 1915-1983 .... DLB-88

Thério, Adrien 1925- DLB-53

Theroux, Paul 1941- DLB-2, 218; CDALB-7

Thesiger, Wilfred 1910-2003 .... DLB-204

They All Came to Paris DS-15

Thibaudeau, Colleen 1925- DLB-88

Thiele, Colin 1920-2006.............. DLB-289

Thielen, Benedict 1903-1965 .... DLB-102

Thiong'o Ngugi wa (see Ngugi wa Thiong'o)

Thirkell, Angela 1890-1961 .... DLB-352

Thiroux d'Arconville, Marie-Geneviève
   1720-1805..................... DLB-314

This Quarter 1925-1927, 1929-1932 ....DS-15

Thoma, Ludwig 1867-1921 . . . . .DLB-66

Thoma, Richard 1902-1974 . . . . .DLB-4

Thomas, Audrey 1935- DLB-60

Thomas, Brandon 1848-1914 . . . . .DLB-344

Thomas, D. M.
   1935- . . . DLB-40, 207, 299; Y-82; CDBLB-8

   The Plagiarism Controversy Y-82

Thomas, Dylan
   1914-1953 . . . . . . .DLB-13, 20, 139; CDBLB-7

   The Dylan Thomas Celebration Y-99

Thomas, Ed 1961- DLB-310

Thomas, Edward
   1878-1917 . . . . DLB-19, 98, 156, 216

   The Friends of the Dymock Poets Y-00

Thomas, Frederick William 1806-1866 . . .DLB-202

Thomas, Gwyn 1913-1981 . . . . DLB-15, 245

Thomas, Isaiah 1750-1831 . . . . . . DLB-43, 73, 187

Thomas, Johann 1624-1679 . . . . .DLB-168

Thomas, John 1900-1932 . . . . .DLB-4

Thomas, Joyce Carol 1938- DLB-33

Thomas, Leslie 1931- DLB-352

Thomas, Lewis 1913-1993 . . . . .DLB-275

Thomas, Lorenzo 1944- DLB-41

Thomas, Norman 1884-1968 . . . . .DLB-303

Thomas, R. S. 1915-2000 . . . . . .DLB-27; CDBLB-8

Isaiah Thomas [publishing house] DLB-49

Thomasîn von Zerclære
   circa 1186-circa 1259 . . . . .DLB-138

Thomason, George 1602?-1666 . . . . .DLB-213

Thomasius, Christian 1655-1728 . . . . .DLB-168

Thompson, Daniel Pierce 1795-1868 . . . . .DLB-202

Thompson, David 1770-1857 . . . . .DLB-99

Thompson, Dorothy 1893-1961 . . . . .DLB-29

Thompson, E. P. 1924-1993 . . . . .DLB-242

Thompson, Flora 1876-1947 . . . . .DLB-240

Thompson, Francis
   1859-1907 . . . . DLB-19; CDBLB-5

Thompson, George Selden (see Selden, George)

Thompson, Henry Yates 1838-1928 . . . . .DLB-184

Thompson, Hunter S. 1939-2005 . . . . . . .DLB-185

Thompson, Jim 1906-1977 . . . . .DLB-226

Thompson, John 1938-1976 . . . . .DLB-60

Thompson, John R. 1823-1873 . . . . DLB-3, 73, 248

Thompson, Judith 1954- DLB-334

Thompson, Lawrance 1906-1973 . . . . . . .DLB-103

Thompson, Maurice 1844-1901 . . . . . .DLB-71, 74

Thompson, Ruth Plumly 1891-1976 . . . . . .DLB-22

Thompson, Thomas Phillips 1843-1933 . . .DLB-99

Thompson, William 1775-1833 . . . . .DLB-158

Thompson, William Tappan
   1812-1882 . . . . .DLB-3, 11, 248

Thomson, Cockburn
   "Modern Style" (1857) [excerpt] DLB-57

Thomson, Edward William 1849-1924 . . . .DLB-92

Thomson, James 1700-1748 . . . . .DLB-95

Thomson, James 1834-1882 . . . . .DLB-35

Thomson, Joseph 1858-1895 . . . . DLB-174

Thomson, Mortimer 1831-1875 . . . . .DLB-11

Thomson, Rupert 1955- DLB-267

Thon, Melanie Rae 1957- DLB-244

Thor Vilhjálmsson 1925- DLB-293

Þórarinn Eldjárn 1949- DLB-293

Þórbergur Þórðarson 1888-1974 . . . . .DLB-293

Thoreau, Henry David 1817-1862 . . . DLB-1, 183, 223, 270, 298; DS-5; CDALB-2

   The Thoreau Society Y-99

   The Thoreauvian Pilgrimage: The
   Structure of an American Cult . . .DLB-223

Thoresen, Magdalene 1819-1903 . . . . .DLB-354

Thorne, William 1568?-1630 . . . . .DLB-281

Thornton, John F.
   [Response to Ken Auletta] Y-97

Thorpe, Adam 1956- DLB-231

Thorpe, Thomas Bangs
   1815-1878 . . . . .DLB-3, 11, 248

Thorup, Kirsten 1942- DLB-214

Thotl, Birgitte 1610-1662 . . . . .DLB-300

Thrale, Hester Lynch
   (see Piozzi, Hester Lynch [Thrale])

The Three Marias: A Landmark Case in
   Portuguese Literary History
   (Maria Isabel Barreno, 1939- ;
   Maria Teresa Horta, 1937- ;
   Maria Velho da Costa, 1938-) DLB-287

Thubron, Colin 1939- DLB-204, 231

Thucydides
   circa 455 B.C.-circa 395 B.C. DLB-176

Thulstrup, Thure de 1848-1930 . . . . .DLB-188

Thümmel, Moritz August von
   1738-1817 .DLB-97

Thurber, James
   1894-1961 . . . . .DLB-4, 11, 22, 102; CDALB-5

Thurman, Wallace 1902-1934 . . . . .DLB-51

   "Negro Poets and Their Poetry" DLB-50

Thwaite, Anthony 1930- DLB-40

   The Booker Prize, Address Y-86

Thwaites, Reuben Gold 1853-1913 . . . . . . .DLB-47

Tibullus circa 54 B.C.-circa 19 B.C. DLB-211

Ticknor, George 1791-1871 . . . . .DLB-1, 59, 140, 235

Ticknor and Fields DLB-49

Ticknor and Fields (revived) DLB-46

Tieck, Ludwig 1773-1853 . . . . .DLB-90; CDWLB-2

Tietjens, Eunice 1884-1944 . . . . .DLB-54

Tikkanen, Märta 1935- DLB-257

Tilghman, Christopher circa 1948 . . . . . . .DLB-244

Tilney, Edmund circa 1536-1610 . . . . .DLB-136

Charles Tilt [publishing house] DLB-106

J. E. Tilton and Company DLB-49

Time-Life Books DLB-46

Times Books .DLB-46

Timothy, Peter circa 1725-1782 . . . . .DLB-43

Timrava 1867-1951 . . . . .DLB-215

Timrod, Henry 1828-1867 . . . . .DLB-3, 248

Tindal, Henrietta 1818?-1879 . . . . .DLB-199

Tindal, Nicholas 1688-1774 . . . . .DLB-336

Tinker, Chauncey Brewster 1876-1963 . . . .DLB-140

Tinsley Brothers DLB-106

Tiptree, James, Jr. 1915-1987 . . . . .DLB-8

Tišma, Aleksandar 1924-2003 . . . . .DLB-181

Titus, Edward William
   1870-1952 . . . . .DLB-4; DS-15

Tiutchev, Fedor Ivanovich 1803-1873 . . . .DLB-205

Tlali, Miriam 1933- DLB-157, 225

Todd, Barbara Euphan 1890-1976 . . . . . . .DLB-160

Tode, Emil (see Õnnepalu, Tõnu)

Todorov, Tzvetan 1939- DLB-242

Todorovski, Gane 1929- DLB-353

Toer, Pramoedya Ananta 1925-2006 . . . . .DLB-348

Tofte, Robert
   1561 or 1562-1619 or 1620 . . . . .DLB-172

Tóibín, Colm 1955- DLB-271

Tokarczuk, Olga 1962- DLB-353

Toklas, Alice B. 1877-1967 . . . . .DLB-4; DS-15

Tokuda Shūsei 1872-1943 . . . . .DLB-180

Toland, John 1670-1722 . . . . .DLB-252, 336

Tolkien, J. R. R.
   1892-1973 . . . . . .DLB-15, 160, 255; CDBLB-6

Toller, Ernst 1893-1939 . . . . .DLB-124

Tollet, Elizabeth 1694-1754 . . . . .DLB-95

Tolson, Melvin B. 1898-1966 . . . . DLB-48, 76

Tolstaya, Tatyana 1951- DLB-285

Tolstoy, Aleksei Konstantinovich
   1817-1875 .DLB-238

Tolstoy, Aleksei Nikolaevich 1883-1945 . .DLB-272

Tolstoy, Leo 1828-1910 . . . . .DLB-238

Tomalin, Claire 1933- DLB-155

Tómas Guðmundsson 1901-1983 . . . . . . .DLB-293

Tomasi di Lampedusa, Giuseppe
   1896-1957 .DLB-177

Tomlinson, Charles 1927- DLB-40

Tomlinson, H. M. 1873-1958 . . . .DLB-36, 100, 195

Abel Tompkins [publishing house] DLB-49

Tompson, Benjamin 1642-1714 . . . . .DLB-24

Tomson, Graham R.
   (see Watson, Rosamund Marriott)

Ton'a 1289-1372 . . . . .DLB-203

Tondelli, Pier Vittorio 1955-1991 . . . . .DLB-196

Tonks, Rosemary 1932- DLB-14, 207

Tonna, Charlotte Elizabeth 1790-1846 . . . .DLB-163

Jacob Tonson the Elder
   [publishing house] DLB-170

Toole, John Kennedy 1937-1969 . . . . Y-81

Toomer, Jean 1894-1967 . . . DLB-45, 51; CDALB-4

Topol, Jáchym 1962- DLB-353

Topsoe, Vilhelm 1840-1881 . . . . DLB-300

Tor Books DLB-46

Torberg, Friedrich 1908-1979 . . . . DLB-85

Torga, Miguel (Adolfo Correira da Rocha)
1907-1995 . . . . DLB-287

Torre, Francisco de la ?-? DLB-318

Torrence, Ridgely 1874-1950 . . . . . . DLB-54, 249

Torrente Ballester, Gonzalo
1910-1999 . . . . DLB-322

Torres-Metzger, Joseph V. 1933- DLB-122

Torres Naharro, Bartolomé de
1485?-1523? DLB-318

El Tostado (see Madrigal, Alfonso Fernández de)

Toth, Susan Allen 1940- Y-86

Richard Tottell [publishing house] DLB-170

"The Printer to the Reader,"
(1557) DLB-167

Tough-Guy Literature DLB-9

Touré, Askia Muhammad 1938- DLB-41

Tourgée, Albion W. 1838-1905 . . . . DLB-79

Tournemir, Elizaveta Sailhas de (see Tur, Evgeniia)

Tourneur, Cyril circa 1580-1626 . . . . DLB-58

Tournier, Michel 1924- DLB-83

Frank Tousey [publishing house] DLB-49

Tower Publications DLB-46

Towers, Joseph 1737-1799 . . . . DLB-336

Towne, Benjamin circa 1740-1793 . . . . . . DLB-43

Towne, Robert 1936- DLB-44

The Townely Plays fifteenth and sixteenth
centuries DLB-146

Townsend, Sue 1946- DLB-271, 352

Townshend, Aurelian
by 1583-circa 1651 . . . . DLB-121

Toy, Barbara 1908-2001 . . . . DLB-204

Tozzi, Federigo 1883-1920 . . . . DLB-264

Tracy, Honor 1913-1989 . . . . DLB-15

Traherne, Thomas 1637?-1674 . . . . DLB-131

Traill, Catharine Parr 1802-1899 . . . . DLB-99

Train, Arthur 1875-1945 . . . . . . DLB-86; DS-16

Tranquilli, Secondino (see Silone, Ignazio)

The Transatlantic Publishing Company . . . DLB-49

The Transatlantic Review 1924-1925 . . . . DS-15

The Transcendental Club
1836-1840 . . . . DLB-1; DLB-223

Transcendentalism DLB-1; DLB-223; DS-5

"A Response from America," by
John A. Heraud DS-5

Publications and Social Movements DLB-1

The Rise of Transcendentalism,
1815-1860 . . . . DS-5

Transcendentalists, American DS-5

"What Is Transcendentalism? By a
Thinking Man," by James
Kinnard Jr. DS-5

transition 1927-1938 . . . . DS-15

Translations (Vernacular) in the Crowns of
Castile and Aragon 1352-1515 . . . . . . DLB-286

Tranströmer, Tomas 1931- DLB-257

Tranter, John 1943- DLB-289

Traubel, Horace 1858-1919 . . . . DLB-345

Travel Writing
American Travel Writing, 1776-1864
(checklist) DLB-183

British Travel Writing, 1940-1997
(checklist) DLB-204

Travel Writers of the Late
Middle Ages DLB-286

(1876-1909) DLB-174

(1837-1875) DLB-166

(1910-1939) DLB-195

Traven, B. 1882?/1890?-1969? DLB-9, 56

Travers, Ben 1886-1980 . . . . DLB-10, 233

Travers, P. L. (Pamela Lyndon)
1899-1996 . . . . DLB-160

Traynor, Joanna 1960- DLB-347

Trediakovsky, Vasilii Kirillovich
1703-1769 . . . . DLB-150

Treece, Henry 1911-1966 . . . . DLB-160

Treitel, Jonathan 1959- DLB-267

Trejo, Ernesto 1950-1991 . . . . DLB-122

Trelawny, Edward John
1792-1881 . . . . DLB-110, 116, 144

Tremain, Rose 1943- DLB-14, 271

Tremblay, Michel 1942- DLB-60

Trenchard, John 1662-1723 . . . . DLB-336

Trent, William P. 1862-1939 . . . . DLB-47, 71

Trescot, William Henry 1822-1898 . . . . . DLB-30

Tressell, Robert (Robert Phillipe Noonan)
1870-1911 . . . . DLB-197

Trevelyan, Sir George Otto
1838-1928 . . . . DLB-144

Trevisa, John circa 1342-circa 1402 . . . . . DLB-146

Trevisan, Dalton 1925- DLB-307

Trevor, William 1928- DLB-14, 139

Triana, José 1931- DLB-305

Trierer Floyris circa 1170-1180 . . . . DLB-138

Trifonov, Iurii Valentinovich
1925-1981 . . . . DLB-302

Trillin, Calvin 1935- DLB-185

Trilling, Lionel 1905-1975 . . . . DLB-28, 63

Trilussa 1871-1950 . . . . DLB-114

Trimmer, Sarah 1741-1810 . . . . DLB-158

Triolet, Elsa 1896-1970 . . . . DLB-72

Tripp, John 1927- DLB-40

Trocchi, Alexander 1925-1984 . . . . DLB-15

Troisi, Dante 1920-1989 . . . . DLB-196

Trollope, Anthony
1815-1882 . . . . DLB-21, 57, 159; CDBLB-4

Novel-Reading: *The Works of Charles
Dickens; The Works of W. Makepeace
Thackeray* (1879) DLB-21

The Trollope Societies Y-00

Trollope, Frances 1779-1863 . . . . DLB-21, 166

Trollope, Joanna 1943- DLB-207

Troop, Elizabeth 1931- DLB-14

Tropicália DLB-307

Trotter, Catharine 1679-1749 . . . . DLB-84, 252

Trotti, Lamar 1898-1952 . . . . DLB-44

Trottier, Pierre 1925- DLB-60

Trotzig, Birgitta 1929- DLB-257

Troupe, Quincy Thomas, Jr. 1943- DLB-41

John F. Trow and Company DLB-49

Trowbridge, John Townsend 1827-1916 . . DLB-202

Trudel, Jean-Louis 1967- DLB-251

True History of the Kelly Gang, 2001 Booker Prize winner,
Peter Carey DLB-326

Truillier-Lacombe, Joseph-Patrice
1807-1863 . . . . DLB-99

Trumbo, Dalton 1905-1976 . . . . DLB-26

Trumbull, Benjamin 1735-1820 . . . . DLB-30

Trumbull, John 1750-1831 . . . . DLB-31

Trumbull, John 1756-1843 . . . . DLB-183

Trunk, Yehiel Teshaia (Yekhiel Yeshayda Trunk)
1888-1961 . . . . DLB-333

Truth, Sojourner 1797?-1883 . . . . DLB-239

Tscherning, Andreas 1611-1659 . . . . DLB-164

Tsubouchi Shōyō 1859-1935 . . . . DLB-180

Tsvetaeva, Marina Ivanovna
1892-1941 . . . . DLB-295

Tuchman, Barbara W.
Tribute to Alfred A. Knopf Y-84

Tucholsky, Kurt 1890-1935 . . . . DLB-56

Tucker, Charlotte Maria
1821-1893 . . . . DLB-163, 190

Tucker, George 1775-1861 . . . . . . DLB-3, 30, 248

Tucker, James 1808?-1866? DLB-230

Tucker, Nathaniel Beverley
1784-1851 . . . . DLB-3, 248

Tucker, St. George 1752-1827 . . . . DLB-37

Tuckerman, Frederick Goddard
1821-1873 . . . . DLB-243

Tuckerman, Henry Theodore 1813-1871 . . . DLB-64

Tullin, Christian Braunmann
1728-1765 . . . . DLB-354

Tumas, Juozas (see Vaizgantas)

Tunis, John R. 1889-1975 . . . . DLB-22, 171

Tunstall, Cuthbert 1474-1559 . . . . DLB-132

Tunström, Göran 1937-2000 . . . . DLB-257

Tuohy, Frank 1925-1999 . . . . DLB-14, 139

Tupper, Martin F. 1810-1889 . . . . DLB-32

Tur, Evgeniia 1815-1892 . . . . DLB-238

al-Turabi, Hasan 1932- DLB-346

Turbyfill, Mark 1896-1991..............DLB-45

Turco, Lewis 1934- Y-84

   Tribute to John Ciardi...............Y-86

Turgenev, Aleksandr Ivanovich
1784-1845 ....DLB-198

Turgenev, Ivan Sergeevich
1818-1883 ....DLB-238

Turgot, baron de l'Aulne, Anne-Robert-Jacques
1727-1781....................DLB-314

   "Memorandum on Local
Government" DLB-314

Turini Bufalini, Francesca 1553-1641.....DLB-339

Turnbull, Alexander H. 1868-1918 ......DLB-184

Turnbull, Andrew 1921-1970...........DLB-103

Turnbull, Gael 1928-2004 ....DLB-40

Turnèbe, Odet de 1552-1581..........DLB-327

Turner, Arlin 1909-1980 ....DLB-103

Turner, Charles (Tennyson)
1808-1879 ....DLB-32

Turner, Ethel 1872-1958................DLB-230

Turner, Frederick 1943- DLB-40

Turner, Frederick Jackson
1861-1932 .... DLB-17, 186

A Conversation between William Riggan
and Janette Turner Hospital Y-02

Turner, Joseph Addison 1826-1868 ....DLB-79

Turpin, Waters Edward 1910-1968 ......DLB-51

Turrini, Peter 1944- DLB-124

Tusquets, Esther 1936- DLB-322

Tutuola, Amos 1920-1997 ...DLB-125; CDWLB-3

Twain, Mark (see Clemens, Samuel Langhorne)

Tweedie, Ethel Brilliana
circa 1860-1940................. DLB-174

A Century of Poetry, a Lifetime of
Collecting: J. M. Edelstein's
Collection of Twentieth-
Century American Poetry............ YB-02

Twombly, Wells 1935-1977 ....DLB-241

Twysden, Sir Roger 1597-1672.........DLB-213

Tyard, Pontus de 1521?-1605...........DLB-327

Ty-Casper, Linda 1931- DLB-312, 348

Tyler, Anne 1941- DLB-6, 143; Y-82; CDALB-7

Tyler, Mary Palmer 1775-1866.........DLB-200

Tyler, Moses Coit 1835-1900........ DLB-47, 64

Tyler, Royall 1757-1826 ....DLB-37

Tylor, Edward Burnett 1832-1917 ......DLB-57

Tynan, Katharine 1861-1931......DLB-153, 240

Tyndale, William circa 1494-1536 ......DLB-132

Tynes, Maxine 1949- DLB-334

Tyree, Omar 1969- DLB-292

U

Uchida, Yoshiko 1921-1992...DLB-312; CDALB-7

Udall, Nicholas 1504-1556...............DLB-62

Ugrešić, Dubravka 1949- DLB-181

Uhland, Ludwig 1787-1862 ....DLB-90

Uhse, Bodo 1904-1963 ....DLB-69

Ujević, Augustin "Tin"
1891-1955 ....DLB-147

Ulenhart, Niclas fl. circa 1600 ....DLB-164

Ulfeldt, Leonora Christina 1621-1698....DLB-300

Ulibarrí, Sabine R. 1919-2003 ....DLB-82

Ulica, Jorge 1870-1926.................DLB-82

Ulitskaya, Liudmila Evgen'evna
1943- DLB-285

Ulivi, Ferruccio 1912- DLB-196

Ulizio, B. George 1889-1969 ....DLB-140

Ulrich von Liechtenstein
circa 1200-circa 1275 ....DLB-138

Ulrich von Zatzikhoven
before 1194-after 1214..............DLB-138

'Umar ibn Abi Rabi'ah 644-712 or 721 ...DLB-311

Unaipon, David 1872-1967 ....DLB-230

Unamuno, Miguel de 1864-1936....DLB-108, 322

Under, Marie 1883-1980 .... DLB-220; CDWLB-4

Underhill, Evelyn 1875-1941 ....DLB-240

Undset, Sigrid 1882-1949 .... DLB-297, 332

Ungaretti, Giuseppe 1888-1970 ....DLB-114

Unger, Friederike Helene
1741-1813 ....DLB-94

United States Book Company DLB-49

Universal Publishing and Distributing
Corporation DLB-46

University of Colorado
Special Collections at the University of
Colorado at Boulder...............Y-98

Indiana University Press Y-02

The University of Iowa
Writers' Workshop Golden Jubilee Y-86

University of Missouri Press Y-01

University of South Carolina
The G. Ross Roy Scottish
Poetry Collection...................Y-89

Two Hundred Years of Rare Books and
Literary Collections at the
University of South Carolina Y-00

The University of South Carolina Press Y-94

University of Virginia
The Book Arts Press at the University
of Virginia....................Y-96

The Electronic Text Center and the
Electronic Archive of Early American
Fiction at the University of Virginia
Library Y-98

University of Virginia Libraries Y-91

University of Wales Press DLB-112

University Press of Florida.................Y-00

University Press of Kansas................Y-98

University Press of Mississippi...............Y-99

Unnur Benediktsdóttir Bjarklind (see Hulda)

Uno Chiyo 1897-1996 ....DLB-180

Unruh, Fritz von 1885-1970......... DLB-56, 118

Unsworth, Barry 1930- DLB-194. 326

Unt, Mati 1944- DLB-232

The Unterberg Poetry Center of the
92nd Street Y Y-98

Untermeyer, Louis 1885-1977 ....DLB-303

T. Fisher Unwin [publishing house]......DLB-106

Upchurch, Boyd B. (see Boyd, John)

Updike, John 1932-2009 ..DLB-2, 5, 143, 218, 227;
Y-80, 82; DS-3; CDALB-6
   John Updike on the Internet............Y-97
   Tribute to Alfred A. Knopf Y-84
   Tribute to John Ciardi.................Y-86

Upīts, Andrejs 1877-1970 ....DLB-220

Uppdal, Kristofer 1878-1961 ....DLB-297

Upton, Bertha 1849-1912 ....DLB-141

Upton, Charles 1948- DLB-16

Upton, Florence K. 1873-1922 ....DLB-141

Upward, Allen 1863-1926 ....DLB-36

Urban, Milo 1904-1982.................DLB-215

Ureña de Henríquez, Salomé 1850-1897 ..DLB-283

Urfé, Honoré d' 1567-1625..............DLB-268

Urista, Alberto Baltazar (see Alurista)

Urquhart, Fred 1912-1995..............DLB-139

Urquhart, Jane 1949- DLB-334

Urrea, Luis Alberto 1955- DLB-209

Urzidil, Johannes 1896-1970 ....DLB-85

U.S.A. (Documentary) DLB-274

Usigli, Rodolfo 1905-1979 ....DLB-305

Usk, Thomas died 1388 ....DLB-146

Uslar Pietri, Arturo 1906-2001 ....DLB-113

Uspensky, Gleb Ivanovich
1843-1902.....................DLB-277

Ussher, James 1581-1656...............DLB-213

Ustinov, Peter 1921-2004................DLB-13

Uttley, Alison 1884-1976 ....DLB-160

Uz, Johann Peter 1720-1796.............DLB-97

V

Vadianus, Joachim 1484-1551 ....DLB-179

Vac, Bertrand (Aimé Pelletier) 1914- DLB-88

Vācietis, Ojārs 1933-1983 ....DLB-232

Vaculík, Ludvík 1926- DLB-232

Vaičiulaitis, Antanas 1906-1992.........DLB-220

Vaičiūnaite, Judita 1937- DLB-232

Vail, Laurence 1891-1968 ....DLB-4

Vail, Petr L'vovich 1949- DLB-285

Vailland, Roger 1907-1965..............DLB-83

Vaižgantas 1869-1933 ....DLB-220

Vajda, Ernest 1887-1954................DLB-44

Valdés, Alfonso de circa 1490?-1532 .....DLB-318

Valdés, Gina 1943- DLB-122

Valdes, Juan de 1508-1541 . . . . DLB-318	Van Vechten, Carl 1880-1964. . . . . . . DLB-4, 9, 51	Verplanck, Gulian C. 1786-1870 . . . . DLB-59
Valdez, Luis Miguel 1940- DLB-122	van Vogt, A. E. 1912-2000 . . . . DLB-8, 251	Vertinsky, Aleksandr 1889-1957. . . . . DLB-317
Valduga, Patrizia 1953- DLB-128	Varela, Blanca 1926- DLB-290	Very, Jones 1813-1880 . . . . DLB-1, 243; DS-5
Vale Press DLB-112	Vargas Llosa, Mario 1936- DLB-145; CDWLB-3	Vesaas, Halldis Moren 1907-1995. . . . . . . DLB-297
Valente, José Angel 1929-2000 . . . . DLB-108	Acceptance Speech for the Ritz Paris Hemingway Award Y-85	Vesaas, Tarjei 1897-1970 . . . . DLB-297
Valenzuela, Luisa 1938- . . DLB-113; CDWLB-3	Varley, John 1947- Y-81	Vian, Boris 1920-1959 . . . . DLB-72, 321
Valera, Diego de 1412-1488 . . . . DLB-286	Varnhagen von Ense, Karl August 1785-1858. . . . . DLB-90	Viazemsky, Petr Andreevich 1792-1878. . . . . DLB-205
Valeri, Diego 1887-1976 . . . . DLB-128	Varnhagen von Ense, Rahel 1771-1833. . . . . DLB-90	Vibe, Johan 1748-1782 . . . . DLB-354
Valerius Flaccus fl. circa A.D. 92 . . . . DLB-211	Varro 116 B.C.-27 B.C.. . . . . DLB-211	Vicars, Thomas 1591-1638. . . . . DLB-236
Valerius Maximus fl. circa A.D. 31 . . . . . DLB-211	Vasilenko, Svetlana Vladimirovna 1956- DLB-285	Vicente, Gil 1465-1536/1540? DLB-287, 318
Valéry, Paul 1871-1945 . . . . DLB-258	Vasiliu, George (see Bacovia, George)	Vickers, Roy 1888?-1965 . . . . DLB-77
Valesio, Paolo 1939- DLB-196	Vásquez, Richard 1928- DLB-209	Vickery, Sukey 1779-1821. . . . . DLB-200
Valgardson, W. D. 1939- DLB-60	Vassa, Gustavus (see Equiano, Olaudah)	Victoria 1819-1901 . . . . DLB-55
Valle, Luz 1899-1971. . . . . DLB-290	Vassalli, Sebastiano 1941- DLB-128, 196	Victoria Press DLB-106
Valle, Víctor Manuel 1950- DLB-122	Vassanji, M. G. 1950- DLB-334	La vida de Lazarillo de Tormes DLB-318
Valle-Inclán, Ramón del 1866-1936 . . . . DLB-134, 322	Vaugelas, Claude Favre de 1585-1650 . . . . DLB-268	Vidal, Gore 1925- DLB-6, 152; CDALB-7
Vallejo, Armando 1949- DLB-122	Vaughan, Henry 1621-1695 . . . . DLB-131	Vidal, Mary Theresa 1815-1873 . . . . DLB-230
Vallejo, César Abraham 1892-1938 . . . . . DLB-290	Vaughan, Thomas 1621-1666. . . . . DLB-131	Vidmer, Richards 1898-1978. . . . . DLB-241
Vallès, Jules 1832-1885 . . . . DLB-123	Vaughn, Robert 1592?-1667 . . . . DLB-213	Viebig, Clara 1860-1952. . . . . DLB-66
Vallette, Marguerite Eymery (see Rachilde)	Vaux, Thomas, Lord 1509-1556. . . . . DLB-132	Vieira, António, S. J. (Antonio Vieyra) 1608-1697 . . . . DLB-307
Valverde, José María 1926-1996 . . . . DLB-108	Vazov, Ivan 1850-1921 . . . . . . DLB-147; CDWLB-4	Viereck, George Sylvester 1884-1962 . . . . . DLB-54
Vampilov, Aleksandr Valentinovich (A. Sanin) 1937-1972 . . . . DLB-302	Vázquez Montalbán, Manuel 1939- DLB-134, 322	Viereck, Peter 1916-2006 . . . . DLB-5
Van Allsburg, Chris 1949- DLB-61	Véa, Alfredo, Jr. 1950- DLB-209	Vietnam War (ended 1975) Resources for the Study of Vietnam War Literature. DLB-9
Van Anda, Carr 1864-1945 . . . . DLB-25	Veblen, Thorstein 1857-1929 . . . . DLB-246	Viets, Roger 1738-1811. . . . . DLB-99
Vanbrugh, Sir John 1664-1726 . . . . DLB-80	Vedel, Anders Sørensen 1542-1616. . . . . . DLB-300	Viewegh, Michal 1962- DLB-353
Vance, Jack 1916?- DLB-8	Vega, Janine Pommy 1942- DLB-16	Vigil-Piñon, Evangelina 1949- DLB-122
Vančura, Vladislav 1891-1942 . . . . DLB-215; CDWLB-4	Veiller, Anthony 1903-1965 . . . . DLB-44	Vigneault, Gilles 1928- DLB-60
Vanderhaege, Guy 1951- DLB-334	Velásquez-Trevino, Gloria 1949- DLB-122	Vigny, Alfred de 1797-1863. . . . . DLB-119, 192, 217
van der Post, Laurens 1906-1996 . . . . DLB-204	Veley, Margaret 1843-1887 . . . . DLB-199	Vigolo, Giorgio 1894-1983 . . . . DLB-114
Van Dine, S. S. (see Wright, Willard Huntington)	Velleius Paterculus circa 20 B.C.-circa A.D. 30 . . . . DLB-211	Vik, Bjorg 1935- DLB-297
Van Doren, Mark 1894-1972 . . . . . DLB-45, 335	Velmar-Janković, Svetlana 1933- DLB-353	The Viking Press DLB-46
van Druten, John 1901-1957. . . . . DLB-10	Veloz Maggiolo, Marcio 1936- DLB-145	Vila-Matas, Enrique 1948- DLB-322
Van Duyn, Mona 1921-2004 . . . . DLB-5	Vel'tman, Aleksandr Fomich 1800-1870. . . . . DLB-198	Vilde, Eduard 1865-1933 . . . . DLB-220
Tribute to James Dickey. Y-97	Venegas, Daniel ?-? DLB-82	Vilikovský, Pavel 1941- DLB-353
Van Dyke, Henry 1852-1933 . . . . . DLB-71; DS-13	Venevitinov, Dmitrii Vladimirovich 1805-1827. . . . . DLB-205	Vilinskaia, Mariia Aleksandrovna (see Vovchok, Marko)
Van Dyke, Henry 1928- DLB-33	Verbitskaia, Anastasiia Alekseevna 1861-1928 . . . . DLB-295	Villa, José García 1908-1997 . . . . DLB-312
Van Dyke, John C. 1856-1932 . . . . DLB-186	Verde, Cesário 1855-1886. . . . . DLB-287	Villanueva, Alma Luz 1944- DLB-122
Vane, Sutton 1888-1963 . . . . DLB-10	Vergil, Polydore circa 1470-1555. . . . . . . DLB-132	Villanueva, Tino 1941- DLB-82
Van Gieson, Judith 1941- DLB-306	Veríssimo, Erico 1905-1975. . . . . DLB-145, 307	Villard, Henry 1835-1900. . . . . DLB-23
Vanguard Press DLB-46	Verlaine, Paul 1844-1896 . . . . DLB-217	Villard, Oswald Garrison 1872-1949 . . DLB-25, 91
van Gulik, Robert Hans 1910-1967 . . . . . . DS-17	Vernacular Translations in the Crowns of Castile and Aragon 1352-1515. . . . . . DLB-286	Villarreal, Edit 1944- DLB-209
van Herk, Aritha 1954- DLB-334	Verne, Jules 1828-1905 . . . . DLB-123	Villarreal, José Antonio 1924- DLB-82
van Itallie, Jean-Claude 1936- DLB-7	*Vernon God Little*, 2003 Booker Prize winner, DBC Pierre DLB-326	Villaseñor, Victor 1940- DLB-209
Van Loan, Charles E. 1876-1919 . . . . . . DLB-171		Villedieu, Madame de (Marie-Catherine Desjardins) 1640?-1683 . . . . DLB-268
Vann, Robert L. 1879-1940. . . . . DLB-29		Villegas, Antonio de ?-? DLB-318
Van Rensselaer, Mariana Griswold 1851-1934 . . . . DLB-47		Villegas de Magnón, Leonor 1876-1955. . . . . DLB-122
Van Rensselaer, Mrs. Schuyler (see Van Rensselaer, Mariana Griswold)		

Villehardouin, Geoffroi de
  circa 1150-1215 .... DLB-208
Villemaire, Yolande 1949- DLB-60
Villena, Enrique de
  ca. 1382/84-1432 .... DLB-286
Villena, Luis Antonio de 1951- DLB-134
Villiers, George, Second Duke
  of Buckingham 1628-1687 .... DLB-80
Villiers de l'Isle-Adam, Jean-Marie
  Mathias Philippe-Auguste,
  Comte de 1838-1889 .... DLB-123, 192
Villon, François 1431-circa 1463? DLB-208
Vinaver, Michel (Michel Grinberg)
  1927- DLB-321
Vine Press DLB-112
Vinje, A. O. 1818-1870 .... DLB-354
Viorst, Judith 1931- DLB-52
Vipont, Elfrida (Elfrida Vipont Foulds,
  Charles Vipont) 1902-1992 .... DLB-160
Viramontes, Helena María 1954- .. DLB-122, 350
Virgil 70 B.C.-19 B.C. DLB-211; CDWLB-1
Vischer, Friedrich Theodor 1807-1887 .... DLB-133
Vitier, Cintio 1921- DLB-283
Vitrac, Roger 1899-1952 .... DLB-321
Vitruvius circa 85 B.C.-circa 15 B.C. DLB-211
Vitry, Philippe de 1291-1361 .... DLB-208
Vittorini, Elio 1908-1966 .... DLB-264
Vivanco, Luis Felipe 1907-1975 .... DLB-108
Vives, Juan Luis 1493-1540 .... DLB-318
Vivian, E. Charles (Charles Henry Cannell,
  Charles Henry Vivian, Jack Mann,
  Barry Lynd) 1882-1947 .... DLB-255
Viviani, Cesare 1947- DLB-128
Vivien, Renée 1877-1909 .... DLB-217
Vizenor, Gerald 1934- DLB-175, 227
Vizetelly and Company DLB-106
Vladimov, Georgii
  1931-2003 .... DLB-302
Voaden, Herman 1903-1991 .... DLB-88
Voß, Johann Heinrich 1751-1826 .... DLB-90
Vogau, Boris Andreevich
  (see Pil'niak, Boris Andreevich)
Vogel, Paula 1951- DLB-341
Vogt, Nils Collett 1864-1937 .... DLB-354
Voigt, Ellen Bryant 1943- DLB-120
Voinovich, Vladimir Nikolaevich
  1932- DLB-302
Vojnović, Ivo 1857-1929 ..... DLB-147; CDWLB-4
Vold, Jan Erik 1939- DLB-297
Volkoff, Vladimir 1932-2005 .... DLB-83
P. F. Volland Company DLB-46
Vollbehr, Otto H. F.
  1872?-1945 or 1946 .... DLB-187
Vollman, William T. 1959- DLB-350
Vologdin (see Zasodimsky, Pavel Vladimirovich)

Voloshin, Maksimilian Aleksandrovich
  1877-1932 .... DLB-295
Volponi, Paolo 1924-1994 .... DLB-177
Voltaire (François-Marie Arouet)
  1694-1778 .... DLB-314
  "An account of the death of the chevalier de
    La Barre" DLB-314
  Candide DLB-314
  Philosophical Dictionary DLB-314
Vonarburg, Élisabeth 1947- DLB-251
von der Grün, Max 1926- DLB-75
Vonnegut, Kurt 1922-2007 .... DLB-2, 8, 152;
                              Y-80; DS-3; CDALB-6
  Tribute to Isaac Asimov Y-92
  Tribute to Richard Brautigan Y-84
Voranc, Prežihov 1893-1950 .... DLB-147
Voronsky, Aleksandr Konstantinovich
  1884-1937 .... DLB-272
Vorse, Mary Heaton 1874-1966 .... DLB-303
Vovchok, Marko 1833-1907 .... DLB-238
Voynich, E. L. 1864-1960 .... DLB-197
Vrkljan, Irena 1930- DLB-353
Vroman, Mary Elizabeth
  circa 1924-1967 .... DLB-33

W

Wace, Robert ("Maistre")
  circa 1100-circa 1175 .... DLB-146
Wackenroder, Wilhelm Heinrich
  1773-1798 .... DLB-90
Wackernagel, Wilhelm 1806-1869 ...... DLB-133
Waddell, Helen 1889-1965 .... DLB-240
Waddington, Miriam 1917-2004 .... DLB-68
Wade, Henry 1887-1969 .... DLB-77
Wagenknecht, Edward 1900-2004 ...... DLB-103
Wägner, Elin 1882-1949 .... DLB-259
Wagner, Heinrich Leopold 1747-1779 .... DLB-94
Wagner, Henry R. 1862-1957 .... DLB-140
Wagner, Richard 1813-1883 .... DLB-129
Wagoner, David 1926- DLB-5, 256
Wah, Fred 1939- DLB-60
Waiblinger, Wilhelm 1804-1830 .... DLB-90
Wain, John 1925-1994
  .... DLB-15, 27, 139, 155; CDBLB-8
  Tribute to J. B. Priestly Y-84
Wainwright, Jeffrey 1944- DLB-40
Waite, Peirce and Company DLB-49
Wakeman, Stephen H. 1859-1924 ..... DLB-187
Wakoski, Diane 1937- DLB-5
Walahfrid Strabo circa 808-849 .... DLB-148
Henry Z. Walck [publishing house] DLB-46
Walcott, Derek
  1930- DLB-117, 332; Y-81, 92; CDWLB-3
  Nobel Lecture 1992: The Antilles:
    Fragments of Epic Memory Y-92

Robert Waldegrave [publishing house] ... DLB-170
Waldis, Burkhard circa 1490-1556? DLB-178
Waldman, Anne 1945- DLB-16
Waldrop, Rosmarie 1935- DLB-169
Walker, Alice 1900-1982 .... DLB-201
Walker, Alice
  1944- DLB-6, 33, 143; CDALB-6
Walker, Annie Louisa (Mrs. Harry Coghill)
  circa 1836-1907 .... DLB-240
Walker, George F. 1947- DLB-60
Walker, John Brisben 1847-1931 .... DLB-79
Walker, Joseph A. 1935-2003 .... DLB-38
Walker, Kath (see Oodgeroo of the Tribe Noonuccal)
Walker, Margaret 1915-1998 .... DLB-76, 152
Walker, Obadiah 1616-1699 .... DLB-281
Walker, Ted 1934-2004 .... DLB-40
Walker, Evans and Cogswell Company ... DLB-49
Wall, John F. (see Sarban)
Wallace, Alfred Russel 1823-1913 ...... DLB-190
Wallace, David Foster 1962-2008 .... DLB-350
Wallace, Dewitt 1889-1981 .... DLB-137
Wallace, Edgar 1875-1932 .... DLB-70
Wallace, Lew 1827-1905 .... DLB-202
Wallace, Lila Acheson 1889-1984 ...... DLB-137
  "A Word of Thanks," From the Initial
    Issue of Reader's Digest
    (February 1922) DLB-137
Wallace, Naomi 1960- DLB-249
Wallace Markfield's "Steeplechase" Y-02
Wallace-Crabbe, Chris 1934- DLB-289
Wallant, Edward Lewis
  1926-1962 .... DLB-2, 28, 143, 299
Waller, Edmund 1606-1687 .... DLB-126
Walling, William English 1877-1936 ..... DLB-345
Walpole, Horace 1717-1797 ..... DLB-39, 104, 213
  Preface to the First Edition of
    The Castle of Otranto (1764) DLB-39, 178
  Preface to the Second Edition of
    The Castle of Otranto (1765) DLB-39, 178
Walpole, Hugh 1884-1941 .... DLB-34
Walrond, Eric 1898-1966 .... DLB-51
Walser, Martin 1927- DLB-75, 124
Walser, Robert 1878-1956 .... DLB-66
Walsh, Ernest 1895-1926 .... DLB-4, 45
Walsh, Robert 1784-1859 .... DLB-59
Walters, Henry 1848-1931 .... DLB-140
Waltharius circa 825 .... DLB-148
Walther von der Vogelweide
  circa 1170-circa 1230 .... DLB-138
Walton, Izaak
  1593-1683 .... DLB-151, 213; CDBLB-1
Walwicz, Ania 1951- DLB-325
Wambaugh, Joseph 1937- DLB-6; Y-83
Wand, Alfred Rudolph 1828-1891 ...... DLB-188

Wandor, Michelene 1940- DLB-310

Waniek, Marilyn Nelson 1946- DLB-120

Wanley, Humphrey 1672-1726 .... DLB-213

War of the Words (and Pictures):
  The Creation of a Graphic Novel Y-02

Warburton, William 1698-1779 .... DLB-104

Ward, Aileen 1919- DLB-111

Ward, Artemus (see Browne, Charles Farrar)

Ward, Arthur Henry Sarsfield (see Rohmer, Sax)

Ward, Douglas Turner 1930- DLB-7, 38

Ward, Mrs. Humphry 1851-1920........ DLB-18

Ward, James 1843-1925 .... DLB-262

Ward, Lynd 1905-1985................. DLB-22

Ward, Lock and Company........... DLB-106

Ward, Nathaniel circa 1578-1652 .... DLB-24

Ward, Theodore 1902-1983 .... DLB-76, 341

Wardle, Ralph 1909-1988............. DLB-103

Ware, Henry, Jr. 1794-1843............. DLB-235

Ware, William 1797-1852 .... DLB-1, 235

Warfield, Catherine Ann 1816-1877 .... DLB-248

Waring, Anna Letitia 1823-1910 .... DLB-240

Frederick Warne and Company [U.K.].... DLB-106

Frederick Warne and Company [U.S.]..... DLB-49

Warner, Anne 1869-1913 .... DLB-202

Warner, Charles Dudley 1829-1900...... DLB-64

Warner, Marina 1946- DLB-194

Warner, Rex 1905-1986 .... DLB-15

Warner, Susan 1819-1885.... DLB-3, 42, 239, 250

Warner, Sylvia Townsend
  1893-1978................. DLB-34, 139

Warner, William 1558-1609 .... DLB-172

Warner Books...................... DLB-46

Warr, Bertram 1917-1943 .... DLB-88

Warren, John Byrne Leicester
  (see De Tabley, Lord)

Warren, Josiah 1798-1874 .... DLB-345

Warren, Lella 1899-1982 .... Y-83

Warren, Mercy Otis 1728-1814...... DLB-31, 200

Warren, Robert Penn 1905-1989
  ..... DLB-2, 48, 152, 320; Y-80, 89; CDALB-6
  Tribute to Katherine Anne Porter Y-80

Warren, Samuel 1807-1877 .... DLB-190

Warszawski, Oser (Oyzer Varshavski)
  1898-1944 .... DLB-333

Die Wartburgkrieg circa 1230-circa 1280 ... DLB-138

Warton, Joseph 1722-1800 .... DLB-104, 109

Warton the Younger, Thomas
  1728-1790............... DLB-104, 109, 336

Warung, Price (William Astley)
  1855-1911.................... DLB-230

Washington, Booker T. 1856?-1915 ..... DLB-345

Washington, George 1732-1799 .... DLB-31

Washington, Ned 1901-1976........... DLB-265

Wassermann, Jakob 1873-1934.......... DLB-66

Wasserstein, Wendy 1950-2006 .... DLB-228

Wassmo, Herbjorg 1942- DLB-297

Wasson, David Atwood 1823-1887 ... DLB-1, 223

Watanna, Onoto (see Eaton, Winnifred)

Waten, Judah 1911?-1985............ DLB-289

Waterhouse, Keith 1929-2009 .... DLB-13, 15

Waterman, Andrew 1940- DLB-40

Waters, Frank 1902-1995 ....DLB-212; Y-86

Waters, Michael 1949- DLB-120

Watkins, Tobias 1780-1855............ DLB-73

Watkins, Vernon 1906-1967 .... DLB-20

Watmough, David 1926- DLB-53

Watson, Colin 1920-1983.............DLB-276

Watson, Ian 1943- DLB-261

Watson, James Wreford (see Wreford, James)

Watson, John 1850-1907.............. DLB-156

Watson, Rosamund Marriott
  (Graham R. Tomson) 1860-1911.... DLB-240

Watson, Sheila 1909-1998 .... DLB-60

Watson, Thomas 1545?-1592.......... DLB-132

Watson, Wilfred 1911-1998 .... DLB-60

W. J. Watt and Company DLB-46

Watten, Barrett 1948- DLB-193

Watterson, Henry 1840-1921............ DLB-25

Watts, Alan 1915-1973 .... DLB-16

Watts, Isaac 1674-1748 .... DLB-95

Franklin Watts [publishing house] DLB-46

Waugh, Alec 1898-1981 .... DLB-191

Waugh, Auberon 1939-2000.... DLB-14, 194; Y-00

Waugh, Evelyn 1903-1966
  .... DLB-15, 162, 195, 352; CDBLB-6

Way and Williams DLB-49

Wayman, Tom 1945- DLB-53

Wearne, Alan 1948- DLB-325

Weatherly, Tom 1942- DLB-41

Weaver, Gordon 1937- DLB-130

Weaver, Robert 1921-2008 .... DLB-88

Webb, Beatrice 1858-1943 .... DLB-190

Webb, Francis 1925-1973 .... DLB-260

Webb, Frank J. fl. 1857................. DLB-50

Webb, James Watson 1802-1884 .... DLB-43

Webb, Mary 1881-1927 .... DLB-34

Webb, Phyllis 1927- DLB-53

Webb, Sidney 1859-1947 .... DLB-190

Webb, Walter Prescott 1888-1963........ DLB-17

Webbe, William ?-1591 .... DLB-132

Webber, Charles Wilkins
  1819-1856?.................... DLB-202

Weber, Max 1864-1920 .... DLB-296

Webling, Lucy (Lucy Betty MacRaye)
  1877-1952 .... DLB-240

Webling, Peggy (Arthur Weston)
  1871-1949.................... DLB-240

Webster, Augusta 1837-1894........ DLB-35, 240

Webster, John
  1579 or 1580-1634?...... DLB-58; CDBLB-1
  The Melbourne Manuscript........... Y-86

Webster, Noah
  1758-1843........ DLB-1, 37, 42, 43, 73, 243

Webster, Paul Francis 1907-1984........ DLB-265

Charles L. Webster and Company....... DLB-49

Weckherlin, Georg Rodolf 1584-1653 ... DLB-164

Wedekind, Frank
  1864-1918 ....DLB-118; CDWLB-2

Weeks, Edward Augustus, Jr.
  1898-1989 .... DLB-137

Weeks, Stephen B. 1865-1918.......... DLB-187

Weems, Mason Locke 1759-1825 ... DLB-30, 37, 42

Weerth, Georg 1822-1856 .... DLB-129

Weidenfeld and Nicolson DLB-112

Weidman, Jerome 1913-1998 .... DLB-28

Weigl, Bruce 1949- DLB-120

Weil, Jiří 1900-1959 .... DLB-299

Weinbaum, Stanley Grauman
  1902-1935 .... DLB-8

Weiner, Andrew 1949- DLB-251

Weintraub, Stanley 1929- DLB-111; Y82

Weise, Christian 1642-1708 .... DLB-168

Weisenborn, Gunther 1902-1969 .... DLB-69, 124

Weiss, John 1818-1879 .... DLB-1, 243

Weiss, Paul 1901-2002 ....DLB-279

Weiss, Peter 1916-1982.......... DLB-69, 124

Weiss, Theodore 1916-2003 .... DLB-5

Weissenberg, Isaac Meir (Yitskhok-Meyer Vaysenberg)
  1878-1938......................DLB-333

Weiß, Ernst 1882-1940................ DLB-81

Weiße, Christian Felix 1726-1804........ DLB-97

Weitling, Wilhelm 1808-1871 .... DLB-129

Welch, Denton 1915-1948 .... DLB-319

Welch, James 1940- DLB-175, 256

Welch, James Colin Ross 1924-1997 .... DLB-352

Welch, Lew 1926-1971? DLB-16

Weldon, Fay 1931-
  .... DLB-14, 194, 319; CDBLB-8

Welhaven, Johan Sebastian 1807-1873 ... DLB-354

Wellek, René 1903-1995................ DLB-63

Weller, Archie 1957- DLB-325

Wells, Carolyn 1862-1942 .... DLB-11

Wells, Charles Jeremiah
  circa 1800-1879 .... DLB-32

Wells, Gabriel 1862-1946 .... DLB-140

Wells, H. G. 1866-1946
  ....DLB-34, 70, 156, 178; CDBLB-6
  H. G. Wells Society Y-98
  Preface to *The Scientific Romances of
  H. G. Wells* (1933) DLB-178

Wells, Helena 1758?-1824 ....DLB-200

Wells, Rebecca 1952- DLB-292

Wells, Robert 1947- DLB-40

Wells-Barnett, Ida B. 1862-1931......DLB-23, 221

Welsh, Irvine 1958- DLB-271

Welty, Eudora 1909-2001 ...... DLB-2, 102, 143;
Y-87, 01; DS-12; CDALB-1

   Eudora Welty: Eye of the Storyteller.......Y-87

   Eudora Welty Newsletter..................Y-99

   Eudora Welty's Funeral................Y-01

   Eudora Welty's Ninetieth Birthday Y-99

   Eudora Welty Remembered in
Two Exhibits....................Y-02

Wendell, Barrett 1855-1921 ....DLB-71

Wentworth, Patricia 1878-1961 ....DLB-77

Wentworth, William Charles
1790-1872 ....DLB-230

Wenzel, Jean-Paul 1947- DLB-321

Werder, Diederich von dem 1584-1657 ...DLB-164

Werfel, Franz 1890-1945 ....DLB-81, 124

Wergeland, Henrik 1808-1845..........DLB-354

Werner, Zacharias 1768-1823............DLB-94

The Werner Company..................DLB-49

Wersba, Barbara 1932- DLB-52

Wescott, Glenway
1901-1987 ....DLB-4, 9, 102; DS-15

Wesker, Arnold
1932- DLB-13, 310, 319; CDBLB-8

Wesley, Charles 1707-1788 ....DLB-95

Wesley, John 1703-1791 ....DLB-104

Wesley, Mary 1912-2002 ....DLB-231

Wesley, Richard 1945- DLB-38

Wessel, Johan Herman 1742-1785 ....DLB-300

A. Wessels and Company DLB-46

Wessobrunner Gebet circa 787-815 ....DLB-148

West, Anthony 1914-1988 ....DLB-15

   Tribute to Liam O'Flaherty.............Y-84

West, Cheryl L. 1957- DLB-266

West, Cornel 1953- DLB-246

West, Dorothy 1907-1998................DLB-76

West, Jessamyn 1902-1984........ DLB-6; Y-84

West, Mae 1892-1980 ....DLB-44, 341

West, Michael Lee 1953- DLB-292

West, Michelle Sagara 1963- DLB-251

West, Morris 1916-1999...............DLB-289

West, Nathanael
1903-1940 ....DLB-4, 9, 28; CDALB-5

West, Paul 1930- DLB-14

West, Rebecca 1892-1983 .... DLB-36; Y-83

West, Richard 1941- DLB-185

West and Johnson DLB-49

Westcott, Edward Noyes 1846-1898 .....DLB-202

The Western Literature Association...........Y-99

The Western Messenger
1835-1841 .... DLB-1; DLB-223

Western Publishing Company DLB-46

Western Writers of America Y-99

The Westminster Review 1824-1914 ....DLB-110

Weston, Arthur (see Webling, Peggy)

Weston, Elizabeth Jane circa 1582-1612...DLB-172

Wetherald, Agnes Ethelwyn 1857-1940 ....DLB-99

Wetherell, Elizabeth (see Warner, Susan)

Wetherell, W. D. 1948- DLB-234

Wetzel, Friedrich Gottlob 1779-1819 ......DLB-90

Weyman, Stanley J. 1855-1928 .....DLB-141, 156

Wezel, Johann Karl 1747-1819 ....DLB-94

Whalen, Philip 1923-2002 ....DLB-16

Whalley, George 1915-1983 ....DLB-88

Wharton, Edith 1862-1937 .... DLB-4, 9, 12,
78, 189; DS-13; CDALB-3

Wharton, Michael Bernard 1913-2006 ...DLB-352

Wharton, William 1925- Y-80

Whately, Mary Louisa 1824-1889.......DLB-166

Whately, Richard 1787-1863 ....DLB-190

   Elements of Rhetoric (1828;
revised, 1846) [excerpt]..........DLB-57

Wheatle, Alex 1963- DLB-347

Wheatley, Dennis 1897-1977 .... DLB-77, 255

Wheatley, Phillis
circa 1754-1784 ....DLB-31, 50; CDALB-2

Wheeler, Anna Doyle 1785-1848?.......DLB-158

Wheeler, Charles Stearns 1816-1843...DLB-1, 223

Wheeler, Monroe 1900-1988..............DLB-4

Wheelock, John Hall 1886-1978 ....DLB-45

   From John Hall Wheelock's
Oral Memoir Y-01

Wheelwright, J. B. 1897-1940 ....DLB-45

Wheelwright, John circa 1592-1679.......DLB-24

Whetstone, George 1550-1587 ....DLB-136

Whetstone, Colonel Pete (see Noland, C. F. M.)

Whewell, William 1794-1866.............DLB-262

Whichcote, Benjamin 1609?-1683 ....DLB-252

Whicher, Stephen E. 1915-1961.........DLB-111

Whipple, Edwin Percy 1819-1886 ......DLB-1, 64

Whitaker, Alexander 1585-1617 ....DLB-24

Whitaker, Daniel K. 1801-1881 ....DLB-73

Whitcher, Frances Miriam
1812-1852 ....DLB-11, 202

White, Andrew 1579-1656................DLB-24

White, Andrew Dickson 1832-1918 ......DLB-47

White, E. B. 1899-1985 ....DLB-11, 22; CDALB-7

White, Edgar B. 1947- DLB-38

White, Edmund 1940- DLB-227

White, Ethel Lina 1887-1944 ....DLB-77

White, Hayden V. 1928- DLB-246

White, Henry Kirke 1785-1806 ....DLB-96

White, Horace 1834-1916 ....DLB-23

White, James 1928-1999 ....DLB-261

White, Patrick 1912-1990 ....DLB-260, 332

White, Phyllis Dorothy James (see James, P. D.)

White, Richard Grant 1821-1885 ....DLB-64

White, T. H. 1906-1964.............DLB-160, 255

White, Walter 1893-1955 ....DLB-51

Wilcox, James 1949- DLB-292

William White and Company DLB-49

White, William Allen 1868-1944........DLB-9, 25

White, William Anthony Parker
(see Boucher, Anthony)

White, William Hale (see Rutherford, Mark)

Whitechurch, Victor L. 1868-1933 ....DLB-70

Whitehead, Alfred North
1861-1947 ....DLB-100, 262

Whitehead, E. A. (Ted Whitehead)
1933- DLB-310

Whitehead, James 1936-2003 ....Y-81

Whitehead, William 1715-1785 ......DLB-84, 109

Whitfield, James Monroe 1822-1871 ......DLB-50

Whitfield, Raoul 1898-1945 ....DLB-226

Whitgift, John circa 1533-1604 ....DLB-132

Whiting, John 1917-1963 ....DLB-13

Whiting, Samuel 1597-1679 ....DLB-24

Whitlock, Brand 1869-1934 ....DLB-12

Whitman, Albery Allson 1851-1901 ......DLB-50

Whitman, Alden 1913-1990 ....Y-91

Whitman, Sarah Helen (Power)
1803-1878 ....DLB-1, 243

Whitman, Walt
1819-1892 ....DLB-3, 64, 224, 250; CDALB-2

Albert Whitman and Company..........DLB-46

Whitman Publishing Company..........DLB-46

Whitney, Geoffrey
1548 or 1552?-1601 ....DLB-136

Whitney, Isabella fl. 1566-1573 ....DLB-136

Whitney, John Hay 1904-1982 ....DLB-127

Whittemore, Reed 1919-1995 ....DLB-5

Whittier, John Greenleaf
1807-1892 ....DLB-1, 243; CDALB-2

Whittlesey House DLB-46

Whyte, John 1941-1992................DLB-334

Wickham, Anna (Edith Alice Mary Harper)
1884-1947 ....DLB-240

Wickram, Georg circa 1505-circa 1561 ...DLB-179

Wicomb, Zoë 1948- DLB-225

Wideman, John Edgar 1941- DLB-33, 143

Widener, Harry Elkins 1885-1912.......DLB-140

Wiebe, Rudy 1934- DLB-60

Wiechert, Ernst 1887-1950..............DLB-56

Wied, Gustav 1858-1914...............DLB-300

Wied, Martina 1882-1957 ....DLB-85

Wiehe, Evelyn May Clowes (see Mordaunt, Elinor)

Wieland, Christoph Martin 1733-1813.... DLB-97	William of Auvergne 1190-1249............ DLB-115	Willis, John circa 1572-1625............ DLB-281
Wienbarg, Ludolf 1802-1872.......... DLB-133	William of Conches circa 1090-circa 1154............. DLB-115	Willis, Nathaniel Parker 1806-1867 ....DLB-3, 59, 73, 74, 183, 250; DS-13
Wieners, John 1934-2002.............. DLB-16	William of Ockham circa 1285-1347.... DLB-115	Willis, Ted 1918-1992................. DLB-310
Wier, Ester 1910-2000 .... DLB-52	William of Sherwood 1200/1205-1266/1271.............. DLB-115	Willkomm, Ernst 1810-1886 .... DLB-133
Wiesel, Elie 1928- DLB-83, 299; Y-86, 87; CDALB-7	The William Charvat American Fiction Collection at the Ohio State University Libraries.................... Y-92	Wills, Garry 1934- DLB-246
Nobel Lecture 1986: Hope, Despair and Memory....................... Y-86		Tribute to Kenneth Dale McCormick Y-97
Wiggin, Kate Douglas 1856-1923........ DLB-42	Williams, Ben Ames 1889-1953........ DLB-102	Wills, W. G. 1828-1891 .... DLB-344
Wiggins, Marianne 1947- DLB-335	Williams, C. K. 1936- DLB-5	Willson, Meredith 1902-1984.......... DLB-265
Wigglesworth, Michael 1631-1705....... DLB-24	Williams, Chancellor 1905-1992........ DLB-76	Willumsen, Dorrit 1940- DLB-214
Wilberforce, William 1759-1833........ DLB-158	Williams, Charles 1886-1945...DLB-100, 153, 255	Wilmer, Clive 1945- DLB-40
Wilbrandt, Adolf 1837-1911............ DLB-129	Williams, Denis 1923-1998............DLB-117	Wilson, A. N. 1950- DLB-14, 155, 194
Wilbur, Richard 1921- .. DLB-5, 169; CDALB-7	Williams, Emlyn 1905-1987.........DLB-10, 77	Wilson, Angus 1913-1991......DLB-15, 139, 155
Tribute to Robert Penn Warren......... Y-89	Williams, Garth 1912-1996............. DLB-22	Wilson, Arthur 1595-1652 .... DLB-58
Wilcox, James 1949- DLB-292	Williams, George Washington 1849-1891 . DLB-47	Wilson, August 1945-2005............. DLB-228
Wild, Peter 1940- DLB-5	Williams, Heathcote 1941- DLB-13	Wilson, Augusta Jane Evans 1835-1909... DLB-42
Wilde, Lady Jane Francesca Elgee 1821?-1896..................... DLB-199	Williams, Helen Maria 1761-1827...... DLB-158	Wilson, Colin 1931- DLB-14, 194
	Williams, Hugo 1942- DLB-40	Tribute to J. B. Priestly................ Y-84
Wilde, Oscar 1854-1900 ....DLB-10, 19, 34, 57, 141, 156, 190, 344; CDBLB-5	Williams, Isaac 1802-1865 .... DLB-32	Wilson, Edmund 1895-1972............ DLB-63
	Williams, Joan 1928-2004............... DLB-6	Wilson, Ethel 1888-1980 .... DLB-68
"The Critic as Artist" (1891) DLB-57	Williams, Joe 1889-1972 .... DLB-241	Wilson, F. P. 1889-1963 .... DLB-201
"The Decay of Lying" (1889)........ DLB-18	Williams, John A. 1925- DLB-2, 33	Wilson, Harriet E. 1827/1828?-1863?........ DLB-50, 239, 243
"The English Renaissance of Art" (1908) DLB-35	Williams, John E. 1922-1994 .... DLB-6	
"L'Envoi" (1882) DLB-35	Williams, Jonathan 1929- DLB-5	Wilson, Harry Leon 1867-1939 .... DLB-9
Oscar Wilde Conference at Hofstra University Y-00	Williams, Joy 1944- DLB-335	Wilson, John 1588-1667................ DLB-24
	Williams, Miller 1930- DLB-105	Wilson, John 1785-1854 .... DLB-110
Wilde, Richard Henry 1789-1847 ...... DLB-3, 59	Williams, Nigel 1948- DLB-231	Wilson, John Anthony Burgess (see Burgess, Anthony)
W. A. Wilde Company................ DLB-49	Williams, Raymond 1921-1988 . DLB-14, 231, 242	
Wilder, Billy 1906-2002 .... DLB-26	Williams, Roger circa 1603-1683 .... DLB-24	Wilson, John Dover 1881-1969 .... DLB-201
Wilder, Laura Ingalls 1867-1957..... DLB-22, 256	Williams, Rowland 1817-1870.......... DLB-184	Wilson, Lanford 1937- DLB-7, 341
Wilder, Thornton 1897-1975 ....DLB-4, 7, 9, 228; CDALB-7	Williams, Samm-Art 1946- DLB-38	Wilson, Margaret 1882-1973 .... DLB-9
	Williams, Sherley Anne 1944-1999 ...... DLB-41	Wilson, Michael 1914-1978 .... DLB-44
Thornton Wilder Centenary at Yale Y-97	Williams, T. Harry 1909-1979 .... DLB-17	Wilson, Mona 1872-1954 .... DLB-149
Wildgans, Anton 1881-1932............ DLB-118	Williams, Tennessee 1911-1983 ....DLB-7, 341; Y-83; DS-4; CDALB-1	Wilson, Robert Charles 1953- DLB-251
Wilding, Michael 1942- DLB-325		Wilson, Robert McLiam 1964- DLB-267
Wiley, Bell Irvin 1906-1980 .... DLB-17	Williams, Terry Tempest 1955- DLB-206, 275	Wilson, Robley 1930- DLB-218
John Wiley and Sons DLB-49	Williams, Ursula Moray 1911-2006..... DLB-160	Wilson, Romer 1891-1930 .... DLB-191
Wilhelm, Kate 1928- DLB-8	Williams, Valentine 1883-1946.......... DLB-77	Wilson, Thomas 1524-1581 .... DLB-132, 236
Wilkes, Charles 1798-1877 .... DLB-183	Williams, William Appleman 1921-1990 .. DLB-17	Wilson, Woodrow 1856-1924........... DLB-47
Wilkes, George 1817-1885 .... DLB-79	Williams, William Carlos 1883-1963 ..... DLB-4, 16, 54, 86; CDALB-4	Effingham Wilson [publishing house].... DLB-154
Wilkins, John 1614-1672.............. DLB-236		Wimpfeling, Jakob 1450-1528 ....DLB-179
Wilkinson, Anne 1910-1961............ DLB-88	The William Carlos Williams Society Y-99	Wimsatt, William K., Jr. 1907-1975....... DLB-63
Wilkinson, Christopher 1941- DLB-310	Williams, Wirt 1921-1986 .... DLB-6	Winchell, Walter 1897-1972 .... DLB-29
Wilkinson, Eliza Yonge 1757-circa 1813 . DLB-200	A. Williams and Company............ DLB-49	J. Winchester [publishing house] DLB-49
Wilkinson, Sylvia 1940- Y-86	Williams Brothers.................... DLB-49	Winckelmann, Johann Joachim 1717-1768 .... DLB-97
Wilkinson, William Cleaver 1833-1920 ... DLB-71	Williamson, David 1942- DLB-289	
Willard, Barbara 1909-1994 .... DLB-161	Williamson, Henry 1895-1977 .... DLB-191	Winckler, Paul 1630-1686............. DLB-164
Willard, Emma 1787-1870............. DLB-239	The Henry Williamson Society Y-98	Wind, Herbert Warren 1916-2005.......DLB-171
Willard, Frances E. 1839-1898 .... DLB-221	Williamson, Jack 1908-2006 .... DLB-8	John Windet [publishing house]........DLB-170
Willard, Nancy 1936- DLB-5, 52	Willingham, Calder Baynard, Jr. 1922-1995 .... DLB-2, 44	Windham, Donald 1920- DLB-6
Willard, Samuel 1640-1707 .... DLB-24		Windsor, Gerard 1944- DLB-325
L. Willard [publishing house] DLB-49	Williram of Ebersberg circa 1020-1085 .. DLB-148	Wing, Donald Goddard 1904-1972 ......DLB-187
Willeford, Charles 1919-1988.......... DLB-226	Willis, Browne 1682-1760............. DLB-336	

Wing, John M. 1844-1917 . . . . .DLB-187

Allan Wingate [publishing house] DLB-112

Winnemucca, Sarah 1844-1921 . . . . .DLB-175

Winnifrith, Tom 1938- DLB-155

Winsloe, Christa 1888-1944 . . . . .DLB-124

Winslow, Anna Green 1759-1780 . . . . . . .DLB-200

Winsor, Justin 1831-1897 . . . . .DLB-47

John C. Winston Company DLB-49

Winters, Yvor 1900-1968 . . . . .DLB-48

Winterson, Jeanette 1959- DLB-207, 261

Winther, Christian 1796-1876 . . . . .DLB-300

Winthrop, John 1588-1649 . . . . .DLB-24, 30

Winthrop, John, Jr. 1606-1676 . . . . .DLB-24

Winthrop, Margaret Tyndal
1591-1647 . . . . .DLB-200

Winthrop, Theodore 1828-1861 . . . . .DLB-202

Winton, Tim 1960- DLB-325

Wirt, William 1772-1834 . . . . .DLB-37

Wise, Francis 1695-1767 . . . . .DLB-336

Wise, John 1652-1725 . . . . .DLB-24

Wise, Thomas James 1859-1937 . . . . .DLB-184

Wiseman, Adele 1928-1992 . . . . .DLB-88

Wishart and Company DLB-112

Wisner, George 1812-1849 . . . . .DLB-43

Wister, Owen 1860-1938 . . . . DLB-9, 78, 186

Wister, Sarah 1761-1804 . . . . .DLB-200

Wither, George 1588-1667 . . . . .DLB-121

Witherspoon, John 1723-1794 . . . . .DLB-31

The Works of the Rev. John Witherspoon
(1800-1801) [excerpts] DLB-31

Withrow, William Henry 1839-1908 . . . . . .DLB-99

Witkacy (see Witkiewicz, Stanisław Ignacy)

Witkiewicz, Stanisław Ignacy
1885-1939 . . . . DLB-215; CDWLB-4

Wittenwiler, Heinrich before 1387-
circa 1414? DLB-179

Wittgenstein, Ludwig 1889-1951 . . . . .DLB-262

Wittig, Monique 1935- DLB-83

Witting, Amy (Joan Austral Levick, née Fraser)
1918-2001 . . . . .DLB-325

Wodehouse, P. G.
1881-1975 . . . . . .DLB-34, 162, 352; CDBLB-6

Worldwide Wodehouse Societies Y-98

Wodrow, Robert 1679-1734 . . . . .DLB-336

Wohmann, Gabriele 1932- DLB-75

Woiwode, Larry 1941- DLB-6

Tribute to John Gardner Y-82

Wolcot, John 1738-1819 . . . . .DLB-109

Wolcott, Roger 1679-1767 . . . . .DLB-24

Wolf, Christa 1929- DLB-75; CDWLB-2

Wolf, Friedrich 1888-1953 . . . . .DLB-124

Wolfe, Gene 1931- DLB-8

Wolfe, Thomas 1900-1938 . . . .
DLB-9, 102, 229; Y-85; DS-2, DS-16; CDALB-5

"All the Faults of Youth and Inexperience":
A Reader's Report on
Thomas Wolfe's *O Lost* Y-01

Emendations for *Look Homeward, Angel* Y-00

Eugene Gant's Projected Works Y-01

Fire at the Old Kentucky Home
[Thomas Wolfe Memorial] Y-98

Thomas Wolfe Centennial
Celebration in Asheville Y-00

The Thomas Wolfe Collection at
the University of North Carolina
at Chapel Hill .Y-97

The Thomas Wolfe Society Y-97, 99

Wolfe, Tom 1931- DLB-152, 185

John Wolfe [publishing house] DLB-170

Reyner (Reginald) Wolfe
[publishing house] DLB-170

Wolfenstein, Martha 1869-1906 . . . . .DLB-221

Wolff, David (see Maddow, Ben)

Wolff, Egon 1926- DLB-305

Wolff, Helen 1906-1994 . . . . .Y-94

Wolff, Tobias 1945- DLB-130

Tribute to Michael M. Rea Y-97

Tribute to Raymond Carver Y-88

Wolfram von Eschenbach
circa 1170-after 1220 . . . . DLB-138; CDWLB-2

Wolfram von Eschenbach's *Parzival:*
Prologue and Book 3 . . . . .DLB-138

Wolker, Jiří 1900-1924 . . . . .DLB-215

Wollstonecraft, Mary 1759-1797
 . . . . .DLB-39, 104, 158, 252; CDBLB-3

Women

Women's Work, Women's Sphere:
Selected Comments from Women
Writers DLB-200

Women Writers in Sixteenth-Century
Spain DLB-318

Wondratschek, Wolf 1943- DLB-75

Wong, Elizabeth 1958- DLB-266

Wong, Nellie 1934- DLB-312

Wong, Shawn 1949- DLB-312

Wongar, B. (Sreten Bozic) 1932- DLB-325

Wood, Anthony à 1632-1695 . . . . .DLB-213

Wood, Benjamin 1820-1900 . . . . .DLB-23

Wood, Charles 1932-1980 . . . . .DLB-13

The Charles Wood Affair:
A Playwright Revived Y-83

Wood, Mrs. Henry 1814-1887 . . . . .DLB-18

Wood, Joanna E. 1867-1927 . . . . .DLB-92

Wood, Sally Sayward Barrell Keating
1759-1855 . . . . .DLB-200

Wood, William fl. seventeenth century DLB-24

Samuel Wood [publishing house] DLB-49

Woodberry, George Edward
1855-1930 . . . . DLB-71, 103

Woodbridge, Benjamin 1622-1684 . . . . . . .DLB-24

Woodbridge, Frederick J. E. 1867-1940 . . .DLB-270

Woodcock, George 1912-1995 . . . . .DLB-88

Woodhull, Victoria C. 1838-1927 . . . . .DLB-79

Woodmason, Charles circa 1720-? DLB-31

Woodress, James Leslie, Jr. 1916- DLB-111

Woods, Margaret L. 1855-1945 . . . . .DLB-240

Woodson, Carter G. 1875-1950 . . . . .DLB-17

Woodward, C. Vann 1908-1999 . . . . .DLB-17

Woodward, Stanley 1895-1965 . . . . .DLB-171

Woodworth, Samuel 1785-1842 . . . . .DLB-250

Wooler, Thomas 1785 or 1786-1853 . . . . .DLB-158

Woolf, David (see Maddow, Ben)

Woolf, Douglas 1922-1992 . . . . .DLB-244

Woolf, Leonard 1880-1969 . . . . . . DLB-100; DS-10

Woolf, Virginia 1882-1941
 . . . . .DLB-36, 100, 162; DS-10; CDBLB-6

"The New Biography," *New York Herald
Tribune,* 30 October 1927 . . . . . . .DLB-149

Woollcott, Alexander 1887-1943 . . . . .DLB-29

Woolman, John 1720-1772 . . . . .DLB-31

Woolner, Thomas 1825-1892 . . . . .DLB-35

Woolrich, Cornell 1903-1968 . . . . .DLB-226

Woolsey, Sarah Chauncy 1835-1905 . . . . . .DLB-42

Woolson, Constance Fenimore
1840-1894 . . . . .DLB-12, 74, 189, 221

Worcester, Joseph Emerson
1784-1865 . . . . .DLB-1, 235

Wynkyn de Worde [publishing house] DLB-170

Wordsworth, Christopher 1807-1885 . . . . .DLB-166

Wordsworth, Dorothy 1771-1855 . . . . . . .DLB-107

Wordsworth, Elizabeth 1840-1932 . . . . . . .DLB-98

Wordsworth, William
1770-1850 . . . . .DLB-93, 107; CDBLB-3

Workman, Fanny Bullock
1859-1925 . . . . .DLB-189

World Literatue Today: A Journal for the
New Millennium Y-01

World Publishing Company DLB-46

World War I (1914-1918) DS-18

The Great War Exhibit and Symposium
at the University of South Carolina . . .Y-97

The Liddle Collection and First World
War Research .Y-97

Other British Poets Who Fell
  in the Great War DLB-216

The Seventy-Fifth Anniversary of
  the Armistice: The Wilfred Owen
  Centenary and the Great War Exhibit
  at the University of Virginia Y-93

World War II (1939–1945)

  Literary Effects of World War II DLB-15

  World War II Writers Symposium
    at the University of South Carolina,
    12–14 April 1995. . . . . Y-95

  WW2 HMSO Paperbacks Society Y-98

R. Worthington and Company. DLB-49

Wotton, Sir Henry 1568-1639 . . . . DLB-121

Wouk, Herman 1915- Y-82; CDALB-7

  Tribute to James Dickey. Y-97

Wreford, James 1915-1990 . . . . DLB-88

Wren, Sir Christopher 1632-1723. . . . . . . DLB-213

Wren, Percival Christopher 1885-1941. . . DLB-153

Wrenn, John Henry 1841-1911 . . . . DLB-140

Wright, C. D. 1949- DLB-120

Wright, Charles 1935- DLB-165; Y-82

Wright, Charles Stevenson 1932- DLB-33

Wright, Chauncey 1830-1875. . . . . .DLB-270

Wright, Frances 1795-1852 . . . . DLB-73

Wright, Harold Bell 1872-1944. . . . . DLB-9

Wright, James 1927-1980
  . . . . DLB-5, 169, 342; CDALB-7

Wright, Jay 1935- DLB-41

Wright, Judith 1915-2000 . . . . DLB-260

Wright, Louis B. 1899-1984 . . . . DLB-17

Wright, Richard 1908-1960
  . . . . DLB-76, 102; DS-2; CDALB-5

Wright, Richard B. 1937- DLB-53

Wright, S. Fowler 1874-1965. . . . . DLB-255

Wright, Sarah Elizabeth 1928- DLB-33

Wright, Stephen 1946- DLB-350

Wright, T. H. "Style" (1877) [excerpt] DLB-57

Wright, Willard Huntington (S. S. Van Dine)
  1887-1939. . . . . DLB-306; DS-16

Wrightson, Patricia 1921- DLB-289

Wrigley, Robert 1951- DLB-256

Writers' Forum. Y-85

Writing

  A Writing Life Y-02

  On Learning to Write Y-88

  The Profession of Authorship:
    Scribblers for Bread. Y-89

  A Writer Talking: A Collage Y-00

Wroth, Lawrence C. 1884-1970 . . . . DLB-187

Wroth, Lady Mary 1587-1653 . . . . DLB-121

Wu Jianren (Wo Foshanren)
  1866-1910 . . . . DLB-328

Wu Zuxiang 1908-1994 . . . . DLB-328

Wumingshi (Bu Baonan) 1917-2002 . . . . . DLB-328

Wurlitzer, Rudolph 1937- DLB-173

Wyatt, Sir Thomas circa 1503-1542 . . . . . DLB-132

Wycherley, William
  1641-1715. . . . . DLB-80; CDBLB-2

Wyclif, John circa 1335-1384 . . . . DLB-146

Wyeth, N. C. 1882-1945. . . . . DLB-188; DS-16

Wyle, Niklas von circa 1415-1479. . . . . . .DLB-179

Wylie, Elinor 1885-1928. . . . . DLB-9, 45

Wylie, Philip 1902-1971 . . . . DLB-9

Wyllie, John Cook 1908-1968 . . . . DLB-140

Wyman, Lillie Buffum Chace
  1847-1929. DLB-202

Wymark, Olwen 1934- DLB-233

Wynd, Oswald Morris (see Black, Gavin)

Wyndham, John (John Wyndham Parkes
  Lucas Beynon Harris) 1903-1969 . . . DLB-255

Wynne-Tyson, Esmé 1898-1972 . . . . DLB-191

X

Xenophon circa 430 B.C.-circa 356 B.C.. . . . .DLB-176

Xiang Kairan (Pingjiang Buxiaoshengj
  Buxiaosheng) 1890-1957 . . . . DLB-328

Xiao Hong 1911-1942 . . . . DLB-328

Xu Dishan (Luo Huasheng)
  1893-1941 . . . . DLB-328

Xu Zhenya 1889-1937 . . . . DLB-328

Y

Yahp, Beth 1964- DLB-325

Yamamoto, Hisaye 1921- DLB-312

Yamanaka, Lois-Ann 1961- DLB-312

Yamashita, Karen Tei 1951- DLB-312

Yamauchi, Wakako 1924- DLB-312

Yang Kui 1905-1985 . . . . DLB-328

Yasuoka Shōtarō 1920- DLB-182

Yates, Dornford 1885-1960. . . . . . DLB-77, 153, 352

Yates, J. Michael 1938- DLB-60

Yates, Richard 1926-1992 . . . . DLB-2, 234; Y-81, 92

Yau, John 1950- DLB-234, 312

Yavorov, Peyo 1878-1914 . . . . DLB-147

Ye Shaojun (Ye Shengtao) 1894-1988 . . . DLB-328

Yearsley, Ann 1753-1806. . . . . DLB-109

Yeats, William Butler 1865-1939
  . . . . DLB-10, 19, 98, 156, 332; CDBLB-5

Yehoash (Yehoyesh; Solomon Bloomgarden
  [Shloyme Blumgarten]) 1872-1927 . . . DLB-333

The W. B. Yeats Society of N.Y. Y-99

Yellen, Jack 1892-1991 . . . . DLB-265

Yep, Laurence 1948- DLB-52, 312

Yerby, Frank 1916-1991 . . . . DLB-76

Yezierska, Anzia 1880-1970. . . . . DLB-28, 221

Yolen, Jane 1939- DLB-52

Yonge, Charlotte Mary 1823-1901 . . . DLB-18, 163

The Charlotte M. Yonge Fellowship Y-98

The York Cycle circa 1376-circa 1569. . . . DLB-146

A Yorkshire Tragedy DLB-58

Thomas Yoseloff [publishing house] DLB-46

Yosifova, Ekaterina 1941- DLB-353

Youd, Sam (see Christopher, John)

Young, A. S. "Doc" 1919-1996 . . . . DLB-241

Young, Al 1939- DLB-33

Young, Arthur 1741-1820 . . . . DLB-158

Young, Dick 1917 or 1918-1987 . . . . .DLB-171

Young, Edward 1683-1765 . . . . DLB-95

Young, Frank A. "Fay" 1884-1957 . . . . . . DLB-241

Young, Francis Brett 1884-1954 . . . . DLB-191

Young, Gavin 1928-2001 . . . . DLB-204

Young, Stark 1881-1963 . . . . . . .DLB-9, 102; DS-16

Young, Waldeman 1880-1938. . . . . DLB-26

William Young [publishing house] DLB-49

Young Bear, Ray A. 1950- DLB-175

Yourcenar, Marguerite 1903-1987 . . . .DLB-72; Y-88

Yovkov, Yordan 1880-1937 . . . DLB-147; CDWLB-4

Yu Dafu 1896-1945. . . . . DLB-328

Yushkevich, Semen 1868-1927 . . . . DLB-317

Yver, Jacques 1520?-1570?. DLB-327

Z

Zachariä, Friedrich Wilhelm 1726-1777 . . . DLB-97

Zagajewski, Adam 1945- DLB-232

Zagoskin, Mikhail Nikolaevich
  1789-1852. . . . . .DLB-198

Zaitsev, Boris 1881-1972. . . . . .DLB-317

Zajc, Dane 1929-2005. . . . . DLB-181

Zālīte, Māra 1952- DLB-232

Zalygin, Sergei Pavlovich 1913-2000 . . . . DLB-302

Zamiatin, Evgenii Ivanovich 1884-1937 . . .DLB-272

Zamora, Bernice 1938- DLB-82

Zamudio, Adela (Soledad) 1854-1928 . . . DLB-283

Zand, Herbert 1923-1970 . . . . DLB-85

Zangwill, Israel 1864-1926 . . . . . .DLB-10, 135, 197

Zanzotto, Andrea 1921- DLB-128

Zapata Olivella, Manuel 1920- DLB-113

Zapoev, Timur Iur'evich
(see Kibirov, Timur Iur'evich)

Zasodimsky, Pavel Vladimirovich
1843-1912......................DLB-238

al-Zayyat, Latifa 1923-1996...........DLB-346

Zebra Books.....................DLB-46

Zebrowski, George 1945- DLB-8

Zech, Paul 1881-1946................DLB-56

Zeidner, Lisa 1955- DLB-120

Zeidonis, Imants 1933- DLB-232

Zeimi (Kanze Motokiyo) 1363-1443 .....DLB-203

Zelazny, Roger 1937-1995 ....DLB-8

Zeng Pu 1872-1935 ....DLB-328

Zenger, John Peter 1697-1746........DLB-24, 43

Zephania, Benjamin 1958- DLB-347

Zepheria........................DLB-172

Zernova, Ruf' 1919-2004 ....DLB-317

Zesen, Philipp von 1619-1689 ....DLB-164

Zhadovskaia, Iuliia Valerianovna
1824-1883......................DLB-277

Zhang Ailing (Eileen Chang)
1920-1995......................DLB-328

Zhang Henshui 1895-1967.............DLB-328

Zhang Tianyi 1906-1985 ....DLB-328

Zhao Shuli 1906-1970 ....DLB-328

Zhukova, Mar'ia Semenovna
1805-1855......................DLB-277

Zhukovsky, Vasilii Andreevich
1783-1852......................DLB-205

Zhvanetsky, Mikhail Mikhailovich
1934- DLB-285

G. B. Zieber and Company DLB-49

Ziedonis, Imants 1933- CDWLB-4

Zieroth, Dale 1946- DLB-60

Zigler und Kliphausen, Heinrich
Anshelm von 1663-1697...........DLB-168

Zil'ber, Veniamin Aleksandrovich
(see Kaverin, Veniamin Aleksandrovich)

Zimmer, Paul 1934- DLB-5

Zinberg, Len (see Lacy, Ed)

Zincgref, Julius Wilhelm 1591-1635 .....DLB-164

Zindel, Paul 1936- DLB-7, 52; CDALB-7

Zinnes, Harriet 1919- DLB-193

Zinov'ev, Aleksandr Aleksandrovich
1922- DLB-302

Zinov'eva-Annibal, Lidiia Dmitrievna
1865 or 1866-1907 ....DLB-295

Zinzendorf, Nikolaus Ludwig von
1700-1760......................DLB-168

Zitkala-Ša 1876-1938 ....DLB-175

Zīverts, Mārtiņš 1903-1990 ....DLB-220

Zlatovratsky, Nikolai Nikolaevich
1845-1911......................DLB-238

Zola, Emile 1840-1902................DLB-123

Zolla, Elémire 1926- DLB-196

Zolotow, Charlotte 1915- DLB-52

Zoshchenko, Mikhail Mikhailovich
1895-1958......................DLB-272

Zschokke, Heinrich 1771-1848..........DLB-94

Zubly, John Joachim 1724-1781 ....DLB-31

Zu-Bolton, Ahmos, II 1935-2005........DLB-41

Zuckmayer, Carl 1896-1977.........DLB-56, 124

Zukofsky, Louis 1904-1978 ....DLB-5, 165

Zupan, Vitomil 1914-1987.............DLB-181

Župančič, Oton 1878-1949... DLB-147; CDWLB-4

zur Mühlen, Hermynia 1883-1951 ....DLB-56

Zurayk, Constantine K. 1909-2000 ......DLB-346

Zweig, Arnold 1887-1968..............DLB-66

Zweig, Stefan 1881-1942 ....DLB-81, 118

Zwicky, Fay 1933- DLB-325

Zwicky, Jan 1955- DLB-334

Zwinger, Ann 1925- DLB-275

Zwingli, Huldrych 1484-1531 ....DLB-179

Ø

Øverland, Arnulf 1889-1968...........DLB-297

ISBN-13: 978-0-7876-8172-2
ISBN-10: 0-7876-8172-5